T0181113

# Lecture Notes in Computer Science 12351

More information about this series at http://www.springer.com/series/7412

Andrea Vedaldi · Horst Bischof ·
Thomas Brox · Jan-Michael Frahm (Eds.)

# Computer Vision – ECCV 2020

16th European Conference
Glasgow, UK, August 23–28, 2020
Proceedings, Part VI

 Springer

*Editors*
Andrea Vedaldi ⓘ
University of Oxford
Oxford, UK

Thomas Brox ⓘ
University of Freiburg
Freiburg im Breisgau, Germany

Horst Bischof ⓘ
Graz University of Technology
Graz, Austria

Jan-Michael Frahm
University of North Carolina at Chapel Hill
Chapel Hill, NC, USA

ISSN 0302-9743          ISSN 1611-3349   (electronic)
Lecture Notes in Computer Science
ISBN 978-3-030-58538-9          ISBN 978-3-030-58539-6   (eBook)
https://doi.org/10.1007/978-3-030-58539-6

LNCS Sublibrary: SL6 – Image Processing, Computer Vision, Pattern Recognition, and Graphics

This Springer imprint is published by the registered company Springer Nature Switzerland AG
The registered company address is: Gewerbestrasse 11, 6330 Cham, Switzerland

# Foreword

Hosting the European Conference on Computer Vision (ECCV 2020) was certainly an exciting journey. From the 2016 plan to hold it at the Edinburgh International Conference Centre (hosting 1,800 delegates) to the 2018 plan to hold it at Glasgow's Scottish Exhibition Centre (up to 6,000 delegates), we finally ended with moving online because of the COVID-19 outbreak. While possibly having fewer delegates than expected because of the online format, ECCV 2020 still had over 3,100 registered participants.

Although online, the conference delivered most of the activities expected at a face-to-face conference: peer-reviewed papers, industrial exhibitors, demonstrations, and messaging between delegates. In addition to the main technical sessions, the conference included a strong program of satellite events with 16 tutorials and 44 workshops.

Furthermore, the online conference format enabled new conference features. Every paper had an associated teaser video and a longer full presentation video. Along with the papers and slides from the videos, all these materials were available the week before the conference. This allowed delegates to become familiar with the paper content and be ready for the live interaction with the authors during the conference week. The live event consisted of brief presentations by the oral and spotlight authors and industrial sponsors. Question and answer sessions for all papers were timed to occur twice so delegates from around the world had convenient access to the authors.

As with ECCV 2018, authors' draft versions of the papers appeared online with open access, now on both the Computer Vision Foundation (CVF) and the European Computer Vision Association (ECVA) websites. An archival publication arrangement was put in place with the cooperation of Springer. SpringerLink hosts the final version of the papers with further improvements, such as activating reference links and supplementary materials. These two approaches benefit all potential readers: a version available freely for all researchers, and an authoritative and citable version with additional benefits for SpringerLink subscribers. We thank Alfred Hofmann and Aliaksandr Birukou from Springer for helping to negotiate this agreement, which we expect will continue for future versions of ECCV.

August 2020

Vittorio Ferrari
Bob Fisher
Cordelia Schmid
Emanuele Trucco

# Preface

Welcome to the proceedings of the European Conference on Computer Vision (ECCV 2020). This is a unique edition of ECCV in many ways. Due to the COVID-19 pandemic, this is the first time the conference was held online, in a virtual format. This was also the first time the conference relied exclusively on the Open Review platform to manage the review process. Despite these challenges ECCV is thriving. The conference received 5,150 valid paper submissions, of which 1,360 were accepted for publication (27%) and, of those, 160 were presented as spotlights (3%) and 104 as orals (2%). This amounts to more than twice the number of submissions to ECCV 2018 (2,439). Furthermore, CVPR, the largest conference on computer vision, received 5,850 submissions this year, meaning that ECCV is now 87% the size of CVPR in terms of submissions. By comparison, in 2018 the size of ECCV was only 73% of CVPR.

The review model was similar to previous editions of ECCV; in particular, it was double blind in the sense that the authors did not know the name of the reviewers and vice versa. Furthermore, each conference submission was held confidentially, and was only publicly revealed if and once accepted for publication. Each paper received at least three reviews, totalling more than 15,000 reviews. Handling the review process at this scale was a significant challenge. In order to ensure that each submission received as fair and high-quality reviews as possible, we recruited 2,830 reviewers (a 130% increase with reference to 2018) and 207 area chairs (a 60% increase). The area chairs were selected based on their technical expertise and reputation, largely among people that served as area chair in previous top computer vision and machine learning conferences (ECCV, ICCV, CVPR, NeurIPS, etc.). Reviewers were similarly invited from previous conferences. We also encouraged experienced area chairs to suggest additional chairs and reviewers in the initial phase of recruiting.

Despite doubling the number of submissions, the reviewer load was slightly reduced from 2018, from a maximum of 8 papers down to 7 (with some reviewers offering to handle 6 papers plus an emergency review). The area chair load increased slightly, from 18 papers on average to 22 papers on average.

Conflicts of interest between authors, area chairs, and reviewers were handled largely automatically by the Open Review platform via their curated list of user profiles. Many authors submitting to ECCV already had a profile in Open Review. We set a paper registration deadline one week before the paper submission deadline in order to encourage all missing authors to register and create their Open Review profiles well on time (in practice, we allowed authors to create/change papers arbitrarily until the submission deadline). Except for minor issues with users creating duplicate profiles, this allowed us to easily and quickly identify institutional conflicts, and avoid them, while matching papers to area chairs and reviewers.

Papers were matched to area chairs based on: an affinity score computed by the Open Review platform, which is based on paper titles and abstracts, and an affinity score computed by the Toronto Paper Matching System (TPMS), which is based on the paper's full text, the area chair bids for individual papers, load balancing, and conflict avoidance. Open Review provides the program chairs a convenient web interface to experiment with different configurations of the matching algorithm. The chosen configuration resulted in about 50% of the assigned papers to be highly ranked by the area chair bids, and 50% to be ranked in the middle, with very few low bids assigned.

Assignments to reviewers were similar, with two differences. First, there was a maximum of 7 papers assigned to each reviewer. Second, area chairs recommended up to seven reviewers per paper, providing another highly-weighed term to the affinity scores used for matching.

The assignment of papers to area chairs was smooth. However, it was more difficult to find suitable reviewers for all papers. Having a ratio of 5.6 papers per reviewer with a maximum load of 7 (due to emergency reviewer commitment), which did not allow for much wiggle room in order to also satisfy conflict and expertise constraints. We received some complaints from reviewers who did not feel qualified to review specific papers and we reassigned them wherever possible. However, the large scale of the conference, the many constraints, and the fact that a large fraction of such complaints arrived very late in the review process made this process very difficult and not all complaints could be addressed.

Reviewers had six weeks to complete their assignments. Possibly due to COVID-19 or the fact that the NeurIPS deadline was moved closer to the review deadline, a record 30% of the reviews were still missing after the deadline. By comparison, ECCV 2018 experienced only 10% missing reviews at this stage of the process. In the subsequent week, area chairs chased the missing reviews intensely, found replacement reviewers in their own team, and managed to reach 10% missing reviews. Eventually, we could provide almost all reviews (more than 99.9%) with a delay of only a couple of days on the initial schedule by a significant use of emergency reviews. If this trend is confirmed, it might be a major challenge to run a smooth review process in future editions of ECCV. The community must reconsider prioritization of the time spent on paper writing (the number of submissions increased a lot despite COVID-19) and time spent on paper reviewing (the number of reviews delivered in time decreased a lot presumably due to COVID-19 or NeurIPS deadline). With this imbalance the peer-review system that ensures the quality of our top conferences may break soon.

Reviewers submitted their reviews independently. In the reviews, they had the opportunity to ask questions to the authors to be addressed in the rebuttal. However, reviewers were told not to request any significant new experiment. Using the Open Review interface, authors could provide an answer to each individual review, but were also allowed to cross-reference reviews and responses in their answers. Rather than PDF files, we allowed the use of formatted text for the rebuttal. The rebuttal and initial reviews were then made visible to all reviewers and the primary area chair for a given paper. The area chair encouraged and moderated the reviewer discussion. During the discussions, reviewers were invited to reach a consensus and possibly adjust their ratings as a result of the discussion and of the evidence in the rebuttal.

After the discussion period ended, most reviewers entered a final rating and recommendation, although in many cases this did not differ from their initial recommendation. Based on the updated reviews and discussion, the primary area chair then made a preliminary decision to accept or reject the paper and wrote a justification for it (meta-review). Except for cases where the outcome of this process was absolutely clear (as indicated by the three reviewers and primary area chairs all recommending clear rejection), the decision was then examined and potentially challenged by a secondary area chair. This led to further discussion and overturning a small number of preliminary decisions. Needless to say, there was no in-person area chair meeting, which would have been impossible due to COVID-19.

Area chairs were invited to observe the consensus of the reviewers whenever possible and use extreme caution in overturning a clear consensus to accept or reject a paper. If an area chair still decided to do so, she/he was asked to clearly justify it in the meta-review and to explicitly obtain the agreement of the secondary area chair. In practice, very few papers were rejected after being confidently accepted by the reviewers.

This was the first time Open Review was used as the main platform to run ECCV. In 2018, the program chairs used CMT3 for the user-facing interface and Open Review internally, for matching and conflict resolution. Since it is clearly preferable to only use a single platform, this year we switched to using Open Review in full. The experience was largely positive. The platform is highly-configurable, scalable, and open source. Being written in Python, it is easy to write scripts to extract data programmatically. The paper matching and conflict resolution algorithms and interfaces are top-notch, also due to the excellent author profiles in the platform. Naturally, there were a few kinks along the way due to the fact that the ECCV Open Review configuration was created from scratch for this event and it differs in substantial ways from many other Open Review conferences. However, the Open Review development and support team did a fantastic job in helping us to get the configuration right and to address issues in a timely manner as they unavoidably occurred. We cannot thank them enough for the tremendous effort they put into this project.

Finally, we would like to thank everyone involved in making ECCV 2020 possible in these very strange and difficult times. This starts with our authors, followed by the area chairs and reviewers, who ran the review process at an unprecedented scale. The whole Open Review team (and in particular Melisa Bok, Mohit Unyal, Carlos Mondragon Chapa, and Celeste Martinez Gomez) worked incredibly hard for the entire duration of the process. We would also like to thank René Vidal for contributing to the adoption of Open Review. Our thanks also go to Laurent Charling for TPMS and to the program chairs of ICML, ICLR, and NeurIPS for cross checking double submissions. We thank the website chair, Giovanni Farinella, and the CPI team (in particular Ashley Cook, Miriam Verdon, Nicola McGrane, and Sharon Kerr) for promptly adding material to the website as needed in the various phases of the process. Finally, we thank the publication chairs, Albert Ali Salah, Hamdi Dibeklioglu, Metehan Doyran, Henry Howard-Jenkins, Victor Prisacariu, Siyu Tang, and Gul Varol, who managed to compile these substantial proceedings in an exceedingly compressed schedule. We express our thanks to the ECVA team, in particular Kristina Scherbaum for allowing open access of the proceedings. We thank Alfred Hofmann from Springer who again serve as the publisher. Finally, we thank the other chairs of ECCV 2020, including in particular the general chairs for very useful feedback with the handling of the program.

August 2020                                                    Andrea Vedaldi
                                                              Horst Bischof
                                                              Thomas Brox
                                                        Jan-Michael Frahm

# Organization

## General Chairs

Vittorio Ferrari      Google Research, Switzerland
Bob Fisher      University of Edinburgh, UK
Cordelia Schmid      Google and Inria, France
Emanuele Trucco      University of Dundee, UK

## Program Chairs

Andrea Vedaldi      University of Oxford, UK
Horst Bischof      Graz University of Technology, Austria
Thomas Brox      University of Freiburg, Germany
Jan-Michael Frahm      University of North Carolina, USA

## Industrial Liaison Chairs

Jim Ashe      University of Edinburgh, UK
Helmut Grabner      Zurich University of Applied Sciences, Switzerland
Diane Larlus      NAVER LABS Europe, France
Cristian Novotny      University of Edinburgh, UK

## Local Arrangement Chairs

Yvan Petillot      Heriot-Watt University, UK
Paul Siebert      University of Glasgow, UK

## Academic Demonstration Chair

Thomas Mensink      Google Research and University of Amsterdam,
                         The Netherlands

## Poster Chair

Stephen Mckenna      University of Dundee, UK

## Technology Chair

Gerardo Aragon Camarasa      University of Glasgow, UK

## Tutorial Chairs

Carlo Colombo            University of Florence, Italy
Sotirios Tsaftaris       University of Edinburgh, UK

## Publication Chairs

Albert Ali Salah         Utrecht University, The Netherlands
Hamdi Dibeklioglu        Bilkent University, Turkey
Metehan Doyran           Utrecht University, The Netherlands
Henry Howard-Jenkins     University of Oxford, UK
Victor Adrian Prisacariu University of Oxford, UK
Siyu Tang                ETH Zurich, Switzerland
Gul Varol                University of Oxford, UK

## Website Chair

Giovanni Maria Farinella  University of Catania, Italy

## Workshops Chairs

Adrien Bartoli           University of Clermont Auvergne, France
Andrea Fusiello          University of Udine, Italy

## Area Chairs

Lourdes Agapito          University College London, UK
Zeynep Akata             University of Tübingen, Germany
Karteek Alahari          Inria, France
Antonis Argyros          University of Crete, Greece
Hossein Azizpour         KTH Royal Institute of Technology, Sweden
Joao P. Barreto          Universidade de Coimbra, Portugal
Alexander C. Berg        University of North Carolina at Chapel Hill, USA
Matthew B. Blaschko      KU Leuven, Belgium
Lubomir D. Bourdev       WaveOne, Inc., USA
Edmond Boyer             Inria, France
Yuri Boykov              University of Waterloo, Canada
Gabriel Brostow          University College London, UK
Michael S. Brown         National University of Singapore, Singapore
Jianfei Cai              Monash University, Australia
Barbara Caputo           Politecnico di Torino, Italy
Ayan Chakrabarti         Washington University, St. Louis, USA
Tat-Jen Cham             Nanyang Technological University, Singapore
Manmohan Chandraker      University of California, San Diego, USA
Rama Chellappa           Johns Hopkins University, USA
Liang-Chieh Chen         Google, USA

| | |
|---|---|
| Timothy Hospedales | University of Edinburgh and Samsung, UK |
| Gang Hua | Wormpex AI Research, USA |
| Slobodan Ilic | Siemens AG, Germany |
| Hiroshi Ishikawa | Waseda University, Japan |
| Jiaya Jia | The Chinese University of Hong Kong, SAR China |
| Hailin Jin | Adobe Research, USA |
| Justin Johnson | University of Michigan, USA |
| Frederic Jurie | University of Caen Normandie, France |
| Fredrik Kahl | Chalmers University, Sweden |
| Sing Bing Kang | Zillow, USA |
| Gunhee Kim | Seoul National University, South Korea |
| Junmo Kim | Korea Advanced Institute of Science and Technology, South Korea |
| Tae-Kyun Kim | Imperial College London, UK |
| Ron Kimmel | Technion-Israel Institute of Technology, Israel |
| Alexander Kirillov | Facebook AI Research, USA |
| Kris Kitani | Carnegie Mellon University, USA |
| Iasonas Kokkinos | Ariel AI, UK |
| Vladlen Koltun | Intel Labs, USA |
| Nikos Komodakis | Ecole des Ponts ParisTech, France |
| Piotr Koniusz | Australian National University, Australia |
| M. Pawan Kumar | University of Oxford, UK |
| Kyros Kutulakos | University of Toronto, Canada |
| Christoph Lampert | IST Austria, Austria |
| Ivan Laptev | Inria, France |
| Diane Larlus | NAVER LABS Europe, France |
| Laura Leal-Taixe | Technical University Munich, Germany |
| Honglak Lee | Google and University of Michigan, USA |
| Joon-Young Lee | Adobe Research, USA |
| Kyoung Mu Lee | Seoul National University, South Korea |
| Seungyong Lee | POSTECH, South Korea |
| Yong Jae Lee | University of California, Davis, USA |
| Bastian Leibe | RWTH Aachen University, Germany |
| Victor Lempitsky | Samsung, Russia |
| Ales Leonardis | University of Birmingham, UK |
| Marius Leordeanu | Institute of Mathematics of the Romanian Academy, Romania |
| Vincent Lepetit | ENPC ParisTech, France |
| Hongdong Li | The Australian National University, Australia |
| Xi Li | Zhejiang University, China |
| Yin Li | University of Wisconsin-Madison, USA |
| Zicheng Liao | Zhejiang University, China |
| Jongwoo Lim | Hanyang University, South Korea |
| Stephen Lin | Microsoft Research Asia, China |
| Yen-Yu Lin | National Chiao Tung University, Taiwan, China |
| Zhe Lin | Adobe Research, USA |

| | |
|---|---|
| Haibin Ling | Stony Brooks, State University of New York, USA |
| Jiaying Liu | Peking University, China |
| Ming-Yu Liu | NVIDIA, USA |
| Si Liu | Beihang University, China |
| Xiaoming Liu | Michigan State University, USA |
| Huchuan Lu | Dalian University of Technology, China |
| Simon Lucey | Carnegie Mellon University, USA |
| Jiebo Luo | University of Rochester, USA |
| Julien Mairal | Inria, France |
| Michael Maire | University of Chicago, USA |
| Subhransu Maji | University of Massachusetts, Amherst, USA |
| Yasushi Makihara | Osaka University, Japan |
| Jiri Matas | Czech Technical University in Prague, Czech Republic |
| Yasuyuki Matsushita | Osaka University, Japan |
| Philippos Mordohai | Stevens Institute of Technology, USA |
| Vittorio Murino | University of Verona, Italy |
| Naila Murray | NAVER LABS Europe, France |
| Hajime Nagahara | Osaka University, Japan |
| P. J. Narayanan | International Institute of Information Technology (IIIT), Hyderabad, India |
| Nassir Navab | Technical University of Munich, Germany |
| Natalia Neverova | Facebook AI Research, France |
| Matthias Niessner | Technical University of Munich, Germany |
| Jean-Marc Odobez | Idiap Research Institute and Swiss Federal Institute of Technology Lausanne, Switzerland |
| Francesca Odone | Università di Genova, Italy |
| Takeshi Oishi | The University of Tokyo, Tokyo Institute of Technology, Japan |
| Vicente Ordonez | University of Virginia, USA |
| Manohar Paluri | Facebook AI Research, USA |
| Maja Pantic | Imperial College London, UK |
| In Kyu Park | Inha University, South Korea |
| Ioannis Patras | Queen Mary University of London, UK |
| Patrick Perez | Valeo, France |
| Bryan A. Plummer | Boston University, USA |
| Thomas Pock | Graz University of Technology, Austria |
| Marc Pollefeys | ETH Zurich and Microsoft MR & AI Zurich Lab, Switzerland |
| Jean Ponce | Inria, France |
| Gerard Pons-Moll | MPII, Saarland Informatics Campus, Germany |
| Jordi Pont-Tuset | Google, Switzerland |
| James Matthew Rehg | Georgia Institute of Technology, USA |
| Ian Reid | University of Adelaide, Australia |
| Olaf Ronneberger | DeepMind London, UK |
| Stefan Roth | TU Darmstadt, Germany |
| Bryan Russell | Adobe Research, USA |

| | |
|---|---|
| Kwang Moo Yi | University of Victoria, Canada |
| Zhaozheng Yin | Stony Brook, State University of New York, USA |
| Chang D. Yoo | Korea Advanced Institute of Science and Technology, South Korea |
| Shaodi You | University of Amsterdam, The Netherlands |
| Jingyi Yu | ShanghaiTech University, China |
| Stella Yu | University of California, Berkeley, and ICSI, USA |
| Stefanos Zafeiriou | Imperial College London, UK |
| Hongbin Zha | Peking University, China |
| Tianzhu Zhang | University of Science and Technology of China, China |
| Liang Zheng | Australian National University, Australia |
| Todd E. Zickler | Harvard University, USA |
| Andrew Zisserman | University of Oxford, UK |

## Technical Program Committee

| | | |
|---|---|---|
| Sathyanarayanan N. Aakur | Samuel Albanie | Pablo Arbelaez |
| Wael Abd Almgaeed | Shadi Albarqouni | Shervin Ardeshir |
| Abdelrahman Abdelhamed | Cenek Albl | Sercan O. Arik |
| Abdullah Abuolaim | Hassan Abu Alhaija | Anil Armagan |
| Supreeth Achar | Daniel Aliaga | Anurag Arnab |
| Hanno Ackermann | Mohammad S. Aliakbarian | Chetan Arora |
| Ehsan Adeli | Rahaf Aljundi | Federica Arrigoni |
| Triantafyllos Afouras | Thiemo Alldieck | Mathieu Aubry |
| Sameer Agarwal | Jon Almazan | Shai Avidan |
| Aishwarya Agrawal | Jose M. Alvarez | Angelica I. Aviles-Rivero |
| Harsh Agrawal | Senjian An | Yannis Avrithis |
| Pulkit Agrawal | Saket Anand | Ismail Ben Ayed |
| Antonio Agudo | Codruta Ancuti | Shekoofeh Azizi |
| Eirikur Agustsson | Cosmin Ancuti | Ioan Andrei Bârsan |
| Karim Ahmed | Peter Anderson | Artem Babenko |
| Byeongjoo Ahn | Juan Andrade-Cetto | Deepak Babu Sam |
| Unaiza Ahsan | Alexander Andreopoulos | Seung-Hwan Baek |
| Thalaiyasingam Ajanthan | Misha Andriluka | Seungryul Baek |
| Kenan E. Ak | Dragomir Anguelov | Andrew D. Bagdanov |
| Emre Akbas | Rushil Anirudh | Shai Bagon |
| Naveed Akhtar | Michel Antunes | Yuval Bahat |
| Derya Akkaynak | Oisin Mac Aodha | Junjie Bai |
| Yagiz Aksoy | Srikar Appalaraju | Song Bai |
| Ziad Al-Halah | Relja Arandjelovic | Xiang Bai |
| Xavier Alameda-Pineda | Nikita Araslanov | Yalong Bai |
| Jean-Baptiste Alayrac | Andre Araujo | Yancheng Bai |
| | Helder Araujo | Peter Bajcsy |
| | | Slawomir Bak |

Mahsa Baktashmotlagh
Kavita Bala
Yogesh Balaji
Guha Balakrishnan
V. N. Balasubramanian
Federico Baldassarre
Vassileios Balntas
Shurjo Banerjee
Aayush Bansal
Ankan Bansal
Jianmin Bao
Linchao Bao
Wenbo Bao
Yingze Bao
Akash Bapat
Md Jawadul Hasan Bappy
Fabien Baradel
Lorenzo Baraldi
Daniel Barath
Adrian Barbu
Kobus Barnard
Nick Barnes
Francisco Barranco
Jonathan T. Barron
Arslan Basharat
Chaim Baskin
Anil S. Baslamisli
Jorge Batista
Kayhan Batmanghelich
Konstantinos Batsos
David Bau
Luis Baumela
Christoph Baur
Eduardo
  Bayro-Corrochano
Paul Beardsley
Jan Bednavr'ik
Oscar Beijbom
Philippe Bekaert
Esube Bekele
Vasileios Belagiannis
Ohad Ben-Shahar
Abhijit Bendale
Róger Bermúdez-Chacón
Maxim Berman
Jesus Bermudez-cameo

Florian Bernard
Stefano Berretti
Marcelo Bertalmio
Gedas Bertasius
Cigdem Beyan
Lucas Beyer
Vijayakumar Bhagavatula
Arjun Nitin Bhagoji
Apratim Bhattacharyya
Binod Bhattarai
Sai Bi
Jia-Wang Bian
Simone Bianco
Adel Bibi
Tolga Birdal
Tom Bishop
Soma Biswas
Mårten Björkman
Volker Blanz
Vishnu Boddeti
Navaneeth Bodla
Simion-Vlad Bogolin
Xavier Boix
Piotr Bojanowski
Timo Bolkart
Guido Borghi
Larbi Boubchir
Guillaume Bourmaud
Adrien Bousseau
Thierry Bouwmans
Richard Bowden
Hakan Boyraz
Mathieu Brédif
Samarth Brahmbhatt
Steve Branson
Nikolas Brasch
Biagio Brattoli
Ernesto Brau
Toby P. Breckon
Francois Bremond
Jesus Briales
Sofia Broomé
Marcus A. Brubaker
Luc Brun
Silvia Bucci
Shyamal Buch

Pradeep Buddharaju
Uta Buechler
Mai Bui
Tu Bui
Adrian Bulat
Giedrius T. Burachas
Elena Burceanu
Xavier P. Burgos-Artizzu
Kaylee Burns
Andrei Bursuc
Benjamin Busam
Wonmin Byeon
Zoya Bylinskii
Sergi Caelles
Jianrui Cai
Minjie Cai
Yujun Cai
Zhaowei Cai
Zhipeng Cai
Juan C. Caicedo
Simone Calderara
Necati Cihan Camgoz
Dylan Campbell
Octavia Camps
Jiale Cao
Kaidi Cao
Liangliang Cao
Xiangyong Cao
Xiaochun Cao
Yang Cao
Yu Cao
Yue Cao
Zhangjie Cao
Luca Carlone
Mathilde Caron
Dan Casas
Thomas J. Cashman
Umberto Castellani
Lluis Castrejon
Jacopo Cavazza
Fabio Cermelli
Hakan Cevikalp
Menglei Chai
Ishani Chakraborty
Rudrasis Chakraborty
Antoni B. Chan

Kwok-Ping Chan
Siddhartha Chandra
Sharat Chandran
Arjun Chandrasekaran
Angel X. Chang
Che-Han Chang
Hong Chang
Hyun Sung Chang
Hyung Jin Chang
Jianlong Chang
Ju Yong Chang
Ming-Ching Chang
Simyung Chang
Xiaojun Chang
Yu-Wei Chao
Devendra S. Chaplot
Arslan Chaudhry
Rizwan A. Chaudhry
Can Chen
Chang Chen
Chao Chen
Chen Chen
Chu-Song Chen
Dapeng Chen
Dong Chen
Dongdong Chen
Guanying Chen
Hongge Chen
Hsin-yi Chen
Huaijin Chen
Hwann-Tzong Chen
Jianbo Chen
Jianhui Chen
Jiansheng Chen
Jiaxin Chen
Jie Chen
Jun-Cheng Chen
Kan Chen
Kevin Chen
Lin Chen
Long Chen
Min-Hung Chen
Qifeng Chen
Shi Chen
Shixing Chen
Tianshui Chen

Weifeng Chen
Weikai Chen
Xi Chen
Xiaohan Chen
Xiaozhi Chen
Xilin Chen
Xingyu Chen
Xinlei Chen
Xinyun Chen
Yi-Ting Chen
Yilun Chen
Ying-Cong Chen
Yinpeng Chen
Yiran Chen
Yu Chen
Yu-Sheng Chen
Yuhua Chen
Yun-Chun Chen
Yunpeng Chen
Yuntao Chen
Zhuoyuan Chen
Zitian Chen
Anchieh Cheng
Bowen Cheng
Erkang Cheng
Gong Cheng
Guangliang Cheng
Jingchun Cheng
Jun Cheng
Li Cheng
Ming-Ming Cheng
Yu Cheng
Ziang Cheng
Anoop Cherian
Dmitry Chetverikov
Ngai-man Cheung
William Cheung
Ajad Chhatkuli
Naoki Chiba
Benjamin Chidester
Han-pang Chiu
Mang Tik Chiu
Wei-Chen Chiu
Donghyeon Cho
Hojin Cho
Minsu Cho

Nam Ik Cho
Tim Cho
Tae Eun Choe
Chiho Choi
Edward Choi
Inchang Choi
Jinsoo Choi
Jonghyun Choi
Jongwon Choi
Yukyung Choi
Hisham Cholakkal
Eunji Chong
Jaegul Choo
Christopher Choy
Hang Chu
Peng Chu
Wen-Sheng Chu
Albert Chung
Joon Son Chung
Hai Ci
Safa Cicek
Ramazan G. Cinbis
Arridhana Ciptadi
Javier Civera
James J. Clark
Ronald Clark
Felipe Codevilla
Michael Cogswell
Andrea Cohen
Maxwell D. Collins
Carlo Colombo
Yang Cong
Adria R. Continente
Marcella Cornia
John Richard Corring
Darren Cosker
Dragos Costea
Garrison W. Cottrell
Florent Couzinie-Devy
Marco Cristani
Ioana Croitoru
James L. Crowley
Jiequan Cui
Zhaopeng Cui
Ross Cutler
Antonio D'Innocente

Rozenn Dahyot
Bo Dai
Dengxin Dai
Hang Dai
Longquan Dai
Shuyang Dai
Xiyang Dai
Yuchao Dai
Adrian V. Dalca
Dima Damen
Bharath B. Damodaran
Kristin Dana
Martin Danelljan
Zheng Dang
Zachary Alan Daniels
Donald G. Dansereau
Abhishek Das
Samyak Datta
Achal Dave
Titas De
Rodrigo de Bem
Teo de Campos
Raoul de Charette
Shalini De Mello
Joseph DeGol
Herve Delingette
Haowen Deng
Jiankang Deng
Weijian Deng
Zhiwei Deng
Joachim Denzler
Konstantinos G. Derpanis
Aditya Deshpande
Frederic Devernay
Somdip Dey
Arturo Deza
Abhinav Dhall
Helisa Dhamo
Vikas Dhiman
Fillipe Dias Moreira
   de Souza
Ali Diba
Ferran Diego
Guiguang Ding
Henghui Ding
Jian Ding

Mingyu Ding
Xinghao Ding
Zhengming Ding
Robert DiPietro
Cosimo Distante
Ajay Divakaran
Mandar Dixit
Abdelaziz Djelouah
Thanh-Toan Do
Jose Dolz
Bo Dong
Chao Dong
Jiangxin Dong
Weiming Dong
Weisheng Dong
Xingping Dong
Xuanyi Dong
Yinpeng Dong
Gianfranco Doretto
Hazel Doughty
Hassen Drira
Bertram Drost
Dawei Du
Ye Duan
Yueqi Duan
Abhimanyu Dubey
Anastasia Dubrovina
Stefan Duffner
Chi Nhan Duong
Thibaut Durand
Zoran Duric
Iulia Duta
Debidatta Dwibedi
Benjamin Eckart
Marc Eder
Marzieh Edraki
Alexei A. Efros
Kiana Ehsani
Hazm Kemal Ekenel
James H. Elder
Mohamed Elgharib
Shireen Elhabian
Ehsan Elhamifar
Mohamed Elhoseiny
Ian Endres
N. Benjamin Erichson

Jan Ernst
Sergio Escalera
Francisco Escolano
Victor Escorcia
Carlos Esteves
Francisco J. Estrada
Bin Fan
Chenyou Fan
Deng-Ping Fan
Haoqi Fan
Hehe Fan
Heng Fan
Kai Fan
Lijie Fan
Linxi Fan
Quanfu Fan
Shaojing Fan
Xiaochuan Fan
Xin Fan
Yuchen Fan
Sean Fanello
Hao-Shu Fang
Haoyang Fang
Kuan Fang
Yi Fang
Yuming Fang
Azade Farshad
Alireza Fathi
Raanan Fattal
Joao Fayad
Xiaohan Fei
Christoph Feichtenhofer
Michael Felsberg
Chen Feng
Jiashi Feng
Junyi Feng
Mengyang Feng
Qianli Feng
Zhenhua Feng
Michele Fenzi
Andras Ferencz
Martin Fergie
Basura Fernando
Ethan Fetaya
Michael Firman
John W. Fisher

Matthew Fisher
Boris Flach
Corneliu Florea
Wolfgang Foerstner
David Fofi
Gian Luca Foresti
Per-Erik Forssen
David Fouhey
Katerina Fragkiadaki
Victor Fragoso
Jean-Sébastien Franco
Ohad Fried
Iuri Frosio
Cheng-Yang Fu
Huazhu Fu
Jianlong Fu
Jingjing Fu
Xueyang Fu
Yanwei Fu
Ying Fu
Yun Fu
Olac Fuentes
Kent Fujiwara
Takuya Funatomi
Christopher Funk
Thomas Funkhouser
Antonino Furnari
Ryo Furukawa
Erik Gärtner
Raghudeep Gadde
Matheus Gadelha
Vandit Gajjar
Trevor Gale
Juergen Gall
Mathias Gallardo
Guillermo Gallego
Orazio Gallo
Chuang Gan
Zhe Gan
Madan Ravi Ganesh
Aditya Ganeshan
Siddha Ganju
Bin-Bin Gao
Changxin Gao
Feng Gao
Hongchang Gao

Jin Gao
Jiyang Gao
Junbin Gao
Katelyn Gao
Lin Gao
Mingfei Gao
Ruiqi Gao
Ruohan Gao
Shenghua Gao
Yuan Gao
Yue Gao
Noa Garcia
Alberto Garcia-Garcia
Guillermo
  Garcia-Hernando
Jacob R. Gardner
Animesh Garg
Kshitiz Garg
Rahul Garg
Ravi Garg
Philip N. Garner
Kirill Gavrilyuk
Paul Gay
Shiming Ge
Weifeng Ge
Baris Gecer
Xin Geng
Kyle Genova
Stamatios Georgoulis
Bernard Ghanem
Michael Gharbi
Kamran Ghasedi
Golnaz Ghiasi
Arnab Ghosh
Partha Ghosh
Silvio Giancola
Andrew Gilbert
Rohit Girdhar
Xavier Giro-i-Nieto
Thomas Gittings
Ioannis Gkioulekas
Clement Godard
Vaibhava Goel
Bastian Goldluecke
Lluis Gomez
Nuno Gonçalves

Dong Gong
Ke Gong
Mingming Gong
Abel Gonzalez-Garcia
Ariel Gordon
Daniel Gordon
Paulo Gotardo
Venu Madhav Govindu
Ankit Goyal
Priya Goyal
Raghav Goyal
Benjamin Graham
Douglas Gray
Brent A. Griffin
Etienne Grossmann
David Gu
Jiayuan Gu
Jiuxiang Gu
Lin Gu
Qiao Gu
Shuhang Gu
Jose J. Guerrero
Paul Guerrero
Jie Gui
Jean-Yves Guillemaut
Riza Alp Guler
Erhan Gundogdu
Fatma Guney
Guodong Guo
Kaiwen Guo
Qi Guo
Sheng Guo
Shi Guo
Tiantong Guo
Xiaojie Guo
Yijie Guo
Yiluan Guo
Yuanfang Guo
Yulan Guo
Agrim Gupta
Ankush Gupta
Mohit Gupta
Saurabh Gupta
Tanmay Gupta
Danna Gurari
Abner Guzman-Rivera

JunYoung Gwak
Michael Gygli
Jung-Woo Ha
Simon Hadfield
Isma Hadji
Bjoern Haefner
Taeyoung Hahn
Levente Hajder
Peter Hall
Emanuela Haller
Stefan Haller
Bumsub Ham
Abdullah Hamdi
Dongyoon Han
Hu Han
Jungong Han
Junwei Han
Kai Han
Tian Han
Xiaoguang Han
Xintong Han
Yahong Han
Ankur Handa
Zekun Hao
Albert Haque
Tatsuya Harada
Mehrtash Harandi
Adam W. Harley
Mahmudul Hasan
Atsushi Hashimoto
Ali Hatamizadeh
Munawar Hayat
Dongliang He
Jingrui He
Junfeng He
Kaiming He
Kun He
Lei He
Pan He
Ran He
Shengfeng He
Tong He
Weipeng He
Xuming He
Yang He
Yihui He

Zhihai He
Chinmay Hegde
Janne Heikkila
Mattias P. Heinrich
Stéphane Herbin
Alexander Hermans
Luis Herranz
John R. Hershey
Aaron Hertzmann
Roei Herzig
Anders Heyden
Steven Hickson
Otmar Hilliges
Tomas Hodan
Judy Hoffman
Michael Hofmann
Yannick Hold-Geoffroy
Namdar Homayounfar
Sina Honari
Richang Hong
Seunghoon Hong
Xiaopeng Hong
Yi Hong
Hidekata Hontani
Anthony Hoogs
Yedid Hoshen
Mir Rayat Imtiaz Hossain
Junhui Hou
Le Hou
Lu Hou
Tingbo Hou
Wei-Lin Hsiao
Cheng-Chun Hsu
Gee-Sern Jison Hsu
Kuang-jui Hsu
Changbo Hu
Di Hu
Guosheng Hu
Han Hu
Hao Hu
Hexiang Hu
Hou-Ning Hu
Jie Hu
Junlin Hu
Nan Hu
Ping Hu

Ronghang Hu
Xiaowei Hu
Yinlin Hu
Yuan-Ting Hu
Zhe Hu
Binh-Son Hua
Yang Hua
Bingyao Huang
Di Huang
Dong Huang
Fay Huang
Haibin Huang
Haozhi Huang
Heng Huang
Huaibo Huang
Jia-Bin Huang
Jing Huang
Jingwei Huang
Kaizhu Huang
Lei Huang
Qiangui Huang
Qiaoying Huang
Qingqiu Huang
Qixing Huang
Shaoli Huang
Sheng Huang
Siyuan Huang
Weilin Huang
Wenbing Huang
Xiangru Huang
Xun Huang
Yan Huang
Yifei Huang
Yue Huang
Zhiwu Huang
Zilong Huang
Minyoung Huh
Zhuo Hui
Matthias B. Hullin
Martin Humenberger
Wei-Chih Hung
Zhouyuan Huo
Junhwa Hur
Noureldien Hussein
Jyh-Jing Hwang
Seong Jae Hwang

Sung Ju Hwang
Ichiro Ide
Ivo Ihrke
Daiki Ikami
Satoshi Ikehata
Nazli Ikizler-Cinbis
Sunghoon Im
Yani Ioannou
Radu Tudor Ionescu
Umar Iqbal
Go Irie
Ahmet Iscen
Md Amirul Islam
Vamsi Ithapu
Nathan Jacobs
Arpit Jain
Himalaya Jain
Suyog Jain
Stuart James
Won-Dong Jang
Yunseok Jang
Ronnachai Jaroensri
Dinesh Jayaraman
Sadeep Jayasumana
Suren Jayasuriya
Herve Jegou
Simon Jenni
Hae-Gon Jeon
Yunho Jeon
Koteswar R. Jerripothula
Hueihan Jhuang
I-hong Jhuo
Dinghuang Ji
Hui Ji
Jingwei Ji
Pan Ji
Yanli Ji
Baoxiong Jia
Kui Jia
Xu Jia
Chiyu Max Jiang
Haiyong Jiang
Hao Jiang
Huaizu Jiang
Huajie Jiang
Ke Jiang

Lai Jiang
Li Jiang
Lu Jiang
Ming Jiang
Peng Jiang
Shuqiang Jiang
Wei Jiang
Xudong Jiang
Zhuolin Jiang
Jianbo Jiao
Zequn Jie
Dakai Jin
Kyong Hwan Jin
Lianwen Jin
SouYoung Jin
Xiaojie Jin
Xin Jin
Nebojsa Jojic
Alexis Joly
Michael Jeffrey Jones
Hanbyul Joo
Jungseock Joo
Kyungdon Joo
Ajjen Joshi
Shantanu H. Joshi
Da-Cheng Juan
Marco Körner
Kevin Köser
Asim Kadav
Christine Kaeser-Chen
Kushal Kafle
Dagmar Kainmueller
Ioannis A. Kakadiaris
Zdenek Kalal
Nima Kalantari
Yannis Kalantidis
Mahdi M. Kalayeh
Anmol Kalia
Sinan Kalkan
Vicky Kalogeiton
Ashwin Kalyan
Joni-kristian Kamarainen
Gerda Kamberova
Chandra Kambhamettu
Martin Kampel
Meina Kan

Christopher Kanan
Kenichi Kanatani
Angjoo Kanazawa
Atsushi Kanehira
Takuhiro Kaneko
Asako Kanezaki
Bingyi Kang
Di Kang
Sunghun Kang
Zhao Kang
Vadim Kantorov
Abhishek Kar
Amlan Kar
Theofanis Karaletsos
Leonid Karlinsky
Kevin Karsch
Angelos Katharopoulos
Isinsu Katircioglu
Hiroharu Kato
Zoltan Kato
Dotan Kaufman
Jan Kautz
Rei Kawakami
Qiuhong Ke
Wadim Kehl
Petr Kellnhofer
Aniruddha Kembhavi
Cem Keskin
Margret Keuper
Daniel Keysers
Ashkan Khakzar
Fahad Khan
Naeemullah Khan
Salman Khan
Siddhesh Khandelwal
Rawal Khirodkar
Anna Khoreva
Tejas Khot
Parmeshwar Khurd
Hadi Kiapour
Joe Kileel
Chanho Kim
Dahun Kim
Edward Kim
Eunwoo Kim
Han-ul Kim

Hansung Kim
Heewon Kim
Hyo Jin Kim
Hyunwoo J. Kim
Jinkyu Kim
Jiwon Kim
Jongmin Kim
Junsik Kim
Junyeong Kim
Min H. Kim
Namil Kim
Pyojin Kim
Seon Joo Kim
Seong Tae Kim
Seungryong Kim
Sungwoong Kim
Tae Hyun Kim
Vladimir Kim
Won Hwa Kim
Yonghyun Kim
Benjamin Kimia
Akisato Kimura
Pieter-Jan Kindermans
Zsolt Kira
Itaru Kitahara
Hedvig Kjellstrom
Jan Knopp
Takumi Kobayashi
Erich Kobler
Parker Koch
Reinhard Koch
Elyor Kodirov
Amir Kolaman
Nicholas Kolkin
Dimitrios Kollias
Stefanos Kollias
Soheil Kolouri
Adams Wai-Kin Kong
Naejin Kong
Shu Kong
Tao Kong
Yu Kong
Yoshinori Konishi
Daniil Kononenko
Theodora Kontogianni
Simon Korman

Adam Kortylewski
Jana Kosecka
Jean Kossaifi
Satwik Kottur
Rigas Kouskouridas
Adriana Kovashka
Rama Kovvuri
Adarsh Kowdle
Jedrzej Kozerawski
Mateusz Kozinski
Philipp Kraehenbuehl
Gregory Kramida
Josip Krapac
Dmitry Kravchenko
Ranjay Krishna
Pavel Krsek
Alexander Krull
Jakob Kruse
Hiroyuki Kubo
Hilde Kuehne
Jason Kuen
Andreas Kuhn
Arjan Kuijper
Zuzana Kukelova
Ajay Kumar
Amit Kumar
Avinash Kumar
Suryansh Kumar
Vijay Kumar
Kaustav Kundu
Weicheng Kuo
Nojun Kwak
Suha Kwak
Junseok Kwon
Nikolaos Kyriazis
Zorah Lähner
Ankit Laddha
Florent Lafarge
Jean Lahoud
Kevin Lai
Shang-Hong Lai
Wei-Sheng Lai
Yu-Kun Lai
Iro Laina
Antony Lam
John Wheatley Lambert

Xiangyuan lan
Xu Lan
Charis Lanaras
Georg Langs
Oswald Lanz
Dong Lao
Yizhen Lao
Agata Lapedriza
Gustav Larsson
Viktor Larsson
Katrin Lasinger
Christoph Lassner
Longin Jan Latecki
Stéphane Lathuilière
Rynson Lau
Hei Law
Justin Lazarow
Svetlana Lazebnik
Hieu Le
Huu Le
Ngan Hoang Le
Trung-Nghia Le
Vuong Le
Colin Lea
Erik Learned-Miller
Chen-Yu Lee
Gim Hee Lee
Hsin-Ying Lee
Hyungtae Lee
Jae-Han Lee
Jimmy Addison Lee
Joonseok Lee
Kibok Lee
Kuang-Huei Lee
Kwonjoon Lee
Minsik Lee
Sang-chul Lee
Seungkyu Lee
Soochan Lee
Stefan Lee
Taehee Lee
Andreas Lehrmann
Jie Lei
Peng Lei
Matthew Joseph Leotta
Wee Kheng Leow

Gil Levi
Evgeny Levinkov
Aviad Levis
Jose Lezama
Ang Li
Bin Li
Bing Li
Boyi Li
Changsheng Li
Chao Li
Chen Li
Cheng Li
Chenglong Li
Chi Li
Chun-Guang Li
Chun-Liang Li
Chunyuan Li
Dong Li
Guanbin Li
Hao Li
Haoxiang Li
Hongsheng Li
Hongyang Li
Houqiang Li
Huibin Li
Jia Li
Jianan Li
Jianguo Li
Junnan Li
Junxuan Li
Kai Li
Ke Li
Kejie Li
Kunpeng Li
Lerenhan Li
Li Erran Li
Mengtian Li
Mu Li
Peihua Li
Peiyi Li
Ping Li
Qi Li
Qing Li
Ruiyu Li
Ruoteng Li
Shaozi Li

Sheng Li
Shiwei Li
Shuang Li
Siyang Li
Stan Z. Li
Tianye Li
Wei Li
Weixin Li
Wen Li
Wenbo Li
Xiaomeng Li
Xin Li
Xiu Li
Xuelong Li
Xueting Li
Yan Li
Yandong Li
Yanghao Li
Yehao Li
Yi Li
Yijun Li
Yikang LI
Yining Li
Yongjie Li
Yu Li
Yu-Jhe Li
Yunpeng Li
Yunsheng Li
Yunzhu Li
Zhe Li
Zhen Li
Zhengqi Li
Zhenyang Li
Zhuwen Li
Dongze Lian
Xiaochen Lian
Zhouhui Lian
Chen Liang
Jie Liang
Ming Liang
Paul Pu Liang
Pengpeng Liang
Shu Liang
Wei Liang
Jing Liao
Minghui Liao

Renjie Liao
Shengcai Liao
Shuai Liao
Yiyi Liao
Ser-Nam Lim
Chen-Hsuan Lin
Chung-Ching Lin
Dahua Lin
Ji Lin
Kevin Lin
Tianwei Lin
Tsung-Yi Lin
Tsung-Yu Lin
Wei-An Lin
Weiyao Lin
Yen-Chen Lin
Yuewei Lin
David B. Lindell
Drew Linsley
Krzysztof Lis
Roee Litman
Jim Little
An-An Liu
Bo Liu
Buyu Liu
Chao Liu
Chen Liu
Cheng-lin Liu
Chenxi Liu
Dong Liu
Feng Liu
Guilin Liu
Haomiao Liu
Heshan Liu
Hong Liu
Ji Liu
Jingen Liu
Jun Liu
Lanlan Liu
Li Liu
Liu Liu
Mengyuan Liu
Miaomiao Liu
Nian Liu
Ping Liu
Risheng Liu

Sheng Liu
Shu Liu
Shuaicheng Liu
Sifei Liu
Siqi Liu
Siying Liu
Songtao Liu
Ting Liu
Tongliang Liu
Tyng-Luh Liu
Wanquan Liu
Wei Liu
Weiyang Liu
Weizhe Liu
Wenyu Liu
Wu Liu
Xialei Liu
Xianglong Liu
Xiaodong Liu
Xiaofeng Liu
Xihui Liu
Xingyu Liu
Xinwang Liu
Xuanqing Liu
Xuebo Liu
Yang Liu
Yaojie Liu
Yebin Liu
Yen-Cheng Liu
Yiming Liu
Yu Liu
Yu-Shen Liu
Yufan Liu
Yun Liu
Zheng Liu
Zhijian Liu
Zhuang Liu
Zichuan Liu
Ziwei Liu
Zongyi Liu
Stephan Liwicki
Liliana Lo Presti
Chengjiang Long
Fuchen Long
Mingsheng Long
Xiang Long

Yang Long
Charles T. Loop
Antonio Lopez
Roberto J. Lopez-Sastre
Javier Lorenzo-Navarro
Manolis Lourakis
Boyu Lu
Canyi Lu
Feng Lu
Guoyu Lu
Hongtao Lu
Jiajun Lu
Jiasen Lu
Jiwen Lu
Kaiyue Lu
Le Lu
Shao-Ping Lu
Shijian Lu
Xiankai Lu
Xin Lu
Yao Lu
Yiping Lu
Yongxi Lu
Yongyi Lu
Zhiwu Lu
Fujun Luan
Benjamin E. Lundell
Hao Luo
Jian-Hao Luo
Ruotian Luo
Weixin Luo
Wenhan Luo
Wenjie Luo
Yan Luo
Zelun Luo
Zixin Luo
Khoa Luu
Zhaoyang Lv
Pengyuan Lyu
Thomas Möllenhoff
Matthias Müller
Bingpeng Ma
Chih-Yao Ma
Chongyang Ma
Huimin Ma
Jiayi Ma

K. T. Ma
Ke Ma
Lin Ma
Liqian Ma
Shugao Ma
Wei-Chiu Ma
Xiaojian Ma
Xingjun Ma
Zhanyu Ma
Zheng Ma
Radek Jakob Mackowiak
Ludovic Magerand
Shweta Mahajan
Siddharth Mahendran
Long Mai
Ameesh Makadia
Oscar Mendez Maldonado
Mateusz Malinowski
Yury Malkov
Arun Mallya
Dipu Manandhar
Massimiliano Mancini
Fabian Manhardt
Kevis-kokitsi Maninis
Varun Manjunatha
Junhua Mao
Xudong Mao
Alina Marcu
Edgar Margffoy-Tuay
Dmitrii Marin
Manuel J. Marin-Jimenez
Kenneth Marino
Niki Martinel
Julieta Martinez
Jonathan Masci
Tomohiro Mashita
Iacopo Masi
David Masip
Daniela Massiceti
Stefan Mathe
Yusuke Matsui
Tetsu Matsukawa
Iain A. Matthews
Kevin James Matzen
Bruce Allen Maxwell
Stephen Maybank

Helmut Mayer
Amir Mazaheri
David McAllester
Steven McDonagh
Stephen J. Mckenna
Roey Mechrez
Prakhar Mehrotra
Christopher Mei
Xue Mei
Paulo R. S. Mendonca
Lili Meng
Zibo Meng
Thomas Mensink
Bjoern Menze
Michele Merler
Kourosh Meshgi
Pascal Mettes
Christopher Metzler
Liang Mi
Qiguang Miao
Xin Miao
Tomer Michaeli
Frank Michel
Antoine Miech
Krystian Mikolajczyk
Peyman Milanfar
Ben Mildenhall
Gregor Miller
Fausto Milletari
Dongbo Min
Kyle Min
Pedro Miraldo
Dmytro Mishkin
Anand Mishra
Ashish Mishra
Ishan Misra
Niluthpol C. Mithun
Kaushik Mitra
Niloy Mitra
Anton Mitrokhin
Ikuhisa Mitsugami
Anurag Mittal
Kaichun Mo
Zhipeng Mo
Davide Modolo
Michael Moeller

Pritish Mohapatra
Pavlo Molchanov
Davide Moltisanti
Pascal Monasse
Mathew Monfort
Aron Monszpart
Sean Moran
Vlad I. Morariu
Francesc Moreno-Noguer
Pietro Morerio
Stylianos Moschoglou
Yael Moses
Roozbeh Mottaghi
Pierre Moulon
Arsalan Mousavian
Yadong Mu
Yasuhiro Mukaigawa
Lopamudra Mukherjee
Yusuke Mukuta
Ravi Teja Mullapudi
Mario Enrique Munich
Zachary Murez
Ana C. Murillo
J. Krishna Murthy
Damien Muselet
Armin Mustafa
Siva Karthik Mustikovela
Carlo Dal Mutto
Moin Nabi
Varun K. Nagaraja
Tushar Nagarajan
Arsha Nagrani
Seungjun Nah
Nikhil Naik
Yoshikatsu Nakajima
Yuta Nakashima
Atsushi Nakazawa
Seonghyeon Nam
Vinay P. Namboodiri
Medhini Narasimhan
Srinivasa Narasimhan
Sanath Narayan
Erickson Rangel
    Nascimento
Jacinto Nascimento
Tayyab Naseer

Lakshmanan Nataraj
Neda Nategh
Nelson Isao Nauata
Fernando Navarro
Shah Nawaz
Lukas Neumann
Ram Nevatia
Alejandro Newell
Shawn Newsam
Joe Yue-Hei Ng
Trung Thanh Ngo
Duc Thanh Nguyen
Lam M. Nguyen
Phuc Xuan Nguyen
Thuong Nguyen Canh
Mihalis Nicolaou
Andrei Liviu Nicolicioiu
Xuecheng Nie
Michael Niemeyer
Simon Niklaus
Christophoros Nikou
David Nilsson
Jifeng Ning
Yuval Nirkin
Li Niu
Yuzhen Niu
Zhenxing Niu
Shohei Nobuhara
Nicoletta Noceti
Hyeonwoo Noh
Junhyug Noh
Mehdi Noroozi
Sotiris Nousias
Valsamis Ntouskos
Matthew O'Toole
Peter Ochs
Ferda Ofli
Seong Joon Oh
Seoung Wug Oh
Iason Oikonomidis
Utkarsh Ojha
Takahiro Okabe
Takayuki Okatani
Fumio Okura
Aude Oliva
Kyle Olszewski

Björn Ommer
Mohamed Omran
Elisabeta Oneata
Michael Opitz
Jose Oramas
Tribhuvanesh Orekondy
Shaul Oron
Sergio Orts-Escolano
Ivan Oseledets
Aljosa Osep
Magnus Oskarsson
Anton Osokin
Martin R. Oswald
Wanli Ouyang
Andrew Owens
Mete Ozay
Mustafa Ozuysal
Eduardo Pérez-Pellitero
Gautam Pai
Dipan Kumar Pal
P. H. Pamplona Savarese
Jinshan Pan
Junting Pan
Xingang Pan
Yingwei Pan
Yannis Panagakis
Rameswar Panda
Guan Pang
Jiahao Pang
Jiangmiao Pang
Tianyu Pang
Sharath Pankanti
Nicolas Papadakis
Dim Papadopoulos
George Papandreou
Toufiq Parag
Shaifali Parashar
Sarah Parisot
Eunhyeok Park
Hyun Soo Park
Jaesik Park
Min-Gyu Park
Taesung Park
Alvaro Parra
C. Alejandro Parraga
Despoina Paschalidou

Nikolaos Passalis
Vishal Patel
Viorica Patraucean
Badri Narayana Patro
Danda Pani Paudel
Sujoy Paul
Georgios Pavlakos
Ioannis Pavlidis
Vladimir Pavlovic
Nick Pears
Kim Steenstrup Pedersen
Selen Pehlivan
Shmuel Peleg
Chao Peng
Houwen Peng
Wen-Hsiao Peng
Xi Peng
Xiaojiang Peng
Xingchao Peng
Yuxin Peng
Federico Perazzi
Juan Camilo Perez
Vishwanath Peri
Federico Pernici
Luca Del Pero
Florent Perronnin
Stavros Petridis
Henning Petzka
Patrick Peursum
Michael Pfeiffer
Hanspeter Pfister
Roman Pflugfelder
Minh Tri Pham
Yongri Piao
David Picard
Tomasz Pieciak
A. J. Piergiovanni
Andrea Pilzer
Pedro O. Pinheiro
Silvia Laura Pintea
Lerrel Pinto
Axel Pinz
Robinson Piramuthu
Fiora Pirri
Leonid Pishchulin
Francesco Pittaluga

Daniel Pizarro
Tobias Plötz
Mirco Planamente
Matteo Poggi
Moacir A. Ponti
Parita Pooj
Fatih Porikli
Horst Possegger
Omid Poursaeed
Ameya Prabhu
Viraj Uday Prabhu
Dilip Prasad
Brian L. Price
True Price
Maria Priisalu
Veronique Prinet
Victor Adrian Prisacariu
Jan Prokaj
Sergey Prokudin
Nicolas Pugeault
Xavier Puig
Albert Pumarola
Pulak Purkait
Senthil Purushwalkam
Charles R. Qi
Hang Qi
Haozhi Qi
Lu Qi
Mengshi Qi
Siyuan Qi
Xiaojuan Qi
Yuankai Qi
Shengju Qian
Xuelin Qian
Siyuan Qiao
Yu Qiao
Jie Qin
Qiang Qiu
Weichao Qiu
Zhaofan Qiu
Kha Gia Quach
Yuhui Quan
Yvain Queau
Julian Quiroga
Faisal Qureshi
Mahdi Rad

Filip Radenovic
Petia Radeva
Venkatesh
  B. Radhakrishnan
Ilija Radosavovic
Noha Radwan
Rahul Raguram
Tanzila Rahman
Amit Raj
Ajit Rajwade
Kandan Ramakrishnan
Santhosh
  K. Ramakrishnan
Srikumar Ramalingam
Ravi Ramamoorthi
Vasili Ramanishka
Ramprasaath R. Selvaraju
Francois Rameau
Visvanathan Ramesh
Santu Rana
Rene Ranftl
Anand Rangarajan
Anurag Ranjan
Viresh Ranjan
Yongming Rao
Carolina Raposo
Vivek Rathod
Sathya N. Ravi
Avinash Ravichandran
Tammy Riklin Raviv
Daniel Rebain
Sylvestre-Alvise Rebuffi
N. Dinesh Reddy
Timo Rehfeld
Paolo Remagnino
Konstantinos Rematas
Edoardo Remelli
Dongwei Ren
Haibing Ren
Jian Ren
Jimmy Ren
Mengye Ren
Weihong Ren
Wenqi Ren
Zhile Ren
Zhongzheng Ren

Zhou Ren
Vijay Rengarajan
Md A. Reza
Farzaneh Rezaeianaran
Hamed R. Tavakoli
Nicholas Rhinehart
Helge Rhodin
Elisa Ricci
Alexander Richard
Eitan Richardson
Elad Richardson
Christian Richardt
Stephan Richter
Gernot Riegler
Daniel Ritchie
Tobias Ritschel
Samuel Rivera
Yong Man Ro
Richard Roberts
Joseph Robinson
Ignacio Rocco
Mrigank Rochan
Emanuele Rodolà
Mikel D. Rodriguez
Giorgio Roffo
Grégory Rogez
Gemma Roig
Javier Romero
Xuejian Rong
Yu Rong
Amir Rosenfeld
Bodo Rosenhahn
Guy Rosman
Arun Ross
Paolo Rota
Peter M. Roth
Anastasios Roussos
Anirban Roy
Sebastien Roy
Aruni RoyChowdhury
Artem Rozantsev
Ognjen Rudovic
Daniel Rueckert
Adria Ruiz
Javier Ruiz-del-solar
Christian Rupprecht

Chris Russell
Dan Ruta
Jongbin Ryu
Ömer Sümer
Alexandre Sablayrolles
Faraz Saeedan
Ryusuke Sagawa
Christos Sagonas
Tonmoy Saikia
Hideo Saito
Kuniaki Saito
Shunsuke Saito
Shunta Saito
Ken Sakurada
Joaquin Salas
Fatemeh Sadat Saleh
Mahdi Saleh
Pouya Samangouei
Leo Sampaio
  Ferraz Ribeiro
Artsiom Olegovich
  Sanakoyeu
Enrique Sanchez
Patsorn Sangkloy
Anush Sankaran
Aswin Sankaranarayanan
Swami Sankaranarayanan
Rodrigo Santa Cruz
Amartya Sanyal
Archana Sapkota
Nikolaos Sarafianos
Jun Sato
Shin'ichi Satoh
Hosnieh Sattar
Arman Savran
Manolis Savva
Alexander Sax
Hanno Scharr
Simone Schaub-Meyer
Konrad Schindler
Dmitrij Schlesinger
Uwe Schmidt
Dirk Schnieders
Björn Schuller
Samuel Schulter
Idan Schwartz

William Robson Schwartz
Alex Schwing
Sinisa Segvic
Lorenzo Seidenari
Pradeep Sen
Ozan Sener
Soumyadip Sengupta
Arda Senocak
Mojtaba Seyedhosseini
Shishir Shah
Shital Shah
Sohil Atul Shah
Tamar Rott Shaham
Huasong Shan
Qi Shan
Shiguang Shan
Jing Shao
Roman Shapovalov
Gaurav Sharma
Vivek Sharma
Viktoriia Sharmanska
Dongyu She
Sumit Shekhar
Evan Shelhamer
Chengyao Shen
Chunhua Shen
Falong Shen
Jie Shen
Li Shen
Liyue Shen
Shuhan Shen
Tianwei Shen
Wei Shen
William B. Shen
Yantao Shen
Ying Shen
Yiru Shen
Yujun Shen
Yuming Shen
Zhiqiang Shen
Ziyi Shen
Lu Sheng
Yu Sheng
Rakshith Shetty
Baoguang Shi
Guangming Shi

Hailin Shi
Miaojing Shi
Yemin Shi
Zhenmei Shi
Zhiyuan Shi
Kevin Jonathan Shih
Shiliang Shiliang
Hyunjung Shim
Atsushi Shimada
Nobutaka Shimada
Daeyun Shin
Young Min Shin
Koichi Shinoda
Konstantin Shmelkov
Michael Zheng Shou
Abhinav Shrivastava
Tianmin Shu
Zhixin Shu
Hong-Han Shuai
Pushkar Shukla
Christian Siagian
Mennatullah M. Siam
Kaleem Siddiqi
Karan Sikka
Jae-Young Sim
Christian Simon
Martin Simonovsky
Dheeraj Singaraju
Bharat Singh
Gurkirt Singh
Krishna Kumar Singh
Maneesh Kumar Singh
Richa Singh
Saurabh Singh
Suriya Singh
Vikas Singh
Sudipta N. Sinha
Vincent Sitzmann
Josef Sivic
Gregory Slabaugh
Miroslava Slavcheva
Ron Slossberg
Brandon Smith
Kevin Smith
Vladimir Smutny
Noah Snavely

Roger
  D. Soberanis-Mukul
Kihyuk Sohn
Francesco Solera
Eric Sommerlade
Sanghyun Son
Byung Cheol Song
Chunfeng Song
Dongjin Song
Jiaming Song
Jie Song
Jifei Song
Jingkuan Song
Mingli Song
Shiyu Song
Shuran Song
Xiao Song
Yafei Song
Yale Song
Yang Song
Yi-Zhe Song
Yibing Song
Humberto Sossa
Cesar de Souza
Adrian Spurr
Srinath Sridhar
Suraj Srinivas
Pratul P. Srinivasan
Anuj Srivastava
Tania Stathaki
Christopher Stauffer
Simon Stent
Rainer Stiefelhagen
Pierre Stock
Julian Straub
Jonathan C. Stroud
Joerg Stueckler
Jan Stuehmer
David Stutz
Chi Su
Hang Su
Jong-Chyi Su
Shuochen Su
Yu-Chuan Su
Ramanathan Subramanian
Yusuke Sugano

Masanori Suganuma
Yumin Suh
Mohammed Suhail
Yao Sui
Heung-Il Suk
Josephine Sullivan
Baochen Sun
Chen Sun
Chong Sun
Deqing Sun
Jin Sun
Liang Sun
Lin Sun
Qianru Sun
Shao-Hua Sun
Shuyang Sun
Weiwei Sun
Wenxiu Sun
Xiaoshuai Sun
Xiaoxiao Sun
Xingyuan Sun
Yifan Sun
Zhun Sun
Sabine Susstrunk
David Suter
Supasorn Suwajanakorn
Tomas Svoboda
Eran Swears
Paul Swoboda
Attila Szabo
Richard Szeliski
Duy-Nguyen Ta
Andrea Tagliasacchi
Yuichi Taguchi
Ying Tai
Keita Takahashi
Kouske Takahashi
Jun Takamatsu
Hugues Talbot
Toru Tamaki
Chaowei Tan
Fuwen Tan
Mingkui Tan
Mingxing Tan
Qingyang Tan
Robby T. Tan

Xiaoyang Tan
Kenichiro Tanaka
Masayuki Tanaka
Chang Tang
Chengzhou Tang
Danhang Tang
Ming Tang
Peng Tang
Qingming Tang
Wei Tang
Xu Tang
Yansong Tang
Youbao Tang
Yuxing Tang
Zhiqiang Tang
Tatsunori Taniai
Junli Tao
Xin Tao
Makarand Tapaswi
Jean-Philippe Tarel
Lyne Tchapmi
Zachary Teed
Bugra Tekin
Damien Teney
Ayush Tewari
Christian Theobalt
Christopher Thomas
Diego Thomas
Jim Thomas
Rajat Mani Thomas
Xinmei Tian
Yapeng Tian
Yingli Tian
Yonglong Tian
Zhi Tian
Zhuotao Tian
Kinh Tieu
Joseph Tighe
Massimo Tistarelli
Matthew Toews
Carl Toft
Pavel Tokmakov
Federico Tombari
Chetan Tonde
Yan Tong
Alessio Tonioni

Andrea Torsello
Fabio Tosi
Du Tran
Luan Tran
Ngoc-Trung Tran
Quan Hung Tran
Truyen Tran
Rudolph Triebel
Martin Trimmel
Shashank Tripathi
Subarna Tripathi
Leonardo Trujillo
Eduard Trulls
Tomasz Trzcinski
Sam Tsai
Yi-Hsuan Tsai
Hung-Yu Tseng
Stavros Tsogkas
Aggeliki Tsoli
Devis Tuia
Shubham Tulsiani
Sergey Tulyakov
Frederick Tung
Tony Tung
Daniyar Turmukhambetov
Ambrish Tyagi
Radim Tylecek
Christos Tzelepis
Georgios Tzimiropoulos
Dimitrios Tzionas
Seiichi Uchida
Norimichi Ukita
Dmitry Ulyanov
Martin Urschler
Yoshitaka Ushiku
Ben Usman
Alexander Vakhitov
Julien P. C. Valentin
Jack Valmadre
Ernest Valveny
Joost van de Weijer
Jan van Gemert
Koen Van Leemput
Gul Varol
Sebastiano Vascon
M. Alex O. Vasilescu

Subeesh Vasu
Mayank Vatsa
David Vazquez
Javier Vazquez-Corral
Ashok Veeraraghavan
Erik Velasco-Salido
Raviteja Vemulapalli
Jonathan Ventura
Manisha Verma
Roberto Vezzani
Ruben Villegas
Minh Vo
MinhDuc Vo
Nam Vo
Michele Volpi
Riccardo Volpi
Carl Vondrick
Konstantinos Vougioukas
Tuan-Hung Vu
Sven Wachsmuth
Neal Wadhwa
Catherine Wah
Jacob C. Walker
Thomas S. A. Wallis
Chengde Wan
Jun Wan
Liang Wan
Renjie Wan
Baoyuan Wang
Boyu Wang
Cheng Wang
Chu Wang
Chuan Wang
Chunyu Wang
Dequan Wang
Di Wang
Dilin Wang
Dong Wang
Fang Wang
Guanzhi Wang
Guoyin Wang
Hanzi Wang
Hao Wang
He Wang
Heng Wang
Hongcheng Wang

Hongxing Wang
Hua Wang
Jian Wang
Jingbo Wang
Jinglu Wang
Jingya Wang
Jinjun Wang
Jinqiao Wang
Jue Wang
Ke Wang
Keze Wang
Le Wang
Lei Wang
Lezi Wang
Li Wang
Liang Wang
Lijun Wang
Limin Wang
Linwei Wang
Lizhi Wang
Mengjiao Wang
Mingzhe Wang
Minsi Wang
Naiyan Wang
Nannan Wang
Ning Wang
Oliver Wang
Pei Wang
Peng Wang
Pichao Wang
Qi Wang
Qian Wang
Qiaosong Wang
Qifei Wang
Qilong Wang
Qing Wang
Qingzhong Wang
Quan Wang
Rui Wang
Ruiping Wang
Ruixing Wang
Shangfei Wang
Shenlong Wang
Shiyao Wang
Shuhui Wang
Song Wang

Tao Wang
Tianlu Wang
Tiantian Wang
Ting-chun Wang
Tingwu Wang
Wei Wang
Weiyue Wang
Wenguan Wang
Wenlin Wang
Wenqi Wang
Xiang Wang
Xiaobo Wang
Xiaofang Wang
Xiaoling Wang
Xiaolong Wang
Xiaosong Wang
Xiaoyu Wang
Xin Eric Wang
Xinchao Wang
Xinggang Wang
Xintao Wang
Yali Wang
Yan Wang
Yang Wang
Yangang Wang
Yaxing Wang
Yi Wang
Yida Wang
Yilin Wang
Yiming Wang
Yisen Wang
Yongtao Wang
Yu-Xiong Wang
Yue Wang
Yujiang Wang
Yunbo Wang
Yunhe Wang
Zengmao Wang
Zhangyang Wang
Zhaowen Wang
Zhe Wang
Zhecan Wang
Zheng Wang
Zhixiang Wang
Zilei Wang
Jianqiao Wangni

Anne S. Wannenwetsch
Jan Dirk Wegner
Scott Wehrwein
Donglai Wei
Kaixuan Wei
Longhui Wei
Pengxu Wei
Ping Wei
Qi Wei
Shih-En Wei
Xing Wei
Yunchao Wei
Zijun Wei
Jerod Weinman
Michael Weinmann
Philippe Weinzaepfel
Yair Weiss
Bihan Wen
Longyin Wen
Wei Wen
Junwu Weng
Tsui-Wei Weng
Xinshuo Weng
Eric Wengrowski
Tomas Werner
Gordon Wetzstein
Tobias Weyand
Patrick Wieschollek
Maggie Wigness
Erik Wijmans
Richard Wildes
Olivia Wiles
Chris Williams
Williem Williem
Kyle Wilson
Calden Wloka
Nicolai Wojke
Christian Wolf
Yongkang Wong
Sanghyun Woo
Scott Workman
Baoyuan Wu
Bichen Wu
Chao-Yuan Wu
Huikai Wu
Jiajun Wu

Jialin Wu
Jiaxiang Wu
Jiqing Wu
Jonathan Wu
Lifang Wu
Qi Wu
Qiang Wu
Ruizheng Wu
Shangzhe Wu
Shun-Cheng Wu
Tianfu Wu
Wayne Wu
Wenxuan Wu
Xiao Wu
Xiaohe Wu
Xinxiao Wu
Yang Wu
Yi Wu
Yiming Wu
Ying Nian Wu
Yue Wu
Zheng Wu
Zhenyu Wu
Zhirong Wu
Zuxuan Wu
Stefanie Wuhrer
Jonas Wulff
Changqun Xia
Fangting Xia
Fei Xia
Gui-Song Xia
Lu Xia
Xide Xia
Yin Xia
Yingce Xia
Yongqin Xian
Lei Xiang
Shiming Xiang
Bin Xiao
Fanyi Xiao
Guobao Xiao
Huaxin Xiao
Taihong Xiao
Tete Xiao
Tong Xiao
Wang Xiao

Yang Xiao
Cihang Xie
Guosen Xie
Jianwen Xie
Lingxi Xie
Sirui Xie
Weidi Xie
Wenxuan Xie
Xiaohua Xie
Fuyong Xing
Jun Xing
Junliang Xing
Bo Xiong
Peixi Xiong
Yu Xiong
Yuanjun Xiong
Zhiwei Xiong
Chang Xu
Chenliang Xu
Dan Xu
Danfei Xu
Hang Xu
Hongteng Xu
Huijuan Xu
Jingwei Xu
Jun Xu
Kai Xu
Mengmeng Xu
Mingze Xu
Qianqian Xu
Ran Xu
Weijian Xu
Xiangyu Xu
Xiaogang Xu
Xing Xu
Xun Xu
Yanyu Xu
Yichao Xu
Yong Xu
Yongchao Xu
Yuanlu Xu
Zenglin Xu
Zheng Xu
Chuhui Xue
Jia Xue
Nan Xue

Tianfan Xue

Xiangyang Xue

Abhay Yadav

Yasushi Yagi

I. Zeki Yalniz

Kota Yamaguchi

Toshihiko Yamasaki

Takayoshi Yamashita

Junchi Yan

Ke Yan

Qingan Yan

Sijie Yan

Xinchen Yan

Yan Yan

Yichao Yan

Zhicheng Yan

Keiji Yanai

Bin Yang

Ceyuan Yang

Dawei Yang

Dong Yang

Fan Yang

Guandao Yang

Guorun Yang

Haichuan Yang

Hao Yang

Jianwei Yang

Jiaolong Yang

Jie Yang

Jing Yang

Kaiyu Yang

Linjie Yang

Meng Yang

Michael Ying Yang

Nan Yang

Shuai Yang

Shuo Yang

Tianyu Yang

Tien-Ju Yang

Tsun-Yi Yang

Wei Yang

Wenhan Yang

Xiao Yang

Xiaodong Yang

Xin Yang

Yan Yang

Yanchao Yang

Yee Hong Yang

Yezhou Yang

Zhenheng Yang

Anbang Yao

Angela Yao

Cong Yao

Jian Yao

Li Yao

Ting Yao

Yao Yao

Zhewei Yao

Chengxi Ye

Jianbo Ye

Keren Ye

Linwei Ye

Mang Ye

Mao Ye

Qi Ye

Qixiang Ye

Mei-Chen Yeh

Raymond Yeh

Yu-Ying Yeh

Sai-Kit Yeung

Serena Yeung

Kwang Moo Yi

Li Yi

Renjiao Yi

Alper Yilmaz

Junho Yim

Lijun Yin

Weidong Yin

Xi Yin

Zhichao Yin

Tatsuya Yokota

Ryo Yonetani

Donggeun Yoo

Jae Shin Yoon

Ju Hong Yoon

Sung-eui Yoon

Laurent Younes

Changqian Yu

Fisher Yu

Gang Yu

Jiahui Yu

Kaicheng Yu

Ke Yu

Lequan Yu

Ning Yu

Qian Yu

Ronald Yu

Ruichi Yu

Shoou-I Yu

Tao Yu

Tianshu Yu

Xiang Yu

Xin Yu

Xiyu Yu

Youngjae Yu

Yu Yu

Zhiding Yu

Chunfeng Yuan

Ganzhao Yuan

Jinwei Yuan

Lu Yuan

Quan Yuan

Shanxin Yuan

Tongtong Yuan

Wenjia Yuan

Ye Yuan

Yuan Yuan

Yuhui Yuan

Huanjing Yue

Xiangyu Yue

Ersin Yumer

Sergey Zagoruyko

Egor Zakharov

Amir Zamir

Andrei Zanfir

Mihai Zanfir

Pablo Zegers

Bernhard Zeisl

John S. Zelek

Niclas Zeller

Huayi Zeng

Jiabei Zeng

Wenjun Zeng

Yu Zeng

Xiaohua Zhai

Fangneng Zhan

Huangying Zhan

Kun Zhan

Xiaohang Zhan
Baochang Zhang
Bowen Zhang
Cecilia Zhang
Changqing Zhang
Chao Zhang
Chengquan Zhang
Chi Zhang
Chongyang Zhang
Dingwen Zhang
Dong Zhang
Feihu Zhang
Hang Zhang
Hanwang Zhang
Hao Zhang
He Zhang
Hongguang Zhang
Hua Zhang
Ji Zhang
Jianguo Zhang
Jianming Zhang
Jiawei Zhang
Jie Zhang
Jing Zhang
Juyong Zhang
Kai Zhang
Kaipeng Zhang
Ke Zhang
Le Zhang
Lei Zhang
Li Zhang
Lihe Zhang
Linguang Zhang
Lu Zhang
Mi Zhang
Mingda Zhang
Peng Zhang
Pingping Zhang
Qian Zhang
Qilin Zhang
Quanshi Zhang
Richard Zhang
Rui Zhang
Runze Zhang
Shengping Zhang
Shifeng Zhang

Shuai Zhang
Songyang Zhang
Tao Zhang
Ting Zhang
Tong Zhang
Wayne Zhang
Wei Zhang
Weizhong Zhang
Wenwei Zhang
Xiangyu Zhang
Xiaolin Zhang
Xiaopeng Zhang
Xiaoqin Zhang
Xiuming Zhang
Ya Zhang
Yang Zhang
Yimin Zhang
Yinda Zhang
Ying Zhang
Yongfei Zhang
Yu Zhang
Yulun Zhang
Yunhua Zhang
Yuting Zhang
Zhanpeng Zhang
Zhao Zhang
Zhaoxiang Zhang
Zhen Zhang
Zheng Zhang
Zhifei Zhang
Zhijin Zhang
Zhishuai Zhang
Ziming Zhang
Bo Zhao
Chen Zhao
Fang Zhao
Haiyu Zhao
Han Zhao
Hang Zhao
Hengshuang Zhao
Jian Zhao
Kai Zhao
Liang Zhao
Long Zhao
Qian Zhao
Qibin Zhao

Qijun Zhao
Rui Zhao
Shenglin Zhao
Sicheng Zhao
Tianyi Zhao
Wenda Zhao
Xiangyun Zhao
Xin Zhao
Yang Zhao
Yue Zhao
Zhichen Zhao
Zijing Zhao
Xiantong Zhen
Chuanxia Zheng
Feng Zheng
Haiyong Zheng
Jia Zheng
Kang Zheng
Shuai Kyle Zheng
Wei-Shi Zheng
Yinqiang Zheng
Zerong Zheng
Zhedong Zheng
Zilong Zheng
Bineng Zhong
Fangwei Zhong
Guangyu Zhong
Yiran Zhong
Yujie Zhong
Zhun Zhong
Chunluan Zhou
Huiyu Zhou
Jiahuan Zhou
Jun Zhou
Lei Zhou
Luowei Zhou
Luping Zhou
Mo Zhou
Ning Zhou
Pan Zhou
Peng Zhou
Qianyi Zhou
S. Kevin Zhou
Sanping Zhou
Wengang Zhou
Xingyi Zhou

Yanzhao Zhou
Yi Zhou
Yin Zhou
Yipin Zhou
Yuyin Zhou
Zihan Zhou
Alex Zihao Zhu
Chenchen Zhu
Feng Zhu
Guangming Zhu
Ji Zhu
Jun-Yan Zhu
Lei Zhu
Linchao Zhu
Rui Zhu
Shizhan Zhu
Tyler Lixuan Zhu

Wei Zhu
Xiangyu Zhu
Xinge Zhu
Xizhou Zhu
Yanjun Zhu
Yi Zhu
Yixin Zhu
Yizhe Zhu
Yousong Zhu
Zhe Zhu
Zhen Zhu
Zheng Zhu
Zhenyao Zhu
Zhihui Zhu
Zhuotun Zhu
Bingbing Zhuang
Wei Zhuo

Christian Zimmermann
Karel Zimmermann
Larry Zitnick
Mohammadreza
    Zolfaghari
Maria Zontak
Daniel Zoran
Changqing Zou
Chuhang Zou
Danping Zou
Qi Zou
Yang Zou
Yuliang Zou
Georgios Zoumpourlis
Wangmeng Zuo
Xinxin Zuo

## Additional Reviewers

Victoria Fernandez
    Abrevaya
Maya Aghaei
Allam Allam
Christine
    Allen-Blanchette
Nicolas Aziere
Assia Benbihi
Neha Bhargava
Bharat Lal Bhatnagar
Joanna Bitton
Judy Borowski
Amine Bourki
Romain Brégier
Tali Brayer
Sebastian Bujwid
Andrea Burns
Yun-Hao Cao
Yuning Chai
Xiaojun Chang
Bo Chen
Shuo Chen
Zhixiang Chen
Junsuk Choe
Hung-Kuo Chu

Jonathan P. Crall
Kenan Dai
Lucas Deecke
Karan Desai
Prithviraj Dhar
Jing Dong
Wei Dong
Turan Kaan Elgin
Francis Engelmann
Erik Englesson
Fartash Faghri
Zicong Fan
Yang Fu
Risheek Garrepalli
Yifan Ge
Marco Godi
Helmut Grabner
Shuxuan Guo
Jianfeng He
Zhezhi He
Samitha Herath
Chih-Hui Ho
Yicong Hong
Vincent Tao Hu
Julio Hurtado

Jaedong Hwang
Andrey Ignatov
Muhammad
    Abdullah Jamal
Saumya Jetley
Meiguang Jin
Jeff Johnson
Minsoo Kang
Saeed Khorram
Mohammad Rami Koujan
Nilesh Kulkarni
Sudhakar Kumawat
Abdelhak Lemkhenter
Alexander Levine
Jiachen Li
Jing Li
Jun Li
Yi Li
Liang Liao
Ruochen Liao
Tzu-Heng Lin
Phillip Lippe
Bao-di Liu
Bo Liu
Fangchen Liu

Hanxiao Liu
Hongyu Liu
Huidong Liu
Miao Liu
Xinxin Liu
Yongfei Liu
Yu-Lun Liu
Amir Livne
Tiange Luo
Wei Ma
Xiaoxuan Ma
Ioannis Marras
Georg Martius
Effrosyni Mavroudi
Tim Meinhardt
Givi Meishvili
Meng Meng
Zihang Meng
Zhongqi Miao
Gyeongsik Moon
Khoi Nguyen
Yung-Kyun Noh
Antonio Norelli
Jaeyoo Park
Alexander Pashevich
Mandela Patrick
Mary Phuong
Bingqiao Qian
Yu Qiao
Zhen Qiao
Sai Saketh Rambhatla
Aniket Roy
Amelie Royer
Parikshit Vishwas
    Sakurikar
Mark Sandler
Mert Bülent Sarıyıldız
Tanner Schmidt
Anshul B. Shah

Ketul Shah
Rajvi Shah
Hengcan Shi
Xiangxi Shi
Yujiao Shi
William A. P. Smith
Guoxian Song
Robin Strudel
Abby Stylianou
Xinwei Sun
Reuben Tan
Qingyi Tao
Kedar S. Tatwawadi
Anh Tuan Tran
Son Dinh Tran
Eleni Triantafillou
Aristeidis Tsitiridis
Md Zasim Uddin
Andrea Vedaldi
Evangelos Ververas
Vidit Vidit
Paul Voigtlaender
Bo Wan
Huanyu Wang
Huiyu Wang
Junqiu Wang
Pengxiao Wang
Tai Wang
Xinyao Wang
Tomoki Watanabe
Mark Weber
Xi Wei
Botong Wu
James Wu
Jiamin Wu
Rujie Wu
Yu Wu
Rongchang Xie
Wei Xiong

Yunyang Xiong
An Xu
Chi Xu
Yinghao Xu
Fei Xue
Tingyun Yan
Zike Yan
Chao Yang
Heran Yang
Ren Yang
Wenfei Yang
Xu Yang
Rajeev Yasarla
Shaokai Ye
Yufei Ye
Kun Yi
Haichao Yu
Hanchao Yu
Ruixuan Yu
Liangzhe Yuan
Chen-Lin Zhang
Fandong Zhang
Tianyi Zhang
Yang Zhang
Yiyi Zhang
Yongshun Zhang
Yu Zhang
Zhiwei Zhang
Jiaojiao Zhao
Yipu Zhao
Xingjian Zhen
Haizhong Zheng
Tiancheng Zhi
Chengju Zhou
Hao Zhou
Hao Zhu
Alexander Zimin

# Contents – Part VI

# Practical Deep Raw Image Denoising on Mobile Devices

Yuzhi Wang[1,2]($\boxtimes$), Haibin Huang[2], Qin Xu[2], Jiaming Liu[2], Yiqun Liu[1], and Jue Wang[2]

[1] Tsinghua University, Beijing, China
justin.w.xd@gmail.com
[2] Megvii Technology, Beijing, China

**Abstract.** Deep learning-based image denoising approaches have been extensively studied in recent years, prevailing in many public benchmark datasets. However, the stat-of-the-art networks are computationally too expensive to be directly applied on mobile devices. In this work, we propose a light-weight, efficient neural network-based raw image denoiser that runs smoothly on mainstream mobile devices, and produces high quality denoising results. Our key insights are twofold: (1) by measuring and estimating sensor noise level, a smaller network trained on synthetic sensor-specific data can out-perform larger ones trained on general data; (2) the large noise level variation under different ISO settings can be removed by a novel *k-Sigma Transform*, allowing a small network to efficiently handle a wide range of noise levels. We conduct extensive experiments to demonstrate the efficiency and accuracy of our approach. Our proposed mobile-friendly denoising model runs at ~70 ms per megapixel on Qualcomm Snapdragon 855 chipset, and it is the basis of the night shot feature of several flagship smartphones released in 2019.

## 1 Introduction

Smartphones have become the go-to devices for consumer photography in recent years. Compared with DSLR cameras, images captured with mobile devices are more easily contaminated with higher level of noise due to the use of relatively low-cost sensors and lenses, especially in low-light scenarios.

Despite decades of development in image denoising technologies, it remains challenging to restore high quality images from extremely noisy ones on mobile devices. Recently, deep neural network (DNN) based denoising methods [10,21,30,36–38,42] have achieved tremendous success and outperformed

This work is supported by The National Key Research and Development Program of China under Grant 2018YFC0831700.

**Electronic supplementary material** The online version of this chapter (https://doi.org/10.1007/978-3-030-58539-6_1) contains supplementary material, which is available to authorized users.

A. Vedaldi et al. (Eds.): ECCV 2020, LNCS 12351, pp. 1–16, 2020.
https://doi.org/10.1007/978-3-030-58539-6_1

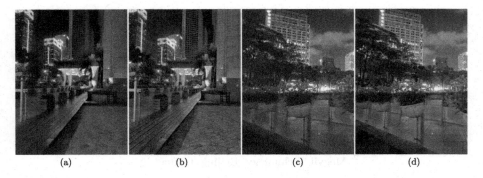

(a)            (b)            (c)            (d)

**Fig. 1.** Our proposed denoising method can run smoothly on smartphones with high quality noise reduction even in low-light conditions (see (b), (d)). In contrast, the default ISP image denoiser produces images with over-smoothed high texture regions (e.g. ground in (a)) and noisy smooth regions (e.g. sky in (c)).

most traditional methods [12,18,39,40,43]. It is however not practical to directly deploy these heavy-weight DNNs on mobile devices due to the limited computational resources available on them.

In this work, we propose a simple yet efficient approach for deep raw image denoising. It can run efficiently on off-the-shelf smartphones with high quality noise reduction. Our key observation is that the noise characteristics for a specific sensor model are consistent and can be measured with sufficient accuracy. By capturing and modeling sensor noise, we can generate synthetic datasets with clean and noisy image pairs, and train a light-weight neural network on them. The trained model remains highly effective on real images captured by the same sensor (i.e. the same smartphone model). Furthermore, based on the parametric sensor noise model, we derive a unique linear transform in luminance space, dubbed as k-Sigma Transform, that maps noisy images captured under different ISO settings into an ISO-invariant signal-noise space, allowing a single network to handle different noise levels in different scenes. We show that this approach is not only theoretically elegant, but in practice is more efficient than training a separate model for each ISO setting, or having one large model trained on images with different noise levels.

To summarize, the main contributions of this work are as follows:

- A systematic approach to estimate sensor noise and train a sensor-specific denoising neural network using properly constructed synthetic data.
- A novel k-Sigma Transform to map noisy images under different ISO settings into a ISO-invariant signal-noise space. Instead of training separate models per ISO or a larger model to cover the variations, the proposed transform allows a single small network trained in this space to handle images with different noise levels.
- A mobile-friendly network architecture for efficient image denoising. We provide in-depth analysis and comparison with different network architectures and denoising methods, demonstrating that our method has compatible

performance with state-of-the-art approaches with significantly less computational resources.

To the best of our knowledge, our solution is the first practical deep-learning-based image denoising approach that has satisfactory efficiency and accuracy on mobile devices. In Fig. 1 we show examplar images captured by an off-the-shelf smartphone that use our approach in low-light photography. Compared with the default ISP image denoising technique, our results contain much more fine details of the scene.

## 2 Related Work

Image denoising is a fundamental task in image processing and computer vision. Classical methods often rely on using sparse image priors, such as non-local means (NLM) [6], sparse coding [2,13,28], 3D transform-domain filtering (BM3D) [12], and others [18,32]. Among them BM3D is usually deemed as the leading method considering its accuracy and robustness. Most of these methods are designed for general noise and do not take advantage of known sensor noise characteristics. Their algorithmic complexity is usually high, making full-fledged implementation difficult on smartphones.

With the recent development of convolutional neural networks (CNNs), training end-to-end denoising CNNs has gained considerable attention. Earlier work that uses multi-layer perceptron (MLP) [7] has achieved comparable results with BM3D. Further improvements have been achieved with the introduction of more advanced network architectures, resulting in a large number of CNN-based denoising methods [10,21,23,30,36–38,41]. These works are primarily focused on novel network structures for improving the accuracy, without paying much attention to their adaptability to mobile devices.

Our work focuses on denoising raw image, i.e., images read out from the sensor in the raw Bayer format before demosaicing and other ISP-processing. On the recently proposed public raw image denoising benchmark datasets [1,3,8], CNN-based methods [8,17,20] have achieved the best results. It is however a very tedious work to construct such high quality real datasets with clean and noisy image pairs. Thus, the problem of synthesizing realistic image noise for training has also been extensively studied, including Gaussian-Poisson noise[16, 27], Gaussian Mixture Model (GMM) [44], in-camera process simulation [25,34], GAN-generated noises [9] and so on. It has been shown that networks properly trained from the synthetic data can generalize well to real data [5,42].

The existing best practice for raw image denoising on mobile devices is to capture and merge multiple frames [19,24,31]. These methods generally require accurate and fast image alignment, which is hard to achieve when moving objects present in the scene. Furthermore, when noise level is high, averaging multiple frames can reduce, but not completely remove the noise, leading to unsatisfactory results. To the best of our knowledge, our proposed method is the first single frame, deep learning-based raw image denoiser specifically designed for mobile devices.

## 3   Method

In this section, we first revisit the general ISO-dependent noise model of camera sensor, and then describe how to estimate noise parameters given a new sensor. We further show how to synthesize ISO-independent training data using the proposed k-Sigma Transform, and use it to train a small neural network that can handle a wide range of noise levels.

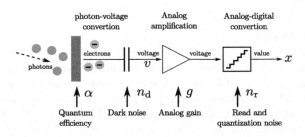

**Fig. 2.** Photon transfer pipeline: multiple noise sources like shot noise, read-out noise and thermal noise are involved along the camera pipeline. Check [14] for more details.

### 3.1   The Noise Model

A camera sensor converts the photons hitting the pixel area during the exposure time into a digitized luminance map. As shown in the photon transfer pipeline shown in Fig. 2, this process contains multiple stages, where each stage introduces specific noise. Let us first consider an ideal system with no noise. Under the linear camera model, at each pixel, the sensor conversion is a linear amplification as:

$$x^* = g\alpha u^*, \tag{1}$$

where $u^*$ is the expected number of photons hitting the pixel area, $\alpha$ is the quantum efficiency factor and $g$ is the analog gain. Now considering the system noise in each step of the pipeline in Fig. 2, we have:

$$x = g(\alpha u + n_{\mathrm{d}}) + n_{\mathrm{r}}, \tag{2}$$

where $u$ denotes the actual collected amount of photons, and $n_d \sim \mathcal{N}(0, \sigma_d^2)$ and $n_r \sim \mathcal{N}(0, \sigma_r^2)$ are Gaussian noise before and after applying the analog gain. Furthermore, it is demonstrated in [14] that $u$ obeys a Poisson distribution of $u^*$, given by

$$u \sim \mathcal{P}(u^*). \tag{3}$$

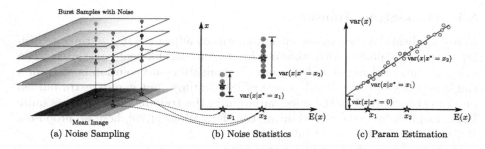

**Fig. 3.** Noise parameter estimation with a burst series of raw images of a static grayscale chart.

Combining Eq. (1) to Eq. (3), we have:

$$x \sim (g\alpha)\mathcal{P}(\frac{x^*}{g\alpha}) + \mathcal{N}(0, g^2\sigma_d^2 + \sigma_r^2). \tag{4}$$

This is consistent with the Poisson-Gaussian noise model that has been extensively studied in previous work [16,27]. This formulation can be further simplified by replacing $k = g\alpha$ and $\sigma^2 = g^2\sigma_d^2 + \sigma_r^2$:

$$x \sim k\mathcal{P}(\frac{x^*}{k}) + \mathcal{N}(0, \sigma^2). \tag{5}$$

Note that both $k$ and $\sigma^2$ are related to $g$, which is determined by the ISO setting of the camera.

## 3.2 Parameter Estimation

To sample the distribution described in Eq. (5), we need an accurate estimation of $k$ and $\sigma$ under a specified ISO setting of a specific sensor. Luckily, as we check the mean and variance over $x$, shown in Eq. (6), we can turn it into the following linear regression problem:

$$\begin{cases} \mathrm{E}(x) &= x^*, \\ \mathrm{Var}(x) &= kx^* + \sigma^2. \end{cases} \tag{6}$$

Similar to [15], we capture a series of raw images of a static grayscale chart in burst mode, depicted in Fig. 3a, and compute $\mathrm{E}(x)$ from the series of luminance values at the same pixel location. Next, as shown in Fig. 3b, we bracket all pixels that have the same estimated luminance, and compute $\mathrm{Var}(x)$ from them. A linear regression is then applied to find the optimal estimation of $k$ and $\sigma^2$, illustrated in Fig. 3c.

### 3.3   The k-Sigma Transform

In real applications the camera will automatically adjust the ISO settings according to the scene illumination, thus one has to consider different noise levels when training the denoising neural network. A straightforward solution is to train a single network to cover a wide range of ISO settings, but it puts extra burden on the network itself as the noise variation in the training data becomes quite large. Inspired by variance stabilizing transformations [4,29], here we propose a k-Sigma Transform to avoid this problem.

Specifically, we define a linear transform

$$f(x) = \frac{x}{k} + \frac{\sigma^2}{k^2}. \tag{7}$$

According to our noise model of Eq. (5),

$$f(x) \sim \mathcal{P}(\frac{x^*}{k}) + \mathcal{N}(\frac{\sigma^2}{k^2}, \frac{\sigma^2}{k^2}). \tag{8}$$

To analyze this distribution, a usual simplification is to treat the Poisson distribution $\mathcal{P}(\lambda)$ as a Gaussian distribution of $\mathcal{N}(\lambda, \lambda)$ [16]. Therefore:

$$
\begin{aligned}
&P(\frac{x^*}{k}) + \mathcal{N}(\frac{\sigma^2}{k^2}, \frac{\sigma^2}{k^2}) \\
&\approx \mathcal{N}(\frac{x^*}{k}, \frac{x^*}{k}) + \mathcal{N}(\frac{\sigma^2}{k^2}, \frac{\sigma^2}{k^2}) \\
&= \mathcal{N}(\frac{x^*}{k} + \frac{\sigma^2}{k^2}, \frac{x^*}{k} + \frac{\sigma^2}{k^2}) \\
&= \mathcal{N}[f(x^*), f(x^*)].
\end{aligned}
\tag{9}
$$

Combining Eq. (8) and Eq. (9), the approximate distribution of $f(x)$ is:

$$f(x) \sim \mathcal{N}[f(x^*), f(x^*)]. \tag{10}$$

Equation (10) indicates that the distribution of $f(x)$ only depends on $f(x^*)$. As shown in Fig. 4, we can train a single network that takes $f(x)$ as input and outputs $f(\hat{x}^*)$ as an estimation of $f(x^*)$. The estimated true image value $x^*$ can then be computed by applying the inverted k-Sigma Transform $f^{-1}(\cdot)$ to $f(\hat{x}^*)$. In other words, we apply ISO-dependent transforms to the input and output of the neural network, so that the network can be trained using normalized data without considering the ISO setting.

## 4   Learning to Denoise

### 4.1   Mobile-Friendly Network Architecture

We further introduce a mobile-friendly convolutional neural network for image denoising, as shown in Fig. 5. We use a U-Net-like [33] architecture with 4 encoder and 4 decoder stages with skip connections, illustrated in Fig. 5a.

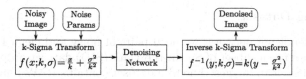

**Fig. 4.** The pipeline of running ISO-independent denoising network with k-Sigma Transform.

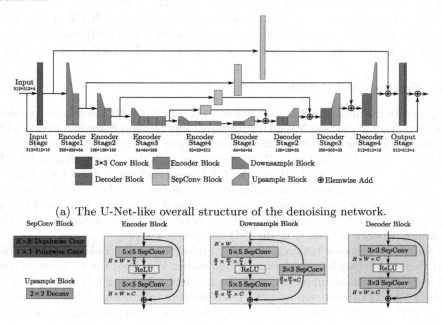

(a) The U-Net-like overall structure of the denoising network.

(b) Detailed stucture of network blocks.

**Fig. 5.** The architecture of the proposed denoising network.

Figure 5b depicts the detailed structures of the network blocks. Specifically, in order to run on mobile devices, we use separable-conv [11] in all encoder and decoder stages to reduce the computation cost, and normal dense convolution layers are only used in the input and output stage. In encoders, we use $5 \times 5$ kernel size to increase receptive field and decrease network depth, and downsample feature maps with stride-2 convolutions. In decoder, we only use $3 \times 3$-speconv and upsample feature maps with $2 \times 2$ deconvolutions. The inputs of each encoder stages are combined into its corresponding decoder stage by element-wise adding, a $3 \times 3$-speconv is adopted in the skip connect to match the channel shape. Finally, the last convolution layer outputs a residual added to the input image as the denoising result.

## 4.2   Training Dataset

To train our denoising network, we need pairs of noisy and clean RAW images. In this paper, we use a subset of See-in-the-Dark (SID) dataset proposed in [8] as the ground truth clean images. The SID dataset contains RAW images captured from a Sony $\alpha$7s II and a Fujifilm X-T2 camera, we choose the 10 s and 30 s long-exposure subset captured by the Sony $\alpha$7s II camera, and manually take out those with visible noise, leaving 214 high quality RAW images.

According to our noise model described in Sect. 3, if clean RAW images were available, we can synthesize noisy images by sampling from a Poisson-Gaussian distribution with estimated noise parameters measured from the target sensor.

## 4.3   Settings and Details

To generate training samples, we randomly crop $1024 \times 1024$-sized bayer patches from the original dataset. We adopt the bayer-aug method described in [26] with random horizontal and vertical flipping and ensure the input bayer pattern is in R-G-G-B order. We then pack the bayer image to $512 \times 512 \times 4$-shaped RGGB tensor. We also randomly adjust the brightness and contrast of the cropped images for data augmentation. Noisy images are then synthesized according to the noise model, with noise parameters of randomly selected ISO value. Finally, we apply k-Sigma Transform to both the noisy and clean images so that the denosing network is trained in the ISO-independent space.

We use $\ell_1$ distance between the noisy and clean images as the loss function, and train the network using Adam [22] optimizer. We adopt the triangular cyclical learning rate scheduling [35] with the maximum learning rate of 1e$-$3, cycle step of $50 \times 214$ iterations, and the base learning rate linearly decays to 1e$-$5 after $4000 \times 214$ iterations. The batch size is set to 1, and the training converges at $8000 \times 214$ iterations.

## 5   Experiments

In this section, we evaluate our denoising method with a real world dataset collected with an OPPO Reno-10x smartphone. This smartphone has three rear cameras, and we use the most commonly used main camera for our test. The sensor of this camera is Sony IMX586 sized at $1/2''$ with 48 megapixels, and the pixel size is $0.8\,\mu$m. This sensor is widely used in many smartphones of 2019, including OPPO Reno series, Xiaomi 9, etc.

### 5.1   Noise Parameters Estimation

We first measure and estimate the noise parameters with the method described in Sect. 3.2. We write a simple app to collect RAW images with Android Camera-2 API, which allows us manually control the camera's ISO and exposure time. To keep a stable light condition, we use an Xrite SpectraLight QC light booth in

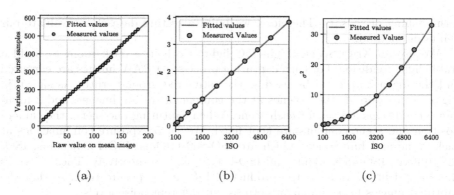

**Fig. 6.** Noise param estimation of Reno-10x smartphone: (a) parameter estimation at ISO-4800 (b) $k$ values at different ISOs (c) $\sigma^2$ at different ISOs.

a dark room. At each ISO and exposure time setting, we adjust the luminance of the light source to avoid over or under exposure, and the final values of the captured image are kept in an appropriate range.

At each ISO setting, 64 RAW images are captured in burst mode, and the mean image is considered as the clean image. With the method described in Sect. 3.2, we can estimate the noise params $k$ and $\sigma^2$ at each specified ISO setting. Figure 6a plots the value-variance curve of the test phone under ISO 4800, where the scattered dots represent the measured variances corresponding to each raw value on the mean image, and the blue line plots the linear regression result of Eq. (6). From the figure we can see that our theoretical noise model can well fit the measurement results. The slope of the fitted line is the estimated noise parameter $\hat{k}$ and the y-intercept value is the estimated noise parameter $\hat{\sigma}^2$.

The adjustable range of IMX586 sensor analog gain is $[1.0, 64.0]$, corresponding to the ISO value of OPPO Reno-10x camera as $[100, 6400]$. According to our noise model Eq. (4), the params $k$ and $\sigma^2$ are linearly, and qudraticly correlated to the ISO value, respectively. We measure and estimate the noise params at each ISO setting, and plot the ISO-$k$ and ISO-$\sigma^2$ curve in Fig. 6. The scattered dots represent the estimated noise params under each ISO setting, and the blue lines in Fig. 6b and Fig. 6c respectively represent the linearly and qudraticly fitted curves, which demostrate that our theoretical model matches the measurements well.

With the ISO-$k$ and ISO-$\sigma^2$ curves well fitted, the noise params under any ISO setting can be easily calculated, and thus satisfying the requirements of both synthesizing training data and applying the k-Sigma transform.

## 5.2   Test Dataset and Metrics

Since our proposed denoising network needs to be trained for specific sensors, we cannot directly use public benchmarks such as SIDD [1] due to the mismatching of sensors. Therefore, we build a testing dataset to evaluate our denoising method.

We use an Xrite SpectraLight QC light booth in a dark room to build a stable light condition. For each capturing process, 64 RAW images are captured and the mean image can be used as the estimated ground truth. As shown in Fig. 7, we capture 4 static scenes as the content of testing images, and 2 luminance conditions are set for each scene. When capturing one scene, the camera position and scene contents are kept fixed. We set 5 exposure combinations at each scene and luminance, which are ISO-800@160ms, ISO-1600@80ms, ISO-3200@40ms, ISO-4800@30ms and ISO-6400@20ms, respectively. These settings share an identical value of the product of ISO and exposure time, so that the captured images have similar brightness but different noise levels.

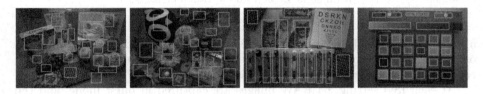

**Fig. 7.** The 4 scenes from the test dataset: the blue boxes represent the regions of interest where image quality metrics are calculated. (Color figure online)

We use peak signal-noise-ratio (PSNR) and structural similarity (SSIM) to measure the performance of denoising methods. The PSNR and SSIM between the denoising results and the clean images are measured in sRGB domain with a simple post processing pipeline, including (1) white balance correction, (2) demosaicking, (3) color correction, and (4) gamma correction. The parameters for white balance correction and color correction are obtained from the metadata of the RAW image. The demosaicking algorithm is pixel-grouping (PPG) and the gamma value is 2.2.

### 5.3   Results

We first show the comparison between our method and the previous state-of-the-art raw image denoising method proposed in [26], which is trained and tested using the SIDD dataset. An extra-large UNet-like network which 1 T multiply-and-cumulate operations (MACs) per megapixel is proposed in [26] and achieved the state-of-the-art performance in NTIRE 2019 denoising challenge. In addition to the UNet-1T architecture, we modify the network by reducing the channel width and layer depth to fit various computation complexities. We train these models with two different data sources: SIDD dataset and the training data generated by our method.

As shown in Fig. 8, because of our accurate noise modeling, the models trained with our synthetic data outperform those trained with the SIDD dataset

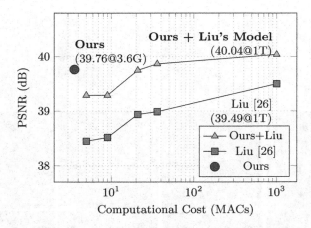

**Fig. 8.** PSNRs at different computation costs of our method, our method using Liu's model [26], and Liu's method. Note that the MACs are in the log space.

**Table 1.** Running time of denoising 1 MP on Qualcomm Snapdragon 855 GPU

| Method | Ours | UNet-5G | UNet-21G | UNet-36G |
|--------|------|---------|----------|----------|
| ms/MP | 70.70 | 79.19 | 292.0 | 383.9 |

by a large margin. Moreover, our mobile-friendly network trained on our synthetic data achieves comparable performance with the UNet-36G with only 10% of its computational complexity (3.6G vs 36.3G). More visual comparisons are provided in Fig. 9.

We further test the actual running time of different models on mobile devices, listed in Table 1. Our mobile-friendly model can process a $1024 \times 1024$ Bayer input with 70.70 ms (aka ∼850 ms for a 12MP full-sized image) on a Qualcomm Snapdragon 855 GPU, while other models with comparable performance require significantly longer time, 292 ms for 21G network and 383 ms for 36G network (aka 4.45 s for 12MP), making them impractical to be deployed on mobile devices.

### 5.4  Ablation Studies

**Data Synthesis Method.** To verify the effectiveness of our data synthesis method, we train our denosing network with four different training datasets, including

- testset overfitting: directly use the inputs and ground truth from the testset as the training data;
- testset with synthetic: use the ground truth of the testset and add synthetic noise as the input;
- testset with noise scaling: use our noise synthesis method but scale the noise parameters to purposely mismatch with the target sensor;

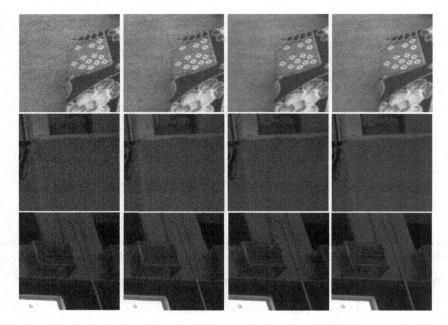

**Fig. 9.** More visual results on our real dataset. From left to right: input image; ground truth; result based on method in [26]; our result. Compared with [26] which generates blurred areas, our method can efficiently reduce the noise as well maintain underlying details. Moreover, our method utilizes a significantly smaller network (3.6G vs 1T).

– SID: synthesize the training set with SID dataset described in Sect. 4.2.

The test results are listed in Table 2. Not surprisingly, the overfitting experiment obtains the highest PSNR of 40.06 dB and SSIM of 0.9335, which sets an upper-bound for this comparison. The testset with our synthetic noise achieves the second best result of 39.97 dB PSNR. When using inaccurate noise parameters by scaling $k$ and $\sigma^2$ by 0.5 or 2.0, the network results in the lowest PSNRs in this experiment. Our method of using the SID dataset achieves 39.76 dB PSNR.

This experiment shows that our noise model and synthetic noise can well match the characteristics of the real input noise, and the testing results can be close to the upper bound performance. Inaccurate noise parameters, even in the overfitting experiment, lead to noticeable performance degradation.

**Robustness to ISO.** We compare several strategies of denoising images of different ISO settings to verify the effectiveness of the k-Sigma Transform. We compare two ways of handling multiple ISO settings: (1) iso-augmentation: randomly choose ISO settings when synthesizing training samples and directly feed them into the denosing network; and (2) concat-variance: the method proposed in [5], where the estimated noise variance are concatenated to the input as 4

**Table 2.** Comparison of training datasets and noise parameters

| Dataset | PSNR (dB) | SSIM |
|---|---|---|
| testset overfitting | 40.06 | 0.9335 |
| testset+synthetic | 39.97 | 0.9337 |
| testset+synthetic scale 0.5 | 36.87 | 0.8850 |
| testset+synthetic scale 2.0 | 39.68 | 0.9301 |
| SID | 39.76 | 0.9310 |

**Table 3.** Strategies of denoising for multiple ISOs

| Method | PSNR (dB) | SSIM |
|---|---|---|
| k-Sigma Transform | 39.76 | 0.9310 |
| concat-variance [5] | 39.65 | 0.9307 |
| iso-augmentation | 39.57 | 0.9299 |
| single-iso-1600 | 35.74 | 0.8072 |
| single-iso-3200 | 38.56 | 0.9089 |
| single-iso-6400 | 38.16 | 0.9167 |

additional channels. In addition, we also test the performance of the single-ISO method, where the training data is synthesized using noise parameters of a single ISO.

The results are listed in Table 3. The concat-variance strategy achieves the PSNR of 39.65 dB, which is about 0.09 dB higher than the iso-augmentation strategy. This means that explicit noise level information can help the model achieve better results than blind denoising. With the proposed k-Sigma Transform, our network achieves the highest PSNR in this experiment. In comparison, all single-ISO methods perform much worse than multi-ISO ones.

Table 4 gives a more detailed analysis of single-ISO methods and our approach, where the PSNRs measured in the testset are grouped into different ISO settings. From the table we can see that when the ISO setting of the testset matches with the single-ISO model, it can produce competitive denoising results. Our method base on the k-Sigma Transform performs consistently well under all ISO settings.

**Table 4.** PSNRs under different ISO settings

|  | ISO-800 | ISO-1600 | ISO-3200 | ISO-4800 | ISO-6400 |
|---|---|---|---|---|---|
| k-Sigma Transform | 43.21 | **41.48** | **39.49** | 38.17 | **36.94** |
| single-iso-1600 | 42.96 | **41.48** | 35.01 | 31.33 | 28.86 |
| single-iso-3200 | 41.79 | 40.87 | **39.51** | 36.97 | 34.08 |
| single-iso-6400 | 39.59 | 38.59 | 38.11 | 37.80 | **36.91** |

# 6   Conclusion

We have presented a new raw image denoiser designed for mobile devices. By accurate sensor noise estimation, we can utilize a light-weight network trained on sensor-specific synthetic data that generalizes well to real noise. We also propose a k-Sigma Transform to process the input and output data, so that denoising can be learned in an ISO-independent space. This allows the network to handle a wide range of noise level without increasing network complexity. Our results show that the proposed method can achieve compatible performance with state-of-the-art methods, which typically employ much larger networks that cannot be directly applied for mobile applications.

In applications, our method can be integrated into existing camera pipeline and replace its denoising component. Since our method can produce high quality denoised raw images, it gives a strong base for the ISP to apply more aggressive post-processing. Our methods have been featured in the night shot mode of several flagship phones released in 2019, with stable and outstanding performance on mobile devices.

In the future, we would like to explore how to further reduce the computational complexity of the proposed method, so that we can apply it on video streams in real-time. Also, we believe it will be interesting and promising to explore deep learning based approaches for raw image processing that can improve or even replace camera's ISP pipeline.

# References

1. Abdelhamed, A., Lin, S., Brown, M.S.: A high-quality denoising dataset for smartphone cameras. In: The IEEE Conference on Computer Vision and Pattern Recognition (CVPR), June 2018
2. Aharon, M., Elad, M., Bruckstein, A., et al.: K-SVD: an algorithm for designing overcomplete dictionaries for sparse representation. IEEE Trans. Sig. Process. **54**(11), 4311 (2006)
3. Anaya, J., Barbu, A.: RENOIR-a dataset for real low-light image noise reduction. J. Vis. Commun. Image Represent. **51**, 144–154 (2018)
4. Anscombe, F.J.: The transformation of Poisson, binomial and negative-binomial data. Biometrika **35**(3/4), 246–254 (1948)
5. Brooks, T., Mildenhall, B., Xue, T., Chen, J., Sharlet, D., Barron, J.T.: Unprocessing images for learned raw denoising. In: Proceedings of the IEEE Conference on Computer Vision and Pattern Recognition, pp. 11036–11045 (2019)
6. Buades, A., Coll, B., Morel, J.M.: A non-local algorithm for image denoising. In: 2005 IEEE Computer Society Conference on Computer Vision and Pattern Recognition (CVPR 2005), vol. 2, pp. 60–65. IEEE (2005)
7. Burger, H.C., Schuler, C.J., Harmeling, S.: Image denoising: can plain neural networks compete with BM3D? In: CVPR (2012)
8. Chen, C., Chen, Q., Xu, J., Koltun, V.: Learning to see in the dark. In: Proceedings of the IEEE Conference on Computer Vision and Pattern Recognition, pp. 3291–3300 (2018)
9. Chen, J., Chen, J., Chao, H., Yang, M.: Image blind denoising with generative adversarial network based noise modeling. In: CVPR (2018)

10. Chen, Y., Pock, T.: Trainable nonlinear reaction diffusion: a flexible framework for fast and effective image restoration. IEEE Trans. Pattern Anal. Mach. Intell. **39**(6), 1256–1272 (2017)
11. Chollet, F.: Xception: deep learning with depthwise separable convolutions, October 2016. http://arxiv.org/abs/1610.02357
12. Dabov, K., Foi, A., Katkovnik, V., Egiazarian, K.: Image restoration by sparse 3D transform-domain collaborative filtering. In: Image Processing: Algorithms and Systems VI, vol. 6812, p. 681207. International Society for Optics and Photonics (2008)
13. Elad, M., Aharon, M.: Image denoising via sparse and redundant representations over learned dictionaries. IEEE Trans. Image Process. **15**(12), 3736–3745 (2006)
14. European Machine Vision Association.: Standard for Characterization of Image Sensors and Cameras (2010). https://doi.org/10.1063/1.1518010
15. Foi, A., Alenius, S., Katkovnik, V., Egiazarian, K.: Noise measurement for raw-data of digital imaging sensors by automatic segmentation of nonuniform targets. IEEE Sens. J. **7**(10), 1456–1461 (2007)
16. Foi, A., Trimeche, M., Katkovnik, V., Egiazarian, K.: Practical Poissonian-Gaussian noise modeling and fitting for single-image raw-data. IEEE Trans. Image Process. **17**(10), 1737–1754 (2008)
17. Gharbi, M., Chaurasia, G., Paris, S., Durand, F.: Deep joint demosaicking and denoising. ACM Trans. Graph. (TOG) **35**(6), 191 (2016)
18. Gu, S., Zhang, L., Zuo, W., Feng, X.: Weighted nuclear norm minimization with application to image denoising. In: CVPR (2014)
19. Hasinoff, S.W., et al.: Burst photography for high dynamic range and low-light imaging on mobile cameras. ACM Trans. Graph. **35**(6), 1–12 (2016). https://doi.org/10.1145/2980179.2980254. http://dl.acm.org/citation.cfm?doid=2980179.2980254
20. Hirakawa, K., Parks, T.W.: Joint demosaicing and denoising. IEEE Trans. Image Process. **15**(8), 2146–2157 (2006)
21. Jain, V., Seung, S.: Natural image denoising with convolutional networks. In: Advances in neural information processing systems, pp. 769–776 (2009)
22. Kingma, D.P., Ba, J.: Adam: a method for stochastic optimization. arXiv preprint arXiv:1412.6980 (2014)
23. Lehtinen, J., et al.: Noise2noise: learning image restoration without clean data. arXiv preprint arXiv:1803.04189 (2018)
24. Liba, O., et al.: Handheld mobile photography in very low light. ACM Trans. Graph. **38**(6) (2019). https://doi.org/10.1145/3355089.3356508
25. Liu, C., Szeliski, R., Kang, S.B., Zitnick, C.L., Freeman, W.T.: Automatic estimation and removal of noise from a single image. IEEE Trans. Pattern Anal. Mach. Intell. **30**(2), 299–314 (2008)
26. Liu, J., et al.: Learning raw image denoising with Bayer pattern unification and Bayer preserving augmentation, April 2019. http://arxiv.org/abs/1904.12945
27. Liu, X., Tanaka, M., Okutomi, M.: Practical signal-dependent noise parameter estimation from a single noisy image. IEEE Trans. Image Process. **23**(10), 4361–4371 (2014)
28. Mairal, J., Bach, F.R., Ponce, J., Sapiro, G., Zisserman, A.: Non-local sparse models for image restoration. In: ICCV, vol. 29, pp. 54–62. Citeseer (2009)
29. Makitalo, M., Foi, A.: Optimal inversion of the Anscombe transformation in low-count Poisson image denoising. IEEE Trans. Image Process. **20**(1), 99–109 (2010)
30. Mao, X., Shen, C., Yang, Y.B.: Image restoration using very deep convolutional encoder-decoder networks with symmetric skip connections. In: NeurIPS (2016)

31. Mildenhall, B., Barron, J.T., Chen, J., Sharlet, D., Ng, R., Carroll, R.: Burst denoising with kernel prediction networks, December 2017. https://arxiv.org/abs/1712.02327

32. Portilla, J., Strela, V., Wainwright, M.J., Simoncelli, E.P.: Image denoising using scale mixtures of Gaussians in the wavelet domain. IEEE Trans. Image Process. **12**(11), 1338–1351 (2003)

33. Ronneberger, O., Fischer, P., Brox, T.: U-Net: convolutional networks for biomedical image segmentation. In: Navab, N., Hornegger, J., Wells, W.M., Frangi, A.F. (eds.) MICCAI 2015. LNCS, vol. 9351, pp. 234–241. Springer, Cham (2015). https://doi.org/10.1007/978-3-319-24574-4_28

34. Shi, G., Zifei, Y., Kai, Z., Wangmeng, Z., Lei, Z.: Toward convolutional blind denoising of real photographs. arXiv preprint arXiv:1807.04686 (2018)

35. Smith, L.N.: Cyclical learning rates for training neural networks. In: 2017 IEEE Winter Conference on Applications of Computer Vision (WACV), pp. 464–472. IEEE (2017)

36. Tai, Y., Yang, J., Liu, X., Xu, C.: MemNet: a persistent memory network for image restoration. In: Proceedings of the IEEE international Conference on Computer Vision, pp. 4539–4547 (2017)

37. Ulyanov, D., Vedaldi, A., Lempitsky, V.: Deep image prior. In: Proceedings of the IEEE Conference on Computer Vision and Pattern Recognition, pp. 9446–9454 (2018)

38. Xie, J., Xu, L., Chen, E.: Image denoising and inpainting with deep neural networks. In: Advances in Neural Information Processing Systems, pp. 341–349 (2012)

39. Xu, J., Zhang, L., Zhang, D., Feng, X.: Multi-channel weighted nuclear norm minimization for real color image denoising. In: ICCV (2017)

40. Yair, N., Michaeli, T.: Multi-scale weighted nuclear norm image restoration. In: CVPR (2018)

41. Zhang, K., Zuo, W., Zhang, L.: FFDNet: toward a fast and flexible solution for CNN based image denoising. IEEE Trans. Image Process. **27**(9), 4608–4622 (2018)

42. Zhou, Y., et al.: When AWGN-based denoiser meets real noises. arXiv preprint arXiv:1904.03485 (2019)

43. Zhou, Y., Liu, D., Huang, T.: Survey of face detection on low-quality images. In: 2018 13th IEEE International Conference on Automatic Face and Gesture Recognition (FG 2018), pp. 769–773. IEEE (2018)

44. Zhu, F., Chen, G., Heng, P.A.: From noise modeling to blind image denoising. In: CVPR (2016)

# SoundSpaces: Audio-Visual Navigation in 3D Environments

Changan Chen[1,4(✉)], Unnat Jain[2,4], Carl Schissler[3],
Sebastia Vicenc Amengual Gari[3], Ziad Al-Halah[1], Vamsi Krishna Ithapu[3],
Philip Robinson[3], and Kristen Grauman[1,4]

[1] UT Austin, Austin, USA
changan@cs.utexas.edu
[2] UIUC, Champaign, USA
[3] Facebook Reality Labs, Pittsburgh, USA
[4] Facebook AI Research, Pittsburgh, USA

**Abstract.** Moving around in the world is naturally a multisensory experience, but today's embodied agents are deaf—restricted to solely their visual perception of the environment. We introduce audio-visual navigation for complex, acoustically and visually realistic 3D environments. By both seeing and hearing, the agent must learn to navigate to a sounding object. We propose a multi-modal deep reinforcement learning approach to train navigation policies end-to-end from a stream of egocentric audio-visual observations, allowing the agent to (1) discover elements of the geometry of the physical space indicated by the reverberating audio and (2) detect and follow sound-emitting targets. We further introduce SoundSpaces: a first-of-its-kind dataset of audio renderings based on geometrical acoustic simulations for two sets of publicly available 3D environments (Matterport3D and Replica), and we instrument Habitat to support the new sensor, making it possible to insert arbitrary sound sources in an array of real-world scanned environments. Our results show that audio greatly benefits embodied visual navigation in 3D spaces, and our work lays groundwork for new research in embodied AI with audio-visual perception. Project: http://vision.cs.utexas.edu/projects/audio_visual_navigation.

## 1 Introduction

Embodied agents perceive and act in the world around them, with a constant loop between their sensed surroundings and their selected movements. Both sights and sounds constantly drive our activity: the laundry machine buzzes

---

C. Chen and U. Jain—Contributed equally.
U. Jain—Work done as an intern at Facebook AI Research.

---

**Electronic supplementary material** The online version of this chapter (https://doi.org/10.1007/978-3-030-58539-6_2) contains supplementary material, which is available to authorized users.

© Springer Nature Switzerland AG 2020
A. Vedaldi et al. (Eds.): ECCV 2020, LNCS 12351, pp. 17–36, 2020.
https://doi.org/10.1007/978-3-030-58539-6_2

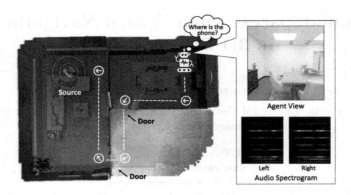

**Fig. 1. Audio source in an unmapped 3D environment**, where an autonomous agent must navigate to the goal. The top-down map is overlaid with the acoustic pressure field heatmap. Our audio-enabled agent gets rich directional information about the goal, since the audio intensity variation is correlated with the shortest path distance. The acoustics also reveal the room's geometry, major structures, and materials. Notice the gradient of the field along the *geodesic* path an agent must use to reach the goal (different from the shortest Euclidean path, which would cut through the inner wall). As a result, the proposed agent enjoys the synergy of both modalities: audio reveals the door as a good intermediate goal, while vision reveals the physical obstacles along the path, such as the furniture in the lefthand room.

to indicate it is done, a crying child draws our attention, the sound of breaking glass may require urgent help.

In embodied AI, the *navigation* task is of particular importance, with applications in search and rescue or service robotics, among many others. Navigation has a long history in robotics, where a premium is placed on rigorous geometric maps [41,81]. More recently, researchers in computer vision are exploring models that loosen the metricity of maps in favor of end-to-end policy learning and learned spatial memories that can generalize to visual cues in novel environments [4,38,39,55,60,74,105].

However, while current navigation models tightly integrate seeing and moving, they are deaf to the world around them. This poses a significant sensory hardship: sound is key to (1) understanding a physical space and (2) localizing sound-emitting targets. As leveraged by blind people and animals who perform sonic navigation, acoustic feedback partially reveals the geometry of a space, the presence of occluding objects, and the materials of major surfaces [26,69]—all of which can complement the visual stream. Meanwhile, targets currently outside the visual range may be detectable *only* by their sound (e.g., a person calling from upstairs, the ringing phone occluded by the sofa, footsteps approaching from behind). Finally, aural cues become critical when visual cues are unreliable (e.g., the lights flicker off) or orthogonal to the agent's task (e.g., a rescue site with rubble that breaks prior visual context).

Motivated by these factors, we introduce *audio-visual navigation* for complex, visually realistic 3D environments. The autonomous agent can both see and hear while attempting to reach its target. We consider two variants of the navigation task: (1) *AudioGoal*, where the target is indicated by the sound it emits, and (2) *AudioPointGoal*, where the agent is additionally directed towards the goal location at the onset. The former captures scenarios where a target initially out of view makes itself known aurally (e.g., phone ringing). The latter augments the popular PointGoal navigation task [4] and captures scenarios where the agent has a GPS pointer towards the target, but should leverage audio-visual cues to navigate the unfamiliar environment and reach it faster.

We propose a multi-modal deep reinforcement learning (RL) approach to train navigation policies end-to-end from a stream of audio-visual observations. Importantly, audio observations must be generated with respect to both the agent's current position and orientation as well as the physical properties of the 3D environment. To do so, we introduce pre-computed audio renderings SoundSpaces for Matterport3D [13] and Replica [77], two public datasets of scanned real-world 3D environments, and we integrate them with the open source Habitat platform [55] for fast 3D simulation (essential for scalable RL). The proposed embodied AI agent learns a policy to choose motions in a novel, unmapped environment that will bring it efficiently to the target while discovering relevant aspects of the latent environment map. See Fig. 1.

Our results show the powerful synergy between audio and vision for navigation. The agent learns to blend both modalities to map novel environments, and doing so yields faster learning at training time and faster, more accurate navigation at inference time. Furthermore—in one of our most exciting results— we demonstrate that for an audio goal, the audio stream competes well with the goal displacement vectors upon which current navigation methods often depend [4,14,35,50,55], while having the advantage of not assuming perfect GPS odometry. Finally, we explore the agent's ability to generalize to not only unseen environments, but also unheard sounds. Our main contributions are:

1. We introduce the task of audio-visual navigation by autonomous agents in complex, visually and acoustically realistic 3D environments.
2. We generalize a state-of-the-art deep RL visual navigation framework to accommodate audio observations and demonstrate its impact on navigation.
3. We introduce SoundSpaces, a first-of-its-kind audio-visual platform for embodied AI. We instrument the 103 environments from Matterport3D [13] and Replica [77] on the Habitat platform [55] with acoustically realistic sound renderings. This allows insertion of an arbitrary sound source and proper sensing of it from arbitrary agent receiver positions. By sharing this new resource publicly, our work can enable other new ideas in this area.
4. We create a benchmark suite of tasks for audio-visual navigation to facilitate future work in this direction.

## 2   Related Work

**Audio-Visual Learning.** The recent surge of research in audio-visual (AV) learning focuses on video rather than embodied perception. This includes interesting directions for synthesizing sounds for video [16,67,104], spatializing sound [31,61], sound source separation [25,30,32,66,103], cross-modal feature learning [29,68,100,101], AV tracking [2,8,9,33], and learning material properties [67]. Unlike prior work that localizes pixels in video frames associated with sounds [6,43,76,82], our goal is to learn navigation policies for agents to actively locate an audio target in a 3D environment. Unlike any of the above, our work addresses embodied navigation, not learning from human-captured video.

**Vision-Based Navigation.** The role of vision for cognitive mapping in *human* navigation is well studied in neuroscience [24,83]. Recent AI agents also aggregate egocentric visual inputs [44,59,80,105,106], often with a spatio-temporal memory [38,42,74,95]. Visual navigation can be tied to other tasks to attain intelligent behavior, such as question answering [21,22,34], active visual recognition [46], and instruction following [5,15]. Our work goes beyond visual perception to incorporate hearing, offering a novel perspective on navigation.

**Audio-Based Navigation.** Cognitive science also confirms that audio is a strong navigational signal [58,79]. Blind and sighted people show comparable skill on spatial navigation [27] and sound localization [36,54,72,87] tasks. Consequently, audio-based AR/VR equipment has been devised for auditory sensory substitution for human users for obstacle avoidance and navigation [37,56]. Additionally, cartoon-like virtual 2D and 3D AV environments can help evaluate human learning of audio cues [19,57,91]. Unlike our proposed platform, these environments are non-photorealistic and they are for *human* navigators; they do not support AI agents or training. Prior studies with autonomous agents in simulated environments are restricted to human-constructed game boards, do not use acoustically correct sound models, and train and test on the same environment [88,93].

**Sound Localization in Robotics.** In robotics, microphone arrays are often used for sound source localization [63–65,71]. Past studies fuse AV cues for surveillance [70,94], speech recognition [99], human robot interaction [1,86], and robotic manipulation tasks [73]. None attempt audio-visual navigation in unmapped environments. Concurrent work explores AV-navigation in computer graphics environments [28]. In contrast to our end-to-end RL agent, their model decouples the task into predicting the goal location from audio and then planning a path to it. Our simulation platform is more realistic for both visuals (real world images in ours vs. computer graphics in [28]) and acoustics (ray tracing/sound penetration/full occlusion model in ours vs. low-cost game audio in [28]), and it offers 5,000× more audio data and 15× more environments. To our knowledge, ours is the first work to demonstrate improved navigation by an AV agent in a visually and acoustically realistic 3D environment, and the first to introduce an end-to-end approach for the problem.

**3D Environments.** Recent research in embodied perception is greatly facilitated by new 3D environments and simulation platforms. Compared to artificial environments like video games [47,48,53,78,96], photorealistic environments portray 3D scenes in which real people and mobile robots would interact. Their realistic meshes can be rendered from agent-selected viewpoints to train and test RL policies for navigation in a reproducible manner [3,7,10,13,51,55,77,97,98]. Many are captured with 3D scanners and real 360 photos, meaning that the views are indeed the perceptual inputs a robot would receive in the real world [3,13,77].

**Fig. 2. Acoustic simulation.** We capture room impulse responses between each location pair within the illustrated grid (here for the 'frl_apartment_0' scene in Replica). In our platform, agents can experience binaural audio at densely sampled locations $\mathcal{L}$ marked with black dots—hearing the sound's intensity, direction, and frequency texture. Heatmaps display audio pressure fields, decreasing from red to blue. **Left**: When a sound source in $\mathcal{S}$ is placed in the center. **Right**: When a source is placed on the stairs. Notice how the sound received by the agent at different positions changes when the sound source moves, and how 3D structures influence the sound propagation. (Color figure online)

None of the commonly used environments and simulators provide audio rendering. We present the first audio-visual simulator for AI agent training and the first study of audio-visual embodied agents in realistic 3D environments.

## 3   SoundSpaces: Enabling Audio in Habitat

Our audio platform augments the Habitat simulator [55], particularly the Matterport3D [13] and Replica [77] datasets hosted within it. Habitat is an open-source 3D simulator with a user-friendly API that supports RGB, depth, and semantic rendering. The API offers fast (over 10 K fps) rendering and support for multiple datasets [12,20,62,77,98]. This has incentivized many embodied AI works to embrace it as the 3D simulator for training navigation and question answering agents [14,35,50,55,89].

We use 85 Matterport3D [13] environments, which are real-world homes and other indoor environments with 3D meshes and image scans. The environments are large, with on average 517 m$^2$ of floorspace. Replica [77] is a dataset of 18 apartment, hotel, office, and room scenes with 3D meshes. By extending these Habitat-compatible 3D assets with our audio simulator, we enable users to take advantage of the efficient Habitat API and easily adopt the audio modality for AI agent training. Our audio platform and data is shared publicly.

Our high-fidelity audio simulator SoundSpaces takes into account important factors for a realistic sound rendering in a 3D environment. We use a state-of-the-art algorithm for room acoustics modeling [11] and a bidirectional path tracing algorithm to model sound reflections in the room geometry [85]. Since materials also influence the sounds received in an environment (e.g., walking across marble floors versus a shaggy carpet), we set the acoustic material properties of major surfaces by mapping the meshes' semantic labels to materials in an existing database [23]. Each material has different absorption, scattering, and transmission coefficients that affect our sound propagation (see Supp). This enables our simulator to model fine-grained acoustic properties like sound propagation through walls.

For each scene, we simulate the acoustics of the environment by precomputing room impulse responses (RIR). The RIR is the transfer function between a sound source and microphone, which varies as a function of the room geometry, materials, and the sound source location [52].

Let $\mathcal{S} = \{(x_i^s, y_i^s, z_i^s)\}_{i=1}^N$ denote the set of $N$ possible sound source positions, and let $\mathcal{L} = \{(x_i^r, y_i^r, z_i^r)\}_{i=1}^N$ denote the set of possible listener positions (i.e., agent microphones). We densely sample a grid of $N$ locations with spatial resolution of 0.5 m (Replica) or 1 m (Matterport). The Replica scenes range in area from 9.5 to 141.5 m$^2$ and thus yield $N \in [38, 566]$; for Matterport the range is 53.1 to 2921.3 m$^2$, with $N \in [20, 2103]$. Points are placed at a vertical height of 1.5 m, reflecting the fixed height of a robotic agent. Then we simulate the RIR for each possible source and listener placement at these locations, $\mathcal{S} \times \mathcal{L}$. Having done so, we can look up any source-listener pair on-the-fly and render the sound, by convolving the desired waveform with the selected RIR. See Fig. 2.

Given our simulations, for any audio source placed in a location $\mathcal{S}_i$ we can generate the ambisonic audio (roughly speaking, the audio equivalent of a 360° image) heard at a particular listener location $\mathcal{L}_j$. We convert the ambisonics to binaural audio [102] in order to represent an agent with two human-like ears, for whom perceived sound depends on the body's relative orientation in the scene.[1] Our platform also permits rendering multiple simultaneous sounds.

Since an agent might not be able to stand at each location in $\mathcal{L}$ due to embodiment constraints (e.g., no climbing on the sofa), we create a graph capturing the reachability and connectivity of these locations. First we remove nodes that are non-navigable, then for each node pair $(i, j)$, we consider the edge $e(i, j)$ as valid if and only if the Euclidean distance between $i$ and $j$ is 0.5 m for Replica or 1 m for Matterport (*i.e.*, nodes $i$ and $j$ are immediate neighbors) and the geodesic and Euclidean distances between them are equal (*i.e.*, no obstacle in between).

All details of our audio simulation are in the Supp. The fidelity of the sound renderings can be experienced in our project page videos.

## 4    Task Definitions: Audio-Visual Navigation

We propose two novel navigation tasks: AudioGoal Navigation and AudioPointGoal Navigation. In AudioGoal, the agent hears an audio source located at the goal—such as a phone ringing—but receives no direct position information about the goal. AudioPointGoal is an audio extension of the PointGoal task studied often in the literature [4,14,35,50,55,97] where the agent hears the source and is told its displacement from the starting position. In all three tasks, to navigate and avoid obstacles, the agent needs to reach the target using sensory inputs alone. That is, no map of the scene is provided to the agent.

---

[1] While algorithms could also run with ambisonic inputs, using binaural sound has the advantage of allowing human listeners to interpret our video results (see Supp video).

*Task Definitions.* For PointGoal [4,55,90], a randomly initialized agent is tasked with navigating to a point goal defined by a displacement vector $(\Delta_x^0, \Delta_y^0)$ relative to the starting position of the agent. For AudioGoal, the agent instead receives audio from the sounding target; the AudioGoal agent does not receive a displacement vector pointing to the target. The observed audio is updated as a function of the location of the agent, the location of the goal, and the structure and materials of the room. In AudioPointGoal, the agent receives the union of information received in the PointGoal and AudioGoal tasks, *i.e.*, audio as well as a point vector. Note that physical obstacles (walls, furniture) typically exist along the displacement vector, which the agent must sense while navigating.

*Agent and Goal Embodiment.* We adopt the standard cylinder embodiment used in Habitat. A target has diameter 0.2 m and height 1.5 m, and, consistent with prior PointGoal work, has no visual presence. While the goal itself does not have a visible embodiment (currently unsupported in Habitat), vision—particularly in the abstraction of depth—is essential to detect and avoid obstacles to move towards the target. Hence, all the tasks have a crucial vision component.

*Action Space.* The action space is: *MoveForward*, *TurnLeft*, *TurnRight*, and *Stop*. The last three actions are always valid. The *MoveForward* action is invalid when the agent attempts to traverse from one node to another without an edge connecting them (as per the graph defined in Sect. 2). If valid, *MoveForward* takes the agent forward by 0.5 m (Replica) or 1 m (Matterport). For all models, there is no actuation noise, *i.e.*, a step executes perfectly or does not execute at all.

*Sensors.* The sensory inputs are binaural sound (absent in PointGoal), GPS (absent in AudioGoal), RGB, and depth. To capture binaural spatial sound, the agent emulates two microphones placed at human height. We assume an idealized GPS sensor, following prior work [14,35,50,55]. However, as we will demonstrate in results, our audio-based learning provides a steady navigation signal that makes it feasible to disable the GPS sensor for the proposed AudioGoal task.

*Episode Specification.* An episode of PointGoal is defined by an arbitrary 1) scene, 2) agent start location, 3) agent start rotation, and 4) goal location. In each episode the agent can reach the target if it navigates successfully. An episode for AudioGoal and AudioPointGoal additionally includes a source audio waveform. The waveform is convolved with the RIR corresponding to the specific scene, goal, agent location and orientation to generate dynamic audio for the agent. We consider a variety of audio sources, both familiar and unfamiliar to the agent (detailed below). An episode is successful if the agent executes the *Stop* action while being exactly at the location of the goal. Agents are allowed a time horizon of 500 actions for all tasks, similar to [14,35,45,50,55].

## 5   Navigation Network and Training

To navigate autonomously, the agent must be able to enter a new yet-unmapped space, accumulate partial observations of the environment over time, and efficiently transport itself to a goal location. Building on recent embodied visual

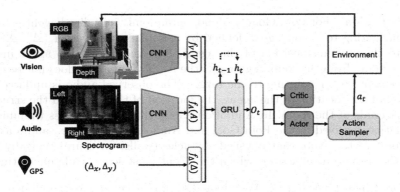

**Fig. 3. Audio-visual navigation network.** Our model uses both acoustic and visual cues from the 3D environment for effective navigation of complex scenes.

navigation work [4,38,39,55,60,105], we take a deep reinforcement learning approach, and we introduce audio to the observation. During training, the agent is rewarded for correctly and efficiently navigating to the target. This yields a policy that maps new multisensory egocentric observations to agent actions.

*Sensory Inputs.* The audio inputs are spectrograms, following literature in audio learning [31,68,103]. Specifically, to represent the agent's binaural audio input (corresponding to the left and right ear), we first compute the Short-Time Fourier Transform (STFT) with a hop length of 160 samples and a windowed signal length of 512 samples, which corresponds to a physical duration of 12 and 32 ms at a sample rate of 44100 Hz (Replica) and 16000 Hz (Matterport). By using the first 1000 milliseconds of audio as input, STFT gives a $257 \times 257$ and a $257 \times 101$ complex-valued matrix, respectively; we take its magnitude and downsample both axes by a factor of 4. For better contrast we take its logarithm. Finally, we stack the left and right audio channel matrices to obtain a $65 \times 65 \times 2$ and a $65 \times 26 \times 2$ tensor, denoted $A$. The visual input $V$ is the RGB and/or depth image, $128 \times 128 \times 3$ and $128 \times 128 \times 1$ tensors, respectively, where 128 is the image resolution for the agent's 90° field of view. The relative displacement vector $\Delta = (\Delta_x, \Delta_y)$ points from the agent to the goal in the 2D ground plane of the scene.

Which specific subset of these three inputs (audio, visual, vector) the agent receives depends on the agent's sensors and the goal's characterization (cf. Sect. 4). The sensory inputs are transformed to a probability distribution over the action space by the policy network, as we describe next.

*Network Architecture.* Next we define the parameterization of the agent's policy $\pi_\theta(a_t|o_t, h_{t-1})$, which selects action $a_t$ given the current observation $o_t$ and aggregated past states $h_{t-1}$, and the value function $V_\theta(o_t, h_{t-1})$, which scores how good the current state is. Here $\theta$ refers to all trainable weights of the network.

Our network architecture is inspired by current RL models in the visual navigation literature [20,45,55,92]. We expand the traditional vision-only navigation model to enable acoustic perception for audio-visual navigation. As highlighted in Fig. 3, we transform $A$ and $V$ by corresponding CNNs $f_A(\cdot)$ and $f_V(\cdot)$. The CNNs have separate weights but the same architecture of conv $8 \times 8$, conv $4 \times 4$, conv $3 \times 3$ and a linear layer, with ReLU activations between each layer. The outputs of the CNNs are vectors $f_A(A)$ and $f_V(V)$ of length $L_A$ and $L_V$, respectively. These are concatenated to the relative displacement vector $\Delta$ and transformed by a gated recurrent unit (GRU) [18]. The GRU operates on the current step's input as well as the accumulated history of states $h_{t-1}$. The GRU updates the history to $h_t$ and outputs the representation of the agent's state $o_t$. Finally, the value of the state $V_\theta(o_t, h_{t-1})$ and the policy distribution $\pi_\theta(a_t | o_t, h_{t-1})$ are estimated using the critic and actor heads of the model. Both are linear layers.

*Training.* We train the network with Proximal Policy Optimization (PPO) [75]. The agent is rewarded for reaching the goal quickly. Specifically, it receives a reward of $+10$ for executing *Stop* at the goal location, a negative reward of $-0.01$ per time step, $+1$ for reducing the geodesic distance to the goal, and the equivalent penalty for increasing it. We add an entropy maximization term to the cumulative reward optimization, for better action space exploration [40, 75].

*Synergy of Audio for Navigation.* Because our agent can both hear and see, it has the potential to not only better localize the target (which emits sound), but also better plan its movements in the environment (whose major structures, walls, furniture, etc. all affect how the sound is perceived). See Fig. 1. The optimal policy would trace a path $\mathcal{P}^*$ corresponding to monotonically decreasing geodesic distance to the goal. Notably, the displacement $\Delta$ does not specify the optimal policy: moving along $\mathcal{P}^*$ decreases the geodesic distance but may decrease or increase the Euclidean distance to the goal at each time step. For example, if the goal is behind the sofa, the agent must move around the sofa to reach it. Importantly, the audio stream $A$ has complementary and potentially stronger information than $\Delta$ in this regard. Not only does the intensity of the audio source reflect the Euclidean distance to the target, but also the geometry of the room captured in the acoustics reveals geodesic distances. As we show in results, the visual and aural inputs are synergistic; neither fares as well on its own.

*Implementation Details.* The lengths of audio, visual, point vector, and final state, *i.e.*, $L_A$, $L_V$, $L_\Delta$, and $L_S$ are 512, 512, 2, and 1026, respectively. We use a single bidirectional GRU with input size 512, hidden size 512, and we use one recurrent layer. We optimize the model using Adam [49] with PyTorch defaults for coefficients for momentum and a learning rate of $2.5e-4$. We discount rewards with a decay of 0.99. We train the network for $30M$ agent steps on Replica and $60M$ on Matterport3D, which amounts to 105 and 210 GPU hours respectively.

## 6   Experiments

Our main objectives are to show:

**O.1** Tackling navigation with both sight and sound *i.e.*, the proposed AudioPointGoal) leads to better navigation and faster learning. This demonstrates that audio has complementary information beyond merely goal coordinates that facilitates navigation.

**O.2** Listening for an audio target in a 3D environment serves as a viable alternative to GPS-based cues. Not only does the proposed AudioGoal agent navigate better than the PointGoal agent, it does so without Point-Goal's assumption of perfect odometry and even with noisy audio sensors. The AudioGoal task has the important advantage of realism: the agent autonomously senses the target in AudioGoal, whereas the target is directly given to the agent via $\Delta$ in PointGoal—a rare scenario in real applications.

**O.3** Audio-visual navigation can generalize to both new environments and new sound sources. In particular, audio-visual agents can navigate better with audio even when the sound sources are unfamiliar.

*Datasets.* Table 1 summarizes SoundSpaces, which includes audio renderings for the Replica and Matterport3D datasets. Each episode consists of a tuple: ⟨scene, agent start location, agent start rotation, goal location, audio waveform⟩. We generate episodes by choosing a scene and a random start and goal location. To eliminate easier episodes, we prune those that are either too short (geodesic distance less than 4) or can be completed by moving mostly in a straight line (ratio of geodesic to Euclidean distance less than 1.1). We ensure that at the onset of each episode the agent can hear the sound, since in some large environments the audio might be inaudible when the agent is very far from the sound source.

*Sound Sources.* Recall that the RIRs can be convolved with an arbitrary input waveform, which allows us to vary the sounds across episodes. We use 102 copyright-free natural sounds of telephones, music, fans, and others (http://www.freesound.org). See Supp video for examples. Unless otherwise specified, the sound source is the telephone ringing. We stress that in all experiments, the environment (scene) at test time is unmapped and has never been seen previously in training. It is valid for sounds heard in training to also be heard at test time, e.g., a phone ringing in multiple environments will sound different depending on both the 3D space and the goal and agent positions. Experiments for O.3 examine the impact of varied train/test sounds.

*Metrics.* We use the success rate normalized by inverse path length (SPL), the standard metric for navigation [4]. We consider an episode successful only if the agent reaches the goal *and* executes the *Stop* action.

*Baselines.* We consider three non-learning baselines adapted from previous work [17,55]: RANDOM chooses an action randomly among {*MoveForward, TurnLeft, TurnRight*}. FORWARD always calls *MoveForward* and if it hits an obstacle, it calls *TurnRight* then resumes going forward and repeats. GOAL FOLLOWER always first orients itself towards the goal and then calls *MoveForward*. All three issue the *Stop* action upon reaching the goal.

**Table 1.** Summary of SoundSpaces dataset properties

| Dataset | # Scenes | Resolution | Sampling Rate | Avg. # Node | Avg. Area | # Training Episodes | # Test Episodes |
|---|---|---|---|---|---|---|---|
| Replica | 18 | 0.5 m | 44100 Hz | 97 | 47.24 m$^2$ | 0.1M | 1000 |
| Matterport3D | 85 | 1 m | 16000 Hz | 243 | 517.34 m$^2$ | 2M | 1000 |

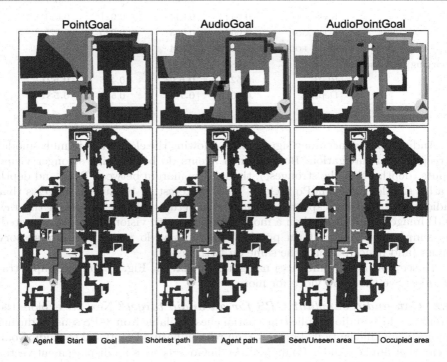

**Fig. 4. Navigation trajectories on top-down maps.** Agent path color fades from dark blue to light blue as time goes by. Green path indicates the shortest geodesic path. **Top:** Replica - The PointGoal agent bumps into the wall several times trying to move towards the target, unable to figure out the target is actually located in another froom. In contrast, the AudioGoal and AudioPointGoal agents better sense the target: the sound travels through the door and the agent leaves the starting room immediately. **Bottom:** Matterport - the AudioGoal agent best avoids backtracking to efficiently reach the target in a large multi-room home.(Color figure online)

***O.1: Does audio help navigation?*** First we evaluate the impact of adding audio sensing to visual navigation by comparing PointGoal and AudioPointGoal agents. Table 2 compares the navigation performance (in SPL) for both agents and the baselines on the test environments. We consider three visual sensing capabilities: no visual input (Blind), raw RGB images, or depth images. (We found RGB+D was no better than depth alone.)

**Table 2.** Adding sound to sight and GPS sensing improves navigation performance significantly. Values are success rate normalized by path length (SPL); higher is better.

|  |  | Replica | | Matterport3D | |
|---|---|---|---|---|---|
|  |  | PointGoal | AudioPoint-Goal | PointGoal | AudioPoint-Goal |
| Baselines | RANDOM | 0.044 | 0.044 | 0.021 | 0.021 |
|  | FORWARD | 0.063 | 0.063 | 0.025 | 0.025 |
|  | GOAL FOLLOWER | 0.124 | 0.124 | 0.197 | 0.197 |
| Varying visual sensor | Blind | 0.480 | **0.681** | 0.426 | **0.473** |
|  | RGB | 0.521 | **0.632** | 0.466 | **0.521** |
|  | Depth | 0.601 | **0.709** | 0.541 | **0.581** |

Audio improves accuracy significantly, showing the clear value in multi-modal perception for navigation. Both learned agents do better with stronger visual inputs (depth being the strongest), though the margin between RGB and depth is a bit smaller for AudioPointGoal. This is interesting because it suggests that audio-visual learning captures geometric structure (like depth) from the raw RGB images more easily than a model equipped with vision alone. As expected, the simple baselines perform poorly because they do not utilize any sensory inputs (and hence perform the same on both tasks).

To see how audio influences navigation behavior, Fig. 4 shows example trajectories. See the Supp video for more.

***O.2: Can audio supplant GPS for an audio target?*** Next we explore the extent to which audio supplies the spatial cues available from GPS sensing during (audio-)visual navigation. This test requires comparing PointGoal to AudioGoal. Recall that unlike (Audio)PointGoal, AudioGoal receives *no* displacement vector pointing to the goal; it can only hear and see.

Figure 5(a) reports the navigation accuracy as a function of GPS quality. The leftmost point uses perfect GPS that tells the PointGoal agents (but not the AudioGoal agent) the exact direction of the goal; for subsequent points, Gaussian noise of increasing variance is added, up to $\sigma = 1.5\,\mathrm{m}$. All agents use depth. While AudioGoal's accuracy is by definition independent of GPS failures, the others suffer noticeably.[2] Furthermore, AudioPointGoal (APG) degrades much more gracefully than PointGoal (PG) in the face of GPS noise. This is evidence that *the audio signal gives similar or even better spatial cues than the PointGoal displacements*—which are likely overly optimistic given the unreliability of GPS in practice and especially indoors. T-SNE [84] visualizations (Fig. 5(b)) reinforce this finding: our learned audio features for AudioGoal naturally encode the distance and angle to the goal. Note that these findings stand even with microphone

---

[2] Replica has more multi-room trajectories, where audio gives clear cues of room entrances/exits (vs. open floor plans in Matterport). This may be why AG is better than PG and APG on Replica.

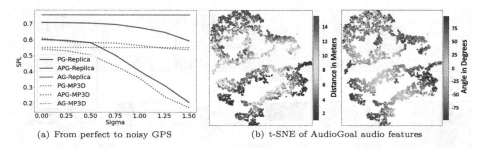

(a) From perfect to noisy GPS                (b) t-SNE of AudioGoal audio features

**Fig. 5. Audio as a learned spatial sensor.** (a) Navigation accuracy with increasing GPS noise. Unlike existing PointGoal agents, our AudioGoal agent does not rely on GPS, and hence is immune to GPS noise. (b) t-SNE projection of audio features, color coded to reveal their correlation with the goal location (left) and direction (right), *i.e.*, source is far (red) or near (violet), and to the left (blue) or right (red) of the agent.(Color figure online)

noise: with 40 dB SNR (bad microphone), SPL only drops marginally from 0.756 to 0.753 and from 0.552 to 0.550 on Replica and Matterport, respectively.

Next we explore whether our AudioGoal agent learned *more* than a pointer to the goal based on the sound intensity. We run a variant of our model in which the audio input consists of only the intensity of the left and right waveforms; the audio CNN is removed, and the rest of the network in Fig. 3 remains the same. This simplified audio input allows the agent to readily learn to follow the intensity gradient. The performance of the AudioGoal-Depth agent drops to an SPL of 0.291 and 0.014 showing that our model (SPL of 0.756 and 0.552 in Fig. 5(a)) does indeed learn additional environment information from the full spectrograms to navigate more accurately. See Supp.

We expect that the audio and visual input vary in their relative impact on the agent's decision making at any given time point, based on the environment context and goal placement. To compute their impact, we ablate each modality in turn by replacing it with its average training sample value, and compare the resulting action probability under our model to that of the action chosen with both modalities. We calculate the importance of each input modality using the absolute difference of logarithmic action probability, normalized by the sum of the two ablations. The greater the change in the selected action, the more impact that modality had on the learned agent's actual choice. Figure 6 and the Supp video show examples of the AV impact scores alongside the egocentric view of the agent at different stages in the trajectory. We see the agent draws dynamically on either or both modalities to inform its motions in the environment.

*O.3: What is the effect of different sound sources?* Next, we analyze the impact of the sound source. First, we explore generalization to novel sounds. We divide the 102 sound clips into 73/11/18 splits for train/val/test, respectively. We train for AudioGoal (AG) and AudioPointGoal (APG), then validate and test on disjoint val and test sounds. In all cases, the test environments are unseen.

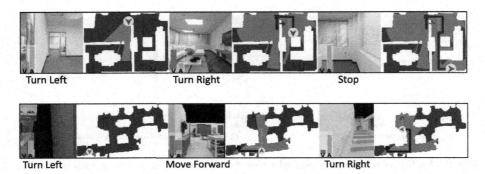

Fig. 6. **Impact of each modality on action selection** for two AudioGoal episodes. We show one episode per row, and three sampled timesteps each. See Fig. 4 for legend. Blue and green bars display the importance of vision and audio, respectively. **Top:** Initially, the agent relies on audio to tell that the goal is on its left and decides to turn left. Later, it uses vision to recognize nobstacles in front of it and decides to turn right. Finally, the agent decides to stop because the sound intensity has peaked. **Bottom:** Initially, the agent decides to turn left, following the audio source. Then the agent uses vision to identify the free space and decides to move forward. Later, the agent relies more on audio to decide to turn right as it hears the target from the right. (Color figure online)

**Table 3.** Navigation performance (SPL) when generalizing to unheard sounds. Higher is better. Results are averaged over 7 test runs; all standard deviations are $\leq 0.01$.

| Dataset | | $PG$ | Same sound | | Varied heard sounds | | Varied unheard sounds | |
|---|---|---|---|---|---|---|---|---|
| | | | $AG$ | $APG$ | $AG$ | $APG$ | $AG$ | $APG$ |
| Replica | Blind | 0.480 | 0.673 | 0.681 | 0.449 | 0.633 | 0.277 | 0.649 |
| | RGB | 0.521 | 0.626 | 0.632 | 0.624 | 0.606 | 0.339 | 0.562 |
| | Depth | 0.601 | 0.756 | 0.709 | 0.645 | 0.724 | 0.454 | 0.707 |
| Matterport3D | Blind | 0.426 | 0.438 | 0.473 | 0.352 | 0.500 | 0.278 | 0.497 |
| | RGB | 0.466 | 0.479 | 0.521 | 0.422 | 0.480 | 0.314 | 0.448 |
| | Depth | 0.541 | 0.552 | 0.581 | 0.448 | 0.570 | 0.338 | 0.538 |

Table 3 shows the results. As we move left to right in the table, the sound generalization task gets harder: from a single heard sound, to variable heard sounds, to variable unheard sounds (see Supp for details on these three test settings). Note, the non-learning baselines are unaffected by changes to the audio and hence are omitted here. Our APG agents almost always outperform the Point-Goal agent, even for unheard test sounds, strengthening the conclusions from Table 2. APG performs fairly similarly on heard and unheard sounds, showing it has learned to balance all three modalities. On the other hand, AG's accuracy declines with varied heard sounds and unheard sounds. While it makes sense that the task of following an unfamiliar sound is harder, we also expect that larger training repositories of more sounds will resolve much of this decline.

## 7 Conclusion

We introduced the task of audio-visual navigation in complex 3D environments. Generalizing a state-of-the-art deep RL navigation engine for this task, we presented encouraging results for audio's role in the visual navigation task. The results show that when linked tightly to the egocentric visual observations, audio enriches not only the directional cues for a sound source, but also the spatial information about the environment—both of which our model successfully leverages for better navigation. Another important contribution of our work is to enable audio rendering for Habitat with the publicly available Replica and Matterport3D environments, which can facilitate future work in the field. Next we are interested in considering multi-agent scenarios, sim2real transfer, moving sound-emitting targets, and navigating in the context of dynamic audio events.

**Acknowledgements.** UT Austin is supported in part by DARPA Lifelong Learning Machines. We thank Alexander Schwing, Dhruv Batra, Erik Wijmans, Oleksandr Maksymets, Ruohan Gao, and Svetlana Lazebnik for valuable discussions and support with the AI-Habitat platform.

## References

1. Alameda-Pineda, X., Horaud, R.: Vision-guided robot hearing. Int. J. Robot. Res. **34**, 437–456 (2015)
2. Alameda-Pineda, X., et al.: Salsa: a novel dataset for multimodal group behavior analysis. IEEE Trans. Pattern Anal. Mach. intell. **38**(8), 1707–1720 (2015)
3. Ammirato, P., Poirson, P., Park, E., Kosecka, J., Berg, A.: A dataset for developing and benchmarking active vision. In: ICRA (2016)
4. Anderson, P., et al.: On evaluation of embodied navigation agents. arXiv preprint arXiv:1807.06757 (2018)
5. Anderson, P., et al.: Vision-and-language navigation: interpreting visually-grounded navigation instructions in real environments. In: CVPR (2018)
6. Arandjelovic, R., Zisserman, A.: Objects that sound. In: ECCV (2018)
7. Armeni, I., Sax, A., Zamir, A.R., Savarese, S.: Joint 2D–3D-Semantic Data for Indoor Scene Understanding. ArXiv e-prints, February 2017
8. Ban, Y., Girin, L., Alameda-Pineda, X., Horaud, R.: Exploiting the complementarity of audio and visual data in multi-speaker tracking. In: ICCV Workshop on Computer Vision for Audio-Visual Media. 2017 IEEE International Conference on Computer Vision Workshops (ICCVW) (2017). https://hal.inria.fr/hal-01577965
9. Ban, Y., Li, X., Alameda-Pineda, X., Girin, L., Horaud, R.: Accounting for room acoustics in audio-visual multi-speaker tracking. In: IEEE International Conference on Acoustics, Speech and Signal Processing (ICASSP) (2018)
10. Brodeur, S., et al.: Home: a household multimodal environment. https://arxiv.org/abs/1711.11017 (2017)

11. Cao, C., Ren, Z., Schissler, C., Manocha, D., Zhou, K.: Interactive sound propagation with bidirectional path tracing. ACM Trans. Graph. (TOG) **35**(6), 1–11 (2016)
12. Chang, A., et al.: Matterport3D: learning from RGB-D data in indoor environments. In: 3DV (2017)
13. Chang, A., et al.: Matterport3D: learning from RGB-D data in indoor environments. In: Proceedings of the International Conference on 3D Vision (3DV) (2017)
14. Chaplot, D.S., Gupta, S., Gupta, A., Salakhutdinov, R.: Learning to explore using active neural mapping. In: ICLR (2020)
15. Chen, H., Suhr, A., Misra, D., Snavely, N., Artzi, Y.: Touchdown: natural language navigation and spatial reasoning in visual street environments. In: CVPR (2019)
16. Chen, L., Srivastava, S., Duan, Z., Xu, C.: Deep cross-modal audio-visual generation. In: Proceedings of the on Thematic Workshops of ACM Multimedia 2017. ACM (2017)
17. Chen, T., Gupta, S., Gupta, A.: Learning exploration policies for navigation. http://arxiv.org/abs/1903.01959
18. Chung, J., Kastner, K., Dinh, L., Goel, K., Courville, A.C., Bengio, Y.: A recurrent latent variable model for sequential data. In: NeurIPS (2015)
19. Connors, E.C., Yazzolino, L.A., Sánchez, J., Merabet, L.B.: Development of an audio-based virtual gaming environment to assist with navigation skills in the blind. J. Vis. Exp. JoVE **73**, e50272 (2013)
20. Das, A., Datta, S., Gkioxari, G., Lee, S., Parikh, D., Batra, D.: Embodied question answering. In: CVPR (2018)
21. Das, A., Gkioxari, G., Lee, S., Parikh, D., Batra, D.: Neural modular control for embodied question answering. In: ECCV (2018)
22. Das, A., et al.: Probing emergent semantics in predictive agents via question answering. In: ICML (2020)
23. Egan, M.D., Quirt, J., Rousseau, M.: Architectural Acoustics. Elsevier, Amsterdam (1989)
24. Ekstrom, A.D.: Why vision is important to how we navigate. Hippocampus **25**, 731–735 (2015)
25. Ephrat, A., et al.: Looking to listen at the cocktail party: a speaker-independent audio-visual model for speech separation. In: SIGGRAPH (2018)
26. Evers, C., Naylor, P.: Acoustic slam. IEEE/ACM Trans. Audio Speech Lang. Process. **26**(9), 1484–1498 (2018)
27. Fortin, M., et al.: Wayfinding in the blind: larger hippocampal volume and supranormal spatial navigation. Brain **131**, 2995–3005 (2008)
28. Gan, C., Zhang, Y., Wu, J., Gong, B., Tenenbaum, J.: Look, listen, and act: towards audio-visual embodied navigation. In: ICRA (2020)
29. Gao, R., Chen, C., Al-Halah, Z., Schissler, C., Grauman, K.: VisualEchoes: spatial image representation learning through echolocation. In: ECCV (2020)
30. Gao, R., Feris, R., Grauman, K.: Learning to separate object sounds by watching unlabeled video. In: Ferrari, V., Hebert, M., Sminchisescu, C., Weiss, Y. (eds.) ECCV 2018. LNCS, vol. 11207, pp. 36–54. Springer, Cham (2018). https://doi.org/10.1007/978-3-030-01219-9_3
31. Gao, R., Grauman, K.: 2.5 D visual sound. In: CVPR (2019)
32. Gao, R., Grauman, K.: Co-separating sounds of visual objects. In: ICCV (2019)
33. Gebru, I.D., Ba, S., Evangelidis, G., Horaud, R.: Tracking the active speaker based on a joint audio-visual observation model. In: Proceedings of the IEEE International Conference on Computer Vision Workshops, pp. 15–21 (2015)

34. Gordon, D., Kembhavi, A., Rastegari, M., Redmon, J., Fox, D., Farhadi, A.: IQA: visual question answering in interactive environments. In: CVPR (2018)
35. Gordon, D., Kadian, A., Parikh, D., Hoffman, J., Batra, D.: SplitNet: Sim2Sim and Task2Task transfer for embodied visual navigation. In: ICCV (2019)
36. Gougoux, F., Zatorre, R.J., Lassonde, M., Voss, P., Lepore, F.: A functional neuroimaging study of sound localization: visual cortex activity predicts performance in early-blind individuals. PLoS Biol. **3**(2), e27 (2005)
37. Gunther, R., Kazman, R., MacGregor, C.: Using 3D sound as a navigational aid in virtual environments. Behav. Inf. Technol. **23**(6), 435–446 (2010). https://doi.org/10.1080/01449290410001723364
38. Gupta, S., Davidson, J., Levine, S., Sukthankar, R., Malik, J.: Cognitive mapping and planning for visual navigation. In: Proceedings of the IEEE Conference on Computer Vision and Pattern Recognition, pp. 2616–2625 (2017)
39. Gupta, S., Fouhey, D., Levine, S., Malik, J.: Unifying map and landmark based representations for visual navigation. arXiv preprint arXiv:1712.08125 (2017)
40. Haarnoja, T., Zhou, A., Abbeel, P., Levine, S.: Soft actor-critic: off-policy maximum entropy deep reinforcement learning with a stochastic actor. In: ICML (2018)
41. Hartley, R., Zisserman, A.: Multiple View Geometry in Computer Vision. Cambridge University Press, Cambridge (2004)
42. Henriques, J.F., Vedaldi, A.: MapNet: an allocentric spatial memory for mapping environments. In: CVPR (2018)
43. Hershey, J.R., Movellan, J.R.: Audio vision: using audio-visual synchrony to locate sounds. In: NeurIPS (2000)
44. Jain, U., et al.: A cordial sync: going beyond marginal policies for multi-agent embodied tasks. In: ECCV (2020)
45. Jain, U., et al.: Two body problem: collaborative visual task completion. In: CVPR (2019)
46. Jayaraman, D., Grauman, K.: End-to-end policy learning for active visual categorization. TPAMI **41**(7), 1601–1614 (2018)
47. Johnson, M., Hofmann, K., Hutton, T., Bignell, D.: The malmo platform for artificial intelligence experimentation. In: International Joint Conference on AI (2016)
48. Kempka, M., Wydmuch, M., Runc, G., Toczek, J., Jakowski, W.: ViZDoom: a doom-based AI research platform for visual reinforcement learning. In: Proceedings of the IEEE Conference on Computational Intelligence and Games (2016)
49. Kingma, D., Ba, J.: A method for stochastic optimization. In: CVPR (2017)
50. Kojima, N., Deng, J.: To learn or not to learn: analyzing the role of learning for navigation in virtual environments. arXiv preprint arXiv:1907.11770 (2019)
51. Kolve, E., et al.: AI2-THOR: an interactive 3D environment for visual AI. arXiv (2017)
52. Kuttruff, H.: Room Acoustics. CRC Press, Boca Raton (2016)
53. Lerer, A., Gross, S., Fergus, R.: Learning physical intuition of block towers by example. In: ICML (2016)
54. Lessard, N., Paré, M., Lepore, F., Lassonde, M.: Early-blind human subjects localize sound sources better than sighted subjects. Nature **395**, 278–280 (1998)
55. Savva, M., et al.: Habitat: a platform for embodied AI research. In: ICCV (2019)
56. Massiceti, D., Hicks, S.L., van Rheede, J.J.: Stereosonic vision: exploring visual-to-auditory sensory substitution mappings in an immersive virtual reality navigation paradigm. PLoS ONE **13**(7), e0199389 (2018)

57. Merabet, L., Sanchez, J.: Audio-based navigation using virtual environments: combining technology and neuroscience. AER J. Res. Pract. Vis. Impair. Blind. **2**, 128–137 (2009)
58. Merabet, L.B., Pascual-Leone, A.: Neural reorganization following sensory loss: the opportunity of change. Nat. Rev. Neurosci. **11**, 44–52 (2010)
59. Mirowski, P., et al.: Learning to navigate in complex environments. In: ICLR (2017)
60. Mishkin, D., Dosovitskiy, A., Koltun, V.: Benchmarking classic and learned navigation in complex 3D environments. arXiv preprint arXiv:1901.10915 (2019)
61. Morgado, P., Nvasconcelos, N., Langlois, T., Wang, O.: Self-supervised generation of spatial audio for 360 video. In: NeurIPS (2018)
62. Murali, A. et al..: PyRobot: an open-source robotics framework for research and benchmarking. arXiv preprint arXiv:1906.08236 (2019)
63. Nakadai, K., Lourens, T., Okuno, H.G., Kitano, H.: Active audition for humanoid. In: AAAI (2000)
64. Nakadai, K., Nakamura, K.: Sound source localization and separation. Wiley Encyclopedia of Electrical and Electronics Engineering (1999)
65. Nakadai, K., Okuno, H.G., Kitano, H.: Epipolar geometry based sound localization and extraction for humanoid audition. In: IROS Workshops. IEEE (2001)
66. Owens, A., Efros, A.A.: Audio-visual scene analysis with self-supervised multisensory features. In: ECCV (2018)
67. Owens, A., Isola, P., McDermott, J., Torralba, A., Adelson, E.H., Freeman, W.T.: Visually indicated sounds. In: CVPR (2016)
68. Owens, A., Wu, J., McDermott, J.H., Freeman, W.T., Torralba, A.: Ambient sound provides supervision for visual learning. In: Leibe, B., Matas, J., Sebe, N., Welling, M. (eds.) ECCV 2016. LNCS, vol. 9905, pp. 801–816. Springer, Cham (2016). https://doi.org/10.1007/978-3-319-46448-0_48
69. Picinali, L., Afonso, A., Denis, M., Katz, B.: Exploration of architectural spaces by blind people using auditory virtual reality for the construction of spatial knowledge. Int. J. Hum.-Comput. Stud. **72**(4), 393–407 (2014)
70. Qin, J., Cheng, J., Wu, X., Xu, Y.: A learning based approach to audio surveillance in household environment. Int. J. Inf. Acquis. **3**, 213–219 (2006)
71. Rascon, C., Meza, I.: Localization of sound sources in robotics: a review. Robot. Auton. Syst. **96**, 184–210 (2017)
72. RoÈder, B., Teder-SaÈlejaÈrvi, W., Sterr, A., RoÈsler, F., Hillyard, S.A., Neville, H.J.: Improved auditory spatial tuning in blind humans. Nature **400**, 162–166 (1999)
73. Romano, J.M., Brindza, J.P., Kuchenbecker, K.J.: ROS open-source audio recognizer: ROAR environmental sound detection tools for robot programming. Auton. Robot. **34**, 207–215 (2013). https://doi.org/10.1007/s10514-013-9323-6
74. Savinov, N., Dosovitskiy, A., Koltun, V.: Semi-parametric topological memory for navigation. In: ICLR (2018)
75. Schulman, J., Wolski, F., Dhariwal, P., Radford, A., Klimov, O.: Proximal policy optimization algorithms. arXiv preprint arXiv:1707.06347 (2017)
76. Senocak, A., Oh, T.H., Kim, J., Yang, M.H., So Kweon, I.: Learning to localize sound source in visual scenes. In: CVPR (2018)
77. Straub, J., et al.: The replica dataset: a digital replica of indoor spaces. arXiv preprint arXiv:1906.05797 (2019)
78. Sukhbaatar, S., Szlam, A., Synnaeve, G., Chintala, S., Fergus, R.: Mazebase: a sandbox for learning from games. arXiv preprint arXiv:1511.07401 (2015)

79. Thinus-Blanc, C., Gaunet, F.: Representation of space in blind persons: vision as a spatial sense? Psychol. Bull. **121**, 20 (1997)
80. Thomason, J., Gordon, D., Bisk, Y.: Shifting the baseline: single modality performance on visual navigation & QA. In: NAACL-HLT (2019)
81. Thrun, S., Burgard, W., Fox, D.: Probabilistic Robotics. MIT Press, Cambridge (2005)
82. Tian, Y., Shi, J., Li, B., Duan, Z., Xu, C.: Audio-visual event localization in unconstrained videos. In: ECCV (2018)
83. Tolman, E.C.: Cognitive maps in rats and men. Psychol. Rev. **55**, 189 (1948)
84. van der Maaten, L., Hinton, G.: Visualizing high-dimensional data using t-SNE. J. Mach. Learn. Res. **9**, 2579–2605 (2008)
85. Veach, E., Guibas, L.: Bidirectional estimators for light transport. In: Sakas, G., Muller, S., Shirley, P. (eds) Photorealistic Rendering Techniques, pp. 145–167. Springer, Heidelberg (1995). https://doi.org/10.1007/978-3-642-87825-1_11
86. Viciana-Abad, R., Marfil, R., Perez-Lorenzo, J., Bandera, J., Romero-Garces, A., Reche-Lopez, P.: Audio-visual perception system for a humanoid robotic head. Sensors **14**, 9522–9545 (2014)
87. Voss, P., Lassonde, M., Gougoux, F., Fortin, M., Guillemot, J.P., Lepore, F.: Early-and late-onset blind individuals show supra-normal auditory abilities in far-space. Curr. Biol. **14**(19), 1734–1738 (2004)
88. Wang, Y., Kapadia, M., Huang, P., Kavan, L., Badler, N.: Sound localization and multi-modal steering for autonomous virtual agents. In: Symposium on Interactive 3D Graphics and Games (2014)
89. Wijmans, E., et al.: Embodied question answering in photorealistic environments with point cloud perception. In: CVPR (2019)
90. Wijmans, E., et al.: Decentralized distributed PPO: solving PointGoal navigation. In: ICLR (2020)
91. Wood, J., Magennis, M., Arias, E.F.C., Gutierrez, T., Graupp, H., Bergamasco, M.: The design and evaluation of a computer game for the blind in the GRAB haptic audio virtual environment. In: Proceedings of Eurohpatics (2003)
92. Wortsman, M., Ehsani, K., Rastegari, M., Farhadi, A., Mottaghi, R.: Learning to learn how to learn: self-adaptive visual navigation using meta-learning. In: CVPR (2019)
93. Woubie, A., Kanervisto, A., Karttunen, J., Hautamaki, V.: Do autonomous agents benefit from hearing? arXiv preprint arXiv:1905.04192 (2019)
94. Wu, X., Gong, H., Chen, P., Zhong, Z., Xu, Y.: Surveillance robot utilizing video and audio information. J. Intell. Robot. Syst. **55**, 403–421 (2009). https://doi.org/10.1007/s10846-008-9297-3
95. Wu, Y., Wu, Y., Tamar, A., Russell, S., Gkioxari, G., Tian, Y.: Bayesian relational memory for semantic visual navigation. In: ICCV (2019)
96. Wymann, B., Espié, E., Guionneau, C., Dimitrakakis, C., Coulom, R., Sumner, A.: TORCS, the open racing car simulator (2013). http://www.torcs.org
97. Xia, F., et al.: Interactive Gibson: a benchmark for interactive navigation in cluttered environments. arXiv preprint arXiv:1910.14442 (2019)
98. Xia, F., Zamir, A.R., He, Z., Sax, A., Malik, J., Savarese, S.: Gibson Env: real-world perception for embodied agents. In: CVPR (2018)
99. Yoshida, T., Nakadai, K., Okuno, H.G.: Automatic speech recognition improved by two-layered audio-visual integration for robot audition. In: 2009 9th IEEE-RAS International Conference on Humanoid Robots, pp. 604–609. IEEE (2009)
100. Aytar, Y., Vondrick, C., Torralba, A.: Learning sound representations from unlabeled video. In: NeurIPS (2016)

101. Aytar, Y., Vondrick, C., Torralba, A.: See, hear, and read: deep aligned representations. arXiv:1706.00932 (2017)
102. Zaunschirm, M., Schörkhuber, C., Höldrich, R.: Binaural rendering of ambisonic signals by head-related impulse response time alignment and a diffuseness constraint. J. Acoust. Soc. Am. **143**, 3616 (2018)
103. Zhao, H., Gan, C., Rouditchenko, A., Vondrick, C., McDermott, J., Torralba, A.: The sound of pixels. In: Ferrari, V., Hebert, M., Sminchisescu, C., Weiss, Y. (eds.) ECCV 2018. LNCS, vol. 11205, pp. 587–604. Springer, Cham (2018). https://doi.org/10.1007/978-3-030-01246-5_35
104. Zhou, Y., Wang, Z., Fang, C., Bui, T., Berg, T.L.: Visual to sound: generating natural sound for videos in the wild. In: CVPR (2018)
105. Zhu, Y., et al.: Visual semantic planning using deep successor representations. In: ICCV (2017)
106. Zhu, Y., et al.: Target-driven visual navigation in indoor scenes using deep reinforcement learning. In: ICRA (2017)

# Two-Stream Consensus Network for Weakly-Supervised Temporal Action Localization

Yuanhao Zhai[1], Le Wang[1(✉)], Wei Tang[2], Qilin Zhang[3], Junsong Yuan[4], and Gang Hua[5]

[1] Xi'an Jiaotong University, Xi'an, Shaanxi, China
lewang@mail.xjtu.edu.cn
[2] University of Illinois at Chicago, Chicago, IL, USA
[3] HERE Technologies, Chicago, IL, USA
[4] State University of New York at Buffalo, Buffalo, NY, USA
[5] Wormpex AI Research, Bellevue, WA, USA

**Abstract.** Weakly-supervised Temporal Action Localization (W-TAL) aims to classify and localize all action instances in an untrimmed video under only video-level supervision. However, without frame-level annotations, it is challenging for W-TAL methods to identify false positive action proposals and generate action proposals with precise temporal boundaries. In this paper, we present a Two-Stream Consensus Network (TSCN) to simultaneously address these challenges. The proposed TSCN features an iterative refinement training method, where a frame-level pseudo ground truth is iteratively updated, and used to provide frame-level supervision for improved model training and false positive action proposal elimination. Furthermore, we propose a new attention normalization loss to encourage the predicted attention to act like a binary selection, and promote the precise localization of action instance boundaries. Experiments conducted on the THUMOS14 and ActivityNet datasets show that the proposed TSCN outperforms current state-of-the-art methods, and even achieves comparable results with some recent fully-supervised methods.

**Keywords:** Temporal action localization · Weakly-supervised learning

## 1 Introduction

The task of Weakly-supervised Temporal Action Localization (W-TAL) aims at simultaneously localizing and classifying all action instances in a long untrimmed video given only video-level categorical labels in the learning phase. Compared to its fully-supervised counterpart, which requires frame-level annotations of all

**Electronic supplementary material** The online version of this chapter (https://doi.org/10.1007/978-3-030-58539-6_3) contains supplementary material, which is available to authorized users.

A. Vedaldi et al. (Eds.): ECCV 2020, LNCS 12351, pp. 37–54, 2020.
https://doi.org/10.1007/978-3-030-58539-6_3

action instances during training, W-TAL greatly simplifies the procedure of data collection and avoids annotation bias of human annotators, therefore has been widely studied [1,18,20,23,24,26–28,30,34,41,43,46] in recent years.

Several W-TAL methods [20,23,26–28,30,41] adopt a Multiple Instance Learning (MIL) framework, where a video is treated as a bag of frames/snippets to perform the video-level action classification. During testing, the trained model slides over time and generates a Temporal-Class Activation Map (T-CAM) [27,49] (*i.e.*, a sequence of probability distributions over action classes at each time step) and an attention sequence that measures the relative importance of each snippet. The action proposals are generated by thresholding the attention value and/or the T-CAM. This MIL framework is usually built on two feature modalities, *i.e.*, RGB frames and optical flow, which are fused in two possible ways. *Early fusion* methods [1,20,23,24,30,34] concatenate the RGB and optical flow features before they are fed into the network, and *late fusion* methods [23,26–28] compute a weighted sum of their respective outputs before generating action proposals. An example of late fusion is shown in Fig. 1.

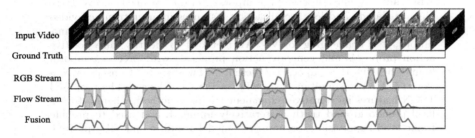

**Fig. 1.** Visualization of two-stream outputs and their late fusion result. The first two rows are an input video and the ground truth action instances, respectively. The last three rows are attention sequences (scaled from 0 to 1) predicted by the RGB stream, the flow stream and their weighted sum (*i.e.*, the fusion result), respectively, and the horizontal and vertical axes denote the time and the intensity of attention values, respectively. The green boxes denote the localization results generated by thresholding the attention at the value of 0.5. By properly combining the two different attention distributions predicted by the RGB and flow streams, the late fusion result achieves a higher true positive rate and a lower false positive rate, and thus has better localization performance (Color figure online)

Despite these recent development, two major challenges still persist. One of the most critical problems that prior W-TAL methods suffer from is the lack of ability to rule out false positive action proposals. Without frame-level annotations, they localize action instances that do not necessarily correspond to the video-level labels. For example, a model may falsely localize the action "swimming" by only checking the existence of water in the scene. Therefore, it is necessary to exploit more fine-grained supervision to guide the learning process. Another problem lies in the generation of action proposals. In previous methods, action proposals are generated by thresholding the activation sequence with a fixed threshold, which is preset empirically. It has a significant impact on the quality of action proposals: a high threshold may result in incomplete action proposals while a low threshold can bring more false positives. But how to get out of this dilemma was rarely studied.

In this paper, we introduce a Two-Stream Consensus Network (TSCN) to address the two aforementioned problems. To eliminate false positive action proposals, we design an iterative refinement training scheme, where a frame-level pseudo ground truth is generated from late fusion attention sequence, and serves as a more precise frame-level supervision to iteratively update two-stream models. Our intuition is simple: late fusion is essentially a voting ensemble of the RGB and flow streams, and if a proper fusion parameter (*i.e.*, the hyperparameter to control the relative importance of two streams) is selected, late fusion can provide more accurate result compared with each individual stream. The advantage of combining these two streams has been demonstrated by the Two-Stream Convolutional Networks [37] for action recognition. As shown in Fig. 1, the two streams produce different activation distributions, which lead to different false positives and false negatives. However, when they are combined, the false positive action proposals that only exist in one stream can be largely eliminated, and a high activation value occurs only when both streams are confident that an action instance exists. Since the late fusion result is of higher quality than single stream result, it can in turn serve as a frame-level pseudo ground truth to supervise and refine both streams. To generate high-quality action proposals, we introduce a new attention normalization loss. It pushes the predicted attention to approach extreme values, *i.e.*, 0 and 1, so as to avoid ambiguity. As a result, simply setting the threshold to 0.5 yields high-quality action proposals.

Formally, given an input video, RGB and optical flow features are first extracted from pre-trained deep networks. Then two-stream base models are trained with video-level labels on RGB and optical flow features, respectively, where the attention normalization loss is used to learn the attention distribution. After obtaining two-stream attention sequences, a frame-level pseudo ground truth is generated based on their weighted sum (*i.e.*, the late fusion attention sequence), and in turn provides frame-level supervision to improve the two-stream models. We iteratively update the pseudo ground truth and refine the two-stream base models, and the normalization term at the same time forces the predicted attention to approach a binary selection. The final localization result is obtained by thresholding the late fusion attention sequence.

To summarize, our contribution is threefold:

- We introduce a Two-Stream Consensus Network (TSCN) for W-TAL. The proposed TSCN uses an iterative refinement training method, where a pseudo ground truth generated from late fusion attention sequence at previous iteration can provide more precise frame-level supervision to current iteration.
- We propose an attention normalization loss function, which forces the attention to act like a binary selection, and thus improves the quality of action proposals generated by the thresholding method.

- Extensive experiments are conducted on two standard benchmarks (*i.e.*, THU-MOS14 and ActivityNet) to demonstrate the effectiveness of the proposed method. Our TSCN significantly outperforms previous state-of-the-art W-TAL methods, and even achieves comparable results to some recent fully-supervised TAL methods.

## 2   Related Work

**Action Recognition.** Traditional methods [7,8,19,39] aim to model spatio-temporal information via hand-crafted features. Two-Stream Convolutional Networks [37] use two separate Convolutional Neural Networks (CNNs) to exploit appearance and motion clues from RGB frames and optical flow, respectively, and use a late fusion method to reconcile the two-stream outputs. [10] focuses on studying different ways to fuse the two streams. The Inflated 3D ConvNet (I3D) [3] expands the 2D CNNs in two-stream networks to 3D CNNs. Several recent methods [5,31,35,40,47] focus on directly learning motion clues from RGB frames instead of calculating optical flow.

**Fully-Supervised Temporal Action Localization.** Fully-supervised TAL requires frame-level annotations of all action instances during training. Several large-scale datasets have been created for this task, such as THUMOS [13,15], ActivityNet [2], and Charades [36]. Many methods [4,6,12,14,22,33,42,48] adopt a two-stage pipeline, *i.e.*, action proposal generation followed by action classification. Several methods [4,6,11,42] adopt the Faster R-CNN [32] framework to TAL. Most recently, some methods [21,22,25] try to generate action proposals with more flexible durations. Zeng *et al.* [45] apply the Graph Convolutional Networks (GCN) [17,38] to TAL to exploit proposal-proposal relations.

**Weakly-Supervised Temporal Action Localization.** W-TAL, which only requires video-level supervision during training, greatly relieves the data annotation efforts, and draws more and more attention from the community recently. Hide-and-Seek [18] randomly hides part of the input video to guide the network to discover other relevant parts. UntrimmedNet [41] consists of a selection module to select the important snippets and a classification module to perform per snippet classification. Sparse Temporal Pooling Network (STPN) [27] improves UntrimmedNet by adding a sparse loss to enforce the sparsity of selected segments. W-TALC [30] jointly optimizes a co-activity similarity loss and a multiple instance learning loss to train the network. AutoLoc [34] is one of the first two-stage methods in W-TAL, and it first generates initial action proposals and then regresses the boundaries of the action proposals with an Outer-Inner-Contrastive loss. CleanNet [24] improves AutoLoc by leveraging the temporal contrast in snippet-level action classification predictions. Liu *et al.* [23] propose a multi-branch network to model different stages of action. Besides, several methods [20,28] focus on modeling the background and achieve state-of-the-art performances.

Recently, RefineLoc [1] uses an iterative refinement method to help the model capture a *complete* action instance. And our method is distinct from RefineLoc in three main aspects. (1) We adopt a late fusion framework, while RefineLoc adopts an early fusion framework. (2) Our pseudo ground truth is generated from two-stream late fusion attention sequences, which provides better localization performance than each single stream, while RefineLoc generates the pseudo ground truth by expanding previous localization results, which might result in coarser and over-complete action proposals. (3) We introduce a new attention normalization loss to explicitly avoid the ambiguity of attention, while RefineLoc has no explicit constraints on attention values.

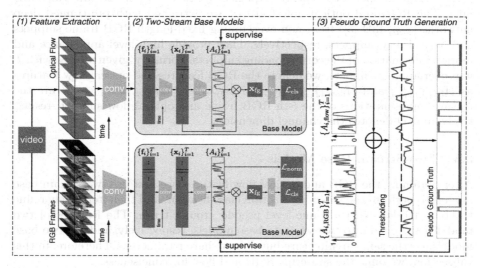

**Fig. 2.** An overview of the proposed Two-Stream Consensus Network, which consists of three parts: (1) RGB and optical flow snippet-level features are extracted with pre-trained models; (2) two-stream base models are separately trained using these RGB and optical flow features; (3) frame-level pseudo ground truth is generated from the two-stream late fusion attention sequence, and in turn provides frame-level supervision to two-stream base models

# 3    Two-Stream Consensus Network

In this section, we first formulate the task of Weakly-supervised Temporal Action Localization (W-TAL), and then describe the proposed Two-Stream Consensus Network (TSCN) in detail. The overall architecture is shown in Fig. 2.

## 3.1    Problem Formulation

Assume we are given a set of training videos. For each video $v$, we only have its video-level categorical label $\mathbf{y}$, where $\mathbf{y} \in \mathbb{R}^C$ is a normalized multi-hot vector, and $C$ is the number of action categories. The goal of temporal action localization is to generate a set of action proposals $\{(t_s, t_e, c, \psi)\}$ for each testing video, where $t_s, t_e, c, \psi$ denote the start time, the end time, the predicted action category and the confidence score of the action proposal, respectively.

### 3.2 Feature Extraction

Following recent W-TAL methods [20, 23, 24, 26–28, 30, 34, 43], we construct TSCN upon snippet-level feature sequences extracted from the raw video volume. The RGB and optical flow features are extracted with pre-trained deep networks (*e.g.*, I3D [3]) from non-overlapping fixed-length RGB frame snippets and optical flow snippets, respectively. They provide high-level appearance and motion information of the corresponding snippets. Formally, given a video with $T$ non-overlapping snippets, we denote the RGB features and optical flow features as $\{\mathbf{f}_{\mathrm{RGB},i}\}_{i=1}^{T}$ and $\{\mathbf{f}_{\mathrm{flow},i}\}_{i=1}^{T}$, respectively, where $\mathbf{f}_{\mathrm{RGB},i}, \mathbf{f}_{\mathrm{flow},i} \in \mathbb{R}^{D}$ are the feature representations of the $i$-th RGB frame and optical flow snippet, respectively, and $D$ denotes the channel dimension.

### 3.3 Two-Stream Base Models

After obtaining the RGB and optical flow features, we first use two-stream base models to perform the video-level action classification, and then iteratively refine the base models with a frame-level pseudo ground truth. The features of two modalities are fed into two separate base models, respectively, and the two base models use the same architecture but do not share parameters. Therefore, in this subsection, we omit the subscript RGB and flow for conciseness.

Since the features are not originally trained for the W-TAL task, we concatenate the $T$ input features $\{\mathbf{f}_i\}_{i=1}^{T}$, and use a set of temporal convolutional layers to generate a set of new features $\{\mathbf{x}_i\}_{i=1}^{T}$, where $\mathbf{x}_i \in \mathbb{R}^{D'}$, and $D'$ denotes the output feature dimension.

As a video may contain background snippets, to perform video-level classification, we need to select snippets that are likely to contain action instances and meanwhile filter out snippets that are likely to contain background. To this end, an attention value $A_i \in (0, 1)$ to measure the likelihood of the $i$-th snippet containing an action is given by a fully-connected (FC) layer:

$$A_i = \sigma\left(\mathbf{w}_A \cdot \mathbf{x}_i + b_A\right), \tag{1}$$

where $\sigma(\cdot)$, $\mathbf{w}_A$, and $b_A$ are the sigmoid function, weight vector and bias of the attention layer. We then perform attention-weighted pooling over the feature sequence to generate a single foreground feature $\mathbf{x}_{\mathrm{fg}}$, and feed it to an FC softmax layer to get the video-level prediction:

$$\mathbf{x}_{\mathrm{fg}} = \frac{1}{\sum_{i=1}^{T} A_i} \sum_{i=1}^{T} A_i \mathbf{x}_i, \tag{2}$$

$$\hat{y}_c = \frac{e^{\mathbf{w}_c \cdot \mathbf{x}_{\text{fg}} + b_c}}{\sum_{i=1}^{C} e^{\mathbf{w}_i \cdot \mathbf{x}_{\text{fg}} + b_i}}, \tag{3}$$

where $\hat{y}_c$ is the probability that the video contains the $c$-th action, and $\mathbf{w}_c$ and $b_c$ are the weight and bias of the FC layer for category $c$. The classification loss function $\mathcal{L}_{\text{cls}}$ is defined as the standard cross entropy loss:

$$\mathcal{L}_{\text{cls}} = -\sum_{c=1}^{C} y_c \log(\hat{y}_c), \tag{4}$$

where $y_c$ denotes the value of label vector $\mathbf{y}$ at index $c$.

Ideally, an attention value is expected to be binary, where 1 indicates the presence of action while 0 indicates background. Recently, several methods [20,28] introduce a background category, and use the background classification to guide the learning of attention. In this work, instead of using background classification, we introduce an attention normalization term to force the attention to approach extreme values:

$$\mathcal{L}_{\text{att}} = \frac{1}{l} \min_{\substack{A \subset \{A_i\} \\ |A| = l}} \sum_{a \in A} a - \frac{1}{l} \max_{\substack{A \subset \{A_i\} \\ |A| = l}} \sum_{a \in A} a, \tag{5}$$

where $l = \max\left(1, \lfloor \frac{T}{s} \rfloor\right)$ and $s$ is a hyperparameter to control the selected snippets. This normalization loss aims to maximize the difference between the average top-$l$ attention values and the average bottom-$l$ attention values, and force the foreground attention to be 1 and background attention to be 0.

Therefore, the overall loss for the base model training is the weighted sum of the classification loss and the attention normalization term:

$$\mathcal{L}_{\text{base}} = \mathcal{L}_{\text{cls}} + \alpha \mathcal{L}_{\text{att}}, \tag{6}$$

where $\alpha$ is a hyperparameter to control the weight of the normalization loss.

In addition, the temporal-class activation map (T-CAM) $\{\mathbf{s}_i\}_{i=1}^{T}$, $\mathbf{s}_i \in \mathbb{R}^C$ is also generated by sliding the classification FC softmax layer over all snippets:

$$s_{i,c} = \frac{e^{\mathbf{w}_c \cdot \mathbf{x}_i + b_c}}{\sum_{j=1}^{C} e^{\mathbf{w}_j \cdot \mathbf{x}_i + b_j}}, \tag{7}$$

where $s_{i,c}$ is the T-CAM value of $i$-th snippet for category $c$.

### 3.4   Pseudo Ground Truth Generation

We iteratively refine the two-stream base models with a frame-level pseudo ground truth. Specifically, we divide the whole training process into several refinement iterations. At refinement iteration 0, only video-level labels are used for training. And at refinement iteration $n+1$, a frame-level pseudo ground truth is generated at refinement iteration $n$, and provides frame-level supervision for the current refinement iteration. However, without *true* ground truth annotations, we can neither measure the quality of the pseudo ground truth, nor guarantee the pseudo ground truth can help the base models achieve higher performance.

Inspired by two-stream late fusion, we introduce a simple yet effective method to generate the pseudo ground truth. Intuitively, locations at which both streams have high activations are likely to contain ground truth action instances; locations at which only one stream has high activations are likely to be either false positive action proposals or true action instances that only one stream can detect; locations at which both streams both have low activations are likely to be the background.

Following this intuition, we use the fusion attention sequence $\{A_{\text{fuse},i}^{(n)}\}_{i=1}^{T}$ at refinement iteration $n$ to generate pseudo ground truth $\{\mathcal{G}_i^{(n+1)}\}_{i=1}^{T}$ for refinement iteration $n+1$, where $A_{\text{fuse},i}^{(n)} = \beta A_{\text{RGB},i}^{(n)} + (1-\beta)A_{\text{flow},i}^{(n)}$, and $\beta \in [0,1]$ is a hyperparameter to control the relative importance of RGB and flow attentions. We introduce two pseudo ground truth generation methods.

**Soft Pseudo Ground Truth** means to directly use the fusion attention values as pseudo labels: $\mathcal{G}_i^{(n+1)} = A_{\text{fuse},i}^{(n)}$. The soft pseudo labels contain the probability of a snippet being the foreground action, but also add uncertainty to the model.

**Hard Pseudo Ground Truth** thresholds the attention sequence to generate a binary sequence:

$$\mathcal{G}_i^{(n+1)} = \begin{cases} 1, & A_{\text{fuse},i}^{(n)} > \theta; \\ 0, & A_{\text{fuse},i}^{(n)} \leq \theta, \end{cases} \qquad (8)$$

where $\theta$ is the threshold value. Setting a large value of $\theta$ will eliminate the action proposals that only one stream has high activations, and therefore reduces the false positive rate. In contrast, setting a small value of $\theta$ will help models to generate more action proposals and achieve a higher recall. Hard pseudo labels remove the uncertainty and provide stronger supervision, but introduce a hyperparameter.

After generating the frame-level pseudo ground truth, we force the attention sequence generated by *each* stream to be similar to the pseudo ground truth with a mean square error (MSE) loss[1]:

$$\mathcal{L}_{\mathcal{G}}^{(n+1)} = \frac{1}{T} \sum_{i=1}^{T} \left( A_i^{(n+1)} - \mathcal{G}_i^{(n+1)} \right)^2. \qquad (9)$$

At refinement iteration $n+1$, the total loss for each stream is

$$\mathcal{L}_{\text{total}}^{(n+1)} = \mathcal{L}_{\text{base}} + \gamma \mathcal{L}_{\mathcal{G}}^{(n+1)}, \qquad (10)$$

where $\gamma$ is a hyperparameter to control the relative importance of two losses.

---

[1] Although it is straightforward to use a cross entropy loss for hard pseudo ground truth, we found in practice that the cross entropy loss and the MSE loss achieve similar performance. To simplify training, we use the MSE loss for both kinds of pseudo ground truth.

## 3.5    Action Localization

During testing, following BaS-Net [20], we first temporally upsample the attention sequence and T-CAM by a factor of 8 via linear interpolation. Then, we select top-$k$ action categories from the fusion video-level prediction $\hat{\mathbf{y}}_{\text{fuse}}$ to perform action localization, where $\hat{\mathbf{y}}_{\text{fuse}} = \beta\hat{\mathbf{y}}_{\text{RGB}} + (1 - \beta)\hat{\mathbf{y}}_{\text{flow}}$. For each of these categories, following our intention that the attention performs a binary selection, we generate action proposals by directly thresholding the attention value at 0.5 and concatenating consecutive snippets. The action proposals are scored via a variant of the Outer-Inner-Constrastive score [34]: instead of using average T-CAM, we use attention weighted T-CAM to measure the outer and inner temporal contrast. Formally, given action proposal $(t_s, t_e, c)$, fusion attention $\{A_{\text{fuse},i}\}_{i=1}^{T}$ and T-CAM $\{\mathbf{s}_{\text{fuse},i}\}_{i=1}^{T}$, where $\mathbf{s}_{\text{fuse},i} = \beta\mathbf{s}_{\text{RGB},i} + (1 - \beta)\mathbf{s}_{\text{flow},i}$, the score $\psi$ is computed as

$$\psi = \frac{\sum_{i=t_s}^{t_e} A_{\text{fuse},i} s_{\text{fuse},i,c}}{t_e - t_s} - \frac{\sum_{i=T_s}^{T_e} A_{\text{fuse},i} s_{\text{fuse},i,c} - \sum_{i=t_s}^{t_e} A_{\text{fuse},i} s_{\text{fuse},i,c}}{T_e - T_s - (t_e - t_s)}, \quad (11)$$

where $T_s = t_s - \frac{L}{4}$, $T_e = t_e + \frac{L}{4}$, and $L = t_e - t_s$. We discard action proposals with confidence scores lower than 0.

## 4    Experiments

### 4.1    Dataset and Evaluation

**THUMOS14 Dataset** [15] contains 200 validation videos and 213 testing videos within 20 categories for the TAL task. We use the 200 validation videos for training, and use the 213 testing videos for evaluation.

**ActivityNet Dataset** [2] has two release versions, *i.e.*, ActivityNet v1.3 and ActivityNet v1.2. ActivityNet v1.3 covers 200 action categories, with a training set of 10,024 videos and a validation set of 4,926 videos. ActivityNet v1.2 is a subset of ActivityNet v1.3, and covers 100 action categories, with 4,819 and 2,383 videos in the training and validation set, respectively [2]. We use the training set and the validation set for training and testing, respectively.

**Evaluation Metrics.** Following the standard protocol on temporal action localization, we evaluate our method with mean Average Precision (mAP) under different Intersection-over-Union (IoU) thresholds. We use the evaluation code provided by ActivityNet[3] to perform the experiments.

---

[2]  In our experiments, there are 9,937 and 4,575 videos in training and validation set of ActivityNet v1.3, respectively, and 4,471 and 2,211 videos in training and validation set of ActivityNet v1.2, respectively, because the rest of the videos are unaccessible from YouTube.

[3]  https://github.com/activitynet/ActivityNet/tree/master/Evaluation.

## 4.2    Implementation Details

Two off-the-shelf feature extraction backbones are used in our experiments, *i.e.*, UntrimmedNet [41] and I3D [3], with snippet lengths of 15 frames and 16 frames, respectively. The two backbones are pre-trained on ImageNet [9] and Kinetics [3], respectively, and are not fine-tuned for fair comparison. The RGB and flow snippet-level features are extracted at the global_pool layer as 1024-D vectors.

The networks are implemented in PyTorch [29]. We use the Adam [16] optimizer with a fixed learning rate 0.0001. We train the base models 200 and 80 epochs at refinement iteration 0, and 100 and 40 epochs for later refinement iterations for ActivityNet and THUMOS14, respectively. We set the maximal number of refinement iterations to 4 for the THUMOS14 dataset, and 24 for the ActivityNet datasets, and choose base models that achieve the lowest loss at the previous refinement iteration to generate the pseudo ground truth. To eliminate fragmentary action proposals, temporal max pooling of kernel size 5 and stride 1 is used on the fusion attention sequence before pseudo ground truth generation on ActivityNet dataset. We use a whole video as a batch. All hyperparameters are determined via grid search: $s = 8$, $\alpha = 0.1$, $\beta = 0.4$, $\gamma = 2$. We set $\theta$ to 0.55 and 0.5 for THUMOS14 and ActivityNet, respectively. We choose top-2 action categories and also reject categories whose fusion classification prediction scores are lower than 0.1 to perform action localization.

## 4.3    Comparison with the State-of-the-Art

**Experiments on THUMOS14.** Table 1 summarizes the performance comparison between the proposed TSCN and state-of-the-art fully-supervised and weakly-supervised TAL methods on the THUMOS14 testing set. With UntrimmedNet features, TSCN outperforms other W-TAL methods by a large margin, and even achieves comparable results to some recent W-TAL methods with I3D features (*e.g.*, Nguyen *et al.* [28] and BaS-Net [20]) at high IoU thresholds.

With I3D features, our performance boosts significantly, and outperforms previous W-TAL methods at most IoU thresholds. We note the proposed TSCN can achieve a comparable performance to some recent fully-supervised methods (*e.g.*, R-C3D [42]). TSCN even outperforms TAL-net [4] at IoU thresholds 0.1 and 0.2. However, as the IoU threshold increases, the performance of TSCN drops significantly, because generating more precise action boundaries need true frame-level ground truth supervision.

**Experiments on ActivityNet.** The performance comparisons on ActivityNet v1.2 and v1.3 are shown in Tables 2 and 3, respectively, where our models are trained with I3D features. The proposed TSCN outperforms previous W-TAL methods at the average mAP at IoU threshold 0.5 : 0.05 : 0.95 on both release versions of ActivityNet, verifying the efficacy of our design intuition.

**Table 1.** Comparison of our method with state-of-the-art TAL methods on the THU-MOS14 testing set. UNT and I3D are abbreviations for UntrimmedNet feature and I3D feature, respectively

| | Method | mAP@IoU (%) | | | | | | | | |
|---|---|---|---|---|---|---|---|---|---|---|
| | | 0.1 | 0.2 | 0.3 | 0.4 | 0.5 | 0.6 | 0.7 | 0.8 | 0.9 |
| Fully-supervised | Yuan et al. [44] | 51.0 | 45.2 | 36.5 | 27.8 | 17.8 | - | - | - | - |
| | CDC [33] | - | - | 40.1 | 29.4 | 23.3 | 13.1 | 7.9 | - | - |
| | R-C3D [42] | 54.5 | 51.5 | 44.8 | 35.6 | 28.9 | - | - | - | - |
| | SSN [48] | 66.0 | 59.4 | 51.9 | 41.0 | 29.8 | - | - | - | - |
| | BSN [22] | - | - | 53.5 | 45.0 | 36.9 | 28.4 | 20.0 | - | - |
| | TAL-Net [4] | 59.8 | 57.1 | 53.2 | 48.5 | 42.8 | 33.8 | 20.8 | - | - |
| | GTAN [25] | 69.1 | 63.7 | 57.8 | 47.2 | 38.8 | - | .- | - | - |
| | BMN [21] | - | - | 56.0 | 47.4 | 38.8 | 29.7 | 20.5 | - | - |
| Weakly-supervised | UntrimmedNet [41] | 44.4 | 37.7 | 28.2 | 21.1 | 13.7 | - | - | - | - |
| | STPN (UNT) [27] | 45.3 | 38.8 | 31.1 | 23.5 | 16.2 | 9.8 | 5.1 | 2.0 | 0.3 |
| | AutoLoc (UNT) [34] | - | - | 35.8 | 29.0 | 21.2 | 13.4 | 5.8 | - | - |
| | W-TALC (UNT) [30] | 49.0 | 42.8 | 32.0 | 26.0 | 18.8 | - | 6.2 | - | - |
| | Liu et al. (UNT) [23] | 53.5 | 46.8 | 37.5 | 29.1 | 19.9 | 12.3 | 6.0 | - | - |
| | RefineLoc (UNT) [1] | - | - | 36.1 | - | 22.6 | - | 5.8 | - | - |
| | CleanNet (UNT) [24] | - | - | 37.0 | 30.9 | 23.9 | 13.9 | 7.1 | - | - |
| | BaS-Net (UNT) [20] | 56.2 | 50.3 | 42.8 | 34.7 | 25.1 | 17.1 | 9.3 | 3.7 | **0.5** |
| | Ours (UNT) | **58.9** | **52.9** | **45.0** | **36.6** | **27.6** | **18.8** | **10.2** | **4.0** | **0.5** |
| | STPN (I3D) [27] | 52.0 | 44.7 | 35.5 | 25.8 | 16.9 | 9.9 | 4.3 | 1.2 | 0.1 |
| | W-TALC (I3D) [30] | 55.2 | 49.6 | 40.1 | 31.1 | 22.8 | - | 7.6 | - | - |
| | Liu et al. (I3D) [23] | 57.4 | 50.8 | 41.2 | 32.1 | 23.1 | 15.0 | 7.0 | - | - |
| | RefineLoc (I3D) [1] | - | - | 40.8 | - | 23.1 | - | 5.3 | - | - |
| | Nguyen et al. (I3D) [28] | 60.4 | 56.0 | 46.6 | 37.5 | 26.8 | 17.6 | 9.0 | 3.3 | 0.4 |
| | BaS-Net (I3D) [20] | 58.2 | 52.3 | 44.6 | 36.0 | 27.0 | 18.6 | **10.4** | **3.9** | 0.5 |
| | Ours (I3D) | **63.4** | **57.6** | **47.8** | **37.7** | **28.7** | **19.4** | 10.2 | 3.9 | **0.7** |

**Table 2.** Comparison of our method with state-of-the-art W-TAL methods on the ActivityNet v1.2 validation set. The Avg column indicates the average mAP at IoU thresholds 0.5:0.05:0.95

| Method | mAP@IoU (%) | | | Avg |
|---|---|---|---|---|
| | 0.5 | 0.75 | 0.95 | |
| UntrimmedNet [41] | 7.4 | 3.2 | 0.7 | 3.6 |
| AutoLoc [34] | 27.3 | 15.1 | 3.3 | 16.0 |
| W-TALC [30] | 37.0 | - | - | 18.0 |
| Liu et al. [23] | 36.8 | 22.0 | 5.6 | 22.4 |
| Ours | **37.6** | **23.7** | **5.7** | **23.6** |

**Table 3.** Comparison of our method with state-of-the-art W-TAL methods on the ActivityNet v1.3 validation set. The Avg column indicates the average mAP at IoU thresholds 0.5:0.05:0.95

| Method | mAP@IoU (%) | | | Avg |
|---|---|---|---|---|
| | 0.5 | 0.75 | 0.95 | |
| STPN [27] | 29.3 | 16.9 | 2.7 | - |
| Liu et al. [23] | 34.0 | 20.9 | **5.7** | 21.2 |
| Nguyen et al. [28] | **36.4** | 19.2 | 2.9 | - |
| Ours | 35.3 | **21.4** | 5.3 | **21.7** |

**Table 4.** Comparison of our method with different attention normalization functions on the THUMOS14 testing set. $\mathcal{L}_{bg}$ is the background classification loss introduced in [28], and $\mathcal{L}_{att}$ is defined in Eq. (5). The var column denotes the average attention variance over the whole testing set

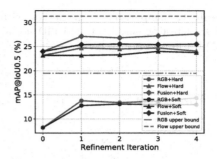

| $\mathcal{L}_{cls}$ | $\mathcal{L}_{bg}$ | $\mathcal{L}_{att}$ | mAP@IoU (%) | | | Var |
|---|---|---|---|---|---|---|
| | | | 0.3 | 0.5 | 0.7 | |
| ✓ | - | - | 29.6 | 16.1 | 4.1 | 0.0440 |
| ✓ | ✓ | - | 34.3 | 19.3 | 6.7 | 0.0599 |
| ✓ | - | ✓ | **40.9** | **24.0** | **8.2** | **0.0937** |
| ✓ | ✓ | ✓ | 40.6 | 23.6 | 7.8 | 0.0886 |

**Fig. 3.** Comparison between models trained with different pseudo ground truth on the THUMOS14 testing set. The upper bounds denote models trained with ground truth actionness sequence

### 4.4   Ablation Study

In this subsection, a set of ablation studies is conducted on the THUMOS14 testing set with UntrimmedNet feature to analyze the efficacy of each component in the proposed TSCN.

**Ablation Study on $\mathcal{L}_{att}$.** The goal of $\mathcal{L}_{att}$ in Eq. (5) is to force the attention values to approach extreme values, and therefore generate a clean foreground feature $\mathbf{x}_{fg}$ and improve action proposal quality. Some recent methods [20,28] introduce background classification to W-TAL. Particularly, background classification loss $\mathcal{L}_{bg}$ [28] is introduced to classify the background, where a background attention is defined as $1 - A_i$, and a background feature is generated via background attention-weighted pooling over all snippets to perform the background classification. Therefore, $\mathcal{L}_{bg}$ is in essence an implicit attention normalization loss. However, one drawback of such background loss is that assigning background labels to all videos will make the value of the background category in the T-CAM increase. We reproduce $\mathcal{L}_{bg}$ in our model, compare it with our proposed $\mathcal{L}_{att}$, and list the results in Table 4. The results reveal that both $\mathcal{L}_{bg}$ and $\mathcal{L}_{att}$ help improve the performance. And the proposed $\mathcal{L}_{att}$ achieves higher attention variance and better localization performance than $\mathcal{L}_{bg}$, demonstrating that the our attention normalization term $\mathcal{L}_{att}$ can better avoid the ambiguity of attention. Surprisingly, with both $\mathcal{L}_{bg}$ and $\mathcal{L}_{att}$, the localization performance is still lower than that with only $\mathcal{L}_{att}$, and we think this is because the noise of background classification reduces the accuracy of action proposal scores.

**Ablation Study on Pseudo Ground Truth.** Figure 3 plots performance comparison between different pseudo ground truth methods at different refinement iterations. Both soft and hard pseudo ground truth help improve the localization performance. The hard pseudo ground truth removes uncertainty to the model, and thus achieves higher performance improvement. However, with the same frame-level supervision, the flow stream outperforms the RGB stream by a large margin. We think this is because of the nature of two modalities: the RGB modality is less sensitive to actions than the optical flow modality. To demonstrate this, we generate a *true* frame-level ground truth actionness sequence (action categories are not used), train our model in the same way as the pseudo ground truth. The results are plotted in Fig. 3 as an upper bound. The results verify our hypothesis and demonstrate that the optical flow modality is more suitable for the action localization task than the RGB modality.

**Table 5.** Comparison between the model trained with only video-level labels and the model trained with hard pseudo ground truth on the THUMOS14 testing set. The label column denotes the supervision used in training, where "video" indicates only video-level labels are leveraged, and "frame" indicates the hard pseudo ground truth is also leveraged during training. Precision, recall and F-measure are calculated under IoU threshold 0.5

| Modality | Label | mAP@IoU (%) | | | | | Precision (%) | Recall (%) | F-measure |
|---|---|---|---|---|---|---|---|---|---|
| | | 0.3 | 0.4 | 0.5 | 0.6 | 0.7 | | | |
| RGB | Video | 19.8 | 13.2 | 8.2 | 4.5 | 1.9 | 10.2 | 20.9 | 0.1371 |
| RGB | Frame | 31.4 | 22.1 | 14.4 | 8.9 | 5.2 | 20.9 | 30.8 | 0.2489 |
| Flow | Video | 40.2 | 32.0 | 23.2 | 15.4 | 7.2 | 25.5 | 43.3 | 0.3207 |
| Flow | Frame | 40.8 | 32.7 | 24.1 | 16.8 | 8.7 | 30.9 | 42.4 | 0.3573 |
| Fusion | Video | 40.9 | 32.4 | 24.0 | 15.9 | 8.2 | 23.6 | 44.4 | 0.3078 |
| Fusion | Frame | 45.0 | 36.5 | 27.6 | 18.8 | 10.2 | 31.3 | 44.6 | 0.3680 |

Table 5 lists the detailed performance comparison between the model trained with only video-level labels and that trained with the hard pseudo ground truth. The results show that pseudo ground truth improves the localization performance for both modalities at all IoU thresholds, and thus improves the performance of the fusion result. Also, the pseudo ground truth greatly improves the precision and recall for the RGB stream and the fusion result, and improves the precision for the flow stream with a minor loss of recall (the overall F-measure improves significantly), which demonstrates that the pseudo ground truth can help eliminate false positive action proposals.

**Qualitative Analysis.** Three representative examples of TAL results are plotted in Fig. 4 to illustrate the efficacy of the proposed pseudo supervision. In the first example of diving and cliff diving, with only video-level labels, the RGB stream provides worse localization result than the flow stream, and thus leads to a noisy fusion attention sequence. The pseudo ground truth guides the RGB stream to identify false positive action proposals and discover true action instances, and further leads to a cleaner fusion attention sequence, where high activations correspond better to the ground truth. In the second example of cricket shot, with only video-level supervision, the RGB stream can only distinguish certain scenes, and fails to separate proximate action instances. In contrast, the flow stream can precisely detect action instances. Therefore, the pseudo ground truth helps the RGB stream to separate consecutive action instances. In the last example of soccer penalty, both streams have high activations on certain false positive temporal locations. Under this circumstance, the false positive action proposals will have higher activations under frame-level pseudo supervision. To eliminate such false positive action proposals, however, need true ground truth supervision. To summarize, the two modalities have their own strengths and limitations: the RGB stream is sensitive to appearance, thus it fails in scenes shot from unusual angles or separating proximate action instances in the same scene; the flow stream is sensitive to motion, and provides more accurate results, but it fails in slow or occluded motion. Qualitative results reveal that the pseudo ground truth helps two streams reach a consensus at most temporal locations. Therefore, the fusion attention sequence becomes cleaner and helps generate more precise action proposals and more reliable confidence scores.

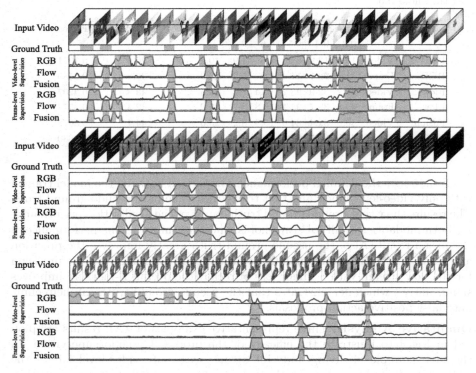

**Fig. 4.** Qualitative results on the THUMOS14 testing set. The eight rows in each example are input video, ground truth action instance, RGB stream, flow stream, and fusion attention sequences from the model trained with only video-level labels and frame-level pseudo ground truth, respectively. Action proposals are represented by green boxes. The horizontal and vertical axes are time and intensity of attention, respectively (Color figure online)

# 5    Conclusions

In this paper, we propose a Two-Stream Consensus Network (TSCN) for W-TAL, which benefits from an iterative refinement training method and a new attention normalization loss. The iterative refinement training uses a novel frame-level pseudo ground truth as fine-grained supervision, and iteratively improves the two-stream base models. The attention normalization loss function reduces the ambiguity of attention values, and thus leads to more precise action proposals. Experiments on two benchmarks demonstrate the proposed TSCN outperforms current state-of-the-art methods, and verify our design intuition.

**Acknowledgement.** This work was supported partly by National Key R&D Program of China Grant 2018AAA0101400, NSFC Grants 61629301, 61773312, and 61976171, China Postdoctoral Science Foundation Grant 2019M653642, Young Elite Scientists Sponsorship Program by CAST Grant 2018QNRC001, and Natural Science Foundation of Shaanxi Grant 2020JQ-069.

# References

1. Alwassel, H., Pardo, A., Heilbron, F.C., Thabet, A., Ghanem, B.: RefineLoc: iterative refinement for weakly-supervised action localization. arXiv preprint arXiv:1904.00227 (2019)
2. Heilbron, F.C., Escorcia, V., Ghanem, B., Niebles, J.C.: Activitynet: a large-scale video benchmark for human activity understanding. In: Proceedings of the IEEE Conference on Computer Vision and Pattern Recognition, pp. 961–970 (2015)
3. Carreira, J., Zisserman, A.: Quo Vadis, action recognition? a new model and the kinetics dataset. In: Proceedings of the IEEE Conference on Computer Vision and Pattern Recognition, pp. 6299–6308 (2017)
4. Chao, Y.W., Vijayanarasimhan, S., Seybold, B., Ross, D.A., Deng, J., Sukthankar, R.: Rethinking the faster R-CNN architecture for temporal action localization. In: Proceedings of the IEEE Conference on Computer Vision and Pattern Recognition, pp. 1130–1139 (2018)
5. Crasto, N., Weinzaepfel, P., Alahari, K., Schmid, C.: MARS: motion-augmented RGB stream for action recognition. In: Proceedings of the IEEE Conference on Computer Vision and Pattern Recognition, pp. 7882–7891 (2019)
6. Dai, X., Singh, B., Zhang, G., Davis, L.S., Chen, Y.Q.: Temporal context network for activity localization in videos. In: Proceedings of the IEEE International Conference on Computer Vision, pp. 5793–5802 (2017)
7. Dalal, N., Triggs, B.: Histograms of oriented gradients for human detection. In: Proceedings of the IEEE Conference on Computer Vision and Pattern Recognition, pp. 886–893 (2005)
8. Dalal, N., Triggs, B., Schmid, C.: Human detection using oriented histograms of flow and appearance. In: Proceedings of the European Conference on Computer Vision, pp. 428–441 (2006)
9. Deng, J., Dong, W., Socher, R., Li, L.J., Li, K., Li, F.F.: ImageNet: a large-scale hierarchical image database. In: Proceedings of the IEEE Conference on Computer Vision and Pattern Recognition, pp. 248–255 (2009)

10. Feichtenhofer, C., Pinz, A., Zisserman, A.: Convolutional two-stream network fusion for video action recognition. In: Proceedings of the IEEE Conference on Computer Vision and Pattern Recognition, pp. 1933–1941 (2016)
11. Gao, J., Yang, Z., Chen, K., Sun, C., Nevatia, R.: TURN TAP: temporal unit regression network for temporal action proposals. In: Proceedings of the IEEE International Conference on Computer Vision, pp. 3628–3636 (2017)
12. Gao, J., Yang, Z., Nevatia, R.: Cascaded boundary regression for temporal action detection. arXiv preprint arXiv:1705.01180 (2017)
13. Gorban, A., et al.: THUMOS challenge: action recognition with a large number of classes (2015)
14. Heilbron, F.C., Barrios, W., Escorcia, V., Ghanem, B.: SCC: semantic context cascade for efficient action detection. In: Proceedings of the IEEE Conference on Computer Vision and Pattern Recognition, pp. 3175–3184 (2017)
15. Jiang, Y.G., et al.: THUMOS challenge: action recognition with a large number of classes (2014)
16. Kingma, D.P., Ba, J.: Adam: a method for stochastic optimization. arXiv preprint arXiv:1412.6980 (2014)
17. Kipf, T.N., Welling, M.: Semi-supervised classification with graph convolutional networks. arXiv preprint arXiv:1609.02907 (2016)
18. Singh, K.K., Lee, Y.J.: Hide-and-seek: forcing a network to be meticulous for weakly-supervised object and action localization. In: Proceedings of the IEEE International Conference on Computer Vision, pp. 3524–3533 (2017)
19. Laptev, I.: On space-time interest points. Int. J. Comput. Vis. **64**, 107–123 (2005)
20. Lee, P., Uh, Y., Byun, H.: Background suppression network for weakly-supervised temporal action localization. In: Proceedings of the AAAI Conference on Artificial Intelligence (2020)
21. Lin, T., Liu, X., Li, X., Ding, E., Wen, S.: BMN: boundary-matching network for temporal action proposal generation. In: Proceedings of the IEEE International Conference on Computer Vision, pp. 3889–3898 (2019)
22. Lin, T., Zhao, X., Su, H., Wang, C., Yang, M.: BSN: boundary sensitive network for temporal action proposal generation. In: Proceedings of the European Conference on Computer Vision, pp. 3–19 (2018)
23. Liu, D., Jiang, T., Wang, Y.: Completeness modeling and context separation for weakly supervised temporal action localization. In: Proceedings of the IEEE Conference on Computer Vision and Pattern Recognition, pp. 1298–1307 (2019)
24. Liu, Z., et al.: Weakly supervised temporal action localization through contrast based evaluation networks. In: Proceedings of the IEEE International Conference on Computer Vision, pp. 3899–3908 (2019)
25. Long, F., Yao, T., Qiu, Z., Tian, X., Luo, J., Mei, T.: Gaussian temporal awareness networks for action localization. In: Proceedings of the IEEE Conference on Computer Vision and Pattern Recognition, pp. 344–353 (2019)
26. Narayan, S., Cholakkal, H., Khan, F.S., Shao, L.: 3C-Net: category count and center loss for weakly-supervised action localization. In: Proceedings of the IEEE International Conference on Computer Vision, pp. 8679–8687 (2019)
27. Nguyen, P., Liu, T., Prasad, G., Han, B.: Weakly supervised action localization by sparse temporal pooling network. In: Proceedings of the IEEE Conference on Computer Vision and Pattern Recognition, pp. 6752–6761 (2018)
28. Nguyen, P.X., Ramanan, D., Fowlkes, C.C.: Weakly-supervised action localization with background modeling. In: Proceedings of the IEEE International Conference on Computer Vision, pp. 5502–5511 (2019)

29. Paszke, A., et al.: PyTorch: an imperative style, high-performance deep learning library. In: Advances in Neural Information Processing Systems, pp. 8024–8035 (2019)
30. Paul, S., Roy, S., Roy-Chowdhury, A.K.: W-TALC: weakly-supervised temporal activity localization and classification. In: Proceedings of the European Conference on Computer Vision, pp. 563–579 (2018)
31. Piergiovanni, A., Ryoo, M.S.: Representation flow for action recognition. In: Proceedings of the IEEE Conference on Computer Vision and Pattern Recognition (2019)
32. Ren, S., He, K., Girshick, R., Sun, J.: Faster R-CNN: towards real-time object detection with region proposal networks. In: Proceedings of Neural Information Processing Systems, pp. 91–99 (2015)
33. Shou, Z., Chan, J., Zareian, A., Miyazawa, K., Chang, S.F.: CDC: convolutional-de-convolutional networks for precise temporal action localization in untrimmed videos. In: Proceedings of the IEEE Conference on Computer Vision and Pattern Recognition, pp. 5734–5743 (2017)
34. Shou, Z., Gao, H., Zhang, L., Miyazawa, K., Chang, S.F.: AutoLoc: weakly-supervised temporal action localization in untrimmed videos. In: Proceedings of the European Conference on Computer Vision, pp. 154–171 (2018)
35. Shou, Z., et al.: DMC-Net: generating discriminative motion cues for fast compressed video action recognition. In: Proceedings of the IEEE Conference on Computer Vision and Pattern Recognition, pp. 1268–1277 (2019)
36. Sigurdsson, G.A., Varol, G., Wang, X., Farhadi, A., Laptev, I., Gupta, A.: Hollywood in homes: crowdsourcing data collection for activity understanding. In: Proceedings of the European Conference on Computer Vision, pp. 510–526 (2016)
37. Simonyan, K., Zisserman, A.: Two-stream convolutional networks for action recognition in videos. In: Proceedings of Neural Information Processing Systems, pp. 568–576 (2014)
38. Tan, M., et al.: Learning graph structure for multi-label image classification via clique generation. In: Proceedings of the IEEE Conference on Computer Vision and Pattern Recognition, pp. 4100–4109 (2015)
39. Wang, H., Kläser, A., Schmid, C., Liu, C.L.: Action recognition by dense trajectories. In: Proceedings of the IEEE Conference on Computer Vision and Pattern Recognition, pp. 3169–3176 (2011)
40. Wang, L., Koniusz, P., Huynh, D.Q.: Hallucinating IDT descriptors and I3D optical flow features for action recognition with CNNS. In: Proceedings of the IEEE International Conference on Computer Vision, pp. 8698–8708 (2019)
41. Wang, L., Xiong, Y., Lin, D., Van Gool, L.: UntrimmedNets for weakly supervised action recognition and detection. In: Proceedings of the IEEE Conference on Computer Vision and Pattern Recognition, pp. 4325–4334 (2017)
42. Xu, H., Das, A., Saenko, K.: R-C3D: region convolutional 3D network for temporal activity detection. In: Proceedings of the IEEE International Conference on Computer Vision, pp. 5783–5792 (2017)
43. Yu, T., Ren, Z., Li, Y., Yan, E., Xu, N., Yuan, J.: Temporal structure mining for weakly supervised action detection. In: Proceedings of the IEEE International Conference on Computer Vision, pp. 5522–5531 (2019)
44. Yuan, Z., Stroud, J.C., Lu, T., Deng, J.: Temporal action localization by structured maximal sums. In: Proceedings of the IEEE Conference on Computer Vision and Pattern Recognition, pp. 3684–3692 (2017)

45. Zeng, R., et al.: Graph convolutional networks for temporal action localization. In: Proceedings of the IEEE International Conference on Computer Vision, pp. 7094–7103 (2019)
46. Zhai, Y., Wang, L., Liu, Z., Zhang, Q., Hua, G., Zheng, N.: Action coherence network for weakly supervised temporal action localization. In: Proceedings of the IEEE International Conference on Image Processing, pp. 3696–3700 (2019)
47. Zhao, Y., Xiong, Y., Lin, D.: Recognize actions by disentangling components of dynamics. In: Proceedings of the IEEE Conference on Computer Vision and Pattern Recognition, pp. 6566–6575 (2018)
48. Zhao, Y., Xiong, Y., Wang, L., Wu, Z., Tang, X., Lin, D.: Temporal action detection with structured segment networks. In: Proceedings of the IEEE International Conference on Computer Vision, pp. 2914–2923 (2017)
49. Zhou, B., Khosla, A., Lapedriza, A., Oliva, A., Torralba, A.: Learning deep features for discriminative localization. In: Proceedings of the IEEE Conference on Computer Vision and Pattern Recognition, pp. 2921–2929 (2016)

# Erasing Appearance Preservation in Optimization-Based Smoothing

Lvmin Zhang[1,2], Chengze Li[3], Yi Ji[2(✉)], Chunping Liu[2(✉)],
and Tien-tsin Wong[3]

[1] Style2Paints Research, Suzhou, China
lvminzhang@acm.org
[2] Soochow University, Suzhou, China
lvminzhang@siggraph.org, {jiyi,cpliu}@suda.edu.cn
[3] The Chinese University of Hong Kong, Hong Kong, China

**Abstract.** Optimization-based Image smoothing is routinely formulated as the game between a smoothing energy and an appearance preservation energy. Achieving adequate smoothing is a fundamental goal of these Image smoothing algorithms. We show that partially "erasing" the appearance preservation facilitate adequate Image smoothing. In this paper, we call this manipulation as Erasing Appearance Preservation (EAP). We conduct an user study, allowing users to indicate the "erasing" positions by drawing scribbles interactively, to verify the correctness and effectiveness of EAP. We observe the characteristics of human-indicated "erasing" positions, and then formulate a simple and effective 0-1 knapsack to automatically synthesize the "erasing" positions. We test our synthesized erasing positions in a majority of Image smoothing methods. Experimental results and large-scale perceptual human judgments show that the EAP solution tends to encourage the pattern separation or elimination capabilities of Image smoothing algorithms. We further study the performance of the EAP solution in many image decomposition problems to decompose textures, shadows, and the challenging specular reflections. We also present examinations of diversiform image manipulation applications like texture removal, retexturing, intrinsic decomposition, layer extraction, recoloring, material manipulation, *etc.* Due to the widespread applicability of Image smoothing, the EAP is also likely to be used in more image editing applications.

**Keyword:** Image smoothing

## 1 Introduction

Image smoothing is one important foundation of image processing. Denoting the input image as $X \in \mathbb{R}^{H \times W \times C}$ and the output image as $Y \in \mathbb{R}^{H \times W \times C}$ (with

**Electronic supplementary material** The online version of this chapter (https://doi.org/10.1007/978-3-030-58539-6_4) contains supplementary material, which is available to authorized users.

© Springer Nature Switzerland AG 2020
A. Vedaldi et al. (Eds.): ECCV 2020, LNCS 12351, pp. 55–70, 2020.
https://doi.org/10.1007/978-3-030-58539-6_4

$\{H, W, C\}$ being the height, width, and channel), one typical formulation for optimization-based Image smoothing could be

$$f(\boldsymbol{X}) = \arg \min_{\boldsymbol{Y}} (\ \underbrace{\sum_p \rho(\boldsymbol{Y})_p}_{\text{smoothing energy}}\ +\ \underbrace{\sum_p L(\boldsymbol{X}, \boldsymbol{Y})_p}_{\text{appearance preservation}}\ ) \qquad (1)$$

where $p$ is pixel position. Herein, the smoothing energy $\rho(\cdot)$ depends on different tasks, which could be total variance [28], L0 gradient counting (L0) [33], L1 piece-wise constraint (L1) [5], Relative Total Variance (RTV) [34], Weighted Least Squares (WLS) [32], *etc*. And, the appearance preservation energy $L(\cdot, \cdot)$ depends on different data likelihoods, which could be L2 distance ($\|\boldsymbol{X} - \boldsymbol{Y}\|_2^2$) [5, 28, 33, 34], Euclidean (or L1) distance ($\|\boldsymbol{X} - \boldsymbol{Y}\|$) [35], other special Laplacian or Poisson distances [7], and so on.

This paper starts with a key assumption: partially "erasing" the appearance preservation energy facilitate adequate Image smoothing. The mathematical form is as follows. We denote all pixel positions as the set $\hbar$. Given an user-indicated set $\mathcal{E}$ of pixel positions to be erased, the remaining pixel positions can be written as the set $\hbar - \mathcal{E}$. We formulate the smoothing problem

$$F(\boldsymbol{X}, \mathcal{E}) = \arg \min_{\boldsymbol{Y}} (\sum_p \rho(\boldsymbol{Y})_p + \sum_{i \in \hbar - \mathcal{E}} L(\boldsymbol{X}, \boldsymbol{Y})_i) \qquad (2)$$

where our assumption is that users can tune the erasing set $\mathcal{E}$ to achieve adequate and satisfying Image smoothing. We conduct an user study, allowing users to draw scribbles to indicate the erasing set $\mathcal{E}$. As shown in Fig. 1, we present the smoothed results from L0, RTV, and L1 algorithms with or without interactive user erasing. Based on this user study, we present discussions as below.

Firstly, such erasing can facilitate more satisfying and adequate smoothing in many practical cases, supported by several evidences: (1) Users can erase their undesired pixels to achieve satisfying smoothing, *e.g.*, in Fig. 1-(a), the user draws scribbles to erase the specular reflections on the car so as to achieve satisfactory car albedo. Figure 1-(b, h, f, j) are similar cases. (2) Users can preserve and emphasize their desired pixels to facilitate adequate smoothing, *e.g.*, in Fig. 1-(d), the user only traces the leaf texture whereas the tree branches remain untouched and emphasized, so as to only preserve the desired tree branch structure and smooth the leave texture adequately. Figure 1-(c, e, g, i, k) are similar cases. (3) Given the typicality of these evidences, we are likely to find more practical cases in other color, texture, object, and illumination manipulation scenarios.

Secondly, this erasing is applicable to a variety of applications, supported by several evidences: (1) This erasing can be used in intrinsic image and illumination editing applications, *e.g.*, in Fig. 1-(h), the user draws scribbles to erase the specularity on the sofa, which can ease further illumination decomposition or editing. Figure 1-(b, f, j) are similar cases. (2) This erasing can be used in texture removal and texture editing applications, *e.g.*, in Fig. 1-(i), the user outlines and

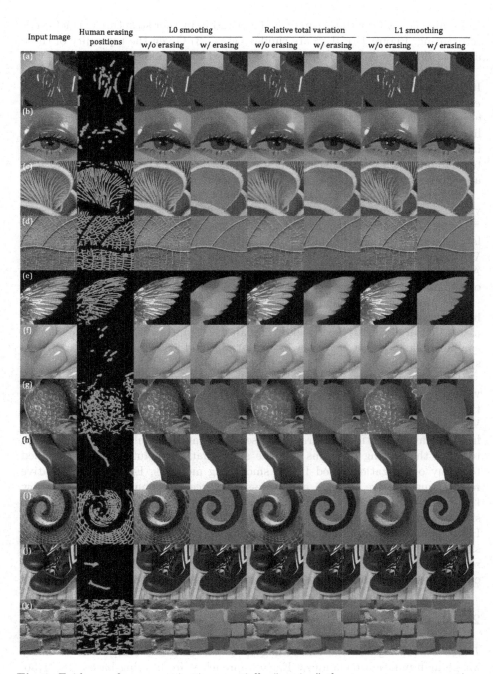

**Fig. 1.** Evidences for our motivation: partially "erasing" the appearance preservation energy facilitate adequate Image smoothing. The user-given erasing pixel position (the set $\mathcal{E}$) are marked with green scribbles. (Color figure online)

eliminate the spider web texture, which can aid in further structure extraction or retexturing. Figure 1-(c, d, g) are similar cases. (3) Given the typicality of these applications, this erasing is likely to be applied to more applications.

Thirdly, the appearance preservation erasing also brings new challenges: (1) It is labor-intensive and time-consuming to indicate the erasing set $\mathcal{E}$ manually, *e.g.*, in Fig. 1-(g), the user have to draw a large number of scribbles to accurately erase the strawberry texture. Figure 1-(c, k) are similar cases.(2) Many real-life Image smoothing applications require fully automatic processing, *e.g.*, many intrinsic image methods are applicable to video processing, and it is unreasonable to manually annotate videos frame-by-frame. Similar challenges also exist in applications like retexturing, materializing, recoloring, relighting, and so on.

Generally, these results verify that partially "erasing" the appearance preservation encourages adequate and satisfying Image smoothing, and achieving such "erasing" can benefit a variety of applications. Nevertheless, the user input is labor-intensive to obtain and is unacceptable in many automatic applications. With the motivation of scalability and applicability, we present the Erasing Appearance Preservation (EAP) problem: solving the erasing set $\mathcal{E}$ in absence of human interaction.

We present a simple and effective solution to the EAP problem. We observe how human indicate their erasing set $\mathcal{E}$ and then use a knapsack model to discover pixels that are likely to be erased by human. Experiments show that our solution can be applied to a variety of downstream tasks, and many state-of-the-art Image smoothing applications can benefit from our solution.

Our contributions are: (1) We motivate the Erasing Appearance Preservation (EAP) problem by verifying the assumption that partially "erasing" the appearance preservation energy facilitate adequate Image smoothing. (2) We present a simple and effective solution to the EAP problem. We observe how human erase the appearance preservation and formulate a 0-1 knapsack to solve the erasing positions. (3) We show that our solution can be applied to many optimization-based Image smoothing methods. Extensive qualitative results, quantitative analysis, and large-scale perceptual human judgments show that this solution facilitates their structure extraction and pattern decomposition capabilities. Furthermore, we study the effectiveness of EAP in various Image smoothing applications, *e.g.*, texture decomposition, intrinsic decomposition, color manipulation, material manipulation, *etc*. Additionally, we show results from our EAP solution in several open problems like adequate texture elimination and the challenging specular reflection decomposition.

## 2   Related Works

*Image Smoothing.* Image smoothing is as an essential component of many image manipulation techniques. Early approaches are filtering-based [18,31,36] and recently optimization methods achieve impressive visual effects, *e.g.*, L0-smoothing [33], L1-smoothing [5], and other energy-based methods [1,11,27,30, 34], to name a few. A wide variety of visual effects can be achieve with Image smoothing, *e.g.*, visual enhancement [26], intrinsic decomposition [5], texture replacement [6], relighting [30], recoloring [29], stylization [14], *etc.*

*Interactive Image Smoothing and Optimization.* Many real-world Image smoothing applications and image optimization techniques allow users to interactively control the optimization, *e.g.*, matting [10], stylization [9], coloring [22], relighting [30], and so on. The existence of these application also verifies the correctness of EAP. The difference is that these approaches are routinely focused on making use of user inputs (like scribbles), whereas we are focused on finding where to "erase" in absence of human interaction for Image smoothing algorithms.

*Image Inpainting and Point-Based imaging.* Image inpainting methods [12, 20, 25] also "erase" pixels to edit image contents. The difference is that we are aimed at solving the unknown erasing positions, whereas image inpainting is aimed at solving the erased content with known erasing positions. Furthermore, point-based imaging literatures [15, 19] compute pixel points to process images. The different is that these methods are aimed at representing images with detected key points (*e.g.*, sparse control points [15]), whereas we are aimed at finding pixels that need to be "erased".

## 3 A Solution to the EAP Problem

Our goal is to solve the "erasing" positions for Image smoothing algorithms. Observing Fig. 1, we have two discoveries: (1) Human is erasing their "undesired" pixels. For example, if the user wants to remove textures, that user will draw scribbles on the undesired texture, *e.g.*, the tree leaf (Fig. 1-(d)) and the spider web (Fig. 1-(i)). (2) Human is preserving their "desired" pixels. For example, if the user wants to preserve salient object structures, that user will prevent drawing scribbles on the objects' structural constitutes, *e.g.*, the nail surface (Fig. 1-(f)) and the strawberry structural outline (Fig. 1-(g)). Motivated by these two discoveries, we can determine where to erase by estimating desired and undesired pixels.

*Estimating How Each Pixel is "Undesired".* Image smoothing routinely penalizes task-specific patterns. These patterns can be textures, shadows, specular reflections, noises, and so on. In many specific applications, these penalized patterns can be viewed as the user undesired patterns. For example, in texture removal applications, the smoothing energy is penalizing textures, and simultaneously, those textures are also undesired by the users. Therefore, we estimate how each pixel is penalized, to reflect how each pixel is undesired. During Image smoothing (Eq. (2)), the more a pixel is penalized, the more its color changes. We can compute the input-output color change to estimate the penalty:

$$V_p = ||X_p - Y_p||_2^2 \tag{3}$$

where $p$ is pixel position and $V_p$ is the estimated penalty. To aid in the robustness of this estimation, we apply some routinely used image processing strategies to ameliorate the formulation: we compute the CIE RGB-to-Lab transform $\tau(\cdot)$, multiply the Gaussian term $w_{ij} = \exp(||\tau(\boldsymbol{X}_i) - \tau(\boldsymbol{Y}_j)||_2^2/2\sigma^2)$, and focus on the local window $l_p$ at $p$. The final equation becomes

$$\boldsymbol{v}_p = \sum_{i \in l_p} \sum_{j \in l_p} w_{ij} ||\tau(\boldsymbol{X}_i) - \tau(\boldsymbol{Y}_j)||_2^2 \tag{4}$$

In this way, this equation represents how each pixel is penalized and undesired in our problem. We provide a detailed verification of this equation using Xu's tests [34] in the supplemental material.

*Estimating How Each Pixel is "Desired".* Image smoothing routinely protects and preserves important image constitutes. For example, texture removal smoothing preserves salient structure, and intrinsic Image smoothing preserves object reflectance or albedo. In many specific applications, these preserved patterns can be viewed as user desired patterns. In most cases, after the Image smoothing process, those preserved patterns tend to show more salient contours than those penalized patterns. For example, after texture removal, the original textured location tend to be flat, and thus have less salient contours than the preserved structure, which may have many color transitions. Therefore, we compute the salient contours for each pixel in the smoothed image $\boldsymbol{Y}$ to estimate how each pixel is preserved, so as to reflect how each pixel is desired:

$$\boldsymbol{w}_p = \epsilon + \sum_{i \in l_p} \sum_{j \in l_p} ||\tau(\boldsymbol{Y}_i) - \tau(\boldsymbol{Y}_j)||_2^2 \tag{5}$$

where $\epsilon$ prevents zero output. When local window $l_p$ is located at salient contours like edges, $w_p$ becomes numerically large. On the contrary, when the colors in $l_p$ are nearly uniform, $w_p$ will decrease to $\epsilon$ as no important pattern can be found. In this way, this equation represents how each pixel is preserved and desired in our problem. We provide a detailed verification in the supplemental material.

*0-1 Knapsack.* Now that we have two estimations for each pixel: the $\boldsymbol{v}_p$ estimates how each pixel is "undesired" whereas the $\boldsymbol{w}_p$ estimates how each pixel is "desired". Naturally, we formulate our problem as a 0-1 knapsack: each pixel is a knapsack item, and each item is then chosen whether to put in the knapsack to achieve the largest possible value, while preserving limited total weights. The item value is $\boldsymbol{v}_p$ and the item weight is $\boldsymbol{w}_p$. Then, the knapsack solves as much undesired pixels as possible, while preserving an amount of desired ones. In this way, we achieve a game between erasing undesired pixels and preserving desired pixels.

The 0-1 knapsack is significant and indispensable in our solution, and it is a must to use both estimations of $\boldsymbol{v}_p$ and $\boldsymbol{w}_p$, supported by three evidences: (1) The determination between erasing undesired pixels and preserving desired pixels can only be formulated as a trade-off. In real-world images, the patterns over pixels are complicated and there is no fixed threshold on $\boldsymbol{v}_p$ or $\boldsymbol{w}_p$ to determine what pixel must be erased or preserved. (2) It is hardly possible for users to accurately

**Algorithm 1:** Solver of EAP.

**Input**: Source Image $X \in \mathbb{R}^{H \times W \times 3}$, $u, \rho(\cdot), t$;
**Output**: Smoothed Image $Y \in \mathbb{R}^{H \times W \times 3}$;

1  Randomly assign 50% pixel positions to $\mathcal{E}$;
2  **for** $(i = 0; i < t; i + +)$ **do**
3     |   $Y \leftarrow F(X, \mathcal{E})$;
4     |   Solve $\mathcal{E}$ using 0-1 knapsack;
5  **end**
6  Output $Y$;

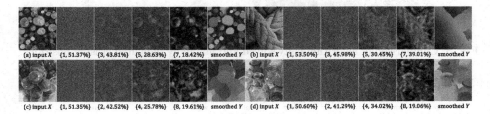

**Fig. 2.** Visualization of erasing set $\mathcal{E}$ (marked in green) during optimization. Each $\{\cdot, \cdot\}$ indicates iteration step and percentage of $\mathcal{E}$ in all positions $\hbar$. (Color figure online)

determine the pixel quantity that should be erased or preserved. Nevertheless, the game of 0-1 knapsack enables a "smart" erasing: given a coarsely indicated knapsack capability, it can adaptively solve how many pixels should be erased. (3) Our later ablative experiments show that, if either one of $v_p$ or $w_p$ is discarded, the performance of our solution will decrease significantly.

To be specific, our maximum knapsack capability is denoted by a manageable scaler $U \in \mathbb{R}$. Considering images vary in scale, for flexibility, we denote $U = HWu$ where $H$ and $W$ are image height and width with $u \in \mathbb{R}$ being an user-given scaler. Finally, this 0-1 knapsack problem of $\{v, w, U\}$ is solved via knapsack dynamic programming. The overall procedures are provided in Algorithm 1. In the supplemental materials, we also include related technical backgrounds of knapsack algorithms and codes of our solver implementations to aid in reproducibility.

*Analysis of the EAP Solution.* Our solution succeeds in solving "undesired" pattern positions. Figure 2-(a,b) shows experiments for texture removal using relative total variance energy [34]. We can find that EAP is capable of discovering textural positions progressively, *i.e.*, pixels of the tree rings and rope twists are gradually recognized. Figure 2-(c, d) are for reflectance extraction using L1 intrinsic energy [5], where specular reflections and shadows are efficiently detected. Furthermore, these experiments convert another important message that the EAP framework is adaptive. Given fixed $u = 0.25$ for all examples in Fig. 2, the final percentage of $\mathcal{E}$ varies significantly over different sources and tasks. This result reflects the fact that EAP can achieve adaptive soft constraints for diversified source images

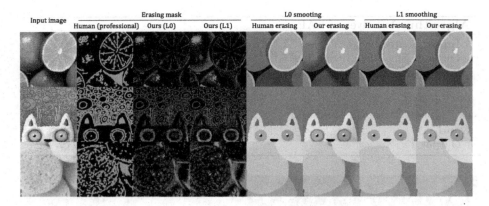

**Fig. 3.** Comparison of algorithmically solved and manually indicated erasing positions.

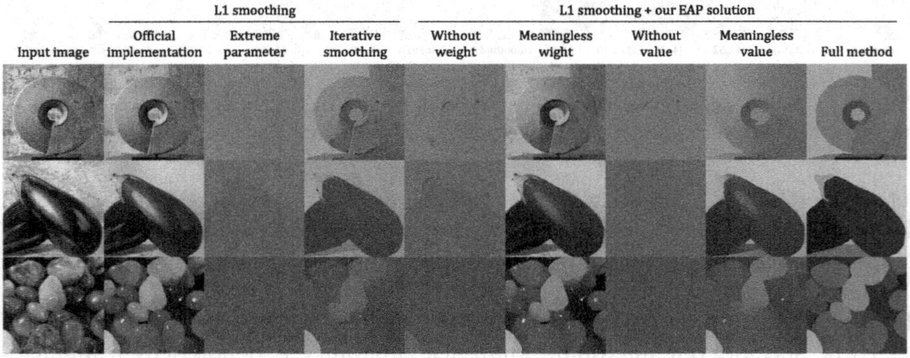

**Fig. 4.** Ablative study with different alternative configurations for L1 smoothing.

and various frontend smoothing energy designed for different tasks. Finally, we also compare our estimated erasing positions to human-indicated erasing points as shown in Fig. 3. We conduct this experiment using both L0 and L1 smoothing. We can see that our solved erasing positions are visually similar to human indication, and our smoothing results are comparable to human performance.

*Ablative Study.* We perform an ablative study as shown in Fig. 4. More ablative results and implementation details are attached in the supplemental material. We mainly focus on L1 smoothing. We first present the L1 smoothing results from the (1) *official implementation,* and then try some existing strategies to facilitate more throughout smoothing without using EAP: (2) *extreme parameter:* using extreme lambda (10.0) in original L1 smoothing, but without using EAP. We can see that this causes the failure cases where the image constitutes are destroyed. (3) *iterative smoothing:* repeating original L1 smoothing multiple times (10 times, same as the later EAP configuration), but without using EAP.

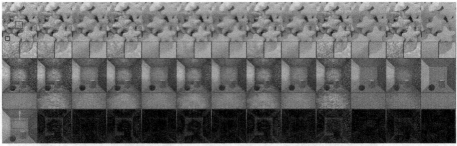

Source    TV(14.07)    ETV(22.60)    RTV(16.32)    ERTV(25.20)    WLS(15.77)    EWLS(24.07)    TREE(15.69)    ETREE(24.38)    L0(13.45)    EL0(27.34)    L1(18.49)    EL1(28.58)

**Fig. 5.** Texture decomposition. Leftmost is the source (ground truth). We show extracted structures and error maps against the ground truth for each method and report PSNR for each instance. Better scores are marked in blue against red baselines. (Color figure online)

We can see that this causes desaturated and low-contrast artifacts. Then, we try different configurations in our EAP solution: (4) *without weight:* not using knapsack weights $w_p$. Instead, we set a fixed threshold (0.1) to the knapsack values, and all pixels above this threshold are viewed as erasing positions. We can see that this causes the image collapsing to a few colors. (5) *meaningless weight:* replacing all knapsack weights $w_p$ with a constant (1.0). We can see that this causes all undesired patterns being preserved in the final result. (6) *without value:* not using knapsack values $v_p$. Instead, we set a fixed threshold (0.1) to the knapsack weights, and all pixels below this threshold are viewed as erasing positions. We can see that this causes all salient counters being eliminated. (7) *meaningless value:* replacing all knapsack value $v_p$ with a constant (1.0). We can see that this can preserve salient constitutes, but the original structure is corrupted. (8) *full method:* our proposed solution, able to facilitate more adequate smoothing without causing other artifacts.

## 4   Image Smoothing Energy Under EAP

Via changing the $\rho(\cdot)$ and $L(\cdot, \cdot)$ term, various smoothing energies can be flexibly implemented in EAP framework. We denote such strategy by prefix **E**, *i.e.*, total variation (TV) will be named as ETV when EAP is applied. Here, we address several widely-used smoothing energies: **WLS** (1977 [32]) weighted least square; **TV** (1992 [28]) total variation; **L0** (2011 [33]) L0 smoothing; **RTV** (2012 [34]) relative total variation; **TREE** (2014 [2]) optimization-based spanning tree; **L1** (2015 [5]) L1 smoothing; **DL1** (2015 [5]) DPGMM (Dirichlet Process Gaussian Mixture Model) L1 reflectance extraction; When applying EAP approaches to these methods, we obtain: **EWLS; ETV; EL0; ERTV; ETREE; EL1; EDL1.** Unless noticed, we set $u = 0.50$, $3 \times 3$ window $l_p$, $\epsilon = 1.00$, $\sigma = 0.10$, and $t = 10$.

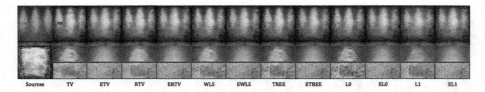

**Fig. 6.** Texture replacement. Leftmost is the source image and the target texture. Results are presented in following cols.

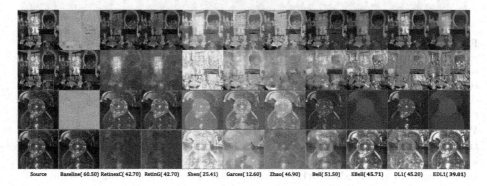

**Fig. 7.** Intrinsic images. IIW-WHDR(%) (lower is better) is reported. Blue EAP scores are compared against red baselines. (Color figure online)

## 5    Applications

*Texture Decomposition and Retexturing.* EAP significantly improves the texture separation capability of optimization-based smoothing methods. Qualitatively, as in the first row of Fig. 5, we compare six appearance-preserving smoothing methods and the respective EAP versions. All EAP-based methods succeed in the complete removal of the challenging dense candy texture, whereas all remaining methods suffer from incomplete texture removal. Quantitatively, as in the second row of Fig. 5, we blend several challenging regular or irregular textures to the Cornell Box to obtain ground truth image pairs with/without textures and evaluate these methods using the PSNR metric. Among all methods, the EAP-based method reports significantly higher PSNR values than others, thus enabling more thorough texture decomposition. More examples are provided in the supplemental material. Figure 6 shows texture replacement examples. The objective is to remove the brick texture on the wall completely (top-left of Fig. 6) and replace it with the new texture of the uncovered wall (bottom-left of Fig. 6) via removing and then swapping texture. All EAP-based methods managed to remove original bricks and swap texture. In contrast, the remaining methods more or less fail in eliminating the original brick texture and cause maroon-spotted artifacts due to incomplete removal of the original red bricks. This phenomenon further validates that EAP improves pattern separation capability of current Image smoothing algorithms.

Source   Baseline( 62.20) RetinexC( 15.70) RetinG( 15.70)   Shen( 25.41)   Garces( 16.02)   Zhao( 14.14)   Bell(25.10)   EBell( 16.10)   DL1( 20.60)   EDL1( 15.21)

**Fig. 8.** Specular reflection removal. IIW-WHDR(%) are reported and blue EAP scores are compared to the red baselines. (Color figure online)

*Intrinsic Images and Illumination Editing.* Intrinsic decomposition [3] aims at extracting reflectance and illumination (shading) maps from single image. Interestingly, many optimization-based intrinsic methods are closely related to Image smoothing, and their objectives can also be viewed as the appearance preservation terms and smoothing (or penalization) terms. To evaluate the performance of EAP in the intrinsic decomposition task, we use typical Bell [4] and DL1 methods as examples as well as their EAP versions EBell and EDL1 in the experiments. More details of involved algorithms and their EAP implementations are provided in the supplemental materials.

Qualitatively, the EAP framework significantly improves structure abstraction and color separation capability of the involved candidates. We provide a challenging example in Fig. 7 with transparent objects and intensive specular reflections. We can see that EBell and EDL1 succeed in separating specular reflection colors and object colors, whereas other methods fail in telling them apart.

Quantitatively, we test on several routine intrinsic metrics: Intrinsic Image in the Wild [4] (IIW) and Shadow Annotation in the Wild [21] (enhanced SAW in [23]). In IIW/SAW tests, humans are invited to annotate pixels based on whether reflectance/shadow colors are similar or not (having offsets), and the human judgments are then compared with the estimations of tested methods. We report scores of optimization-based methods [4,5,16,17,21,30,37] in Table 1. We can see that the EAP framework can significantly improve the quantitative performance of Bell and DL1 with the controllable parameter $u$ (the 0-1 Knapsack capability). Given the typicality of Bell and DL1, the EAP framework is likely to improve more optimization-based intrinsic decomposition methods.

On the other hand, although recent IIW/SAW benchmarks are dominated by deep learning methods [13,23,24,38] (CGIntrinsics [23] 99.11% AP and GloSH [38] 15.2% WHDR), optimization methods are still widely used methods. IIW/SAW only evaluates the quantitative accuracy of the reflectance and shadows but ignores the real-life usability of decomposed layers in image editing tasks like relighting, retexturing, rematerializing, *etc.* In Fig. 7, it is obvious that Garces [16] is not suitable for image editing despite its best IIW-WHDR score. Another example of specular reflection removal in Fig. 8 shows that only EAP-based methods manage to eliminate specular reflections, but in the meanwhile, the unusable Zhao [37] reports the best IIW score.

To evaluate image editing performance of intrinsic methods, we introduce real humans to help with the evaluation. We apply state of the art deep learning

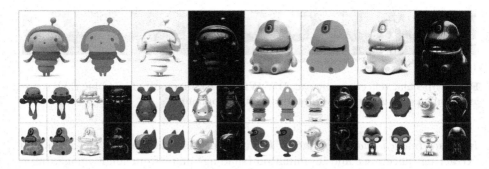

**Fig. 9.** Qualitative results on image decomposition. We visualize decomposed layers using our EAP-based method EDL1.

**Fig. 10.** Comparisons of specular reflections extracted for image decomposition task using different smoothing algorithms.

methods [23,38], optimization methods [4,5], and their EAP versions to decompose 100 scenes into layers, and then apply their layers to two typical illumination editing tasks: shadow enhancement and specular reflection removal. In this way, we obtain 600 results with enhanced shadows and 600 results with specular reflections eliminated. We employ Amazon Mechanical Turk (AMT) to rank the visual quality of these results and report the obtained ranking in Table 2. Interestingly, traditional optimization algorithms outperform learning-based models in both tasks, and EAP-based optimization outperforms standard optimizations. We provide 1200 raw results and 1200 raw AMT ranks in the supplement. This strong evidence shows that EAP achieves beyond state of the art performance in intrinsic decomposition based image manipulation.

*Advanced Illumination Decomposition.* Both natural images and artistic illustrations may contain complex lighting conditions, and the lighting in digital paintings could be arbitrarily drawn for aesthetic purposes. Advanced decomposition method [8] supports extracting multiple illumination layers and assign specular reflections into separated layers when reflectance maps are given. Notably, this technique alone is not functional for image decomposition, and it requires users to input the smoothed image structure. In this task, we use Image smoothing methods to provide such smoothed image structures for layer decomposition. We compare DL1, Bell, and our revamped EDL1. We provide qualitative results in

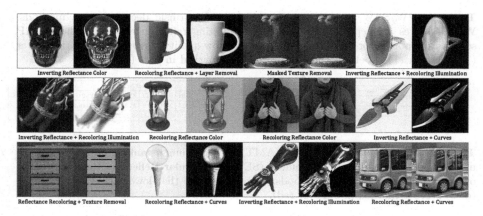

**Fig. 11.** EAP-based image manipulation. We show various image editing use cases with EDL1 layer decomposition method.

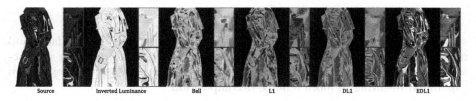

**Fig. 12.** Comparison of black-to-white rematerialization via inverting reflectance colors extracted with or without EAP.

Fig. 9. These results show that our method is capable of decomposing challenging hard shadows and specular reflections simultaneously. On the contrary, as in Fig. 10, previous methods are almost not likely to achieve visually satisfactory decomposition because appearance preservation prevents them from completely separating desired patterns.

*Decomposition-Based Image Manipulation.* A wide variety of intrinsic decomposition based image manipulation applications can be greatly benefited from the EAP framework. Figure 11 shows qualitative results of use cases like reflectance/illumination recoloring, retexturing, curve tuning, *etc.* Related technical backgrounds are provided in the supplementary materials.

We discuss the significance of EAP using recoloring examples. One of the most difficult case in recoloring is to invert the scene reflectance while preserving the original illumination. Specular materials and complicated lighting conditions can make this case even more challenging. Figure 12 shows an example to turn the black coat into white while preserving the specular latex material, by inverting the reflectance colors extracted using Bell, L1, DL1, and EAP-based EDL1 method. We also include a naive luminance inverting method. Because the appearance preservation terms of previous methods tend to prevent thorough

**Table 1.** IIW/SAW test for optimization-based intrinsic decomposition methods. WHDR scores are reported for IIW test evaluating reflectance quality whereas AP scores are reported for SAW test evaluating shadow quality. Arrows indicate that lower (↓) or higher (↑) is better. Top 1 (or 2) score is marked in blue (or red).

| Method | C-R [21] | Zhao [37] | Garces [16] | RetinexC [17] | Shen [30] | Bell [4] | DL1 [5] |
|---|---|---|---|---|---|---|---|
| WHDR% ↓ | 36.6 | 23.8 | 24.8 | 26.9 | 31.8 | 20.6 | 17.7 |
| AP% ↑ | 75.5 | 89.72 | 92.39 | 85.26 | 91.4 | 92.18 | 93.57 |

| Method | EAP + Bell [4] | | | | | EAP + DL1 [5] | | | | |
|---|---|---|---|---|---|---|---|---|---|---|
| u | 0.01 | 0.05 | 0.10 | 0.25 | 0.50 | 0.01 | 0.05 | 0.10 | 0.25 | 0.50 |
| WHDR% ↓ | 20.4 | 20.9 | 19.9 | 25.3 | 44.7 | 17.9 | 16.2 | 16.9 | 20.4 | 52.5 |
| AP% ↑ | 92.97 | 92.17 | 94.43 | 86.25 | 77.52 | 93.69 | 94.17 | 95.21 | 88.41 | 65.47 |

**Table 2.** Amazon Mechanical Turk (AMT) average human ranking on image manipulation tasks of Shadow Enhancement (SE) and Specular Reflection Removal (SRR) over intrinsic decomposition methods. Arrows indicate that lower (↓) is better. Top 1 (or 2) score is marked in blue (or red).

| Method | CGIntrinsics [23] | GLoSH [38] | Bell [4] | EAP + Bell [4] | DL1 [5] | EAP + DL1 [5] |
|---|---|---|---|---|---|---|
| SE ↓ | 5.70 ± 0.46 | 5.30 ± 0.46 | 3.55 ± 0.50 | 1.71 ± 0.45 | 3.45 ± 0.50 | 1.29 ± 0.45 |
| SRR ↓ | 5.22 ± 0.41 | 5.77 ± 0.44 | 3.54 ± 0.52 | 1.66 ± 0.47 | 3.47 ± 0.50 | 1.34 ± 0.47 |

specular decomposition, their results suffer from visible hole-like artifacts and non-saturated artifacts. On the contrary, EDL1 succeeded in producing satisfactory results because the EAP technique greatly enhances the pattern separation capability, resulting in more reliable decomposition.

## 6    Conclusion

This paper presents the Erasing Appearance Preservation (EAP) problem that partially "erase" the appearance preservation energy to facilitate adequate Image smoothing. We conduct an user study to verify the effectiveness and correctness of EAP. We also presents a method to synthesize the erasing positions automatically. Qualitative, quantitative, and perceptual evidences show that EAP can facilitate the pattern separation and structure extraction capabilities of a majority of optimization-based Image smoothing algorithms. We extensively study the performance of the EAP framework in smoothing-based image decomposition problems for textures, shadows, and the challenging specular reflections. Diversiform image manipulation applications like texture decomposition, intrinsic decomposition, color/material manipulation, and many others are also studied with the EAP solution. Due to the widespread applicability of Image smoothing in visual editing, the EAP method is likely to benefit more applications.

## References

1. Bach, F., et al.: Structured sparsity through convex optimization. Stat. Sci. **27**(4), 450–468 (2012)
2. Bao, L., Song, Y., Yang, Q., Yuan, H., Wang, G.: Tree filtering efficient structure preserving smoothing with a minimum spanning tree. IEEE Trans. Image Process. (2014)

3. Barrow, H.G., Tenenbaum, J.M.: Recovering intrinsic scene characteristics from images. In: Hanson, A., Riseman, E. (eds.) Computer Vision Systems, pp. 3–26. Academic Press (1978)
4. Bell, S., Bala, K., Snavely, N.: Intrinsic images in the wild. ACM Trans. Graph. **33**(4), 1–12 (2014)
5. Bi, S., Han, X., Yu, Y.: An L1 image transform for edge preserving smoothing and scene level intrinsic decomposition. ACM Trans. Graph. **34**(4), 1–12 (2015)
6. Bousseau, A., Paris, S., Durand, F.: User-assisted intrinsic images. ACM Trans. Graph. (2009)
7. Buzug, M, T.: Computed Tomography. Springer, Heidelberg (2008). https://doi.org/10.1007/978-3-540-39408-2
8. Carroll, R., Ramamoorthi, R., Agrawala, M.: Illumination decomposition for material recoloring with consistent interreflections. ACM Trans. Graph. (2011)
9. Champandard, A.J.: Semantic style transfer and turning two-bit doodles into fine artworks. CoRR abs/1603.01768 (2016)
10. Chen, Q., Li, D., Tang, C.K.: KNN matting. IEEE Trans. Pattern Anal. Mach. Intell. **35**(9), 2175–2188 (2013)
11. Cho, H., Lee, H., Kang, H., Lee, S.: Bilateral texture filtering. ACM Trans. Graph. **33**(4), 1–8 (2014)
12. Criminisi, A., Perez, P., Toyama, K.: Region filling and object removal by exemplar-based image inpainting. IEEE Trans. Image Process. **13**(9), 1200–1212 (2004)
13. Fan, Q., Yang, J., Hua, G., Chen, B., Wipf, D.: Revisiting deep intrinsic image decompositions. In: CVPR (2018)
14. Fan, Q., Yang, J., Wipf, D., Chen, B., Tong, X.: Image smoothing via unsupervised learning. ACM Trans. Graph. **37**(6), 1–14 (2018)
15. Galić, I., Weickert, J., Welk, M., Bruhn, A., Belyaev, A., Seidel, H.P.: Image compression with anisotropic diffusion. J. Math. Imaging Vis. **31**(2–3), 255–269 (2008)
16. Garces, E., Munoz, A., Lopez-Moreno, J., Gutierrez, D.: Intrinsic images by clustering. In: Computer Graphics Forum (2012)
17. Grosse, R., Johnson, M.K., Adelson, E.H., Freeman, W.T.: Ground truth dataset and baseline evaluations for intrinsic image algorithms. In: ICCV (2019)
18. He, K., Sun, J., Tang, X.: Guied image filtering. TPAMI **35**(6), 1397–1409 (2013)
19. Hoeltgen, L., Setzer, S., Weickert, J.: An optimal control approach to find sparse data for laplace interpolation. In: Heyden, A., Kahl, F., Olsson, C., Oskarsson, M., Tai, X.-C. (eds.) EMMCVPR 2013. LNCS, vol. 8081, pp. 151–164. Springer, Heidelberg (2013). https://doi.org/10.1007/978-3-642-40395-8_12
20. Iizuka, S., Simo-Serra, E., Ishikawa, H.: Globally and locally consistent image completion. ACM Trans. Graph. (Proc. of SIGGRAPH 2017) **36**(4), 107:1–107:14 (2017)
21. Kovacs, B., Bell, S., Snavely, N., Bala, K.: Shading annotations in the wild. In: CVPR (2017)
22. Levin, A., Lischinski, D., Weiss, Y.: Colorization using optimization. In: ACM SIGGRAPH 2004 Papers, SIGGRAPH 2004, pp. 689–694. Association for Computing Machinery, New York (2004)
23. Li, Z., Snavely, N.: CGIntrinsics: better intrinsic image decomposition through physically-based rendering. In: Ferrari, V., Hebert, M., Sminchisescu, C., Weiss, Y. (eds.) ECCV 2018. LNCS, vol. 11207, pp. 381–399. Springer, Cham (2018). https://doi.org/10.1007/978-3-030-01219-9_23
24. Li, Z., Snavely, N.: Learning intrinsic image decomposition from watching the world. In: CVPR (2018)

25. Liu, G., Reda, F.A., Shih, K.J., Wang, T.C., Tao, A., Catanzaro, B.: Image inpainting for irregular holes using partial convolutions. In: The European Conference on Computer Vision (ECCV) (2018)
26. Min, D., Choi, S., Lu, J., Ham, B., Sohn, K., Do, M.N.: Fast global image smoothing based on weighted least squares. IEEE Trans. Image Process. **23**(12), 5638–5653 (2014)
27. Prasath, V.S., Vorotnikov, D., Pelapur, R., Jose, S., Seetharaman, G., Palaniappan, K.: Multiscale Tikhonovtotal variation image restoration using spatially varying edge coherence exponent. IEEE Trans. Image Process. **24**(12), 5220–5235 (2015)
28. Rudin, L., Osher, S., Fatemi, E.: Nonlinear total variation based noise removal algorithms. Phys. D: Nonlinear Phenomena **60**(1–4), 259–268 (1992)
29. Serra, M., Penacchio, O., Benavente, R., Vanrell, M.: Names and shades of color for intrinsic image estimation. In: CVPR (2012)
30. Shen, J., Yang, X., Jia, Y., Li, X.: Intrinsic images using optimization. In: CVPR (2011)
31. Tomasi, C.: Bilateral filtering for gray and color images. In: ICCV (1998)
32. Holland, P.W., Welsch, R.E.: Robust regression using iteratively reweighted least-squares. Commun. Stat. Theory Methods **6**(9), 813–827 (1977)
33. Xu, L., Lu, C., Xu, Y., Jia, J.: Image smoothing via L0 gradient minimization. ACM Trans. Graph. (2011)
34. Xu, L., Yan, Q., Xia, Y., Jia, J.: Structure extraction from texture via relative total variation. ACM Trans. Graph. **31**(6), 1–10 (2012)
35. Yang, J., Zhang, Y., Yin, W.: An efficient TVL1 algorithm for deblurring multichannel images corrupted by impulsive noise. SIAM J. Sci. Comput. **31**(4), 2842–2865 (2009)
36. Yin, H., Gong, Y., Qiu, G.: Side window filtering. In: CVPR (2019)
37. Zhao, Q., Tan, P., Dai, Q., Shen, L., Wu, E., Lin, S.: A closed-form solution to retinex with nonlocal texture constraints. TPAMI **34**(7), 1437–1444 (2012)
38. Zhou, H., Yu, X., Jacobs, D.W.: Glosh: global-local spherical harmonics for intrinsic image decomposition. In: ICCV (2019)

# Counterfactual Vision-and-Language Navigation via Adversarial Path Sampler

Tsu-Jui Fu[1]([✉]), Xin Eric Wang[2], Matthew F. Peterson[1], Scott T. Grafton[1], Miguel P. Eckstein[1], and William Yang Wang[1]

[1] UC Santa Barbara, Santa Barbara, USA
tsu-juifu@ucsb.edu,
{peterson,scott.grafton,miguel.eckstein}@psych.ucsb.edu
william@cs.ucsb.edu
[2] UC Santa Cruz, Santa Cruz, USA
xwang366@ucsc.edu

**Abstract.** Vision-and-Language Navigation (VLN) is a task where agents must decide how to move through a 3D environment to reach a goal by grounding natural language instructions to the visual surroundings. One of the problems of the VLN task is data scarcity since it is difficult to collect enough navigation paths with human-annotated instructions for interactive environments. In this paper, we explore the use of counterfactual thinking as a human-inspired data augmentation method that results in robust models. Counterfactual thinking is a concept that describes the human propensity to create possible alternatives to life events that have already occurred. We propose an adversarial-driven counterfactual reasoning model that can consider effective conditions instead of low-quality augmented data. In particular, we present a model-agnostic adversarial path sampler (APS) that learns to sample challenging paths that force the navigator to improve based on the navigation performance. APS also serves to do pre-exploration of unseen environments to strengthen the model's ability to generalize. We evaluate the influence of APS on the performance of different VLN baseline models using the room-to-room dataset (R2R). The results show that the adversarial training process with our proposed APS benefits VLN models under both seen and unseen environments. And the pre-exploration process can further gain additional improvements under unseen environments.

## 1 Introduction

Vision-and-language navigation (VLN) [3,8] is a complex task that requires an agent to understand natural language, encode visual information from the surrounding environment, and associate critical visual features of the scene and

**Electronic supplementary material** The online version of this chapter (https://doi.org/10.1007/978-3-030-58539-6_5) contains supplementary material, which is available to authorized users.

© Springer Nature Switzerland AG 2020
A. Vedaldi et al. (Eds.): ECCV 2020, LNCS 12351, pp. 71–86, 2020.
https://doi.org/10.1007/978-3-030-58539-6_5

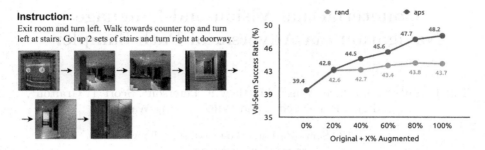

**Fig. 1.** The comparison between randomly-sampled (rand) and APS-sampled (aps) under validation-seen set for Seq2Seq over different ratios of augmented path used.

appropriate actions with the instructions to achieve a specified goal (usually to move through a 3D environment to a target destination).

To accomplish the VLN task, the agent learns to align linguistic semantics and visual understanding and also make sense of dynamic changes in vision-and-language interactions. One of the primary challenges of the VLN task for artificial agents is data scarcity; for instance, while there are more than 200 K possible paths in the Room-to-Room (R2R) dataset [3], the R2R training data comprises only 14 K sampled paths. This scarcity of data makes learning the optimal match between vision and language within the interactive environments quite challenging.

Meanwhile, humans often lack extensive experience with joint access to visual experience and accompanying language instructions for navigating novel or unfamiliar environments, yet the human mind can navigate environments despite this data scarcity by incorporating mechanisms such as counterfactual reasoning [30] and self-recovered missing information. For example, if a human follows an instruction to "turn right" and they see a door in front of them, they can also consider what they may have encountered had they turned left instead. Or, if we stop in front of the dining table instead of walking away from it, what should the instruction be? The premise, then, is that counterfactual reasoning can improve performance in a VLN task through exploration and consideration of alternative actions that the agent did not actually make. This may allow the agent to operate in data-scarce scenarios by bootstrapping familiarity of environments and the links between instructions and multiple action policy options.

Counterfactual thinking has been used to increase the robustness of models for various tasks [12,24]. However, no explicitly counterfactual models have been applied to the VLN task specifically. Speaker-Follower [11], which applies a back-translated speaker model to reconstruct the instructions for randomly-sampled paths as augmented training examples, is probably the VLN model that comes closest to instantiating counterfactual thinking.

While the use of augmented training examples by the Speaker-Follower agent resembles a counterfactual process, the random sampling method is too arbitrary. Figure 1 reports the performance of the model trained with randomly-sampled augmented data (the line in a light color) over different ratios of the augmented path used. It shows that the success rate stops increasing once augmented paths account for 60% or more of the training data [19]. Since those paths are all randomly sampled, it can limit the benefit of counterfactual thinking to data augmentation.

In this paper, we propose the use of adversarial-driven counterfactual thinking where the model learns to consider effective counterfactual conditions instead of sampling ample but uninformative data. We introduce a model-agnostic adversarial path sampler (APS) that learns how to generate augmented paths for training examples that are challenging, and thus effective, for the target navigation model. During the adversarial training process, the navigator is trying to accomplish augmented paths from APS and thus optimized for a better navigation policy, while the APS aims at producing increasingly challenging paths, which are therefore more effective than randomly-sampled paths.

Moreover, empowered by APS, the model can adapt to unseen environments in a practical setting—environment-based pre-exploration, where when deployed to a new environment, the robot can first pre-explore and get familiar with it, and then perform natural language guided tasks within this environment.

Experimental results on the R2R dataset show that the proposed APS can be integrated into a diverse collection of VLN models, improving their performance under both seen and unseen environments. In summary, our contributions are four-fold:

- We integrate counterfactual thinking into the vision-and-language navigation task, and propose the adversarial path sampler (APS) to progressively sample challenging and effective paths to improve the navigation policy.
- The proposed APS method is model-agnostic and can be easily integrated into various navigation models.
- Extensive experiments on the R2R dataset validate that the augmented paths generated by APS are not only useful in seen environments but also capable of generalizing the navigation policy better in unseen environments.
- We demonstrate that APS can also be used to adapt the navigation policy to unseen environments under environment-based pre-exploration.

## 2  Related Work

**Vision-and-Language Navigation.** Navigation in 3D environments based on natural language instruction has recently been investigated by many studies [3, 8,11,16,20–22,25,26,29,32–35]. For vision-and-language navigation (VLN), fine-grained human-written instructions are provided as guidance to navigate a robot in indoor environments. But data scarcity is a critical issue in VLN due to the high cost of data collection.

In order to augment more data for training, the Speaker-Follower model [11] applies a back-translated speaker model to generate instructions for randomly-sampled paths. In spite of obtaining some improvements from those extra paths, a recent study [19] shows that only a limited number of those augmented paths are useful and after using 60% of the augmented data, the improvement diminishes with additional augmented data. In this paper, we present a model-agnostic adversarial path sampler that progressively produces more challenging paths via an adversarial learning process with the navigator, therefore forcing the navigation policy to be improved as the augmented data grows.

**Counterfactual Thinking.** Counterfactual thinking is a concept that describes the human propensity to create possible alternatives to life events that have already occurred. Humans routinely ask questions such as: "What if ...?" or "If there is only ..." to consider the outcomes of different scenarios and apply inferential reasoning to the process. In the field of data science, counterfactual thinking has been used to make trained models explainable and more robust [12, 14,24]. Furthermore, counterfactual thinking is also applied to augment training targets [6,9,39]. Although previous studies have shown some improvements over different tasks, they all implement counterfactual thinking arbitrarily without a selection process to sample counterfactual data that might optimize learning. This can limit the effectiveness of counterfactual thinking. In this paper, we combine the adversarial training with counterfactual conditions to guide models that might lead to robust learning. In this way, we can maximize the benefit of counterfactual thinking.

**Adversarial Training.** Adversarial training refers to the process by which two models try to detrimentally influence each other's performance and as a result, both models improve by competing against each other. Adversarial training has been successfully used to guide the target during model training [1,10,13,18,27, 37]. Apart from leading the training target, adversarial training is also applied to data augmentation [5,38]. While previous studies just generate large amounts of augmented examples using a fixed pre-trained generator. In this paper, the generator is updated along with the target model and serves as a path sampler which samples challenging paths for effective data augmentation.

**Pre-exploration Under Unseen Environments.** Pre-exploration under unseen environments is a popular method to bridge the gap between seen and unseen environments. Speaker-Follower [11] adopts a state-factored beam search for several candidate paths and then selects the best one. RCM [33] introduces self-imitation learning (SIL) that actively optimized the navigation model to maximize the cross-matching score between the generated path and the original instruction. Nevertheless, beam search requires multiple runs for each inference, and SIL utilizes the original instructions in the unseen environments for optimization. EnvDrop [32] conducts pre-exploration by sampling shortest paths from unseen environments and augments them with back-translation, which however utilizes the meta-information of unseen environments (*e.g.*, the shortest path planner that the robot is not supposed to use).

## 3   Methodology

### 3.1   Background

**Visual-and-Language Navigation (VLN).** At each time step $t$, the environment presents the image scene $s_t$. After stepping an action $a_t$, the environment will transfer to next image scene $s_{t+1}$:

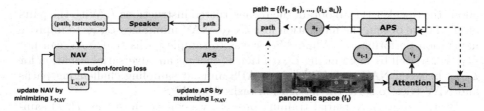

**Fig. 2.** The learning framework of our adversarial path sampler (APS), where Speaker is the back-translated speaker model and NAV is the navigation model.

**Fig. 3.** The architecture of the adversarial path sampler (APS).

$$s_{t+1} = \text{Environment}(s_t, a_t). \qquad (1)$$

To carry out a VLN task, the navigation model steps a serious of actions $\{a_t\}_{t=1}^{T}$ to achieve the final goal described in the instruction. Though previous studies propose different architectures of navigation model (NAV), in general, NAV is a recurrent action selector based on the visual feature of the image scene, navigation instruction, and previous history:

$$
\begin{aligned}
f_t &= \text{VisualFeature}(s_t), \\
a_t &= \text{softmax}(\text{NAV}(f_t, I, h_t)),
\end{aligned}
\qquad (2)
$$

where $f_t$ is the visual feature of the image scene $s_t$ at time step $t$, $I$ is the navigation instruction, $h_t$ represents the previous history of image scenes, and $a_t$ is the probability of each action to step at time step $t$. With $a_t$, we can decide which action to step based on greedy decoding (step the action with the highest probability).

In this work, we experiment under navigator with 3 different architectures, Seq2Seq [3], Speaker-Follower [11], and RCM [33].

**Back-Translated Speaker Model.** Introduced in Speaker-Follower [11], the back-translated speaker model (Speaker) generates the instruction of a navigation path:

$$I = \text{Speaker}(\{(f_1, a_1), (f_2, a_2), ..., (f_L, a_L)\}), \qquad (3)$$

where $f_t$ is the visual feature of the image scene, $a_t$ is the action taken at time step $t$, $L$ represents the length of the navigation path, and $I$ is the generated instruction. Speaker is trained with pairs of navigation paths and human-annotated instructions in the training data. With Speaker, we can sample various paths in the environments and augment their instructions.

### 3.2 Overview

The overall learning framework of our model-agnostic adversarial path sampler (APS) is illustrated in Fig. 2. At first, APS samples batch of paths $P$ and we adopt the Speaker [11] to obtain the reconstructed instructions $I$. With the pairs of $(P, I)$, we obtain the navigation loss $\mathcal{L}_{\text{NAV}}$. NAV minimizes $\mathcal{L}_{\text{NAV}}$ to improve navigation performance. While APS learns to sample paths that NAV can not perform so well by maximizing $\mathcal{L}_{\text{NAV}}$. Hence, there is an adversarial situation for $\mathcal{L}_{\text{NAV}}$ between NAV and APS, where APS aims at sampling challenging paths and NAV tries to solve the navigation tasks from APS.

By the above adversarial training process, we collect all of the $(P, I)$ sampled from APS to compose the adversarial augmented data which can be more helpful to NAV than randomly-sampled one. Both Speaker and NAV are pretrained using the original training set and Speaker keeps fixed during adversarial training. We collect all $(P, I)$ sampled from APS as APS-sampled augmented path and further train NAV. More detail can be seen in Sect. 3.4.

## 3.3   Architecture of APS

As shown in Fig. 3, the proposed APS is a recurrent action sampler $\pi_{\text{APS}}$ which samples series of actions $\{a_t\}_{t=1}^T$ (with the scene images $\{f_t\}_{t=1}^T$ presented from the environment) and combines as the path output, where $f_t$ means the visual feature (e.g., extracted from the convolutional neural networks). For the panoramic image scene, $f_{t,j}$ represents the visual feature of the image patch at viewpoint $j$ at time step $t$.

At each time step $t$, the history of previous visual feature and $a_{t-1}$ is encoded as $h_t$ by a long short-term memory (LSTM) [17] encoder:

$$h_t = \text{LSTM}([v_t, a_{t-1}], h_{t-1}), \tag{4}$$

where $a_{t-1}$ is the action taken at previous step and $v_t$ is the weighted sum of visual feature of each image path for the panoramic image scene. $v_t$ is calculated using the attention [7] between the history $h_{t-1}$ and the image patches $\{f_{t,j}\}_{j=1}^m$:

$$\begin{aligned} v_t &= \text{Attention}(h_{t-1}, \{f_{t,j}\}_{j=1}^m) \\ &= \sum_j \text{softmax}(h_{t-1}W_h(f_{t,j}W_f)^T)f_{t,j}, \end{aligned} \tag{5}$$

where $W_h$ and $W_f$ are learnable projection matrics. The above equation of $v_t$ is for panoramic scene with $m$ viewpoints. APS also supports the navigator which uses visuomotor view as input (e.g., Seq2Seq [3]) and the single visual feature $f_t$ is seen as $v_t$ directly.

Finally, APS decides which action to step based on the history $h_t$ and action embedding $u$:

$$a_t = \text{softmax}(h_t W_c(u_k W_u^T)), \tag{6}$$

where $u_k$ is the action embedding of the $k$-th navigable direction. $W_c$ and $W_u$ are learnable projection matrics.

**Algorithm 1.** Training Process of Adversarial Path Sampler

---

1: NAV: the target navigation model
2: Speaker: the back-translated instruction model
3: APS: the adversarial path sampler
4: $\text{aug}_{\text{aps}}$: collected APS-sampled augmented data
5:
6: Pre-train NAV with original training set
7: Pre-train Speaker with original navigation path
8: Initialize APS
9: $\text{aug}_{\text{aps}} \leftarrow \varnothing$
10:
11: **while** DO_APS **do**
12:     $P = \{(f_1, a_1), (f_2, a_2), ..., (f_L, a_L)\} \leftarrow$ APS samples
13:     $I \leftarrow$ back-translated by Speaker with $P$
14:     $\mathcal{L}_{\text{NAV}} \leftarrow$ student-forcing loss of NAV using $(P, I)$
15:
16:     Update NAV by minimizing $\mathcal{L}_{\text{NAV}}$
17:     Update APS by maximizing $\mathcal{L}_{\text{NAV}}$ using Policy Gradient
18:     $\text{aug}_{\text{aps}} \leftarrow \text{aug}_{\text{aps}} \cup (P, I)$
19: **end while**
20:
21: Train NAV with $\text{aug}_{\text{aps}}$
22: Fine-tune NAV with original training set

---

### 3.4 Adversarial Training of APS

After each unrolling of APS, we comprise the navigation history $\{a_t\}_{t=1}^T$ and $\{f_{t,j}\}_{j=1}^m$ to obtain the path $P$. To be consistent with the original training data whose navigation paths are all shortest paths [3], we transform the sampled paths by APS into shortest paths[1] (same start and end nodes as in the sampled paths). Then we employ the Speaker model [11] to produce one instruction $I$ for each sampled path $P$, and eventually obtain a set of new augmented pairs $(P, I)$. We train the navigation model (NAV) with $(P, I)$ using student-forcing [3]. The training loss ($\mathcal{L}_{\text{NAV}}$) can be seen as an indicator of NAV's performance under $(P, I)$: the higher $\mathcal{L}_{\text{NAV}}$ is, the worse NAV performs. Hence, in order to create increasingly challenging paths to improve the navigation policy, we define the loss function $\mathcal{L}_{\text{APS}}$ of APS as:

$$\mathcal{L}_{\text{APS}} = -\mathbb{E}_{p(\text{P};\pi_{\text{APS}})}\mathcal{L}_{\text{NAV}}. \tag{7}$$

Since the path sampling process is not differentiable, we adopt policy gradient [31] and view $\mathcal{L}_{\text{NAV}}$ as the reward $R$ to optimize the APS objective. According to the REINFORCE algorithm [36], the gradient is computed as following:

---

[1] Note that transforming the sampled paths into shortest paths can only be done under seen environments. For pre-exploration under unseen environments, we directly use the sampled paths because the shortest path planner should not be exploited in unseen environments.

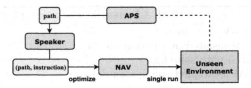

**Fig. 4.** The optimization flow of environment-based pre-exploration under unseen environments. APS samples paths from the unseen environment to optimize NAV and make it more adaptive. Then, NAV runs each instruction in a single turn.

$$\nabla_{\pi_{\text{APS}}} \mathcal{L}_{\text{APS}} \approx -\sum_{t=1}^{T} [\nabla_{\pi_{\text{APS}}} \log p(a_t | a_{1:t-1}; \pi_{\text{APS}}) R]$$
$$\approx -\sum_{t=1}^{T} [\nabla_{\pi_{\text{APS}}} \log p(a_t | a_{1:t-1}; \pi_{\text{APS}})(R - b)], \tag{8}$$

where $b$ is the baseline estimation to reduce the variance and we treat $b$ as the mean of all previous losses. Note that APS is model-agnostic and can be easily integrated into different navigation models, since it only considers the training loss from a navigation model regardless of its model architecture.

Algorithm 1 illustrates the training process of APS. APS aims at maximizing the navigation loss $\mathcal{L}_{\text{NAV}}$ of NAV to create more challenging paths, while NAV tries to minimize $\mathcal{L}_{\text{NAV}}$ to do better navigation:

$$\min_{\text{NAV}} \max_{\text{APS}} \mathcal{L}_{\text{NAV}}. \tag{9}$$

After collecting the challenging paths augmented by APS, we train NAV on them and finally fine-tune NAV with the original training set. The detailed analysis of APS-sampled augmented data is shown in Sect. 4.3.

### 3.5   Environment-Based Pre-exploration

Pre-exploration is a technique that adapts the navigation model to unseen environments. The navigator can explore the unfamiliar environment first and increase the chance to carry out the navigation instructions under unseen environments. For previous pre-exploration methods like beam search [11] or self-imitation learning (SIL) [33], they are instruction-based which optimizes for each instruction. This will make the navigation path excessive long since it first runs many different paths and then selects the possible best one.

In the real world, when we deploy a robot into a new environment, it might pre-explore and get familiar with the environment, and then efficiently execute the tasks following natural language instructions within this environment. So unlike previous approaches [32,33] that either optimize the given instructions or assume access to all the unseen environments at once, we propose to use our APS method to do the environment-based pre-exploration where the agent pre-explore an environment only for the tasks within the same environment with no

**Table 1.** R2R results for Seq2Seq, Speaker-Follower, and RCM under testing set. Models are trained without augmented data, with randomly-sampled augmented path ($\text{aug}_{\text{rand}}$), with APS-sampled augmented path ($\text{aug}_{\text{aps}}$), and under pre-exploration in unseen environments. Note that those results are run in single turn and with greedy action decoding.

| Model | Test (VLN Challenge Leaderboard) | | | |
| --- | --- | --- | --- | --- |
| | NE ↓ | OSR ↑ | SR ↑ | SPL ↑ |
| Seq2Seq [3] | 7.9 | 26.6 | 20.4 | 18.0 |
| + $\text{aug}_{\text{rand}}$ | 7.8 | 26.2 | 21.0 | 18.8 |
| + $\text{aug}_{\text{aps}}$ | **7.5** | 30.1 | **22.5** | 19.3 |
| + $\text{aug}_{\text{aps}}$ + pre-exploration | **6.7** | 29.4 | **23.2** | 20.8 |
| Speaker-Follower [11] | 7.0 | 41.2 | 30.9 | 24.0 |
| + $\text{aug}_{\text{rand}}$ | 6.6 | 43.4 | 34.8 | 29.2 |
| + $\text{aug}_{\text{aps}}$ | **6.5** | 44.2 | **36.1** | 28.8 |
| + $\text{aug}_{\text{aps}}$ + pre-exploration | **5.9** | 46.4 | **37.6** | 32.4 |
| RCM [33] | 6.7 | 43.5 | 35.9 | 33.1 |
| + $\text{aug}_{\text{rand}}$ | 5.9 | 52.4 | 44.5 | 40.8 |
| + $\text{aug}_{\text{aps}}$ | **5.8** | 53.9 | **45.1** | 40.9 |
| + $\text{aug}_{\text{aps}}$ + pre-exploration | **5.5** | 55.6 | **45.9** | 40.9 |

prior knowledge of it. Under an unseen environment, we adopt APS to sample multiple paths ($P'$) and generate the instructions ($I'$) of the sampled paths[2] with the Speaker model [11]. We then use ($P'$, $I'$) to optimize NAV to adapt to the unseen environment as illustrated in Fig. 4. Note that during pre-exploration, we only optimize NAV and let APS fixed[3]. We also present a detailed analysis of our proposed environment-based pre-exploration method in Sect. 4.3.

# 4  Experiments

## 4.1  Experimental Setup

**R2R Dataset.** We evaluate the proposed method on the Room-to-Room (R2R) dataset [3] for vision-and-language navigation. R2R is built upon the Matterport3D [4], which contains 90 different environments that are split into 61 for training and validation-seen, 11 for validation-unseen, and 18 for testing sets.

---

[2] Note that the shortest-path information is not used during pre-exploration.

[3] We have tried to update APS simultaneously with NAV during pre-exploration, but it turns out that under a previous unseen environment without any regularization of human-annotated paths, APS tends to sample too difficult paths to accomplish, e.g., back and forth or cycles. However, those paths will not improve NAV and may even hurt the performance. To avoid this kind of dilemma, we keep APS fixed under the pre-exploration.

**Table 2.** R2R results for Seq2Seq, Speaker-Follower, and RCM under validation-seen and validation-unseen sets.

| Model | Val-Seen | | | | Val-Unseen | | | |
|---|---|---|---|---|---|---|---|---|
| | NE ↓ | OSR ↑ | SR ↑ | SPL ↑ | NE ↓ | OSR ↑ | SR ↑ | SPL ↑ |
| Seq2Seq [3] | 6.0 | 51.7 | 39.4 | 33.8 | 7.8 | 27.7 | 22.1 | 19.1 |
| + aug$_{rand}$ | 5.3 | 58.1 | 43.7 | 37.2 | 7.7 | 28.9 | 22.6 | 19.9 |
| + aug$_{aps}$ | **5.0** | **60.8** | **48.2** | **40.1** | **7.1** | **32.7** | **24.2** | **20.4** |
| + aug$_{aps}$ + pre-exploration | - | | | | **6.6** | **37.8** | **27.0** | **24.6** |
| Speaker-Follower [11] | 5.0 | 61.6 | 51.7 | 44.4 | 6.9 | 40.7 | 29.9 | 21.0 |
| + aug$_{rand}$ | 3.7 | 74.2 | 66.4 | 59.8 | 6.6 | 46.6 | 36.1 | 28.8 |
| + aug$_{aps}$ | **3.3** | **74.9** | **68.2** | **62.5** | **6.1** | **46.7** | **38.8** | **32.1** |
| + aug$_{aps}$ + pre-exploration | - | | | | **5.2** | **49.1** | **42.0** | **35.7** |
| RCM [33] | 5.7 | 53.8 | 47.0 | 44.3 | 6.8 | 43.0 | 35.0 | 31.4 |
| + aug$_{rand}$ | 4.1 | 66.9 | 61.9 | 58.6 | 5.7 | 52.4 | 45.6 | 41.8 |
| + aug$_{aps}$ | **3.9** | **69.3** | **63.2** | **59.5** | **5.4** | **56.6** | **47.7** | **42.8** |
| + aug$_{aps}$ + pre-exploration | - | | | | **5.3** | 56.2 | **48.0** | **42.8** |

There are 7,189 paths and each path has 3 human-written instructions. The validation-seen set shares the same environments with the training set. In contrast, both the validation-unseen and the testing sets contain distinct environments that do not appear during training.

**Evaluation Metrics.** To compare with the existing methods, we report the same used evaluation metrics: Navigation Error (NE), Oracle Success Rate (OSR), Success Rate (SR), and Success Rate weighted by Path Length (SPL). NE is the distance between the agent's final position and goal location. OSR is the success rate at the closest point to the goal that the agent has visited. SR is calculated as the percentage of the final position within 3 m from the goal location. SPL, defined in [2], is the success rate weighted by path length which considers both effectiveness and efficiency.

**Baselines.** We experiment with the effectiveness of the model-agnostic APS on 3 kinds of baselines:

- **Seq2Seq** [3], the attention-based seq2seq model that is trained with student forcing (or imitation learning) under the visuomotor view and action space;
- **Speaker-Follower** [11], the compositional model that is trained with student forcing under the panoramic view and action space;
- **RCM** [33], the model that integrates cross-modal matching loss, and is trained using reinforcement learning under the panoramic view and action space.

In the following sections, we use the notations as:

- aug$_{rand}$: the randomly-sampled augmented path;

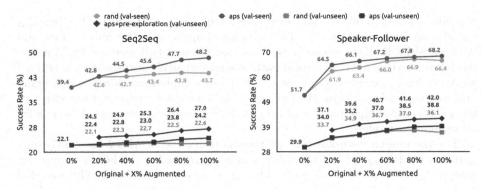

**Fig. 5.** The comparison between randomly-sampled and APS-sampled under validation-seen and validation-unseen sets for Seq2Seq and Speaker-Follower over different ratios of augmented path used.

- $aug_{aps}$: the APS-sampled augmented path;
- $model_{rand}$: the model trained with $aug_{rand}$;
- $model_{aps}$: the model trained with $aug_{aps}$.

For example, Speaker-Follower$_{aps}$ is the Speaker-Follower model trained with the APS-sampled augmented path.

For each baseline, we report the results of the model trained without any augmented data, trained with $aug_{rand}$, and trained with $aug_{aps}$. For the unseen environments, we also report the results under the pre-exploration.

**Implementation Details.** To follow the previous studies [3,11,33], we adopt ResNet-152 [15] to extract visual features (2048d) for all scene images without fine-tuning; for the navigation instructions, the pre-trained GloVe embeddings [28] are used for initialization and then fine-tuned with the model training. For baseline models, we apply the same batch size 100, LSTM with 512 hidden units, learning rate 1e−4, RL learning rate 1e−5, and dropout rate 0.5. For our proposed APS, the hidden unit of LSTM is also 512, the action embedding size is 128, and the learning rate is 3e−5. We adopt the learning rate 1e−5 under the pre-exploration for the unseen environments. All models are optimized via Adam optimizer [23] with weight decay 5e−4.

For $aug_{rand}$, we use the same 17 K paths as Speaker-Follower [11]. To compare fairly, APS also adversarially samples the same amounts of paths for data augmentation. The navigation models are first trained using augmented data for 50 K iterations and then fine-tuned with original instructions for 20 K iterations.

## 4.2 Quantitative Results

Tables 1 and 2 present the R2R results for Seq2Seq [3], Speaker-Follower [11], and RCM [33] under validation-seen, validation-unseen, and testing sets. All models are trained without augmented data, with $aug_{rand}$, and with $aug_{aps}$. First, we can observe that under validation-seen set, $Seq2Seq_{aps}$ outperforms $Seq2Seq_{rand}$ on all evaluation metrics, e.g., 4.5% absolute improvement on Sucess Rate and 2.9% on SPL. Similar trends can be found for Speaker-Follower and RCM where models trained with APS-sampled paths comprehensively surpass models trained with randomly-sampled paths. Since APS can sample increasingly challenging and custom-made paths for the navigator, APS-sampled paths are more effective than randomly-sample paths and bring in larger improvements on all metrics for all navigation models.

For the unseen environments, all models trained with APS consistently outperform $model_{rand}$ with 1.6%–2.7% success rate under validation-unseen set and 0.6%–1.5% under testing set. The improvement shows that APS-sampled paths are not only helpful under the seen environments, but also strengthens the model's generalizability under the unseen environments. The results under validation-seen, validation-unseen, and testing sets demonstrate that our proposed APS can further improve the baseline models in all terms of visuomotor view, panoramic view, imitation learning, and reinforcement learning.

And under the pre-exploration, all models gain further improvement, especially on SPL for Seq2Seq and Speaker-Follower due to the prior exploration experience which can shorten the navigation path length.

| Model | train | As Testing Set | |
| --- | --- | --- | --- |
| | | $aug_{rand}$ | $aug_{aps}$ |
| Seq2Seq | 71.3 | 20.3 | 17.7 |
| $Seq2Seq_{rand}$ | **81.4** | 26.4 | 23.8 |
| $Seq2Seq_{aps}$ | 78.5 | **27.3** | **24.8** |

| Model | As Testing Set | |
| --- | --- | --- |
| | $aug_{rand}$ | $aug_{aps}$ |
| $RCM_{rand}$ | 33.3 | 31.1 |
| $RCM_{aps}$ | **38.9** | **37.9** |

**Fig. 6.** The success rate under training, randomly-sampled augmented ($aug_{rand}$), and APS-sampled augmented ($aug_{aps}$) sets for Seq2Seq and RCM.

### 4.3  Ablation Study

**Random Path Sampling vs. Adversarial Path Sampling.** To investigate the advantage of APS, we perform a detailed comparison between randomly-sampled and APS-sampled data. Figure 5 presents the R2R success rate over different ratios of augmented data used for Seq2Seq and Speaker-Follower. The trend line in light color shows that $Seq2Seq_{rand}$ cannot gain additional improvement when using more than 60% augmented data. However, for our proposed APS, the sampled augmented path can keep benefiting the model when more data used and achieve 4.5% and 1.6% improvement under validation-seen and validation-unseen sets, respectively. Since $aug_{rand}$ is sampled in advance, the help to the model is limited. While, our proposed APS adversarially learns to sample challenging paths that force the navigator to keep improving. A similar trend can be found for Speaker-Follower where the improvement of Speaker-Follower$_{rand}$ is also stuck but Speaker-Follower$_{aps}$ can lead to even better performance.

**Difficulty and Usefulness of the APS-sampled Paths.** For a more intuitive view of the difficulty and usefulness of the APS-sampled paths, we conduct experiments shown in Table 6 to quantitatively compare them with randomly-sample paths. As you can see, the APS-sampled paths seem to be the most challenging as all models perform worst on them. These paths can in turn help train a more robust navigation model (Seq2Seq$_{aps}$) that outperforms the model trained with randomly sampled paths. Moreover, Seq2Seq$_{aps}$ even performs better on aug$_{rand}$ than Seq2Seq$_{rand}$ which shows that aug$_{aps}$ is not only challenging but also covers useful paths over aug$_{rand}$.

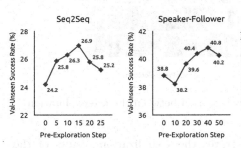

**Fig. 7.** The success rate under validation-unseen set under different pre-exploration steps for Seq2Seq and Speaker-Follower.

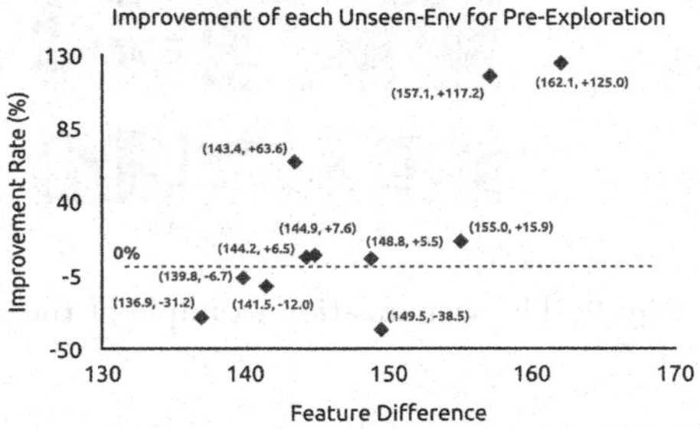

**Fig. 8.** The improvement of success rate over the scene feature difference under the pre-exploration.

**Pre-exploration.** Table 2 has shown the improvement brought from the pre-exploration. While, those paths in training, validation, and testing sets are all shortest path but the paths sampled from our APS under unseen environments are not promised to be the shortest. With more pre-exploration steps, the model has more opportunities to explore the unseen environment but at the same time, those too complicated paths sampled from APS may hurt the model. Figure 7 presents the success rate under different pre-exploration steps. It shows a trade-off between the model performance and the iterations of the pre-exploration. For Seq2Seq, 15 steps of pre-exploration come out the best result and 40 steps are most suitable for Speaker-Follower.

We also analyze the performance under the pre-exploration under each unseen environments. Figure 8 demonstrates the improvement of the success rate over the scene feature difference. Each point represents a distinct validation-unseen environment. The feature difference under each unseen environment is calculated as the mean of the L2-distance between the visual feature of all scenes from that environment and all scenes in the training environments. In general, most of the unseen environments gain improvement under the pre-exploration. We also find a trend that under the environment which has a larger feature difference, it can improve more under the pre-exploration. It shows that under more different environments, the pre-exploration can be more powerful which makes it practical to be more adaptive and generalized to real-life unseen environments.

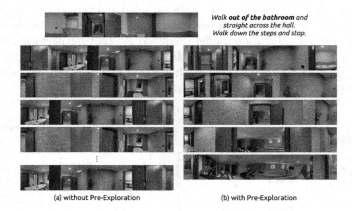

*Walk **out of the bathroom** and straight across the hall. Walk down the steps and stop.*

(a) without Pre-Exploration          (b) with Pre-Exploration

**Fig. 9.** The visualization example of the comparison between the pre-exploration.

**Qualitative Results.** Figure 9 demonstrates the visualization results of the navigation path without and with pre-exploration for the instruction *"Walk out of the bathroom"*. Under the unseen environment, it is difficult to find out a path to get out of the unfamiliar bathroom, and as is shown in Fig. 9(a), the model without pre-exploration is stuck inside. In contrast, with the knowledge learned during the pre-exploration phase, the model can successfully walk out of the bathroom and eventually achieve the final goal.

## 5    Conclusion

In this paper, we integrate counterfactual thinking into the vision-and-language navigation (VLN) task to solve the data scarcity problem. We realize counterfactual thinking via adversarial learning where we introduce an adversarial path sampler (APS) to only consider useful counterfactual conditions. The proposed APS is model-agnostic and proven effective in producing challenging but useful paths to boost the performances of different VLN models. Due to the power of reasoning, counterfactual thinking has gradually received attention in different fields. We believe that our adversarial training method is an effective solution to realize counterfactual thinking in general, which can possibly benefit more tasks.

**Acknowledgments.** Research was sponsored by the U.S. Army Research Office and was accomplished under Contract Number W911NF-19-D-0001 for the Institute for

Collaborative Biotechnologies. The views and conclusions contained in this document are those of the authors and should not be interpreted as representing the official policies, either expressed or implied, of the U.S. Government. The U.S. Government is authorized to reproduce and distribute reprints for Government purposes notwithstanding any copyright notation herein.

# References

1. Agmon, N.: Robotic strategic behavior in adversarial environments. In: IJCAI (2017)
2. Anderson, P., et al.: On evaluation of embodied navigation agents. arXiv:1807.06757 (2018)
3. Anderson, P., et al.: Vision-and-language navigation: interpreting visually-grounded navigation instructions in real environments. In: CVPR (2018)
4. Angel, C., e al.: Matterport3D: learning from RGB-D data in indoor environments. In: 3DV (2017)
5. Antoniou, A., Storkey, A., Edwards, H.: Data augmentation generative adversarial networks. arXiv:1711.04340 (2017)
6. Ashual, O., Wolf, L.: Specifying object attributes and relations in interactive scene generation. In: ICCV (2019)
7. Bahdanau, D., Cho, K., Bengio, Y.: Neural machine translation by jointly learning to align and translate. In: ICLR (2015)
8. Chen, H., Suhr, A., Misra, D., Snavely, N., Artzi, Y.: Touchdown: natural language navigation and spatial reasoning in visual street environments. In: CVPR (2019)
9. Chen, L., Zhang, H., Xiao, J., He, X., Pu, S., Chang, S.F.: Counterfactual critic multi-agent training for scene graph generation. In: ICCV (2019)
10. Chou, C.J., Chien, J.T., Chen, H.T.: Self adversarial training for human pose estimation. In: APSIPA (2018)
11. Fried, D., et al.: Speaker-follower models for vision-and-language navigation. In: NeurIPS (2018)
12. Garg, S., Perot, V., Limtiaco, N., Taly, A., Chi, E.H., Beutel, A.: Counterfactual fairness in text classification through robustness. In: AIES (2019)
13. Goodfellow, I.J., et al.: Generative adversarial networks. In: NeurIPS (2014)
14. Goyal, Y., Wu, Z., Ernst, J., Batra, D., Parikh, D., Lee, S.: Counterfactual visual explanations. In: ICML (2019)
15. He, K., Zhang, X., Ren, S., Sun, J.: Deep residual learning for image recognition. In: CVPR (2016)
16. Hemachandra, S., Duvallet, F., Howard, T.M., Stentz, A., Roy, N., Walter, M.R.: learning models for following natural language directions in unknown environments. In: ICRA (2015)
17. Hochreiter, S., Schmidhuber, J.: Long short-term memory. In: Neural Computation (1997)
18. Hong, Z.W., Fu, T.J., Shann, T.Y., Chang, Y.H., Lee, C.Y.: Adversarial active exploration for inverse dynamics model learning. In: CoRL (2019)
19. Huang, H., Jain, V., Mehta, H., Baldridge, J., Ie, E.: Multi-modal discriminative model for vision-and-language navigation. In: NAACL Workshop (2019)
20. Huang, H., Jain, V., Mehta, H., Ku, A., Magalhaes, G., Baldridge, J., Ie, E.: Transferable representation learning in vision-and-language navigation. In: ICCV (2019)

21. Jain, V., Magalhaes, G., Ku, A., Vaswani, A., Ie, E., Baldridge, J.: Stay on the path: instruction fidelity in vision-and-language navigation. arXiv:1905.12255 (2019)
22. Ke, L., et al.: Tactical Rewind: self-correction via backtracking in vision-and-language navigation. In: CVPR (2019)
23. Kingma, D.P., Ba, J.: Adam: a method for stochastic optimization. In: ICLR (2015)
24. Kusner, M., Loftus, J., Russell, C., Silva, R.: Counterfactual fairness. In: NeurIPS (2017)
25. Ma, C.Y., et al.: Self-monitoring navigation agent via auxiliary progress estimation. In: ICLR (2019)
26. Ma, C.Y., Wu, Z., AlRegib, G., Xiong, C., Kira, Z.: The regretful agent: heuristic-aided navigation through progress estimation. In: CVPR (2019)
27. Miyato, T., Dai, A.M., Goodfellow, I.: Adversarial training methods for semi-supervised text classification. In: ICLR (2017)
28. Pennington, J., Socher, R., Manning, C.: Glove: global vectors for word representation. In: EMNLP (2014)
29. Qi, Y., et al.: REVERIE: remote embodied visual referring expression in real indoor environments. In: CVPR (2020)
30. Roese, N.J.: Counterfactual thinking. Psychol. Bull. **121**(1), 133–148 (1997)
31. Sutton, R.S., McAllester, D., Singh, S., Mansour, Y.: Policy gradient methods for reinforcement learning with function approximation. In: NeurIPS (2000)
32. Tan, H., Yu, L., Bansal, M.: Learning to navigate unseen environments: back translation with environmental dropout. In: NAACL (2019)
33. Wang, X., et al.: Reinforced cross-modal matching and self-supervised imitation learning for vision-language navigation. In: CVPR (2019)
34. Wang, X., Jain, V., Ie, E., Wang, W., Kozareva, Z., Ravi, S.: Environment-agnostic multitask learning for natural language grounded navigation. In: ECCV (2020)
35. Wang, X., Xiong, W., Wang, H., Wang, W.Y.: Look before you leap: bridging model-free and model-based reinforcement learning for planned-ahead vision-and-language navigation. In: Ferrari, V., Hebert, M., Sminchisescu, C., Weiss, Y. (eds.) Computer Vision—ECCV 2018. Lecture Notes in Computer Science, vol. 11220, pp. 38–55. Springer, Cham (2018). https://doi.org/10.1007/978-3-030-01270-0_3
36. Williams, R.J.: Simple statistical gradient-following algorithms for connectionist reinforcement learning. Mach. Learn. **8**, 229–256 (1992)
37. Wu, Y., Bamman, D., Russell, S.: Adversarial training for relation extraction. In: EMNLP (2017)
38. Zhang, R., Che, T., Ghahramani, Z., Bengio, Y., Song, Y.: MetaGAN: an adversarial approach to few-shot learning. In: NeurIPS (2018)
39. Zmigrod, R., Mielke, S.J., Wallach, H., Cotterell, R.: Counterfactual data augmentation for mitigating gender stereotypes in languages with rich morphology. In: ACL (2019)

# Guided Deep Decoder: Unsupervised Image Pair Fusion

Tatsumi Uezato[1]([✉])[iD], Danfeng Hong[2,3][iD], Naoto Yokoya[1,4][iD], and Wei He[1][iD]

[1] RIKEN AIP, Tokyo, Japan
{tatsumi.uezato,naoto.yokoya,wei.he}@riken.jp
[2] German Aerospace Center, Wessling, Germany
danfeng.hong@dlr.de
[3] Univ. Grenoble Alpes, CNRS, Grenoble INP, GIPSA-Lab, Grenoble, France
[4] The University of Tokyo, Tokyo, Japan

**Abstract.** The fusion of input and guidance images that have a tradeoff in their information (e.g., hyperspectral and RGB image fusion or pansharpening) can be interpreted as one general problem. However, previous studies applied a task-specific handcrafted prior and did not address the problems with a unified approach. To address this limitation, in this study, we propose a guided deep decoder network as a general prior. The proposed network is composed of an encoder-decoder network that exploits multi-scale features of a guidance image and a deep decoder network that generates an output image. The two networks are connected by feature refinement units to embed the multi-scale features of the guidance image into the deep decoder network. The proposed network allows the network parameters to be optimized in an unsupervised way without training data. Our results show that the proposed network can achieve state-of-the-art performance in various image fusion problems.

**Keywords:** Deep image prior · Deep decoder · Image fusion · Hyperspectral image · Super-resolution · Pansharpening

## 1 Introduction

Some image fusion tasks address the fusion of image pairs in the same modality. The tasks consider a pair of images that capture the same region but have a tradeoff between the two images (Fig. 1). For example, a low spatial resolution hyperspectral (LR-HS) image has greater spectral resolution at lower spatial resolution [39]. However, an RGB image acquires much lower spectral resolution at higher spatial resolution. Likewise, panchromatic and multispectral (MS) images have a tradeoff between spatial and spectral resolution [29]. No-flash images capture ambient illumination, but are very noisy, while flash images capture artificial

**Electronic supplementary material** The online version of this chapter (https://doi.org/10.1007/978-3-030-58539-6_6) contains supplementary material, which is available to authorized users.

© Springer Nature Switzerland AG 2020
A. Vedaldi et al. (Eds.): ECCV 2020, LNCS 12351, pp. 87–102, 2020.
https://doi.org/10.1007/978-3-030-58539-6_6

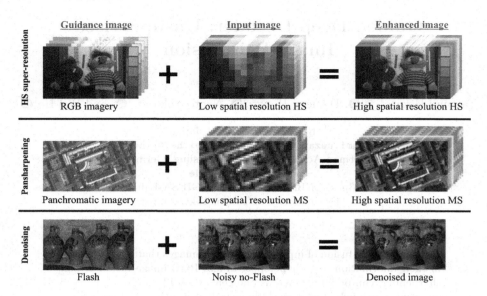

**Fig. 1.** Illustration of image pair fusion of the same modality.

light, but are less noisy [23]. Image fusion enables an image that overcomes the tradeoff to be generated. Hyperspectral super-resolution or pansharpening aims to generate a high resolution (HR) HS or MS image. The denoising of a no-flash image with a flash image can be also interpreted as a special case of image fusion.

Although these tasks share a common goal (i.e., enhancing input images with the help of guidance images), the tasks have been studied independently. This occurs because a different handcrafted prior is considered to incorporate the specific property of an output image. In HS super-resolution, a prior exploiting the low-rankness of HS has been extensively used [7,18,40]. In pansharpening, a prior representing a spatial smoothness has been considered [22]. The denoising task assumes that the spatial structure of a restored image is similar to that of a guidance image [23]. While these handcrafted priors share the same goal, the priors need to be designed for each task to exploit the specific properties of data. It is highly desirable to develop a prior applicable to various image fusion problems.

Deep learning (DL) approaches avoid the assumption of explicit priors for each specific task. Although network architectures themselves need to be handcrafted, properly designed network architectures have shown to solve various problems [14,25]. Most DL approaches rely on training data. However, for pansharpening and hyperspectral super-resolution, it is difficult to collect a large size of training data including reference (i.e., HR-HS or HR-MS) because of the cost or hardware limitation. Thus, previous studies [26,36] have frequently used synthetic data for training, which may have limited generalization performance. In addition, different sensors provide different spectral response functions. Networks trained on data acquired by a particular sensor may not work well on new data acquired by a different sensor.

A natural question arises: is it possible to use DL approaches without training data? Ulyanov *et al.* [28] have shown that network architectures have inductive bias and can be used as deep image prior (DIP) without any training data. This intriguing property of DIP has been successfully used for various problems [12,27,38]. In [28], the guided denoising task of flash and no-flash image pair has been addressed using a no-flash image as an input and a flash image as an output. Although this approach can be potentially used to address the problems shown in Fig. 1, the network architecture does not fully exploit the semantic features or image details of a guidance image. It is still unclear how the network architecture is conditioned on the features of a guidance image. Although DIP has great potential, the uncertainties limit DIP to achieve state-of-the-art (SOTA) performance in various image fusion problems.

As discussed above, previous studies face two major problems (task-specific handcrafted priors and requirement of training data) to address various image fusion problems in a unified framework. In this study, we propose a new network architecture, called a guided deep decoder (GDD), that overcomes the problems and can achieve SOTA performance in different image fusion problems. Specifically, the proposed network architecture is composed of two networks where one encoder-decoder network is designed to extract multi-scale semantic features from a guidance image, while another deep decoder network generates an output image from random noise. The two networks are connected by feature refinement units incorporating attention gates to embed the multi-scale features of the guidance image into the deep decoder network.

The contributions of this paper are as follows. (1) We propose a new unsupervised DL method that does not require training data and can be adapted to different image fusion tasks in a unified framework. We achieve SOTA results for various image fusion problems. (2) We propose a new network architecture as a regularizer for unsupervised image fusion problems. The attention gates used in the proposed architecture guide the generation of an output image using the multi-scale semantic features from a guidance image. The guidance of the multi-scale features can lead to an effective regularizer for an ill-posed optimization problem.

## 2    Related Work

Most of the previous works have independently addressed one of the image fusion problems shown in Fig. 1, although the common goal is to generate an image that overcomes the tradeoff. This study focuses on the data acquired in the same modality and is different from the image fusion problems of different modalities where the sensor captures different physical quantities (e.g., fusion of RGB images and depth maps [20]). To address the ill-posed fusion problems, similar approaches have been developed for different image fusion tasks.

**Classical Approach:** The classical approach is to specifically design a handcrafted prior for each task. For example, handcrafted priors exploiting the low-rankness or sparsity of HS have been developed for HS and MS image fusion problems [16,17,34,40]. In panchromatic and MS image fusion, the handcrafted priors, which assume that the spatial details of PAN are similar to those of MS, have been widely used [6,10,19,22]. In addition, flash and no-flash image fusion uses a prior that promotes similar spatial details between the paired image [23]. The classical approach can reconstruct an enhanced image without any training data by explicitly assuming prior knowledge. However, the priors designed for a specific task may not be effective when they are applied to other tasks. In addition, an optimization method needs to be tailored for a different prior.

**Supervised DL Approach:** DL methods that use training data have recently achieved SOTA performance in different image fusion problems. DL methods are usually built upon a popular network (e.g., [14,25]). In the HS and RGB image fusion, DL methods use LR-HS and RGB images as an input and an HR-HS image as an output and learn the mapping function between the inputs and the output [8,36]. Similarly, in pansharpening, the methods consider panchromatic and LR-MS images as an input and HR-MS as an output and learn the mapping function [26,35,37]. As long as training data are available, DL methods can be potentially applied to different image fusion problems in a unified framework by slightly changing the network architecture or the loss function. However, it may be difficult to acquire training data, including reference data, for HS or MS images because of the cost or hardware limitation.

**Unsupervised DL Approach:** To bridge the gap between the classical and supervised DL approaches, an unsupervised DL approach has been considered in some studies. The unsupervised DL methods have been developed to address the HS and RGB image fusion problem [11,24]. In [11,24], the network architecture has been specifically designed to exploit the property of the HS image and different handcrafted priors have been combined to achieve optimal performance. However, it may not achieve SOTA performance in other tasks because of the specifically designed network and handcrafted priors. DIP that can apply DL in an unsupervised way has been recently developed by [28] and has been applied for a variety of problems [12,27,38]. Although DIP can be potentially applied for various image fusion problems, it has not been explored yet. The simple application of DIP cannot achieve SOTA performance in different image fusion tasks, which is shown in the following experiments. Our study borrows the idea of DIP and proposes a robust network architecture that achieves SOTA performance in these tasks.

## 3  Methodology

### 3.1  Problem Formulation

Let us denote a low resolution or noisy input image $\mathbf{Y} \in \mathbb{R}^{C \times w \times h}$ and a guidance image $\mathbf{G} \in \mathbb{R}^{c \times W \times H}$ where $C$, $W$, and $H$ represent the number of channels, the image width, and the image height, respectively. When considering HS super-resolution or pansharpening, $w \ll W$, $h \ll H$, and $c \ll C$. In the unsupervised

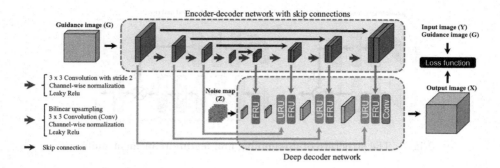

**Fig. 2.** The structure of a guided deep decoder. The semantic features are extracted from the guidance image by the U-net like encoder-decoder network. The blue layers represent the features of the encoder. The red layers represent the features of the decoder. The green layers represent the features of the deep decoder network. The semantic features of G are used to guide the features of the deep decoder in the upsampling and feature refinement units (URU and FRU). (Color figure online)

image fusion problem, the corresponding output $\mathbf{X} \in \mathbb{R}^{C \times W \times H}$ can be estimated by solving the following optimization problem:

$$\min_{\mathbf{X}} \mathcal{L}\left(\mathbf{X}, \mathbf{Y}, \mathbf{G}\right) + \mathcal{R}\left(\mathbf{X}\right), \tag{1}$$

where $\mathcal{L}$ is a loss function that is different for each task. Because the problem is ill-posed, existing methods commonly add the handcrafted regularization term $\mathcal{R}$. However, the task-specific regularization term (e.g., low-rank property of HS images) cannot be easily applied to other tasks. Instead of using the handcrafted regularization terms, DIP estimates $\mathbf{X}$ using a convolutional neural network (CNN)-based mapping function as:

$$\mathbf{X} = f_\theta\left(\mathbf{Z}\right), \tag{2}$$

where $f_\theta$ represents the mapping function with the network parameters $\theta$, $\mathbf{Z}$ is the input representing the random code tensor. The optimization problem can be rewritten as:

$$\min_\theta \mathcal{L}\left(f_\theta\left(\mathbf{Z}\right), \mathbf{Y}, \mathbf{G}\right). \tag{3}$$

In this formulation, only one input image $\mathbf{Y}$ and a guidance image $\mathbf{G}$ are used for the optimization problem; thus, training data are *not* required. $\mathbf{X}$ is regularized by the implicit prior of the network architecture. Different types of architectures can lead to different regularizers. The architecture that effectively incorporates multi-scale spatial details and semantic features of the guidance image can be a powerful regularizer for the optimization problem. In the following section, we propose a new architecture, called the guided deep decoder, as a regularizer that can be used for various image fusion problems.

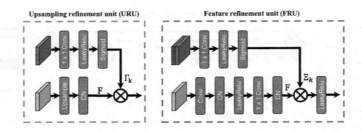

**Fig. 3.** The structure of upsampling and feature refinement units.

## 3.2  Guided Deep Decoder (GDD)

GDD is composed of an encoder-decoder network with skip connections and a deep decoder network, as shown in Fig. 2. The encoder-decoder network is similar to the architecture of U-net [25] and produces the features of a guidance image at multiple scales. The multi-scale features represent hierarchical semantic features of the guidance image from low to high levels. The semantic features are used to guide the parameter estimation in the deep decoder. Let $\mathbf{\Gamma}_k$ denote the features of the encoder at the $k$th scale, $\mathbf{\Xi}_k$ denotes the $k$th-scale features in the decoder part of the encoder-decoder network. The mapping function is conditioned on the multi-scale features as $f_\theta\left(\mathbf{Z}\mid\mathbf{\Gamma}_1,\cdots,\mathbf{\Gamma}_K,\mathbf{\Xi}_1,\cdots,\mathbf{\Xi}_K\right)$. The multi-scale features are incorporated in the deep decoder by the two proposed units shown in Fig. 3.

**Upsampling Refinement Unit (URU).** Upsampling is a vital part of DIP [4]. Bilinear or nearest neighbor upsampling promotes piecewise constant patches or smoothness across all channels [15]. However, the prior is too strong to recover exact spatial structures or boundaries of an image. Although this problem is alleviated using skip connections, the spatial details of a guidance image are still lost in the features of the decoder. URU incorporates an attention gate for weighting the features derived after upsampling and channel-wise normalization (CN) in the deep decoder. The features from the guidance image are gated by a $1 \times 1$ convolution (Conv), a leaky rectified linear unit (LeakyRelu), and a sigmoid activation layer (Sigmoid) to preserve the spatial locality of the features and generate the conditional weights. Given the features of the deep decoder $\mathbf{F}$, the transformation is carried out as:

$$\mathbf{URU}\left(\mathbf{F}\mid\mathbf{\Gamma}_k\right) = \mathbf{F} \otimes \mathbf{\Gamma}_k, \tag{4}$$

where $\otimes$ represents the element-wise multiplication. Note that the dimensions of $\mathbf{F}$ and $\mathbf{\Gamma}_k$ are the same at each scale. Both channel-wise and spatial-wise conditional weights are considered in URU.

**Feature Refinement Unit (FRU).** FRU is different from URU in that the features of the deep decoder are weighted by the high-level semantic features of the guidance image. FRU promotes the semantic alignment with the features of the guidance image, while URU promotes similar spatial locality. Using an attention gate, the high-level features are gated by a $1 \times 1$ convolution, a leaky rectified linear unit, and a sigmoid activation layer to generate the conditional weights. FRU transforms the features of the deep decoder as follows:

$$\mathbf{FRU}\left(\mathbf{F}|\Xi_k\right) = \mathbf{F} \otimes \Xi_k. \tag{5}$$

Note that the dimensions of $\mathbf{F}$ and $\Xi_k$ are the same at each scale. The features of the deep decoder are weighted in URU and FRU, which leads to a deep prior that can more explicitly exploit the spatial details or semantic features of the guidance image than DIP.

## 3.3 Loss Function

The loss function is different for each task. In this section, the loss functions used for HS super-resolution, pansharpening, and denoising are discussed.

**HS Super-Resolution.** When fusing RGB and HS images, the loss function is usually designed to preserve the spectral information from the HS image while keeping the spatial information from the RGB image. For simplicity, the matrix forms of $\mathbf{X}, \mathbf{Y}, \mathbf{G}$ are denoted as $\tilde{\mathbf{X}} \in \mathbb{R}^{C \times WH}$, $\tilde{\mathbf{Y}} \in \mathbb{R}^{C \times wh}$, and $\tilde{\mathbf{G}} \in \mathbb{R}^{c \times WH}$, respectively. Given the estimated HR-HS $\tilde{\mathbf{X}}$, the loss function can be defined as:

$$\mathcal{L}\left(\mathbf{X}, \mathbf{Y}, \mathbf{G}\right) = \mu \|\tilde{\mathbf{X}}\mathbf{S} - \tilde{\mathbf{Y}}\|_F^2 + \|\mathbf{R}\tilde{\mathbf{X}} - \tilde{\mathbf{G}}\|_F^2, \tag{6}$$

where $\|\cdot\|_F$ is the Frobenius norm, $\mathbf{S}$ is the spatial downsampling with blurring and $\mathbf{R}$ is the spectral response function that integrates the spectra into R, G, B channels. The first term encourages the spectral similarity between the spatially downsampled $\mathbf{X}$ and $\mathbf{Y}$. The second term encourages the spatial similarity between the spectrally downsampled $\mathbf{X}$ and $\mathbf{G}$. $\mu$ is a scalar controlling the balance between the two terms. The loss function has been widely used with the handcrafted priors in the HS super-resolution [18,40] because the optimization problem is highly ill-posed. Our approach differs from those used in previous studies because it uses GDD as a regularizer.

**Pansharpening.** Like HS super-resolution, pansharpening also considers two terms that balance the tradeoff between spatial and spectral information. Although the first term in (6) can be also used for the loss function of pansharpening, the second term may not be effective. This is because the spectral response function of the pansharpening image may partially cover the spectral range captured by the MS image. Thus, the second term cannot effectively measure the spatial similarity between panchromatic and MS images. To address the problem, the second term measuring the spatial similarity is defined as follows:

$$\mathcal{L}\left(\mathbf{X}, \mathbf{Y}, \mathbf{G}\right) = \mu \|\tilde{\mathbf{X}}\mathbf{S} - \tilde{\mathbf{Y}}\|_F^2 + |\mathbf{D}\nabla\tilde{\mathbf{X}} - \nabla\tilde{\mathbf{G}}|, \tag{7}$$

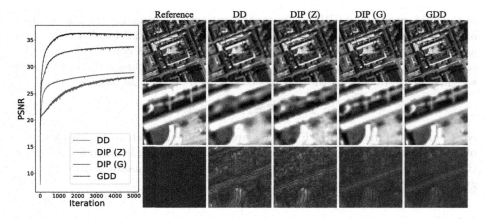

**Fig. 4.** Comparison of DD, DIP, and GDD. The left figure shows PSNR at different iterations. The right figure shows the images derived at the 5000 iterations. From top to bottom, RGB images, enlarged RGB images, and the error maps of the compared methods.

where $\tilde{\mathbf{Y}}$ is the MS image, $\tilde{\mathbf{G}}$ is the panchromatic image expanded to the same number of bands of $\tilde{\mathbf{X}}$, $\nabla\tilde{\mathbf{X}}$ is the image gradient of $\tilde{\mathbf{X}}$, $\nabla\tilde{\mathbf{G}}$ is the image gradient of $\tilde{\mathbf{G}}$, $|\cdot|$ is the $l_1$ norm, and $\mathbf{D}$ is the diagonal matrix to weight each channel of $\nabla\tilde{\mathbf{X}}$ so that the magnitude of $\tilde{\mathbf{X}}$ is scaled to that of $\nabla\tilde{\mathbf{G}}$. Note that $\mathbf{D}$ can be learned with other parameters within the GDD optimization framework. The $l_1$ norm is chosen because this norm more explicitly encourages the edges of the output and guidance images to be similar than other norms (e.g., $l_2$ norm). The first term encourages the spectral similarity while the second term promotes the spatial similarity. A similar loss function has been also explored in [5].

**Denoising.** For the denoising of the no-flash image, the following loss function was used:

$$\mathcal{L}\left(\mathbf{X}, \mathbf{Y}\right) = \|\tilde{\mathbf{X}} - \tilde{\mathbf{Y}}\|_F^2, \tag{8}$$

where $\tilde{\mathbf{Y}}$ is the no-flash image. Only $\tilde{\mathbf{X}}, \tilde{\mathbf{Y}}$ are considered in the loss function. $\tilde{\mathbf{G}}$ is considered only in the network architecture because in the detail transfer of the flash and no-flash images, the spatial structures or colors are not necessarily consistent [23]. To fairly compare the results derived by DIP [28], we adopt the same loss function.

Different handcrafted priors are usually considered with task-specific loss functions. As a result, an optimization framework can be also different for each task. Our approach is different from the previous studies in that GDD is used as a common prior for all of the tasks in a unified optimization framework.

# 4    Comparison Between DD, DIP, and GDD

In this section, we show the comparison between a deep decoder (DD), DIP, and GDD to discuss how GDD outperforms the compared methods. Extensive experiments, including other applications, are shown in the following section. Figure 4 shows peak signal-to-noise ratio (PSNR) at different iterations. DD uses a tensor representing random noise as an input. DD corresponds to the deep decoder part in GDD. DD is considered for comparison to validate whether the features guided by the encoder-decoder network are really useful. DIP (Z) represents the deep image prior that uses a random tensor as an input, while DIP (G) uses a guidance image (i.e., panchromatic imagery) as an input in the encoder-decoder network. Because DD considers only the decoder part, the information lost in the process of upsampling cannot be recovered. DIP(Z) can use the features derived by a skip connection as a bias term and try to compensate for the lost information. This led to slightly better results of DIP(Z). GDD and DIP (G) that incorporate the guidance image produced high PSNR at early iterations. This shows that the use of the guidance image leads to the high quality of the HR-MS image at fewer iterations. Although both GDD and DIP (G) use the guidance image, GDD considerably outperformed DIP in terms of PSNR. Figure 4 also shows the RGB images of the reconstructed images, the enlarged RGB, and the corresponding error maps. The enlarged RGB image derived from DD is blurred. The image derived by DIP (Z) is also blurred and the texture is not correctly recovered. In the highly ill-posed optimization problem, the deep prior that does not incorporate the guidance image cannot produce satisfactory results. DIP (G) performs better than DD or DIP (Z). However, the small objects or boundaries of the image are missing in the reconstructed image. GDD preserved the small objects or boundaries more explicitly than DIP (G), which led to smaller errors. In addition, GDD produced smaller errors in the homogeneous regions of the objects.

**Reasons Why GDD Is a Good Regularizer.** We argue that GDD works as a better regularizer than DIP (G) for the following two reasons:

1. **Upsampling refinement:** The bilinear upsampling used in DIP and GDD causes a strong bias to promote piecewise smoothness and tends to wash away the small objects or boundaries. GDD differs from DIP because it uses an attention gate to weight the features derived by the upsampling. The attention gate enables the small objects or boundaries to be aware by the conditional weights shown in Fig. 5. Owing to attention gates, GDD can reconstruct spatial details.
2. **Feature refinement at multiple scales:** DIP uses the guidance image as an input in the hourglass architecture. In DIP, the features of each layer in the decoder part of the architecture are conditioned using only the features of the previous layer. GDD enables the features of each layer in the decoder part to be conditioned on the semantic features from the guidance image at multiple scales. The attention gates at multiple scales emphasize salient features within each layer, leading to the semantic alignment between the output image and the guidance image.

**Fig. 5.** Examples of the conditional weights of different channels used in the attention gates.

## 5 Experiments

In this section, we show how GDD works as a regularizer for different image fusion problems. Because of the limited space, only the selected results are shown in the main document. Additional results are shown in the supplementary material. The network architecture of GDD has been fixed for all of the following experiments to validate the robustness of GDD as a regularizer. It is possible to carefully tune the network architecture for each task. However, we believe that the fixed network architecture that works well for different tasks is more important than a carefully tuned architecture that obtains the best performance only for a specific task. In the following experiments, DIP used the guidance image as an input and the same loss function with GDD for fair comparison.

### 5.1 Hyperspectral Super-Resolution

**Dataset.** The CAVE dataset[1] was chosen for the experiments because it has been extensively used to evaluate HS super-resolution methods [7, 11, 24, 36]. The CAVE dataset consists of HR-HS images that were acquired in 32 indoor scenes with controlled illumination. Each HR-HS image has the spatial size of $256 \times 256$ with 31 bands representing the reflectance of materials in the scene. We followed the experimental setup of [36], *i.e.*, the generation of the LR-HS image from the HR-HS image by averaging over $32 \times 32$ pixel blocks and the generation of the RGB image by spectral downsampling on the basis of the spectral response function. The proposed GDD does not require training data. However, for fair comparison with the supervised DL method, we chose 12 images for the test, and the rest of the images were used for training as done in [36].

**Compared Methods.** The compared SOTA methods include the matrix/ tensor related methods (CNMF [40], BSR [1], NSSR [9] and NLSTF [7]), the supervised DL method (MHF [36]), and the unsupervised DL methods (UDL [11], uSDN [24] and DIP [28]). Among all methods, only MHF required training data.

To quantitatively validate the results, four different criteria were used. The criteria are the root mean square error (RMSE), spectral angle (SA), structural similarity (SSIM [33]), and the relative dimensionless global error in synthesis (ERGAS [31]).

---

[1] http://www1.cs.columbia.edu/CAVE/databases/.

Reference  CNMF     BSR     NSSR    NLSTF    UDL     uSDN      MHF      DIP      GDD

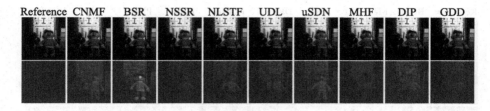

**Fig. 6.** First row: reference and RGB images of the reconstructed HS. The selected results are from *chart and staffed toy* in the CAVE data. Second row: The corresponding error maps.

**Results.** Table 1 shows the average results of all test images. The performance of BSR and uSDN was worse than those of other methods because the two methods do not assume that the downsampling matrix is available *a priori*. GDD outperformed other unsupervised HS super-resolution methods and was even competitive with the trained DL method (i.e., MHF). This shows that the proposed network architecture is an effective regularizer for the HS super-resolution problem. Figure 6 shows the RGB images of the reconstructed HS images and the error maps. In general, GDD produced lower errors than other methods. The noticeable difference between DIP and GDD is that the errors of DIP are significantly larger at the edges of the image than those of GDD. This implies that GDD properly incorporates the spatial details or semantic features of the guidance image, leading to the edge-preserving image.

**Table 1.** Quantitative results of different metrics on the CAVE dataset. ↓ shows lower is better while ↑ shows higher is better.

|        | CNMF   | BSR     | NLSTF  | NSSR   | UDL    | uSDN    | MHF    | DIP    | GDD        |
|--------|--------|---------|--------|--------|--------|---------|--------|--------|------------|
| RMSE↓  | 3.4557 | 5.2030  | 2.9414 | 2.4247 | 2.7971 | 4.9289  | 2.0827 | 3.1589 | **2.0213** |
| ERGAS↓ | 0.5347 | 0.7318  | 0.4144 | 0.3696 | 0.3650 | 0.7723  | 0.3062 | 0.4597 | **0.3041** |
| SA↓    | 7.0801 | 13.1719 | 8.9825 | 7.4138 | 6.9816 | 12.4995 | 6.0100 | 7.6734 | **5.5740** |
| SSIM↑  | 0.9760 | 0.9524  | 0.9805 | 0.9770 | 0.9733 | 0.9385  | **0.9874** | 0.9621 | 0.9869     |

## 5.2  Pansharpening

**Dataset.** Four different image scenes covering agriculture, urban, forest or mixtures of these were chosen for the experiments. The images were acquired by the WorldView-2. Each MS image is composed of 8 bands representing spectral reflectance. The spatial resolution of the MS image is 2 m while that of the panchromatic image is 0.5 m. Each panchromatic image has one band that partially covers the spectral range of the MS image. Synthetic MS and panchromatic images were generated by spatially downsampling the original resolution MS and panchromatic images by the factor of 4. Bicubic downsampling was used. The

Reference  BDSD  MTF-GLP  SIRF  DRPNN  PanNet  PNN  PNN+  DIP  GDD

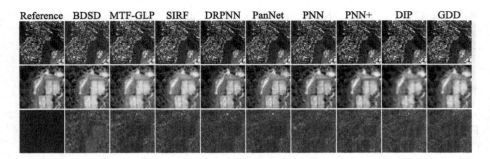

**Fig. 7.** First row: RGB images of the pansharpened MS images. Second row: The enlarged RGB images. Third row: The corresponding error maps.

original resolution MS image was used as reference data. This is the common approach called Wald's protocol [30] to generate reference data because reference data (i.e., HR-MS image) are not available [10,37].

**Compared Methods.** The compared SOTA methods include three unsupervised pansharpening methods (BDSD [13], MTF-GLP [29], SIRF [5]) and four supervised DL methods (DRPNN [35], PanNet [37], PNN [21], PNN+ [26]). The supervised DL methods achieved the SOTA performance. However, the generalization performance of the supervised DL methods is still limited if training data are acquired by a different sensor or in different regions. Training data must be carefully prepared for the supervised DL methods. In this study, we divided each image scene into training and test data acquired by the same sensor. This produces a favorable condition for the supervised DL methods and can be used to validate whether the unsupervised GDD can be comparable to the supervised DL methods.

To qualitatively validate the performance of the methods, the synthetic data (i.e., reduced spatial resolution images) and real data (i.e., original spatial resolution images) were used. Four different criteria were used for evaluation. Similar to the experiments of the HS super-resolution, ERDAS and SA were also considered in pansharpening. In addition, the eight-band extension of average universal image quality index (Q8 [3,32]), and spatial correlation coefficient (SCC [41]) were used for evaluation. In pansharpening, there are also criteria to validate the performance of the methods on the original spatial resolution images without using reference data. The criteria include a spectral quality index ($\mathbf{D}_\lambda$) and a spatial quality index ($\mathbf{D}_S$), and the joint spectral and spatial quality with no reference (QNR [2]). The criteria were used to validate the methods using real data (i.e., original spatial resolution of images).

**Results.** Table 2 shows the average results of all test images. When using the synthetic data with reference data, GDD outperformed other existing methods in terms of all criteria. This showed that GDD reconstructed an HR-MS image that has better quality of both spectral and spatial information. Figure 7 shows RGB of the reconstructed MS images, the enlarged RGB images, and the corresponding error maps. Although PanNet, PNN, or DRPNN generated sharp edges in the reconstructed images, the spectral information was distorted, which led to the colors that are different from the reference. DIP produced blurred results especially at the edges of the reconstructed images. GDD preserved the spectral information while producing similar spatial details with reference data. This led to lower errors in the reconstructed image. Real images (original resolution images) were also used to evaluate the reconstructed images, as shown in Table 2. DIP produced the lowest value in terms of $D_\lambda$. This shows that the spectra reconstructed by DIP are most similar to the spectra of the LR-MS image. PNN+ produced the lowest value in terms of $D_s$. This shows that the spatial details reconstructed by PNN+ are the most similar to the spatial details of the pansharpening image. GDD performed better than the other methods in terms of QNR. GDD properly balanced the tradeoff between spectral and spatial resolution, which led to the better value of QNR.

**Table 2.** Average results of different image scenes for pansharpening. Synthetic represents evaluation with reference at lower resolution. Real represents evaluation with no reference at original resolution. ↓ shows lower is better while ↑ shows higher is better.

| | | BDSD | MTF-GLP | SIRF | DRPNN | PanNet | PNN | PNN+ | DIP | GDD |
|---|---|---|---|---|---|---|---|---|---|---|
| Synthetic | Q8↑ | 0.8879 | 0.9074 | 0.8935 | 0.9144 | 0.9164 | 0.9073 | 0.9231 | 0.9171 | **0.9469** |
| | SA↓ | 5.9425 | 5.4838 | 5.9248 | 5.3690 | 5.4475 | 6.5587 | 5.7963 | 4.6514 | **4.0254** |
| | ERGAS↓ | 4.6554 | 4.1339 | 3.9836 | 3.6549 | 3.9762 | 4.1547 | 3.7432 | 3.5274 | **2.6879** |
| | SCC↑ | 0.9071 | 0.9021 | 0.8970 | 0.9316 | 0.8868 | 0.9131 | 0.9048 | 0.8965 | **0.9418** |
| Real | QNR↑ | 0.9077 | 0.9157 | 0.9071 | 0.8648 | 0.8833 | 0.9253 | 0.9492 | 0.9446 | **0.9517** |
| | $D_\lambda$↓ | 0.0423 | 0.0391 | 0.0538 | 0.0320 | 0.0574 | 0.0316 | 0.0250 | **0.0188** | 0.0202 |
| | $D_s$↓ | 0.0531 | 0.0469 | 0.0414 | 0.1066 | 0.0629 | 0.0447 | **0.0264** | 0.0374 | 0.0288 |

## 5.3 Denoising

In this section, the reconstruction of a flash image with the help of a no-flash image was addressed to show another application of GDD. The no-flash image acquires an image under ambient illumination where the image can be noisy because of the low-light conditions [23]. However, the flash image acquires an image under artificial light where the image is noise-free and the spatial details of the image are recorded. However, the lighting characteristics are unnatural, and unwanted shadows or artifacts may be produced in the flash image. The objective of this application is to reconstruct a clean no-flash image using the features of a flash image. In this application, true reference data cannot be available. Although an image with long exposure may be used as a reference [23], the magnitude or characteristics of illumination are not necessarily the same as those of the true reference. In this study, the reconstructed images are qualitatively

| Flash | No-Flash | JB | DIP | GDD |
|-------|----------|----|----|-----|

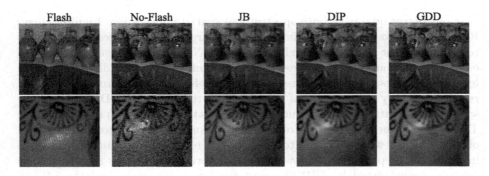

**Fig. 8.** The reconstructed images of the no-flash image with the help of the flash image.

evaluated according to [28]. In [28], DIP that uses the flash image as an input and the no-flash image as an output was successfully applied to the problem. We qualitatively examined if the architecture used in GDD was as effective as DIP.

Figure 8 shows that the reconstructed images of the no-flash image. DIP and GDD removed the artifacts more clearly than the joint bilateral method (JB) [23]. GDD produced more explicit boundaries of the image than DIP while preserving the natural colors of the image. This shows that GDD performed at least as well as DIP for the no-flash image reconstruction.

## 6   Conclusion

We proposed an unsupervised image fusion method that was based on GDD. GDD is a network architecture-based regularizer and can be used to solve different image fusion problems that have been independently studied so far. The network architecture can better exploit spatial details and semantic features of a guidance image. This is achieved by considering an encoder-decoder network that extracts spatial details and semantic features of a guidance image. The multi-scale attention gates enable the extracted semantic features to guide a deep decoder network that generates an output image. This approach achieved the SOTA performance in the different image fusion problems. It pushes the boundaries of the current studies that address only one specific problem. The promising results open up the possibility of a network architecture-based prior that can be used for general purpose including various image fusion problems.

## References

1. Akhtar, N., Shafait, F., Mian, A.: Bayesian sparse representation for hyperspectral image super resolution. In: CVPR, pp. 3631–3640 (2015)
2. Alparone, L., Aiazzi, B., Baronti, S., Garzelli, A., Nencini, F., Selva, M.: Multi-spectral and panchromatic data fusion assessment without reference. Photogramm. Eng. Remote Sens. **74**(2), 193–200 (2008)

3.  Alparone, L., Baronti, S., Garzelli, A., Nencini, F.: A global quality measurement of pan-sharpened multispectral imagery. IEEE Geosci. Remote Sens. Lett. 1(4), 313–317 (2004)
4.  Chakrabarty, P., Maji, S.: The spectral bias of the deep image prior. In: NeurIPS Workshops (2019)
5.  Chen, C., Li, Y., Liu, W., Huang, Z.: SIRF: simultaneous satellite image registration and fusion in a unified framework. IEEE Trans. Image Process. 24(11), 4213–4224 (2015)
6.  Chen, C., Li, Y., Liu, W., Huang, J.: Image fusion with local spectral consistency and dynamic gradient sparsity. In: CVPR (2014)
7.  Dian, R., Fang, L., Li, S.: Hyperspectral image super-resolution via non-local sparse tensor factorization. In: CVPR, pp. 3862–3871 (2017)
8.  Dian, R., Li, S., Guo, A., Fang, L.: Deep hyperspectral image sharpening. IEEE Trans. Neural Netw. Learn. Syst. 29(11), 5345–5355 (2018)
9.  Dong, W., et al.: Hyperspectral image super-resolution via non-negative structured sparse representation. IEEE Transactions on Image Processing 25(5) (2016)
10. Fu, X., Lin, Z., Huang, Y., Ding, X.: A variational pan-sharpening with local gradient constraints. In: CVPR (2019)
11. Fu, Y., Zhang, T., Zheng, Y., Zhang, D., Huang, H.: Hyperspectral image super-resolution with optimized rgb guidance. In: Proceedings of the IEEE Conference on Computer Vision and Pattern Recognition. pp. 11661–11670 (2019)
12. Gandelsman, Y., Shocher, A., Irani, M.: "Double-Dip": unsupervised image decomposition via coupled deep-image-priors. In: CVPR (2019)
13. Garzelli, A., Nencini, F., Capobianco, L.: Optimal MMSE pan sharpening of very high resolution multispectral images. IEEE Trans. Geosci. Remote Sens. 46(1), 228–236 (2007)
14. He, K., Zhang, X., Ren, S., Sun, J.: Deep residual learning for image recognition. In: CVPR, pp. 770–778 (2016)
15. Heckel, R., Hand, P.: Deep decoder: Concise image representations from untrained non-convolutional networks. In: ICLR (2019)
16. Kawakami, R., Matsushita, Y., Wright, J., Ben-Ezra, M., Tai, Y., Ikeuchi, K.: High-resolution hyperspectral imaging via matrix factorization. In: CVPR, pp. 2329–2336 (2011)
17. Kwon, H., Tai, Y.W.: RGB-guided hyperspectral image upsampling. In: Proceedings of the IEEE International Conference on Computer Vision, pp. 307–315 (2015)
18. Lanaras, C., Baltsavias, E., Schindler, K.: Hyperspectral super-resolution by coupled spectral unmixing. In: ICCV (2015)
19. Liu, P., Xiao, L., Li, T.: A variational pan-sharpening method based on spatial fractional-order geometry and spectral–spatial low-rank priors. IEEE Trans. Geosci. Remote Sens. 56, 1788–1802 (2018)
20. Lutio, R.d., D'Aronco, S., Wegner, J.D., Schindler, K.: Guided super-resolution as pixel-to-pixel transformation. In: ICCV (2019)
21. Masi, G., Cozzolino, D., Verdoliva, L., Scarpa, G.: Pansharpening by convolutional neural networks. Remote Sensing 8(7), 594 (2016)
22. Palsson, F., Sveinsson, J.R., Ulfarsson, M.O.: A new pansharpening algorithm based on total variation. IEEE Geosci. Remote Sens. Lett. 11, 318–322 (2014)
23. Petschnigg, G., Szeliski, R., Agrawala, M., Cohen, M., Hoppe, H., Toyama, K.: Digital photography with flash and no-flash image pairs. ACM Trans. Graph. 23(3), 664 (2004)
24. Qu, Y., Qi, H., Kwan, C.: Unsupervised sparse Dirichlet-net for hyperspectral image super-resolution. In: CVPR (2018)

25. Ronneberger, O., Fischer, P., Brox, T.: U-Net: convolutional networks for biomedical image segmentation. In: Navab, N., Hornegger, J., Wells, W.M., Frangi, A.F. (eds.) MICCAI 2015. LNCS, vol. 9351, pp. 234–241. Springer, Cham (2015). https://doi.org/10.1007/978-3-319-24574-4_28
26. Scarpa, G., Vitale, S., Cozzolino, D.: Target-adaptive CNN-based pansharpening. IEEE Trans. Geosci. Remote Sens. **56**(9), 5443–5457 (2018)
27. Sidorov, O., Hardeberg, J.Y.: Deep hyperspectral prior: denoising, inpainting, super-resolution. In: ICIP (2019)
28. Ulyanov, D., Vedaldi, A., Lempitsky, V.: Deep image prior. In: CVPR (2018)
29. Vivone, G., et al.: A critical comparison among pansharpening algorithms. IEEE Trans. Geosci. Remote Sens. **53**(5), 2565–2586 (2014)
30. Wald, L., Ranchin, T., Mangolini, M.: Fusion of satellite images of different spatial resoltuions: assessing the quality of resulting images. Photogrammetric engineering and remote sensing **63**(6), 691–699 (1997)
31. Wald, L.: Quality of high resolution synthesised images: is there a simple criterion? In: Third Conference Fusion of Earth Data: Merging Point Measurements, Raster Maps and Remotely Sensed Images, pp. 99–103. SEE/URISCA (2000)
32. Wang, Z., Bovik, A.C.: A universal image quality index. IEEE Signal Process. Lett. **9**(3), 81–84 (2002)
33. Wang, Z., Bovik, A.C., Sheikh, H.R., Simoncelli, E.P., et al.: Image quality assessment: from error visibility to structural similarity. IEEE Trans. Image Process. **13**(4), 600–612 (2004)
34. Wei, Q., Dobigeon, N., Tourneret, J., Bioucas-Dias, J., Godsill, S.: R-FUSE: robust fast fusion of multiband images based on solving a Sylvester equation. IEEE Signal Process. Lett. **23**(11), 1632–1636 (2016)
35. Wei, Y., Yuan, Q., Shen, H., Zhang, L.: Boosting the accuracy of multispectral image pansharpening by learning a deep residual network. IEEE Geosci. Remote Sens. Lett. **14**(10), 1795–1799 (2017)
36. Xie, Q., Zhou, M., Zhao, Q., Meng, D., Zuo, W., Xu, Z.: Multispectral and hyperspectral image fusion by MS/HS fusion net. In: CVPR (2019)
37. Yang, J., Fu, X., Hu, Y., Huang, Y., Ding, X., Paisley, J.: PanNet: a deep network architecture for pan-sharpening. In: ICCV. pp. 1753–1761 (2017)
38. Yokota, T., Kawai, K., Sakata, M., Kimura, Y., Hontani, H.: Dynamic pet image reconstruction using nonnegative matrix factorization incorporated with deep image prior. In: ICCV (2019)
39. Yokoya, N., Grohnfeldt, C., Chanussot, J.: Hyperspectral and multispectral data fusion: a comparative review of the recent literature. IEEE Geosci. Remote Sens. Mag. **5**(2), 29–56 (2017)
40. Yokoya, N., Yairi, T., Iwasaki, A.: Coupled nonnegative matrix factorization unmixing for hyperspectral and multispectral data fusion. IEEE Trans. Geosci. Remote Sens. **50**(2), 528–537 (2012)
41. Zhou, J., Civco, D., Silander, J.: A wavelet transform method to merge landsat TM and SPOT panchromatic data. Int. J. Remote Sens. **19**(4), 743–757 (1998)

# Filter Style Transfer Between Photos

Jonghwa Yim[1], Jisung Yoo[1(✉)], Won-joon Do[1], Beomsu Kim[2],
and Jihwan Choe[3]

[1] Visual Solution Lab., Samsung Electronics, Suwon, South Korea
{jonghwa.yim,jisung.yoo,wonjoon.do}@samsung.com
[2] Visual Solution Lab., Samsung Electronics, Seoul, South Korea
bs8207.kim@samsung.com
[3] Visual Solution Lab., Samsung Electronics, Bucheon, South Korea
jihwan.choe@samsung.com

**Abstract.** Over the past few years, image-to-image style transfer has risen to the frontiers of neural image processing. While conventional methods were successful in various tasks such as color and texture transfer between images, none could effectively work with the custom filter effects that are applied by users through various platforms like Instagram. In this paper, we introduce a new concept of style transfer, Filter Style Transfer (FST). Unlike conventional style transfer, new technique FST can extract and transfer custom filter style from a filtered style image to a content image. FST first infers the original image from a filtered reference via image-to-image translation. Then it estimates filter parameters from the difference between them. To resolve the ill-posed nature of reconstructing the original image from the reference, we represent each pixel color of an image to class mean and deviation. Besides, to handle the intra-class color variation, we propose an uncertainty based weighted least square method for restoring an original image. To the best of our knowledge, FST is the first style transfer method that can transfer custom filter effects between FHD image under 2 ms on a mobile device without any textual context loss.

**Keywords:** Photorealistic style transfer · Filter style transfer · Image-to-image translation

## 1  Introduction

Stylizing an image with characteristics of other stylized images has long been a difficult problem in Computer Vision. Beyond simple editings, people's desire to grand artistic feelings to their pictures has increased. For this reason, a tool that can stylize their photos in a unique way is highly desired.

**Electronic supplementary material** The online version of this chapter (https://doi.org/10.1007/978-3-030-58539-6_7) contains supplementary material, which is available to authorized users.

A. Vedaldi et al. (Eds.): ECCV 2020, LNCS 12351, pp. 103–119, 2020.
https://doi.org/10.1007/978-3-030-58539-6_7

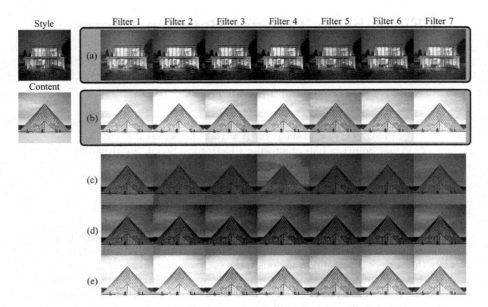

**Fig. 1. Filter style transfer results.** Given reference images with arbitrary filters applied (a), the filter styles can be transferred to a new image with our model. While (b) is the ground-truth, (c)–(e) show the results of color transfer [24], photorealistic style transfer: WCT2 [32], and ours, respectively.

There have been several studies addressing technical solutions for image-to-image style or content transfer. Reinhard et al. [24] is one of the pioneering attempts where mean and variance of RGB color distribution from a source image were used to apply the color scheme to a target image, but with limited success obtaining enough similarity between two images. Others [23, 26–28] tried to improve results by using various mathematical approaches to treat color distribution but failed to consider the semantics of pictures during the process. Moreover, their methods transferred objects' inherent colors as well, limiting their methods in the assumption that scene components of the two images must be similar.

More recently, taking advantage of the advent of Deep Neural Network, more sophisticated applications of image-to-image style transfer became possible. Style transfer [7] encoded not only color but also shapes and textures. After that, many following works branched out to further improve the accuracy and efficiency of the style transfer. Some researches [12, 20, 35] were related to domain transfer, which transfers styles between different image domains such as semantic-labels to street-scene, aerial to map, and sketch to photo. However, since most domain transfer approaches aimed to move input images' distributions close to the target domain, the output of them does not explicitly reflect the style of a single image. Some other researches [18, 21, 25, 32] introduced methods to transfer photorealistic styles from a single style image, but they required a large dataset for training leading to a high computational cost. Even with the high processing time, they often displayed undesirable transfers of colors and textures due to fundamentally implicit actions of deep neural networks. In this case, it is difficult to identify causes and solutions, which is a significant hurdle when commercializing the approaches.

Meanwhile, some researches suggested automated photograph editing to enhance the overall quality [1–5, 8, 11, 14, 15, 22, 29, 30] or control exposure [10, 31, 33, 34]. All of these researches showed considerable progress on automated image editing, but they also required large datasets to train an image enhancement model. More importantly, they only followed a predefined editing rule like High Dynamic Range (HDR). Some focused on the extraction of photo-editing-parameters directly [1, 2, 8, 22], while [5] focused on learning image enhancement using GAN [9] to generate HDR output. A method in [2] suggested parameter extraction from a neural network, but it was not a single-stage and showed limited performance. Also, efforts to model polynomial functions in the previous studies [1, 2] may suffer from high-order variables' fitting issues as well as they still limited their methods to predefined editing rules. There have been a few efforts to adopt reinforcement learning [10, 33] to train enhancement policies. Despite all the efforts, all the aforementioned methods were not able to extract filter parameters from an already stylized image and require the original version of the stylized image to enhance the target image. Such limitations prevented previous studies from fully satisfying commercial needs.

With the increased accessibility of mobile phones and the internet, these days, people spend even more time on social media. As a result, many photo-editing applications have been developed and are widely used with various stylizing filters to give special effects on photos taken. To the best of our knowledge, however, there has not been an attempt to extract custom filter effects from a stylized photo. In this study, a mathematical formulation of custom filter extraction and its application to new photos are presented (Fig. 1). FST is quite efficient without requiring expensive computing time, even in a low-end mobile device; so the application can be easily adopted and used in our fast-moving social networking environment.

## 2  Method Overview

Figure 2 shows an overview of the proposed method in this research. It comprises extracting custom photo filters from a single reference image ($I$) and applying them to a new one ($X$). Our method restores the original image ($\hat{I}$) from $I$, which is called *defilterization* in this paper. Then, using two images, a filter parameter $w$ is obtained, which is called *filter style estimation*. Lastly, using $w$, a designed filter function $f_w$ can be used to filter the user's original image ($X$) to newly-stylized image ($Y$).

## 3  Defilterization

In Fig. 2, the stylized reference input $I$ is a projected image from the original image $\acute{I}$ using the filter-applying function $f_w$, leading to

$$I = f_w(\acute{I}). \tag{1}$$

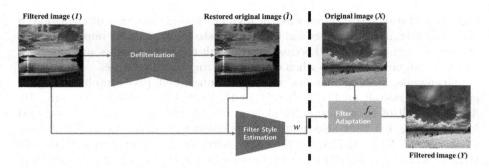

**Fig. 2. System overview to extract the photo editing parameter and apply it to the new input images.** $I$ is a filtered or edited image that we want to extract filter style and $w$ represents the parameters of the filter style of $I$. The system is initially black-box and must be designed appropriately to infer standalone parameters.

To determine $f_w$, the relationship between the pair of the original image $Í$ and stylized image $I$ needs to be investigated. From (1), we know that

$$Í = f_w^{-1}(I) \tag{2}$$

Assume that there is a collection $S$ of $M$ stylized images, $S = \{I_1, I_2, \ldots, I_M\}$. Each image $I$ consists of $K$ object segments, like the sky, cow, grass, etc., and each object segment can be represented its vectorized form $\boldsymbol{o}$, such that

$$I = \{\boldsymbol{o}_1, \boldsymbol{o}_2, \boldsymbol{o}_3, \ldots, \boldsymbol{o}_K\} \tag{3}$$

where $\boldsymbol{o}_k$ is a vector of colors of the flattened pixels in the $k$-th object segment. Then the original image of $I$ can also be represented as a set of the original object segments, such that

$$Í = \{\acute{\boldsymbol{o}}_1, \acute{\boldsymbol{o}}_2, \acute{\boldsymbol{o}}_3, \ldots, \acute{\boldsymbol{o}}_K\} \tag{4}$$

where $\acute{\boldsymbol{o}}_k$ is the original colors before stylized. If an implicit object, $\acute{\boldsymbol{o}}_k$, has some class label, $cls$, and its mean color can be obtained by averaging all pixel colors in $cls$ throughout the dataset $S$, then, $\acute{\boldsymbol{o}}_k$ can be expressed with the mean color value of the class, $\tilde{\boldsymbol{o}}_{k,cls}$, and pixel-wise color deviations, $\Delta_{k,cls}$. Note that we start to explain from the implicit object level to introduce the class label and its mean color. Also, there is a numerical error term $\epsilon_k$ due to imperfect restoration of original object colors. Therefore $\acute{\boldsymbol{o}}_k$ can be expressed as

$$\acute{\boldsymbol{o}}_k = \tilde{\boldsymbol{o}}_{k,cls} + \Delta_{k,cls} = f_w^{-1}(\boldsymbol{o}_k) + \epsilon_k. \tag{5}$$

The distance between the restored image, $f_w^{-1}(I)$, and the true original, $Í$, can be described as the sum of the squared distance between restored and true objects.

$$Distance(f_w^{-1}(I), Í) = \sum_{k=1}^{K} \|f_w^{-1}(\boldsymbol{o}_k) - \acute{\boldsymbol{o}}_k\|^2 \tag{6}$$

Then our problem to find the original image becomes a minimization problem. At a pixel level, the objective function of the minimization process becomes

$$\underset{f_w^{-1}}{\arg\min} \frac{1}{N} \sum_{k=1}^{K} \left[ \sum_{c \in o_k} \left( f_w^{-1}(c) - \acute{c} \right)^2 \right], \tag{7}$$

where $N$ is the number of pixels in $I$. The sum of the differences of $o_k$ can be reformulated by merging two summations in (7). Then, the distance is a sum of the squared difference between $f_w^{-1}(c)$ and $\acute{c}$. Converting (5) into pixel-level representation and substituting $\acute{c}$ into its mean and deviations lead to

$$\underset{f_w^{-1}}{\arg\min} \frac{1}{N} \sum_{c \in I} \left( f_w^{-1}(c) - \tilde{c}_{cls} - \Delta_{c,cls} \right)^2 \tag{8}$$

where $\tilde{c}_{cls}$ is an element of $\tilde{o}_{k,cls}$. Since the objective function (7) and (8) corresponds to the error criterion of the neural network, especially autoencoder, where the pixel differences can be calculated after forward-passing the input image, we now let $f_w^{-1}$ be an autoencoder network and train to infer $\acute{c}$ over the dataset $S$. Then we can expect that the trained autoencoder can restore the original image considering implicit semantic, $cls$. Thus, the objective function over the entire dataset $S$ of $M$ equal-sized images is

$$\underset{f_w^{-1}}{\arg\min} \sum_{m=1}^{M} \left[ \sum_{c \in I_m} \left( f_w^{-1}(c) - \tilde{c}_{cls} - \Delta_{c,cls} \right)^2 \right]. \tag{9}$$

By definition, $\sum_{c \in S_{cls}} \Delta_{c,cls} = 0$ where $S_{cls}$ is a subset of $S$ that belongs to a class label $cls$. With this definition, after some calculation, Eq. (9) becomes

$$\underset{f_w^{-1}}{\arg\min} \sum_{m=1}^{M} \left[ \sum_{c \in I_m} \left( \left( f_w^{-1}(c) - \tilde{c}_{cls} \right)^2 + 2\epsilon_c \Delta_{c,cls} - \Delta_{c,cls}^2 \right) \right]. \tag{10}$$

Since $\Delta^2$ is a constant for a given dataset $S$, the minimization becomes

$$\underset{f_w^{-1}}{\arg\min} \sum_{m=1}^{M} \left[ \sum_{c \in I_m} \left( \left( f_w^{-1}(c) - \tilde{c}_{cls} \right)^2 + 2\epsilon_c \Delta_{c,cls} \right) \right]. \tag{11}$$

Then $f_w^{-1}$ learns to restore image toward the mean, between the mean and original. Therefore, one can geometrically assume that $\epsilon_c$ at the optimum point is smaller than and proportional to $\Delta_{c,cls}$. Since deducing $\Delta_{cls}$ solely from a single image is an ill-posed problem, our method minimizes the influence of the inevitable error $\epsilon_c$ by collecting pixels during regression in Sect. 4.1.

## 4    Filter Style Estimation

### 4.1    Filter Parameterization

Most of the image filtering and editing can be built with three operations - brightness, contrast, and color controls. Even though there are some local operations such as Vignetting, for simplicity, we have not considered those in this study. In general the three primary operations can be expressed as linear or polynomial functions for input image $x$ and output image $y$;

$$\text{Brightness} \qquad y_1 = x + c \qquad\qquad (12)$$

$$\text{Contrast} \qquad y_2 = ax + b \qquad\qquad (13)$$

$$\text{Color} \qquad y_3 = \sum_{i=1}^{\alpha} \left( e_i x_i^3 + f_i x_i^2 + g_i x_i \right) \qquad\qquad (14)$$

where $\alpha$ is the number of color channels, three (i.e. RGB) in our case. After adding up $y_1$, $y_2$, and $y_3$ and expressing parameters as $\beta$, the three operations becomes

$$y_\gamma = \beta_{\gamma,0} + \sum_{i=1}^{3} \left( \beta_{\gamma,i1} x_i + \beta_{\gamma,i2} x_i^2 + \beta_{\gamma,i3} x_i^3 \right). \qquad (15)$$

Note that we repeatedly calculate $y_\gamma$ over the output color channel, i.e. $\gamma \in \{R, G, B\}$. Hereafter, we omit $\gamma$ for brevity. Since (15) represents global editing operations, using this, we model the parametric function $f_\beta^*$ of $f_w$ in the regarding $\beta$. Thus, with the original and the reference image, we can approach filter parameter extraction, obtaining $\beta$ in (15), as a nonlinear regression problem operated at every pixel of an image. Hence the minimization target $E(\beta)$ is

$$E(\beta) = \sum_{n=1}^{N} \left( y_n - f_\beta^*(\acute{x}_n) \right)^2 \qquad\qquad (16)$$

where $(\acute{x}, y)$ is a color pair in $(\acute{I}, I)$. After applying (5), (16) becomes (17). In a normalized color domain, recalling the geometrical interpretation of (11), $\epsilon$ becomes small, and thus the high order of $\epsilon$ becomes negligibly small. After some calculation and with the assumption that $\epsilon$ is proportional to $\Delta$, (17) becomes

$$E(\beta) = \sum_{n=1}^{N} \left( y_n - f_\beta^*(f_w^{-1}(y_n) + \epsilon_n) \right)^2 \qquad\qquad (17)$$

$$\approx \sum_{n=1}^{N} \left( y_n - f_\beta^*(f_w^{-1}(y_n)) \right)^2. \qquad\qquad (18)$$

Since high order terms of $\epsilon_n$ are ignored, (18) is a rough approximation on a single image. Due to the ill-posed nature of the problem, instead, we propose uncertainty-based regression in Sect. 4.2 to alleviate the error of rough approximation. To this end, we set the problem to weighted least squares and solved it using quasi-Newton optimization. Note that Eq. (18) works well when $\sum_{c \in I} \Delta_{c,cls}$ is close to 0.

Additionally, our method can also provide results similar to color transfer, depending on filter parameters. If there are insufficient samples in the RGB color domain in a stylized image, it would not be easy to infer the coefficients to cover the absence of samples. In this case, if the Channel Correlation term (CC) is added, those colors can be transferred to other colors correlated with RG, RB, GB values as below.

$$y_\gamma = \beta_{\gamma,0} + \sum_{i=1}^{3} \left( \beta_{\gamma,i1} x_i + \beta_{\gamma,i2} x_i^2 + \beta_{\gamma,i3} x_i^3 \right) + \beta_{\gamma,1} x_1 x_2 + \beta_{\gamma,2} x_1 x_3 + \beta_{\gamma,3} x_2 x_3$$

(19)

Then the result becomes more like color transfer than FST. For example, in Fig. 3, green color is absent in stylized image. Therefore, green is transferred to another color in the result. More details will be presented in Sect. 5.4.

**Fig. 3. The result comparison with and without correlation term.** (a) is an input image. (b) is a stylized reference image. (c) and (d) are FST results using (15) and (19), respectively.

## 4.2 Uncertainty-Based Adaptive Filter Regression

After training $f_w^{-1}$, for any single filtered style image, we depend on a trained neural network to get the restored image and to regress the approximate function $f_\beta^*$. In the process, there are high order terms of $\epsilon$ that causes the filter estimation error in the previous section. Due to the lack of evidence to directly minimize the error, we propose a roundabout method using the uncertainty of the inference and lower the weight where $\epsilon$ is expected high.

The error term is inherently non-negligible in our case since the function inferred $\Delta_{c,cls}$ solely from a single image. To be more specific, in the single inference of $I$, from each pixel $c$, the uncertainty of $f_w^{-1}(c)$ would be high when the implicit class variance $Var(\Delta_{c,cls})$ is high over the entire set $S$ (aleatoric uncertainty). That means if the variance of the deviation of $cls$ is high over $S$, the function $f_w^{-1}(c)$ is likely to give larger $\epsilon$. Moreover, $f_w^{-1}(c)$ would be more uncertain as $\Delta_{c,cls}$ is increased (epistemic uncertainty). In this case, the weight of unsure pixels should be lower when regressing the approximate function, $f_\beta^*$.

The error term is independent over pixels. Therefore, we compute variance term same as combined uncertainty, a combination of epistemic uncertainty from Mean Standard Deviation (Mean STD) in the earlier study [6] and aleatoric uncertainty in [16] in recovering the original image. Then for every pixel, the inverse of uncertainty, written as $\boldsymbol{\Omega}^{-1}$, is used as a weight of the least squares criterion. Then the general form of the solution to our regression problem is

$$\boldsymbol{\beta} = (\boldsymbol{X}^T \boldsymbol{\Omega}^{-1} \boldsymbol{X})^{-1} \boldsymbol{X}^T \boldsymbol{\Omega}^{-1} \boldsymbol{y} \tag{20}$$

In practice, our uncertainty-based regression can be achieved by multiplying $\boldsymbol{\Omega}^{-1/2}$ to both of the $\boldsymbol{X}$ and $\boldsymbol{y}$ followed by quasi-Newton optimization. Note that $\boldsymbol{X}$ and $\boldsymbol{y}$ are the design matrix that consists of stacked polynomial vectors of the restored original colors and the vector of the filtered colors, respectively.

## 4.3   Regularization

With the methods described in previous sections, we are now able to estimate the parameters of filter style from single image input. However, there are two problems with this unrefined algorithm. Firstly, when we do not have enough plots around each extremum of color space, the regression function is left to vary dramatically outside of plots. Like the blue line shown in Fig. 4, a polynomial function curves very fast without the basis of plots, leading the extrema transformed to unfavorable values. So, for the new user input image $X$, stylized image $Y$ often show clipping or extreme colors around the extremes. The second problem is that the output can sometimes be visually unnatural as the regression function severely deviates from linear, leaving the regression process vulnerable to specific colors, which are exceptionally scarce but saturated in the pairs of the stylized and inferred original.

To relieve the above symptoms, we design and add regularization term in the regression function. To deal with the first phenomenon, we regularize the function to be close to $(0, 0)$, $(1, 1)$, respectively, when the color range is normalized. Hence, an L2 penalty is added and penalizes the function when it starts to diverge from 1 and 0. For each output channel $\gamma$,

$$R_{1,\gamma} = \beta_{\gamma,0}^2 + \left\{ \left[ \beta_{\gamma,0} + \sum_{i=1}^{3} (\beta_{\gamma,i1} + \beta_{\gamma,i2} + \beta_{\gamma,i3}) \right] - 1 \right\}^2 \tag{21}$$

After adding (21), the nonlinear function looks like a red line instead of a blue line in Fig. 4.

For the second symptom, we add an L2 penalty on the coefficients of high order terms. Empirically we found out that imposing the L2 penalty only on different sources of colors is visually good, rather than imposing L2 on all color sources.

$$R_{2,\gamma} = \sum_{i \neq \gamma} \left( \beta_{\gamma,i2}^2 + \beta_{\gamma,i3}^2 \right) \tag{22}$$

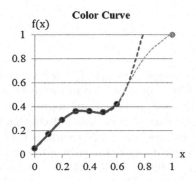

Fig. 4. **An example of a nonlinear function that has unfavorable extrema matching in a color transfer curve.** Since there is no color sample near $x = 1$, the function can diverge as shown by the blue dotted line. Instead, we can add a regularization term to guide nonlinear function into a red line. (Color figure online)

After adding two regularization terms (21) and (22), the error of regression function becomes

$$\acute{E}(\boldsymbol{\beta}_\gamma) = E(\boldsymbol{\beta}_\gamma) + \lambda R(\boldsymbol{\beta}_\gamma), \text{ where} \tag{23}$$

$$R(\boldsymbol{\beta}_\gamma) = \beta_{\gamma,0}^2 + \left\{ \left[ \beta_{\gamma,0} + \sum_{i=1}^{3} (\beta_{\gamma,i1} + \beta_{\gamma,i2} + \beta_{\gamma,i3}) \right] - 1 \right\}^2 + \sum_{i \neq \gamma} \left( \beta_{\gamma,i2}^2 + \beta_{\gamma,i3}^2 \right) \tag{24}$$

In Fig. 5, we show the difference in result images by introducing our regularization term. In this figure, the result when regularization weight is 0 shows clipping around the ground region, while the full use of the regularization does not exhibit this behavior. Note that $\lambda$ can be obtained by grid-search.

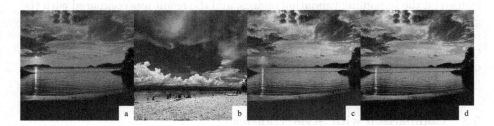

Fig. 5. **An example of the regularization effect.** Regularization term yields a stable result where there is less or no clipping. (a) is an input image, (b) is a filtered style image, and (c) and (d) are results of FST without and with regularization terms, respectively.

# 5    Experiment

## 5.1    Dataset

To generalize the defilterization network $f_w^{-1}$ for various scenes, we require a large-scale dataset with lots of classes. One of the most popular image datasets, MSCOCO [19], is widely used and contains more than 110K images with 80 object categories. However, this dataset does not contain filtered images. Therefore, to generate filtered images, we applied various types of real and arbitrary synthetic photo filters to the dataset. Initially, a filtered dataset was generated by posing 26 real Instagram filters using publicly available source code in CSS-gram [17]. In addition, synthetic filtered images were added by posing random color, contrast, and brightness six times. Based on this dataset, we trained the defilterization network and tested our proposed method.

To check the dataset dependency, we also prepared 99 private photos and 17 unseen real filters from one of the camera application in Android Play Store. As shown in the experiment in the next section, the proposed method, FST, can successfully transfer filter effects from a single image to the new input, even the filters unseen in the training phase.

## 5.2    Evaluation

Firstly we prepared the architecture of image-to-image translation, introduced in [13], as a defilterization function $f_w^{-1}$. Then, we trained $f_w^{-1}$ using the combined dataset and fully synthetic dataset (self-supervised learning) until the test MSE is saturated. Note that the filter transferred output would show better results with a better choice of defilterization network and more synthetic dataset generation, but we leave it as further work.

To validate our proposed method, we randomly chose 100 images from the MSCOCO validation set, and selected 18 real filters out of 26 filters to generate 1800 filtered images. We excluded eight filters that have a noticeable vignetting effect, which is outside of the scope of the current study. Then, FST was performed on the remaining validation images, and the result was compared with the ground truth images, which were directly generated by applying filters. Quantitative and qualitative results are given in Table 1 and Fig. 6, respectively. To further test our method on unseen dataset, we also evaluated the proposed method on private photos with 43 filters (17 unseen filters and 26 Instagram filters). The result is given in Table 2.

## 5.3    Comparison with Style Transfer

Our problem definition is inherently different from conventional style transfer researches. Style transfer seeks the transfer of texture, color, and even abstract concepts, while our method targets the transfer of photo editing or filter effects applied to an image. Although photorealistic stylization approaches [18,32] show

**Table 1. Quantitative evaluation.** The MSCOCO validation set with 18 Instagram filters is used for evaluation. Our method supports a few variations. Our method can have (R): regularization, (AU): Aleatoric uncertainty, (U): combined uncertainty, (CC): color correlation. Note that for WCT2, we gave option that uses features from decoder and skip-connection since it performs the best. Note that lower $\Delta E_{00}^*$ (a.k.a., Delta-E 2000) is better.

| Methods | PSNR | $\Delta E_{00}^*$ |
|---|---|---|
| **Ours** | **25.226** | **6.660** |
| **Ours (w. U, CC)** | **24.931** | **6.725** |
| **Ours (w. AU)** | **25.438** | **6.427** |
| **Ours (w. U)** | **25.495** | **6.394** |
| **Ours (w. R, U)** | **26.093** | **6.148** |
| WCT2 [32] | 16.473 | 17.516 |
| Color Transfer [24] | 7.325 | 34.914 |

**Table 2.** Quantitative evaluation on private photos with 43 filters.

| Methods | Ours (w. R, AU) | Ours (w. R, U) | WCT2 [32] | Color Transfer [24] |
|---|---|---|---|---|
| PSNR | **25.814** | **25.850** | 17.234 | 6.985 |
| $\Delta E_{00}^*$ | **5.881** | **5.854** | 15.723 | 35.123 |

| Style Original | Filtered Style | Input | Output | Ground Truth |

**Fig. 6. Qualitative results of FST.** We also included the originals of filtered style images, which were not given during inference.

attractive results in terms of structure preservation, they tend to directly transfer color distribution from the style to content images, not transferring filter information of the style image. Nonetheless, we compared our proposed FST with photorealistic style transfer, since style transfer is the most similar task.

To validate the effectiveness of the proposed method, we compare it with two types of photorealistic style transfer methods based on conventional linear color distribution transfer [24] and structure-preserved style transfer based on a high-frequency component skip, which is the state-of-the-art in photorealistic style transfer [32]. As shown in Fig. 7, both approaches tend to directly reflect the color distribution of the style image to the content image while FST transfers filter style only. In case of color transfer, if style image consists of achromatic colors mostly, it often generates visually unpleasing and questionable results. Furthermore, in terms of computational complexity, while conventional style transfer techniques take several hundred milliseconds, our solution can transfer filter style to the content image in less than a few milliseconds. Moreover, FST can transfer stylish effects as well as unseen filters. Detailed results are shown in Fig. 8.

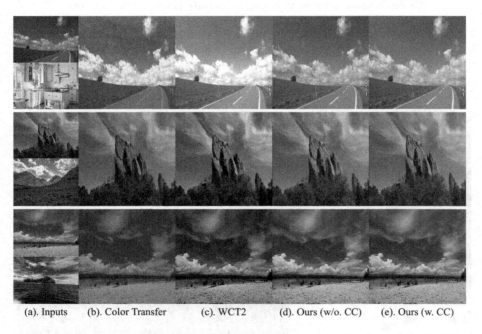

(a). Inputs  (b). Color Transfer  (c). WCT2  (d). Ours (w/o. CC)  (e). Ours (w. CC)

**Fig. 7. The results of FST with channel correlation.** Given (a) an input pair (top: content, bottom: style), the results of (b) color transfer [24], (c) WCT2 [32], (d) and (e) ours (FST) are shown. With CC (color correlation) term, the proposed method can also transfer colors of contents, whitish color in the first row, green forests in the second row, and bluish color in the third row, for example. (Color figure online)

Content     Style     Output     Content     Style     Output

**Fig. 8.** More results from the proposed FST using stylish photos.

## 5.4 Application

**A Trade-Off Between Filter and Color Style.** In Sect. 4.1, the approximate filter-applying function is modeled as a polynomial form (15) to transfer filter styles. However, in addition to filter style, more dramatic effects may be required upon requests. In this case, by adding a correlation term to filter-applying function as shown in (19), FST can transfer some colors that are not present in the reference style image to neighbor colors at the expense of quantitative accuracy. As shown in Fig. 3, results look more like color style transfer than the original FST.

**Real-Time Filter Transfer on Mobile Device.** Along with the satisfactory results of our method, it is designed to run real-time on a mobile environment, where there is a severe restriction on computational power. FST takes most of its time on filter parameter extraction, and it costs as much as the inference time of autoencoder, plus nonlinear regression. However, once the parameters are obtained, transferring the filter style onto the new input can be done almost instantly. The processing times are firstly measured on a PC, and compared with WCT2 and Color Transfer. Results are given in Table 3. Furthermore, in a mobile environment, our approach performs with 900 ms on average on Qualcomm Snapdragon 855 to process an FHD image. The processing time on a smartphone is given in Table 4. Note that once the filter is extracted, RGB Look Up Table (LUT) can be precomputed and stored on the device to shorten the processing time. Then, in the run-time, pixels are matched to new values using LUT to generate a stylized output image, which requires less than 2ms to transfer FHD images.

**Table 3. Run-time comparison on a PC.** Steps are divided into two; filter extraction and application. Tests were done using the machine with Python Numpy, Nvidia GTX 1080ti, and Intel i7-8700 CPU. We used $256 \times 256$ image for filter extraction and $1920 \times 1080$ (FHD) for filter application. Note that excluding Epistemic Uncertainty (EU) in the proposed method can shorten the time required for filter extraction. We used 10 MC dropouts for EU.

| Methods | Filter extraction | Filter application |
|---|---|---|
| **Ours (w/o. EU)** | **28 ms** | **86 ms** |
| **Ours (full ver.)** | **132 ms** | **86 ms** |
| WCT2 [32] | 16ms | 943ms |
| Color Transfer [24] | 49 ms (single stage) | |

**Table 4. Run-time on a smartphone.** We also measured our method in a mobile environment, Samsung Galaxy S10. We used $256 \times 256$ image for filter extraction and $1920 \times 1080$ (FHD) for filter application. The filter application is much faster than the PC version since the mobile version uses GPU parallel processing, while the PC version partially uses Numpy CPU. Note that we excluded EU from the mobile version.

| Methods | Filter extraction | Filter application |
|---|---|---|
| **Ours, mobile version** | **900 ms** | **2 ms** |

# 6    Conclusion and Future Work

To the best of our knowledge, this is the first study on the real-time filter transfer between two real photos. Our approach resolves a new task called FST (Filter Style Transfer), transferring custom filter operation between images, which is different from previous works of style transfer. Although style transfer methods yield reasonable outputs in some cases, it does not consistently generate pleasant outputs in every case and may require an additional effort on tuning the result. Moreover, arbitrary photorealistic style transfer still provides degraded or ruined texture, which is not desirable in photo filter extraction.

In a mobile environment, once filter parameters acquired, FST consistently runs within 2 ms to transfer FHD previews in camera applications, which shows exceptional real-time performance. Moreover, our solution can also perform similar to color transfer depending on the regression function, but it still creates more natural output than any other existing color transfer method.

In the proposed method, a defilterization network can be replaced by any other network structures. However, note that the performance of the network directly relates to the performance of filter transfer. In the future, we therefore plan to work on improving the performance of the defilterization network to extract the originals from filtered images more accurately. For implicit learning of semantical objects, it may require to train class labels explicitly as well as decoder part. If the defilterization network can perfectly extract the original image, the final result of the filter transfer would be more reliable.

# References

1. Bianco, S., Cusano, C., Piccoli, F., Schettini, R.: Content-preserving tone adjustment for image enhancement. In: Proceedings of the IEEE Conference on Computer Vision and Pattern Recognition Workshops (2019)
2. Bianco, S., Cusano, C., Piccoli, F., Schettini, R.: Learning parametric functions for color image enhancement. In: Tominaga, S., Schettini, R., Trémeau, A., Horiuchi, T. (eds.) CCIW 2019. LNCS, vol. 11418, pp. 209–220. Springer, Cham (2019). https://doi.org/10.1007/978-3-030-13940-7_16
3. Bychkovsky, V., Paris, S., Chan, E., Durand, F.: Learning photographic global tonal adjustment with a database of input/output image pairs. In: CVPR 2011, pp. 97–104. IEEE (2011)
4. Chandakkar, P.S., Li, B.: Joint regression and ranking for image enhancement. In: 2017 IEEE Winter Conference on Applications of Computer Vision (WACV), pp. 235–243. IEEE (2017)
5. Chen, Y.S., Wang, Y.C., Kao, M.H., Chuang, Y.Y.: Deep photo enhancer: unpaired learning for image enhancement from photographs with GANs. In: Proceedings of the IEEE Conference on Computer Vision and Pattern Recognition, pp. 6306–6314 (2018)
6. Gal, Y., Islam, R., Ghahramani, Z.: Deep Bayesian active learning with image data. In: Proceedings of the 34th International Conference on Machine Learning-Volume, vol. 70, pp. 1183–1192. JMLR. org (2017)
7. Gatys, L.A., Ecker, A.S., Bethge, M.: Image style transfer using convolutional neural networks. In: Proceedings of the IEEE Conference on Computer Vision and Pattern Recognition, pp. 2414–2423 (2016)
8. Gharbi, M., Chen, J., Barron, J.T., Hasinoff, S.W., Durand, F.: Deep bilateral learning for real-time image enhancement. ACM Trans. Graph. (TOG) 36(4), 1–12 (2017)
9. Goodfellow, I., et al.: Generative adversarial nets. In: Advances in Neural Information Processing Systems, pp. 2672–2680 (2014)
10. Hu, Y., He, H., Xu, C., Wang, B., Lin, S.: Exposure: a white-box photo post-processing framework. ACM Trans. Graph. (TOG) 37(2), 1–17 (2018)
11. Ignatov, A., Kobyshev, N., Timofte, R., Vanhoey, K., Van Gool, L.: DSLR-quality photos on mobile devices with deep convolutional networks. In: Proceedings of the IEEE International Conference on Computer Vision, pp. 3277–3285 (2017)
12. Isola, P., Zhu, J.Y., Zhou, T., Efros, A.A.: Image-to-image translation with conditional adversarial networks. In: Proceedings of the IEEE Conference on Computer Vision and Pattern Recognition, pp. 1125–1134 (2017)
13. Johnson, J., Alahi, A., Fei-Fei, L.: Perceptual losses for real-time style transfer and super-resolution. In: Leibe, B., Matas, J., Sebe, N., Welling, M. (eds.) ECCV 2016. LNCS, vol. 9906, pp. 694–711. Springer, Cham (2016). https://doi.org/10.1007/978-3-319-46475-6_43
14. Kang, S.B., Kapoor, A., Lischinski, D.: Personalization of image enhancement. In: 2010 IEEE Computer Society Conference on Computer Vision and Pattern Recognition, pp. 1799–1806. IEEE (2010)
15. Kaufman, L., Lischinski, D., Werman, M.: Content-aware automatic photo enhancement. Comput. Graph. Forum 31(8), 2528–2540 (2012). Wiley Online Library

16. Kendall, A., Gal, Y.: What uncertainties do we need in Bayesian deep learning for computer vision? In: Advances in Neural Information Processing Systems, pp. 5574–5584 (2017)
17. Kravets, U.: CSSGram (2016). https://github.com/una/CSSgram
18. Li, Y., Liu, M.Y., Li, X., Yang, M.H., Kautz, J.: A closed-form solution to photorealistic image stylization. In: Proceedings of the European Conference on Computer Vision (ECCV). pp. 453–468 (2018)
19. Lin, T.-Y., et al.: Microsoft COCO: common objects in context. In: Fleet, D., Pajdla, T., Schiele, B., Tuytelaars, T. (eds.) ECCV 2014. LNCS, vol. 8693, pp. 740–755. Springer, Cham (2014). https://doi.org/10.1007/978-3-319-10602-1_48
20. Liu, M.Y., Breuel, T., Kautz, J.: Unsupervised image-to-image translation networks. In: Advances in Neural Information Processing Systems, pp. 700–708 (2017)
21. Luan, F., Paris, S., Shechtman, E., Bala, K.: Deep photo style transfer. In: Proceedings of the IEEE Conference on Computer Vision and Pattern Recognition, pp. 4990–4998 (2017)
22. Omiya, M., Simo-Serra, E., Iizuka, S., Ishikawa, H.: Learning photo enhancement by black-box model optimization data generation. In: SIGGRAPH Asia 2018 Technical Briefs, p. 7. ACM (2018)
23. Pitié, F., Kokaram, A.C., Dahyot, R.: Automated colour grading using colour distribution transfer. Comput. Vis. Image Underst. **107**(1–2), 123–137 (2007)
24. Reinhard, E., Adhikhmin, M., Gooch, B., Shirley, P.: Color transfer between images. IEEE Comput. Graph. Appl. **21**(5), 34–41 (2001)
25. Sheng, L., Lin, Z., Shao, J., Wang, X.: Avatar-Net: multi-scale zero-shot style transfer by feature decoration. In: Proceedings of the IEEE Conference on Computer Vision and Pattern Recognition, pp. 8242–8250 (2018)
26. Tai, Y.W., Jia, J., Tang, C.K.: Local color transfer via probabilistic segmentation by expectation-maximization. In: 2005 IEEE Computer Society Conference on Computer Vision and Pattern Recognition (CVPR 2005), vol. 1, pp. 747–754. IEEE (2005)
27. Welsh, T., Ashikhmin, M., Mueller, K.: Transferring color to greyscale images. In: Proceedings of the 29th Annual Conference on Computer Graphics and Interactive Techniques, pp. 277–280 (2002)
28. Xiao, X., Ma, L.: Color transfer in correlated color space. In: Proceedings of the 2006 ACM International Conference on Virtual Reality Continuum and Its Applications, pp. 305–309 (2006)
29. Yan, J., Lin, S., Bing Kang, S., Tang, X.: A learning-to-rank approach for image color enhancement. In: Proceedings of the IEEE Conference on Computer Vision and Pattern Recognition, pp. 2987–2994 (2014)
30. Yan, Z., Zhang, H., Wang, B., Paris, S., Yu, Y.: Automatic photo adjustment using deep neural networks. ACM Trans. Graph. (TOG) **35**(2), 1–15 (2016)
31. Yang, H., Wang, B., Vesdapunt, N., Guo, M., Kang, S.B.: Personalized exposure control using adaptive metering and reinforcement learning. IEEE Trans. Vis. Comput. Graph. **25**(10), 2953–2968 (2018)
32. Yoo, J., Uh, Y., Chun, S., Kang, B., Ha, J.W.: Photorealistic style transfer via wavelet transforms. In: Proceedings of the IEEE International Conference on Computer Vision, pp. 9036–9045 (2019)
33. Yu, R., Liu, W., Zhang, Y., Qu, Z., Zhao, D., Zhang, B.: DeepExposure: learning to expose photos with asynchronously reinforced adversarial learning. In: Advances in Neural Information Processing Systems, pp. 2149–2159 (2018)

34. Yuan, L., Sun, J.: Automatic exposure correction of consumer photographs. In: Fitzgibbon, A., Lazebnik, S., Perona, P., Sato, Y., Schmid, C. (eds.) ECCV 2012. LNCS, vol. 7575, pp. 771–785. Springer, Heidelberg (2012). https://doi.org/10.1007/978-3-642-33765-9_55
35. Zhu, J.Y., et al.: Toward multimodal image-to-image translation. In: Advances in Neural Information Processing Systems, pp. 465–476 (2017)

# JGR-P2O: Joint Graph Reasoning Based Pixel-to-Offset Prediction Network for 3D Hand Pose Estimation from a Single Depth Image

Linpu Fang[1], Xingyan Liu[1], Li Liu[2], Hang Xu[3], and Wenxiong Kang[1(✉)]

[1] South China University of Technology, Guangzhou, China
auwxkang@scut.edu.cn
[2] Center for Machine Vision and Signal Analysis, University of Oulu, Oulu, Finland
[3] Huawei Noah's Ark Lab, Hong Kong, China

**Abstract.** State-of-the-art single depth image-based 3D hand pose estimation methods are based on dense predictions, including voxel-to-voxel predictions, point-to-point regression, and pixel-wise estimations. Despite the good performance, those methods have a few issues in nature, such as the poor trade-off between accuracy and efficiency, and plain feature representation learning with local convolutions. In this paper, a novel pixel-wise prediction-based method is proposed to address the above issues. The key ideas are two-fold: (a) explicitly modeling the dependencies among joints and the relations between the pixels and the joints for better local feature representation learning; (b) unifying the dense pixel-wise offset predictions and direct joint regression for end-to-end training. Specifically, we first propose a graph convolutional network (GCN) based joint graph reasoning module to model the complex dependencies among joints and augment the representation capability of each pixel. Then we densely estimate all pixels' offsets to joints in both image plane and depth space and calculate the joints' positions by a weighted average over all pixels' predictions, totally discarding the complex post-processing operations. The proposed model is implemented with an efficient 2D fully convolutional network (FCN) backbone and has only about 1.4M parameters. Extensive experiments on multiple 3D hand pose estimation benchmarks demonstrate that the proposed method achieves new state-of-the-art accuracy while running very efficiently with around a speed of 110 fps on a single NVIDIA 1080Ti GPU (This work was supported in part by the National Natural Science Foundation of China under Grants 61976095, in part by the Science and Technology Planning Project of Guangdong Province under Grant 2018B030323026. This work was also partially supported by the Academy of Finland.). The code is available at https://github.com/fanglinpu/JGR-P2O.

**Electronic supplementary material** The online version of this chapter (https://doi.org/10.1007/978-3-030-58539-6_8) contains supplementary material, which is available to authorized users.

A. Vedaldi et al. (Eds.): ECCV 2020, LNCS 12351, pp. 120–137, 2020.
https://doi.org/10.1007/978-3-030-58539-6_8

**Keywords:** 3D hand pose estimation · Depth image · Graph neural network

# 1 Introduction

Vision-based 3D hand pose estimation aims to locate hand joints in 3D space from input hand images, which serves as one of the core techniques in contactless human computer interaction applications, such as virtual reality, augmented reality and robotic gripping [11,23]. Recent years have witnessed significant advances [6,8,20,22,48] in this area with the availability of consumer depth cameras, such as Microsoft Kinect and Intel RealSense, and the success of deep learning technology in the computer vision community. However, accurate and real-time 3D hand pose estimation is still a challenging task due to the high articulation complexity of the hand, severe self-occlusion between different fingers, poor quality of depth images, etc.

In this paper, we focus on the problem of 3D hand pose estimation from a single depth image. At present, the state-of-the-art approaches to this task rely on deep learning technology, especially deep convolutional neural networks (CNNs). The main reasons are two-fold. On one hand, public available large datasets [34,37,39, 49] with fully labeled 3D hand poses provide a large number of training data for these data-hungry methods. On the other hand, CNNs with well-designed network structures provide very effective solutions to challenging visual learning tasks and have been demonstrated to outperform traditional methods by a large margin in various computer vision tasks, including 3D hand pose estimation.

Best performing deep learning-based methods are detection-based, which formulate 3D hand pose parameters as volumetric heat-maps or extended 3D heat-maps together with offset vector fields and estimate them in a dense prediction manner with fully convolutional networks (FCNs) or PointNet [30,31]. Contrary to their regression-based counterparts that directly map the depth images to 3D hand pose parameters and severely suffer from the problem of highly non-linear mapping, the detection-based methods can learn better feature representations by pose reparameterization and have proven to be more effective for both human pose estimation [4,29] and hand pose estimation [10,22,43].

By analyzing previous detection-based methods, we find that they suffer from several drawbacks in nature, which can be improved to boost performance. First, they bear the problem of poor trade-off between accuracy and efficiency. For example, the V2V [22] uses 3D CNNs to estimate volumetric heat-maps, which is very parameter-heavy and computationally inefficient. The pixel-wise and point-wise prediction-based methods [10,43] take the advantages of 2D CNNs or PointNet to regress dense 3D estimations. In spite of the higher efficiency, these methods achieve lower estimation precision empirically, and the complex post-processing operations still degrade the computational efficiency. Second, they consist of non-differentiable post-processing operations, such as taking maximum and taking neighboring points, preventing fully end-to-end training and causing inevitable quantization errors. In addition, the models are trained with non-adaptive Gaussian heat-maps or joint-centered heat-maps, which may be suboptimal. Finally, the feature representation for each element (e.g., a voxel, a pixel or a point) is only learned by local convolutions ignoring the global context information. However, modeling the dependencies among joints and the relations between the elements and the joints helps to learn more abundant contextual information and better local feature representations.

To cope with these problems, we propose a novel joint graph reasoning based pixel-to-offset prediction network (JGR-P2O) for 3D hand pose estimation, which aims at directly regressing joints' positions from single depth images. Specifically, we decompose the 3D hand pose into joints' 2D image plane coordinates and depth values, and estimate these parameters in an ensemble way, fully exploiting the 2.5D property of depth images. The proposed method consists of two key modules, i.e., GCN-based joint graph reasoning module and pixel-to-offset prediction module. The joint graph reasoning module aims at learning a better feature representation for each pixel, which is vital for dense prediction. First, the features of joints are generated by summarizing the global information encoded in local features. Second, the dependencies among joints are modeled by graph reasoning to obtain stronger feature representations of joints. Finally, the evolved joints' features are mapped back to local features accordingly enhancing the local feature representations. The pixel-to-offset prediction module densely estimates all the pixels' offsets to joints in both image plane and depth space. And the joints' positions in both image plane space and depth space are calculated by a weighted average over all the pixels' predictions. In this way, we discard the complex post-processing operations used in [10,43], which improves not only the computational efficiency but also the estimation robustness.

Note that our JGR-P2O can obtain joints' positions directly from single depth images without extra post-processing operations. It generates intermediate dense offset vector fields, and can also be fully end-to-end trained under the direct supervision of joints' positions, fully sharing the merits of both detection-based and regression-based methods. It also explicitly models the dependencies among joints and the relations between the pixels and the joints to augment the local feature representations. The whole model is implemented with an efficient 2D FCN backbone and has only about 1.4M parameters. It generally outperforms the previous detection-based methods on effectiveness and efficiency simultaneously. Overall, the proposed method provides some effective solutions to the problems encountered by previous detection-based methods.

To sum up, the main contributions of this paper are as follows:

- We propose an end-to-end trainable pixel-to-offset module by leveraging the 2.5D property of depth images to unify the dense pixel-wise offset predictions and direct joint regression.
- We propose a GCN-based joint graph reasoning module to explicitly model the dependencies among joints and the relations between the pixels and the joints to augment the local feature representations.
- We conduct extensive experiments on multiple most common 3D hand pose estimation benchmarks (i.e., ICVL [37], NYU [39], and MSRA [34]). The

results demonstrate that the proposed method achieves new state-of-the-art accuracy with only about 1.4M parameters while running very efficiently with around a speed 110 fps on single NVIDIA 1080Ti GPU.

## 2  Related Work

This paper focuses on the problem of estimating 3D hand pose from a single depth image. The approaches to this problem can be categorized into discriminative methods [7,9,34,44], generative methods [14,32,40] and hybrid methods [25,27,28,38,42,47,50]. In this section, we focus on the discussions of the deep learning-based discriminative and hybrid methods related closely to our work. These methods can be further classified into regression-based methods, detection-based methods, hierarchical and structured methods. Please refer to [35,36,48] for more detailed review. Furthermore, we also introduce some GCN-based works that related to our method.

**Regression-Based Methods.** Regression-based methods [3,7,9,12,25,26] aim at directly regressing 3D hand pose parameters such as 3D coordinates or joint angles. Oberweger et al. [25,26] exploit a bottleneck layer to learn a pose prior for constraining the hand pose. Guo et al. [12] propose a tree-structured Region Ensemble Network (REN) to regressing joints' 3D coordinates directly. Instead of using depth images as inputs, other works focus on 3D input representations, fully utilizing the depth information. Ge et al. [7,9] apply 3D CNNs and PointNet [30,31] for estimating 3D hand joint positions directly, which use 3D volumetric representation and 3D point cloud as inputs respectively. Despite the simplicity, the global regression manner within the fully-connected layers incurs highly non-linear mapping, which may reduce the estimation performance. However, our method adopts the dense prediction manner to regress the offsets from pixels to joints, effectively maintaining the local spatial context information.

**Detection-Based Methods.** Detection-based methods [8,10,22,43] work in dense local prediction manner via setting a heat map for each joint. Early works [8,39] firstly detect the joints' positions in 2D plain based on the estimated 2D heat-maps and then translate them into 3D coordinates by complex optimization-based post-processing. Recent works [10,22,43] directly detect 3D joint positions from 3D heat-maps with much more simple post-processing. Moon et al. [22] propose a Voxel-to-Voxel prediction network (V2V) for both 3D hand and human pose estimation. Wan et al. [43] and Ge et al. [10] formulate 3D hand pose as 3D heat-maps and unit vector fields and estimate these parameters by dense pixel-wise and point-wise regression respectively. Despite the good performance, these methods have some drawbacks, such as the poor trade-off between accuracy and efficiency and local feature representations. With the proposed pixel-to-offset prediction module and GCN-based joint graph reasoning module, our method can effectively solve these problems.

**Hierarchical and Structured Methods.** These methods aim at incorporating hand part correlations or pose constraints into the model. Hierarchical methods

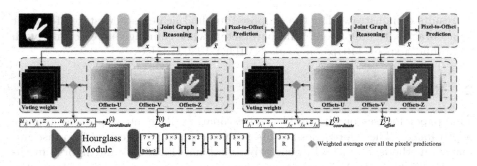

**Fig. 1.** An overview of our JGR-P2O. The abbreviations C, P, R indicate convolutional layer with BN and ReLU, pooling layer and residual module respectively. Given a hand depth image, the backbone module first extracts the intermediate local feature representation $X$, which is then augmented by the proposed GCN-based joint graph reasoning module producing the augmented local feature representation $\bar{X}$. Finally, the proposed pixel-to-offset prediction module predicts three offset maps for each joint where each pixel value indicates the offset from the pixel to the joint along one of the axes in the UVZ coordinate system. The joint's UVZ coordinates are calculated as the weighted average over all the pixels' predictions. Two kinds of losses, coordinate-wise regression loss $L_{coordinate}$ and pixel-wise offset regression loss $L_{offset}$, are proposed to guide the learning process. We stack together two hourglasses to enhance the learning power, feeding the output from the previous module as the input into the next while exerting intermediate supervision at the end of each module.

[2,6,20] divide the hand joints into different subsets and use different network branches to extract local pose features for each subset. Then all the local pose features are combined together forming the global hand pose representation for final pose estimation. Structured methods [20,25,26,50] impose physical hand motion constraints into the model, which are implemented by embedding constraint layers in the CNN model [25,26,50] or adding specific items in the loss function [50]. Different from these methods, the proposed GCN-based joint graph reasoning module aims at augmenting the local feature representation by learning the dependencies among joints and the relations between the pixels and the joints.

**Related GCN-Based Works.** Graph CNNs (GCNs) generalize CNNs to graph-structured data. Approaches in this field are often classified into two categories: spectral based methods [5,15] that start with constructing the frequency filtering, and spatial based methods [21,41] that generalize the convolution to a patch operator on groups of node neighbors. Recently, some works use GCNs for 3D pose estimation [1] and skeleton-based action recognition [16,33,46]. And some works [18,19] use GCN-based methods to augment the local feature representation for dense prediction. Inspired by these works, we also define the connections between hand joints as a graph and apply a GCN to learn their dependencies. Moreover, we design several different joint graph structures for comprehensive comparison studies.

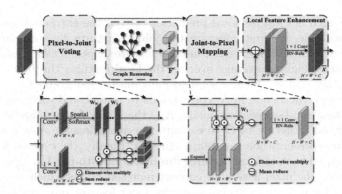

**Fig. 2.** Flowchart of our proposed GCN-based joint graph reasoning module. Given the intermediate feature representation $X$ extracted from the backbone module, it first generates the joints' feature representation $F$ by a pixel-to-joint voting mechanism where each joint is represented as the weighted average over all the local features. Then we define the connections between joints as a graph and map the joints' features to the corresponding graph nodes. The joints' features are propagated within the graph by graph reasoning, obtaining the enhanced joints' feature $F^e$. Next, the $F^e$ is mapped back to local features by a joint-to-pixel mapping mechanism that is the inverse operation of the pixel-to-joint voting, generating the joint context representations for all pixels. Finally, the original feature representation and the joint context representation are fused together obtaining enhanced local feature representation.

## 3    The Proposed Method

### 3.1    Overview

The proposed JGR-P2O casts the problem of 3D hand pose estimation as dense pixel-to-offset predictions, fully exploiting the 2.5D property of depth images. It takes a depth image as input and outputs the joints' positions in image plain (i.e., uv coordinates) and depth space (i.e., z coordinates) directly. An overview of the JGR-P2O can be found in Fig. 1. We use the high-efficient hourglass network [24] as the backbone to extract intermediate local feature representation. Then the proposed joint graph reasoning module models the dependencies among joints and the relations between the pixels and the joints enhancing the intermediate local feature representation. Finally, the pixel-to-offset module estimates the offsets from pixels to joints and aggregates all the pixels' predictions to obtain final joints' positions. Following [24], we stack together two hourglasses to enhance the learning power, feeding the output from the previous module as the input into the next while exerting intermediate supervision at the end of each module.

### 3.2    GCN-Based Joint Graph Reasoning Module

Inspired by the symbolic graph reasoning (SGR) [19], we propose the joint graph reasoning module to augment the intermediate local feature representation for each pixel, which is vital for local prediction. Given the extracted feature map from the backbone, we first generate the joints' features by summarizing the global context information encoded in local features. Specifically, joints are represented as the weighted average over all the local features through a pixel-to-joint voting mechanism. Then a joint-to-joint undirected graph $G = <\mathcal{N}, \mathcal{E}>$ is defined, where each node in $\mathcal{N}$ corresponds to a joint and each edge $e_{i,j} \in \mathcal{E}$ encodes relationship between two joints. And the joints' features are propagated with the defined structure of $G$ to capture the dependencies among joints and enhance their representation capabilities further. Finally, the evolved joints' features are mapped back to local features through a joint-to-pixel mapping mechanism, obtaining the pixel-wise joint context representations which are combined with original local features to enhance the local feature representations. The detailed pipeline of this module can be found in Fig. 2.

**Pixel-to-Joint Voting.** We seek to obtain joints' visual representations based on the global context information encoded in local features. Specifically, each joint has its informative pixels, the representations of which are aggregated to form the joint's feature. In this paper, we compute the joints' features by a pixel-to-joint voting mechanism. Given the feature map $X \in \mathbb{R}^{H \times W \times C}$ after the backbone network, where $H$, $W$ and $C$ denote the height, width and number of channels of the feature map respectively. First, the voting weights from pixels to joints are computed as:

$$W = \Phi(\phi(X)), \qquad (1)$$

where $\phi(\cdot)$ is a transformation function implemented by a $1 \times 1$ convolution, $\Phi$ is the spatial softmax normalization, and $W \in \mathbb{R}^{H \times W \times N}$ is the voting tensor where the $kth$ channel $\mathbf{W}_k \in \mathbb{R}^{H \times W}$ represents the voting matrix for joint $k$. Then the feature representation for joint $k$ is calculated as the weighted average over all the transformed pixel-wise representations:

$$\mathbf{f}_k = \sum_i w_{ki} \varphi(\mathbf{x}_i), \qquad (2)$$

where $\mathbf{x}_i$ is the representation of pixel $p_i$, $\varphi(\cdot)$ is a transformation function implemented by a $1 \times 1$ convolution layer, and $w_{ki}$, an element of $\mathbf{W}_k$, is the voting weight for pixel $p_i$. We also define the whole representation of all $N$ joints as $\mathbf{F} = [\mathbf{f}_1^T; \ldots; \mathbf{f}_N^T]$.

**Graph Reasoning.** Given the joints' features and the defined joint-to-joint undirected graph $G$, it is natural to use a GCN to model the dependencies among joints and augment the joints' feature representations further. Following GCN defined in [15], we perform graph reasoning over representation $\mathbf{F}$ of all joints with matrix multiplication, resulting the evolved joint features $\mathbf{F}^e$:

$$\mathbf{F}^e = \sigma(\mathbf{A}^e \mathbf{F} \mathbf{W}^e), \qquad (3)$$

where $\mathbf{W}^e \in \mathbb{R}^{C \times C}$ is a trainable transformation matrix, $\mathbf{A}^e \in \mathbb{R}^{N \times N}$ is the connection weight matrix defined according to the edge connections in $\mathcal{E}$, and $\sigma(\cdot)$ is a nonlinear function (we use ReLU function for $\sigma(\cdot)$ in this paper). To demonstrate the generalization capability of the GCN-based joint graph reasoning module, we try three different methods to construct graph structure (i.e., the definition of $\mathbf{A}^e$) in this paper.

**Skeleton Graph.** The most intuitive method is to define the edge connections as hard weights (i.e., $\{0, 1\}$) based on the physical connections between joints in the hand skeleton. Then the connection weight matrix is defined as the normalized form as in [15]: $\mathbf{A}^e = \tilde{\mathbf{D}}^{-\frac{1}{2}} (\mathbf{A} + \mathbf{I}_N) \tilde{\mathbf{D}}^{-\frac{1}{2}}$, where $\mathbf{A}$ is the adjacency matrix defined in the hand skeleton, $\mathbf{I}_N$ is the identity matrix, and $\tilde{\mathbf{A}} = \mathbf{A} + \mathbf{I}_N$ defines a undirected graph with added self-connections. $\tilde{\mathbf{D}}$ is the diagonal node degree matrix of $\tilde{\mathbf{A}}$ with $\tilde{\mathbf{D}}_{ii} = \sum_j \tilde{\mathbf{A}}_{ij}$.

**Feature Similarity.** The connection weight between two joints can be calculated as the similarity of their visual representations: $a^e_{ij} = \frac{exp(\upsilon(\mathbf{f}_i)^T \psi(\mathbf{f}_j))}{\sum_{j=1}^{N} exp(\upsilon(\mathbf{f}_i)^T \psi(\mathbf{f}_j))}$, where $\upsilon$ and $\psi$ are two liner transformation functions implemented by two fully-connected layers. Note that each sample has a unique graph learned by this data-dependent method.

**Parameterized Matrix.** In this way, $\mathbf{A}^e$ is defined as a parameterized matrix whose elements are optimized together with the other parameters in the training process, that is, the graph is completely learned according to the training data.

**Joint-to-Pixel Mapping.** The evolved joint features can be used to augment the local feature representations. Specifically, the pixel-wise joint context representations are first calculated by mapping the evolved joint features back to local features and then combined with original pixel-wise representations to compute the augmented local feature representations. We use the inverse operation of pixel-to-joint voting, i.e., joint-to-pixel mapping, to calculate the pixel-wise joint context representation. For pixel $p_i$, we first compute its context representation of joint $k$ as: $\mathbf{c}_{ik} = w_{ik} \mathbf{f}^e_k$, where $\mathbf{f}^e_k$ is the evolved feature of joint $k$, and $w_{ik}$ is the mapping weight from joint $k$ to pixel $p_i$, which is the same as the voting weight $w_{ki}$ in formula (2). Then the mean of set $\{\mathbf{c}_{ik}; k = 1, \ldots N\}$ is used to calculate the final pixel-wise joint context representation for pixel $p_i$:

$$\mathbf{c}_i = \rho \left( \frac{1}{N} \sum_k \mathbf{c}_{ik} \right), \tag{4}$$

where $\rho$ is a transformation function implemented by a $1 \times 1$ convolution with BN and ReLU.

**Local Feature Enhancement.** Finally, we aggregate the original feature representation $\mathbf{x}_i$ and joint context representation $\mathbf{c}_i$ to obtain the augmented feature representation for pixel $p_i$:

$$\bar{\mathbf{x}}_i = \tau \left( [\mathbf{c}_i^T, \mathbf{x}_i^T]^T \right),\qquad(5)$$

where $\tau$ is a transformation function used to fuse the original feature representation and joint context representation, and implemented by a $1 \times 1$ convolution with BN and ReLU. The combination of the augmented features of all the pixels constitutes the augmented feature map $\bar{\boldsymbol{X}}$, which is used as the input to the pixel-to-offset prediction module.

### 3.3   Pixel-to-Offset Prediction Module

A depth image consists of pixels' 2D image plane coordinates and depth values (i.e., UVZ coordinates), which are the most direct information for determining the positions of hand joints. In this paper, we also decompose the 3D hand pose into joints' 2D image plane coordinates and depth values, and estimate these parameters in an ensemble way. More concretely, a pixel's UVZ coordinates and its offset vector to a joint can determine the joint's position in the UVZ coordinate system. That is, instead of predicting the joint's UVZ coordinates directly, we can detour estimate the offset vector from the pixel to the joint since the pixel's UVZ coordinates can be obtained from the depth image directly. To achieve robust estimation, we aggregate the predictions of all the pixels to obtain the position of the joint. Formally, for a certain joint $k$, we predict three offset values for each pixel representing the offset vector in the UVZ coordinate system from the pixel to joint $k$, resulting in three offset maps. Then the UVZ coordinates $(u_{j_k}, v_{j_k}, z_{j_k})$ of joint $k$ is obtained by a weighted average over all the pixels' predictions:

$$\begin{cases} u_{j_k} = \sum_i w_{ki} \left( u_{p_i} + \Delta u_{ki} \right) \\ v_{j_k} = \sum_i w_{ki} \left( v_{p_i} + \Delta v_{ki} \right), \\ z_{j_k} = \sum_i w_{ki} \left( z_{p_i} + \Delta z_{ki} \right) \end{cases}\qquad(6)$$

where $(u_{p_i}, v_{p_i}, z_{p_i})$ indicate the UVZ coordinates of pixel $p_i$, $(\Delta u_{ki}, \Delta v_{ki}, \Delta z_{ki})$ represent the predicted offset values from pixel $p_i$ to joint $k$. $w_{ki}$ is the normalized prediction weight of pixel $p_i$, indicating its importance for locating the joint $k$, which is set to be same as the voting weight introduced in Sect. 3.2.1. The pixel-to-offset prediction module is implemented by a $1 \times 1$ convolution layer that takes the augmented local feature representation $\bar{\boldsymbol{X}}$ as input and output $3N$ offset maps for all the $N$ joints directly.

Note that our P2O module is much simpler than the estimation scheme of A2J [45] where two different branches are design to estimate the joints' UV coordinates and Z coordinates, respectively. In addition, A2J uses a single feature in high-level feature maps to predict multiple estimations for a set of anchor points, which may distract the model's representation learning as well as increasing the parameters. The experimental results also demonstrates the superiority of our method over the A2J.

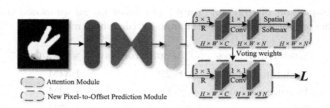

**Fig. 3.** The flowchart of the attention-based baseline model. The JGR module is replaced with an attention module to calculate the weights of pixels for locating the joints. The attention module consists of a $3 \times 3$ Residual block, a $1 \times 1$ Conv layer, and a spatial softmax operation. We also add a $3 \times 3$ Residual block to the original pixel-to-offset prediction module. This figure only depicts the one-stage version of the attention-based baseline model. In practice, we employ the two-stage version for comparison.

### 3.4 Training Strategy

The predicted joints' coordinates are calculated as in formula (6). According to the ground truth 3D hand pose, we can construct a coordinate-wise regression loss:

$$L_{coordinate} = \sum_k \sum_c L_\delta \left(c_{j_k} - c_{j_k}^*\right), \tag{7}$$

where $c_{j_k}$ is one of the predicted UVZ coordinates of joint $k$, and $c_{j_k}^*$ is the corresponding ground truth coordinate. We choose the Huber loss function $L_\delta$ as the regression loss function since it is less sensitive to outliers in data than squared error loss function. Moreover, we can also explicitly supervise the generation process of offset maps by constructing a pixel-wise offset regression loss:

$$L_{offset} = \sum_k \sum_i \sum_c L_\delta \left(\Delta c_{ki} - \Delta c_{ki}^*\right), \tag{8}$$

where $\Delta c_{ki}$ is the offset value from pixel $p_i$ to joint $k$ along one of axes in the UVZ coordinate system, and $\Delta c_{ki}^*$ is the corresponding ground truth offset value. The pixel-wise offset regression loss can be seen as a regularization term for learning better local feature representation. Note that we normalize the ground truth coordinates and offset values to be within the range $[-1, 1]$, the pixel's UV coordinates and Z coordinates (i.e., depth values) are also normalized to be within the range $[0, 1]$ and $[-1, 1]$ respectively. Therefore, the estimated offset maps and joints' coordinates are also the normalized versions. We use a downsampled input depth image with the same resolution as the predicted offset map to calculate these parameters. Following [24], we boost the learning capability of the network architecture by stacking multiple hourglasses with identical structures, feeding the output from the previous module as the input into the next while exerting intermediate supervision at the end of each module. The final loss for the whole network is defined as follows:

**Table 1.** Comparison of different graph structures in the proposed JGR module. #Params indicates the number of parameters of the whole model.

| Graph structures | Mean error (mm) | #Params |
|---|---|---|
| Skeleton graph | **8.29** | 1.37M |
| Feature similarity | 8.45 | 1.43M |
| Parameterized matrix | 8.36 | 1.37M |

**Table 2.** Effectiveness of individual components of the proposed method.

| Component | | | Mean error (mm) |
|---|---|---|---|
| P2O | Offset loss | JGR | |
| ✓ | | | 10.83 |
| ✓ | ✓ | | $10.54^{-0.29}$ |
| ✓ | ✓ | ✓ | $\mathbf{8.29}^{-2.25}$ |

$$L = \sum_{s=1}^{S} L_{coordinate}^{(s)} + \beta L_{offset}^{(s)}. \tag{9}$$

where $L_{coordinate}^{(s)}$ and $L_{offset}^{(s)}$ are the coordinate-wise regression loss and pixel-wise offset regression loss at the $sth$ stage, $\beta = 0.0001$ is the weight factor for balancing the proposed two kinds of losses, and $S = 2$ is the total number of the stacked hourglasses. The whole network architecture is trained in an end-to-end style with the supervision of this loss.

## 4   Experiments

### 4.1   Datasets and Settings

We evaluate our proposed JGR-P2O on three common 3D hand pose estimation datasets: ICVL dataset [37], NYU dataset [39], and MSRA dataset [34]. The ICVL dataset 330K training 1.5K testing depth images that are captured with an Intel Realsense camera. The ground truth hand pose of each image consists of $N = 16$ joints. The NYU dataset was captured with three Microsoft Kinects from different views. Each view consists 72K training 8K testing depth images. There are 36 joints in each annotated hand pose. Following most previous works, we only use view 1 and $N = 14$ joints for training and testing in all experiments. The MSRA dataset consists 76K training images captured from 9 subjects with 17 gestures, using Intel's Creative Interactive Camera. Each image is annotated with a hand pose with $N = 21$ joints. We use the leave-one-subject-out cross-validation strategy [34] for evaluation.

We employ two most commonly used metrics to evaluate the performance of 3D hand pose estimation. The first one is the mean 3D distance error (in mm)

**Table 3.** Comparison of different numbers of stacked hourglass module.

| #Hourglasses | Mean error (mm) | #Params |
|---|---|---|
| 1 | 8.63 | 0.72M |
| 2 | 8.29 | 1.37M |
| 3 | 8.27 | 2.02M |

**Table 4.** Comparison with different baselines on NYU.

| Model | Mean error (mm) | #Params |
|---|---|---|
| Baseline with attention module | 8.72 | 1.42M |
| Baseline with DHM module | 8.69 | 1.37M |
| Ours | **8.29** | 1.37M |

averaged over all joints and all test images. The second one is the percentage of success frames in which the worst joint 3D distance error is below a threshold.

All experiments are conducted on a single server with four NVIDIA 1080Ti GPU using Tensorflow. For inputs to the JGR-P2O, we crop a hand area from the original image using a method similar to the one proposed in [25] and resize it to a fixed size of 96 × 96. The depth values are normalized to $[-1, 1]$ for the cropped image. For training, Adam with weight decay of 0.00005 and batch size of 32 is used to optimize all models. Online data augmentation is used, including in-plane rotation ($[-180, 180]$ degree), 3D scaling ($[0.9, 1,1]$), and 3D translation ($[-10, 10]$ mm). The initial learning rate is set to be 0.0001, reduced by a factor of 0.96 every epoch. We train 8 epochs for the ICVL training set and 58 epochs for the other training sets.

## 4.2  Ablation Studies

We firstly conduct ablation studies to demonstrate the effectiveness of various components of the proposed JGR-P2O. The ablation studies are conducted on the NYU dataset since it is more challenge than the other two.

**Comparison of Different Graph Structures.** Table 1 reports the performance of different graph structures in the proposed joint graph reasoning module. It can be seen that different graph structures can obtain similar estimation precision, indicating that the proposed joint graph reasoning module has strong generalization capability. In the following experiments, we choose the skeleton graph as the default graph structure for the joint graph reasoning module since it is more interpretable and best-performed.

**Effectiveness of Individual Components.** The results in Table 2 show how much each component improves the estimation performance along with the combinations of other components. The simplest baseline that combines the backbone network and a P2O module, denoted as P2O in Table 2, estimates the

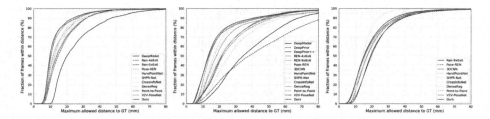

**Fig. 4.** Comparison with previous state-of-the-art methods. The percentages of success frames over different error thresholds are presented in this figure. Left: ICVL dataset, Middle: NYU dataset, Right: MSRA dataset.

joint's positions with the average summation over all pixels' predictions and obtains highest estimation error. Adding the pixel-wise offset regression loss for training decreases estimation error by 0.29 mm. Finally, the JGR module helps to greatly decrease the estimation error by 2.25 mm.

**Number of Hourglass Modules.** The results of using different numbers of hourglass modules are reported in Table 3. It can be seen that with only one hourglass, the proposed JGR-P2O would achieve relatively low mean 3D distance errors (8.63 mm) on the NYU dataset. Increasing the number of hourglasses can improve the estimation precision, but three hourglasses can only obtain negligible improvement. In this paper, we stack only two hourglasses to balance accuracy and efficiency.

### 4.3 Comparison with Different Baselines

To demonstrate the effectiveness of the proposed JGR and P2O module, we compare them with related baseline methods. The results are shown in Table 4.

**JGR vs. Attention.** To verify the effectiveness of the proposed JGR module, we design an attention-based baseline model where the JGR module is replaced with an attention module to calculate the weights of pixels for locating the joints. The flowchart of the baseline model can be found in Fig. 3. As shown in Table 4, the JGR module outperforms the attention module by reducing the mean 3D distance error 0.43 mm on the NYU dataset, while having fewer parameters. It demonstrates that the JGR module is indeed useful for better local feature learning.

**P2O vs. Differentiable Heat-Map (DHM).** To demonstrate the effectiveness of the proposed P2O module, we compare our model with a model by replacing the P2O module with the DHM module proposed in [13]. DHM implicitly learns the joints' depth maps and heatmap distributions, while our P2O explicitly estimates the offsets from pixels to joints. It can be seen from Table 4 that our P2O module surpasses the DHM module by reducing the mean 3D distance error 8.69 mm to 8.29 mm on NYU, which demonstrates the superiority of the proposed P2O module.

**Table 5.** Comparison with previous state-of-the-art methods on the ICVL, NYU and MSRA dataset. Mean error indicates the average 3D distance error. Type DR and DP indicate the direct regression-based method and dense prediction-based method, respectively. #Params indicates the parameter quantity of the whole network. Speed indicates the running speed during testing.

| Method | Mean error (mm) | | | Type | #Params | Speed (fps) |
|---|---|---|---|---|---|---|
| | ICVL | NYU | MSRA | | | |
| DeepModel [50] | 11.56 | 17.04 | – | DR | – | – |
| DeepPrior [26] | 10.40 | 19.73 | – | DR | – | – |
| DeepPrior++ [25] | 8.10 | 12.24 | 9.50 | DR | – | 30.0 |
| REN-4x6x6 [12] | 7.63 | 13.39 | – | DR | – | – |
| REN-9x6x6 [12] | 7.31 | 12.69 | 9.70 | DR | – | – |
| Pose-REN [2] | 6.79 | 11.81 | 8.65 | DR | – | – |
| 3DCNN [9] | – | 14.1 | 9.60 | DR | 104.9M | 215 |
| HandPointNet [7] | 6.94 | 10.54 | 8.50 | DR | 2.58M | 48.0 |
| SHPR-Net [3] | 7.22 | 10.78 | 7.76 | DR | – | – |
| CrossInfoNet [6] | 6.73 | 10.08 | 7.86 | DR | 23.8M | 124.5 |
| DenseReg [43] | 7.30 | 10.2 | **7.20** | DP | 5.8M | 27.8 |
| Point-to-Point [10] | 6.30 | 9.10 | 7.70 | DP | 4.3M | 41.8 |
| V2V-PoseNet [22] | 6.28 | 8.42 | 7.59 | DP | 457.5M | 3.5 |
| Point-to-Pose Voting [17] | – | 8.99 | – | DP | – | 80.0 |
| A2J [45] | 6.46 | 8.61 | – | DP | 44.7M | 105.1 |
| JGR-P2O (Ours) | **6.02** | **8.29** | 7.55 | DP | 1.4M | 111.2 |

## 4.4   Comparison with State-of-the-Art

We compare our proposed JGR-P2O with state-of-the-art deep learning-based methods, including both dense prediction-based methods: dense regression network (DenseReg) [43], Point-to-Point [10], Point-to-Pose Voting [17], A2J [45], and V2V [22], and direct regression-based methods: model-based method (Deep-Model) [50], DeepPrior [26], improved DeepPrior (DeepPrior++) [25], region ensemble network (Ren-4x6x6 and Ren-9x6x6 [12]), Pose-guided REN (Pose-Ren) [2], 3DCNN [9], HandPointNet [7], SHPR-Net [3] and CrossInfoNet [6]. The percentages of success frames over different error thresholds and mean 3D distance errors are shown in Fig. 4 and Table 5, respectively.

It can be seen that dense prediction-based methods are generally superior to direct regression-based methods. As shown in Table 5, our method can achieve the lowest mean estimation errors (6.02 mm and 8.29 mm) on the ICVL and NYU dataset. Figure 4 also shows that the proportions of success frames of our method are highest when the error thresholds are lower 30 mm and 50 mm on the ICVL and NYU dataset, respectively. Our method obtains the second-lowest estimation error (7.55 mm) on the MSRA dataset, which is only 0.35 mm higher than the estimation error (7.20 mm) of DenseReg [43].

Table 5 also shows that our method has the minimum model size and fastest running speed, compared with state-of-the-art dense prediction-based methods. Specifically, the total parameter quantity of our network is only 1.4M, and the running speed of our method is 111.2 fps, including 2.0 ms for reading and pre-processing image, and 7.0 ms for network inference on a NVIDIA 1080Ti GPU.

More experimental analysis including qualitative results can be found in the supplementary material.

## 5    Conclusions

In this work, we propose a new prediction network (JGR-P2O) for 3D hand pose estimation from single depth images. Within JGR-P2O the GCN-based joint graph reasoning module can help to learn better local feature representation by explicitly modeling the dependencies among joints and the relations between pixels and joints, and the pixel-to-offset prediction module unifies the dense pixel-wise offset predictions and direct joint regression for end-to-end training, fully exploiting the 2.5D property of depth images. Extensive experiments demonstrate the superiority of the JGR-P2O concerning for both accuracy and efficiency.

## References

1. Cai, Y., et al.: Exploiting spatial-temporal relationships for 3D pose estimation via graph convolutional networks. In: Proceedings of the IEEE International Conference on Computer Vision, pp. 2272–2281 (2019)
2. Chen, X., Wang, G., Guo, H., Zhang, C.: Pose guided structured region ensemble network for cascaded hand pose estimation. Neurocomputing **395**, 138–149 (2019)
3. Chen, X., Wang, G., Zhang, C., Kim, T.K., Ji, X.: SHPR-Net: deep semantic hand pose regression from point clouds. IEEE Access **6**, 43425–43439 (2018)
4. Chu, X., Yang, W., Ouyang, W., Ma, C., Yuille, A.L., Wang, X.: Multi-context attention for human pose estimation. In: Proceedings of the IEEE Conference on Computer Vision and Pattern Recognition, pp. 1831–1840 (2017)
5. Defferrard, M., Bresson, X., Vandergheynst, P.: Convolutional neural networks on graphs with fast localized spectral filtering. In: Advances in Neural Information Processing Systems, pp. 3844–3852 (2016)
6. Du, K., Lin, X., Sun, Y., Ma, X.: CrossInfoNet: multi-task information sharing based hand pose estimation. In: Proceedings of the IEEE Conference on Computer Vision and Pattern Recognition, pp. 9896–9905 (2019)
7. Ge, L., Cai, Y., Weng, J., Yuan, J.: Hand PointNet: 3D hand pose estimation using point sets. In: Proceedings of the IEEE Conference on Computer Vision and Pattern Recognition, pp. 8417–8426 (2018)
8. Ge, L., Liang, H., Yuan, J., Thalmann, D.: Robust 3D hand pose estimation in single depth images: from single-view CNN to multi-view CNNs. In: Proceedings of the IEEE Conference on Computer Vision and Pattern Recognition, pp. 3593–3601 (2016)

9. Ge, L., Liang, H., Yuan, J., Thalmann, D.: 3D convolutional neural networks for efficient and robust hand pose estimation from single depth images. In: Proceedings of the IEEE Conference on Computer Vision and Pattern Recognition, pp. 1991–2000 (2017)

10. Ge, L., Ren, Z., Yuan, J.: Point-to-point regression PointNet for 3D hand pose estimation. In: Ferrari, V., Hebert, M., Sminchisescu, C., Weiss, Y. (eds.) ECCV 2018. LNCS, vol. 11217, pp. 489–505. Springer, Cham (2018). https://doi.org/10.1007/978-3-030-01261-8_29

11. Guleryuz, O.G., Kaeser-Chen, C.: Fast lifting for 3D hand pose estimation in AR/VR applications. In: 2018 25th IEEE International Conference on Image Processing (ICIP), pp. 106–110. IEEE (2018)

12. Guo, H., Wang, G., Chen, X., Zhang, C.: Towards good practices for deep 3D hand pose estimation. arXiv preprint arXiv:1707.07248 (2017)

13. Iqbal, U., Molchanov, P., Breuel, T., Gall, J., Kautz, J.: Hand pose estimation via latent 2.5D heatmap regression. In: Ferrari, V., Hebert, M., Sminchisescu, C., Weiss, Y. (eds.) ECCV 2018. LNCS, vol. 11215, pp. 125–143. Springer, Cham (2018). https://doi.org/10.1007/978-3-030-01252-6_8

14. Khamis, S., Taylor, J., Shotton, J., Keskin, C., Izadi, S., Fitzgibbon, A.: Learning an efficient model of hand shape variation from depth images. In: Proceedings of the IEEE Conference on Computer Vision and Pattern Recognition, pp. 2540–2548 (2015)

15. Kipf, T.N., Welling, M.: Semi-supervised classification with graph convolutional networks. arXiv preprint arXiv:1609.02907 (2016)

16. Li, M., Chen, S., Chen, X., Zhang, Y., Wang, Y., Tian, Q.: Actional-structural graph convolutional networks for skeleton-based action recognition. In: Proceedings of the IEEE Conference on Computer Vision and Pattern Recognition, pp. 3595–3603 (2019)

17. Li, S., Lee, D.: Point-to-pose voting based hand pose estimation using residual permutation equivariant layer. In: Proceedings of the IEEE Conference on Computer Vision and Pattern Recognition, pp. 11927–11936 (2019)

18. Li, Y., Gupta, A.: Beyond grids: learning graph representations for visual recognition. In: Advances in Neural Information Processing Systems, pp. 9225–9235 (2018)

19. Liang, X., Hu, Z., Zhang, H., Lin, L., Xing, E.P.: Symbolic graph reasoning meets convolutions. In: Advances in Neural Information Processing Systems, pp. 1853–1863 (2018)

20. Madadi, M., Escalera, S., Baró, X., Gonzalez, J.: End-to-end global to local CNN learning for hand pose recovery in depth data. arXiv preprint arXiv:1705.09606 (2017)

21. Monti, F., Boscaini, D., Masci, J., Rodola, E., Svoboda, J., Bronstein, M.M.: Geometric deep learning on graphs and manifolds using mixture model CNNs. In: Proceedings of the IEEE Conference on Computer Vision and Pattern Recognition, pp. 5115–5124 (2017)

22. Moon, G., Yong Chang, J., Mu Lee, K.: V2V-PoseNet: voxel-to-voxel prediction network for accurate 3D hand and human pose estimation from a single depth map. In: Proceedings of the IEEE Conference on Computer Vision and Pattern Recognition, pp. 5079–5088 (2018)

23. Mueller, F., Mehta, D., Sotnychenko, O., Sridhar, S., Casas, D., Theobalt, C.: Real-time hand tracking under occlusion from an egocentric RGB-D sensor. In: Proceedings of the IEEE International Conference on Computer Vision, pp. 1284–1293 (2017)

24. Newell, A., Yang, K., Deng, J.: Stacked hourglass networks for human pose estimation. In: Leibe, B., Matas, J., Sebe, N., Welling, M. (eds.) ECCV 2016. LNCS, vol. 9912, pp. 483–499. Springer, Cham (2016). https://doi.org/10.1007/978-3-319-46484-8_29

25. Oberweger, M., Lepetit, V.: DeepPrior++: improving fast and accurate 3D hand pose estimation. In: Proceedings of the IEEE International Conference on Computer Vision, pp. 585–594 (2017)

26. Oberweger, M., Wohlhart, P., Lepetit, V.: Hands deep in deep learning for hand pose estimation. arXiv preprint arXiv:1502.06807 (2015)

27. Oberweger, M., Wohlhart, P., Lepetit, V.: Training a feedback loop for hand pose estimation. In: Proceedings of the IEEE International Conference on Computer Vision, pp. 3316–3324 (2015)

28. Oberweger, M., Wohlhart, P., Lepetit, V.: Generalized feedback loop for joint hand-object pose estimation. IEEE Trans. Pattern Anal. Mach. Intell. **42**, 1898–1912 (2019)

29. Pavlakos, G., Zhou, X., Derpanis, K.G., Daniilidis, K.: Coarse-to-fine volumetric prediction for single-image 3D human pose. In: Proceedings of the IEEE Conference on Computer Vision and Pattern Recognition, pp. 7025–7034 (2017)

30. Qi, C.R., Su, H., Mo, K., Guibas, L.J.: PointNet: deep learning on point sets for 3D classification and segmentation. In: Proceedings of the IEEE Conference on Computer Vision and Pattern Recognition, pp. 652–660 (2017)

31. Qi, C.R., Yi, L., Su, H., Guibas, L.J.: PointNet++: deep hierarchical feature learning on point sets in a metric space. In: Advances in Neural Information Processing Systems, pp. 5099–5108 (2017)

32. Remelli, E., Tkach, A., Tagliasacchi, A., Pauly, M.: Low-dimensionality calibration through local anisotropic scaling for robust hand model personalization. In: Proceedings of the IEEE International Conference on Computer Vision, pp. 2535–2543 (2017)

33. Shi, L., Zhang, Y., Cheng, J., Lu, H.: Two-stream adaptive graph convolutional networks for skeleton-based action recognition. In: Proceedings of the IEEE Conference on Computer Vision and Pattern Recognition, pp. 12026–12035 (2019)

34. Sun, X., Wei, Y., Liang, S., Tang, X., Sun, J.: Cascaded hand pose regression. In: Proceedings of the IEEE Conference on Computer Vision and Pattern Recognition, pp. 824–832 (2015)

35. Supancic, J.S., Rogez, G., Yang, Y., Shotton, J., Ramanan, D.: Depth-based hand pose estimation: data, methods, and challenges. In: Proceedings of the IEEE International Conference on Computer Vision, pp. 1868–1876 (2015)

36. Supančič, J.S., Rogez, G., Yang, Y., Shotton, J., Ramanan, D.: Depth-based hand pose estimation: methods, data, and challenges. Int. J. Comput. Vis. **126**(11), 1180–1198 (2018)

37. Tang, D., Jin Chang, H., Tejani, A., Kim, T.K.: Latent regression forest: structured estimation of 3D articulated hand posture. In: Proceedings of the IEEE Conference on Computer Vision and Pattern Recognition, pp. 3786–3793 (2014)

38. Tang, D., et al.: Opening the black box: hierarchical sampling optimization for hand pose estimation. IEEE Trans. Pattern Anal. Mach. Intell. **41**, 2161–2175 (2018)

39. Tompson, J., Stein, M., Lecun, Y., Perlin, K.: Real-time continuous pose recovery of human hands using convolutional networks. ACM Trans. Graph. (ToG) **33**(5), 169 (2014)

40. Tzionas, D., Ballan, L., Srikantha, A., Aponte, P., Pollefeys, M., Gall, J.: Capturing hands in action using discriminative salient points and physics simulation. Int. J. Comput. Vis. **118**(2), 172–193 (2016)
41. Veličković, P., Cucurull, G., Casanova, A., Romero, A., Lio, P., Bengio, Y.: Graph attention networks. arXiv preprint arXiv:1710.10903 (2017)
42. Wan, C., Probst, T., Van Gool, L., Yao, A.: Crossing nets: combining GANs and VAEs with a shared latent space for hand pose estimation. In: Proceedings of the IEEE Conference on Computer Vision and Pattern Recognition, pp. 680–689 (2017)
43. Wan, C., Probst, T., Van Gool, L., Yao, A.: Dense 3D regression for hand pose estimation. In: Proceedings of the IEEE Conference on Computer Vision and Pattern Recognition, pp. 5147–5156 (2018)
44. Wan, C., Yao, A., Van Gool, L.: Hand pose estimation from local surface normals. In: Leibe, B., Matas, J., Sebe, N., Welling, M. (eds.) ECCV 2016. LNCS, vol. 9907, pp. 554–569. Springer, Cham (2016). https://doi.org/10.1007/978-3-319-46487-9_34
45. Xiong, F., et al.: A2J: anchor-to-joint regression network for 3D articulated pose estimation from a single depth image. In: Proceedings of the IEEE International Conference on Computer Vision, pp. 793–802 (2019)
46. Yan, S., Xiong, Y., Lin, D.: Spatial temporal graph convolutional networks for skeleton-based action recognition. In: Thirty-Second AAAI Conference on Artificial Intelligence (2018)
47. Ye, Q., Yuan, S., Kim, T.-K.: Spatial attention deep net with partial PSO for hierarchical hybrid hand pose estimation. In: Leibe, B., Matas, J., Sebe, N., Welling, M. (eds.) ECCV 2016. LNCS, vol. 9912, pp. 346–361. Springer, Cham (2016). https://doi.org/10.1007/978-3-319-46484-8_21
48. Yuan, S., et al.: Depth-based 3D hand pose estimation: from current achievements to future goals. In: Proceedings of the IEEE Conference on Computer Vision and Pattern Recognition, pp. 2636–2645 (2018)
49. Yuan, S., Ye, Q., Garcia-Hernando, G., Kim, T.K.: The 2017 hands in the million challenge on 3D hand pose estimation. arXiv preprint arXiv:1707.02237 (2017)
50. Zhou, X., Wan, Q., Zhang, W., Xue, X., Wei, Y.: Model-based deep hand pose estimation. arXiv preprint arXiv:1606.06854 (2016)

# Dynamic Group Convolution for Accelerating Convolutional Neural Networks

Zhuo Su[1], Linpu Fang[2], Wenxiong Kang[2], Dewen Hu[3], Matti Pietikäinen[1], and Li Liu[3,1(✉)]

[1] Center for Machine Vision and Signal Analysis, University of Oulu, Oulu, Finland
li.liu@oulu.fi
[2] South China University of Technology, Guangzhou, China
[3] National University of Defense Technology, Changsha, China

**Abstract.** Replacing normal convolutions with group convolutions can significantly increase the computational efficiency of modern deep convolutional networks, which has been widely adopted in compact network architecture designs. However, existing group convolutions undermine the original network structures by cutting off some connections permanently resulting in significant accuracy degradation. In this paper, we propose dynamic group convolution (DGC) that adaptively selects which part of input channels to be connected within each group for individual samples on the fly. Specifically, we equip each group with a small feature selector to automatically select the most important input channels conditioned on the input images. Multiple groups can adaptively capture abundant and complementary visual/semantic features for each input image. The DGC preserves the original network structure and has similar computational efficiency as the conventional group convolution simultaneously. Extensive experiments on multiple image classification benchmarks including CIFAR-10, CIFAR-100 and ImageNet demonstrate its superiority over the existing group convolution techniques and dynamic execution methods. The code is available at https://github.com/zhuogege1943/dgc.

**Keywords:** Group convolution · Dynamic execution · Efficient network architecture

## 1 Introduction

Deep convolutional neural networks (CNNs) have achieved significant successes in a wide range of computer vision tasks including image classification [5], object

---

Z. Su and L. Fang—Equal contributions.

---

**Electronic supplementary material** The online version of this chapter (https://doi.org/10.1007/978-3-030-58539-6_9) contains supplementary material, which is available to authorized users.

A. Vedaldi et al. (Eds.): ECCV 2020, LNCS 12351, pp. 138–155, 2020.
https://doi.org/10.1007/978-3-030-58539-6_9

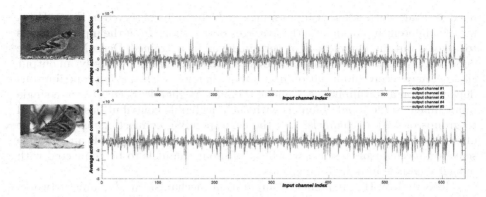

**Fig. 1.** The average contributions from the input channels to several output channels at a certain layer in a trained DenseNet [20] are depicted. The X-axis and Y-axis indicate the input channels and their average contributions to the output channels. For a pair of input and output channel, an activation map is firstly obtained by convolution with the corresponding filter, and the average contribution from this input channel to the output channel is calculated as the average value of the activation map. It can be seen that such contributions vary a lot across different input-output pairs, which is the main observation behind the motivation of the proposed DGC.

detection [30], and semantic segmentation [36]. Earlier studies [11,20] found that deeper and wider networks could obtain better performance, which results in a large number of huge and complex models being designed in the community. However, these models are very compute-intensive making them impossible to be deployed on edge devices with strict latency requirements and limited computing resources. In recent years, more and more researchers turn to study network compression techniques or design computation-efficient architectures to solve this troublesome.

Group convolution, which was first introduced in AlexNet [25] for accelerating the training process across two GPUs, has been comprehensively applied in computation-efficient network architecture designs [4,37,45,52,55]. Standard group convolution equally split the input and output channels in a convolution layer into $G$ mutually exclusive groups while performing normal convolution operation within individual groups, which reduces the computation burden by $G$ times in theory. The predefined group partition in standard group convolution may be suboptimal, recent studies [19,48] further propose learnable group convolution that learns the connections between input and output features in each group during the training process.

By analyzing the existing group convolutions, it can be found that they have two key disadvantages: (1) They weaken the representation capability of the normal convolution by introducing sparse neuron connections and suffer from decreasing performance especially for those difficult samples; (2) They have fixed neuron connection routines, regardless of the specific properties of individual inputs. However, the dependencies among input and output channels are not fixed and vary with different input images, which can be observed in Fig. 1. Here, for two different input images, the average contributions from the input channels to several output channels at a certain layer in a trained DenseNet [20] are depicted. Two interesting phenomenons can be found in Fig. 1. Firstly, an output channel may receive information from input channels with varying contributions depending on a certain image, some of them are negligible. Secondly, for a single input image, some input channels with such negligible contributions correspond to groups of output channels, *i.e.*, the corresponding connections could be cut off without influences on the final results. It indicates that it needs an adaptive selection mechanism to select which set of input channels to be connected with output channels in individual groups.

Motivated by the dynamical computation mechanism in dynamic networks [9,17,29], in this paper, we propose dynamic group convolution (DGC) to adaptively select the most related input channels for each group while keeping the full structure of the original networks. Specifically, we introduce a tiny auxiliary feature selector for each group to dynamically decide which part of input channels to be connected based on the activations of all of input channels. Multiple groups can capture different complementary visual/semantic features of input images, making the DGC powerful to learn plentiful feature representations. Note that the computation overhead added by the auxiliary feature selectors are negligible compared with the speed-up provided by the sparse group convolution operations. In addition, the proposed DGC is compatible with various exiting deep CNNs and can be easily optimized in an end-to-end fashion.

We embed the DGC into popular deep CNN models including ResNet [11], CondenseNet [19] and MobileNetV2 [44], and evaluate its effectiveness on three common image recognition benchmarks: CIFAR-10, CIFAR-100 and ImageNet. The experimental results indicate the DGC outperforms the exiting group convolution techniques and dynamic execution methods.

## 2    Related Work

**Efficient Architecture Design.** As special cases of sparsely connected convolution, group convolution and its extreme version, *i.e.* depth-wise separable convolution, are most popular modules employed in efficient architecture designs. AlexNet [25] firstly uses group convolution to handle the problem of memory limitation. ResNeXt [52] further applies group convolution to implement a set of transformations and demonstrates its effectiveness. A series of subsequent researches use group convolution or depth-wise separable convolution to design computation-efficient CNNs [15,37,44,45,54,55]. Instead of predefining the connection models, CondenseNet [19] and FLGC [48] propose to automatically learn the connections of group convolution during the training process. All these exiting group convolutions have fixed connections during inference, inevitably weakening the representation capability of the original normal convolutions due to the sparse structures. Our proposed DGC can effectively solve this

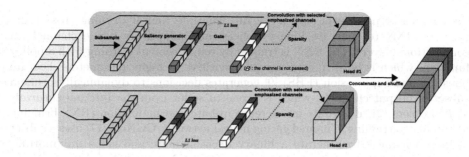

**Fig. 2.** Overview of a DGC layer. For a simple illustration, we set the number of channels as 8 for both input and output volume and the number of heads as 2. Each head is responsible for generating half of the output volume, with different part of the input volume, by respectively using a saliency guided channel selector (gate). Here, white blocks after the gate represents the corresponding channel would not take part in the convolution. (Color figure online)

troublesome by employing dynamic execution strategy that keeps sparse computation without undermining original network structures.

**Network Compression.** Generally, compression methods can be categorized into five types: quantization [1,3,7,31,43], knowledge distillation [14,23,32,41, 53], low-rank decomposition [6,22,38,56], weight sparsification [10,26,51], and filter pruning [13,27,34,40]. Quantization methods accelerate deep CNNs by replacing high-precision float point operations with low-precision fixed point ones, which usually incurs significantly accuracy drop. Knowledge distillation methods aim to learn a small student model by mimicking the output or feature distributions of a larger teacher model. Low-rank decomposition methods reduce the computation by factorizing the convolution kernels. Weight sparsification methods removes individual connections between neural nodes resulting in irregular models, while filter pruning methods, which our method is most related to, directly cut off entire filters keeping the regular architectures. Generally, those compression methods usually need several rounds to obtain the final compact models. On the contrary, the proposed DGC can be easily optimized with any exiting networks in an end-to-end manner. Note that the filter pruning removes some channels after training, which loses the capabilities of the original CNNs permanently, while our method keeps the capabilities by the dynamic channel selection scheme.

**Dynamic Network.** In contrast to the one-size-fit-all paradigm, dynamic networks [8,18,28,33,42,49,50] dynamically execute different modules across a deep network for individual inputs. One kind of method [2,18,42] sets multiple classifiers at different places in a deep network and apply early exiting strategy to implement dynamic inference. Another line of work [8,28,29,33,47,49,50] learns auxiliary controllers or gating units to decide which parts of layers or channels could be skipped for extracting intermediate feature representations. Among those dynamic execution methods, our proposed DGC is mostly motivated by the channel or pixel-level ones [9,17,29]. Runtime Neural Pruning (RNP) [29] learns a RNN to generate binary policies and adaptively prune channels in convolutional layers. The RNN is trained by reinforcement learning with a policy function, which is hard to converge and sensitive to hyper-parameters. Feature boosting and suppression (FBS) [9] generates decisions to dynamically prune a subset of output channels, which is prone to suffer from the *internal covariate shift* problem [21] due to its interference in batch normalization (BN), bringing instability to training. Channel gating neural network (CGNet) [17] uses a subset of input channels to generate a binary decision map, and skips unimportant computation in the rest of input channels. The CGNet actually works in a semi-dynamic way and uses a complex approximating non-differentiable gate function to learn the binary decisions. In contrast to these methods, our proposed DGC works better to achieve stable training with dynamic channel selection, and can be easily optimized using common SGD algorithms.

## 3    Dynamic Group Convolution

### 3.1    Group Convolution and Dynamic Channel Pruning Revisiting

Consider how a CNN layer works with groups, which can be generalized as:

$$\boldsymbol{x}' = [\hat{f}(\boldsymbol{x}^1), \hat{f}(\boldsymbol{x}^2), \dots, \hat{f}(\boldsymbol{x}^N)], \tag{1}$$

$$\hat{f}(\boldsymbol{x}^i) = f(\boldsymbol{x}^i, \boldsymbol{\theta}^i) \cdot \pi(\boldsymbol{x}^i, \boldsymbol{\phi}^i), \tag{2}$$

where $\boldsymbol{x} \in \mathbb{R}^{C \times H \times W}$, $\boldsymbol{x}' \in \mathbb{R}^{C' \times H' \times W'}$ are the input and output of the current layer respectively, $\boldsymbol{x}^i \subseteq \boldsymbol{x}$ is a subset of input channels that is divided into the *ith* group, $N$ is the number of groups, $f$ executes the conventional convolution using parameter $\boldsymbol{\theta}$, while the meaning of $\pi$ is case-dependent, with its parameter $\boldsymbol{\phi}$, which would be discussed below.

In a standard convolution layer, $N = 1$ and $\pi \equiv \mathbf{1}$. While a standard group convolution (SGC) evenly allocates equal number of channels in $\boldsymbol{x}$ to each group with hard assignments, thus reducing the computation cost by $N$ times. On the other hand, studies show that although complemented with channel permutation before performing group convolution, SGC is not always optimal [19,48], and introduce a learning strategy to soften the hard assignments, leading to a better group allocation. Such soft assignments allow each channel in $\boldsymbol{x}$ to automatically choose its fitted group(s). To achieve the soft assignments, common methods are to add a group-lasso loss to induce group-level weights sparsity or a learnable binary decision matrix [19,48]. However, these methods can not be easily transferred to dynamic versions due to their "staticness".

In a convolution layer with dynamic execution [8,9,17,29] and $N = 1$, a on-the-fly gate score or saliency is pre-calculated through a prediction function (represented as $\pi$ in (2)) for each output cell that needs to be computed by $f$. The cell could be an output channel [9,29] or a pixel in the output feature maps [8,17]. Computation of the output cell in $f$ is skipped if the corresponding saliency is small enough. Denoting the saliency vector (output of $\pi$, with size equal to the number of output cells) as $g$, sparsity for $g$ is implemented by reinforcement learning in [29], which is hard to be optimized. [8,9] associate $g$ with a lasso loss, which is in fact a L1 norm regularization:

$$L_{lasso} = \|g_1, g_2, \ldots\|_1 . \tag{3}$$

In [8], $\pi$ and $f$ are homogeneous functions (both are convolutions and compute tensors with the same shape), halving $\phi$ and doubling $\theta$ can always lead to decrease in (3), making the lasso loss meaningless. [9] regards $g$, where $g \in \mathbb{R}^{1 \times C'}$, as a replacement of the BN scaling factors, so the following BN layer is modified by eliminating the scaling parameters. In such case, function $\pi$ need to be carefully designed and trained due to the *internal covariate shift* problem [21] (will be analyzed in the next section).

Different from the above mentioned dynamic execution methods that skips computations for some output cells, the dynamic mechanism in DGC conducts $g$ on the input channels to sparsify their connections with the output channels, while keeping the shape of the output volume unchanged. Embedding into group executions, DGC actually performs like the multi-head self-attention mechanism proposed in [46]. Thereby, the Eq. 2 is modified as:

$$\hat{f}(\boldsymbol{x}^i) = f(\boldsymbol{x}^i \cdot \pi(\boldsymbol{x}^i, \boldsymbol{\phi}^i), \boldsymbol{\theta}^i). \tag{4}$$

In this case, the scale-sensitive problem can be easily removed by connecting an untouched BN layer (see Sect. 3.2). Note that in practical computation, $\boldsymbol{\theta}^i$ is also partially selected according to the selected channels in $\boldsymbol{x}^i$ (see Eq. 7).

## 3.2 Group-Wise Dynamic Execution

An illustration of the framework of a DGC layer can be seen in Fig. 2. We split the output channels into multiple groups, each of them is generated by an auxiliary head that equips with an input channel selector to decide which part of input channels should be selected for convolution calculation (see the blue and green areas in Fig. 2). First, the input channel selector in each head adopts a gating strategy to dynamically determine the most important subset of input channels according to their importance scores generated by a saliency generator. Then, the normal convolution is conducted based on the selected subset of input channels generating the output channels in each head. Finally, the output channels from different heads are concatenated and shuffled, which would be connected to a BN layer and non-linear activation layer.

**Saliency Generator.** The saliency generator assigns each input channel a score representing its importance. Each head has a specific saliency generator, which encourages different heads to use different subpart of the input channels and achieve diversified feature representations. In this paper, we follow the design of the SE block in [16] to design the saliency generator. For the *ith* head, the saliency vector $\boldsymbol{g}^i$ is calculated as:

$$\boldsymbol{g}^i = \pi(\boldsymbol{x}^i, \boldsymbol{\phi}^i) = \pi(\boldsymbol{x}, \boldsymbol{\phi}^i) = (W^i(p(\boldsymbol{x})) + \boldsymbol{\beta}^i)_+, \tag{5}$$

where $g^i \in \mathbb{R}^{1 \times C}$ represents the saliency vector for the input channels, $(z)_+$ denotes the ReLU activation, $p$ reduces each feature map in $x$ into a single scalar, such as global average pooling as we used in our experiments, $\beta^i$ and $W^i$ are trainable parameters representing the biases and a two-step transformation function mapping $\mathbb{R}^{1 \times C} \mapsto \mathbb{R}^{1 \times C/d} \mapsto \mathbb{R}^{1 \times C}$ with $d$ being the squeezing rate. Note that $x^i$ in Eq. 4 is equal to the whole input volume $x$ here, meaning all the input channels would be considered as candidates in each of the heads.

**Gating Strategy.** Once the saliency vector is obtained, the next step is to determine which part of the input channels should join the following convolution in the current head. We can either use a head-wise or globally network-wise threshold that decides a certain number of passed gates out of all for each head in a DGC layer. We adopt the head-wise threshold here for simplicity and the global threshold will be discussed in Sect. 4.3.

Given a target pruning rate $\xi$, the head-wise threshold $\tau^i$ in $ith$ head meets the equation where $|\mathcal{S}|$ means the length of set $\mathcal{S}$:

$$\xi = \frac{|\{g^i \mid g^i < \tau^i, g^i \in g^i\}|}{|\{g^i \mid g^i \in g^i\}|}. \tag{6}$$

The saliency goes with two streams, $i.e.$, any of channels in the input end with its saliency smaller than the threshold is screened out, while anyone in the remaining channels is amplified with its corresponding $g$, leading to a group of selected emphasized channels $y^i \in \mathbb{R}^{(1-\xi)C \times H \times W}$. Assuming the number of heads is $\mathcal{H}$, the convolution in the $ith$ head is conducted with $y^i$ and the corresponding filters $w^i$ ($w^i \subset \theta^i$, $\theta^i \in \mathbb{R}^{k \times k \times C \times \frac{C'}{\mathcal{H}}}$ and $k$ is the kernel size):

$$\hat{x}^i = x[v, :, :], \quad \hat{g}^i = g^i[v], \quad w^i = \theta^i[:, :, v, :], \quad v = \mathcal{I}_{top}\lceil(1-\xi)C\rceil(g^i)$$
$$x'^i = \hat{f}(x^i) = f(\underbrace{x \cdot \pi(x, \phi^i)}_{\text{before pruning}}, \theta^i) = f(\underbrace{\hat{x}^i \cdot \hat{g}^i}_{\text{after pruning}}, w^i) = f(y^i, w^i) = y^i \otimes w^i,$$

$$\tag{7}$$

where $\mathcal{I}_{top}\lceil k\rceil(z)$ returns the indices of the k largest elements in $z$, the output $x'^i \in \mathbb{R}^{\frac{C'}{\mathcal{H}} \times H' \times W'}$, $\otimes$ means the regular convolution. At the end of the DGC layer, individual outputs gathered from multiple heads are simply concatenated and shuffled, producing $x'$. The gating strategy is unbiased for weights updating since all the channels own the equal chance to be selected.

To induce sparsity, we also add a lasso loss following Eq. 3 as

$$L_{lasso} = \lambda \frac{1}{\mathcal{L}\mathcal{H}} \sum_{l=1}^{\mathcal{L}} \sum_{i=1}^{\mathcal{H}} \left\| g^{l,i} \right\|_1 \tag{8}$$

to the total loss, where $\mathcal{L}$ is the number of DGC layers and $\lambda$ is a pre-defined parameter.

**Computation Cost.** Regular convolution using the weight tensor $\theta$ with kernel size $k$ takes $k^2 C'CH'W'$ *multiply-accumulate operations* (MACs). In a DGC layer for each head, the saliency generator and convolution part costs $\frac{2C^2}{d}$ and

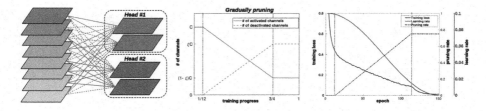

**Fig. 3.** The training process of a DGC network. We gradually increase the number of deactivated input channels in each DGC layer with three stages, using a cosine shape learning rate, to make the first stage (first 1/12 of the training epochs, where no channels are pruned) warm up the network, the second stage perform gradual pruning, and the last stage (last 1/4 epochs) fine-tune the sparsified structure. The right figure shows an example of training process on the CIFAR-10 dataset, with pruning rate 0.75 and total 150 epochs. The blue curve shows that even after entering the second stage, the training loss smoothly drops towards 0. (Color figure online)

$k^2(1 - \xi)C\frac{C'}{\mathcal{H}}H'W'$ MACs respectively. Therefore, the overall MAC saving of a DGC layer is:

$$(k^2CC'H'W')/(\mathcal{H}(k^2(1-\xi)C\frac{C'}{\mathcal{H}}H'W'+\frac{2C^2}{d})) = 1/((1-\xi)+\frac{2\mathcal{H}C}{dk^2C'H'W'}) \approx 1/(1-\xi).$$

As a result, the number of heads $\mathcal{H}$ has negligible influence on the total computation cost.

**Invariant to Scaling.** As discussed in Sect. 3.1, [9] implements a convolution layer (including normalization and non-linear activation) by replacing BN scaling factors with the saliency vector:

$$\mathfrak{L}(\boldsymbol{x}) = (\boldsymbol{g} \cdot \mathsf{norm}(\mathsf{conv}(\boldsymbol{x},\boldsymbol{\theta})) + \boldsymbol{\beta})_+,$$

where $\mathsf{norm}(z)$ normalizes each output channel with mean 0 and variance 1. Since $\boldsymbol{g} = \pi(\boldsymbol{x},\boldsymbol{\phi})$ is dynamically generated, scaling in $\boldsymbol{\phi}$ first leads to scale change in $\boldsymbol{g}$ and then in $\mathfrak{L}(\boldsymbol{x})$, thus each sample has a self-dependent distribution, leading to the *internal covariate shift* problem during training on the whole dataset [21]. In contrast, the inference with a DGC layer is defined as (we denote $\boldsymbol{y}^i$ as $\boldsymbol{y}$ and $\boldsymbol{w}^i$ as $\boldsymbol{w}$ for convenience):

$$\mathfrak{L}(\boldsymbol{x}) = (\mathsf{batchnorm}(\mathsf{conv}(\boldsymbol{y},\boldsymbol{w})))_+.$$

Combining Eq. 7 and above equation, scaling in $\boldsymbol{\phi}$ leads to scale change in $\boldsymbol{g}$ while stops at $\boldsymbol{y}$. With the following batch normalization, the ill effects of the internal covariate shift can be effectively removed [21].

**Training DGC Networks.** We train our DGC network from scratch by an end-to-end manner, without the need of model pre-training. During backward propagation, for $\boldsymbol{\theta}$ which accompanies a decision process, gradients are calculated only for weights connected to selected channels during the forward pass, and safely set as 0 for others thanks to the unbiased gating strategy. To avoid abrupt changes in training loss while pruning, we gradually deactivate input channels along the training process with a cosine shape learning rate (see Fig. 3).

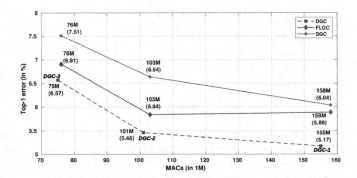

**Fig. 4.** Comparison with SGC and FLGC based on MobileNetV2 on CIFAR-10. For DGC, the width multiplier and the positions of the downsample layers are adjusted to obtain models with matched MACs comparing with SGC and FLGC. For DGC-1 and DGC-2, the downsample layers are set on the first layer of the *3rd* and *5th* block. While the first layer of the *2nd* and *4th* block are set as the downsample layers for DGC-3. DGC-1 sets the width multiplier to be 1, while both DGC-2 and DGC-3 set the width multiplier to be 0.75. The results of SGC and FLGC are copied from the FLGC paper [48].

## 4    Experiments

### 4.1    Experimental Settings

We evaluate the proposed DGC on three common image classification benchmarks: CIFAR-10, CIFAR-100 [24], and ImageNet (ILSVRC2012) [5]. The two CIFAR datasets both include 50K training images and 10K test images with 10 classes for CIFAR-10 and 100 classes for CIFAR-100. The ImageNet dataset consists of 1.28 million training images and 50K validation images from 1000 classes. For evaluations, we report detailed accuracy/MACs trade-off against different methods on both CIFAR and ImageNet dataset.

We choose previous popular models including ResNet [11], CondenseNet [19] and MobileNetV2 [44] as the baseline models and embed our proposed DGC into them for evaluations.

*ResNet with DGC.* ResNet is one of the most powerful models that has been extensively applied in many visual tasks. In this paper, we use the ResNet18 as the baseline model and replace the two $3 \times 3$ convolution layers in each residual block with the proposed DGC.

*MobileNetV2 with DGC.* MobileNetV2 [44] is a powerful efficient network architecture, which is designed for mobile applications. To further improve its efficiency, we replace the last $1 \times 1$ point-wise convolution layer in each inverted residual block with our proposed DGC.

*CondenseNet with DGC.* CondenseNet is also a popular efficient model, which combines the dense connectivity in DenseNet [20] with a learned group

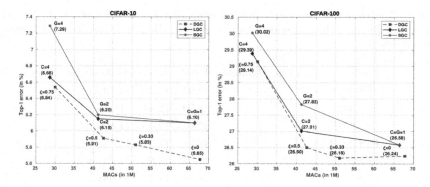

**Fig. 5.** Comparison with SGC and LGC based on CondenseNet on CIFAR-10 (left) and CIFAR-100 (right). The groups (heads) is set as 4 for both LGC and DGC. We change the pruning rate $\xi$ in DGC, *condensation factor* $C$ in LGC and the number of groups $G$ in SGC to control the model computation costs. Noting that for LGC and SGC, when $C = G = 1$, the two models actually share the same structure, corresponding to our DGC version when $\xi = 0$. While a DGC layer works in a self-attention way with $\mathcal{H}$ auxiliary saliency generators, making it better than its vanilla counterparts.

convolution (LGC) module. We compare against the LGC by replacing it with the proposed DGC.

All experiments are conducted using Pytorch [39] deep learning library. For both datasets, the standard data augmentation scheme is adopted as in [19]. All models are optimized using stochastic gradient descent (SGD) with Nesterov momentum with a momentum weight of 0.9, and the weight decay is set to be $10^{-4}$. Mini batch size is set as 64 and 256 for CIFAR and ImageNet, respectively. The cosine shape learning rate (Fig. 3) starts from 0.1 for ResNet/CondenseNet and 0.05 for MobileNetV2. Models are trained for 300 epochs on CIFAR and 150 epochs on ImageNet for MobileNetV2, 150 epochs on CIFAR and 120 epochs on ImageNet for CondenseNet, and 120 epochs for ResNet on ImageNet. By default we use 4 groups (heads) in each DGC layer.

## 4.2   Results on Cifar

We compare DGC with both SGC and previous state-of-the-art learnable group convolutions including CondenseNet [19] and FLGC [48] on CIFAR datasets to demonstrate the effectiveness of its dynamic selecting mechanism. We use MobileNetV2 as backbone and conduct comparison with SGC and FLGC. For comparison with CondenseNet, we employ the proposed modified DenseNet structure in CondenseNet with 50 layers as the baseline model.

**MobileNetV2.** We compare the proposed DGC with SGC and FLGC on CIFAR-10. Like the FLGC, we replace the last $1 \times 1$ convolution layer in each inverted residual block with the proposed DGC. For SGC and FLGC, models with different MACs are obtained by adjusting the number of groups in group

**Table 1.** Comparison of Top-1 and Top-5 classification error with state-of-the-art filter pruning and dynamic channel selection methods using ResNet-18 as the baseline model on ImageNet.

| Model | Group | Dynamic | Top-1 | Top-5 | MAC saving |
|-------|-------|---------|-------|-------|------------|
| SFP [12] | | | 32.90 | 12.22 | (1.72×) |
| NS [35] | | | 32.79 | 12.61 | (1.39×) |
| DCP [57] | | | 32.65 | 12.40 | (1.89×) |
| FPGM [13] | | | 31.59 | 11.52 | (1.53×) |
| LCCN [8] | | ✓ | 33.67 | 13.06 | (1.53×) |
| FBS [9] | | ✓ | 31.83 | 11.78 | (1.98×) |
| CGNet [17] | ✓ | ✓ | 31.70 | – | (2.03×) |
| **DGC** | ✓ | ✓ | **31.22** | **11.38** | **(2.04×)** |
| DGC-G | ✓ | ✓ | 31.37 | 11.56 | (2.08×) |

convolution layers. For our proposed DGC, we adjust the width multiplier and the positions of the downsample convolution layers (*i.e.*, with stride equals to 2) to obtain models with matched MACs. The pruning rate $\xi$ is set to be 0.65 for each head and 4 heads are employed in a DGC layer. The results are shown in Fig. 4. It can be seen that both DGC and FLGC outperforms SGC, while DGC can achieve lowest top-1 errors with less computation costs. Note that the group structures are still fixed in FLGC after training, which ignores the properties of single inputs and results in poor connections for some of them. By introducing dynamic feature selectors, our proposed DGC can adaptively select most related input channels for each group conditioned on the individual input images. The results indeed demonstrate the superiority of DGC compared with FLGC. Specifically, DGC achieves lower top-1 errors and computation cost (for example, 5.17% *vs.* 5.89% and 155M *vs.* 158M).

**CondenseNet.** We compare the proposed DGC with SGC and CondenseNet on both CIFAR-10 and CIFAR-100. CondenseNet adopts a LGC strategy to sparsify the compute-intensive $1 \times 1$ convolution layers and uses the group-lasso regularizer to gradually prune less important connections during training. The final model after training is also fixed like FLGC. We replace all the LGC layers in CondenseNet with the SGC or DGC structures under similar computation costs for comparison. The results are shown in Fig. 5. It also shows both DGC and LGC perform better than SGC due to the learnable soft channel assignments for groups. Meanwhile, DGC can perform better than LGC with less or similar MACs (for example, 5.83% *vs.* 6.10% and 51M *vs.* 66M on CIFAR-10, 26.18% *vs.* 26.58% and 51M *vs.* 66M on CIFAR-100), demonstrating that the dynamic computation scheme in DGC is superior to the static counterpart in LGC.

**Table 2.** Comparison of Top-1 and Top-5 classification error with state-of-the-art efficient CNNs on ImageNet.

| Model | Top-1 | Top-5 | MACs |
|---|---|---|---|
| MobileNetV1 [15] | 29.4 | 10.5 | 569M |
| ShuffleNet [55] | 29.1 | 10.2 | 524M |
| NASNet-A (N = 4) [58] | 26.0 | 8.4 | 564M |
| NASNet-B (N = 4) [58] | 27.2 | 8.7 | 488M |
| NASNet-C (N = 3) [58] | 27.5 | 9.0 | 558M |
| IGCV3-D [45] | 27.8 | – | 318M |
| MobileNetV2 [44] | 28.0 | 9.4 | 300M |
| CondenseNet [19] | 26.2 | 8.3 | 529M |
| CondenseNet-SGC | 29.0 | 9.9 | 529M |
| CondenseNet-FLGC [48] | 25.3 | 7.9 | 529M |
| MobileNetV2-DGC | 29.3 | 10.2 | 245M |
| CondenseNet-DGC | 25.4 | 7.8 | 549M |
| CondenseNet-DGC-G | 25.2 | 7.8 | 543M |

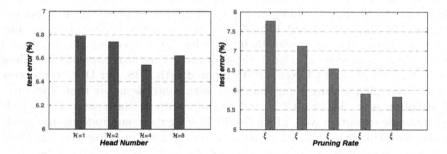

**Fig. 6.** Ablation study on head numbers and pruning rates (Color figure online)

### 4.3   Results on ImageNet

To further demonstrate the effectiveness of the proposed DGC, we compare it with state-of-the-art filter pruning and channel-level dynamic execution methods using ResNet18 as the baseline model on ImageNet. We also embed the DGC into the CondenseNet [19] and MobileNetV2 [44] (*i.e.*, CondenseNet-DGC and MobileNetV2-DGC) to compare with state-of-the-art efficient CNNs. For CondenseNet-DGC/SGC, the same structure as CondenseNet in [19] is used with LGC replaced by DGC/SGC. For MobileNetV2-DGC, the last $1 \times 1$ convolution layers in all inverted residual blocks in the original MobileNetV2 are replaced with DGC layers. We set $\mathcal{H} = 4$, $\xi = 0.75$ and $\lambda = 10^{-5}$ for all models. The results are reported in Tables 1 and 2. Here, for further exploration, we additionally adopt a global threshold (see appendix for detail) to give more

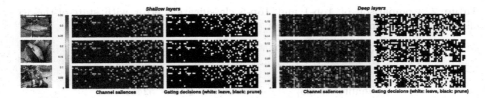

**Fig. 7.** Visualization of network sparse patterns for different input images. Each row represents a particular image. We compare the saliency vectors in shallow (*the 5–8th DGC layers*) and deep (*the 33–36th DGC layers*) DGC layers of the CondenseNet-DGC structure used in Sect. 4.3 and also output their corresponding pruning decisions as white-black pixels. In each saliency map (with 64 columns and 16 rows), columns mean different channels, each row indicates a certain head for a layer and every 4 rows represent a DGC layer since $\mathcal{H} = 4$.

flexibility to the DGC network. The corresponding models are noted with a suffix "*G*". Different from the head-wise threshold, the global threshold is learnt during training and used in testing (like parameters in BN layers), therefore the actual pruning rate is slightly different to the target $\xi$.

Table 1 shows that our method outperforms all of the compared static filter pruning methods while achieving higher speed-up. For example, when compared with previous best-performed FPGM [13] that achieves 1.53× speed-up, our method decreases the top-1 error by 0.37% with 2.04× speed-up. It can also be seen that our method is superior to those dynamic execution methods including LCCN [8], FBS [9], and CGNet [17]. Compared with FBS, our DGC can better achieve diversified feature representations with multiple heads that work in a self-attention way. As for LCCN and CGNet, both of them work in a pixel-level dynamic execution way, which results in irregular computations and needs specific algorithms or devices for computation acceleration. However, our DGC directly removes some part of input channels for each group, which can be easily implemented like SGC.

It can be found from Table 2 that the proposed DGC performs well when embedded into the state-of-the-art efficient CNNs. Specifically, DGC can further speed up the MobileNetV2 by 1.22× (245M *vs.* 300M) with only 1.3% degradation of top-1 error. In addition, DGC outperforms both SGC and CondenseNet's LGC, and obtains comparable accuracy when compared with FLGC. Finally, our MobileNetV2-DGC even achieves comparable accuracy compared with MobileNetV1 and ShuffleNet while reducing the computation cost more than doubled.

### 4.4 Ablation and Visualization

**Number of Heads.** We use a 50-layer CondenseNet-DGC network structure on the CIFAR-10 dataset as the basis to observe the effects of number of heads ($\mathcal{H} = 1, 2, 4, 8$). The network is trained for 150 epochs and the pruning rate $\xi$ is

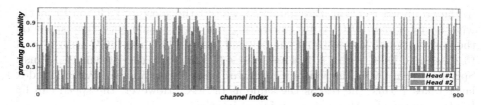

**Fig. 8.** Channel pruning probabilities. We track the last 900 input channels in *the 33rd DGC layer* of the CondenseNet-DGC structure used in Sect. 4.3 on the validation set of ImageNet dataset for the first two (out of four) heads (blue and red colors). For each channel each head, the probability is calculated as the percentage of images which deactivate the channel in this head during their inferences. (Color figure online)

set to 0.75. Blue bars in Fig. 6 shows the Top-1 error under varying head numbers. It can be seen that the performance is firstly improved with the increase of head number, reaching the peak at $\mathcal{H} = 4$, and then slightly drops when $\mathcal{H} = 8$. We conjecture that under similar computation costs, using more heads helps capture diversified feature representations (also see Fig. 8), while a big head number may also bring extra difficulty in training effectiveness.

**Pruning Rate.** We follow the above structure but fix $\mathcal{H} = 4$ and adjust the pruning rate ($\xi = 7/8, 5/6, 3/4, 1/2, 1/3$). The right part in Fig. 6 shows the performance changes. Generally, with a higher pruning rate, more channels are deactivated during inference thus with less computation cost, but at the same time leading to an increasing error rate.

***Dynamicness*** **and** ***Adaptiveness*** **of DGC Networks.** Figure 7 visualizes the saliency vectors and corresponding sparse patterns of the CondenseNet-DGC structure used in Sect. 4.3 for different input images. We can see that shallower layers share the similar sparse patterns, since they tend to catch the basic and less abstract image features, while deeper layers diverge different images into different sparse patterns, matching our observation in Sect. 1. On the other hand, similar images tend to produce similar patterns, and vice versa, which indicates the *adaptiveness* property of DGC networks.

In addition, We also visualize the pruning probability of channels in one of the deep layers in Fig. 8. We track the first two heads and show the *jumping* channels whose pruning probability is neither 0 nor 1 (noting that those *freezing* channels with probability 0 or 1 can still be jumping in the other two heads). Firstly, We can see that each head owns a particular pruning pattern but complementary with the other, indicating features can be captured from multiple perspectives with different heads. Secondly, the existence of *jumping* channels reveals the *dynamicness* of the DGC network, which will adaptively ignite its channels depending on certain input samples (more results can be seen in appendix).

**Computation Time.** Following [19,48], the inference speed of DGC can be made close to SGC by embedding a dynamic index layer right before each convolution that reorders the indices of input channels and filters according to the group information. Based on this, we test the speed of DGC on Resnet18 with an Intel i7-8700 CPU by calculating the average inference time spent on the convolutional layers, using the original model (11.5 ms), SGC with $G = 4$ (5.1 ms), and DGC with $\xi = 3/4$ and $\mathcal{H} = 4$ (7.8 ms = 5.1 ms + 0.8 ms + 1.9 ms). Specifically, in DGC, the saliency generator takes 0.8 ms and the dynamic index layer takes 1.9 ms, the rest is the same as of SGC. However, the speed can be further improved with a more careful optimization.

## 5   Conclusion

In this paper, we propose a novel group convolution method named DGC, which improves the existing group convolutions that have fixed connections during inference by introducing the dynamic channel selection scheme. The proposed DGC has the following three-fold advantages over existing group convolutions and previous state-of-the-art channel/pixel-level dynamic execution methods: (1) It conducts sparse group convolution operations while keeping the capabilities of the original CNNs; (2) It dynamically executes sample-dependent convolutions with multiple complementary heads using a self-attention based decision strategy; (3) It can be embedded into various exiting CNNs and the resulted models can be stably and easily optimized in an end-to-end manner without the need of pre-training.

**Acknowledgement.** This work was partially supported by the Academy of Finland under grant 331883 and the National Natural Science Foundation of China under Grant 61872379. The authors also wish to acknowledge CSC IT Center for Science, Finland, for computational resources.

## References

1. Banner, R., Nahshan, Y., Soudry, D.: Post training 4-bit quantization of convolutional networks for rapid-deployment. In: Advances in Neural Information Processing Systems, pp. 7948–7956 (2019)
2. Bolukbasi, T., Wang, J., Dekel, O., Saligrama, V.: Adaptive neural networks for efficient inference. In: Proceedings of the 34th International Conference on Machine Learning, vol. 70, pp. 527–536. JMLR.org (2017)
3. Cao, S., et al.: SeerNet: predicting convolutional neural network feature-map sparsity through low-bit quantization. In: Proceedings of the IEEE Conference on Computer Vision and Pattern Recognition, pp. 11216–11225 (2019)
4. Chollet, F.: Xception: deep learning with depthwise separable convolutions. In: Proceedings of the IEEE Conference on Computer Vision and Pattern Recognition, pp. 1251–1258 (2017)
5. Deng, J., Dong, W., Socher, R., Li, L.J., Li, K., Fei-Fei, L.: ImageNet: a large-scale hierarchical image database. In: 2009 IEEE Conference on Computer Vision and Pattern Recognition, pp. 248–255. IEEE (2009)
6. Denton, E.L., Zaremba, W., Bruna, J., LeCun, Y., Fergus, R.: Exploiting linear structure within convolutional networks for efficient evaluation. In: Advances in Neural Information Processing Systems, pp. 1269–1277 (2014)

7. Ding, Y., Liu, J., Xiong, J., Shi, Y.: On the universal approximability and complexity bounds of quantized ReLU neural networks. arXiv preprint arXiv:1802.03646 (2018)
8. Dong, X., Huang, J., Yang, Y., Yan, S.: More is less: a more complicated network with less inference complexity. In: Proceedings of the IEEE Conference on Computer Vision and Pattern Recognition, pp. 5840–5848 (2017)
9. Gao, X., Zhao, Y., Dudziak, Ł., Mullins, R., Xu, C.Z.: Dynamic channel pruning: feature boosting and suppression. arXiv preprint arXiv:1810.05331 (2018)
10. Han, S., Pool, J., Tran, J., Dally, W.: Learning both weights and connections for efficient neural network. In: Advances in Neural Information Processing Systems, pp. 1135–1143 (2015)
11. He, K., Zhang, X., Ren, S., Sun, J.: Deep residual learning for image recognition. In: Proceedings of the IEEE Conference on Computer Vision and Pattern Recognition, pp. 770–778 (2016)
12. He, Y., Kang, G., Dong, X., Fu, Y., Yang, Y.: Soft filter pruning for accelerating deep convolutional neural networks. arXiv preprint arXiv:1808.06866 (2018)
13. He, Y., Liu, P., Wang, Z., Hu, Z., Yang, Y.: Filter pruning via geometric median for deep convolutional neural networks acceleration. In: Proceedings of the IEEE Conference on Computer Vision and Pattern Recognition, pp. 4340–4349 (2019)
14. Heo, B., Kim, J., Yun, S., Park, H., Kwak, N., Choi, J.Y.: A comprehensive overhaul of feature distillation. In: Proceedings of the IEEE International Conference on Computer Vision, pp. 1921–1930 (2019)
15. Howard, A.G., et al.: MobileNets: efficient convolutional neural networks for mobile vision applications. arXiv preprint arXiv:1704.04861 (2017)
16. Hu, J., Shen, L., Sun, G.: Squeeze-and-excitation networks. In: Proceedings of the IEEE Conference on Computer Vision and Pattern Recognition, pp. 7132–7141 (2018)
17. Hua, W., Zhou, Y., De Sa, C.M., Zhang, Z., Suh, G.E.: Channel gating neural networks. In: Advances in Neural Information Processing Systems, pp. 1884–1894 (2019)
18. Huang, G., Chen, D., Li, T., Wu, F., van der Maaten, L., Weinberger, K.Q.: Multi-scale dense networks for resource efficient image classification. arXiv preprint arXiv:1703.09844 (2017)
19. Huang, G., Liu, S., Van der Maaten, L., Weinberger, K.Q.: CondenseNet: an efficient DenseNet using learned group convolutions. In: Proceedings of the IEEE Conference on Computer Vision and Pattern Recognition, pp. 2752–2761 (2018)
20. Huang, G., Liu, Z., Van Der Maaten, L., Weinberger, K.Q.: Densely connected convolutional networks. In: Proceedings of the IEEE Conference on Computer Vision and Pattern Recognition, pp. 4700–4708 (2017)
21. Ioffe, S., Szegedy, C.: Batch normalization: accelerating deep network training by reducing internal covariate shift. arXiv preprint arXiv:1502.03167 (2015)
22. Jaderberg, M., Vedaldi, A., Zisserman, A.: Speeding up convolutional neural networks with low rank expansions. arXiv preprint arXiv:1405.3866 (2014)
23. Jin, X., et al.: Knowledge distillation via route constrained optimization. In: Proceedings of the IEEE International Conference on Computer Vision, pp. 1345–1354 (2019)
24. Krizhevsky, A., Hinton, G., et al.: Learning multiple layers of features from tiny images (2009)
25. Krizhevsky, A., Sutskever, I., Hinton, G.E.: ImageNet classification with deep convolutional neural networks. In: Advances in Neural Information Processing Systems, pp. 1097–1105 (2012)

26. Lee, N., Ajanthan, T., Torr, P.H.: SNIP: single-shot network pruning based on connection sensitivity. arXiv preprint arXiv:1810.02340 (2018)
27. Li, Y., et al.: Exploiting kernel sparsity and entropy for interpretable CNN compression. In: Proceedings of the IEEE Conference on Computer Vision and Pattern Recognition, pp. 2800–2809 (2019)
28. Liang, X.: Learning personalized modular network guided by structured knowledge. In: Proceedings of the IEEE Conference on Computer Vision and Pattern Recognition, pp. 8944–8952 (2019)
29. Lin, J., Rao, Y., Lu, J., Zhou, J.: Runtime neural pruning. In: Advances in Neural Information Processing Systems, pp. 2181–2191 (2017)
30. Lin, T.-Y., et al.: Microsoft COCO: common objects in context. In: Fleet, D., Pajdla, T., Schiele, B., Tuytelaars, T. (eds.) ECCV 2014. LNCS, vol. 8693, pp. 740–755. Springer, Cham (2014). https://doi.org/10.1007/978-3-319-10602-1_48
31. Liu, C., et al.: Circulant binary convolutional networks: enhancing the performance of 1-bit DCNNs with circulant back propagation. In: Proceedings of the IEEE Conference on Computer Vision and Pattern Recognition, pp. 2691–2699 (2019)
32. Liu, J., et al.: Knowledge representing: efficient, sparse representation of prior knowledge for knowledge distillation. In: Proceedings of the IEEE Conference on Computer Vision and Pattern Recognition Workshops (2019)
33. Liu, L., Deng, J.: Dynamic deep neural networks: optimizing accuracy-efficiency trade-offs by selective execution. In: Thirty-Second AAAI Conference on Artificial Intelligence (2018)
34. Liu, Y., Dong, W., Zhang, L., Gong, D., Shi, Q.: Variational Bayesian dropout with a hierarchical prior. In: Proceedings of the IEEE Conference on Computer Vision and Pattern Recognition, pp. 7124–7133 (2019)
35. Liu, Z., Li, J., Shen, Z., Huang, G., Yan, S., Zhang, C.: Learning efficient convolutional networks through network slimming. In: Proceedings of the IEEE International Conference on Computer Vision, pp. 2736–2744 (2017)
36. Long, J., Shelhamer, E., Darrell, T.: Fully convolutional networks for semantic segmentation. In: Proceedings of the IEEE Conference on Computer Vision and Pattern Recognition, pp. 3431–3440 (2015)
37. Ma, N., Zhang, X., Zheng, H.-T., Sun, J.: ShuffleNet V2: practical guidelines for efficient CNN architecture design. In: Ferrari, V., Hebert, M., Sminchisescu, C., Weiss, Y. (eds.) Computer Vision – ECCV 2018. LNCS, vol. 11218, pp. 122–138. Springer, Cham (2018). https://doi.org/10.1007/978-3-030-01264-9_8
38. Minnehan, B., Savakis, A.: Cascaded projection: end-to-end network compression and acceleration. In: Proceedings of the IEEE Conference on Computer Vision and Pattern Recognition, pp. 10715–10724 (2019)
39. Paszke, A., et al.: PyTorch: an imperative style, high-performance deep learning library. In: Advances in Neural Information Processing Systems, pp. 8024–8035 (2019)
40. Peng, H., Wu, J., Chen, S., Huang, J.: Collaborative channel pruning for deep networks. In: International Conference on Machine Learning, pp. 5113–5122 (2019)
41. Phuong, M., Lampert, C.: Towards understanding knowledge distillation. In: International Conference on Machine Learning, pp. 5142–5151 (2019)
42. Phuong, M., Lampert, C.H.: Distillation-based training for multi-exit architectures. In: Proceedings of the IEEE International Conference on Computer Vision, pp. 1355–1364 (2019)
43. Sakr, C., Shanbhag, N.: Per-tensor fixed-point quantization of the back-propagation algorithm. arXiv preprint arXiv:1812.11732 (2018)

44. Sandler, M., Howard, A., Zhu, M., Zhmoginov, A., Chen, L.C.: MobileNetV2: inverted residuals and linear bottlenecks. In: Proceedings of the IEEE Conference on Computer Vision and Pattern Recognition, pp. 4510–4520 (2018)
45. Sun, K., Li, M., Liu, D., Wang, J.: IGCV3: interleaved low-rank group convolutions for efficient deep neural networks. In: BMVC (2018)
46. Vaswani, A., et al.: Attention is all you need. In: Advances in Neural Information Processing Systems, pp. 5998–6008 (2017)
47. Veit, A., Belongie, S.: Convolutional networks with adaptive inference graphs. In: Ferrari, V., Hebert, M., Sminchisescu, C., Weiss, Y. (eds.) ECCV 2018. LNCS, vol. 11205, pp. 3–18. Springer, Cham (2018). https://doi.org/10.1007/978-3-030-01246-5_1
48. Wang, X., Kan, M., Shan, S., Chen, X.: Fully learnable group convolution for acceleration of deep neural networks. In: Proceedings of the IEEE Conference on Computer Vision and Pattern Recognition, pp. 9049–9058 (2019)
49. Wang, X., Yu, F., Dou, Z.-Y., Darrell, T., Gonzalez, J.E.: SkipNet: learning dynamic routing in convolutional networks. In: Ferrari, V., Hebert, M., Sminchisescu, C., Weiss, Y. (eds.) ECCV 2018. LNCS, vol. 11217, pp. 420–436. Springer, Cham (2018). https://doi.org/10.1007/978-3-030-01261-8_25
50. Wu, Z., et al.: BlockDrop: dynamic inference paths in residual networks. In: Proceedings of the IEEE Conference on Computer Vision and Pattern Recognition, pp. 8817–8826 (2018)
51. Xiao, X., Wang, Z., Rajasekaran, S.: AutoPrune: automatic network pruning by regularizing auxiliary parameters. In: Advances in Neural Information Processing Systems, pp. 13681–13691 (2019)
52. Xie, S., Girshick, R., Dollár, P., Tu, Z., He, K.: Aggregated residual transformations for deep neural networks. In: Proceedings of the IEEE Conference on Computer Vision and Pattern Recognition, pp. 1492–1500 (2017)
53. Yoo, J., Cho, M., Kim, T., Kang, U.: Knowledge extraction with no observable data. In: Advances in Neural Information Processing Systems, pp. 2701–2710 (2019)
54. Zhang, T., Qi, G.J., Xiao, B., Wang, J.: Interleaved group convolutions. In: Proceedings of the IEEE International Conference on Computer Vision, pp. 4373–4382 (2017)
55. Zhang, X., Zhou, X., Lin, M., Sun, J.: ShuffleNet: an extremely efficient convolutional neural network for mobile devices. In: Proceedings of the IEEE Conference on Computer Vision and Pattern Recognition, pp. 6848–6856 (2018)
56. Zhang, X., Zou, J., Ming, X., He, K., Sun, J.: Efficient and accurate approximations of nonlinear convolutional networks. In: Proceedings of the IEEE Conference on Computer Vision and pattern Recognition, pp. 1984–1992 (2015)
57. Zhuang, Z., et al.: Discrimination-aware channel pruning for deep neural networks. In: Advances in Neural Information Processing Systems, pp. 875–886 (2018)
58. Zoph, B., Vasudevan, V., Shlens, J., Le, Q.V.: Learning transferable architectures for scalable image recognition. In: Proceedings of the IEEE Conference on Computer Vision and Pattern Recognition, pp. 8697–8710 (2018)

# RD-GAN: Few/Zero-Shot Chinese Character Style Transfer via Radical Decomposition and Rendering

Yaoxiong Huang[1,2], Mengchao He[2], Lianwen Jin[1(✉)], and Yongpan Wang[2]

[1] School of Electronic and Information Engineering,
South China University of Technology, Guangzhou, China
`hwang.yaoxiong@gmail.com, lianwen.jin@gmail.com`
[2] Alibaba Group, Hangzhou, China
`mengchao.hmc@alibaba-inc.com, yongpan@taobao.com`

**Abstract.** Style transfer has attracted much interest owing to its various applications. Compared with English character or general artistic style transfer, Chinese character style transfer remains a challenge owing to the large size of the vocabulary (70224 characters in GB18010-2005) and the complexity of the structure. Recently some GAN-based methods were proposed for style transfer; however, they treated Chinese characters as a whole, ignoring the structures and radicals that compose characters. In this paper, a novel radical decomposition-and-rendering-based GAN (RD-GAN) is proposed to utilize the radical-level compositions of Chinese characters and achieves few-shot/zero-shot Chinese character style transfer. The RD-GAN consists of three components: a radical extraction module (REM), radical rendering module (RRM), and multi-level discriminator (MLD). Experiments demonstrate that our method has a powerful few-shot/zero-shot generalization ability by using the radical-level compositions of Chinese characters.

**Keywords:** GAN · Style transfer · Radical decomposition · Few-Shot/Zero-Shot learning

## 1 Introduction

With the development of deep learning, character recognition has reached an unprecedented stage of development; however, it is very data-dependent. In many cases, such as in historical documents, character samples are expensive/difficult to obtain. One of the most efficient ways to obtain character samples is to generate character data via style transfer. Unfortunately, character generation remains a relatively under-explored problem compared with the automatic recognition of characters [24,34]. This unbalanced progress is detrimental to the development of optical character recognition.

Recently, there have been many attempts to generate simple characters such as English and Latin characters [13,21]; however, Chinese character generation

© Springer Nature Switzerland AG 2020
A. Vedaldi et al. (Eds.): ECCV 2020, LNCS 12351, pp. 156–172, 2020.
https://doi.org/10.1007/978-3-030-58539-6_10

has not been explored extensively. Compared with English or Latin character generation, Chinese character generation is much more challenging owing to the following characteristics. First, Chinese characters share an extremely large vocabulary. To address this issue, [61] generated Chinese characters by introducing a Recurrent Neural Network (RNN)-based model and learned a low-dimensional character label embedding. However, this method can only generate characters that the model has seen. Unfortunately, it is almost impossible to obtain all of the categories' samples from a fixed style. Generating unseen Chinese characters remains an urgent problem.

Moreover, Chinese characters contain a large number of glyphs with complicated content and characteristic style that vary from the shapes of the component and the stroke styles. Recent works such as "Rewrite" [2] and its advanced version "zi2zi" [3] generated Chinese characters by learning to map the source style to a target style with thousands of character pairs for strong supervision. However, these methods still cannot generate unseen Chinese characters.

Finally, unlike the photo-to-artwork task, Chinese characters have a complex and flexible structure. Subtle errors in the skeleton and stroke are obvious and unacceptable. Some attempts have been made in Chinese character generation by assembling components of radicals and strokes [48,52,55]. However, these performed poorly for two reasons: 1) they are largely dependent on the performance of radical/stroke extraction while perfect automatic radical/stroke extraction is almost impossible in real applications; and 2) they pay more attention to the rendering of the radical/stroke while ignoring their internal relationship.

Although Chinese characters comprise an extremely large vocabulary, more than 10,000 characters can be composed by approximately 1000 radicals [46]. Meanwhile, all Chinese characters can be decomposed into a unique radical string. When people learn Chinese characters, they first learn the radicals and structures that form characters. By learning radicals and structures, the difficulty of learning to read and write Chinese characters decreases significantly.

Compelled by the above observations, we propose a novel radical decomposition-and-rendering-based GAN (RD-GAN) for Chinese character style transfer that can efficiently generate unseen Chinese characters with a few samples. The RD-GAN consists of three components: a radical extraction module (REM) to extract the radical roughly, radical rendering module (RRM) that learns how to render the radical with stroke details in the target style, and multi-level discriminator (MLD) that guarantees the global structure and local details of the generated character images. The advantages of the proposed RD-GAN can be summarized as follows:

- Owing to the specificity of the relationship between characters and radicals, we can use only a few samples to generate unseen Chinese characters efficiently. This can largely reduce the difficulty and labor of collecting training data.
- By decomposing Chinese characters into radicals, the rendering difficulty decreases significantly.

- Owing to the multi-level discriminator, we can generate stylized Chinese characters that not only have good details but also have more realistically combined components.
- RD-GAN can generate realistic character samples for training character classifiers with few real data. Experiments show that our method can effectively transfer unseen Chinese characters and obtain better performance than recent state-of-the-art methods.

## 2    Related Work

### 2.1    Image-to-Image Translation

Image-to-image translation learns the mapping from the input image to the output image and covers many tasks such as edge/contour extraction [38,50], semantic segmentation [28,36], artistic style transfer [9,19], and image colorization [31,59]. Pix2pix [16] used a conditional GAN based network that needs a significant amount of paired data for training. To alleviate the problem of obtaining data pairs, unpaired image-to-image translation frameworks [26,27,63] have been proposed. Liu et al. [26] made a shared-latent space assumption that a pair of corresponding images in different domains can be mapped to the same latent representation in a shared-latent space. After that, authors [27] extended [26] to an unsupervised image-to-image translation problem. Then, authors [63] proposed the cycle-consistent adversarial network (CycleGAN), which performs well for many vision and graphics tasks. Meanwhile, supervised GAN-based methods require numerous image pairs, while unsupervised methods often cause blurred and incorrect construction. In this paper, we propose a novel radical decomposition-and-rendering GAN that focuses on training a generative model with as few samples as possible.

### 2.2    Character Style Transfer

Recent studies considered character style transfer as an image translation task. A popular project named "Rewrite" [2] implemented a simple traditional flavor top-down Convolutional Neural Network (CNN) to transfer a standard font to another stylized font. After that, its advanced version, named "zi2zi" [3], implemented the font style transfer of Chinese characters by learning to map the source style to a target style with thousands of character pairs. Upchurch et al. [43] adopted a supervised method and assigned each character a one-hot label. In addition, Lyu et al. [32] proposed an auto-encoder-guided GAN network (AEGN) to synthesize calligraphy images with specified styles from standard Chinese font images. Easyfont [23] extracted strokes from given Chinese characters and learned to generate corresponding strokes for other characters in the same style. Jiang et al. [18] integrated the domain knowledge of Chinese characters with deep generative networks to ensure that high-quality glyphs with correct structures can be synthesized. MC-GAN [4] synthesizes ornamented glyphs from images of a few example glyphs in the same style by predicting the coarse glyph shapes and texture of the final glyphs.

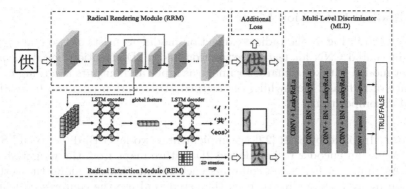

**Fig. 1.** Overview of the proposed method for Chinese character style transfer. Standard font Chinese character images are firstly fed into the radical rendering module to obtain the output stylized images. The output stylized images and the corresponding target images are then transmitted to the radical extraction module to obtain a 2D-attention map. With the 2D-attention map, we crop the corresponding radical regions from the output images. Finally, output images and cropped images are fed to the multi-level discriminator to improve the distributional similarity between the output images and the corresponding target images.

### 2.3 Attention Mechanism

The attention mechanism was first proposed in machine translation [5,44] to enable a model to automatically search for parts of a source sentence for prediction. Then, the method rapidly became popular in applications such as (visual) question answering [30,54], image caption generation [29,51,54], speech recognition [6,20], and scene text recognition [7,22,40]. Most important, the attention mechanism can also be applied to 2D predictions, such as mathematical expression recognition [56,57], paragraph recognition [8,49], and radical recognition [45]. Thanks to the characteristics of the attention mechanism, we implement a 2D attention mechanism for rough radical extraction.

## 3 Proposed Methodology

### 3.1 Overview

Given a standard-font Chinese character image $I_C$ with content $C$, our proposed system $f$ aims to generate another stylized character image $I'_C$ with the same content as realistically as possible. The proposed RD-GAN is a network for few-shot/zero-shot Chinese character image generation. As illustrated in Fig. 1, the proposed RD-GAN consists of three components. The **Radical Extraction Module** splits an image into different parts to empower our system with few-shot/zero-shot learning. The **Radical Rendering Module** outputs stylized character images based on stroke/radical details. Finally, a **multi-level discriminator** is adopted to pay more attention to both local details and global context.

## 3.2    Radical Extraction Module

As presented in Fig. 1, the radical extraction module consists of two main parts: a weight-shared CNN for feature extraction and a 2D-attention based encoder-decoder model. It takes a character image as input and outputs a varying length sequence of radicals. Meanwhile, the learned 2D-attention map can be used for radical decomposition.

**Encoder.** Inspired by SAR [22], we implement a two-layer Bi-directional LSTM (BLSTM) as an encoder to handle the 2D feature maps from the weight-shared CNN. As shown in Fig. 2, we compress each column feature along the vertical direction by average-pooling at each time step, and use the compressed feature to update the hidden state $h_t$. After $T$ steps, which is the width of the 2D feature maps, the final hidden state of the encoder $f_g$ is output as the global feature of our input character image, and is fed to the following decoder.

**Decoder.** The decoder is another BLSTM model with two layers. Most traditional 2D attention models [8,56] consider only local information and treat each location independently, neglecting the relationship between pixels in adjacent areas. We follow the concept of [22] to take neighborhood information into consideration.

Initially, the global feature $f_g$ is fed into the decoder BLSTM. The decoder iteratively updates the attention mechanism and outputs the current prediction(radical) according to the previous output $y_{t-1}$ and hidden state $s_{t-1}$:

$$\hat{s}_t = BLSTM(y_{t-1}, s_{t-1}) \tag{1}$$

$$c_t = f_{attn}(\hat{s}_t, F) \tag{2}$$

$$s_t = BLSTM(c_t, \hat{s}_t) \tag{3}$$

$$y_t = \psi(s_t) \tag{4}$$

where $\psi(.)$ is a linear transformation, and $f_{attn}$ is a neighborhood-considered 2D attention mechanism as follows:

$$e_{ij} = W^{attn} \cdot tanh(W^s \hat{s}_t + W^p p_{ij} + \sum_{x=i-1}^{i+1} \sum_{y=j-1}^{j+1} W^h_{xy} p_{xy}) \tag{5}$$

$$\alpha_{ij} = \frac{e_{ij}}{\sum_{ij} e_{ij}} \tag{6}$$

$$c_t = \sum_{ij} \alpha_{ij} p_{ij} \tag{7}$$

Note that, $W^{attn}, W^s, W^p$, and $W^h$ are all learnable parameters; $p_{ij}$ is the local feature vector at position $(i, j)$ in the input 2D feature map $F$; and $i, j$ are range from 0 to the width and height of $F$, respectively. According to the response of 2D attention map, we can roughly separate the corresponding radicals for subsequent processes.

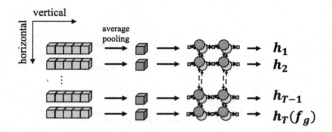

**Fig. 2.** Illustration of the BLSTM encoder. $T$ represents the width of 2D feature map. At each time step, column feature is compressed by a vertical average-pooling and the final hidden state of the encoder is fed to the following decoder.

### 3.3    Radical Rendering Module

The overall network architecture of the radical rendering module is shown in Fig. 3. The RRM is composed of a downsampling module and an upsampling module. Lateral connections are employed to preserve more details. Fed with a standard-font Chinese character image, the RRM generates a stylized character image with complete strokes and radicals.

It is typically considered that higher-level features share stronger semantics, while lower-level features exhibit semantically weak features but include more detailed information [39] such as texture and position information. Therefore, we introduce a lateral connection to mix up semantics features with detailed geometric features. As shown in Fig. 4, this lateral connection contains two pathways, named SE-pathway and up-sample pathway, respectively.

| index | Layer(Weight-Shared CNN) | output shape (C×H×W) | | index | Layer(Up-Sample) | output shape (C×H×W) |
|---|---|---|---|---|---|---|
| 0 | input: character image | 1×96×96 | | 18 | output: stylized image | 1×96×96 |
| 1 | num: 64, kernel: 3×3, pad: (h:1, w:1), stride: (h:1, w:1) | 64×96×96 | | 17 | 1, 1×1, (0,0), (1,1) | 1×96×96 |
| | | | | 16 | ratio: 2×2 | 64×96×96 |
| 2 | 64, 3×3, (1,1), (1,1) | 64×96×96 | | 15 | [64, 3×3, (1,1), (1,1)] ×2 | 64×48×48 |
| 3 | kernel: 2×2, stride: 2×2 | 64×48×48 | ⟺ | 14 | ratio: 2×2 | 128×48×48 |
| 4 | [128, 3×3, (1,1), (1,1)] ×2 | 128×48×48 | | 13 | [128, 3×3, (1,1), (1,1)] ×2 | 128×24×24 |
| 5 | 2×1, 2×2 | 128×24×24 | ⟺ | 12 | ratio: 2×2 | 256×24×24 |
| 6 | [256, 3×3, (1,1), (1,1)] ×2 | 256×24×24 | | 11 | [256, 3×3, (1,1), (1,1)] ×2 | 256×12×12 |
| 7 | 2×1, 2×2 | 256×12×12 | ⟺ | 10 | ratio: 2×2 | 512×12×12 |
| 8 | 512, 3×3, (1,1), (1,1) | 512×12×12 | | 9 | 2×1, 2×2 | 512×6×6 |

| convolution layer | max pooling layer | up-sample layer | ⟺ lateral connection |

**Fig. 3.** Illustration of the radical rendering module. It is a convolutional neural network with an encoder decoder structure and lateral connection. Specially, the encoder part is shared with radical extraction module as feature extractor.

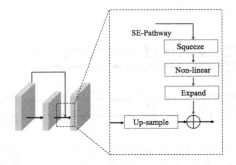

**Fig. 4.** Illustration of the lateral connection.

**SE-Pathway.** Unlike [15], our operation is performed in the channel dimension. First, the squeeze layer reduces the feature dimensions by using a $1 \times 1$ convolution for information fusion from different channels and less computation. Then, we implement a non-linear layer including two deformable convolutions and ReLU activation function to achieve large receptive fields. Last, an expand layer is used to enlarge the feature map channels by a $1 \times 1$ convolution as the reverse of the squeeze layer.

**Up-Sample Pathway.** To enlarge the feature map, we utilize a bilinear sampling operation followed by two same-size ($3 \times 3$) convolutional layers. This can avoid checkerboard artifacts more effectively than deconvolution. The up-sampled feature maps are then element-wise summed with the corresponding ones from the SE-Pathway. Inspired by [10], we use ELU as non-linear activation function because it can handle large negative responses and thereby stabilize the training process.

### 3.4 Multi-level Discriminator

To differentiate fake images from real ones, the original GANs [12] discriminate the results based on the entire image level. However, as mentioned before, Chinese characters have complex and flexible structures, which make the discriminator difficult to focus on. To determine whether the images we generate are realistic enough to lead the RRM to generate more realistic images, we proposed a multi-level discriminator. Here, "multi-level" includes both the geometry level and structure level.

**Geometry Level.** As noted in [41], any local patch sampled from the generated image should have statistics similar to those of a real image patch. Specifically, following the PatchGAN [16], we execute our discriminator to classify whether each $N \times N$ patch in an image is real or fake. We run this discriminator convolutationally across the image, averaging all responses to provide the ultimate output of the discriminator. We define the loss as follows:

$$L_D^g = -\frac{1}{N^2} \sum_{n=1}^{N^2} (1-y)log(\xi_n) \tag{8}$$

where $y$ and $\xi$ are the label of the image and the discriminator prediction, respectively. In our experiments, $N$ is set to 6.

**Structure Level.** All Chinese characters can be decomposed into a unique radical set. A perfectly generated Chinese character image should have well refined strokes and more realistically combined components. Therefore, we penalize both the entire image and the radical patches. Given the 2D-attention map $\mathcal{M}_t$ at timestep $t$ and input image $\mathcal{I}$, we define the structure level loss as follows:

$$L_D^s = -(1-y)[log(D^s(\mathcal{I})) + \sum_{t=1}^{T} log(D^s(\mathcal{I} \otimes \mathbb{I}\{\mathcal{M}_t > \theta\}))] \tag{9}$$

where $\mathbb{I}\{\cdot\} = 1$ when the condition is true and zero otherwise. Besides, $D^s$ represents a convolutional network with binary classification outputs, $\theta$ denotes the threshold set to 0.5 and $\otimes$ is element-wise multiplication.

By combining the above two loss terms, we come to the overall adversarial training objective:

$$L_a = L_D^g + L_D^s \tag{10}$$

### 3.5 Additional Loss Function

We aim to generate stylized Chinese character images as realistically as possible. This includes both per-pixel reconstructed accuracy as well as radical composition, i.e. how smoothly the radical regions can harmonize with their surrounding context. Inspired by recent image processing tasks (neural style transfers [11] and text eraser [60]), three additional losses are applied to our system as follows:

**L2 Loss($L_2$).** To obtain an output image that is both invariant to content and complete in describing a Chinese character, we can simply minimize the difference between the output image $I_C'$ and target image $\hat{I}_C$ in an explicit fashion:

$$L_2 = \|I_C' - \hat{I}_C\|_2 \tag{11}$$

**Total Variation Loss($L_{tv}$).** For image generation, a common problem is that model tends to generate noisy images. To solve this problem, we adopt $L_{tv}$ [19] for global denoising, as defined below:

$$L_{tv} = \sum_{ij} \|I_C'[i,j] - I_C'[i+1,j]\|_1 + \|I_C'[i,j] - I_C'[i,j+1]\|_1 \tag{12}$$

Here, $i,j$ indicates the position of the pixel.

**Content Loss($L_c$).** As noted in [19], the loss function measured for different high-level features is effective for feature reconstruction. To better generate images from different levels, we introduce content loss to penalize the discrepancy between the features of the output images and the corresponding ground truth images on certain layers in the CNN. We feed the output images and ground truth images to a pre-trained model and force the response in the corresponding layer to be matched. The content loss can be formulated as follows:

$$L_c = \sum_{n=1}^{N-1} \|\phi_n(\boldsymbol{I'_C}) - \phi_n(\boldsymbol{\hat{I}_C})\|_1 \tag{13}$$

where $N$ and $\phi_n(.)$ are the layer index we choose and the feature responding in layer $n$, respectively. Following [60], we compute the content loss at layers pool1, pool2, and pool3 of a pretrained VGG16 [42].

Combining all of the above loss terms, we come to the overall training objective for our Chinese character style transfer model:

$$L = L_a + \alpha_1 L_2 + \alpha_2 L_{tv} + \alpha_3 L_c \tag{14}$$

where $\alpha_1$, $\alpha_2$, and $\alpha_3$ are weighting coefficients that are empirically set to 0.5, 0.5, and 0.1 in our experiments, respectively.

## 4   Experiments

### 4.1   Dataset

In the following experiments, a historical document dataset named TKH Dataset [53] is used to quantitatively and qualitatively evaluate the performance of Chinese character style transfer. TKH has 1000 manually annotated Tripitaka paragraph images composed of approximately 320,000 character instances. There are two benefits to using this dataset: 1) The Chinese characters in historical documents are much closer to handwritten characters, which vary in the shapes of the components and the stroke styles. This is more useful in verifying the robustness and effectiveness of our method for difficult styles. 2) There are many strange and unusual characters in historical documents and they are an ideal testbed for few-shot/zero-shot learning.

To meet the requirements of different experiments and metrics, the entire dataset is partitioned into three subsets: $\mathcal{D}1$, where both the training set and test set have the same category (1473 classes in the same style) with 50 samples for each category; $\mathcal{D}2$, a subset of $\mathcal{D}1$ with only 5 samples for each category in the training set; and $\mathcal{D}3$, where images in the test set (213 classes) are never seen in the training set (1260 classes) but share the same radical sets. The three datasets represent different levels of challenges, e.g., supervised learning, few-shot learning, and zero-shot learning.

## 4.2   Experiment Setup

We use TrueType fonts to render the corresponding characters in black with font style Song as standard font character images. Both the standard font character images and target character images are resized to $96 \times 96$ before being fed to the model. We set the initial learning rate as 0.0001 and train the model end-to-end with the Adam optimization method until the output is stable.

Radicals are viewed as a part of the semantics and are shared by different characters [35]. Many studies have examined the reasonable splitting of Chinese characters into radical sets. [33] extracted 1118 substructures from 4284 characters to build a radical lexicon, and [46] extended this lexicon to 9820 characters. In our experiments, we adopt the radical lexicon in project [1] and filter out the symbols and single-structure characters in the dataset that cannot be decomposed into smaller parts. There are 1473 characters with 576 radicals for experiments. In our experiments, we train an REM with 150,000 samples generated by [17] and achieve an accuracy of 98.7% as tested on synthetic data.

Although the most commonly used metric for determining the quality of generative models is the inception score [37], it is not suitable for Chinese character style transfer [25]. To impartially compare the proposed method with other recent works, we calculate the L1 loss, Root Mean Square Error (RMSE) and the structural similarity (SSIM) [47] between the generated images and target images. In addition, one of the most important purposes of Chinese character style transfer is to improve the classifier performance. Therefore, we compare the performance among classifiers trained with different generation methods. We adopt a character recognizer with 1473 classes as follows:

$76 \times 76 Input - 32C3 - MP2 - 64C3 - MP2 - 128C3 - 128C3 - MP2 - 256C3 - 256C3 - MP2 - 384C3 - 384C3 - FC1024 - FC1473 - Output$

where $xCy$ represents a convolutional layer with kernel number of $x$ and kernel size of $y \times y$, $MPx$ denotes a max-pooling layer with kernel size of $x$, and $FCx$ is a fully connected layer of kernel number of $x$.

## 4.3   Experimental Results

**Comparison with State-of-the-Art Methods.** In this subsection, we compare our model with the following methods for Chinese character style transfer from the perspective of supervised learning, few-shot learning, and zero-shot learning:

1) Pix2pix [16]: Pix2pix is a conditional GAN based image translation network and is optimized by L1 distance loss and adversarial loss.
2) Cycle-GAN [63]: Cycle-GAN not only learns the mapping from the input image to the output image, but also learns a loss function to reverse this mapping. It is noted that Cycle-gan only requires unpaired data.
3) MC-GAN [4]: MC-GAN is the first end-to-end solution to synthesizing ornamented glyphs from images of a few example glyphs in the same style.
4) Zi2zi [3]: Zi2zi is an application and extension of the pix2pix model to Chinese characters with the addition of category embedding.

5) EMD [62]: EMD is a generalized style transfer network that attempts to separate the representations for style and content.

**Supervised Learning:** In this part, all methods are trained with paired images in $\mathcal{D}1$. The results are displayed in Fig. 5 (a). We observe that for supervised learning, our proposed method outperforms Pix2pix and Cycle-GAN and is slightly better than the results of Zi2zi and EMD. It is noted that Cycle-GAN has the worst performance, as it can only generate parts of characters or sometimes unreasonable structures. This may be because it only learns the domain mappings without the domain knowledge [62]. Zi2zi and EMD can learn how to map standard fonts to stylized fonts through an abundant number of paired images, as in our method. For quantitative analysis, we conducted experiments three times with different initializations. The average results are displayed in the last three columns in Fig. 5 (a). We can observe that our method performs best and achieves the lowest L1 loss, RMSE and the highest SSIM.

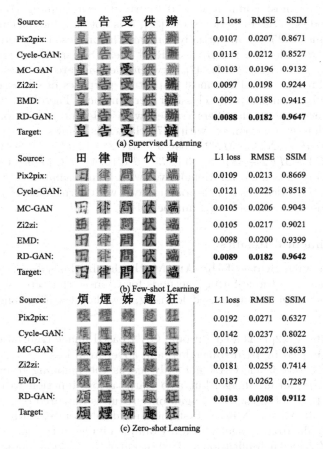

**Fig. 5.** Comparison among previous methods and proposed method.

**Table 1.** Character recognition accuracy trained with different generation methods

| Generation Methods | Accuracy(%) |
|---|---|
| $\mathcal{D}1$(Real data only) | 82.45 |
| $\mathcal{D}1$+synthtext2014 [17] | 83.25 |
| $\mathcal{D}1$+pix2pix [16] | 84.74 |
| $\mathcal{D}1$+zi2zi [3] | 85.63 |
| $\mathcal{D}1$+EMD [62] | 87.21 |
| $\mathcal{D}1$+RD-GAN | 88.11 |

**Few-Shot Learning:** We train our model and other methods with $\mathcal{D}2$, in which there are only five samples for each category. The results are presented in Fig. 5 (b). As shown in the figure, our method and EMD still exhibit good performance, while the performance of Zi2zi drops sharply. It is unrealistic for Zi2zi to transfer font style for 1473 categories trained with only 5 samples for each category. However, by decomposing Chinese characters into radicals, the number of categories we need to learn is reduced from 1473 to 576. This significantly reduces the difficulty of our task. In addition, all Chinese characters share the same radical lexicon, which means a radical will appear in both character A and character B. Therefore, a sufficient number of radical samples can be used for our training. The quantitative comparison results including the L1 loss, RMSE, and SSIM are also shown in the last three columns of Fig. 5 (b). Note that our model achieves the best performance among all of the methods and there is almost no degradation in performance even when training with only five samples, which demonstrates the effectiveness of our method.

**Zero-Shot Learning:** As an extreme case, all methods are trained with $\mathcal{D}3$. The categories in the test set were never seen during training. Both qualitative and quantitative analyses are presented in Fig. 5 (c). As shown in Fig. 5 (c), our model can still deal with unseen categories in the training set. However, images generated by other methods are messy, and their content may not be recognized. This is because these methods treat Chinese characters as a whole and cannot generate unseen Chinese characters. Differently, we cannot see the entire characters but all radicals in the test set can be explored during training, giving our method the ability of zero-shot learning.

In conclusion, most of the state-of-the-art methods require many paired images to train, which may difficult to collect images for some special fonts or categories such as historical documents. In addition, these methods can only transfer character font styles for categories appearing in the training set, and with no ability to generate unseen categories. However, our method can generalize stylized characters given only a few reference images. In addition, the experiments indicated the strong few-shot/zero-shot learning ability of our method owing to the relationship between characters and radicals.

| Source | baseline | +LC | +MLD | +AL | Target |
|--------|----------|-----|------|-----|--------|
| 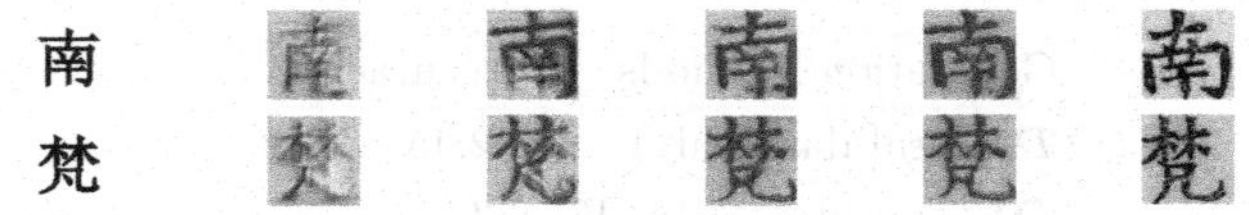 南 | 南 | 南 | 南 | 南 | 南 |
| 梵 | 梵 | 梵 | 梵 | 梵 | 梵 |

| | baseline | +LC | +MLD | +AL |
|--------|----------|--------|--------|--------|
| L1 loss | 0.0118 | 0.0102 | 0.0092 | 0.0088 |
| RMSE | 0.0210 | 0.0201 | 0.0189 | 0.0182 |
| SSIM | 0.8591 | 0.9144 | 0.9635 | 0.9647 |

**Fig. 6.** Effect of different components in our method. LC, MLD and AL represent lateral connection, multi-level discriminator and additional loss, respectively.

**Classifier Performance.** In this part, we train a character classifier using 50,000 synthetic character images generated by different methods and test the classifier on $\mathcal{D}1$. Table 1 lists the classification accuracy using different generation methods. We can observe that the character classifier trained with samples generated by our method performs much better than others. This is also consistent with the results of the quantitative and qualitative analyses mentioned above. It further reflects the outstanding ability of our method to generate data to promote the classifier performance.

## 4.4    Ablation Studies

In this section, we analyze the influence of the factors influencing the model performance, including the lateral connection, multi-level discriminator, and additional loss.

**Lateral Connection:** To evaluate the effectiveness of the lateral connection during image generation, we compare the results with and without lateral connections in Fig. 6. As shown in the figure, images generated with lateral connections exhibit much better details and obtain a lower L1 loss. This indicates that the lateral connections can effectively learn more detailed information to reconstruct stylized images.

**Multi-level Discriminator:** Radical decomposition and reconstruction are the key features of the proposed RD-GAN model. The multi-level discriminator is one of the indispensable components. To evaluate the influence of the discriminator, we conduct experiments using the multi-level discriminator and single-level discriminator, which treat images as a whole. The results are displayed in Fig. 6. We can observe that images generated with a multi-level discriminator have a better stroke/radical rendering. Besides, they obtain higher SSIM, which indicates that the character structure is better reconstructed.

**Additional Loss:** In addition, we conduct experiments with additional loss. Figure 6 displays the image generation results with and without additional loss. It noted that the generated images have more local details, less noise, and better reconstruction with lower L1 Loss, RMSE and higher SSIM.

**Fig. 7.** Experimental results on face transfer. Images from top to buttom: input images and output results.

## 4.5 Generalization to Face Transfer

As Chinese characters are composed of multiple radicals, the face is also composed of multiple parts including the eyes, nose, and mouth. In this section, an experiment on face transfer is conducted to test the generalization ability of RD-GAN. We evaluate our method on a well-known face dataset named Ms-celeb-1m [14]. In the experiment, we choose pairs of photos taken for the same person but from different perspectives for training. Besides, we implement MTCNN [58] instead of REM to extract the components of the face. The qualitative results are shown in Fig. 7. We can observe that the generated images effectively retain the face information and details, which further reflects the generalization and effectiveness of our method.

## 5    Conclusion

In this paper, we proposed a novel Chinese character style transfer model named RD-GAN that shows powerful few-shot/zero-shot generalization ability. The main idea is that all Chinese characters share the same radical lexicon, and that the REM decomposes Chinese characters into radical parts. Then, according to the radical parts, the RRM renders the radicals with stroke details in the target style. Finally, an MLD was proposed to guarantee the global structure and local details of the generated characters. To the best of our knowledge, RD-GAN is the first method that can generate Chinese character images of unseen categories with roughly radical decomposition. We evaluated the proposed method on Chinese character style transfer task, and extensive experiment demonstrated its effectiveness.

**Acknowledgement.** This research is supported in part by NSFC (Grant No.: 61936003), GD-NSF (no. 2017A030312006), Alibaba Innovative Research Foundation (no. D8200510), and Fundamental Research Funds for the Central Universities (no. D2190570).

# References

1. Cjkvi. https://github.com/cjkvi/cjkvi-ids
2. Rewrite. https://github.com/kaonashi-tyc/Rewrite
3. Zi2zi. https://github.com/kaonashi-tyc/zi2zi
4. Azadi, S., Fisher, M., Kim, V., Wang, Z., Shechtman, E., Darrell, T.: Multi-content GAN for few-shot font style transfer (2017)
5. Bahdanau, D., Cho, K., Bengio, Y.: Neural machine translation by jointly learning to align and translate. arXiv preprint arXiv:1409.0473 (2014)
6. Bahdanau, D., Chorowski, J., Serdyuk, D., Brakel, P., Bengio, Y.: End-to-end attention-based large vocabulary speech recognition. In: ICASSP (2016)
7. Bai, F., Cheng, Z., Niu, Y., Pu, S., Zhou, S.: Edit probability for scene text recognition. In: CVPR (2018)
8. Bluche, T.: Joint line segmentation and transcription for end-to-end handwritten paragraph recognition. In: NIPS (2016)
9. Chen, T.Q., Schmidt, M.: Fast patch-based style transfer of arbitrary style. arXiv preprint arXiv:1612.04337 (2016)
10. Clevert, D.A., Unterthiner, T., Hochreiter, S.: Fast and accurate deep network learning by exponential linear units (ELUs). arXiv preprint arXiv:1511.07289 (2015)
11. Gatys, L.A., Ecker, A.S., Bethge, M.: A neural algorithm of artistic style. arXiv preprint arXiv:1508.06576 (2015)
12. Goodfellow, I., et al.: Generative adversarial nets. In: NIPS (2014)
13. Graves, A.: Generating sequences with recurrent neural networks. arXiv preprint arXiv:1308.0850 (2013)
14. Guo, Y., Zhang, L., Hu, Y., He, X., Gao, J.: MS-Celeb-1M: a dataset and benchmark for large-scale face recognition. In: Leibe, B., Matas, J., Sebe, N., Welling, M. (eds.) ECCV 2016. LNCS, vol. 9907, pp. 87–102. Springer, Cham (2016). https://doi.org/10.1007/978-3-319-46487-9_6
15. Hu, J., Shen, L., Sun, G.: Squeeze-and-excitation networks. In: CVPR (2018)
16. Isola, P., Zhu, J.Y., Zhou, T., Efros, A.A.: Image-to-image translation with conditional adversarial networks. In: CVPR (2017)
17. Jaderberg, M., Simonyan, K., Vedaldi, A., Zisserman, A.: Synthetic data and artificial neural networks for natural scene text recognition. arXiv preprint arXiv:1406.2227 (2014)
18. Jiang, Y., Lian, Z., Tang, Y., Xiao, J.: SCFont: structure-guided Chinese font generation via deep stacked networks. In: AAAI (2019)
19. Johnson, J., Alahi, A., Fei-Fei, L.: Perceptual losses for real-time style transfer and super-resolution. In: Leibe, B., Matas, J., Sebe, N., Welling, M. (eds.) ECCV 2016. LNCS, vol. 9906, pp. 694–711. Springer, Cham (2016). https://doi.org/10.1007/978-3-319-46475-6_43
20. Kim, S., Hori, T., Watanabe, S.: Joint CTC-attention based end-to-end speech recognition using multi-task learning. In: ICASSP (2017)
21. Lake, B.M., Salakhutdinov, R., Tenenbaum, J.B.: Human-level concept learning through probabilistic program induction. Science **350**, 1332–1338 (2015)
22. Li, H., Wang, P., Shen, C., Zhang, G.: Show, attend and read: a simple and strong baseline for irregular text recognition. In: AAAI (2019)
23. Lian, Z., Zhao, B., Chen, X., Xiao, J.: EasyFont: a style learning-based system to easily build your large-scale handwriting fonts. ACM Trans. Graph. (TOG) **38**, 1–18 (2018)

24. Lian, Z., Zhao, B., Xiao, J.: Automatic generation of large-scale handwriting fonts via style learning. In: SIGGRAPH ASIA 2016 Technical Briefs (2016)
25. Lin, Q., Liang, L., Huang, Y., Jin, L.: Learning to generate realistic scene Chinese character images by multitask coupled GAN. In: Lai, J.-H., Liu, C.-L., Chen, X., Zhou, J., Tan, T., Zheng, N., Zha, H. (eds.) PRCV 2018. LNCS, vol. 11258, pp. 41–51. Springer, Cham (2018). https://doi.org/10.1007/978-3-030-03338-5_4
26. Liu, M.Y., Breuel, T., Kautz, J.: Unsupervised image-to-image translation networks. In: NIPS (2017)
27. Liu, M.Y., Tuzel, O.: Coupled generative adversarial networks. In: NIPS (2016)
28. Long, J., Shelhamer, E., Darrell, T.: Fully convolutional networks for semantic segmentation. In: CVPR (2015)
29. Lu, J., Xiong, C., Parikh, D., Socher, R.: Knowing when to look: adaptive attention via a visual sentinel for image captioning. In: CVPR (2017)
30. Lu, J., Yang, J., Batra, D., Parikh, D.: Hierarchical question-image co-attention for visual question answering. In: NIPS (2016)
31. Luan, Q., Wen, F., Cohen-Or, D., Liang, L., Xu, Y.Q., Shum, H.Y.: Natural image colorization. In: Proceedings of the 18th Eurographics Conference on Rendering Techniques (2007)
32. Lyu, P., Bai, X., Yao, C., Zhu, Z., Huang, T., Liu, W.: Auto-encoder guided GAN for Chinese calligraphy synthesis. In: ICDAR, vol. 1 (2017)
33. Ma, L.L., Liu, C.L.: A new radical-based approach to online handwritten Chinese character recognition. In: ICPR (2008)
34. Miyazaki, T., et al.: Automatic generation of typographic font from small font subset. IEEE Comput. Graph. Appl. **40**, 99–111 (2019)
35. Myers, J.: Knowing Chinese character grammar. Cognition **147**, 127–132 (2016)
36. Noh, H., Hong, S., Han, B.: Learning deconvolution network for semantic segmentation. In: ICCV (2015)
37. Salimans, T., Goodfellow, I., Zaremba, W., Cheung, V., Radford, A., Chen, X.: Improved techniques for training GANs. In: NIPS (2016)
38. Shen, W., Zhao, K., Jiang, Y., Wang, Y., Zhang, Z., Bai, X.: Object skeleton extraction in natural images by fusing scale-associated deep side outputs. In: CVPR (2016)
39. Shen, X., Chen, Y.C., Tao, X., Jia, J.: Convolutional neural pyramid for image processing. In: CVPR (2017)
40. Shi, B., Yang, M., Wang, X., Lyu, P., Yao, C., Bai, X.: ASTER: an attentional scene text recognizer with flexible rectification. IEEE Trans. Pattern Anal. Mach. Intell. **41**, 2035–2048 (2018)
41. Shrivastava, A., Pfister, T., Tuzel, O., Susskind, J., Wang, W., Webb, R.: Learning from simulated and unsupervised images through adversarial training. In: CVPR (2017)
42. Simonyan, K., Zisserman, A.: Very deep convolutional networks for large-scale image recognition. arXiv preprint arXiv:1409.1556 (2014)
43. Upchurch, P., Snavely, N., Bala, K.: From a to z: supervised transfer of style and content using deep neural network generators. arXiv preprint arXiv:1603.02003 (2016)
44. Vaswani, A., et al.: Attention is all you need. In: NIPS (2017)
45. Wang, T., et al.: Decoupled attention network for text recognition. In: AAAI (2020)
46. Wang, T.Q., Yin, F., Liu, C.L.: Radical-based Chinese character recognition via multi-labeled learning of deep residual networks. In: ICDAR (2017)

47. Wang, Z., Bovik, A.C., Sheikh, H.R., Simoncelli, E.P.: Image quality assessment: from error visibility to structural similarity. IEEE Trans. Image Process. **13**, 600–612 (2004)
48. Wen, C., Chang, J., Zhang, Y.: Handwritten Chinese font generation with collaborative stroke refinement. arXiv preprint arXiv:1904.13268 (2019)
49. Wigington, C., Tensmeyer, C., Davis, B., Barrett, W., Price, B., Cohen, S.: Start, follow, read: end-to-end full-page handwriting recognition. In: ECCV (2018)
50. Xie, S., Tu, Z.: Holistically-nested edge detection. In: ICCV (2015)
51. Xu, K., et al.: Show, attend and tell: neural image caption generation with visual attention. In: ICML (2015)
52. Xu, S., Jin, T., Jiang, H., Lau, F.C.: Automatic generation of personal Chinese handwriting by capturing the characteristics of personal handwriting. In: IAAI (2009)
53. Yang, H., Jin, L., Huang, W., Yang, Z., Lai, S., Sun, J.: Dense and tight detection of Chinese characters in historical documents: datasets and a recognition guided detector. IEEE Access **6**, 30174–30183 (2018)
54. Yang, Z., He, X., Gao, J., Deng, L., Smola, A.: Stacked attention networks for image question answering. In: CVPR (2016)
55. Yiming Gao, J.W.: GAN-based unpaired Chinese character image translation via skeleton transformation and stroke rendering. In: AAAI (2020)
56. Zhang, J., Du, J., Dai, L.: Track, attend, and parse (TAP): an end-to-end framework for online handwritten mathematical expression recognition. IEEE Trans. Multimedia **21**, 221–233 (2018)
57. Zhang, J., et al.: Watch, attend and parse: an end-to-end neural network based approach to handwritten mathematical expression recognition. Pattern Recogn. **71**, 196–206 (2017)
58. Zhang, K., Zhang, Z., Li, Z., Qiao, Y.: Joint face detection and alignment using multitask cascaded convolutional networks. IEEE Signal Process. Lett. **23**, 1499–1503 (2016)
59. Zhang, R., Isola, P., Efros, A.A.: Colorful image colorization. In: Leibe, B., Matas, J., Sebe, N., Welling, M. (eds.) ECCV 2016. LNCS, vol. 9907, pp. 649–666. Springer, Cham (2016). https://doi.org/10.1007/978-3-319-46487-9_40
60. Zhang, S., Liu, Y., Jin, L., Huang, Y., Lai, S.: EnsNet: Ensconce text in the wild. In: AAAI (2019)
61. Zhang, X.Y., Yin, F., Zhang, Y.M., Liu, C.L., Bengio, Y.: Drawing and recognizing Chinese characters with recurrent neural network. IEEE Trans. Pattern Anal. Mach. Intell. **40**, 849–862 (2017)
62. Zhang, Y., Zhang, Y., Cai, W.: Separating style and content for generalized style transfer. In: CVPR (2018)
63. Zhu, J.Y., Park, T., Isola, P., Efros, A.A.: Unpaired image-to-image translation using cycle-consistent adversarial networks. In: ICCV (2017)

# Object-Contextual Representations
# for Semantic Segmentation

Yuhui Yuan[1,2,3], Xilin Chen[1,2], and Jingdong Wang[3(✉)]

[1] Key Lab of Intelligent Information Processing of Chinese Academy of Sciences
(CAS), Institute of Computing Technology, CAS, Beijing, China
xlchen@ict.ac.cn
[2] University of Chinese Academy of Sciences, Beijing, China
[3] Microsoft Research Asia, Beijing, China
{yuhui.yuan,jingdw}@microsoft.com

**Abstract.** In this paper, we study the context aggregation problem in semantic segmentation. Motivated by that the label of a pixel is the category of the object that the pixel belongs to, we present a simple yet effective approach, object-contextual representations, characterizing a pixel by exploiting the representation of the corresponding object class. First, we learn object regions under the supervision of the ground-truth segmentation. Second, we compute the object region representation by aggregating the representations of the pixels lying in the object region. Last, we compute the relation between each pixel and each object region, and augment the representation of each pixel with the object-contextual representation which is a weighted aggregation of all the object region representations. We empirically demonstrate our method achieves competitive performance on various benchmarks: Cityscapes, ADE20K, LIP, PASCAL-Context and COCO-Stuff. Our submission "HRNet + OCR + SegFix" achieves the 1st place on the Cityscapes leaderboard by the ECCV 2020 submission deadline. Code is available at: https://git.io/openseg and https://git.io/HRNet.OCR.

**Keywords:** Semantic segmentation · Context aggregation

## 1   Introduction

Semantic segmentation is a problem of assigning a class label to each pixel for an image. It is a fundamental topic in computer vision and is critical for various practical tasks such as autonomous driving. Deep convolutional networks since FCN [46] have been the dominant solutions. Various studies have been conducted, including high-resolution representation learning [7,54], contextual aggregation [6,78] that is the interest of this paper, and so on.

**Electronic supplementary material** The online version of this chapter (https://doi.org/10.1007/978-3-030-58539-6_11) contains supplementary material, which is available to authorized users.

© Springer Nature Switzerland AG 2020
A. Vedaldi et al. (Eds.): ECCV 2020, LNCS 12351, pp. 173–190, 2020.
https://doi.org/10.1007/978-3-030-58539-6_11

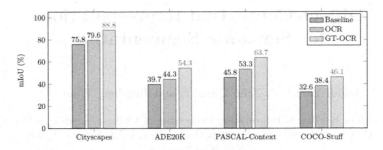

**Fig. 1. Illustrating the effectiveness of our OCR scheme.** GT-OCR estimates the ideal object-contextual representations through exploiting the ground-truth, which is the upper-bound of our method. OCR reports the performance of our proposed object-contextual representations. The three methods, Baseline, OCR and GT-OCR, use the dilated ResNet-101 with output stride 8 as the backbone. We evaluate their (single-scale) segmentation results on Cityscapes val, ADE20K val, PASCAL-Context test and COCO-Stuff test separately. (Color figure online)

The context of one position typically refers to a set of positions, e.g., the surrounding pixels. The early study is mainly about the spatial scale of contexts, i.e., the spatial scope. Representative works, such as ASPP [6] and PPM [78], exploit multi-scale contexts. Recently, several works, such as DANet [16], CFNet [75] and OCNet [70], consider the relations between a position and its contextual positions, and aggregate the representations of the contextual positions with higher weights for similar representations.

We propose to investigate the contextual representation scheme along the line of exploring the relation between a position and its context. The motivation is that *the class label assigned to one pixel is the category of the object*[1] *that the pixel belongs to.* We aim to augment the representation of one pixel by exploiting the representation of the object region of the corresponding class. The empirical study, shown in Fig. 1, verifies that such a representation augmentation scheme, when the ground-truth object region is given, dramatically improves the segmentation quality[2].

Our approach consists of three main steps. First, we divide the contextual pixels into a set of soft object regions with each corresponding to a class, i.e., a coarse soft segmentation computed from a deep network (e.g., ResNet [23] or HRNet [54]). Such division is learned under the supervision of the ground-truth segmentation. Second, we estimate the representation for each object region by aggregating the representations of the pixels in the corresponding object region. Last, we augment the representation of each pixel with the object-contextual representation (OCR). The OCR is the weighted aggregation of all the object region representations with the weights calculated according to the relations between pixels and object regions.

---

[1] We use "object" to represent both "things" and "stuff" following [14,53].
[2] See Sect. 3.4 for more details.

The proposed OCR approach differs from the conventional multi-scale context schemes. Our OCR differentiates the same-object-class contextual pixels from the different-object-class contextual pixels, while the multi-scale context schemes, such as ASPP [6] and PPM [78], do not, and only differentiate the pixels with different spatial positions. Figure 2 provides an example to illustrate the differences between our OCR context and the multi-scale context. On the other hand, our OCR approach is also different from the previous relational context schemes [16,62,70,73,75]. Our approach structures the contextual pixels into object regions and exploits the relations between pixels and object regions. In contrast, the previous relational context schemes consider the contextual pixels separately and only exploit the relations between pixels and contextual pixels [16,70,75] or predict the relations only from pixels without considering the regions [73].

We evaluate our approach on various challenging semantic segmentation benchmarks. Our approach outperforms the multi-scale context schemes, e.g., PSPNet, DeepLabv3, and the recent relational context schemes, e.g., DANet, and the efficiency is also improved. Our approach achieves competitive performance on five benchmarks: 84.5% on Cityscapes test, 45.66% on ADE20K val, 56.65% on LIP val, 56.2% on PASCAL-Context test and 40.5% on COCO-Stuff test. Besides, we extend our approach to Panoptic-FPN [29] and verify the effectiveness of our OCR on the COCO panoptic segmentation task, e.g., Panoptic-FPN + OCR achieves 44.2% on COCO val.

## 2   Related Work

**Multi-scale Context.** PSPNet [78] performs regular convolutions on pyramid pooling representations to capture the multi-scale context. The DeepLab series [5,6] adopt parallel dilated convolutions with different dilation rates (each rate captures the context of a different scale). The recent works [22,67,70,82] propose various extensions, e.g., DenseASPP [67] densifies the dilated rates to cover larger scale ranges. Some other studies [7,17,41] construct the encoder-decoder structures to exploit the multi-resolution features as the multi-scale context.

**Relational Context.** DANet [16], CFNet [75] and OCNet [70] augment the representation for each pixel by aggregating the representations of the contextual pixels, where the context consists of all the pixels. Different from the global context [45], these works consider the relation (or similarity) between the pixels, which is based on the self-attention scheme [60,62], and perform a weighted aggregation with the similarities as the weights.

Double Attention and its related work [8,9,24,34,37,39,72,73] and ACFNet [73] group the pixels into a set of regions, and then augment the pixel representations by aggregating the region representations with the consideration of their context relations predicted by using the pixel representation.

Our approach is a relational context approach and is related to Double Attention and ACFNet. The differences lie in the region formation and the pixel-region

(a) ASPP                    (b) OCR

**Fig. 2. Illustrating the multi-scale context with the ASPP as an example and the OCR context for the pixel marked with ■.** (a) ASPP: The context is a set of sparsely sampled pixels marked with ■, ■. The pixels with different colors correspond to different dilation rates. Those pixels are distributed in both the object region and the background region. (b) Our OCR: The context is expected to be a set of pixels lying in the object (marked with color blue). The image is chosen from ADE20K. (Color figure online)

relation computation. Our approach learns the regions with the supervision of the ground-truth segmentation. In contrast, the regions in previous approaches except ACFNet are formed unsupervisedly. On the other hand, the relation between a pixel and a region is computed by considering both the pixel and region representations, while the relation in previous works is only computed from the pixel representation.

**Coarse-to-Fine Segmentation.** Various coarse-to-fine segmentation schemes have been developed [15, 18, 27, 32, 33, 58, 83] to gradually refine the segmentation maps from coarse to fine. For example, [33] regards the coarse segmentation map as an additional representation and combines it with the original image or other representations for computing a fine segmentation map.

Our approach in some sense can also be regarded as a coarse-to-fine scheme. The difference lies in that we use the coarse segmentation map for generating a contextual representation instead of directly used as an extra representation. We compare our approach with the conventional coarse-to-fine schemes in the supplementary material.

**Region-Wise Segmentation.** There exist many region-wise segmentation methods [1, 2, 20, 21, 49, 59, 63] that organize the pixels into a set of regions (usually super-pixels), and then classify each region to get the image segmentation result. Our approach does not classify each region for segmentation and instead uses the region to learn a better representation for the pixel, which leads to better pixel labeling.

## 3    Approach

Semantic segmentation is a problem of assigning one label $l_i$ to each pixel $p_i$ of an image $I$, where $l_i$ is one of $K$ different classes.

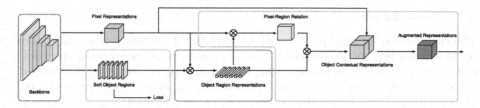

**Fig. 3. Illustrating the pipeline of OCR.** (i) form the soft object regions in the *pink dashed box*. (ii) estimate the object region representations in the *purple dashed box*; (iii) compute the object contextual representations and the augmented representations in the *orange dashed box*. See Sects 3.2 and 3.3 for more details. (Color figure online)

## 3.1 Background

**Multi-scale context.** The ASPP [5] module captures the multi-scale context information by performing several parallel dilated convolutions with different dilation rates [5,6,69]:

$$\mathbf{y}_i^d = \sum_{\mathbf{p}_s = \mathbf{p}_i + d\Delta_t} \mathbf{K}_t^d \mathbf{x}_s. \tag{1}$$

Here, $\mathbf{p}_s = \mathbf{p}_i + d\Delta_t$ is the $s$th sampled position for the dilation convolution with the dilation rate $d$ (e.g., $d = 12, 24, 36$ in DeepLabv3 [6]) at the position $\mathbf{p}_i$. $t$ is the position index for a convolution, e.g., $\{\Delta_t = (\Delta_w, \Delta_h) | \Delta_w = -1, 0, 1, \Delta_h = -1, 0, 1\}$ for a $3 \times 3$ convolution. $\mathbf{x}_s$ is the representation at $\mathbf{p}_s$. $\mathbf{y}_i^d$ is the output representation at $\mathbf{p}_i$ for the $d$th dilated convolution. $\mathbf{K}_t^d$ is the kernel parameter at position $t$ for for the $d$th dilated convolution. The output multi-scale contextual representation is the concatenation of the representations output by the parallel dilated convolutions.

The multi-scale context scheme based on dilated convolutions captures the contexts of multiple scales without losing the resolution. The pyramid pooling module in PSPNet [78] performs regular convolutions on representations of different scales, and also captures the contexts of multiple scales but loses the resolution for large scale contexts.

**Relational Context.** The relational context scheme [16,70,75] computes the context for each pixel by considering the relations:

$$\mathbf{y}_i = \rho(\sum_{s \in \mathcal{I}} w_{is} \delta(\mathbf{x}_s)), \tag{2}$$

where $\mathcal{I}$ refers to the set of pixels in the image, $w_{is}$ is the relation between $\mathbf{x}_i$ and $\mathbf{x}_s$, and may be predicted only from $\mathbf{x}_i$ or computed from $\mathbf{x}_i$ and $\mathbf{x}_s$. $\delta(\cdot)$ and $\rho(\cdot)$ are two different transform functions as done in self-attention [60]. The global context scheme [45] is a special case of relational context with $w_{is} = \frac{1}{|\mathcal{I}|}$.

## 3.2   Formulation

The class label $l_i$ for pixel $p_i$ is essentially the label of the object that pixel $p_i$ lies in. Motivated by this, we present an object-contextual representation approach, characterizing each pixel by exploiting the corresponding object representation.

The proposed object-contextual representation scheme (1) structurizes all the pixels in image I into $K$ soft object regions, (2) represents each object region as $\mathbf{f}_k$ by aggregating the representations of all the pixels in the $k$th object region, and (3) augments the representation for each pixel by aggregating the $K$ object region representations with consideration of its relations with all the object regions:

$$\mathbf{y}_i = \rho(\sum_{k=1}^{K} w_{ik}\delta(\mathbf{f}_k)), \tag{3}$$

where $\mathbf{f}_k$ is the representation of the $k$th object region, $w_{ik}$ is the relation between the $i$th pixel and the $k$th object region. $\delta(\cdot)$ and $\rho(\cdot)$ are transformation functions.

**Soft Object Regions.** We partition the image I into $K$ soft object regions $\{\mathbf{M}_1, \mathbf{M}_2, \ldots, \mathbf{M}_K\}$. Each object region $\mathbf{M}_k$ corresponds to the class $k$, and is represented by a 2D map (or coarse segmentation map), where each entry indicates the degree that the corresponding pixel belongs to the class $k$.

We compute the $K$ object regions from an intermediate representation output from a backbone (e.g., ResNet or HRNet). During training, we learn the object region generator under the supervision from the ground-truth segmentation using the cross-entropy loss.

**Object Region Representations.** We aggregate the representations of all the pixels weighted by their degrees belonging to the $k$th object region, forming the $k$th object region representation:

$$\mathbf{f}_k = \sum_{i \in \mathcal{I}} \tilde{m}_{ki}\mathbf{x}_i. \tag{4}$$

Here, $\mathbf{x}_i$ is the representation of pixel $p_i$. $\tilde{m}_{ki}$ is the normalized degree for pixel $p_i$ belonging to the $k$th object region. We use spatial softmax to normalize each object region $\mathbf{M}_k$.

**Object Contextual Representations.** We compute the relation between each pixel and each object region as below:

$$w_{ik} = \frac{e^{\kappa(\mathbf{x}_i, \mathbf{f}_k)}}{\sum_{j=1}^{K} e^{\kappa(\mathbf{x}_i, \mathbf{f}_j)}}. \tag{5}$$

Here, $\kappa(\mathbf{x}, \mathbf{f}) = \phi(\mathbf{x})^{\top}\psi(\mathbf{f})$ is the unnormalized relation function, $\phi(\cdot)$ and $\psi(\cdot)$ are two transformation functions implemented by $1 \times 1$ conv $\rightarrow$ BN $\rightarrow$ ReLU. This is inspired by self-attention [60] for a better relation estimation.

The object contextual representation $\mathbf{y}_i$ for pixel $p_i$ is computed according to Eq. 3. In this equation, $\delta(\cdot)$ and $\rho(\cdot)$ are both transformation functions implemented by $1 \times 1$ conv $\rightarrow$ BN $\rightarrow$ ReLU, and this follows non-local networks [62].

**Augmented Representations.** The final representation for pixel $p_i$ is updated as the aggregation of two parts, (1) the original representation $\mathbf{x}_i$, and (2) the object contextual representation $\mathbf{y}_i$:

$$\mathbf{z}_i = g([\mathbf{x}_i^\top \; \mathbf{y}_i^\top]^\top). \tag{6}$$

where $g(\cdot)$ is a transform function used to fuse the original representation and the object contextual representation, implemented by $1 \times 1$ conv $\to$ BN $\to$ ReLU. The whole pipeline of our approach is illustrated in Fig. 3.

*Comments:* Some recent studies, e.g., Double Attention [8] and ACFNet [73], can be formulated similarly to Eq. 3, but differ from our approach in some aspects. For example, the region formed in Double Attention do not correspond to an object class, and the relation in ACFNet [73] is computed only from the pixel representation w/o using the object region representation.

### 3.3   Architecture

**Backbone.** We use the dilated ResNet-101 [23] (with output stride 8) or HRNet-W48 [54] (with output stride 4) as the backbone. For dilated ResNet-101, there are two representations input to the OCR module. The first representation from Stage 3 is for predicting coarse segmentation (object regions). The other representation from Stage 4 goes through a $3 \times 3$ convolution (512 output channels), and then is fed into the OCR module. For HRNet-W48, we only use the final representation as the input to the OCR module.

**OCR Module.** We implement the above formulation of our approach as the OCR module, as illustrated in Fig. 3. We use a linear function (a $1 \times 1$ convolution) to predict the coarse segmentation (soft object region) supervised with a pixel-wise cross-entropy loss. All the transform functions, $\psi(\cdot)$, $\phi(\cdot)$, $\delta(\cdot)$, $\rho(\cdot)$, and $g(\cdot)$, are implemented as $1 \times 1$ conv $\to$ BN $\to$ ReLU, and the first three output 256 channels and the last two output 512 channels. We predict the final segmentation from the final representation using a linear function and we also apply a pixel-wise cross-entropy loss on the final segmentation prediction.

### 3.4   Empirical Analysis

We conduct the empirical analysis experiments using the dilated ResNet-101 as the backbone on Cityscapes `val`.

**Object Region Supervision.** We study the influence of the object region supervision. We modify our approach through removing the supervision (i.e., loss) on the soft object regions (within the pink dashed box in Fig. 3), and adding another auxiliary loss in the stage-3 of ResNet-101. We keep all the other settings the same and report the results in the left-most 2 columns of Table 1. We can see that the supervision for forming the object regions is crucial for the performance.

**Table 1. Influence of object region supervision and pixel-region relation estimation scheme.** We can find both the object region supervision and our pixel-region relation scheme are important for the performance.

| Object region supervision | | Pixel-region relations | | |
|---|---|---|---|---|
| w/o supervision | w/ supervision | DA scheme | ACF scheme | Ours |
| 77.31% | **79.58%** | 79.01% | 78.02% | **79.58%** |

**Pixel-Region Relations.** We compare our approach with other two mechanisms that do not use the region representation for estimating the pixel-region relations: (i) Double-Attention [8] uses the pixel representation to predict the relation; (ii) ACFNet [73] directly uses one intermediate segmentation map to indicate the relations. We use DA scheme and ACF scheme to represent the above two mechanisms. We implement both methods by ourselves and only use the dilated ResNet-101 as the backbone without using multi-scale contexts (the results of ACFNet is improved by using ASPP [73]).

The comparison in Table 1 shows that our approach gets superior performance. The reason is that we exploit the pixel representation as well as the region representation for computing the relations. The region representation is able to characterize the object in the specific image, and thus the relation is more accurate for the specific image than that only using the pixel representation.

**Ground-Truth OCR.** We study the segmentation performance using the ground-truth segmentation to form the object regions and the pixel-region relations, called GT-OCR, to justify our motivation. (i) Object region formation using the ground-truth: set the confidence of pixel $i$ belonging to $k$th object region $m_{ki} = 1$ if the ground-truth label $l_i \equiv k$ and $m_{ki} = 0$ otherwise. (ii) Pixel-region relation computation using the ground-truth: set the pixel-region relation $w_{ik} = 1$ if the ground-truth label $l_i \equiv k$ and $w_{ik} = 0$ otherwise. We have illustrated the detailed results of GT-OCR on four different benchmarks in Fig. 1.

# 4    Experiments: Semantic Segmentation

## 4.1    Datasets

**Cityscapes.** The Cityscapes dataset [11] is tasked for urban scene understanding. There are totally 30 classes and only 19 classes are used for parsing evaluation. The dataset contains 5K high quality pixel-level finely annotated images and 20K coarsely annotated images. The finely annotated 5K images are divided into $2,975/500/1,525$ images for training, validation and testing.

**ADE20K.** The ADE20K dataset [80] is used in ImageNet scene parsing challenge 2016. There are 150 classes and diverse scenes with $1,038$ image-level labels. The dataset is divided into $20K/2\,K/3K$ images for training, validation and testing.

**LIP.** The LIP dataset [19] is used in the LIP challenge 2016 for single human parsing task. There are about 50K images with 20 classes (19 semantic human part classes and 1 background class). The training, validation, and test sets consist of 30K, 10K, 10K images respectively.

**PASCAL-Context.** The PASCAL-Context dataset [48] is a challenging scene parsing dataset that contains 59 semantic classes and 1 background class. The training set and test set consist of $4,998$ and $5,105$ images respectively.

**COCO-Stuff.** The COCO-Stuff dataset [3] is a challenging scene parsing dataset that contains 171 semantic classes. The training set and test set consist of 9K and 1K images respectively.

### 4.2   Implementation Details

**Training Setting.** We initialize the backbones using the model pre-trained on ImageNet and the OCR module randomly. We perform the polynomial learning rate policy with factor $(1 - (\frac{iter}{iter_{max}})^{0.9})$, the weight on the final loss as 1, the weight on the loss used to supervise the object region estimation (or auxiliary loss) as 0.4. We use INPLACE-ABN$^{\text{sync}}$ [52] to synchronize the mean and standard-deviation of BN across multiple GPUs. For the data augmentation, we perform random flipping horizontally, random scaling in the range of $[0.5, 2]$ and random brightness jittering within the range of $[-10, 10]$. We perform the same training settings for the reproduced approaches, e.g., PPM, ASPP, to ensure the fairness. We follow the previous works [6,74,78] for setting up the training for the benchmark datasets.

☐ *Cityscapes:* We set the initial learning rate as 0.01, weight decay as 0.0005, crop size as $769 \times 769$ and batch size as 8 by default. For the experiments evaluated on val/test set, we set training iterations as 40K/100K on train/train+val set separately. For the experiments augmented with extra data: (i) w/ coarse, we first train our model on train + val for 100K iterations with initial learning rate as 0.01, then we fine-tune the model on coarse set for 50K iterations and continue fine-tune our model on train+val for 20K iterations with the same initial learning rate 0.001. (ii) w/ coarse + Mapillary [49], we first pre-train our model on the Mapillary train set for 500K iterations with batch size 16 and initial learning rate 0.01 (achieves 50.8% on Mapillary val), then we fine-tune the model on Cityscapes following the order of train + val (100K iterations) $\rightarrow$ coarse (50K iterations) $\rightarrow$ train + val (20K iterations), we set the initial learning rate as 0.001 and the batch size as 8 during the above three fine-tuning stages on Cityscapes.

☐ *ADE20K:* We set the initial learning rate as 0.02, weight decay as 0.0001, crop size as $520 \times 520$, batch size as 16 and and training iterations as 150K if not specified.

☐ *LIP:* We set the initial learning rate as 0.007, weight decay as 0.0005, crop size as $473 \times 473$, batch size as 32 and training iterations as 100K if not specified.

**Table 2. Comparison with multi-scale context scheme.** We use ★ to mark the result w/o using Cityscapes `val` for training. We can find OCR consistently outperforms both PPM and ASPP across different benchmarks under the fair comparisons.

| Method | Cityscapes (w/o coarse) | Cityscapes (w/ coarse) | ADE20K | LIP |
|---|---|---|---|---|
| PPM [78] | 78.4%★ | 81.2% | 43.29% | – |
| ASPP [6] | – | 81.3% | – | – |
| PPM (Our impl.) | 80.3% | 81.6% | 44.50% | 54.76% |
| ASPP (Our impl.) | 81.0% | 81.7% | 44.60% | 55.01% |
| OCR | **81.8%** | **82.4%** | **45.28%** | **55.60%** |

**Table 3. Comparison with relational context scheme.** Our method consistently performs better across different benchmarks. Notably, Double Attention is sensitive to the region number choice and we have fine-tuned this hyper-parameter as 64 to report its best performance.

| Method | Cityscapes (w/o coarse) | Cityscapes (w/ coarse) | ADE20K | LIP |
|---|---|---|---|---|
| CC-Attention [26] | 81.4% | - | 45.22% | - |
| DANet [16] | 81.5% | - | - | - |
| Self Attention (Our impl.) | 81.1% | 82.0% | 44.75% | 55.15% |
| Double Attention (Our impl.) | 81.2% | 82.0% | 44.81% | 55.12% |
| OCR | **81.8%** | **82.4%** | **45.28%** | **55.60%** |

**Table 4. Complexity comparison.** We use input feature map of size $[1 \times 2048 \times 128 \times 128]$ to evaluate their complexity during inference. The numbers are obtained on a single P40 GPU with CUDA 10.0. All the numbers are the smaller the better. Our OCR requires the least GPU memory and the least runtime.

| Method | Parameters▲ | Memory▲ | FLOPs ▲ | Time▲ |
|---|---|---|---|---|
| PPM (Our impl.) | 23.1M | 792M | 619G | 99ms |
| ASPP (Our impl.) | 15.5M | 284M | 492G | 97ms |
| DANet (Our impl.) | 10.6M | 2339M | 1110G | 121ms |
| CC-Attention (Our impl.) | 10.6M | 427M | 804G | 131ms |
| Self-Attention (Our impl.) | 10.5M | 2168M | 619G | 96ms |
| Double Attention (Our impl.) | **10.2M** | 209M | **338G** | 46ms |
| OCR | 10.5M | **202M** | 340G | **45ms** |

☐ *PASCAL-Context:* We set the initial learning rate as 0.001, weight decay as 0.0001, crop size as $520 \times 520$, batch size as 16 and training iterations as 30K if not specified.

☐ *COCO-Stuff:* We set the initial learning rate as 0.001, weight decay as 0.0001, crop size as $520 \times 520$, batch size as 16 and training iterations as 60K if not specified.

### 4.3   Comparison with Existing Context Schemes

We conduct the experiments using the dilated ResNet-101 as the backbone and use the same training/testing settings to ensure the fairness.

**Multi-scale Contexts.** We compare our OCR with the multi-scale context schemes including PPM [78] and ASPP [6] on three benchmarks including Cityscapes `test`, ADE20K `val` and LIP `val` in Table 2. Our reproduced PPM/ASPP outperforms the originally reported numbers in [6,78]. From Table 2, it can be seen that our OCR outperforms both multi-scale context schemes by a large margin. For example, the absolute gains of OCR over PPM (ASPP) for the four comparisons are 1.5% (0.8%), 0.8% (0.7%), 0.78% (0.68%), 0.84% (0.5%). To the best of our knowledge, these improvements are already significant considering that the baselines (with dilated ResNet-101) are already strong and the complexity of our OCR is much smaller.

**Relational Contexts.** We compare our OCR with various relational context schemes including Self-Attention [60,62], Criss-Cross attention [26] (CC-Attention), DANet [16] and Double Attention [8] on the same three benchmarks including Cityscapes `test`, ADE20K `val` and LIP `val`. For the reproduced Double Attention, we fine-tune the number of the regions (as it is very sensitive to the hyper-parameter choice) and we choose 64 with the best performance. More detailed analysis and comparisons are illustrated in the supplementary material. According to the results in Table 3, it can be seen that our OCR outperforms these relational context schemes under the fair comparisons. Notably, the complexity of our OCR is much smaller than most of the other methods.

**Complexity.** We compare the efficiency of our OCR with the efficiencies of the multi-scale context schemes and the relational context schemes. We measure the increased parameters, GPU memory, computation complexity (measured by the number of FLOPs) and inference time that are introduced by the context modules, and do not count the complexity from the backbones. The comparison in Table 4 shows the superiority of the proposed OCR scheme.

☐ *Parameters*: Most relational context schemes require less parameters compared with the multi-scale context schemes. For example, our OCR only requires 1/2 and 2/3 of the parameters of PPM and ASPP separately.

☐ *Memory*: Both our OCR and Double Attention require much less GPU memory compared with the other approaches (e.g., DANet, PPM). For example, our GPU memory consumption is 1/4, 1/10, 1/2, 1/10 of the memory consumption of PPM, DANet, CC-Attention and Self-Attention separately.

☐ *FLOPs*: Our OCR only requires 1/2, 7/10, 3/10, 2/5 and 1/2 of the FLOPs based on PPM, ASPP, DANet, CC-Attention and Self-Attention separately.

☐ *Running time*: The runtime of OCR is very small: only 1/2, 1/2, 1/3, 1/3 and 1/2 of the runtime with PPM, ASPP, DANet, CC-Attention and Self-Attention separately.

In general, *our OCR is a much better choice if we consider the balance between performance, memory complexity, GFLOPs and running time.*

## 4.4    Comparison with State-of-the-Art

Considering that different approaches perform improvements on different base-lines to achieve the best performance, we categorize the existing works to two groups according to the baselines that they apply: (i) *simple baseline:* dilated ResNet-101 with stride 8; (ii) *advanced baseline:* PSPNet, DeepLabv3, multi-grid (MG), encoder-decoder structures that achieve higher resolution outputs with stride 4 or stronger backbones such as WideResNet-38, Xception-71 and HRNet.

For fair comparison with the two groups fairly, we perform our OCR on a simple baseline (dilated ResNet-101 with stride 8) and an advanced baseline (HRNet-W48 with stride 4). Notably, our improvement with HRNet-W48 (over ResNet-101) is comparable with the gain of the other work based on advanced baseline methods. For example, DGCNet [76] gains 0.7% with Multi-grid while OCR gains 0.6% with stronger backbone on Cityscapes test. We summarize all the results in Table 5 and illustrate the comparison details on each benchmark separately as follows.

**Cityscapes.** Compared with the methods based on the simple baseline on Cityscape test w/o using the coarse data, our approach achieves the best per-formance 81.8%, which is already comparable with some methods based on the advanced baselines, e.g, DANet, ACFNet. Our approach achieves better perfor-mance 82.4% through exploiting the coarsely annotated images for training.

For comparison with the approaches based on the advanced baselines, we perform our OCR on the HRNet-W48, and pre-train our model on the Mapillary dataset [49]. Our approach achieves 84.2% on Cityscapes test. We further apply a novel post-processing scheme SegFix [71] to refine the boundary quality, which brings 0.3% ↑ improvement. Our final submission "HRNet + OCR + SegFix" achieves 84.5%, which ranks the 1$^{st}$ place on the Cityscapes leaderboard by the time of our submission. In fact, we perform PPM and ASPP on HRNet-W48 separately and empirically find that directly applying either PPM or ASPP does not improve the performance and even degrades the performance, while our OCR consistently improves the performance.

Notably, the very recent work [56] sets a new state-of-the-art performance 85.4% on Cityscapes leaderboard via combining our "HRNet + OCR" and a new hierarchical multi-scale attention mechanism.

**ADE20K.** From Table 5, it can be seen that our OCR achieves competi-tive performance (45.28% and 45.66%) compared with most of the previous approaches based on both simple baselines and advanced baselines. For exam-ple, the ACFNet [22] exploits both the multi-scale context and relational context to achieve higher performance. The very recent ACNet [17] achieves the best per-formance through combining richer local and global contexts.

**LIP.** Our approach achieves the best performance 55.60% on LIP val based on the simple baselines. Applying the stronger backbone HRNetV2-W48 fur-ther improves the performance to 56.65%, which outperforms the previous

**Table 5. Comparison with state-of-the-art.** We use M to represent multi-scale context and R to represent relational context. Red, Green, Blue represent the top-3 results. We use ♭, † and ‡ to mark the result w/o using Cityscapes `val`, the method using Mapillary dataset and the method using the Cityscapes video dataset separately

| Method | Baseline | Stride | Context schemes | Cityscapes (w/o coarse) | Cityscapes (w/ coarse) | ADE20K | LIP | PASCAL Context | COCO-Stuff |
|---|---|---|---|---|---|---|---|---|---|
| Simple baselines | | | | | | | | | |
| PSPNet [78] | ResNet-101 | 8× | M | 78.4♭ | 81.2 | 43.29 | - | 47.8 | - |
| DeepLabv3 [6] | ResNet-101 | 8× | M | - | 81.3 | - | - | - | - |
| PSANet [79] | ResNet-101 | 8× | R | 80.1 | 81.4 | 43.77 | - | - | - |
| SAC [77] | ResNet-101 | 8× | M | 78.1 | - | 44.30 | - | - | - |
| AAF [28] | ResNet-101 | 8× | R | 79.1♭ | - | - | - | - | - |
| DSSPN [40] | ResNet-101 | 8× | - | 77.8 | - | 43.68 | - | - | 38.9 |
| DepthSeg [31] | ResNet-101 | 8× | - | 78.2 | - | - | - | - | - |
| MMAN [47] | ResNet-101 | 8× | - | - | - | - | 46.81 | - | - |
| JPPNet [38] | ResNet-101 | 8× | M | - | - | - | 51.37 | - | - |
| EncNet [74] | ResNet-101 | 8× | - | - | - | 44.65 | - | 51.7 | - |
| GCU [37] | ResNet-101 | 8× | R | - | - | 44.81 | - | - | - |
| APCNet [22] | ResNet-101 | 8× | M,R | - | - | 45.38 | - | 54.7 | - |
| CFNet [75] | ResNet-101 | 8× | R | 79.6 | - | 44.89 | - | 54.0 | - |
| BFP [12] | ResNet-101 | 8× | R | 81.4 | - | - | - | 53.6 | - |
| CCNet [26] | ResNet-101 | 8× | R | 81.4 | - | 45.22 | - | - | - |
| ANNet [82] | ResNet-101 | 8× | M,R | 81.3 | - | 45.24 | - | 52.8 | - |
| OCR | ResNet-101 | 8× | R | 81.8 | 82.4 | 45.28 | 55.60 | 54.8 | 39.5 |
| Advanced baselines | | | | | | | | | |
| DenseASPP [67] | DenseNet-161 | 8× | M | 80.6 | - | - | - | - | - |
| DANet [16] | ResNet-101 + MG | 8× | R | 81.5 | - | 45.22 | - | 52.6 | 39.7 |
| DGCNet [76] | ResNet-101 + MG | 8× | R | 82.0 | - | - | - | 53.7 | - |
| EMANet [34] | ResNet-101 + MG | 8× | R | - | - | - | - | 53.1 | 39.9 |
| SeENet [51] | ResNet-101 + ASPP | 8× | M | 81.2 | - | - | - | - | - |
| SGR [39] | ResNet-101 + ASPP | 8× | R | - | - | 44.32 | - | 52.5 | 39.1 |
| OCNet [70] | ResNet-101 + ASPP | 8× | M,R | 81.7 | - | 45.45 | 54.72 | - | - |
| ACFNet [73] | ResNet-101 + ASPP | 8× | M,R | 81.8 | - | - | - | - | - |
| CNIF [61] | ResNet-101 + ASPP | 8× | M | - | - | - | 56.93 | - | - |
| GALD [35] | ResNet-101 + ASPP | 8× | M,R | 81.8 | 82.9 | - | - | - | - |
| GALD† [35] | ResNet-101 + CGNL + MG | 8× | M,R | - | 83.3 | - | - | - | - |
| Mapillary [52] | WideResNet-38 + ASPP | 8× | M | - | 82.0 | - | - | - | - |
| GSCNN† [55] | WideResNet-38 + ASPP | 8× | M | 82.8 | - | - | - | - | - |
| SPGNet [10] | 2× ResNet-50 | 4× | - | 81.1 | - | - | - | - | - |
| ZigZagNet [41] | ResNet-101 | 4× | M | - | - | - | - | 52.1 | - |
| SVCNet [13] | ResNet-101 | 4× | R | 81.0 | - | - | - | 53.2 | 39.6 |
| ACNet [17] | ResNet-101 + MG | 4× | M,R | 82.3 | - | 45.90 | - | 54.1 | 40.1 |
| CE2P [44] | ResNet-101 + PPM | 4× | M | - | - | - | 53.10 | - | - |
| VPLR†‡ [81] | WideResNet-38 + ASPP | 4× | M | - | 83.5 | - | - | - | - |
| DeepLabv3+ [7] | Xception-71 | 4× | M | - | 82.1 | - | - | - | - |
| DPC [4] | Xception-71 | 4× | M | 82.7 | - | - | - | - | - |
| DUpsampling [57] | Xception-71 | 4× | M | - | - | - | - | 52.5 | - |
| HRNet [54] | HRNetV2-W48 | 4× | - | 81.6 | - | - | 55.90 | 54.0 | - |
| OCR | HRNetV2-W48 | 4× | R | 82.4 | 83.0 | 45.66 | 56.65 | 56.2 | 40.5 |
| OCR† | HRNetV2-W48 | 4× | R | 83.6 | 84.2 | - | - | - | - |

approaches. The very recent work CNIF [61] achieves the best performance (56.93%) through injecting the hierarchical structure knowledge of human parts. Our approach potentially benefit from such hierarchical structural knowledge. All the results are based on only flip testing without multi-scale testing[3].

---

[3] Only few methods adopt multi-scale testing. For example, CNIF [61] gets the improved performance from 56.93% to 57.74%.

**PASCAL-Context.** We evaluate the performance over 59 categories following [54]. It can be seen that our approach outperforms both the previous best methods based on simple baselines and the previous best methods based on advanced baselines. The HRNet-W48 + OCR approach achieves the best performance 56.2%, significantly outperforming the second best, e.g., ACPNet (54.7%) and ACNet (54.1%).

**COCO-Stuff.** It can be seen that our approach achieves the best performance, 39.5% based ResNet-101 and 40.5% based on HRNetV2-48.

**Qualitative Results.** We illustrate the qualitative results in the supplementary material due to the limited pages.

## 5     Experiments: Panoptic Segmentation

To verify the generalization ability of our method, we apply OCR scheme on the more challenging panoptic segmentation task [30], which unifies both the instance segmentation task and the semantic segmentation task.

**Dataset.** We choose the COCO dataset [42] to study the effectiveness of our method on panoptic segmentation. We follow the previous work [29] and uses all 2017 COCO images with 80 thing and 53 stuff classes annotated.

**Training Details.** We follow the default training setup of "COCO Panoptic Segmentation Baselines with Panoptic FPN (3× learning schedule)"[4] in Detectron2 [64]. The reproduced Panoptic FPN reaches higher performance than the original numbers in the paper [29] (Panoptic FPN w/ ResNet-50, PQ: 39.2%/Panoptic FPN w/ ResNet-101, PQ: 40.3%) and we choose the higher reproduced results as our baseline.

In our implementation, we use the original prediction from the semantic segmentation head (within Panoptic-FPN) to compute the soft object regions and then we use a OCR head to predict a refined semantic segmentation map. We set the loss weights on both the original semantic segmentation head and the OCR head as 0.25. All the other training settings are kept the same for fair comparison. We directly use the same OCR implementation (for the semantic segmentation task) without any tuning.

**Results.** In Table 6, we can see that OCR improves the PQ performance of Panoptic-FPN (ResNet-101) from 43.0% to 44.2%, where the main improvements come from better segmentation quality on the *stuff* region measured by mIoU and $PQ^{St}$. Specifically, our OCR improves the mIoU and $PQ^{St}$ of Panoptic-FPN (ResNet-101) by 1.0% and 2.3% separately. In general, the performance of "Panoptic-FPN + OCR" is very competitive compared to various recent methods [43,65,68]. We also report the results of Panoptic-FPN with PPM and ASPP to illustrate the advantages of our OCR in the supplementary material.

---

[4] https://github.com/facebookresearch/detectron2/blob/master/MODEL_ZOO.md.

**Table 6. Panoptic segmentation results on COCO val 2017.** The performance of Panoptic-FPN [29] is reproduced based on the official open-source Detectron2 [64] and we use the 3× learning rate schedule by default. Our OCR consistently improves the PQ performance with both backbones.

| Backbone | Method | AP | $PQ^{Th}$ | mIoU | $PQ^{St}$ | PQ |
|---|---|---|---|---|---|---|
| ResNet-50 | Panoptic-FPN | 40.0 | 48.3 | 42.9 | 31.2 | 41.5 |
| | Panoptic-FPN + OCR | 40.4 *(+0.4)* | 48.6 *(+0.3)* | 44.3 *(+1.4)* | 33.9 *(+2.7)* | 42.7 *(+1.2)* |
| ResNet-101 | Panoptic-FPN | 42.4 | 49.7 | 44.5 | 32.9 | 43.0 |
| | Panoptic-FPN + OCR | 42.7 *(+0.3)* | 50.2 *(+0.5)* | 45.5 *(+1.0)* | 35.2 *(+2.3)* | 44.2 *(+1.2)* |

# 6  Conclusions

In this work, we present an object-contextual representation approach for semantic segmentation. The main reason for the success is that the label of a pixel is the label of the object that the pixel lies in and the pixel representation is strengthened by characterizing each pixel with the corresponding object region representation. We empirically show that our approach brings consistent improvements on various benchmarks.

**Acknowledgement.** This work is partially supported by Natural Science Foundation of China under contract No. 61390511, and Frontier Science Key Research Project CAS No. QYZDJ-SSW-JSC009.

# References

1. Arbeláez, P., Hariharan, B., Gu, C., Gupta, S., Bourdev, L., Malik, J.: Semantic segmentation using regions and parts. In: CVPR (2012)
2. Caesar, H., Uijlings, J., Ferrari, V.: Region-based semantic segmentation with end-to-end training. In: ECCV (2016)
3. Caesar, H., Uijlings, J., Ferrari, V.: COCO-Stuff: thing and stuff classes in context. In: CVPR (2018)
4. Chen, L.C., et al.: Searching for efficient multi-scale architectures for dense image prediction. In: NIPS (2018)
5. Chen, L.C., Papandreou, G., Kokkinos, I., Murphy, K., Yuille, A.L.: DeepLab: semantic image segmentation with deep convolutional nets, atrous convolution, and fully connected CRFS. PAMI **40**(4), 834–848 (2018)
6. Chen, L.C., Papandreou, G., Schroff, F., Adam, H.: Rethinking atrous convolution for semantic image segmentation. arXiv:1706.05587 (2017)
7. Chen, L.C., Zhu, Y., Papandreou, G., Schroff, F., Adam, H.: Encoder-decoder with atrous separable convolution for semantic image segmentation. In: ECCV (2018)
8. Chen, Y., Kalantidis, Y., Li, J., Yan, S., Feng, J.: A2-nets: double attention networks. In: NIPS (2018)
9. Chen, Y., Rohrbach, M., Yan, Z., Yan, S., Feng, J., Kalantidis, Y.: Graph-based global reasoning networks. arXiv:1811.12814 (2018)
10. Cheng, B., et al.: SPGNet: semantic prediction guidance for scene parsing. In: ICCV (2019)
11. Cordts, M., et al.: The cityscapes dataset for semantic urban scene understanding. In: CVPR (2016)

12. Ding, H., Jiang, X., Liu, A.Q., Thalmann, N.M., Wang, G.: Boundary-aware feature propagation for scene segmentation. In: ICCV (2019)
13. Ding, H., Jiang, X., Shuai, B., Liu, A.Q., Wang, G.: Semantic correlation promoted shape-variant context for segmentation. In: CVPR (2019)
14. Farabet, C., Couprie, C., Najman, L., LeCun, Y.: Learning hierarchical features for scene labeling. PAMI **35**(8), 1915–1929 (2012)
15. Fieraru, M., Khoreva, A., Pishchulin, L., Schiele, B.: Learning to refine human pose estimation. In: CVPRW (2018)
16. Fu, J., Liu, J., Tian, H., Fang, Z., Lu, H.: Dual attention network for scene segmentation. arXiv:1809.02983 (2018)
17. Fu, J., et al.: Adaptive context network for scene parsing. In: ICCV (2019)
18. Gidaris, S., Komodakis, N.: Detect, replace, refine: deep structured prediction for pixel wise labeling. In: CVPR (2017)
19. Gong, K., Liang, X., Zhang, D., Shen, X., Lin, L.: Look into person: self-supervised structure-sensitive learning and a new benchmark for human parsing. In: CVPR (2017)
20. Gould, S., Fulton, R., Koller, D.: Decomposing a scene into geometric and semantically consistent regions. In: ICCV (2009)
21. Gu, C., Lim, J.J., Arbelaez, P., Malik, J.: Recognition using regions. In: CVPR (2009)
22. He, J., Deng, Z., Zhou, L., Wang, Y., Qiao, Y.: Adaptive pyramid context network for semantic segmentation. In: CVPR (2019)
23. He, K., Zhang, X., Ren, S., Sun, J.: Deep residual learning for image recognition. In: CVPR (2016)
24. Huang, L., Yuan, Y., Guo, J., Zhang, C., Chen, X., Wang, J.: Interlaced sparse self-attention for semantic segmentation. arXiv preprint arXiv:1907.12273 (2019)
25. Huang, Y.H., Jia, X., Georgoulis, S., Tuytelaars, T., Van Gool, L.: Error correction for dense semantic image labeling. In: CVPRW (2018)
26. Huang, Z., Wang, X., Huang, L., Huang, C., Wei, Y., Liu, W.: CCNet: criss-cross attention for semantic segmentation. In: ICCV (2019)
27. Islam, M.A., Naha, S., Rochan, M., Bruce, N., Wang, Y.: Label refinement network for coarse-to-fine semantic segmentation. arXiv:1703.00551 (2017)
28. Ke, T.W., Hwang, J.J., Liu, Z., Yu, S.X.: Adaptive affinity fields for semantic segmentation. In: Ferrari, V., Hebert, M., Sminchisescu, C., Weiss, Y. (eds.) Computer Vision – ECCV 2018. Lecture Notes in Computer Science, vol. 11205, pp. 605–621. Springer, Cham (2018). https://doi.org/10.1007/978-3-030-01246-5_36
29. Kirillov, A., Girshick, R., He, K., Dollár, P.: Panoptic feature pyramid networks. In: CVPR (2019)
30. Kirillov, A., He, K., Girshick, R., Rother, C., Dollár, P.: Panoptic segmentation. In: CVPR (2019)
31. Kong, S., Fowlkes, C.C.: Recurrent scene parsing with perspective understanding in the loop. In: CVPR (2018)
32. Kuo, W., Angelova, A., Malik, J., Lin, T.Y.: ShapeMask: learning to segment novel objects by refining shape priors (2019)
33. Li, K., Hariharan, B., Malik, J.: Iterative instance segmentation. In: CVPR (2016)
34. Li, X., Zhong, Z., Wu, J., Yang, Y., Lin, Z., Liu, H.: Expectation-maximization attention networks for semantic segmentation. In: ICCV (2019)
35. Li, X., Zhang, L., You, A., Yang, M., Yang, K., Tong, Y.: Global aggregation then local distribution in fully convolutional networks. BMVC (2019)
36. Li, X., Liu, Z., Luo, P., Change Loy, C., Tang, X.: Not all pixels are equal: difficulty-aware semantic segmentation via deep layer cascade. In: CVPR (2017)

37. Li, Y., Gupta, A.: Beyond grids: learning graph representations for visual recognition. In: NIPS (2018)
38. Liang, X., Gong, K., Shen, X., Lin, L.: Look into person: joint body parsing & pose estimation network and a new benchmark. PAMI (2018)
39. Liang, X., Hu, Z., Zhang, H., Lin, L., Xing, E.P.: Symbolic graph reasoning meets convolutions. In: NIPS (2018)
40. Liang, X., Zhou, H., Xing, E.: Dynamic-structured semantic propagation network. In: CVPR (2018)
41. Lin, D., et al.: ZigZagNet: fusing top-down and bottom-up context for object segmentation. In: CVPR (2019)
42. Lin, T.Y., et al.: Microsoft COCO: common objects in context. In: Fleet, D., Pajdla, T., Schiele, B., Tuytelaars, T. (eds.) Computer Vision – ECCV 2014. Lecture Notes in Computer Science, vol. 8693, pp. 740–755. Springer, Cham (2014). https://doi.org/10.1007/978-3-319-10602-1_48
43. Liu, H., et al.: An end-to-end network for panoptic segmentation. In: CVPR (2019)
44. Liu, T., et al.: Devil in the details: Towards accurate single and multiple human parsing. arXiv:1809.05996 (2018)
45. Liu, W., Rabinovich, A., Berg, A.C.: ParseNet: looking wider to see better. arXiv:1506.04579 (2015)
46. Long, J., Shelhamer, E., Darrell, T.: Fully convolutional networks for semantic segmentation. In: CVPR (2015)
47. Luo, Y., Zheng, Z., Zheng, L., Tao, G., Junqing, Y., Yang, Y.: Macro-micro adversarial network for human parsing. In: Ferrari, V., Hebert, M., Sminchisescu, C., Weiss, Y. (eds.) Computer Vision – ECCV 2018. Lecture Notes in Computer Science, vol. 11213, pp. 424–440. Springer, Cham (2018). https://doi.org/10.1007/978-3-030-01240-3_26
48. Mottaghi, R., et al.: The role of context for object detection and semantic segmentation in the wild. In: CVPR (2014)
49. Neuhold, G., Ollmann, T., Rota Bulo, S., Kontschieder, P.: The mapillary vistas dataset for semantic understanding of street scenes. In: CVPR (2017)
50. Nigam, I., Huang, C., Ramanan, D.: Ensemble knowledge transfer for semantic segmentation. In: WACV (2018)
51. Pang, Y., Li, Y., Shen, J., Shao, L.: Towards bridging semantic gap to improve semantic segmentation. In: ICCV (2019)
52. Rota Bulò, S., Porzi, L., Kontschieder, P.: In-place activated batchnorm for memory-optimized training of DNNs. In: CVPR (2018)
53. Shetty, R., Schiele, B., Fritz, M.: Not using the car to see the sidewalk-quantifying and controlling the effects of context in classification and segmentation. In: CVPR (2019)
54. Sun, K., et al.: High-resolution representations for labeling pixels and regions. arXiv:1904.04514 (2019)
55. Takikawa, T., Acuna, D., Jampani, V., Fidler, S.: Gated-SCNN: gated shape CNNs for semantic segmentation. In: ICCV (2019)
56. Tao, A., Sapra, K., Catanzaro, B.: Hierarchical multi-scale attention for semantic segmentation. arXiv:2005.10821 (2020)
57. Tian, Z., He, T., Shen, C., Yan, Y.: Decoders matter for semantic segmentation: data-dependent decoding enables flexible feature aggregation. In: CVPR (2019)
58. Tu, Z., Bai, X.: Auto-context and its application to high-level vision tasks and 3D brain image segmentation. PAMI 32(10), 1744–1757 (2010)
59. Uijlings, J.R., Van De Sande, K.E., Gevers, T., Smeulders, A.W.: Selective search for object recognition. IJCV 104, 154–171 (2013)

60. Vaswani, A., et al.: Attention is all you need. In: NIPS (2017)
61. Wang, W., Zhang, Z., Qi, S., Shen, J., Pang, Y., Shao, L.: Learning compositional neural information fusion for human parsing. In: ICCV (2019)
62. Wang, X., Girshick, R., Gupta, A., He, K.: Non-local neural networks. In: CVPR (2018)
63. Wei, Y., Feng, J., Liang, X., Cheng, M.M., Zhao, Y., Yan, S.: Object region mining with adversarial erasing: a simple classification to semantic segmentation approach. In: CVPR (2017)
64. Wu, Y., Kirillov, A., Massa, F., Lo, W.Y., Girshick, R.: Detectron2. https://github. com/facebookresearch/detectron2 (2019)
65. Xiong, Y., et al.: UPSNet: a unified panoptic segmentation network. In: CVPR (2019)
66. Xu, J., Chen, K., Lin, D.: MMSegmenation. https://github.com/open-mmlab/ mmsegmentation (2020)
67. Yang, M., Yu, K., Zhang, C., Li, Z., Yang, K.: DenseASPP for semantic segmentation in street scenes. In: CVPR (2018)
68. Yang, Y., Li, H., Li, X., Zhao, Q., Wu, J., Lin, Z.: SogNet: scene overlap graph network for panoptic segmentation. arXiv:1911.07527 (2019)
69. Yu, F., Koltun, V.: Multi-scale context aggregation by dilated convolutions. In: ICLR (2016)
70. Yuan, Y., Wang, J.: OCNet: object context network for scene parsing. arXiv:1809.00916 (2018)
71. Yuan, Y., Xie, J., Chen, X., Wang, J.: SegFix: model-agnostic boundary refinement for segmentation. In: Vedaldi, A., Bischof, H., Brox, T., Frahm, J.M. (eds.) Computer Vision – ECCV 2020. Lecture Notes in Computer Science, vol. 12357, pp. 489–506. Springer, Cham (2020). https://doi.org/10.1007/978-3-030-58610-2_29
72. Yue, K., Sun, M., Yuan, Y., Zhou, F., Ding, E., Xu, F.: Compact generalized non-local network. In: NIPS (2018)
73. Zhang, F., et al.: ACFNet: attentional class feature network for semantic segmentation. In: ICCV (2019)
74. Zhang, H., et al.: Context encoding for semantic segmentation. In: CVPR (2018)
75. Zhang, H., Zhang, H., Wang, C., Xie, J.: Co-occurrent features in semantic segmentation. In: CVPR (2019)
76. Zhang, L., Li, X., Arnab, A., Yang, K., Tong, Y., Torr, P.H.: Dual graph convolutional network for semantic segmentation. In: BMVC (2019)
77. Zhang, R., Tang, S., Zhang, Y., Li, J., Yan, S.: Scale-adaptive convolutions for scene parsing. In: ICCV (2017)
78. Zhao, H., Shi, J., Qi, X., Wang, X., Jia, J.: Pyramid scene parsing network. In: CVPR (2017)
79. Zhao, H., et al.: PSANet: point-wise spatial attention network for scene parsing. In: Ferrari, V., Hebert, M., Sminchisescu, C., Weiss, Y. (eds.) Computer Vision – ECCV 2018. Lecture Notes in Computer Science, vol. 11213, pp. 270–286. Springer, Cham (2018). https://doi.org/10.1007/978-3-030-01240-3_17
80. Zhou, B., Zhao, H., Puig, X., Fidler, S., Barriuso, A., Torralba, A.: Scene parsing through ade20k dataset. In: CVPR (2017)
81. Zhu, Y., et al.: Improving semantic segmentation via video propagation and label relaxation. In: CVPR (2019)
82. Zhu, Z., Xu, M., Bai, S., Huang, T., Bai, X.: Asymmetric non-local neural networks for semantic segmentation. In: ICCV (2019)
83. Zhu, Z., Xia, Y., Shen, W., Fishman, E., Yuille, A.: A 3D coarse-to-fine framework for volumetric medical image segmentation. In: 3DV (2018)

# Efficient Spatio-Temporal Recurrent Neural Network for Video Deblurring

Zhihang Zhong[1], Ye Gao[2], Yinqiang Zheng[3(✉)], and Bo Zheng[2]

[1] The University of Tokyo, Tokyo 113-8656, Japan
zhong@race.t.u-tokyo.ac.jp
[2] Tokyo Research Center, Huawei, Tokyo, Japan
{jeremy.gao,bozheng.jp}@huawei.com
[3] National Institute of Informatics, Tokyo 101-8430, Japan
yqzheng@nii.ac.jp

**Abstract.** Real-time video deblurring still remains a challenging task due to the complexity of spatially and temporally varying blur itself and the requirement of low computational cost. To improve the network efficiency, we adopt residual dense blocks into RNN cells, so as to efficiently extract the spatial features of the current frame. Furthermore, a global spatio-temporal attention module is proposed to fuse the effective hierarchical features from past and future frames to help better deblur the current frame. For evaluation, we also collect a novel dataset with paired blurry/sharp video clips by using a co-axis beam splitter system. Through experiments on synthetic and realistic datasets, we show that our proposed method can achieve better deblurring performance both quantitatively and qualitatively with less computational cost against state-of-the-art video deblurring methods.

**Keywords:** Video deblurring · RNN · Network efficiency · Attention · Dataset

## 1 Introduction

Nowadays, video recording usually suffers from the quality issues caused by motion blur. This is especially true in poorly illuminated environment, where one has to lengthen the exposure time for sufficient brightness. A great variety of video deblurring methods have been proposed, which have to deal with two competing goals, i.e., to improve the deblurring quality and to reduce the computational cost. The latter is of critical importance for low-power mobile devices, like smartphones.

To properly make use of the spatio-temporal correlation of the video signal is the key to achieve better performance on video deblurring. The CNN-based

**Electronic supplementary material** The online version of this chapter (https://doi.org/10.1007/978-3-030-58539-6_12) contains supplementary material, which is available to authorized users.

A. Vedaldi et al. (Eds.): ECCV 2020, LNCS 12351, pp. 191–207, 2020.
https://doi.org/10.1007/978-3-030-58539-6_12

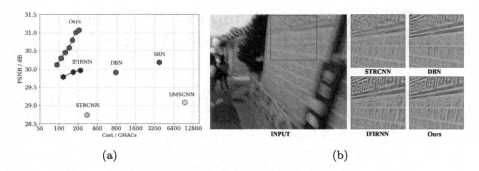

(a)                                          (b)

**Fig. 1.** A comparison of network efficiency on video deblurring. SRN [32], DMSCNN [22] are state-of-the-art (SoTA) methods for image deblurring, and STRCNN [30], DBN [13], IFIRNN [23] are SoTA methods for video deblurring. (a) shows the computational cost required for processing a frame of 720P(1280 × 720) video and the corresponding performance of each model on GOPRO [22] dataset in terms of GMACs and PSNR, respectively. (b) shows the deblurred image generated by SoTA video deblurring methods and ours.

methods [30, 34] make an inference of the deblurred frame by stacking neighboring frames with current frame as input to the CNN framework. The RNN-based methods, like [13, 23, 35, 43], employ recurrent neural network architecture to transfer the effective information frame by frame for deblurring. However, how to utilize spatio-temporal dependency of video for deblurring more efficiently still needs to be explored. The CNN-based methods are usually cumbersome in dealing with spatio-temporal dependency of concatenated neighboring frames, and the existing RNN-based methods have limited capacity to transfer the effective information temporally. Thus, they suffer from either the huge computational cost, or the ineffectiveness of deblurring.

In this work, we propose an efficient spatio-temporal recurrent neural network (denoted as ESTRNN) to solve the above issues. We mainly focus on the network efficiency of video deblurring methods, which directly reflects on the deblurring performance of the method under the limited computational resources, as Fig. 1a. It shows that our method can achieve much better performance with less computational cost against SoTA deblurring methods. Due to making full use of spatio-temporal dependency of the video signal, our method is exceptionally good at restoring the details of the blurry frame compared with SoTA video deblurring methods, as shown in Fig. 1b.

To make a more computational efficient video deblurring method, we develop our method through amelioration of basic RNN architecture from three aspects: 1) In temporal domain, the high-level features generated by RNN cell are more informative, which are more suitable for temporal feature fusion (see Fig. 2) than using channel-concatenated neighboring frames as input. Another advantage of using neighboring high-level features for temporal fusion is that it reuses the intermediate results of deblurring process of other frames, which helps to improve the overall network efficiency; 2) it is obvious that not all high-level features from neighboring frames are beneficial to deblurring of the current frame. Thus, it is worth designing an attention mechanism [1] that allows the method to focus on more informative part of high-level features from other frames. To this end, we propose a novel global spatio-temporal attention module (see Sect. 3.3) for efficiently temporal feature fusion; 3) Regarding the spatial domain, how to extract the spatial features from the current frame will affect the quality of information transmitted in temporal domain. In other words, well generated spatial features of each frame are a prerequisite for ensuring good temporal feature fusion. Therefore, we integrate the residual dense blocks (RDB [41]) as backbone into RNN cell to construct our RDB cell (see Sect. 3.2). The high-level hierarchical features generated by RDB cell is more computationally efficient with richer spatial information.

Our contributions in this work are summarized as follows:

- To the best of our knowledge, this is the first work making use of the high-level features of RNN cell from future and past frames for deblurring the current frame in the video.
- To efficiently utilize the high-level features from neighboring frames, we propose a global spatio-temporal attention module for temporal feature fusion.
- To improve the efficiency of extracting spatial features from the current frame, we adopt residual dense blocks into our RNN cell to generate more informative hierarchical features.
- Besides the conventional synthetic video deblurring dataset, such as REDS [21] and GOPRO [22], we also use a beam splitter system [14] to capture realistic blurry/sharp video pairs for evaluation. Our realistic dataset will be released to facilitate further researches.
- The experimental results demonstrate that our method achieves better deblurring performance both quantitatively and qualitatively than SoTA video deblurring methods with less computational cost.

## 2   Related Works

### 2.1   Video Deblurring

In recent years, video deblurring technologies become significant for daily life media editing and for advanced processing such as SLAM [17], 3D reconstruction [29] and visual tracking [36]. Research focus starts to shift from early single non-blind image deblurring [28,31,44] and single blind image deblurring [3,6,20,25,38] to the more challenging video deblurring task.

Typically, the blur in a video has different sizes and intensities in different position of each frame. In the early work of video deblurring, [18] and [2] attempt to automatically segment a moving blurred object from the background and assume a uniform blur model for them. Then, in view of the different kinds of blur in different regions of an image, [37] tries to segment an image into various layers and generate segment-wise blur kernels for deblurring. More recently, there are some researches that estimate pixel-wise blur kernel with segmentation [27], or without segmentation [11,12]. However, these kernel based methods are quite expensive in computation and usually rely on human knowledge. An inaccurate blur kernel will result in severe artifacts in deblurred image.

To overcome the above issues, recently researchers start to work on deep learning methods for video deblurring. CNN-based methods are used to handle the inter-frame relationship of video signal, such as [30], which makes the estimation of deblurred frame by using channel-concatenated neighboring frames. Usually, alignment of neighboring frames is required for these methods, which is quite computationally expensive. They realize it by traditional way like optical flow [26] or the network itself such as using deformable convolutional operation [4] in [34]. Some researchers tend to focus on RNN-based methods because of their excellent performance for time-series signal. RNN-based methods do not need to perform the explicit alignment and the model could manage it implicitly through hidden states. For example, [35] employs RNN architecture to reuse the features extracted from the past frame, and [13] improves the performance of deblurring by blending the hidden states in temporal domain. Then, [23] iteratively updates the hidden state via reusing RNN cell parameters and achieves SoTA video deblurring performance while operating in real time.

In this paper, we adopt a RNN framework similar to [23]. Our method is different from [23] in that we integrate RDB into the RNN cell in order to exploit the potential of the RNN cell through feature reusing and generating hierarchical features for the current frame. Furthermore, we propose a GSA module to selectively merge effective hierarchical features from both past and future frames, which enables our model to utilize the spatio-temporal information more efficiently.

## 2.2   Attention Mechanism

Allocating more computational resources towards the most informative components of a signal is a wise strategy to enhance system performance under the situation of limited resources. Such a selectively focusing mechanism originated from natural language processing (NLP) is named as attention mechanism [1,33,39], which has demonstrated to be very effective in many areas including image restoration task [34,40]. Inspired by the success of attention mechanism in image restoration task, [34] proposed their attention module to assign pixel-level aggregation weights on each neighboring frame for video deblurring. The principle of their attention module is the same as the original idea from NLP that a neighboring frame that is more similar to the reference one in an embedding space should be paid more attention. However, we believe that considering the situation of video deblurring, the method should pay attention to the useful features (the lost information), rather than the similar features from neighboring features. Therefore, we propose a global spatio-temporal attention module, which allows our method to efficiently fuse the effective features from both past and future frames for deblurring the current frame.

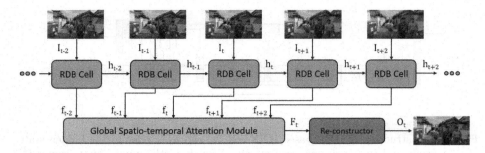

**Fig. 2.** Framework of proposed efficient spatio-temporal recurrent neural network. $I_t$ refers to the $t^{th}$ input blurry frame; $h_t$ and $f_t$ refer to the extracted hidden state and hierarchical features of RDB-based RNN cell (see Sect. 3.2) from $t^{th}$ frame; $F_t$ refers to the fused features generated by GSA module (see Sect. 3.3) for $t^{th}$ frame; $O_t$ refers to the $t^{th}$ deblurred frame by the proposed method.

# 3   Proposed Method

In this section, we will first give an overview of the proposed method first in Sect. 3.1. Then we will go into details of RDB cell and GSA module in Sect. 3.2 and Sect. 3.3, respectively.

## 3.1   Overview

According to the characteristics of blur in the video, it may keep varying temporally and spatially, which makes deblurring problem intractable. In turn, it is possible that the blurred information in the current frame is relatively clear and complete in the past frames and future frames. When using RNN-based method to implement video deblurring, high-level features of the current frame will be generated to make the inference of deblurred image. Actually, some parts of the high-level features are worth saving and reusing for making up the loss information for other frames. Therefore, distributing part of computational resources to fuse informative features in past and future frames could be a method to effectively improve the efficiency of the neural network. Furthermore, how to improve RNN cell itself to extract high-level features with better spatial structure is critical to enhancing the efficiency of the neural network. Starting from the above viewpoints, we integrate multiple residual dense blocks into RNN cell to generate hierarchical features and propose a global spatio-temporal attention module for feature fusion of neighboring frames.

The whole video deblurring process of our method is shown as Fig. 2. We denote the input frames of blurry video and corresponding output frames as $\{I_t\}$ and $\{O_t\}$ respectively, where $t \in \{1 \cdots T\}$. Through RDB-based RNN cell, the model could get hierarchical features for each frame as $\{f_t\}$. To get the inference of latent frame $O_t$, the global spatio-temporal attention module takes current hierarchical feature $f_t$ with two past and two future features

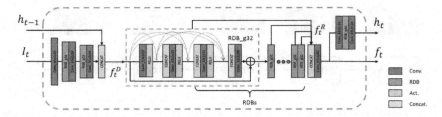

**Fig. 3.** The structure of RDB-based RNN cell. $h_t$ and $h_{t-1}$ refer to the hidden state of past frame and current frame, respectively; $I_t$ refers to the input blurry frame; $f_t^D$ refers to the features after downsampling module; $f_t^R$ refers to the feature set generated by series of RDB modules; $f_t$ refers to the hierarchical features generated by the RDB cell; As for the details of each layer and RDB module, $k$, $s$, $c$ and $g$ denote kernel size, stride, channels and growth rate, respectively.

$(f_{t-2}, f_{t-1}, f_{t+1}, f_{t+2})$ as input to perform feature fusion and generate $F_t$ as output. Finally, through re-constructor module, the model can get the latent frame $O_t$.

## 3.2    RDB Cell: RDB-Based RNN Cell

We adopt residual dense block (RDB) [41,42] into the RNN cell, which is named as RDB cell. The dense connections of RDB inherited from dense block (DB) [10] let each layer receive feature maps from all the previous layers by concatenating them together in channels. The output channels of each layer in RDB will keep the same size, which allows collective features to be reused and save the computational resources. Moreover, through local feature fusion, RDB could generate hierarchical features from convolutional layers in different depth with different size of receptive fields, which could provide better information for image reconstruction.

The structure of RDB-based RNN cell is shown as Fig. 3. First, the current input frame $I_t$ will be downsampled and concatenated with last hidden state $h_{t-1}$ to get shallow feature maps $f_t^D$ as

$$f_t^D = CAT(DS(I_t), h_{t-1}) \tag{1}$$

where $CAT(\cdot)$ refers to concatenation operation; $DS(\cdot)$ refers to downsampling operation in the cell which consists of $5 \times 5$ convolutional layers and RDB module. Then, $f_t^D$ will be fed into a series of RDB modules. For each RDB module, the output is represented as $f_t^R = \{f_t^{R_1}, \cdots, f_t^{R_N}\}$, where $N$ refers to the number of RDB modules. RDB cell could get the global hierarchical features $f_t$ by fusing the concatenation of local hierarchical features $f_t^R$ with $1 \times 1$ convolutional layer as follows:

$$f_t = Conv(CAT(f_t^R)) \tag{2}$$

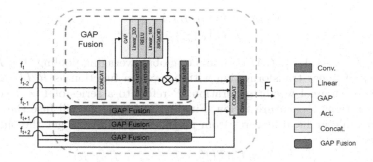

**Fig. 4.** The structure of global spatio-temporal attention module. $f_{t-2}$, $f_{t-1}$, $f_{t+1}$, $f_{t+2}$ and $f_t$ refer to the hierarchical features of corresponding neighboring frames in the past or future and the current frame, respectively; *linear* refers to fully convolutional layer; $GAP$ refers to global average pooling layer; $F_t$ refers to the output of the GSA module, integrating the effective components of hierarchical features from each past and future frame by GAP Fusion module

where $Conv(\cdot)$ refers to convolutional operation. Then, the hidden state $h_t$ could be updated as follows:

$$h_t = H(f_t) \tag{3}$$

where $H$ refers to the hidden state generation function, consisting of $3 \times 3$ convolutional layer and RDB module. In short, while processing each frame in the video, the inputs of RDB cell are current blur frame and previous hidden state. Then, RDB cell will generate the hierarchical features of this frame and update the hidden state as well.

### 3.3    GSA: Global Spatio-Temporal Attention Module

The structure of GSA module is shown as Fig. 4. This module aims to extract and fuse the effective components of hierarchical features from future and past frames. Intuitively, the frames which are closer to the current frame in time domain are more likely to have useful information for deblurring of current frame. In the situation of real-time video deblurring, considering that the requirement of low computational cost for each output frame, the number of neighboring hierarchical features that will be fused into current frame should be limited. Furthermore, considering that delaying output by only several frames is usually acceptable, the hierarchical features from the future frames are available for the feature fusion. Therefore, the input of GSA will be hierarchical features of two frames before and two frames after the current frame as $\{f_{t-2}, f_{t-1}, f_t, f_{t+1}, f_{t+2}\}$. Inspired by Squeeze-and-Excitation (SE) block in [9], a submodule named global averaging pooling fusion is proposed, which takes features of current frame and a neighboring frame as input to filter out effective hierarchical features $f^e_{t+i}$ from the neighboring frame as follows:

$$f^c_{t+i} = CAT(f_t, f_{t+i}) \qquad (4)$$

$$f^e_{t+i} = L(GAP(f^c_{t+i})) \otimes P(f^c_{t+i}) \qquad (5)$$

where $i \in \{-2, -1, 1, 2\}$; $GAP(\cdot)$ refers to global averaging pooling [19]; $L$ refers to a series of linear transformation with activation function as $ReLU$ [24] and $Sigmoid$ for channel weight generation; $P$ refers to a series of $1 \times 1$ convolutional operations for feature fusion. Finally, GSA module will fuse the $f_t$ with all effective hierarchical features from neighboring frames to get the output $F_t$ as follows:

$$F_t = Conv(CAT(f^e_{t-2}, f^e_{t-1}, f^e_{t+1}, f^e_{t+2}, f_t)) \qquad (6)$$

The output $F_t$ of GSA module will be upsampled by deconvolutional layers [5] in re-constructor module for generating latent image for the current frame.

## 4 Experiment Results

### 4.1 Implementation Details

**Synthesized Dataset.** We test our model ESTRNN on two public datasets that made by averaging high-FPS video as GOPRO [22] and REDS [21]. We choose the same GOPRO version as [23]. There are 22 training sequences and 11 evaluation sequences in GOPRO with 2103 training samples and 1111 evaluation samples respectively. As for REDS, there are 240 training sequences and 30 evaluation sequences with 100 frames for each sequence. Due to the huge size of REDS dataset and limited computational resources, we train our model and other SoTA models only on first-half training sequences of REDS (120 sequences) for comparison.

**Beam-Splitter Dataset (BSD).** At present, there are still very limited methods for building a video deblurring dataset. The mainstream way is to average several consecutive short-exposure images in order to mimic the phenomenon of blur caused by relatively long exposure time [15]. This kind of method requires a high-speed camera to capture high-FPS video and then synthesizes pairs of sharp and blurry videos based on the high-FPS video. Video deblurring datasets such as DVD [30], GOPRO [22] and REDS [21] were born by the above method. However, it is questionable whether such a synthetic way truly reflects the blur in real scenarios. In here, we provide a new solution for building video deblurring dataset by using a beam splitter system with two synchronized cameras, as shown in Fig. 5. In our solution, by controlling the length of exposure time and strength of exposure intensity during video shooting as shown in Fig. 5b, the system could obtain a pair of sharp and blurry video samples by shooting video one time.

In this work, we captured beam-splitter datasets (BSD) with two different recording frequency as 15 fps and 30 fps, respectively. For each frequency, there are 24 sequences of short video with 50 frames for each. We let the exposure time of camera $C1$ and camera $C2$ as 16 ms and 2 ms to capture blurry and sharp

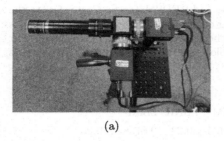
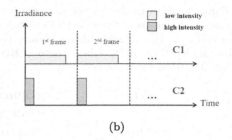

(a)                                              (b)

**Fig. 5.** A beam splitter system for building video deblurring dataset. (a) is the profile of our beam splitter system. $C1$ and $C2$ refer to two cameras with same configurations for generating blur and sharp videos, respectively; (b) shows the exposure scheme of $C1$ and $C2$ to generate blurry/sharp video pairs.

videos, respectively. The intensity of irradiance of $C1$ is $\frac{1}{8}$ of $C2$, in order to keep the total irradiance intensity equalized. This is physically implemented by inserting a 12.5% neutral density filter in the front of $C1$. The video resolution is $720P$ ($1280 \times 720$). 75% sequences (18) will be randomly selected for training, and the rest sequences (6) will be used for testing.

**Training Setting.** To be fair, we try our best to keep the hyper-parameters as same for each model. We train each model for 500 epochs by ADAM optimizer [16] ($\beta_1 = 0.9, \beta_2 = 0.999$) with initial learning rate as $10^{-4}$ (decay rate as 0.5, decay step as 200 epochs). We use RGB patches of size $256 \times 256$ in subsequence of 10 frames as input to train the models. Also, same data augmentation processes are taken for each model, including $90°$, horizontal and vertical flips. Mini-batch size is set to 4 for single GPU (V100) training. For synthentic dataset GOPRO and REDS, the loss function is uniformly defined as $\mathcal{L}2$ loss; while for the proposed dataset BSD, we use $\mathcal{L}1$ for each model as follows:

$$\mathcal{L}2 = \frac{1}{TCHW} \sum_{t}^{T} \|O_t - O_t^{GT}\|_2^2, \tag{7}$$

$$\mathcal{L}1 = \frac{1}{TCHW} \sum_{t}^{T} \|O_t - O_t^{GT}\|_1 \tag{8}$$

where $T$, $C$, $H$, $W$ denote the number of frames and the number of channel, height, width for each frame; $O_t^{GT}$ refers to the ground truth of the $t^{th}$ frame. Source code and dataset will be released on https://github.com/zzh-tech/ESTRNN.

### 4.2    Results

**GOPRO.** First, we compare our method with the SoTA video deblurring methods on GOPRO dataset. We implement 7 variants of our model with different

**Table 1.** Quantitative results on both GOPRO and REDS datasets. Cost refers to the computational cost of the model for deblurring one frame of HD(720P) video in terms of GMACs. The meaning of cost is same for other tables and figures in this paper. For our model, $B_{\#}$ and $C_{\#}$ denote the # of RDB blocks in RDB cell and the # of channels for each RDB block, respectively

| Model | GOPRO | | REDS | | Cost |
|---|---|---|---|---|---|
| | PSNR | SSIM | PSNR | SSIM | |
| STRCNN [13] | 28.74 | 0.8465 | 30.23 | 0.8708 | 276.20 |
| DBN [30] | 29.91 | 0.8823 | 31.55 | 0.8960 | 784.75 |
| IFIRNN ($c2h1$) [23] | 29.79 | 0.8817 | 31.29 | 0.8913 | 116.29 |
| IFIRNN ($c2h2$) [23] | 29.92 | 0.8838 | 31.35 | 0.8929 | 167.09 |
| IFIRNN ($c2h3$) [23] | 29.97 | 0.8859 | 31.36 | 0.8942 | 217.89 |
| ESTRNN ($B_9C_{60}$) | 30.12 | 0.8837 | 31.64 | 0.8930 | 92.57 |
| ESTRNN ($B_9C_{65}$) | 30.30 | 0.8892 | 31.63 | 0.8965 | 108.20 |
| ESTRNN ($B_9C_{70}$) | 30.45 | 0.8909 | 31.94 | 0.8968 | 125.55 |
| ESTRNN ($B_9C_{75}$) | 30.58 | 0.8923 | 32.06 | 0.9022 | 143.71 |
| ESTRNN ($B_9C_{80}$) | 30.79 | 0.9016 | 32.33 | 0.9060 | 163.61 |
| ESTRNN ($B_9C_{85}$) | 31.01 | 0.9013 | 32.34 | 0.9074 | 184.25 |
| ESTRNN ($B_9C_{90}$) | 31.07 | 0.9023 | 32.63 | 0.9110 | 206.70 |

**Table 2.** Quantitative results on BSD dataset

| Model | BSD | PSNR | SSIM | Cost |
|---|---|---|---|---|
| IFIRNN ($c2h3$) | 15 fps | 34.50 | 0.8703 | 217.89 |
| ESTRNN ($B_9C_{80}$) | 15 fps | 35.06 | 0.8739 | 206.70 |
| IFIRNN ($c2h3$) | 30 fps | 34.28 | 0.8796 | 217.89 |
| ESTRNN ($B_9C_{80}$) | 30 fps | 34.80 | 0.8835 | 206.70 |

computational cost by modifying the number of channels ($C_{\#}$) of base model and keeping the number of RDB blocks ($B_{\#}$) as 9. The larger $C_{\#}$ is, the higher computational cost it needs. We report the deblurring performance and the corresponding computational cost for processing one frame in the video of all compared models in terms of PSNR [8], SSIM and GMACs, respectively, in Table 1. From the perspective of quantitative analysis, it is clear that our model can achieve higher PSNR and SSIM value with less computational cost, which means our model has higher network efficiency. To further validate the deblurring performance of proposed model, we also show the deblurred image generated by each model, as illustrated in Fig. 6. We can see the proposed model can restore sharper image with more details, such as the textures of tiles on the path and the characters on the poster.

(a) Blur

(b) Deblur (Ours)

(c) Blur     (d) STRCNN     (e) DBN     (f) IFIRNN     (g) Ours     (h) GT

**Fig. 6.** Visual comparisons on testing dataset of GOPRO [22].

**REDS.** We also do the comparison on REDS, which has more diverse scenes from different places. From Table 1, we can see our model $B_9C_{90}$ achieves best results as 32.63 PSNR with only around 200 GMACs computational cost for one $720P$ frame. Even our small model $B_9C_{60}$ with cost less than 100 GMACs can achieve same level performance as $c2h3$ of IFIRNN, the computational cost of which is as twise as the former. On the qualitative results as Fig. 7, the proposed model can significantly reduce ambiguous parts for the deblurred frame and the restored details such as the texture of the wall, characters and human body are closer to the ground truth.

**BSD.** We further compare our model $B_9C_{80}$ with IFIRNN $c2h3$ on our beam splitter video deblurring dataset, shown as Table 2. The proposed model is superior to the SoTA with around 0.5 dB more gain under same level of computational cost, on both $15fps$ and $30fps$ BSD dataset. The deblurring results are shown in

(a) Blur                     (b) Deblur (Ours)

(c) Blur    (d) STRCNN    (e) DBN    (f) IFIRNN    (g) Ours    (h) GT

**Fig. 7.** Visual comparisons on testing dataset of REDS [21].

Fig. 8, which proves the effectiveness of our method on realistic video deblurring dataset.

**Network Efficiency Analysis.** We collect the computational cost for one frame as well as the performance (PSNR) of the SoTA lightweight image [32] and video deblurring models on GOPRO dataset, as shown in Fig. 1. The proposed model includes 7 red nodes that represent different variants of our ESTRNN from $B_9C_{60}$ to $B_9C90$ in Table 1. Also, the three blue nodes represent different variants of IFIRNN as $c2h1$, $c2h2$ and $c2h3$. Because the computational cost of different models varies drastically, we take $log_{10}$(GMACs) as abscissa unit to better display the results. An ideal model with high network efficiency will locate at upper-left corner of the coordinate. The proposed models are closer to the upper-left corner than the existing image or video deblurring models, which reflects the high network efficiency of our model.

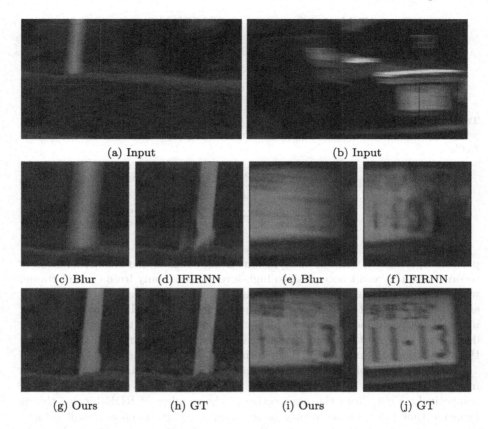

(a) Input                                          (b) Input

(c) Blur          (d) IFIRNN                (e) Blur          (f) IFIRNN

(g) Ours          (h) GT                    (i) Ours          (j) GT

**Fig. 8.** Visual comparisons on testing dataset of our BSD.

**Table 3.** Ablation study of ESTRNN. Fusion refers to the fusion strategy that utilizes the high level features from neighboring frames

| Model | Fusion | RDB Cell | GSA | PSNR | Cost |
|---|---|---|---|---|---|
| $B_9 C_{110}$ | ✗ | ✗ | ✗ | 30.29 | 163.48 |
| $B_9 C_{100}$ | ✓ | ✗ | ✗ | 30.46 | 165.59 |
| $B_9 C_{100}$ | ✗ | ✓ | ✗ | 30.51 | 168.56 |
| $B_9 C_{90}$ | ✓ | ✓ | ✗ | 30.55 | 161.28 |
| $B_9 C_{85}$ | ✗ | ✓ | ✓ | 30.69 | 162.69 |
| $B_9 C_{80}$ | ✓ | ✓ | ✓ | 30.79 | 163.61 |

**Ablation Study.** We conduct an ablation study to demonstrate the effectiveness of the high-level feature fusion strategy, RDB cell, as well as GSA module, as shown in Table 3. When ablating the modules, we keep the computational cost almost unchanged by adjusting the number of channels ($C_\#$) for fair com-

**Table 4.** Effectiveness of # of RDB blocks

|        | $B_3C_{80}$ | $B_6C_{80}$ | $B_9C_{80}$ | $B_{12}C_{80}$ | $B_{15}C_{80}$ |
|--------|-------------|-------------|-------------|----------------|----------------|
| PSNR   | 29.74       | 30.31       | 30.79       | 31.03          | 31.27          |
| Cost   | 123.03      | 143.32      | 163.31      | 183.90         | 204.19         |

**Table 5.** Effectiveness of # of neighboring frames used by GSA module. $F_\#$ and $P_\#$ refers to the number of future and past frames used by the model. The base model is $B_9C_{80}$

|        | $F_0P_1$ | $F_0P_2$ | $F_0P_3$ | $F_1P_1$ | $F_2P_2$ | $F_3P_3$ |
|--------|----------|----------|----------|----------|----------|----------|
| PSNR   | 30.54    | 30.57    | 30.69    | 30.58    | 30.79    | 30.82    |
| Cost   | 119.93   | 133.75   | 148.31   | 133.75   | 163.61   | 196.42   |

parison. Specifically, without using fusion strategy means that the model directly reconstructs the result according to high-level features only from current frame; without RDB cell, the model will use residual block [7] instead, in the same way as [22] does; without GSA module, high-level features will be directly concatenated in channel dimension. The results clearly demonstrate that each module or design can improve the deblurring efficiency, because each module can improve the overall performance of model when the computational cost keeps unchanged.

We further explore the effectiveness of the number of RDB blocks and the number of past and future frames used by the model as Table 4 and Table 5, respectively. First, from the perspective of the number of RDB blocks, this is intuitive that more blocks which means more computational cost will achieve better performance. If we compare the variant $B_{15}C_{80}$ with variant $B_9C_{90}$ in Table 1 which has almost same computational cost, we can find that it is better to increase the number of RDB blocks rather than the channels, when the number of channels is relatively enough. As for the number of neighboring frames, Table 5 shows that, considering the increased computational cost, the benefit of using more neighboring frames as $F_3P_3$ is relatively small. Besides, the results of $F_0P_1$, $F_0P_2$ and $F_0P3$ show that the proposed model can still achieve comparative good results even without high-level features borrowed from future frames.

## 5   Conclusions

In this paper, we proposed a novel RNN-based method for more computational efficient video deblurring. Residual dense block was adopted to the RNN cell to generate hierarchical features from current frame for better restoration. Moreover, to make full use of the spatio-temporal correlation, our model utilized the global spatio-temporal fusion module for fusing the effective components of hierarchical features from past and future frames. The experimental results show that our model is more computational efficient for video deblurring, which can achieve much better performance with less computational cost. Furthermore, we also propose a new method for generating more realistic video deblurring dataset by using a beam splitter based capture system.

# References

1. Bahdanau, D., Cho, K., Bengio, Y.: Neural machine translation by jointly learning to align and translate. arXiv preprint arXiv:1409.0473 (2014)
2. Bar, L., Berkels, B., Rumpf, M., Sapiro, G.: A variational framework for simultaneous motion estimation and restoration of motion-blurred video. In: 2007 IEEE 11th International Conference on Computer Vision, pp. 1–8. IEEE (2007)
3. Chakrabarti, A.: A neural approach to blind motion deblurring. In: Leibe, B., Matas, J., Sebe, N., Welling, M. (eds.) ECCV 2016. LNCS, vol. 9907, pp. 221–235. Springer, Cham (2016). https://doi.org/10.1007/978-3-319-46487-9_14
4. Dai, J., et al.: Deformable convolutional networks. In: Proceedings of the IEEE International Conference on Computer Vision, pp. 764–773 (2017)
5. Dumoulin, V., Visin, F.: A guide to convolution arithmetic for deep learning. ArXiv e-prints, March 2016
6. Goldstein, A., Fattal, R.: Blur-kernel estimation from spectral irregularities. In: Fitzgibbon, A., Lazebnik, S., Perona, P., Sato, Y., Schmid, C. (eds.) ECCV 2012. LNCS, vol. 7576, pp. 622–635. Springer, Heidelberg (2012). https://doi.org/10.1007/978-3-642-33715-4_45
7. He, K., Zhang, X., Ren, S., Sun, J.: Deep residual learning for image recognition. In: Proceedings of the IEEE Conference on Computer Vision and Pattern Recognition, pp. 770–778 (2016)
8. Hore, A., Ziou, D.: Image quality metrics: PSNR vs. SSIM. In: 2010 20th International Conference on Pattern Recognition, pp. 2366–2369. IEEE (2010)
9. Hu, J., Shen, L., Sun, G.: Squeeze-and-excitation networks. In: Proceedings of the IEEE Conference on Computer Vision and Pattern Recognition, pp. 7132–7141 (2018)
10. Huang, G., Liu, Z., Van Der Maaten, L., Weinberger, K.Q.: Densely connected convolutional networks. In: Proceedings of the IEEE Conference on Computer Vision and Pattern Recognition, pp. 4700–4708 (2017)
11. Hyun Kim, T., Mu Lee, K.: Segmentation-free dynamic scene deblurring. In: Proceedings of the IEEE Conference on Computer Vision and Pattern Recognition, pp. 2766–2773 (2014)
12. Hyun Kim, T., Mu Lee, K.: Generalized video deblurring for dynamic scenes. In: Proceedings of the IEEE Conference on Computer Vision and Pattern Recognition, pp. 5426–5434 (2015)
13. Hyun Kim, T., Mu Lee, K., Scholkopf, B., Hirsch, M.: Online video deblurring via dynamic temporal blending network. In: Proceedings of the IEEE International Conference on Computer Vision, pp. 4038–4047 (2017)
14. Jiang, H., Zheng, Y.: Learning to see moving objects in the dark. In: Proceedings of the IEEE International Conference on Computer Vision, pp. 7324–7333 (2019)
15. Kim, T.H., Nah, S., Lee, K.M.: Dynamic scene deblurring using a locally adaptive linear blur model. arXiv preprint arXiv:1603.04265 (2016)
16. Kingma, D.P., Ba, J.: Adam: a method for stochastic optimization. arXiv preprint arXiv:1412.6980 (2014)

17. Lee, H.S., Kwon, J., Lee, K.M.: Simultaneous localization, mapping and deblurring. In: 2011 International Conference on Computer Vision, pp. 1203–1210. IEEE (2011)
18. Levin, A.: Blind motion deblurring using image statistics. In: Advances in Neural Information Processing Systems, pp. 841–848 (2007)
19. Lin, M., Chen, Q., Yan, S.: Network in network. arXiv preprint arXiv:1312.4400 (2013)
20. Michaeli, T., Irani, M.: Blind deblurring using internal patch recurrence. In: Fleet, D., Pajdla, T., Schiele, B., Tuytelaars, T. (eds.) ECCV 2014. LNCS, vol. 8691, pp. 783–798. Springer, Cham (2014). https://doi.org/10.1007/978-3-319-10578-9_51
21. Nah, S., et al.: Ntire 2019 challenge on video deblurring and super-resolution: dataset and study. In: Proceedings of the IEEE Conference on Computer Vision and Pattern Recognition Workshops (2019)
22. Nah, S., Hyun Kim, T., Mu Lee, K.: Deep multi-scale convolutional neural network for dynamic scene deblurring. In: Proceedings of the IEEE Conference on Computer Vision and Pattern Recognition, pp. 3883–3891 (2017)
23. Nah, S., Son, S., Lee, K.M.: Recurrent neural networks with intra-frame iterations for video deblurring. In: Proceedings of the IEEE Conference on Computer Vision and Pattern Recognition, pp. 8102–8111 (2019)
24. Nair, V., Hinton, G.E.: Rectified linear units improve restricted Boltzmann machines. In: Proceedings of the 27th International Conference on Machine Learning (ICML-10), pp. 807–814 (2010)
25. Nimisha, T.M., Kumar Singh, A., Rajagopalan, A.N.: Blur-invariant deep learning for blind-deblurring. In: Proceedings of the IEEE International Conference on Computer Vision, pp. 4752–4760 (2017)
26. Pérez, J.S., Meinhardt-Llopis, E., Facciolo, G.: Tv-l1 optical flow estimation. Image Process. On Line **2013**, 137–150 (2013)
27. Ren, W., Pan, J., Cao, X., Yang, M.H.: Video deblurring via semantic segmentation and pixel-wise non-linear kernel. In: Proceedings of the IEEE International Conference on Computer Vision, pp. 1077–1085 (2017)
28. Schuler, C.J., Christopher Burger, H., Harmeling, S., Scholkopf, B.: A machine learning approach for non-blind image deconvolution. In: Proceedings of the IEEE Conference on Computer Vision and Pattern Recognition, pp. 1067–1074 (2013)
29. Seok Lee, H., Mu Lee, K.: Dense 3D reconstruction from severely blurred images using a single moving camera. In: Proceedings of the IEEE Conference on Computer Vision and Pattern Recognition, pp. 273–280 (2013)
30. Su, S., Delbracio, M., Wang, J., Sapiro, G., Heidrich, W., Wang, O.: Deep video deblurring for hand-held cameras. In: Proceedings of the IEEE Conference on Computer Vision and Pattern Recognition, pp. 1279–1288 (2017)
31. Sun, L., Cho, S., Wang, J., Hays, J.: Good image priors for non-blind deconvolution. In: Fleet, D., Pajdla, T., Schiele, B., Tuytelaars, T. (eds.) ECCV 2014. LNCS, vol. 8692, pp. 231–246. Springer, Cham (2014). https://doi.org/10.1007/978-3-319-10593-2_16
32. Tao, X., Gao, H., Shen, X., Wang, J., Jia, J.: Scale-recurrent network for deep image deblurring. In: Proceedings of the IEEE Conference on Computer Vision and Pattern Recognition, pp. 8174–8182 (2018)
33. Vaswani, A., et al.: Attention is all you need. In: Advances in Neural Information Processing Systems, pp. 5998–6008 (2017)
34. Wang, X., Chan, K.C., Yu, K., Dong, C., Change Loy, C.: Edvr: video restoration with enhanced deformable convolutional networks. In: Proceedings of the IEEE Conference on Computer Vision and Pattern Recognition Workshops (2019)

35. Wieschollek, P., Hirsch, M., Scholkopf, B., Lensch, H.: Learning blind motion deblurring. In: Proceedings of the IEEE International Conference on Computer Vision, pp. 231–240 (2017)
36. Wu, Y., Ling, H., Yu, J., Li, F., Mei, X., Cheng, E.: Blurred target tracking by blur-driven tracker. In: 2011 International Conference on Computer Vision, pp. 1100–1107. IEEE (2011)
37. Wulff, J., Black, M.J.: Modeling blurred video with layers. In: Fleet, D., Pajdla, T., Schiele, B., Tuytelaars, T. (eds.) ECCV 2014. LNCS, vol. 8694, pp. 236–252. Springer, Cham (2014). https://doi.org/10.1007/978-3-319-10599-4_16
38. Xu, L., Jia, J.: Two-phase kernel estimation for robust motion deblurring. In: Daniilidis, K., Maragos, P., Paragios, N. (eds.) ECCV 2010. LNCS, vol. 6311, pp. 157–170. Springer, Heidelberg (2010). https://doi.org/10.1007/978-3-642-15549-9_12
39. Yang, J., Nguyen, M.N., San, P.P., Li, X.L., Krishnaswamy, S.: Deep convolutional neural networks on multichannel time series for human activity recognition. In: Twenty-Fourth International Joint Conference on Artificial Intelligence (2015)
40. Zhang, Y., Li, K., Li, K., Wang, L., Zhong, B., Fu, Y.: Image super-resolution using very deep residual channel attention networks. In: Proceedings of the European Conference on Computer Vision (ECCV), pp. 286–301 (2018)
41. Zhang, Y., Tian, Y., Kong, Y., Zhong, B., Fu, Y.: Residual dense network for image super-resolution. In: Proceedings of the IEEE Conference on Computer Vision and Pattern Recognition, pp. 2472–2481 (2018)
42. Zhang, Y., Tian, Y., Kong, Y., Zhong, B., Fu, Y.: Residual dense network for image restoration. IEEE Trans. Pattern Anal. Mach. Intell. (2020)
43. Zhou, S., Zhang, J., Pan, J., Xie, H., Zuo, W., Ren, J.: Spatio-temporal filter adaptive network for video deblurring. In: Proceedings of the IEEE International Conference on Computer Vision, pp. 2482–2491 (2019)
44. Zoran, D., Weiss, Y.: From learning models of natural image patches to whole image restoration. In: 2011 International Conference on Computer Vision, pp. 479–486. IEEE (2011)

# The Semantic Mutex Watershed
# for Efficient Bottom-Up Semantic
# Instance Segmentation

Steffen Wolf[1]([✉]), Yuyan Li[1], Constantin Pape[1,2], Alberto Bailoni[1],
Anna Kreshuk[2], and Fred A. Hamprecht[1]

[1] HCI/IWR, Heidelberg University, Heidelberg, Germany
{steffen.wolf,yuyan.li,constantin.pape,alberto.bailoni,
fred.hamprecht}@iwr.uni-heidelberg.de
[2] EMBL, Heidelberg, Germany
{constantin.pape,anna.kreshuk}@embl.de

**Abstract.** Semantic instance segmentation is the task of simultaneously partitioning an image into distinct segments while associating each pixel with a class label. In commonly used pipelines, segmentation and label assignment are solved separately since joint optimization is computationally expensive. We propose a greedy algorithm for joint graph partitioning and labeling derived from the efficient Mutex Watershed partitioning algorithm. It optimizes an objective function closely related to the Asymmetric Multiway Cut objective and empirically shows efficient scaling behavior. Due to the algorithm's efficiency it can operate directly on pixels without prior over-segmentation of the image into superpixels. We evaluate the performance on the Cityscapes dataset (2D urban scenes) and on a 3D microscopy volume. In urban scenes, the proposed algorithm combined with current deep neural networks outperforms the strong baseline of 'Panoptic Feature Pyramid Networks' by Kirillov *et al.* (2019). In the 3D electron microscopy images, we show explicitly that our joint formulation outperforms a separate optimization of the partitioning and labeling problems.

## 1 Introduction

Image segmentation literature distinguishes *semantic segmentation* - associating each pixel with a class label - and *instance segmentation*, i.e. detecting and segmenting individual objects while ignoring the background. The joint task of simultaneously assigning a class label to each pixel and grouping pixels to instances has been addressed under different names, including semantic instance segmentation, scene parsing [42], image parsing [43], holistic scene understanding

---

S. Wolf and Y. Li—Authors contributed equally.

---

**Electronic supplementary material** The online version of this chapter (https://doi.org/10.1007/978-3-030-58539-6_13) contains supplementary material, which is available to authorized users.

A. Vedaldi et al. (Eds.): ECCV 2020, LNCS 12351, pp. 208–224, 2020.
https://doi.org/10.1007/978-3-030-58539-6_13

[47] or instance-separating semantic segmentation [29]. Recently, a new metric and evaluation approach to such problems has been introduced under the name of *panoptic segmentation* [19].

From a graph theory perspective, semantic instance segmentation corresponds to the simultaneous partitioning and labeling of a graph. Most greedy graph partitioning algorithms are defined on graphs encoding attractive interactions only. Clusters are then formed through agglomeration or division until a user-defined termination criterion is met (often a threshold or a desired number of clusters). These algorithms perform pure instance segmentation. The semantic labels for the segmented instances need to be generated independently.

If repulsive - as well as attractive - forces are defined between the nodes of the graph, partitioning can be formulated as a Multicut problem [2]. In this formulation clusters emerge naturally without the need for a termination criterion. Furthermore, the Multicut problem can be extended to include the labeling of the graph, delivering a semantic instance segmentation from a joint optimization of partitioning and labeling [24].

We propose to solve the joint partitioning and labeling problem by an efficient algorithm which we term Semantic Mutex Watershed (SMWS), inspired by the Mutex Watershed [44]. In more detail, in this contribution we:

- propose a fast algorithm for joint graph partitioning and labeling
- prove that the algorithm (exactly) minimizes an objective function closely related to the Asymmetric Multiway Cut objective
- demonstrate competitive performance on natural and biological images.

## 2    Related Work

**Semantic Segmentation.** State-of-the-art semantic segmentation algorithms are based on convolutional neural networks (CNNs) which are trained end-to-end. The networks commonly follow the design principles of image classification networks (*e.g.* [16,23,40]), replacing the fully connected layers at the end with convolutional layers to form a fully convolutional network [32]. This architecture can be further extended to include encoder-decoder paths [39], dilated or atrous convolutions [5,49] and pyramid pooling modules [6,50].

**Instance Segmentation.** Many instance segmentation methods use a detection or a region proposal framework as their basis; object segmentation masks are then predicted inside region proposals. A cascade of multiple networks is employed by [11], each solving a specific subtask to find the instance labeling. Mask-RCNN [15] builds on the bounding box prediction capabilities of Faster-RCNN [38] to simultaneously produce masks and class predictions. An extension of this method with an additional semantic segmentation branch has been proposed in [18] as a single network for semantic instance segmentation.

In contrast to the region-based methods, proposal-free algorithms often start with a pixel-wise representation which is then clustered into instances [12,21,48]. Alternatively, the distance transform of instance masks can be predicted and clustered by thresholding [3].

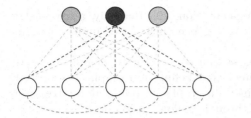 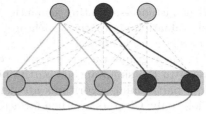

**Fig. 1.** *Left:* An example of an extended graph. Nodes on the top are terminal nodes whereby each color represents a label class. The associated semantic edges are colored correspondingly. The internal nodes are on the bottom with attractive (green) and repulsive (red) edges between them. *Right:* Semantic instance segmentation. Edges that are part of the active set are shown in bold. Clusters are depicted in grey. Note that two adjacent nodes with the same label are not necessarily clustered together. (Color figure online)

**Graph-Based Segmentation.** Graph-based methods, used independently or in combination with machine learning on pixels, form another popular basis for image segmentation algorithms [13]. In this case, the graph is built from pixels or superpixels of the image and the instance segmentation problem becomes a graph partitioning problem. When the number of instances is not known in advance and repulsive interactions are present between the graph nodes, graph partitioning can in turn be formulated as a Multicut or correlation clustering problem [2]. This NP-hard problem can be solved reasonably fast for small problem sizes with integer linear programming solvers [1] or approximate algorithms [4,36]. A modified Multicut objective is introduced by [44] together with the Mutex Watershed - an efficient clustering algorithm for its optimization.

The Multicut objective can be extended to solve a joint graph partitioning and labeling problem [17]. One such extension is the Asymmetric Multiway Cut [24] that is used for simultaneous instance and semantic segmentation. This formulation has been applied to natural images by [20] and to biological images by [22].

The Node Labeling Multicut Problem (NLMP) [29] further generalizes this problem to larger feasible sets, extending the range of applications to human pose estimation and multiple object tracking. In practice, the computational complexity of the NLMP only allows for approximate solutions, possibly combined with reducing the problem size by over-segmentation into superpixels.

Similar to the semantic segmentation use case, CNNs can be used to predict pixel and superpixel affinities which serve as edge weights in the graph partitioning problem [28,31,33].

## 3 The Semantic Mutex Watershed

In this section, we introduce an extension to the Mutex Watershed algorithm for semantic instance segmentation. To this end, we build a graph of image

---

**Semantic Mutex Watershed**

---

$\mathbf{SMWS}(\mathcal{G}(V, E'),\ w : E' \to \mathbb{R},\ \text{boolean connect\_all})$:

  $A^+ \leftarrow \emptyset;\quad A^- \leftarrow \emptyset$

  **for** $(i, j) = e \in E'$ *in descending order of* $|w_e|$ **do**

    **if** $e \in E^+$ **then**

      **if not** $\text{mutex}(i, j; A^+, A^-)$

      **and not** $\text{differentclass}(i, j, A^+, A^S)$ **then**

        **if not** $\text{connected}(i, j; A^+)$ **or** connect\_all **then**

          $\text{merge}(i, j)$: $A^+ \leftarrow A^+ \cup e$

            // merge $i$ and $j$ and inherit the mutual

            // exclusions from the parent clusters

    **else if** $e \in E^-$ **then**

      **if not** $\text{connected}(i, j; A^+)$ **then**

        $\text{addmutex}(i, j)$: $A^- \leftarrow A^- \cup e$

          // add mutual exclusion between $i$ and $j$

    **else if** $e \in E^S$ **then**

      **if** $class(i, A^+, A^S) = \emptyset$ **or** $class(i, A^+, A^S) = l_j$ **then**

        assignLabel(i, j): $A \leftarrow A \cup e$

  **return** $A$

---

**Algorithm 1:** The Semantic Mutex Watershed algorithm. The differences to the Mutex Watershed are marked in blue.

pixels (voxels) or superpixels and formulate the semantic instance segmentation problem as the joint graph partitioning and labeling.

**Weighted Graph with Terminal Nodes.** To partition an undirected weighted graph $G = G(V, E, w)$ into instances Wolf *et al.* [44] separate the set of edges into two sets: *attractive edges* $E^+ = \{e \in E \mid w_e >= 0\}$ and *repulsive edges* $E^- = \{e \in E \mid w_e < 0\}$, based on their weight. These are used in the Mutex Watershed to find a graph partitioning. To model label assignments, we will augment this graph with additional nodes and edges and refer to $V$ as *internal nodes* and edges $E = E^+ \cup E^-$ as *internal edges*.

Semantic instance segmentation is achieved by clustering the internal nodes and assigning a semantic label $l \in \{l_0, ..., l_k\}$ to each cluster. We extend $G$ by $k$ *terminal* nodes $\{t_0, ..., t_k\} \in T$ where each $t_i$ is associated with a label $l_i$. Every internal node $v \in V$ is connected to every $t$ by a weighted *semantic edge* $e \in E^S$. Here, a large *semantic weight* $w_{ut} \subseteq \mathbb{R}^+$ implies a strong association of internal node $u$ with the label of the terminal node $t \in T$. The extended graph thus becomes $\mathcal{G}(V', E', w')$ with $V' = V \cup T$, $E' = E \cup E^S$ and $w' = w \cup \{w_{ut} \mid \forall t \in T,\ \forall u \in V\}$. Figure 1 shows an example of such an extended graph.

## 3.1   The Semantic Mutex Watershed Algorithm

We will now extend the Mutex Watershed Algorithm to the extended graph $\mathcal{G}$ for joint graph partitioning and labeling. The algorithm finds a clustering and label assignment described by a set of *active* edges: $A \subseteq E'$ where $A^+ := A \cap E^+$, $A^- := A \cap E^-$ and $A^S := A \cap E^S$ encode clusters, mutual exclusions and label assignments, respectively. For example, $(u, v) \in A^+$ assigns nodes $u$ and $v$ to the same cluster. Similarly, $(u, t_k) \in A^S$ assigns node $u$ to class $k$. However, not all possible $A$ represent a consistent partitioning and labeling. To ensure consistency, we will make the following definitions:

We define two internal nodes $i, j \in V$ as connected if they are connected by active attractive edges, i.e.

$$\forall i, j \in V : \tag{1}$$

$$\Pi_{i \to j} = \{\text{paths } \pi \text{ from } i \text{ to } j \text{ with } \pi \subseteq E'\} \tag{2}$$

$$\text{connected}(i, j; A^+) \Leftrightarrow \exists \text{ path } \pi \in \Pi_{i \to j} \text{ with } \pi \subseteq A^+ \tag{3}$$

$$\text{cluster}(i; A^+) = \{i\} \cup \{j \mid \text{connected}(i, j; A^+)\} \tag{4}$$

and the mutual exclusion between two nodes as

$$\text{mutex}(i, j; A^+, A^-) \Leftrightarrow \exists e = (k, l) \in A^- \text{ with} \tag{5}$$

$$k \in \text{cluster}(i; A^+) \text{ and} \tag{6}$$

$$l \in \text{cluster}(j; A^+) \text{ and} \tag{7}$$

$$\text{cluster}(i; A^+) \neq \text{cluster}(j; A^+) \tag{8}$$

Two nodes are thus mutual exclusive if they are connected by a path from $i$ to $j$ with exactly one repulsive edge.

Furthermore, a label $l_j$ is assigned to a node $i$ if this node is connected to the corresponding terminal node $t_j$ by attractive and semantic edges:

$$\text{class}(i, A^+, A^S) = l_j \Leftrightarrow \exists \pi \in \Pi_{i \to j} \text{ with } \pi \subseteq A^+ \cup A^S. \tag{9}$$

For unlabeled nodes $i$, where $\text{class}(i, A^+, A^S) \neq c \quad \forall c \in \{l_0, ..., l_k\}$, we use the notation $\text{class}(i, A^+, A^S) = \emptyset$ and use it to define the following predicate

$$\text{differentclass}(i, j, A^+, A^S) \quad \Leftrightarrow \quad \text{class}(i, A^+, A^S) \neq \text{class}(j, A^+, A^S) \text{ and} \tag{10}$$

$$\text{class}(i, A^+, A^S) \neq \emptyset \text{ and} \tag{11}$$

$$\text{class}(j, A^+, A^S) \neq \emptyset \tag{12}$$

The graph partitioning assignments $A^+ \cup A^-$ must be chosen such that the clustering and labeling is consistent. This means:

1. Nodes engaged in a mutual exclusion constraint cannot be in the same cluster [44]:

$$\text{mutex}(i, j; A^+, A^-) \Rightarrow \text{not connected}(i, j; A^+) \tag{13}$$

2. Nodes in the same cluster must have the same label, or equivalently:

$$\text{connected}(i,j;A^+) \Rightarrow \text{not differentclass}(i,j,A^+,A^S) \qquad (14)$$

**Algorithm.** The Semantic Mutex Watershed algorithm is an extension of the Mutex Watershed algorithm introduced by Wolf *et al.* [44]. It augments the partitioning of the latter with a consistent labeling. The algorithm is shown in Algorithm 1 with the additions to [44] highlighted. In the following we explain the syntax and procedure of the shown pseudocode.

For each edge $e \in E'$ it will be decided if it should be added to the active set $A$. The decisions are made in descending order of the absolute edge-weights and follow rules depending on the type of each edge:

*Attractive Edges:* The edge is added if the incident nodes are not mutual exclusive and not labeled differently. We call this a merge because the two incident nodes will be connected afterwards.
*Repulsive Edges:* The edge is added if the incident nodes are not connected.
*Semantic Edges:* The edge is added if the node is either unlabeled or already has the same label as the edge's terminal node.

Note, that the set $A$ never violates Eqs. (13) and (14) during the procedure. Therefore, after following these rules, the set of attractive edges in the final set $A \cap E^+$ form clusters in the graph $G$, which are each connected to a single terminal node indicating the labeling. Figure 1(b) shows a simple example of such an active set. Note, that the Mutex Watershed algorithm is embedded in the Semantic Mutex Watershed for the special case when there are zero or one label ($|T| \in \{0,1\}$).

**Efficient Implementation with Maximum-Spanning-Trees.** The SMWS is similar to the efficient Kruskal's maximum spanning tree algorithm [25] and can feasibly be applied to pixel-graphs of large images and even image volumes. Our implementation utilizes an efficient union-find data structure; mutual exclusions are realized through a hash table.

### 3.2  The Semantic Mutex Watershed Objective

The Semantic Mutex Watershed, introduced in the previous section, operates on a graph with terminal nodes identical to the graph for the Asymmetric Multiway Cut (AMWC) [24]. In this section we prove that the Semantic Mutex Watershed optimizes a precise objective and show how it relates to the Asymmetric Multiway Cut objective. To this end, we will extend the proof by [44] to the Semantic Mutex Watershed. Let us first recall their definitions of *dominant powers* and *conflicted cycles*.

**Dominant Power.** Let $\mathcal{G} = (V', E', w)$ be an edge-weighted graph, with unique weights $w : E' \to \mathbb{R}$. We call $p \in \mathbb{N}^+$ a dominant power if:

$$|w_e|^p > \sum_{t \in E',\, w_t < w_e} |w_t|^p \qquad \forall e \in E', \qquad (15)$$

Note that there exists a dominant power for any finite set of edges, since for any $e \in E$ we can divide (15) by $w_e^p$ and observe that the normalized weights $w_t^p / w_e^p$ (and any finite sum of these weights) converges to 0 when $p$ tends to infinity.

**Conflicted Cycles.** We call a cycle of $\mathcal{G}$ conflicted w.r.t. $(\mathcal{G}, w)$ if it contains precisely one repulsive edge $e \in E^-$, s.t. $w_e < 0$. We denote by $\mathcal{C}^-(\mathcal{G}, w) \subseteq \mathcal{C}(\mathcal{G}, w)$ the set of all conflicted cycles. Furthermore, given a set of edges $A \subseteq E$, we denote by $\mathcal{C}^-(A, \mathcal{G}, w) \subseteq \mathcal{C}^-(\mathcal{G}, w)$ the set of conflicted cycles involving only edges in $A$. If there are no conflicted cycles $\mathcal{C}^-(G, A, w) = \emptyset$ then $A$ implies a consistent graph partitioning [26]. In other words, ensuring that there are no conflicted cycles ensures that two nodes that are mutual exclusive can not be connected.

Furthermore, we define the set $\mathcal{P}(A)$ of all paths $\pi$ that connect two distinct terminal nodes through attractive and semantic edges:

$$\mathcal{P}(A) := \{ \pi \mid \pi \in \Pi_{t \to t'}, \pi \in A \cap (E^+ \cup E^S), t, t' \in T, t \neq t' \} \qquad (16)$$

The algorithm must never connect two terminal nodes through such a path, thus we define the **label constraint** $\mathcal{P}(A) = \emptyset$. This ensures the consistency between the partitioning and labeling.

**Lemma 1 (Optimality of the Semantic Mutex Watershed).** *Let* $\mathcal{G} = (V', E', w) = (V \cup T, E \cup E^S, w)$ *be an edge-weighted graph extended by terminal nodes* $T$, *with unique weights* $w' : E' \to \mathbb{R}$, $w_t > 0 \forall t \in T$ *and* $p \in \mathbb{R}^+$ *a dominant power. The edge indicator given by the Semantic Mutex Watershed*

$$x^{\mathbf{SMWS}} := \mathbb{1}$$

*is the optimal solution to the integer linear program*

$$\underset{x \in \{0,1\}^{|E'|}}{\arg\min} \sum_{e \in E'} |w_e|^p x_e \qquad (17)$$

$$\text{s.t.} \quad \mathcal{C}^-(G, A, w) = \emptyset, \qquad (18)$$

$$\mathcal{P}(A) = \emptyset, \qquad (19)$$

$$\text{with} \quad A := \{ e \in E \mid x_e = 0 \}. \qquad (20)$$

*Proof.* This proof is completely analogous to the optimality proof of the Mutex Watershed (see Theorems 4.1 in [44]) and even identical for $T = \emptyset$. The SMWS finds the optimal solution because it enjoys the properties *optimal substructure* and *greedy choice*. Showing the optimal substructure of the Mutex Watershed does not rely on the specific constraints in the ILP. Thus it can also be applied with the additional constraint in Eq. (19), giving the ILP Eqs. (17) to (20) optimal substructure.

In every iteration the SMWS adds the feasible edge $e$ with the largest weight to the active set. Due to the dominant power, its energy contribution is larger than for any combination of edges $e'$ with $w'_e < w_e$. Thus, SMWS has the greedy choice property [10]. It follows by induction that the SMWS algorithm finds the globally optimal solution to the SMWS objective.

**Relation to the Asymmetric Multiway Cut.** To understand the relation of the Semantic Mutex Watershed to the Asymmetric Multiway Cut we will transform the SMWS problem (Eqs. (17) to (20)) into an ILP with the same minimal energy solution as the AMWC.

First, let us review the AMWC [24] as an ILP:

$$\underset{y \in \{0,1\}^{|E'|}}{\arg\min} \sum_{e \in E'} \text{sign}(w_e)|w_e|^P y(x,e) \tag{21}$$

$$\text{subject to} \quad y_e \leq \sum_{e' \in C \setminus \{e\}} y_{e'} \qquad\qquad \forall C \in \text{cycles }(G) \forall e \in C \tag{22}$$

$$\sum_{t \in T} y_{tv} = |T| - 1, \qquad\qquad\qquad \text{if } T \neq \emptyset, \forall v \in V \setminus T \tag{23}$$

$$y_{tt'} = 1, \qquad\qquad\qquad\qquad \forall t, t' \in T, t \neq t'c, f \tag{24}$$

$$y_{tu} + y_{uv} \geq y_{tv}, \qquad\qquad\qquad \forall (u,v) \in E, t \in T \tag{25}$$

$$y_{tv} + y_{uv} \geq y_{tu}, \qquad\qquad\qquad \forall (u,v) \in E, t \in T. \tag{26}$$

We have reformulated the objective by [24] slightly, to highlight the relations of the following cases: For $p = 1$ and $T \neq \emptyset$, this ILP corresponds to the Asymmetric Multiway Cut. Without semantic classes (*i.e.* $T = \emptyset$) Eqs. (23) to (26) are superfluous and the problem reduces to the Multi Cut for $p = 1$ and the Mutex Watershed objective when $p$ is large enough to be dominant [44].

We will now show, for $T \neq \emptyset$ and dominant $p$, that Eqs. (21) to (26) can be solved to optimality with the SMWS. To this end, we identify the indicator variables $x$ in Eq. (17) with the AMWC indicators $y$.

For attractive and semantic edges both indicators represent the same graph partitions and class assignments. In particular, given the associated indicators $x$ and $y$ of any graph partitioning and labeling, $x_e = y(x,e) \quad \forall e \in E^+ \cup E^S$ holds. For repulsive edges $e^- \in E^-$ however, $x_{e^-}$ indicates a mutex edge and therefore a necessary cut, hence $y_{e^-} = 1 - x_{e^-}$. Additionally, the Asymmetric Multiway Cut introduces repulsive edges between terminal nodes and constrains them to be always cut. In conclusion we can translate between both indicators with

$$y(x,e) = \begin{cases} x_e & \text{if } e \in E^+ \cup E^S \\ 1 - x_e & \text{if } e \in E^- \\ 1 & \text{if } e \in (T \times T) \end{cases} \tag{27}$$

Using Eq. (27) we translate the SMWS objective Eq. (17)

$$\sum_{e \in E'} |w_e|^P x_e = \sum_{e \in E^+} |w_e|^P y(x,e) + \underbrace{\left( \sum_{e \in E^-} 1 \right)}_{\mathcal{L}_{\text{triv}}} - \sum_{e \in E^-} |w_e|^P y(x,e) + \sum_{e \in E^S} |w_e|^P y(x,e) \tag{28}$$

$$= \sum_{e \in E'} \text{sign}(w_e)|w_e|^P y(x,e) + \mathcal{L}_{\text{triv}} \tag{29}$$

Note that the constant $\mathcal{L}_{\text{triv}}$ does not affect the minimum energy solution.

Second, we will add the constraints

$$\sum_{t \in T} y_{tv} = |T| - 1 \qquad\qquad \forall v \in V \qquad (30)$$

$$y_e \leq \sum_{e' \in C \setminus \{e\}} y_{e'} \qquad \forall C \in \text{ cycles } (G) \forall e \in C \qquad (31)$$

to the Semantic Mutex Watershed ILP Eqs. (17) to (19) and observe, since $y(x^{\mathbf{SMWS}})$ always fulfills Eqs. (30) and (31). Therefore, $y(x^{\mathbf{SMWS}})$ also minimizes Eq. (17) subject to the tighter constraints Eqs. (19), (20), (30) and (31). Using Eq. (30) and Lemma 2 (see Appendix A) we can replace the path constraints Eq. (19) by

$$\mathcal{P}(A) = \emptyset \quad \Leftrightarrow \quad \sum_{e \in P} y(x, e) \geq 1 \qquad \forall P \in \pi_{t \rightsquigarrow t'} \ \forall t, t' \in T, \ t \neq t' \quad (32)$$

$$\Leftrightarrow \quad y_{ut} + y_{uv} + y_{vt'} \geq 1 \quad \forall (u,v) \in E \ \forall t, t' \in T, \ t \neq t' \quad (33)$$

$$\Leftrightarrow \quad y_{tu} + y_{uv} \geq y_{tv}, \qquad\qquad \forall uv \in E, t \in T \quad (34)$$

$$y_{tv} + y_{uv} \geq y_{tu}, \qquad\qquad \forall uv \in E, t \in T. \quad (35)$$

We conclude that $y(x^{\mathbf{SMWS}})$ minimizes the objective Eqs. (21) to (26) highlighting the close connection to the Asymmetric Mutiway Cut objective. In fact, although unlikely in practical applications, for graphs $\mathcal{G}$ where $d = 1$ is a dominant power, the Semantic Mutex Watershed solves the Asymmetric Mutiway Cut to optimality.

## 4    Experiments

We will now demonstrate how to apply the SMWS algorithm to semantic instance segmentation of 2D and 3D images. We show how existing CNNs can be used as graph weight estimators and compare different sources of edge weights on the Cityscapes dataset. Additionally, we apply the SMWS to a 3D electron microscopy volume and demonstrate its efficiency and scalability. Our SMWS implementation is available at www.github.com/constantinpape/affogato.

### 4.1    Affinity Generation with Neural Networks

The only input to the SMWS are the graph weights; it does not require any hyperparamters such as thresholds. Consequently, its segmentation quality relies on good estimates of the graph weights $w'$. In this section we present how state-of-the-art CNNs can be used as sources for these weights.

**Affinity Learning.** Affinities are commonly used in instance segmentation; for many modern algorithms CNNs are trained to directly predict pixel affinities. A common approach is to employ a stencil pattern that describes for each pixel which neighbours to consider for the affinity computation. Regularly spaced, multi-scale stencil patterns are widely used for natural images [31,33] and bio-medical data [28,45]. These affinities are usually in the interval $[0,1]$ and can be interpreted as pseudo-probabilities. We use these affinities directly as weights for the attractive edges and invert them to get the repulsive edge weights. Therefore the set of affinities from a single source (e.g. a single CNN) forms a weighted graph an which the SMWS can be applied. When multiple sources of affinities are used, each one adds a new set of weighted edges to the graph. If two sources yield different weights for the same edge, only the maximum absolute weight for this edge will be considered by the SMWS algorithm.

**Mask-RCNN** produces overlapping masks that have to be resolved for a consistent panoptic segmentation. We achieve this with the SMWS by deriving affinities from the foreground probabilities of each mask. A straightforward approach is to compute the (attractive) affinity $a(i,j)$ of two pixels as their joint foreground probability, weighted by the classification score $s$: $a(i,j) = s\,p(i)\,p(j)$.

We find that sparse repulsive edges work well in practice, as they lead to faster inference and reduced over-segmentation on the instance boundaries. For this reason, we sample random points from all pairs of masks and add (repulsive) edges with weight proportional to a soft intersection over union of two masks $m$ and $n$: $w_{nm} = 1 - \frac{\sum_{q \in V} p_m(q)p_n(q)}{\sum_{q \in V} \max\,(p_m(q),\,p_n(q))}$.

**Semantic Segmentation CNNs.** State of the art CNNs [7,50] achieve high quality results on semantic segmentation tasks. The output of the last softmax layer usually used in these networks can be interpreted as the normalized probability of each pixel belonging to each class. Thus, we can use these predictions directly as semantic weights. Additionally, we derive affinities of two pixels $i$ and $j$ from the stuff class probabilities, using their joint probability of being in each stuff class $c$, i.e.: $a_c(i,j) = p_c(i)\,p_c(j)$.

### 4.2 Panoptic Segmentation on Cityscapes

We apply the SMWS on the challenging task of panoptic segmentation on the Cityscapes dataset [9]. We illustrate how the different sources of affinities can be used and combined and show their different strengths and weaknesses.

**Dataset.** The Cityscapes dataset consists of urban street scene images taken from a driver's perspective. It has 5k densely annotated images separated into train (2975), val (500) and test (1525) set. We report all results on the validation set. There are 19 classes with 11 stuff classes and 8 thing classes.

**Implementation Details.** To derive graph weights, we use multiple neural networks trained for affinity, semantic class probability and bounding box prediction (see Subsect. 4.1). First, we train two Deeplab 3+ [7] networks to predict semantic class probabilities and affinities on the full image resolution. We adopt the training procedure of [7], for both networks. For the affinities we employ the stencil pattern by [31] and train with the Sorensen Dice Loss [45]. The training

218    S. Wolf et al.

| image | our prediction | groundtruth |
|-------|----------------|-------------|

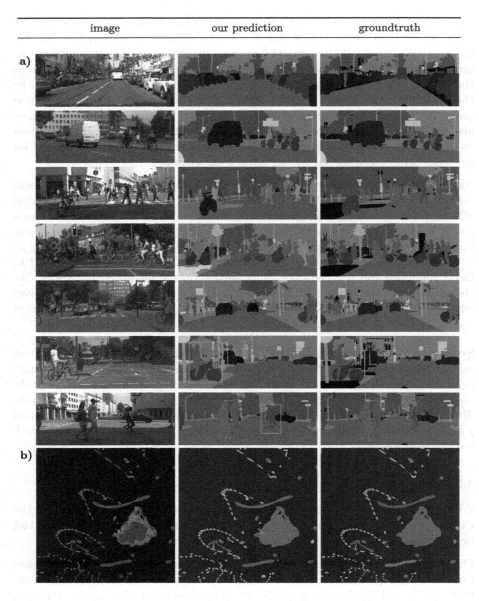

**Fig. 2. a)** Semantic instance segmentation. Results on Cityscapes using semantic unaries (Deeplab 3+ network) and affinities derived from Mask-RCNN foreground probability. Colors indicate predicted semantic classes with variations for separate instances. The last two rows show failure cases highlighted in green. Cyclists and their bicycle often form separate components with few to no graph connections between them resulting in a common failure for graph-based segmentation in general, and the SMWS in particular. **b)** Results for the 3D sponge dataset. Cell-bodies are colored in blue, microvilli in green and flagella in red. (Color figure online)

**Table 1.** Panoptic segmentation quality PQ of the SMWS on top of diverse sources of graph weights.

| MRCNN[15] | | GMIS[31] | | DEEPLAB[7] | | | Cityscapes | | |
|---|---|---|---|---|---|---|---|---|---|
| att | rep | att | rep | att | rep | sem | PQ | PQ$^{Th}$ | PQ$^{St}$ |
| ✓ | ✓ | | | | | ✓ | 59.3 | 50.6 | 65.7 |
| | | ✓ | ✓ | | | ✓ | 58.6 | 48.8 | 65.7 |
| | | ✓ | ✓ | | | ✓ | 56.1 | 42.8 | 65.7 |
| ✓ | ✓ | ✓ | ✓ | ✓ | ✓ | ✓ | 48.7 | 38.7 | 55.9 |
| | | ✓ | ✓ | ✓ | ✓ | ✓ | 47.3 | 35.5 | 55.9 |
| | | | | ✓ | ✓ | ✓ | 46.3 | 33.1 | 56.0 |

**Table 2.** Comparison of panoptic segmentation quality on Cityscapes and Sponge dataset. For Cityscapes, the SMWS uses attractive and repulsive graph weights derived from a Masked-RCNN and semantic class probabilities predicted by a Deeplab 3+ network. For Sponge the weights are estimated by two 3D-U-Nets.

| Cityscapes | PQ | PQ$^{Th}$ | PQ$^{St}$ |
|---|---|---|---|
| AdaptIS [41] | 62.0 | 64.4 | 64.4 |
| SSAP [14] | 61.1 | 55.0 | - |
| SMWS | 59.3 | 50.6 | 65.7 |
| UPSNet [46] | 59.3 | 54.6 | 62.7 |
| AUNet [30] | 59.0 | 54.8 | 62.1 |
| PFPN [18] | 58.1 | 52.0 | 62.5 |

| Sponge | PQ | PQ$^{Th}$ | PQ$^{St}$ |
|---|---|---|---|
| SMWS | **51.6** | **62.1** | 20.0 |
| MWS-MAX | 48.1 | 56.2 | **23.8** |
| CC$_{sem}$ | 43.4 | 55.6 | 06.7 |
| CC$_{aff}$ | 24.3 | 27.7 | 13.9 |

is done with a batch size of 12, 70k training iterations and without test time augmentations. We will refer to these networks as DEEPLAB in Table 1.

Additionally, we, use a more sophisticated method for affinity prediction and a second Deeplab 3+ network trained on re-scaled crops (GMIS in Table 1). This method was proposed by [31], who kindly provided their trained models allowing us to use their affinities. Their clustering utilizes a threshold, which we use as the splitting point between attractive and repulsive edge weights, i.e. affinities below the threshold are inverted and all affinities are scaled to [0, 1].

Finally, we train a Mask-RCNN with the training procedure described in [15] using the implementation from [34]. We derive graph weights, as described in Subsect. 4.1, for attractive edges in a regular 8-neighborhood with distances of {1, 2, 4} pixels, and for repulsive edges between pairs of masks. To avoid the large combinatorial number of all pixel pairs between masks, we restrict the repulsive edges to 5 random pixel per mask. The affinities from this procedure are referred to as MRCNN in Table 1.

**Study of Affinity Sources.** We evaluate the semantic instance segmentation performance of the SMWS in terms of the "panoptic" metric using different combinations of the graph weight sources discussed above. In Table 1 we compare the PQ metric on the Cityscapes dataset. The best performance can be achieved with a combination of Mask-RCNN affinities and Deeplab 3+ for semantic predictions outperforming the strong baseline of [18] listed in Table 2 and shown in Fig. 2. We find that Mask-RCNN affinities are more reliable in detecting small objects and connecting fragmented instances. Note that PQ measures detection quality, weighted by the segmentation quality of the found instances, hence the detection strength of the Mask-RCNN shines through. Using all sources together leads to a performance drop of 10 % points below the best result. We believe this is due to the greedy nature of the SMWS which selects the strongest of all provided edges. This example demonstrates how important it is to carefully select and train the algorithm input.

### 4.3    Semantic Instance Segmentation of 3D EM Volumes

Semantic instance segmentation is an important task in bio-medical image analysis where classes naturally arise through cellular ultra-structure. We use a 3D EM image dataset to compare the SMWS to algorithms that separately optimize instance segmentation and semantic class assignment.

**Dataset.** The dataset consists of two FIBSEM volumes of a sponge choanocyte chamber. The data was acquired in [35] to study proto-neural cells in sponges using the segmentation approach introduced in [37]. These cells filter nutrients from water by creating a flow with the beating of a flagellum and absorbing the nutrients through microvilli that surround the flagellum in a collar [27] (see Fig. 2). To investigate this process in detail, a precise semantic instance segmentation of the cell-bodies, flagella and microvilli is needed. The dataset consists of three EM image volumes of size $96 \times 896 \times 896$ pixel ($2 \times 18 \times 18\,\mu$m).

**Implementation Details.** We predict affinities with two separate 3D U-Nets [8] to derive graph edge weights and semantic class probabilities respectively. We adopt the training procedure by [45], which uses the Dice Coefficient as the loss function. Two volumes are used for training and one for testing.

**Results.** We implement baseline approaches which start from the same network predictions, but do not perform joint labeling and partitioning. We compare to instance segmentation with the Mutex Watershed, followed by assigning instances the semantic label of the strongest semantic edge (MWS-MAX). As a further baseline, we compute connected components of the semantic predictions ($CC_{\text{sem}}$) and short-range affinities ($CC_{\text{aff}}$). The PQ values in Table 2 show that the SMWS outperforms the baselines approaches that separately optimize instance segmentation and semantic class assignment. Additionally, we measure the runtime of the SMWS on crops of the EM-volume with varying number of voxels, shown in Fig. 3). The inference on the full volume (with $\sim 5 \cdot 10^7$ voxels) takes 65 s. In the analyzed volume domain the runtime appears to scale linearly with the number of volxels, suggesting that even larger volumes can be processed in reasonable time. We also compare the runtime of the SMWS with an NLMP solver introduced in [29] and find that it is about 5 orders of magnitude faster with only marginally decreased segmentation quality.

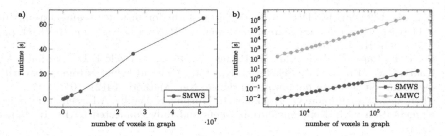

**Fig. 3.** Runtime scaling of the SMWS. **a)** The runtime of the SMWS is evaluated on different volume sizes of the 3D Sponge dataset. We find an almost linear relation between runtime and number of voxels. **b)** Runtime comparison of **(blue)** the SMWS (minimizing (17) with $p \to \infty$) with **(orange)** a KLj\*r solver [29] (minimizing the AMWC objective [24], (17) with $p = 1$). The runtime is evaluated on 2D slices of the 3D Sponge dataset with varying size. On the largest feasible slice the SMWS is marginally less accurate with $PQ = 49.2$ (compared to AMWC $PQ = 52.0$), but 5 orders of magnitude faster. We use the implementation of [29] for the AMWC optimization. (Color figure online)

## 5    Conclusion

We introduced a new method for joint partitioning and labeling of weighted graphs as a generalization of the Mutex Watershed algorithm. This algorithm optimally solves an objective function closely related to the objective of the Asymmetric Multiway Cut problem. Our experiments demonstrate that the SMWS with graph edge weights predicted by convolutional neural networks outperform strong baselines on natural and biological images. Any improvement in the CNN performance will translate directly to an improvement of the SMWS results. However, we also observe that the extreme value selection used by the SMWS to assign edges to the active set can lead to sub-optimal performance when diverse edge weights sources are combined. Empirically, the algorithm scales almost linearly with the number of graph edges $N$ making it applicable to large images and volumes without prior over-segmentation into superpixels.

**Acknowledgements.** Funded in part by the Deutsche Forschungsgemeinschft (DFG, German Research Foundation) – Projektnummer 240245660 - SFB 1129.

## References

1. Andres, B., et al.: Globally optimal closed-surface segmentation for connectomics. In: Fitzgibbon, A., Lazebnik, S., Perona, P., Sato, Y., Schmid, C. (eds.) ECCV 2012. LNCS, vol. 7574, pp. 778–791. Springer, Heidelberg (2012). https://doi.org/10.1007/978-3-642-33712-3_56
2. Andres, B., Kappes, J.H., Beier, T., Köthe, U., Hamprecht, F.A.: Probabilistic image segmentation with closedness constraints. In: 2011 International Conference on Computer Vision, pp. 2611–2618. IEEE (2011)

3. Bai, M., Urtasun, R.: Deep watershed transform for instance segmentation. In: 2017 IEEE Conference on Computer Vision and Pattern Recognition (CVPR), pp. 2858–2866. IEEE (2017)
4. Beier, T., Pape, C., Rahaman, N., Prange, T., Berg, S., Bock, D.D., Cardona, A., Knott, G.W., Plaza, S.M., Scheffer, L.K., et al.: Multicut brings automated neurite segmentation closer to human performance. Nat. Methods **14**(2), 101 (2017)
5. Chen, L.C., Papandreou, G., Kokkinos, I., Murphy, K., Yuille, A.L.: semantic image segmentation with deep convolutional nets and fully connected CRFs. In: ICLR (2016)
6. Chen, L., Papandreou, G., Schroff, F., Adam, H.: Rethinking atrous convolution for semantic image segmentation. CoRR arXiv:abs/1706.05587 (2017)
7. Chen, L.C., Zhu, Y., Papandreou, G., Schroff, F., Adam, H.: Encoder-decoder with atrous separable convolution for semantic image segmentation. In: Ferrari, V., Hebert, M., Sminchisescu, C., Weiss, Y. (eds.) Computer Vision – ECCV 2018. Lecture Notes in Computer Science, vol. 11211, pp. 833–851. Springer, Cham (2018). https://doi.org/10.1007/978-3-030-01234-2_49
8. Çiçek, O., Abdulkadir, A., Lienkamp, S.S., Brox, T., Ronneberger, O.: 3D U-Net: learning dense volumetric segmentation from sparse annotation. In: Ourselin, S., Joskowicz, L., Sabuncu, M., Unal, G., Wells, W. (eds.) Medical Image Computing and Computer-Assisted Intervention – MICCAI 2016. Lecture Notes in Computer Science, vol. 9901, pp. 424–432. Springer, Cham (2016). https://doi.org/10.1007/978-3-319-46723-8_49
9. Cordts, M., et al.: The Cityscapes dataset for semantic urban scene understanding. arXiv:1604.01685 (2016)
10. Cormen, T.H., Leiserson, C.E., Rivest, R.L., Stein, C.: Introduction to Algorithms, 3rd edn. The MIT Press, Cambridge (2009)
11. Dai, J., He, K., Sun, J.: Instance-aware semantic segmentation via multi-task network cascades. In: 2016 IEEE Conference on Computer Vision and Pattern Recognition (CVPR), pp. 3150–3158. IEEE (2016)
12. Fathi, A., et al.: Semantic instance segmentation via deep metric learning. arXiv:1703.10277 (2017)
13. Felzenszwalb, P.F., Huttenlocher, D.P.: Efficient graph-based image segmentation. Int. J. Comput. Vis. **59**(2), 167–181 (2004)
14. Gao, N., et al.: SSAP: single-shot instance segmentation with affinity pyramid. In: Proceedings of the IEEE International Conference on Computer Vision, pp. 642–651 (2019)
15. He, K., Gkioxari, G., Dollár, P., Girshick, R.: Mask R-CNN. In: 2017 IEEE International Conference on Computer Vision (ICCV), pp. 2980–2988 (2017)
16. He, K., Zhang, X., Ren, S., Sun, J.: Deep residual learning for image recognition. In: 2016 IEEE Conference on Computer Vision and Pattern Recognition (CVPR), pp. 770–778 (2016)
17. Kappes, J.H., Speth, M., Andres, B., Reinelt, G., Schn, C.: Globally Optimal image partitioning by multicuts. In: Boykov, Y., Kahl, F., Lempitsky, V., Schmidt, F.R. (eds.) EMMCVPR 2011. LNCS, vol. 6819, pp. 31–44. Springer, Heidelberg (2011). https://doi.org/10.1007/978-3-642-23094-3_3
18. Kirillov, A., Girshick, R., He, K., Dollár, P.: Panoptic feature pyramid networks. In: Proceedings of the IEEE Conference on Computer Vision and Pattern Recognition, pp. 6399–6408 (2019)
19. Kirillov, A., He, K., Girshick, R., Rother, C., Dollár, P.: Panoptic segmentation. In: Proceedings of the IEEE Conference on Computer Vision and Pattern Recognition, pp. 9404–9413 (2019)

20. Kirillov, A., Levinkov, E., Andres, B., Savchynskyy, B., Rother, C.: InstanceCut: from edges to instances with multiCut. In: CVPR, vol. 3, p. 9 (2017)
21. Kong, S., Fowlkes, C.C.: Recurrent pixel embedding for instance grouping. In: 2018 IEEE Conference on Computer Vision and Pattern Recognition, CVPR 2018, Salt Lake City, UT, USA, June 18–22, 2018, pp. 9018–9028. IEEE Computer Society (2018)
22. Krasowski, N., Beier, T., Knott, G., Kothe, U., Hamprecht, F.A., Kreshuk, A.: Neuron segmentation with high-level biological priors. IEEE Trans. Med. Imaging **37**(4), 829–839 (2018)
23. Krizhevsky, A., Sutskever, I., Hinton, G.E.: ImageNet classification with deep convolutional neural networks. Commun. ACM **60**(6), 84–90 (2017)
24. Kroeger, T., Kappes, J.H., Beier, T., Koethe, U., Hamprecht, F.A.: Asymmetric cuts: joint image labeling and partitioning. In: Jiang, X., Hornegger, J., Koch, R. (eds.) GCPR 2014. LNCS, vol. 8753, pp. 199–211. Springer, Cham (2014). https://doi.org/10.1007/978-3-319-11752-2_16
25. Kruskal, J.B.: On the shortest spanning subtree of a graph and the traveling salesman problem. Proc. Am. Math. Soc. **7**(1), 48–50 (1956)
26. Lange, J.H., Karrenbauer, A., Andres, B.: Partial optimality and fast lower bounds for weighted correlation clustering. In: International Conference on Machine Learning, pp. 2898–2907 (2018)
27. Langenbruch, P.F., Weissenfels, N.: Canal systems and choanocyte chambers in freshwater sponges (porifera, spongillidae). Zoomorphology **107**(1), 11–16 (1987)
28. Lee, K., Zung, J., Li, P., Jain, V., Seung, H.S.: Superhuman accuracy on the SNEMI3D connectomics challenge. CoRR arXiv:abs/1706.00120 (2017). http://arxiv.org/abs/1706.00120
29. Levinkov, E., et al.: Joint graph decomposition & node labeling: problem, algorithms, applications. In: 2017 IEEE Conference on Computer Vision and Pattern Recognition (CVPR), pp. 1904–1912. IEEE (2017)
30. Li, Y., et al.: Attention-guided unified network for panoptic segmentation. In: Proceedings of the IEEE Conference on Computer Vision and Pattern Recognition, pp. 7026–7035 (2019)
31. Liu, Y., Yang, S., Li, B., Zhou, W., Xu, J., Li, H., Lu, Y.: Affinity derivation and graph merge for instance segmentation. In: Ferrari, V., Hebert, M., Sminchisescu, C., Weiss, Y. (eds.) ECCV 2018. LNCS, vol. 11207, pp. 708–724. Springer, Cham (2018). https://doi.org/10.1007/978-3-030-01219-9_42
32. Long, J., Shelhamer, E., Darrell, T.: Fully convolutional networks for semantic segmentation. In: Proceedings of the IEEE Conference on Computer Vision and Pattern Recognition, pp. 3431–3440 (2015)
33. Maire, M., Narihira, T., Yu, S.X.: Affinity CNN: learning pixel-centric pairwise relations for figure/ground embedding. In: Proceedings of the IEEE Conference on Computer Vision and Pattern Recognition, pp. 174–182 (2016)
34. Massa, F., Girshick, R.: Maskrcnn-benchmark: fast, modular reference implementation of instance segmentation and object detection algorithms in PyTorch (2018)
35. Musser, J.M., et al.: Profiling cellular diversity in sponges informs animal cell type and nervous system evolution. BioRxiv, p. 758276 (2019)
36. Pape, C., Beier, T., Li, P., Jain, V., Bock, D.D., Kreshuk, A.: Solving large multicut problems for connectomics via domain decomposition. In: 2017 IEEE International Conference on Computer Vision Workshops (ICCVW), pp. 1–10. IEEE (2017)
37. Pape, C., et al.: Leveraging domain knowledge to improve microscopy image segmentation with lifted multicuts. Front. Comput. Sci. **1**, 6 (2019)

38. Ren, S., He, K., Girshick, R., Sun, J.: Faster R-CNN: towards real-time object detection with region proposal networks. In: Advances in Neural Information Processing Systems, vol. 28, pp. 91–99. Curran Associates, Inc. (2015)
39. Ronneberger, O., Fischer, P., Brox, T.: U-net: convolutional networks for biomedical image segmentation. In: Navab, N., Hornegger, J., Wells, W., Frangi, A. (eds.) Medical Image Computing and Computer-Assisted Intervention – MICCAI 2015. Lecture Notes in Computer Science, vol. 9351, pp. 234–241. Springer, Cham (2015). https://doi.org/10.1007/978-3-319-24574-4_28
40. Simonyan, K., Zisserman, A.: Very deep convolutional networks for large-scale image recognition. In: 3rd International Conference on Learning Representations, ICLR 2015, Conference Track Proceedings (2015)
41. Sofiiuk, K., Barinova, O., Konushin, A.: AdaptiS: adaptive instance selection network. In: Proceedings of the IEEE International Conference on Computer Vision, pp. 7355–7363 (2019)
42. Tighe, J., Niethammer, M., Lazebnik, S.: Scene parsing with object instance inference using regions and per-exemplar detectors. Int. J. Comput. Vis. **112**(2), 150–171 (2014). https://doi.org/10.1007/s11263-014-0778-5
43. Tu, Z., Chen, X., Yuille, A.L., Zhu, S.C.: Image parsing: unifying segmentation, detection, and recognition. Int. J. Comput. Vis. **63**(2), 113–140 (2005)
44. Wolf, S., et al.: The mutex watershed and its objective: efficient, parameter-free image partitioning. IEEE Trans. Pattern Anal. Mach. Intell. (2020)
45. Wolf, S., et al.: The mutex watershed: efficient, parameter-free image partitioning. In: Ferrari, V., Hebert, M., Sminchisescu, C., Weiss, Y. (eds.) ECCV 2018. LNCS, vol. 11208, pp. 571–587. Springer, Cham (2018). https://doi.org/10.1007/978-3-030-01225-0_34
46. Xiong, Y., et al.: UPSNet: a unified panoptic segmentation network. In: Proceedings of the IEEE Conference on Computer Vision and Pattern Recognition, pp. 8818–8826 (2019)
47. Yao, J., Fidler, S., Urtasun, R.: Describing the scene as a whole: Joint object detection, scene classification and semantic segmentation. In: 2012 IEEE Conference on Computer Vision and Pattern Recognition, pp. 702–709. IEEE (2012)
48. Yu, C., Wang, J., Peng, C., Gao, C., Yu, G., Nong, S.: Learning a discriminative feature network for semantic segmentation. In: 2018 IEEE/CVF Conference on Computer Vision and Pattern Recognition, pp. 1857–1866 (2018)
49. Yu, F., Koltun, V.: Multi-scale context aggregation by dilated convolutions. In: 4th International Conference on Learning Representations, ICLR 2016, Conference Track Proceedings (2016)
50. Zhao, H., Shi, J., Qi, X., Wang, X., Jia, J.: Pyramid scene parsing network. In: IEEE Conference on Computer Vision and Pattern Recognition (CVPR), pp. 2881–2890 (2017)

# Photon-Efficient 3D Imaging
# with A Non-local Neural Network

Jiayong Peng, Zhiwei Xiong$^{(\boxtimes)}$, Xin Huang, Zheng-Ping Li, Dong Liu,
and Feihu Xu

University of Science and Technology of China, Hefei, China
zwxiong@ustc.edu.cn

**Abstract.** Photon-efficient imaging has enabled a number of applications relying on single-photon sensors that can capture a 3D image with as few as one photon per pixel. In practice, however, measurements of low photon counts are often mixed with heavy background noise, which poses a great challenge for existing computational reconstruction algorithms. In this paper, we first analyze the long-range correlations in both spatial and temporal dimensions of the measurements. Then we propose a non-local neural network for depth reconstruction by exploiting the long-range correlations. The proposed network achieves decent reconstruction fidelity even under photon counts (and signal-to-background ratio, SBR) as low as 1 photon/pixel (and 0.01 SBR), which significantly surpasses the state-of-the-art. Moreover, our non-local network trained on simulated data can be well generalized to different real-world imaging systems, which could extend the application scope of photon-efficient imaging in challenging scenarios with a strict limit on optical flux. Code is available at https://github.com/JiayongO-O/PENonLocal.

**Keywords:** Photon-efficient imaging · Long-range correlation · Non-local network · Depth reconstruction

## 1 Introduction

Active 3D imaging systems have broad applications including biology, robotics, vehicle navigation and remote sensing. Typically, a large number of photons per pixel (ppp), e.g., $10^3$ ppp in a 1 megapixel image, is required to suppress the background noise inherent in the optical detection process [18]. Important progress has been made for image sensors, where single-photon detectors [17] and arrays [38,46] can provide extraordinary optical sensitivity and timing resolution. Together with the advanced computational algorithms, new photon-counting light detection and ranging (LiDAR) systems, which detect only a single photon

---

**Electronic supplementary material** The online version of this chapter (https://doi.org/10.1007/978-3-030-58539-6_14) contains supplementary material, which is available to authorized users.

A. Vedaldi et al. (Eds.): ECCV 2020, LNCS 12351, pp. 225–241, 2020.
https://doi.org/10.1007/978-3-030-58539-6_14

per pixel on average [21], have demonstrated dramatic improvements in photon efficiency [3]. However, in certain scenarios, such as remote sensing of a dynamic scene at a long standoff distance [24,31], non-line-of-sight imaging [28,30,39], as well as microscope imaging of delicate biological samples [22,41], limitations on the optical flux and integration time preclude the collection of the effective signal photons. Consequently, the raw measurements with extremely low photon counts and low signal-to-background ratio (SBR) pose great challenges on the reconstruction algorithms.

Recently, a number of algorithms have been proposed for 3D imaging with a small number of photons [2,3,21,26,35,43,44]. One of the earliest attempts is first-photon imaging [21], in which 3D structures and reflectivity can be recovered from the first detected photon at each pixel. Afterwards, there emerge other approaches dealing with the measurements captured with array detectors [7,36,44]. By exploiting scene structures, recent algorithms [2,35,43,44] build probabilistic models for individual photon detections and use photon-by-photon processing to remove the detections that are likely to be background noise. These algorithms are more effective in low-light scenarios where conventional histogram techniques [1,6] perform poorly. Still, their performance degrades significantly with the decrease of photon counts and SBR [35].

As in various computer vision tasks [13,14,23,34], deep learning has boosted computational imaging [5,10,33,42,48,49], encouraging remarkable progress in this field. Lindell et al. [26] first introduce deep learning to single photon 3D imaging under a sensor fusion configuration, which utilizes an additional high-resolution intensity measurement. However, the intensity image of the target scene is usually not available in practice, which restricts the application scope of this method. On the other hand, the deep neural network lacks specific designs to cope with the large-volume yet sparse photon-efficient measurements, making it less competitive to the state-of-the-art non-learning-based method [35].

In this paper, we first analyze that the photon-efficient measurements contain long-range correlations in both spatial and temporal dimensions. Then we propose an end-to-end deep learning method for depth reconstruction from the measurements with utilization of the long-range correlations. Since the measured raw photon counts are contaminated with background noise, we build our network from a denoising backbone [8,9]. Most importantly, we integrate the non-local operator to exploit the correlations within the measurements. To make it sufficiently effective for large-volume 3D measurements, we deploy a subsequent downsampling operation along the temporal dimension in the feature space, which promotes the reconstruction performance by further enlarging the receptive field for the backbone network. As a general assumption in previous literature [26,35,43,44], we focus on low photon flux regimes, which copes with our long-distance imaging system where the returning photons are weak. Comprehensive simulations demonstrate the significantly improved accuracy of our non-local network over state-of-the-art methods, and this advantage is even larger under extremely low photon counts (e.g., 1 ppp) and low SBR (e.g., 0.01). In addition, the network trained on simulated data achieves superior performance for outdoor scenes (over ranges up to 21 km, with about 1 ppp and 0.1 SBR) captured by our long-distance imaging system. This advantage is demonstrated again on real-world measurements from another indoor imaging system.

The main contributions of this work can be summarized into three aspects:

(1) An end-to-end network for depth reconstruction from photon-efficient measurements, especially those with extremely low photon counts and low SBR;
(2) Analysis of long-range correlations in the measurements and exploitation of the correlations with our specifically designed non-local neural network;
(3) Superior reconstruction performance on both simulated and real-world measurements and improved generalization capability to unseen noise levels as well as across different imaging systems.

## 2  Related Work

**Single-Photon Sensors.** Photon-efficient imaging has attracted increasing attention recently. To name a few, O'Toole et al. [29] design an imaging system which builds on single-photon avalanche diode (SPAD) sensors to capture multi-path responses with active illuminations. Instead of capturing the distance, Ingle et al. [19] propose the passive free-running SPAD imaging, which uses SPADs to acquire 2D intensity images without any active light source. The captured intensity images are with unprecedented dynamic range under ambient lighting. Gupta et al. [16] study the correlations between photon flux and the distortion of captured temporal waveform. They then derive a closed form expression for the optimal flux of a SPAD-based LiDAR system, and propose a simple adaptive approach to achieve the optimal flux. Furthermore, Gupta et al. [15] propose an asynchronous single-photon 3D imaging system to mitigate the distortions caused by the ambient light.

**Computational Reconstruction Algorithms.** Depth reconstruction from photon-efficient measurements is an active research topic. As an embodiment of maximum likelihood estimation, conventional log-matched filter [4] can be effective for high-light scenarios with a large number of data samples. To tackle with decreased photon counts and SBR, Shin et al. [43] develop a robust method for estimating depth and reflectivity using fixed dwell time per pixel. They [44] also develop an array-specific algorithm to recover depth and reflectivity by exploiting both the transverse smoothness and longitudinal sparsity of the natural scenes. Rapp et al. [35] introduce a novel method that emphasizes the unmixing of contributions from signal and noise sources, which achieves promising results. With exploitation of high-resolution intensity images, Lindell et al. [26] propose a deep learning-based method for photon-efficient 3D imaging under a sensor fusion configuration. These advanced algorithms can promote the reconstruction performance in low-light scenarios. Still, their performance degrades significantly under extremely low photon counts and low SBR due to a lack of specifically designed mechanism, which hinders the application of photon-efficient imaging in challenging scenarios.

**Image Denoising and Non-local Mechanism.** As a representative image denoising method, BM3D [11] searches similar patches in a global manner to exploit the non-local correlations in the whole image. Our work is inspired by this simple yet effective idea, together with the observation that the raw photon-efficient measurements have long-range correlations across both spatial and temporal dimensions. To accomplish the depth reconstruction task with an advanced architecture, we build our network on the basis of the deep boosting denoising model [8,9] as well as the non-local operator [47,50]. The latter has been demonstrated effective in various tasks, such as super-resolution [12] and sequence learning [27]. However, different from ordinary images and videos, the photon-efficient measurements are in large 3D volume, sparse in temporal dimension and contaminated with heavy noise. To the best of our knowledge, this is the first time that the non-local mechanism is adopted to deal with such high dimensional and sparse measurements. Our specifically designed non-local neural network excavates the long-range correlations in both spatial and temporal dimensions and significantly improves the depth reconstruction performance especially in the challenging low photon counts and low SBR scenarios.

## 3    The Proposed Method

### 3.1    Forward Model

We depict an image formation model for SPAD-based pulsed LiDAR imaging system, which is then used to generate simulated data for training our network. Such a system generally contains a pulsed laser source and a SPAD detector, as shown in Fig. 1(a). The pulsed laser source transmits periodic short light pulses $s(t)$ with repetition period $T_r$ to illuminate the scene in a raster-scanned manner. To avoid distance aliasing, we assume $T_r > 2z_{max}/c$, where $z_{max}$ is the maximum scene depth and $c$ is the speed of light. The SPAD detector observes the reflected light pulses by detecting at most one photon per pulse repetition period, and builds a temporal histogram with recorded photons.

Note that the system operates in low photon flux regimes, which is a general assumption in previous literature [26,35,43,44]. This means that the returning photons are very weak (far less than 1 photon) within each repetition period $T_r$ and the pile-up effect [16,32] can be negligible. Thus for each illumination position $(i, j)$, the photon flux arrived at the detector at time interval $n$ can be described as

$$r_{i,j}[n] = \int_{n\Delta t}^{(n+1)\Delta t} \Phi_{i,j} \cdot s\left(t - \frac{2z_{i,j}}{c}\right)dt + b_\gamma, \tag{1}$$

where $r_{i,j}[n]$ denotes the photon flux arrived at the detector at time interval $n$, $\Delta t$ is the bins of duration, and $\Phi_{i,j}$ encapsulates the distance fall-off, scene reflectance and BRDF. $s(t)$ denotes the transmitted light pulses and $z_{i,j}$ is the scene depth of illumination position $(i, j)$. $b_\gamma$ denotes the photon flux caused by the ambient light with optical frequency $\gamma$.

For a SPAD detector, the arrived photon flux is attenuated by the detector's quantum efficiency $\eta \in [0, 1)$, which describes the probability that an incident

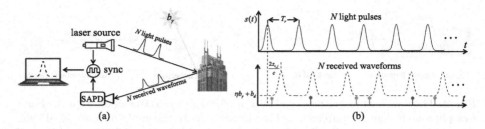

**Fig. 1.** (a) SPAD-based pulsed LiDAR imaging system, which contains a pulsed laser source and a SPAD detector. (b) In low photon flux regimes, the photon detections within $N$ illumination periods can be described as the sum of signal photon detections (red) and background photon detections (blue). The signal photon detections are from the light pulses with the same distribution and they are correlated with each other, while the background photon detections are randomly distributed and not correlated (Color figure online)

photon can be detected by the device [37]. Besides, the detector has a non-zero dark count $b_d$ (numbers of false detections) as well. Therefore, the number of photons measured by the SPAD detector in response to $N$ illumination periods of light pulses can be represented by a temporal histogram

$$\mathbf{h}_{i,j}[n] \sim \mathbf{P}\{N[\eta r_{i,j}[n] + b_d]\}, \tag{2}$$

where $\mathbf{h}_{i,j}[n]$ represents the temporal histogram at time interval $n$ for position $(i, j)$ within $N$ illumination periods of light pulses. The measurements are modeled as a Poisson process $\mathbf{P}$ with a time-varying arrival function.

### 3.2  Long-Range Correlations

As shown in Fig. 1(b), in temporal dimension, the photon detections within $N$ illumination periods can be described as the sum of signal photon detections (red) and background photon detections (blue) under low photon flux regimes. The signal photon detections are from the light pulses with the same distributions and thus they are correlated with each other. However, the background photon detections are randomly distributed in time, which have no correlations with each other or the signal photon detections. Since the signal photons will reach the SPAD at any timestamps, the correlations should be considered across the whole temporal dimension. In spatial dimension, for most natural scenes, the neighborhoods that have similar geometry have correlations with each other. Since these neighborhoods may appear at any spatial positions, the correlations should be considered across the whole spatial dimension. Thus, the photon-efficient measurements have correlations in both spatial and temporal dimensions.

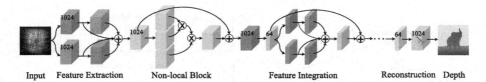

Input     Feature Extraction          Non-local Block          Feature Integration          Reconstruction Depth

**Fig. 2.** The flowchart of our proposed network for depth reconstruction from the input raw photon-efficient measurements. The cuboids denote features which are in 3D volume (spatial and temporal). The temporal dimension of features is 1024 originally, and 64 after downsampling. Note that we only show one channel of features for simplification. The red, blue, and green colors denote the 3D convolution, dilated convolution and deconvolution with kernel size of $3 \times 3 \times 3$, respectively. The gray color denotes the 3D convolution with kernel size of $1 \times 1 \times 1$. "+" and "×" with circular blocks denote the concatenation and matrix multiplication, respectively. Each layer (except for the last one) adopts ReLU as the activation function, which is omitted here for simplification. For more details about our network, please refer to the supplementary material (Color figure online)

### 3.3    Network Architecture

Aiming at high fidelity depth reconstruction from photon-efficient measurements especially those with extremely low photon counts and low SBR, we propose an end-to-end deep neural network with dedicated components to exploit the long-range correlations within the measurements. The flowchart of our proposed network is shown in Fig. 2, the backbone of which is an advanced denoising model called dense dilated fusion network [8,9].

Given a photon-efficient measurement for depth reconstruction, the first step is to extract features with a *feature extraction* block. After that, a *non-local* block is adopted to capture long-range spatial-temporal correlations within the measurement. Then, a *feature integration* block, that contains a downsampling operator and several 3D dilated dense fusion sub-blocks, is performed to downsample features in temporal dimensions and integrate them across channels. The last *reconstruction* block first estimates the denoised histogram $\widehat{\mathbf{h}}$, then generates the 2D depth map by reporting the bin index of the maximum value of $\widehat{\mathbf{h}}$.

In order to make our network training more efficient, we adopt two loss terms to constrain the network. One is the Kullback-Leibler (KL) divergence at each spatial position $(i, j)$ between the denoised histogram $\widehat{\mathbf{h}}$ and the normalized groundtruth histogram $\mathbf{h}$, which can be written as

$$D_{KL}(\mathbf{h}_{i,j}, \widehat{\mathbf{h}}_{i,j}) = \sum_n \mathbf{h}_{i,j}[n] \log \frac{\mathbf{h}_{i,j}[n]}{\widehat{\mathbf{h}}_{i,j}[n]}. \tag{3}$$

The other is a total variation (TV) term for regularization on the output 2D depth map, which is to improve the robustness of the network. We apply a differentiable argmax operator $S$ to $\widehat{\mathbf{h}}$ to find the bin index of the maximum value through a simple weighted sum calculation for each spatial location $(i, j)$

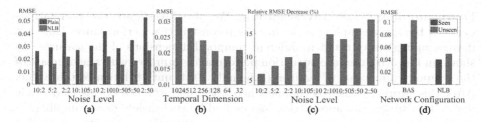

**Fig. 3.** (a) Performance comparisons of different network configurations against noise levels. (b) Reconstruction performance against temporal dimension of features after downsampling. (c) Improvements of NLB over BAS against noise levels. (d) Quantitative comparisons of NLB and BAS in generalization to unseen noise levels

$$S(\widehat{\mathbf{h}}_{i,j}) = \sum_n n \cdot \widehat{\mathbf{h}}_{i,j}[n]. \tag{4}$$

Thus the final loss function to train our depth reconstruction network is

$$L(\mathbf{h}, \widehat{\mathbf{h}}) = \sum_{i,j} D_{KL}(\mathbf{h}_{i,j}, \widehat{\mathbf{h}}_{i,j}) + \lambda TV(S(\widehat{\mathbf{h}})), \tag{5}$$

where $\lambda$ is a hyper-parameter giving the ratio of the two loss terms.

### 3.4 Non-local Block

Since the photon-efficient measurements contain long-range correlations in both spatial and temporal dimensions, we propose our non-local block to exploit the correlations. Due to the high dimensionality and sparsity of the measurements, integrating the non-local block and making it sufficiently effective is non-trivial. Thus, we deploy a downsampling operation along the temporal dimension in the feature space after the non-local block to make the training efficient for such high dimensional and sparse 3D measurements.

**Global Information Exploration.** The global information across both spatial and temporal dimensions explored by our non-local block remarkably improves the reconstruction performance, especially in low photon counts and low SBR scenarios. To verify this, we conduct an ablation between two networks: "Plain" denotes the backbone network [8,9], "NLB" denotes our non-local neural network exploiting both spatial and temporal correlations. Here we report some intermediate results. As shown in Fig. 3(a), our non-local neural network achieves performance improvements on each noise level, and the improvements are more prominent in low photon counts and low SBR (e.g., 49% on 2:50) compared with that in higher ones (e.g., 42% on 10:2), which demonstrates the effectiveness of our non-local network. Note that the less the photon counts are, the more difficult the reconstruction is. For example, it is much more challenging to reconstruct on 2:2 than 10:10, although they are with the same SBR.

**Downsampling Scale Investigation.** We also investigate the correlations between the downsampling scale and the reconstruction performance. Different downsampling scales result in different temporal dimensions of the features. As shown in Fig. 3(b), the reconstruction performance improves with the decrease of the temporal dimension of features (originally 1024) until it hits a certain value. After this turning point (64 channels here), the performance begins to degrade due to the substantial information loss caused by such heavy downsampling. In the following simulation and experiments, we uniformly set the downsampling scale to 16 (corresponding to 64 channels) in our network, which guarantees superior performance as well as training efficiency.

**A Closer Look at the Low End.** As demonstrated above, the long-range spatial-temporal dependencies within the raw measurements can be effectively captured by our non-local block. Here we take a closer look at the performance improvement, where the network containing the downsampling operator but not the non-local block is adopted as the baseline (denoted as "BAS"). In this way, we can see the role of the non-local block in our network more clearly. Specifically, we compare the improvements of our non-local neural network (with both non-local block and downsampling, denoted as "NLB") over the above baseline on various noise levels. As shown in Fig. 3(c), the non-local block itself achieves a notable improvement on each noise level, and the improvements are more prominent in low photon counts and low SBR (e.g., 18% on 2:50) compared with those in high ones (e.g., 6% on 10:2), which demonstrates the effectiveness of the non-local block itself.

**Generalization Capability Improvement.** Due to the exploration of the global information across both spatial and temporal dimensions, the non-local block also helps to improve the generalization capability of the network to unseen noise levels. To verify this, we first train two networks, i.e., BAS and NLB, on a dataset with a large range of noise levels (9 typical noise levels plus 3 extremely low SBR cases, see Sect. 4.3 for more details), and the obtained models are denoted as "Seen". The two networks are then retrained on a dataset with a small range of noise levels (the 9 typical noise levels in the previous large range), and the obtained models are denoted as "Unseen". We compare the performance of the above models on the test data in the 3 extremely low SBR cases. As shown in Fig. 3(d), the performance of the BAS network degrades 60% when a trained model generalizes to unseen noise levels, while the NLB network only drops 24% in the same situation. It thus demonstrates the effectiveness of the non-local block, once again.

In summary, our non-local block effectively captures the long-range spatial-temporal dependencies within 3D photon-efficient measurements, which is beneficial for depth reconstruction especially in low photon counts and low SBR scenarios. Moreover, it helps improve the generalization capability of the network to unseen noise levels.

# 4    Experiments

## 4.1    Data Simulation and Evaluation Metric

We simulate SPAD measurements for a variety of scenes and illumination conditions using RGB-D images from the NYU v2 dataset [45] captured with the Microsoft Kinect sensor, by sampling the corresponding inhomogeneous Poisson process in Eq. 2. To vary the signal and background noise levels across the dataset, we simulate an average of 2, 5, and 10 signal photons detected per pixel, with 2, 10, and 50 background photons at each signal level. Each measurement has 1024 bins for every histogram on a certain spatial position with a bin size of 80 ps, and a detected illumination pulse with a full width at half maximum (FWHM) of 400 ps. A total of 13800 and 2800 measurements are generated from the NYU v2 dataset for training and validation, respectively. The test data is simulated on a set of 8 scenes from the Middlebury dataset [40] under different noise levels. The evaluation metric is the generally used root mean square error (RMSE) between the recovered depth map and the ground truth, which is averaged over 8 test scenes under a number of selected noise levels.

## 4.2    Implementation Details

We implement our method using PyTorch, and make comparisons with conventional log-matched filter (LM Filter) [4] and several state-of-the-art approaches including Shin et al. [44], Rapp et al. [35], and Lindell et al. [26] (Lindell_I and Lindell denote the networks trained with and without intensity maps, respectively) on both simulated and real-world measurements. The implementation of these methods follows their publicly available codes. For our network, we adopt eight 3D dilated dense fusion sub-blocks in the feature integration block, and the hyper-parameter $\lambda$ in the loss function is set to $10^{-5}$. We train the networks in [26] with the same training data as ours, during which we extract patches of size $32 \times 32 \times 1024$, with a batch size of 4. We initialize the network randomly and use the ADAM [20] solver with $\beta_1 = 0.9$, $\beta_2 = 0.999$ and a learning rate of $10^{-4}$ with a learning rate decay of 0.9 after each epoch. The training is conducted on NVIDIA 1080Ti GPU, which takes about 35 h for the network to converge. Limited by the large GPU memory required for 3D convolution especially in [26], we test on the measurements with a relatively low spatial resolution of $72 \times 88$ and a uniform temporal resolution of 1024 (unless noted otherwise), yet higher spatial resolution input can be processed in a patch-by-patch manner.

## 4.3    Simulation Results

**Quantitative Evaluation.** We first evaluate our method on the 8 test scenes under 9 typical noise levels generally reported in literature (10:2, 5:2, 2:2, 10:10, 5:10, 2:10, 10:50, 5:50, 2:50) with comparison of LM Filter [4], Shin et al. [44], Rapp et al. [35], and Lindell et al. [26]. The quantitative results are listed in the upper part of Table 1. As can be seen, our method achieves the best performance

**Table 1.** Quantitative comparisons of several depth reconstruction methods under different noise levels (signal photon: noise photon). All results are reported as an average root mean square error (RMSE) over the test set containing 8 scenes with spatial resolution of 72 × 88. Lindell_I and Lindell denote that the networks in [26] are trained with and without intensity maps, respectively

| Noise levels | LM Filter | Shin | Rapp | Lindell | Lindell_I | Ours |
|---|---|---|---|---|---|---|
| 10:2 | 0.8023 | 0.0274 | 0.0226 | 0.0296 | 0.0278 | **0.0147** |
| 5:2 | 1.8994 | 0.0380 | 0.0268 | 0.0346 | 0.0334 | **0.0160** |
| 2:2 | 3.7632 | 0.0677 | 0.0376 | 0.0470 | 0.0454 | **0.0216** |
| 10:10 | 1.2328 | 0.0385 | 0.0232 | 0.0303 | 0.0286 | **0.0150** |
| 5:10 | 2.5967 | 0.0532 | 0.0282 | 0.0354 | 0.0342 | **0.0165** |
| 2:10 | 4.8231 | 0.0892 | 0.0570 | 0.0485 | 0.0479 | **0.0218** |
| 10:50 | 1.7839 | 0.0764 | 0.0267 | 0.0317 | 0.0295 | **0.0153** |
| 5:50 | 3.4985 | 0.1060 | 0.0359 | 0.0380 | 0.0345 | **0.0185** |
| 2:50 | 5.7514 | 0.1514 | 0.0890 | 0.0748 | 0.0681 | **0.0266** |
| Ave. | 2.9057 | 0.0720 | 0.0385 | 0.0411 | 0.0388 | **0.0184** |
| 3:100 | 5.4568 | 1.2593 | 0.0614 | 0.0655 | 0.0487 | **0.0250** |
| 2:100 | 6.2437 | 1.3648 | 0.1163 | 0.2435 | 0.1311 | **0.0328** |
| 1:100 | 6.9180 | 2.1753 | 0.6605 | 1.3650 | 1.2702 | **0.0893** |
| Ave. | 6.2062 | 1.5998 | 0.2794 | 0.5580 | 0.4833 | **0.0490** |

in terms of all noise levels and significantly surpasses previous approaches. Compared with the two most recent methods Rapp and Lindell, our method improves the reconstruction performance by a large margin (over 50%), which indicates the effectiveness of exploiting long-range correlations within the measurements using the non-local block.

**A Closer Look at the Low End.** To further evaluate the performance of our method under extremely low photon counts and low SBR, we conduct simulations with noise levels of 3:100, 2:100, and 1:100, which are seldom investigated before since they are too challenging[1]. The results are listed in the lower part of Table 1. Quantitatively, our method achieves 82% and 89% improvements over the second and third best, respectively. Specifically, the performance of Rapp and Lindell decrease dramatically from 2:100 to 1:100, while our method behaves much better with an elegant degradation. Note that, the three noise levels are not involved in the training data. It demonstrates the generalization capability of our network to unseen test data, which is essential to guarantee that the network trained from simulated data is applicable to real-world scenarios.

---

[1] Note that we enlarge the illumination periods $N$ to ensure that the returning photons in each period are weak enough so that our image formation model in Eq. 2 can still be valid without suffering from the pile-up effect in simulating these noise levels.

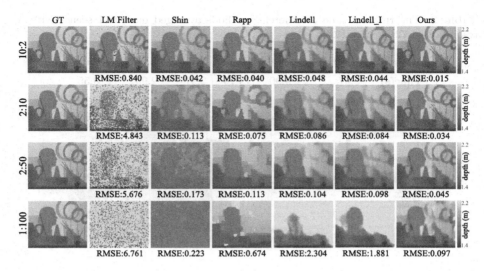

**Fig. 4.** Comparisons of several depth reconstruction methods for the *Art* scene on different noise levels: 10:2, 2:10, 2:50, and 1:100. Depth maps are with a spatial resolution of 72 × 88. GT denotes the groundtruth depth map provided in the dataset

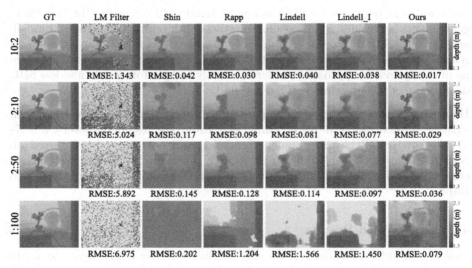

**Fig. 5.** Comparisons of several depth reconstruction methods for the *Reindeer* scene on different noise levels: 10:2, 2:10, 2:50, and 1:100. Depth maps are with a spatial resolution of 72 × 88. GT denotes the groundtruth depth map provided in the dataset

**Qualitative Evaluation.** We provide qualitative comparisons of depth reconstruction for different methods on various noise levels, with two exemplar scenes shown in Fig. 4 and Fig. 5. As can be seen, existing state-of-the-art methods recover accurate depth maps under high SBR (e.g., 10:2), but they all fail to

**Table 2.** The running time of different methods averaged on 8 test scenes with a resolution of $72 \times 88 \times 1024$

| Methods | LM Filter | Shin | Rapp | Lindell | Lindell_I | Ours |
|---------|-----------|------|------|---------|-----------|------|
| Time(s) | 8.47 | 9.90 | 19.19 | 2.91 | 2.95 | 0.55 |

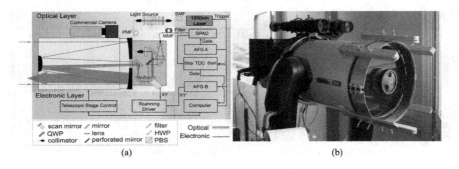

(a)                                                                    (b)

**Fig. 6.** (a) Imaging optics. (b) Photo of imaging setup

recover decent depth under SBR as low as 1:100 (0.01). Specifically, LM Filter generates noisy results, Shin loses informative depth information, Rapp, Lindell, and Lindell_I fail to recover structures of the scene. In contrast, our method still reconstructs decent depth even in this challenging case. The distinct improvement over previous approaches under extremely low photon counts and low SBR demonstrates the superiority of our method.

**Running Time.** We further compare the running time of our method with existing approaches. LM Filter, Shin, and Rapp are tested on Intel Core i7-6700k @4GHz CPU, while Lindell, Lindell_I, and our method are tested on NVIDIA 1080Ti GPU. As shown in Table 2, our method is much faster than others, achieving nearly 6 and 35 times acceleration compared with Lindell and Rapp.

## 4.4    Real-World Results

Besides the simulated test set, we also conduct outdoor experiments to verify the performance of our method in real-world scenarios. Our long-distance coaxial single-photon imaging setup is shown in Fig. 6. The laser transmitted from the collimator, passing through the perforated mirror and the scanning mirror, comes out from the telescope. The photons reflected by the target are collected with the same telescope, then delivered through the scanning mirror, perforated mirror and polarization beam splitter, detected by the single photon detector at last. This system was initially proposed in [25] yet with a traditional reconstruction algorithm. For more details about the imaging system, please refer to the supplementary material.

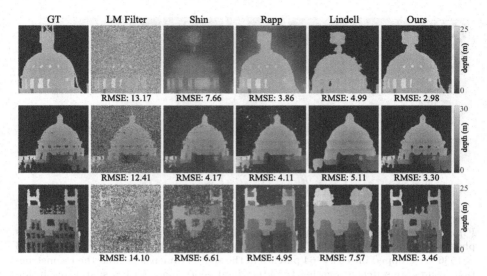

**Fig. 7.** The reconstruction results for three outdoor scenes. First row: a *Hotel*, that locates 1 km away with a spatial resolution of 320 × 320, SBR = 0.1, and about 1 ppp. Second row: a *Castle*, that locates 4 km away with a spatial resolution of 256 × 256, SBR = 0.9, and about 1 ppp. Third row: a tall building named *K11*, that locates 21 km away with a spatial resolution of 128 × 128, SBR = 0.1, and about 1 ppp. GT denotes the groundtruth depth maps captured by our system with a long acquisition time. Limited by the GPU memory, the input measurements are cropped into 64 × 64 patches in the spatial dimensions, and the reconstruction results are stitched together to obtain final depth maps with the same spatial resolution as the inputs

We capture three different scenes over 1 km, 4 km and 21 km away, respectively, and make comparisons among different depth reconstruction methods. Here the networks of Lindell and ours are both trained on the aforementioned simulated dataset in Sect. 4.1, which are adopted to process the real-world measurements directly. The qualitative comparisons are shown in Fig. 7. As can be seen, both LM Filter and Shin fail to reconstruct the main structures of the scenes, resulting heavy noise or missing components. For Rapp and Lindell, they fail to reconstruct the fine structures in the scenes. For example, they can hardly reconstruct the windows in the second and third scenes. In contrast, our network recovers both main and fine structures in the scenes even under heavy noise. For a further comparison, we also provide quantitative results in terms of RMSE computed with the groundtruth depth maps which are captured by our system with a long acquisition time. The quantitative results clearly demonstrate the superior performance of our method over previous approaches.

In addition to our long-distance coaxial single-photon imaging system, we also test on real-world measurements captured by another indoor single-photon imaging prototype [26], which consists of synchronization electronics, off-the-shelf optical and optomechanical components, a standard vision camera, a picosec-

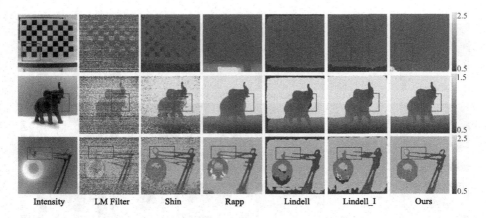

**Fig. 8.** The reconstruction results for real-world scenes captured by an indoor single-photon imaging prototype [26]. The input measurements with a resolution of 256 × 256 × 1536 are cropped into 64 × 64 patches in the spatial dimensions, and the reconstruction results are stitched together to obtain final depth maps with a spatial resolution of 256 × 256

ond laser, and a linear array of 256 SPADs. The qualitative comparisons are shown in Fig. 8, which demonstrate the superiority of the proposed method over previous approaches again. Specifically, as marked by the red boxes, one can easily observe grid-like errors in the first scene, a bump-like error below the elephant's head in the second scene, and missing structures in the third scene for different methods in comparison, yet our method gets rid of these errors. In the last scene, our method makes the lamp circle larger which is an error due to the extremely high brightness of the lamp (see the intensity image). However, other methods also encounter errors in this region which are even more severe. It is worth mentioning that the networks used in the above two single-photon imaging systems are trained on the same simulated dataset, which demonstrates the generalization capability of our method across different imaging systems.

## 5   Conclusion

We analyze the long-range correlations across spatial and temporal dimensions within the photon-efficient measurements and propose an end-to-end deep neural network for depth reconstruction from the measurements by exploiting the correlations with the non-local block and the downsampling operator. Comprehensive simulations demonstrate the significantly improved accuracy of the proposed method over existing state-of-the-art approaches, and this advantage is even larger under extremely low photon counts (e.g., 1 ppp) and low SBR (e.g., 0.01). In addition to the superior performance on simulated data, our method also generalizes well in real-world experiments ranging up to 21 km, with about 1 ppp and 0.1 SBR. We believe that the proposed method could extend the application scope of photon-efficient imaging especially in challenging scenarios, e.g., long-range imaging at a few hundreds of kilometers, non-line-of-sight imaging, and biological imaging with a strict limit on optical flux.

**Acknowledgements.** We acknowledge funding from National Key R&D Program of China under Grants 2017YFA0700800 and 2018YFB0504300, National Natural Science Foundation of China under Grants 61671419 and 61771443, the Shanghai Municipal Science and Technology Major Project (2019SHZDZX01), the Shanghai Science and Technology Development Funds (18JC1414700), and the Fundamental Research Funds for the Central Universities (WK2340000083).

# References

1. Abreu, E., Lightstone, M., Mitra, S.K., Arakawa, K.: A new efficient approach for the removal of impulse noise from highly corrupted images. IEEE Trans. Image Process. **5**(6), 1012–1025 (1996)
2. Altmann, Y., Ren, X., Mccarthy, A., Buller, G., Mclaughlin, S.: Lidar waveform based analysis of depth images constructed using sparse single-photon data. IEEE Trans. Comput. Imaging **25**(5), 1935–1946 (2016)
3. Altmann, Y., McLaughlin, S., Padgett, M.J., Goyal, V.K., Hero, A.O., Faccio, D.: Quantum-inspired computational imaging. Science **361**(6403), 2298 (2018)
4. Bar-David, I.: Communication under the poisson regime. IEEE Trans. Inf. Theory **15**(1), 31–37 (1969)
5. Barbastathis, G., Ozcan, A., Situ, G.: On the use of deep learning for computational imaging. Optica **6**(8), 921–943 (2019)
6. Buller, G.S., Wallace, A.M., Mccarthy, A., Lamb, R.A.: Ranging and three-dimensional imaging using time-correlated single-photon counting. IEEE J. Sel. Top. Quantum Electron. **13**(4), 1006–1015 (2007)
7. Chan, S., et al.: Long-range depth imaging using a single-photon detector array and non-local data fusion. Sci. Rep. **9**(1), 8075 (2019)
8. Chen, C., Xiong, Z., Tian, X., Wu, F.: Deep boosting for image denoising. In: Ferrari, V., Hebert, M., Sminchisescu, C., Weiss, Y. (eds.) ECCV 2018, Part XI. LNCS, vol. 11215, pp. 3–19. Springer, Cham (2018). https://doi.org/10.1007/978-3-030-01252-6_1
9. Chen, C., Xiong, Z., Tian, X., Zha, Z.J., Wu, F.: Real-world image denoising with deep boosting. IEEE Transactions on Pattern Analysis and Machine Intelligence (2019)
10. Cheng, Z., Xiong, Z., Liu, D.: Light field super-resolution by jointly exploiting internal and external similarities. IEEE Trans. Circuits Syst. Video Technol. **30**(8), 2604–2616 (2019)
11. Dabov, K., Foi, A., Katkovnik, V., Egiazarian, K.: Image denoising by sparse 3-D transform-domain collaborative filtering. IEEE Trans. Image Process. **16**(8), 2080–2095 (2007)
12. Dai, T., Cai, J., Zhang, Y., Xia, S.T., Zhang, L.: Second-order attention network for single image super-resolution. In: IEEE Conference on Computer Vision and Pattern Recognition, pp. 11065–11074 (2019)
13. Dong, C., Loy, C.C., He, K., Tang, X.: Image super-resolution using deep convolutional networks. IEEE Trans. Pattern Anal. Mach. Intell. **38**(2), 295–307 (2015)
14. Girshick, R.: Fast R-CNN. In: IEEE International Conference on Computer Vision, pp. 1440–1448 (2015)

15. Gupta, A., Ingle, A., Gupta, M.: Asynchronous single-photon 3D imaging. In: IEEE International Conference on Computer Vision, pp. 7909–7918 (2019)
16. Gupta, A., Ingle, A., Velten, A., Gupta, M.: Photon-flooded single-photon 3D cameras. In: IEEE Conference on Computer Vision and Pattern Recognition, pp. 6770–6779 (2019)
17. Hadfield, R.H.: Single-photon detectors for optical quantum information applications. Nat. Photonics **3**(12), 696 (2009)
18. Holst, G.C.: CCD Arrays, Cameras, and Displays. SPIE Optical Engineering, Bellingham (1998)
19. Ingle, A., Velten, A., Gupta, M.: High flux passive imaging with single-photon sensors. In: IEEE Conference on Computer Vision and Pattern Recognition, pp. 6760–6769 (2019)
20. Kingma, D.P., Ba, J.: Adam: A method for stochastic optimization. arXiv preprint arXiv:1412.6980 (2014)
21. Kirmani, A., et al.: First-photon imaging. Science **343**(6166), 58–61 (2014)
22. Köllner, M., Wolfrum, J.: How many photons are necessary for fluorescence-lifetime measurements? Chem. Phys. Lett. **200**(1–2), 199–204 (1992)
23. Krizhevsky, A., Sutskever, I., Hinton, G.E.: ImageNet classification with deep convolutional neural networks. In: International Conference on Neural Information Processing Systems, pp. 1097–1105 (2012)
24. Li, Z.P., et al.: Single-photon computational 3D imaging at 45 km. Photon. Res. **8**(9), 1532–1540 (2020)
25. Li, Z.P., et al.: All-time single-photon 3D imaging over 21 km. In: Conference on Lasers and Electro-Optics, p. SM1N.1 (2019)
26. Lindell, D.B., O'Toole, M., Wetzstein, G.: Single-photon 3D imaging with deep sensor fusion. ACM Trans. Graph. **37**(4), 113 (2018)
27. Liu, P., Chang, S., Huang, X., Tang, J., Cheung, J.C.K.: Contextualized non-local neural networks for sequence learning. In: Association for the Advancement of Artificial Intelligence, pp. 6762–6769 (2019)
28. Liu, X., et al.: Non-line-of-sight imaging using phasor-field virtual wave optics. Nature **572**(7771), 620–623 (2019)
29. O'Toole, M., Heide, F., Lindell, D.B., Zang, K., Diamond, S., Wetzstein, G.: Reconstructing transient images from single-photon sensors. In: IEEE Conference on Computer Vision and Pattern Recognition, pp. 1539–1547 (2017)
30. O'Toole, M., Lindell, D.B., Wetzstein, G.: Confocal non-line-of-sight imaging based on the light-cone transform. Nature **555**(7696), 338 (2018)
31. Pawlikowska, A.M., Halimi, A., Lamb, R.A., Buller, G.S.: Single-photon three-dimensional imaging at up to 10 kilometers range. Opt. Express **25**(10), 11919–11931 (2017)
32. Pediredla, A.K., Sankaranarayanan, A.C., Buttafava, M., Tosi, A., Veeraraghavan, A.: Signal processing based pile-up compensation for gated single-photon avalanche diodes. arXiv preprint arXiv:1806.07437 (2018)
33. Peng, J., Xiong, Z., Liu, D., Chen, X.: Unsupervised depth estimation from light field using a convolutional neural network. In: International Conference on 3D Vision, pp. 295–303 (2018)
34. Peng, J., Xiong, Z., Wang, Y., Zhang, Y., Liu, D.: Zero-shot depth estimation from light field using a convolutional neural network. IEEE Trans. Comput. Imaging **6**, 682–696 (2020)
35. Rapp, J., Goyal, V.K.: A few photons among many: unmixing signal and noise for photon-efficient active imaging. IEEE Trans. Comput. Imaging **3**(3), 445–459 (2017)

36. Ren, X., et al.: High-resolution depth profiling using a range-gated CMOS SPAD quanta image sensor. Opt. Express **26**(5), 5541–5557 (2018)
37. Renker, D.: Geiger-mode avalanche photodiodes, history, properties and problems. Nucl. Instrum. Methods Phys. Res. **567**(1), 48–56 (2006)
38. Richardson, J.A., Grant, L.A., Henderson, R.K.: Low dark count single-photon avalanche diode structure compatible with standard nanometer scale CMOS technology. IEEE Photon. Technol. Lett. **21**(14), 1020–1022 (2009)
39. Saunders, C., Murray-Bruce, J., Goyal, V.K.: Computational periscopy with an ordinary digital camera. Nature **565**(7740), 472 (2019)
40. Scharstein, D., Pal, C.: Learning conditional random fields for stereo. In: IEEE Conference on Computer Vision and Pattern Recognition, pp. 1–8 (2007)
41. Schwartz, D.E., Charbon, E., Shepard, K.L.: A single-photon avalanche diode array for fluorescence lifetime imaging microscopy. IEEE J. Solid-State Circuits **43**(11), 2546–2557 (2008)
42. Shi, Z., Chen, C., Xiong, Z., Liu, D., Wu, F.: HSCNN+: Advanced CNN-based hyperspectral recovery from RGB images. In: Proceedings of the IEEE Conference on Computer Vision and Pattern Recognition Workshops (2018)
43. Shin, D., Kirmani, A., Goyal, V.K., Shapiro, J.H.: Photon-efficient computational 3-D and reflectivity imaging with single-photon detectors. IEEE Trans. Comput. Imaging **1**(2), 112–125 (2015)
44. Shin, D., et al.: Photon-efficient imaging with a single-photon camera. Nat. Commun. **7**, 12046 (2016)
45. Silberman, N., Hoiem, D., Kohli, P., Fergus, R.: Indoor segmentation and support inference from RGBD images. In: Fitzgibbon, A., Lazebnik, S., Perona, P., Sato, Y., Schmid, C. (eds.) ECCV 2012, Part V. LNCS, vol. 7576, pp. 746–760. Springer, Heidelberg (2012). https://doi.org/10.1007/978-3-642-33715-4_54
46. Villa, F., et al.: CMOS imager with 1024 SPADs and TDCs for single-photon timing and 3D time-of-flight. IEEE J. Sel. Top. Quantum Electron. **20**(6), 364–373 (2014)
47. Wang, X., Girshick, R., Gupta, A., He, K.: Non-local neural networks. In: IEEE Conference on Computer Vision and Pattern Recognition, pp. 7794–7803 (2018)
48. Xiong, Z., Shi, Z., Li, H., Wang, L., Liu, D., Wu, F.: HSCNN: CNN-based hyperspectral image recovery from spectrally undersampled projections. In: Proceedings of the IEEE International Conference on Computer Vision Workshops (2017)
49. Yao, M., Xiong, Z., Wang, L., Liu, D., Chen, X.: Spectral-depth imaging with deep learning based reconstruction. Opt. Express **27**(26), 38312–38325 (2019)
50. Yue, K., Sun, M., Yuan, Y., Zhou, F., Ding, E., Xu, F.: Compact generalized non-local network. In: International Conference on Neural Information Processing Systems, pp. 6510–6519 (2018)

# GeLaTO: Generative Latent Textured Objects

Ricardo Martin-Brualla[1]([✉]), Rohit Pandey[2], Sofien Bouaziz[2],
Matthew Brown[1], and Dan B. Goldman[1]

[1] Google Research, Seattle, USA
rmbrualla@google.com, mtbr@google.com, dgo@google.com
[2] Google Research, Mountain View, CA, USA
rohitpandey@google.com, sofien@google.com

**Abstract.** Accurate modeling of 3D objects exhibiting transparency, reflections and thin structures is an extremely challenging problem. Inspired by billboards and geometric proxies used in computer graphics, this paper proposes Generative Latent Textured Objects (GeLaTO), a compact representation that combines a set of coarse shape proxies defining low frequency geometry with learned neural textures, to encode both medium and fine scale geometry as well as view-dependent appearance. To generate the proxies' textures, we learn a joint latent space allowing category-level appearance and geometry interpolation. The proxies are independently rasterized with their corresponding neural texture and composited using a U-Net, which generates an output photorealistic image including an alpha map. We demonstrate the effectiveness of our approach by reconstructing complex objects from a sparse set of views. We show results on a dataset of real images of eyeglasses frames, which are particularly challenging to reconstruct using classical methods. We also demonstrate that these coarse proxies can be handcrafted when the underlying object geometry is easy to model, like eyeglasses, or generated using a neural network for more complex categories, such as cars.

**Keywords:** 3D modeling · 3D reconstruction · Generative modeling

## 1 Introduction

Recent research in category-level view and shape interpolation has largely focused on generative methods [20] due to their ability to generate realistic and high resolution images. To close the gap between generative models and 3D reconstruction approaches, we present a method that embeds a generative model in a compact 3D representation based on textured-mapped proxies.

Texture-mapped proxies have been used as a substitute for complex geometry since the early days of computer graphics. Because manipulating and rendering

**Electronic supplementary material** The online version of this chapter (https://doi.org/10.1007/978-3-030-58539-6_15) contains supplementary material, which is available to authorized users.

© Springer Nature Switzerland AG 2020
A. Vedaldi et al. (Eds.): ECCV 2020, LNCS 12351, pp. 242–258, 2020.
https://doi.org/10.1007/978-3-030-58539-6_15

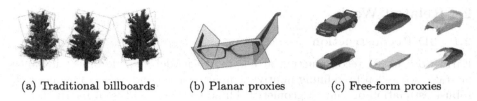

(a) Traditional billboards    (b) Planar proxies    (c) Free-form proxies

**Fig. 1.** Inspired by (a) traditional computer graphics billboards [12], our representation uses (b) planar proxies for classes with well-bounded geometric variations like eyeglasses, and (c) free-form 3D patches for generic classes like cars.

geometric proxies is much less computationally intensive than corresponding detailed geometry, this representation has been especially useful to represent objects with highly complex appearance such as clouds, trees, and grass [10, 36]. Even today, with the availability of powerful graphics processing units, real-time game engines offer geometric representations with multiple levels of detail that can be swapped in and out with distance, using texture maps to supplant geometry at lower levels of detail.

This concept can be adapted to deep learning, for which the capacity of a network that can learn complex geometry might be larger than the capacity needed to learn its surface appearance under multiple viewpoints. Inspired by texture-mapped proxies, we propose a representation consisting of four parts: ① a 3D proxy geometry that coarsely approximates the object geometry; ② a view-dependent deep texture encoding the object's surface light field, including view-dependent effects like specular reflections, and geometry that lies away from the proxy surface; ③ a generative model for these deep textures that can be used to smoothly interpolate between models, or to reconstruct unseen object instances within the category; ④ a U-Net to re-render and composite all the Neural Proxies into a final RGB image and a transparency mask.

To evaluate our approach we capture a dataset of 85 eyeglasses frames and demonstrate that our compact representation is able to generate realistic reconstructions even for these complex objects featuring transparencies, reflections and thin features. In particular, we use three planar proxies to model eyeglasses and show that using our generative model, we can reconstruct an instance with more accuracy and 3× fewer input views compared to a model optimized exclusively for that instance. We also show compelling interpolations between instances of the dataset, and a prototype virtual try-on system for eyeglasses. Finally, we qualitatively evaluate our representation on cars from the ShapeNet dataset [7], for which we use five free-form parameterized textured mesh proxies learnt to model car shapes [15].

To summarize, our main contributions are: ① a novel compact representation to capture the appearance and geometry of complex real world objects; ② a re-rendering and compositing step that can handle transparent objects; ③ a learned latent space allowing category-level interpolation; ④ few-shot reconstruction, using a network pre-trained on a corpus of the corresponding object category.

## 2    Related Work

### 2.1    3D Reconstruction

Early work in 3D reconstruction attempted to model a single object instance or static scene [34] by refining multiview image correspondences [13] along with robust estimation of camera geometry. These methods work well for rigid, textured scenes but are limited by assumptions of Lambertian reflectance. Later work attempts to address this, for example using active illumination to capture reflectance [44], known backgrounds to reason about transparency [38], or special markers on the scanner to recognise mirrors [45]. Thin structures present special challenges, which Liu et al. [25] address by fusing of RGBD observations over multiple views. Even with such specifically engineered solutions, reconstruction of thin structures, reflection and transparency remain open research problems, and strong object or scene priors are desirable to enable accurate 3D reconstruction.

Recent progress in deep learning has renewed efforts to develop scene priors and object category models. Kar et al. [19] learn a linear shape basis for 3D keypoints for each category, using a variant of NRSfM [6]. Kanazawa et al. [18] learn category models using a fixed deformable mesh, with a silhouette based loss function trained via a differentiable mesh renderer. Later work to regress mesh coordinates directly from the image, trained via cycle consistency, showed generalization across deformations for a class-specific mesh [23]. Chen et al. represent view dependent effects by learning surface lightfields [8]. Implicit surface models [9,28,32] use a fully connected network to represent the signed surface distance as a function of 3D coordinate.

### 2.2    Neural Rendering

Neural rendering techniques relax the requirement to produce a fully specified physical model of the object or scene, generating instead an intermediate representation that requires a neural network to render. We refer the reader to the comprehensive survey of Tewari et al. [41]. Recent works use volumetric representations that can be learned on a voxel grid [27,39], or modeled directly as a function taking 3D coordinates as input [30,40]. These methods tend to be computationally expensive and have limited real-time performance (except for [27]). Neural textures [43] jointly learn features on a texture map along with a U-Net. IGNOR [42] incorporates view dependent effects by modelling the difference between true appearance and a diffuse reprojection. Such effects are difficult to predict given the scene knowledge, so GAN based loss functions are often used to render realistic output. Deep Appearance Models [26] use a conditional variational autoencoder to generate view-dependent texture maps of faces. Image-to-image translation (pix2pix) [16] is often used as a general baseline. HoloGAN learns a 3D object representation such that sampled reprojections under a transform fool a discriminator [31]. Point-cloud representations are also popular for neural rerendering [29,33] or to optimize neural features on the point cloud itself [2].

# 3  Generative Latent Textured Objects

Our representation is inspired by proxy geometry used in computer graphics. We encode the geometric structure using a set of coarse proxy surfaces shown in Fig. 1, and shape, albedo, and view dependent effects using view-dependent neural textures. The neural textures are parameterized using a generative model that can produce a variety of shape and appearances.

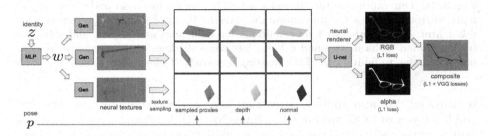

**Fig. 2.** Network architecture. See Sect. 3.2 for details.

## 3.1  Model

Given a collection of objects of a particular class, we define a latent code for each instance $i$ as $\mathbf{z}_i \in \mathbb{R}^n$. We assume that a coarse geometry consisting of a set of $K$ proxies $\{P_{i,1}, \ldots, P_{i,K}\}$, i.e. triangular meshes with UV-coordinates, is available. Our network computes a neural texture $T_{i,j} = \mathrm{Gen}_j(\mathbf{w}_i)$ for each instance and proxy, where $\mathbf{w}_i = \mathrm{MLP}(\mathbf{z}_i)$ is a non-linear reparametrization of the latent code $\mathbf{z}_i$ using an MLP. The image generators $\mathrm{Gen}_j(\cdot)$ are decoders, that take a latent code as input and generate a feature map. To render an output view, we rasterize a deferred shading deep buffer from each proxy consisting of the depth, normal and UV coordinates. We then sample the corresponding neural texture using the deep buffer UV coordinates for each proxy. The deep buffers are finally processed by a U-Net [37] that generates four output channels, three color channels interpreted as color premultiplied by alpha [35], and a separate alpha channel. We use color values premultiplied by alphas because color in pixels with low alpha tends to be particularly noisy in the extracted mattes and distracts the network when using reconstruction losses on the RGB components.

## 3.2  Training and Architecture Details

Our network architecture is depicted in Fig. 2. We use the Generative Latent Optimization (GLO) framework [5] to train our network end to end using simple $\ell_1$ and perceptual reconstruction losses [17]. We use reconstruction $\ell_1$ losses on the premultiplied RGB values, alphas, and a composite on a neutral gray

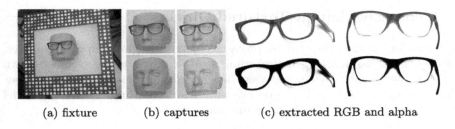

(a) fixture            (b) captures            (c) extracted RGB and alpha

**Fig. 3.** (a) Our capture fixture includes a backlit mannequin head and white acrylic plate, surrounded by a Calibu calibration pattern [3], all of which are actuated by a robot arm. We capture (b) four conditions for each pose and object, and solve for (c) foreground alpha mattes and colors. Note some shadows of the eyeglasses remain unmasked, due to limitations of the matting approach. (Color figure online)

background. We also apply a perceptual loss on the composite using the 2nd and 5th layers of VGG pretrained on ImageNet [11]. We found adversarial losses lead to worse results, and we apply no regularization losses on the latent codes.

The latent codes $\mathbf{z}$ for each class are randomly initialized, and we use the Adam [21] optimizer with a learning rate of $1e^{-5}$. We use neural textures of 9 channels, and $\mathbf{z}$ and $\mathbf{w}$ are 8 and 512 dimensions respectively. We generate results at a $512 \times 512$ resolution for the eyeglasses dataset and $256 \times 256$ for ShapeNet. The latent transformation MLP has 4 layers of 256 features, and the rendering U-Net contains 5 down- and up-sampling blocks with 2 convolutions each, and uses BlurPool layers [47], see more details in the supplementary.

## 4  Dataset

The *de facto* standard for evaluating category-level object reconstruction approaches is the ShapeNet dataset [7]. Shapenet objects can be rendered under different viewpoints, generating RGB images with ground truth poses, and masks for multiple objects of the same category.

Although using a synthetic dataset can help in analyzing 3D reconstruction algorithms, synthetically rendered images do not capture the complexities of real-world data. To evaluate our approach we acquire a challenging dataset of eyeglasses frames. We choose this object category because eyeglasses are physically small and have well-bounded geometric variations, making them easy to photograph under controlled settings, but they still exhibit complex structures and materials, including transparency, reflections, and thin geometric features.

### 4.1  Eyeglasses Frames

We collect a dataset of 85 eyeglasses frames under different viewpoints and fixed illumination. To capture the frames, we design a robotic fixture to sample $24 \times 24$ viewpoints spanning approximately $\pm 24°$ in yaw and azimuth (Fig. 3a). The fixture includes a Calibu pattern [3] with 3 vertical and 5 horizontal rows, enabling

**Table 1.** Ablation study comparing multiple baselines on view interpolation of seen instances, and of few-shot reconstruction using $N = 3$ input views, where we fine-tune the whole network together with the latent code. The VAE model is inferior in both tasks, and our approach improves upon DNR in few-shot reconstruction because our textured proxies are not masked by z-buffering.

| Model | View interpolation | | | Few-shot reconstruction | | |
|---|---|---|---|---|---|---|
| | VAE | DNR | Ours | VAE | DNR | Ours |
| PSNR | 39.70 | 41.21 | 41.32 | 35.59 | 36.14 | 37.19 |
| PSNR$_M$ | 21.79 | 23.29 | 23.42 | 17.94 | 18.65 | 19.64 |
| SSIM | 0.9897 | 0.9916 | 0.9917 | 0.9793 | 0.9819 | 0.9842 |
| Mask IoU | 0.9379 | 0.9556 | 0.9556 | 0.8686 | 0.8725 | 0.9012 |

accurate pose estimation. The fixture center features a hollow 3D printed mannequin head and contains a light inside. For each pose, we capture an image with this backlight on and off (Fig. 3b). We perform difference matting by subtracting the backlit images – which contain fewer shadows – from a reference backlit frame without glasses. We then solve for foreground and background using the closed-form matting approach of Levin et al. [24] (Fig. 3c). The robot's pose is repeatable within 0.5 pixels, enabling precise difference matting.

We generate 3 planar billboards to model each eyeglasses instance: front, left and right. We first compute a coarse visual hull for each object using the extracted alpha masks. We then specify a region of interest in axis-aligned head coordinates, and extract a plane that best matches the surface seen from the corresponding direction. See the supplementary for a more detailed description. We use 5 instances for testing few-shot reconstruction and train on the rest.

Note that this dataset contains two types of artifacts due to the simple acquisition setup: ① shadows cast by the glasses onto the 3D head pollute the alpha mattes and RGB images; ② depending of the viewpoint, the 3D head can occlude part of the glasses frames, resulting in missing temples. We find however that these artifacts do not affect the overall evaluation of our approach.

### 4.2   ShapeNet

We also train GeLaTO using cars from ShapeNet [7]. We generate the proxies using the auto-encoder version of AtlasNet [15] which takes as input a point cloud. We train a 5 patches/proxies model generating triangular meshes based on a $24 \times 24$ uniform grid sampling. Note that the proxies generated by AtlasNet can overlap, but our model is robust thanks to the U-Net compositing step.

## 5   Evaluation

We evaluate GeLaTO on a number of tasks on the eyeglasses dataset, and then show qualitative results on ShapeNet cars. We compare our representation

VAE

DNR

Ours

GT

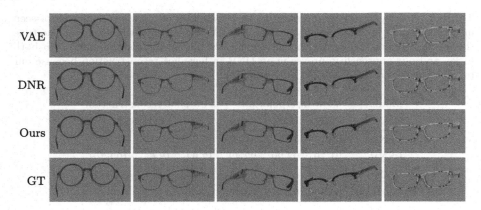

**Fig. 4.** Comparison of view interpolation results for our model and the baselines.

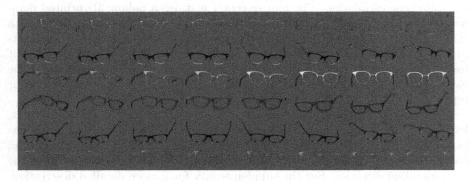

**Fig. 5.** View interpolation results from our model for a variety of glasses.

against baselines inspired by neural textures [43] using the same proxy geometry. In particular, we modify deferred neural rendering (DNR) in two ways: we parameterize the texture using a generator network, without loss of performance, and concatenate deep buffer channels consisting of normal and depth information to the sampled neural texture, instead of multiplying the sampled neural texture by the viewing direction vector. A key difference of our method is that Thies et al. render a deferred rendering buffer with *z-buffering* before the U-Net, whereas our method *stacks* the deferred rendering buffers of each texture proxy before the U-Net. Thus our network is able to "see through" transparent layers to other surfaces behind the frontmost proxy. We evaluate a second baseline that uses a Variational Auto-Encoder (VAE) [22] instead of GLO [5] to model the distribution of instances, where the encoder is a MLP that takes as input a one-hot encoding of the instance id (more details in the supplementary).

**Fig. 6.** Examples of instance interpolation of VAE and our model using GLO.

### 5.1 View Interpolation

We first evaluate our method on the view interpolation task, and show that textured proxies can model complex geometry and view-dependent effects. We train a network on 98% of the views of the training set of the eyeglasses dataset, and test on the remaining 2%. Quantitative results in Table 1 show that our model slightly improves upon the DNR baseline, and is significantly better than VAE. We report PSNR and SSIM on the whole image, $PSNR_M$ evaluated within 7 pixels of alpha > 0.1 values, and IoU of the alpha channel thresholded at 0.5.

Figure 4 qualitatively compares the view interpolation results. VAE results are overly smoothed, and our approach captures more high-frequency details compared to DNR. Figure 5 contains interpolations of the eyeglasses seen from multiple viewpoints, showcasing strong view-dependent effects due to shiny or metallic metallic materials, and reconstructions of transparent glasses that are predominantly composed of specular reflections (last example).

### 5.2 Instance Interpolation

Our generative model allows interpolations in the latent space of objects, effectively building a deformable model of shape and appearance, reminiscent of 3D morphable models [4]. We visualize such interpolations in Fig. 6, in which the latent code **z** is linearly interpolated while the proxy geometry is kept constant. VAE models are commonly thought to have better interpolation abilities than GLO, because the injected noise regularizes the latent space. However, we find GLO offers better interpolations in our setup. VAE interpolations tend to be less visually monotonic, like in the last example where a white border appears and then disappears on the left side of the frame, and often contain spurious structures like the double rim on the second example. The supplementary video shows the effects of interpolating the neural texture and proxy geometry independently.

VAE        DNR        Ours        GT

**Fig. 7.** Comparison of few-shot reconstruction using $N = 3$ input views.

**Table 2.** Reconstruction results with varying numbers of input images $N$ for unseen instances, for the DNR baseline without the category model, finetuning our category-level model, and NeRF. Fine-tuning the category model provides similar quality to DNR with $> 3\times$ fewer input views, and provides $\sim 3$ dB improvement with the same number of input views. NeRF generates better results with $N \geq 30$ views, but is significantly slower to train and render novel views.

| | DNR [43] | | Ours | | | | NeRF [30] | | | |
|---|---|---|---|---|---|---|---|---|---|---|
| | Trained from scratch | | Finetuning category model | | | | Trained from scratch | | | |
| | N = 30 | N = 100 | N = 3 | N = 10 | N = 30 | N = 100 | N = 3 | N = 10 | N = 30 | N = 100 |
| PSNR | 38.75 | 40.05 | 36.53 | 39.35 | 41.61 | 43.42 | 31.20 | 37.21 | 43.32 | **45.28** |
| PSNR$_M$ | 21.48 | 22.43 | 19.01 | 21.78 | 24.00 | 25.80 | 15.41 | 21.25 | 27.49 | **29.80** |
| SSIM | 0.9858 | 0.9897 | 0.9824 | 0.9890 | 0.9921 | 0.9942 | 0.9600 | 0.9845 | 0.9947 | 0.9962 |
| Mask IoU | 0.9293 | 0.9407 | 0.8864 | 0.9350 | 0.9585 | 0.9682 | N/A | N/A | N/A | N/A |

### 5.3   Few-Shot Reconstruction

Because we have parameterized the space of textures, we can think of reconstructing a particular instance by finding the right latent code $\mathbf{z}$ that reproduces the input views. This can be done either using an encoder network, or by optimization via gradient descent on a reconstruction loss. These approaches are unlikely to yield good results in isolation, because the dimensionality of the object space can be arbitrarily large compared to the dimensionality of the latent space, e.g., when objects exhibit a print of a logo or text. As noted by Abdal et al. [1], optimizing intermediate parameters of the networks instead can yield better results, like the transformed latent space $\mathbf{w}$, the neural texture space, or even optimizing all the network parameters, i.e. fine-tuning the whole network.

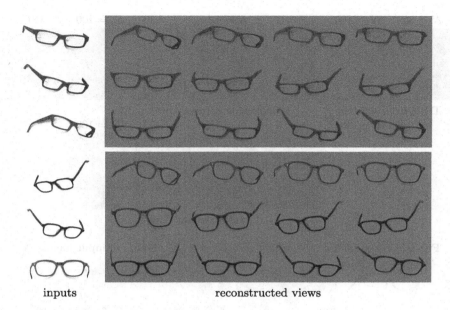

inputs                    reconstructed views

**Fig. 8.** Results for few-shot reconstruction using $N = 3$ views. Left: Input views. Right: Reconstructed views using our method after fine-tuning on the input views. Notice that although the first instance is only captured from the left, our network still is able to reconstruct other viewpoints effectively. We are also able to capture view-dependent effects as seen on the bridge region of the glasses.

Thus, given a set of views $\{I_1, \ldots, I_k\}$ with corresponding poses $\{\mathbf{p}_1 \ldots \mathbf{p}_k\}$ and proxy geometry $\{P_1, \ldots, P_K\}$, we define a new latent code $\mathbf{z}$ and set the reconstruction process as optimization

$$\mathbf{z}^\star, \boldsymbol{\theta}^\star = \arg\min_{\mathbf{z}, \boldsymbol{\theta}} \sum_k \|I^k - \text{Net}(\mathbf{z}, \mathbf{p}_k, \boldsymbol{\theta})\|_1,$$

where $\text{Net}(\cdot, \cdot, \cdot)$ is the end to end network depicted in Fig. 2 parameterized by the latent code $\mathbf{z}$, the pose $\mathbf{p}$, and the network parameters $\boldsymbol{\theta}$.

In Table 1, we quantitatively evaluate reconstructions of 5 unseen instances using only $N = 3$ input images, by fine-tuning all network parameters together with the latent code, and show qualitative results in Fig. 7. We use the same baselines as in Sect. 5.1, and report statistics across the 5 instances. We halt the optimization at 1000 steps, because running the optimization to convergence overfits to only the visible data, reducing the performance on unseen views. We observe that the VAE model is inferior, and that stacking the proxy inputs in our model performs better compared to z-buffering in DNR, because the eyeglasses' arms can be occluded by the front proxy, preventing the optimization of the side textured proxy. Figure 8 shows the input images and reconstructed views using our model, illustrating accurate reproduction of view-dependent effects on the bridge and novel views from an unseen side of the glasses.

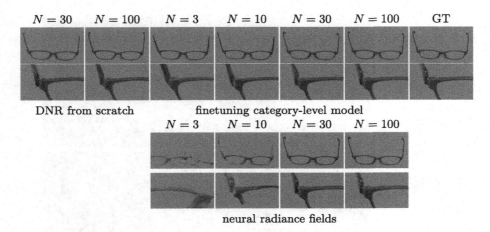

**Fig. 9.** Unseen instance reconstruction varying the number of input images $N$.

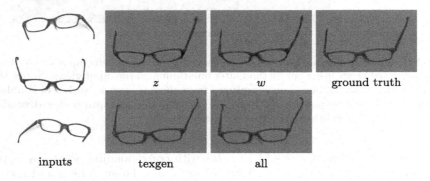

**Fig. 10.** Differences depending on where the model is being fit. The shape is best fit under **w**, although the texture does not match, and better overall reconstruction is achieved when all network parameters are fine-tuned.

To demonstrate the power of our representation, we compare reconstructions of unseen objects with increasing number of input images $N$, using our GeLaTO, and the DNR baseline described in Sect. 5.1, that is exclusively trained on the unseen instance. Similar to Thies et al. [43], we optimize the neural texture for 30k and 100k steps for $N = 30$ and $N = 100$ respectively. We also compare with Neural Radiance Fields (NeRF) [30], a concurrent novel-view synthesis technique that uses a volumetric approach that does not require proxy geometry. Table 2 and Fig. 8 show that our representation achieves better results than the DNR baseline with more than 3× less input images. Using the same number of input images, our reconstructions have PSNR score ∼3 dB higher than the model trained from scratch. Compared to NeRF, our model is more accurate with few views, although NeRF is significantly better with denser sampling. Moreover, training the DNR baseline takes 50 and 150 min on 15 GPUs for $N = 30$ and

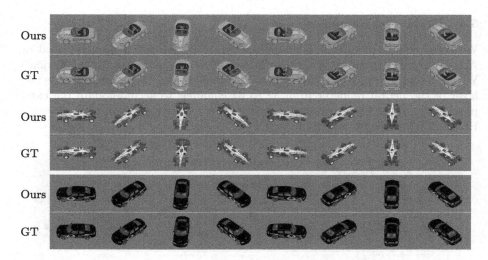

**Fig. 11.** Reconstruction results on ShapeNet cars using textured proxies based on AtlasNet reconstructions. See supplementary video for more results.

$N = 100$ respectively, whereas fine-tuning GeLaTO takes less than 4 min on a single GPU. Training NeRF takes 4 hours on 4 GPUs and rendering a single using NeRF takes several seconds, making it unsuitable for real-time rendering, while DNR and GeLaTO render new views under 20 ms on a NVidia 1080 Ti.

**Table 3.** Comparison of reconstructions when fitting in different spaces. $z$ is the instance latent code, $w$ is the transformed latent code, texture refers to fitting also the parameters of the texture generators, and all refers to fine-tuning the neural rendering network as well.

| Fit variables | $z$ | $w$ | Texture | All |
|---|---|---|---|---|
| PSNR | 31.30 | 36.50 | 37.12 | **37.19** |
| $PSNR_M$ | 13.85 | 18.85 | 19.59 | **19.64** |
| SSIM | 0.9638 | 0.9833 | 0.9841 | **0.9842** |
| Mask IoU | 0.7242 | **0.9152** | 0.8984 | 0.9012 |

Finally, we evaluate the choice of which variables to optimize during few-shot reconstruction in Table 3, and show comparative qualitative results in Fig. 10. Optimizing the transformed latent code **w** reconstructs the shape best as measured by the mask IoU, albeit with a strong color mismatch. Fine-tuning all the network parameters generates the best results as measured by PSNR.

## 5.4   Results on ShapeNet

We show results of modeling ShapeNet cars using textured proxies based on AtlasNet reconstructions. We train a model on 100 car instances using 500 views. We use 5 textured proxies, with a $128 \times 128$ resolution each, and increase the first layer of the neural renderer from 32 to 64 channels to accommodate the extra proxies' channels. Figure 11 shows unseen view reconstruction results, scoring a PSNR of 30.99 dB on a held-out set.

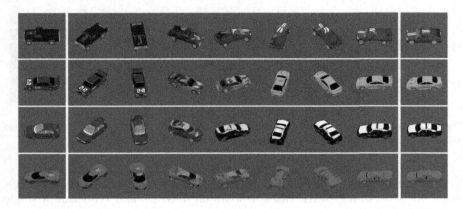

**Fig. 12.** Instance interpolations on ShapeNet. Left: reconstructed view of start instance. Middle: latent texture code interpolation while keeping proxy geometry constant. Right: target instance reconstruction using its proxy geometry.

**Fig. 13.** Learnt neural textures for eyeglasses and cars. Left top: reconstructed view, left bottom: ground truth, right: neural textures. Note the high frequency details encoding the eyeglasses' shape and the number decal on the car.

Figure 12 shows smooth latent interpolation of the latent code of the textured proxies while maintaining the proxy geometry of the first car. Although the proxy geometry is different between instances, Groueix et al. [15] observe that the semantically similar areas of the car are modeled consistently by the same parts

**Fig. 14.** Virtual try-on application for eyeglasses frames, in which a user without eyewear can virtually place reconstructed glasses on themselves. The eyeglasses are generated by our model given the user's head pose, and composited on the user's view. See supplementary video for more results.

of the AtlasNet patches, allowing our model to generate plausible renderings when modifying only the neural texture. Using the proxy geometry of the first instance creates some artifacts, like the white stripes on the first example that are tilted compared to the car's main axis. The eyeglasses interpolation results are more realistic due to a smaller degree of variability in the object class. Please see the supplementary video for more results.

### 5.5  Neural Textures

We visualize the learned neural textures in Fig. 13, showing the first three channels as red, green and blue. They contain high frequency details of the object, such as the eyeglasses shape and decals on the car.

### 5.6  Limitations

Our model has several limitations. When seen from the side, planar proxies almost disappear when rasterized to the target view, creating artifacts on the eyeglasses arms in view interpolations, as seen for a few instances in the supplementary video. Another type of artifacts stems from inaccurate matting in the captured dataset, as seen by the remaining skin color shadows in row 4 of Fig. 4 and the incomplete transparent eyeframe in row 6. In the case of few-shot reconstruction, a major limitation of our model is the requirement of known pose and proxy geometry, which can be tackled as a general 6D pose estimation in the case of planar billboard proxies.

## 6  Application: Virtual Try-On

Our generative model of eyeglasses frames can enable the experience of virtually trying-on a pair of eyeglasses [46]. Additionally, the learned latent space allows a user to modify the appearance and shape of eyeglasses by modifying the input latent code. We prototype such a system in Fig. 14, where we capture a video of a user at close distance who is not wearing eyewear, track their head pose using [14], place the textured proxies on the head frame of reference, render the neural proxies to into a RGBA eyeglasses layer and finally composite it onto the frame. Our neural renderer network is sufficiently lightweight – running under 20 ms on a NVidia 1080Ti – that such a system could be made to run interactively.

# 7   Conclusion

We present a novel compact and efficient representation for jointly modeling shape and appearance. Our approach uses coarse proxy geometry and generative latent textures. We show that by jointly modeling an object collection, we can perform latent interpolations between seen instances, and reconstruct unseen instances at high quality with as few as 3 input images. We show results on a dataset consisting of real images and alpha mattes of eyeglasses frames, containing strong view-dependent effects and semi-transparent materials, and on ShapeNet cars. The current approach assumes known proxy geometry and pose; modeling the distribution of proxy geometry and estimating both its parameters and pose on a given image remains as future work.

# References

1. Abdal, R., Qin, Y., Wonka, P.: Image2StyleGAN: how to embed images into the StyleGAN latent space? In: 2019 IEEE/CVF International Conference on Computer Vision (ICCV), October 2019. https://doi.org/10.1109/iccv.2019.00453
2. Aliev, K.A., Ulyanov, D., Lempitsky, V.: Neural point-based graphics (2019)
3. Autonomous Robotics and Perception Group: Calibu Camera Calibration Library. http://github.com/arpg/calibu
4. Blanz, V., Vetter, T.: A morphable model for the synthesis of 3D faces. In: Proceedings of the 26th Annual Conference on Computer Graphics and Interactive Techniques, pp. 187–194 (1999)
5. Bojanowski, P., Joulin, A., Lopez-Pas, D., Szlam, A.: Optimizing the latent space of generative networks. In: Dy, J., Krause, A. (eds.) Proceedings of the 35th International Conference on Machine Learning, Proceedings of Machine Learning Research (2018)
6. Bregler, C., Hertzmann, A., Biermann, H.: Recovering non-rigid 3D shape from image streams. In: Proceedings IEEE Conference on Computer Vision and Pattern Recognition, CVPR 2000 (Cat. No. PR00662), vol. 2, pp. 690–696. IEEE (2000)
7. Chang, A.X., et al.: ShapeNet: an information-rich 3D model repository. Technical report, arXiv:1512.03012 [cs.GR], Stanford University – Princeton University – Toyota Technological Institute at Chicago (2015)
8. Chen, A., et al.: Deep surface light fields. In: Proceedings of the ACM Computer Graphics Interactive Techniques, vol. 1, no. 1, July 2018
9. Chen, Z., Zhang, H.: Learning implicit fields for generative shape modeling. In: Proceedings of the IEEE/CVF Conference on Computer Vision and Pattern Recognition (CVPR), June 2019

10. Décoret, X., Durand, F., Sillion, F.X., Dorsey, J.: Billboard clouds for extreme model simplification. ACM Trans. Graph. **22**(3), 689–696 (2003). https://doi.org/10.1145/882262.882326

11. Deng, J., Dong, W., Socher, R., Li, L.J., Li, K., Fei-Fei, L.: ImageNet: a large-scale hierarchical image database. In: 2009 IEEE Conference on Computer Vision and Pattern Recognition, pp. 248–255. IEEE (2009)

12. Fuhrmann, A., Umlauf, E., Mantler, S.: Extreme model simplification for forest rendering, pp. 57–66, January 2005

13. Furukawa, Y., Ponce, J.: Accurate, dense, and robust multiview stereopsis. IEEE Trans. Pattern Anal. Mach. Intell. **32**(8), 1362–1376 (2010)

14. Google: AR Core Augmented Faces. https://developers.google.com/ar/develop/ios/augmented-faces/overview

15. Groueix, T., Fisher, M., Kim, V.G., Russell, B., Aubry, M.: AtlasNet: a papier-Mâché approach to learning 3D surface generation. In: Proceedings IEEE Conference on Computer Vision and Pattern Recognition (CVPR) (2018)

16. Isola, P., Zhu, J., Zhou, T., Efros, A.A.: Image-to-image translation with conditional adversarial networks. In: 2017 IEEE Conference on Computer Vision and Pattern Recognition (CVPR), July 2017

17. Johnson, J., Alahi, A., Fei-Fei, L.: Perceptual losses for real-time style transfer and super-resolution. In: Leibe, B., Matas, J., Sebe, N., Welling, M. (eds.) ECCV 2016. LNCS, vol. 9906, pp. 694–711. Springer, Cham (2016). https://doi.org/10.1007/978-3-319-46475-6_43

18. Kanazawa, A., Tulsiani, S., Efros, A.A., Malik, J.: Learning category-specific mesh reconstruction from image collections. In: ECCV (2018)

19. Kar, A., Tulsiani, S., Carreira, J., Malik, J.: Category-specific object reconstruction from a single image. In: 2015 IEEE Conference on Computer Vision and Pattern Recognition (CVPR), June 2015

20. Karras, T., Laine, S., Aila, T.: A style-based generator architecture for generative adversarial networks. In: 2019 IEEE/CVF Conference on Computer Vision and Pattern Recognition (CVPR), June 2019. https://doi.org/10.1109/cvpr.2019.00453

21. Kingma, D.P., Ba, J.: Adam: a method for stochastic optimization. arXiv preprint arXiv:1412.6980 (2014)

22. Kingma, D.P., Welling, M.: Auto-encoding variational Bayes. arXiv preprint arXiv:1312.6114 (2013)

23. Kulkarni, N., Gupta, A., Tulsiani, S.: Canonical surface mapping via geometric cycle consistency. In: The IEEE International Conference on Computer Vision (ICCV), October 2019

24. Levin, A., Lischinski, D., Weiss, Y.: A closed-form solution to natural image matting. IEEE Trans. Pattern Anal. Mach. Intell. **30**(2), 228–242 (2008)

25. Liu, L., Chen, N., Ceylan, D., Theobalt, C., Wang, W., Mitra, N.J.: CurveFusion: reconstructing thin structures from RGBD sequences. ACM Trans. Graph. **37**(6), 1–2 (2018)

26. Lombardi, S., Saragih, J., Simon, T., Sheikh, Y.: Deep appearance models for face rendering. ACM Trans. Graph. **37**(4), 1–3 (2018)

27. Lombardi, S., Simon, T., Saragih, J., Schwartz, G., Lehrmann, A., Sheikh, Y.: Neural volumes: learning dynamic renderable volumes from images. ACM Trans. Graph. **38**(4), (2019). https://doi.org/10.1145/3306346.3323020

28. Mescheder, L., Oechsle, M., Niemeyer, M., Nowozin, S., Geiger, A.: Occupancy networks: learning 3D reconstruction in function space. In: Proceedings IEEE Conference on Computer Vision and Pattern Recognition (CVPR) (2019)

258 R. Martin-Brualla et al.

29. Meshry, M., et al.: Neural rerendering in the wild. In: The IEEE Conference on Computer Vision and Pattern Recognition (CVPR), June 2019
30. Mildenhall, B., Srinivasan, P.P., Tancik, M., Barron, J.T., Ramamoorthi, R., Ng, R.: NeRF: representing scenes as neural radiance fields for view synthesis (2020)
31. Nguyen-Phuoc, T., Li, C., Theis, L., Richardt, C., Yang, Y.L.: HoloGAN: unsupervised learning of 3D representations from natural images. In: The IEEE International Conference on Computer Vision (ICCV), October 2019
32. Park, J.J., Florence, P., Straub, J., Newcombe, R., Lovegrove, S.: DeepSDF: learning continuous signed distance functions for shape representation. In: Proceedings of the IEEE Conference on Computer Vision and Pattern Recognition, pp. 165–174 (2019)
33. Pittaluga, F., Koppal, S.J., Bing Kang, S., Sinha, S.N.: Revealing scenes by inverting structure from motion reconstructions. In: Proceedings of the IEEE Conference on Computer Vision and Pattern Recognition, pp. 145–154 (2019)
34. Pollefeys, M., et al.: Visual modeling with a hand-held camera. Int. J. Comput. Vision **59**(3), 207–232 (2004)
35. Porter, T., Duff, T.: Compositing digital images. SIGGRAPH Comput. Graph. **18**(3), 253–259 (1984)
36. Rohlf, J., Helman, J.: Iris performer: a high performance multiprocessing toolkit for real-time 3D graphics. In: Proceedings of the 21st Annual Conference on Computer Graphics and Interactive Techniques, SIGGRAPH 1994 (1994)
37. Ronneberger, O., Fischer, P., Brox, T.: U-Net: convolutional networks for biomedical image segmentation. In: Navab, N., Hornegger, J., Wells, W.M., Frangi, A.F. (eds.) MICCAI 2015. LNCS, vol. 9351, pp. 234–241. Springer, Cham (2015). https://doi.org/10.1007/978-3-319-24574-4_28
38. Shan, Q., Agarwal, S., Curless, B.: Refractive height fields from single and multiple images. In: 2012 IEEE Conference on Computer Vision and Pattern Recognition, pp. 286–293, June 2012
39. Sitzmann, V., Thies, J., Heide, F., Nießner, M., Wetzstein, G., Zollhöfer, M.: DeepVoxels: learning persistent 3D feature embeddings. In: Proceedings Computer Vision and Pattern Recognition (CVPR). IEEE (2019)
40. Sitzmann, V., Zollhöfer, M., Wetzstein, G.: Scene representation networks: continuous 3D-structure-aware neural scene representations. In: Advances in Neural Information Processing Systems, pp. 1119–1130 (2019)
41. Tewari, A., et al.: State of the art on neural rendering. In: Computer Graphics Forum (EG STAR 2020) (2020)
42. Thies, J., Zollhöfer, M., Theobalt, C., Stamminger, M., Nießner, M.: IGNOR: image-guided neural object rendering. arXiv 2018 (2018)
43. Thies, J., Zollhöfer, M., Nießner, M.: Deferred neural rendering: image synthesis using neural textures. ACM Trans. Graph. **38**(4), 1–2 (2019)
44. Tunwattanapong, B., et al.: Acquiring reflectance and shape from continuous spherical harmonic illumination. ACM Trans. Graph. **32**(4) (2013)
45. Whelan, T., et al.: Reconstructing scenes with mirror and glass surfaces. ACM Trans. Graph. **37**(4) (2018)
46. Zhang, Q., Guo, Y., Laffont, P., Martin, T., Gross, M.: A virtual try-on system for prescription eyeglasses. IEEE Comput. Graph. Appl. **37**(4), 84–93 (2017). https://doi.org/10.1109/MCG.2017.3271458
47. Zhang, R.: Making convolutional networks shift-invariant again. arXiv preprint arXiv:1904.11486 (2019)

# Improving Vision-and-Language Navigation with Image-Text Pairs from the Web

Arjun Majumdar[1(✉)], Ayush Shrivastava[1], Stefan Lee[3], Peter Anderson[1], Devi Parikh[1,2], and Dhruv Batra[1,2]

[1] Georgia Institute of Technology, Atlanta, USA
arjun.majumdar@gatech.edu
[2] Facebook AI Research, Menlo Park, USA
[3] Oregon State University, Corvallis, USA

**Abstract.** Following a navigation instruction such as *'Walk down the stairs and stop at the brown sofa'* requires embodied AI agents to ground referenced scene elements referenced (e.g. *'stairs'*) to visual content in the environment (pixels corresponding to *'stairs'*). We ask the following question – can we leverage abundant 'disembodied' web-scraped vision-and-language corpora (e.g. Conceptual Captions) to learn the visual groundings that improve performance on a relatively data-starved embodied perception task (Vision-and-Language Navigation)? Specifically, we develop VLN-BERT, a visiolinguistic transformer-based model for scoring the compatibility between an instruction ( *'...stop at the brown sofa'*) and a trajectory of panoramic RGB images captured by the agent. We demonstrate that pretraining VLN-BERT on image-text pairs from the web before fine-tuning on embodied path-instruction data significantly improves performance on VLN – outperforming prior state-of-the-art in the fully-observed setting by 4 absolute percentage points on success rate. Ablations of our pretraining curriculum show each stage to be impactful – with their combination resulting in further gains.

**Keywords:** Vision-and-language navigation · Transfer learning · Embodied AI

## 1 Introduction

Consider the navigation instruction in Fig. 1, *'Walk through the bedroom and out of the door into the hallway. Walk down the hall along the banister rail through the open door. Continue into the bedroom with a round mirror on the wall and*

---

P. Anderson—Now at Google.

---

**Electronic supplementary material** The online version of this chapter (https://doi.org/10.1007/978-3-030-58539-6_16) contains supplementary material, which is available to authorized users.

A. Vedaldi et al. (Eds.): ECCV 2020, LNCS 12351, pp. 259–274, 2020.
https://doi.org/10.1007/978-3-030-58539-6_16

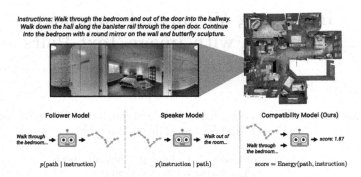

**Fig. 1.** We propose a compatibility model (right) for path selection in vision-and-language navigation (VLN). In contrast to the follower (left) and speaker (center) models that have typically been used in prior work, our model takes a path and instruction pair as input and produces a score that reflects their alignment. Based on this model we describe a training curriculum that leverages internet data in the form of image-caption pairs to improve performance on VLN.

*butterfly sculpture.'* In vision-and-language navigation (VLN) [4], agents must interpret such instructions to navigate through photo-realistic environments. In this instance, the agent needs to exit the bedroom, walk past something called a *'banister rail'* and find the bedroom containing a *'round mirror'* and *'butterfly sculpture.'* But what if the agent has never seen a butterfly before, let alone a sculpture of one? To solve this task, an agent needs to determine if the visual evidence along a path matches the descriptions provided in the instructions. As such, the ability to ground references to objects and scene elements like *'butterfly sculpture'* and *'banister rail'* is central to success. Existing work has focused on learning this grounding solely from a task-specific training dataset of path-instruction pairs [3,8,13,20,21,28,30,31] – which are expensive, laborious, and time-consuming to collect at scale and thus tend to be relatively small (e.g. the VLN dataset contains around 14k path-instruction pairs for training). As an alternative, we propose learning visual grounding from freely-available internet data, such as the web images with alt-text captured in the Conceptual Captions dataset [24], containing around 3.3M image-text pairs.

Conceptually, transfer learning from large-scale web data to embodied AI tasks such as VLN is an attractive alternative to collecting more data. Empirically, however, the effectiveness of this strategy remains open to question. Unlike web images, which are highly-curated and with clear aesthetic biases, embodied data contains content and viewpoints that are not widely published online. As shown in Fig. 2, an embodied agent may perceive doors via a close-up view of a door frame rather than as a carefully composed image of a (typically closed) door. In VLN, image framing is a consequence of the agent's position rather than an aesthetic choice made by a photographer. Consequently, in this paper we investigate this question – to what degree can visual grounding learned on static web images be transferred to the embodied VLN task? That is, can 'dis-embodied' web data be used to improve visual grounding for embodied agents?

**Fig. 2.** Images from the Conceptual Captions (CC) [24] (top) and Matterport3D (MP3D) [5] (bottom) datasets illustrate the differences between the two domains. Images from CC are typically well-lit, well-composed and aesthetically pleasing, while for MP3D images (used in VLN) the framing depends on the position of the agent (e.g. a couch (left) in CC is typically viewed head-on, whereas in MP3D they may be hidden to the side as an agent navigates past them).

To answer this question, we introduce VLN-BERT, a joint visiolinguistic transformer-based compatibility model for scoring the alignment between an instruction and an agent's observations along a trajectory. We structure VLN-BERT to enable straight-forward transfer learning from a model from prior work on general visiolinguistic representation learning [18], and explore a training curriculum that incorporates both large-scale internet data and embodied path-instruction pairs. VLN-BERT is sequentially trained using 1) language-only data (Wikipedia and BooksCorpus [34] as in BERT [7]), 2) web image-text pairs (Conceptual Captions [24] as in ViLBERT [18]), and 3) path-instruction pairs from the VLN dataset [4]. Following this protocol the model progressively learns to represent language, then to ground visual concepts, and finally to ground visual concepts alongside action descriptions. We evaluate VLN-BERT on a path selection task in VLN, demonstrating that this training procedure leads to significant gains over prior work (4 absolute percentage points on leaderboard success rate).

*Contributions.* Concretely, we make the following main contributions:

- We develop VLN-BERT, a visiolinguistic transformer-based model for scoring path-instruction pairs. We show that VLN-BERT outperforms strong single-model baselines from prior work on the path selection task – increasing success rate (SR) by 4.6 absolute percentage points.
- We demonstrate that in an ensemble of diverse models VLN-BERT improves SR by 3.0 absolute percentage points on "unseen" validation, leading to a SR of 73% on the VLN leaderboard (4 absolute percentage points higher than previously published work)[1].
- We ablate the proposed training curriculum, and find that each stage contributes significantly to the final outcome, with a cumulative benefit that is greater than the sum of the individual effects. Notably, we find that pretrain-

---

[1] evalai.cloudcv.org/web/challenges/challenge-page/97/leaderboard/270.

ing on image-text pairs from the web provides a significant boost in path selection performance – improving SR by 9.2 absolute percentage points.

## 2   Related Work

***Path Selection in VLN.*** In VLN [4], an agent is required to follow a navigation instruction from a start location to a goal. While most existing works focus on the setting in which the test environments are previously unseen, many also consider the scenario in which the test environment is previously explored and stored in memory (i.e., fully observable). In this setting, a high-probability path is typically generated by performing beam search through the environment and ranking paths according to either: (1) their probability under a 'follower' model [3,8,13,20,21,30,31], as in Fig. 1 (left), or (2) by how well they explain the instruction according to a 'speaker' (instruction generation) model [8,28], as in Fig. 1 (center). In contrast, we use beam search with an existing agent model [28] to generate a set of candidate paths, which we then evaluate using our discriminative path-instruction compatibility model, as in Fig. 1 (right).

***Data Augmentation and Auxiliary Tasks in VLN.*** To compensate for the small size of existing VLN datasets, previous works have investigated various data augmentation strategies and auxiliary tasks. Many papers report results trained on augmented data including instructions synthesized by a speaker model [8,20,21,28]. Tan et al. [28] use environmental dropout to mimic additional training environments to improve generalization. Li et al. [17] incorporate language-only pretraining using a BERT model. Several existing papers [11,30] and one concurrent hitherto-unpublished work [10] consider path-instruction compatibility as an auxiliary loss function or reward for VLN agents. We focus on path-instruction compatibility in the context of transfer learning from large-scale internet data, which has not been previously explored.

***Vision-and-Language Pretraining.*** There has been significant recent progress towards learning transferable joint representations of images and text [15,16,18,26,27,32]. Using BERT-like [7] self-supervised objectives and Transformer [29] architectures, these models have achieved state-of-the-art results on multiple vision-and-language tasks by pretraining on aligned image-and-text data collected from the web [24] and transferring the base architecture to other tasks such as VQA [9], referring expressions [12], and caption-based image retrieval [6]. However, these tasks are all based on single images. The extent to which these pretrained models can generalize from human-composed and curated internet images to embodied AI tasks has not been investigated. In this work we propose a training curriculum to handle potential domain-shift and augment a previous model architecture to process panoramic image sequences, extending the progress in vision-and-language to vision-and-language navigation (VLN).

# 3 Preliminaries: Self-supervised Learning from the Web

Recent works have demonstrated that high-capacity models trained under self-supervised objectives on large-scale web data can learn strong, generalizable representations for both language and images [7,15,16,18,26,27,32]. We build upon these works as a basis for transfer and describe them briefly here.

***Language Modeling with BERT.*** The BERT [7] model is a large transformer-based [29] architecture for language modeling. The input to the model is sequences of tokenized words augmented with positional embeddings and outputs a representation for each. For example, a two sentence input could be written as

$$\texttt{<CLS>} \; w_1^{(1)}, \ldots, w_{L_1}^{(1)} \; \texttt{<SEP>} \; w_1^{(2)}, \ldots, w_{L_2}^{(2)} \; \texttt{<SEP>} \tag{1}$$

where CLS, and SEP are special tokens. To train this approach, [7] introduce two self-supervised objectives – *masked language modelling* and *next sentence prediction*. Given two input sentences from a text corpus, the masked language modelling objective masks out some percentage of tokens and tasks the model to predict their values given the remaining tokens as context. The next sentence prediction objective requires the model to predict whether the two sentences follow each other in the original corpus or not. BERT is then trained under these objectives on large language corpuses from the web (Wikipedia and BooksCorpus [34]). This model forms the basis for both our approach and the visiolinguistic representation learning discussed next.

***Visiolinguistic Representations Learning with ViLBERT.*** Extending BERT, ViLBERT [18] (and a number of similar approaches [15,16,18,26,27,32]) focuses on learning joint visiolinguistic representations from paired image-text data, specifically web images and their associated alt-text collected in the Conceptual Captions dataset [24]. ViLBERT is composed of two BERT-like processing streams that operate on visual and textual inputs, respectively. The input to the visual stream is composed of image regions (generated by an object detector [2,22] pretrained on Visual Genome [14]) that act as "words" in the visual domain. Concretely, given a single image $I$ consisting of a set of image regions $\{v_1, \ldots, v_k\}$ and a text sequence (i.e. a caption) $w_1, \ldots, w_L$, we can write the input to ViLBERT as the sequence

$$\texttt{<IMG>} \; v_1, \ldots, v_k \; \texttt{<CLS>} \; w_1, \ldots, w_L \; \texttt{<SEP>} \tag{2}$$

where IMG, CLS, and SEP are special tokens marking the different modality subsequences. The two streams are connected using co-attention [19] transformer layers, which attend from the visual stream over language stream and vice versa. Notably, the language stream of ViLBERT is designed to mirror BERT such that it can be initialized by a pretrained BERT model. After processing, the model produces a contextualized output representation for each input token.

In analogy to the training objectives in BERT, ViLBERT introduces the *masked multimodal modelling* and *multimodal alignment tasks*. In the first, a random subset of language tokens and image regions are masked and must be

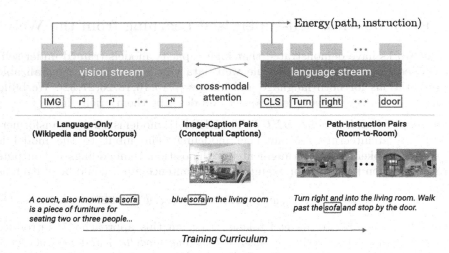

**Fig. 3.** We propose VLN-BERT (top), a visiolinguistic transformer-based model similar to the model from [18], to process image regions from a sequence of panoramas and words from an instruction. We demonstrate that with the proposed training curriculum (bottom) visual grounding learned from image-text pairs from the web (center) can be transferred to significantly improve performance in VLN.

predicted given the remaining context. For image regions, this amounts to predicting a distribution over object classes present in the masked region. Masked text tokens are handled as in BERT. The multimodal alignment objective trains the model to determine if an image-text pair matches, i.e. if the text describes the image content. Individual token outputs are used to predict masked inputs in the masking objective, and the IMG and CLS tokens are used for the image-caption alignment objective. We build upon this model extensively in this work.

## 4   Approach

### 4.1   Vision-and-Language Navigation as Path Selection

In the Vision-and-Language Navigation (VLN) [4] task, agents are placed in an environment specified as a navigation-graph $G = \{\mathcal{V}, \mathcal{E}\}$. Nodes $v \in \mathcal{V}$ represent different positions within the environment, and are represented by 360-degree panoramas taken at that viewpoint. Meanwhile, edges delineate navigable paths between panorama positions. The agent is provided with a navigation instruction $x$ that describes the shortest-path between a starting position $v_s$ and goal position $v_g$ (as illustrated in the bottom right of Fig. 3). Agents are considered to have succeeded if they traverse a path $\tau = [v_s, v_1, v_2, \ldots, v_N]$ with a final position $v_N$ that is 3 m of the goal $v_g$.

Much of the work in VLN focuses on this problem as an exploration task in new environments; however, many practical deployments of robotic agents would be long-term in relatively fixed environments (e.g. an assistant operating in a single home). In this paper, we consider the setting in which the environment is previously explored with the navigation-graph and panoramas are stored in the agent's memory. This setting has been studied in prior work [8,13,20,28, 30] and is operationalized by providing the agent unrestricted access to the Matterport3D Simulator [4] during inference such that it can consider arbitrarily many valid paths originating from the starting position $v_s$, before selecting one to follow.

In this setting, the navigation task becomes one of identifying the path best aligned with the instructions. Concretely, given a set of valid paths $\mathcal{T}$ with the same starting position $v_s$ and an instruction $x$, the problem of navigation is to identify a trajectory $\tau^*$ such that

$$\tau^* = \operatorname*{argmax}_{\tau \in \mathcal{T}} \ f(\tau, x) \tag{3}$$

for some compatibility function $f$ that determines if the trajectory follows the instruction and terminates near the goal. The two major challenges are how to learn a compatibility function $f$ and how to efficiently search through the large set of possible paths. Given that our focus is on transfer learning, we address the first challenge within a simple path selection setting. Specifically, we consider a small set of paths $\mathcal{T}' = \{\tau^1, \tau^2, \ldots, \tau^M\}$ for each instruction, which are generated using beam-search with a greedy instruction-following agent [28], and task $f$ with selecting the path that best aligns with the instruction from this set. Future work might explore how $f$ could be further used as a heuristic to efficiently search through the larger, exhaustive set of candidate paths $\mathcal{T}$.

## 4.2    Modeling Instruction-Path Compatibility

To formalize the task, we consider a function $f$ that maps a trajectory $\tau$ and an instruction $x$ to compatibility score $f(\cdot, \cdot)$. We model $f(\tau, x)$ as a visiolinguistic transformer-based model denoted as VLN-BERT. The architecture of VLN-BERT is structural similar to ViLBERT [18]; this is by design because it enables straight-forward transfer of visual grounding learned from large-scale web data. Specifically, we make a number of VLN-specific adaptations to ViLBERT, but they are all structured as augmentations (adding modules) rather than ablations (removing existing network components) so that pretrained weights can be transferred to initialize large portions of the model.

***Representing Trajectories and Instructions.*** Predicting path-instruction compatibility requires jointly reasoning over a sequence of observations and a sequence of instruction words. As in prior work [8], a trajectory is represented as a sequence of panoramic images (as in Fig. 3 bottom right) with positional information – i.e. $\tau = [(I_1, p_1), \ldots, (I_N, p_N)]$ where $(I_i)$ are panoramas and $(p_i)$ are poses. Further, we represent each panorama $I_i$ as a set of image regions $\{r_1^{(i)}, \ldots, r_K^{(i)}\}$. Let an instruction $x$ be a sequence of tokens $w_1, \ldots, w_L$. We can thus write a path-instruction pair for VLN-BERT as the input sequence

$$\texttt{<IMG>} \ r_1^{(1)}, \ldots, r_K^{(1)}, \ldots, \texttt{<IMG>} \ r_1^{(N)}, \ldots, r_K^{(N)}, \ \texttt{<CLS>} \ w_1, \ldots, w_L \ \texttt{<SEP>} \tag{4}$$

where `IMG`, `CLS`, and `SEP` are special tokens as before.

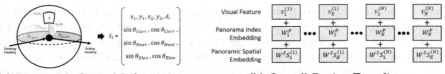

(a) Panoramic Spatial Information          (b) Overall Region Encoding

**Fig. 4.** We encode spatial information for each region to include not only the region position, but also its relation to the trajectory path (a). We form overall region encoding by summing visual features, an embedding indicating the index of the source panorama in the trajectory, and an embedding of panoramic spatial information (b).

The transformer models on which VLN-BERT (as well as BERT and ViL-BERT) is based are inherently invariant to sequence order – only representing interactions between inputs as a function of their values. The common practice to introduce this information is to add positional embeddings to the input token representations. For language, this is straight-forward and amounts to an index-in-sequence encoding. Panorama trajectories on the other have significantly more complex relationships. While the panoramas themselves are a sequence, there are also geometric relationships between them (e.g. two panoramas being 1.2 meters apart at 10 degrees off north). Further, each individual image region not only has a position in the image (as modelled in ViLBERT) but also an angle relative to the heading of an agent as it traverses the trajectory. These are important considerations for language-guided navigation – after all, something on your left going one way is on your right if you go in the opposite direction. Being able to reason about the order of panoramas and the relative heading of image content is integral for following instructions like *'Go down the hallway on the right then stop when you see a table on your left.'*.

To address this, as visualized in Fig. 4(a), we encode the spatial location of each image region $r_i$ in terms of its location in the panorama (top-left and bottom-right corners in normalized coordinates as well as area of the image covered), its elevation relative to the horizon, and its heading relative to the agents current and next viewing directions. All angles are encoded as $[\cos(\theta), \sin(\theta)]$. The resulting 11-dimensional vector $S_i$ is projected into 2048 dimensions using a learned projection $W^S$. To capture the sequential order of the panoramas within a trajectory, we project the scalar panorama index to 2048 dimensions using a learned embedding $W^P$. As shown in Fig. 4(b), the complete visual input representation for the image region is the element-wise sum of the visual features, panorama index embedding, and panoramic spatial embedding.

***Extracting Image Regions from Panoramas.*** To extract image regions $\{v_1^{(i)}, \ldots, v_k^{(i)}\}$ from each panorama, we generate $600 \times 600$ pixel perspective projections using an 80 degree field of view at the 36 discrete heading and elevation directions used in previous work [4]. Similarly to ViLBERT, we use the bottom-up attention model [2, 22] pretrained on Visual Genome [14] to extract a set of image regions and features from each perspective image. Since the perspective images have substantial overlap we remove redundant regions within each panorama. First, we discard regions that are centred more than 20 degrees away from the center of the image (i.e. we discard regions along the boarders). We assume that the discarded regions will be captured in a neighboring perspective image (spaced at 30 degree heading increments), with more visual context. Next, we examine pairs of image regions within each panorama in order of decreasing feature similarity. We discard the region in the pair with the lower bottom-up attention class detection score, until a maximum of 100 regions per panorama remain. We define similarity as the cosine distance between image features to which we add the absolute difference in region heading and elevation. Including heading and elevation differences ensures that visually similar features found in different regions of the panorama are unlikely to be classified as redundant.

***Training for Path Selection.*** To train VLN-BERT for path selection, we consider a 4-way multiple-choice task. Given an instruction $x$, we sample four trajectories out of which only one is successful $\{\tau_1^+, \tau_2^-, \tau_3^-, \tau_4^-\}$. We run VLN-BERT on each instruction-trajectory pair and extract their corresponding final representations. We denote these outputs for the CLS and the first IMG token as $h_{\texttt{CLS}}$ and $h_{\texttt{IMG}}$ respectively and compute a compatibility score $s_i$ as

$$s_i = f(\tau_i, x) = W \left( h_{\texttt{CLS}}^{(i)} \odot h_{\texttt{IMG}}^{(i)} \right) \qquad (5)$$

where $\odot$ denotes element-wise multiplication and $W$ is a learned transformation matrix. Scores, normalized via a softmax, are supervised with cross-entropy loss,

$$\mathbf{p} = \text{softmax}(\mathbf{s}) \qquad (6)$$

$$\mathcal{L}\left(x, \{\tau_1^+, \tau_2^-, \tau_3^-, \tau_4^-\}\right) = \text{CrossEntropy}\left(\mathbf{p}, \mathbf{1}[\tau_1^+]\right) \qquad (7)$$

where $\mathbf{1}[\tau_1^+]$ is a 1-hot vector with mass at the index of $\tau^+$. At inference, we simply sort trajectories by their compatibility scores $s_i$.

***Mining Negative Examples.*** We find that choosing an appropriate set of path-instruction pairs is important for performance. Ideally, samples would span the space of all possible pairs, including hard negatives. The question is how to find varied path-instruction pairs with semantically meaningful differences? We find that using beam search with an instruction-following model yields a diverse set of paths that are effective for training. Specifically, we sample up to 30 beams per instruction from the follower model of Tan et al. [28] and label the path as successful if it meets the VLN success criteria (i.e. $< 3m$ from the goal). Finally, one positive and three negatives pairs are sampled at random for training.

### 4.3   Internet-to-Embodied Transfer Learning

While VLN-BERT can be trained from scratch, we designed the model to specifically enable transfer learning from language [7] and visiolinguistic [18] models trained on large-scale web corpora. This transfer is especially important due to the data-sparsity in VLN dataset (containing ~14k path-instruction training pairs) and has a natural bias towards describing only objects present in training environments. In this section, we describe a pretraining curriculum for transferring models learned on 'disembodied' web data to the embodied VLN task.

We summarize the pretraining process in Fig. 3. In total, we consider three stages focused on learning language, visual grounding, and action grounding.

- **Stage 1: Language.** We initialize the language stream of our model with weights from a BERT [7] model trained on Wikipedia and the BooksCorpus [34] under the masked language modelling and next sentence prediction objectives. Directly training on the path selection task after this stage is analogous to introducing a BERT encoder to represent instructions.
- **Stage 2: Visual Grounding.** Starting from a pretrained BERT model, Lu et al. train both streams of ViLBERT on the Conceptual Captions dataset [24] under the masked multimodal language modelling and multimodal alignment objectives. In this stage, we initialize model weights with a ViLBERT model trained in this manner. Training directly from this stage provides an initialization that can associate descriptions with image regions.
- **Stage 3: Action Grounding.** In the final stage, we pair paths and instructions from VLN and train the model under the masked multimodal modelling objective from [18]. While the previous stage learns to ground visual concepts, this stage additionally exposes the model to actions and their trajectory-based referents. For example, correctly predicting a masked instruction phrase like *'turn _____'* or *'stop at the _____'* requires the model to reason about the agent's path from the visual inputs and positional encodings.

Finally, we fine-tune VLN-BERT as described in the previous section.

## 5   Experiments

Our experiments primarily address following questions:

1. *Does pretraining on web image-text pairs improve VLN performance?*
2. *How does the performance of VLN-BERT compare with strong baselines?*
3. *Does VLN-BERT consider relevant image regions to produce alignment scores?*

### 5.1   Dataset

We conduct experiments using the Room-to-Room (R2R) navigation task [4] based on the Matterport3D dataset [5]. R2R contains human-annotated path-instruction pairs that are divided into training, seen and unseen validation, and unseen testing sets. To generate a dataset for path selection we run beam search on the instruction-follower model from [28], to produce a set of up to 30 candidate paths for each instruction in R2R. We find that with a beam size of 30 over 99% of the candidate sets contain one path that reaches the goal, which places an acceptable upper bound on path selection performance. In all of the experiments that follow, results are reported for selecting one path from the set of candidates.

## 5.2    Evaluation Metrics

We compare the performance of different models using standard VLN metrics.

- **Success rate (SR)** measures the percentage of selected paths that stop 3 m of the goal. In path selection this is our primary metric of interest.
- **Oracle Success rate (SR)** measures the percentage of selected paths with any position that passes 3 m of the goal.
- **Navigation error (NE)** measures the average distance of the shortest path from the last position in the selected path to the goal position.
- **Path length (PL)** measures the average length of the selected path.
- **Success rate weighted by path length (SPL)**, as defined in [1], provides a measure of success normalized by the ratio between the length of the shortest path and the selected path.

Note that for path selection we calculate metrics using only the selected path, which corresponds with the pre-explored environment setting. However, for the VLN leaderboard results we follow the required approach of prepending the exploration path to the selected path (which affects path length based metrics).

## 5.3    Training Baseline Models

We compare with the follower and speaker models from [28], which achieve state-of-the-art performance on the VLN test set in an ensemble model setting. The only auxiliary dataset used to train these baseline models is ImageNet [23] (used to pretrain an image feature extractor). All of the other components are trained from scratch (including word embeddings). Data augmentation, via environmental dropout [28], is used to train the follower model and greatly improves performance. We report results using code and weights provided by Tan et al. [28].

## 5.4    Results

***Does Pretraining on Web Image-Text Pairs Improve VLN Performance?*** To answer this question we dissect our proposed training curriculum as indicated in Table 1, and find that in general each stage of training does contribute to performance. First, we find that our model has limited performance learning from scratch, achieving only 30.5% SR (compared with the 54.7% SR achieved by the speaker model from [28]). However, language-only pretraining, which corresponds to initializing our model with BERT [7] weights, improves performance substantially to 45.2% SR (an improvement of 14.7 absolute percentage points) – indicating that language understanding plays an important role in VLN.

Next, we find that both pretraining on image-text pairs from the Conceptual Captions [24] (visual grounding) and pretraining on path-instruction pairs from VLN [4] (action grounding) similarly improve success rate (by 4.5 and 4.9 absolute percentage points, respectively) when used independently. However, when the two pretraining stages are combined in series the improvement jumps to 14.1

**Table 1.** We compare the contribution from the different stages of pretraining. We find that stage 2 and 3 both contribute significantly to task performance (improving Val Unseen Success Rate (SR) by ~15–20 absolute percentage points over the no pretraining baseline – rows 3 and 4 vs. 1), with their full combination providing further synergistic gains (row 5). Notably, skipping the visual grounding stage (but still doing the others) results in a 9 absolute percentage point drop in Val Unseen SR (compare rows 4 and 5) – demonstrating the importance of internet-to-embodied transfer of visual grounding.

| | | Pretraining Stage | | Val Seen | | | | | Val Unseen | | | | |
|---|---|---|---|---|---|---|---|---|---|---|---|---|---|
| # | Language Only | Visual Grounding | Action Grounding | PL | NE↓ | SPL↑ | OSR↑ | SR↑ | PL | NE↓ | SPL↑ | OSR↑ | SR↑ |
| 1 | (no pretraining) | | | 10.78 | 6.78 | 0.35 | 54.22 | 37.55 | 10.29 | 6.81 | 0.27 | 50.62 | 30.52 |
| 2 | ✓ | | | 10.33 | 4.89 | 0.55 | 69.31 | 58.73 | 9.59 | 5.47 | 0.41 | 57.34 | 45.17 |
| 3 | ✓ | ✓ | | 10.42 | 4.48 | 0.58 | 71.57 | 62.16 | 9.70 | 4.96 | 0.45 | 62.79 | 49.64 |
| 4 | ✓ | | ✓ | 10.51 | 4.28 | 0.60 | 72.65 | 63.82 | 9.81 | 5.05 | 0.46 | 62.75 | 50.02 |
| 5 | ✓ | ✓ | ✓ | 10.28 | 3.73 | 0.66 | 76.47 | 70.20 | 9.60 | 4.10 | 0.55 | 69.22 | 59.26 |

(VLN-BERT)

absolute percentage points in success rate or 9.2 absolute percentage points over the next best setting. The substantial level of improvement that results from our full training curriculum suggests that not only does pretraining on webly-supervised image-text pairs from [24] improve path selection performance, but it also constructively supports the action grounding stage (Stage 3) of pretraining.

*How Does VLN-BERT Compare with Strong Baseline Methods?* The results in Table 2 compare path selection performance of VLN-BERT with the state-of-the-art speaker and follower models from [28]. We evaluate path selection using the set of up to 30 candidate paths generated with beam search using the follower from [28]. For the follower model results this amounts to taking the top beam from the candidate set. In the single model setting we see that VLN-BERT, trained with our full curriculum, achieves 59.3% SR, which is 4.6 absolute percentage points better than either of the other two methods.

In the pre-explored setting, the speaker and follower models are typically linearly combined (using a hyperparameter selected through grid search on val unseen) to further improve path selection performance [8,28]. In the ensemble models section of Table 2, the speaker + follower line (row 4) represents our execution of the state-of-the-art ensemble model from [28]. In rows 5–7, we consider three model ensembles composed of a speaker, follower, and one additional model (again linearly combined with hyperparameters selected via grid search on val unseen). We find that adding another (randomly seeded) speaker or follower model yields modest improvements of 1.2 and 2.7 absolute percentage points in SR (rows 5 and 6). In contrast, adding VLN-BERT results in a 5.7 absolute percentage point boost in SR (row 7), which is 3.0 absolute percentage points higher on success rate than the next best ensemble.

**Table 2.** Results comparing VLN-BERT with the follower and speaker from [28]. Notably, in the ensemble models setting, combining VLN-BERT with the speaker and follower results in a 3 absolute percentage point improvement in Val Unseen Success Rate (SR) over the next best three-model ensemble (compare rows 6 and 7).

| | # | Re-ranking Model | Val Seen | | | | Val Unseen | | | | |
|---|---|---|---|---|---|---|---|---|---|---|---|
| | | | PL | NE ↓ | SPL ↑ | OSR ↑ | SR ↑ | PL | NE ↓ | SPL ↑ | OSR ↑ | SR ↑ |
| Single Models | 1 | follower (flw) [28] | 10.40 | 3.68 | 0.62 | 74.12 | 65.10 | 9.57 | 5.20 | 0.49 | 58.79 | 52.36 |
| | 2 | speaker (spk) [28] | 11.19 | 3.80 | 0.56 | 77.25 | 60.69 | 10.71 | 4.25 | 0.49 | **72.07** | 54.66 |
| | 3 | VLN-BERT | 10.28 | 3.73 | 0.66 | 76.47 | 70.20 | 9.60 | **4.10** | **0.55** | 69.22 | **59.26** |
| Ensemble Models | 4 | spk + flw [28] | 10.69 | 2.72 | 0.70 | 82.94 | 74.22 | 10.10 | 3.32 | 0.63 | 76.63 | 67.90 |
| | 5 | spk + flw + flw | 10.73 | 2.72 | 0.71 | 83.33 | 74.71 | 10.12 | 3.22 | 0.64 | 77.56 | 69.14 |
| | 6 | spk + flw + spk | 10.77 | 2.45 | 0.73 | 85.98 | 76.86 | 10.17 | 2.99 | 0.65 | 79.28 | 70.58 |
| | 7 | spk + flw + VLN-BERT | 10.61 | 2.35 | 0.78 | 86.57 | 81.86 | 10.00 | **2.76** | **0.68** | 81.91 | **73.61** |

**Table 3.** Leaderboard results on Test Unseen for methods using beam search.

| Re-ranking Model | Test Unseen | | | | |
|---|---|---|---|---|---|
| | PL | NE ↓ | SPL ↑ | OSR ↑ | SR ↑ |
| Speaker-Follower [8] | 1,257 | 4.87 | 0.01 | 96 | 53 |
| Tactical Rewind [13] | 197 | 4.29 | **0.03** | 90 | 61 |
| Self-Monitoring [20] | 373 | 4.48 | 0.02 | 97 | 61 |
| Reinforced Cross-Modal Matching [30] | 358 | 4.03 | 0.02 | 96 | 63 |
| Environmental Dropout [28] | 687 | 3.26 | 0.01 | **99** | 69 |
| Auxiliary Tasks† [33] | 41 | 3.24 | 0.21 | 81 | 71 |
| VLN-BERT | 687 | **3.09** | 0.01 | **99** | **73** |

†indicates unpublished/concurrent work

In Table 3 we report results on the VLN test set via the VLN leaderboard, using the three-model ensemble that includes a speaker, follower, and VLN-BERT. The ensemble achieves a success rate of 73%, which is 4 absolute percentage points greater than previously published work [28], and 2 absolute percentage points greater than concurrent, unpublished work [33].

***Does VLN-BERT Consider Relevant Image Regions to Produce Alignment Scores?*** To gain insight into the visual grounding learned by VLN-BERT, we visualize which panoramic image regions affect the compatibility score. This analysis is performed using a simple gradient-based visualization technique [25]. We take the gradient of our learned score $f(x, \tau)$ with respect to the feature representation for each region from each panorama, and sum this 2048-dimensional gradient vector over the feature dimension to produce a scalar measure of region importance. To gain further insight, we analyze how the region importance varies when the instruction is perturbed by removing parts of the description.

Two examples of this analysis are illustrated in Fig. 5. The left panel provides the original and modified versions of the instructions. The middle panel illustrates the region importance histograms and the top-5 regions that influence the compatibility score for the original instructions. The right panel provides the equivalent illustrations for the modified instructions. The words and regions

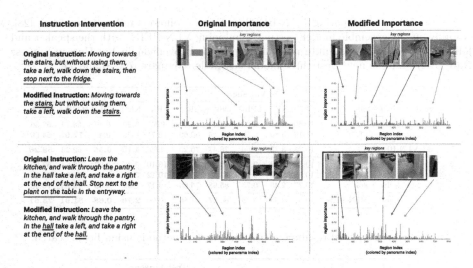

**Fig. 5.** We compare region importance histograms under instruction ablations – removing a phrase or sentence. Region importance is calculated by taking the gradient of the compatibility score with respect to image region features. The images above each histogram correspond to the most influential regions (i.e. the peaks in the histogram). The underlined instruction phrases correspond with the regions outlined in green and purple. In the top example, removing the reference to the *'fridge'* (in green) shifts the importance to other regions along the path (i.e. the *'stairs'* in purple), suggesting that VLN-BERT considers visually relevant image regions to score path-instruction pairs. (Color figure online)

highlighted in green provide a qualitative assessment of the visual grounding learned by VLN-BERT. Next, we remove a part of the original instruction that refers to a high-importance region, producing the modified versions of the instructions. The purple highlights demonstrate that after the instructions have been modified, VLN-BERT appropriately shifts importance to remaining scene elements referenced in the instructions. For example, in the first row regions containing a *'fridge'* are important for the original instruction, whereas for the modified instruction the importance shifts to the *'stairs'*.

## 6  Conclusion

In this work, we demonstrated internet-to-embodied transfer of visual concept grounding – leveraging large-scale image-text data from the web to improve a discriminative path-instruction alignment model for VLN. In our path re-ranking setting, this model improves over prior work and our ablations show each stage of our transfer curriculum contributes significantly.

**Acknowledgements.** The Georgia Tech effort was supported in part by NSF, AFRL, DARPA, ONR YIPs, ARO PECASE, Amazon. The views and conclusions contained herein are those of the authors and should not be interpreted as necessarily representing the official policies or endorsements, either expressed or implied, of the U.S. Government, or any sponsor.

# References

1. Anderson, P., et al.: On evaluation of embodied navigation agents. arXiv preprint arXiv:1807.06757 (2018)
2. Anderson, P., et al.: Bottom-up and top-down attention for image captioning and visual question answering. In: CVPR (2018)
3. Anderson, P., Shrivastava, A., Parikh, D., Batra, D., Lee, S.: Chasing ghosts: instruction following as Bayesian state tracking. In: Advances in Neural Information Processing Systems, pp. 369–379 (2019)
4. Anderson, P., et al.: Vision-and-language navigation: interpreting visually-grounded navigation instructions in real environments. In: Proceedings of the IEEE Conference on Computer Vision and Pattern Recognition (2018)
5. Chang, A., et al.: Matterport3D: Learning from RGB-D data in indoor environments. In: International Conference on 3D Vision (3DV) (2017)
6. Chen, X., et al.: Microsoft coco captions: data collection and evaluation server. arXiv preprint arXiv:1504.00325 (2015)
7. Devlin, J., Chang, M.W., Lee, K., Toutanova, K.: Bert: pre-training of deep bidirectional transformers for language understanding. arXiv preprint arXiv:1810.04805 (2018)
8. Fried, D., et al.: Speaker-follower models for vision-and-language navigation. In: Advances in Neural Information Processing Systems, pp. 3314–3325 (2018)
9. Goyal, Y., Khot, T., Summers-Stay, D., Batra, D., Parikh, D.: Making the V in VQA matter: elevating the role of image understanding in visual question answering. In: Conference on Computer Vision and Pattern Recognition (CVPR) (2017)
10. Hao, W., Li, C., Li, X., Carin, L., Gao, J.: Towards learning a generic agent for vision-and-language navigation via pre-training. arXiv preprint arXiv:2002.10638 (2020)
11. Huang, H., Jain, V., Mehta, H., Baldridge, J., Ie, E.: Multi-modal discriminative model for vision-and-language navigation. arXiv preprint arXiv:1905.13358 (2019)
12. Kazemzadeh, S., Ordonez, V., Matten, M., Berg, T.L.: Referit game: referring to objects in photographs of natural scenes. In: EMNLP (2014)
13. Ke, L., et al.: Tactical rewind: self-correction via backtracking in vision-and-language navigation. In: Proceedings of the IEEE Conference on Computer Vision and Pattern Recognition, pp. 6741–6749 (2019)
14. Krishna, R., et al.: Visual genome: connecting language and vision using crowd-sourced dense image annotations. arXiv preprint arXiv:1602.07332 (2016)
15. Li, G., Duan, N., Fang, Y., Jiang, D., Zhou, M.: Unicoder-VL: a universal encoder for vision and language by cross-modal pre-training. arXiv preprint arXiv:1908.06066 (2019)
16. Li, L.H., Yatskar, M., Yin, D., Hsieh, C.J., Chang, K.W.: VisualBERT: a simple and performant baseline for vision and language. arXiv preprint arXiv:1908.03557 (2019)
17. Li, X., et al.: Robust navigation with language pretraining and stochastic sampling. arXiv preprint arXiv:1909.02244 (2019)

18. Lu, J., Batra, D., Parikh, D., Lee, S.: ViLBERT: pretraining task-agnostic visiolinguistic representations for vision-and-language tasks. In: Advances in Neural Information Processing Systems, pp. 13–23 (2019)
19. Lu, J., Yang, J., Batra, D., Parikh, D.: Hierarchical question-image co-attention for visual question answering. In: Advances in Neural Information Processing Systems, pp. 289–297 (2016)
20. Ma, C.Y., et al.: Self-monitoring navigation agent via auxiliary progress estimation. arXiv preprint arXiv:1901.03035 (2019)
21. Ma, C.Y., Wu, Z., AlRegib, G., Xiong, C., Kira, Z.: The regretful agent: heuristic-aided navigation through progress estimation. In: Proceedings of the IEEE Conference on Computer Vision and Pattern Recognition, pp. 6732–6740 (2019)
22. Ren, S., He, K., Girshick, R., Sun, J.: Faster R-CNN: towards real-time object detection with region proposal networks. In: Advances in Neural Information Processing Systems (NIPS) (2015)
23. Russakovsky, O., et al.: ImageNet large scale visual recognition challenge. Int. J. Comput. Vis. **115**(3), 211–252 (2015)
24. Sharma, P., Ding, N., Goodman, S., Soricut, R.: Conceptual captions: a cleaned, hypernymed, image alt-text dataset for automatic image captioning. In: Proceedings of the 56th Annual Meeting of the Association for Computational Linguistics (Volume 1: Long Papers), pp. 2556–2565 (2018)
25. Simonyan, K., Vedaldi, A., Zisserman, A.: Deep inside convolutional networks: visualising image classification models and saliency maps. arXiv preprint arXiv:1312.6034 (2013)
26. Su, W., et al.: VL-BERT: pre-training of generic visual-linguistic representations. arXiv preprint arXiv:1908.08530 (2019)
27. Tan, H., Bansal, M.: LXMERT: learning cross-modality encoder representations from transformers. In: EMNLP (2019)
28. Tan, H., Yu, L., Bansal, M.: Learning to navigate unseen environments: back translation with environmental dropout. arXiv preprint arXiv:1904.04195 (2019)
29. Vaswani, A., et al.: Attention is all you need. In: Advances in Neural Information Processing Systems, pp. 5998–6008 (2017)
30. Wang, X., et al.: Reinforced cross-modal matching and self-supervised imitation learning for vision-language navigation. In: Proceedings of the IEEE Conference on Computer Vision and Pattern Recognition, pp. 6629–6638 (2019)
31. Wang, X., Xiong, W., Wang, H., Yang Wang, W.: Look before you leap: bridging model-free and model-based reinforcement learning for planned-ahead vision-and-language navigation. In: Proceedings of the European Conference on Computer Vision (ECCV), pp. 37–53 (2018)
32. Zhou, L., Palangi, H., Zhang, L., Hu, H., Corso, J.J., Gao, J.: Unified vision-language pre-training for image captioning and VQA. arXiv preprint arXiv:1909.11059 (2019)
33. Zhu, F., Zhu, Y., Chang, X., Liang, X.: Vision-language navigation with self-supervised auxiliary reasoning tasks. arXiv preprint arXiv:1911.07883 (2019)
34. Zhu, Y., et al.: Aligning books and movies: towards story-like visual explanations by watching movies and reading books. In: Proceedings of the IEEE International Conference on Computer Vision, pp. 19–27 (2015)

# Directional Temporal Modeling
# for Action Recognition

Xinyu Li$^{(\boxtimes)}$, Bing Shuai, and Joseph Tighe

Amazon Web Service, Seattle, USA
{xxnl,bshuai,tighej}@amazon.com

**Abstract.** Many current activity recognition models use 3D convolutional neural networks (e.g. I3D, I3D-NL) to generate local spatial-temporal features. However, such features do not encode clip-level ordered temporal information. In this paper, we introduce a channel independent directional convolution (CIDC) operation, which learns to model the temporal evolution among local features. By applying multiple CIDC units we construct a light-weight network that models the clip-level temporal evolution across multiple spatial scales. Our CIDC network can be attached to any activity recognition backbone network. We evaluate our method on four popular activity recognition datasets and consistently improve upon state-of-the-art techniques. We further visualize the activation map of our CIDC network and show that it is able to focus on more meaningful, action related parts of the frame.

**Keywords:** Action recognition · Temporal modeling · Directional convolution

## 1 Introduction

Action recognition has made significant progress in recent years [6,14,19,21,35], with most of these methods leveraging 3D convolutions to learn spatial-temporal features. Most operate by taking as the input a video clip (a set of contiguous frames extracted from a video), and passing it through a 3D feature backbone. After the final convolutional block, the temporal dimension of feature map is typically down-sampled by a factor of $t$ (e.g. 8). At this point the feature map at each temporal position represents a $t$ frame sub-clip. The spatial-temporal feature map is passed to a global average pooling layer to summarize its salient features, and this pooled feature is used to derive the activity class label.

Even though 3D feature extraction backbones [35] and their derivatives (e.g. I3D-NL [35]) have proven to be effective, there are two major issues: (1) while the 3D convolutions in these networks have a temporal receptive field that spans the full clip, the effective receptive fields have been shown to actually be quite

**Electronic supplementary material** The online version of this chapter (https://doi.org/10.1007/978-3-030-58539-6_17) contains supplementary material, which is available to authorized users.

© Springer Nature Switzerland AG 2020
A. Vedaldi et al. (Eds.): ECCV 2020, LNCS 12351, pp. 275–291, 2020.
https://doi.org/10.1007/978-3-030-58539-6_17

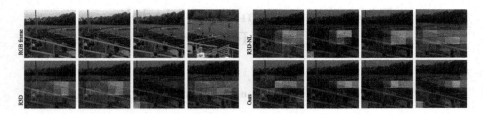

**Fig. 1.** We show a video clip (32 frames) and the spatial activation maps for the representative frame of every sub-clip (8 frames). I3D and I3D-NL not only activates related image regions of "althelets hurdling", but also activates "audiences moving" in the background. In contrast, our proposed model has clip-level motion understanding, thus it largely focuses on image region of interest that explains the action "althelets hurdling". Video examples are from Kinetics-400 dataset.

local [20] and thus lack full clip level motion understanding and (2) the temporal ordering/relationships between sub-clips is lost by the global average pooling of the feature maps.

To this end, we propose a novel channel independent directional convolution (CIDC) operation that captures temporal order information between sub-clips. Specifically, our CIDC unit encodes a feature vector that progressively aggregates the backbone features over the full extent of the input video clip. In other words, the first element in our method's output represents only the first few frames of the input clip, the middle element: the first half of the clip, and the last element: the full clip. We perform this operation bidirectionally (both forwards and backwards) to better capture the complete temporal order information of the video clip.

We use our CIDC unit to construct a light-weight CIDC network that can be attached to any activity recognition backbone (e.g. I3D, I3D-NL) to explicitly aggregate clip-level motion information. Our CIDC network is formed by stacking multiple CIDC units on top of the last three blocks of any action recognition backbone network. Our network is able to aggregate multiple spatial-temporal feature maps from different scales to effectively encode different types of motion.

As can be seen in Fig. 1, although the I3D and I3D-NL feature encoders are able to focus on the image areas correlated with the activity, they also activate on image regions where irrelevant object motion happens (i.e audience moving in the background). In contrast, the proposed network is able to understand the longer-term clip-level motion, therefore it precisely localizes the key area of the video for the action of interest (i.e. athletes hurdling).

We test our multi-scale CIDC network on four datasets: UCF-101 [26], HMDB-51 [16], Something-Something V2 [11] and Kinetics-400 [2]. Our model consistently improves state-of-the-art activity recognition models, demonstrating the effectiveness of the proposed method. Overall, our contributions are:

1. A novel channel independent directional convolution (CIDC) unit that aggregates features temporally and maintains the relative temporal order in the generated feature.

2. A multi-scale CIDC network that learns video clip-level temporal feature from different spatial and temporal scales.

3. An in-depth analysis and visualization of CIDC network that shows it is able to leverage clip-level temporal association to better focus on action-related features.

The rest of this paper is organized as follows. Section 2 discusses the related work. Section 3 elaborates the technical details of the proposed multi-scale CIDC networks. Section 4 presents our experimental results. Section 5 concludes the paper.

## 2   Related Work

*Feature Representation for Activity Recognition.* In order to represent an action, the video-level feature encoder needs to summarize the information about the objects, scenes as well as target object motions in the videos. First, researchers use ConvNet-2D [7,14,19,25,34] to extract feature for every frame, and aggregate frame-wise features to video-level feature. In order to encode motion information, two stream ConvNet-2D [7,14,25,34] are used, in which optical flow images [22] are directly taken as input to complement visual appearance information from RGB-stream Convnet-2D. Recently, ConvNet-3D [3,6,21,29–31,35,39] extends ConvNet-2D to spatial-temporal domain, handling both spatial and temporal dimensions similarly. It achieves successes on action recognition in terms of its model efficiency and model capacity. TSM [19] and TAM [5] propose to perform temporal modeling by shifting the feature channel along temporal dimension. SlowFast [6] models the action with a motion (fast) branch and a visual appearance (slow) branch, and it achieves the state-of-the-art performance. LFB [37] adopts a self-attention block to aggregate video-level features [37]. In this paper, we propose a novel light-weight CIDC network to learn clip-level temporal association, which is important for action recognition. More importantly, the proposed CIDC network is complementary to previous works that usually captures local spatio-temporal information.

*Temporal Modelling in Activity Recognition.* Temporal modelling is considered to be essential for action recognition [6,19,37]. LSTMs [13] are firstly used to model temporal associations among features extracted by 2D networks [4,17,18,40]. However, its results are not as good as expected in helping activity recognition [6,19,37]. The temporal rank pooling is another way to model the evolution of actions in sequential order [1,8,9]. Temporal rank pooling requires flattened features, which may compromises the spatial arrangement of the features, which makes it not feasible to insert the temporal rank pooling in the middle of the network. Furthermore, self-attention block [24,32] is used to aggregate spatial-temporal features, and it helps improving the action recognition performance [10,35]. In this paper, we propose channel independent directional convolution (CIDC) network to model clip-level temporal associations. We empirically show that our CIDC network outperforms LSTM and self-attention block in improving action recognition accuracy.

## 3    Methodology

A typical action recognition network takes as input a video clip (a set of $n$ contiguous video frames), and passes it through a 3D feature backbone (e.g. I3D, I3D-NL [35]) to create a feature map ($\mathbf{F}^{C \times T \times W \times H}$), where $T$ indicates the temporal length, $C$ the number of channels and $W \times H$ the width and height. While the 3D convolutions that create this feature map do have a temporal receptive field that spans the full clip ($T$), the effective receptive fields of convolutional features have been shown to generate local, sub-clip descriptors [20], rather descriptors that capture the long term temporal evolution of the full clip. Unfortunately, most networks at this point perform global average pooling over the spatial-temporal dimensions, thus throwing away any information of how the action evolves over the entirety of the clip. In this section we present our method to overcome this limitation by explicitly modeling the temporal evolution over the full clip.

### 3.1    Channel Independent Directional Convolution

To explicitly encode the temporal evolution of the clip, we introduce our novel **directional convolution** operation. This operation can be thought of as set of 2D convolution over the spatial dimensions that progressively add more temporal context. The first convolution of this set only operates on the first temporal element of the clip volume. The subsequent spatial convolutions progressively incorporate more of the temporal extent of the clip until the final convolution considers the whole clip. Considering that different channels in the feature map represent different visual components, applying the same directional convolution across all channels restricts the temporal modelling capacity of the network. Thus, we instead apply this directional convolution independently per channel, and we refer to the complete operation as a **channel independent directional convolution** or CIDC. In the following section we present how we implement our proposed CIDC.

**Channel Independent Directional Convolution Implementation.** We implement our proposed CIDC operator as 2D convolutions that operate on each channel ($C$) independently and treat the temporal dimension ($T$) as the channels normally would be. Consider the input feature map $\mathbf{F}_c$ as the feature map for the $c^{\text{th}}$ channel where $\mathbf{F}_c \in \mathbb{R}^{T \times W \times H}$. We convolve it with $T'$ filters $\mathbf{w}^c = [\mathbf{w}_1^c; \dots \mathbf{w}_t^c; \dots ; \mathbf{w}_{T'}^c]$ to produce a feature map $\mathbf{F}'_c \in \mathbb{R}^{T' \times W \times H}$:

$$\mathbf{F}'_c = \text{concat })\mathbf{w}_t^c * \mathbf{F}_c )_{t \in 1..T} \tag{1}$$

and then concatenate all $c$ features maps to produce $\mathbf{F}' \in \mathbb{R}^{T' \times C \times W \times H}$, which is our generated spatial-temporal feature map. This brings us close to the operator outline in Sect. 3.1, but if we apply such a convolution naively over feature maps we do not have any guarantees that it will capture the temporal evolution of the full clip.

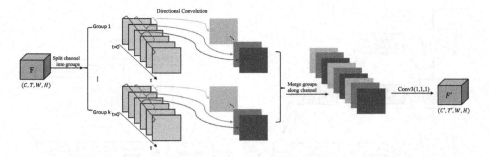

**Fig. 2.** Graphical illustration of a single Channel Independent Directional Convolution (CIDC) unit.

To create our CIDC operator we force the upper triangle of each $\mathbf{w}^c$ to be zeros. By doing so the output features gradually represent larger portions of the video: the first element only has the context of the first sub-clip of the video clip, the center element has the context of the first half of the video clip and the last element has the context of the whole video clip. The operation is straight forward to implement when $T = T'$ but when this condition is not met (when we perform temporal re-sampling) it is less obvious. We cover this case in detail in Sect. 3.3, as it turns out the efficient implementation of this operation can deal with this dimension miss match trivially.

Our method has the added benefit that by changing the output temporal dimension $T'$, we are able to "softly" manipulate the temporal dimension. This is important, as it avoids the significant information loss due to temporal pooling or temporal convolution with strides that current 3D backbones use.

To have an efficient implementation of the above algorithm, instead of splitting the operation into $C$ separate operators, we combine the temporal and channel dimensions and maintain the channel independence by using grouped convolutions [15,38] where the number of groups is $C$. In this work we only use $1 \times 1$ filter sizes for $w$ as our main focus is on the temporal, not spatial modeling but there is nothing that specifically restricts one to this choice. After this operation, we also apply a standard channel-wise 3D convolution with kernel size of 1 to learn the semantic features after temporal aggregation (Fig. 2).

## 3.2   Multi-scale CIDC Network

Although the spatial-temporal feature map $\mathbf{F}$ encodes sub-clip level motion information, it lacks longer-time clip-level motion understanding. To encode this, it is important to get rid of distracting motion information from irrelevant objects. Even though in some case, background objects or their motion information can help action recognition, we argue that the model should focus on the motion of the target objects in order to achieve deeper video understanding (e.g. spatial-temporal action detection, etc.).

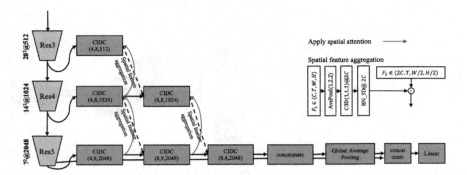

**Fig. 3.** The architecture of multi-scale CIDC network, in which it aggregates multiple spatial-scale feature maps. The dotted line arrows denotes spatial feature aggregation operation from higher-resolution feature maps to lower-resolution ones. The solid line arrow indicates the spatial attention propagation operation. CIDC($T_1, T_2, C$) refers to a CIDC unit with $T_1$ input temporal length, $T_2$ output temporal lenght and $C$ channels.

To this end, we construct our CIDC network (Fig. 3) by stacking multiple CIDC units and attaching it to a backbone network. The resulting output feature map of our CIDC network is compact, has temporally ordered information and more importantly, it aggregates the clip-level temporal information. Therefore, the network can leverage such information to activate image regions that can consistently explain the actions (athletes `hurdling` in Fig. 1) in the video clips rather than to attend to short-term background motions (audiences `moving` due to camera motion in Fig. 1). The output of our network ($\mathbf{F}_{CIDC}$) has the same dimensions ($C \times T \times W \times H$) as the backbone output $\mathbf{F}$ before average pooling.

We expect these two features to be complementary, and we fuse $\mathbf{F}$ and $\mathbf{F}_{CIDC}$ before they are passed to a final classification layer. We define,

$$\mathbf{F}_{out} = \mathcal{S}(\mathbf{F}, \mathbf{F}_{CIDC}) \qquad (2)$$

where $\mathcal{S}$ is the fusion function. We explore the following fusion functions: (1), concatenation $\mathbf{F}_{out} = [\mathbf{F}; \mathbf{F}_{CIDC}]_d$, where $d$ indicates the dimension along which the concatenation operation happens; (2), summation $\mathbf{F}_{out} = \mathbf{F} + \mathbf{F}_{CIDC}$.

**Multi-scale Aggregation.** Inspired by HRNet [27,28], our CIDC network consists of multiple CIDC branches attached to different scale feature maps, with cross-scale links. Instead of applying bi-directional cross scale aggregation, as in HR-Net, we only pass early stage feature maps (with higher resolution) to later stage feature maps (with lower resolution). To achieve this aggregation, our feature aggregation unit performs the necessary dimensionality reduction to ensure that feature vectors are compatible and applies an element-wise addition to fuse these two feature maps. The dimentionality reduction is performed by

2D spatial average pooling, followed by 3D $1 \times 1 \times 1$ convolution. The details of this multi-scale aggregation operator is illustrated in Fig. 3.

**Spatial-Attention Propagation.** It has been shown that self attention from the later stage feature maps is an effective way to aggregate semantic context from across the scene and focus on the key elements of the scene [33]. We leverage this idea by using activation maps on the later stage feature maps to weight the early stage features. This guides our CIDC module to focus on the temporal evolution of the semantically important parts of the video clip. We propose to propagate attention maps from later stage feature maps to early stage ones, and use them to generate task-attentive feature maps before they are fed to CIDC network. Formally,

$$\mathbf{F}'_x = \text{Bilinear}(\text{att}(\mathbf{F})) \odot \mathbf{F}_x + \mathbf{F}_x \qquad (3)$$

where $\mathbf{F} \in \mathbb{R}^{C \times T \times W \times H}$ and $\mathbf{F}_x$ corresponds to later stage and early stage feature maps respectively, $\odot$ is the element-wise multiplication operator, $att(\mathbf{F}_{(t,i,j)} = sigmoid(mean(\mathbf{F}_{(t,i,j)}))$ and *Bilinear* denotes the bilinear interpolation operation that is used to upsample the spatial attention maps.

### 3.3   Implementation Details

**Efficient CIDC Unit.** While conceptually our CIDC unit is straight forward, if implemented as separate convolutions for each time step (sub-clip feature) it would be very inefficient. Instead we use the intuition that our unit is equivalent to a standard $1 \times 1$ convolution with the upper triangle portion of the weights set to zero. However simply performing this operation poses issues for stable learning through SGD, and so here we present our normalization strategy to perform this operation efficiently, while keeping it stable during training.

To be as efficient as possible, we would ideally construct the weights of convolution kernel ($\mathbf{w}$ from Eq. 1) in such a way that $t$-th row of $\mathbf{w}_t^c$ abides by the conditions of Eq. 1: $\mathbf{w}_t^c(t + 1 : T) = 0$ and that is compatible with SGD optimization. In other words, Eq. 1 is a differentiable operation that is compatible with the SGD family of training. To achieve this we take advantage of the fact that we are using a softmax operation to normalize each row $\mathbf{w}_t^c$. Modify Eq. 1 as follows, adding $-\inf$ to each element of $\mathbf{w}_t^c[t + 1 : T]$:

$$\mathbf{F}'_c = [\mathbf{w}_t^c * \mathbf{F}_c]_{t \in 1..T} \qquad (4)$$
$$\mathbf{w}_t^c = \text{softmax}(\mathbf{k}_t^c - [\inf \cdot \text{triu}(\mathbf{k})]_t^c) \qquad (5)$$

where $\mathbf{k}$ is the learnable parameters, $\mathbf{k}_t^c$ is the $t^{\text{th}}$ row of $\mathbf{k}^c$, and $\mathbf{w}$ is computed from $\mathbf{k}$ that are passed through a softmax operation. By adding $-\inf$ to the upper triangle matrix of $\mathbf{k}$ we mask the convolution kernel and achieve our directional temporal convolution. We further linearly normalize the numerical values of weights in the lower-triangular portion of kernel $\mathbf{w}$ to the range of $[-1, 1]$. When $T' \neq T$, we first generate a square upper triangle matrix and rescale it to $T' \times T$ using bilinear interpolation. Finally, the uni-directional convolution can be extended to bi-directional by flipping the input data along temporal dimension as is done in bi-directional LSTMs [23].

**Training Details.** We first pre-train the backbone network or initialize backbone from pre-trained models, and then train our multi-scale CIDC network. We start training with a learning rate of 0.01, and decay it by a factor of 10 at epoch 40 and 80 respectively. In total the model is trained for 100 epoches. We use stochastic gradient descent (SGD) with momentum of 0.9 and weight decay of $1e-4$ to train the network. In order to mitigate over-fitting, we add a dropout layer of rate of 0.6 for fully connected layers in CIDC network. During training, we sample a random clip of length of 32 frames by skipping ever other frame (on average 15 fps). We perform scale augmentation by randomly resizing the shorter size of training clip to between 256 and 320 pixels, and then randomly crop a video clip with spatial size of $224 \times 224$ pixels. Meanwhile, we apply random horizontal flips to the video clip at 0.5 probability.

During inference, we follow [6] to first uniformly sample 10 clips from each video, and then resize the shorter side of every testing clip to 256 pixels. We then uniformly take three crops (with spatial size of $256 \times 256$) along its longer side, and finally we derive the prediction by taking average of predictions of all these 30 clips. Our experiments are conducted using the pytorch framework.

## 4  Experiments

### 4.1  Dataset

We evaluate our model on four commonly used datasets.

**UCF 101.** [26] includes 101 categories of human actions. It contains more 13 K videos with an average length of 180 frames per video. Following previous works [19,34], we report the top-1 classification accuracy on the validation videos based on split 1.

**HMDB 51.** [16] has a total of 6766 videos organized as 51 distinct action categories. The dataset has three splits and we report the top-1 classification accuracy on split 1 by following previous works [19,34].

**Something something V2.** [11] dataset consists of 174 actions and contains approximately 220,847 videos. Following other works [34], we report top-1 and top-5 classification accuracy on validation set. Something-Something dataset requires strong temporal modeling because many activities cannot be inferred based on spatial features only (e.g. open something, Covering something with something).

**Kinetics 400.** [2] consists of approximately 240k training and 20k validation videos videos trimmed to 10 s from 400 human action categories. Similar to other works, we report top-1 and top-5 classification accuracy on validation set.

**Table 1.** Result comparison on UCF101 and HMDB51 datasets. We only compare with methods that use ResNet-50 as backbone and take as input the RGB video. All models are pre-trained on Kinetics-400 dataset.

| Model | Conv | FLOPs | Param | HMDB51 | UCF101 |
|---|---|---|---|---|---|
| R2D [12] | 2D | 42G | 24M | 69.0 | 92.6 |
| R2D-NL [36] | 2D | 64G | 31M | 72.5 | 93.3 |
| TSN [34] | 2D | 19G | 11M | 64.7 | 91.7 |
| TSM [19] | 2D | 64G | 24M | 73.5 | 95.9 |
| I3D [36] | 3D | 65G | 44M | 69.1 | 92.9 |
| I3D-NL [36] | 3D | 94G | 62M | 72.2 | 94.6 |
| Ours (R2D) | 2D | 72G | 85M | 72.6 | 95.6 |
| Ours (R2D-NL) | 2D | 91G | 90M | 73.3 | 95.9 |
| Ours (I3D) | 3D | 92G | 87M | **74.9** | **97.2** |
| Ours (I3D-NL) | 3D | 121G | 103M | **75.2** | **97.9** |

## 4.2   Comparison with State-of-the-art

*UCF101 and HMDB51.* We summarize the results in Table 1. Our proposed method achieves state-of-the-art performance on both datasets. Our method improves upon both 2D and 3D baselines, both with and without non-local attention blocks. We see the biggest error reduction using our method on 3D networks, where our method reduces error by 11% to 19% on HMDB51 and **61%** on UCF101.

*Kinetics-400.* We compare our model with state-of-the-art methods in Table 2. The results for non-local [35] and Slowfast network [6] are obtained by running the model definition and weights provided by Gluon CV on our copy of the Kinetics 400 dataset. It is important to note that there is a consistent performance discrepancy between our reproduced results and those reported in [6, 35]. We believe that this is due to inconsistencies in the data as videos go missing from Kinetics 400 over time. The results in Table 2 show that the proposed multi-scale CIDC network again, consistently improves upon state-of-the-art methods for both 2D and 3D networks.

*Something-something V2.* We compare our method with state-of-the-art methods in Table 3. Our method achieves very competitive results. By digging into the results, we observe that the proposed multi-scale CIDC network reduces the error on the baseline networks (R2D, I3D) by **7.3%** and **13.2%** respectively. This demonstrates that CIDC network learns important temporal information that is complementary to 3D convolutions.

**Table 2.** Result comparison on Kinetics-400 dataset. For fair comparison, we only compare with methods that use ResNet-50.

| Model | Conv | FLOPs | Top1 | Top5 |
|---|---|---|---|---|
| TSN [34] | 2D | 19G | 70.6 | 89.2 |
| R2D [35] | 2D | 42G | 70.2 | 88.7 |
| R2D-NL [35] | 2D | 64G | 72.4 | 89.8 |
| I3D[35] | 3D | 65G | 73.8 | 91.1 |
| I3D-NL [35] | 3D | 94G | 75.2 | 91.9 |
| TSM [19] | 2D | 65G | 74.1 | 92.2 |
| bLVNet [5] | 3D | 93G | 74.3 | 91.2 |
| SF 4 × 16 [6] | 3D | 36G | 75.3 | 91.1 |
| Ours (R2D) | 2D | 72G | 72.2 | 90.1 |
| Ours (R2D-NL) | 2D | 91G | 72.8 | 90.5 |
| Ours (I3D) | 3D | 92G | 74.5 | 91.3 |
| Ours (I3D-NL) | 3D | 121G | 75.6 | 92.4 |
| Ours (Slowonly) | 3D | 101G | 75.5 | 92.1 |

**Table 3.** Result comparison on Something-Something V2 dataset. We only compare with methods that use ResNet-50 as backbone and take as input the RGB video. MS-TRN stands for multi-scale TRN and TS-TRN denotes two-stream TRN.

| Model | Conv | FLOPs | Top1 | Top5 |
|---|---|---|---|---|
| TSN [19,34] | 2D | 19G | 30.0 | 60.5 |
| MS-TRN [41] | 2D | 33G | 48.8 | 77.6 |
| TS-TRN [41] | 2D | 42G | 55.5 | 83.1 |
| Fine-grain [21] | 3D | 69G | 53.4 | 81.1 |
| TSM [19] | 2D | 65G | 63.4 | 88.5 |
| bLVNet [5] | 3D | 48G | 61.7 | 88.1 |
| R2D [35] | 2D | 42G | 35.5 | 65.4 |
| I3D[35] | 3D | 65G | 49.6 | 78.2 |
| Ours (R2D) | 2D | 72G | 40.2 | 68.6 |
| Ours (I3D) | 3D | 92G | 56.3 | 83.7 |

## 4.3   Ablation Study

We carefully perform the ablation study on one of the most challenging and largest-scale action classification dataset – Kinetics-400 as well as on UCF-101 and HMDB-51 datasets. To facilitate the studies, we adopt I3D-50 as our feature backbone unless specified. Results are summarized in Table 4.

*CIDC Multi-scale is Effective.* We first look at the effect that the multi-scale and spatial attention have on the model performance. We attach a single-scale CIDC network on top of the final feature map produced by the I3D-50 backbone; then we add our multi-scale version; and finally add our spatial attention. We present these results in Table 4(a). Each component provides a non-trivial boost in the final performance. These results show that by substituting single CIDC with its multi-scale alternative (w/ or w/o spatial attention propagation), we observe a healthy performance boost, which demonstrates the benefit of aggregating early stage feature maps.

*Directional Temporal Modeling is Important.* In order to understand the significance of directional temporal modeling, we instantiate the directional convolution in CIDC unit with three different configurations: (1), non-direction, where there is no temporal masking applied to the temporal convolution kernel. (2), uni-direction, where we apply temporal masking to the convolution kernel to make temporal modeling directional. and (3), bi-direction, where we apply the directional temporal modeling to both feature and temporally inverted feature, and concatenate the feature together along temporal axis. The performance of their corresponding multi-scale CIDC networks are listed in Table 4(b). As shown, the model with bi-directional CIDC unit performs best, and it reduces error relative

**Table 4.** Ablation experiments on UCF-101, HMDB-51 and Kinetics-400 (K400) datasets. Top-1 classification accuracy is reported.

(a) Result comparison with CIDC networks with different configurations.

| Model | UCF | HMDB | K400 |
|---|---|---|---|
| I3D-50 | 92.9 | 69.1 | 73.8 |
| + single-scale CIDC | 95.2 | 73.6 | 74.0 |
| + Multi-scale CIDC | 95.9 | 74.1 | 74.4 |
| + Spatial attention | 97.2 | 74.9 | 74.5 |

(b) Result comparison of using different directional modeling units.

| Model | UCF | HMDB | K400 |
|---|---|---|---|
| I3D-50 | 92.9 | 69.1 | 73.8 |
| non-direction | 94.1 | 72.5 | 73.9 |
| uni-direction | 95.5 | 73.1 | 74.2 |
| bi-direction | 97.2 | 74.9 | 74.5 |

**Table 5.** Ablation experiments on UCF-101, HMDB-51 and Kinetics-400 datasets. Top-1 classification accuracy is reported.

(a) Result comparison among different temporal modeling methods.

| Model | UCF | HMDB | Kinetics |
|---|---|---|---|
| I3D | 92.9 | 69.1 | 73.8 |
| LSTM | 63.2 | 31.3 | 63.4 |
| self-attention | 94.7 | 69.7 | 74.2 |
| CIDC | 95.3 | 73.6 | 74.5 |

(b) Result comparison among feature fusion functions $\mathcal{S}$ on Kinetics-400.

| Model | Acc% |
|---|---|
| I3D | 73.8 |
| concatenate along $t$ | 74.5 |
| concatenate along $c$ | 74.1 |
| sum | 73.7 |

to its non-directional alternative by a significant percentage: 52.5% 8.7% 2.2% on UCF-101, HMDB-51 nad Kinetics-400 respectively. These results validate the importance of directional temporal modeling in activity recognition. We notice that the performance improvement on UCF and HMDB dataset is more significant than that on Kinetics. We conjecture that it is because many videos in kinetics can be simply recognized by spotting key objects, thus undercutting the benefits of directional temporal modelling.

*Other Temporal Modeling Methods are Less Effective.* We compare against two related clip-level temporal modelling methods – self-attention and LSTM in Table 5. In detail, we attach a network with 2-layer LSTM for temporal features with 512 LSTM unit on each layer (by performing 2D spatial pooling layer on spatial-temporal feature map **F** in Eq. 1). Meanwhile, we attach a network with 2-layer self-attention block on top of spatial-temporal feature map **F**. We used the vanilla self-attention [32]. Following previous work [35], we first flatten the spatio-temporal feature map and then use 3D convolution instead of linear layer used in [32] for linear projection. Their outputs are concatenated accordingly with the spatial-temporal feature map **F** before and after global pooling. As shown in Table 5 (a), LSTM network does not perform well, even being outperformed by baseline I3D. This result is consistent with the observations in

Carreira etc. [3]. Even though self-attention network improves over I3D, it trails behind our proposed CIDC network. These results demonstrate that the proposed network is effective at learning clip-level motion information for action recognition.

*Feature Fusion Function S.* We experiment with different feature fusion functions $S$ in Eq. 2, and we summarize their results on Kinetics-400 in Table 5 (b). Overall, feature concatenation across temporal dimension $F_{out} = [F; F_{CIDC}]_t$ performs the best. We thus use this feature fusion function in our CIDC network.

*Performance Across Different Backbones.* As shown in Table 1, 2, and 3, the proposed multi-scale CIDC network substantially boosts the top-1 accuracy both for 2-D (R-2D, R2D-NL) and 3-D (R-3D, I3D-NL, Slowfast) feature backbones on all four datasets. It shows that the temporal associations learned by the proposed CIDC network generalizes well to different state-of-the-art activity recognition models. It is particularly important to note that our method improves upon even backbones that contain similar temporal mechanisms (R2D-NL, I3D-NL). This shows that not only is our temporal modeling strategy powerful but also complementary to other common temporal modeling techniques.

### 4.4   Error Analysis

In order to understand which classes are impacted most by the proposed method, we compare per-class errors on Kinetics 400 dataset between I3D and our model. In Table 6 (a), we show the 5 action classes that are most positively and negatively impacted. We observe that our model improves the recognition performance for actions that exhibit large target object motions, e.g. "waxing legs, climbing trees, whereas the model is confused for those actions that involves less obvious target object motions, e.g. "strumming guitar, yawning". Given that the proposed model is to learn the clip-level temporal information, it's easier for the model to differentiate actions that exhibit large motions. We noticed the "garbage collection" and "springboard diving" should have noticeable motion but didn't benefit from our CIDC module. After watch the videos in these classes, we noticed the "garbage collection" is often related to the garbage truck rather than the collection motion and the diving often has the camera motion with the athlete which makes the motion subtle. We also explore how our model performs for several challenging activity pairs whose visual appearance looks similar except the motion patterns exhibited by the targets are easily distinguishable (e.g. "swimming breast stroke" vs "swimming butterfly stroke"). As results shown in Table 6 (b), our model significantly improves the recognition accuracy for all those activities over I3D.

**Table 6.** Quantitative analysis on Kinetics-400 dataset. The performance gain is defined as the disparity of the top-1 accuracy between CIDC network and that of I3D.

(a) Top 5 activity classes that are positively and negatively impacted by introducing CIDC network over I3D.

| Top 5 (+) | Accuracy gain | Top 5 (-) | Accuracy gain |
|---|---|---|---|
| waxing legs | +24% | kissing | -17% |
| celebrating | +23% | garbage collecting | -17% |
| rock scissors paper | +22% | strumming guitar | -17% |
| climbing tree | +21% | yawning | -16% |
| ironing | +20% | springboard diving | -14% |

(b) The activity recognition accuracy gains of attaching CIDC network to I3D for activity pairs which share similar visual appearance.

| Activity pair | Accuracy gain |
|---|---|
| waxing legs / shaving legs | +24% / +11% |
| (swimming) breast stroke / butterfly stroke | +22% / +9% |
| washing hair / curling hair | +20% / +11% |
| long jump / triple jump | +10% / +6% |
| bending metal / welding | +12% / +8% |

### 4.5 Visualizing CIDC Activations

We visualize the feature maps from I3D, I3D-NL and our CIDC network on videos from Kinetics-400 dataset. We generate the spatial activation map based on $att(F)$ in Eq. 3 and show some representative examples in Fig. 4. From the visualized spatial attention maps, we can infer that: 1. I3D is only able to attend to image regions that are related to understanding actions but does not pick out the specific action in the scene. The top right of Fig. 4 illustrates this as image regions related to the object "potato" and the action "peeling" are both activated by I3D to detect the "peeling_potato" action, even though the potatoes that are highlighted have nothing to do with the pealing action. 2. I3D-NL further narrows down these attention maps to focus on image regions that highly correlate with the action labels. Take action "clapping" in Fig. 4 as an example, some of the background object "person" that does not perform the action "clapping" is deactivated. 3. Finally as examples in Fig. 4 show, the proposed CIDC network only activates image regions that can explain the actions (e.g. "clapping" and "peeling"). This demonstrates that the 3D convolution is sensitive to motion across adjacent frames, however, without clip level contextual information, the 3D convolution is not able to distinguish whether the motion is related to action. As a result, the 3D convolution is likely to pick up all of the moving target. The CIDC network learns clip-level motion and has the contextual information about action target and irrelevant motion and thus tend to

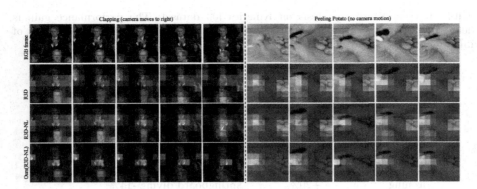

**Fig. 4.** We show two video clips (32 frames) and the spatial activation maps for the representative frame of every sub-clip (8 frames). I3D and I3D-NL network not only activates related image regions of "clapping" and "peeling", but also activates image regions that include irrelevant "people moving" due to camera motion and irrelevant potato in the background respectively. In contrast, our proposed model largely focuses on image region of interest that explains the action "clapping" and "peeling". Examples are from Kinetics-400 dataset.

focus better on the action related features. 4. On Fig. 1 and Fig. 4, the activation maps show the spatial attention propagation fires on both background and action related regions, and thus it is the CIDC unit that is able to focus on action related regions only

## 5    Conclusion

In this paper, we first introduce the channel independent directional convolution (CIDC) unit, which learns temporal association among local features in a temporally directional fashion. Thus, it is able to encode the temporal ordering information of actions into feature maps. Moreover, we propose a light-weight network (based on CIDC units) that models the video clip-level temporal association of local spatial/spatial-temporal features. We test our method on four datasets and achieved the state-of-the-art performance. Our ablation study validates that the proposed CIDC is more effective at temporal modelling in action recognition. Furthermore, we visualize the activation map of CIDC network and show that it generally focuses on moving target that performs the actions.

## References

1. Bilen, H., Fernando, B., Gavves, E., Vedaldi, A., Gould, S.: Dynamic image networks for action recognition. In: Proceedings of the IEEE Conference on Computer Vision and Pattern Recognition, pp. 3034–3042 (2016)

2. Carreira, J., Zisserman, A.: Quo vadis, action recognition? A new model and the kinetics dataset. In: 2017 IEEE Conference on Computer Vision and Pattern Recognition (CVPR), pp. 4724–4733, July 2017. https://doi.org/10.1109/CVPR.2017.502

3. Carreira, J., Zisserman, A.: Quo vadis, action recognition. A new model and the kinetics dataset. CoRR, abs/1705.07750 2, 3 (2017)

4. Donahue, J., et al.: Long-term recurrent convolutional networks for visual recognition and description. In: Proceedings of the IEEE Conference on Computer Vision and Pattern Recognition, pp. 2625–2634 (2015)

5. Fan, Q., Chen, C.F.R., Kuehne, H., Pistoia, M., Cox, D.: More is less: learning efficient video representations by temporal aggregation modules. In: Advances in Neural Information Processing Systems, vol. 33 (2019)

6. Feichtenhofer, C., Fan, H., Malik, J., He, K.: SlowFast networks for video recognition. In: Proceedings of the IEEE International Conference on Computer Vision, pp. 6202–6211 (2019)

7. Feichtenhofer, C., Pinz, A., Zisserman, A.: Convolutional two-stream network fusion for video action recognition. In: Proceedings of the IEEE Conference on Computer Vision and Pattern Recognition, pp. 1933–1941 (2016)

8. Fernando, B., Gavves, E., Oramas, J., Ghodrati, A., Tuytelaars, T.: Rank pooling for action recognition. IEEE Trans. Pattern Anal. Mach. Intell. 39(4), 773–787 (2016)

9. Fernando, B., Gavves, E., Oramas, J.M., Ghodrati, A., Tuytelaars, T.: Modeling video evolution for action recognition. In: Proceedings of the IEEE Conference on Computer Vision and Pattern Recognition, pp. 5378–5387 (2015)

10. Girdhar, R., Carreira, J., Doersch, C., Zisserman, A.: Video action transformer network. In: Proceedings of the IEEE Conference on Computer Vision and Pattern Recognition, pp. 244–253 (2019)

11. Goyal, R., et al.: The something something video database for learning and evaluating visual common sense. In: ICCV, vol. 1, p. 3 (2017)

12. He, K., Zhang, X., Ren, S., Sun, J.: Deep residual learning for image recognition. In: Proceedings of the IEEE Conference on Computer Vision and Pattern Recognition, pp. 770–778 (2016)

13. Hochreiter, S., Schmidhuber, J.: Long short-term memory. Neural Comput. 9(8), 1735–1780 (1997)

14. Karpathy, A., Toderici, G., Shetty, S., Leung, T., Sukthankar, R., Fei-Fei, L.: Large-scale video classification with convolutional neural networks. In: Proceedings of the IEEE Conference on Computer Vision and Pattern Recognition, pp. 1725–1732 (2014)

15. Krizhevsky, A., Sutskever, I., Hinton, G.E.: ImageNet classification with deep convolutional neural networks. In: Advances in Neural Information processing Systems, pp. 1097–1105 (2012)

16. Kuehne, H., Jhuang, H., Garrote, E., Poggio, T., Serre, T.: HMDB: a large video database for human motion recognition. In: 2011 International Conference on Computer Vision, pp. 2556–2563. IEEE (2011)

17. Li, X., et al.: Progress estimation and phase detection for sequential processes. Proc. ACM Interact. Mob. Wearable Ubiquit. Technol. 1(3), 73 (2017)

18. Li, Z., Gavrilyuk, K., Gavves, E., Jain, M., Snoek, C.G.: Videolstm convolves, attends and flows for action recognition. Comput. Vis. Image Underst. 166, 41–50 (2018)

19. Lin, J., Gan, C., Han, S.: TSM: temporal shift module for efficient video under-standing. In: Proceedings of the IEEE International Conference on Computer Vision (2019)
20. Luo, W., Li, Y., Urtasun, R., Zemel, R.: Understanding the effective receptive field in deep convolutional neural networks. In: Advances in Neural Information Processing Systems, pp. 4898–4906 (2016)
21. Martinez, B., Modolo, D., Xiong, Y., Tighe, J.: Action recognition with spatial-temporal discriminative filter banks. In: Proceedings of the IEEE International Conference on Computer Vision (2019)
22. Pérez, J.S., Meinhardt-Llopis, E., Facciolo, G.: Tv-l1 optical flow estimation. Image Process. On Line **2013**, 137–150 (2013)
23. Schuster, M., Paliwal, K.K.: Bidirectional recurrent neural networks. IEEE Trans. Signal Process. **45**(11), 2673–2681 (1997)
24. Shen, T., Zhou, T., Long, G., Jiang, J., Pan, S., Zhang, C.: DiSAN: directional self-attention network for RNN/CNN-free language understanding. In: Thirty-Second AAAI Conference on Artificial Intelligence (2018)
25. Simonyan, K., Zisserman, A.: Two-stream convolutional networks for action recognition in videos. In: Advances in Neural Information Processing Systems, pp. 568–576 (2014)
26. Soomro, K., Zamir, A.R., Shah, M.: A dataset of 101 human action classes from videos in the wild. Center for Research in Computer Vision (2012)
27. Sun, K., Xiao, B., Liu, D., Wang, J.: Deep high-resolution representation learning for human pose estimation. In: CVPR (2019)
28. Sun, K., et al.: High-resolution representations for labeling pixels and regions. CoRR abs/1904.04514 (2019)
29. Taylor, G.W., Fergus, R., LeCun, Y., Bregler, C.: Convolutional learning of spatio-temporal features. In: Daniilidis, K., Maragos, P., Paragios, N. (eds.) ECCV 2010. LNCS, vol. 6316, pp. 140–153. Springer, Heidelberg (2010). https://doi.org/10.1007/978-3-642-15567-3_11
30. Tran, D., Bourdev, L., Fergus, R., Torresani, L., Paluri, M.: Learning spatiotem-poral features with 3D convolutional networks. In: Proceedings of the IEEE International Conference on Computer Vision, pp. 4489–4497 (2015)
31. Tran, D., Wang, H., Torresani, L., Ray, J., LeCun, Y., Paluri, M.: A closer look at spatiotemporal convolutions for action recognition. In: Proceedings of the IEEE Conference on Computer Vision and Pattern Recognition, pp. 6450–6459 (2018)
32. Vaswani, A., et al.: Attention is all you need. In: Advances in Neural Information Processing Systems, pp. 5998–6008 (2017)
33. Wang, F., et al.: Residual attention network for image classification. In: Proceedings of the IEEE Conference on Computer Vision and Pattern Recognition, pp. 3156–3164 (2017)
34. Wang, L., et al.: Temporal segment networks: towards good practices for deep action recognition. In: Leibe, B., Matas, J., Sebe, N., Welling, M. (eds.) ECCV 2016. LNCS, vol. 9912, pp. 20–36. Springer, Cham (2016). https://doi.org/10.1007/978-3-319-46484-8_2
35. Wang, X., Girshick, R., Gupta, A., He, K.: Non-local neural networks. In: Proceedings of the IEEE Conference on Computer Vision and Pattern Recognition, pp. 7794–7803 (2018)
36. Wang, X., Gupta, A.: Videos as space-time region graphs. In: Proceedings of the European Conference on Computer Vision (ECCV), pp. 399–417 (2018)

37. Wu, C.Y., Feichtenhofer, C., Fan, H., He, K., Krahenbuhl, P., Girshick, R.: Long-term feature banks for detailed video understanding. In: Proceedings of the IEEE Conference on Computer Vision and Pattern Recognition, pp. 284–293 (2019)
38. Xie, S., Girshick, R., Dollár, P., Tu, Z., He, K.: Aggregated residual transformations for deep neural networks. In: Proceedings of the IEEE Conference on Computer Vision and Pattern Recognition, pp. 1492–1500 (2017)
39. Xie, S., Sun, C., Huang, J., Tu, Z., Murphy, K.: Rethinking spatiotemporal feature learning: speed-accuracy trade-offs in video classification. In: Proceedings of the European Conference on Computer Vision (ECCV), pp. 305–321 (2018)
40. Yue-Hei Ng, J., Hausknecht, M., Vijayanarasimhan, S., Vinyals, O., Monga, R., Toderici, G.: Beyond short snippets: deep networks for video classification. In: Proceedings of the IEEE Conference on Computer Vision and Pattern Recognition, pp. 4694–4702 (2015)
41. Zhou, B., Andonian, A., Oliva, A., Torralba, A.: Temporal relational reasoning in videos. In: Proceedings of the European Conference on Computer Vision (ECCV), pp. 803–818 (2018)

# Shonan Rotation Averaging: Global Optimality by Surfing $SO(p)^n$

Frank Dellaert[1]([✉])([iD]), David M. Rosen[2], Jing Wu[1], Robert Mahony[3]([iD]), and Luca Carlone[2]

[1] Georgia Institute of Technology, Atlanta, GA, USA
{fd27,jingwu}@gatech.edu
[2] Massachusetts Institute of Technology, Cambridge, MA, USA
{dmrosen,lcarlone}@mit.edu
[3] Australian National University, Canberra, Australia
Robert.Mahony@anu.edu.au

**Abstract.** Shonan Rotation Averaging is a fast, simple, and elegant rotation averaging algorithm that is guaranteed to recover globally optimal solutions under mild assumptions on the measurement noise. Our method employs semidefinite relaxation in order to recover provably globally optimal solutions of the rotation averaging problem. In contrast to prior work, we show how to solve large-scale instances of these relaxations using manifold minimization on (only slightly) higher-dimensional rotation manifolds, re-using existing high-performance (but *local*) structure-from-motion pipelines. Our method thus preserves the speed and scalability of current SFM methods, while recovering *globally* optimal solutions.

## 1 Introduction

*Rotation averaging* is the problem of estimating a set of $n$ unknown orientations $\mathbf{R}_1, \ldots, \mathbf{R}_n \in \mathrm{SO}(d)$ from noisy measurements $\bar{\mathbf{R}}_{ij} \in \mathrm{SO}(d)$ of the *relative rotations* $\mathbf{R}_i^{-1}\mathbf{R}_j$ between them [17,18]. This problem frequently arises in geometric reconstruction; in particular, it occurs as a sub-problem in bundle adjustment [3,34], structure from motion [29], multi-camera rig calibration [25], and sensor network localization [35]. The development of *fast* and *reliable* algorithms for solving the rotation averaging problem is therefore of great practical interest.

While there are numerous (inequivalent) ways of formalizing the rotation averaging problem in common use [18], unfortunately all of them share the common features of (a) *high dimensionality*, due to the typically large number $n$ of orientations $\mathbf{R}_i$ to be estimated, and (b) *non-convexity*, due to the non-convexity

---

F. Dellaert and D. M. Rosen—Equal contribution.

---

**Electronic supplementary material** The online version of this chapter (https://doi.org/10.1007/978-3-030-58539-6_18) contains supplementary material, which is available to authorized users.

A. Vedaldi et al. (Eds.): ECCV 2020, LNCS 12351, pp. 292–308, 2020.
https://doi.org/10.1007/978-3-030-58539-6_18

of the space of rotations itself. In consequence, *all* of these approaches lead to optimization problems that are computationally hard to solve in general.

In this work, we address rotation averaging using *maximum likelihood estimation*, as this provides strong statistical guarantees on the quality of the resulting estimate [11,19]. We consider the maximum likelihood estimation problem:

$$\max_{R \in \mathrm{SO}(d)^n} \sum_{(i,j) \in \mathcal{E}} \kappa_{ij} \mathrm{tr}\left( R_i \bar{R}_{ij} R_j^\mathsf{T} \right), \tag{1}$$

where the $\kappa_{ij} \geq 0$ are concentration parameters for an assumed Langevin noise model [5,9,27]. Our goal in this paper is to develop a *fast* and *scalable* optimization method that is capable of computing *globally* optimal solutions of the rotation averaging problem (1) in practice, despite its non-convexity.

We propose a new, straightforward algorithm, *Shonan Rotation Averaging*, for finding *globally optimal* solutions of problem (1). At its core, our approach simply applies the standard Gauss-Newton or Levenberg-Marquardt methods to a *sequence* of successively *higher-dimensional* rotation averaging problems

$$\max_{Q \in \mathrm{SO}(p)^n} \sum_{(i,j) \in \mathcal{E}} \kappa_{ij} \mathrm{tr}\left( Q_i P \bar{R}_{ij} P^\mathsf{T} Q_j^\mathsf{T} \right), \tag{2}$$

for increasing $p \geq d$. Note that the only difference between (1) and (2) is the $p \times d$ projection matrix $P \triangleq [\mathbf{I}_d; 0]$, which adapts the measurement matrix $\bar{R}_{ij}$ to the higher-dimensional rotations $Q_i$. We start by running local optimization on (2) with $p = d$, and if this fails to produce a globally-optimal solution, we increase the dimension $p$ and try again. Under mild conditions on the noise, we prove that this simple approach succeeds in recovering a *globally* optimal solution of the rotation averaging problem (1).

A primary contribution of this work is to show how the fast optimization approach developed in [26,27] can be adapted to run directly on the manifold of rotations (rather than the Stiefel manifold), implemented using the venerable Gauss-Newton or Levenberg-Marquardt methods. This approach enables Shonan Averaging to be easily implemented in high-performance optimization libraries commonly used in robotics and computer vision [2,12,22].

## 2   Related Work

By far the most common approach to addressing smooth optimization problems in computer vision is to apply standard first- or second-order nonlinear optimization methods to compute a critical point of the objective function [24]; this holds in particular for the rotation averaging problem (see [18] generally). This approach is very attractive from the standpoint of computational efficiency, as the low per-iteration cost of these techniques (exploiting the sparsity present in real-world problems) enables these methods to scale gracefully to very large problem sizes; indeed, it is now possible to process reconstruction problems (of which rotation averaging is a crucial part) involving *millions* of images on a single machine [15,20]. However, this computational efficiency comes at the expense of *reliability*, as the use of *local* optimization methods renders this approach susceptible to convergence to bad (significantly suboptimal) local minima.

To address this potential pitfall, several recent lines of work have studied the convergence behavior of local search techniques applied to the rotation averaging problem. One thrust proposes various initialization techniques that attempt to start the local search in low-cost regions of the state space, thereby favoring convergence to the true (global) minimum [6,10,23,30]. Another direction investigates the size of the locally convex region around the global minimizer, in order to understand when local search is likely to succeed [18,38]. A third class of approaches attempts to evaluate the *absolute* quality of a candidate solution $\hat{R}$ by employing Lagrangian duality to derive an *upper bound* on $\hat{R}$'s (global) suboptimality [9,16]. Interestingly, while these last two works employ different representations for rotations ([16] uses quaternions, whereas [9] uses rotation matrices), *both* of the resulting dual problems are semidefinite programs [37], and *both* of these duals are observed to be *tight* unless the measurements $\bar{R}_{ij}$ are contaminated by large amounts of noise; this fact enables the *certification* of optimality of a global minimizer $R^*$.

Motivated by the striking results reported in [9,16], a recent line of work proposes to recover *globally* optimal solutions of the rotation averaging problem from a solution of the Lagrangian dual. Both [16] and [9] propose to compute such solutions using an off-the-shelf SDP solver; however, as general-purpose SDP methods do not scale well with the problem size, this approach is limited to problems involving only a few hundred states. More recently, [13,14] proposed a block-coordinate-descent method specifically tailored to the dual of (1), and showed that this method was 1–2 orders of magnitude faster than the standard SDP algorithm SeDuMi [32]; however, the reported results were still limited to problems involving at most ≈300 states. Finally, [27] presents a global optimization approach for pose-graph SLAM based upon the *dual* of the Lagrangian dual (also an SDP), together with a fast optimization scheme that is capable of solving problems involving tens of thousands of poses in a few seconds. However, this optimization approach uses a truncated-Newton Riemannian optimization method [1] employing an *exact* model Hessian, and so cannot be deployed using the Gauss-Newton framework [24] that forms the basis of standard optimization libraries commonly used in computer vision applications [2,12,22].

Our method builds on the approach of [27], but adapts the optimization scheme to run directly on the manifold of rotations using the Gauss-Newton method or a trust-region variant like Levenberg-Marqardt. In this way, it is able to leverage the availability of high-performance software libraries [2,12,22] for performing *local* search on problems of the form (2) while preserving *global optimality* guarantees. In addition, working with the rotation manifold SO($p$), for $p \geq 3$ avoids introducing new, unfamiliar objects like Stiefel manifolds in the core algorithm. The result is a simple, intuitive method for globally optimal rotation averaging that improves upon the scalability of current global methods [13] by an order of magnitude.

## 3  Gauss-Newton for Rotation Averaging

This section reviews how the Gauss-Newton (GN) algorithm is applied to find a first-order critical point of the rotation averaging problem (1). We first rewrite (1) in terms of minimizing a sum of Frobenius norms:

$$\min_{\boldsymbol{R} \in \mathrm{SO}(d)^n} \sum_{(i,j) \in \mathcal{E}} \kappa_{ij} \left\| \boldsymbol{R}_j - \boldsymbol{R}_i \bar{\boldsymbol{R}}_{ij} \right\|_{\mathrm{F}}^2 . \tag{3}$$

This can in turn be vectorized as:

$$\min_{\boldsymbol{R} \in \mathrm{SO}(d)^n} \sum_{(i,j) \in \mathcal{E}} \kappa_{ij} \left\| \mathrm{vec}(\boldsymbol{R}_j) - \mathrm{vec}(\boldsymbol{R}_i \bar{\boldsymbol{R}}_{ij}) \right\|_2^2 \tag{4}$$

where "vec" is the column-wise vectorization of a matrix, and we made use of the fact that $\| \boldsymbol{M} \|_{\mathrm{F}}^2 = \| \mathrm{vec}(\boldsymbol{M}) \|_2^2$.

Problem (4) does not admit a simple closed-form solution. Therefore, given a feasible point $\boldsymbol{R} = (\boldsymbol{R}_1, \dots, \boldsymbol{R}_n) \in \mathrm{SO}(d)^n$, we will content ourselves with identifying a set of tangent vectors $\boldsymbol{\omega}_1, \dots, \boldsymbol{\omega}_n \in \mathfrak{so}(d)$ along which we can *locally perturb* each rotation $\boldsymbol{R}_i$:

$$\boldsymbol{R}_i \leftarrow \boldsymbol{R}_i e^{[\boldsymbol{\omega}_i]} \tag{5}$$

to *decrease* the value of the objective; here $[\boldsymbol{\omega}_i]$ is the $d \times d$ skew-symmetric matrix corresponding to the hat operator of the Lie algebra $\mathfrak{so}(d)$ associated with the rotation group $\mathrm{SO}(d)$. We can therefore reformulate problem (4) as:

$$\min_{\boldsymbol{\omega} \in \mathfrak{so}(d)^n} \sum_{(i,j) \in \mathcal{E}} \kappa_{ij} \left\| \mathrm{vec}(\boldsymbol{R}_j e^{[\boldsymbol{\omega}_j]}) - \mathrm{vec}(\boldsymbol{R}_i e^{[\boldsymbol{\omega}_i]} \bar{\boldsymbol{R}}_{ij}) \right\|_2^2 . \tag{6}$$

In effect, Eq. (6) replaces the optimization over the *rotations* $\boldsymbol{R}_i$ in (4) by an optimization over the *tangent vectors* $\boldsymbol{\omega}_i \in \mathfrak{so}(d)$. This is advantageous because $\mathfrak{so}(d)$ is a *linear* space, whereas $\mathrm{SO}(d)$ is not. However, we still cannot solve (6) directly, as the $\boldsymbol{\omega}_i$ enter the objective through the (nonlinear) exponential map.

However, we can *locally approximate* the exponential map to first order as $e^{[\boldsymbol{\nu}]} \approx \mathbf{I} + [\boldsymbol{\nu}]$. Therefore, for any matrix $\boldsymbol{A}$ we have

$$\mathrm{vec}(\bar{\boldsymbol{R}} e^{[\boldsymbol{\nu}]} \boldsymbol{A}) \approx \mathrm{vec}(\bar{\boldsymbol{R}}(\mathbf{I} + [\boldsymbol{\nu}])\boldsymbol{A}) \tag{7}$$

$$= \mathrm{vec}(\bar{\boldsymbol{R}} \boldsymbol{A}) + \mathrm{vec}(\bar{\boldsymbol{R}}[\boldsymbol{\nu}]\boldsymbol{A}) \tag{8}$$

$$= \mathrm{vec}(\bar{\boldsymbol{R}} \boldsymbol{A}) + (\boldsymbol{A}^{\mathsf{T}} \otimes \bar{\boldsymbol{R}})\mathrm{vec}([\boldsymbol{\nu}]), \tag{9}$$

where we made use of a well-known property of the Kronecker product $\otimes$. We can also decompose the skew-symmetric matrix $[\boldsymbol{\nu}]$ in terms of the coordinates $\nu^k$ of the vector $\boldsymbol{\nu}$ according to:

$$\mathrm{vec}([\boldsymbol{\nu}])) = \mathrm{vec}(\sum \nu^k \boldsymbol{G}_k) = \sum \nu^k \mathrm{vec}(\boldsymbol{G}_k) = \bar{\boldsymbol{G}}_d \boldsymbol{\nu} \tag{10}$$

where $G_k$ is the $k$th generator of the Lie algebra $\mathfrak{so}(d)$, and $\bar{G}_d$ is the matrix obtained by concatenating the vectorized generators $\text{vec}(G_k)$ column-wise.

The (local) Gauss-Newton model of the rotation averaging problem (1) is obtained by substituting the linearizations (7)–(9) and decomposition (10) into (6) to obtain a *linear least-squares* problem in the tangent vectors $\omega_i$:

$$\min_{\omega \in \mathfrak{so}(d)^n} \sum_{(i,j) \in \mathcal{E}} \kappa_{ij} \left\| F_j \omega_j - H_i \omega_i - b_{ij} \right\|_2^2, \tag{11}$$

where the Jacobians $F_j$ and $H_i$ and the right-hand side $b_{ij}$ can be calculated as

$$F_j \doteq (\mathbf{I} \otimes \bar{R}_j)\bar{G}_d \tag{12}$$

$$H_i \doteq (\bar{R}_{ij}^\mathsf{T} \otimes \bar{R}_i)\bar{G}_d \tag{13}$$

$$b_{ij} \doteq \text{vec}(\bar{R}_i \bar{R}_{ij} - \bar{R}_j). \tag{14}$$

The *local model* problem (11) can be solved efficiently to produce an optimal *correction* $\omega^\star \in \mathfrak{so}(d)^n$. (To do so one can use either direct methods, based on sparse matrix factorization, or preconditioned conjugate gradient (PCG). As an example, to produce the results in Sect. 5 we use PCG with a block-Jacobi preconditioner and a Levenberg-Marquardt trust-region method.) This correction is then applied to *update* the state $R$ as in Eq. (5). Typically, this is done in conjunction with a trust-region control strategy to prevent taking a step that leaves the neighborhood of $R$ in which the local linear models (11)–(14) well-approximate the objective. The above process is then repeated to generate a *sequence* $\{\omega\}$ of such corrections, each of which improves the objective value, until some termination criterion is satisfied.

We emphasize that while the Gauss-Newton approach is sufficient to *locally improve* on an initial estimate, but because of non-convexity the final iterate returned by this method is **not** guaranteed to be a minimizer of (1).

## 4    Shonan Rotation Averaging

### 4.1    A Convex Relaxation for Rotation Averaging

The main idea behind Shonan Averaging is to develop a *convex relaxation* of (1) (which can be solved *globally*), and then exploit this relaxation to search for good solutions of the rotation averaging problem. Following [27, Sect. 3], in this section we derive a convex relaxation of (1) whose minimizers in fact provide *exact, globally optimal* solutions of the rotation averaging problem subject to mild conditions on the measurement noise.

To begin, we rewrite problem (1) in a more compact, matricized form as:

$$f_{\mathrm{MLE}}^* = \min_{R \in \mathrm{SO}(d)^n} \text{tr}\left(\bar{L} R^\mathsf{T} R\right), \tag{15}$$

where $R = (R_1, \ldots, R_n)$ is the $d \times dn$ matrix of rotations $R_i \in \mathrm{SO}(d)$, and $\bar{L}$ is a symmetric $(d \times d)$-block-structured matrix constructed from the measurements

$\bar{R}_{ij}$. The matrix $\bar{L}$, known as the *connection Laplacian* [31], is the generalization of the standard (scalar) graph Laplacian to a graph having matrix-valued data $\bar{R}_{ij}$ assigned to its edges.

Note that $R$ enters the objective in (15) only through the product $R^{\mathsf{T}}R$; this is a rank-$d$ positive-semidefinite matrix (since it is an outer product of the rank-$d$ matrix $R$), and has a $(d \times d)$-block-diagonal comprised entirely of identity matrices (since the blocks $R_i$ of $R$ are rotations). Our convex relaxation of (15) is derived simply by replacing the rank-$d$ product $R^{\mathsf{T}}R$ with a *generic* positive-semidefinite matrix $Z$ having identity matrices along its $(d \times d)$-block-diagonal:

$$f^*_{\mathrm{SDP}} = \min_{Z \succeq 0} \mathrm{tr}\left(\bar{L}Z\right)$$

$$\text{s.t. } \mathrm{BlockDiag}_{d \times d}(Z) = (\mathbf{I}_d, \dots, \mathbf{I}_d). \tag{16}$$

Problem (16) is a *semidefinite program* (SDP) [37]: it requires the minimization of a linear function of a positive-semidefinite matrix $Z$, subject to a set of linear constraints. Crucially, since the set of positive-semidefinite matrices is a convex cone, SDPs are *always* convex, and can therefore be solved *globally* in practice. Moreover, since by construction (15) and (16) share the same objective, and the feasible set of (16) contains every matrix of the form $R^{\mathsf{T}}R$ with $R$ feasible in (15), we can regard (16) as a convexification of (15) obtained by *expanding the latter's feasible set*. It follows immediately that $f^*_{\mathrm{SDP}} \leq f^*_{\mathrm{MLE}}$. Furthermore, if it so happens that a minimizer $Z^\star$ of (16) admits a factorization of the form $Z^\star = R^{\star\mathsf{T}}R^\star$ with $R^\star \in \mathrm{SO}(d)^n$, then it is clear that $R^\star$ is also a (global) minimizer of (15), since it attains the lower-bound $f^*_{\mathrm{SDP}}$ for (15)'s optimal value $f^*_{\mathrm{MLE}}$. The key fact that motivates our interest in the relaxation (16) is that this favorable situation *actually occurs*, provided that the noise on the observations $\bar{R}_{ij}$ is not too large. More precisely, the following result is a specialization of [27, Proposition 1] to the rotation averaging problem (15).

**Theorem 1.** *Let $L$ denote the connection Laplacian for problem (15) constructed from the true (noiseless) relative rotations $R_{ij} \triangleq R_i^{-1}R_j$. Then there exists a constant $\beta \triangleq \beta(L)$ (depending upon $L$) such that, if $\|\bar{L} - L\|_2 \leq \beta$:*

*(i)   The semidefinite relaxation (16) has a unique solution $Z^\star$, and*
*(ii)  $Z^\star = R^{\star\mathsf{T}}R^\star$, where $R^\star \in \mathrm{SO}(d)^n$ is a globally optimal solution of the rotation averaging problem (15).*

## 4.2   Solving the Semidefinite Relaxation: The Riemannian Staircase

In this section, we describe a specialized optimization procedure that enables the fast solution of large-scale instances of the semidefinite relaxation (16), following the approach of [27, Sec. 4.1].

Theorem 1 guarantees that in the (typical) case that (16) is exact, the *solution* $Z^\star$ that we seek admits a concise description in the factored form $Z^\star = R^{\star\mathsf{T}}R^\star$ with $R^\star \in \mathrm{SO}(d)^n$. More generally, even in those cases where exactness fails, minimizers $Z^\star$ of (16) generically have a rank $p$ not much greater than $d$, and therefore admit a symmetric rank decomposition $Z^\star = S^{\star\mathsf{T}} S^\star$ for $S^\star \in \mathbb{R}^{p \times dn}$ with $p \ll dn$. We exploit the existence of such low-rank solutions by adopting the approach of [8], and replacing the decision variable $Z$ in (16) with a symmetric rank-$p$ product of the form $S^\mathsf{T} S$. This substitution has the effect of dramatically reducing the size of the search space, as well as rendering the positive-semidefiniteness constraint *redundant*, since $S^\mathsf{T} S \succeq 0$ for *any* $S$. The resulting *rank-restricted* version of (16) is thus a standard *nonlinear program* with decision variable the low-rank factor $S$:

$$f^*_{\text{SDPLR}}(p) = \min_{S \in \mathbb{R}^{p \times dn}} \text{tr}\left(\bar{L} S^\mathsf{T} S\right)$$
$$\text{s.t. BlockDiag}_{d \times d}(S^\mathsf{T} S) = (\mathbf{I}_d, \ldots, \mathbf{I}_d). \tag{17}$$

The identity block constraints in (17) are equivalent to the $p \times d$ block-columns $S_i$ of $S$ being orthonormal $d$-frames in $\mathbb{R}^p$. The set of all orthonormal $d$-frames in $\mathbb{R}^p$ is a matrix manifold, the **Stiefel manifold** $\text{St}(d, p)$ [1]:

$$\text{St}(d, p) \doteq \{ M \in \mathbb{R}^{p \times d} \mid M^\mathsf{T} M = \mathbf{I}_d \}. \tag{18}$$

We can therefore rewrite (17) as a low-dimensional *unconstrained* optimization over a product of $n$ Stiefel manifolds:

$$f^*_{\text{SDPLR}}(p) = \min_{S \in \text{St}(d,p)^n} \text{tr}\left(\bar{L} S^\mathsf{T} S\right). \tag{19}$$

Now, let us compare the rank-restricted relaxation (19) with the original rotation averaging problem (15) and its semidefinite relaxation (16). Since any matrix $R_i$ in the (special) orthogonal group satisfies conditions (18) with $p = d$, we have the set of inclusions:

$$\text{SO}(d) \subset \text{O}(d) = \text{St}(d, d) \subset \cdots \subset \text{St}(d, p) \subset \cdots \tag{20}$$

Therefore, we can regard the rank-restricted problems (19) as a *hierarchy* of relaxations (indexed by the rank parameter $p$) of (15) that are intermediate between (15) and (16) for $d < p < r$, where $r$ is the lowest rank of any solution of (16). Indeed, if (16) has a minimizer of rank $r$, then it is clear by construction that for $p \geq r$ any (global) minimizer $S^\star$ of (19) corresponds to a minimizer $Z^\star = S^{\star\mathsf{T}} S^\star$ of (16). However, unlike (16), the rank-restricted problems (19) are no longer convex, since we have reintroduced the (nonconvex) orthogonality constraints in (18). It may therefore not be clear that anything has really been gained by relaxing problem (15) to problem (19), since it seems that we may have just replaced one difficult (nonconvex) optimization problem with another. The key fact that justifies our interest in the rank-restricted relaxations (19) is the following remarkable result [7, Corollary 8]:

**Theorem 2.** *If $S^\star \in \text{St}(d, p)^n$ is a rank-deficient second-order critical point of* (19)*, then $S^\star$ is a global minimizer of* (19)*, and $Z^\star = S^{\star\mathsf{T}} S^\star$ is a global minimizer of the semidefinite relaxation* (16)*.*

This result immediately suggests the following simple algorithm (the **Riemannian staircase** [7]) for recovering solutions $Z^\star$ of (16) from (19): for some small relaxation rank $p \geq d$, find a second-order critical point $S^\star$ of problem (19) using a local search technique. If $S^\star$ is rank-deficient, then Theorem 2 proves that $S^\star$ is a *global* minimizer of (19), and $Z^\star = S^{\star\mathsf{T}}S^\star$ is a solution of (16). Otherwise, increase the rank parameter $p$ and try again. In the worst possible case, we might have to take $p$ as large as $dn + 1$ before finding a rank-deficient solution. However, in practice typically only one or two "stairs" suffice – just a *bit* of extra room in (19) vs. (15) is all one needs!

Many popular optimization algorithms only guarantee convergence to *first-order* critical points because they use only limited second-order information [24]. This is the case for the Gauss-Newton and Levenberg-Marquardt methods in particular, where the model Hessian is positive-semidefinite by construction. Fortunately, there is a simple procedure that one can use to test the global optimality of a *first*-order critical point $S^\star$ of (19), and (if necessary) to construct a *direction of descent* that we can use to "nudge" $S^\star$ away from stationarity before restarting local optimization at the next level of the Staircase [4].

**Theorem 3.** *Let* $S^\star \in St(d,p)^n$ *be a first-order critical point of* (19), *define*

$$C \triangleq \bar{L} - \frac{1}{2}\,\mathrm{BlockDiag}_{d \times d}\left(\bar{L}S^{\star\mathsf{T}}S^\star + S^{\star\mathsf{T}}S^\star\bar{L}\right), \tag{21}$$

*and let* $\lambda_{min}$ *be the minimum eigenvalue of* $C$, *with corresponding eigenvector* $v_{min} \in \mathbb{R}^{dn}$. *Then:*

(*i*) *If* $\lambda_{min} \geq 0$, *then* $S^\star$ *is a global minimizer of* (19), *and* $Z^\star = S^{\star\mathsf{T}}S^\star$ *is a global minimizer of* (16).

(*ii*) *If* $\lambda_{min} < 0$, *then the higher-dimensional lifting* $S^+ \triangleq \left[S^\star; 0\right] \in St(d, p + 1)^n$ *of* $S^\star$ *is a stationary point for the rank-restricted relaxation* (19) *at the next level* $p + 1$ *of the Riemannian Staircase, and* $\dot{S}^+ \triangleq \left[0; v_{min}^\mathsf{T}\right] \in T_{S^+}(St(d, p + 1)^n)$ *is a second-order descent direction from* $S^+$.

*Remark 1 (Geometric interpretation of Theorems 1–3).* With $C$ defined as in (21), part (i) of Theorem 3 is simply the standard necessary and sufficient conditions for $Z^\star = S^{\star\mathsf{T}}S^\star$ to be a minimizer of (16) [37]. $C$ *also* gives the action of the Riemannian Hessian of (19) on tangent vectors; therefore, if $\lambda_{\min}(C) < 0$, the corresponding direction of negative curvature $\dot{S}^+$ defined in part (ii) of Theorem 3 provides a second-order descent direction from $S^+$. Theorem 2 is an analogue of Theorem 3(i). Finally, Theorem 1 follows from the fact that the certificate matrix $C$ depends continuously upon both the data $\bar{L}$ and $S^\star$, and is *always* valid for $S^\star = R^\star$ in the noiseless case; one can then employ a continuity argument to show that $C$ *remains* a valid certificate for $Z^\star = R^{\star\mathsf{T}}R^\star$ as a minimizer of (16) for sufficiently small noise; see [28, Appendix C] for details.

---

**Algorithm 1.** Rounding procedure for solutions of (19)

---

**Input:** A minimizer $S \in \mathrm{St}(d,p)^n$ of (19).
**Output:** A feasible point $\hat{R} \in \mathrm{SO}(d)^n$ for (1).
1: **function** ROUNDSOLUTION($S$)
2:      Compute a rank-$d$ truncated SVD $U_d \Xi_d V_d^\mathsf{T}$ for $S$ and assign $\hat{R} \leftarrow \Xi_d V_d^\mathsf{T}$.
3:      Set $N_+ \leftarrow |\{\hat{R}_i \mid \det(\hat{R}_i) > 0\}|$.
4:      **if** $N_+ < \lceil \frac{n}{2} \rceil$ **then**
5:           $\hat{R} \leftarrow \mathrm{Diag}(1, \dots, 1, -1)\hat{R}$.
6:      **end if**
7:      **for** $i = 1, \dots, n$ **do**
8:           Set $\hat{R}_i \leftarrow$ NEARESTROTATION($\hat{R}_i$) (see [36])
9:      **end for**
10:      **return** $\hat{R}$
11: **end function**

---

### 4.3    Rounding the Solution

Algorithm 1 provides a truncated SVD procedure to extract a feasible point $\hat{R} \in \mathrm{SO}(d)^n$ for the original rotation averaging problem (1) from the optimal factor $S^\star \in \mathrm{St}(d,p)^n$ obtained via the rank-restricted relaxation (19). We need to ensure that $\hat{R}$ is a *global minimizer* of (1) whenever the semidefinite relaxation (16) is *exact*, and is at least an *approximate* minimizer otherwise. The factor $R$ of a symmetric factorization $Z = R^\mathsf{T} R$ is only unique up to left-multiplication by some $A \in \mathrm{O}(d)$. The purpose of lines 3–6 is to choose a representative $\hat{R}$ with a majority of $d \times d$ blocks $\hat{R}_i$ satisfying $\det(\hat{R}_i) > 0$, since these should *all* be rotations in the event (16) is exact [27, Sect. 4.2].

### 4.4    From Stiefel Manifolds to Rotations

In this section we show how to reformulate the low-rank optimization (19) as an optimization over the product $\mathrm{SO}(p)^n$ of rotations of $p$-dimensional space. This is convenient from an implementation standpoint, as affordances for performing optimization over rotations are a standard feature of many high-performance optimization libraries commonly used in robotics and computer vision [2,12,22].

The main idea underlying our approach is the simple observation that since the columns of a rotation matrix $Q \in \mathrm{SO}(p)$ are orthonormal, then in particular the first $d$ columns $Q_{[1:d]}$ form an orthonormal $d$-frame in $p$-space, i.e., the submatrix $Q_{[1:d]}$ is itself an element of $\mathrm{St}(d,p)$. Let us define the following projection, which simply extracts these first $d$ columns:

$$\pi : \mathrm{SO}(p) \to \mathrm{St}(d,p)$$
$$\pi(Q) = QP \tag{22}$$

where $P = [\mathbf{I}_d; 0]$ is the $p \times d$ projection matrix appearing in (2). It is easy to see that $\pi$ is surjective for any $p > d$:[1] given any element $S = [s_1, \dots, s_d] \in \mathrm{St}(d,p)$,

---

[1] In the case that $d = p$, $\mathrm{St}(p,p) \supset \mathrm{SO}(p)$, and it is impossible for $\pi$ to be surjective.

we can construct a rotation $Q \in \pi^{-1}(S)$ simply by extending $\{s_1, \ldots s_d\}$ to an orthonormal basis $\{s_1, \ldots, s_d, v_1, \ldots, v_{p-d}\}$ for $\mathbb{R}^p$ using the Gram-Schmidt process, and (if necessary) multiplying the final element $v_{p-d}$ by $-1$ to ensure that this basis has a positive orientation; the matrix $Q = [s_1, \ldots, s_d, v_1, \ldots, v_{p-d}] \in \mathrm{SO}(p)$ whose columns are the elements of this basis is then a rotation satisfying $\pi(Q) = S$. Conversely, if $Q \in \pi^{-1}(S)$, then by (22) $Q = [S, V]$ for some $V \in \mathbb{R}^{p \times (p-d)}$; writing the orthogonality constraint $Q^\mathsf{T} Q = \mathbf{I}_p$ in terms of this block decomposition then produces:

$$Q^\mathsf{T} Q = \begin{bmatrix} S^\mathsf{T} S & S^\mathsf{T} V \\ V^\mathsf{T} S & V^\mathsf{T} V \end{bmatrix} = \begin{bmatrix} \mathbf{I}_d & 0 \\ 0 & \mathbf{I}_{p-d} \end{bmatrix}. \tag{23}$$

It follows from (23) that the preimage of any $S \in \mathrm{St}(d, p)$ under the projection $\pi$ in (22) is given explicitly by:

$$\pi^{-1}(S) = \left\{ [S, V] \mid V \in \mathrm{St}(p - d, p), \; S^\mathsf{T} V = 0, \; \det([S, V]) = +1 \right\}. \tag{24}$$

Equations (22) and (24) provide a means of representing $\mathrm{St}(d, p)$ using $\mathrm{SO}(p)$: given any $S \in \mathrm{St}(d, p)$, we can represent it using one of the rotations in (24) in which it appears as the first $d$ columns, and conversely, given any $Q \in \mathrm{SO}(p)$, we can extract its corresponding Stiefel manifold element using $\pi$. We can extend this relation to *products* of rotations and Stiefel manifolds in the natural way:

$$\begin{aligned} \Pi &: \mathrm{SO}(p)^n \to \mathrm{St}(d, p)^n \\ \Pi(Q_1, \ldots, Q_n) &= (\pi(Q_1), \ldots, \pi(Q_n)) \end{aligned} \tag{25}$$

and $\Pi$ is likewise surjective for $p > d$.

The projection $\Pi$ enables us to "pull back" the rank-restricted optimization (19) on $\mathrm{St}(d, p)^n$ to an equivalent optimization problem on $\mathrm{SO}(p)^n$. Concretely, if $f : \mathrm{St}(d, p)^n \to \mathbb{R}$ is the objective of (19), then we simply define the objective $\tilde{f}$ of our "lifted" optimization over $\mathrm{SO}(p)^n$ to be the pullback of $f$ via $\Pi$:

$$\begin{aligned} \tilde{f} &: \mathrm{SO}(p)^n \to \mathbb{R} \\ \tilde{f}(Q) &= f \circ \Pi(Q). \end{aligned} \tag{26}$$

Comparing (19), (25), and (26) reveals that the pullback of the low-rank optimization (19) to $\mathrm{SO}(p)^n$ is exactly the Shonan Averaging problem (2).

**Theorem 4.** *Let $p > d$. Then:*

(i) *The rank-restricted optimization (19) and the Shonan Averaging problem (2) attain the same optimal value.*

(ii) $Q^\star \in \mathrm{SO}(p)^n$ *minimizes (2) if and only if $S^\star = \Pi(Q^\star)$ minimizes (19).*

Similarly, we also have the following analogue of Theorem 3 for problem (2):

**Theorem 5.** *Let $Q^\star = (Q_1^\star, \ldots, Q_n^\star) \in \mathrm{SO}(p)^n$ be a first-order critical point of problem (2), and $S^\star = (S_1^\star, \ldots, S_n^\star) = \Pi(Q^\star) \in \mathrm{St}(d, p)^n$. Then:*

---

**Algorithm 2.** Shonan Rotation Averaging

---

**Input:** An initial point $Q \in SO(p)^n$ for (2), $p \geq d$.
**Output:** A feasible estimate $\hat{R} \in SO(d)^n$ for the rotation averaging problem (1), and
the lower bound $f^*_{\text{SDP}}$ for problem (1)'s optimal value.

1: **function** SHONANAVERAGING($Q$)
2:   **repeat**                                                   ▷ Riemannian Staircase
3:       $Q \leftarrow$ LOCALOPT($Q$)                             ▷ Find critical point of (2)
4:       Set $S \leftarrow \Pi(Q)$                                ▷ Project to St$(d,p)^n$
5:       Construct the certificate matrix $C$ in (21), and
         compute its minimum eigenpair ($\lambda_{\min}, v_{\min}$).
6:       **if** $\lambda_{\min} < 0$ **then**                     ▷ $Z = S^\mathsf{T}S$ is *not* optimal
7:           Set $p \leftarrow p + 1$ and $Q_i \leftarrow \begin{pmatrix} Q_i & 0 \\ 0 & 1 \end{pmatrix} \forall i.$          ▷ Ascend to next level
8:           Construct descent direction $\dot{Q}$ as in (28).
9:           $Q \leftarrow$ LINESEARCH($Q, \dot{Q}$)              ▷ Nudge $Q$
10:      **end if**
11:  **until** $\lambda_{\min} \geq 0$                            ▷ $Z = S^\mathsf{T}S$ solves (16)
12:  Set $f^*_{\text{SDP}} \leftarrow \text{tr}\left(\bar{L}S^\mathsf{T}S\right)$.
13:  Set $\hat{R} \leftarrow$ ROUNDSOLUTION($S$).
14:  **return** $\left\{\hat{R}, f^*_{\text{SDP}}\right\}$
15: **end function**

---

(i) $S^\star$ *is a first-order critical point of the rank-restricted optimization* (19).
(ii) *Let $C$ be the certificate matrix defined in* (21), $\lambda_{min}$ *its minimum eigenvalue,
and $v = (v_1, \ldots, v_n) \in \mathbb{R}^{dn}$ a corresponding eigenvector. If $\lambda_{\min} < 0$, then
the point $Q^+ \in SO(p+1)^n$ defined elementwise by:*

$$Q_i^+ = \begin{bmatrix} Q_i^\star & 0 \\ 0 & 1 \end{bmatrix} \in SO(p+1) \tag{27}$$

*is a first-order critical point of problem* (2) *in dimension $p + 1$, and the
tangent vector $\dot{Q}^+ \in T_{Q^+}(SO(p+1)^n)$ defined blockwise by:*

$$\dot{Q}_i^+ = Q_i^+ \begin{bmatrix} 0 & -v_i \\ v_i^\mathsf{T} & 0 \end{bmatrix} \in T_{Q_i^+}(SO(p+1)) \tag{28}$$

*is a second-order descent direction from $Q^+$.*

Theorems 4 and 5 are proved in Appendix ?? of the supplementary material.

## 4.5   The Complete Algorithm

Combining the results of the previous sections gives the complete *Shonan Averaging* algorithm (Algorithm 2). (We employ Levenberg-Marquardt to perform the fast local optimization required in line 3 – see Appendix ?? for details).

When applied to an instance of rotation averaging, Shonan Averaging returns a feasible point $\hat{R} \in SO(d)^n$ for the maximum likelihood estimation (1), and a

Table 1. Shonan Averaging results for the SLAM benchmark datasets

|  | $n$ | $m$ | Shonan Averaging | | | | |
|---|---|---|---|---|---|---|---|
|  |  |  | $p$ | $\lambda_{min}$ | $f^*_{SDP}$ | Opt. time [s] | Min. eig. time [s] |
| smallGrid | 125 | 297 | 5 | $-9.048 \times 10^{-6}$ | $4.850 \times 10^2$ | $2.561 \times 10^{-1}$ | $2.613 \times 10^{-1}$ |
| sphere | 2500 | 4949 | 6 | $-1.679 \times 10^{-4}$ | $5.024 \times 10^0$ | $1.478 \times 10^1$ | $1.593 \times 10^1$ |
| torus | 5000 | 9048 | 5 | $-2.560 \times 10^{-4}$ | $1.219 \times 10^4$ | $7.819 \times 10^1$ | $8.198 \times 10^1$ |
| garage | 1661 | 6275 | 5 | $1.176 \times 10^{-4}$ | $2.043 \times 10^{-1}$ | $1.351 \times 10^1$ | $1.420 \times 10^1$ |
| cubicle | 5750 | 16869 | 5 | $-9.588 \times 10^{-5}$ | $3.129 \times 10^1$ | $1.148 \times 10^2$ | $1.208 \times 10^2$ |

lower bound $f^*_{SDP} \leq f^*_{MLE}$ for problem (1)'s optimal value. This lower bound provides an *upper* bound on the suboptimality of *any* feasible point $R \in SO(d)^n$ as a solution of problem (1) according to:

$$f(\bar{L}R^\mathsf{T}R) - f^*_{SDP} \geq f(\bar{L}R^\mathsf{T}R) - f^*_{MLE}. \tag{29}$$

Furthermore, if the relaxation (16) is exact, the estimate $\hat{R}$ returned by Algorithm 2 *attains* this lower bound:

$$f(\bar{L}\hat{R}^\mathsf{T}\hat{R}) = f^*_{SDP}. \tag{30}$$

Consequently, verifying *a posteriori* that (30) holds provides a *certificate* of $\hat{R}$'s *global* optimality as a solution of the rotation averaging problem (1).

## 5   Experimental Results

In this section we evaluate Shonan Averaging's performance on (a) several large-scale problems derived from standard pose-graph SLAM benchmarks, (b) small randomly generated synthetic datasets, and (c) several structure from motion (SFM) datasets used in earlier work. The experiments were performed on a desktop computer with a 6-core Intel i5-9600K CPU @ 3.70 GHz running Ubuntu 18.04. Our implementation of Shonan Averaging (SA) is written in C++, using the GTSAM library [12] to perform the local optimization. The fast minimum-eigenvalue computation described in [26, Sect. III-C] is implemented using the symmetric Lanczos algorithm from the Spectra library[2] to compute the minimum eigenvalue required in line 5. We initialize the algorithm with a randomly-sampled point $Q \in SO(p)^n$ at level $p = 5$, and require that the minimum eigenvalue satisfy $\lambda_{min} \geq -10^{-4}$ at termination of the Riemannian Staircase.

The results for the pose-graph SLAM benchmarks demonstrate that Shonan Averaging is already capable of recovering *certifiably globally optimal* solutions of large-scale real-world rotation averaging problems in tractable time. For these experiments, we have extracted the rotation averaging problem (1) obtained by simply ignoring the translational parts of the measurements. Table 1 reports

---

[2] https://Spectralib.org/.

**Table 2.** Synthetic results for varying problem sizes $n$ and noise levels $\sigma$. SA = Shonan, BD = block coordinate descent from [13], LM = Levenberg-Marquardt.

| n, $\sigma$ | Method | Error | Time (s) | Success |
|---|---|---|---|---|
| n = 20 $\sigma$ = 0.2 | SA | 0.000% | 0.030 | 100% |
|  | BD | 1.397% | 0.374 | 60% |
|  | LM | −0.001% | 0.003 | 80% |
| n = 20 $\sigma$ = 0.5 | SA | 0.000% | 0.037 | 100% |
|  | BD | 0.014% | 0.446 | 40% |
|  | LM | −0.001% | 0.004 | 20% |
| n = 50 $\sigma$ = 0.2 | SA | 0.000% | 0.141 | 100% |
|  | BD | 0.291% | 6.261 | 60% |
|  | LM | −0.039% | 0.011 | 20% |
| n = 50 $\sigma$ = 0.5 | SA | 0.000% | 0.194 | 100% |
|  | BD | −7.472% | 6.823 | 60% |
|  | LM | −0.008% | 0.014 | 40% |
| n = 100 $\sigma$ = 0.2 | SA | 0.000% | 0.403 | 100% |
|  | BD | nan% | nan | 0% |
|  | LM | −0.014% | 0.016 | 20% |
| n = 100 $\sigma$ = 0.5 | SA | 0.000% | 0.373 | 100% |
|  | BD | 3.912% | 32.982 | 20% |
|  | LM | −0.142% | 0.023 | 60% |
| n = 200 $\sigma$ = 0.2 | SA | 0.000% | 1.275 | 100% |
|  | BD | nan% | nan | 0% |
|  | LM | −0.102% | 0.049 | 60% |
| n = 200 $\sigma$ = 0.5 | SA | 0.000% | 1.845 | 100% |
|  | BD | nan% | nan | 0% |
|  | LM | −0.293% | 0.046 | 40% |

the size of each problem (the number of unknown rotations $n$ and relative measurements $m$), together with the relaxation rank $p$ at the terminal level of the Riemannian Staircase, the optimal value of the semidefinite relaxation (16) corresponding to the recovered low-rank factor $S^\star$, and the total elapsed computation times for the local optimizations in line 3 and minimum-eigenvalue computations in line 5 of Algorithm 2, respectively. We remark that the datasets torus in Table 1 is *1–2 orders of magnitude larger* than the examples reported in previous work on direct globally-optimal rotation averaging algorithms [13,16].

We attribute Shonan Averaging's improved scalability to its use of superlinear *local* optimization in conjunction with the Riemanian Staircase; in effect, this strategy provides a means of "upgrading" a fast *local* method to a fast *global* one. This enables Shonan Averaging to leverage existing heavily-optimized, scalable,

Table 3. Results on SFM problems from the YFCC dataset.

| Dataset | Method | Error | Time | Success |
|---------|--------|-------|------|---------|
| reichstag (n = 71, m = 2554) | SA | 0.000% | 0.197 | 100% |
| | BD | 0.000% | 0.247 | 100% |
| | LM | 0.001% | 0.085 | 80% |
| pantheon_interior (n = 186, m = 10000) | SA | 0.000% | 0.971 | 100% |
| | BD | 0.000% | 1.823 | 100% |
| | LM | 0.001% | 0.313 | 100% |

and high-performance software libraries for superlinear *local* optimization [2,12, 22] as the main computational engine of the algorithm (cf. line 3 of Algorithm 2), while preserving the guarantee of *global* optimality.

The synthetic results confirm that Shonan Averaging always converges to the true (*global*) minimizer, and significantly outperforms the block coordinate descent method from [13,14] as soon as the number of unknown rotations becomes large. We followed the approach for generating the data from [13], generating 4 sets of problem instances of increasing size, for two different noise levels. We generated 3D poses on a circular trajectory, forming a cycle graph. Relative rotation measurements were corrupted by composing with a random axis-angle perturbation, where the axis was chosen randomly and the angle was generated from a normal distribution with a standard deviation $\sigma = 0.2$ or $\sigma = 0.5$. Initialization for all three algorithms was done randomly, with angles uniform random over the range $(-\pi, \pi)$. We compare our results with two baselines: (LM) Levenberg-Marquardt on the $SO(3)^n$ manifold, also implemented in GTSAM, which is fast but not expected to find the global minimizer; (BD): the block coordinate descent method from [13,14]. Because no implementation was available, we re-implemented it in Python, using a $3 \times 3$ SVD decomposition at the core. However, our implementation differs in that we establish optimality using the eigenvalue certificate from Shonan.

The synthetic results are shown in Table 2. In the table we show the percentage of the cases in which either method found a global minimizer, either as certified by the minimum eigenvalue $\lambda_{\min} \geq -10^{-4}$, or being within 5% of the optimal cost. Shonan Averaging ("SA" in the table) finds an optimal solution every time as certified by $\lambda_{\min}$. Levenberg-Marquardt is fast but finds global minima in only about 40% to 60% of the cases. Finally, the block coordinate descent method (BD) is substantially slower, and does not always converge within the allotted time. We found that in practice BD converges very slowly and it takes a long time for the algorithm to converge to the same value as found by SA or LM. In the table we have shown the relative error and running time (in seconds), both averaged over 5 runs. For $n = 100$ and $n = 200$ the BD method did often not converge to the global optimum within reasonable time.

Finally, Table 3 shows results on two datasets derived by Heinly et al. [21] from the large-scale YFCC-100M dataset [21,33]. The relative measurements for these were derived from the SFM solution provided with the data, and corrupted with noise as before, using $\sigma = 0.2$. All three methods agree on the globally optimal solution, and the timing data shows the same trend as in Table 2.

# 6 Conclusion

In this work we presented Shonan Rotation Averaging, a fast, simple, and elegant algorithm for rotation averaging that is *guaranteed* to recover globally optimal solutions under mild conditions on the measurement noise. Our approach applies a fast *local* search technique to a *sequence* of higher-dimensional lifts of the rotation averaging problem until a globally optimal solution is found. Shonan Averaging thus leverages the speed and scalability of existing high-performance *local* optimization methods already in common use, while enabling the recovery of *provably optimal* solutions.

# References

1. Absil, P.-A., Mahony, R., Sepulchre, R.: Optimization Algorithms on Matrix Manifolds. Princeton University Press, Princeton (2007)
2. Agarwal, S., Mierle, K.: Ceres Solver: Tutorial & Reference. Google Inc., Menlo Park (2012)
3. Agarwal, S., Snavely, N., Seitz, S.M., Szeliski, R.: Bundle adjustment in the large. In: Daniilidis, K., Maragos, P., Paragios, N. (eds.) ECCV 2010. LNCS, vol. 6312, pp. 29–42. Springer, Heidelberg (2010). https://doi.org/10.1007/978-3-642-15552-9_3
4. Boumal, N.: A Riemannian low-rank method for optimization over semidefinite matrices with block-diagonal constraints. arXiv preprint arXiv:1506.00575 (2015)
5. Boumal, N., Singer, A., Absil, P.A.: Cramer-Rao bounds for synchronization of rotations. Inf. Infer. **3**(1), 1–39 (2014)
6. Boumal, N., Singer, A., Absil, P.-A.: Robust estimation of rotations from relative measurements by maximum likelihood. In: 52nd IEEE Conference on Decision and Control, pp. 1156–1161. IEEE (2013)
7. Boumal, N., Voroninski, V., Bandeira, A.: The non-convex Burer-Monteiro approach works on smooth semidefinite programs. In: Advances in Neural Information Processing Systems (NIPS), pp. 2757–2765 (2016)
8. Burer, S., Monteiro, R.: A nonlinear programming algorithm for solving semidefinite programs via low-rank factorization. Math. Program. **95**(2), 329–357 (2003)
9. Carlone, L., Rosen, D.M., Calafiore, G.C., Leonard, J.J., Dellaert, F.: Lagrangian duality in 3D SLAM: verification techniques and optimal solutions. In: IEEE/RSJ International Conference on Intelligent Robots and Systems (IROS), pp. 125–132 (2015). (pdf) (code) (datasets: (web)) (supplemental material: (pdf))
10. Carlone, L., Tron, R., Daniilidis, K., Dellaert, F.: Initialization techniques for 3D SLAM: a survey on rotation estimation and its use in pose graph optimization. In: IEEE International Conference on Robotics and Automation (ICRA), pp. 4597–4604 (2015). (pdf) (code) (supplemental material: (pdf))
11. Cover, T.M., Thomas, J.A.: Elements of Information Theory. John Wiley & Sons, New York (1991)

12. Dellaert, F.: Factor graphs and GTSAM: a hands-on introduction. Technical report GT-RIM-CP&R-2012-002, Georgia Institute of Technology, September 2012
13. Eriksson, A., Olsson, C., Kahl, F., Chin, T.-J.: Rotation averaging and strong duality. In: IEEE Conference on Computer Vision and Pattern Recognition (CVPR) (2018)
14. Eriksson, A., Olsson, C., Kahl, F., Chin, T.-J.: Rotation averagingwith the chordal distance: global minimizers and strong duality. IEEE Trans. Pattern Anal. Mach. Intell. (2019)
15. Frahm, J.-M., et al.: Building Rome on a cloudless day. In: Daniilidis, K., Maragos, P., Paragios, N. (eds.) ECCV 2010. LNCS, vol. 6314, pp. 368–381. Springer, Heidelberg (2010). https://doi.org/10.1007/978-3-642-15561-1_27
16. Fredriksson, J., Olsson, C.: Simultaneous multiple rotation averaging using Lagrangian duality. In: Lee, K.M., Matsushita, Y., Rehg, J.M., Hu, Z. (eds.) ACCV 2012. LNCS, vol. 7726, pp. 245–258. Springer, Heidelberg (2013). https://doi.org/10.1007/978-3-642-37431-9_19
17. Govindu, V.M.: Combining two-view constraints for motion estimation. In: Proceedings of the 2001 IEEE Computer Society Conference on Computer Vision and Pattern Recognition, CVPR 2001, vol. 2. IEEE (2001)
18. Hartley, R., Trumpf, J., Dai, Y., Li, H.: Rotation averaging. IJCV **103**(3), 267–305 (2013)
19. Hartley, R., Zisserman, A.: Multiple View Geometry in Computer Vision. Cambridge University Press, Cambridge (2000)
20. Heinly, J., Schonberger, J.L., Dunn, E., Frahm, J.-M.: Reconstructing the world* in six days*(as captured by the Yahoo 100 million image dataset). In: Proceedings of the IEEE Conference on Computer Vision and Pattern Recognition, pp. 3287–3295 (2015)
21. Heinly, J., Schonberger, J.L., Dunn, E., Frahm, J.-M.: Reconstructing the world* in six days *(as captured by the Yahoo 100 million image dataset). In: The IEEE Conference on Computer Vision and Pattern Recognition (CVPR), June 2015
22. Kümmerle, R., Grisetti, G., Strasdat, H., Konolige, K., Burgard, W.: G2O: a general framework for graph optimization. In: Proceedings of the IEEE International Conference on Robotics and Automation (ICRA), May 2011
23. Martinec, D., Pajdla, T.: Robust rotation and translation estimation in multiview reconstruction. In: IEEE Conference on Computer Vision and Pattern Recognition (CVPR), pp. 1–8 (2007)
24. Nocedal, J., Wright, S.J.: Numerical Optimization. Springer Series in Operations Research. Springer, Heidelberg (1999)
25. Pless, R.: Using many cameras as one. In: IEEE Conference on Computer Vision and Pattern Recognition (CVPR), vol. 2, pp. 587–593 (2003)
26. Rosen, D.M., Carlone, L.: Computational enhancements for certifiably correct SLAM. In: IEEE/RSJ International Conference on Intelligent Robots and Systems (IROS) (2017). Workshop on "Introspective Methods for Reliable Autonomy", (pdf)
27. Rosen, D.M., Carlone, L., Bandeira, A.S., Leonard, J.J.: SE-Sync: a certifiably correct algorithm for synchronization over the Special Euclidean group. In: International Workshop on the Algorithmic Foundations of Robotics (WAFR), San Francisco, CA, December 2016. (pdf), (pdf) (code), best paper award
28. Rosen, D.M., Carlone, L., Bandeira, A.S., Leonard, J.J.: SE-Sync: a certifiably correct algorithm for synchronization over the Special Euclidean group. Int. J. Robot. Res. (2018). Accepted, arxiv preprint: 1611.00128, (pdf)

308     F. Dellaert et al.

29. Schonberger, J.L., Frahm, J.-M.: Structure-from-motion revisited. In: Proceedings of the IEEE Conference on Computer Vision and Pattern Recognition, pp. 4104–4113 (2016)
30. Singer, A.: Angular synchronization by eigenvectors and semidefinite programming. Appl. Comput. Harmon. Anal. **30**, 20–36 (2010)
31. Singer, A., Wu, H.-T.: Vector diffusion maps and the connection Laplacian. Commun. Pure Appl. Math. **65**, 1067–1144 (2012)
32. Sturm, J.F.: Using SeDuMi 1.02, a MATLAB toolbox for optimization over symmetric cones. Optim. Softw. **11**(1–4), 625–653 (1999)
33. Thomee, B., et al.: YFCC100M: the new data in multimedia research. Commun. ACM **59**(2), 64–73 (2016)
34. Triggs, B., McLauchlan, P.F., Hartley, R.I., Fitzgibbon, A.W.: Bundle adjustment—a modern synthesis. In: Triggs, B., Zisserman, A., Szeliski, R. (eds.) IWVA 1999. LNCS, vol. 1883, pp. 298–372. Springer, Heidelberg (2000). https://doi.org/10.1007/3-540-44480-7_21
35. Tron, R., Vidal, R., Terzis, A.: Distributed pose averaging in camera networks via consensus on SE(3). In: 2008 Second ACM/IEEE International Conference on Distributed Smart Cameras, pp. 1–10. IEEE (2008)
36. Umeyama, S.: Least-squares estimation of transformation parameters between two point patterns. IEEE Trans. Pattern Anal. Mach. Intell. **13**(4), 376–380 (1991)
37. Vandenberghe, L., Boyd, S.: Semidefinite programming. SIAM Rev. **38**(1), 49–95 (1996)
38. Wilson, K., Bindel, D., Snavely, N.: When is rotations averaging hard? In: Leibe, B., Matas, J., Sebe, N., Welling, M. (eds.) ECCV 2016. LNCS, vol. 9911, pp. 255–270. Springer, Cham (2016). https://doi.org/10.1007/978-3-319-46478-7_16

# Semantic Curiosity for Active Visual Learning

Devendra Singh Chaplot[1]([⊠]), Helen Jiang[1], Saurabh Gupta[2],
and Abhinav Gupta[1]

[1] Carnegie Mellon University, Pittsburgh, USA
{chaplot,helenjia,abhinavg}@cs.cmu.edu
[2] UIUC, Champaign, USA
saurabhg@illinois.edu

**Abstract.** In this paper, we study the task of embodied interactive learning for object detection. Given a set of environments (and some labeling budget), our goal is to learn an object detector by having an agent select what data to obtain labels for. How should an exploration policy decide which trajectory should be labeled? One possibility is to use a trained object detector's failure cases as an external reward. However, this will require labeling millions of frames required for training RL policies, which is infeasible. Instead, we explore a self-supervised approach for training our exploration policy by introducing a notion of semantic curiosity. Our semantic curiosity policy is based on a simple observation – the detection outputs should be consistent. Therefore, our semantic curiosity rewards trajectories with inconsistent labeling behavior and encourages the exploration policy to explore such areas. The exploration policy trained via semantic curiosity generalizes to novel scenes and helps train an object detector that outperforms baselines trained with other possible alternatives such as random exploration, prediction-error curiosity, and coverage-maximizing exploration.

**Keywords:** Embodied learning · Active visual learning · Semantic curiosity · Exploration

## 1 Introduction

Imagine an agent whose goal is to learn how to detect and categorize objects. How should the agent learn this task? In the case of humans (especially babies), learning is quite interactive in nature. We have the knowledge of what we know

---

D. S. Chaplot and H. Jiang—Equal Contribution.
Webpage: https://devendrachaplot.github.io/projects/SemanticCuriosity.

---

**Electronic supplementary material** The online version of this chapter (https://doi.org/10.1007/978-3-030-58539-6_19) contains supplementary material, which is available to authorized users.

A. Vedaldi et al. (Eds.): ECCV 2020, LNCS 12351, pp. 309–326, 2020.
https://doi.org/10.1007/978-3-030-58539-6_19

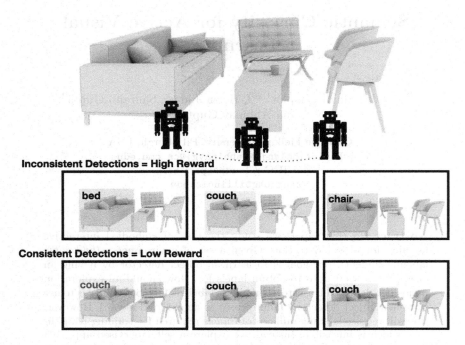

**Fig. 1. Semantic Curiosity:** We propose semantic curiosity to learn exploration for training object detectors. Our semantically curious policy attempts to take actions such that the object detector will produce inconsistent outputs.

and what we don't, and we use that knowledge to guide our future experiences/supervision. Compare this to how current algorithms learn – we create datasets of random images from the internet and label them, followed by model learning. The model has no control over what data and what supervision it gets – it is resigned to the static biased dataset of internet images. Why does current learning look quite different from how humans learn? During the early 2000s, as data-driven approaches started to gain acceptance, the computer vision community struggled with comparisons and knowing which approaches work and which don't. As a consequence, the community introduced several benchmarks from BSDS [34] to VOC [18]. However, a negative side effect of these benchmarks was the use of static training and test datasets. While the pioneering works in computer vision focused on active vision and interactive learning, most of the work in the last two decades focuses on static internet vision. But as things start to work on the model side, we believe it is critical to look at the big picture again and return our focus to an embodied and interactive learning setup (Fig. 1).

In an embodied interactive learning setup, an agent has to perform actions such that observations generated from these actions can be useful for learning to perform the semantic task. Several core research questions need to be answered: (a) what is the policy of exploration that generates these observations? (b) what should be labeled in these observations - one object, one frame, or the whole trajectory? (c) and finally, how do we get these labels? In this paper, we focus on the first task – what should the exploration policy be to generate observations which can be useful in training an object detector? Instead of using labels, we focus on learning these trajectories in an unsupervised/self-supervised manner. Once the policy has been learned, we use the policy in novel (previously unseen) scenes to perform actions. As observations are generated, we assume that an oracle will densely label all the objects of interest in the trajectories.

So what are the characteristics of a good exploration policy for visual learning, and how do we learn it? A good semantic exploration policy is one which generates observations of objects and not free-space or the wall/ceiling. But not only should the observations be objects, but a good exploration policy should also observe many unique objects. Finally, a good exploration policy will move to parts of the observation space where the current object detection model fails or does not work. Given these characteristics, how should we define a reward function that could be used to learn this exploration policy? Note, as one of the primary requirements, we assume the policy is learned in a self-supervised manner – that is, we do not have ground-truth objects labeled which can help us figure out where the detections work or fail.

Inspired by recent work in intrinsic motivation and curiosity for training policies without external rewards [37,38], we propose a new intrinsic reward called semantic curiosity that can be used for the exploration and training of semantic object detectors. In the standard curiosity reward, a policy is rewarded if the predicted future observation does not match the true future observation. The loss is generally formulated in the pixel-based feature space. A corresponding reward function for semantic exploration would be to compare semantic predictions with the current model and then confirm with ground-truth labels – however, this requires external labels (and hence is not self-supervised anymore). Instead, we formulate semantic curiosity based on the meta-supervisory signal of consistency in semantic prediction – that is, if our model truly understands the object, it should predict the same label for the object even as we move around and change viewpoints. Therefore, we exploit consistency in label prediction to reward our policies. Our semantic curiosity rewards trajectories which lead to inconsistent labeling behavior of the same object by the semantic classifier. Our experiments indicate that training an exploration policy via semantic curiosity generalizes to novel scenes and helps train an object detector which outperforms baselines trained with other possible alternatives such as random exploration, pixel curiosity, and free space/map curiosity. We also perform a large set of experiments to understand the behavior of a policy trained with semantic curiosity.

## 2   Related Work

We study the problem of how to sample training data in embodied contexts. This is related to active learning (picking what sample to label), active perception (how to move around to gain more information), intrinsic motivation (picking what parts of the environment to explore). Learning in embodied contexts can also leverage spatio-temporal consistency. We survey these research areas below.

**Active Perception.** Active perception [5] refers to the problem of actively moving the sensors around at *test time* to improve performance on the task by gaining more information about the environment. This has been instantiated in the context of object detection [1], amodal object detection [56], scene completion [29], and localization [11,22]. We consider the problem in a different setting and study how to efficiently move around to best *learn* a model. Furthermore, our approach to learn this movement policy is self-supervised and does not rely on end-task rewards, which were used in [11,29,56].

**Active Learning.** Our problem is more related to that of active learning [45], where an agent actively acquires labels for unlabeled data to improve its model at the fastest rate [24,44,57]. This has been used in a number of applications such as medical image analysis [30], training object detectors [50,55], video segmentation [21], and visual question answering [36]. Most works tackle the setting in which the unlabeled data has already been collected. In contrast, we study learning a policy for efficiently acquiring effective unlabeled data, which is complementary to such active learning efforts.

**Intrinsic Rewards.** Our work is also related to work on exploration in reinforcement learning [3,28,42,48]. The goal of these works is to effectively explore a Markov Decision Process to find high reward paths. A number of works formulate this as a problem of maximizing an intrinsic reward function which is designed to incentivize the agent to seek previously unseen [19] or poorly understood [37] parts of the environment. This is similar to our work, as we also seek poorly understood parts of the environment. However, we measure this understanding via multi-view consistency in semantics. This is in a departure from existing works that measure it in 2D image space [37], or consistency among multiple models [38]. Furthermore, our focus is not effective exhaustive exploration, but exploration for the purpose of improving semantic models.

**Spatio-Temporal Smoothing at Test Time.** A number of papers use spatio-temporal consistency at test time for better and more consistent predictions [7, 23]. Much like the distinction from active perception, our focus is using it to generate better data at train time.

**Spatio-Temporal Consistency as Training Signal.** Labels have been propagated in videos to simplify annotations [51], improve prediction performance given limited data [4,6], as well as collect images [15]. This line of work leverages spatio-temporal consistency to propagate labels for more efficient labeling. Researchers have also used multi-view consistency to learn about 3D shape from weak supervision [49]. We instead leverage spatio-temporal consistency as a cue to identify what the model does not know. [46] is more directly related, but we tackle the problem in an embodied context and study how to navigate to gather the data, rather than analyzing passive datasets for what labels to acquire.

**Visual Navigation and Exploration.** Prior work on visual navigation can broadly be categorized into two classes based on whether the location of the goal is known or unknown. Navigation scenarios, where the location of the goal is known, include the most common *pointgoal* task where the coordinate to the goal is given [26,40]. Another example of a task in this category is vision and language navigation [2] where the path to the goal is described in natural language. Tasks in this category do not require exhaustive exploration of the environment as the location of the goal is known explicitly (coordinates) or implicitly (path).

Navigation scenarios, where the location of the goal is not known, include a wide variety of tasks. These include navigating to a fixed set of objects [10, 17,26,31,35,53], navigating to an object specified by language [13,27] or by an image [12,58], and navigating to a set of objects in order to answer a question [16, 25]. Tasks in this second category essentially involve efficiently and exhaustively exploring the environment to search the desired object. However, most of the above approaches overlook the exploration problem by spawning the target a few steps away from the goal and instead focus on other challenges. For example, models for playing FPS games [10,17,31,53] show that end-to-end RL policies are effective at reactive navigation and short-term planning such as avoiding obstacles and picking positive reward objects as they randomly appear in the environment. Other works show that learned policies are effective at tackling challenges such as perception (in recognizing the visual goal) [12,58], grounding (in understanding the goal described by language) [13,27] or reasoning (about visual properties of the target object) [16,25]. While end-to-end reinforcement learning is shown to be effective in addressing these challenges, they are ineffective at exhaustive exploration and long-term planning in a large environment as the exploration search space increases exponentially as the distance to the goal increases.

Some very recent works explicitly tackle the problem of exploration by training end-to-end RL policies maximizing the explored area [9,14,20]. The difference between these approaches and our method is twofold: first, we train semantically-aware exploration policies as compared spatial coverage maximization in some prior works [9,14], and second, we train our policy in an unsupervised fashion, without requiring any ground truth labels from the simulator as compared to prior works trained using rewards based on ground-truth labels [20].

## 3 Overview

Our goal is to learn an exploration policy such that if we use this policy to generate trajectories in a novel scene (and hence observations) and train the object detector from the trajectory data, it would provide a robust, high-performance detector. In literature, most approaches use on-policy exploration; that is, they use the external reward to train the policy itself. However, training an action policy to sample training data for object recognition requires labeling objects. Specifically, these approaches would use the current detector to predict objects and compare them to the ground-truth; they reward the policy if the predictions do not match the ground-truth (the policy is being rewarded to explore regions where the current object detection model fails). However, training such a policy via semantic supervision and external rewards would have a huge bottleneck of supervision. Given that our RL policies require millions of samples (in our case, we train using 10M samples), using ground-truth supervision is clearly not the

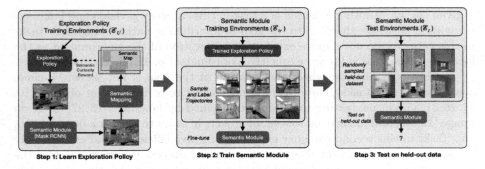

**Fig. 2. Embodied Active Visual Learning:** We use semantic curiosity to learn an exploration policy on $\mathcal{E}_U$ scenes. The exploration policy is learned by projecting segmentation masks on the top-down view to create semantic maps. The entropy of semantic map defines the inconsistency of the object detection module. The learned exploration policy is then used to generate training data for the object detection/segmentation module. The labeled data is then used to finetune and evaluate the object detection/segmentation.

way. What we need is an intrinsic motivation reward that can help train a policy which can help sample training data for object detectors.

We propose a semantic curiosity formulation. Our work is inspired by a plethora of efforts in active learning [45] and recent work on intrinsic reward using disagreement [38]. The core idea is simple – a good object detector has not only high mAP performance but is also consistent in predictions. That is, the detector should predict the same label for different views of the same object. We use this meta-signal of consistency to train our action policy by rewarding trajectories that expose inconsistencies in an object detector. We measure inconsistencies by measuring temporal entropy of prediction – that is, if an object is labeled with different classes as the viewpoint changes, it will have high temporal entropy. The trajectories with high temporal entropy are then labeled via an oracle and used as the data to retrain the object detector (See Fig. 2).

## 4    Methodology

Consider an agent $\mathcal{A}$ which can perform actions in environments $\mathcal{E}$. The agent has an exploration policy $a_t = \pi(x_t, \theta)$ that predicts the action that the agent must take for current observation $x_t$. $\theta$ represents the parameters of the policy that have to be learned. The agent also has an object detection model $\mathcal{O}$ which takes as input an image (the current observation) and generates a set of bounding boxes along with their categories and confidence scores.

The goal is to learn an exploration policy $\pi$, which is used to sample $N$ trajectories $\tau_1...\tau_N$ in a set of novel environments (and get them semantically labeled). When used to train an object detector, this labeled data would yield a high-performance object detector. In our setup, we divide the environments into

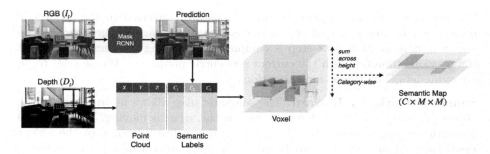

**Fig. 3. Semantic Mapping.** The Semantic Mapping module takes in a sequence of RGB ($I_t$) and Depth ($D_t$) images and produces a top-down Semantic Map.

three non-overlapping sets ($\mathcal{E}_U, \mathcal{E}_{tr}, \mathcal{E}_t$) – the first set is the set of environments where the agent will learn the exploration policy $\pi$, the second set is the object detection training environments where we use $\pi$ to sample trajectories and label them, and the third set is the test environment where we sample random images and test the performance of the object detector on those images.

### 4.1 Semantic Curiosity Policy

We define semantic curiosity as the temporal inconsistency in object detection and segmentation predictions from the current model. We use a Mask RCNN to obtain the object predictions. In order to associate the predictions across frames in a trajectory, we use a semantic mapping module as described below.

**Semantic Mapping.** The Semantic Mapping module takes in a sequence of RGB ($I_t$) and Depth ($D_t$) images and produces a top-down semantic map ($M_t^{Sem}$) represented by a 3-dimensional tensor $C \times M \times M$, where $M$ is the length of the square top-down map, and $C$ is the number of semantic categories. Each element $(c, i, j)$ in this semantic map is 1 if the Mask RCNN predicted the object category $c$ at coordinates $(i, j)$ on the map in any frame during the whole trajectory and 0 otherwise. Figure 3 shows how the semantic map is generated for a single frame. The input RGB frame ($I_t$) is passed through a current Mask RCNN to obtain object segmentation predictions, while the Depth frame is used to calculate the point cloud. Each point in the point cloud is associated with its semantic labels based on Mask RCNN predictions. Note that these are not ground-truth labels, as each pixel is assigned the category of the highest-confidence Mask RCNN segmentation prediction on the corresponding pixel. The point cloud with the associated semantic labels is projected to a 3-dimensional voxel map using geometric computations. The voxel representation is converted to a top-down map by max-pooling the values across the height. The resulting 2D map is converted to a 3-dimensional Semantic Map, such that each channel represents an object category.

The above gives a first-person egocentric projection of the semantic map at each time-step. The egocentric projections at each time step are used to compute a geocentric map over time using a spatial transformation technique similar to

Chaplot et al. [9]. The egocentric projections are converted to the geocentric projections by doing a spatial transformation based on the agent pose. The semantic map at each time step is computed by pooling the semantic map at the previous timestep with the current geocentric prediction. Please refer to [9] for more details on these transformations.

**Semantic Curiosity Reward.** The semantic map allows us to associate the object predictions across different frames as the agent is moving. We define the semantic curiosity reward based on the temporal inconsistency of the object predictions. If an object is predicted to have different labels across different frames, multiple channels in the semantic map at the coordinates corresponding to the object will have 1s. Such inconsistencies are beneficial for visual learning in downstream tasks, and hence, favorable for the semantic curiosity policy. Thus, we define the cumulative semantic curiosity reward to be proportional to the sum of all the elements in the semantic map. Consequently, the semantic curiosity reward per step is just the increase in the sum of all elements in the semantic map as compared to the previous time step:

$$r_{SC} = \lambda_{SC} \Sigma_{(c,i,j) \in (C,M,M)} (M_t^{Sem}[c,i,j] - M_{t-1}^{Sem}[c,i,j])$$

where $\lambda_{SC}$ is the semantic curiosity reward coefficient. Summation over the channels encourages exploring frames with temporally inconsistent predictions. Summation across the coordinates encourages exploring as many objects with temporally inconsistent predictions as possible.

The proposed Semantic Curiosity Policy is trained using reinforcement learning to maximize the cumulative semantic curiosity reward. Note that although the depth image and agent pose are used to compute the semantic reward, we train the policy only on RGB images.

## 5   Experimental Setup

We use the Habitat simulator [41] with three different datasets for our experiments: Gibson [54], Matterport [8] and Replica [47]. While the RGB images used in our experiments are visually realistic as they are based on real-world reconstructions, we note that the agent pose and depth images in the simulator are noise-free unlike the real-world. Prior work has shown that both depth and agent pose can be estimated effectively from RGB images under noisy odometry [9]. In this paper, we assume access to perfect agent pose and depth images, as these challenges are orthogonal to the focus of this paper. Furthermore, these assumptions are only required in the unsupervised pre-training phase for calculating the semantic curiosity reward and not at inference time when our trained semantic-curiosity policy (based only on RGB images) is used to gather exploration trajectories for training the object detector.

In a perfectly interactive learning setup, the current model's uncertainty will be used to sample a trajectory in a new scene, followed by labeling and updating the learned visual model (Mask-RCNN). However, due to the complexity of this online training mechanism, we show results on batch training. We use a pre-trained COCO Mask-RCNN as an initial model and train the exploration policy on that model. Once the exploration policy is trained, we collect trajectories in the training environments and then obtain the labels on these trajectories. The labeled examples are then used to fine-tune the Mask-RCNN detector.

## 5.1 Implementation Details

**Exploration Policy:** We train our semantic curiosity policy on the Gibson dataset and test it on the Matterport and Replica datasets. We train the policy on the set of 72 training scenes in the Gibson dataset specified by Savva et al. [41]. Our policy is trained with reinforcement learning using Proximal Policy Optimization [43]. The policy architecture consists of convolutional layers of a pre-trained ResNet18 visual encoder, followed by two fully connected layers and a GRU layer leading to action distribution as well as value prediction. We use 72 parallel threads (one for each scene) with a time horizon on 100 steps and 36 mini batches per PPO epoch. The curiosity reward coefficient is set to $\lambda_{SC} = 2.5 \times 10^{-3}$. We use an entropy coefficient of 0.001, the value loss coefficient of 0.5. We use Adam optimizer with a learning rate of $1 \times 10^{-5}$. The maximum episode length during training is 500 steps.

**Fine-tuned Object Detector:** We consider 5 classes of objects, chosen because they overlap with the COCO dataset [33] and correspond to objects commonly seen in an indoor scene: chair, bed, toilet, couch, and potted plant. To start, we pre-train a Faster-RCNN model [39] with FPN [32] using ResNet-50 as the backbone on the COCO dataset labeled with these 5 overlapping categories. We then fine-tuned our models on the trajectories collected by the exploration policies for 90000 iterations using a batch size of 12 and a learning rate of 0.001, with annealing by a factor of 0.1 at iterations 60000 and 80000. We use the Detectron2 codebase [52] and set all other hyperparameters to their defaults in this codebase. We compute the AP50 score (i.e., average precision using an IoU threshold of 50) on the validation set every 5000 iterations.

## 5.2 Baselines

We use a range of baselines to gather exploration trajectories and compare them to the proposed Semantic Curiosity policy:

- **Random.** A baseline sampling actions randomly.
- **Prediction Error Curiosity.** This baseline is based on Pathak et al. [37], which trains an RL policy to maximize error in a forward prediction model.
- **Object Exploration.** Object Exploration is a naive baseline where an RL policy is trained to maximize the number of pre-trained Mask R-CNN detections. The limitation of simply maximizing the number of detections is that the policy can learn to look at frames with more objects but might not learn to look at different objects across frames or objects with low confidence.

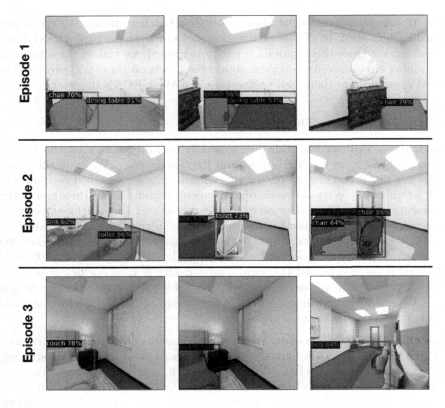

**Fig. 4. Temporal Inconsistency Examples.** Figure showing example trajectories sampled from the semantic curiosity exploration policy. We highlight the segmentation/detection inconsistencies of Mask RCNN. By obtaining labels for these images, the Mask RCNN pipeline improves the detection performance significantly.

- **Coverage Exploration.** This baseline is based on Chen et al. [14], where an RL policy is trained to maximize the total explored area.
- **Active Neural SLAM.** This baseline is based on Chaplot et al. [9] and uses a modular and hierarchical system to maximize the total explored area.

After training the proposed policy and the baselines in the Gibson domain, we use them directly (without fine-tuning) in the Matterport and Replica domains. We sample trajectories using each exploration policy, using the images and ground-truth labels to train an object detection model.

## 6   Analyzing Learned Exploration Behavior

Before we measure the quality of the learned exploration policy for the task of detection/segmentation, we first want to analyze the behavior of the learned policy. This will help characterize the quality of data that is gathered by the

**Table 1. Analysis.** Comparing the proposed Semantic Curiosity policy with the baselines along different exploration metrics.

| Method name | Semantic curiosity reward | Explored area | Number of object detections |
|---|---|---|---|
| Random | 1.631 | 4.794 | 82.83 |
| Curiosity [37] | 2.891 | 6.781 | 112.24 |
| Object exploration reward | 2.168 | 6.082 | 382.27 |
| Coverage Exploration [14] | 3.287 | 10.025 | 203.73 |
| Active Neural SLAM [9] | 3.589 | 11.527 | 231.86 |
| Semantic Curiosity | 4.378 | 9.726 | 291.78 |

**Table 2. Quality of object detection on training trajectories.** We also analyze the training trajectories in terms of how well the pre-trained object detection model works on the trajectories. We want the exploration policy to sample hard data where the pre-trained object detector fails. Data on which the pre-trained model already works well would not be useful for fine-tuning. Thus, lower performance is better.

| Method name | Chair | Bed | Toilet | Couch | Potted plant | Average |
|---|---|---|---|---|---|---|
| Random | 46.7 | 28.2 | 46.9 | 60.3 | 39.1 | 44.24 |
| Curiosity [37] | 49.4 | 18.3 | 1.8 | 67.7 | 49.0 | 37.42 |
| Object Exploration | 54.3 | 24.8 | 5.7 | 76.6 | 49.6 | 42.2 |
| Coverage Exploration [14] | 48.5 | 23.1 | 69.2 | 66.3 | 48.0 | 51.02 |
| Active Neural SLAM [9] | 51.3 | 20.5 | 49.4 | 59.7 | 45.6 | 45.3 |
| Semantic Curiosity | 51.6 | 14.6 | 14.2 | 65.2 | 50.4 | 39.2 |

exploration policy. We will compare the learned exploration policy against the baselines described above. For all the experiments below, we trained our policy on Gibson scenes and collected statistics in 11 Replica scenes.

Figure 4 shows some examples of temporal inconsistencies in trajectories sampled using the semantic curiosity exploration policy. The pre-trained Mask-RCNN detections are also shown in the observation images. Semantic curiosity prefers trajectories with inconsistent detections. In the top row, the chair and couch detector fire on the same object. In the middle row, the chair is misclassified as a toilet and there is inconsistent labeling in the last trajectory. The bed is misclassified as a couch. By selecting these trajectories and obtaining their labels from an oracle, our approach learns to improve the object detection module.

Table 1 shows the behavior of all of the policies on three different metrics. The first metric is the semantic curiosity reward itself which measures uncertain detections in the trajectory data. Since our policy is trained for this reward, it gets the highest score on the sampled trajectories. The second metric is the amount of explored area. Both [14] and [9] optimize this metric and hence perform the best (they cover a lot of area but most of these areas will either not have objects or not enough contradictory overlapping detections). The third metric is the number of objects in the trajectories. The object exploration baseline optimizes for this reward and hence performs the best but it does so without exploring diverse areas or uncertain detections/segmentations. If we look at the three metrics together it

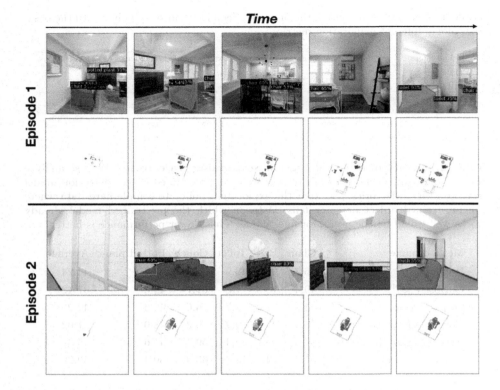

**Fig. 5. Example trajectories.** Figure showing example trajectories sampled from the semantic curiosity exploration policy. In each episode the top row shows the first-person images seen by the agent and the pre-trained Mask R-CNN predictions. The bottom rows show a visualization of the semantic map where colors denote different object categories. Different colors for the same object indicate that the same object is predicted to have different categories from different view points. (Color figure online)

is clear that our policy has the right tradeoff – it explores a lot of area but still focuses on areas where objects can be detected. Not only does it find a large number of object detections, but our policy also prefers inconsistent object detections and segmentations. In Fig. 5, we show some examples of trajectories seen by the semantic curiosity exploration along with the semantic map. It shows examples of the same object having different object predictions from different viewpoints and also the representation in the semantic map. In Figure 6, we show a qualitative comparison of maps and objects explored by the proposed model and all the baselines. Example trajectories in this figure indicate that the semantic curiosity policy explores more unique objects with higher temporal inconsistencies.

Next, we analyze the trajectories created by different exploration policies during the object detection training stage. Specifically, we want to analyze the kind of data that is sampled by these trajectories. How is the performance of a pre-trained detector on this data? If the pre-trained detector already works well

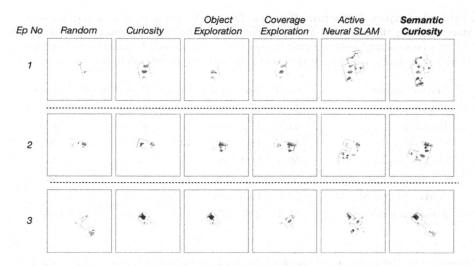

**Fig. 6. Qualitative Comparison.** Figure showing map and objects explored by the proposed Semantic Curiosity policy and the baselines in 3 example episodes. Semantic Curiosity Policy explores more unique objects with higher temporal inconsistency (denoted by different colors for the same object).

on the sampled trajectories, we would not see much improvement in performance by fine-tuning with this data. In Table 2, we show the results of this analysis for these trajectories. As the results indicate, the mAP50 score is low for the data obtained by the semantic curiosity policy.[1] As the pre-trained object detector fails more on the data sampled by semantic curiosity, labeling this data would intuitively improve the detection performance.

## 7   Actively Learned Object Detection

Finally, we evaluate the performance of our semantic curiosity policy for the task of object detection. The semantic curiosity exploration policy is trained on 72 Gibson scenes. The exploration policy is then used to sample data on 50 Matterport scenes. Finally, the learned object detector is tested on 11 Matterport scenes. For each training scene, we sample 5 trajectories of 300 timesteps leading to 75,000 total training images with ground-truth labels. For test scenes, we randomly sample images from test scenes.

In Table 3, we report the top AP50 scores for each method. Our results demonstrate that the proposed semantic curiosity policy obtains higher quality data for performing object detection tasks over alternative methods of exploration. First, we outperform the policy that tries to see maximum coverage area

---

[1] Note that curiosity-based policy has the lowest mAP because of outlier toilet category.

**Table 3. Object Detection Results.** Object detection results in the Matterport domain using the proposed Semantic Curiosity policy and the baselines. We report AP50 scores on randomly sampled images in the test scenes. Training on data gathered from the semantic curiosity trajectories results in improved object detection scores.

| Method name | Chair | Bed | Toilet | Couch | Potted plant | Average |
|---|---|---|---|---|---|---|
| PreTrained | 41.8 | 17.3 | 34.9 | 41.6 | 23.0 | 31.72 |
| Random | 51.7 | 17.2 | 43.0 | 45.1 | 30.0 | 37.4 |
| Curiosity [37] | 48.4 | 18.5 | 42.3 | 44.3 | 32.8 | 37.26 |
| Object Exploration | 50.3 | 16.4 | 40.0 | 39.7 | 29.9 | 35.26 |
| Coverage Exploration [14] | 50.0 | 19.1 | 38.1 | 42.1 | 33.5 | 36.56 |
| Active Neural SLAM [9] | 53.1 | 19.5 | 42.0 | 44.5 | 33.4 | 38.5 |
| Semantic Curiosity | 52.3 | 22.6 | 42.9 | 45.7 | 36.3 | **39.96** |

(and hence the most novel images). Second, our approach also outperforms the policy that detects a lot of objects. Finally, apart from outperforming the random policy, visual curiosity [37], and coverage; we also outperform the highly-tuned approach of [9]. The underlying algorithm is tuned on this data and was the winner of the RGB and RGBD challenge in Habitat.

## 8   Conclusion and Future Work

We argue that we should go from object detection and segmentation driven by static datasets to a more embodied active learning setting. In this setting, an agent can move in the scene and create its own datapoints. An oracle labels these datapoints and helps the agent learn a better semantic object detector. This setting is closer to how humans learn to detect and recognize objects. In this paper, we focus on the exploration policy for sampling images to be labeled. We ask a basic question – how should an autonomous agent explore to learn how to detect objects?

We propose semantic curiosity as a reward to train the exploration policy. Semantic curiosity encourages trajectories which will lead to inconsistent detection behavior from an object detector. Our experiments indicate that exploration driven by semantic curiosity shows all of the good characteristics of an exploration policy: uncertain/high entropy detections, attention to objects rather than the entire scene and also high coverage for diverse training data. We also show that an object detector trained on trajectories from a semantic curiosity policy leads to the best performance compared to a plethora of baselines. For future work, this paper is just the first step in embodied active visual learning. It assumes perfect odometry, localization and zero trajectory labeling costs. It also assumes that the trajectories will be labeled – a topic of interest would be to sample trajectories with which minimal labels can learn the best detector. Finally, the current approach is demonstrated in simulators - it will be interesting to see whether the performance can transfer to real-world robots.

**Acknowledgements.** This work was supported by IARPA DIVA D17PC00340, ONR MURI, ONR Grant N000141812861, ONR Young Investigator, DARPA MCS, and NSF Graduate Research Fellowship. We would also like to thank NVIDIA for GPU support.
**Licenses for referenced datasets:**
Gibson: http://svl.stanford.edu/gibson2/assets/GDS_agreement.pdf
Matterport3D: http://kaldir.vc.in.tum.de/matterport/MP_TOS.pdf
Replica: https://raw.githubusercontent.com/facebookresearch/Replica-Dataset/master/LICENSE.

# References

1. Ammirato, P., Poirson, P., Park, E., Košecká, J., Berg, A.C.: A dataset for developing and benchmarking active vision. In: 2017 IEEE International Conference on Robotics and Automation (ICRA). pp. 1378–1385. IEEE (2017)
2. Anderson, P., et al.: Vision-and-language navigation: interpreting visually-grounded navigation instructions in real environments. In: Proceedings of the IEEE Conference on Computer Vision and Pattern Recognition, pp. 3674–3683 (2018)
3. Auer, P.: Using confidence bounds for exploitation-exploration trade-offs. J. Mach. Learn. Res. 3(Nov), 397–422 (2002)
4. Badrinarayanan, V., Galasso, F., Cipolla, R.: Label propagation in video sequences. In: 2010 IEEE Computer Society Conference on Computer Vision and Pattern Recognition, pp. 3265–3272. IEEE (2010)
5. Bajcsy, R.: Active perception. Proc. IEEE **76**(8), 966–1005 (1988)
6. Bengio, Y., Delalleau, O., Le Roux, N.: Label propagation and quadratic criterion. In: Semi-Supervised Learning (2006)
7. Chandra, S., Couprie, C., Kokkinos, I.: Deep spatio-temporal random fields for efficient video segmentation. In: Proceedings of the IEEE Conference on Computer Vision and Pattern Recognition, pp. 8915–8924 (2018)
8. Chang, A., et al.: Matterport3D: learning from RGB-D data in indoor environments. International Conference on 3D Vision (3DV) (2017). http://kaldir.vc.in.tum.de/matterport/MP_TOS.pdf
9. Chaplot, D.S., Gandhi, D., Gupta, S., Gupta, A., Salakhutdinov, R.: Learning to explore using active neural SLAM. In: ICLR (2020). https://openreview.net/forum?id=HklXn1BKDH
10. Chaplot, D.S., Lample, G.: Arnold: an autonomous agent to play fps games. In: Thirty-First AAAI Conference on Artificial Intelligence (2017)
11. Chaplot, D.S., Parisotto, E., Salakhutdinov, R.: Active neural localization. In: International Conference on Learning Representations (2018). https://openreview.net/forum?id=ry6-G_66b
12. Chaplot, D.S., Salakhutdinov, R., Gupta, A., Gupta, S.: Neural topological SLAM for visual navigation. In: CVPR (2020)
13. Chaplot, D.S., Sathyendra, K.M., Pasumarthi, R.K., Rajagopal, D., Salakhutdinov, R.: Gated-attention architectures for task-oriented language grounding. In: Thirty-Second AAAI Conference on Artificial Intelligence (2018)
14. Chen, T., Gupta, S., Gupta, A.: Learning exploration policies for navigation. In: International Conference on Learning Representations (2019). https://openreview.net/forum?id=SyMWn05F7
15. Chen, X., Shrivastava, A., Gupta, A.: NEIL: extracting visual knowledge from web data. In: Proceedings of the IEEE International Conference on Computer Vision, pp. 1409–1416 (2013)

16. Das, A., Datta, S., Gkioxari, G., Lee, S., Parikh, D., Batra, D.: Embodied question answering. In: CVPR (2018)
17. Dosovitskiy, A., Koltun, V.: Learning to act by predicting the future. In: ICLR (2017)
18. Everingham, M., Van Gool, L., Williams, C.K.I., Winn, J., Zisserman, A.: The PASCAL Visual Object Classes Challenge 2007 (VOC2007) Results. http://www.pascal-network.org/challenges/VOC/voc2007/workshop/index.html
19. Eysenbach, B., Gupta, A., Ibarz, J., Levine, S.: Diversity is all you need: learning skills without a reward function. In: International Conference on Learning Representations (2019). https://openreview.net/forum?id=SJx63jRqFm
20. Fang, K., Toshev, A., Fei-Fei, L., Savarese, S.: Scene memory transformer for embodied agents in long-horizon tasks. In: CVPR (2019)
21. Fathi, A., Balcan, M.F., Ren, X., Rehg, J.M.: Combining self training and active learning for video segmentation. In: Proceedings of the British Machine Vision Conference, Georgia Institute of Technology (2011)
22. Fox, D., Burgard, W., Thrun, S.: Active Markov localization for mobile robots. Robot. Auton. Syst. 25(3–4), 195–207 (1998)
23. Gadde, R., Jampani, V., Gehler, P.V.: Semantic video CNNs through representation warping. In: Proceedings of the IEEE International Conference on Computer Vision, pp. 4453–4462 (2017)
24. Gal, Y., Islam, R., Ghahramani, Z.: Deep Bayesian active learning with image data. In: Proceedings of the 34th International Conference on Machine Learning, vol. 70, pp. 1183–1192. JMLR.org (2017)
25. Gordon, D., Kembhavi, A., Rastegari, M., Redmon, J., Fox, D., Farhadi, A.: IQA: visual question answering in interactive environments. In: Proceedings of the IEEE Conference on Computer Vision and Pattern Recognition, pp. 4089–4098 (2018)
26. Gupta, S., Davidson, J., Levine, S., Sukthankar, R., Malik, J.: Cognitive mapping and planning for visual navigation. In: Proceedings of the IEEE Conference on Computer Vision and Pattern Recognition, pp. 2616–2625 (2017)
27. Hermann, K.M., et al.: Grounded language learning in a simulated 3D world. arXiv preprint arXiv:1706.06551 (2017)
28. Jaksch, T., Ortner, R., Auer, P.: Near-optimal regret bounds for reinforcement learning. J. Mach. Learn. Res. 11(Apr), 1563–1600 (2010)
29. Jayaraman, D., Grauman, K.: Learning to look around: intelligently exploring unseen environments for unknown tasks. In: Proceedings of the IEEE Conference on Computer Vision and Pattern Recognition, pp. 1238–1247 (2018)
30. Kuo, W., Häne, C., Yuh, E., Mukherjee, P., Malik, J.: Cost-sensitive active learning for intracranial hemorrhage detection. In: Frangi, A.F., Schnabel, J.A., Davatzikos, C., Alberola-López, C., Fichtinger, G. (eds.) MICCAI 2018. LNCS, vol. 11072, pp. 715–723. Springer, Cham (2018). https://doi.org/10.1007/978-3-030-00931-1_82
31. Lample, G., Chaplot, D.S.: Playing FPS games with deep reinforcement learning. In: Thirty-First AAAI Conference on Artificial Intelligence (2017)
32. Lin, T.Y., Dollár, P., Girshick, R., He, K., Hariharan, B., Belongie, S.: Feature pyramid networks for object detection. In: Proceedings of the IEEE Conference on Computer Vision and Pattern Recognition, pp. 2117–2125 (2017)
33. Lin, T.-Y., et al.: Microsoft COCO: common objects in context. In: Fleet, D., Pajdla, T., Schiele, B., Tuytelaars, T. (eds.) ECCV 2014. LNCS, vol. 8693, pp. 740–755. Springer, Cham (2014). https://doi.org/10.1007/978-3-319-10602-1_48

34. Martin, D., Fowlkes, C., Tal, D., Malik, J.: A database of human segmented natural images and its application to evaluating segmentation algorithms and measuring ecological statistics. In: Proceedings of 8th International Conference on Computer Vision, vol. 2, pp. 416–423, July 2001
35. Mirowski, P., et al.: Learning to navigate in complex environments. ICLR (2017)
36. Misra, I., Girshick, R., Fergus, R., Hebert, M., Gupta, A., van der Maaten, L.: Learning by asking questions. In: CVPR (2018)
37. Pathak, D., Agrawal, P., Efros, A.A., Darrell, T.: Curiosity-driven exploration by self-supervised prediction. In: Proceedings of the IEEE Conference on Computer Vision and Pattern Recognition Workshops, pp. 16–17 (2017)
38. Pathak, D., Gandhi, D., Gupta, A.: Self-supervised exploration via disagreement. In: ICML (2019)
39. Ren, S., He, K., Girshick, R., Sun, J.: Faster R-CNN: towards real-time object detection with region proposal networks. In: Advances in Neural Information Processing Systems, pp. 91–99 (2015)
40. Savva, M., Chang, A.X., Dosovitskiy, A., Funkhouser, T., Koltun, V.: MINOS: multimodal indoor simulator for navigation in complex environments. arXiv:1712.03931 (2017)
41. Savva, M., et al.: Habitat: a platform for embodied AI research. In: ICCV (2019)
42. Schmidhuber, J.: A possibility for implementing curiosity and boredom in model-building neural controllers. In: Proceedings of the International Conference on Simulation of Adaptive Behavior: From Animals to Animats, pp. 222–227 (1991)
43. Schulman, J., Wolski, F., Dhariwal, P., Radford, A., Klimov, O.: Proximal policy optimization algorithms. arXiv preprint arXiv:1707.06347 (2017)
44. Sener, O., Savarese, S.: Active learning for convolutional neural networks: a coreset approach. In: International Conference on Learning Representations (2018). https://openreview.net/forum?id=H1aIuk-RW
45. Settles, B.: Active learning literature survey. Technical report, University of Wisconsin-Madison Department of Computer Sciences (2009)
46. Siddiqui, Y., Valentin, J., Nießner, M.: ViewAL: active learning with viewpoint entropy for semantic segmentation. In: Proceedings of the IEEE/CVF Conference on Computer Vision and Pattern Recognition, pp. 9433–9443 (2020)
47. Straub, J., et al.: The replica dataset: a digital replica of indoor spaces. arXiv preprint arXiv:1906.05797 (2019). https://github.com/facebookresearch/Replica-Dataset/blob/master/LICENSE
48. Sutton, R.S., Barto, A.G.: Reinforcement Learning: An Introduction. MIT Press (1998). http://www.cs.ualberta.ca/~sutton/book/the-book.html
49. Tulsiani, S., Zhou, T., Efros, A.A., Malik, J.: Multi-view supervision for single-view reconstruction via differentiable ray consistency. TPAMI (2019)
50. Vijayanarasimhan, S., Grauman, K.: Large-scale live active learning: training object detectors with crawled data and crowds. Int. J. Comput. Vis. **108**(1–2), 97–114 (2014)
51. Vondrick, C., Patterson, D., Ramanan, D.: Efficiently scaling up crowdsourced video annotation. Int. J. Comput. Vis. 1–21 (2013). http://dx.doi.org/10.1007/s11263-012-0564-1
52. Wu, Y., Kirillov, A., Massa, F., Lo, W.Y., Girshick, R.: Detectron2 (2019). https://github.com/facebookresearch/detectron2
53. Wu, Y., Tian, Y.: Training agent for first-person shooter game with actor-critic curriculum learning. In: ICLR (2017)

54. Xia, F., Zamir, A.R., He, Z.Y., Sax, A., Malik, J., Savarese, S.: Gibson Env: real-world perception for embodied agents. In: 2018 IEEE Conference on Computer Vision and Pattern Recognition (CVPR). IEEE (2018). http://svl.stanford.edu/gibson2/assets/GDS_agreement.pdf

55. Yang, J., Lu, J., Lee, S., Batra, D., Parikh, D.: Visual curiosity: learning to ask questions to learn visual recognition. In: Conference on Robot Learning, pp. 63–80 (2018)

56. Yang, J., et al.: Embodied amodal recognition: learning to move to perceive objects. In: Proceedings of the IEEE International Conference on Computer Vision, pp. 2040–2050 (2019)

57. Yoo, D., Kweon, I.S.: Learning loss for active learning. In: Proceedings of the IEEE Conference on Computer Vision and Pattern Recognition, pp. 93–102 (2019)

58. Zhu, Y., et al.: Target-driven visual navigation in indoor scenes using deep reinforcement learning. In: 2017 IEEE International Conference on Robotics and Automation (ICRA), pp. 3357–3364. IEEE (2017)

# Multi-Temporal Recurrent Neural Networks for Progressive Non-uniform Single Image Deblurring with Incremental Temporal Training

Dongwon Park⬛, Dong Un Kang⬛, Jisoo Kim⬛, and Se Young Chun$^{(\boxtimes)}$⬛

Department of Electrical Engineering, UNIST, Ulsan, Republic of Korea
{dong1,qkrtnskfk23,rlawltn1053,sychun}@unist.ac.kr

**Abstract.** Blind non-uniform image deblurring for severe blurs induced by large motions is still challenging. Multi-scale (MS) approach has been widely used for deblurring that sequentially recovers the downsampled original image in low spatial scale first and then further restores in high spatial scale using the result(s) from lower spatial scale(s). Here, we investigate a novel alternative approach to MS, called multi-temporal (MT), for non-uniform single image deblurring by exploiting time-resolved deblurring dataset from high-speed cameras. MT approach models severe blurs as a series of small blurs so that it deblurs small amount of blurs in the original spatial scale progressively instead of restoring the images in different spatial scales. To realize MT approach, we propose progressive deblurring over iterations and incremental temporal training with temporally augmented training data. Our MT approach, that can be seen as a form of curriculum learning in a wide sense, allows a number of state-of-the-art MS based deblurring methods to yield improved performances without using MS approach. We also proposed a MT recurrent neural network with recurrent feature maps that outperformed state-of-the-art deblurring methods with the smallest number of parameters.

## 1 Introduction

Non-uniform single image deblurring is still a challenging *ill-posed* inverse problem to recover the original sharp image from a blurred image with or without estimating unknown non-uniform blur kernels. One approach to tackle this problem is to simplify the given problem by assuming uniform blur and to recover both image and blur kernel [7,11,37,45]. However, uniform blur is not accurate

---

D. Park and D. U. Kang—Equal contribution. Code is available at https://github.com/Dong1P/MTRNN.

---

**Electronic supplementary material** The online version of this chapter (https://doi.org/10.1007/978-3-030-58539-6_20) contains supplementary material, which is available to authorized users.

© Springer Nature Switzerland AG 2020
A. Vedaldi et al. (Eds.): ECCV 2020, LNCS 12351, pp. 327–343, 2020.
https://doi.org/10.1007/978-3-030-58539-6_20

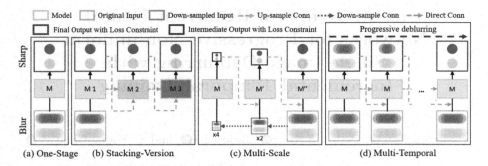

**Fig. 1.** Pipelines of four approaches for deblurring: (a) one-stage (OS) [2,23,24], (b) stacking version (SV) [32,47], (c) multi-scale (MS) [12,31,41] and (d) our proposed multi-temporal (MT). In SV, the models M1, M2, M3 are independent. In MS, the models M, M', M" used to be independent, but recent works used strongly dependent models with parameter sharing. Our MT uses the identical model M over all iterations.

enough to approximate real blur, and thus there has been much research to extend the blur model from uniform to non-uniform in a limited way compared to the full dense matrix [14–16,33,42,44]. Other non-uniform blur models have been investigated such as additional segmentations within which simple blur models were used [8,18] or motion estimation based deblurs [19,20]. Recently, deep-learning-based approaches have been proposed with excellent quantitative results and fast computation time. There are largely two different ways of using deep neural networks (DNNs) for deblurring. One is to use DNNs to explicitly estimate non-uniform blurs [4,6,36,40] and the other is to use DNNs to directly estimate the sharp image without estimating blurs [21,31,39,41,43,46].

Focusing on DNN based non-uniform single image deblurring, there are three different approaches as illustrated in Fig. 1: (a) one-stage (OS) attempts to recover the original image from blurred image in the original spatial scale [2,23,24] (b) stacking-version (SV) uses independent models multiple times and each model attempts to restore the original image from blurred or intermediate deblurred image in the original scale iteratively [32,47] and (c) multi-scale (MS) (or coarse-to-fine) exploits multiple downsampled images in different spatial scales and recovers the downsampled original images in the lowest scale first and then to restore the original images in the original scale at the end [12,31,41]. This approach has been the most popular among state-of-the-art methods [12,41].

OS approach in Fig. 1(a) is straightforward and the model M is supervised to yield the original sharp image in the original high spatial scale at once. SV approach in Fig. 1(b) uses multiple independent models M1, M2, M3 and possibly more. Each model is supervised to yield the original sharp image in the original high spatial scale. However, each model has different input, either a given blurred image or an intermediate deblurring result of the previous model. Later models refine the deblurring results for improved performance, but with the price of increased network parameters.

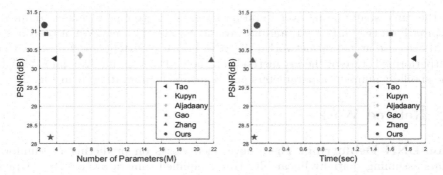

**Fig. 2.** Number of parameters (Million) and Time (Sec) vs. PSNR (dB) evaluated on the GoPro dataset. Our proposed MT-RNN method (Ours) yielded the best PSNR with the smallest parameters, real-time computation among state-of-the-art image deblurring methods such as Tao [41], Kupyn [24], Aljadaany [2], Gao [12] and Zhang [47].

MS approach in Fig. 1(c) also uses multiple models like SV approach, but the models are supervised to yield the original or down-scaled images in the different spatial scales. It is well-known that blurs become relatively smaller as image scale decreases and recovering image from intermediate result of deblurring is easier than restoring image from given blurred image. Thus, MS approach breaks a challenging deblurring problem for severe blur into multiple easy problems (dealing with small blur in low spatial scale or deblurring from intermediate result of deblurring in high spatial scale) that can be seen as a form of curriculum learning [5] in a wide sense. However, since edge information is important for reliable deblurring [7,45], performing deblurring in low spatial scales using MS approach could be a potential drawback. Note that MS approach requires incremental spatial training with spatially augmented training data (*i.e.*, downsampled sharp and blurred images). MS approach used to require large number of network parameters for different spatial scales [31], but recently many state-of-the-art MS based methods are using shared network parameters over spatial scales [12,41]. The models at different spatial scales are strongly dependent.

Here, we investigate a novel alternative approach to MS, called multi-temporal (MT), for non-uniform single image deblurring by exploiting time-resolved deblurring dataset from high-speed cameras like the popular GoPro dataset [31]. We model severe blurs as a series of small blurs so that MT approach deblurs small amount of blurs in the original spatial scale progressively instead of restoring the images in different spatial scales as illustrated in Fig. 1(d). Our MT approach, that can be seen as another form of curriculum learning [5] in a wide sense, also breaks down a challenging deblurring problem into a series of easy deblurring problems with small blurs. Note that unlike MS approach, each deblurring sub-problem in MT approach is still in the original spatial scale so that high-frequency information can be used for reliable deblurring [7,45].

To realize MT approach, we propose progressive deblurring over iterations and incremental temporal training. Our scheme does not require special parameter sharing across spatial scales like [12], but allows natural parameter sharing in the same spatial scale over iterations, yielding better performance than MS approach on the GoPro [31] and its variant, Su [39] datasets. We also proposed a MT recurrent neural network (MT-RNN) with recurrent feature maps that outperformed state-of-the-art methods on the GoPro [31], Lai [25] datasets with the smallest number of parameters and real-time computation as in Fig. 2.

## 2  Related Works

**Non-DNN Deblurring:** There have been works on predicting non-uniform blurs assuming spatially linear blur [15], simplified camera motion [14], parameterized model [42], filter flow [16], $l_0$ sparsity [44], and dark channel prior [33]. There have also been some works to exploit multiple images from videos [26], to utilize segmentation by assuming uniform blur on each segmentation area [8], to segment motion blur using optimization [18], to simplify motion model as local linear using MS approach [19], and to use bidirectional optical flows [20].

**DNN Image Deblurring:** Blind image/video deblurring employed DNNs for original sharp images from blurred input images. Xu *et al.* proposed a direct estimation of the sharp image with optimization to approximate deconvolution by a series of convolutions using DNNs [46]. Aljadaany *et al.* proposed a learning of both image prior and data fidelity for deblurring [2]. Kupyn *et al.* [24] proposes generative adversarial network based on feature pyramid and relativistic discriminator [29] with a least-square loss [17]. Zhang *et al.* proposed a multi-patch hierarchical network for different feature levels on the same spatial resolution [47]. They also proposed a stacked multi-patch network without parameter sharing. Nah *et al.* proposed a MS network with Gaussian pyramid [31] and Tao *et al.* proposed convolution long short-term memory (LSTM)-based MS DNN [41]. Gao *et al.* proposed MS parameter sharing and nested skip connections [12].

**Curriculum Learning:** MS approach for deblurring [12, 31, 38, 41] can be seen as a form of curriculum learning [5], tackling a challenging deblurring problem with less challenging sub-problems in lower spatial scales. At each scale, DNN is trained more effectively so that it helped to achieve state-of-the-art performances. Li [27] trained the model to generate the intermediate goals using Gaussian blurs and to progressively perform image super-resolution. Our MT approach is another form of curriculum learning, but breaks the deblurring problem in a different way. We exploit temporal information to generate intermediate goals with *non-uniform* blurs in the original spatial scale, while MS is generating intermediate goals with *uniform* blurs in lower scales or in the original scale.

**RNN Video Deblurring:** There have been video deblurring works to exploit temporal information: blending temporal information in spatio-temporal RNN [21], taking temporal information into account with RNN of several deblur blocks [43] and accumulating video information across frames [39]. Zhou [49] proposed spatio-temporal variant RNN. RNN utilizes previous frames effectively such as convolutional LSTM [41]. Similar to SV, Nah [32] proposed RNN with intra-frame iterations by reusing RNN cell parameters. RNN based video deblurring and our MT-RNN share similar architectures. However, the former has inputs across frames while our MT-RNN has inputs over deblurring sub-problems.

**Deblurring Dataset:** The importance of image deblurring dataset has been raised with remarkable progress of image deblurring. Several existing popular uniform deblurring dataset [13, 22, 40] are sythesized by blur kernel. In [13, 22, 40], single sharp image is convolved with a set of motion kernels for blurred image. Recently, several works [12, 30, 31, 41] generated dynamic motion blurred image by averaging consecutive video frames captured by high frame rate camera.

# 3   Temporal Data Augmentation

Unlike MS approach [12, 31, 41] to augment training data with down-sampling that could be sub-optimal for reliable deblurring [7, 45], we propose temporal training data augmentation for deblurring. Most deblurring training datasets were obtained from high-speed cameras [31, 38, 39], thus our MT augmentation scheme for intermediate goals and inputs can be widely applicable.

## 3.1   Motion Blur Dataset

Recent non-uniform deblurring datasets were generated by the integration of the sharp images [31, 38, 39]. The blurred image $y \in R^{M \times N}$ from a sequence of images $x \in R^{M \times N}$ can be constructed as follows:

$$y = g \left( \frac{1}{T} \int_{t=0}^{T} x(t) dt \right) \approx g \left( \frac{1}{n} \sum_{i=0}^{n} x[i] \right) \tag{1}$$

where $T$ and $x(t)$ denote an exposure time and a sharp image at time $t$ in continuous domain, $n$ and $x[i]$ denote the number of images and the $i$th sharp image in discrete domain, and $g$ is a camera response function (CRF). We denote the dataset of blurred images $y$ from $n$ frames as Temporal Level $n$ (TL$n$).

For example, motion blur datasets in [31, 38, 39] were captured by GoPro Hero camera (240 frame per sec) and 7–13 frames were averaged to yield a blurred image where a mid-frame image was selected as a ground truth image. Thus, the training/test datasets of [31] (called the GoPro dataset) consist of TL7, TL9, TL11 and TL13 with the ground truth of TL1.

## 3.2   Temporal Data Augmentation for MT Approach

Our MT approach requires more intermediate goals and inputs. Our temporal data augmentation further generates more blurred images to complete the whole training set with TL$n$ where $n$ is an odd number. For the GoPro dataset [31], we temporally augmented the data to generate TL1 (ground truth), TL3, ..., TL13 (we denote them Temporal GoPro or T-GoPro dataset). Unlike previous works using TL7-13 for the inputs of training, our MT exploits TL3-13 for both inputs and intermediate goals of training as proposed in the next section.

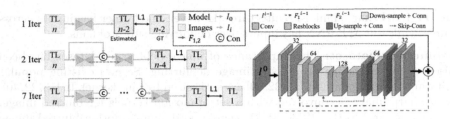

**Fig. 3.** (Left) Pipeline of incremental temporal training with our proposed MT-RNN, (Right) proposed neural network architecture of MT-RNN.

## 4 Multi-Temporal (MT) Approach

Figure 1(d) illustrates the concept of our MT approach that progressively predicts intermediate deblurred image (*e.g.*, predicting TL$(n-2)$ from TL$n$) to finally yield the desired sharp image that is close to the ground truth (TL1). As illustrated in Fig. 1, our proposed MT approach is different from others such as OS (*e.g.*, predicting TL1 from TL$n$), SV (*e.g.*, predicting TL1 from TL$n$ or intermediate results from previous network), and MS (*e.g.*, predicting downsampled TL1 from downsampled TL$n$ or intermediate results from previous scale). Here, we present incremental temporal training for our MT approach to use intermediate goals (*e.g.*, TL$(n-2)$). Then, we propose the MT-RNN with recurrent feature maps as a representative implementation of our MT approach for progressive deblurring. Lastly, we briefly discuss empirical convergence of our MT-RNN.

### 4.1 Incremental Temporal Training

Our MT approach conjectures that it is easier to predict TL5 from TL7 than to directly estimate TL1 from TL7, which seems reasonable (see supplementary material for further details). Curriculum learning approach can be used and incremental temporal training uses various temporally augmented dataset as intermediate goals as illustrated in Fig. 3 (left).

At the first iteration, a network is trained with randomly selected blurred images TL$n$ (*e.g.*, 7, 9, 11, 13) as inputs and with corresponding less blurred images TL$(n-2)$ as intermediate goals using $L1$ loss. At the next iteration, the estimated image from the previous iteration is taken as input and corresponding less blurred images TL$(n-4)$ as intermediate goals. This process is continued if intermediate goals become the final goals with TL1. Finally, 1–3 more iterations are done with the same final goals TL1. The max iteration for training was set to be 7 to reduce the overall training time. Temporal step (TS) is defined to be the difference between the input TL and the output TL over 1 iteration for training. Unless specified, we set TS $= 2$ based on the ablation studies in Table 1.

Our model uses identical parameters and training was performed independently for all iterations. This allows us to train the DNN with limited memory and to reduce the size of network without special parameter sharing.

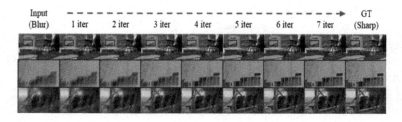

**Fig. 4.** Progressively deblurred images over iterations using our proposed MT-RNN.

## 4.2   MT-RNN for Progressive Deblurring

**Baseline MS Deblurring:** Among MS based deblurrings [31,38,41], the DNN of Tao [41] shares parameters over scales that can be modeled as follows:

$$\{\hat{I}^j, h^j\} = \text{DNN}_{\text{Tao}}(U(I^j), U(\hat{I}^{j+1}), U(h^{j+1}); \theta_{\text{Tao}}) \qquad (2)$$

where $j$ refers to a spatial scale where $j = 1$ represents the original high spatial scale, $I^j$ and $\hat{I}^j$ are blurred and estimated images at the $j$th scale, respectively, $\text{DNN}_{\text{Tao}}$ is the MS based DNN and $\theta_{Tao}$ is a set of parameters in the network, $I^j$ is a down-sampled image from $I^1$ if $j > 1$, $h$ is an intermediate feature map of convolutional LSTM, and $U$ is a up-sampling operation by bilinear interpolation. Due to the encoder-decoder structure of U-Net [35], a base network of Tao [41], the receptive field of the DNN of Tao was relatively large, which is desirable for good deblurring performance. Thus, the DNN of Tao [41] was chosen as the base model for our proposed MT-RNN as illustrated in Fig. 3 (right).

**Proposed MT-RNN:** We propose MT-RNN with recurrent feature maps that can be modeled as follows:

$$\{\hat{I}^i, F_1^i, F_2^i\} = \text{DNN}_{\text{Ours}}(\hat{I}^{i-1}, I^0, F_1^{i-1}, F_2^{i-1}; \theta_{\text{Ours}}) \qquad (3)$$

where $i$ refers to an iteration number, $F_1^{i-1}$ and $F_2^{i-1}$ are recurrent feature maps from the $(i - 1)$th decoder, $I^0$ is an input blurred image(TL$n$), $\hat{I}^{i-1}$ and $\hat{I}^i$ are predicted images at the $i$th iteration, respectively. Since the network utilizes previous feature maps, the output recurrent feature maps $F_1^i$ and $F_2^i$ are fed into the feature skip connection layer in the next iteration. $\text{DNN}_{\text{Ours}}$ is our MT-RNN and $\theta_{\text{Ours}}$ is a set of network parameters to be trained as shown in Fig. 3 (right) with feature extraction layers and residual blocks of 32, 64, 128 channels at the top, middle and bottom encoder-decoders, respectively [31,41].

For our proposed MT-RNN, we made a number of modifications on the DNN of Tao [41]. Firstly, changing kernel size from $5 \times 5$ to $3 \times 3$ was responsible for 0.13dB improvement in PSNR and substantially decreased number of parameters by 26%. Secondly, residual skip connection for input was responsible for 0.15dB improvement in PSNR. Figure 4 illustrates progressive deblurring of our proposed MT-RNN over iterations. Figure 5 quantitatively shows that our proposed MT approach recovers frequency components over iterations unlike SV approach.

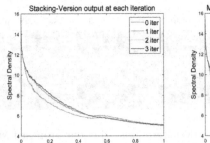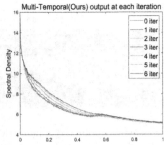

**Fig. 5.** Output spectral densities at each iteration for SV and our MT approaches. MT approach progressively recovers frequency components while SV approach does not.

**Recurrent Feature Maps:** Recurrent features $F^{i-1}$ are from the last residual block of each decoder and are concatenated with the feature maps of previous encoder at feature extraction layer as illustrated in Fig. 3 (right):

$$F^i_{enc} = Cat(F^{i-1}, f^i) \tag{4}$$

where $f^i$ is the feature map of previous encoder at the $i$th iteration. Estimated image $\hat{I}^{i-1}$ is concatenated with $I^0$:

$$I^i_{cat} = Cat(\hat{I}^{i-1}, I^0) \tag{5}$$

and then the encoder takes the $I^i_{cat}$ and $F^i_{encoder}$ as inputs.

Similar to other works of Tao [41] using convolutional LSTM for passing intermediate feature maps to the next spatial scale or of Nah [32] using hidden state $h_{t-1}$ in RNN cell, our MT-RNN uses intermediate feature maps $F^{i-1}$ from decoder that may include information about blur patterns and intermediate results for $I^i$. Using recurrent feature maps $F^{i-1}$ was responsible for improved performance by 0.31 dB.

**Residual Learning:** Kupyn [24], Gao [12] and Zhou [49] utilized residual learning for deblurring. We conducted an ablation study for residual learning. In Fig. 3, our proposed network takes $I^0$ and $\hat{I}^{i-1}$ as inputs and residual skip connection is linked to $I^0$. The linked $I^0$ was responsible for improved performance over $\hat{I}^{i-1}$ as summarized in Table 1.

### 4.3   Convergence of Progressive MT-RNN

Determining the number of iterations for MT-RNN is important for performance. We studied iteration vs. PSNR/SSIM for the network that was trained only with one type of TL images (e.g., TL13) for all TL7, 9, 11, 13. Training was performed until the 7th iteration for all cases. As illustrated in Fig. 6, all networks yielded increased PSNR/SSIM over iterations until 5th/6th iterations, and then decreased performances beyond the trained iteration. We set the number of iterations to be 6 for all experiments of our proposed MT-RNN. In all cases with different TL images, our proposed MT-RNN methods outperform state-of-the-art MS methods (Tao [41]) as in Fig. 6 (solid lines vs. dotted lines).

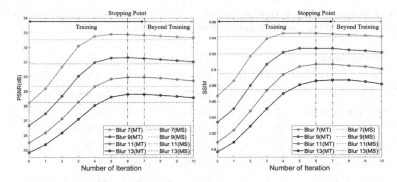

**Fig. 6.** Iteration vs. PSNR/SSIM for our proposed MT-RNN trained with one of TL7, 9, 11, 13. Corresponding MS models are also trained only with each TL.

# 5   Experiments

**Datasets.** The GoPro dataset [31] consists of 3,214 blurred images with the size of 1280 × 720 that are divided into 2,103 training images and 1,111 test images. In both training and test sets, TL7, 9, 11, 13 images were evenly distributed. We generated our T-GoPro dataset that includes more intermediate TL images (TL3, 5) with 5,500 training, 110 validation and 1,200 test images. Note that this new training dataset does not include any video from the original GoPro test dataset.

Su dataset [39] consists of 71 videos (6,708 images) with the size of 1,920 × 1080 or 1,280 × 720 from multiple devices. They are divided into 61 training and 10 test videos. Lastly, qualitative comparison was performed on Lai dataset [25] whose image sizes are varying within 351–1,024 × 502–1,024.

**Implementation Details.** For fair comparisons, we evaluated our proposed method and state-of-the-art methods on the same machine with NVIDIA Titan V GPU using PyTorch During training, the Adam optimizer was used with learning rate $2 \times 10^{-4}$, $\beta_1 = 0.9$, $\beta_2 = 0.999$ and $\epsilon = 10^{-8}$. Patch size was set to be $256 \times 256$ and data augmentations such as random crop, horizontal flip and $90°$ rotation were used. Note that since the number of channel is changed by concatenation replacing the original add operation of skip connection [41], $1 \times 1$ convolution was used. PSNR and SSIM were used for evaluations. Run time was recorded with batch size 1 and data-loading time was not counted.

For Tables 1, 2, 3, the training iteration was $92 \times 10^3$ with reduced learning rate by half every $46 \times 10^3$ iterations. Both our T-GoPro dataset and the original GoPro dataset [31] were used. For Table 3, Su dataset [39] was used only for test. For Table 4 and Fig. 7, the total iteration was $46 \times 10^4$ with reduced learning rate by half every $46 \times 10^3$ iterations. The GoPro dataset [31] and the Lai dataset [25] were used for quantitative and qualitative evaluations.

**Table 1.** Ablation studies with temporal step (TS), residual learning (ResL) and recurrent feature map (RFM) with training $92 \times 10^3$ iterations.

| Test dataset | | | | T-GoPro | | GoPro [31] | |
|---|---|---|---|---|---|---|---|
| TS | Iteration | ResL | RFM | PSNR | SSIM | PSNR | SSIM |
| (a) **2** | **6** | $I^0$ | o | **30.74** dB | **0.917** | **29.98** dB | **0.908** |
| (b) n/a | 1 (OS) | $I^0$ | n/a | 29.93 dB | 0.904 | 29.26 dB | 0.895 |
| (c) 4 | 4 | $I^0$ | o | 30.44 dB | 0.913 | 29.85 dB | 0.889 |
| (d) 2 | 6 | $I^0$ | x | 30.43 dB | 0.911 | 29.70 dB | 0.888 |
| (e) 2 | 6 | $\hat{I}^{i-1}$ | o | 30.05 dB | 0.905 | 29.41 dB | 0.896 |
| (f) 2 | 6 | x | o | 30.57 dB | 0.913 | 29.90 dB | 0.905 |

## 5.1  Ablation Studies for MT-RNN Designs

There are a number of components that affect the performance of our MT-RNN and we performed ablation studies on the T-GoPro and GoPro datasets to select the best possible combinations of the components: temporal step (TS), residual learning (ResL) and recurrent feature map (RFM). All results are summarized in Table 1 with our MT-RNN in the first row (a).

Table 1 (a), (b), (c) are corresponding to the ablation study for temporal step (TS). The row (b) is one-step approach, thus there is no TS as well as no recurrent feature map (RFM). The row (c) is the case with TS = 4, yielding improved performance over OS. In (c), iteration was set to be 4 to account for large TS as compared to our proposed MT-RNN with TS = 2. Note that (a), (c) are our MT approaches with different TS parameters and they outperformed one-step (OS) approach on both T-GoPro and GoPro datasets.

Table 1 (a), (d) are corresponding to the ablation study for recurrent feature map (RFM). It turned out that using RFM increased performances in MT-RNN by 0.31dB on the T-GoPro dataset and by 0.28dB on the original GoPro dataset.

Lastly, Table 1 (a), (e), (f) are corresponding to the ablation study for residual learning (ResL). It seems that using the original blurred image in the residual learning is important for improved performances as compared to using the previous output image in the residual learning. ResL in MT-RNN was the least important component among all three components according to the performance results in Table 1 (a), (f), especially for the original GoPro dataset.

## 5.2  Empirical Comparisons of OS, SV, MS and MT Approaches

We performed empirical comparison studies for different deblurring approaches as illustrated in Fig. 1: one-stage (OS), stacking version (SV), multi-scale (MS) and our multi-temporal (MT). Table 2 summarizes the performances of different approaches in PSNR (dB), SSIM and the number of parameters (Million).

Firstly, Table 2 (g), (h), (i), (j) are comparing the performances of OS, SV, MS and MT approaches where OS, MS and MT contain the same amount of network

**Table 2.** Empirical comparisons among different deblurring approaches with training $92 \times 10^3$ iterations: one-stage (OS), stacking version (SV), multi-scale (MS) and our proposed multi-temporal (MT). MT has 0.041 M more parameters (1.58% increase) than MS does due to recurrent feature map (RFM). MS w/ TL3-5 was trained with the training set of MT for inputs (*i.e.*, more training data) to yield ground truth images.

| Test dataset | T-GoPro | | GoPro [31] | | Param |
|---|---|---|---|---|---|
| Approach | PSNR | SSIM | PSNR | SSIM | |
| (g) OS | 29.93 dB | 0.904 | 29.26 dB | 0.895 | 2.594 M |
| (h) SV | 30.38 dB | 0.912 | 29.71 dB | 0.903 | 7.890 M |
| (i) MS | 30.25 dB | 0.908 | 29.50 dB | 0.898 | 2.594 M |
| (j) MT w/o RFM | 30.43 dB | 0.911 | 29.70 dB | 0.888 | 2.594 M |
| (k) **MT** | **30.82** dB | **0.917** | **30.04** dB | **0.908** | 2.635 M |
| (l) MS + MT | 30.58 dB | 0.915 | 29.87 dB | 0.905 | 2.637 M |
| (m) MS w/ TL3-5 | 30.04 dB | 0.906 | 29.27 dB | 0.893 | 2.594 M |

parameters. Note that the original MT contains 0.041 M more parameters (1.58% increase) than MS does due to recurrent feature map (RFM), thus we removed RFM in MT (called MT w/o RFM) to have the same number of parameters. Even though RFM was an important component for improved performance as shown in Table 1, our proposed MT approach without RFM still outperformed OS and MS approaches with the same number of parameters in most cases and yielded comparable performances to SV with 3 times less parameters. With RFM, MT approach yielded state-of-the-art performances on both T-GoPro and GoPro datasets in all metrics over all the other approaches as shown in Table 2 (k).

Table 2 (l) are the results of the case to combine MS and MT (with RFM). MS + MT still outperformed all other approaches, but was not able to achieve better performance than the original MT approach. Lastly, Table 2 (m) are

**Table 3.** Performance comparisons for state-of-the-art methods: Kupyn [24], Zhang [47] and Gao [12] before/after converting the original approach (OS/MS) into our MT approach with training $92 \times 10^3$ iterations. Evaluations were performed on T-GoPro, GoPro [31] and Su [39] datasets. Converting into MT approach does not change the number of parameters much since RFM was not used. PSNR in dB.

| Test dataset | | T-GoPro | | GoPro [31] | | Su [39] | | Param |
|---|---|---|---|---|---|---|---|---|
| Method | Approach | PSNR | SSIM | PSNR | SSIM | PSNR | SSIM | (M) |
| Kupyn [24] | OS | 28.27 | 0.870 | 27.58 | 0.858 | 28.32 | 0.865 | 3.28 |
| **Kupyn*** | MT | **28.36** | **0.872** | **27.70** | **0.860** | **28.53** | **0.868** | 3.28 |
| Zhang [47] | OS | 30.25 | 0.908 | 29.591 | 0.900 | 28.59 | 0.866 | 5.42 |
| **Zhang*** | MT | **30.91** | **0.918** | **30.21** | **0.910** | **29.56** | **0.892** | 5.43 |
| Gao [12] | MS | 30.70 | 0.916 | 29.930 | 0.907 | 29.73 | 0.897 | 3.87 |
| **Gao*** | MT | **31.01** | **0.921** | **30.32** | **0.915** | **29.79** | **0.898** | 3.40 |

the results of MS approach to be trained with the original dataset along with additional dataset (TL3-5) that was used for training MT approaches (called MS w/TL3-5). It turned out that using more data for training in MS degraded the performance of the original MS approach trained without TL3-5. In other words, using more training data only seems to help appropriate approaches such as MT, not any approaches such as MS.

We further investigated on different deblurring approaches by converting the original approach into our MT: for Kupyn [24] and Zhang [47], OS approach was converted into MT approach (called Kupyn* and Zhang*) and for Gao [12], MS approach was converted into MT (called Gao*). Note that the number of parameters in Gao was decreased by converting into MT since independent feature extraction modules at different scales was removed except for the original scale. As shown in Table 3, in all cases on all datasets, MT conversions of state-of-the-art methods yielded improved performances in PSNR and SSIM over original deblurring approaches. These results demonstrated the superior performances of our proposed MT approaches over other deblurring approaches.

### 5.3   Benchmark Results

We performed benckmark studies on the popular GoPro dataset [31]. Our proposed MT-RNN method was trained with our T-GoPro dataset that is generated using temporal data augmentation of the original GoPro dataset and then it was evaluated on the GoPro test dataset (1,111 images) that other previous methods were also evaluated on. The total training iteration was $4 \times 10^4$. Table 4

**Table 4.** Benchmarks on the GoPro test dataset [31] for PSNR, SSIM, parameter size, run time and training datasets. The 1st, 2nd and 3rd best performances are highlighted with red, blue and green. The run times of [19,40,44] and [2] are from their papers.

| Method | PSNR | SSIM | Param | Run time | Training sets |
|---|---|---|---|---|---|
| Xu [44] | 25.10 dB | 0.890 | - | 13.41 s | - |
| Kim [19] | 23.64 dB | 0.824 | - | 1 h | - |
| Sun [40] | 24.64 dB | 0.843 | - | 20 min | [10] |
| Gong [13] | 27.19 dB | 0.908 | - | - | [3,28] |
| Ram [34] | 28.94 dB | 0.922 | - | - | [9,28,31] |
| Nah [31] | 29.08 dB | 0.914 | 21.0 M | 0.91 s | [31] |
| Kupyn [23] | 28.70 dB | 0.958 | - | 0.15 s | [28,31] |
| Tao [41] | 30.26 dB | 0.934 | 3.8 M | 0.34 s | [31] |
| Kupyn [24] | 28.17 dB | 0.925 | 3.3 M | 0.03 s | [28,31] |
| Zhang [47] | 30.21 dB | 0.934 | 21.7 M | 0.02 s | [31,39] |
| Aljadaany [2] | 30.35 dB | 0.961 | 6.7 M | 1.20 s | [1,22,31] |
| Gao [12] | 30.92 dB | 0.942 | 2.84 M | 1.01 s | [31] |
| **Ours** | 31.15 dB | 0.945 | 2.6 M | 0.07 s | Temporal [31] |

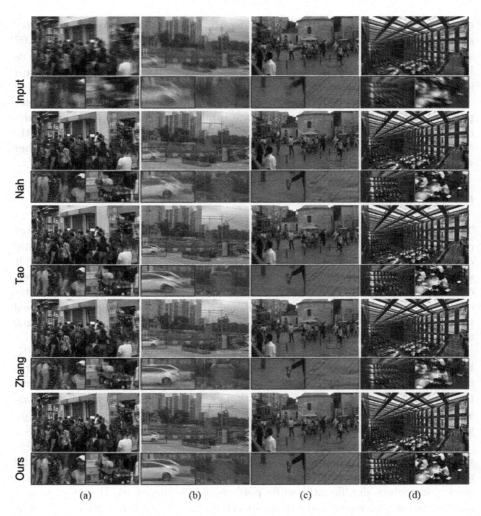

**Fig. 7.** Visual comparisons among state-of-the-art methods and our proposed MT-RNN on GoPro dataset [31] for (a), (b), (c) and on Lai dataset [25] for (d). Four input blurred images are on the 1st row, deblurred images of Nah [31] on the 2nd row, deblurring results of Tao [41] on the 3rd row, results of Zhang [48] on the 4th row. Our results using MT-RNN are on the 5th row (bottom row). Our proposed method yielded deblurred images that are visually better than the results of state-of-the-art methods for all 4 image cases for fine details.

summarized the reported performances of state-of-the-art methods in the literature in PSNR (dB), SSIM as well as other information such as the number of parameters, run time and used training sets. Our MT-RNN yielded the highest PSNR (31.15 dB) with the smallest number of parameters (2.6 M) thanks to our MT approach to use the identical network over all iterations and effective curriculum learning approach to break challenging problem into easy sub-problems. Moreover, our MT-RNN is real-time - its run time is only 0.07 second, which is advantageous over other state-of-the-art methods such as Kupyn [23], Aljadaany [2] or Gao [12]. Figure 2 summarized the results of Table 4 in graphs.

Figure 7 shows deblurred results on GoPro and Lai datasets for visual comparisons. The images on the first row are input blurred images and the results of Nah [31], Tao [41], Zhang [47], and our MT-RNN are on the 2nd, 3rd, 4th, 5th rows of Fig. 7, respectively, showing that our MT-RNN outperforms other state-of-the-art methods visually on both GoPro and Lai test datasets.

## 6   Discussion

The GoPro training dataset has been the most popular dataset for single image deblurring works as shown in Table 4, but most works also used additional dataset such as Microsoft COCO dataset [28] for improved performance. Thus, it seems disadvantageous to use the GoPro dataset [31] only for training. However, our proposed MT-RNN was able to achieve better performance than other state-of-the-art methods without using additional dataset. Even though we increased the training set size by temporal data augmentation, as shown in Table 2 (m), this increased training dataset is not always helpful for performance boost.

In Fig. 6, MT-RNN yielded increased PSNR over early iterations (usually, before 6th or 7th iterations) and then yielded decreased PSNR for later iterations. This seems to be related to the generalization of deep learning and thus this issue is beyond the scope of this work. Deep learning beyond training scenarios often fails to yield expected, reliable results. Active stopping criterion (e.g., gating unit in [32]) can potentially improve the performance of our MT-RNN.

Many state-of-the-art MS based single image deblurring methods exploit network weights across different spatial scales by parameter sharing [41] or partial networks weight sharing [12]. Weight sharing allows to reduce the number of network parameters significantly while performance is increased. However, weight sharing across scales seems to require special techniques and they are usually slow in computation. Our MT approach can be seen as natural weight sharing across temporal iterations without special methods. Thus, our MT approach seems to yield fast computation and high performance. We observed that the performance of MT was substantially decreased without weight sharing over iterations.

## 7   Conclusion

We investigate a novel alternative approach to MS, called MT, for non-uniform image deblurring by exploiting time-resolved deblurring dataset from high-speed cameras. Our proposed MT approach with progressive deblurring, incremental temporal training and MT-RNN yielded improved performance over previous deblurring approaches (OS, SV, MS) and outperformed state-of-the-art deblurring methods with the smallest number of parameters and real-time computation.

**Acknowledgement.** This work was supported partly by Basic Science Research Program through the National Research Foundation of Korea(NRF) funded by the Ministry of Education(NRF-2017R1D1A1B05035810), the Technology Innovation Program or Industrial Strategic Technology Development Program (10077533, Development of robotic manipulation algorithm for grasping/assembling with the machine learning using visual and tactile sensing information) funded by the Ministry of Trade, Industry & Energy (MOTIE, Korea), and a grant of the Korea Health Technology R&D Project through the Korea Health Industry Development Institute (KHIDI), funded by the Ministry of Health & Welfare, Republic of Korea (grant number: HI18C0316).

# References

1. Agustsson, E., Timofte, R.: NTIRE 2017 challenge on single image super-resolution: dataset and study. In: CVPRW (2017)
2. Aljadaany, R., Pal, D.K., Savvides, M.: Douglas-Rachford networks: learning both the image prior and data fidelity terms for blind image deconvolution. In: CVPR (2019)
3. Arbelaez, P., Maire, M., Fowlkes, C., Malik, J.: Contour detection and hierarchical image segmentation. IEEE T-PAMI **33**, 898–916 (2011)
4. Bahat, Y., Efrat, N., Irani, M.: Non-uniform Blind Deblurring by Reblurring. In: ICCV (2017)
5. Bengio, Y., Louradour, J., Collobert, R., Weston, J.: Curriculum learning. In: ICML (2009)
6. Chakrabarti, A.: A neural approach to blind motion deblurring. In: Leibe, B., Matas, J., Sebe, N., Welling, M. (eds.) ECCV 2016. LNCS, vol. 9907, pp. 221–235. Springer, Cham (2016). https://doi.org/10.1007/978-3-319-46487-9_14
7. Cho, S., Lee, S.: Fast motion deblurring. ACM Trans. Graph. **28**, 1–8 (2009)
8. Couzinie-Devy, F., Sun, J., Alahari, K., Ponce, J.: Learning to estimate and remove non-uniform image blur. In: CVPR (2013)
9. Deng, J., Dong, W., Socher, R., Li, L.J., Li, K., Fei-Fei, L.: ImageNet: a large-scale hierarchical image database. In: CVPR (2009)
10. Everingham, M., Van Gool, L., Williams, C.K., Winn, J., Zisserman, A.: The PASCAL visual object classes (VOC) challenge. IJCV **88**, 303–338 (2010)
11. Fergus, R., Singh, B., Hertzmann, A., Roweis, S.T., Freeman, W.T.: Removing camera shake from a single photograph. ACM Trans. Graph. **25**, 787–794 (2006)
12. Gao, H., Tao, X., Shen, X., Jia, J.: Dynamic scene deblurring with parameter selective sharing and nested skip connections. In: CVPR (2019)
13. Gong, D., et al.: From motion blur to motion flow: a deep learning solution for removing heterogeneous motion blur. In: CVPR (2017)
14. Gupta, A., Joshi, N., Lawrence Zitnick, C., Cohen, M., Curless, B.: Single image deblurring using motion density functions. In: Daniilidis, K., Maragos, P., Paragios, N. (eds.) ECCV 2010. LNCS, vol. 6311, pp. 171–184. Springer, Heidelberg (2010). https://doi.org/10.1007/978-3-642-15549-9_13
15. Harmeling, S., Hirsch, M., Schölkopf, B.: Space-variant single-image blind deconvolution for removing camera shake. In: NIPS (2010)
16. Hirsch, M., Schuler, C.J., Harmeling, S., Schölkopf, B.: Fast removal of non-uniform camera shake. In: ICCV (2011)
17. Jolicoeur-Martineau, A.: The relativistic discriminator: a key element missing from standard GAN. arXiv preprint arXiv:1807.00734 (2018)

18. Kim, T.H., Ahn, B., Lee, K.M.: Dynamic scene deblurring. In: ICCV (2013)
19. Kim, T.H., Lee, K.M.: Segmentation-free dynamic scene deblurring. In: CVPR (2014)
20. Kim, T.H., Lee, K.M.: Generalized video deblurring for dynamic scenes. In: CVPR (2015)
21. Kim, T.H., Lee, K.M., Schölkopf, B., Hirsch, M.: Online video deblurring via dynamic temporal blending network. In: ICCV (2017)
22. Köhler, R., Hirsch, M., Mohler, B., Schölkopf, B., Harmeling, S.: Recording and playback of camera shake: benchmarking blind deconvolution with a real-world database. In: Fitzgibbon, A., Lazebnik, S., Perona, P., Sato, Y., Schmid, C. (eds.) ECCV 2012. LNCS, vol. 7578, pp. 27–40. Springer, Heidelberg (2012). https://doi.org/10.1007/978-3-642-33786-4_3
23. Kupyn, O., Budzan, V., Mykhailych, M., Mishkin, D., Matas, J.: DeblurGAN: blind motion deblurring using conditional adversarial networks. In: CVPR (2018)
24. Kupyn, O., Martyniuk, T., Wu, J., Wang, Z.: DeblurGAN-v2: deblurring (orders-of-magnitude) faster and better. In: ICCV (2019)
25. Lai, W.S., Huang, J.B., Hu, Z., Ahuja, N., Yang, M.H.: A comparative study for single image blind deblurring. In: CVPR (2016)
26. Li, Y., Kang, S.B., Joshi, N., Seitz, S.M., Huttenlocher, D.P.: Generating sharp panoramas from motion-blurred videos. In: CVPR (2010)
27. Li, Z., Yang, J., Liu, Z., Yang, X., Jeon, G., Wu, W.: Feedback network for image super-resolution. In: CVPR (2019)
28. Lin, T.-Y., et al.: Microsoft COCO: common objects in context. In: Fleet, D., Pajdla, T., Schiele, B., Tuytelaars, T. (eds.) ECCV 2014. LNCS, vol. 8693, pp. 740–755. Springer, Cham (2014). https://doi.org/10.1007/978-3-319-10602-1_48
29. Mao, X., Li, Q., Xie, H., Lau, R.Y., Wang, Z., Smolley, S.P.: Least squares generative adversarial networks. In: ICCV (2017)
30. Nah, S., Baik, S., Hong, S., Moon, G., Son, S., Timofte, R., Lee, K.M.: NTIRE 2019 challenge on video deblurring and super-resolution: dataset and study. In: CVPRW (2019)
31. Nah, S., Kim, T.H., Lee, K.M.: Deep multi-scale convolutional neural network for dynamic scene deblurring. In: CVPR (2017)
32. Nah, S., Son, S., Lee, K.M.: Recurrent neural networks with intra-frame iterations for video deblurring. In: CVPR (2019)
33. Pan, J., Sun, D., Pfister, H., Yang, M.H.: Blind image deblurring using dark channel prior. In: CVPR (2016)
34. Ramakrishnan, S., Pachori, S., Gangopadhyay, A., Raman, S.: Deep generative filter for motion deblurring. In: ICCVW (2017)
35. Ronneberger, O., Fischer, P., Brox, T.: U-Net: convolutional networks for biomedical image segmentation. In: Navab, N., Hornegger, J., Wells, W.M., Frangi, A.F. (eds.) MICCAI 2015. LNCS, vol. 9351, pp. 234–241. Springer, Cham (2015). https://doi.org/10.1007/978-3-319-24574-4_28
36. Schuler, C.J., Hirsch, M., Harmeling, S., Schölkopf, B.: Learning to deblur. IEEE Trans. Pattern Anal. Mach. Intell. 38, 1439–1451 (2016)
37. Shan, Q., Jia, J., Agarwala, A.: High-quality motion deblurring from a single image. ACM Trans. Graph. 27, 1–10 (2008)
38. Shen, Z., et al.: Human-aware motion deblurring. In: ICCV (2019)
39. Su, S., Delbracio, M., Wang, J., Sapiro, G., Heidrich, W., Wang, O.: Deep video deblurring for hand-held cameras. In: CVPR (2017)
40. Sun, J., Cao, W., Xu, Z., Ponce, J.: Learning a convolutional neural network for non-uniform motion blur removal. In: CVPR (2015)

41. Tao, X., Gao, H., Shen, X., Wang, J., Jia, J.: Scale-recurrent network for deep image deblurring. In: CVPR (2018)
42. Whyte, O., Sivic, J., Zisserman, A., Ponce, J.: Non-uniform deblurring for shaken images. In: CVPR (2010)
43. Wieschollek, P., Hirsch, M., Schölkopf, B., Lensch, H.P.A.: Learning blind motion deblurring. In: ICCV (2017)
44. Xu, L., Zheng, S., Jia, J.: Unnatural l0 sparse representation for natural image deblurring. In: CVPR (2013)
45. Xu, L., Jia, J.: Two-phase kernel estimation for robust motion deblurring. In: Daniilidis, K., Maragos, P., Paragios, N. (eds.) ECCV 2010. LNCS, vol. 6311, pp. 157–170. Springer, Heidelberg (2010). https://doi.org/10.1007/978-3-642-15549-9_12
46. Xu, L., Ren, J.S., Liu, C., Jia, J.: Deep convolutional neural network for image deconvolution. In: NIPS (2014)
47. Zhang, H., Dai, Y., Li, H., Koniusz, P.: Deep stacked hierarchical multi-patch network for image deblurring. In: CVPR (2019)
48. Zhang, Y., Li, K., Li, K., Wang, L., Zhong, B., Fu, Y.: Image super-resolution using very deep residual channel attention networks. In: ECCV (2018)
49. Zhou, S., Zhang, J., Pan, J., Xie, H., Zuo, W., Ren, J.: Spatio-temporal filter adaptive network for video deblurring. arXiv preprint arXiv:1904.12257 (2019)

# ProgressFace: Scale-Aware Progressive Learning for Face Detection

Jiashu Zhu$^{(\boxtimes)}$, Dong Li, Tiantian Han, Lu Tian, and Yi Shan

Xilinx Inc., Beijing, China
{jiashuz,dongl,hantian,lutian,yishan}@xilinx.com

**Abstract.** Scale variation stands out as one of key challenges in face detection. Recent attempts have been made to cope with this issue by incorporating image/feature pyramids or adjusting anchor sampling/matching strategies. In this work, we propose a novel scale-aware progressive training mechanism to address large scale variations across faces. Inspired by curriculum learning, our method gradually learns large-to-small face instances. The preceding models learned with easier samples (i.e., large faces) can provide good initialization for succeeding learning with harder samples (i.e., small faces), ultimately deriving a better optimum of face detectors. Moreover, we propose an auxiliary anchor-free enhancement module to facilitate the learning of small faces by supplying positive anchors that may be not covered according to the criterion of IoU overlap. Such anchor-free module will be removed during inference and hence no extra computation cost is introduced. Extensive experimental results demonstrate the superiority of our method compared to the state-of-the-arts on the standard FDDB and WIDER FACE benchmarks. Especially, our ProgressFace-Light with MobileNet-0.25 backbone achieves 87.9% AP on the hard set of WIDER FACE, surpassing largely RetinaFace with the same backbone by 9.7%. Code and our trained face detection models are available at https://github.com/jiashu-zhu/ProgressFace.

**Keywords:** Face detection · Progressive learning · Anchor-free methods

## 1 Introduction

Face detection is an important task in computer vision with extensive subsequent research fields (e.g., face recognition and face tracking) and practical applications including intelligent surveillance for smart city and face unlock/beautification in smartphones. Owing to the great development of convolutional neural networks (CNNs), deep face detectors have achieved outstanding performance compared to the conventional hand-crafted features and classifiers. Typical methods

**Electronic supplementary material** The online version of this chapter (https://doi.org/10.1007/978-3-030-58539-6_21) contains supplementary material, which is available to authorized users.

© Springer Nature Switzerland AG 2020
A. Vedaldi et al. (Eds.): ECCV 2020, LNCS 12351, pp. 344–360, 2020.
https://doi.org/10.1007/978-3-030-58539-6_21

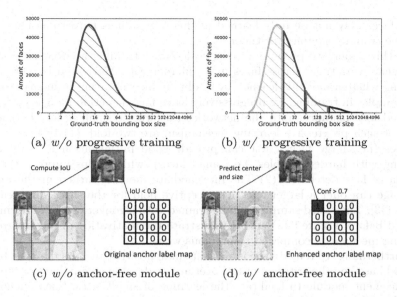

(a) *w/o* progressive training      (b) *w/* progressive training

(c) *w/o* anchor-free module      (d) *w/* anchor-free module

**Fig. 1.** Illustration of our motivations. With progressive learning, we train faces with different scales in a large-to-small order instead of feeding them into network at the same time. In (b), the different colors mean the groups of face instances with different sizes. Blue represents the faces with largest sizes, green represents the second largest, and so on. With anchor-free enhancement module, small positive anchors are recovered for training. (Color figure online)

include two-stage and one-stage anchor-based detectors. The predominant two-stage methods [37] first generate a set of candidate region proposals and then refine them for final detection. One-stage detectors [30] aim to directly classify and regress the pre-defined anchors without the extra proposal generation step.

Face detection, acting as a special case of object detection, has inherited effective techniques from generic detection methods but still suffers from large scale variations across face instances. Previous attempts have been made to alleviate this issue. (1) Multi-scale image pyramids [17] or multi-level feature pyramids [29] are exploited to cope with large ranges of face scales. Image pyramids augment training samples for varying face scales, while feature pyramids offer multi-granularity feature representations for detecting faces with different scales. (2) Various anchor sampling and matching strategies are developed including designing suitable anchor stride [57], adjusting anchor layout [53] or balancing samples at different scales [34]. While these existing methods have shown promising results, they remain two main limitations as follows. First, even though multi-scale training or anchor sampling methods can balance face instances with a large scale range to an extent, those faces with different scales are fed into the network for training at the same time. It might be difficult to obtain a good optimum from learning such complex and varying samples. Second, discrete anchors are tiled on feature maps and are classified as positive and negative based on the metric of intersection-over-union (IoU) overlap. However, small faces may not be fully learned in this way as it is hard to assign precise positive training samples for them.

In this paper, we propose a novel scale-aware training approach to address large scale variations across faces in a different way. Motivated by curriculum learning where a model is learned by gradually incorporating from easy to complex samples in training, we progressively learn face detection models by feeding grouped face instances into the network in a large-to-small order. The advantages of such progressive learning mechanism are two-fold. (1) Learning easier samples (i.e., large faces) first can provide good initialization for subsequent learning with harder samples (i.e., small faces), which helps improve the final optima of face detectors. (2) The intermediate models learned in the preceding stage can offer a larger effective receptive field for the succeeding learning stages [33]. Thus hard samples will be trained with stronger context information learned before. Figure 1 (a) and (b) illustrate the motivation of our progressive learning mechanism compared to previous work.

Furthermore, to remedy the issue that small positive anchors may not be discovered based on the criterion of IoU overlap, we develop an auxiliary anchor-free enhancement module to facilitate the learning of small faces. Such anchor-free module will be removed during inference and hence no extra computation cost will be introduced. Figure 1(c) and (d) illustrate our motivations on how to remedy the miss of positive anchors for small faces. We also attempt to improve bounding box regression by estimating uncertainty caused by ambiguous annotations. To this end, we learn to predict localization variance for each predicted bounding box.

We extensively evaluate the proposed method, named ProgressFace, on the standard face detection benchmarks of FDDB and WIDER FACE. Our method achieves competitive performance with the state-of-the-art face detectors. Specifically, our ProgressFace with ResNet-152 obtains 98.7% TPR at 1,000 FPs on FDDB and 91.8% AP on the hard set of WIDER FACE, both performing favorably against the state-of-the-arts. Equipped with a light-weight MobileNet-0.25 backbone, we achieve 87.9% AP on the hard set of WIDER FACE, surpassing RetinaFace largely by 9.7%.

The main contributions of this paper are summarized as follows:

- We propose a novel scale-aware progressive learning method for face detection by gradually incorporating large-to-small face instances in training. Such mechanism effectively alleviates the issue of large scale variations and helps improve the quality of feature representations for detecting faces with different scales.
- We propose an anchor-free enhancement module to facilitate the learning of small faces. It serves the anchor-based detection branch with more small positive anchors. This anchor-free module will be removed during inference and does not introduce extra computation cost.
- Our empirical evaluations demonstrate the superiority of the proposed method compared to the state-of-the-arts on both FDDB and WIDER FACE benchmarks. Especially, with the same light-weight MobileNet-0.25 as backbone, our ProgressFace outperforms RetinaFace by a large margin.

## 2     Related Work

### 2.1     Generic Object Detection

In the deep learning era, generic object detection has achieved impressive performance due to the powerful representations learned by CNNs. The basic idea of detecting objects is casting this problem as classifying and regressing candidate bounding boxes in images. On the one hand, R-CNN [10] proposes to first generate candidate region proposals and then refine them in the deep network. This two-stage detection method has been improved by a broad range of following work, including reducing redundant calculation of RoI features with spatial pyramid pooling [12], RoIPooling [12] or RoIAlign [11], generating region proposals by RPN [37], improving efficiency by position-sensitive score maps [4], and improving performance by cascade procedure with increasing IoU thresholds [2]. On the other hand, one-stage methods [32] directly classify and refine the pre-defined anchors without region proposal generation. Attempts also have been made to further improve the performance by incorporating additional context information [7], tackling foreground-background class imbalance [30] and developing an anchor refinement module [51].

In contrast to anchor mechanism, an emerging line of recent work attempts to cast object detection as keypoint estimation [22,24,44,48,55,56], instead of enumerating possible locations, scales and aspect ratios by pre-defined anchor boxes. There are different designs in these anchor-free methods for object detection such as finding object centers and regressing to their sizes [18,55], detecting and grouping bounding box corners [24,56], modeling all points [44] or shrunk points [22] in boxes as positive. Different from [46], we integrate an auxiliary anchor-free enhancement module to boost the learning of small faces in this work.

### 2.2     Face Detection

Face detection has derived benefit from the development of generic object detection. Traditional Harr-AdaBoost [45] and DPM [6] algorithms have trailed deep face detectors. Most of recent face detectors are built upon the anchor-based detection paradigm [37]. Additional attempts have been made to further improve the performance of face detection including integration of context module [17,28,43], adjustment from anchor sampling or matching strategies [53] and utilization of multi-task learning with auxiliary supervision [5,50]. Scale variation is one of key challenges in face detection (e.g., the range of face sizes on WIDER FACE could be 2~1289). Existing methods tackle the issue in the following aspects. (1) Multi-scale image pyramids are exploited to select specific scales or normalize different scales for training [17,36,40,41]. (2) Multi-level feature pyramids provide features with different spatial resolutions to help detect faces of different sizes [28,43,52]. The detection output can be drawn from multiple feature maps without [32] or with [29] feature fusion. (3) Various anchor sampling or matching strategies are employed for detecting small faces, including data-anchor-sampling [27,28,43], high overlaps between anchors and ground-truth faces based on EMO score [57], scale compensation anchor matching strategy [53], two-stage anchor refinement [3] and balanced anchor sampling [34]. In this work, we propose a different mechanism to handle large scale variations in face detection by progressively training faces with different scales.

### 2.3  Curriculum Learning and Progressive Learning

Our work is related to curriculum learning [1] in which samples are not randomly presented but organized in a meaningful order for training. Bengio et al. [1] propose this learning paradigm and its intuition comes from the learning process of humans that gradually incorporates easy-to-hard samples. Self-paced learning further improves curriculum learning by joint optimization of original objective and curriculum design [23], which has been applied to many vision tasks such as visual tracking [42], image search [20] and object discovery [25]. Progressive methods also share similar inspirations with curriculum learning in other problem contexts [26,31] by decomposing complex problems into simpler ones. Our work resembles these learning regimes but we apply free curriculum (i.e., object sizes) to address the issue of large scale variations in the face detection task.

## 3  Approach

### 3.1  Anchor-Based Face Detection Baseline

**Backbone.** We build our backbone of face detection network based on feature pyramid network (FPN) [29], which can incorporate low-level details and high-level semantics. We denote $\{C_i\}|_{i=1}^n$ as the last feature map before reducing the spatial resolution in a typical network. Naturally, $C_i$ has the $\frac{1}{2^i}$ resolution of input image. Feature pyramids $\{P_i\}|_{i=l}^h$ are extracted by top-down pathways and lateral connections between the $l$-th and $h$-th layers. $P_i$ has the same spatial size with the corresponding feature map $C_i$. Following [43], we build the FPN structure starting from an intermediate layer instead of top layers ($h < n$). Besides, in order to reduce the complexity of FPN structure, we do not incorporate feature maps with too large resolutions ($l > 1$). Feature pyramids $\{P_i\}$ are used as detection outputs and each has an output stride $R = 2^i$.

**Anchor Design.** We takes anchors with IoU $> 0.5$ to at least one ground-truth face as positive and those with IoU $< 0.3$ to all ground-truth faces as negative (i.e., background). Unlike RPN in generic object detection, we restrict the aspect ratios of anchors as one since faces have relatively rigid shape. We set the base anchor size $s_b = 16$, which means the minimum area of anchor boxes is $s_b^2 = 256$. We tile anchors on all the feature pyramids $\{P_i\}|_{i=l}^h$. Specifically, suppose we have feature pyramids $\{P_3, P_4, P_5\}$ and each level $P_i$ has two anchor scales, we will use anchor scales $\{1, 2\}$ in $P_3$, $\{4, 8\}$ in $P_4$ and $\{16, 32\}$ in $P_5$. This results in 6 sizes of anchor boxes ($s \times s_b, s \in \{1, 2, 4, 8, 16, 32\}, s_b = 16$) in the 640 $\times$ 640 input image.

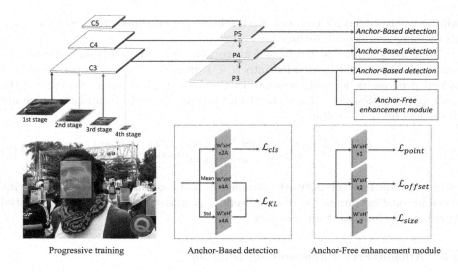

**Fig. 2.** Overall architecture of the proposed method. See Sect. 3 for details.

**Multi-task Loss.** Following previous anchor-based detectors [30,43,53], we optimize the objective of detection by simultaneously classifying and regressing anchor boxes. Such multi-task loss will be minimized for each anchor $i$:

$$\mathcal{L} = \mathcal{L}_{\mathrm{cls}}(p_i, p_i^*) + \lambda \cdot p_i^* \mathcal{L}_{\mathrm{reg}}(t_i, t_i^*) \tag{1}$$

The classification loss $\mathcal{L}_{\mathrm{cls}}(p_i, p_i^*)$ is a binary cross-entropy loss to classify positive and negative samples (i.e., faces and background), where $p_i$ is the predicted probability of anchor $i$ being a face and $p_i^*$ represents its ground-truth label (1 for positive and 0 for negative). The localization loss $\mathcal{L}_{\mathrm{reg}}(t_i, t_i^*)$ is a smooth-L1 loss [9], where $t_i$ represents the 4-D coordinate parameters of a predicted box and $t_i^*$ is the ground-truth bounding box. $\lambda$ is used to balance these two losses and is set to 0.25 in our experiments.

### 3.2 Progressive Training Framework

Figure 2 illustrates the overall architecture of our method. Inspired by curriculum learning [1], we propose a progressive training mechanism for face detection by gradually incorporating large-to-small samples. We use the free curriculum, i.e. size of face instances, to guide the entire learning process. Specifically, we first group faces with different scales based on the valid scale range on each level of feature pyramids $P_i$. Then these grouped faces are gradually fed into the network for training in a large-to-small order. For example, in the first stage, we use the smaller anchor scale of $P_5$ (i.e., 16) to determine the minimum area of ground-truth faces to be addressed, i.e., $(16 \times s_b)^2$. Thus, face instances with the area of $[(16 \times s_b)^2, +\infty]$ will be valid for training in this stage. In the next stage, the smaller anchor scale of $P_4$ is 4 and thus faces with the area of $[(4 \times s_b)^2, (16 \times s_b)^2]$

will be newly added for training. Such scheme is performed stage by stage until all training samples are included.

Suppose we have $K$ levels of feature pyramids for detection outputs, the training samples will be divided into $K + 1$ groups according to the aforementioned progressive learning scheme. In the $k$-th training stage, we exploit the same optimization objective as Eq. 1 and retrain network parameters which are initialized by the last stage:

$$\mathcal{L}^{(k)} = \mathcal{L}(p_i, p_i^*, t_i, t_i^* | \Theta^{(k-1)}), \ t = 1, 2, \dots, K + 1.$$
$$\Theta^{(k-1)} = \arg \min_\Theta \mathcal{L}^{(k-1)}$$
$$(2)$$

where $\Theta$ indicates the network parameters to be optimized. To avoid getting stuck in local optima induced by subsets of partial samples, we raise the initial learning rate for each training stage.

### 3.3  Anchor-Free Enhancement Module

In the anchor-based face detection baseline, the anchor scale affects face sizes which can be handled. A metric of IoU overlap is often used to define positive and negative samples. For example, anchors with IoU >0.5 to ground-truth faces are taken as positive. Such procedure may lead to two main limitations for matching small faces. First, in order to cover more small faces, we need more anchors with smaller size or denser layouts, which will incur extensive computation cost and more imbalanced distributions of positive and negative samples. Second, it is difficult to cover small ground-truth faces and prone to miss the corresponding positive anchors based on this metric. Typically, if the base anchor size is set to 16 and IoU threshold is set to 0.5, faces with area $< 16^2 \times 0.5 = 128$ will be ignored for training[1] if no other scale-aware augmentation strategies are used. Although multi-scale training can be applied to mitigate this issue, it is not efficient especially when the scale range of faces is extremely large.

To remedy the problem of missing small positive anchors in the anchor-based paradigm, we propose an anchor-free enhancement module to facilitate the training of small faces. Specifically, we append an auxiliary anchor-free branch to the feature map $P_l$ with the highest spatial resolution in FPN. The anchor-based branch will generate a label map of $W' \times H' \times A$ to classify anchors, where $W'$ and $H'$ mean the spatial shape of $P_l$ and $A$ represents the amount of anchors for each location. The anchor-free branch will provide more positive anchors by predicting the face centers and regressing their sizes, which leads to an enhanced anchor label map for better training the anchor-based branch.

We train the anchor-free branch by modeling faces as points inspired by CenterNet [55] in generic object detection. Specifically, denote $Y \in [0, 1]^{\frac{W}{R} \times \frac{H}{R}}$ as a predicted heatmap where $R$ is the output stride of the feature map, $W$ and $H$ are the size of input image. $Y_{xy} = 1$ means the detected point $(x, y)$ is a face

---

[1] Faces with area <128 accounts for ~29% in WIDER FACE.

center and $Y_{xy} = 0$ is background. The training objective of classifying points is pixel-wise logistic regression with focal loss [30]:

$$\mathcal{L}_{\text{point}} = \frac{1}{N} \sum_{x=1}^{\frac{W}{R}} \sum_{y=1}^{\frac{H}{R}} \begin{cases} -(1 - Y_{xy})^{\alpha} log(Y_{xy}) & \text{if } Y_{xy}^* = 1 \\ -(1 - Y_{xy}^*)^{\beta} (Y_{xy})^{\alpha} log(1 - Y_{xy}) & \text{otherwise} \end{cases} \quad (3)$$

where $Y_{xy}^*$ is a Gaussian kernel softly representing the ground-truth face center, $\alpha$ and $\beta$ are hyper-parameters of focal loss, and N is the number of face centers. We use $\alpha = 2$ and $\beta = 4$ in our experiments. To restore the error of discretizing each face center point $(x_k, y_k)$ by the output stride, we use L1 loss to train the offset $o_k$:

$$\mathcal{L}_{\text{offset}} = \frac{1}{N} \sum_{k=1}^{N} |o_k - o_k^*|, \text{where } o_k^* = (\frac{x_k}{R} - \lfloor \frac{x_k}{R} \rfloor, \frac{y_k}{R} - \lfloor \frac{y_k}{R} \rfloor) \quad (4)$$

For each ground-truth bounding box $(x_1^k, y_1^k, x_2^k, y_2^k)$, we also regress to the size by L1 loss:

$$\mathcal{L}_{\text{size}} = \frac{1}{N} \sum_{k=1}^{N} |s_k - s_k^*|, \text{where } s_k = (\frac{x_2^k - x_1^k}{R}, \frac{y_2^k - y_1^k}{R}) \quad (5)$$

We use the following multi-task loss as the training objective to optimize our anchor-free branch:

$$\mathcal{L} = \mathcal{L}_{\text{point}} + \lambda_1 \cdot \mathcal{L}_{\text{offset}} + \lambda_2 \cdot \mathcal{L}_{\text{size}} \quad (6)$$

where $\lambda_1 = 1$ and $\lambda_2 = 0.1$ are used in our experiments.

This anchor-free enhancement module is activated in the last stage of progressive training when small faces are incorporated. At each iteration, points with predicted probabilities $Y_{xy} > T$ will be set as complementary positive anchors. We use $T = 0.7$ in our experiments. For inference, this anchor-free module will be removed and no extra computation cost will be introduced.

### 3.4 Uncertainty Estimation in Face Localization

To improve the robustness and interpretability of deep neural networks, uncertainty estimation has been investigated in Bayesian deep learning by learning a distribution over network weights [21]. Recently, it has also been applied in vision tasks such as face recognition [38] and generic object detection [14]. In this work, we find that ambiguities exist in ground-truth bounding boxes as shown in Fig. 3(a) and attempt to further improve the quality of face localization by estimating uncertainty.

To address the problem, we estimate the variance of a predicted location for each ground-truth bounding box. In detail, we formulate each possible bounding box location as a Gaussian distribution:

$$P(x) = \frac{1}{\sqrt{2\pi\sigma^2}} e^{-\frac{(x - \hat{x})^2}{2\sigma^2}} \quad (7)$$

(a)                                     (b)

**Fig. 3.** (a) Examples of ambiguous ground-truth bounding boxes including occlusion and inaccurate annotations across different face scales in the WIDER FACE dataset. (b) Each predicted bounding box can be modeled with a Gaussian distribution. More accurate location has the smaller variance.

where the mean of gaussian $\hat{x}$ represents the predicted bounding box and the standard deviation $\sigma$ represents the estimated uncertainty. Each ground-truth bounding box $x^*$ can be formulated as a Dirac delta function (i.e., Gaussian distribution with $\sigma \to 0$).

$$P_G(x) = \delta(x - x^*) \tag{8}$$

Then the objective is minimizing the KL divergence between the predicted and ground-truth bounding boxes:

$$\mathcal{L}_{\text{KL}} = D_{\text{KL}}(P_G(x) \parallel P(x)) \propto \frac{(x^* - \hat{x})^2}{2\sigma^2} + \frac{\log(\sigma^2)}{2} \tag{9}$$

Following [14], we predict $\alpha = \log \sigma^2$ instead of $\sigma$ to avoid gradient explosion and exploit a similar smooth-L1 loss for training:

$$\mathcal{L}_{\text{KL}} = \begin{cases} \frac{e^{-\alpha}}{2}(x^* - \hat{x})^2 + \frac{1}{2}\alpha & |x^* - \hat{x}| \leq 1 \\ e^{-\alpha}(|x^* - \hat{x}| - \frac{1}{2}) + \frac{1}{2}\alpha & |x^* - \hat{x}| > 1 \end{cases} \tag{10}$$

The improved bounding box regression loss (Eq. 10) is applied to each progressive training stage and each feature map in FPN. Unlike [14], we only rely on the standard bounding box voting [8] to vote for a more accurate location without using the predicted location variance.

## 4   Experiments

### 4.1   Datasets and Evaluation Metrics

**WIDER FACE Dataset.** The WIDER FACE dataset [47] consists of $32,203$ images and $393,703$ annotated faces, 158,989 of which are in the *train* set, 39,496 in the *validation* set, and the rest are held out in the *test* set. Each subset has three levels of detection difficulty: *Easy*, *Medium* and *Hard*. It is one of the most challenging face benchmarks with large variations in scale, pose, expression, occlusion and illumination. We use the *train* set of WIDER FACE to train our face detector and perform evaluations on the *validation* and *test* sets.

**FDDB Dataset.** The FDDB dataset [19] contains 2,845 images and 5,171 annotated faces with different image resolutions, occlusions and poses. We use this dataset for test only.

**Evaluation Metrics.** We use the standard average precision (AP) metric to evaluate the performance of face detectors on the WIDER FACE dataset. For FDDB, we draw the receiver operating characteristic (ROC) curves and compute the true positive rate (TPR) when the amount of false positives (FP) is equal to 1,000. For both AP and TPR metrics, a predicted bounding box is considered as correct if it has an IoU $> 0.5$ with a ground-truth face annotation.

## 4.2 Implementation Details

We summarize other techniques used in our method as follows. We use the five facial landmarks on WIDER FACE provided by [5] to train a auxiliary landmark prediction task with smooth-L1 loss. Thus the multi-task loss in Eq. 1 is improved with an extra term for landmark prediction and its loss weight is set to 0.1 in our experiments. We use online hard example mining (OHEM) [39] and constrain the ratio of positive and negative anchors to 1 : 3. We employ context modules [35] on each level of feature pyramid to incorporate more context information and increase the receptive field. We also apply deformable convolution [58] in the feature pyramids as well as context modules.

For data augmentation, we randomly resize an original image from a predefined scale set and randomly crop a fixed size of 640 × 640 with random flipping as input for training.

We evaluate our method with both ResNet-152 [13] and MobileNet-0.25 [16] backbones. We construct 5 levels of feature pyramids for ResNet-152 (P2-6) and 3 levels of feature pyramids for MobileNet-0.25 (P3-5). Both backbones are pre-trained on the ImageNet classification task. We use the MobileNet-0.25 backbone to conduct ablation studies.

We train the face detection networks with a batch size of 32 on 4 NVIDIA Tesla P100 GPUs. We use Adam to optimize the last stage of progressive training in which the anchor-free module is activated. The initial learning rate is set to 5e−4 and decreased 10× twice during training. We use SGD to optimize the other training stages with momentum of 0.9 and weight decay of $5 \times 10^{-4}$. In each stage (except the last one), an initial learning rate of 1e−2 is used and decreased 10× twice. We train for 380 epochs and cost 3 days to obtain the final face detector with the MobileNet-0.25 backbone. For inference, we apply the multi-scale testing strategy [5,35,53] in which the short side of image is resized to $\{500, 800, 1100, 1400, 1700\}$. All of our experiments are conducted on MXNet. Code and our trained face detection models are available at https://github.com/jiashu-zhu/ProgressFace.

354      J. Zhu et al.

## 4.3   Comparisons to the State-of-the-Arts

**Table 1.** Performance comparisons on the WIDER FACE *validation* set. * indicates the work which is under review or not formally published. For fair comparisons, FLOPs are computed with the same 640 × 480 input size for all the methods.

| Methods | Backbone | *Easy* | *Medium* | *Hard* | Params | FLOPs |
|---|---|---|---|---|---|---|
| MTCNN [50] | Customized | 0.851 | 0.820 | 0.607 | 0.50M | 4.65G |
| Faceboxes-3.2x [52] | Customized | 0.798 | 0.802 | 0.715 | 1.01M | 2.84G |
| LFFD v2* [15] | Customized | 0.837 | 0.835 | 0.729 | 1.45M | 6.87G |
| LFFD v1* [15] | Customized | 0.910 | 0.881 | 0.780 | 2.15M | 9.25G |
| RetinaFace* [5] | MobileNet-0.25 | 0.914 | 0.901 | 0.782 | 0.31M | 0.57G |
| RetinaFace* [5] + DCNv2 [58] | MobileNet-0.25 | 0.922 | 0.910 | 0.795 | 0.60M | 1.23G |
| ProgressFace-Light | MobileNet0.25 | **0.949** | **0.935** | **0.879** | 0.66M | 1.35G |
| S³FD [53] | VGG-16 | 0.928 | 0.913 | 0.840 | 22.46M | 96.60G |
| SSH [35] | VGG-16 | 0.927 | 0.915 | 0.844 | 19.75M | 99.98G |
| PyramidBox [43] | VGG-16 | 0.956 | 0.946 | 0.887 | 57.18M | 236.58G |
| FA-RPN [36] | ResNet-50 | 0.950 | 0.942 | 0.889 | – | – |
| DSFD [27] | VGG-16 | 0.960 | 0.953 | 0.900 | 141.38M | 140.19G |
| SRN [3] | ResNet-50 | 0.964 | 0.953 | 0.902 | – | – |
| VIM-FD* [54] | DenseNet-121 | 0.967 | 0.957 | 0.907 | – | – |
| PyramidBox++* [28] | VGG-16 | 0.965 | 0.959 | 0.912 | – | – |
| AInnoFace* [49] | ResNet-152 | **0.970** | 0.961 | **0.918** | – | – |
| RetinaFace* [5] | ResNet-152 | 0.969 | 0.961 | **0.918** | – | – |
| ProgressFace | ResNet-152 | 0.968 | **0.962** | **0.918** | 68.63M | 123.91G |

**Results on WIDER FACE.** Table 1 compares our method with the state-of-the-art approaches on the WIDER FACE *validation* set. Taking the lightweight MobileNet-0.25 as backbone, our ProgressFace-Light only requires 1.35G FLOPs and achieves 87.9% AP on the hard set, significantly surpassing the previous methods. Especially, we outperform RetinaFace with the same backbone by a large margin of 9.7%. For fair comparisons, we also reimplement RetinaFace with DCNv2 [58], which has similar FLOPs with ours. Compared to the improved RetinaFace, we also achieve superior performance (87.9% vs. 79.5%). On the easy and medium sets, our method consistently outperforms the other light-weight face detectors. Taking ResNet-152 as backbone, our ProgressFace achieves detection AP of 96.8%, 96.2%, 91.8% with respect to the easy, medium and hard sets, which is competitive with the state-of-the-art methods. Detailed precision-recall curves on the *validation* set are shown in Fig. 4. On the *test* set, we obtain similar results of 95.9% (easy), 95.7% (medium) and 91.5% (hard). Detailed precision-recall curves on the *test* set are presented in the supplementary material. We also show some detection results on the WIDER FACE *validation* set in Fig. 5. Our method can detect faces in a wide variety of scales, illuminations, poses, scenes and occlusion.

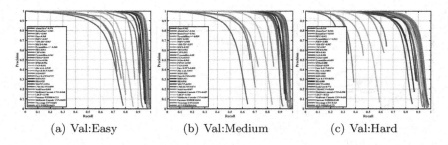

| (a) Val:Easy | (b) Val:Medium | (c) Val:Hard |

**Fig. 4.** Precision-recall curves on the WIDER FACE *validation* set. * indicates the work which is under review or not formally published.

**Fig. 5.** Sample detection results by our method on the WIDER FACE *validation* set.

**Results on FDDB.** For evaluations on the FDDB benchmark, we use the trained model on the *train* set of WIDER FACE with the ResNet-152 backbone. Our ProgressFace achieves 98.7% TPR when the amount of false positives is equal to 1,000, which is comparable with existing methods. Detailed ROC curves are presented in the supplementary material.

### 4.4 Ablation Study

**Contributions from Algorithmic Components.** We first conduct ablation experiments to show the relative contributions of each algorithmic component in the proposed method. Table 2 compares the baseline with our method in different settings on the WIDER FACE *validation* set. Based on the MobileNet-0.25 backbone, we implement a strong baseline with 85.1% AP on the hard set. With the proposed progressive training mechanism, the performance can be improved by 0.7~0.9% on the three sets. The results demonstrate that training with samples in the large-to-small order helps learn better face detectors. By applying KL loss for uncertainty estimation in the bounding box regression step, we can obtain a 0.5% gain on the hard set (86.3% vs. 85.8%). After integrating our anchor-free enhancement module, the performance can be further improved, especially on the hard set (87.9% vs. 86.3%). Such results validate the effectiveness of this auxiliary anchor-free module.

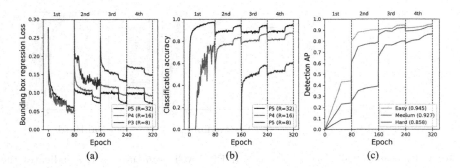

**Fig. 6.** (a) Loss curve for bounding box regression loss during training. (b) Classification accuracy during training. (c) Detection AP performance during validation.

**Table 2.** Ablation experiments of our methods on the WIDER FACE *validation* set. PT: Progressive training scheme. UE: Uncertainty estimation by KL loss. AF: Anchor-free enhancement module.

| Baseline | PT | UE | AF | Easy | Medium | Hard |
|---|---|---|---|---|---|---|
| ✓ | | | | 0.937 | 0.918 | 0.851 |
| ✓ | ✓ | | | 0.945 | 0.927 | 0.858 |
| ✓ | ✓ | ✓ | | 0.946 | 0.929 | 0.863 |
| ✓ | ✓ | | ✓ | 0.949 | 0.933 | 0.876 |
| ✓ | ✓ | ✓ | ✓ | **0.949** | **0.935** | **0.879** |

**Discussions on Progressive Training.** To further examine the effect of progressive training on the performance, we also train the same epochs for the baseline method. The results show that training longer only introduces a slight performance boost on the hard set (85.3% vs. 85.1%). With the same training epochs, the progressive learning scheme still can obtain another 0.5% improvement (85.8% vs. 85.3%). In addition, we show the bounding box regression loss, classification accuracy during training and detection performance during validation in Fig. 6. We observe that the validation performance increases with gradually incorporating easy-to-hard samples stage by stage. Even though easy samples encounter the potential risk of overfitting in the early stage, incorporation of more complex samples in the subsequent stage will mitigate this issue. Moreover, in order to avoid getting stuck in the intermediate sub-optimal solutions, we increase the initial learning rate of each stage when new samples are added into training.

**Anchor-Based vs. Anchor-Free.** To better understand the effect of our anchor-free enhancement module, we conduct three sets of ablation experiments in Table 3 to investigate the effects of different optimization methods, different levels of feature pyramids and different test schemes. (1) In the first group of

**Table 3.** Ablation experiments of anchor-based and anchor-free methods.

| Methods | | *Easy* | *Medium* | *Hard* |
|---|---|---|---|---|
| Optimization methods | Anchor-based only | 0.937 | 0.918 | 0.851 |
| | Anchor-free only | 0.879 | 0.870 | 0.813 |
| | Anchor-based + Anchor-free | 0.939 | 0.920 | 0.860 |
| Feature pyramids | Anchor-based + Anchor-free ($P_3$) | 0.949 | 0.935 | 0.879 |
| | Anchor-based + Anchor-free ($P_4$) | 0.946 | 0.930 | 0.867 |
| | Anchor-based + Anchor-free ($P_5$) | 0.944 | 0.930 | 0.864 |
| Test schemes | Anchor-based only | 0.949 | 0.935 | 0.879 |
| | Anchor-free only | 0.889 | 0.882 | 0.828 |
| | Anchor-based + Anchor-free | 0.947 | 0.932 | 0.876 |

Table 3, the results show training with anchor-based branches only outperforms training with anchor-free only. We accordingly choose the anchor-based method as our strong baseline. After combining these two optimization methods, the performance is better than either of them, which validates the motivation of our anchor-free enhancement module. (2) We add the anchor-free module to different levels of feature pyramids and compare their performance. Implementing such module on the lowest feature map $P_3$ in FPN obtains the best performance. The results validate our observations that small positive anchors tend to be missed on the low feature map. We also try adding anchor-free modules to each anchor-based branch and no more gains are obtained. (3) After training the anchor-based face detector with the anchor-free enhancement module together, we compare different test schemes. We found that only using the output of anchor-based branches is responsible for good results. Simply combining the output of anchor-based and anchor-free branches will not be a good choice because their generated scores tend to have different distributions.

## 5    Conclusion

In this paper, we propose a novel scale-aware progressive training mechanism to address large scale variations for face detection. Inspired by curriculum learning, our method gradually learns large-to-small face instances during training. We propose an auxiliary anchor-free enhancement module to facilitate the learning of small faces. We also apply KL loss to further improve bounding box regression by estimating uncertainty caused by ambiguous annotations. Extensive experimental results demonstrate the superiority of our method on the standard FDDB and WIDER FACE benchmarks. Especially, our ProgressFace with the MobileNet-0.25 backbone achieves 87.9% AP on the hard set of WIDER FACE, surpassing RetinaFace largely with the same backbone by 9.7%.

# References

1. Bengio, Y., Louradour, J., Collobert, R., Weston, J.: Curriculum learning. In: ICML (2009)
2. Cai, Z., Vasconcelos, N.: Cascade R-CNN: delving into high quality object detection. In: CVPR (2018)
3. Chi, C., Zhang, S., Xing, J., Lei, Z., Li, S.Z., Zou, X.: Selective refinement network for high performance face detection. In: AAAI (2019)
4. Dai, J., Li, Y., He, K., Sun, J.: R-FCN: object detection via region-based fully convolutional networks. In: NeurIPS (2016)
5. Deng, J., Guo, J., Zhou, Y., Yu, J., Kotsia, I., Zafeiriou, S.: Retinaface: single-stage dense face localisation in the wild. arXiv preprint arXiv:1905.00641 (2019)
6. Felzenszwalb, P.F., Girshick, R.B., McAllester, D., Ramanan, D.: Object detection with discriminatively trained part-based models. TPAMI **32**(9), 1627–1645 (2009)
7. Fu, C.Y., Liu, W., Ranga, A., Tyagi, A., Berg, A.C.: DSSD: deconvolutional single shot detector. arXiv preprint arXiv:1701.06659 (2017)
8. Gidaris, S., Komodakis, N.: Object detection via a multi-region and semantic segmentation-aware CNN model. In: ICCV (2015)
9. Girshick, R.: Fast R-CNN. In: ICCV (2015)
10. Girshick, R., Donahue, J., Darrell, T., Malik, J.: Rich feature hierarchies for accurate object detection and semantic segmentation. In: CVPR (2014)
11. He, K., Gkioxari, G., Dollár, P., Girshick, R.: Mask R-CNN. In: ICCV (2017)
12. He, K., Zhang, X., Ren, S., Sun, J.: Spatial pyramid pooling in deep convolutional networks for visual recognition. TPAMI **37**(9), 1904–1916 (2015)
13. He, K., Zhang, X., Ren, S., Sun, J.: Deep residual learning for image recognition. In: CVPR (2016)
14. He, Y., Zhu, C., Wang, J., Savvides, M., Zhang, X.: Bounding box regression with uncertainty for accurate object detection. In: CVPR (2019)
15. He, Y., Xu, D., Wu, L., Jian, M., Xiang, S., Pan, C.: LFFD: a light and fast face detector for edge devices. arXiv preprint arXiv:1904.10633 (2019)
16. Howard, A.G., et al.: Mobilenets: efficient convolutional neural networks for mobile vision applications. arXiv preprint arXiv:1704.04861 (2017)
17. Hu, P., Ramanan, D.: Finding tiny faces. In: CVPR (2017)
18. Huang, L., Yang, Y., Deng, Y., Yu, Y.: Densebox: unifying landmark localization with end to end object detection. arXiv preprint arXiv:1509.04874 (2015)
19. Jain, V., Learned-Miller, E.: FDDB: a benchmark for face detection in unconstrained settings. Technical report, UMass Amherst technical report (2010)
20. Jiang, L., Meng, D., Mitamura, T., Hauptmann, A.G.: Easy samples first: self-paced reranking for zero-example multimedia search. In: ACM MM (2014)
21. Kendall, A., Gal, Y.: What uncertainties do we need in Bayesian deep learning for computer vision? In: NeurIPS (2017)
22. Kong, T., Sun, F., Liu, H., Jiang, Y., Shi, J.: Foveabox: beyond anchor-based object detector. arXiv preprint arXiv:1904.03797 (2019)
23. Kumar, M.P., Packer, B., Koller, D.: Self-paced learning for latent variable models. In: NeurIPS (2010)
24. Law, H., Deng, J.: CornerNet: detecting objects as paired keypoints. In: Ferrari, V., Hebert, M., Sminchisescu, C., Weiss, Y. (eds.) Computer Vision – ECCV 2018. LNCS, vol. 11218, pp. 765–781. Springer, Cham (2018). https://doi.org/10.1007/978-3-030-01264-9_45

25. Lee, Y.J., Grauman, K.: Learning the easy things first: self-paced visual category discovery. In: CVPR (2011)
26. Li, D., Huang, J.B., Li, Y., Wang, S., Yang, M.H.: Weakly supervised object localization with progressive domain adaptation. In: CVPR (2016)
27. Li, J., et al.: DSFD: dual shot face detector. In: CVPR (2019)
28. Li, Z., Tang, X., Han, J., Liu, J., He, R.: Pyramidbox++: high performance detector for finding tiny face. arXiv preprint arXiv:1904.00386 (2019)
29. Lin, T.Y., Dollár, P., Girshick, R., He, K., Hariharan, B., Belongie, S.: Feature pyramid networks for object detection. In: CVPR (2017)
30. Lin, T.Y., Goyal, P., Girshick, R., He, K., Dollár, P.: Focal loss for dense object detection. In: ICCV (2017)
31. Liu, C., et al.: Progressive neural architecture search. In: Ferrari, V., Hebert, M., Sminchisescu, C., Weiss, Y. (eds.) ECCV 2018. LNCS, vol. 11205, pp. 19–35. Springer, Cham (2018). https://doi.org/10.1007/978-3-030-01246-5_2
32. Liu, W., et al.: SSD: single shot multibox detector. In: Leibe, B., Matas, J., Sebe, N., Welling, M. (eds.) ECCV 2016. LNCS, vol. 9905, pp. 21–37. Springer, Cham (2016). https://doi.org/10.1007/978-3-319-46448-0_2
33. Luo, W., Li, Y., Urtasun, R., Zemel, R.: Understanding the effective receptive field in deep convolutional neural networks. In: NeurIPS (2016)
34. Ming, X., Wei, F., Zhang, T., Chen, D., Wen, F.: Group sampling for scale invariant face detection. In: CVPR (2019)
35. Najibi, M., Samangouei, P., Chellappa, R., Davis, L.S.: SSH: single stage headless face detector. In: ICCV (2017)
36. Najibi, M., Singh, B., Davis, L.S.: FA-RPN: floating region proposals for face detection. In: CVPR (2019)
37. Ren, S., He, K., Girshick, R., Sun, J.: Faster R-CNN: towards real-time object detection with region proposal networks. TPAMI **39**(6), 1137–1149 (2015)
38. Shi, Y., Jain, A.K.: Probabilistic face embeddings. In: ICCV (2019)
39. Shrivastava, A., Gupta, A., Girshick, R.: Training region-based object detectors with online hard example mining. In: CVPR (2016)
40. Singh, B., Davis, L.S.: An analysis of scale invariance in object detection snip. In: CVPR (2018)
41. Singh, B., Najibi, M., Davis, L.S.: Sniper: efficient multi-scale training. In: NeurIPS (2018)
42. Supancic, J.S., Ramanan, D.: Self-paced learning for long-term tracking. In: CVPR (2013)
43. Tang, X., Du, D.K., He, Z., Liu, J.: PyramidBox: a context-assisted single shot face detector. In: Ferrari, V., Hebert, M., Sminchisescu, C., Weiss, Y. (eds.) ECCV 2018. LNCS, vol. 11213, pp. 812–828. Springer, Cham (2018). https://doi.org/10.1007/978-3-030-01240-3_49
44. Tian, Z., Shen, C., Chen, H., He, T.: FCOS: fully convolutional one-stage object detection. In: ICCV (2019)
45. Viola, P., Jones, M.J.: Robust real-time face detection. IJCV **57**(2), 137–154 (2004). https://doi.org/10.1023/B:VISI.0000013087.49260.fb
46. Wang, J., Yuan, Y., Li, B., Yu, G., Jian, S.: SFace: an efficient network for face detection in large scale variations. arXiv preprint arXiv:1804.06559 (2018)
47. Yang, S., Luo, P., Loy, C.C., Tang, X.: Wider face: a face detection benchmark. In: CVPR (2016)
48. Yu, J., Jiang, Y., Wang, Z., Cao, Z., Huang, T.: Unitbox: an advanced object detection network. In: ACMMM (2016)

49. Zhang, F., Fan, X., Ai, G., Song, J., Qin, Y., Wu, J.: Accurate face detection for high performance. arXiv preprint arXiv:1905.01585 (2019)
50. Zhang, K., Zhang, Z., Li, Z., Qiao, Y.: Joint face detection and alignment using multitask cascaded convolutional networks. IEEE Signal Process. Lett. **23**(10), 1499–1503 (2016)
51. Zhang, S., Wen, L., Bian, X., Lei, Z., Li, S.Z.: Single-shot refinement neural network for object detection. In: CVPR (2018)
52. Zhang, S., Zhu, X., Lei, Z., Shi, H., Wang, X., Li, S.Z.: Faceboxes: a cpu real-time face detector with high accuracy. In: IJCB (2017)
53. Zhang, S., Zhu, X., Lei, Z., Shi, H., Wang, X., Li, S.Z.: S3FD: single shot scale-invariant face detector. In: ICCV (2017)
54. Zhang, Y., Xu, X., Liu, X.: Robust and high performance face detector. arXiv preprint arXiv:1901.02350 (2019)
55. Zhou, X., Wang, D., Krähenbühl, P.: Objects as points. arXiv preprint arXiv:1904.07850 (2019)
56. Zhou, X., Zhuo, J., Krahenbuhl, P.: Bottom-up object detection by grouping extreme and center points. In: CVPR (2019)
57. Zhu, C., Tao, R., Luu, K., Savvides, M.: Seeing small faces from robust anchor's perspective. In: CVPR (2018)
58. Zhu, X., Hu, H., Lin, S., Dai, J.: Deformable convnets v2: more deformable, better results. In: CVPR (2019)

# Learning Multi-layer Latent Variable Model via Variational Optimization of Short Run MCMC for Approximate Inference

Erik Nijkamp[1(✉)], Bo Pang[1], Tian Han[2], Linqi Zhou[1], Song-Chun Zhu[1], and Ying Nian Wu[1]

[1] University of California, Los Angeles, USA
{enijkamp,bopang,linqi.zhou}@ucla.edu, {sczhu,ywu}@stat.ucla.edu
[2] Stevens Institute of Technology, Hoboken, USA
than6@stevens.edu

**Abstract.** This paper studies the fundamental problem of learning deep generative models that consist of multiple layers of latent variables organized in top-down architectures. Such models have high expressivity and allow for learning hierarchical representations. Learning such a generative model requires inferring the latent variables for each training example based on the posterior distribution of these latent variables. The inference typically requires Markov chain Monte Caro (MCMC) that can be time consuming. In this paper, we propose to use noise initialized nonpersistent short run MCMC, such as finite step Langevin dynamics initialized from the prior distribution of the latent variables, as an approximate inference engine, where the step size of the Langevin dynamics is variationally optimized by minimizing the Kullback-Leibler divergence between the distribution produced by the short run MCMC and the posterior distribution. Our experiments show that the proposed method outperforms variational auto-encoder (VAE) in terms of reconstruction error and synthesis quality. The advantage of the proposed method is that it is simple and automatic without the need to design an inference model.

## 1 Introduction

Deep generative models have seen many applications such as image and video synthesis, and unsupervised or semi-supervised learning. Such models usually consist of one or more layers of latent variables organized in top-down architectures. Learning such latent variable models from training examples is a fundamental problem, and this paper studies this problem for top-down models with

E. Nijkamp and B. Pang—Equal contribution.

**Electronic supplementary material** The online version of this chapter (https://doi.org/10.1007/978-3-030-58539-6_22) contains supplementary material, which is available to authorized users.

A. Vedaldi et al. (Eds.): ECCV 2020, LNCS 12351, pp. 361–378, 2020.
https://doi.org/10.1007/978-3-030-58539-6_22

multiple layers of latent variables. Such models have high expressivity and allow for learning hierarchical representations.

Learning latent variable models requires inferring the latent variables based on their joint posterior distribution, i.e., the conditional distribution of the latent variables given each observed example. The inference typically requires Markov chain Monte Carlo (MCMC) such as Langevin dynamics [22] or Hamiltonian Monte Carlo (HMC) [24]. Such MCMC posterior sampling can be time consuming and difficult to scale up. The convergence of MCMC sampling in finite time is also questionable, especially if the posterior distribution is multi-modal.

An alternative to MCMC posterior sampling is variational inference, such as variational auto-encoder (VAE) [20,29], which learns an extra inference network that maps each input example to the approximate posterior distribution. Despite the success of VAE, it has the following shortcomings. (1) It requires a separate inference model with a separate set of parameters. These parameters are to be learned together with the parameters of the generative model. (2) The design of the inference model is not automatic, especially for generative models with multiple layers of latent variables, which may have complex relationships governed by their joint posterior distribution. It is a highly non-trivial task to design an inference model to adequately capture the explaining-away competitions and bottom-up and top-down interactions between layers of latent variables [23,32].

The goal of this paper is to completely do away with a separate inference model. Specifically, we propose to use noise initialized non-persistent short run MCMC [25], such as finite step Langevin dynamics, as an approximate inference engine. In the learning process, for each training example, we always initialize such a short run MCMC from the prior distribution of the latent variables, such as Gaussian or uniform noise distribution, and run a fixed finite number (e.g., 25) of steps. Thus the short run MCMC is non-persistent. In agreement with the philosophy of variational inference, we accept the approximate nature of short run MCMC, and we optimize the step size, or in general, algorithmic hyper-parameters of the short run MCMC, by minimizing the Kullback-Leibler divergence between the approximate distribution produced by the short run MCMC and the posterior distribution. This is a variational optimization, except that the variational parameter is the step size. Our experiments show that the proposed method outperforms VAE for multi-layer latent variable models in terms of reconstruction error and synthesis quality.

One major advantage of the proposed method is that it is simple and automatic. For models with multiple layers of latent variables that may be organized in complex top-down architectures, the gradient computation in Langevin dynamics is automatic on modern deep learning platforms. Such dynamics naturally integrates explaining-away competitions and bottom-up and top-down interactions between multiple layers of latent variables. It thus enables researchers to explore flexible generative models without dealing with the challenging task of designing and learning the inference models.

One class of generative models that are of particular interest are biologically plausible models, such as Boltzmann machine [1] and the generation model of the Helmholtz machine [15], where each node is a latent variable. With such a large number of latent variables, designing an inference network to regulate the bottom-up and top-down flows of information as well as lateral inhibitions becomes a daunting task. However, short run MCMC is automatic, natural, and biologically plausible as it may be related to attractor dynamics [2,17,27].

## 2  Contributions and Related Work

The following are contributions of our paper.

- We propose short run MCMC for approximate inference of latent variables in deep generative models.
- We provide a method to determine the optimal step size, or in general, hyper-parameters of the short run MCMC.
- We demonstrate learning of multi-layer latent variable models with high quality samples and reconstructions.

The following are themes related to our work.

(1) *Variational inference.* As mentioned above, VAE [9,20,29,32] is the prominent method for learning generator network. Our short run MCMC can be considered an inference model, except that it is intrinsic to the generative model in that it is based on the parameters of the generative model. Thus there is little mismatch between the inference process and the generative model, even at the beginning stage of the learning algorithm. Only algorithmic hyper-parameters such as step size are optimized by variational criterion. It is particularly convenient for models with multiple layers of latent variables, whereas designing variational inference models for such generative models can be a highly non-trivial task.

(2) *Alternating back-propagation.* [11] proposes to learn the generator network by maximum likelihood, and the learning algorithm iterates the following two steps: (a) inferring the latent variables by Langevin dynamics that samples from the posterior distribution of the latent variables. (b) updating the model parameters based on the inferred latent variables. Both steps involve gradient computations based on back-propagation. Similar training scheme has been developed and extended to model flexible latent prior as in [26,28] and spatial-temporal data as in [10,35]. [4] also leverages Langevin dynamics for posterior sampling which is however initialized from samples produced by an inference network. In the training stage, in step (a), the Langevin dynamics is initialized from the samples produced in the previous learning epoch. This is usually called persistent chain in the literature [34]. In our work, in step (a), we always initialize the finite-step (e.g., 25-step) Langevin updates from the prior noise distribution. This can be called non-persistent chain. The following are advantages of our method based on non-persistent short run MCMC as compared to methods based on persistent chain. (1) The short run MCMC can be viewed as an inference model whose hyper-parameters can be optimized based on variational criterion. This strikes a middle ground between MCMC and variational inference. (2) Theoretical underpinning of the learning method based on short run MCMC is much cleaner. (3) In both training and testing stages, the same short run MCMC is used.

(3) *Short run MCMC for energy-based model.* Recently [25] proposes to learn short run MCMC for energy-based model (EBM). An EBM is in the form of an unnormalized probability density function, where the log-density or the energy function is parametrized by a bottom-up neural network. [25] shows that it is possible to learn noise initialized non-persistent short run MCMC such as 100-step Langevin dynamics that can generate images of high synthesis quality. Our method follows a similar strategy, but it is intended for approximately sampling from the posterior distribution of latent variables.

(4) *Attractor dynamics.* In computational neuroscience, the dynamics of the neuron activities is often modeled by attractor dynamics [2,17,27]. However, the objective function of the attractor dynamics is often implicit, thus it is unclear what is the computational problem that the attractor dynamics is solving. For the attractor dynamics to be implemented in real time, the dynamics is necessarily a short run dynamics. Our short run MCMC is guided by a top-down model with a well-defined posterior distribution of the latent variables. It may be connected to the attractor dynamics and help us understand the latter. We shall explore this direction in future work.

## 3   Top-Down Model with Multi-layer Latent Variables

### 3.1   Joint, Marginal, and Posterior Distributions

Let $x$ be the observed example, such as an image. Let $z$ be the latent variables, which may consist of latent variables at multiple layers organized in a top-down architecture.

The joint distribution of $(x, z)$ is $p_\theta(x, z)$, where $\theta$ consists of model parameters. The marginal distribution of $x$ is $p_\theta(x) = \int p_\theta(x, z)dz$. Given $x$, the inference of $z$ can be based on the posterior distribution $p_\theta(z|x) = p_\theta(x, z)/p_\theta(x)$.

The generator network assumes a $d$-dimensional noise vector $z$ at the top-layer. The prior distribution $p(z)$ is known, such as $z \sim \mathcal{N}(0, I_d)$, where $I_d$ is the $d$-dimensional identity matrix. Given $z$, $x = g_\theta(z) + \epsilon$, where $g_\theta(z)$ is a top-down convolutional neural network (sometimes called deconvolutional network due to the top-down nature), where $\theta$ consists of all the weight and bias terms of this top-down network. $\epsilon$ is usually assumed to be Gaussian white noise with mean 0 and variance $\sigma^2$. Thus $p_\theta(x|z)$ is such that $[x|z] \sim \mathcal{N}(g_\theta(z), \sigma^2 I_D)$, where $D$ is the dimensionality of $x$. For this model

$$\log p_\theta(x, z) = \log[p(z)p_\theta(x|z)] \tag{1}$$

$$= -\frac{1}{2}\left[\|z\|^2 + \|x - g_\theta(z)\|^2/\sigma^2\right] + c, \tag{2}$$

where $c$ is a constant independent of $\theta$.

In this paper, we are mainly concerned with multi-layer generator network. While it is computationally convenient to have a single latent noise vector at the top layer, it does not account for the fact that patterns can appear at multiple layers of compositions or abstractions (e.g., face → (eyes, nose, mouth) → (edges, corners) $\rightarrow$ pixels), where variations and randomness occur at multiple layers. To capture such a hierarchical structure, it is desirable to introduce multiple layers of latent variables organized in a top-down architecture. Specifically, we have $z = (z_l, l = 1, ..., L)$, where layer $L$ is the top layer, and layer 1 is the bottom layer above $x$. For notational simplicity, we let $x = z_0$. We can then specify $p_\theta(z)$ as

$$p_\theta(z) = p_\theta(z_L) \prod_{l=0}^{L-1} p_\theta(z_l | z_{l+1}).$$ 

(3)

One concrete example is $z_L \sim \mathcal{N}(0, I)$, $[z_l | z_{l+1}] \sim \mathcal{N}(\mu_l(z_{l+1}), \sigma_l^2(z_{l+1}))$, $l = 0, ..., L-1$. where $\mu_l()$ and $\sigma_l^2()$ are the mean vector and the diagonal variance-covariance matrix of $z_l$ respectively, and they are functions of $z_{l+1}$. $\theta$ collects all the parameters in these functions. $p_\theta(x, z)$ can be obtained similarly as in Eq. (2).

### 3.2   Learning and Inference

Let $p_{\text{data}}(x)$ be the data distribution that generates the example $x$. The learning of parameters $\theta$ of $p_\theta(x)$ can be based on $\min_\theta \text{KL}(p_{\text{data}}(x) \| p_\theta(x))$, where $\text{KL}(p \| q) = E_p[\log(p(x)/q(x))]$ is the Kullback-Leibler divergence between $p$ and $q$ (or from $p$ to $q$ since $\text{KL}(p \| q)$ is asymmetric). If we observe training examples $\{x_i, i = 1, ..., n\} \sim p_{\text{data}}(x)$, the above minimization can be approximated by maximizing the log-likelihood

$$L(\theta) = \frac{1}{n} \sum_{i=1}^{n} \log p_\theta(x_i),$$

(4)

which leads to the maximum likelihood estimate (MLE).

The gradient of the log-likelihood, $L'(\theta)$, can be computed according to the following identity:

$$\frac{\partial}{\partial \theta} \log p_\theta(x) = \frac{1}{p_\theta(x)} \frac{\partial}{\partial \theta} p_\theta(x)$$

(5)

$$= \int \frac{\partial}{\partial \theta} \log p_\theta(x, z) \frac{p_\theta(x, z)}{p_\theta(x)} dz$$

(6)

$$= E_{p_\theta(z|x)} \left[ \frac{\partial}{\partial \theta} \log p_\theta(x, z) \right].$$

(7)

The above expectation can be approximated by Monte Carlo samples from $p_\theta(z|x)$. The MLE learning can be accomplished by gradient descent. Each learning iteration updates $\theta$ by

$$\theta_{t+1} = \theta_t + \eta_t \frac{1}{n} \sum_{i=1}^{n} E_{p_{\theta_t}(z_i|x_i)} \left[ \frac{\partial}{\partial \theta} \log p_\theta(x_i, z_i) \mid_{\theta=\theta_t} \right],$$

(8)

where $\eta_t$ is the step size or learning rate, and $E_{p_{\theta_t}(z_i|x_i)}$ can be approximated by Monte Carlo sampling from $p_{\theta_t}(z_i|x_i)$.

## 4  Short Run MCMC for Approximate Inference

### 4.1  Langevin Dynamics

Sampling from $p_\theta(z|x)$ usually requires MCMC. One convenient MCMC is Langevin dynamics [22], which iterates

$$z_{k+1} = z_k + s\frac{\partial}{\partial z}\log p_\theta(z_k|x) + \sqrt{2s}\epsilon_k, \qquad (9)$$

where $\epsilon_k \sim \mathcal{N}(0,I)$, $k$ indexes the time step of the Langevin dynamics, and $s$ is the step size. The Langevin dynamics consists of a gradient descent term on $-\log p(z|x)$. In the case of generator network, it amounts to gradient descent on $\|z\|^2/2 + \|x - g_\theta(z)\|^2/2\sigma^2$, which is penalized reconstruction error. The Langevin dynamics also consists of a white noise diffusion term $\sqrt{2s}\epsilon_k$ to create randomness for sampling from $p_\theta(z|x)$.

For small step size $s$, the marginal distribution of $z_k$ will converge to $p_\theta(z|x)$ as $k \to \infty$ regardless of the initial distribution of $z_0$. More specifically, let $q_k(z)$ be the marginal distribution of $z_k$ of the Langevin dynamics, then $\mathrm{KL}(q_k(z)\|p_\theta(z|x))$ decreases monotonically to 0, that is, by increasing $k$, we reduce $\mathrm{KL}(q_k(z)\|p_\theta(z|x))$ monotonically [5].

### 4.2  Noise Initialized Short Run MCMC

It is impractical to run long chains to sample from $p_\theta(z|x)$. We thus propose the following short run MCMC as inference dynamics, with a fixed small $K$ (e.g., $K = 25$),

$$z_0 \sim p(z), z_{k+1} = z_k + s\frac{\partial}{\partial z}\log p_\theta(z_k|x) + \sqrt{2s}\epsilon_k, \quad k = 1, ..., K, \qquad (10)$$

where $p(z)$ is the prior noise distribution of $z$.

We can write the above short run MCMC as

$$z_0 \sim p(z), \ z_{k+1} = z_k + sR(z_k) + \sqrt{2s}\epsilon_k, \quad k = 1, ..., K, \qquad (11)$$

$R(z) = \frac{\partial}{\partial z}\log p_\theta(z|x)$, where we omit $x$ and $\theta$ in $R(z)$ for simplicity of notation. For finite $K$, this dynamics is a $K$-layer noise-injected residual network [12], or $K$-step noise-injected RNN [16,31]. It may also be compared to flow-based inference model [6–8,19,21], except we do not learn a separate inference model.

To further simplify the notation, we may write the short run MCMC as

$$z_0 \sim p(z), \ z_K = F(z_0, \epsilon), \qquad (12)$$

where $\epsilon = (\epsilon_k, k = 1, ..., K)$, and $F$ composes the $K$ steps of Langevin updates.

Let the distribution of $z_K$ be $q_s(z)$, where we include the notation $s$ to make it explicit that the distribution of $z_K$ depends on the step size $s$. Recall that the distribution of $z_K$ also depends on $x$ and $\theta$, so that in full notation, we may write $q_s(z)$ as $q_{s,\theta}(z|x)$.

For short run MCMC (10), the gradient term usually dominates the noise term, and most of the randomness comes from $z_0 \sim p(z)$. Given $\epsilon$, $z_K$ is a deterministic transformation of $z_0$. Assuming this transformation is invertible, and let $z_0 = F^{-1}(z_k, \epsilon)$. Let $q_s(z|\epsilon)$ be the conditional distribution of $z_K$ given $\epsilon$. By change of variable,

$$q_s(z|\epsilon) = p(F^{-1}(z, \epsilon))|\det(dF^{-1}(z, \epsilon)/dz)|. \tag{13}$$

Then

$$q_s(z) = \int q_s(z|\epsilon)p(\epsilon)d\epsilon = \mathrm{E}_{p(\epsilon)}[q_s(z|\epsilon)], \tag{14}$$

which can be approximated by Monte Carlo sampling from $p(\epsilon)$, i.e., the iid $\mathcal{N}(0, I)$ distribution.

For our method, we never need to compute $F^{-1}$, because we only need to compute $\mathrm{E}[h(z_K)] = \mathrm{E}_{q_s(z)}[h(z)]$ for a given function $h$, and

$$\mathrm{E}_{q_s(z)}[h(z)] = \mathrm{E}_{p(z_0)p(\epsilon)}[h(F(z_0, \epsilon))]. \tag{15}$$

In particular, we need to compute the entropy of $q_s(z)$ for variational optimization of step size $s$. The entropy is the negative of

$$\mathrm{E}_{q_s(z)}[\log q_s(z)] = \mathrm{E}_{p(z_0)p(\epsilon)}[\log \mathrm{E}_{p(\epsilon)}(q_s(F(z_0, \epsilon)|\epsilon))] \tag{16}$$

$$= \mathrm{E}_{p(z_0)p(\epsilon)}[\log \mathrm{E}_{p(\epsilon)}(p(z_0)/|\det(dF(z_0, \epsilon)/dz_0)|)], \tag{17}$$

where the expectations can be approximated by Monte Carlo sampling from the known prior distribution of $z_0$ and the known noise distribution of $\epsilon$. In the above computation, we need to compute the determinant of the Jacobian $dF(z_0, \epsilon)/dz_0$. Fortunately, on modern deep learning platforms, such computation is easily feasible even if the dimension of $z_0$ is very high. Specifically, after computing the matrix $dF(z_0, \epsilon)/dz_0$, we can compute the eigenvalues of $dF(z_0, \epsilon)/dz_0$, so that the log-determinant is the sum of the log of the eigenvalues.

As to the invertibility of $F$, in our experience, the eigenvalues of $dF(z_0, \epsilon)/dz_0$ are always away from 0, suggesting that $z_K = F(z_0, \epsilon)$ is locally invertible. Moreover, different $z_0$ always lead to different $z_K = F(z_0, \epsilon)$, suggesting that $F$ is globally invertible. Again, our method does not require inverting $F$.

## 4.3    Variational Optimization of Step Size

We want to optimize the step size $s$ so that $q_s(z)$ best approximates the posterior $p_\theta(z|x)$. This can be accomplished by

$$\min_s \mathrm{KL}(q_s(z)\|p_\theta(z|x)). \tag{18}$$

This is similar to variational approximation, with step size $s$ being the variational parameter.

$$\mathrm{KL}(q_s(z)\|p_\theta(z|x)) = \mathrm{E}_{q_s(z)}[\log q_s(z) - \log p_\theta(x, z)] + \log p_\theta(x), \tag{19}$$

where the last term $\log p_\theta(x)$ is independent of $s$. The computation of the first two terms is explained in the previous subsection. See Eqs. (15) and (17).

While we can optimize the step size $s$ for each example $x$, in our work, we optimize over an overall $s$ that is shared by all the examples. Reverting to the full notation $q_{s,\theta}(z|x)$ for $q_s(z)$, this means we minimizes

$$\frac{1}{n}\sum_{i=1}^{n}\mathrm{KL}(q_{s,\theta}(z_i|x_i)\|p_\theta(z_i|x_i)) \tag{20}$$

over $s$. The minimization can be accomplished by a grid search, or by gradient descent (the gradient is still computable on modern deep learning platforms).

Instead of using a constant step size $s$ for all $k$, we may also optimize over varying step sizes $s_k, k = 1, ..., K$. We leave it to future work.

The main computational burden in optimizing algorithmic hyper-parameters such as step size comes from the computation of the entropy of $q_{s,\theta}(z_i|x_i)$. In this paper, we compute it rigorously to make the learning principled. In future work, we shall explore efficient approximate methods to optimize short run MCMC.

## 4.4   Learning with Short Run MCMC

A learning iteration consists of the following two steps. (1) Update $s$ by minimizing (20). (2) Update $\theta$ by

$$\theta_{t+1} = \theta_t + \eta_t \frac{1}{n}\sum_{i=1}^{n}\mathrm{E}_{q_{s,\theta_t}(z_i|x_i)}\left[\frac{\partial}{\partial\theta}\log p_\theta(x_i, z_i)\mid_{\theta=\theta_t}\right], \tag{21}$$

where $\eta_t$ is the learning rate, $\mathrm{E}_{q_{s,\theta_t}(z_i|x_i)}$ (here we use the full notation $q_{s,\theta}(z|x)$ instead of the abbreviated notation $q_s(z)$) can be approximated by sampling from $q_{s,\theta_t}(z_i|x_i)$ using the noise initialized $K$-step Langevin dynamics. Compared to MLE learning algorithm (8), we replace $p_{\theta_t}(z|x)$ by $q_{s,\theta}(z|x)$, and fair Monte Carlo samples from $q_{s,\theta}(z|x)$ can be obtained by short run MCMC.

The learning procedure is summarized in Algorithm 1. Note, we only optimize $s$ every $T_s$ iterations, so that it does not incur much computational burden.

---

**Algorithm 1:** Learning with short run MCMC.

---

**input**  : Training examples $\{x_i\}_{i=1}^{n}$, learning iterations $T$, step size updating interval $T_s$, learning rate $\eta$, initial parameters $\theta_0$, batch size $m$, number of steps $K$, initial step size $s$.

**output:** Parameters $\theta_T$.

**for** $t = 0 : T - 1$ **do**

    1. Draw observed examples $\{x_i\}_{i=1}^{m}$.
    2. Draw latent vectors $\{z_{i,0} \sim p(z)\}_{i=1}^{m}$.
    3. Infer $\{z_{i,K}\}_{i=1}^{m}$ by $K$ steps of dynamics (10) with step size $s$.
    4. Update $\theta$ according to (21).
    5. Every $T_s$ iterations, update $s$ by minimizing (20).

---

## 4.5    Theoretical Underpinning

Given $\theta_t$, the updating Eq. (21) is a one step gradient ascent on

$$Q_s(\theta) = \frac{1}{n} \sum_{i=1}^{n} \mathrm{E}_{q_{s,\theta_t}(z_i|x_i)} \left[ \log p_\theta(x_i, z_i) \right]. \tag{22}$$

Compared to the log-likelihood in MLE learning, $L(\theta) = \frac{1}{n} \sum_{i=1}^{n} \log p_\theta(x)$,

$$Q_s(\theta) = L(\theta) + \frac{1}{n} \sum_{i=1}^{n} \mathrm{E}_{q_{s,\theta_t}(z_i|x_i)} \left[ \log p_\theta(z_i|x_i) \right] \tag{23}$$

$$= L(\theta) - \frac{1}{n} \sum_{i=1}^{n} \mathrm{KL}(q_{s,\theta_t}(z_i|x_i) \| p_\theta(z_i|x_i)) \tag{24}$$

$$+ \frac{1}{n} \sum_{i=1}^{n} \mathrm{E}_{q_{s,\theta_t}(z_i|x_i)} \left[ \log q_{s,\theta_t}(z_i|x_i) \right]. \tag{25}$$

Since the last term has nothing to do with $\theta$, gradient ascent on $Q_s(\theta)$ is equivalent to gradient ascent of $\tilde{Q}_s(\theta) = L(\theta) - \frac{1}{n} \sum_{i=1}^{n} \mathrm{KL}(q_{s,\theta_t}(z_i|x_i) \| p_\theta(z_i|x_i))$, which is a lower bound of $L(\theta)$. $\tilde{Q}_s(\theta)$ is a perturbation of $L(\theta)$. At $\theta_t$, the optimization over $s$ by minimizing (20) is to minimize this perturbation.

Thus a learning iteration can be interpreted as a joint maximization of $\tilde{Q}_s(\theta)$ over $s$ and $\theta$. Specifically, step (1) maximizes $\tilde{Q}_s(\theta)$ over $s$ given $\theta = \theta_t$, and step (2) seeks to maximize $\tilde{Q}_s(\theta)$ over $\theta$ given $s$. This is similar to variational inference with $s$ being the variational parameter.

The fixed point of the learning algorithm (21) solves the following estimating equation:

$$\frac{1}{n} \sum_{i=1}^{n} \mathrm{E}_{q_{s,\theta}(z_i|x_i)} \left[ \frac{\partial}{\partial\theta} \log p_\theta(x_i, z_i) \right] = 0. \tag{26}$$

If we approximate $\mathrm{E}_{q_{s,\theta_t}(z_i|x_i)}$ by Monte Carlo samples from $q_{s,\theta_t}(z_i|x_i)$, then the learning algorithm becomes Robbins-Monro algorithm for stochastic approximation [30]. For fixed $s$, its convergence to the fixed point follows from regular conditions of Robbins-Monro. We expect that the optimized $s$ will also converge to a fixed value.

It is worth stressing that $q_{s,\theta_t}(z_i|x_i)$ is the distribution under the short run MCMC. Thus fair samples can be obtained from $q_{s,\theta_t}(z_i|x_i)$ by running $K$ steps of short run MCMC. In contrast, the MLE estimating equation is $\frac{1}{n} \sum_{i=1}^{n} \mathrm{E}_{p_\theta(z_i|x_i)} \left[ \frac{\partial}{\partial\theta} \log p_\theta(x_i, z_i) \right] = 0$, where $p_\theta(z_i|x_i)$ is the posterior distribution. The MLE learning algorithm (8) requires sampling from $p_{\theta_t}(z_i|x_i)$, which can be impractical, especially for multi-modal posterior distribution, where the mixing rate of MCMC can be very slow.

In our method, our estimate is defined by the solution to the estimating Eq. (26), which is a perturbation of the MLE estimating equation. We accept this bias, so that the learning algorithm can be justified as a Robbins-Monro algorithm, whose convergence can be easily established. Thus both the target and the convergence of our learning algorithm are theoretically sound.

The bias of the learned $\theta$ based on short run MCMC relative to the MLE depends on the gap between $q_{s,\theta}(z|x)$ and $p_\theta(z|x)$. We suspect that this bias may actually be beneficial in the following sense. The gradient ascent of $Q_s(\theta)$ seeks to increase $L(\theta)$ while decreasing $\frac{1}{n}\sum_{i=1}^{n}\text{KL}(q_{s,\theta_t}(z_i|x_i)\|p_\theta(z_i|x_i))$. The latter tends to bias the learned model so that its posterior distribution $p_\theta(z_i|x_i)$ is close to the short run MCMC $q_{s,\theta_t}(z_i|x_i)$, i.e., our learning method may bias the model to make inference by short run MCMC accurate.

## 5    Experiments

In this section, we will demonstrate (1) realistic synthesis, (2) faithful reconstructions of observed images, (3) inpainting of occluded images, (4) learning of hierarchical representations, (5) variational grid search and gradient descent on the step size, and, (6) ablation on latent layers and Langevin steps. The baselines are trained with ladder variational autoencoder [32] for multi-layer latent variable models. We refer to the Appendix and the reference implementation[1] for details.

### 5.1    Synthesis

We evaluate the learned generator $g_\theta(z)$ by examining the fidelity of generated examples quantitatively on various datasets. Figure 1 depicts generated samples by our method and Ladder-VAE of size $64 \times 64$ pixels on the CelebA dataset. Figure 2 depicts generated samples of size $32 \times 32$ pixels for various datasets with $K = 25$ short run MCMC inference steps. Table 1 compares the Fréchet Inception Distance (FID) [14] with Inception v3 classifier [33] on $40,000$ generated examples for the comparable multi-layer latent variable models Ladder-VAE [32] and Glow [21] for which levels may be comparable with layers of latent variables. Even though our method is specifically crafted for multi-layer latent-variable models, Table 2 compares short run MCMC on training single-layer latent-variable models with ABP [11], GLO [3], VAE [20], and VAE with MADE [8]. Despite its simplicity, short run MCMC is competitive with elaborate means of inference in VAE models and flow-based models, such as Glow [21].

### 5.2    Reconstruction

We evaluate the accuracy of the learned short run MCMC inference dynamics $q_{s,\theta_t}(z|x_i)$ by reconstructing test images. In contrast to traditional MCMC posterior sampling with persistent chains, short run inference with small $K$ allows not only for efficient learning on training examples, but also the same dynamics

---

[1] https://enijkamp.github.io/project_short_run_inference/.

(a) Ladder-VAE with $L = 5$.　　　(b) Short run inference with $K$

**Fig. 1.** Generated samples for models with $L = 5$ layers on CelebA ($64 \times 64 \times 3$).

(a) MNIST ($28 \times 28$).　(b) SVHN ($32 \times 32 \times 3$).　(c) CelebA ($32 \times 32 \times 3$).

**Fig. 2.** Generated samples for $K = 25$ inference steps with $L = 5$ layers.

**Table 1.** Comparison of generators $g_\theta(z)$ with latent layers $L$ learned by Ladder-VAE and short run inference with respect to MSE of reconstructions and FID of generated samples for MNIST, SVHN, and CelebA ($32 \times 32 \times 3$).

| Models | MNIST | | SVHN | | CelebA | |
|---|---|---|---|---|---|---|
| | MSE | FID | MSE | FID | MSE | FID |
| Glow, $L = 3$ | – | – | – | 65.27 | – | 39.84 |
| Ladder-VAE, $L = 1$ | 0.020 | – | 0.019 | 46.78 | 0.031 | 69.90 |
| Ladder-VAE, $L = 3$ | 0.018 | – | 0.015 | 41.72 | 0.029 | 58.33 |
| Ladder-VAE, $L = 5$ | 0.018 | – | 0.014 | 39.26 | 0.028 | 53.40 |
| Ours, $L = 1$ | 0.019 | – | 0.018 | 44.86 | 0.019 | 45.74 |
| Ours, $L = 3$ | 0.017 | – | 0.015 | 39.02 | 0.018 | 41.15 |
| Ours, $L = 5$ | 0.015 | – | 0.011 | 35.23 | 0.011 | 36.84 |

**Table 2.** Comparison of generators $g_\theta(z)$ with latent layers $L = 1$ with respect to FID of generated samples for SVHN and CelebA ($32 \times 32 \times 3$).

| | ABP [11] | GLO [3] | VAE [20] | VAE+IAF [8] | Ours |
|---|---|---|---|---|---|
| SVHN | 49.71 | 65.52 | 46.78 | 50.41 | 44.86 |
| CelebA | 51.50 | 50.70 | 69.90 | 53.78 | 45.74 |

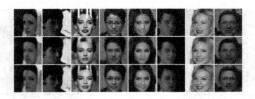

**Fig. 3.** Comparison of reconstructions between Ladder-VAE samples and our method on CelebA ($64 \times 64 \times 3$) with $L = 5$. *Top*: original test images. *Middle*: reconstructions from VAE. *Bottom*: reconstructions by short run inference.

**Fig. 4.** Inpainting on CelebA ($64 \times 64 \times 3$) with $L = 5$ for varying occlusion masks. *Top*: original test images. *Middle*: occluded images. *Bottom*: inpainted test images by short run MCMC inference.

can be recruited for testing examples. Figure 3 compares the reconstructions of learned generators with $L = 5$ layers by Ladder-VAE and short run inference on CelebA ($64 \times 64 \times 3$). The fidelity of reconstructions by short run MCMC inference appears qualitatively improved over VAE, which is quantitatively confirmed by a consistently lower MSE in Table 1.

### 5.3   Inpainting

Our method can "inpaint" occluded image regions. To recover the occluded pixels, the only required modification of (10) involves the computation of $\|x - g_\theta(z)\|^2/\sigma^2$. For a fully observed image, the term is computed by the summation over all pixels. For partially observed images, we only compute the summation over the observed pixels. Figure 4 depicts test images taken from the CelebA dataset for which a mask randomly occludes pixels in various patterns.

### 5.4   Hierarchical Representation

Multi-layer latent variable models not only demonstrate improved expressiveness over single-layer ones but also allow for learning the hierarchical structure. [36] argues that an alternative parameterization of the multi-layer generator promotes disentangled hierarchical features. We train a three-layer model with this parameterization using short run inference on SVHN. As shown in Fig. 5, the three-layer latent variables capture disentangled representations, which are background color, digit identity, general structure from bottom to top layer.

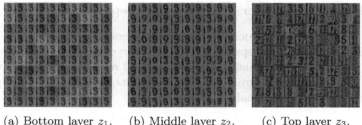

(a) Bottom layer $z_1$.      (b) Middle layer $z_2$.      (c) Top layer $z_3$.

**Fig. 5.** Generated samples from a three-layer generator where each sub-figure corresponds to samples drawn when fixing the latent variables $z$ of all layers except for one. (a) The bottom layer represents background color. (b) The second layer represents digit identity. (c) The top layer represents general structure. (Color figure online)

## 5.5   Variational Optimization of Step Size

The step size $s$ in (10) may be optimized such that $q_s(z)$ best approximates the posterior $p_\theta(z|x)$. That is, we can optimize the step size $s$ by minimizing $\mathrm{KL}(q_s(z)\|p_\theta(z|x))$ via a grid search or gradient descent. As outlined in Sect. 4.3, we require $dF(z_0, \epsilon)/dz_0$. In reverse-mode auto-differentiation, we construct the Jacobian one row at a time by evaluating vector-Jacobian products. Then, we evaluate the eigenvalues of $dF(z_0, \epsilon)/dz_0$. As both steps are computed in a differentiable manner, we may compute the gradient with respect to $s$.

Figure 6a and b depict the optimal step size $s$ over learning iterations $t$ determined by grid-search with $s \in \{0.01, 0.02, \ldots, 0.15\}$ and gradient descent on (20). For both grid-search and gradient descent the step size settles near 0.05 after a few learning iterations. Figure 6c details the optimization objective of $s$, $\mathrm{E}_{q_s(z)}[\log q_s(z) - \log p_\theta(x, z)]$, with respect to individual step sizes $s$.

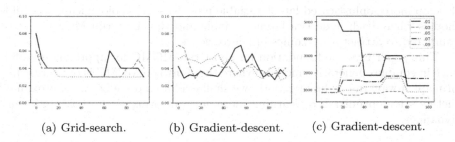

(a) Grid-search.      (b) Gradient-descent.      (c) Gradient-descent.

**Fig. 6.** (a) and (b) step size $s$ over epochs $T$ for three individual runs with varying random seed. (c) $\mathrm{E}_{q_s(z)}[\log q_s(z) - \log p_\theta(x, z)]$ for step sizes $s$ over epochs $T$.

## 5.6   Influence of Number of Layers and Steps

Tables 3a and b show the influence of the latent layers $L$ for the generator network $g_\theta(z)$ and the number of steps $K$ in the inference dynamics (10), respectively. Increasing $L$ improves the quality of synthesis and reconstruction. Increasing $K$ up to 25 steps results in significant improvements, while $K > 25$ appears to affect the scores only marginally.

**Table 3.** Influence of number of layers $L$ and number of short run inference steps $K$ on (a) CelebA ($64 \times 64 \times 3$) and (b) CelebA ($32 \times 32 \times 3$).

| | $L$ | | | | $K$ | | | | |
|---|---|---|---|---|---|---|---|---|---|
| | 1 | 3 | 5 | | 5 | 10 | 25 | 50 | 400 |
| FID | 61.03 | 52.19 | 47.95 | FID | 82.79 | 67.38 | 36.84 | 35.39 | 35.16 |
| MSE | 0.020 | 0.018 | 0.015 | MSE | 0.045 | 0.037 | 0.011 | 0.010 | 0.010 |

(a) Varying $L$ with $K = 25$.     (b) Varying $K$ with $L = 5$.

## 6   Conclusion

This paper proposes to use short run MCMC to infer latent variables in deep generative models, where the tuning parameters such as step size of the short run MCMC are optimized by a variational criterion. It thus combines the strengths of both MCMC and variational inference. Unlike variational auto-encoder, there is no need to design an extra inference model, which is usually a challenging task for models with multiple layers of latent variables.

The short run MCMC is easily affordable on the current computing platforms and can be easily scaled up to big training data. It will enable the researchers to develop more sophisticated latent variable models, such as biologically plausible models where each node is a latent variable and the short run MCMC can be compared to attractor dynamics in neuroscience.

This paper lays the foundation for short run MCMC for approximate inference in complex generative models, where the short run MCMC is optimized in a principled way. In our further work, we shall explore more efficient approximate methods for optimizing or learning more general forms of short run inference dynamics.

**Acknowledgments.** The work is supported by NSF DMS-2015577, DARPA XAI N66001-17-2-4029, ARO W911NF1810296, ONR MURI N00014-16-1-2007, and XSEDE grant ASC170063. We thank NVIDIA for the donation of Titan V GPUs. We thank Eric Fischer for the assistance with experiments.

# A    Appendix

## A.1    Experiment Details

All the training image datasets are resized and scaled to $[-1, 1]$ with no further pre-processing. We train the models with $T = 3 \times 10^5$ parameter updates optimized by Adam [18]. The learning rate $\eta$ decays step-wise $(1 \times 10^4, 5 \times 10^5, 1 \times 10^5)$ for each $1 \times 10^5$ iterations. If not stated otherwise, we use $K = 25$ short run inference steps and $\sigma$ is gradually annealed to 0.15.

## A.2    Model Specification

For the multi-layer generator model, we have $z = (z_l, l = 1, \ldots, L)$ for which layer $L$ is the top layer, and layer 1 is the bottom layer close to $x$. For simplicity, let $x = z_0$. Then, $p_\theta(z) = p_\theta(z_L) \prod_{l=0}^{L-1} p_\theta(z_l \mid z_{l+1})$. In our case, we have $z_L \sim \mathcal{N}(0, I)$, $[z_l | z_{l+1}] \sim \mathcal{N}(\mu_l(d_l(p_l(z_{l+1}))), \sigma_l^2(d_l(p_l(z_{l+1})))), l = 0, ..., L - 1$. where $\mu_l()$ and $\sigma_l^2()$ are the mean vector and the diagonal variance-covariance matrix of $z_l$ respectively, and they are functions of $d_l(p_l(z_{l+1}))$ where $d_l$ are deterministic layers and $p_l$ are projection layer to preserve dimensionality. $d_l$ is defined as two subsequent *conv2d* layers with *GeLU* [13] activation functions and skip connection. $p_l$ is a linear layer with subsequent *transpose_conv2d*. $\mu_l$ and $\sigma_l$ are a pair of *conv2d* and *linear* layers to project to dimensionality of $z_l$. Then, $z_l = \mu_l(d_l(p_l(z_{l+1}))) + \sigma_l(d_l(p_l(z_{l+1}))) \otimes \epsilon_l$ where $\epsilon_l \sim \mathcal{N}(0, I_{d_l})$. The final deterministic block $o_0$ is a *transpose_conv2d* layer projecting to the desired dimensionality of $x$. The range of $x$ is bounded by $tanh()$.

Table 4 illustrates a specification with $L = 3$ latent layers, latent dimensions $d_3 = 32$, $d_2 = 64$, $d_1 = 128$ for $z_3$, $z_2$, $z_1$, respectively, and $n_f = 64$ channels.

**Table 4.** Specification of multi-layer generator model with $L = 3$ layers, latent dimensions $d_3 = 32$, $d_2 = 64$, $d_1 = 128$ for $z_3$, $z_2$, $z_1$, respectively, and $n_f = 64$ channels.

| $l$ | Operation | Dimensions |
|---|---|---|
| 3 | $z_3 \sim N(0, I_{d_3})$ | $[n, d_3, 1, 1]$ |
| 2 | $z_{3,p} = p_2(z_3)$ | $[n, n_f, 16, 16]$ |
| 2 | $z_{3,d} = d_2(z_{3,p})$ | $[n, n_f, 16, 16]$ |
| 2 | $z_2 = \mu_2(z_{3,d}) + \sigma_2(z_{3,d}) \otimes \epsilon_2$ | $[n, d_2, 1, 1]$ |
| 1 | $z_{2,p} = p_1(z_2)$ | $[n, n_f, 16, 16]$ |
| 1 | $z_{2,d} = d_1(z_{2,p}) + z_{3,d}$ | $[n, n_f, 16, 16]$ |
| 1 | $z_1 = \mu_1(z_{2,d}) + \sigma_1(z_{2,d}) \otimes \epsilon_1$ | $[n, d_1, 1, 1]$ |
| 0 | $z_{1,p} = p_0(z_1)$ | $[n, n_f, 16, 16]$ |
| 0 | $z_{1,d} = d_0(z_{1,p}) + z_{2,d}$ | $[n, n_f, 16, 16]$ |
| 0 | $x = tanh(o_0(z_{1,d}))$ | $[n, 3, 32, 32]$ |

## A.3    Training of Baselines

For ladder variational autoencoder [32], the generator model is defined in Table 4. The training follows the one outlined in [32]. We train the model with $T = 3 \times 10^5$ parameter updates optimized by Adam [18].

For GLO [3] and ABP [11], our model in Table 4 was reduced to a single-layer variational autoencoder.

For GLO, we used a re-implementation[2] in PyTorch. As outlined in [3], after training the model, the inferred latent vectors, $z$, were used to fit a multivariate Gaussian distribution from which $z$ was drawn for sampling. The hyperparameters are as follows: $code\_dim = 128$, $n\_pca = 64 * 64 * 3 * 2$, $loss = l2$.

For ABP, 40 steps of persistent Markov Chains were used. The hyperparameters are as follows: 40 MCMC steps, Langevin discretization step size of 0.3, $\sigma = 0.3$, Adam [18] optimizer.

For Glow [21], the model was trained using the official code[3] with our datasets and the evaluation was performed with our implementation of the Fréchet Inception Distance (FID) [14] with Inception v3 classifier [33] on $40,000$ generated example. The hyperparameters are as follows: $dal = 0$, $n\_batch\_train = 64$, $optimizer = adamax$, $n\_levels = 3$, $width = 512$, $depth = 16$, $n\_bits\_x = 8$, $learntop = False$, $flow\_coupling = 0$.

# References

1. Ackley, D.H., Hinton, G.E., Sejnowski, T.J.: A learning algorithm for Boltzmann machines. Cogn. Sci. **9**(1), 147–169 (1985). https://doi.org/10.1207/s15516709cog0901_7
2. Amit, D.J.: Modeling Brain Function: The World of Attractor Neural Networks, 1st edn. Cambridge University Press, Cambridge (1989). http://www.worldcat.org/oclc/19922497
3. Bojanowski, P., Joulin, A., Lopez-Paz, D., Szlam, A.: Optimizing the latent space of generative networks. In: Dy, J.G., Krause, A. (eds.) Proceedings of the 35th International Conference on Machine Learning, ICML 2018, Stockholmsmässan, Stockholm, Sweden, 10–15 July 2018. Proceedings of Machine Learning Research, vol. 80, pp. 599–608. PMLR (2018). http://proceedings.mlr.press/v80/bojanowski18a.html
4. Chen, C., Li, C., Chen, L., Wang, W., Pu, Y., Duke, L.C.: Continuous-time flows for efficient inference and density estimation. In: Dy, J., Krause, A. (eds.) Proceedings of the 35th International Conference on Machine Learning. Proceedings of Machine Learning Research, PMLR, Stockholmsmässan, Stockholm, Sweden, 10–15 July 2018, vol. 80, pp. 824–833 (2018). http://proceedings.mlr.press/v80/chen18d.html
5. Cover, T.M., Thomas, J.A.: Elements of Information Theory, 2nd edn. Wiley, Hoboken (2006). http://www.elementsofinformationtheory.com/
6. Dinh, L., Krueger, D., Bengio, Y.: NICE: non-linear independent components estimation. In: 3rd International Conference on Learning Representations, ICLR 2015, San Diego, CA, USA, 7–9 May 2015, Workshop Track Proceedings (2015). http://arxiv.org/abs/1410.8516

---

[2] https://github.com/tneumann/minimal_glo.
[3] https://github.com/openai/glow.

7. Dinh, L., Sohl-Dickstein, J., Bengio, S.: Density estimation using real NVP. In: 5th International Conference on Learning Representations, ICLR 2017, Toulon, France, 24–26 April 2017, Conference Track Proceedings (2017). https://openreview.net/forum?id=HkpbnH9lx

8. Germain, M., Gregor, K., Murray, I., Larochelle, H.: Made: masked autoencoder for distribution estimation. In: International Conference on Machine Learning, pp. 881–889 (2015)

9. Gregor, K., Danihelka, I., Graves, A., Rezende, D.J., Wierstra, D.: DRAW: a recurrent neural network for image generation. In: Proceedings of the 32nd International Conference on Machine Learning, ICML 2015, Lille, France, 6–11 July 2015, pp. 1462–1471 (2015). http://proceedings.mlr.press/v37/gregor15.html

10. Han, T., Lu, Y., Wu, J., Xing, X., Wu, Y.N.: Learning generator networks for dynamic patterns. In: 2019 IEEE Winter Conference on Applications of Computer Vision (WACV), pp. 809–818. IEEE (2019)

11. Han, T., Lu, Y., Zhu, S., Wu, Y.N.: Alternating back-propagation for generator network. In: Proceedings of the Thirty-First AAAI Conference on Artificial Intelligence, San Francisco, California, USA, 4–9 February 2017, pp. 1976–1984 (2017). http://aaai.org/ocs/index.php/AAAI/AAAI17/paper/view/14784

12. He, K., Zhang, X., Ren, S., Sun, J.: Deep residual learning for image recognition. In: 2016 IEEE Conference on Computer Vision and Pattern Recognition, CVPR 2016, Las Vegas, NV, USA, 27–30 June 2016, pp. 770–778. IEEE Computer Society (2016). https://doi.org/10.1109/CVPR.2016.90

13. Hendrycks, D., Gimpel, K.: Bridging nonlinearities and stochastic regularizers with Gaussian error linear units. CoRR abs/1606.08415 (2016). http://arxiv.org/abs/1606.08415

14. Heusel, M., Ramsauer, H., Unterthiner, T., Nessler, B., Hochreiter, S.: GANs trained by a two time-scale update rule converge to a local Nash equilibrium. In: Advances in Neural Information Processing Systems 30: Annual Conference on Neural Information Processing Systems 2017, Long Beach, CA, USA, 4–9 December 2017, pp. 6626–6637 (2017)

15. Hinton, G.E., Dayan, P., Frey, B.J., Neal, R.M.: The wake-sleep algorithm for unsupervised neural networks. Science 268(5214), 1158–1161 (1995)

16. Hochreiter, S., Schmidhuber, J.: Long short-term memory. Neural Comput. 9(8), 1735–1780 (1997). https://doi.org/10.1162/neco.1997.9.8.1735

17. Hopfield, J.J.: Neural networks and physical systems with emergent collective computational abilities. In: Proceedings of the National Academy of Sciences, vol. 79, pp. 2554–2558. National Acad Sciences (1982)

18. Kingma, D.P., Ba, J.: Adam: a method for stochastic optimization. In: 3rd International Conference on Learning Representations, ICLR 2015, San Diego, CA, USA, 7–9 May 2015, Conference Track Proceedings (2015). http://arxiv.org/abs/1412.6980

19. Kingma, D.P., Salimans, T., Welling, M.: Improving variational inference with inverse autoregressive flow. CoRR abs/1606.04934 (2016). http://arxiv.org/abs/1606.04934

20. Kingma, D.P., Welling, M.: Auto-encoding variational bayes. In: 2nd International Conference on Learning Representations, ICLR 2014, Banff, AB, Canada, 14–16 April 2014, Conference Track Proceedings (2014). http://arxiv.org/abs/1312.6114

21. Kingma, D.P., Dhariwal, P.: Glow: generative flow with invertible 1x1 convolutions. In: Advances in Neural Information Processing Systems, pp. 10215–10224 (2018)

22. Langevin, P.: On the theory of Brownian motion (1908)

23. Maaløe, L., Fraccaro, M., Liévin, V., Winther, O.: Biva: a very deep hierarchy of latent variables for generative modeling. In: Advances in Neural Information Processing Systems, pp. 6551–6562 (2019)
24. Neal, R.M.: MCMC using Hamiltonian dynamics. In: Handbook of Markov Chain MonteCarlo, vol. 2 (2011)
25. Nijkamp, E., Hill, M., Zhu, S.C., Wu, Y.N.: Learning non-convergent non-persistent short-run MCMC toward energy-based model. In: Advances in Neural Information Processing Systems 33: Annual Conference on Neural Information Processing Systems 2019, NeurIPS 2019, Vancouver, Canada, 8–14 December (2019)
26. Pang, B., Han, T., Nijkamp, E., Zhu, S.C., Wu, Y.N.: Learning latent space energy-based prior model. arXiv preprint arXiv:2006.08205 (2020)
27. Poucet, B., Save, E.: Attractors in memory. Science 308(5723), 799–800 (2005)
28. Qiu, Y., Wang, X.: Almond: adaptive latent modeling and optimization via neural networks and Langevin diffusion. J. Am. Stat. Assoc. 1–13 (2019)
29. Rezende, D.J., Mohamed, S., Wierstra, D.: Stochastic backpropagation and approximate inference in deep generative models. In: Proceedings of the 31th International Conference on Machine Learning, ICML 2014, Beijing, China, 21–26 June 2014, pp. 1278–1286 (2014). http://proceedings.mlr.press/v32/rezende14.html
30. Robbins, H., Monro, S.: A stochastic approximation method. Ann. Math. Stat. 22, 400–407 (1951)
31. Rumelhart, D.E., Hinton, G.E., Williams, R.J.: Learning representations by back-propagating errors. Nature 323(6088), 533–536 (1986)
32. Sønderby, C.K., Raiko, T., Maaløe, L., Sønderby, S.K., Winther, O.: Ladder variational autoencoders. In: Advances in Neural Information Processing Systems 29: Annual Conference on Neural Information Processing Systems 2016, Barcelona, Spain, 5–10 December 2016, pp. 3738–3746 (2016), http://papers.nips.cc/paper/6275-ladder-variational-autoencoders
33. Szegedy, C., Vanhoucke, V., Ioffe, S., Shlens, J., Wojna, Z.: Rethinking the inception architecture for computer vision. In: 2016 IEEE Conference on Computer Vision and Pattern Recognition, CVPR 2016, Las Vegas, NV, USA, 27–30 June 2016, pp. 2818–2826 (2016). https://doi.org/10.1109/CVPR.2016.308
34. Tieleman, T.: Training restricted Boltzmann machines using approximations to the likelihood gradient. In: Machine Learning, Proceedings of the Twenty-Fifth International Conference (ICML 2008), Helsinki, Finland, 5–9 June 2008, pp. 1064–1071 (2008). https://doi.org/10.1145/1390156.1390290
35. Xie, J., Gao, R., Zheng, Z., Zhu, S., Wu, Y.N.: Learning dynamic generator model by alternating back-propagation through time. In: The Thirty-Third AAAI Conference on Artificial Intelligence, AAAI 2019, The Thirty-First Innovative Applications of Artificial Intelligence Conference, IAAI 2019, The Ninth AAAI Symposium on Educational Advances in Artificial Intelligence, EAAI 2019, Honolulu, Hawaii, USA, 27 January–1 February 2019, pp. 5498–5507 (2019). https://doi.org/10.1609/aaai.v33i01.33015498
36. Zhao, S., Song, J., Ermon, S.: Learning hierarchical features from deep generative models. In: Precup, D., Teh, Y.W. (eds.) Proceedings of the 34th International Conference on Machine Learning, ICML 2017, Sydney, NSW, Australia, 6–11 August 2017. Proceedings of Machine Learning Research, vol. 70, pp. 4091–4099. PMLR (2017). http://proceedings.mlr.press/v70/zhao17c.html

# CoTeRe-Net: Discovering Collaborative Ternary Relations in Videos

Zhensheng Shi[1], Cheng Guan[1], Liangjie Cao[1], Qianqian Li[1],
Ju Liang[1], Zhaorui Gu[1], Haiyong Zheng[1(✉)], and Bing Zheng[1,2(✉)]

[1] Underwater Vision Lab, Ocean University of China, Qingdao, China
{shizhensheng,guancheng,caoliangjie,
liqianqian5957,liangjie8257}@stu.ouc.edu.cn,
{guzhaorui,zhenghaiyong,bingzh}@ouc.edu.cn
[2] Sanya Oceanographic Institution, Ocean University of China, Sanya, China
http://ouc.ai

**Abstract.** Modeling relations is crucial to understand videos for action and behavior recognition. Current relation models mainly reason about relations of invisibly implicit cues, while important relations of visually explicit cues are rarely considered, and the collaboration between them is usually ignored. In this paper, we propose a novel relation model that discovers relations of both implicit and explicit cues as well as their collaboration in videos. Our model concerns *Co*llaborative *Te*rnary *Re*lations (CoTeRe), where the ternary relation involves channel ($C$, for implicit), temporal ($T$, for implicit), and spatial ($S$, for explicit) relation ($R$). We devise a flexible and effective CTSR module to collaborate ternary relations for 3D-CNNs, and then construct CoTeRe-Nets for action recognition. Extensive experiments on both ablation study and performance evaluation demonstrate that our CTSR module is significantly effective with approximate 3% gains and our CoTeRe-Nets outperform state-of-the-art approaches on three popular benchmarks. Boosts analysis and relations visualization also validate that relations of both implicit and explicit cues are discovered with efficacy by our method. Our code is available at https://github.com/zhenglab/cotere-net.

**Keywords:** Video understanding · Action recognition · Relation model

## 1 Introduction

We carve our world into relations between things [36]. The ability to discover relations between entities and their properties is central to our cognition of the world [17,20]. Consider an action of *"something colliding with something and both come to a halt"*, in contrast to the action of *"moving something and something closer to each other"*, identifying *"colliding"* and *"halt"* requires to reason about invisibly implicit dependencies and interactions, while recognizing *"moving"* and *"something"* needs to exploit visually explicit temporal motions

© Springer Nature Switzerland AG 2020
A. Vedaldi et al. (Eds.): ECCV 2020, LNCS 12351, pp. 379–396, 2020.
https://doi.org/10.1007/978-3-030-58539-6_23

and spatial objects. Thus, we understand these two actions from the videos via fusing these two requirements in our mind, and we argue that they correspond to relations of implicit and explicit cues respectively.

Discovering relations between entities is crucial to understand action and behavior from videos [9,11,30,32]. Existing relation models [4,53,63] for recognizing actions from videos typically discover the relations by reasoning about invisibly implicit temporal or channel cues, like dependencies and interactions. While, many efforts have been devoted to detect visually explicit temporal motions [5,50,51] or spatial objects [47,55], such as optical flow and visual attention, due to their effectiveness to recognize human actions. However, discovering the relations of these visually explicit cues is rarely considered. In addition, the collaboration between relations of implicit and explicit cues is usually ignored.

In this work, going further in modeling relations on the implicit level, we discover relations via leveraging both implicit and explicit cues to represent videos for understanding actions better. Our proposed relation model discovers the collaborative ternary relations in videos, dubbed **CoTeRe**, where the ternary relation involves channel (**C**, for implicit), temporal (**T**, for implicit), and spatial (**S**, for explicit) relation (**R**). Specifically, the channel relations take in charge of reasoning about implicit cues among different perspectives of global information over spatiotemporal scope, and the temporal relations are responsible for reasoning about implicit temporal dependencies between video frames, while the spatial relations are in charge of exploiting explicit spatiotemporal topological information visually. Finally, we collaborate the ternary relation for fusing implicit and explicit cues to better understand actions from videos.

Our **contributions** include: (a) A novel relation model discovering relations of both implicit and explicit cues in videos. (b) A flexible and effective CTSR module to collaborate the ternary relation for 3D-CNNs. (c) CoTeRe-Nets achieving state-of-the-art performance with a significant gain on action recognition especially in densely-labeled and fine-grained situations.

## 2    Related Works

### 2.1    Video Representation

Early contributions in video representation have focused on developing hand-designed spatiotemporal features [48,49]. Since the breakthrough of Convolutional Neural Networks (CNNs) [24] for image representation [12,14,21,41–43], many works have tried to design effective architectures for spatiotemporal representation in videos [2,18,38,44,51,52]. Karpathy *et al.* [18] first introduced CNN to represent videos. Then, two-stream [6,38] and 3D-CNN [15,44] led two mainstreams of video representation. Two-stream methods mainly used video RGB data and motion features like optical flow to learn representation [6,28,51,60]. C3D [44] devised a 3D convolutional filter and I3D [2] inflated 2D convolutional filters into their 3D counterparts to learn spatiotemporal representation. The recent 3D-CNN methods, such as P3D [33], S3D [57], and R(2+1)D [46], gained superior performance under better video representation by factorizing the 3D convolutional filter into separate spatial and temporal operations.

Some recent works on video representation focused on better leveraging temporal information to improve the performance [3,5,37,50,52,62,63]. TrajectoryNet [62] incorporated trajectory convolution for integrating features along temporal dimension to replace the existing temporal convolution. SlowFast networks [5] proposed a SlowFast concept with a slow pathway and a fast pathway to capture spatial semantics and finer motions respectively.

### 2.2 Relation Models

Recently, relation models have been adopted in the area of visual question answering [25,36], object detection/recognition [8,13], and intuitive physics [1, 54]. In the case of action recognition, a lot of efforts have been made on modeling pairwise human-object and object-object relations[11,23,35,58,59].

The latest works attempted to employ relational structures [36] for video representation and manifested that exploiting spatiotemporal relations is significant for video analysis [4,50,53,63]. ARTNet [50] decoupled spatial and temporal modeling into two parallel branches. TRN [63] was designed to learn and reason about temporal relations between video frames at multiple time scales. Wang *et al.* [53] proposed to represent videos as space-time region graphs connected by similarity relations and spatial-temporal relations. STC [4] modeled correlations between channels of a 3D-CNN with respect to temporal and spatial features.

### 2.3 Comparison to Our Approach

Compared to existing relation models for video representation, our approach aims to discover relations of both implicit and explicit cues for channel-temporal-spatial ternary collaboration, which significantly differs from previous works that capture only one or two scopes of relations with only implicit cues. We devise a novel CTSR module to discover collaborative ternary relations in videos, which is lightweight and flexible yet effective, and can be applied to any 3D-CNN architecture. Experiments demonstrate that our approach is able to not only outperform state-of-the-art on three action recognition datasets but also represent relations of implicit and explicit cues effectively (see Sect. 4).

## 3    Collaborative Ternary Relations Networks

We construct CoTeRe-Net by integrating CTSR modules (Fig. 1), which is designed on hierarchical mechanism with three levels: aggregation, relation and collaboration, for discovering collaborative ternary relations. CTSR module is lightweight and flexible, thus can be applied to any 3D-CNN architecture.

A CTSR module is a computational unit with the transformation mapping an input $\mathbf{X} \in \mathbb{R}^{C \times T \times H \times W}$ to collaborative relations $\mathbf{Z}^{\varsigma} \in \mathbb{R}^{C \times T \times H \times W}$, as shown in Fig. 1. The input of CTSR module $\mathbf{X}$ is a set of feature maps:

$$\mathbf{X} = [\mathbf{x}_1, \mathbf{x}_2, \cdots, \mathbf{x}_C] \in \mathbb{R}^{C \times T \times H \times W}, \tag{1}$$

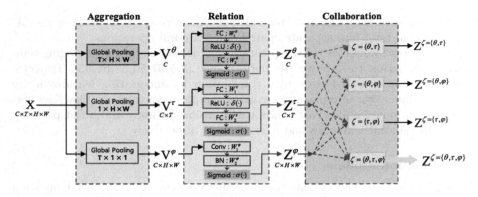

**Fig. 1.** CTSR module. A CTSR module is a computational unit designed on hierarchical mechanism with three levels: aggregation, relation, and collaboration. Aggregation level takes **X** as input and outputs relational descriptors **V**. Relation level analyzes descriptors for yielding ternary relation **Z**. Collaboration level builds upon relations to generate collaborative representation $\mathbf{Z}^\varsigma$.

where $\mathbf{x}_c \in \mathbb{R}^{T \times H \times W}$ $(c = 1, 2, \cdots, C)$ denotes the $c$-th channel of feature maps, $C$, $T$, $H$, and $W$ represent the channel number, temporal depth, height, and width of feature map, respectively.

We symbolize the ternary as channel $\theta$, temporal $\tau$, and spatial $\varphi$, and we define them relying on the scope of corresponding operation dimension, channel $C$, temporal $C \times T$, and spatial $C \times H \times W$, respectively. As shown in Fig. 1, aggregation level of CTSR module takes **X** as input and outputs three relational descriptors $\mathbf{V}^\theta$, $\mathbf{V}^\tau$, and $\mathbf{V}^\varphi$. These descriptors are then fed into relation level for yielding the ternary relation $\mathbf{Z}^\theta$, $\mathbf{Z}^\tau$, and $\mathbf{Z}^\varphi$. Finally collaboration level builds upon the ternary relation to generate channel-temporal-spatial collaborative representation $\mathbf{Z}^\varsigma$ $(\varsigma = \{\theta, \tau, \varphi\})$.

### 3.1 Aggregation Level

Aggregation level is at the first of CTSR module, and is designed to aggregate the channel, temporal, and spatial features separately from the input features **X**, yielding the corresponding relational descriptor **V**. We employ global pooling with different dimensions of kernel for aggregating different scopes of meaningful and non-linear relational descriptors.

**Channel Aggregation.** The input **X** is pooled on $T \times H \times W$ kernel over spatiotemporal scope, for aggregating channel descriptors $\mathbf{V}^\theta$:

$$\mathbf{V}^\theta = \left[\mathbf{v}_1^\theta, \mathbf{v}_2^\theta, \cdots, \mathbf{v}_C^\theta\right] \in \mathbb{R}^C, \tag{2}$$

and the $c$-th channel descriptors $\mathbf{v}_c^\theta$ are aggregated by:

$$\mathbf{v}_c^\theta = \frac{1}{T \times H \times W} \sum_{t=1}^{T} \sum_{h=1}^{H} \sum_{w=1}^{W} \mathbf{x}_c\left(t, h, w\right). \tag{3}$$

where $(t, h, w)$ represents the spatiotemporal position in volume.

**Temporal Aggregation.** Similarly, temporal descriptors $\mathbf{V}^\tau$ are aggregated by pooling the input $\mathbf{X}$ on $1 \times H \times W$ kernel over temporal scope:

$$\mathbf{V}^\tau = [\mathbf{v}_1^\tau, \mathbf{v}_2^\tau, \cdots, \mathbf{v}_C^\tau] \in \mathbb{R}^{C \times T}, \tag{4}$$

and the $c$-th temporal descriptors $\mathbf{v}_c^\tau$ are aggregated by:

$$\mathbf{v}_c^\tau = \frac{1}{H \times W} \sum_{h=1}^{H} \sum_{w=1}^{W} \mathbf{x}_c\left(t, h, w\right). \tag{5}$$

**Spatial Aggregation.** In the same way, we aggregate spatial descriptors $\mathbf{V}^\varphi$ using $T \times 1 \times 1$ kernel to pool the input $\mathbf{X}$:

$$\mathbf{V}^\varphi = [\mathbf{v}_1^\varphi, \mathbf{v}_2^\varphi, \cdots, \mathbf{v}_C^\varphi] \in \mathbb{R}^{C \times H \times W}, \tag{6}$$

and the $c$-th spatial descriptors $\mathbf{v}_c^\varphi$ are aggregated by:

$$\mathbf{v}_c^\varphi = \frac{1}{T} \sum_{t=1}^{T} \mathbf{x}_c\left(t, h, w\right). \tag{7}$$

## 3.2   Relation Level

Relation level is designed to extract ternary relation $\mathbf{Z}$ from aggregated relational descriptor $\mathbf{V}$ based on gating mechanism. For channel-temporal-spatial ternary relational descriptors, we devise different operations to obtain corresponding ternary relation, involving implicit and explicit cues.

**Channel Relations.** Channel descriptors $\mathbf{V}^\theta \in \mathbb{R}^C$ consist of $C$ descriptors. Thus, we feed these $C$ descriptors into multi-layer perceptron (MLP) with one hidden layer to obtain non-linear channel relations, and then they are passed through the sigmoid for activating the final channel relations $\mathbf{Z}^\theta$. Channel relations are expressed as:

$$\mathbf{Z}^\theta = \sigma\left(\mathbf{W}_2^\theta \delta\left(\mathbf{W}_1^\theta \mathbf{V}^\theta\right)\right) = \left[\mathbf{z}_1^\theta, \mathbf{z}_2^\theta, \cdots, \mathbf{z}_C^\theta\right] \in \mathbb{R}^C, \tag{8}$$

where $\delta$ and $\sigma$ refer to Sigmoid and ReLU functions respectively, $\mathbf{W}_1^\theta \in \mathbb{R}^{\frac{C}{r} \times C}$ and $\mathbf{W}_2^\theta \in \mathbb{R}^{C \times \frac{C}{r}}$ represent MLP weights and $r$ is reduction ratio of MLP. In such a way, MLP is essentially implemented for implicit relation reasoning [36].

**Temporal Relations.** Temporal descriptors $\mathbf{V}^\tau \in \mathbb{R}^{C \times T}$ are $T$ descriptors for each channel. Thus, we obtain temporal relations $\mathbf{Z}^\tau$ in the similar way as channel relations $\mathbf{Z}^\theta$, that is, we also employ MLP followed by sigmoid activation on temporal descriptors $\mathbf{V}^\tau$. Temporal relations are expressed by:

$$\mathbf{Z}^\tau = \sigma\left(\mathbf{W}_2^\tau \delta\left(\mathbf{W}_1^\tau \mathbf{V}^\tau\right)\right) = \left[\mathbf{z}_1^\tau, \mathbf{z}_2^\tau, \cdots, \mathbf{z}_C^\tau\right] \in \mathbb{R}^{C \times T}, \tag{9}$$

where $\mathbf{W}_1^\tau \in \mathbb{R}^{\frac{(C \times T)}{\tau} \times (C \times T)}$ and $\mathbf{W}_2^\tau \in \mathbb{R}^{(C \times T) \times \frac{(C \times T)}{\tau}}$ are MLP weights. Here MLP actually performs implicit relation reasoning temporally.

**Spatial Relations.** Spatial descriptors $\mathbf{V}^\varphi \in \mathbb{R}^{C \times T \times W}$ are $T \times W$ spatial representations for each channel, which are different from channel and temporal descriptors. Thereby we adopt spatial $3 \times 3$ convolution and batch normalization (BN) on spatial descriptors $\mathbf{V}^\varphi$ to extract spatial relations. The final spatial relations $\mathbf{Z}^\varphi$ are also obtained through sigmoid activation, and can be expressed as:

$$\mathbf{Z}^\varphi = \sigma \left( \mathbf{W}_2^\varphi \left( \mathbf{W}_1^\varphi \mathbf{V}^\varphi \right) \right) = [\mathbf{z}_1^\varphi, \mathbf{z}_2^\varphi, \cdots, \mathbf{z}_C^\varphi] \in \mathbb{R}^{C \times H \times W}, \tag{10}$$

where $\mathbf{W}_1^\varphi \in \mathbb{R}^{C \times 3 \times 3}$ and $\mathbf{W}_2^\varphi \in \mathbb{R}^C$ are weights of convolutional and BN layers respectively. By spatial aggregation and relation, in essence, the simple convolution plays a role in exploiting explicit cues.

### 3.3   Collaboration Level

Based upon ternary relation $\mathbf{Z}$, we collaborate channel-temporal-spatial relations at the last of CTSR module. The designed collaboration level will discover collaborative ternary relations $\mathbf{Z}^\zeta$ among channel-temporal-spatial relations $\mathbf{Z}$:

$$\mathbf{Z}^\zeta = \left[ \mathbf{z}_1^\zeta, \mathbf{z}_2^\zeta, \cdots, \mathbf{z}_C^\zeta \right] \in \mathbb{R}^{C \times T \times H \times W}, \tag{11}$$

where $\zeta \subseteq \{\theta, \tau, \varphi\}$ is the collaborative set of ternary relation $\{\theta, \tau, \varphi\}$.

Spatiotemporal features in volume are essentially channel-level in CNN architecture. We thereby employ channel-wise relation on each spatiotemporal relation for collaboration, and the $c$-th collaborative ternary relations $\mathbf{z}_c^{\zeta \subseteq \{\theta, \tau, \varphi\}}$ can be computed by:

$$\mathbf{z}_c^{\zeta \subseteq \{\theta, \tau, \varphi\}} = \mathbf{z}_c^\theta \cdot \left( \tilde{\mathbf{z}}_c^\tau (t, h, w) + \tilde{\mathbf{z}}_c^\varphi (t, h, w) \right), \tag{12}$$

$$\begin{cases} \mathbf{z}_c^\theta = \mathbf{1}^C, & \text{if } \theta \notin \zeta, \\ \tilde{\mathbf{z}}_c^\tau = \mathbf{0}^{C \times T \times H \times W}, & \text{if } \tau \notin \zeta, \\ \tilde{\mathbf{z}}_c^\varphi = \mathbf{0}^{C \times T \times H \times W}, & \text{if } \varphi \notin \zeta, \end{cases} \tag{13}$$

where $\tilde{\mathbf{z}}_c^\tau \in \mathbb{R}^{C \times T \times H \times W}$ and $\tilde{\mathbf{z}}_c^\varphi \in \mathbb{R}^{C \times T \times H \times W}$ denote that $\mathbf{z}_c^\tau \in \mathbb{R}^{C \times T}$ and $\mathbf{z}_c^\varphi \in \mathbb{R}^{C \times H \times W}$ are broadcasted to the size of $C \times T \times H \times W$, respectively.

Noting that, we have empirically evaluated the performance of addition on the ternary relations, and it does perform worse (about 0.3% lower) than our way formulated in Eq. 12. Except for collaborative ternary relations $\mathbf{Z}^{\zeta = \{\theta, \tau, \varphi\}}$, we can choose arbitrary two elements from the set $\{\theta, \tau, \varphi\}$ to acquire corresponding collaborative dual relations in videos, $\mathbf{Z}^{\zeta = \{\theta, \tau\}}$ refers to collaborative channel and temporal relations, $\mathbf{Z}^{\zeta = \{\theta, \varphi\}}$ concerns collaborative channel and spatial relations, and $\mathbf{Z}^{\zeta = \{\tau, \varphi\}}$ involves collaborative temporal and spatial relations.

Finally, the discovered collaborative ternary relations $\mathbf{Z}^\zeta$ are used to render the input features $\mathbf{X}$ via element-wise product, yielding the output features:

$$\mathbf{Y} = \mathbf{Z}^\zeta \cdot \mathbf{X} \in \mathbb{R}^{C \times T \times H \times W}. \tag{14}$$

**Table 1.** Network details of CoTeRe-ResNet-18 architecture. CoTeRe-ResNet-18 equips 3D ResNet-18 backbone with our CTSR modules.

| Layer name | Output size | 3D ResNet-18 | CoTeRe-ResNet-18 |
|---|---|---|---|
| $\text{conv}_1$ | $32 \times 56 \times 56$ | $3 \times 7 \times 7$, 64, stride $1 \times 2 \times 2$ | |
| $\text{res}_{2\_x}$ | $32 \times 56 \times 56$ | $\begin{bmatrix} 3 \times 3 \times 3, 64 \\ 3 \times 3 \times 3, 64 \end{bmatrix} \times 2$ | $\begin{bmatrix} 3 \times 3 \times 3, 64 \\ 3 \times 3 \times 3, 64 \\ \text{CTSR}, 64 \end{bmatrix} \times 2$ |
| $\text{res}_{3\_x}$ | $16 \times 28 \times 28$ | $\begin{bmatrix} 3 \times 3 \times 3, 128 \\ 3 \times 3 \times 3, 128 \end{bmatrix} \times 2$ | $\begin{bmatrix} 3 \times 3 \times 3, 128 \\ 3 \times 3 \times 3, 128 \\ \text{CTSR}, 128 \end{bmatrix} \times 2$ |
| $\text{res}_{4\_x}$ | $8 \times 14 \times 14$ | $\begin{bmatrix} 3 \times 3 \times 3, 256 \\ 3 \times 3 \times 3, 256 \end{bmatrix} \times 2$ | $\begin{bmatrix} 3 \times 3 \times 3, 256 \\ 3 \times 3 \times 3, 256 \\ \text{CTSR}, 256 \end{bmatrix} \times 2$ |
| $\text{res}_{5\_x}$ | $4 \times 7 \times 7$ | $\begin{bmatrix} 3 \times 3 \times 3, 512 \\ 3 \times 3 \times 3, 512 \end{bmatrix} \times 2$ | $\begin{bmatrix} 3 \times 3 \times 3, 512 \\ 3 \times 3 \times 3, 512 \end{bmatrix} \times 2$ |
| $\text{pool}_5$ | $1 \times 1 \times 1$ | Spatiotemporal avg pool, fc layer with softmax | |

### 3.4 Network Architecture

**Plug-in CTSR Module.** To render collaborative ternary relations from learned 3D feature representations, we plug our CTSR module into 3D residual block following 3D convolutions, constructing our CoTeRe-ResNet for videos.

**An Exemplar: CoTeRe-ResNet-18.** We construct CoTeRe-Net by equipping 3D-CNN backbones with our CTSR modules. In current implementation, we develop a CoTeRe-Net by plugging CTSR modules into 3D ResNet-18 architecture, and the resulted architecture is coined as CoTeRe-ResNet-18. Since motion modeling may be partially useful in the early layers, while it might be not necessary at higher levels of semantic abstraction (late layers) [46], thus we integrate CTSR modules on $\text{res}_2$, $\text{res}_3$, and $\text{res}_4$ layers, and leave $\text{res}_5$ layer unchanged. In this way, we can also better balance between model capacity and processing efficiency.

**Implementation Details.** Table 1 lists the details of our CoTeRe-ResNet-18 architecture, which takes $32 \times 112 \times 112$ volumes as input. We adopt one spatial downsampling at $\text{conv}_1$ implemented by convolutional striding of $1 \times 2 \times 2$, and three spatiotemporal downsamplings at $\text{res}_{2\_1}$, $\text{res}_{3\_1}$, and $\text{res}_{4\_1}$ with convolutional striding of $2 \times 2 \times 2$ respectively. We then apply a spatiotemporal average pooling with kernel size of $4 \times 7 \times 7$ on the final convolution at $\text{res}_5$, followed by a FC layer predicting the classification.

**Variant CoTeRe-Nets.** As illustrated in Sect. 3.3 and Fig. 1, different choices of set $\{\theta, \tau, \varphi\}$ refer to different collaborations of ternary relation, corresponding to different variants of CTSR modules as well. Thereby we can construct different variants of CoTeRe-Nets equipped by different variants of CTSR modules. These variant CoTeRe-Nets can be used to well study the efficacy of the ternary relation and their collaborations. Thus, in our implementation, we also build these variant CoTeRe-Nets for ablative study to explore the proposed collaborative ternary relations.

## 4    Experiments

### 4.1    Datasets and Setups

**Something-Something V1 and V2** [10]. V1 contains 108,499 short video clips in 174 action labels with simple textual descriptions, which is densely-labelled and fine-grained. V2 is the update of V1, and it contains 220,847 short video clips and also 174 same action labels with V1.

**UCF101** [40] **and HMDB51** [22]. UCF101 contains 13,320 videos divided into 101 action categories, ranging from daily life activities to unusual sports. HMDB51 contains 6,766 videos divided into 51 action categories.

**Training Details.** We perform data augmentation on both temporal and spatial scopes. We randomly sample 32 consecutive frames with sampling step 1 for Something-Something V1 and V2, 2 for UCF101 and HMDB51. The input frames are cropped via multi-scale random cropping and then resized to $112 \times 112$. The cropping window size is $d \times d$, where $d$ is the multiplication of input shorter side length and scale factors in $[0.8, 1]$ for Something-Something V1 and V2, $[0.7, 0.875]$ for UCF101 and HMDB51. We train and evaluate our models on a computer with 4 NVIDIA RTX 2080Ti GPUs, and set batch size to 8 with freezing BatchNorm parameters in training procedure for studying variant network settings (the batch size can be acctually set to 32 and it will gain within 0.5% performance compared to batch size 8). The network is trained by SGD with momentum 0.9 and weight decay 0.0001. The detailed training procedures for different experiments are explained in the specific sections. All the experiments are implemented by PyTorch framework (version 1.3).

**Evaluation Metric.** We report top-1 accuracy for all the experiments. We perform multiple clips testing for the evaluation at test time, temporal clips are uniformly sampled from each video, and spatial crops are then sampled from each frame of these clips. For UCF101 and HMDB51, we uniformly sample 10 temporal clips from the full length of the video, and use 3 spatial crops (two sides and the center). For Something-Something V1 and V2, temporal clips are uniformly sampled with the start frame in $[0, L - 32]$ ($L$ is the full length of the video), and are uniformly sampled 5 spatial crops (from left to right). We also perform spatial fully-convolutional inference [39,52] by scaling the shorter side of each video frame to 128 while maintaining the aspect ratios. The final prediction is the average softmax scores of all clips.

**Table 2.** Ablation study of 12 variant CoTeRe-Nets. Each of our ternary relation contributes to accuracy gain of action recognition, and collaborative dual relations contribute more than the single one of ternary relation with further accuracy gains. Our CoTeRe-Net model performs the best, validating the efficacy of CTSR module for discovering relations of both implicit and explicit cues.

| model | $\zeta$ | $r$ | top-1 | params | FLOPs |
|---|---|---|---|---|---|
| 3D ResNet-18 | - | - | 43.1 | 1× | 1× |
| CoTeRe-ResNet-18 | $\{\theta\}$ | 4 | 43.3 | 1.011× | 1× |
| CoTeRe-ResNet-18 | $\{\theta\}$ | 2 | 43.5 | 1.021× | 1× |
| CoTeRe-ResNet-18 | $\{\theta\}$ | 1 | 44.2 | 1.042× | 1× |

(a) Analysis of channel relations.

| model | $\zeta$ | $r$ | top-1 | params | FLOPs |
|---|---|---|---|---|---|
| 3D ResNet-18 | - | - | 43.1 | 1× | 1× |
| CoTeRe-ResNet-18 | $\{\tau\}$ | 128 | 43.3 | 1.012× | 1× |
| CoTeRe-ResNet-18 | $\{\tau\}$ | 64 | 43.7 | 1.024× | 1× |
| CoTeRe-ResNet-18 | $\{\tau\}$ | 32 | 44.5 | 1.048× | 1× |

(b) Analysis of temporal relations.

| model | $\zeta$ | Conv | top-1 | params | FLOPs |
|---|---|---|---|---|---|
| 3D ResNet-18 | - | - | 43.1 | 1× | 1× |
| CoTeRe-ResNet-18 | $\{\varphi\}$ | 1 × 1 | 43.4 | 1.005× | 1.001× |
| CoTeRe-ResNet-18 | $\{\varphi\}$ | 3 × 3 | 44.7 | 1.047× | 1.009× |

(c) Analysis of spatial relations.

| model | $\zeta$ | top-1 | params | FLOPs |
|---|---|---|---|---|
| 3D ResNet-18 | - | 43.1 | 1× | 1× |
| CoTeRe-ResNet-18 | $\{\theta,\tau\}$ | 44.9 | 1.090× | 1× |
| CoTeRe-ResNet-18 | $\{\theta,\varphi\}$ | 45.0 | 1.089× | 1.009× |
| CoTeRe-ResNet-18 | $\{\tau,\varphi\}$ | 45.4 | 1.094× | 1.009× |
| CoTeRe-ResNet-18 | $\{\theta,\tau,\varphi\}$ | **45.8** | 1.136× | 1.009× |

(d) Analysis of collaborative relations.

## 4.2  Ablation Study

We conduct ablative experiments on Something-Something V1 dataset [10]. We use 3D ResNet-18 as backbone, and construct variant CoTeRe-ResNet-18 models for analysis. Models are trained from scratch, and the training procedure takes 50 epochs total, with an initial learning rate 0.01 and reduces by a factor 0.1 at 40 and 45 epochs.

**Analysis of Channel Relations.** We first ablatively analyze the efficacy of channel relations by setting $\zeta = \{\theta\}$ (see Sect. 3.4). For channel relations $\mathbf{Z}^\theta \in \mathbb{R}^C$, we design a MLP-based gate to reason about relations of implicit cues among different perspectives of global information over spatiotemporal scope (see Sect. 3.2). We thereby study the impact of reduction ratio $r$ of MLPs. Due to only $C$ dimension of channel relations, we employ three different sizes of $r = \{4, 2, 1\}$ for evaluation, and the results of these CoTeRe-ResNet-18 models are reported in Table 2a. As it can be observed, by decreasing reduction ratio of MLPs, top-1 accuracy of CoTeRe-ResNet-18 models increases, but at the cost of more parameters as well. Considering the balance between accuracy gain and computational cost, we use $r = 1$ for MLPs contributing to channel relations. Moreover, in contrast to the baseline, we can see that channel relations do help to improve the performance of recognizing actions from videos.

**Analysis of Temporal Relations.** Similarly, we conduct ablative study to analyze the efficacy of temporal relations by setting $\zeta = \{\tau\}$. As to temporal relations $\mathbf{Z}^\tau \in \mathbb{R}^{C \times T}$, we adopt similar MLP-based gate design to reason about relations of implicit dependencies between video frames at multiple time scales. Thus we also study the impact of reduction ratio $r$ of MLPs. Differing from channel relations, temporal relations are $C \times T$ dimensional, such that we employ three different sizes of $r = \{128, 64, 32\}$, and evaluation results of these CoTeRe-ResNet-18 models are reported in Table 2b. Similar conclusion can be drawn according to the analysis of $r$ for channel relations. Considering that we can only obtain 0.6% gains with $r = 64$ while the number of parameters only increases 0.048 times with $r = 32$, we thus set $r = 32$ for MLPs conducing to temporal relations. Comparing to baseline, our temporal relations are also beneficial to gain accuracy of action recognition.

**Analysis of Spatial Relations.** Then, we investigate the efficacy of spatial relations by setting $\zeta = \{\varphi\}$. Spatial relations concern explicit spatiotemporal topological information that differs from implicit cues, hence we devise a different convolution-based gate for relation discovery (see Sect. 3.2). For the setting of convolution, we study the impact of kernel size with commonly used $1 \times 1$ and $3 \times 3$, and evaluation results are reported in Table 2c. Since $1 \times 1$ convolution only contributes 0.3% gains, we choose $3 \times 3$ convolution with only 0.047 times parameters and 0.009 times FLOPs increase but 1.6% gains on top-1 accuracy. Furthermore, CoTeRe-ResNet-18 with spatial relations involved outperforms baseline 3D ResNet-18 model, indicating efficacy of spatial relations.

**Analysis of Collaborative Relations.** Except for analyzing each single one of our ternary relation, we also study collaborative dual relations, for validating the efficacy of our collaboration level (see Sect. 3.3). By setting $\zeta$ to $\{\theta, \tau\}$, $\{\theta, \varphi\}$, and $\{\tau, \varphi\}$, we can get three variants of CoTeRe-ResNet-18 models with collaborative dual relations. While, the full CoTeRe-ResNet-18 model with collaborative ternary relations is built by $\zeta = \{\theta, \tau, \varphi\}$. The evaluation results of these four models are reported in Table 2d.

Observing the whole evaluation of Table 2, it is obvious that each of ternary relation makes a contribution to accuracy gain, and collaborative dual relations contribute more than single one of relations with further gains on top-1 accuracy. Overall, the model with collaborative ternary relations performs the best among these variants, verifying the effectiveness of our CTSR module for discovering relations of both implicit and explicit cues for better video representation.

### 4.3  Boosts Analysis

We show class-wise boosts over baseline with our ternary relation in Fig. 2. It can be seen that, **(1)** channel relations help to gain performance of recognizing actions that require implicit reasoning, such as classes with *pretending* behavior, indicating the efficacy of discovered channel relations with implicit cues; **(2)** temporal relations contribute more to understand actions with implicit temporal cues (dependencies and interactions), *e.g.*, recognizing *spreading*, *putting* and *hitting* actions needs temporal reasoning between video frames; **(3)** spatial relations benefit action recognition with explicit spatiotemporal topological

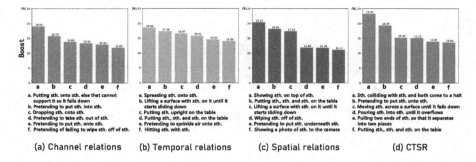

**Fig. 2.** Class-wise boosts of our ternary relation with respect to the baseline. Refer to Sect. 4.3 for further details.

information, for instance, *showing* and *wiping* actions mainly concern relations of objects and motions; **(4)** some fine-grained actions, like *lifting a surface with sth. on it until it starts sliding down* and *putting sth., sth. and sth. on the table*, contain both implicit temporal dependencies and explicit visual objects, thus require both temporal and spatial relations for boosting; **(5)** while CTSR takes advantages of the ternary relations for both implicit reasoning and explicit discovery spatiotemporally, such as, identifying *something colliding with something and both come to a halt* from *moving something and something closer to each other* needs relations of temporal dependencies and visual objects with reasoning information (for *colliding* and *halt*). Therefore, these boosts demonstrate that our ternary relation facilitates the model to discover relations of both implicit and explicit cues which do help to understand actions in videos.

Actually, relations in videos for recognizing actions are much more complex and elusive than that we can imagine, thus ternary relation might still not be elaborate enough to discriminate them, *e.g.*, *pretending* is such an elusive action, and it appears to be boosted by each of ternary relation and CTSR as well. So more effort is still needed for further exploring, and we hope that our work opens up new avenues for video understanding.

### 4.4 Relations Visualization

We visualize ternary relation on $res_2$ layer of CoTeRe-ResNet-18 in Fig. 3. For channel relations $\mathbf{Z}^\theta \in \mathbb{R}^C$ (Eq. 8), we use 2D chart to show scores of channels. For temporal relations $\mathbf{Z}^\tau \in \mathbb{R}^{C \times T}$ (Eq. 9), we also use 2D chart to show scores of temporal frames under certain channels. For spatial relations $\mathbf{Z}^\varphi \in \mathbb{R}^{C \times H \times W}$ (Eq. 10), we thereby use 3D chart to show scores of spatial widths and heights.

The top of Fig. 3 represents channel descriptors (red curve) and our discovered channel relations (blue curve), it's clear to see the changes indicating relation discovery, and high relation score reflects rich relation while low relation score implies poor relation. We take a closer look at two obvious positive changes at $8^{th}$ and $18^{th}$ channel, and two obvious negative changes at $29^{th}$ and $32^{th}$ channel, to observe their corresponding temporal and spatial relations, shown in the

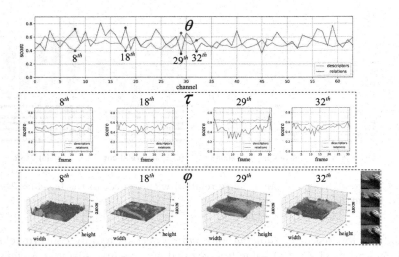

**Fig. 3.** Visualization of our ternary relation. From top to bottom: channel relations, temporal relations, and spatial relations. All scores are obtained by adopting sigmoid functions. Refer to Sects. 4.4 and 3 for further details. (Color figure online)

middle and bottom of Fig. 3 respectively. We can see that the trend and direction of changes for temporal relation discovery are the same as those for channel relation discovery, demonstrating that both of the $8^{th}$ and $18^{th}$ channel discover significant relations of implicit cues while both of the $29^{th}$ and $32^{th}$ channel discover insignificant relations of implicit cues. By contrast, visualization of spatial relations indicates that, the $8^{th}$ and $18^{th}$ channel don't have more relations of visually explicit motion and object information, but the $29^{th}$ and $32^{th}$ channel have, and high relation scores match with the objects and motion trajectory in the right clip spatially. These visualizations further interpret that our channel and temporal relations refer to implicit cues while our spatial relations concern explicit cues, thus they are supplementary for representing videos better.

### 4.5   Experiments on Something-Something V1 and V2

We use ResNet-34 backbone network with separable R(2+1)D [46] to construct CoTeRe-ResNet-34, by implementing CTSR modules on res$_2$, res$_3$, and res$_4$ layers. We implement our CoTeRe-ResNet-34 on Kinetics-400 [19] to produce the pre-train models: Kinetics (top-1: 75.3, train Kinetics from scratch for 200 epochs), IG-65M+Kinetics (top-1: 80.2, finetune Kinetics on the released IG-65M [7] pre-trained model for 40 epochs). Besides, we also similarly build CoTeRe-ResNet-18 pre-trained on Kinetics (top-1: 70.6) for fair comparison with previous works. For the experiments on Something-Something V1 and V2, the training procedure is different from ablation study in Sect. 4.2 when uses IG-65M+Kinetics pre-train, which takes 30 epochs with initial learning rate 0.001 and reduces by a factor 0.1 at 20 and 25 epochs.

**Table 3.** Comparison with state-of-the-arts on Something-Something V1 and V2.

| Model | Backbone | Pre-train | FLOPs | Top-1(V1) | Top-1(V2) |
|---|---|---|---|---|---|
| 3D-CNN [10] | C3D | Sports1M | N/A | 11.5 | N/A |
| TRN* [63] | BNInception | ImageNet | N/A | 42.0 | 55.5 |
| NL I3D+GCN [53] | ResNet-50 | ImageNet+Kinetics | 158G | 46.1 | N/A |
| TrajectoryNet* [62] | ResNet-18 | Kinetics | N/A | 47.8 | N/A |
| ECO* [64] | ResNet-18 | Kinetics | N/A | 49.5 | N/A |
| S3D-G [57] | Inception | ImageNet | 71.4G | 48.2 | N/A |
| GST [29] | ResNet-50 | ImageNet | 59G | 48.6 | 62.6 |
| TRN Dual Attn.* [56] | BNInception | ImageNet | N/A | N/A | 58.4 |
| CPNet [27] | ResNet-34 | ImageNet | N/A | N/A | 57.7 |
| ir-CSN [45] | ResNet-152 | – | 96.7G | 49.3 | N/A |
| Ghadiyaram et al. [7] | ResNet-152 | IG-65M | 252G | 51.6 | N/A |
| STM [16] | ResNet-50 | ImageNet | 66.5G | 50.7 | 64.2 |
| TSM* [26] | ResNet-50 | Kinetics | 65.8G | 52.6 | 66.0 |
| MARS* [3] | ResNeXt-101 | Kinetics | N/A | 53.0 | N/A |
| Martinez et al. [31] | ResNet-152 | ImageNet | N/A | 53.4 | N/A |
| Our baseline | ResNet-34 | – | 76.3G | 47.2 | 60.8 |
| Our CoTeRe-Net | ResNet-34 | – | 77.9G | 49.7 | 63.2 |
| Our CoTeRe-Net | ResNet-18 | Kinetics | 41.1G | 50.5 | 63.9 |
| Our CoTeRe-Net | ResNet-34 | Kinetics | 77.9G | 52.8 | 66.2 |
| Our CoTeRe-Net | ResNet-34 | IG65M+Kinetics | 77.9G | **53.9** | **67.1** |

*more complicated models with extra information (trajectory features or optical flow).
"N/A" means that the paper didn't report the corresponding evaluation value.

Table 3 reports comparison results of top-1 accuracy on Something-Something V1 and V2 datasets, from which we make the following observations: First, our approach outperforms baseline model considerably, by improving top-1 accuracy from 47.2 to 49.7 (V1) and 60.8 to 63.2 (V2) using ResNet-34 without pre-train, which also beats the latest ir-CSN [45] (49.7 vs. 49.3 on V1); Second, our approach with a ResNet-18 backbone pre-trained on Kinetics improves over previous state-of-the-art (with the same settings) by 1% (V1) in top-1 accuracy (50.5 vs. 49.5, ECO [64]); Third, we further improve our performance by training on deeper backbone ResNet-34 and larger pre-training datasets IG-65M+Kinetics, and substantially increase top-1 accuracy by 6.7% (V1) and 6.3% (V2) against baseline model, achieving state-of-the-art performance on both V1 and V2 datasets. Also note that Martinez et al. [31] uses a much deeper ResNet-152 backbone to achieve competitive top-1 accuracy (53.4), while we have not tried it, we expect a similar improvement, referring to boosts of 50.5 to 52.8 (V1) and 63.9 to 66.2 (V2) by only changing backbone from ResNet-18 to ResNet-34, which can further boost our performance. Our CoTeRe-Nets also show competitive computational cost via FLOPs comparison.

**Table 4.** Comparison with state-of-the-arts on UCF101 and HMDB51.

| Model | Backbone | Pre-train | UCF101 | HMDB51 |
|---|---|---|---|---|
| IDT [49] | – | – | 86.4 | 61.7 |
| C3D-RGB [44] | – | Sports1M | 85.2 | N/A |
| Two-stream [38] | – | ImageNet | 88.0 | 59.4 |
| TSN [51] | BNInception | ImageNet | 94.2 | 69.4 |
| P3D [33] | ResNet-152 | ImageNet | 93.7 | N/A |
| ARTNet with TSN [50] | ResNet-18 | Kinetics | 94.3 | 70.9 |
| Attention Cluster [28] | ResNet-152 | ImageNet | 94.6 | 69.2 |
| I3D-RGB [2] | Inception | ImageNet+Kinetics | 95.6 | 74.8 |
| STC-Net [4] | ResNeXt-101 | ImageNet+Kinetics | 95.8 | 72.6 |
| Zhao et al. [61] | BNInception | ImageNet+Kinetics | 95.9 | N/A |
| R(2+1)D-RGB [46] | ResNet-34 | Sports1M+Kinetics | 96.8 | 74.5 |
| S3D-G [57] | Inception | ImageNet+Kinetics | 96.8 | 75.9 |
| LGD-3D-RGB [34] | ResNet-101 | ImageNet+Kinetics | 97.0 | 75.7 |
| Our CoTeRe-Net | ResNet-18 | Kinetics | 94.5 | 71.3 |
| Our CoTeRe-Net | ResNet-34 | Kinetics | 96.4 | 75.0 |
| Our CoTeRe-Net | ResNet-34 | IG-65M+Kinetics | **97.6** | **76.0** |

Our state-of-the-art results on these two challenging datasets demonstrate the strength of our CoTeRe-Net and highlight the importance of discovering collaborative ternary relations for action recognition from videos.

### 4.6    Experiments on UCF101 and HMDB51

We also conduct experiments on two classic action recognition benchmarks: UCF101 [40] and HMDB51 [22]. The training procedure takes 40 epochs total, with an initial learning rate 0.001 for Kinetics pre-train and 0.0001 for IG-65M+Kinetics, and reduces by a factor 0.1 at 15 and 30 epochs.

We compare against single RGB models, and Table 4 reports results of top-1 accuracy on these two datasets. Compared to the models with similar or deeper backbone and same pre-train, our CoTeRe-ResNets pre-trained on Kinetics achieve superior performance (top-1 accuracy) on UCF101 and HMDB51. Also our CoTeRe-ResNet-34 pre-trained on IG-65M+Kinetics achieves state-of-the-art performance over existing models with similar settings but much deeper backbones.

## 5    Conclusion

We propose a novel relation model for discovering collaborative ternary relations in videos. Both boosts analysis and relations visualization validate the efficacy of our CTSR module for representing relations from videos. Both ablation study and evaluation comparison verify the effectiveness of our CoTeRe-Net models on action recognition. To the best of our knowledge, our work is one of the first to model relations involving both implicit and explicit cues for video representation. Nevertheless, relations between things are much more complex and elusive than that we can imagine, thus more effort is still needed for further exploring, and we hope that our work opens up new avenues for video understanding.

**Acknowledgment.** This work was supported by the National Natural Science Foundation of China under grant numbers 61771440 and 41776113.

# References

1. Battaglia, P., Pascanu, R., Lai, M., Rezende, D.J., et al.: Interaction networks for learning about objects, relations and physics. In: NIPS, pp. 4502–4510 (2016)
2. Carreira, J., Zisserman, A.: Quo vadis, action recognition? A new model and the Kinetics dataset. In: CVPR, pp. 6299–6308 (2017)
3. Crasto, N., Weinzaepfel, P., Alahari, K., Schmid, C.: MARS: motion-augmented RGB stream for action recognition. In: CVPR, pp. 7882–7891 (2019)
4. Diba, A., et al.: Spatio-temporal channel correlation networks for action classification. In: Ferrari, V., Hebert, M., Sminchisescu, C., Weiss, Y. (eds.) ECCV 2018. LNCS, vol. 11208, pp. 299–315. Springer, Cham (2018). https://doi.org/10.1007/978-3-030-01225-0_18
5. Feichtenhofer, C., Fan, H., Malik, J., He, K.: Slowfast networks for video recognition. In: ICCV, pp. 6202–6211 (2019)
6. Feichtenhofer, C., Pinz, A., Zisserman, A.: Convolutional two-stream network fusion for video action recognition. In: CVPR, pp. 1933–1941 (2016)
7. Ghadiyaram, D., Tran, D., Mahajan, D.: Large-scale weakly-supervised pre-training for video action recognition. In: CVPR, pp. 12046–12055 (2019)
8. Gkioxari, G., Girshick, R., Dollár, P., He, K.: Detecting and recognizing human-object interactions. In: CVPR, pp. 8359–8367 (2018)
9. Gkioxari, G., Girshick, R., Malik, J.: Actions and attributes from wholes and parts. In: ICCV, pp. 2470–2478 (2015)
10. Goyal, R., et al.: The "something something" video database for learning and evaluating visual common sense. In: ICCV, pp. 5842–5850 (2017)
11. Gupta, A., Kembhavi, A., Davis, L.S.: Observing human-object interactions: using spatial and functional compatibility for recognition. IEEE TPAMI **31**(10), 1775–1789 (2009)
12. He, K., Zhang, X., Ren, S., Sun, J.: Deep residual learning for image recognition. In: CVPR, pp. 770–778 (2016)
13. Hu, H., Gu, J., Zhang, Z., Dai, J., Wei, Y.: Relation networks for object detection. In: CVPR, pp. 3588–3597 (2018)
14. Ioffe, S., Szegedy, C.: Batch normalization: accelerating deep network training by reducing internal covariate shift. arXiv preprint arXiv:1502.03167 (2015)
15. Ji, S., Xu, W., Yang, M., Yu, K.: 3D convolutional neural networks for human action recognition. IEEE TPAMI **35**(1), 221–231 (2013)
16. Jiang, B., Wang, M., Gan, W., Wu, W., Yan, J.: STM: spatiotemporal and motion encoding for action recognition. In: ICCV, pp. 2000–2008 (2019)

17. Johnson, J., Hariharan, B., van der Maaten, L., Fei-Fei, L., Lawrence Zitnick, C., Girshick, R.: CLEVR: a diagnostic dataset for compositional language and elementary visual reasoning. In: CVPR, pp. 2901–2910 (2017)
18. Karpathy, A., Toderici, G., Shetty, S., Leung, T., Sukthankar, R., Fei-Fei, L.: Large-scale video classification with convolutional neural networks. In: CVPR, pp. 1725–1732 (2014)
19. Kay, W., et al.: The Kinetics human action video dataset. arXiv preprint arXiv:1409.1556 (2017)
20. Kemp, C., Tenenbaum, J.B.: The discovery of structural form. PNAS **105**(31), 10687–10692 (2008)
21. Krizhevsky, A., Sutskever, I., Hinton, G.E.: ImageNet classification with deep convolutional neural networks. In: NIPS, pp. 1097–1105 (2012)
22. Kuehne, H., Jhuang, H., Garrote, E., Poggio, T., Serre, T.: HMDB: a large video database for human motion recognition. In: ICCV, pp. 2556–2563 (2011)
23. Kumar, M.P., Koller, D.: Efficiently selecting regions for scene understanding. In: CVPR, pp. 3217–3224 (2010)
24. LeCun, Y., Bottou, L., Bengio, Y., Haffner, P.: Gradient-based learning applied to document recognition. Proc. IEEE **86**(11), 2278–2324 (1998)
25. Li, L., Gan, Z., Cheng, Y., Liu, J.: Relation-aware graph attention network for visual question answering. In: ICCV, pp. 10313–10322 (2019)
26. Lin, J., Gan, C., Han, S.: TSM: temporal shift module for efficient video understanding. In: ICCV, pp. 7083–7093 (2019)
27. Liu, X., Lee, J.Y., Jin, H.: Learning video representations from correspondence proposals. In: CVPR, pp. 4273–4281 (2019)
28. Long, X., Gan, C., de Melo, G., Wu, J., Liu, X., Wen, S.: Attention clusters: purely attention based local feature integration for video classification. In: CVPR, pp. 7834–7843 (2018)
29. Luo, C., Yuille, A.L.: Grouped spatial-temporal aggregation for efficient action recognition. In: ICCV, pp. 5512–5521 (2019)
30. Ma, C.Y., Kadav, A., Melvin, I., Kira, Z., AlRegib, G., Graf, H.P.: Attend and interact: Higher-order object interactions for video understanding. In: CVPR, pp. 6790–6800 (2018)
31. Martinez, B., Modolo, D., Xiong, Y., Tighe, J.: Action recognition with spatial-temporal discriminative filter banks. In: ICCV, pp. 5482–5491 (2019)
32. Ni, B., Yang, X., Gao, S.: Progressively parsing interactional objects for fine grained action detection. In: CVPR, pp. 1020–1028 (2016)
33. Qiu, Z., Yao, T., Mei, T.: Learning spatio-temporal representation with Pseudo-3D residual networks. In: ICCV, pp. 5533–5541 (2017)
34. Qiu, Z., Yao, T., Ngo, C.W., Tian, X., Mei, T.: Learning spatio-temporal representation with local and global diffusion. In: CVPR, pp. 12056–12065 (2019)
35. Russell, B.C., Freeman, W.T., Efros, A.A., Sivic, J., Zisserman, A.: Using multiple segmentations to discover objects and their extent in image collections. In: CVPR, vol. 2, pp. 1605–1614 (2006)
36. Santoro, A., et al.: A simple neural network module for relational reasoning. In: NIPS, pp. 4967–4976 (2017)
37. Shou, Z., et al.: DMC-Net: generating discriminative motion cues for fast compressed video action recognition. In: CVPR, pp. 1268–1277 (2019)
38. Simonyan, K., Zisserman, A.: Two-stream convolutional networks for action recognition in videos. In: NIPS, pp. 568–576 (2014)
39. Simonyan, K., Zisserman, A.: Very deep convolutional networks for large-scale image recognition. arXiv preprint arXiv:1409.1556 (2014)

40. Soomro, K., Zamir, A.R., Shah, M.: UCF101: a dataset of 101 human actions classes from videos in the wild. arXiv preprint arXiv:1212.0402 (2012)
41. Szegedy, C., Ioffe, S., Vanhoucke, V., Alemi, A.A.: Inception-v4, Inception-ResNet and the impact of residual connections on learning. In: AAAI, pp. 4278–4284 (2017)
42. Szegedy, C., et al.: Going deeper with convolutions. In: CVPR, pp. 1–9 (2015)
43. Szegedy, C., Vanhoucke, V., Ioffe, S., Shlens, J., Wojna, Z.: Rethinking the inception architecture for computer vision. In: CVPR, pp. 2818–2826 (2016)
44. Tran, D., Bourdev, L., Fergus, R., Torresani, L., Paluri, M.: Learning spatiotemporal features with 3D convolutional networks. In: ICCV, pp. 4489–4497 (2015)
45. Tran, D., Wang, H., Torresani, L., Feiszli, M.: Video classification with channel-separated convolutional networks. In: ICCV, pp. 5552–5561 (2019)
46. Tran, D., Wang, H., Torresani, L., Ray, J., LeCun, Y., Paluri, M.: A closer look at spatiotemporal convolutions for action recognition. In: CVPR, pp. 6450–6459 (2018)
47. Wang, F., et al.: Residual attention network for image classification. In: CVPR, pp. 3156–3164 (2017)
48. Wang, H., Kläser, A., Schmid, C., Liu, C.L.: Action recognition by dense trajectories. In: CVPR, pp. 3169–3676 (2011)
49. Wang, H., Schmid, C.: Action recognition with improved trajectories. In: ICCV, pp. 3551–3558 (2013)
50. Wang, L., Li, W., Li, W., Van Gool, L.: Appearance-and-relation networks for video classification. In: CVPR, pp. 1430–1439 (2018)
51. Wang, L., et al.: Temporal segment networks: towards good practices for deep action recognition. In: Leibe, B., Matas, J., Sebe, N., Welling, M. (eds.) ECCV 2016. LNCS, vol. 9912, pp. 20–36. Springer, Cham (2016). https://doi.org/10.1007/978-3-319-46484-8_2
52. Wang, X., Girshick, R., Gupta, A., He, K.: Non-local neural networks. In: CVPR, pp. 7794–7803 (2018)
53. Wang, X., Gupta, A.: Videos as space-time region graphs. In: Ferrari, V., Hebert, M., Sminchisescu, C., Weiss, Y. (eds.) ECCV 2018. LNCS, vol. 11209, pp. 413–431. Springer, Videos as space-time region graphs (2018). https://doi.org/10.1007/978-3-030-01228-1_25
54. Watters, N., Zoran, D., Weber, T., Battaglia, P., Pascanu, R., Tacchetti, A.: Visual interaction networks: learning a physics simulator from video. In: NIPS, pp. 4539–4547 (2017)
55. Woo, S., Park, J., Lee, J.-Y., Kweon, I.S.: CBAM: convolutional block attention module. In: Ferrari, V., Hebert, M., Sminchisescu, C., Weiss, Y. (eds.) ECCV 2018. LNCS, vol. 11211, pp. 3–19. Springer, Cham (2018). https://doi.org/10.1007/978-3-030-01234-2_1
56. Xiao, T., Fan, Q., Gutfreund, D., Monfort, M., Oliva, A., Zhou, B.: Reasoning about human-object interactions through dual attention networks. In: ICCV, pp. 3919–3928 (2019)
57. Xie, S., Sun, C., Huang, J., Tu, Z., Murphy, K.: Rethinking spatiotemporal feature learning: speed-accuracy trade-offs in video classification. In: Ferrari, V., Hebert, M., Sminchisescu, C., Weiss, Y. (eds.) ECCV 2018. LNCS, vol. 11219, pp. 318–335. Springer, Cham (2018). https://doi.org/10.1007/978-3-030-01267-0_19
58. Yao, B., Fei-Fei, L.: Modeling mutual context of object and human pose in human-object interaction activities. In: CVPR, pp. 17–24 (2010)
59. Yao, J., Fidler, S., Urtasun, R.: Describing the scene as a whole: joint object detection. In: CVPR. Citeseer (2012)

60. Yue-Hei Ng, J., Hausknecht, M., Vijayanarasimhan, S., Vinyals, O., Monga, R., Toderici, G.: Beyond short snippets: deep networks for video classification. In: CVPR, pp. 4694–4702 (2015)
61. Zhao, Y., Xiong, Y., Lin, D.: Recognize actions by disentangling components of dynamics. In: CVPR, pp. 6566–6575 (2018)
62. Zhao, Y., Xiong, Y., Lin, D.: Trajectory convolution for action recognition. In: NeurIPS, pp. 2208–2219 (2018)
63. Zhou, B., Andonian, A., Oliva, A., Torralba, A.: Temporal relational reasoning in videos. In: Ferrari, V., Hebert, M., Sminchisescu, C., Weiss, Y. (eds.) ECCV 2018. LNCS, vol. 11205, pp. 831–846. Springer, Cham (2018). https://doi.org/10.1007/978-3-030-01246-5_49
64. Zolfaghari, M., Singh, K., Brox, T.: ECO: efficient convolutional network for online video understanding. In: Ferrari, V., Hebert, M., Sminchisescu, C., Weiss, Y. (eds.) ECCV 2018. LNCS, vol. 11206, pp. 713–730. Springer, Cham (2018). https://doi.org/10.1007/978-3-030-01216-8_43

# Modeling the Effects of Windshield Refraction for Camera Calibration

Frank Verbiest[1](✉), Marc Proesmans[1], and Luc Van Gool[1,2]

[1] Center for Processing Speech and Images, ESAT-PSI, KU Leuven,
Leuven, Belgium
`frank.verbiest@esat.kuleuven.be`
[2] Computer Vision Lab, D-ITET, ETH Zürich, Zürich, Switzerland

**Abstract.** In this paper, we study the effects of windshield refraction for autonomous driving applications. These distortion effects are surprisingly large and can not be explained by traditional camera models. Instead of using a generalized camera approach, we propose a novel approach to jointly optimize a traditional camera model, and a mathematical representation of the windshield's surface. First, using the laws of geometric optics, the refraction is modeled using a local spherical approximation to the windshield's geometry. Next, a spline-based model is proposed as a refinement to better adapt to deviations from the ideal shape and manufacturing variations. By jointly optimizing refraction and camera parameters, the projection error can be significantly reduced. The proposed models are validated on real windshield observations and custom setups to compare recordings with and without windshield, with accurate laser scan measurements as 3D ground truth.

## 1 Introduction

Camera calibration is an important topic in computer vision. It is the basis of general image based scene analysis, multi-view 3D reconstruction, visual based robotics, etc. For autonomous driving, a proper calibration of the cameras is important to map the free-space around the car, and estimate distances and relative velocities of the surrounding traffic. Contrary to prototype vehicles with roof mounted equipment, the placement of the cameras in commercial cars has to be both functional and aesthetically pleasing, and that often means behind the car windshield. The effect of refraction by a windshield, illustrated in Fig. 1, is significant, and prompts the need to understand the image formation process. Little can be found on the effects of real windshields though, neither on curved surfaces in general for that matter. Hanel *et al.* [7] investigate the influence of a car windshield on depth calculation with stereo camera setups, and show that the difference in base length values can be highly significant. But the paper focuses on observation differences, not the solution.

**Electronic supplementary material** The online version of this chapter (https://doi.org/10.1007/978-3-030-58539-6_24) contains supplementary material, which is available to authorized users.

© Springer Nature Switzerland AG 2020
A. Vedaldi et al. (Eds.): ECCV 2020, LNCS 12351, pp. 397–412, 2020.
https://doi.org/10.1007/978-3-030-58539-6_24

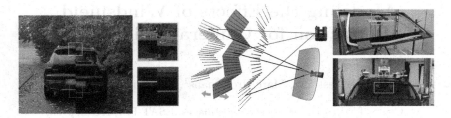

**Fig. 1.** Windshield refraction. Left: the split image shows the images captured without and with windshield, resp. The effect is visible as a mostly vertical shift. Right: our evaluation setups, an example of a camera behind a separately mounted windshield, and a camera mounted behind the windshield of car.

Over the years, a wealth of camera models and calibration methods have been investigated. Amongst others, Sturm *et al.* [21] provide an extensive overview of camera models, such as pinholes, fisheyes, catadioptric cameras, including a variety of distortion models. For image formation processes involving refraction or reflection, existing work can be roughly subdivided in two main approaches. On the one hand there are the generalized camera models that avoid explicit modeling of these processes. Grossberg and Nayer [6] proposed a ray-based camera model where each pixel has an associated 3D ray. To densely calibrate all pixels, they use a structured light-type approach using calibration reference planes with know positions. Many used the concept in complex optical setups, especially in underwater photography to account for refraction by housing or water tanks [5,13,22]. Ramalingam and Sturm *et al.* [17,18,20] utilize three calibration planes with unknown pose, but the method only applies to known, class specific, ray-distributions. Nishimura *et al.* [14] proposed to use the intersection of the calibration planes and realize a simple linear algorithm that applies to any ray-distribution. Miraldo *et al.* [12] introduced an RBF interpolation technique to densify the ray space when the measurements are sparse, assuming the rays vary smoothly across space.

Next to generalized camera models, there are some approaches that use an explicit formulation of refraction based on Snell's law. Chari and Sturm [3] analysed the multi-view relationships between cameras when the scene contains a single refractive planar surface separating two different media. Agrawal *et al.* [2] investigated the effects of multi-layered flat refractive geometry, evaluated by means of a water tank. Pedersen *et al.* [16] evaluated the effects of refraction on underwater 3D reconstruction, where the water-housing-air interfaces are considered flat. Kunz and Singh [11] examine refraction of hemispherical pressure housing interfaces in an underwater context, in particular the effects where the camera mount is offset from the ideal center of the housing. Recently, the work by Pavel *et al.* [15] is one of the few to explicitly model refraction through a curved surface. They compare simulated and real checkerboard data viewed through a conic/tubular shaped glass, and estimate the geometry parameters of the surface via model inversion employing an RBF neural network.

Although generalized camera models are a natural choice for solving this particular problem, we consider two issues. First, they do not easily scale to larger settings, especially when dense measurements are needed. The calibration volume in our setting easily covers several meters across to lessen the effects of extrapolation when operating at larger distances. Secondly, by design these approaches make abstraction of the different internal components of the setup, so they do not attempt to explain the image formation process.

In this paper, we propose an approach where the image formation process is modeled by an explicit formulation of the refraction through a curved surface, together with a traditional camera model (Sect. 2). First, using the laws of geometric optics, the refraction is modeled as a local spherical approximation to the geometry of the windshield (Sect. 3). We show that this approximation allows to reduce a non-trivial 3D problem to a mathematical formulation that is easy to solve numerically. By jointly optimizing the refraction and camera parameters, we obtain the surface's radius, position, and the intrinsics and extrinsics of the camera behind the windshield. Second, to better adapt to deviations from the ideal spherical model and possible manufacturing variations, a spline-based refraction model is proposed as a refinement of the former (Sect. 4).

The mathematical analysis offers new insights into the relationship between the windshield curvature, the scene depth and the observed distortion in the image plane after projection. We will show that the refraction model compares favorably to the generalized approach. Also, we show that the image formation process is well approximated by a (traditional) pinhole camera model by means of a correction, which is advantageous because of their ease of use, since such models are well documented and widely supported. The proposed methodology is verified with real windshields, both separately mounted, and in real car scenarios. For this study, we use a 3D laser measurement system to create ground truth samples in 3D space and verify the projections in image space (Sect. 5).

## 2   Projection Model

Let us assume a basic pinhole camera model [8]. In this model, the image projection $\mathbf{m} = [x \, y]^\top$ of a 3D point $\mathbf{M} = [X \, Y \, Z]^\top$ can be written as,

$$\begin{bmatrix} \mathbf{m} \\ 1 \end{bmatrix} \simeq \mathbf{K}\mathbf{R}^\top(\mathbf{M} - \mathbf{t}), \tag{1}$$

where $\mathbf{K}$, $\mathbf{R}$ and $\mathbf{t}$ are the calibration matrix, rotation matrix, and translation vector of the camera, respectively ($\simeq$ denotes equality up to a non-zero scalar multiple). To introduce radial distortion and refraction in the basic pinhole camera model, we rewrite Eq. (1) as,

$$\begin{bmatrix} \mathbf{m} \\ 1 \end{bmatrix} = \mathbf{K}\begin{bmatrix} \mathbf{q} \\ 1 \end{bmatrix} \tag{2}$$

$$\text{with} \quad \begin{bmatrix} \mathbf{q} \\ 1 \end{bmatrix} \simeq \mathbf{p} \quad \text{and} \quad \mathbf{p} = \mathbf{R}^\top(\mathbf{M} - \mathbf{t}), \tag{3}$$

where the point $\mathbf{p}$ corresponds to the point $\mathbf{M}$ but converted to the camera coordinate frame and the point $\mathbf{q} = [u\,v]^{\top}$ is the "normalized" projection before conversion to image coordinates by Eq. (2). We introduce radial distortion by modifying Eq. (2) as follows,

$$\begin{bmatrix} \mathbf{m} \\ 1 \end{bmatrix} = \mathbf{K} \begin{bmatrix} \mathcal{D}(\mathbf{q}) \\ 1 \end{bmatrix}, \tag{4}$$

with $\mathcal{D}([u\,v]^{\top}) = d \cdot [u\,v]^{\top}$ and $d = (1 + \kappa_1 r^2 + \kappa_2 r^4 + \ldots)$ and $r^2 = u^2 + v^2$ and $\kappa_1, \kappa_2, \ldots$ are parameters of radial distortion. To take into account the effects of refraction, we introduce the function $\mathcal{R}()$ in Eq. (3) as follows,

$$\begin{bmatrix} \mathbf{q} \\ 1 \end{bmatrix} \simeq \mathcal{R}(\mathbf{p}). \tag{5}$$

Considering the projection of point $\mathbf{p}$, we expect the function $\mathcal{R}(\mathbf{p})$ to return any point on the line of sight after refraction, *i.e.*, the line of sight as perceived by the camera.

## 3   Spherical Refraction

For a camera mounted directly behind a windshield, we approximate the local geometry of the windshield by a sphere with an appropriate position, radius, thickness and material index. The projection of a point through a refracting medium boils down to finding the ray projected back from the camera, which after refraction passes through that point. This is non-trivial, however, under the spherical assumption it is possible to reduce the 3D problem to a 2D problem that can be solved numerically.

### 3.1   Plane of Refraction

Consider the spherical geometry shown in Fig. 2, where $\mathbf{p}$ is the point that must projected, $\mathbf{c}$ is the center of the sphere, and $\mathbf{t}$ is the center of projection of the camera. Together, the points $\mathbf{p}$, $\mathbf{c}$ and $\mathbf{t}$, in general position, define a unique plane. Since the plane passes through the center of the sphere, it cuts the sphere in two halves. For reasons of symmetry, it then follows that all refraction takes place in this plane, called the *plane of refraction*, thereby reducing the 3D projection problem to a 2D problem. For the special cases where $\mathbf{c}$ coincides with the origin $\mathbf{t}$ or the points $\mathbf{p}$, $\mathbf{c}$ and $\mathbf{t}$ are collinear, a unique plane does not exist. However, it can be verified that in these cases the refraction has no effect and therefore the pinhole camera can be used as is. Given a plane of refraction, a *refraction coordinate frame* can be defined with its origin in $\mathbf{c}$, the x-axis pointing from $\mathbf{c}$ to $\mathbf{t}$, the y-axis in the plane of refraction and perpendicular to the x-axis, and the z-axis perpendicular to the x- and y-axis, as illustrated in Fig. 2.

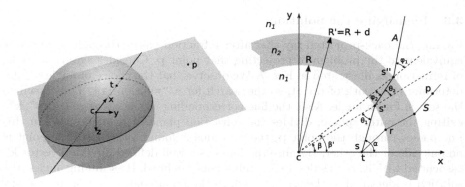

**Fig. 2.** Spherical geometry: All refraction takes place in the plane defined by the points **p**, **c**, and **t**, *i.e.*, the *plane of refraction*.

## 3.2  Planar Ray Refraction

Using Snell's law of refraction, we describe the refraction of rays projected back from the camera. Assume everything is expressed in the refraction coordinate frame and consider the configuration in the plane of refraction, *i.e.*, the xy-plane, as shown in Fig. 2, where $\mathbf{p} = [p_1\ p_2]^\top$ is the point that must be projected, $\mathbf{t} = [t_1\ 0]^\top$ is the camera projection center, $\mathbf{c} = [0\ 0]^\top$ is the center of the spheres, $R$ is the radius of the sphere, $d$ is the thickness of the glass, and $n_1$ and $n_2$ are the refraction indices of air and glass, respectively. Since we are only interested in the xy-plane, where the z-coordinate is 0, it is more convenient to work with 2D points instead, keeping in mind that the corresponding 3D points are readily obtained by adding a z-coordinate with value 0.

We describe the refraction of ray $A$ in Fig. 2. Let $(\mathbf{s}, \mathbf{k})$, $(\mathbf{s}', \mathbf{k}')$ and $(\mathbf{s}'', \mathbf{k}'')$ be the starting points and direction vectors for each of the successive ray segments, respectively. The first ray segment originates in the camera projection center $\mathbf{t}$, where it makes an angle $\alpha$ with the x-axis, so $\mathbf{s} = \mathbf{t}$ and $\mathbf{k} = [\cos\alpha\ \sin\alpha]^\top$. Then, it intersects the inner sphere and is refracted. Points on the line associated with the first ray segment are given by, $\mathbf{m} = \mathbf{s} + \lambda\mathbf{k}$ , where $\lambda$ parametrizes the line. The intersections with the inner sphere are obtained by solving the quadratic equation, $\|\mathbf{s} + \lambda\mathbf{k}\|^2 = R^2$ for $\lambda$. For a starting point $\mathbf{s}$ strictly inside the sphere, there is a positive $\lambda_+ > 0$ and a negative $\lambda_- < 0$ solution. The solution $\lambda_+$ is picked since it corresponds to an intersection that is on the forward travel path of the ray. The starting point of the second ray segment is given by this intersection, so $\mathbf{s}' = [s_1'\ s_2']^\top = \mathbf{s} + \lambda_+\mathbf{k}$. Since $\theta_1 = \alpha - \beta$ with $\beta = \mathrm{atan2}\,(s_2', s_1')$, the angle $\theta_2$ can be obtained from Snell's law of refraction $n_1 \sin\theta_1 = n_2 \sin\theta_2$. The direction vector of the second ray segment is then given by $\mathbf{k}' = [\cos(\beta+\theta_2)\ \sin(\beta+\theta_2)]^\top$. For the ray segment exiting the outer sphere, the starting point $\mathbf{s}''$ and direction vector $\mathbf{k}''$ are obtained using similar steps.

## 3.3   Identifying the Solution

Finding the back-projected ray that after refraction passes through a point **p** is equivalent to the problem of projecting that point **p**. Consider again the plane of refraction as illustrated in Fig. 2. We observe that the choice of angle $\alpha$ fully determines the path of ray $A$, so the search for a "solution" ray boils down to the search for an angle. Also, the line corresponding to the ray segment $(\mathbf{s}'', \mathbf{k}'')$ exiting the outer sphere, divides the refraction plane in two sides. When this line passes through the point **p**, the solutions is found, otherwise, the point is on one side or the other. Because the line has a well defined direction vector $\mathbf{k}''$ associated with it, both sides are unambiguously defined. By scanning angles, the solution is identified as the angle for which the point changes sides. In practice, it is more convenient to work with a signed distance function, where the sign of the returned value determines which side of the line a point is on and the absolute value gives the point-to-line distance. The zero-crossing of this function corresponds to the solution. Let $\mathbf{k}'' = [k_1'' \, k_2'']^\top$, the distance function is defined as the projection of the vector $(\mathbf{p} - \mathbf{s}'')$ onto the direction perpendicular to $\mathbf{k}''$,

$$f(\alpha) = (\mathbf{p} - \mathbf{s}'')^\top \begin{bmatrix} -k_2'' \\ k_1'' \end{bmatrix}. \tag{6}$$

The *Regula-Falsi* method [23] is used for finding the root of $f(\alpha)$. This iterative method requires that we specify an interval for which the solution is known to lie in. Let $\mathbf{p} = [p_1 \, p_2]^\top$. For a point **p** in the upper half-plane, *i.e.*, $p_2 > 0$, it is clear that a unique solution can be found in the interval $(0, \pi)$ and that $f(0)f(\pi) < 0$. Similarly, for a point **p** in the lower half-plane, *i.e.*, $p_2 < 0$, the search interval is set to $(\pi, 2\pi)$. For a point **p** on the x-axis, *i.e.*, $p_2 = 0$, the ray is not refracted, so the solutions for $p_1 > 0$ and $p_1 < 0$ are given by $\alpha = 0$ and $\alpha = \pi$, respectively.

In Fig. 2, the solution is given by ray $S$, which intersects the inner sphere at point **r**. Since the point **r** is on line of sight as perceived by the camera, it can serve as the definition for the function $\mathcal{R}()$ in Eq. (5), where it should be noted that the function $\mathcal{R}()$ is expected to return points expressed in the camera coordinate frame. Automatic differentiation techniques (*e.g.*, Ceres [1]) are used to evaluate the derivatives for the above procedure.

## 3.4   Qualitative Assessment

This section intends to illustrate the effects of refraction on the image formation process when a windshield is placed in front of the camera. Consider a traditional pinhole camera and a back-projected ray for this camera. The points $\mathbf{M} = [X \, Y \, Z]^\top$ along this back-projected ray all project to a point $\mathbf{m} = [x \, y]^\top$. The offsets $\Delta x$ and $\Delta y$ are defined as the horizontal and vertical offsets/corrections to the projection **m** as a result of introducing the spherical refraction model. We investigate these offsets for points along the back-projected ray as a function of depth $Z$, the radius of the sphere, and the position of **m** in the image.

Consider a prototypical configuration for a camera mounted behind the windshield. The image has width $w = 1920$ and height $h = 1200$. The camera

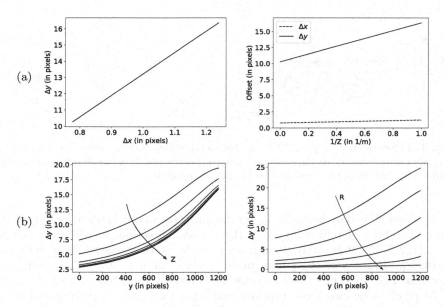

**Fig. 3.** Offset analysis. (a) Left: vertical offsets $\Delta y$ plotted against horizontal offsets $\Delta x$ for different depths. Right: horizontal offsets $\Delta x$ and vertical offsets $\Delta y$ plotted against the inverse depth $\frac{1}{Z}$. (b) Left: vertical offset $\Delta y$ plotted against vertical positions $y$ for different depths $Z \in \{1, 2, 5, 10, 20, 50, 100\}$ (in m), and $R = 3$ (in m). Right: vertical offset $\Delta y$ for different radii $R \in \{1, 2, 5, 10, 50, +\infty\}$ (in m), and $Z = 10$ (in m).

has focal length $f = 2200$ (in pixels), principal point in the middle of the image, and no radial distortion. The sphere has radius $R = 3$ (in m), thickness $d = 0.005$ (in m), and the refraction indices for air and glass are $n_1 = 1$ and $n_2 = 1.5$, respectively. The sphere position, in camera coordinates, is given by $\mathbf{c} = [0 \ (R - l)\sin\alpha \ - (R - l)\cos\alpha]^\top$, where $l = 0.05$ (in m) is the distance of the camera center to the glass, and $\alpha = 70$ (in degrees) is the angle the vector $\mathbf{c}$ makes with the negative z-axis, *i.e.*, the orientation of the windshield. We arbitrarily select the point $\mathbf{m} = [\frac{3}{4}w, \frac{3}{4}h]^\top$ for analysis. In Fig. 3a, the vertical offsets $\Delta y$ are plotted against the horizontal offset $\Delta x$, for different depths $Z$. We observe that they form a line and that the offsets in the vertical direction are much larger. The fact that they form a line is unsurprising since, for a single image point, the back-projection and the different projections all take place in the same plane of refraction, whose intersection with the image plane presents as a line. Alternatively, globally the pinhole camera cannot model the effects of refraction, but locally in the image it can be a good approximation. So, the "offset" lines can be seen as epipolar lines resulting from the epipolar geometry formed by the such a local camera and the back-projection camera. Also, it is expected that as the depth is increased the resulting offsets along the epipolar line show an approximately inverse proportional relationship, which is confirmed in Fig. 3a, where the offsets $\Delta x$ and $\Delta y$ are plotted against the inverse depth

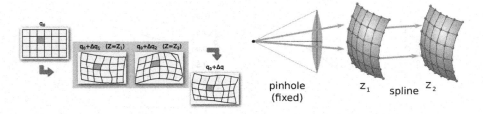

**Fig. 4.** The correction $\Delta q(q_0, Z)$ to $q_0$ due to refraction is decomposed in two simpler 2D only corrections terms $\Delta q_1(q_0)$ and $\Delta q_2(q_0)$ corresponding to two different depths. Right: illustration of the ray-based refraction using splines.

$Z$. However, this only holds for larger distances (as in our application). To illustrate the effect of refraction along the vertical direction, for different depths $Z \in \{1, 2, 5, 10, 20, 50, 100\}$ (in m), we plot the vertical offsets $\Delta y$ against the vertical positions $y$ of the points $\mathbf{m} = [\frac{1}{2}w, y]^\top$ for $y \in [0, h]$. The results are shown in Fig. 3b. The offsets increase substantially from top to bottom, up to $\sim 20$ pixels. The closer the rays are making a right angle with the surface of the sphere (*i.e.*, closer to the x-axis in Fig. 2), the lower the effect of refraction, which for this configuration happens to be the case for points near the top of the image. Also, we observe that the highly non-linear offset curves converge for increasing depth. Similarly, the effect of the radius is shown in Fig. 3b for $R \in \{1, 2, 5, 10, 50, +\infty\}$ (in m) and $Z = 10$ (in m). The important conclusions here is that the effect of refraction is substantial for even moderate amounts of curvature, *e.g.*, for $R = 5$ (in m) the vertical offset can go up to $\sim 10$ pixels. For a flat surface, *i.e.*, $R = \infty$ (in m), the effect is small and constant.

## 4    Spline Refraction

The previous section described the joint optimization of both a pinhole camera and spherical refraction model. In this section, we deal with the fact that the local windshield geometry may not be perfectly spherical, and that possible manufacturing variations are difficult to model. We propose a more generic refraction model as a refinement of the former (the pinhole camera parameters are kept fixed). This correction is decomposed in simpler parts that are each represented by spline-based functions (see Fig. 4).

### 4.1    Decomposition

Consider the normalized projection $q_0$ if there had been no refraction, which, using Eq. (3), can be expressed as,

$$\begin{bmatrix} q_0 \\ 1 \end{bmatrix} \simeq \mathbf{p}. \tag{7}$$

The introduction of a correction $\Delta\mathbf{q}$ to the projection $\mathbf{q_0}$ allows to define the refraction function $\mathcal{R}()$ from Eq. (5) as follows,

$$\mathcal{R}(\mathbf{p}) = \begin{bmatrix} \mathbf{q_0} + \Delta\mathbf{q} \\ 1 \end{bmatrix}, \tag{8}$$

where the correction $\Delta\mathbf{q}$ is a displacement in the normalized image plane due to refraction. The correction $\Delta\mathbf{q}$ is a function of the point $\mathbf{p}$, or equivalently, a function of the projection $\mathbf{q_0}$ and the depth $Z$.

Based on observations made for the spherical model (see Sect. 3.4), we assume that, for a fixed point $\mathbf{q_0}$, the corrections for different depths form a line parametrized by inverse depth. Two corrections are needed to form a line. Assume the function $\Delta\mathbf{q}(\mathbf{q_0}, Z)$ is available, then by evaluation for two different depths $Z_1$ and $Z_2$, we obtain the corrections $\Delta\mathbf{q_1}(\mathbf{q_0}) = \Delta\mathbf{q}(\mathbf{q_0}, Z_1)$ and $\Delta\mathbf{q_2}(\mathbf{q_0}) = \Delta\mathbf{q}(\mathbf{q_0}, Z_2)$. Then based on the above assumptions, the correction $\Delta\mathbf{q}(\mathbf{q_0}, Z)$ is approximated as,

$$\Delta\mathbf{q}(\mathbf{q_0}, Z) \approx \frac{\Delta\mathbf{q_1}(\mathbf{q_0})\left(\frac{1}{Z_2}-\frac{1}{Z}\right)+\Delta\mathbf{q_2}(\mathbf{q_0})\left(\frac{1}{Z}-\frac{1}{Z_1}\right)}{\left(\frac{1}{Z_2}-\frac{1}{Z_1}\right)} \tag{9}$$

where $\Delta\mathbf{q_1}(\mathbf{q_0})$ and $\Delta\mathbf{q_2}(\mathbf{q_0})$ are defined over the normalized image only. Essentially, the original correction term is decomposed in two simpler 2D only corrections terms, see Fig. 4. Next, the corrections $\Delta\mathbf{q_1}(\mathbf{q_0})$ and $\Delta\mathbf{q_2}(\mathbf{q_0})$ are modeled using spline-based functions $\mathbf{f_1}(\mathbf{q_0}; \boldsymbol{\theta}_1)$ and $\mathbf{f_2}(\mathbf{q_0}; \boldsymbol{\theta}_2)$, respectively, where the parameter vectors $\boldsymbol{\theta}_1$ and $\boldsymbol{\theta}_2$ are the subject of optimization during a calibration procedure. The final spline-based correction term is then given by,

$$\Delta\mathbf{q}(\mathbf{q_0}, Z) \approx \frac{\mathbf{f_1}(\mathbf{q_0};\theta_1)\left(\frac{1}{Z_2}-\frac{1}{Z}\right)+\mathbf{f_2}(\mathbf{q_0};\theta_2)\left(\frac{1}{Z}-\frac{1}{Z_1}\right)}{\left(\frac{1}{Z_2}-\frac{1}{Z_1}\right)} \tag{10}$$

We arbitrarily select $Z_1 = 1$ and $Z_2 = +\infty$.

## 4.2   Cubic Spline Representation

Each of the spline-based functions $\mathbf{f_1}(\mathbf{q})$ and $\mathbf{f_2}(\mathbf{q})$ from the previous section has two scalar components (a horizontal and vertical component). Let the function $s(\mathbf{q})$, or $s(u, v)$, denote such a component, where $\mathbf{q} = [u\, v]^\top$ is the normalized projection. The function $s(u, v)$ consists of a 2D grid of connected bi-cubic spline patches, where neighbouring patches share function values and derivatives at their corners to ensure continuity across patches.

A single bi-cubic patch function $p(u, v)$ is written as,

$$p(u, v) = [u^3\, u^2\, u\, 1]\, \mathbf{C}\, [v^3\, v^2\, v\, 1]^\top, \tag{11}$$

where the coefficients of the $4 \times 4$ matrix $\mathbf{C}$ are completely determined by the function values $s$ and the derivatives $\frac{\partial s}{\partial u}$, $\frac{\partial s}{\partial v}$, and $\frac{\partial^2 s}{\partial u \partial v}$ stored at the four corners of the patch. Indeed, matching the function $p(u, v)$ with these values yields 16 linear equations in the 16 coefficients. The function values and derivatives that are shared across patches are used as parameters in an optimization. Because the above spline representation has many parameters, regularization is required to prevent over-fitting. Smoothness is enforced using thin-plate constraints on each patch $p(u,v)$, $E = \iint_\Omega \left( \left( \frac{\partial^2 p}{\partial u^2} \right)^2 + 2\left( \frac{\partial^2 p}{\partial u \partial v} \right)^2 + \left( \frac{\partial^2 p}{\partial v^2} \right)^2 \right) du\, dv$, where $\Omega$ is the domain of the patch. It is easy to confirm that this can be written as, $E = \mathbf{z}^\top \mathbf{A} \mathbf{z}$, where $\mathbf{z}$ is a 16-vector that holds the function values and derivatives of the four corners of the patch, and $\mathbf{A}$ is a fixed $16 \times 16$ symmetric positive semi-definite matrix. The cost for the function $s(u,v)$ is the sum over of all patches.

## 5    Experiments

### 5.1    Acquisition

The acquisition setup used to obtain accurate real-world 2D-3D correspondences for camera calibration is shown in Fig. 1. Here, a 3D laser measurement device (Leica 3D Disto) scans the scene using a laser dot, where for each position of the laser an image is taken. The 2D image features are obtained by sub-pixel measurement of the observed laser 'blobs' in the images. The scene consists of movable panels to provide sufficient depth variation. Typically, around 500 points are measured for each of the 3 to 4 panel positions.

An important argument in considering this approach is that it allows to get rid of any uncertainty on the 3D measurements in our evaluation and thus any possible interference/interchange between camera parameters and feature point locations is avoided. It is useful to note that our measurement approach also relates to methods using structured light or chess board panels with known postures [5,6,12,13,22], but given our working volumes, the laser is less bulky.

### 5.2    Calibration Procedure

Once the 2D-3D correspondences are known, we can proceed with the calibration process. As a first step, we ignore refraction and determine the intrinsics and extrinsics of the pinhole camera behind the windshield through the use of the minimal solver [10] inside a RANSAC [4] loop. The initial camera is then refined by minimizing the reprojection error using non-linear least squares [1] with a robust loss function (M-estimators [9]). The scale parameters for the robust loss function is set to the *Median Absolute Deviation* (MAD) [19] of the residuals.

Next, the parameters of the spherical refraction model are initialized to represent a typical configuration (*e.g.*, see assessment above) relative to the previously determined camera. Initially, this relative configuration is kept fixed, while the parameters of the camera are optimized by robustly minimizing the reprojection error. This brings the camera closer to its expected solution. Finally, by jointly optimizing the parameters of the camera and the spherical refraction model, the calibration is obtained. Note, in practice we fix the thickness of the windshield ($d = 5.3\,\mathrm{mm}$) and the refraction indices of glass and air ($n_{air} = 1$ and $n_{glass} = 1.5$), as they can be measured beforehand.

**Table 1.** Comparisons on camera intrinsics (P = pinhole, WS = windshield, BC = Brown-Conrady, SPH = spherical refraction, SPL = spline refraction)

|  | CamA P | WS-P | WS-BC | WS-SPH | WS-SPL | CamA' P | WS-P | WS-BC | WS-SPH | WS-SPL |
|---|---|---|---|---|---|---|---|---|---|---|
| $f$ | **1841.2** | 1852.1 | *1865.5* | **1842.3** | / | **2173.8** | 2193.3 | *2223.8* | **2174.2** | / |
| $c_x$ | 940.9 | 939.6 | *1190.1* | 941.3 | / | 968.3 | 965.8 | *1433.5* | 961.9 | / |
| $c_y$ | 708.6 | 706.2 | *675.0* | 710.7 | / | 604.8 | 593.6 | *564.1* | 600.2 | / |
| $\sigma_{MAD}$ | 0.137 | 1.44 | 0.312 | 0.199 | 0.095 | 0.135 | 2.47 | 0.57 | 0.264 | 0.11 |

**Fig. 5.** 3D view on the extrinsics. From left to right: WS-P, WS-BC, WS-SPH (grey = ground truth, green = calculated) (Color figure online)

Finally, we keep the camera parameters fixed and optimize the parameters of a spline-based refraction model, again, by robustly minimizing the reprojection error, and the parameters initialized to 0. We typically use $4 \times 4$ spline patches. To prevent over-fitting, a thin-plate regularization term is used, so that the cost function becomes $E = E_{reproj.} + \lambda E_{thinplate}$, where $\lambda$ controls the amount of regularization. The $\lambda$ is determined automatically by splitting the 2D-3D correspondences in a training set and a test set. The training set is used during optimization, and the resulting parameters are verified against the test set to find the optimal $\lambda$, *i.e.*, minimal cost on the test set.

### 5.3   Comparison With and Without Windshield

In this paragraph, we provide a number of numerical results on the proposed approach, using a variety of visualizations. For the illustrations , we chose a few prototypical example cameras, for the separate windshield setup (CamA) and in the real automotive context (CamB). Yet, we've observed that the results are very similar for various setups and windshields that we have experimented with so far. In total about 6 different cameras with various focal lengths have been used on 4 different windshields.

Table 1 and Fig. 5 display some interesting observations when determining the camera intrinsics and extrinsics as viewed behind a windshield. The table lists two 2Mpix PointGrey cameras CamA and CamA' with different focal lengths. The ground truth in the resp. first columns, are the measurements based on observations without windshield. The next three columns indicate the intrinsics when minimizing the pinhole alone (step 1 in Sect. 5.2), a Brown-Conrady camera model, and the spherical refraction method (step 2 in Sect. 5.2). The parameters of the Brown-Conrady model have been defined to cover both radial and tangential

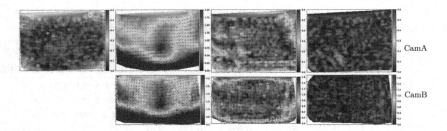

**Fig. 6.** Projection error maps, Ground truth comparison from left to right: (1) without WS (2) with WS, no refraction (3) with WS, spherical refraction (4) with WS. Top row: separate windshield setup. Bottom row: automotive setup.

distortion of lens systems, however in this context, these additional parameters tend to interchange information between focal length, distortion parameters and principal point to try to "explain" the distortion. The re-projection error drops ($\sigma_{MAD}$), however, the numbers clearly deviate from the actual cameras. Using the spherical refraction model though, the parameters come very close to the original. Using the spline refraction model, the re-projection error drops even more (cfr. sequel), but the camera parameters are not affected during this stage (Sect. 5.2).

Figure 5 provides a few 3D impressions of the results. The ground truth cone is in gray, it is the camera without windshield. The green cones are the ones when fitting the measurements behind windshield with resp. the pinhole alone, the Brown-Conrady model, and the spherical refraction method. The visualization confirms the observations above, the Brown-Conrady model tends to overcompensate, the spherical method provides the best fit.

Figure 6 shows the re-projections plots for the different stages of the calibration process described in Sect. 5.2. They show the error between the actual observed image coordinates of the 3D (laser) measurements, and the projected image coordinates. The top row shows the results when using the separately mounted windshield (CamA). The left image shows the error plot of the camera, the ground truth calculation without windshield, the 3 consecutive images show the error plots when fitting the data as observed behind the windshield, with resp. the pinhole alone, with the spherical refraction model, and finally with the spline refraction model. As indicated before and expected, the non-linear vertical shift can not be explained by the pinhole alone. When introducing the spherical refraction, the error already reduces dramatically. And finally, when introducing the spline approach, the average error rate $\sigma_{MAD}$ drops from a pixel error 1.44 down to 0.199 and further to <0.1 pixel. These numbers are also indicated in the Table 1 (CamA). The bottom row of Fig. 6 shows the results for a real automotive setup. Since the camera was mounted inside the car, one can not compare to the situtation without windshield, but the resemblance of the plots with the experiments above is striking. For this particular case CamB, $\sigma_{MAD}$ drops from close to 2.1 pixel error, over 0.54, arriving at slightly around 0.23 pixel. A useful footnote in this context is that the lower resolution of these cameras (1.3Mpix), and the bayer effects

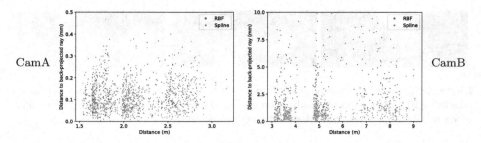

CamA    CamB

**Fig. 7.** Comparison with generalized calibration: distance between the original measurements, and the back-projected ray assigned to the measurements.

have more impact on the subpixel accuracy of the measurements, and consequently the average error.

### 5.4  Comparison with Generalized Calibration

Generalized camera models are natural candidates to solve problem involving refraction. Actually, our method can be seen as a class-specific ray-pixel mapping, whereas in earlier work the ray distribution is governed by specific smoothness constraints, ours is governed by the refraction of the spherical surface we introduced. We will show that the mathematical formulation of the joint camera-refraction model imposes better constraints on the ray distribution. And our approach compares favorably to the generalized approach.

Given the fact that our laser measurement space is sparse, we used the RBF-based ray interpolation method [12] as a proper representative. In Fig. 7, we considered two cameras CamA and CamB, also used in Fig. 6. We subdivided the measurements (for each camera about 1300 samples) in a training (800) and test set (500), where the training set is used for the calibration process, and the test set for evaluation. For the generalized method, we used the interpolation function $\phi(r) = \sqrt{\gamma^2 + r^2}$. We executed several runs where each time 50 control centers are randomly chosen, and we looped over the shape parameter $\gamma$ to find the optimal solution. For our approach, we use the ray representation of the spline refraction model: the forward projection (see Sect. 4) of a plane at a distance $Z$ to the camera yields a 3D point for each 2D point in the image plane. The rays are defined by two such planes at different distances.

Our evaluation criterion is as follows. For each 2D-3D measurement pair $(\mathbf{m}, \mathbf{M})$, we define the error as the distance between the original measurement $\mathbf{M}$, and the back-projected ray assigned to the 2D point $\mathbf{m}$. Figure 7 plots these errors against the distance of the original measurements. The RMSE for both methods for the higher resolution camera CamA are 0.147817 mm (SPL) and 0.159189 mm (RBF). Those for the automotive camera CamB are 1.31364 mm (SPL) and 6.19127 mm (RBF). As can be observed by the figure and the numbers, the errors are in favor of the spline refraction approach and are especially noticeable for the automotive camera. A possible reason is that the larger noise

**Fig. 8.** Left: image of a stereo pair of type CamB, middle: stereo disparity when using (traditional) camera pinhole calibration and rectification. Right: stereo disparity when using rectification after spline based refraction modeling.

levels for these cameras are better handled by an explicit noise model for the projection – such as our Maximum Likelihood Estimation (MLE) formulation above (Sect. 5.2) – as opposed to the set of algebraic equations (set to be 0) used by [12] that may well fit the noise itself and distort the ray distribution.

### 5.5   Windshield Image Undistortion and Rectification

One would not easily associate the concept of image undistortion with complex image formation processes involving refraction. Yet, following the discussion in Sect. 4, we have shown that the effects of windshield refraction can be approximated by a image plane distortion on the pinhole camera model, and furthermore, we can settle for a given Z since the dependency on depth decreases rapidly for large Z's (Fig. 3b). This can be advantaguous when there is a need to use camera models in traditional computer vision pipelines. We evaluated this approximation on an automotive CamB type stereo setup behind the windshield. Figure 8 shows the effect of rectification on the stereo disparity. When only using the pinhole model calibration, there will misalignments between the images which disturbs the disparity calculation. When using our refractive undistortion, the improvement is substantial.

## 6   Conclusion

We have proposed two models of refraction to deal with the distortion effects due to a windshield placed in front of a camera. The spherical refraction model shows that with using even a simple geometry it is possible to significantly reduce the re-projection error, as well as, accurately determine the camera behind the windshield as demonstrated by ground-truth experiments. This strengthens our believe that the approach is valid. The spline-based refraction is more generic in approach and reduces the error even further, and can deal with variations otherwise difficult to model. A potential comment is that our calibration is confined to a specialized lab setting. So, as an indication for future research, we will investigate the integration of our spherical model in a structure-from-motion based calibration approach. As a final note, we invite the reader to view our observations also in the context of other applications that involve refraction through curved surfaces.

**Acknowledgement.** This work was supported by the TRACE project with Toyota Motors Europe (TME).

# References

1. Agarwal, S., Mierle, K., Others: Ceres solver. http://ceres-solver.org
2. Agrawal, A., Ramalingam, S., Taguchi, Y., Chari, V.: A theory of multilayer flat refractive geometry. In: 2012 IEEE Conference on Computer Vision and Pattern Recognition (CVPR), pp. 3346–3353. IEEE (2012) (2012)
3. Chari, V., Sturm, P.: Multiple-view geometry of the refractive plane. In: 20th British Machine Vision Conference, pp. 1–11 (2009). In BMVA
4. Fischler, M.A., Bolles, R.C.: Random sample consensus: a paradigm for model fitting with applications to image analysis and automated cartography. Commun. ACM **24**(6), 381–395 (1981)
5. Gregson, J., Krimerman, M., Hullin, M.B., Heidrich, W.: Stochastic tomography and its applications in 3D imaging of mixing fluids. ACM Trans. Graph. (Proc. SIGGRAPH 2012) **31**(4), 52:1–52:10 (2012)
6. Grossberg, M.D., Nayar, S.K.: The raxel imaging model and ray-based calibration. Int. J. Comput. Vis. **61**(2), 119–137 (2005)
7. Hanel, A., Hoegner, L., Stilla, U.: Towards the influence of a car windshield on depth calculation with a stereo camera system. In: ISPRS - International Archives of the Photogrammetry, Remote Sensing and Spatial Information Sciences XLI-B5, pp. 461–468 (2016)
8. Hartley, R.I., Zisserman, A.: Multiple View Geometry in Computer Vision, Second edn. Cambridge University Press, Cambridge (2004)
9. Huber, P.J.: Robust Statistic. In: Lovric, M. (ed.) International Encyclopedia of Statistical Science, pp. 1248-1251. Springer, Heidelberg (2011). https://doi.org/10.1007/978-3-642-04898-2_594
10. Kukelova, Z., Bujnak, M., Pajdla, T.: Real-time solution to the absolute pose problem with unknown radial distortion and focal length. In: Proceedings of the 2013 IEEE International Conference on Computer Vision (ICCV 2013), Washington, DC, USA, pp. 2816–2823 (2013)
11. Kunz, C., Singh, H.: Hemispherical refraction and camera calibration in underwater vision. In: OCEANS2008, pp. 1–7 (2008)
12. Miraldo, P., Araujo, H.: Calibration of smooth camera models. IEEE Trans. Pattern Anal. Mach. Intell. **35**(9), 2091–2103 (2013)
13. Narasimhan, S., Nayar, S., Sun, B., Koppal, S.: Structured light in scattering media. In: Proceedings of ICCV, pp. 420–427 (2005)
14. Nishimura, M., Nobuhara, S., Matsuyama, T., Shimizu, S., Fujii, K.: A linear generalized camera calibration from three intersecting reference planes. In: Proceedings of ICCV, pp. 2354–2362 (2015)
15. Pável, S., Sándor, C., Csató, L.: Distortion estimation through explicit modeling of the refractive surface. In: Tetko, I.V., Kůrková, V., Karpov, P., Theis, F. (eds.) ICANN 2019. LNCS, vol. 11729, pp. 17–28. Springer, Cham (2019). https://doi.org/10.1007/978-3-030-30508-6_2
16. Pedersen, M., Bengtson, S.H., Gade, R., Madsen, N., Moeslund, T.B.: Camera calibration for underwater 3D reconstruction based on ray tracing using Snell's law. In: CVPR Workshops (CVPRW), pp. 1410–1417 (2018)
17. Ramalingam, S., Lodha, S., Sturm, P.: A generic structure-from-motion framework. Comput. Vis. Image Understand. **103**, 218–228 (2006)

18. Ramalingam, S., Sturm, P., Lodha, S.: Towards complete generic camera calibration. IEEE Conference on Computer Vision and Pattern Recognition, San Diego, USA, pp. 1093–1098 (2005)
19. Rousseeuw, P.J., Croux, C.: Alternatives to the median absolute deviation. J. Am. Stat. Assoc. **88**(424), 1273–1283 (1993)
20. Sturm, P., Ramalingam, S.: A generic concept for camera calibration. In: Pajdla, T., Matas, J. (eds.) ECCV 2004. LNCS, vol. 3022, pp. 1–13. Springer, Heidelberg (2004). https://doi.org/10.1007/978-3-540-24671-8_1
21. Sturm, P., Ramalingam, S., Tardif, J.P., Gasparini, S., Barreto, J.: Camera models and fundamental concepts used in geometric computer vision. Found. Trends ®Comput. Graph. Vis. **6**(1–2), 1–183 (2011)
22. Trifonov, B., Bradley, D., Heidrich, W.: Tomographic reconstruction of transparent objects. In: Eurographics Conference on Rendering Techniques (2006)
23. Wikipedia: False position method – Wikipedia, the free encyclopedia (2018). https://en.wikipedia.org/wiki/False_position_method

# Unsupervised Domain Adaptation for Semantic Segmentation of NIR Images Through Generative Latent Search

Prashant Pandey(✉)(ID), Aayush Kumar Tyagi(ID), Sameer Ambekar(ID), and A. P. Prathosh(ID)

Indian Institute of Technology Delhi, New Delhi, India
getprashant57@gmail.com, aayush16081@iiitd.ac.in,
ambekarsameer@gmail.com, prathoshap@iitd.ac.in

**Abstract.** Segmentation of the pixels corresponding to human skin is an essential first step in multiple applications ranging from surveillance to heart-rate estimation from remote-photoplethysmography. However, the existing literature considers the problem only in the visible-range of the EM-spectrum which limits their utility in low or no light settings where the criticality of the application is higher. To alleviate this problem, we consider the problem of skin segmentation from the Near-infrared images. However, Deep learning based state-of-the-art segmentation techniques demands large amounts of labelled data that is unavailable for the current problem. Therefore we cast the skin segmentation problem as that of target-independent Unsupervised Domain Adaptation (UDA) where we use the data from the Red-channel of the visible-range to develop skin segmentation algorithm on NIR images. We propose a method for target-independent segmentation where the 'nearest-clone' of a target image in the source domain is searched and used as a proxy in the segmentation network trained only on the source domain. We prove the existence of 'nearest-clone' and propose a method to find it through an optimization algorithm over the latent space of a Deep generative model based on variational inference. We demonstrate the efficacy of the proposed method for NIR skin segmentation over the state-of-the-art UDA segmentation methods on the two newly created skin segmentation datasets in NIR domain despite not having access to the target NIR data. Additionally, we report state-of-the-art results for adaption from Synthia to Cityscapes which is a popular setting in Unsupervised Domain Adaptation for semantic segmentation. The code and datasets are available at https://github.com/ambekarsameer96/GLSS.

**Keywords:** Unsupervised domain adaptation · Semantic segmentation · Near IR dataset · VAE

P. Pandey and A. K. Tyagi—Equal contribution.

**Electronic supplementary material** The online version of this chapter (https://doi.org/10.1007/978-3-030-58539-6_25) contains supplementary material, which is available to authorized users.

A. Vedaldi et al. (Eds.): ECCV 2020, LNCS 12351, pp. 413–429, 2020.
https://doi.org/10.1007/978-3-030-58539-6_25

# 1  Introduction

## 1.1  Background

Human skin segmentation is the task of finding pixels corresponding to skin from images or videos. It serves as a necessary pre-processing step for multiple applications like video surveillance, people tracking, human computer interaction, face detection and recognition, facial gesture detection and monitoring heart rate and respiratory rate [7,32,33,38] using remote photoplethysmography. Most of the research efforts on skin detection have focused on visible spectrum images because of the challenges that it poses including, illumination change, ethnicity change and presence of background/clothes similar to skin colour. These factors adversely affect the applications where skin is used as conjugate information. Further, the algorithms that rely on visible spectrum images cannot be employed in the low/no light conditions especially during night times where the criticality of the application like human detection is higher. These problems which are encountered in visible spectrum domain can be overcome by considering the images taken in the Near-infrared (NIR) domain [24] or hyper spectral imaging [35]. The information about the skin pixels is invariant of factors such as illumination conditions, ethnicity etc., in these domains. Moreover, most of the surveillance cameras that are used world-wide are NIR imaging devices. Thus, it is meaningful to pursue the endeavour of detecting the skin pixels from the NIR images.

## 1.2  Problem Setting and Contributions

The task of detection of skin pixels from an image is typically cast as a segmentation problem. Most of the classical approaches relied on the fact that the skin-pixels have a distinctive color pattern [13,19] compared to other objects. In recent years, harnessing the power of Deep learning, skin segmentation problem has been dealt with using deep neural networks that show significant performance enhancement over the traditional methods [21,30,40], albeit generalization across different illuminations still remains a challenge. While there exists sufficient literature on skin segmentation in the visible-spectrum, there is very little work done on segmenting the skin pixels in the NIR domain. Further, all the state-of-the-art Deep learning based segmentation algorithms demand large-scale annotated datasets to achieve good performance which is available in the case of visible-spectrum images but not the NIR images. Thus, building a fully-supervised skin segmentation network from scratch is not feasible for the NIR images because of the unavailability of the large-scale annotated data. However, the underlying concept of 'skin-pixels' is the same across the images irrespective of the band in which they were captured. Additionally, the NIR and the Red-channel of the visible-spectrum are close in terms of their wavelengths. Owing to these observations, we pose the following question in this paper - Can the labelled data (source) in the visible-spectrum (Red-channel) be used to perform skin segmentation in the NIR domain (target) [37]?

We cast the problem of skin segmentation from NIR images as a target-independent Unsupervised Domain Adaptation (UDA) task [36] where we consider the Red-channel of the visible-spectrum images as the source domain and NIR images as the target domain. The state-of-the-art UDA techniques demand access to the target data, albeit unlabelled, to adapt the source domain features to the target domain. In the present case, we do not assume existence of any data from the target domain, even unlabelled. This is an important desired attribute which ensures that a model trained on the Red-channel does not need any retraining with the data from NIR domain. The core idea is to sample the 'nearest-clone' in the source domain to a given test image from the target domain. This is accomplished through a simultaneous sampling-cum-optimization procedure using a latent-variable deep neural generative network learned on the source distribution. Thus, given a target sample, its 'nearest-clone' from the source domain is sampled and used as a proxy in the segmentation network trained only on the samples of the source domain. Since the segmentation network performs well on the source domain, it is expected to give the correct segmentation mask on the 'nearest-clone' which is then assigned to the target image. Specifically, the core contributions of this work are listed as follows:

1. We cast the problem of skin segmentation from NIR images as a UDA segmentation task where we use the data from the Red-channel of the visible-range of the EM-spectrum to develop skin segmentation algorithm on NIR images.
2. We propose a method for target-independent segmentation where the 'nearest-clone' of a target image in the source domain is searched and used as a proxy in the segmentation network trained only on the source domain.
3. We theoretically prove the existence of the 'nearest-clone' given that it can be sampled from the source domain with infinite data points.
4. We develop a joint-sampling and optimization algorithm using variational inference based generative model to search for the 'nearest-clone' through implicit sampling in the source domain.
5. We demonstrate the efficacy of the proposed method for NIR skin segmentation over the state-of-the-art UDA segmentation methods on the two newly created skin segmentation datasets in NIR domain. The proposed method is also shown to reach SOTA performance on standard segmentation datasets like Synthia [41] and Cityscapes [10].

## 2   Related Work

In this section, we first review the existing methods for skin segmentation in the visible-range followed by a review of UDA methods for segmentation.

### 2.1   Skin Segmentation in Visible-Range

Methods for skin segmentation can be grouped into three categories, i.e. (i) Thresholding based methods [13,25,39], (ii) Traditional machine learning techniques to learn a skin color model [29,51], (iii) Deep learning based methods to learn an end-to-end model for skin segmentation [2,7,15,42,50]. The thresholding based methods focus on defining a specified range in different color representation spaces like (HSV)[34] and orthogonal color space (YCbCr)[3,18] to differentiate skin pixels. Traditional machine learning can be further divided into pixel based and region based methods. In pixel based methods, each pixel is classified as skin or non-skin without considering the neighbours [45] whereas region based approaches use spatial information to identify similar regions [8]. In recent years, Fully convolutional neural networks (FCN) are employed to solve the problem [30]. [40] proposed a UNet architecture, consisting of an encoder-decoder structure with backbones like InceptionNet[43] and ResNet [14]. Holistic skin segmentation [12] combine inductive transfer learning and UDA. They term this technique as cross domain pseudo-labelling and use it in an iterative manner to train and fine tune the model on the target domain. [15] propose mutual guidance to improve skin detection with the usage of body masks as guidance. They use dual task neural network for joint detection with shared encoder and two decoders for detecting skin and body simultaneously. While all these methods offer different advantages, they do not generalize to low-light settings with NIR images, which we aim to solve through UDA.

## 2.2   Domain Adaptation for Semantic Segmentation

Unsupervised Domain Adaptation aims to improve the performance of deep neural networks on a target domain, using labels only from a source domain. UDA for segmentation task can be grouped into following categories:

**Adversarial Training Based Methods:** These methods use the principles of adversarial learning [16], which generally consists of two networks. One predicts the segmentation mask of the input image coming from either source or target distribution while the other network acts as discriminator which tries to predict the domain of the images. AdaptSegNet [46] exploits structural similarity between the source and target domains in a multi-level adversarial network framework. ADVENT [47] introduce entropy-based loss to directly penalize low-confident predictions on target domain. Adversarial training is used for structural adaptation of the target domain to the source domain. CLAN [31] considers category-level joint distribution and aligns each class with an adaptive adversarial loss. They reduce the weight of the adversarial loss for category-level aligned features while increasing the adversarial force for those that are poorly aligned. DADA [48] uses the geometry of the scene by simultaneously aligning the segmentation and depth-based information of source and target domains using adversarial training.

**Feature-Transformation Based Methods:** These methods are based on the idea of learning image-level or feature-level transformations between the source and the target domains. CyCADA [1] adapts between domains using both generative image space alignment and latent representation space alignment. Image level adaptation is achieved with cycle loss, semantic consistency loss and pixel-level GAN loss while feature level adaptation employs feature-level GAN loss and task loss between true and predicted labels. DISE [4] aims to discover a domain-invariant structural feature by learning to disentangle domain-invariant structural information of an image from its domain-specific texture information. BDL [26] involves two separated modules a) image-to-image translation model b) segmentation adaptation model, in two directions namely 'translation-to-segmentation' and 'segmentation-to-translation'.

# 3 Proposed Method

Most of the UDA methods assume access to the unlabelled target data which may not be available at all times. In this work, we propose a UDA segmentation technique by learning to find a data point from the source that is arbitrarily close (called the 'nearest-clone') to a given target point so that it can used as a proxy in the segmentation network trained only on the source data. In the subsequent sections, we describe the methodology used to find the 'nearest-clone' from the source distribution to a given target point.

## 3.1 Existence of Nearest Source Point

To start with, we show that for a given target data point, there exists a corresponding source data point, that is arbitrarily close to, provided that infinite data points can be sampled from the source distribution. Mathematically, let $\mathcal{P}_s(\mathbf{x})$ denotes the source distribution and $\mathcal{P}_t(\mathbf{x})$ denotes any target distribution that is similar but not exactly same as $\mathcal{P}_s$ (Red-channel images are source and NIR images are target). Let the underlying random variable on which $\mathcal{P}_s$ and $\mathcal{P}_t$ are defined form a separable metric space $\{\mathcal{X}, \mathcal{D}\}$ with $\mathcal{D}$ being some distance metric. Let $\mathcal{S}_n = \{\mathbf{x}_1, \mathbf{x}_2, \mathbf{x}_3, ...., \mathbf{x}_n\}$ be i.i.d points drawn from $\mathcal{P}_s(\mathbf{x})$ and $\tilde{\mathbf{x}}$ be a point from $\mathcal{P}_t(\mathbf{x})$. With this, the following lemma shows the existence of the 'nearest-clone'.

**Lemma 1.** *If $\tilde{\mathbf{x}}_\mathcal{S} \in \mathcal{S}_n$ is the point such that $\mathcal{D}\{\tilde{\mathbf{x}}, \tilde{\mathbf{x}}_\mathcal{S}\} < \mathcal{D}\{\tilde{\mathbf{x}}, \mathbf{x}\} \ \forall \mathbf{x} \in \mathcal{S}_n$, as $n \to \infty$ (in $\mathcal{S}_n$), $\tilde{\mathbf{x}}_\mathcal{S}$ converges to $\tilde{\mathbf{x}}$ with probability 1.*

*Proof.* Let $\mathbb{B}_r(\tilde{\mathbf{x}}) = \{\mathbf{x} : \mathcal{D}\{\tilde{\mathbf{x}}, \mathbf{x}\} \le r\}$ be a closed ball of radius $r$ around $\tilde{\mathbf{x}}$ under the metric $\mathcal{D}$. Since $\mathcal{X}$ is a separable metric space [11],

$$\mathbf{Prob}(\mathbb{B}_r(\tilde{\mathbf{x}})) \triangleq \int_{\mathbb{B}_r(\tilde{\mathbf{x}})} \mathcal{P}_s(\mathbf{x}) \, d\mathbf{x} > 0, \forall r > 0, \tag{1}$$

With this, for any $\delta > 0$, the probability that none of the points in $\mathcal{S}_n$ are within the ball $\mathbb{B}_\delta(\tilde{\mathbf{x}})$ of radius $\delta$ is:

$$\mathbf{Prob}\left[\min_{i=1,2..,n} \mathcal{D}\{\mathbf{x}_i, \tilde{\mathbf{x}}\} \ge \delta\right] = \left[1 - \mathbf{Prob}(\mathbb{B}_\delta(\tilde{\mathbf{x}}))\right]^n \tag{2}$$

Therefore, the probability of $\tilde{\mathbf{x}}_\mathcal{S}$ (the closest point to $\tilde{\mathbf{x}}$) lying within $\mathbb{B}_\delta(\tilde{\mathbf{x}})$ is:

$$\mathbf{Prob}\Big[\tilde{\mathbf{x}}_\mathcal{S} \in \mathbb{B}_\delta(\tilde{\mathbf{x}})\Big] = 1 - \big[1 - \mathbf{Prob}\big(\mathbb{B}_\delta(\tilde{\mathbf{x}})\big)\big]^n \qquad (3)$$

$$= 1 \;\; as \; n \to \infty \qquad (4)$$

Thus, given any infinitesimal $\delta > 0$, with probability 1, $\exists \; \tilde{\mathbf{x}}_\mathcal{S} \in \mathcal{S}_n$ ('nearest-clone') that is within $\delta$ distance from $\tilde{\mathbf{x}}$ as $n \to \infty$ $\qquad\qquad\qquad\qquad\qquad$ $\square$

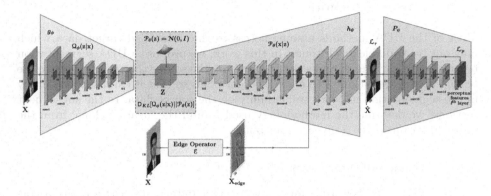

**Fig. 1.** VAE training. Edges of an input image are concatenated with the features from the decoder $h_\theta$. Encoder and decoder parameters $\phi$, $\theta$ are optimized with reconstruction loss $\mathcal{L}_r$, KL-divergence loss $\mathbb{D}_{KL}$ and perceptual loss $\mathcal{L}_p$. Perceptual model $P_\psi$ is trained on source samples. A zero mean and unit variance isotropic Gaussian prior is imposed on the latent space $\mathbf{z}$.

While Lemma 1 guarantees the existence of a 'nearest-clone', it demands the following two conditions:

– It should be possible to sample infinitely from the source distribution $\mathcal{P}_s$.
– It should be possible to search for the 'nearest-clone' in the $\mathcal{P}_s$, for a target sample $\tilde{\mathbf{x}}$ under the distance metric $\mathcal{D}$.

We propose to employ Variational Auto-encoding based sampling models on the source distribution to simultaneously sample and find the 'nearest-clone' through an optimization over the latent space.

## 3.2 Variational Auto-encoder for Source Sampling

Variational Auto-Encoders (VAEs) [23] are a class of latent-variable generative models that are based on the principles of variational inference where the variational distribution, $\mathcal{Q}_\phi(\mathbf{z}|\mathbf{x})$ is used to approximate the intractable true posterior $\mathcal{P}_\theta(\mathbf{z}|\mathbf{x})$. The log-likelihood of the observed data is decomposed into two terms,

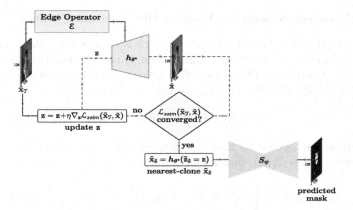

**Fig. 2.** Latent Search procedure during inference with GLSS. The latent vector **z** is initialized with a random sample drawn from $\mathcal{N}(0,1)$. Iterations over the latent space **z** are performed to minimize the $\mathcal{L}_{ssim}$ loss between the input target image $\tilde{\mathbf{x}}_{\mathcal{T}}$ and the predicted target image $\hat{\mathbf{x}}$ (blue dotted lines). After convergence of $\mathcal{L}_{ssim}$ loss, the optimal latent vector $\tilde{\mathbf{z}}_{\mathcal{S}}$, generates the closest clone $\tilde{\mathbf{x}}_{\mathcal{S}}$ which is used to predict the mask of $\tilde{\mathbf{x}}_{\mathcal{T}}$ using the segmentation network $S_\psi$. (Color figure online)

an irreducible non-negative KL-divergence between $\mathcal{P}_\theta(\mathbf{z}|\mathbf{x})$ and $\mathcal{Q}_\phi(\mathbf{z}|\mathbf{x})$ and the Evidence Lower Bound (ELBO) term which is given by Eq. 5.

$$\ln \mathcal{P}_\theta(\mathbf{x}) = \mathcal{L}(\theta, \phi) + \mathbb{D}_{KL}[\mathcal{Q}_\phi(\mathbf{z}|\mathbf{x})||\mathcal{P}_\theta(\mathbf{z}|\mathbf{x})] \tag{5}$$

where,

$$\mathcal{L}(\theta, \phi) = \mathbb{E}_{\mathcal{Q}_\phi(\mathbf{z}|\mathbf{x})}[\ln(\mathcal{P}_\theta(\mathbf{x}|\mathbf{z}))] - \mathbb{D}_{KL}[\mathcal{Q}_\phi(\mathbf{z}|\mathbf{x})||\mathcal{P}_\theta(\mathbf{z})] \tag{6}$$

The non-negative KL-term in Eq. 5 is irreducible and thus, $\mathcal{L}(\theta, \phi)$ serves as a lower bound on the data log-likelihood which is maximized in a VAE by parameterizing $\mathcal{Q}_\phi(\mathbf{z}|\mathbf{x})$ and $\mathcal{P}_\phi(\mathbf{x}|\mathbf{z})$ using probabilistic encoder $g_\phi$ (that outputs the parameters $\mu_{\mathbf{z}}$ and $\sigma_{\mathbf{z}}$ of a distribution) and decoder $h_\theta$ neural networks. The latent prior $\mathcal{P}_\theta(\mathbf{z})$ is taken to be arbitrary prior on **z** which is usually a 0 mean and unit variance Gaussian distribution. After training, the decoder network is used as a sampler for $\mathcal{P}_s(\mathbf{x})$ in a two-step process: (i) Sample $\mathbf{z} \sim \mathcal{N}(0, I)$, (ii) Sample **x** from $\mathcal{P}_\theta(\mathbf{x}|\mathbf{z})$. The likelihood term in Eq. 5 is approximated using norm based losses and it is known to result in blurry images. Therefore, we use the perceptual loss [20] along with the standard norm based losses. Further, since the edges in images are generally invariant across the source and target domains, we extract edge of the input image and use it in the decoder of the VAE via a skip connection, as shown in Fig. 1. This is shown to reduce the blur in the generated images. Figure 1 depicts the entire VAE architecture used for training on the source data.

### 3.3  VAE Latent Search for Finding the 'Nearest-Clone'

As described, the objective of the current work is to search for the nearest point in the source distribution, given a sample from target distribution. The decoder $h_\theta$ of a VAE trained on the source distribution $\mathcal{P}_s(\mathbf{x})$, outputs a new sample using the Normally distributed latent sample as input. That is,

$$\forall \mathbf{z} \sim \mathcal{N}(0, I), \hat{\mathbf{x}} = h_\theta(\mathbf{z}) \sim \mathcal{P}_s(\hat{\mathbf{x}}) \qquad (7)$$

With this, our goal is to find the 'nearest-clone' to a given target sample. That is, given a $\tilde{\mathbf{x}} \sim \mathcal{P}_t(\mathbf{x})$, find $\tilde{\mathbf{x}}_S$ as follows:

$$\tilde{\mathbf{x}}_S = h_\theta(\tilde{\mathbf{z}}_S) : \left\{ \mathcal{D}\{\tilde{\mathbf{x}}, \tilde{\mathbf{x}}_S\} < \mathcal{D}\{\mathbf{x}, \tilde{\mathbf{x}}\} \ \forall \mathbf{x} = h_\theta(\mathbf{z}) \sim \mathcal{P}_s(\mathbf{x}) \right. \qquad (8)$$

Since $\mathcal{D}$ is pre-defined and $h_\theta(\mathbf{z})$ is a deep neural network, finding $\tilde{\mathbf{x}}_S$ can be cast as an optimization problem over $\mathbf{z}$ with minimization of $\mathcal{D}$ as the objective. Mathematically,

$$\tilde{\mathbf{z}}_S = \arg\min_{\mathbf{z}} \mathcal{D}\big(\tilde{\mathbf{x}}, h_\theta(\mathbf{z})\big) \qquad (9)$$

$$\tilde{\mathbf{x}}_S = h_\theta(\tilde{\mathbf{z}}_S) \qquad (10)$$

The optimization problem is Eq. 9 can be solved using gradient-descent based techniques on the decoder network $h_{\theta*}$ ($\theta^*$ are the parameters of the decoder network trained only on the source samples $\mathcal{S}_n$) with respect to $\mathbf{z}$. This implies that given any input target image, the optimization problem in Eq. 9 will be solved to find its 'nearest-clone' in the source distribution which is used as a proxy in the segmentation network trained only on $\mathcal{S}_n$. We call the iterative procedure of finding $\tilde{\mathbf{x}}_S$ through optimization using $h_{\theta*}$ as the Latent Search (LS). Finally, inspired by the observations made in [17], we propose to use structural similarity index (SSIM) [49] based loss $\mathcal{L}_{ssim}$ for $\mathcal{D}$ to conduct the Latent Search. Unlike norm based losses, SSIM loss helps in preservation of structural information which is needed for segmentation. Figure 2 depicts the complete inference procedure employed in the proposed method named as the Generative Latent Search for Segmentation (GLSS).

## 4  Implementation Details

### 4.1  Training

Architectural details of the VAE used are shown in Fig. 1. Sobel operator is used to extract the edge information of the input image which is concatenated with one of the layers of the Decoder via a *tanh* non linearity as shown in Fig. 1. The VAE is trained using (i) the Mean squared error reconstruction loss $\mathcal{L}_r$ and KL divergence $\mathbb{D}_{KL}$ and (ii) the perceptual loss $\mathcal{L}_p$ for which the features are extracted from the $l^{\text{th}}$ layer (a hyper-parameter) of the DeepLabv3+ [6]

(Xception backbone [9]) and the UNet [40] (EfficientNet backbone [44]) segmentation networks. The segmentation network ($S_\psi$ in Fig. 2) is either DeepLabv3+ or UNet and is trained on the source dataset. For traning $S_\psi$, we use combination of binary cross-entropy ($\mathcal{L}_{bce}$) and dice coefficient loss ($\mathcal{L}_{dise}$) for UNet with RMSProp (lr = 0.001) as optimizer and binary focal loss ($\mathcal{L}_{focal}$) [28] with $\gamma = 2.0$, $\alpha = 0.75$ and RMSProp (lr = 0.01) as optimizer for DeepLabv3+. For the VAE, the hidden layers of Encoder and Decoder networks use Leaky ReLU and *tanh* as activation functions with the dimensionality of the latent space being 64. VAE is trained using standard gradient descent procedure with RMSprop ($\alpha = 0.0001$) as optimizer. We train VAE for 100 to 150 epochs with batchsize 64.

## 4.2   Inference

Once the VAE is trained on the source dataset, given an image $\tilde{\mathbf{x}}_\mathcal{T}$ from the target distribution, the Latent Search algorithm searches for an optimal latent vector $\tilde{\mathbf{z}}_\mathcal{S}$ that generates its 'nearest-clone' $\tilde{\mathbf{x}}_\mathcal{S}$ from $\mathcal{P}_S$. The search is performed by minimizing the SSIM loss $\mathcal{L}_{ssim}$ between the input target image $\tilde{\mathbf{x}}_\mathcal{T}$ and the VAE-reconstructed target image, using a gradient-descent based optimization procedure such as ADAM [22] with $\alpha = 0.1$, $\beta_1 = 0.9$ and $\beta_2 = 0.99$. The Latent Search is performed for $K$ (hyper-parameter) iterations over the latent space of the source for a given target image. Finally, the segmentation mask for the input target sample is assigned the same as the one given by the segmentation network $S_\psi$, which is trained on source data, on the 'nearest-clone' $\tilde{\mathbf{x}}_\mathcal{S}$. Latent Search for one sample takes roughly 450 ms and 120 ms on SNV and Hand Gesture datasets respectively. Please refer supplementary material for more details.

## 5   Experiment and Results

### 5.1   Datasets

We consider the Red-channel of the COMPAQ dataset [21] as our source data. It consists of 4675 RGB images with the corresponding annotations of the skin. Since there is no publicly available dataset with NIR images and corresponding skin segmentation labels, we create and use two NIR datasets (publicly available) as targets. The first one named as the Skin NIR Vision (SNV), consists of 800 images of multiple human subjects taken in different scenes, captured using a WANSVIEW 720P camera in the night-vision mode. The captured images cover wide range of scenarios for skin detection task like presence of multiple humans, backgrounds similar to skin color, different illuminations, saturation levels and different postures of subjects to ensure diversity. Additionally, we made use of the publicly available multi-modal Hand Gesture dataset[1] as another target dataset which we call as Hand Gesture dataset. This dataset covers 16 different hand-poses of multiple subjects. We randomly sampled 500 images in order to cover

---

[1]  https://www.gti.ssr.upm.es/data/MultiModalHandGesture_dataset.

illumination changes and diversity in hand poses. Both SNV and Hand Gesture datasets are manually annotated with precision.

## 5.2    Benchmarking on SNV and Hand Gesture Datasets

To begin with, we performed supervised segmentation experiments on both SNV and Hand Gesture datasets with 80–20 train-test split using SOTA segmentation algorithms.

**Table 1.** Benchmarking Skin NIR Vision (SNV) dataset and Hand Gesture dataset on standard segmentation architectures with 80–20 train-test split.

| Method | SNV | | Hand Gesture | |
|---|---|---|---|---|
| | IoU | Dice | IoU | Dice |
| FPN [27] | 0.792 | 0.895 | 0.902 | 0.950 |
| UNet [40] | 0.798 | 0.890 | 0.903 | 0.950 |
| DeepLabv3+ [6] | 0.750 | 0.850 | 0.860 | 0.924 |
| Linknet [5] | 0.768 | 0.872 | 0.907 | 0.952 |
| PSPNet [52] | 0.757 | 0.850 | 0.905 | 0.949 |

Table 1 shows the standard performance metrics such as IoU and Dice-coefficient calculated using FPN [27], UNet [40], LinkNet [5], PSPNet [52], all with EfficientNet [44] as backbone and DeepLabv3+ [6] with Xception network [9] as backbone. It is seen that SNV dataset (IoU $\approx$ 0.79) is slightly complex as compared to Hand Gesture dataset (IoU $\approx$ 0.90).

**Table 2.** Empirical analysis of GLSS along with standard UDA methods. IoU and Dice-coefficient are computed for both SNV and Hand Gesture datasets using UNet and DeepLabv3+ as segmentation networks.

| Models | SNV | | | | Hand Gesture | | | |
|---|---|---|---|---|---|---|---|---|
| | UNet | | DeepLabv3+ | | UNet | | DeepLabv3+ | |
| | IoU | Dice | IoU | Dice | IoU | Dice | IoU | Dice |
| Source Only | 0.295 | 0.426 | 0.215 | 0.426 | 0.601 | 0.711 | 0.505 | 0.680 |
| AdaptSegnet [46] | 0.315 | 0.435 | 0.230 | 0.435 | 0.641 | 0.716 | 0.542 | 0.736 |
| Advent [47] | 0.341 | 0.571 | 0.332 | 0.540 | 0.612 | 0.729 | 0.508 | 0.689 |
| CLAN [31] | 0.248 | 0.442 | 0.225 | 0.426 | 0.625 | 0.732 | 0.513 | 0.692 |
| BDL [26] | 0.320 | 0.518 | 0.301 | 0.509 | 0.647 | 0.720 | 0.536 | 0.750 |
| DISE [4] | 0.341 | 0.557 | 0.339 | 0.532 | 0.672 | 0.789 | 0.563 | 0.769 |
| DADA [48] | 0.332 | 0.534 | 0.314 | 0.521 | 0.643 | 0.743 | 0.559 | 0.761 |
| Ours (GLSS) | **0.406** | **0.597** | **0.385** | **0.597** | **0.736** | **0.844** | **0.698** | **0.824** |

## 5.3  Baseline UDA Experiments

**SNV and Hand Gesture Dataset:** We have performed the UDA experiments with the SOTA UDA algorithms using Red-channel of the COMPAQ Dataset [21] as the source and SNV and Hand Gesture as the target. Table 2 compares the performance of proposed GLSS algorithm with six SOTA baselines along with the Source Only case (without any UDA). We have used entire target dataset for IoU and Dice-coefficient evaluation. Two architectures, DeepLabv3+ and UNet,

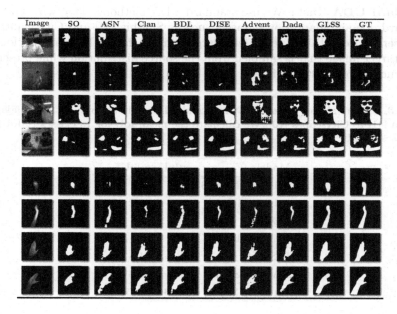

**Fig. 3.** Qualitative comparison of predicted segmentation skin masks on SNV and Hand Gesture datasets with standard UDA methods. Top four rows shows skin masks for SNV dataset and the last four are the masks for Hand Gesture dataset. It is evident that GLSS predicted masks are very close to the GT masks as compared to other UDA methods. (SO = Source Only, ASN = AdaptSegNet [46], GT = Ground Truth).

are employed for the segmentation network $(S_\psi)$. It can be seen that although all the UDA SOTA methods improve upon the Source Only performance, GLSS offers significantly better performance despite not using any data from the target distribution. Hence, it may be empirically inferred that GLSS is successful in producing the 'nearest-clone' through implicit sampling from the source distribution and thereby reducing the domain shift. It is also observed that the performance of the segmentation network $S_\psi$ does not degrade on the source data with GLSS. The predicted masks with DeepLabv3+ are shown in Fig. 3 for SNV and Hand Gesture datasets, respectively. It can be seen that GLSS is able to capture fine facial details like eyes, lips and body parts like hands, better as compared to SOTA methods. It is also seen that the predicted masks for

Hand Gesture dataset are sharper in comparison to other methods. Most of the methods work with the assumption of spatial and structural similarity between the source and target data. Since our source and target datasets do not have similar backgrounds, the methods that make such assumptions perform poorer on our datasets. We observed that for methods like BDL, the image translation between NIR images and Red channel images is not effective for skin segmentation task.

**Standard UDA Task:** We use standard UDA methods along with GLSS on standard domain adaptation datasets such as Synthia [41] and Cityscapes [10]. As observed from Table 3, even with large domain shift, GLSS finds a clone for every target image that is sampled from the source distribution while preserving the structure of the target image.

**Table 3.** Empirical analysis of GLSS on standard domain adaptaion task of adapting Synthia [41] to Cityscapes [10]. We calculate the mean IoU for 13 classes (mIoU) and 16 classes (mIoU*).

| Models | mIoU | mIoU* |
|---|---|---|
| AdaptsegNet [46] | 46.7 | – |
| Advent [47] | 48.0 | 41.2 |
| BDL [26] | 51.4 | – |
| CLAN [31] | 47.8 | – |
| DISE [4] | 48.8 | 41.5 |
| DADA [48] | 49.8 | 42.6 |
| Ours (GLSS) | **52.3** | **44.5** |

## 5.4   Ablation Study

We have conducted several ablation experiments on GLSS using both SNV and Hand Gesture datasets using DeepLabv3+ as segmentation networks ($S_\psi$) to ascertain the utility of different design choices we have made in our method.

**Effect of Number of Iterations on LS:** The inference of GLSS involves a gradient-based optimization through the decoder network $h_{\theta^*}$ to generate the 'nearest-clone' for a given target image. In Fig. 4, we show the skin masks of the transformed target images after every 30 iterations. It is seen that with the increasing number of iterations, the predicted skin masks improves using GLSS as the 'nearest-clones' are optimized during the Latent Search procedure. We plot the IoU as a function of the number of iterations during Latent Search as shown in Fig. 5 where it is seen that it saturates around 90–100 iterations that are used for all the UDA experiments described in the previous section.

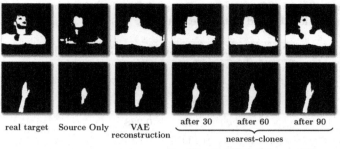

real target    Source Only    VAE
reconstruction          after 30    after 60    after 90
                                    nearest-clones

iterations over the latent space of source

**Fig. 4.** Illustration of Latent Search in GLSS. Real target is a ground truth mask. Source Only masks are obtained from target samples by training segmentation network $S_\psi$ on source dataset. Prior to the LS, skin masks are obtained from VAE reconstructed target samples. It is evident that predicted skin masks improve as the LS progresses. The predicted masks for the 'nearest-clones' are shown after every 30 iterations.

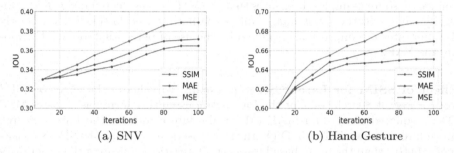

(a) SNV                    (b) Hand Gesture

**Fig. 5.** Performance of gradient-based Latent Search during inference on target SNV and Hand Gesture images using different objective functions; MSE, MAE, SSIM loss. DeepLabv3+ is employed as segmentation network. It is evident that the losses saturate at around 90–100 iterations.

**Effect of Edge Concatenation:** As discussed earlier, edges extracted using Sobel filter on input images are concatenated with one of the layers of decoder for both training and inference. It is seen from Table 4 that IoU improves for both the target datasets with concatenation of edges. It is observed that without the edge concatenation, the generated images ('nearest-clones') are blurry thus the segmentation network fails to predict sharper skin masks.

**Table 4.** Ablation of different components of GLSS during training and inference; Edge, perceptual loss $\mathcal{L}_p$ and Latent Search (LS).

| Edge | $\mathcal{L}_p$ | LS | SNV IoU | Hand Gesture IoU |
|------|------|------|---------|------------------|
|      |      |      | 0.112   | 0.227            |
| ✓    |      |      | 0.178   | 0.560            |
|      | ✓    |      | 0.120   | 0.250            |
|      |      | ✓    | 0.128   | 0.238            |
| ✓    | ✓    |      | 0.330   | 0.615            |
|      | ✓    | ✓    | 0.182   | 0.300            |
| ✓    |      | ✓    | 0.223   | 0.58             |
| ✓    | ✓    | ✓    | 0.385   | 0.698            |

**Effect of Perceptual Loss $\mathcal{L}_p$:** We have introduced a perceptual model $P_\psi$, trained on source samples. It ensures that the VAE reconstructed image is semantically similar to the input image unlike the norm based losses. Table 4 clearly demonstrates the improvement offered by the use of perceptual loss while training the VAE.

**Effect of SSIM for Latent Search:** Finally, to validate the effect of SSIM loss for Latent Search, we plot the IoU metric using two norm based losses MSE (Mean squared error) and MAE (Mean absolute error) for the Latent Search procedure as shown in Fig. 5. On both the datasets, it is seen that SSIM is consistently better than the norm based losses at all iterations affirming the superiority of the SSIM loss in preserving the structures while finding the 'nearest-clone'.

# 6    Conclusion

In this paper, we addressed the problem of skin segmentation from NIR images. Owing to the non-existence of large-scale labelled NIR datasets for skin segmentation, the problem is casted as Unsupervised Domain Adaptation where we use the segmentation network trained on the Red-channel images from a large-scale labelled visible-spectrum dataset for UDA on NIR data. We propose a novel method for UDA without the need for the access to the target data (even unlabelled). Given a target image, we sample an image from the source distribution that is 'closest' to it under a distance metric. We show that such a 'closest' sample exists and describe a procedure using an optimization algorithm over the latent space of a VAE trained on the source data. We demonstrate the utility of the proposed method along with the comparisons with SOTA UDA segmentation methods on the skin segmentation task on two NIR datasets that were created. Also, we reach SOTA performance on Synthia and Cityscapes datasets for semantic segmentation of urban scenes.

# References

1. CyCADA: cycle consistent adversarial domain adaptation. In: International Conference on Machine Learning (ICML) (2018)
2. Al-Mohair, H.K., Saleh, J., Saundi, S.: Impact of color space on human skin color detection using an intelligent system. In: 1st WSEAS International Conference on Image Processing and Pattern Recognition (IPPR 2013), vol. 2 (2013)
3. Brancati, N., De Pietro, G., Frucci, M., Gallo, L.: Human skin detection through correlation rules between the YCb and YCr subspaces based on dynamic color clustering. Comput. Vis. Image Underst. **155**, 33–42 (2017)
4. Chang, W.L., Wang, H.P., Peng, W.H., Chiu, W.C.: All about structure: adapting structural information across domains for boosting semantic segmentation. In: Proceedings of the IEEE Conference on Computer Vision and Pattern Recognition, pp. 1900–1909 (2019)
5. Chaurasia, A., Culurciello, E.: LinkNet: exploiting encoder representations for efficient semantic segmentation. In: 2017 IEEE Visual Communications and Image Processing (VCIP), pp. 1–4. IEEE (2017)
6. Chen, L.-C., Zhu, Y., Papandreou, G., Schroff, F., Adam, H.: Encoder-decoder with atrous separable convolution for semantic image segmentation. In: Ferrari, V., Hebert, M., Sminchisescu, C., Weiss, Y. (eds.) ECCV 2018. LNCS, vol. 11211, pp. 833–851. Springer, Cham (2018). https://doi.org/10.1007/978-3-030-01234-2_49
7. Chen, W., Wang, K., Jiang, H., Li, M.: Skin color modeling for face detection and segmentation: a review and a new approach. Multimedia Tools Appl. **75**(2), 839–862 (2016). https://doi.org/10.1007/s11042-014-2328-0
8. Chen, W.C., Wang, M.S.: Region-based and content adaptive skin detection in color images. Int. J. Pattern Recogn. Artif. Intell. **21**(05), 831–853 (2007)
9. Chollet, F.: Xception: deep learning with depthwise separable convolutions. In: Proceedings of the IEEE Conference on Computer Vision and Pattern Recognition, pp. 1251–1258 (2017)
10. Cordts, M., et al.: The cityscapes dataset for semantic urban scene understanding. In: Proceedings of the IEEE Conference on Computer Vision and Pattern Recognition, pp. 3213–3223 (2016)
11. Cover, T., Hart, P.: Nearest neighbor pattern classification. IEEE Trans. Inf. Theory **13**(1), 21–27 (1967)
12. Dourado, A., Guth, F., de Campos, T.E., Weigang, L.: Domain adaptation for holistic skin detection. arXiv preprint arXiv:1903.06969 (2019)
13. Erdem, C., Ulukaya, S., Karaali, A., Erdem, A.T.: Combining Haar feature and skin color based classifiers for face detection. In: 2011 IEEE International Conference on Acoustics, Speech and Signal Processing (ICASSP), pp. 1497–1500. IEEE (2011)
14. He, K., Zhang, X., Ren, S., Sun, J.: Deep residual learning for image recognition. In: Proceedings of the IEEE Conference on Computer Vision and Pattern Recognition, pp. 770–778 (2016)
15. He, Y., et al.: Semi-supervised skin detection by network with mutual guidance. In: Proceedings of the IEEE International Conference on Computer Vision, pp. 2111–2120 (2019)
16. Hoffman, J., Wang, D., Yu, F., Darrell, T.: FCNs in the wild: pixel-level adversarial and constraint-based adaptation. arXiv preprint arXiv:1612.02649 (2016)
17. Hore, A., Ziou, D.: Image quality metrics: PSNR vs. SSIM. In: 2010 20th International Conference on Pattern Recognition, pp. 2366–2369. IEEE (2010)

18. Hsu, R.L., Abdel-Mottaleb, M., Jain, A.K.: Face detection in color images. IEEE Trans. Pattern Anal. Mach. Intell. **24**(5), 696–706 (2002)
19. Huynh-Thu, Q., Meguro, M., Kaneko, M.: Skin-color-based image segmentation and its application in face detection. In: MVA, pp. 48–51 (2002)
20. Johnson, J., Alahi, A., Fei-Fei, L.: Perceptual losses for real-time style transfer and super-resolution. In: Leibe, B., Matas, J., Sebe, N., Welling, M. (eds.) ECCV 2016. LNCS, vol. 9906, pp. 694–711. Springer, Cham (2016). https://doi.org/10.1007/978-3-319-46475-6_43
21. Jones, M.J., Rehg, J.M.: Statistical color models with application to skin detection. Int. J. Comput. Vis. **46**(1), 81–96 (2002). https://doi.org/10.1023/A:1013200319198
22. Kingma, D.P., Ba, J.: Adam: a method for stochastic optimization. arXiv preprint arXiv:1412.6980 (2014)
23. Kingma, D.P., Welling, M.: Auto-encoding variational Bayes. arXiv preprint arXiv:1312.6114 (2013)
24. Kong, S.G., Heo, J., Abidi, B.R., Paik, J., Abidi, M.A.: Recent advances in visual and infrared face recognition-a review. Comput. Vis. Image Underst. **97**(1), 103–135 (2005)
25. Kovac, J., Peer, P., Solina, F.: Human skin color clustering for face detection, vol. 2. IEEE (2003)
26. Li, Y., Yuan, L., Vasconcelos, N.: Bidirectional learning for domain adaptation of semantic segmentation. arXiv preprint arXiv:1904.10620 (2019)
27. Lin, T.Y., Dollár, P., Girshick, R., He, K., Hariharan, B., Belongie, S.: Feature pyramid networks for object detection. In: Proceedings of the IEEE Conference on Computer Vision and Pattern Recognition, pp. 2117–2125 (2017)
28. Lin, T.Y., Goyal, P., Girshick, R., He, K., Dollár, P.: Focal loss for dense object detection. In: Proceedings of the IEEE International Conference on Computer Vision, pp. 2980–2988 (2017)
29. Liu, Q., Peng, G.: A robust skin color based face detection algorithm. In: 2010 2nd International Asia Conference on Informatics in Control, Automation and Robotics (CAR 2010), vol. 2, pp. 525–528. IEEE (2010)
30. Long, J., Shelhamer, E., Darrell, T.: Fully convolutional networks for semantic segmentation. In: Proceedings of the IEEE Conference on Computer Vision and Pattern Recognition, pp. 3431–3440 (2015)
31. Luo, Y., Zheng, L., Guan, T., Yu, J., Yang, Y.: Taking a closer look at domain shift: category-level adversaries for semantics consistent domain adaptation. In: Proceedings of the IEEE Conference on Computer Vision and Pattern Recognition, pp. 2507–2516 (2019)
32. Mahmoodi, M.R.: High performance novel skin segmentation algorithm for images with complex background. arXiv preprint arXiv:1701.05588 (2017)
33. Mahmoodi, M.R., Sayedi, S.M.: A comprehensive survey on human skin detection. Int. J. Image Graph. Sig. Process. **8**(5), 1–35 (2016)
34. Moallem, P., Mousavi, B.S., Monadjemi, S.A.: A novel fuzzy rule base system for pose independent faces detection. Appl. Soft Comput. **11**(2), 1801–1810 (2011)
35. Pan, Z., Healey, G., Prasad, M., Tromberg, B.: Face recognition in hyperspectral images. IEEE Trans. Pattern Anal. Mach. Intell. **25**(12), 1552–1560 (2003)
36. Pandey, P., Prathosh, A.P., Kyatham, V., Mishra, D., Dastidar, T.R.: Target-independent domain adaptation for WBC classification using generative latent search. arXiv preprint arXiv:2005.05432 (2020)

37. Pandey, P., Prathosh, A., Kohli, M., Pritchard, J.: Guided weak supervision for action recognition with scarce data to assess skills of children with autism. In: Proceedings of the AAAI Conference on Artificial Intelligence, vol. 34, pp. 463–470 (2020)

38. Prathosh, A., Praveena, P., Mestha, L.K., Bharadwaj, S.: Estimation of respiratory pattern from video using selective ensemble aggregation. IEEE Trans. Sig. Process. **65**(11), 2902–2916 (2017)

39. Qiang-rong, J., Hua-lan, L.: Robust human face detection in complicated color images. In: 2010 2nd IEEE International Conference on Information Management and Engineering, pp. 218–221. IEEE (2010)

40. Ronneberger, O., Fischer, P., Brox, T.: U-Net: convolutional networks for biomedical image segmentation. In: Navab, N., Hornegger, J., Wells, W.M., Frangi, A.F. (eds.) MICCAI 2015. LNCS, vol. 9351, pp. 234–241. Springer, Cham (2015). https://doi.org/10.1007/978-3-319-24574-4_28

41. Ros, G., Sellart, L., Materzynska, J., Vazquez, D., Lopez, A.M.: The synthia dataset: a large collection of synthetic images for semantic segmentation of urban scenes. In: Proceedings of the IEEE Conference on Computer Vision and Pattern Recognition, pp. 3234–3243 (2016)

42. Seow, M.J., Valaparla, D., Asari, V.K.: Neural network based skin color model for face detection. In: 2003 Proceedings of the 32nd Applied Imagery Pattern Recognition Workshop, pp. 141–145. IEEE (2003)

43. Szegedy, C., Vanhoucke, V., Ioffe, S., Shlens, J., Wojna, Z.: Rethinking the inception architecture for computer vision. In: Proceedings of the IEEE Conference on Computer Vision and Pattern Recognition, pp. 2818–2826 (2016)

44. Tan, M., Le, Q.V.: EfficientNet: rethinking model scaling for convolutional neural networks. arXiv preprint arXiv:1905.11946 (2019)

45. Taqa, A.Y., Jalab, H.A.: Increasing the reliability of skin detectors. Sci. Res. Essays **5**(17), 2480–2490 (2010)

46. Tsai, Y.H., Hung, W.C., Schulter, S., Sohn, K., Yang, M.H., Chandraker, M.: Learning to adapt structured output space for semantic segmentation. In: Proceedings of the IEEE Conference on Computer Vision and Pattern Recognition, pp. 7472–7481 (2018)

47. Vu, T.H., Jain, H., Bucher, M., Cord, M., Pérez, P.: ADVENT: adversarial entropy minimization for domain adaptation in semantic segmentation. In: CVPR (2019)

48. Vu, T.H., Jain, H., Bucher, M., Cord, M., Pérez, P.: DADA: depth-aware domain adaptation in semantic segmentation. In: Proceedings of the IEEE International Conference on Computer Vision, pp. 7364–7373 (2019)

49. Wang, Z., Bovik, A.C., Sheikh, H.R., Simoncelli, E.P.: Image quality assessment: from error visibility to structural similarity. IEEE Trans. Image Process. **13**(4), 600–612 (2004)

50. Wu, Q., Cai, R., Fan, L., Ruan, C., Leng, G.: Skin detection using color processing mechanism inspired by the visual system (2012)

51. Zaidan, A., Ahmad, N.N., Karim, H.A., Larbani, M., Zaidan, B., Sali, A.: On the multi-agent learning neural and Bayesian methods in skin detector and pornography classifier: an automated anti-pornography system. Neurocomputing **131**, 397–418 (2014)

52. Zhao, H., Shi, J., Qi, X., Wang, X., Jia, J.: Pyramid scene parsing network. In: Proceedings of the IEEE Conference on Computer Vision and Pattern Recognition, pp. 2881–2890 (2017)

# PROFIT: A Novel Training Method for sub-4-bit MobileNet Models

Eunhyeok Park[1] and Sungjoo Yoo[2]([✉])

[1] Inter-university Semiconductor Research Center (ISRC), Seoul National University,
Seoul, Korea
canusglow@gmail.com
[2] Department of Computer Science and Engineering,
Neural Processing Research Center (NPRC), Seoul National University, Seoul, Korea
sungjoo.yoo@gmail.com

**Abstract.** 4-bit and lower precision mobile models are required due to the ever-increasing demand for better energy efficiency in mobile devices. In this work, we report that the activation instability induced by weight quantization (AIWQ) is the key obstacle to sub-4-bit quantization of mobile networks. To alleviate the AIWQ problem, we propose a novel training method called PROgressive-Freezing Iterative Training (PROFIT), which attempts to freeze layers whose weights are affected by the instability problem stronger than the other layers. We also propose a differentiable and unified quantization method (DuQ) and a negative padding idea to support asymmetric activation functions such as h-swish. We evaluate the proposed methods by quantizing MobileNet-v1, v2, and v3 on ImageNet and report that 4-bit quantization offers comparable (within 1.48% top-1 accuracy) accuracy to full precision baseline. In the ablation study of the 3-bit quantization of MobileNet-v3, our proposed method outperforms the state-of-the-art method by a large margin, 12.86% of top-1 accuracy. The quantized model and source code is available at https://github.com/EunhyeokPark/PROFIT.

**Keywords:** Mobile network · Quantization · Activation distribution · h-swish activation

## 1 Introduction

Neural networks are widely adopted in various embedded applications, e.g., smartphones, AR/VR devices, and drones. Such applications are characterized by stringent constraints in latency (for real-time constraints) and energy consumption (because of battery). Thus, it is imperative to optimize neural networks in terms of latency and energy consumption, while maintaining the quality of the neural networks, e.g., accuracy.

**Electronic supplementary material** The online version of this chapter (https://doi.org/10.1007/978-3-030-58539-6_26) contains supplementary material, which is available to authorized users.

© Springer Nature Switzerland AG 2020
A. Vedaldi et al. (Eds.): ECCV 2020, LNCS 12351, pp. 430–446, 2020.
https://doi.org/10.1007/978-3-030-58539-6_26

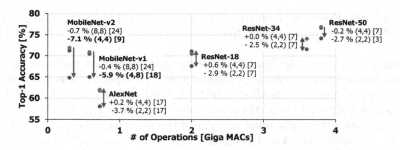

**Fig. 1.** Recent results of quantization studies. The blue dots represent full-precision accuracy and the red dots quantized accuracy. The tuple (a, w) represents the bit-width of activation and weight, respectively. (Color figure online)

Quantization is one of the most effective optimization techniques. By reducing the bit-width of activations and weights, the performance and energy efficiency can be improved by executing more computations with the same amount of memory accesses and computation resources (e.g., the silicon chip area and battery). The 8-bit computation is already popular [32,33,36,38], and NVIDIA recently announced that tensor core supports 4-bit precision which gives more than 50% of performance improvement on ResNet-50 [25]. We expect 4-bit and lower precision computation will become more and more important and make further contributions to the energy efficiency and real-time characteristics of future deep learning applications [26,28,30,35,36].

In order to support the up-coming hardware acceleration, there have been active studies on sub-4-bit quantization [3,4,15,17,21,27,39–42]. These studies show that deep networks, e.g., AlexNet or ResNet-18 for ImageNet classification [5], can be quantized into sub-4 bits with negligible accuracy loss, as shown in Fig. 1. However, these out-dated networks are prohibitively expensive to use in mobile devices. In mobile devices, it is imperative to quantize the optimized networks, e.g., MobileNet-v2 [29] or MobileNet-v3 [13].

However, the previous quantization methods do not work well on the advanced optimized networks. These networks adopt novel structures like depthwise separable convolution [14], inverted residual block with linear expansion layer [29], squeeze-excitation module, and h-swish activation function [13]. These structures have less redundancy and are vulnerable to quantization, and the h-swish activation function generates an asymmetric distribution. Previous quantization methods did not consider the optimizations, thus having a significant accuracy degradation in the sub-4-bit quantization of the advanced networks.

In this study, we propose two novel ideas that enable 4-bit quantization for the optimized networks. First, we report that the primary reason for the accuracy loss in sub-4-bit quantization is the activation instability induced by weight quantization (AIWQ). Weight quantization can skew the statistics of the output activation, i.e., the mean and variance, at every iteration during fine-tuning. This adversely affects the following layers and finally prevents the network from converging to a good optimal point in low-precision quantization. In order to address this problem, we propose a novel training method called

**PRO**gressively-**F**reezing **I**terative **T**raining (PROFIT) that minimizes the effects of AIWQ by progressively freezing the weights sensitive to AIWQ during training.

Second, we identify the limitations of the state-of-the-art trainable methods of linear quantization in terms of asymmetric activation support, and we propose a novel quantization method called differentiable and unified quantization (DuQ) and negative padding. Many advanced networks begin to adopt the activation functions allowing a small amount of the negative value, e.g., hard swish (h-swish) of MobileNet-v3 and Gaussian error linear unit (GeLU) of BERT [6]. These activation functions increase accuracy with minimal overhead. However, they produce asymmetric output distributions. Existing quantization methods are only designed to support symmetric or non-negative distributions; therefore, they are unsuitable for the asymmetric distributions. The proposed DuQ method resolves the above problems without limiting the value range while minimizing both rounding and truncation errors in a differentiable manner. Furthermore, the novel negative padding idea contributes to accuracy improvement by appropriately utilizing the quantization levels under an asymmetric distribution.

## 2    Related Work

The neural network architecture has been continuously improved while increasing accuracy at a lower computation cost. MobileNet-v1 [14] and -v2 [29] introduced a depth-wise separable convolution and an inverted residual structure respectably. MNasNet was designed based on AutoML, which automates the network architecture search, considering the computation cost [34]. MobileNet-v3 is the state-of-the-art network, which was designed from MNasNet by improving it with the h-swish activation function and squeeze-excitation modules [13]. Compared to the conventional deep networks like AlexNet [20], VGG [31], and ResNet [11], the recent networks have adopted optimized structures for better accuracy at a low computation cost. However, such optimized structures render quantization challenging, especially for 4-bit and lower precision quantization.

Several studies have been proposed for sub-4-bit quantization. [27] and [39] are the representative studies showing that neural networks can be quantized into sub-4-bits with marginal accuracy loss. [42] proposed progressive quantization, which reduces the precision in a progressive manner. [3,4,7,9,17] and [23] show that networks for large-scale datasets, e.g., ResNet [11] for ImageNet [5], can be quantized into sub-4-bits without accuracy loss. Recently, [8] and [24] are focused on post-training 8-bit quantization, and showed that quantization introduces a bias shift, which acts as the main cause of accuracy degradation. The previous works show the potential of aggressive quantization in terms of sub-4-bits (with fine-tuning) for AlexNet and ResNet, or 8-bit quantization (without fine-tuning) for MobileNet-v2. In this study, we focus on the 4-bit and lower precision quantization (with fine-tuning) for recently optimized networks such as MobileNet-v2 and -v3.

Many of the previous quantization methods utilize hand-crafted loss, e.g., L2 distance between full-precision and quantized data [3]. For a lower precision,

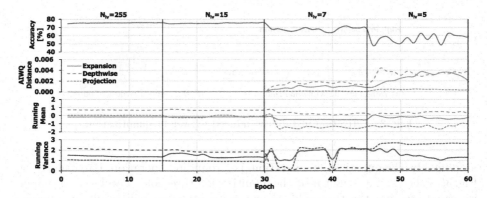

**Fig. 2.** Top-1 accuracy [%], AIWQ distance, and the running mean, and the running variance during fine-tuning for quantization where $N_{lv}$ represents the number of available quantization levels. Running mean and variance are extracted from the arbitrary channels of batch normalization layer after the depth-wise convolution in the 2nd inverted residual module of MobileNet-v3.

it is desirable to learn the quantization interval of the loss of the target task, e.g., cross-entropy loss for classification. In [3,4,17] and [7], the quantization interval is learned via backpropagation. In this study, we also propose DuQ with a negative padding idea that learns the quantization interval by utilizing the gradients and asymmetric activations better than the previous methods.

## 3   AIWQ and PROFIT

In this section, we first demonstrate that the AIWQ problem is strongly correlated with the accuracy degradation at low precision. Then, we present a metric to measure the activation instability and propose a training method called PROFIT that controls the training of each layer to minimize the effect of AIWQ based on the presented metric.

### 3.1   Observation

Figure 2 (Accuracy) shows the accuracy of MobileNet-v3 for the Cifar-100 dataset [19]. The accuracy is measured during fine-tuning in progressive weight quantization [42], where the number of quantization levels of the weights $N_{lv}$ are gradually reduced from 255 to 5 while using full-precision activation. The accuracy curves in Fig. 2 show that, in each precision case, e.g., $N_{lv} = 15$, the test accuracy is gradually recovered as the fine-tuning advances. However, when the number of available quantization levels reduces to 7 or lower, the accuracy significantly oscillates and fails to converge.

From our analysis, that will be given in the next subsection, this is mainly due to the activation instability during fine-tuning, as shown in Fig. 3. The challenge is that the effects of the weight update, due to backpropagation, could be

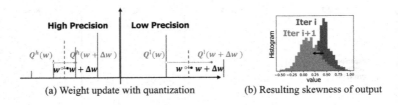

(a) Weight update with quantization          (b) Resulting skewness of output

**Fig. 3.** Activation instability induced by weight quantization.

amplified by the quantization operation, i.e., rounding operation. Particularly, as Fig. 3(a) shows, if a weight near the quantization threshold is updated to change its value crossing the threshold, then the quantization will result in different quantized weight values before and after the weight update. Thus, the results of the convolution operation will change due to the weight update and quantization. As Fig. 3(b) shows, this skews the statistics of the output activation, which affects the following layers, including the normalization layers; therefore, yielding inaccurate running mean and variance in these layers. The inaccurate running mean and variance, obtained during training, degrades the test accuracy as illustrated in Fig. 2 because they are utilized in the normalization layers during the test but can't represent the actual statistics of the activation.

At lower precision, the activation instability induced by weight quantization (AIWQ) becomes more significant because the space between two adjacent quantization levels ($\sim 1/2^{\texttt{bit-width}}$) becomes large. Thus, the lower the precision gets, the more the activation instability can be incurred.[1] Besides, please note that the AIWQ problem is also found in conventional neural networks. However, because these networks use full convolution as their building block having more than hundreds of accumulation per output, the quantization error is likely to be amortized based on the law of large numbers. This makes the networks robust to quantize, but they also suffer from instability when the precision lower.

## 3.2   Activation Instability Metric

We present a metric to quantify the per-layer activation instability and use it to (1) prove that AIWQ is correlated with the test accuracy of the low-precision model (in Fig. 2) and (2) utilize the per-layer sensitivity when determining the order of freezing the weights during training (to be explained in Sect. 3.3).

In order to measure per-layer activation instability, a desirable solution would be to calculate the KL divergence between two distributions of the outputs before ($p_o^t$) and after ($q_o^t$) a training iteration $t$. We first calculate the per-output channel

---

[1] Note that, in higher (lower) precision, there will be more (less) occurrences of smaller (larger) amounts of activation instability. Our study empirically shows that a few occurrences of large activation instability at low precision tend to have a higher impact on the test accuracy than many occurrences of small activation instabilities at high precision.

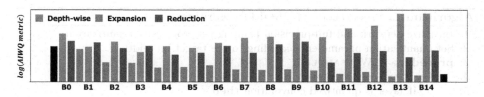

**Fig. 4.** Layer-wise AIWQ metric measured at MobileNet-V3 on Imagenet. Bx refers to x-th building block of MobileNet-v3. Please note that y-axis is in log-scale thus the layer-wise sensitivity is highly vary depending on layer index.

KL divergence between $p_o^t$ and $q_o^t$. Then, as shown below, we compute the layer-wise AIWQ metric $D^l$ by averaging the per-output channel KL divergence across all the output channels of the current layer in the current training batch.

$$D^l = E_o^t[D_{KL}(p_o^t \parallel q_o^t)]. \tag{1}$$

We simplify the computation of the KL divergence by adopting a second-order model which considers the mean and variance of per-channel output distribution because the computation of the KL divergence is expensive, and the second-order model proves sufficient for our goal of evaluating the relative order between layers.[2] Figure 4 shows the AIWQ metric of MobileNet-v3 on ImageNet. As the figure shows, depth-wise convolution layers tend to exhibit a large AIWQ while some reduction (point-wise $1 \times 1$ convolution) layers also give a larger AIWQ than the depth-wise layers in the early layers.

Recall Fig. 2, which illustrates how the AIWQ metric varies during fine-tuning. The AIWQ increases in the 7- and 5-level quantization, which empirically proves that weight quantization at low precision can incur significant perturbation of the convolution output, i.e., makes the output activation unstable. As shown in the figure, such an instability causes the running mean and variance[3] to fluctuate, which prevents us from obtaining good running mean and variance during training. When comparing the accuracy, the AIWQ metric, and the mean and variance in Fig. 2, they are closely correlated at low precision, i.e., $N_{lv} = 5$. In the following subsection, we use the AIWQ metric to schedule which layers to freeze first during the fine-tuning, which contributes to reducing the AIWQ, hence improving the test accuracy.

### 3.3 PROFIT

We propose a novel training method which aims at minimizing the AIWQ effect to improve the accuracy of low precision networks. Our basic idea is progres-

---

[2] Note that in [8,24] the first-order momentum, i.e., the channel-wise mean is utilized to evaluate the difference in the output distributions. From our observation, the channel-wise variance is also significantly skewed by the AIWQ, and significantly affects the accuracy via normalization. AIWQ metric is designed to consider the two important momenta, the mean and variance, concurrently with an affordable cost.

[3] We show the mean and variance on three sampled output channels in Fig. 2.

---

**Algorithm 1.** Pseudo code of PROFIT algorithm

---

1: Initialize network and full-precision training (+ progressive quantization)
2: Set quantization parameters according to the target bit-width.
3: **procedure** AIWQ SAMPLING
4:     **for** layer ∈ network.layers **do**
5:         **if** layer is quantized convolution **then**
6:             metric_map[layer] = 0
7:     **for** i ∈ sampling iterations **do**
8:         **for** layer ∈ network.layers **do**
9:             layer.forward()
10:            **if** layer is quantized convolution **then**
11:                metric_map[layer] += layer.AIWQ_metric
12:        network.update()
13: AIWQ_list ← sort_by_value(metric_map, order=descending)
14: $N_{layers}$ ← len(AIWQ_list)
15: **procedure** PROFIT
16:     **for** n ∈ $N_{PROFIT}$ **do**
17:         **for** e ∈ Profit_Epoch **do**
18:             network.training_epoch()
19:         begin ← $n * N_{layers}/N_{PROFIT}$, end ← $(n+1) * N_{layers}/N_{PROFIT}$
20:         freeze_target_layers ← AIWQ_list[begin:end]
21:         **for** layer ∈ freeze_target_layers **do**
22:             layer.learning_rate ← 0
23:     **for** e ∈ BN_Epoch **do**
24:         network.training_epoch()

---

sively freezing (the weights of) the most sensitive layer to AIWQ to remove the fluctuation source, thus allowing the rest of the layers to converge to a more optimal point. We determine the layer-wise order of the weight freezing considering the per-layer AIWQ metric in Eq. 1. Algorithm 1 shows how our method, called **PRO**gressively-**F**reezing **I**terative **T**raining (PROFIT), works. When PROFIT is triggered, we start a sampling stage where we evaluate the per-layer AIWQ metric for each layer. After the sampling stage, we perform fine-tuning in an initial stage without freezing weights. Subsequently, after sorting all the weight layers in terms of the per-layer metric, we perform weight freezing stages by selecting the most sensitive layers (the ones having the largest AIWQ metric values) and freezing their weights. As shown in the algorithm, we iteratively perform $N_{PROFIT}$ freezing stages. Thus, in each stage, $N_{layers}/N_{PROFIT}$ ($N_{layers}$ is the total number of quantized layers) are selected from the sorted layer list and their weights are frozen. Then, we perform training for all un-frozen layers. After finishing the additional training stage, we select the next set of un-frozen sensitive layers (another $N_{layers}/N_{PROFIT}$ layers) and repeat the same procedure until there is no more un-frozen layer left. Finally, we perform an additional training stage (typically, 3–5 epochs) for the normalization layers while freezing all the other layers. This further stabilizes the statics of the normalization layers.

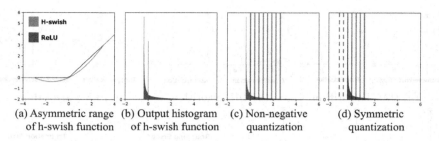

(a) Asymmetric range    (b) Output histogram    (c) Non-negative    (d) Symmetric
   of h-swish function      of h-swish function      quantization         quantization

**Fig. 5.** Characteristics of h-swish function and corresponding non-negative and symmetric quantization.

As will be shown in our experimental results, PROFIT improves the accuracy of low precision networks by significantly reducing the effect of AIWQ.

## 4   Quantization for Asymmetric Distributions

In many advanced networks, the activation functions allow a small number of negative values, e.g., h-swish of MobileNet-v3 and GeLU of BERT, are becoming more popular. These functions increase the accuracy with minimal computation overhead, thus gradually expanding their scope of use. However, they have a critical limitation in terms of quantization. Because of the negative range, the output has an asymmetric distribution. Even though the negative range is small, many values are concentrated in that area, as shown in Fig. 5. These negative values should be carefully considered to maintain accuracy at low precision.

However, existing quantization methods are only designed for symmetric or non-negative output. In such a case, when we apply quantization to only the non-negative output of the h-swish function, many negative values are ignored (Fig. 5(c)). On the contrary, when we apply symmetric quantization, some of the quantization levels, allocated for large negative values, are wasted, and a significant truncation error is incurred due to the narrower value range for positive values (Fig. 5(d)). In either case, there is a significant loss in accuracy.

In order to quantize the asymmetric distribution with minimal accuracy loss, we propose two ideas: DuQ and negative padding. First, we propose a quantization algorithm called Differentiable and Unified Quantization (DuQ) that resolves the above problems without limiting the value range while minimizing the rounding and truncation errors in a differentiable manner. Second, we propose negative padding that allows us to avoid wasting quantization levels, hence improving accuracy at low precision.

### 4.1   Limitations of State-of-the-Art Methods

Our goal is to realize differentiable quantization, which minimizes the task loss of the asymmetric distribution of activation. There are three representative methods, parameterized clipping activation function (PACT) [3], quantization interval learning (QIL) [17], and learned step size quantization (LSQ) [7]. In all the

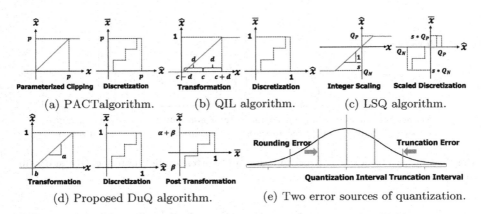

(a) PACTalgorithm.      (b) QIL algorithm.      (c) LSQ algorithm.

(d) Proposed DuQ algorithm.      (e) Two error sources of quantization.

**Fig. 6.** Quantization algorithm details.

methods, the differentiable parameters and quantization intervals are updated through backpropagation to minimize the task loss.

Both PACT and QIL have a critical limitation in supporting new activation functions because the transformation stage or parameterized clipping stage forces the activation data to be mapped to $[0, 1]$ in [17] or $[0, p]$ in [3], as shown in Fig. 6(a) and (b). Thus, it is not applicable to activation functions with asymmetric distributions. In the case of LSQ, as shown in Fig. 6(c), a trainable scale parameter $s$ is adopted, and the hand-crafted parameters utilize the number of negative quantization levels $Q_N$ and that of positive ones $Q_P$. LSQ also handles either symmetric ($Q_N = Q_P = 2^{bit-1} - 1$) or non-negative ($Q_N = 0, Q_P = 2^{bit} - 1$) distributions. Additionally, because the user predetermines the number of quantization levels for negative and positive ranges, it has a limitation in handling various distributions across the layers.

### 4.2   Proposed Method: DuQ

Our proposed method, called DuQ, learns the quantization and truncation intervals through back-propagation. This is an extension of QIL with scale ($\alpha$) and shift($\beta$) parameters that remove the limitation of QIL, i.e., the limited output range of $[0, 1]$.

The two stages of transformation (Eq. 2) and discretization (Eq. 3) are identical to those of QIL except that the slope $a$ and offset $b$ are used in the transformation stage instead of the center $c$ and width $d$ in QIL. As Eqs. 2 and 4 show, we use the softplus function for $a$ and $\alpha$ to make them positive values for improving the stability of the transformation stage. Equation 3 represents the discretization stage, where $N_{lv}$ is the number of quantization levels.

$$\hat{x} = clip((x - b)/a', 0, 1), \ a' = softplus(a), \tag{2}$$

$$\bar{x} = round((N_{lv} - 1) \cdot \hat{x})/(N_{lv} - 1), \tag{3}$$

$$\tilde{x} = \alpha' \cdot \bar{x} + \beta, \ \alpha' = softplus(\alpha). \tag{4}$$

Our proposed DuQ method allows us to utilize the full value range of activation including the negative ones, and to achieve that, the discretized data can be mapped to an arbitrary range through a scale $\alpha$ and offset $\beta$, in the post-transformation stage, as shown in Eq. 4 as shown in Fig. 6(d). One additional advantage is DuQ utilizes all the gradients across the entire activation data. PACT only utilizes the gradients from the truncation interval (the value range larger than the truncation threshold), while QIL only utilizes the gradients from the quantization interval (between the minimum and maximum quantization levels). Both utilize only a portion of the backpropagated error. However, DuQ utilizes all the gradients to learn a good quantization interval considering the trade-off between rounding and truncation errors, as Fig. 6(e) shows.

### 4.3  Negative Padding

DuQ is flexible enough to support asymmetric distributions. However, many of existing hardware accelerators support only symmetric and non-negative integer types. We propose a idea called negative padding to accelerate the quantized network having asymmetric distributions on such hardware accelerators.

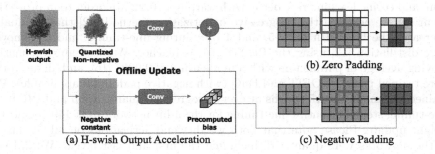

**Fig. 7.** Negative padding for h-swish function.

Even though the output of the h-swish function has an asymmetric distribution, it has a constant minimal value, $-0.375$. As shown in Fig. 7(a), by shifting the activations by the minimal value, the activations can be broken down into two components, constant negative ones, and shifted non-negative ones. The output corresponding to the constant negative feature can be calculated offline, and the output corresponding to the input-dependent non-negative activations can be efficiently calculated by the hardware accelerator. By combining those two outputs, we can obtain the output. Note that, because of the linearity of the convolution and matrix multiplication, the output is correct.

However, because of conventional zero padding, the output corresponding to constant negative input activations has inconsistent values on the edges, as shown in Fig. 7(b). We need to store the spatial position-dependent values, which can increase the cost of memory access and computation. This problem can be solved by adopting negative padding instead of zero padding (Fig. 7(c)). When we pad the edge of the activation with the constant minimal value of the h-swish function, i.e., $-0.375$, the output has an identical value for all the features in the same spatial dimension. This constant output enables the pre-computed result to be mapped by the efficient channel-wise bias-add operator, thereby minimizing computational/storage costs.

The proposed negative padding makes the minimum quantization level of input activation zero. Thus, the proposed method can also be beneficial to zero skipping solutions like zero activation-skipping hardware accelerators [1,37] to improve the inference speed. Please note that the negative padding is applicable to any non-linear activation function, which has asymmetric distributions with a constant minimal value.

## 5    Experiments

We implemented the proposed methods in PyTorch 1.4 and demonstrated their effectiveness by measuring the accuracy of the quantized networks. We applied quantization to well-known optimized CNNs, MobileNet-v1 to v3 and MNasNet-A1. The networks were trained on 4-GPU with a 256 batch, SGD with momentum, and cosine learning rate decay with warmup [10,22]. In order to improve the accuracy, we adopted the progressive quantization method [42] that gradually decreases the bit-width to 8, 5, and 4 bits during fine-tuning, and use knowledge distillation [12] using the ResNet-101 as teacher. We used an exponential moving average of parameters with a momentum of 0.9997 [16], and all networks were trained using PROFIT and DuQ (with negative padding if applicable). We trained the model for 15 epochs at every progressive quantization and PROFIT fine-tuning step. The entire fine-tuning for the 4-bit network took 140 epochs for weight update. Please note that both weights and activations on all the layers of the networks were quantized, including the first and last layers. We did not apply quantization only for the input image of the first convolution layer and the activation of the squeeze-excitation module.

### 5.1    Accuracy on ImageNet Dataset

In Table 1, the accuracy of quantized networks under our proposed methods are shown. In the table, 'Full' represents our reproduction of the original training procedure. 'Full+' adopts teacher-student and weight averaging algorithms on top of 'Full'. Compared to the full precision accuracy ('Full+' in the table), our 4-bit models give comparable accuracy at a top-1 accuracy loss of 1.48%. To the best of the authors' knowledge, this is the SOTA result on the 4-bit quantization of MobileNet-v3 including the first and last layers. From the table, it is also evident that compared with full-precision ('Full+'), our method loses only less than 0.5% of top-1 accuracy on 4-bit MobileNet-v1 and v2.

**Table 1.** Top-1/Top-5 accuracy [%] of the quantized networks on ImageNet.

|          | MobileNet-v1   | MobileNet-v2   | MobileNet-v3   | MNasNet-A1    |
|----------|----------------|----------------|----------------|----------------|
| Full     | 68.848/88.740  | 71.328/90.016  | 74.728/92.136  | 73.130/91.276  |
| Full+    | 69.552/89.138  | 71.944/90.470  | 75.296/92.446  | 73.396/91.464  |
| 8-bit    | 70.164/89.370  | 72.352/90.636  | 75.166/92.498  | 73.742/91.756  |
| 5-bit    | 69.866/89.058  | 72.192/90.498  | 74.690/92.092  | 73.378/91.244  |
| 4-bit    | 69.056/88.412  | 71.564/90.398  | 73.812/91.588  | 72.244/90.584  |

## 5.2   Comparison with the Existing Works

We compare the accuracy of MobileNet-v1 and v2 with the existing works in Table 2 where (a, w) represent a-bit activation and w-bit weight quantization and c and l channel-wise and layer-wise quantization, respectively. * represents the post-training quantization. Compared to [18], our 4-bit layer-wise quantization gives comparable accuracy to the 8-bit models of previous work, and better accuracy than the channel-wise 8/4-bit models. Furthermore, our 4-bit MobileNet-v2 model outperforms the previous best 4-bit model [9] by 6.76%, and it outperforms even the 8-bit models of existing works [8,24].

## 5.3   Ablation Study

In the ablation study, we compared the existing methods and our proposed method on the 4-bit quantization of MobileNet-v3 on ImageNet. Moreover, to decompose the effect of each of our methods, we evaluated the effect on the existing method and our own method. Note that we use DuQ with negative padding by default except DuQ, Sym (zero-padding with symmetric quantization) and DuQ, Non (zero-padding with non-negative quantization). We used two existing methods, QIL [17] and PACT with SAWB [3]. When we applied the QIL algorithm to 4-bit MobileNet-v3, the fine-tuning failed to converge. It is because QIL has a critical limitation that its output range is bounded from 0 to 1, which is detrimental to the squeeze-excitation layer and h-swish activation function. As shown in Table 3, PACT gives 70.16% of top-1 accuracy with a 5.14% accuracy drop from full-precision accuracy ('Full+' in Table 1). Our proposed methods are beneficial to the existing method. By applying PROFIT to PACT, we can obtain 2.78% accuracy improvement, as shown in the table. DuQ outperforms PACT by 1.53% (= 69.504% − 67.978%). Under teacher-student and progressive quantization, our solution (DuQ + PROFIT) gives 3.65% (= 73.812% − 70.160%) accuracy gain over PACT.

In order to evaluate the effect of incremental weight freezing, we also applied only the last stage of PROFIT that stabilizes the normalization layers by fine-tuning after freezing all the convolution layers. This option ($\triangle$ in the table) gives approximately half the gain of PROFIT, which confirms that PROFIT is essential in minimizing the effect of AIWQ.

**Table 2.** Top-1 accuracy [%] comparison of existing works on MobileNet-v1 (MV1) and MobileNet-v2 (MV2).

|  | MV1 | MV2 |
|---|---|---|
| (8, 8), c [18] | 70.7 | 71.1 |
| (8, 8), l [18] | 70.0 | 70.9 |
| (8, 4), c [18] | 64.0 | 58.0 |
| (4, 8), c [18] | 65.0 | 62.0 |
| (4, 4), l [9] | – | 64.80 |
| (8, 8), l [8]* | 70.10 | 70.60 |
| (8, 8), l [24]* | 70.5 | 71.2 |
| (5, 5), l, ours | 69.866 | 72.192 |
| (4, 4), l, ours | 69.056 | 71.564 |

**Table 3.** Top-1/Top-5 accuracy [%] of 4-bit MobileNet-v3 on ImageNet. TS represents teacher-student, PG progressive quantization and PF PROFIT.

| Algorithm | TS | PG | PF | Accuracy |
|---|---|---|---|---|
| QIL |  |  |  | Fail |
| PACT |  |  |  | 67.978/88.204 |
| PACT | ✓ | ✓ |  | 70.160/89.576 |
| PACT | ✓ | ✓ | ✓ | 72.948/90.892 |
| DuQ |  |  |  | 69.504/88.946 |
| DuQ | ✓ |  |  | 71.006/90.018 |
| DuQ | ✓ | ✓ |  | 71.466/90.200 |
| DuQ | ✓ | ✓ | ✓ | 73.812/91.588 |
| DuQ |  |  | ✓ | 72.260/90.772 |
| DuQ | ✓ | ✓ | △ | 72.826/91.068 |
| DuQ, Sym |  |  |  | 68.480/88.496 |
| DuQ, Non |  |  |  | 68.724/88.566 |
| PACT3b | ✓ | ✓ |  | 57.086/80.898 |
| PACT3b | ✓ | ✓ | ✓ | 66.458/87.360 |
| DuQ3b | ✓ | ✓ |  | 65.674/86.480 |
| DuQ3b | ✓ | ✓ | ✓ | 69.942/89.340 |

The table also shows the effect of negative padding. Comparing DuQ (with negative padding) with DuQ, Sym and DuQ, Non, negative padding gives 1.02% and 0.78% of accuracy improvement, respectably. In addition, with negative padding, 27.5% of activations of h-swish output can be mapped to zero, thus the conventional zero-skipping accelerator can additionally improve performance and energy efficiency without the modification of the network. When we reduce the bit-width down to 3-bit (PACT3b and DuQ3b in Table 3), our proposed methods bring more accuracy improvement. Compared to the conventional PACT, our methods (DuQ+PROFIT) give 12.86% (= 69.942% − 57.086%) improvement.

The conventional models also suffer from the AIWQ problem in more aggressive quantization, and PROFIT is helpful to improve accuracy. With PROFIT, ResNet-18 can be quantized into 3-bit without accuracy loss and 2-bit with 2.31% accuracy loss compared to the baseline model accuracy, which is the state-of-the-art result as far as we know.

## 5.4   Computation Cost and Model Size Analysis

We compared the computation overhead and memory efficiency over the accuracy of the quantized network (Fig. 8). We used the bit-operations (BOPS) metric [2] that estimates the computation cost based on the required silicon area

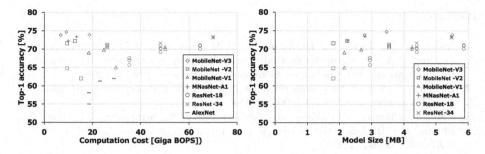

**Fig. 8.** Comparison of accuracy and estimated computation cost based on the HW accelerator model (the bit-operations (BOPS), [2]), and comparison of accuracy and model size of the quantized network. The tuple (a, w) represents the bit-width of activation and weight, respectively. The red markers represent our results, and the blue markers the results of state-of-the-art methods [3,7–9,13,17,18,24].

of the hardware accelerator for the quantized network. In terms of computation, our quantized model offers much higher efficiency with the same accuracy. For instance, at accuracy higher than 73%, our 4-bit MobileNet-v3 model takes 2.77× less computation cost than the previous best 8-bit MobileNet-v3 model [13]. Compared to 3-bit ResNet-34 [7], we reduce the cost by up to 10.3×. In terms of the model size, our model gives higher accuracy within the same memory constraint. For instance, the 4-bit MobileNet-v2 model shows 6.76% higher accuracy than the previous best model (4-bit MobileNet-v2 [9]) within the model size constraint of 2 MB, and the 4-bit MobileNet-v3 model gives 6.21% higher accuracy (versus 2-bit ResNet-18 [7]) at 3 MB. These benefits come from our proposed method and the efficiency of the advanced network structure.

## 6 Conclusion

We proposed a novel training method called PROFIT, a quantization method called DuQ, and negative padding. PROFIT aims at minimizing the effect of activation instability induced by weight quantization, and DuQ and negative padding enable the quantization of asymmetric distribution in optimized networks. Based on the proposed methods, we can quantize the optimized networks into 4 bits with less than 1.5% (MobileNet-v3) and 0.5% (MobileNet-v1/2) of top-1 accuracy loss. We anticipate that our proposed methods can contribute to advancing towards sub-4-bit precision computation on mobile and edge devices.

**Acknowledgement.** This work was supported by Samsung Electronics, the National Research Foundation of Korea grants, NRF-2016M3A7B4909604 and NRF-2016M3C4A7952587 funded by the Ministry of Science, ICT & Future Planning (PE Class Heterogeneous High Performance Computer Development). We appreciate valuable comments from Dr. Andrew G. Howard and Dr. Jaeyoun Kim at Google.

# References

1. Albericio, J., Judd, P., Hetherington, T.H., Aamodt, T.M., Jerger, N.D.E., Moshovos, A.: Cnvlutin: ineffectual-neuron-free deep neural network computing. In: International Symposium on Computer Architecture (ISCA) (2016)
2. Baskin, C., et al.: UNIQ: uniform noise injection for non-uniform quantization of neural networks. arXiv:1804.10969 (2018)
3. Choi, J., Chuang, P.I., Wang, Z., Venkataramani, S., Srinivasan, V., Gopalakrishnan, K.: Bridging the accuracy gap for 2-bit quantized neural networks. arXiv:1807.06964 (2018)
4. Choi, J., Wang, Z., Venkataramani, S., Chuang, P.I., Srinivasan, V., Gopalakrishnan, K.: PACT: parameterized clipping activation for quantized neural networks. arXiv:1805.06085 (2018)
5. Deng, J., Dong, W., Socher, R., Li, L., Li, K., Li, F.: ImageNet: a large-scale hierarchical image database. In: Computer Vision and Pattern Recognition (CVPR) (2009)
6. Devlin, J., Chang, M., Lee, K., Toutanova, K.: BERT: pre-training of deep bidirectional transformers for language understanding. In: Human Language Technologies (NAACL-HLT). North American Chapter of the Association for Computational Linguistics (2019)
7. Esser, S.K., McKinstry, J.L., Bablani, D., Appuswamy, R., Modha, D.S.: Learned step size quantization. arXiv:1902.08153) (2019)
8. Finkelstein, A., Almog, U., Grobman, M.: Fighting quantization bias with bias. arXiv:1906.03193 (2019)
9. Gong, R., et al.: Differentiable soft quantization: bridging full-precision and low-bit neural networks. arXiv:1908.05033 (2019)
10. Goyal, P., et al.: Accurate, large minibatch SGD: training imagenet in 1 hour. arXiv:1706.02677 (2017)
11. He, K., Zhang, X., Ren, S., Sun, J.: Deep residual learning for image recognition. In: Computer Vision and Pattern Recognition (CVPR) (2016)
12. Hinton, G.E., Vinyals, O., Dean, J.: Distilling the knowledge in a neural network. arXiv:1503.02531 (2015)
13. Howard, A., et al.: Searching for MobileNetV3. In: International Conference on Computer Vision (ICCV) (2019)
14. Howard, A.G., et al.: MobileNets: efficient convolutional neural networks for mobile vision applications. arXiv:1704.04861 (2017)
15. Hubara, I., Courbariaux, M., Soudry, D., El-Yaniv, R., Bengio, Y.: Quantized neural networks: training neural networks with low precision weights and activations. J. Mach. Learn. Res. (JMLR) 18(1), 6869–6898 (2017)
16. Izmailov, P., Podoprikhin, D., Garipov, T., Vetrov, D.P., Wilson, A.G.: Averaging weights leads to wider optima and better generalization. In: Uncertainty in Artificial Intelligence (UAI) (2018)
17. Jung, S., et al.: Learning to quantize deep networks by optimizing quantization intervals with task loss. In: Computer Vision and Pattern Recognition (CVPR) (2019)
18. Krishnamoorthi, R.: Quantizing deep convolutional networks for efficient inference: a whitepaper. arXiv:1806.08342 (2018)
19. Krizhevsky, A., Nair, V., Hinton, G.: The cifar-10 dataset (2014). https://www.cs.toronto.edu/~kriz/cifar.html. Accessed 03 Mar 2020

20. Krizhevsky, A., Sutskever, I., Hinton, G.E.: ImageNet classification with deep convolutional neural networks. In: Neural Information Processing Systems (NeurIPS) (2012)
21. Liu, Z., Wu, B., Luo, W., Yang, X., Liu, W., Cheng, K.-T.: Bi-Real Net: enhancing the performance of 1-bit CNNs with improved representational capability and advanced training algorithm. In: Ferrari, V., Hebert, M., Sminchisescu, C., Weiss, Y. (eds.) ECCV 2018. LNCS, vol. 11219, pp. 747–763. Springer, Cham (2018). https://doi.org/10.1007/978-3-030-01267-0_44
22. Loshchilov, I., Hutter, F.: SGDR: stochastic gradient descent with warm restarts. In: International Conference on Learning Representations (ICLR) (2017)
23. Mishra, A.K., Nurvitadhi, E., Cook, J.J., Marr, D.: WRPN: wide reduced-precision networks. In: International Conference on Learning Representations (ICLR) (2018)
24. Nagel, M., van Baalen, M., Blankevoort, T., Welling, M.: Data-free quantization through weight equalization and bias correction. arXiv:1906.04721 (2019)
25. INT4 precision for AI inference (2019). https://devblogs.nvidia.com/int4-for-ai-inference/. Accessed 03 Mar 2020
26. Park, E., Kim, D., Yoo, S.: Energy-efficient neural network accelerator based on outlier-aware low-precision computation. In: International Symposium on Computer Architecture (ISCA) (2018)
27. Rastegari, M., Ordonez, V., Redmon, J., Farhadi, A.: XNOR-Net: ImageNet classification using binary convolutional neural networks. In: Leibe, B., Matas, J., Sebe, N., Welling, M. (eds.) ECCV 2016. LNCS, vol. 9908, pp. 525–542. Springer, Cham (2016). https://doi.org/10.1007/978-3-319-46493-0_32
28. Samsung low-power NPU solution for AI deep learning (2019). https://news.samsung.com/global/samsung-electronics-introduces-a-high-speed-low-power-npu-solution-for-ai-deep-learning. Accessed 03 Mar 2020
29. Sandler, M., Howard, A.G., Zhu, M., Zhmoginov, A., Chen, L.: MobileNetV2: inverted residuals and linear bottlenecks. In: Computer Vision and Pattern Recognition (CVPR) (2018)
30. Sharma, H., et al.: Bit fusion: bit-level dynamically composable architecture for accelerating deep neural networks. In: International Symposium on Computer Architecture (ISCA) (2018)
31. Simonyan, K., Zisserman, A.: Very deep convolutional networks for large-scale image recognition. In: International Conference on Learning Representations (ICLR) (2015)
32. Snapdragon neural processing engine SDK (2017). https://developer.qualcomm.com/docs/snpe/index.html. Accessed 03 Mar 2020
33. Song, J., et al.: 7.1 an 11.5 TOPS/W 1024-MAC butterfly structure dual-core sparsity-aware neural processing unit in 8nm flagship mobile SoS. In: International Solid-State Circuits Conference (ISSCC) (2019)
34. Tan, M., et al.: MnasNet: platform-aware neural architecture search for mobile. In: Computer Vision and Pattern Recognition (CVPR) (2019)
35. Tulloch, A., Jia, Y.: High performance ultra-low-precision convolutions on mobile devices. arXiv:1712.02427 (2017)
36. Tulloch, A., Jia, Y.: Quantization and training of neural networks for efficient integer-arithmetic-only inference. In: Conference on Computer Vision and Pattern Recognition (CVPR) (2018)
37. Wang, T., Xiong, J., Xu, X., Shi, Y.: SCNN: a general distribution based statistical convolutional neural network with application to video object detection. In: Association for the Advancement of Artificial Intelligence (AAAI) (2019)

38. Wu, H.: NVIDIA low precision inference on GPU. In: GPU Technology Conference (2019)
39. Zhou, S., Ni, Z., Zhou, X., Wen, H., Wu, Y., Zou, Y.: DoReFa-Net: Training low bitwidth convolutional neural networks with low bitwidth gradients. arXiv:1606.06160 (2016)
40. Zhou, S., Wang, Y., Wen, H., He, Q., Zou, Y.: Balanced quantization: an effective and efficient approach to quantized neural networks. J. Comput. Sci. Technol. **32**, 667–682 (2017). https://doi.org/10.1007/s11390-017-1750-y
41. Zhu, C., Han, S., Mao, H., Dally, W.J.: Trained ternary quantization. In: International Conference on Learning Representations (ICLR) (2017)
42. Zhuang, B., Shen, C., Tan, M., Liu, L., Reid, I.D.: Towards effective low-bitwidth convolutional neural networks. In: Computer Vision and Pattern Recognition (CVPR) (2018)

# Visual Relation Grounding in Videos

Junbin Xiao[1], Xindi Shang[1], Xun Yang[1], Sheng Tang[2], and Tat-Seng Chua[1(✉)]

[1] Department of Computer Science, National University of Singapore,
Singapore, Singapore
{junbin,shangxin,chuats}@comp.nus.edu.sg, xunyang@nus.edu.sg
[2] Institute of Computing Technology, Chinese Academy of Sciences, Beijing, China
ts@ict.ac.cn

**Abstract.** In this paper, we explore a novel task named visual Relation Grounding in Videos (vRGV). The task aims at spatio-temporally localizing the given relations in the form of *subject-predicate-object* in the videos, so as to provide supportive visual facts for other high-level video-language tasks (*e.g.*, video-language grounding and video question answering). The challenges in this task include but not limited to: (1) both the subject and object are required to be spatio-temporally localized to ground a query relation; (2) the temporal dynamic nature of visual relations in videos is difficult to capture; and (3) the grounding should be achieved without any direct supervision in space and time. To ground the relations, we tackle the challenges by collaboratively optimizing two sequences of regions over a constructed hierarchical spatio-temporal region graph through relation attending and reconstruction, in which we further propose a message passing mechanism by spatial attention shifting between visual entities. Experimental results demonstrate that our model can not only outperform baseline approaches significantly, but also produces visually meaningful facts to support visual grounding. (Code is available at https://github.com/doc-doc/vRGV).

## 1 Introduction

Visual grounding aims to establish precise correspondence between textual query and visual contents by localizing in the images or videos the relevant visual facts depicted by the given language. It was originally tackled in language-based visual fragment-retrieval [9,12,13], and has recently attracted widespread attention as a task onto itself. While lots of the existing efforts are made on referring expression grounding in static images [8,19,22,23,28,41,42,44], recent research attempts to study visual grounding in videos by finding the objects either in individual frames [10,32,47] or in video clips spatio-temporally [1,3,46]. Nonetheless, all these works focus on grounding in videos the objects depicted by natural language sentences. Although the models have shown success on the corresponding

**Electronic supplementary material** The online version of this chapter (https://doi.org/10.1007/978-3-030-58539-6_27) contains supplementary material, which is available to authorized users.

© Springer Nature Switzerland AG 2020
A. Vedaldi et al. (Eds.): ECCV 2020, LNCS 12351, pp. 447–464, 2020.
https://doi.org/10.1007/978-3-030-58539-6_27

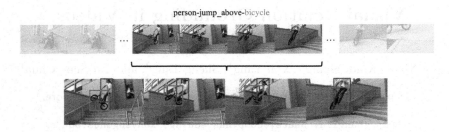

**Fig. 1.** Illustration of the vRGV task. For the query relation *person-jump_above-bicycle* and an untrimmed video containing the relation, the objective is to find a video segment along with two trajectories corresponding to the subject (red box) and object (green box) that match the query relation. (Color figure online)

datasets, they lack transparency to tell which parts of the sentence help to disambiguate the object from the others, and thus hard to explain whether they truly understand the contents or just vaguely learn from data statistics. Furthermore, the models fail to effectively reason about the visual details (*e.g.*, relational semantics), and thus would generalize poorly on unseen scenarios.

To achieve understandable visual analytics, many works have showed the importance of comprehending the interactions and relationships between objects [8,16,31]. To this end, we explore explicit relations in videos by proposing a novel task of visual Relation Grounding in Videos (vRGV). The task takes a relation in the form of *subject-predicate-object* as query, and requires the models to localize the related visual subject and object in a video by returning their trajectories. As shown in Fig. 1, given a query relation *person-jump_above-bicycle* and an untrimmed video containing that relation, the task is to find in the video the subject (person in white) and object (bicycle) trajectory pairs that hold the query relationship *jump_above*.[1] Considering that annotating fine-grained region-relation pairs in videos is complicated and labor-intensive [30], we define the task as weakly-supervised grounding where only video-relation correspondences are available. That is, the models only know that a relation exists but do not know where and when it is present in the video during training.

vRGV retains and invokes several challenges associated with video visual relation and visual grounding. First, unlike existing video grounding [1,3] which is to localize a specific object according to its natural language description, in visual relation grounding, the models are required to jointly localize a pair of visual entities (subject and object) conditioned on their local relationships. Second, unlike a coarsely global description, relations are more fine-grained and change over time, *i.e.*, even a same object would have different relationships with different objects at different time. For example, the enduring relations (*e.g.*, *person-drive-car*) may exist for a long time but the transient ones (*e.g.*, *person-get_off-car*) may disappear quickly. Besides, static relationships like spatial locations and

---

[1] The word 'untrimmed' is regarding to relation. We refer to relation as the complete triplet *subject-predicate-object*, and relationship as the *predicate* only.

states (*e.g.*, *hold* and *hug*) can be grounded at frame level, whereas the dynamic ones such as *lift_up* and *put_down* can only be grounded based on a short video clip. Such dynamic nature of relations in videos will cause great challenge for spatio-temporal modeling. Third, the requirement for weakly-supervision also challenges the models to learn to ground the relation without reliance on any spatial (bounding boxes) and temporal (time spans) supervisions.

To address the above challenges, we devise a model of video relation grounding by reconstruction. Concretely, we incorporate a query relation into a given video which is modeled as a hierarchical spatio-temporal region graph, for the purpose of identifying the related subject and object from region proposals in multi-temporal granularity. For weakly-supervised video relation grounding during training, we optimize the localization by reconstructing the query relation with the subject and object identified by textual clues and attention shift. During inference, we dynamically link the subject and object which contribute most to the re-generated relations into trajectories as the grounding result. Our insight is that visual relations are data representations of clear structural information, and there is a strong cross-modal correspondence between the textual subject-object and the visual entities in the videos. Thus, it is reasonable to ground the relevant subject and object by re-generating the relation.

Our main contributions are: (1) we define a novel task, visual Relation Grounding in Videos (vRGV), to provide a new benchmark for the research on video visual relation and underpin high-level video-language tasks; (2) we propose an approach for weakly-supervised video relation grounding, by collaboratively optimizing two sequences of regions over a hierarchical spatio-temporal region graph through relation attending and reconstruction; and (3) we propose a novel message passing mechanism based on spatial attention shifting between visual entities, to spatially pinpoint the related subject and object.

## 2    Related Work

In this section, we briefly recap the history in visual relation, visual grounding and video modeling, which are either similar in spirit to the task definition or technically relevant to our approach.

**Visual Relation.** Early attempts on visual relation either leveraged object co-occurrence and spatial relationships for object segmentation [4], or focused on human-centric relationships for understanding human-object interactions [40]. Recently, many works started to study visual relations as a task onto itself to facilitate cognitive visual reasoning. Lu *et al.* [20] firstly formulated visual relations as three separated parts of *object_1-predicate-object_2*, and classified visual relationships as spatial, comparative, preposition and verb predicates. Krishna *et al.* [16] formalized visual relations as a scene graph for image structural representation, in which visual entities are corresponding to nodes and connected by edges depicted by object relationships. Shang *et al.* [31] introduced visual relations from images to videos (video scene graph). Apart from the relations in static images, they added relationships that are featured with dynamic information (*e.g.*, *chase* and *wave*), so as to emphasize spatio-temporal reasoning of fine-grained video contents. According to their definition, a valid relation in videos requires both the subject and object to appear together in each frame of a certain video clip.

While a handful of works have successfully exploited relations to improve visual grounding [8] and visual question answering [21], relation as an independent problem is mostly tackled in the form of detection task and the advancements are mostly made in the image domain [17,20,45]. In contrast, relation as a detection task in video domain has earned little attention, partly due to the great challenges in joint video object detection and relation prediction with insufficient video data [26,35]. In this paper, instead of blindly detecting all visual objects and relations in videos, we focuses on the inverse side of the problem by spatio-temporally grounding a given relation in a video.

**Visual Grounding.** Visual grounding has emerged as a subject under intense study in referring expression comprehension [8,15,22,23,28,41,42,44]. Mao *et al.* [22] first explored referring expression grounding by using the framework of Convolutional Neural Network (CNN) and Long-Short Term Memory (LSTM) network [7] for image and sentence modeling. They achieved grounding by extracting region proposals and then finding the region that can generate the sentence with maximum posterior probability. Similarly, Rohrbach *et al.* [28] explored image grounding by reconstruction to enable grounding in a weakly-supervised scenario. Krishna *et al.* [15] explored referring relationships in images by iterative message passing between subjects and objects. While these works focus on image grounding, more recent efforts [1,3,10,32,39,46,47] also attempted to ground objects in videos. Zhou *et al.* [47] explored weakly-supervised grounding of descriptive nouns in separate frames in a frame-weighted retrieval fashion. Huang *et al.* [10] proposed to grounding referring expression in temporally aligned instructional videos. Chen *et al.* [3] proposed to perform spatio-temporal object grounding with video-level supervision, which aims to localize an object tube described by a natural language sentence. They pre-extracted the action tubes, and then rank and return the tube of maximal similarity with the query sentence. Instead of grounding a certain object in trimmed videos by a global object description [3], we are interested in localizing a couple of objects conditioned upon their relationships in untrimmed videos, which is more challenging and meaningful in reasoning real-world visual contents.

**Video Modeling.** Over the decades, modeling the spatio-temporal nature of video has been the core of research in video understanding. Established hand-crafted feature like iDT [37] and deep CNN based features like C3D [34], two-Stream [33] and I3D [2], have shown their respective strengths in different models. However, all these features mainly capture motion information in a short time interval (*e.g.*, 16 frames as the popular setting in C3D). To enable both long and short-term dependency capturing, researchers [36,43] also attempted to model the video as an ordered frame sequence using Recurrent Neural Networks (RNNs). While RNN can deal with dynamic video length in principle, it was reported that the preferable number of frames with regard to a video should be ranged from 30 to 80 [24,36]. As a result, Pan *et al.* [24] further proposed a hierarchical recurrent neural encoder to achieve temporal modeling in multiple granularity. Yet, they focused on generating a global description of the video by extracting frame-level CNN feature, which can hardly be applied to relation understanding where fine-grained regional information is indispensable. Recently, there is a tendency of modeling videos as spatio-temporal graphs [11,26,35,38], where the nodes correspond to regions and edges to spatial-temporal relationships. Nonetheless, all of them model the video as a flat and densely connected graph. Instead, we retain the temporal structure (ordered frames and clips) of videos by modeling it as a hierarchical spatio-temporal region graph with sparse directed connections.

## 3  Method

Recall that our goal is to ground relations in the given videos, which is formulated by giving a relation coupled with videos containing that relation, and returning two trajectories for each video, corresponding to the subject and object participating in the query relation[2]. We formally define the task as follows.

**Task Definition:** Given a set of query relations in form of $\mathcal{R} = \{<S-P-O>\}$ and a set of untrimmed videos $\mathcal{V}$ (where $S$, $P$, $O$ denote the *subject*, *predicate* and *object* respectively), and each specific query relation $\mathcal{R}_i$ is coupled with several videos from $\mathcal{V}$ which contain that relation, the task is to spatio-temporally localize in the videos the respective subjects and objects by returning their trajectories $T_s, T_o$. The trajectory $T$ is given by a sequence of bounding boxes tied to a certain visual entity across a video segment. For weakly-supervised grounding, there is no spatial (bounding box) and temporal supervisions (time spans) from the dataset during training.

### 3.1  Solution Overview

Given a video of $N$ frames, we first extract $M$ region proposals for each frame. Thus, a video can be represented by a set of regions $V = \{B_{i,j} \mid i \in [1, N], j \in [1, M]\}$, and a trajectory $T = \{B_i \mid i \in [k, l], k \in [1, N], l \in [k, N]\}$ can be a sequence of bounding boxes in the video. Our approach will learn to ground a given relation $R$ by finding two trajectories $T_s, T_o$ that indicate the subject and object of the relation. According to the task definition, we resolve the problem by maximizing the following posterior probability:

$$T_s^*, T_o^* = \arg\max_{T_s, T_o} P(R \mid T_s, T_o) * P(T_s, T_o \mid V, R), \tag{1}$$

where $P(T_s, T_o \mid V, R)$ aims to attend to the most relevant trajectories in $V$ given the relation $R$, and $P(R \mid T_s, T_o)$ attempts to reconstruct the same

---

[2] If there are more than one instances that match the query relation in a video, it is a correct grounding by returning any one of them.

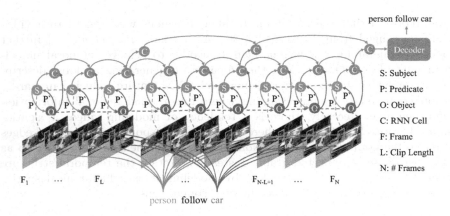

**Fig. 2.** Schematic diagram of video relation grounding by reconstruction. The model takes the query relation as guidance to pinpoint regions of subjects and objects over the hierarchical spatio-temporal region graph, where the regions correspond to nodes which are spatially connected by visual relationships and are temporally connected by hierarchical RNN over different frames and clips.

relation $R$ based on the relevant trajectories it attended to. During inference, our approach will output the trajectories ($T_s^*$ and $T_o^*$) that contribute mostly to the re-generated relation to accomplish grounding.

The key idea of our approach is to ground the relation through reconstruction by capturing the intuition that there is a clear correspondence between subject-object in textual relation and visual instances. However, unlike image grounding [28] which can directly model and return the region proposals, effective trajectory proposals are unavailable in this task due to the complicated dynamics of the relations in videos. To achieve the optimization in Eq. (1), we model the trajectory proposals implicitly over a hierarchical spatio-temporal region graph and online-optimize them through relation attending and reconstruction. As shown in Fig. 2, two sequences of regions corresponding to the query subject and object will be identified from the video (region graph) and jointly embedded into the final graph representation which will be fed to the decoder to reconstruct the relation. The reconstruction loss from the decoder will be back-propagated to the graph encoder, to penalize the incorrect object pairs with respect to the relation. During inference, we dynamically link the regions which response significantly to the reconstructed relations into explicit trajectories to accomplish the grounding, where the importance of the regions are determined by spatial and temporal attention over the hierarchical space-time region graph. In this way, our model can in principle ground visual relations in multi-temporal granularity without the bottleneck of off-line trajectory proposal extraction [3].

We next elaborate how to learn to spatio-temporally attend to the correct sequences of regions for a given relation, and then how to obtain the final trajectories based on the attention values, to accomplish the grounding.

## 3.2  Message Passing by Attention Shifting

**Spatial Attention.** This unit takes as input all the region proposals $B = \{B_j \mid j \in [1, M]\}$ in a frame and the query relation $R = <S - P - O>$. It learns two spatial attentions $(\alpha_s^{M \times 1}, \alpha_o^{M \times 1})$ corresponding to the subject and object. Concretely, the spatial attention unit (SAU) is formulated as:

$$\alpha_s = SAU(f(B), g(S)), \quad \alpha_o = SAU(f(B), g(O)), \tag{2}$$

in which $g(\cdot)$ returns the textual word feature for subject (S) or object (O), and is achieved by embedding the respective GloVe [25] vector: $g(S) = Emb(GloVe(S))$. Besides, $f(\cdot)$ means feature extraction for the region proposals. In our implementation, we utilize several kinds of feature related to the object appearances, relative locations and sizes, which are not only important in visual relation understanding, but also crucial in identifying the same object in different frames.

The object appearance is captured by the ROI-aligned feature from object detection models, *i.e.*, $f_{app} = CNN(B_j)$. The object relative location and size are useful to identify the spatial and comparative relationships, and are given by $f_B = [\frac{x_{min}}{W}, \frac{y_{min}}{H}, \frac{x_{max}}{W}, \frac{y_{max}}{H}, \frac{area}{W*H}]$, in which $W, H$ are respectively the width, height of the frame and $area$ is the area of the bounding box represented by the top-left $(x_{min}, y_{min})$ and bottom-right $(x_{max}, y_{max})$ coordinates. The final feature of a region proposal $f(B_j)$ is thus obtained by element-wise addition of the transformed visual appearance feature $f_{app}$ and bounding box feature $f_B$. The transform operation is achieved by linear mapping with ReLU activation.

We take the subject $S$ as an example to introduce how to obtain the representation $f_s$ and attention distribution $\alpha_s$ for it (similar way to obtain $\alpha_o$ and $f_o$ for object $O$). Given the textual subject representation $g(S)$ and each region proposal $f(B_j)$, the attention score $s_j$ is obtained by

$$s_j = W_2 tanh(W_1[f(B_j), \ g(S)] + b_1), \tag{3}$$

in which $W_1, b_1, W_2$ are model parameters. Then, the attention distribution over different region $B_j$, and the final representation for subject $S$ are give by

$$\alpha_{s_j} = softmax(s_j) = \frac{exp(s_j)}{\sum_{z=1}^{M} exp(s_z)}, \quad f_s = \sum_{j=0}^{M} \alpha_{s_j} f(B_j). \tag{4}$$

**Attention Shifting.** Although the aforementioned attention unit is capable of identifying the subjects and objects semantically related to the query relations, they are not necessarily the exact visual entities that hold the relationships. Take the instance in Fig. 2 as an example, there is one *person* but several *cars* on the street, and only one *car* match the relationship *follow* with the *person*. It is the relationship *follow* that helps to disambiguate the *car* of interest from the other *cars*. Another intuition is that, given the subject *person* and relationship *follow*, the searching space of the object *car* can be narrowed to the areas in front of the *person*, and vice versa.

As shown in Fig. 2, we capture these insights by modeling the relationships as attention shifting (message passing) between the visual entities, so as to accurately pinpoint the subject and object participating in the query relation. Specifically, we learn two independent transfer matrices $W_{so}$ and $W_{os}$ tied to the forward relationship ($P$, message from subject to object) and backward relationship ($P'$, message from object to subject) respectively.

$$f_{so} = ReLU(W_{so}\alpha_s), \quad f_{os} = ReLU(W_{os}\alpha_o). \tag{5}$$

The transferred location feature from subject (object) to object (subject) will be added to the attention based object (subject) feature:

$$f_s = f_s + f_{os}, \quad f_o = f_o + f_{so}. \tag{6}$$

Finally, the subject and object representations will be concatenated and transformed to obtain the node input at time step i, *i.e.*, $f_i = W_3([f_s, f_o]) + b_3$, where $W_3$, $b_3$ are learnable parameters.

### 3.3    Hierarchical Temporal Attention

To cope with the temporal dynamics of video relations, we devise two relation-aware hierarchical temporal attention units $TAU_1$ and $TAU_2$ (which work in a way similar to $SAU$) over the frames and clips respectively. As shown in Fig. 2, a video is firstly divided into $H = \frac{N}{L}$ short clips of length $L$. The frame-wise temporal attention $\beta^{l1}$ (of dimension $N$) is obtained by

$$\beta^{l1} = TAU_1(f^{l1}, \; f_H^{l2}), \tag{7}$$

in which $f^{l1}$ denotes the sequence of frame-wise feature, and is achieved by sequence modeling the subject and object concatenated feature $f$

$$f_i^{l1} = LSTM_{l1}(f_{1,\cdots,i}), \; i \in [1, N]. \tag{8}$$

Besides, $f_H^{l2}$ denotes the output at the last time step of the clip-level neural encoder, which is obtained by

$$f_H^{l2} = LSTM_{l2}((\beta_i^{l2} f_i^c)_{i=1,\cdots,H}), \tag{9}$$

where $f^c$ denotes the sequence of clip-level inputs which are obtained by selecting the output of the first layer of LSTM at every L steps, *i.e.*, $f^c = \{f_i^{l1} \mid i \in \{1, L, \cdots, N\}\}$. $\beta^{l2}$ (of dimension $H$) is the clip-level temporal attention distribution, and is obtained by

$$\beta^{l2} = TAU_2(f^c, \; f_R), \tag{10}$$

where $f_R$ denotes the query relation which is obtained by concatenating the GloVe feature of each part in the relation (average for phrase) and further transformed to the same dimension space as feature vectors in $f^c$.

### 3.4   Train and Inference

During training, we drive the final graph embedding by an attention-guided pooling of the node representations across the video, $i.e.$, $feat_v = \sum \beta^{l1} f^{l1}$. The graph embedding will be fed to the decoder to re-generate the query relation. The decoder part of our model is similar to [28] by treating the relation as a textual phrase and reconstruct it by a single LSTM layer. The model was trained with the cross-entropy loss

$$L_{rec} = -\frac{1}{n_{vr}} \sum_{n=1}^{n_{vr}} \sum_{t=1}^{n_w} logP(R_t|R_{0:t-1}, \ feat_v), \qquad (11)$$

where $R_t$ denotes the $t^{th}$ word in the relation. $n_{vr}$ and $n_w$ denote the number of video-relation samples and number of words in the relation respectively.

During inference, we base on the learned spatio-temporal attention values to achieve the relation-aware trajectories. First, we temporally threshold to obtain a set of candidate sub-segments for each relation-video instance in the test set. The segments are obtained by grouping the successive frames in the remaining frame set after thresholding with value $\sigma$, $i.e.$, $B = \{B_{i,1:M}|\beta_i >= \sigma\}$, in which $B_i$ denotes regions in frame $i$. $\beta$ is temporal attention value obtained by $\beta = \beta^{l1} + \beta^{l2}$. Note that the clip-level attention value will be propagated to all frames belonging to that clip. (Refer to appendix for more details.)

Then, for each sub-segment, we define a linking score $s(B_{i,p}, B_{i+1,q})$ between regions of successive frames (after sampling)

$$s(B_{i,p}, B_{i+1,q}) = \alpha_{i,p} + \alpha_{i+1,q} + \lambda \cdot IoU(B_{i,p}, B_{i+1,q}), \qquad (12)$$

where $\alpha$ is the spatial attention value, it can be $\alpha_s$ (subject) or $\alpha_o$ (object) depending on the linking visual instances. $IoU$ denotes the overlap between two bounding boxes, and $\lambda = \frac{1}{D}$ is a balancing term related to the distance ($D \in [1, 10]$) of the two successive frames. By defining $\lambda$, we trust more on the attention score when the distance between the two frames are larger. Our idea is to link the regions which response strongly to the subject or object, and their spatial extent overlaps significantly. The final trajectory can thus be achieved by finding the optimal path over the segment

$$T^* = \arg\max_{T} \frac{1}{K-1} \sum_{i=1}^{K-1} s(B_{i,p}, B_{i+1,q}), \qquad (13)$$

where $T$ is a certain linked region sequence of length $K$ for the subject or object. Similar to [5], we solve the optimization problem using Viterbi algorithm. Finally, the linking scores associated with the subject and object are averaged to obtain the score for the corresponding sub-segment. The grounding is achieved by returning the segment (subject-object trajectory pair) of maximal score.

# 4    Experiments

## 4.1    Dataset and Evaluation

We conduct experiments on the challenging video relation dataset ImageNet-VidVRD [31]. It contains 1000 videos selected from ILSVRC-VID [29], and is annotated with over 30,000 relation instances covering 35 object classes and 132 predefined predicates. Our preliminary investigation shows that over 99% of relations do not appear throughout the video, with 92% (67%) appearing in less than 1/2 (1/5) length of the video, and the shortest relation only exists in 1 s, while the longest relation lasts for 40 s. Besides, each video contains 2 to 22 objects (3 on average), excluding those un-related objects which also matter due to the weakly-supervised setting. The dataset statistics are listed in Table 1, others details are given in the appendix. Note that the object trajectories are provided but are not used during training.

**Table 1.** Statistics of ImageNet-VidVRD.

| Dataset | | #Videos | #Objects | #Predicates | #Relations | #Instances |
|---|---|---|---|---|---|---|
| ImageNet-VidVRD [31] | Train | 800 | 35 | 132 | 2961 | 25,917 |
| | Val | 200 | 35 | 132 | 1011 | 4,835 |

We report accuracy (in percentage) as the grounding performance. Specifically, for each query relation, there might be one or more videos, with each having one or more visual instances corresponding to that relation. For a video-relation pair, a true-positive grounding is confirmed if the returned subject-object trajectory has an overlap ratio of larger than 0.5 with one of the ground-truth visual relation instances. The overlap is measured by the temporal Intersection over Union (tIoU), which is based on the average number of three different spatial IoU thresholds (*i.e.*, sIoU = 0.3, 0.5 and 0.7). Aside from the joint accuracy for the whole relation ($Acc_R$), we also separately report the accuracy for the subject ($Acc_S$) and object ($Acc_O$) for better analysis of algorithms.

## 4.2    Implementation Details

For each video-relation instance, we uniformly sample N = 120 frames from the video and further divide them into H = 10 clips of length L = 12 frames, and extract M = 40 region proposals for each frame. We apply Faster R-CNN [27] with ResNet-101 [6] as backbone (pretrained on MS-COCO [18]) to extract the region proposals, along with the 2048-D regional appearance feature. The final dimension of each region representation is transformed to 256. For each word in the textual relation, we obtain the 300-D GloVe feature and then embed it

**Table 2.** Results of visual relation grounding in videos. We add bold and underline to highlight the best and second-best results under each metric respectively.

| Methods | sIoU = 0.3 | | | sIoU = 0.5 | | | sIoU = 0.7 | | | Average | | |
|---------|------------|--|--|------------|--|--|------------|--|--|---------|--|--|
| | $Acc_S$ | $Acc_O$ | $Acc_R$ | $Acc_S$ | $Acc_O$ | $Acc_R$ | $Acc_S$ | $Acc_O$ | $Acc_R$ | $Acc_S$ | $Acc_O$ | $Acc_R$ |
| T-Rank $V_1$ [3] | 33.55 | 27.52 | 17.25 | 22.61 | 12.79 | 4.49 | 6.31 | 3.30 | 0.76 | 20.27 | 10.68 | 3.99 |
| T-Rank $V_2$ [3] | 34.35 | 21.71 | 15.06 | 23.00 | 9.18 | 3.82 | 7.06 | 2.09 | 0.50 | 20.83 | 7.35 | 3.16 |
| Co-occur* [15] | 27.84 | 25.62 | 18.44 | 23.50 | 20.40 | 13.81 | 17.02 | 14.93 | 7.29 | 22.99 | 19.33 | 12.80 |
| Co-occur [15] | 31.31 | 30.65 | 21.79 | 28.02 | 27.69 | 18.86 | <u>21.99</u> | <u>21.64</u> | <u>13.16</u> | 25.90 | 25.23 | 16.48 |
| vRGV* (ours) | <u>37.61</u> | <u>37.75</u> | <u>27.54</u> | <u>32.17</u> | <u>32.32</u> | <u>21.43</u> | 21.34 | 21.02 | 10.62 | <u>31.64</u> | <u>30.92</u> | <u>20.54</u> |
| vRGV (ours) | **42.31** | **41.31** | **29.95** | **37.11** | **37.52** | **24.77** | **29.71** | **29.72** | **17.09** | **36.77** | **36.30** | **24.58** |

to 256 dimension space. The hidden size for the encoder and decoder LSTM is 512. Besides, the models are trained using Adam [14] optimization algorithm based on an initial learning rate of 1e−4 and batch size of 32. We train the model with maximal 20 epochs, and use dropout rate 0.2 and early stopping to alleviate over-fitting. During inference, we first obtain the spatial and temporal grounding results on the basis of all the sampled frames, and then propagate the adjacent bounding boxes to the missing frames based on linear interpolation (see appendix for details). The temporal attention threshold is set to 0.04, and is greedily searched on a validation split of the training data.

### 4.3    Compared Baselines

As there is no existing method for the vRGV task, we adapt several related works as our baselines. (1) **Object Co-occurrence**, it was applied in [15] for referring relationship in images. We can equivalently achieve it in the video scenario by removing all the predicates in our model and only grounding the two categories. This baseline is to study how much the object co-occurrence will contribute to the relation grounding performance. (2) **Trajectory Ranking**. We adapt the method proposed in video language grounding (namely WSSTG [3]) to the relation scenario. This can be achieved by regarding the relation as a natural language sentence and transforming grounding to sentence matching with the pre-extracted object tubes. Specifically, we consider two implementation variants: (a) $V_1$, which optimizes the similarity between each trajectory proposal and the query relation during training, and outputs the top-2 ranked trajectories as the grounded subject and object during inference; and (b) $V_2$, which concatenates the trajectories pair-wisely to compare their similarity with the query sentence during training, and returns the top-1 trajectory-pair as grounded results during inference. (More details can be found in the appendix.)

### 4.4    Result Analysis

Table 2 shows the performance comparisons between our approach and the baselines, where vRGV* (similar for Co-occur*) denotes our model variant that

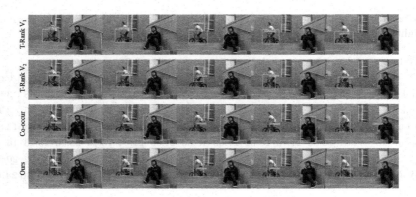

**Fig. 3.** Qualitative results on the query relation *bicycle-move_beneath-person*.

**Table 3.** Model ablation results on ImageNet-VidVRD.

| Models | sIoU = 0.3 | | | sIoU = 0.5 | | | sIoU = 0.7 | | | Average | | |
|---|---|---|---|---|---|---|---|---|---|---|---|---|
| | $Acc_S$ | $Acc_O$ | $Acc_R$ | $Acc_S$ | $Acc_O$ | $Acc_R$ | $Acc_S$ | $Acc_O$ | $Acc_R$ | $Acc_S$ | $Acc_O$ | $Acc_R$ |
| vRGV | **42.31** | **41.31** | **29.95** | **37.11** | **37.52** | **24.77** | **29.71** | **29.72** | **17.09** | **36.77** | **36.30** | **24.58** |
| W/o Msg | 34.72 | 33.23 | 23.96 | 31.60 | 29.15 | 19.43 | 22.56 | 21.36 | 11.78 | 29.41 | 27.46 | 17.63 |
| W/o Clip | 41.08 | 39.64 | 27.15 | 36.31 | 35.05 | 21.77 | 28.19 | 27.11 | 13.72 | 35.05 | 34.03 | 20.58 |
| W/o TAU | 32.99 | 32.76 | 20.34 | 22.36 | 19.99 | 7.61 | 15.29 | 13.27 | 4.83 | 21.75 | 19.26 | 7.06 |

greedily links the regions of maximal attention score in each frame by setting $\lambda$ in Eq. (12) to 0. We conduct this experiment to validate that our model is capable of learning the object identity across different frames, because we implicitly model and optimize the trajectories on the spatio-temporal graph. When the model is complemented with explicit object locations during post-linking, it can achieve better performances as shown in the bottom row.

From the results, we can see that our methods significantly outperform the baselines, and both methods adapted from WSSTG [3] (*i.e.*, T-Rank $V_1$ and T-Rank $V_2$) perform poorly on this task. We speculate the reasons are two folds: (1) the method in WSSTG is designed for single object grounding, they fail to jointly ground two visual entities and further to disambiguate between subject and object (see Fig. 3). In our approach, we collaboratively optimize two sequences of objects on the spatio-temporal graph with relation attending and message passing mechanisms, and thus cope well with the joint grounding problem. This is supported by the observation that the two baselines [3] obtain relatively closer results to ours on separate grounding accuracy ($Acc_S$), but much lower results than ours regarding the joint accuracy $Acc_R$; (2) The method in WSSTG aims for object grounding in trimmed video clips, and it pre-extracts relation agnostic object tube proposals and keeps them unchanged during training. In contrast, our approach enables online optimization of object trajectories regarding relation and post-generates relation-aware trajectory pairs. Thus, we can generate better

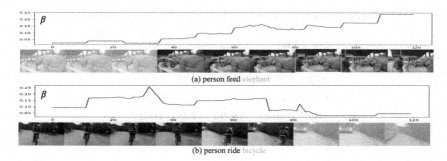

Fig. 4. Qualitative results based on temporal threshold 0.04.

trajectories tailored for relations. This is supported by the observation that the two baselines can get closer results to ours at a relatively lower overlap threshold, but their results degenerate significantly at higher thresholds. (Please also refer to our results on different temporal overlap thresholds shown in the appendix.)

Another observation is that T-Rank $V_2$ performs better than T-Rank $V_1$ in grounding the subject ($Acc_S$), but gets much worse results in terms of object ($Acc_O$) and hence acts poorly on the joint grounding results for relations ($Acc_R$). This indicates that the two objects in the top-ranked trajectory pair usually do not correspond to the subject and object mentioned in the sentence, and they are more likely the redundant proposals of the main objects. As shown in Fig. 3, the model T-Rank $V_2$ can successfully find the subject *bicycle*, but fails to localize the object *person*. We think the reason is that WSSTG [3] is oriented for grounding the main object in a natural language sentence (*i.e.*, the subject), and when concatenating the representations of two trajectories, it can enhance the representation for the main object, but not sure for other supportive objects. According to the results, it even confuses the model and thus jeopardizes the grounding performance for the object ($Acc_O$).

Relatively, the co-occurrence baseline performs better than [3] on this task. Yet, its performances are still worse than ours (Co-occur* v.s. vRGV* and Co-occur v.s. vRGV). This demonstrates that the "predicate" in the relation is crucial in precisely disambiguating the subjects and objects. As shown in Fig. 3, the occurrence baseline wrongly grounds the person sitting as the object, whereas our method successfully grounds the object to the person riding the bicycle. We also note that the co-occurrence baseline beats our weak model variant under the metric with threshold 0.7 (Co-occur v.s. vRGV*), which in fact, shows the superiority of our overall framework for joint grounding of two objects. Also, it indicates the importance of object locations in generating better trajectories.

### 4.5  Model Ablations

We ablate our model in Table 3 to study the contribution of each component. Results in the 2nd row are obtained by removing the message passing module. We can see that the performance $Acc_R$ drops from 24.58% to 17.63%. This is mainly because the model without explicit message communication between subject and

**Table 4.** Results of zero-shot visual relation grounding.

| Methods | $Acc_S$ | $Acc_O$ | $Acc_R$ |
|---------|---------|---------|---------|
| T-Rank $V_1$ [3] | 4.05 | 4.08 | 1.37 |
| T-Rank $V_2$ [3] | 7.09 | 4.13 | 1.37 |
| Co-occur [15] | 11.60 | 10.99 | 7.38 |
| vRGV (ours) | **18.94** | **17.23** | **10.27** |

object cannot cope well with the scenario where there are multiple visual entities of same category present in the video. Another reason could be that the ablated model is weak in detecting objects under complex conditions (*e.g.*, occlusion and blur) without the contextual information from their partners.

Results in the 3rd row are obtained by removing the clip-level attention. We do this ablation to prove the importance of the hierarchical structure of our model. Note that the temporal threshold $\sigma$ for this experiment is set to 0.0001, because we only have the frame-level attention $\beta^{l1}$. Comparing with results in the first row, we can see the results drop under all criteria without the hierarchical structure. When we further remove the frame-level attention (shown in the 4th row), and thus delete the whole temporal attention unit (TAU), the results degrade significantly from 24.58% to 7.06%. This is because our model will blindly link the objects throughout the video regardless of relation without the temporal grounding module. These findings demonstrate the importance of relation-aware temporal grounding in untrimmed videos.

We also analyze the temporal threshold $\sigma$ by changing it from 0.01 to 0.05, the corresponding results $Acc_R$ are 24.51%, 24.76%, 24.43%, 24.58% and 22.94%. From the results, we can see that there is no significant difference when the threshold changes from 0.01 to 0.05, and the best result is achieved at the threshold of 0.02. We show some qualitative results in Fig. 4 based on temporal threshold of 0.04 (More results can be found in the appendix), from which we can see that our model can ground the subjects and objects in the videos when the query relations exist.

### 4.6   Zero-Shot Evaluation

In this section, we analyze the models' capability of grounding the new (unseen during training) relation triplets. Specifically, in zero-shot relation grounding, we consider the case that the complete relation triplet is never seen, but their separate components (*e.g.*, *subject*, *predicate* or *object*) are known during training. For example, the model may have seen the relation triplets *person-ride-bicycle* and *person-run_behind-car* during training, but it never knows *bicycle-run_behind-car*. As a result, we can find 432 relation instances of 258 unseen relation triplets in 73 videos from the test set.

As shown in Table 4, our approach still outperforms the baselines in the zero-shot setting. We attribute such strength of our approach under zero-shot scenario to two reasons. First, we decompose the relation and separately embed the words corresponding to the subject and object into a semantic space during relation embedding. This is different from modeling the relation holistically using LSTM as in [3], which lacks flexibility and is hard to learn with limited training data. Second, we treat the relation as a natural language in the reconstruction stage, which enhances the model's ability in visual reasoning through forcing it to infer the remaining words conditioned on the related visual content and the previously generated words in the relation.

## 5    Conclusion

In this paper, we defined a novel task of visual relation grounding in videos which is of significance in underpinning other high-level video-language tasks. To solve the challenges in the task, we proposed a weakly-supervised video relation grounding method by modeling the video as hierarchical spatio-temporal region graph, and collaboratively optimizing two region sequences over it by incorporating relation as textual clues and passing messages by spatial attention shift. Our experiments demonstrated the effectiveness of the proposed approach. Future efforts can either be made on how to jointly ground the subject and object in videos conditioned on their interactions, or how to better capture the temporal dynamics of relations in videos. In addition, it is also important to explore how to better optimize the video graph model based on video-level supervisions only. Another promising direction could be utilizing relation to boost video language grounding and video question answering.

**Acknowledgement.** This research is supported by the National Research Foundation, Singapore under its International Research Centres in Singapore Funding Initiative. Any opinions, findings and conclusions or recommendations expressed in this material are those of the author(s) and do not reflect the views of National Research Foundation, Singapore.

## References

1. Balajee Vasudevan, A., Dai, D., Van Gool, L.: Object referring in videos with language and human gaze. In: Proceedings of the IEEE Conference on Computer Vision and Pattern Recognition, pp. 4129–4138 (2018)
2. Carreira, J., Zisserman, A.: Quo vadis, action recognition? A new model and the kinetics dataset. In: Proceedings of the IEEE Conference on Computer Vision and Pattern Recognition, pp. 6299–6308 (2017)
3. Chen, Z., Ma, L., Luo, W., Wong, K.Y.K.: Weakly-supervised spatio-temporally grounding natural sentence in video. In: ACL (2019)
4. Galleguillos, C., Rabinovich, A., Belongie, S.: Object categorization using co-occurrence, location and appearance. In: 2008 IEEE Conference on Computer Vision and Pattern Recognition, pp. 1–8. IEEE (2008)
5. Gkioxari, G., Malik, J.: Finding action tubes. In: Proceedings of the IEEE Conference on Computer Vision and Pattern Recognition, pp. 759–768 (2015)

6. He, K., Zhang, X., Ren, S., Sun, J.: Deep residual learning for image recognition. In: Proceedings of the IEEE Conference on Computer Vision and Pattern Recognition, pp. 770–778 (2016)
7. Hochreiter, S., Schmidhuber, J.: Long short-term memory. Neural Comput. **9**(8), 1735–1780 (1997)
8. Hu, R., Rohrbach, M., Andreas, J., Darrell, T., Saenko, K.: Modeling relationships in referential expressions with compositional modular networks. In: Proceedings of the IEEE Conference on Computer Vision and Pattern Recognition, pp. 1115–1124 (2017)
9. Hu, R., Xu, H., Rohrbach, M., Feng, J., Saenko, K., Darrell, T.: Natural language object retrieval. In: Proceedings of the IEEE Conference on Computer Vision and Pattern Recognition, pp. 4555–4564 (2016)
10. Huang, D.A., Buch, S., Dery, L., Garg, A., Fei-Fei, L., Niebles, J.C.: Finding "it": weakly-supervised reference-aware visual grounding in instructional videos. In: IEEE Conference on Computer Vision and Pattern Recognition (CVPR), pp. 5948–5957. IEEE (2018)
11. Jain, A., Zamir, A.R., Savarese, S., Saxena, A.: Structural-RNN: deep learning on spatio-temporal graphs. In: Proceedings of the IEEE Conference on Computer Vision and Pattern Recognition, pp. 5308–5317 (2016)
12. Karpathy, A., Fei-Fei, L.: Deep visual-semantic alignments for generating image descriptions. In: Proceedings of the IEEE Conference on Computer Vision and Pattern Recognition, pp. 3128–3137 (2015)
13. Karpathy, A., Joulin, A., Fei-Fei, L.F.: Deep fragment embeddings for bidirectional image sentence mapping. In: Advances in Neural Information Processing Systems, pp. 1889–1897 (2014)
14. Kingma, D.P., Ba, J.: Adam: a method for stochastic optimization. arXiv preprint arXiv:1412.6980 (2014)
15. Krishna, R., Chami, I., Bernstein, M., Fei-Fei, L.: Referring relationships. In: Proceedings of the IEEE Conference on Computer Vision and Pattern Recognition, pp. 6867–6876 (2018)
16. Krishna, R., et al.: Visual genome: connecting language and vision using crowd-sourced dense image annotations. Int. J. Comput. Vis. **123**(1), 32–73 (2017). https://doi.org/10.1007/s11263-016-0981-7
17. Liang, K., Guo, Y., Chang, H., Chen, X.: Visual relationship detection with deep structural ranking. In: Thirty-Second AAAI Conference on Artificial Intelligence (2018)
18. Lin, T.-Y., et al.: Microsoft COCO: common objects in context. In: Fleet, D., Pajdla, T., Schiele, B., Tuytelaars, T. (eds.) ECCV 2014. LNCS, vol. 8693, pp. 740–755. Springer, Cham (2014). https://doi.org/10.1007/978-3-319-10602-1_48
19. Liu, X., Li, L., Wang, S., Zha, Z.J., Meng, D., Huang, Q.: Adaptive reconstruction network for weakly supervised referring expression grounding. In: Proceedings of the IEEE International Conference on Computer Vision, pp. 2611–2620 (2019)
20. Lu, C., Krishna, R., Bernstein, M., Fei-Fei, L.: Visual relationship detection with language priors. In: Leibe, B., Matas, J., Sebe, N., Welling, M. (eds.) ECCV 2016. LNCS, vol. 9905, pp. 852–869. Springer, Cham (2016). https://doi.org/10.1007/978-3-319-46448-0_51
21. Lu, P., Ji, L., Zhang, W., Duan, N., Zhou, M., Wang, J.: R-VQA: learning visual relation facts with semantic attention for visual question answering. In: Proceedings of the 24th ACM SIGKDD International Conference on Knowledge Discovery & Data Mining, pp. 1880–1889. ACM (2018)

22. Mao, J., Huang, J., Toshev, A., Camburu, O., Yuille, A.L., Murphy, K.: Generation and comprehension of unambiguous object descriptions. In: Proceedings of the IEEE Conference on Computer Vision and Pattern Recognition, pp. 11–20 (2016)
23. Nagaraja, V.K., Morariu, V.I., Davis, L.S.: Modeling context between objects for referring expression understanding. In: Leibe, B., Matas, J., Sebe, N., Welling, M. (eds.) ECCV 2016. LNCS, vol. 9908, pp. 792–807. Springer, Cham (2016). https://doi.org/10.1007/978-3-319-46493-0_48
24. Pan, P., Xu, Z., Yang, Y., Wu, F., Zhuang, Y.: Hierarchical recurrent neural encoder for video representation with application to captioning. In: Proceedings of the IEEE Conference on Computer Vision and Pattern Recognition, pp. 1029–1038 (2016)
25. Pennington, J., Socher, R., Manning, C.D.: GloVe: global vectors for word representation. In: Empirical Methods in Natural Language Processing (EMNLP), pp. 1532–1543 (2014)
26. Qian, X., Zhuang, Y., Li, Y., Xiao, S., Pu, S., Xiao, J.: Video relation detection with spatio-temporal graph. In: Proceedings of the 27th ACM International Conference on Multimedia, pp. 84–93. ACM (2019)
27. Ren, S., He, K., Girshick, R., Sun, J.: Faster R-CNN: towards real-time object detection with region proposal networks. In: Advances in Neural Information Processing Systems, pp. 91–99 (2015)
28. Rohrbach, A., Rohrbach, M., Hu, R., Darrell, T., Schiele, B.: Grounding of textual phrases in images by reconstruction. In: Leibe, B., Matas, J., Sebe, N., Welling, M. (eds.) ECCV 2016. LNCS, vol. 9905, pp. 817–834. Springer, Cham (2016). https://doi.org/10.1007/978-3-319-46448-0_49
29. Russakovsky, O., et al.: ImageNet large scale visual recognition challenge. Int. J. Comput. Vis. (IJCV) **115**(3), 211–252 (2015). https://doi.org/10.1007/s11263-015-0816-y
30. Shang, X., Di, D., Xiao, J., Cao, Y., Yang, X., Chua, T.S.: Annotating objects and relations in user-generated videos. In: ACM International Conference on Multimedia Retrieval, Ottawa, ON, Canada, June 2019
31. Shang, X., Ren, T., Guo, J., Zhang, H., Chua, T.S.: Video visual relation detection. In: Proceedings of the 25th ACM International Conference on Multimedia, pp. 1300–1308. ACM (2017)
32. Shi, J., Xu, J., Gong, B., Xu, C.: Not all frames are equal: weakly-supervised video grounding with contextual similarity and visual clustering losses. In: Proceedings of the IEEE Conference on Computer Vision and Pattern Recognition, pp. 10444–10452 (2019)
33. Simonyan, K., Zisserman, A.: Two-stream convolutional networks for action recognition in videos. In: Advances in Neural Information Processing Systems, pp. 568–576 (2014)
34. Tran, D., Bourdev, L., Fergus, R., Torresani, L., Paluri, M.: Learning spatiotemporal features with 3D convolutional networks. In: Proceedings of the IEEE International Conference on Computer Vision, pp. 4489–4497 (2015)
35. Tsai, Y.H.H., Divvala, S., Morency, L.P., Salakhutdinov, R., Farhadi, A.: Video relationship reasoning using gated spatio-temporal energy graph. In: Proceedings of the IEEE Conference on Computer Vision and Pattern Recognition, pp. 10424–10433 (2019)
36. Venugopalan, S., Rohrbach, M., Donahue, J., Mooney, R., Darrell, T., Saenko, K.: Sequence to sequence-video to text. In: Proceedings of the IEEE International Conference on Computer Vision, pp. 4534–4542 (2015)

37. Wang, H., Schmid, C.: Action recognition with improved trajectories. In: Proceedings of the IEEE International Conference on Computer Vision, pp. 3551–3558 (2013)
38. Wang, X., Gupta, A.: Videos as space-time region graphs. In: Proceedings of the European Conference on Computer Vision (ECCV), pp. 399–417 (2018)
39. Yamaguchi, M., Saito, K., Ushiku, Y., Harada, T.: Spatio-temporal person retrieval via natural language queries. In: Proceedings of the IEEE International Conference on Computer Vision, pp. 1453–1462 (2017)
40. Yao, B., Fei-Fei, L.: Modeling mutual context of object and human pose in human-object interaction activities. In: 2010 IEEE Computer Society Conference on Computer Vision and Pattern Recognition, pp. 17–24. IEEE (2010)
41. Yu, L., et al.: MAttNet: modular attention network for referring expression comprehension. In: Proceedings of the IEEE Conference on Computer Vision and Pattern Recognition, pp. 1307–1315 (2018)
42. Yu, L., Poirson, P., Yang, S., Berg, A.C., Berg, T.L.: Modeling context in referring expressions. In: Leibe, B., Matas, J., Sebe, N., Welling, M. (eds.) ECCV 2016. LNCS, vol. 9906, pp. 69–85. Springer, Cham (2016). https://doi.org/10.1007/978-3-319-46475-6_5
43. Yue-Hei Ng, J., Hausknecht, M., Vijayanarasimhan, S., Vinyals, O., Monga, R., Toderici, G.: Beyond short snippets: deep networks for video classification. In: Proceedings of the IEEE Conference on Computer Vision and Pattern Recognition, pp. 4694–4702 (2015)
44. Zhang, H., Niu, Y., Chang, S.F.: Grounding referring expressions in images by variational context. In: Proceedings of the IEEE Conference on Computer Vision and Pattern Recognition, pp. 4158–4166 (2018)
45. Zhang, J., Kalantidis, Y., Rohrbach, M., Paluri, M., Elgammal, A.M., Elhoseiny, M.: Large-scale visual relationship understanding. In: AAAI (2019)
46. Zhang, Z., Zhao, Z., Zhao, Y., Wang, Q., Liu, H., Gao, L.: Where does it exist: spatio-temporal video grounding for multi-form sentences. In: Proceedings of the IEEE Conference on Computer Vision and Pattern Recognition (2020)
47. Zhou, L., Louis, N., Corso, J.J.: Weakly-supervised video object grounding from text by loss weighting and object interaction. arXiv preprint arXiv:1805.02834 (2018)

# Weakly Supervised 3D Human Pose and Shape Reconstruction with Normalizing Flows

Andrei Zanfir, Eduard Gabriel Bazavan[(✉)], Hongyi Xu, William T. Freeman,
Rahul Sukthankar, and Cristian Sminchisescu

Google Research, Zurich, Switzerland
{andreiz,egbazavan,hongyixu,wfreeman,sukthankar,sminchisescu}@google.com

**Abstract.** Monocular 3D human pose and shape estimation is challenging due to the many degrees of freedom of the human body and the difficulty to acquire training data for large-scale supervised learning in complex visual scenes. In this paper we present practical semi-supervised and self-supervised models that support training and good generalization in real-world images and video. Our formulation is based on kinematic latent normalizing flow representations and dynamics, as well as differentiable, semantic body part alignment loss functions that support self-supervised learning. In extensive experiments using 3D motion capture datasets like CMU, Human3.6M, 3DPW, or AMASS, as well as image repositories like COCO, we show that the proposed methods outperform the state of the art, supporting the practical construction of an accurate family of models based on large-scale training with diverse and incompletely labeled image and video data.

**Keywords:** 3D human sensing · Normalizing flows · Semantic alignment

## 1 Introduction

Recovering 3D human pose and shape from monocular RGB images is important for motion and behavioral analysis, robotics, self-driving cars, computer graphics, and the gaming industry. Considerable progress has been made recently in increasing the size of datasets, in the level of detail of human body modeling, and the use of deep learning. A difficulty is the somewhat limited diversity of supervision available in the 3D domain. Many datasets offer 2D human body joint annotations or semantic body part segmentation masks for images collected in the wild, but lack 3D annotations. Motion capture datasets in turn offer large and diverse 3D annotations but their image backgrounds, clothing or

---

**Electronic supplementary material** The online version of this chapter (https://doi.org/10.1007/978-3-030-58539-6_28) contains supplementary material, which is available to authorized users.

© Springer Nature Switzerland AG 2020
A. Vedaldi et al. (Eds.): ECCV 2020, LNCS 12351, pp. 465–481, 2020.
https://doi.org/10.1007/978-3-030-58539-6_28

body shape variation is not as high. Multi-task models, or models able to learn using limited forms of supervision, represent a potential solution to the current 3D supervision limitations. However, the number of human body shapes and poses observed in images collected in the wild is large, so strong pose, shape priors and expressive loss functions appear necessary in order to make learning feasible. In this paper we address some of these challenges by designing a family of normalizing flow based kinematic priors, together with semantic alignment losses that make large scale weakly and self-supervised learning more accurate and efficient. *The introduction and integration of these components, new in the framework of human sensing, with strong results, is one of the main contributions of this work.* An evaluation (with ablation studies) on large scale datasets like Human3.6M, COCO, 3DPW, indicates good weakly supervised performance for 3D reconstruction. Our proposed priors and loss functions are amenable to both integration into deep learning losses and to direct non-linear state optimization (refinement) of a model given a random seed or initialization from a learnt predictor.

**Mindset.** Our use of different data sources is practically minded, as we aim towards large scale operation in the wild. Hence we rely on all types of supervision and data sources available. We often start with models trained in the lab, e.g. using Human3.6M and those are *supervised*. We also use 3D motion capture repositories like CMU in order to construct kinematic (output) priors and that component alone would make our approach *semi-supervised*. Finally, we make use of large scale predict-and-reproject losses for unlabeled datasets like MS COCO, which makes our approach, at least to an extent *self-supervised*. Whatever model curriculum used, we aim, long-term, to converge on self-supervised operation. We work with a semi-supervised output prior and model ignition is based on supervision in the lab. By convention, we call this regime *weakly-supervised*.

**Related Work.** There is considerable work in 3D human pose estimation based on 2D keypoints, semantic segmentation of body parts, and 3D joint positions [9,25,26,32,35,37]. More recently, there has been significant interest in 3D human pose and shape estimation [1,6,13,19,36,42], with some in the form of a reduced parametric model [30] decoded by 2D predictions, volumetric variants [39] or direct vertex prediction combined with 3D model fitting [10,44]. Learning under weak supervision represents the next frontier, considered in this work as well. [43] learns a discriminator in order to transfer knowledge gained on a 3D dataset to a 2D one. [46] train a shared representation for both 2D and 3D pose estimation, with a regularizer operating on body segments in order to preserve statistics. [12] use a discriminator as prior, with adversarial training, and mixes 3D supervision and image labels. [27] uses segmentations as an intermediate layer, defines a loss on 2D and 3D joints, and rely on rotation matrices instead of angle-axis representation. [31] uses a differentiable renderer (OpenDR) to compute a silhouette loss with a limited basin of attraction. This is only used for finetuning the network, but the authors report not having observed significant gains. [38] rely on a segmentation loss defined on silhouettes, not on the body parts, and rely on multiple views and temporal constraints for learning.

A variety of methods rely on priors for 3D optimization starting from an initial estimate provided by a neural network and/or by relying on image features like keypoints or silhouettes. [2] fit a Gaussian mixture model to motion capture data from CMU [11] and use it during optimization. We will evaluate this prior in our work. SPIN [18] alternates rounds of training with estimation of new targets using optimization (we will compare in Sect. 3).

Multiple differentiable rendering models [14,22,34] have been proposed recently, in more general settings. Such models are elegant and offer the promise of optimizing photo-realistic losses in the long run. The challenge is in defining an end-to-end model that embeds the difficult assignment problem between the model predictions (rasterized or not) and the image features in ways that are both differentiable and amenable to larger basins of attraction. Our semantic alignment loss is not technically a rendering model, but is differentiable and offers large basins of attraction, supported by explicit, long-range semantic body part correspondences. Gradients can be propagated for points that are not rendered (i.e. points that fail the z-test) and the operation is parallelizable and easy to implement.

## 2   Methodology

**3D Pose and Shape Representations.** We use a statistical body model [21, 41] to represent the pose and the shape of the human body. Given a monocular RGB image, our objective is to infer the pose state variables $\boldsymbol{\theta} \in \mathbb{R}^{N_j \times 3}$ and shape $\boldsymbol{\beta} \in \mathbb{R}^{N_s}$. A posed mesh $\mathbf{M}(\boldsymbol{\theta}, \boldsymbol{\beta})$ has $N_v$ associated 3D vertices $\mathbf{V} = \{\mathbf{v}_i, i = 1 \ldots N_v\}$. By dropping dependency on parameters we sometimes denote $\mathbf{M}(\mathbf{V}, k)$ the subset of vertices associated with body part index $k$ (e.g. torso or head).

For prediction and optimization tasks we experiment with several kinematic representations. The angle-axis gives good results in connection with deep learning architectures [12,44]. The representation consists of a set of $N_j$ angle-axis variables $\boldsymbol{\theta} = \{\boldsymbol{\theta}_1, \boldsymbol{\theta}_2, \ldots, \boldsymbol{\theta}_{N_j}\}, \boldsymbol{\theta}_i \in \mathbb{R}^3$, where the norm of $\boldsymbol{\theta}_i$ is the rotation angle in radians and $\frac{\boldsymbol{\theta}_i}{\|\boldsymbol{\theta}_i\|}$ is the unit length 3D axis of rotation.

We also explore a new 6D over-parameterization of rotations [47], given by the first two columns of the rotation matrix. We test this parameterization in the context of optimization, by building a prior and minimizing a cost function over the compound space of 6D kinematic rotations.[1]

### 2.1   3D Normalizing Flow-Based Representations

**Existing Work on 3D Human Priors.** The method of [2] builds a density model to favor more probable poses over improbable ones. They use a mixture

---

[1] We have also considered quaternions, but our experiments showed these to be inferior even to angle-axis (AA), by at least 10%.

with 8 Gaussian modes $N(\boldsymbol{\mu}_j, \boldsymbol{\Sigma}_j)$, fitted to 1 million CMU poses. During optimization, the prior is evaluated to produce the log-likelihood of the pose. For numerical stability and to avoid excessive averaging effects, an approximation based on choosing the closest mode is used, which is not smooth, and may still lead to instability during mode switching.

For neural network models, [12] proposed a factorized adversarial network to learn the admissible rotation manifold of 3D poses, by relying on $N_j + 1$ discriminators, one for each joint, and one for the whole pose. The rotation limits for each joint are expected to be learned implicitly by each of the $N_j$ discriminators, while the last one measures the probability of the combined pose. Learning rotation matrices (as opposed to angle-axis based) discriminators, is beneficial in avoiding the non-continuous nature of the angle-axis representation, but trades off increasing representational redundancy and consequently dimensionality.

Another approach has been pursued by [29], where the authors use a variational auto-encoder for 3D poses. The reconstruction loss is the mean per-vertex error between the input posed mesh and the reconstructed one. The latent representation can be used as a prior, by querying the log-likelihood of a given pose. Our experiments with VAEs constructed on top of kinematic representations (joint angles, rotations) showed that those have poor performance compared to our proposed models. The more sophisticated approaches used in VPoser [29] rely on losses defined on meshes rather than kinematics, but meshes inevitably introduce artefacts due to e.g. imperfect skinning. Moreover, VAEs need to balance two terms – the reconstruction loss and a KL divergence, which leads to a compromise: either the latent space is not close to Gaussian or/and decoding is imperfect. Our normalizing flow approach ensures that reconstruction loss is perfect (by the bijectivity of NFlow's construction) and during training we only optimize against the simpler Gaussian latent space objective.

**Normalizing Flow Priors.** In this paper we propose different normalizing flow-based prior representations, to our knowledge used for the first time in modeling 3D human pose. A normalizing flow [4, 5, 15, 33] is a sequence of invertible transformations applied to the original distribution. The end-result is a warped (latent) space with a potentially simple and tractable density function, e.g. $\mathbf{z} \sim \mathcal{N}(0; \mathbf{I})$). We consider $\boldsymbol{\theta} \sim p^*(\boldsymbol{\theta})$ sampled from an unknown distribution. One way to learn it is to use a dataset $\mathcal{D}$ (e.g. from CMU or Human3.6M) and maximize data log-likelihood with respect to a parametric model $p_\phi(\boldsymbol{\theta})$

$$\max_{\phi} \sum_{\theta \in \mathcal{D}} \log p_\phi(\boldsymbol{\theta}) \tag{1}$$

where $\phi$ are the parameters of the generative model. If we choose $\mathbf{z} = \mathbf{f}_\phi(\boldsymbol{\theta})$ where $\mathbf{f}_\phi$ is a component-wise invertible transformation, one can rewrite the log-probability under a change of variables

$$\log p_\phi(\boldsymbol{\theta}) = \log p_\phi(\mathbf{z}) + \log |\det(d\mathbf{z}/d\boldsymbol{\theta})| \tag{2}$$

Dropping the subscript $\phi$, if $\mathbf{f}$ is the composition of multiple bijections $\mathbf{f}_i$, with intermediate output $\mathbf{h}_i$, (2) becomes

$$\log p_\phi(\boldsymbol{\theta}) = \log p_\phi(\mathbf{z}) + \sum_{i=1}^{K} \log |\det(d\mathbf{h}_i/d\mathbf{h}_{i-1})| \tag{3}$$

where $\mathbf{h}_0 = \boldsymbol{\theta}$ and $\mathbf{h}_K = \mathbf{z}$, and $p_\phi(\mathbf{z}) = \mathcal{N}(\mathbf{z}; \mathbf{0}, \mathbf{I})$ is chosen as a spherical multivariate Gaussian distribution. State-of-the-art flow architectures are based on auto-regressive versions, such as the Masked Autoregressive Flow (MAF) [28], Inverse Autoregressive Flow (IAF) [16], NICE [4], MADE [7] or Real-NVP [5]. In our experiments, we found MAF/IAF/MADE to be too slow given our representation and dataset size, with no measurable improvement over a Real-NVP. A Real-NVP step takes as input a variable $\mathbf{x}$ and outputs the transformed variable $\mathbf{y}$, under the following rules

$$\mathbf{y}_{1:d} = \mathbf{x}_{1:d}, \quad \mathbf{y}_{d+1:D} = \mathbf{x}_{d+1:D} \odot \exp \mathbf{s} + \mathbf{t}, \tag{4}$$

where $\mathbf{s}$ and $\mathbf{t}$ are shift-and-scale vectors that can be modelled as neural network outputs, i.e. $(\mathbf{s}, \mathbf{t}) = \mathrm{NN}(\mathbf{x}_{1:d})$, and $d$ is the splitting location of the current $D$-dimensional variable. The '$\odot$' operator represents the pointwise product, while 'exp' is the exponential function. In order to chain multiple Real-NVP steps, one has to ensure that order is not constant, otherwise the first $d$-dimensions would not be transformed. Typically, $\mathbf{x}$ is permuted before the operation. Because, in our case, $\boldsymbol{\theta}$ has moderate although sufficiently large size, we introduce a trainable, fully-connected layer before each NVP step. This is fast and results in better models. We also experiment with a lower capacity model, which replaces the Real-NVP with a simple parametric ReLU, as activation function. We do not use batch normalization. We found that we can trade a bit of accuracy (given by RealNVP) for a standard MLP that is faster and requires less memory. For the same network depth, the Real-NVP variant had 2x the number of parameters, and had marginal performance benefits (2%). More details can be found in the Sup. Mat.

For optimization-based inference or neural network training, we can parameterize the problem either in the latent (warped) space, or in the ambient (original) kinematic space, given the exact connection between them. Our empirical studies show that directly predicting (or optimizing) the latent representation always yields better results over working in the ambient space (see Table 1).

In Fig. 1 we show a sample pose interpolation in latent space.

**Optimization.** To optimize normalizing flow representations, we assume normalization variable $\boldsymbol{\theta}$, Gaussian variable $\mathbf{z} = \mathbf{f}(\boldsymbol{\theta})$, and $\boldsymbol{\theta} = \mathbf{f}^{-1}(\mathbf{z})$, given that $\mathbf{f}$ is bijective. We define the normalizing flow prior as the negative log-likelihood in ambient $\psi_{nf}(\mathbf{f}(\boldsymbol{\theta})) = -\log p_\phi(\mathbf{f}(\boldsymbol{\theta}))$ or, equivalently in latent space, $\psi_{nf}(\mathbf{z}) = -\log p_\phi(\mathbf{z})$. Then, for any objective function or loss defined as $L(\boldsymbol{\theta}, \boldsymbol{\beta})$, we have either the option of working (i.e. predicting or optimizing) in the **ambient space** and back-projecting in the latent space at each step

$$\arg \min_{\boldsymbol{\theta}, \boldsymbol{\beta}} L(\boldsymbol{\theta}, \boldsymbol{\beta}) + \psi_{nf}(\mathbf{f}(\boldsymbol{\theta})) \tag{5}$$

**Fig. 1.** From left to right: interpolation in latent space for normalizing flow, for two (begin and end) normal random codes. Notice smooth results, plausible human poses.

or the option to operate in the **latent space** directly

$$\arg \min_{\mathbf{z}, \boldsymbol{\beta}} L(\mathbf{f}^{-1}(\mathbf{z}), \boldsymbol{\beta}) + \psi_{nf}(\mathbf{z}) \tag{6}$$

Both approaches are differentiable and we will evaluate them in Sect. 3.

## 2.2  Differentiable Semantic Alignment Loss

In order to be able to efficiently learn using weak supervision (e.g. just images of people), one needs a measure of prediction quality during the different phases of model training. In this work we explore forms of structured feedback by considering detailed correspondences between the different body part vertices of our 3D human body mesh (projected in the image), and the semantic human body part segmentation produced by another neural network.

As presented by [44], an Iterated Closest Point (ICP)-style cost for body part alignment can be designed in 2D (for 3D this is quite common e.g. [45]). Given a set of $N_b$ body parts, their semantic image segmentation $\{\mathbf{S}_i \subset \mathbb{R}^2\}$ and associated mesh vertices of similar type $\{\mathbf{M}(\mathbf{V}, k) \subset \mathbb{R}^3\}$ (i.e. the 3D vertex set of body part $k$), a distance between the set of semantic segmentation regions and the 3D mesh vertex projections (using an operator $\Pi$) can be defined as the first term of (7). This term encourages pixels of a particular semantic body type (e.g. torso, head or left lower arm) to attract projected model vertices with the same body part label. Depending on the sizes of the image regions with particular labels, and the corresponding number of vertices, the minimum of this function is not necessarily achieved only when all vertices are inside the body part. Consequently, we add a complementary loss, encouraging good overlap between model projections and image regions of corresponding semantics.

$$L_{BA}(\mathbf{S}, \mathbf{V}) = \sum_{k=1}^{N_b} \sum_{\mathbf{p} \in \mathbf{S}_k} \min_{\mathbf{v} \in \mathbf{M}(\mathbf{V}, k)} \|\mathbf{p} - \Pi(\mathbf{v})\| + \sum_{k=1}^{N_b} \sum_{\mathbf{v} \in \mathbf{M}(\mathbf{V}, k)} \min_{\mathbf{p} \in \mathbf{S}_k} \|\mathbf{p} - \Pi(\mathbf{v})\| \tag{7}$$

We will refer to the two terms as the forward semantic segmentation loss and the backward loss, respectively. Compared to state-of-the-art differentiable rendering techniques like [14], this loss has exact gradients, because we express it as an explicit objective connecting semantic image masks and mesh vertex projections. Furthermore, our method is designed for categorical masks and only defined for regions explained by the vertex projections of our model, rather than all the image pixels. The process is naturally parallelizable, and we offer a GPU implementation.

### 2.3 Network Architecture

Our architecture is based on a multistage deep convolutional neural network to predict human body joints, semantic segmentation of body parts, as well as 3D body pose and shape. The network consists of multiple modules, and has multiple losses, each corresponding to a different prediction task, but it can be run with a subset of the losses under different levels of supervision ranging from full to none. The first module takes as input the image and outputs keypoint (body joint) heatmaps [3]. We extract the joint positions from the heatmaps and obtain $\mathbf{J}_{2d} = \{\mathbf{J}_i, i = 1 \ldots N_j\}$. The next module computes semantic body part segmentations by processing images and the keypoint heatmaps obtained by the keypoint prediction module. The outputs are semantic segmentation heatmaps for each body part (see Fig. 2), $\mathbf{S} = \{\mathbf{S}_i, i = 1 \ldots N_b\}$. The last module predicts pose and shape parameters. It takes as input the outputs from previous modules and produces $\{\boldsymbol{\theta}, \boldsymbol{\beta}\}$. For the camera, we adopt a perspective projection model. We fix the intrinsics and estimate translation by means of fitting the predicted 3D skeleton to 2D joint detections (that step alone requires a weak perspective approximation, see Sup. Mat.).

**Fig. 2.** From left to right: Original image, ground truth semantic body part segmentation mask from MSCOCO 2014, predicted segmentation mask, projected semantic mask of our 3D mesh.

**3D Pose and Shape.** The goal of the 3D pose layers is to predict the pose and shape parameters $\{\boldsymbol{\theta}, \boldsymbol{\beta}\}$. The associated network is similar to the ones of the previous two modules. A stack of convolutional stages is created with losses on each stage to reinforce the weights and avoid vanishing gradients [3,40]. The architecture of each 3D regressor stage is composed of a stack of $5 \times$ 2D convolutional layers with 128 feature maps, $7 \times 7$ kernels, `relu` activations, followed by another 2D convolutional module with 128 layers and $1 \times 1$ kernels. The last layer is a 2D convolutional layer, has no activation function and the number of heatmaps is equal to the number of predicted parameters. Two separate dense layers are used to output $\{\boldsymbol{\theta}, \boldsymbol{\beta}\}$.

**Supervised and Weakly Supervised Losses.** We train our network by using a combination of fully and weakly supervised losses. The fully supervised training regime assumes complete ground truth on pose, shape. A predicted posed mesh $\mathbf{M}(\boldsymbol{\theta}, \boldsymbol{\beta})$ with $N_v$ associated vertices $\mathbf{V} = \{\mathbf{v}_i, i = 1 \ldots N_v\}$ has ground truth $\mathbf{M}(\widehat{\boldsymbol{\theta}}, \widehat{\boldsymbol{\beta}})$ with vertices $\{\widehat{\mathbf{v}}_i\}$. We define the following MSE losses, respectively, on the mesh

$$L_V = \frac{1}{N_v} \sum_{i=1}^{N_v} \|\mathbf{v}_i - \widehat{\mathbf{v}}_i\|_2^2 \tag{8}$$

pose and shape parameters

$$L_\theta = \frac{1}{N_j} \sum_{i=1}^{N_j} \left\|\boldsymbol{\theta}_i - \widehat{\boldsymbol{\theta}}_i\right\|_2^2, \quad L_\beta = \frac{1}{N_s} \sum_{i=1}^{N_s} \left\|\boldsymbol{\beta}_i - \widehat{\boldsymbol{\beta}}_i\right\|_2^2 \tag{9}$$

The supervised loss combines previously defined losses

$$L_{fs} = L_V + L_\theta + L_\beta \tag{10}$$

For the weakly supervised case, the predicted mesh $\mathbf{M}(\boldsymbol{\theta}, \boldsymbol{\beta})$ is projected into the image. Denote the projected skeleton joints by $\mathbf{J}_{2d} = \{\mathbf{J}_i\}$, the estimated (or ground truth) 2D joint positions by $\widehat{\mathbf{J}}_{2d} = \{\widehat{\mathbf{J}}_i\}$, and the semantic body part segmentation maps by $\widehat{\mathbf{S}} = \{\widehat{\mathbf{S}}_i, i = 1 \ldots N_b\}$. The weakly supervised regime assumes access to large 3D mocap datasets, e.g. CMU – in order to construct kinematic priors – but without the corresponding images. Additionally we also rely on images in the wild, with only 2D body joint or semantic segmentation maps ground truth. Our weakly-supervised model relies on all practically useful data in order to bootstrap a self-supervised system at later stages. Hence we do not discard 3D data when we have it, and aim to use it to circumvent the missing link: images in the wild with 3D pose and shape ground truth. Then, one can define weakly supervised losses for *keypoint alignment:* $L_{KA} = \frac{1}{N_j} \sum_{i=1}^{N_j} \left\|\mathbf{J}_i - \widehat{\mathbf{J}}_i\right\|_2^2$, *semantic body-part alignment:* $L_{BA}\left(\widehat{\mathbf{S}}, \mathbf{V}\right)$, and *the prior:* $L_\psi = \psi_{nf}\left(\mathbf{f}(\boldsymbol{\theta})\right)$ (or $\psi_{nf}(\mathbf{z})$ when working in the latent space). The weakly supervised loss is a combination of multiple losses, plus a term that regularizes the shape parameters

$$L_{ws} = L_{KA} + L_{BA} + L_\psi + \|\boldsymbol{\beta}\|_2^2 \tag{11}$$

The total loss will be $L_{total} = L_{fs} + L_{ws}$. For a graceful transition between supervision regimes, during fully supervised training we use $L_{total}$, then switch to $L_{ws}$ in the weakly supervised phase.

**Fig. 3. Reconstruction results of models trained weakly-supervised using COCO (best seen in color).** Starting from a network fully supervised on H80K (**red**), we fine-tune with a weakly-supervised loss (**green**) and a normalizing flow kinematic prior. Notice considerable improvement in both alignment and the perceptual 3D estimates. Last column shows a different view angle for the WS estimate. (Color figure online)

## 3   Experiments

**Datasets.** We run our fully supervised experiments on the Human80K (H80K) – a representative subset sampled from Human3.6M (H3.6M) [8]. We also use H80K in order to train pose priors and for optimization experiments. We report errors in the form of MPJPE (mean per-joint position error) and MPVPE (mean per-vertex position error) all in 3D.

We split the training set of H80K (composed of $\approx 54,000$ images) into train, eval and test. As there are no publicly available statistical body model fittings for H80K data, we had to build them ourselves. Based on the ground truth 3D joint positions $\widehat{\mathbf{J}}_{3D}$ (this is used to retrieve pose $\widehat{\boldsymbol{\theta}}$) and the available 3D subject scans (used to retrieve shape $\widehat{\boldsymbol{\beta}}$) provided with the dataset, we optimize a fitting objective (solved using BFGS). We then project the 3D meshes associated to motion captured body configurations in each frame, to obtain ground truth 2D annotations, $\widehat{\mathbf{J}}_{2d}$ and $\widehat{\mathbf{S}}_{2d}$. We thus have full supervision on H80K in the form of $\left(\widehat{\boldsymbol{\theta}}, \widehat{\boldsymbol{\beta}}, \widehat{\mathbf{J}}_{2d}, \widehat{\mathbf{S}}_{2d}\right)$ for each image in the training set.

We also use CMU [11] and AMASS [23] to train 3D pose priors. Both datasets have publicly available kinematic model fittings and we used the $\widehat{\boldsymbol{\theta}}$ values to train our normalizing pose model $p_\phi(\boldsymbol{\theta})$. This results in priors over ambient and latent spaces, $\psi_{nf}(\mathbf{f}(\boldsymbol{\theta}))$ and $\psi_{nf}(\mathbf{z})$, respectively. Similar models were trained for H80K.

For weakly supervised learning 'in the wild', we use a subset of 15,000 images from COCO 2014 [20]. The dataset has no 3D ground truth, but offers 2D annotations for human body joints $\widehat{\mathbf{J}}_{2d}$, as well semantic segmentation of body parts $\widehat{\mathbf{S}}_{2d}$. We split the data in 14,000 examples for training and 1,000 for testing, and use it for building the weakly supervised models. We refer to models trained using 2D body joints and semantic body part losses as KA and BA, respectively.

**Optimization with Different Priors and Losses.** In order to analyze the impact of priors and semantic segmentation losses on optimization, we choose H80K where ground-truth is available for all components including 3D camera, pose and shape. We perform non-linear optimization with the objective function as defined in (11), where $L_\psi$ is changed to accommodate all the various priors, and $L_{KA}$ and $L_{BA}$ are studied both together and independently.

We evaluate different prior types: i) $\psi_{gmm}(\boldsymbol{\theta})$ – GMM [2], ii) $\psi_{nf}(\mathbf{f}(\boldsymbol{\theta}))$ and $\psi_{nf}(\mathbf{z})$ – normalizing flow in ambient and latent space, as given by (5), and (6), using either the angle-axis or the 6D representation, iii) $\psi_{VPoser}(\mathbf{z})$ – the variational auto-encoder VPoser of [29], iv) $\psi_{hmr}(\boldsymbol{\theta})$ – the discriminator of [12].

We also evaluate different datasets (CMU, H80K, AMASS) for prior construction, different loss functions based on either body joints/keypoints or semantic segmentation of body parts (KA and BA). To directly compare with VPoser, we train a light-weight normalizing flow prior ($\approx 93,000$ parameters compared to $\approx 344,000$ for VPoser), with the same operating speed, and constructed on the same dataset (AMASS) and train/test splits.

To isolate confounding factors, optimization is performed using the ground-truth 2D joints (KA) and body part labels (BA), under a perspective projection model, by using the loss defined at (11). Optimization relies on BFGS with analytical Jacobians, obtained through automatic differentiation. We start with four different initializations and report the solution with the smaller loss (N.B. this does not require observing the ground truth). We consider four different global rotations, and initialize parameters with **0**, for pose (either in ambient or latent space) and shape.

We test the model on 500 images and report results in Table 1. The best results are achieved by normalizing flow priors when optimization is performed in latent space. By using both keypoint and body part alignment-based self-supervision, the results improve. The 6D rotation representation has a slight edge over the angle-axis. The light-weight normalizing flow trained on AMASS is the best performer, surpassing VPoser even at a third of its capacity. Note that we do not have to balance two terms (the reconstruction loss and the KL-divergence), as normalizing flows support exact latent-variable inference. Additionally, VPoser requires posing meshes *during training*, whereas normalizing flow models do not.

**Table 1.** Optimization-based pose and shape estimation experiments with evaluation on the ground truth of H80K dataset. Priors are learned on the training sets of CMU, AMASS or H80K. The HMR discriminator has the largest errors, as it was arguably designed for use with deep neural network losses, and not for model fitting. Optimizing in latent space (using normalizing flows) and semantic alignment always helps. The 6D representation performs slightly better than angle-axis. The best performers are objective functions that include normalizing flow priors trained on H80K or AMASS. VPoser performs slightly worse than our normalizing flow prior, even though it also encodes and decodes 6D rotations. *Notation:* AA = angle-axis representation, 6D = 6 dimensions rotation representation, RM = rotation matrices, KA = keypoint alignment, BA = body alignment.

| Method | Error (cm) |
|---|---|
| *prior, dataset, representation, features* | MPJPE/MPVPE |
| $\psi_{gmm}(\boldsymbol{\theta})$, CMU, AA, KA | 7.9/10.4 |
| $\psi_{gmm}(\boldsymbol{\theta})$, CMU, AA, KA + BA | 6.9/9.6 |
| $\psi_{VPoser}(\mathbf{z})$, AMASS, 6D, KA | 4.6/6.7 |
| $\psi_{nf}(\mathbf{z})$, AMASS, 6D, KA | **4.3/6.0** |
| $\psi_{hmr}(\boldsymbol{\theta})$, H3.6M, RM, KA | 11.9/15.3 |
| $\psi_{nf}(\mathbf{f}(\boldsymbol{\theta}))$, CMU, AA, KA | 6.2/8.4 |
| $\psi_{nf}(\mathbf{f}(\boldsymbol{\theta}))$, CMU, AA, KA + BA | 6.0/8.1 |
| $\psi_{nf}(\mathbf{z})$, CMU, AA, KA | 5.0/7.1 |
| $\psi_{nf}(\mathbf{z})$, CMU, AA, KA + BA | 4.9/6.9 |
| $\psi_{nf}(\mathbf{f}(\boldsymbol{\theta}))$, CMU, 6D, KA | 6.1/8.4 |
| $\psi_{nf}(\mathbf{f}(\boldsymbol{\theta}))$, CMU, 6D, KA + BA | 5.8/8.0 |
| $\psi_{nf}(\mathbf{z})$, CMU, 6D, KA | 5.1/6.8 |
| $\psi_{nf}(\mathbf{z})$, CMU, 6D, KA + BA | 4.8/6.6 |
| $\psi_{nf}(\mathbf{f}(\boldsymbol{\theta}))$, H80K, AA, KA | 5.4/7.5 |
| $\psi_{nf}(\mathbf{z})$, H80K, AA, KA | 4.4/6.1 |

**Table 2.** Ablations on H80K, reported as MPJPE/MPVPE metrics in millimeters. Notice the impact of weakly supervised losses (WS), especially in the fully supervised (FS) regime with small training sets, as well as for the model initialized randomly (column two, 0% supervision).

| Percentage Supervised | 0% | 20% | 40% | 60% | 80% | 100% |
|---|---|---|---|---|---|---|
| FS (mm) | 649/677 | 117/136 | 101/118 | 93/109 | 86/102 | 83/97.15 |
| WS (mm) | | **123/140** | **97/111** | **92/108** | **90/106** | **85/101** | 84/98.85 |

**Fully to Weakly Supervised Transfer Learning.** We present experiments and ablation studies showing how the weakly supervised training of shape and pose parameters $(\theta, \beta)$ can be successful in conjunction with the proposed normalizing flow priors and self-supervised losses.

For this study, we split H80K into two parts where we keep 5 subjects for training (S1, S5, S6, S7 and S8) and two subjects (S9, S11) for testing.

We further split the training set into partitions of 20%, 40%, 60%, 80%, 100%. We initially train the network fully supervised (FS) on the specific partition of the data using $L_{fs}$ loss. We train the fully supervised model for 30 epochs, then continue in a weakly supervised (WS) regime based on $L_{ws}$ on all the data. In Table 2 we report MPJPE/MPVPE for the ablation study. Notice that in all cases weak supervision improves performance whenever additional image data is available.

We also check that our methodology compares favorably to a similar method HMR [12] which we retrained on H80K. In this case our model achieves 84 mm MPJE whereas HMR has 88 mm.[2] We were not able to train on their split and retargeting of H3.6M, as their training data was not available.

**Weakly Supervised Transfer for Images in the Wild.** In order to validate our network predictions beyond a motion capture laboratory, 'in the wild', we refined the network on the subset of COCO which has body part labelling available. We started with a network pre-trained on H80K, then continued training on COCO using the complete loss. As ground truth 3D is not available for COCO, we monitor errors between ground truth and estimated 2D projections of the 3D model joints, and the IoU semantic body part alignment metrics. As shown in Fig. 4, in all cases the pixel error of the projected 2D joints decreased consistently, as a result of weakly supervised fine tuning. A similar trend can be seen for the IoU metric computed for body part alignment, illustrating the importance of a segmentation loss. We explicitly run two configurations, one in which we only use the keypoints alignment (KA) and another based on body part alignment (KA+BA).

A potentially interesting question is whether the 3D prediction is affected by a self-supervised refinement. We run experiments on 3DPW [24] which consists

---

[2] Based on HMR's Github repository, we identify a total of $\approx$27M trainable parameters. Our model has 6 stages, each with $5 \times 7 \times 7 \times 128 \times 128$ parameters resulting in $\approx$24M trainable parameters.

**Table 3.** Results on the 3DPW test set for two regimes: **static** and **video**. FS is fully supervised, FS+OPT are predictions from FS with optimization. FS+WS are results for self-supervised refinement of the FS model on MS COCO. 'S' stands for smoothing in the video regime. MPJPE is the mean per joint position error, whereas MPJPE-PA is the error after Procrustes alignment. **Static:** we observe that the self-supervised training did not affect the performance of the 3D predictions. The semantic alignment loss reduces error more than only keypoints alignment. Perceptually, image alignment is also much better for BA than KA, even when it does not immediately produce significant 3D quantitative improvements. **Video:** the best performer is our FS+WS (KA+BA) model, further optimized over 16 frames with the temporal smoothing term.

|  | Method | MPJPE (mm) | MPJPE-PA (mm) |
|---|---|---|---|
| **STATIC** | HMR [12] | - | 81.3 |
| | Kanazawa et al. [13] | - | 72.6 |
| | SPIN [18] (static fits) | - | 66.3 |
| | SPIN [18] (best) | - | 59.2 |
| | FS | 95 | 61.3 |
| | FS+OPT (KA) | 95 | 60.3 |
| | FS+OPT (KA+BA) | 91.4 | 58.87 |
| | FS+WS (KA+BA) | **90.0** | **57.1** |
| **VIDEO** | VIBE [17](16 frames) | 82.9 | 51.9 |
| | FS+OPT(KA+BA+S, 16 frames) | 82.8 | 52.2 |
| | FS+WS+OPT(KA+BA+S, 4 frames) | 84.5 | 54.5 |
| | FS+WS+OPT(KA+BA+S, 8 frames) | 82.0 | 51.4 |
| | FS+WS+OPT(KA+BA+S, 16 frames) | **80.2** | **49.8** |

of $\approx 60,000$ images containing one or more humans performing various actions in the wild. The subjects were recorded using IMUs so shape and pose parameters were recovered. We used the training data as supervision, and evaluate on the test set. We report results for a model trained only with full supervision, as well as results of refining the fully supervised (feed-forward) estimate by further optimizing the KA, and KA+BA losses against the predicted 2D outputs (keypoint and body part alignment). After training the network in the weakly supervised regime we obtain better accuracy, showing that 3D prediction quality is preserved. We show the results in Table 3. To the best of our knowledge, these are the lowest errors reported so far on the 3DPW test set in a static setting.

**Temporal Optimization.** We also experiment in the temporal setting, on batches of 4, 8 and 16 consecutive frames drawn from the 3DPW dataset. Starting from the best results obtained per frame in the static setting, we do a whole batch optimization. Different from the $L_{ws}$ objective, now the shape parameters are tied across frames, with an additional term that enforces smoothness between adjacent temporal pose parameters (in latent space):

$$L_{smooth} = \sum_{t=2}^{N_f} \left\| \mathbf{z}^t - \mathbf{z}^{t-1} \right\|_2^2 \qquad (12)$$

The weight for this term is set to be 50× the weight of the prior, as we expect a lower variance for pose dynamics. We compare our method with the recent work of [17], showing the results in Table 3. As in the static setting, these are also the lowest errors reported so far.

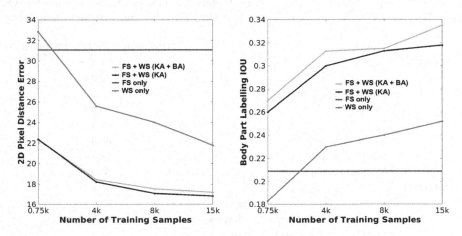

**Fig. 4.** *Left and Right*: Weakly supervised experiments on COCO with different loss combinations (KA, KA+BA) and different amounts of training data. The baseline is obtained by running the network trained fully supervised on H80K. WS Only is trained only on COCO.

## 4    Conclusions

We have presented large scale weakly supervised deep learning-based models for 3D human pose and shape estimation from monocular images and video. Key to scalability is unlocking the ability to exploit human statistics implicitly available in large, diverse image repositories, which however do not come with detailed 3D pose or shape supervision. Key to making such approaches feasible, in terms of identifying model parameters with good generalization performance, is the ability to design training losses that are tightly controlled by both the existing prior knowledge on human pose and shape, and by the image and video evidence.

We introduce latent normalizing flow representations and dynamical models, as well as fully differentiable, structured, semantic body party alignment (reprojection) loss functions which provide informative feedback for self-supervised learning. In extensive, large-scale experiments, using both motion capture datasets like CMU, Human3.6M, AMASS, or 3DPW, as well as 'in the wild' repositories like COCO, we show that our proposed methodology achieves state-of-the-art results in both images and video, supporting the claim that constructing accurate models based on large-scale weak supervision 'in the wild' is possible.

# References

1. Arnab, A., Doersch, C., Zisserman, A.: Exploiting temporal context for 3D human pose estimation in the wild. In: Proceedings of the IEEE Conference on Computer Vision and Pattern Recognition, pp. 3395–3404. IEEE (2019)
2. Bogo, F., Kanazawa, A., Lassner, C., Gehler, P., Romero, J., Black, M.J.: Keep it SMPL: automatic estimation of 3D human pose and shape from a single image. In: Leibe, B., Matas, J., Sebe, N., Welling, M. (eds.) ECCV 2016. LNCS, vol. 9909, pp. 561–578. Springer, Cham (2016). https://doi.org/10.1007/978-3-319-46454-1_34
3. Cao, Z., Simon, T., Wei, S., Sheikh, Y.: Realtime multi-person 2D pose estimation using part affinity fields. In: Proceedings of the IEEE conference on computer vision and pattern recognition, pp. 7291–7299. IEEE (2017)
4. Dinh, L., Krueger, D., Bengio, Y.: Nice: non-linear independent components estimation. arXiv preprint arXiv:1410.8516 (2014)
5. Dinh, L., Sohl-Dickstein, J., Bengio, S.: Density estimation using real nvp. arXiv preprint arXiv:1605.08803 (2016)
6. Doersch, C., Zisserman, A.: Sim2real transfer learning for 3D human pose estimation: motion to the rescue. In: Advances in Neural Information Processing Systems, pp. 12929–12941 (2019)
7. Germain, M., Gregor, K., Murray, I., Larochelle, H.: Made: masked autoencoder for distribution estimation. In: International Conference on Machine Learning, pp. 881–889 (2015)
8. Ionescu, C., Papava, D., Olaru, V., Sminchisescu, C.: Human3.6M: large scale datasets and predictive methods for 3D human sensing in natural environments. IEEE Trans. Pattern Anal. Mach. Intell. **36**(7), 1325–1339 (2014)
9. Iskakov, K., Burkov, E., Lempitsky, V., Malkov, Y.: Learnable triangulation of human pose. In: Proceedings of the IEEE International Conference on Computer Vision, pp. 7718–7727 (2019)
10. Jackson, A.S., Manafas, C., Tzimiropoulos, G.: 3D human body reconstruction from a single image via volumetric regression. In: Proceedings of the European Conference on Computer Vision (ECCV) (2018)
11. Joo, H., Simon, T., Sheikh, Y.: Total capture: a 3D deformation model for tracking faces, hands, and bodies. In Proceedings of the IEEE conference on computer vision and pattern recognition, pp. 8320–8329 (2018)
12. Kanazawa, A., Black, M.J., Jacobs, D.W., Malik, J.: End-to-end recovery of human shape and pose. In: Proceedings of the IEEE Conference on Computer Vision and Pattern Recognition, pp. 7122–7131 (2018)
13. Kanazawa, A., Zhang, J.Y., Felsen, P., Malik, J.: Learning 3D human dynamics from video. In: Proceedings of the IEEE Conference on Computer Vision and Pattern Recognition, pp. 5614–5623 (2019)
14. Kato, H., Ushiku, Y., Harada, T.: Neural 3d mesh renderer. In: Proceedings of the IEEE Conference on Computer Vision and Pattern Recognition, pp. 3907–3916 (2018)
15. Kingma, D.P., Dhariwal, P.: Glow: generative flow with invertible $1 \times 1$ convolutions. In: Advances in neural information processing systems, pp. 10215–10224 (2018)
16. Kingma, D.P., Salimans, T., Jozefowicz, R., Chen, X., Sutskever, I., Welling, M.: Improved variational inference with inverse autoregressive flow. In: Advances in neural information processing systems, pp. 4743–4751 (2016)

17. Kocabas, M., Athanasiou, N., Black, M.J.: Vibe: video inference for human body pose and shape estimation. arXiv preprint arXiv:1912.05656 (2019)
18. Kolotouros, N., Pavlakos, G., Black, M.J., Daniilidis, K.: Learning to reconstruct 3D human pose and shape via model-fitting in the loop. In: Proceedings of the IEEE International Conference on Computer Vision, pp. 2252–2261 (2019)
19. Kolotouros, N., Pavlakos, G., Daniilidis, K.: Convolutional mesh regression for single-image human shape reconstruction. In: Proceedings of the IEEE Conference on Computer Vision and Pattern Recognition, pp. 4501–4510 (2019)
20. Lin, T.-Y., et al.: Microsoft COCO: common objects in context. In: Fleet, D., Pajdla, T., Schiele, B., Tuytelaars, T. (eds.) ECCV 2014. LNCS, vol. 8693, pp. 740–755. Springer, Cham (2014). https://doi.org/10.1007/978-3-319-10602-1_48
21. Loper, M., Mahmood, N., Romero, J., Pons-Moll, G., Black, M.J.: SMPL: a skinned multi-person linear model. ACM Trans. Graph. (TOG) 34(6), 1–16 (2015)
22. Loper, M.M., Black, M.J.: OpenDR: an approximate differentiable renderer. In: Fleet, D., Pajdla, T., Schiele, B., Tuytelaars, T. (eds.) ECCV 2014. LNCS, vol. 8695, pp. 154–169. Springer, Cham (2014). https://doi.org/10.1007/978-3-319-10584-0_11
23. Mahmood, N., Ghorbani, N., Troje, N.F., Pons-Moll, G., Black, M.J.: Amass: archive of motion capture as surface shapes. arXiv preprint arXiv:1904.03278 (2019)
24. von Marcard, T., Henschel, R., Black, M., Rosenhahn, B., Pons-Moll, G.: Recovering accurate 3D human pose in the wild using imus and a moving camera. In: Proceedings of the European Conference on Computer Vision (ECCV), pp. 601–617 (2018)
25. Martinez, J., Hossain, R., Romero, J., Little, J.J.: A simple yet effective baseline for 3d human pose estimation. In: ICCV (2017)
26. Mehta, D., et al.: Vnect: real-time 3D human pose estimation with a single rgb camera. ACM Trans. Graph. (TOG) 36(4), 1–14 (2017)
27. Omran, M., Lassner, C., Pons-Moll, G., Gehler, P.V., Schiele, B.: Neural body fitting: unifying deep learning and model-based human pose and shape estimation. In: 2018 international conference on 3D vision (3DV), pp. 484–494 IEEE (2018)
28. Papamakarios, G., Pavlakou, T., Murray, I.: Masked autoregressive flow for density estimation. In: Advances in Neural Information Processing Systems, pp. 2338–2347 (2017)
29. Pavlakos, G., et al.: Expressive body capture: 3d hands, face, and body from a single image. In: Proceedings of the IEEE Conference on Computer Vision and Pattern Recognition, pp. 10975–10985. IEEE (2019)
30. Pavlakos, G., Zhou, X., Derpanis, K.G., Daniilidis, K.: Coarse-to-fine volumetric prediction for single-image 3D human pose. In: Proceedings of the IEEE Conference on Computer Vision and Pattern Recognition, pp. 7025–7034 IEEE (2017)
31. Pavlakos, G., Zhu, L., Zhou, X., Daniilidis, K.: Learning to estimate 3D human pose and shape from a single color image. In: Proceedings of the IEEE Conference on Computer Vision and Pattern Recognition, pp. 459–468. IEEE (2018)
32. Popa, A., Zanfir, M., Sminchisescu, C.: Deep multitask architecture for integrated 2D and 3D human sensing. In: Proceedings of the IEEE Conference on Computer Vision and Pattern Recognition, pp. 6289–6298. IEEE (2017)
33. Rezende, D.J., Mohamed, S.: Variational inference with normalizing flows. arXiv preprint arXiv:1505.05770 (2015)

34. Rhodin, H., Robertini, N., Richardt, C., Seidel, H.P., Theobalt, C.: A versatile scene model with differentiable visibility applied to generative pose estimation. In: Proceedings of the IEEE International Conference on Computer Vision, pp. 765–773 (2015)
35. Rogez, G., Schmid, C.: Mocap-guided data augmentation for 3D pose estimation in the wild. In: Advances in neural information processing systems, pp. 3108–3116 (2016)
36. Sun, Y., Ye, Y., Liu, W., Gao, W., Fu, Y., Mei, T.: Human mesh recovery from monocular images via a skeleton-disentangled representation. In: Proceedings of the IEEE International Conference on Computer Vision, pp. 5349–5358 (2019)
37. Tekin, B., Marquez Neila, P., Salzmann, M., Fua, P.: Learning to fuse 2D and 3D image cues for monocular body pose estimation. In: Proceedings of the IEEE International Conference on Computer Vision. pp. 3941–3950 (2017)
38. Tung, H.Y., Tung, H.W., Yumer, E., Fragkiadaki, K.: Self-supervised learning of motion capture. In: Advances in Neural Information Processing Systems, pp. 5236–5246 (2017)
39. Varol, G., et al.: BodyNet: volumetric inference of 3D human body shapes. In: Proceedings of the European Conference on Computer Vision (ECCV), pp. 20–36 (2018)
40. Wei, S.E., Ramakrishna, V., Kanade, T., Sheikh, Y.: Convolutional pose machines. In: Proceedings of the IEEE conference on Computer Vision and Pattern Recognition, pp. 4724–4732. IEEE (2016)
41. Xu, H., Bazavan, E.G., Zanfir, A., Freeman, W.T., Sukthankar, R., Sminchisescu, C.: Ghum & ghuml: generative 3D human shape and articulated pose models. In: Proceedings of the IEEE/CVF Conference on Computer Vision and Pattern Recognition, pp. 6184–6193 (2020)
42. Xu, Y., Zhu, S.C., Tung, T.: Denserac: joint 3D pose and shape estimation by dense render-and-compare. In: Proceedings of the IEEE International Conference on Computer Vision, pp. 7760–7770. IEEE (2019)
43. Yang, W., Ouyang, W., Wang, X., Ren, J., Li, H., Wang, X.: 3D human pose estimation in the wild by adversarial learning. In: Proceedings of the IEEE Conference on Computer Vision and Pattern Recognition, pp. 5255–5264. IEEE (2018)
44. Zanfir, A., Marinoiu, E., Sminchisescu, C.: Monocular 3d pose and shape estimation of multiple people in natural scenes-the importance of multiple scene constraints. In: Proceedings of the IEEE Conference on Computer Vision and Pattern Recognition, pp. 2148–2157. IEEE (2018)
45. Zhang, C., Pujades, S., Black, M.J., Pons-Moll, G.: Detailed, accurate, human shape estimation from clothed 3D scan sequences. In: Proceedings of the IEEE Conference on Computer Vision and Pattern Recognition, pp. 4191–4200. IEEE(2017)
46. Zhou, X., Huang, Q., Sun, X., Xue, X., Wei, Y.: Towards 3D human pose estimation in the wild: a weakly-supervised approach. In: Proceedings of the IEEE International Conference on Computer Vision, pp. 398–407. IEEE (2017)
47. Zhou, Y., Barnes, C., Lu, J., Yang, J., Li, H.: On the continuity of rotation representations in neural networks. arXiv preprint arXiv:1812.07035 (2018)

# Controlling Style and Semantics in Weakly-Supervised Image Generation

Dario Pavllo[(✉)], Aurelien Lucchi, and Thomas Hofmann

Department of Computer Science, ETH Zurich, Zürich, Switzerland
`dario.pavllo@inf.ethz.ch`

**Abstract.** We propose a weakly-supervised approach for conditional image generation of complex scenes where a user has fine control over objects appearing in the scene. We exploit sparse semantic maps to control object shapes and classes, as well as textual descriptions or attributes to control both local and global style. In order to condition our model on textual descriptions, we introduce a semantic attention module whose computational cost is independent of the image resolution. To further augment the controllability of the scene, we propose a two-step generation scheme that decomposes background and foreground. The label maps used to train our model are produced by a large-vocabulary object detector, which enables access to unlabeled data and provides structured instance information. In such a setting, we report better FID scores compared to fully-supervised settings where the model is trained on ground-truth semantic maps. We also showcase the ability of our model to manipulate a scene on complex datasets such as COCO and Visual Genome.

## 1 Introduction

Deep generative models such as VAEs [23] and GANs [9] have made it possible to learn complex distributions over various types of data, including images and text. For images, recent technical advances [1,13,20,28,29,49] have enabled GANs to produce realistically-looking images for a large number of classes. However, these models often do not provide high-level control over image characteristics such as appearance, shape, texture, or color, and they fail to accurately model multiple (or compound) objects in a scene, thus limiting their practical applications. A related line of research aims at disentangling factors of variation [21]. While these approaches can produce images with varied styles by injecting noise at different levels, the style factors are learned without any oversight, leaving the user with a loose handle on the generation process. Furthermore, their applicability has only been demonstrated for single-domain images (e.g. faces, cars, or birds). Some conditional approaches allow users to control the style of an image using

**Electronic supplementary material** The online version of this chapter (https://doi.org/10.1007/978-3-030-58539-6_29) contains supplementary material, which is available to authorized users.

A. Vedaldi et al. (Eds.): ECCV 2020, LNCS 12351, pp. 482–499, 2020.
https://doi.org/10.1007/978-3-030-58539-6_29

**Fig. 1.** Our approach enables control over the style of a scene and its objects via high-level attributes or textual descriptions. It also allows for image manipulation through the mask, including moving, deleting, or adding object instances. The decomposition of the background and foreground (top-right corner) facilitates local changes in a scene.

either attributes [12,46] or natural language [45,50,51], but again, these methods only show compelling results on single-domain datasets.

One key aspect in generative modeling is the amount of required semantic information: i) *weak conditioning* (e.g. a sentence that describes a scene) makes the task underconstrained and harder to learn, potentially resulting in incoherent images on complex datasets. On the other hand, ii) *rich semantic information* (e.g. full segmentation masks) yields the best generative quality, but requires more effort from an artist or annotator. The applications of such richly-conditioned models are numerous, including art, animation, image manipulation, and realistic texturing of video games. Existing works in this category [4,17,31,32,44] typically require hand-labeled segmentation masks with per-pixel class annotations. Unfortunately, this is not flexible enough for downstream applications such as image manipulation, where the artist is faced with the burden of modifying the semantic mask coherently. Common transformations such as moving, deleting, or replacing an object require instance information (usually not available) and a strategy for infilling the background. Moreover, these models present little-to-no high-level control over the style of an image and its objects.

Our work combines the merits of both weak conditioning and strong semantic information, by relying on both mask-based generation – using a variant we call *sparse masks* – and text-based generation – which can be used to control the style of the objects contained in the scene as well as its global aspects. Figure 1 conceptualizes our idea. Our approach uses a large-vocabulary object detector to obtain annotations, which are then used to train a generative model in a weakly-supervised fashion. The input masks are sparse and retain instance information – making them easy to manipulate – and can be inferred from images or videos in-the-wild. We additionally contribute a conditioning scheme for controlling the style of the scene and its instances, either using high-level attributes or natural language with an attention mechanism. Unlike prior approaches, our attention model is applied directly to semantic maps (making it easily interpretable) and its computational cost does not depend on the image resolution, enabling its use in high-resolution settings. This conditioning module is general enough to be plugged into existing architectures. We also tackle another issue of existing generative models: local changes made to an object (such as moving or deleting) can affect the scene globally due to the learned correlations between classes. While these entangled representations improve scene coherence, they do not allow the user to modify a local part of a scene without affecting the rest. To this end, our approach relies on a multi-step generation process where we first generate a *background image* and then we generate foreground objects conditioned on the former. The background can be frozen while manipulating foreground objects.

Finally, we evaluate our approach on COCO [2,5,26] and Visual Genome [25], and show that our weakly-supervised setting can achieve better FID scores [13] than fully-supervised counterparts trained on ground-truth masks, and weakly-supervised counterparts where the model is trained on dense maps obtained from an off-the-shelf semantic segmentation model, while being more controllable and scalable to large unlabeled datasets. We show that this holds both in presence and in absence of style control.

Code is available at https://github.com/dariopavllo/style-semantics.

## 2   Related Work

The recent success of GANs has triggered interest for conditional image synthesis from categorical labels [1,28,29,49], text [33,45,50,51], semantic maps [17,31, 44], and conditioning images from other domains [17,53].

**Image Generation from Semantic Maps.** In this setting, a semantic segmentation map is translated into a natural image. Non-adversarial approaches are typically based on perceptual losses [4,32], whereas GAN architectures are based on patch-based discriminators [17], progressive growing [20,44], and conditional batch normalization where the semantic map is fed to the model at different resolutions [31]. Similarly to other state-of-the-art methods, our work is also based on this paradigm. Most approaches are trained on hand-labeled masks (limiting their application in the wild), but [31] shows one example where the model is weakly supervised on masks inferred using a semantic segmentation model [3]. Our model is also weakly supervised, but instead of a semantic segmentation model we use an object detector – which allows us to maintain instance information during manipulations, and results in *sparse masks*. While early work focused on class semantics, recent methods support some degree of style control. E.g. [44] trains an instance autoencoder and allows the user to choose a latent code from among a set of modes, whereas [31] trains a VAE to control the global style of a generated image by copying the style of a *guide* image. Both these methods, however, do not provide fine-grained style control (e.g. changing the color of an object to *red*). Another recent trend consists in

Ground-truth mask  Manipulated mask  Fill with "road"  Semantic seg.  Sparse mask  Instance map  Manipulated mask

Generated  Fill with "no class"  Fill with "building"  Generated  Ground-truth image  Generated  Generated

**Fig. 2. Left:** when manipulating a ground-truth mask (e.g. deleting one bus), one is left with the problem of infilling the background which is prone to ambiguities (e.g. selecting a new class as either road or building). Furthermore, in existing models, local changes affect the scene globally due to learned correlations. **Middle:** in the wild, ground-truth masks are not available (neither are instance maps). One can infer maps using a semantic segmentation model, but these are often noisy and lack instance information (in the example above, we observe that the two buses are merged). **Right:** our weakly-supervised sparse mask setting, which combines fine-detailed masks with instance information. The two-step decomposition ensures that changes are localized.

generating images from structured layouts, which are transformed into semantic maps as an intermediate step to facilitate the task. In this regard, there is work on generation from bounding-box layouts [14,15,40,52] and scene graphs [18]. Although these approaches tackle a harder task, they generate low-resolution images and are not directly relatable to our work, which tackles controllability among other aspects.

**Semantic Control.** Existing approaches do not allow for easy manipulation of the semantic map because they present no interface for encoding existing images. In principle, it is possible to train a weakly-supervised model on maps inferred from a semantic segmentation model, as [31] does for landscapes. However, as we show in Sect. 4.2, the results in this setting are notably worse than fully-supervised baselines. Furthermore, manipulations are still challenging because instance information is not available. Since the label masks are *dense*, even simple transformations such as deleting or moving an object would create holes in the semantic map that need to be adjusted by the artist (Fig. 2). *Dense* masks also make the task too constrained with respect to background aspects of the scene (e.g. sky, land, weather), which leaves less room for style control. Semantic control can also be framed as an unpaired image-to-image translation task [30], but this requires ground-truth masks for both source and target instances, and can only translate between two classes.

**Text-Based Generation.** Some recent models condition the generative process on text data. These are often based on autoregressive architectures [34] and GANs [33,45,50,51]. Learning to generate images from text using GANs is known to be difficult due to the task being unconstrained. In order to ease the training process, [50,51] propose a two-stage architecture named *StackGAN*. To avoid the instability associated with training a language model jointly with a GAN, they use a pretrained sentence encoder [24] that encodes a caption into a fixed-length vector which is then fed to the model. More advanced architectures such as *AttnGAN* [45] use an attention mechanism which we discuss in one of the next paragraphs. These approaches show interesting results on single-domain datasets (birds, flowers, etc.) but are less effective on complex datasets such as *COCO* [26] due to the intrinsic difficulty of generating coherent scenes from text alone. Some works [19,48] have demonstrated that generative models can benefit from taking as input multiple diverse textual descriptions per image. Finally, we are not aware of any prior work that conditions the generative process on *both* text and semantic maps (our setting).

**Multi-step Generation.** Approaches such as [38,47] aim at disentangling background and foreground generation. While fully-unsupervised disentanglement is provably impossible [27], it is still achievable through some form of inductive bias – either in the model architecture or in the loss function. While [47] uses spatial transformers to achieve separation, [38] uses object bounding boxes. Both methods show compelling results on single-domain datasets that depict a centered object, but are not directly applicable to more challenging datasets. For composite scenes, [42] generates foreground objects sequentially to counteract merging effects. In our work, we are not interested in full disentanglement (i.e. we do not assume independence between background and foreground), but merely in separating the two steps while keeping them interpretable. Our model still exploits correlations among classes to maximize visual quality, and is applied to datasets with complex scenes. Finally, there has also been work on interactive generation using dialogue [6,8,36].

**Attention Models in GANs.** For unconditional models (or models conditioned on simple class labels), self-attention GANs [1,49] use visual-visual attention to improve spatial coherence. For generation from text, [45] employ sentence-visual attention coupled with an LSTM encoder, but only in the generator. In the discriminator, the caption is enforced through a supervised loss based on features extracted from a pretrained Inception [41] network. We introduce a new form of attention (*sentence-semantic*) which is applied to semantic maps instead of convolutional feature maps, and whose computational cost is independent of the image resolution. It is applied both to the generator and the discriminator, and on the sentence side it features a transformer-based [43] encoder.

# 3   Approach

## 3.1   Framework

Our main interest is conditional image generation of complex scenes where a user has fine control over the objects appearing in the scene. Prior work has focused on generating objects from ground-truth masks [17,31,44,53] or on generating outdoor scenes based on simple hand-drawn masks [31]. While the former approach requires a significant labeling effort, the latter is not directly suitable for complex datasets such as COCO-Stuff [2], whose images consist of a large number of classes with complex (hard to draw) shapes. We address these problems by introducing a new model that is conditioned on sparse masks – to control object shapes and classes – and on text/attributes to control style and textures. This gives the ability to a user to produce scenes through a variety of image manipulations (such as moving, scaling or deleting an instance, adding an instance from another image or from a database of shapes) as well as style manipulations controlled using either high-level attributes on individual instances (e.g. *red*, *green*, *wet*, *shiny*) or using text that refers to objects as well as global context (e.g. "a red car at night"). In the latter case, visual-textual correlations are not explicitly defined but are learned in an unsupervised way.

**Sparse Masks.** Instead of training a model on precise segmentation masks as in [17,31,44], we use a mask generated automatically from a large-vocabulary object detector. Compared to a weakly-supervised setting based on semantic segmentation, this process introduces less artifacts (see Appendix A.4 in the supplementary material) and has the benefit of providing information about each instance (which may not always be available otherwise), including parts of objects which would require significant manual effort to label in a new dataset. In general, our set of classes comprises countable objects (person, car, etc.), parts of objects (light, window, door, etc.), as well as uncountable classes (grass, water, snow), which are typically referred to as "stuff" in the COCO terminology [2]. For the latter category, an object detector can still provide useful sparse information about the background, while keeping the model autonomous to fill-in the gaps. We describe the details of our object detection setup in Sect. 4.1.

**Two-Step Generation.** In the absence of constraints, conditional models learn class correlations observed in the training data. For instance, while dogs typically stand on green grass, zebras stand on yellow grass. While this feature is useful for maximizing scene coherence, it is undesirable when only a local change in the image is wanted. We observed similar global effects on other local transformations, such as moving an object or changing its attributes, and generally speaking, small perturbations of the input can result in large variations of the output. We show a few examples in the Appendix A.4. To tackle this issue, we propose a variant of our architecture which we call *two-step* model and which consists of two concatenated generators (Fig. 3, right). The first step (generator $G_1$) is responsible for generating a *background* image, whereas the second step (generator $G_2$) generates a *foreground* image conditioned on the background image. The definition of what constitutes background and foreground is arbitrary: our choice is to separate by class: static/uncountable objects (e.g. buildings, roads, grass, and other surfaces) are assigned to *background*, and moving/countable objects are assigned to *foreground*. Some classes can switch roles depending on the parent class, e.g. *window* is *background* by default, but it becomes *foreground* if it is a child of a foreground object such as a car.

When applying a local transformation to a foreground object, the background can conveniently be frozen to avoid global changes. As a side benefit, this also results in a lower computational cost to regenerate an image. Unlike work on disentanglement [38,47] which enforces that the background is independent of the foreground without necessarily optimizing for visual quality, our goal is to enforce separation while maximizing qualitative results. In our setting, $G_1$ is exposed to both background and foreground objects, but its architecture is designed in a way that foreground information is not rendered, but only used to induce a bias in the background (see Sect. 3.2).

**Attributes.** Our method allows the user to control the style of individual instances using high-level attributes. These attributes refer to appearance factors such as colors (e.g. white, black, red), materials (wood, glass), and even modifiers that are specific to classes (leafless, snowy), but not shape or size, since these two are determined by the mask. An object can also combine multiple attributes (e.g. black and white) or have none – in this case, the generator would pick a predefined mode. This setup gives the user a lot of flexibility to manipulate a scene, since the attributes need not be specified for every object.

**Captions.** Alternatively, one can consider conditioning style using natural language. This has the benefit of being more expressive, and allows the user to control global aspects of the scene (e.g. time of the day, weather, landscape) in addition to instance-specific aspects. While this kind of conditioning is harder to learn than plain attributes, in Sect. 3.2 we introduce a new attention model that shows compelling results without excessively increasing the model complexity.

## 3.2   Architecture

We design our conditioning mechanisms to have sufficient generality to be attached to existing conditional generative models. In our experiments, we choose *SPADE* [31] as the backbone for our conditioning modules, which to our knowledge represents the state of the art. As in [31], we use a multi-scale discriminator [44], a perceptual loss in the generator using a pretrained VGG network [37], and a feature matching loss in the discriminator [44].

**One-Step Model.** Since this model (Fig. 3, left) serves as a baseline, we keep its backbone as close as possible to the reference model of [31]. We propose to

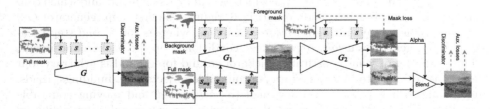

**Fig. 3. Left:** One-step model. **Right:** two-step model. The background generator $G_1$ takes as input a *background mask* (processed by $S$-blocks) and the full mask (processed by $S_{avg}$-blocks, where positional information is removed). The foreground generator takes as input the output of $G_1$ and a *foreground mask*. Finally, the two outputs are alpha-blended. For convenience, we do not show attributes/text in this figure.

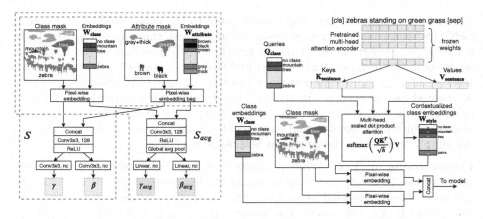

**Fig. 4. Left:** Conditioning block with attributes. Class and attribute embeddings are concatenated and processed to generate the conditional batch normalization gain and bias. In the attribute mask, embeddings take the contour of the instance to which they refer. In $G_1$ of the two-step model, where $S$ and $S_{avg}$ are both used, the embedding weights are shared. **Right:** Attention mechanism for conditioning style via text. The sentence (of length $n = 7$ including delimiters) is fed to a pretrained attention encoder, and each token is transformed into a key and a value using two trainable linear layers. The queries are learned for each class, and the attention yields a set of contextualized class embeddings that are concatenated to the regular semantic embeddings.

insert the required information about attributes/captions in this architecture by modifying the input layer and the conditional batch normalization layers of the generator, which is where semantic information is fed to the model. We name these $S$-blocks (short for *semantic-style* block).

**Semantic-Style Block.** For class semantics, the input sparse mark is fed to a pixel-wise embedding layer to convert categorical labels into 64D embeddings (including the empty space, which is a special class "no class"). To add style information, we optionally concatenate another 64D representation to the class embedding (pixel-wise); we explain how we derive this representation in the next two paragraphs. The resulting feature map is convolved with a $3 \times 3$ kernel, passed through a ReLU non-linearity and convolved again to produce two feature maps $\gamma$ and $\beta$, respectively, the conditional batch normalization gain and bias. The normalization is then computed as $\mathbf{y} = \mathrm{BN}(\mathbf{x}) \odot (1 + \gamma) + \beta$, where $\mathrm{BN}(\mathbf{x})$ is the parameter-free batch normalization. The last step is related to [31] and other architectures based on conditional batch normalization. Unlike [31], however, we do not use $3 \times 3$ convolutions on one-hot representations in the input layer. This allows us to scale to a larger number of classes without significantly increasing the number of parameters. We apply the same principle to the discriminators.

**Conditioning on Attributes.** For attributes, we adopt a *bag-of-embeddings* approach where we learn a 64D embedding for each possible attribute, and all attribute embeddings assigned to an instance are broadcast to the contour of the instance, summed together, and concatenated to the class embedding. Figure 4 (left) ($S$-block) depicts this process. To implement this efficiently, we create a multi-hot *attribute mask* (1 in the locations corresponding to the attributes assigned to the instance, 0 elsewhere) and feed it through a $1 \times 1$ convolutional layer with $N_{attr}$ input channels and 64 output channels. Attribute embeddings are shared among classes and are not class-specific. This helps the model generalize better (e.g. colors such as "white" apply both to vehicles and animals), and we empirically observe that implausible combinations (e.g. leafless person) are simply ignored by the generator without side effects.

**Conditioning on Text.** While previous work has used fixed-length vector representations [50,51] or one-layer attention models coupled with RNNs [45], the diversity of our scenes led us to use a more powerful encoder entirely based on self-attention [43]. We encode the image caption using a pretrained BERT$_{base}$ model [7] (110M parameters). It is unreasonable to attach such a model to a GAN and fine-tune it, both due to excessive memory requirements and due to potential instabilities. Instead, we freeze the pretrained model and encode the sentence, extract its hidden representation after the last or second-to-last layer (we compare these in Sect. 4.2), and train a custom multi-head attention layer for our task. This paradigm, which is also suggested by [7], has proven successful on a variety of NLP downstream tasks, especially when these involve small datasets or limited vocabularies. Furthermore, instead of storing the language model in memory, we simply pre-compute the sentence representations and cache them.

Next, we describe the design of our trainable attention layer (Fig. 4, right). Our attention mechanism is different from the commonly-used sentence-visual attention [45], where attention is directly applied to convolutional feature maps inside the generator. Instead, we propose a form of sentence-semantic attention which is computationally efficient, interpretable, and modular. It can be concatenated to conditioning layers in the same way as we concatenate attributes. Compared to sentence-visual attention, whose cost is $\mathcal{O}(nd^2)$ (where $n$ is the sentence length and $d \times d$ is the feature map resolution), our method has a cost of $\mathcal{O}(nc)$ (where $c$ is the number of classes), i.e. it is independent of the image resolution. We construct a set of $c$ *queries* (i.e. one for each class) of size $h = 64$ (where $h$ is the attention head size). We feed the hidden representations of each token of the sentence to two linear layers, one for the *keys* and one for the *values*. Finally, we compute a scaled dot-product attention [43], which yields a set of $c$ *values*. To allow the conditioning block to attend to multiple parts of the sentence, we use 6 or 12 attention heads (ablations in Sect. 4.2), whose output values are concatenated and further transformed through a linear layer. This process can be thought of as generating *contextualized class embeddings*, i.e. class embeddings customized according to the sentence. For instance, given a semantic map that depicts a car and the caption "a red car and a person", the query corresponding to the visual class *car* would most likely attend to "red car", and the corresponding value will induce a bias in the model to add redness to the position of the car. Finally, the *contextualized class embeddings* are applied to the semantic mask via pixel-wise matrix multiplication with one-hot vectors, and concatenated to the *class embeddings* in the same way as attributes. In the current formulation, this approach is unable to differentiate between instances of the same class. We propose a possible mitigation in Sect. 5.

**Two-Step Model.** It consists of two concatenated generators. $G_1$ generates the background, i.e. it models $p(x_{bg})$, whereas $G_2$ generates the foreground conditioned on the background, i.e. $p(x_{fg}|x_{bg})$. One notable difficulty in training such a model is that background images are never observed in the training set (we only observe the final image), therefore we cannot use an intermediate discriminator for $G_1$. Instead, we use a single, final discriminator and design the architecture in a way that the gradient of the discriminator (plus auxiliary losses) is redirected to the correct generator. The convolutional nature of $G_1$ would then ensure that the background image does not contain visible holes. A natural choice is *alpha blending*, which is also used in [38,47]. $G_2$ generates an RGB foreground image plus a transparency mask (*alpha* channel), and the final image is obtained by pasting the foreground onto the background via linear blending:

$$x_{\text{final}} = x_{bg} \cdot (1 - \alpha_{fg}) + x_{fg} \cdot \alpha_{fg} \tag{1}$$

where $x_{\text{final}}$, $x_{bg}$, and $x_{fg}$ are RGB images, and $\alpha_{fg}$ is a 1-channel image bounded in $[0,1]$ by a sigmoid. Readers familiar with highway networks [39] might notice a similarity to this approach in terms of gradients dynamics. If $\alpha_{fg} = 1$, the gradient is completely redirected to $x_{fg}$, while if $\alpha_{fg} = 0$, the gradient is redirected to $x_{bg}$. This scheme allows us to train both generators in an end-to-end fashion using a single discriminator, and we can also preserve auxiliary losses (e.g. VGG loss) which [31] has shown to be very important for convergence. To incentivize separation between classes as defined in Sect. 3.1, we supervise $\alpha_{fg}$ using a binary cross-entropy loss, and decay this term over time (see Sect. 4.1).

$G_2$ uses the same $S$-blocks as the ones in the one-step model, but here they take a *foreground mask* as input (Fig. 3, right). $G_1$, on the other hand, must exploit foreground information without rendering it. We therefore devise a further variation of input conditioning that consists of two branches: (i) the first branch ($S$-block) takes a *background mask* as input and processes it as usual to produce the batch normalization gain $\gamma$ and bias $\beta$. (ii) the second branch ($S_{avg}$-block, Fig. 4 left) takes the full mask as input (background plus foreground), processes it, and applies global average pooling to the feature map to remove information about localization. This way, foreground information is only used to bias $G_1$ and cannot be rendered at precise spatial locations. After pooling, it outputs $\gamma_{avg}$ and $\beta_{avg}$. (iii) The final conditional batch normalization is computed as:

$$\mathbf{y} = \text{BN}(\mathbf{x}) \odot (1 + \gamma + \gamma_{avg}) + \beta + \beta_{avg} \tag{2}$$

Finally, the discriminator $D$ takes the full mask as input (background plus foreground). Note that, if $G_1$ took the full mask as input without information reduction, it would render visible "holes" in the output image due to gradients never reaching the foreground zones of the mask, which is what we are trying to avoid. The Appendix A.1 provides more details about our architectures, and A.2 shows how $G_2$ can be used to generate one object at a time to fully disentangle foreground objects from each other (although this is unnecessary in practice).

## 4   Experiments

For consistency with [31], we always evaluate our model on the COCO-Stuff validation set [2], but we train on a variety of training sets:

**COCO-Stuff (COCO2017)** [2,26] contains 118k training images with captions [5]. We train with and without captions. COCO-Stuff extends COCO2017 with ground-truth semantic maps, but for our purposes the two datasets are equivalent since we do not exploit ground-truth masks.

**Visual Genome (VG)** [25] contains 108k images that partially overlap with COCO ($\approx$50%). VG does not have a standard train/test split, therefore we leave out 10% of the dataset to use as a validation set (IDs ending with 9), and use the rest as a training set from which we remove images that overlap with the COCO-Stuff validation set. We extract the attributes from the scene graphs.

**Visual Genome augmented (VG+).** VG augmented with the 123k images from the COCO unlabeled set. The total size is 217k images after removing exact duplicates. The goal is to evaluate how well our method scales to large unlabeled datasets. We train without attributes and without captions.

For all experiments, we evaluate the *Fréchet Inception Distance* (FID) [13] (precise implementation details of the FID in the Appendix A.3). Furthermore, we report our results in Sect. 4.2 and provide additional qualitative results in A.4.

### 4.1   Implementation Details

**Semantic Maps.** To construct the input semantic maps, we use the semi-supervised implementation of Mask R-CNN [11,35] proposed by [16]. It is trained on bounding boxes from Visual Genome (3000 classes) and segmentation masks from COCO (80 classes), and learns to segment classes for which there are no ground-truth masks. We discard the least frequent classes, and, since some VG concepts overlap (e.g. car, vehicle) leading to spurious detections, we merge these classes and end up with a total of $c = 280$ classes (plus a special class for "no class"). We set the threshold of the object detector to 0.2, and further refine the predictions by running a class-agnostic non-maximum-suppression (NMS) step on the detections whose mask intersection-over-union (IoU) is greater than 0.7. We also construct a transformation hierarchy to link children to their parents in the semantic map (e.g. headlight of a car) so that they can be manipulated as a whole; further details in the Appendix A.1. We select the 256 most frequent attributes, manually excluding those that refer to shapes (e.g. *short, square*).

**Training.** We generate images at $256 \times 256$ and keep our experimental setting and hyperparameters as close as possible to [31] for a fair comparison. For the two-step model, we provide supervision on the alpha blending mask and decay

COCO Mask     Generated     Sparse mask     Generated     Ground truth     Generation from hand-drawn sparse sketches

**Fig. 5. Left:** the larger set of labels in our sparse masks improves fine details. These masks are easy to obtain with a semi-supervised object detector, and would otherwise be too hard to hand-label. **Right:** sparse masks are also easy to sketch by hand.

this loss term over time, observing that the model does not re-entangle background and foreground. This gives $G_2$ some extra flexibility in drawing details that are not represented by the mask (reflections, shadows). Hyperparameters and additional training details are specified in the Appendix A.1.

## 4.2 Results

**Quantitative.** We show the FID scores for the main experiments in Table 1 (left). While improving FID scores is not the goal of our work, our weakly-supervised sparse mask baseline (#3) interestingly outperforms both the fully-supervised baseline on SPADE [31] (#1) and the weakly-supervised baseline (#2) trained on dense semantic maps. These experiments adopt an identical architecture and training set, no style input, and differ only in the type of input mask. For #2 we obtain the semantic maps from *DeepLab-v2* [3], a state-of-the-art semantic segmentation model pretrained on COCO-Stuff. Our improvement is partly due to masks better representing fine details (such as windows, doors, lights, wheels) in compound objects, which are not part of the COCO class set. In Fig. 5 (left) we show some examples. Moreover, the experiment on the *augmented* Visual Genome dataset highlights that our model benefits from extra unlabeled images (#4). Rows #5–9 are trained with style input. In particular, we observe that these outperform the baseline even when they use a two-step architecture (which is more constrained) or are trained on a different training set (VG instead of COCO). Row #6–7 draw their text embeddings from the last BERT layer and adopt 12 attention heads (the default), whereas #5 draws its embeddings from the 2nd-last layer, uses 6 heads, and performs slightly better.

**Qualitative.** In Fig. 6 we show qualitative results as well as examples of manipulations, either through attributes or text. Additional examples can be seen in the Appendix A.4, including latent space interpolation [22]. In A.5, we visualize the attention mechanism. Finally, we observe that sketching sparse masks by hand is very practical (Fig. 5, right) and provides an easier interface than dense semantic maps (in which the class of every pixel must be manually specified). The supplementary video (see Appendix A.7) shows how these figures are drawn.

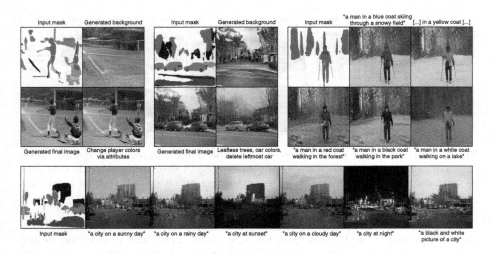

**Fig. 6.** Qualitative results (256 × 256). **Top-left** and **top-middle**: two-step generation with manipulation of attributes and instances. **Top-right:** manipulating style (both context and instances) via text. **Bottom:** manipulating global style via text.

**Style Randomization.** Since we represent style explicitly, at inference we can randomize the style of an image by drawing attributes from a per-class empirical distribution. This is depicted in Fig. 7, and has the additional advantage of being interpretable and editable (attributes can be refined manually after sampling). The two-step decomposition also allows users to specify different sampling strategies for the background and foreground; more details in the Appendix A.2.

**Ablation Study.** While Table 1 (left) already includes a partial ablation study where we vary input conditioning and some aspects of the attention module, in Table 1 (right) we make this more explicit and include additional experiments.First, we train a model on a sparsified COCO dataset by only keeping the "things" classes and discarding the "stuff" classes. This setting (I) performs significantly worse than #1 (which uses all classes), motivating the use of a large class vocabulary. Next, we ablate conditioning via text (baseline #6, which adopts the default hyperparameters of BERT). In (II), we augment the discriminator with ground-truth attributes to provide a stronger supervision signal for the generator (we take the attributes from Visual Genome for the images that overlap between the two datasets). The improvement is marginal, suggesting that our model can learn visual-textual correlations without explicit supervision. In (III), we draw the token representations from the second-to-last layer instead of the last, and in (IV) we further reduce the number of attention heads from 12 to 6. Both III and IV result in an improvement of the FID, which justifies the hyperparameters chosen in #5. Finally, we switch to attribute conditioning (baseline #9). In (IV), we remove foreground information at inference from the $S_{avg}$ block of the first generator $G_1$ (we feed the background mask twice in $S$ and $S_{avg}$). The FID degrades significantly, suggesting that $G_1$ effectively exploits

**Table 1. Left:** FID scores for the main experiments; lower is better. The first line represents the SPADE baseline [31]. For the models trained on VG, we also report FID scores on our VG validation set. (†) indicates that the model is weakly-supervised, (6h) denotes "6 attention heads", $L_{n-1}$ indicates that the text embeddings are drawn from the second-to-last BERT layer. **Right:** ablation study with extra experiments.

| # | Training set | Test set(s) | Type | Mask input | Style input | FID |
|---|---|---|---|---|---|---|
| 1 | COCO-train | COCO-val | 1-step [31] | Ground truth | None | 22.64 |
| 2 | COCO-train | COCO-val | 1-step † | Semantic seg. | None | 23.97 |
| 3 | COCO-train | COCO-val | 1-step † | Sparse (ours) | None | 20.02 |
| 4 | VG+ (aug.) | COCO-val/VG-val | 1-step † | Sparse (ours) | None | **18.93**/13.23 |
| 5 | COCO-train | COCO-val | 1-step † | Sparse (ours) | Text (6h, $L_{n-1}$) | 19.65 |
| 6 | COCO-train | COCO-val | 1-step † | Sparse (ours) | Text (12h, $L_n$) | 20.63 |
| 7 | COCO-train | COCO-val | 2-step † | Sparse (ours) | Text (12h, $L_n$) | 20.64 |
| 8 | VG | COCO-val/VG-val | 1-step † | Sparse (ours) | Attributes | 21.13/15.12 |
| 9 | VG | COCO-val/VG-val | 2-step † | Sparse (ours) | Attributes | 20.83/14.88 |

| | Ref. | Experiment | FID ($\Delta$) |
|---|---|---|---|
| I | #1 | COCO "things" only | 32.31 (+9.67) |
| II | #6 | 12h, $L_n$, attr. in $D$ | 20.44 (-0.19) |
| III | #6 | 12h, $L_{n-1}$ | 19.77 (-0.86) |
| IV | #6 | 6h, $L_{n-1}$ | 19.65 (-0.98) |
| V | #9 | No f.g. info in $S_{avg}$ | 25.16 (+4.33) |
| VI | #9 | Attr. randomization | 20.64 (-0.19) |

**Fig. 7.** Random styles by sampling attributes from a per-class empirical distribution.

foreground information to bias the result. In (V) we show that randomizing style at inference (previous paragraph) is not detrimental to the FID, but in fact seems to be slightly beneficial, probably due to the greater sample diversity.

**Robustness and Failure Cases.** Input masks can sometimes be noisy due to spurious object detections on certain classes. Since these are also present at train time, weakly-supervised training leads to some degree of noise robustness, but sometimes the artifacts are visible in the generated images. We show some positive/negative examples in the Appendix Fig. 14. In principle, mask noise can be reduced by using a better object detector. We also observe that our setup tends to work better on outdoor scenes and sometimes struggles with fine geometric details in indoor scenes or photographs shot from a close range.

## 5   Conclusion

We introduced a weakly-supervised approach for the conditional generation of complex images. The generated scenes can be controlled through various manipulations on the sparse semantic maps, as well as through textual descriptions or attribute labels. Our method enables a high level of semantic/style control while benefiting from improved FID scores. From a qualitative point-of-view, we have demonstrated a wide variety of manipulations that can be applied to an image.

Furthermore, our weakly supervised setup opens up opportunities for large-scale training on unlabeled datasets, as well as generation from hand-drawn sketches.

There are several ways one could pursue to further enrich the set of tools used to manipulate the generation process. For instance, the current version of our attention mechanism cannot differentiate between instances belonging to the same class and does not have direct access to positional information. While incorporating such information is beyond the scope of this work, we suggest that this can be achieved by appending a *positional embedding* to the attention queries. In the NLP literature, the latter is often learned according to the position of the word in the sentence [7, 43], but images are 2D and therefore do not possess such a natural order. Additionally, this would require captions that are more descriptive than the ones in COCO, which typically focus on actions instead of style. Finally, in order to augment the quality of sparse maps, we would like to train the object detector on a higher-quality, large-vocabulary dataset [10].

**Acknowledgments.** This work was partly supported by the Swiss National Science Foundation (SNF) and Research Foundation Flanders (FWO), grant #176004. We thank Graham Spinks and Sien Moens for helpful discussions.

# References

1. Brock, A., Donahue, J., Simonyan, K.: Large scale GAN training for high fidelity natural image synthesis. arXiv preprint arXiv:1809.11096 (2019)
2. Caesar, H., Uijlings, J., Ferrari, V.: COCO-Stuff: thing and stuff classes in context. In: Proceedings of the IEEE Conference on Computer Vision and Pattern Recognition (CVPR), pp. 1209–1218 (2018)
3. Chen, L.C., Papandreou, G., Kokkinos, I., Murphy, K., Yuille, A.L.: Deeplab: semantic image segmentation with deep convolutional nets, atrous convolution, and fully connected crfs. IEEE Trans. Pattern Anal. Mach. Intell. (TPAMI) **40**(4), 834–848 (2018)
4. Chen, Q., Koltun, V.: Photographic image synthesis with cascaded refinement networks. In: IEEE International Conference on Computer Vision (ICCV), pp. 1511–1520 (2017)
5. Chen, X., et al.: Microsoft COCO captions: data collection and evaluation server. arXiv preprint arXiv:1504.00325 (2015)
6. Cheng, Y., Gan, Z., Li, Y., Liu, J., Gao, J.: Sequential attention GAN for interactive image editing via dialogue. arXiv preprint arXiv:1812.08352 (2018)
7. Devlin, J., Chang, M.W., Lee, K., Toutanova, K.: Bert: pre-training of deep bidirectional transformers for language understanding. arXiv preprint arXiv:1810.04805 (2018)
8. El-Nouby, A., et al.: Tell, draw, and repeat: generating and modifying images based on continual linguistic instruction. In: IEEE International Conference on Computer Vision (ICCV), pp. 10304–10312 (2019)
9. Goodfellow, I., et al.: Generative adversarial nets. arXiv preprint arXiv:1411.1784 (2014)
10. Gupta, A., Dollar, P., Girshick, R.: LVIS: a dataset for large vocabulary instance segmentation. In: Proceedings of the IEEE Conference on Computer Vision and Pattern Recognition (CVPR), pp. 5356–5364 (2019)

11. He, K., Gkioxari, G., Dollár, P., Girshick, R.: Mask R-CNN. In: Proceedings of the IEEE International Conference on Computer Vision (ICCV), pp. 2961–2969 (2017)
12. He, Z., Zuo, W., Kan, M., Shan, S., Chen, X.: Attgan: facial attribute editing by only changing what you want. IEEE Trans. Image Process. **28**(11), 5464–5478 (2019)
13. Heusel, M., Ramsauer, H., Unterthiner, T., Nessler, B., Hochreiter, S.: GANs trained by a two time-scale update rule converge to a local Nash equilibrium. In: Advances in Neural Information Processing Systems, pp. 6626–6637 (2017)
14. Hinz, T., Heinrich, S., Wermter, S.: Generating multiple objects at spatially distinct locations. arXiv preprint arXiv:1901.00686 (2019)
15. Hong, S., Yang, D., Choi, J., Lee, H.: Inferring semantic layout for hierarchical text-to-image synthesis. In: Proceedings of the IEEE Conference on Computer Vision and Pattern Recognition (CVPR), pp. 7986–7994 (2018)
16. Hu, R., Dollár, P., He, K., Darrell, T., Girshick, R.: Learning to segment every thing. In: Proceedings of the IEEE Conference on Computer Vision and Pattern Recognition (CVPR), pp. 4233–4241 (2018)
17. Isola, P., Zhu, J.Y., Zhou, T., Efros, A.A.: Image-to-image translation with conditional adversarial networks. In: Proceedings of the IEEE Conference on Computer Vision and Pattern Recognition (CVPR), pp. 1125–1134 (2017)
18. Johnson, J., Gupta, A., Fei-Fei, L.: Image generation from scene graphs. In: Proceedings of the IEEE Conference on Computer Vision and Pattern Recognition (CVPR), pp. 1219–1228 (2018)
19. Joseph, K., Pal, A., Rajanala, S., Balasubramanian, V.N.: C4Synth: cross-caption cycle-consistent text-to-image synthesis. In: IEEE Winter Conference on Applications of Computer Vision (WACV), pp. 358–366. IEEE (2019)
20. Karras, T., Aila, T., Laine, S., Lehtinen, J.: Progressive growing of GANs for improved quality, stability, and variation. arXiv preprint arXiv:1710.10196 (2018)
21. Karras, T., Laine, S., Aila, T.: A style-based generator architecture for generative adversarial networks. In: Proceedings of the IEEE Conference on Computer Vision and Pattern Recognition (CVPR), pp. 4401–4410 (2019)
22. Kilcher, Y., Lucchi, A., Hofmann, T.: Semantic interpolation in implicit models. arXiv preprint arXiv:1710.11381 (2018)
23. Kingma, D.P., Welling, M.: Auto-encoding variational Bayes. arXiv preprint arXiv:1312.6114 (2014)
24. Kiros, R., et al.: Skip-thought vectors. In: Advances in Neural Information Processing Systems, pp. 3294–3302 (2015)
25. Krishna, R., et al.: Visual genome: connecting language and vision using crowd-sourced dense image annotations. Int. J. Comput. Vis. (IJCV) **123**(1), 32–73 (2017)
26. Lin, T.-Y., et al.: Microsoft COCO: common objects in context. In: Fleet, D., Pajdla, T., Schiele, B., Tuytelaars, T. (eds.) ECCV 2014. LNCS, vol. 8693, pp. 740–755. Springer, Cham (2014). https://doi.org/10.1007/978-3-319-10602-1_48
27. Locatello, F., Bauer, S., Lucic, M., Gelly, S., Schölkopf, B., Bachem, O.: Challenging common assumptions in the unsupervised learning of disentangled representations. In: International Conference on Machine Learning, pp. 4114–4124 (2019)
28. Miyato, T., Kataoka, T., Koyama, M., Yoshida, Y.: Spectral normalization for generative adversarial networks. arXiv preprint arXiv:1802.05957 (2018)
29. Miyato, T., Koyama, M.: cGANs with projection discriminator. arXiv preprint arXiv:1802.05637 (2018)
30. Mo, S., Cho, M., Shin, J.: Instance-aware image-to-image translation. arXiv preprint arXiv:1812.10889 (2019)

31. Park, T., Liu, M.Y., Wang, T.C., Zhu, J.Y.: Semantic image synthesis with spatially-adaptive normalization. In: Proceedings of the IEEE Conference on Computer Vision and Pattern Recognition (CVPR), pp. 2337–2346 (2019)
32. Qi, X., Chen, Q., Jia, J., Koltun, V.: Semi-parametric image synthesis. In: Proceedings of the IEEE Conference on Computer Vision and Pattern Recognition, pp. 8808–8816 (2018)
33. Reed, S., Akata, Z., Yan, X., Logeswaran, L., Schiele, B., Lee, H.: Generative adversarial text to image synthesis. arXiv preprint arXiv:1605.05396 (2016)
34. Reed, S., van den Oord, A., Kalchbrenner, N., Bapst, V., Botvinick, M., de Freitas, N.: Generating interpretable images with controllable structure. Open Rev. (2016)
35. Ren, S., He, K., Girshick, R., Sun, J.: Faster R-CNN: towards real-time object detection with region proposal networks. In: Advances in Neural Information Processing Systems, pp. 91–99 (2015)
36. Sharma, S., Suhubdy, D., Michalski, V., Kahou, S.E., Bengio, Y.: Chatpainter: improving text to image generation using dialogue. arXiv preprint arXiv:1802.08216 (2018)
37. Simonyan, K., Zisserman, A.: Very deep convolutional networks for large-scale image recognition. arXiv preprint arXiv:1409.1556 (2014)
38. Singh, K.K., Ojha, U., Lee, Y.J.: FineGAN: unsupervised hierarchical disentanglement for fine-grained object generation and discovery. In: Proceedings of the IEEE Conference on Computer Vision and Pattern Recognition, pp. 6490–6499 (2019)
39. Srivastava, R.K., Greff, K., Schmidhuber, J.: Highway networks. arXiv preprint arXiv:1505.00387 (2015)
40. Sun, W., Wu, T.: Image synthesis from reconfigurable layout and style. In: Proceedings of the IEEE International Conference on Computer Vision (ICCV), pp. 10531–10540 (2019)
41. Szegedy, C., Vanhoucke, V., Ioffe, S., Shlens, J., Wojna, Z.: Rethinking the inception architecture for computer vision. In: Proceedings of the IEEE Conference on Computer Vision and Pattern Recognition (CVPR), pp. 2818–2826 (2016)
42. Turkoglu, M.O., Thong, W., Spreeuwers, L., Kicanaoglu, B.: A layer-based sequential framework for scene generation with GANs. Proc. AAAI Conf. Artif. Intell. **33**, 8901–8908 (2019)
43. Vaswani, A., et al.: Attention is all you need. In: Advances in Neural Information Processing Systems, pp. 5998–6008 (2017)
44. Wang, T.C., Liu, M.Y., Zhu, J.Y., Tao, A., Kautz, J., Catanzaro, B.: High-resolution image synthesis and semantic manipulation with conditional GANs. In: Proceedings of the IEEE Conference on Computer Vision and Pattern Recognition (CVPR), pp. 8798–8807 (2018)
45. Xu, T., et al.: AttnGAN: fine-grained text to image generation with attentional generative adversarial networks. In: Proceedings of the IEEE Conference on Computer Vision and Pattern Recognition (CVPR), pp. 1316–1324 (2018)
46. Yan, X., Yang, J., Sohn, K., Lee, H.: Attribute2Image: conditional image generation from visual attributes. In: Leibe, B., Matas, J., Sebe, N., Welling, M. (eds.) ECCV 2016. LNCS, vol. 9908, pp. 776–791. Springer, Cham (2016). https://doi.org/10.1007/978-3-319-46493-0_47
47. Yang, J., Kannan, A., Batra, D., Parikh, D.: LR-GAN: layered recursive generative adversarial networks for image generation. arXiv preprint arXiv:1703.01560 (2017)
48. Yin, G., Liu, B., Sheng, L., Yu, N., Wang, X., Shao, J.: Semantics disentangling for text-to-image generation. In: Proceedings of the IEEE Conference on Computer Vision and Pattern Recognition (CVPR), pp. 2327–2336 (2019)

49. Zhang, H., Goodfellow, I., Metaxas, D., Odena, A.: Self-attention generative adversarial networks. In: International Conference on Machine Learning (ICML), pp. 7354–7363 (2019)
50. Zhang, H., et al.: StackGAN: text to photo-realistic image synthesis with stacked generative adversarial networks. In: Proceedings of the IEEE International Conference on Computer Vision (ICCV), pp. 5907–5915 (2017)
51. Zhang, H., Xu, T., Li, H., Zhang, S., Wang, X., Huang, X., Metaxas, D.N.: StackGAN++: realistic image synthesis with stacked generative adversarial networks. IEEE Trans. Pattern Anal. Mach. Intell. (TPAMI) **41**(8), 1947–1962 (2018)
52. Zhao, B., Meng, L., Yin, W., Sigal, L.: Image generation from layout. In: Proceedings of the IEEE Conference on Computer Vision and Pattern Recognition (CVPR), pp. 8584–8593 (2019)
53. Zhu, J.Y., Park, T., Isola, P., Efros, A.A.: Unpaired image-to-image translation using cycle-consistent adversarial networks. In: Proceedings of the IEEE International Conference on Computer Vision (ICCV), pp. 2223–2232 (2017)

# Jointly Learning Visual Motion and Confidence from Local Patches in Event Cameras

Daniel R. Kepple[1(✉)], Daewon Lee[1], Colin Prepsius[1], Volkan Isler[1],
Il Memming Park[2], and Daniel D. Lee[1]

[1] Samsung AI Center, New York, USA
{d.kepple,daewon.l,c.prepscius,ibrahim.i,daniel.d.lee}@samsung.com
[2] Department of Neurobiology and Behavior, Stony Brook University,
New York, USA
memming.park@stonybrook.edu

**Abstract.** We propose the first network to jointly learn visual motion and confidence from events in spatially local patches. Event-based sensors deliver high temporal resolution motion information in a sparse, non-redundant format. This creates the potential for low computation, low latency motion recognition. Neural networks which extract global motion information, however, are generally computationally expensive. Here, we introduce a novel shallow and compact neural architecture and learning approach to capture reliable visual motion information along with the corresponding confidence of inference. Our network makes a prediction of the visual motion at each spatial location using only local events. Our confidence network then identifies which of these predictions will be accurate. In the task of recovering pan-tilt ego velocities from events, we show that each individual confident local prediction of our network can be expected to be as accurate as state of the art optimization approaches which utilize the full image. Furthermore, on a publicly available dataset, we find our local predictions generalize to scenes with camera motions and the presence of independently moving objects. This makes the output of our network well suited for motion based tasks, such as the segmentation of independently moving objects. We demonstrate on a publicly available motion segmentation dataset that restricting predictions to confident regions is sufficient to achieve results that exceed state of the art methods.

## 1 Introduction

Individual pixels in an event-based camera report only when there is an above-threshold change in the log light intensity in its field of view [1–3]. Such an

**Electronic supplementary material** The online version of this chapter (https://doi.org/10.1007/978-3-030-58539-6_30) contains supplementary material, which is available to authorized users.

operation can be performed extremely quickly, without influence from neighboring pixels, and with minimal influence of the absolute light intensity [4]. This creates inherent advantages, e.g., low latency vision without requiring high power or being constrained to uniform, well-lit environments. This makes event-based cameras attractive for motion based tasks which require precise timing and are ideally invariant under extreme changes in lighting conditions [5–9]. Other advantages of event based vision, such as its potential for vision with low computational cost owing to its sparse, asynchronous output, can only be realized with the development of novel data processing techniques.

Here, we suggest a neural network which takes advantage of event-based vision's potential for low computation in the context of visual motion. Rather than computing dense optical flow, we extend the philosophy of event-based sensing to sparsely recover visual motion information. We simultaneously predict both a region's local flow and its reliability for visual motion predictions. Downstream processes, such as camera pose estimation or motion segmentation, can then use the sparse, confident visual motion information. Similar to biological vision systems [10–14], we compute this visual motion as the projection of optical flow on preferred axes, rather than as a true optical flow.

Our solution therefore has two parts: prediction of the visual motion in each small spatial region, and prediction of the confidence of each region's visual motion prediction. We demonstrate that because our solution is fully local, it can be learned under uniform visual motion conditions and generalize to make reliable predictions in dramatically different conditions, such as those with independently moving objects or unseen motions.

Our contributions are:

1. **Compact visual motion network:** Our formulation has two orders of magnitude fewer parameters than networks which solve similar problems [15, 16]. This makes our network attractive for employment in systems with limited resources.
2. **Accurate local visual motion predictions:** Our network produces confident, fully local predictions which can be expected to as accurate as methods which use the entire image.
3. **Improved performance in downstream tasks:** We show that our sparse predictions still enable motion segmentation and camera pose estimation that competes with state of the art methods.
4. **Novel training approach:** Despite training on the limited domain of pan/tilt camera motions in front of a computer monitor, we show that our network generalizes to realistic datasets with challenging lighting and full 6DOF camera motion.
5. **New dataset:** We have collected a large-scale dataset with 10,000 diverse scenes with precisely controlled known camera movements in static environments.

## 2  Related Work

In this paper, we consider the problem of recovering visual motion in a scene with an event-based system. This is often considered in the context of optical flow, for which event-based neural networks have been proposed with some success [15–18]. Such networks, however, are deep and require heavy computation to provide a dense optical flow. Furthermore, in part due to the challenge of getting labelled optical flow in dynamic scenes, these networks, with the exception of [17], cannot handle the presence of independently moving objects.

In the realm of optimization, there are also approaches to capture visual motion with event-cameras [17,19–21]. Many of these utilize the approach of Contrast Maximization [19]. This approach takes advantage of the edge detection of event-sensors, and the assumption that flows are uniform on small spatiotemporal scales. Events in local regions are warped back in time according to a proposed velocity, and the velocity whose warped image most accurately reconstructs an edge is identified. While this approach requires less computation than a deep network, warped images are still costly to compute. Furthermore, extension of this approach to scenes with independently moving objects requires computing a warped image for each object, compounding computational costs [21].

In keeping with the philosophy of event sensors, we aim for a network which can get visual motion information quickly and at low computational cost. Rather than sacrificing the accuracy of our predictions, we will identify local regions in which accurate visual motion predictions can be cheaply computed. Towards this goal, we propose a novel training framework to enable a network to selectively learn from a large number of examples where some are assumed to be uninformative of the target. Our formulation is most related to Mixture of Experts models [22] and attention networks [23].

In traditional vision, the idea of limiting the domain of one predictor to subregions determined by another has had success in the form of Region Proposal Networks (RPN) [24–26]. Our proposal differs significantly from these approaches by necessity. RPNs are trained using ground truth labels – that is, the true locations of objects in the images are known and used in training. In our case, the ground truth reliability of a subregion in predicting optical flow projections is unknown. Therefore, we developed a novel, joint training procedure to address this problem.

## 3  Method

### 3.1  Event Cameras

Unlike traditional cameras which communicate the light intensity at every pixel synchronously according to a frame rate, event-based cameras report the list of pixel locations whose light intensity has changed, the sign of that change, and precise time the change is detected [1–3]. More formally, event-based sensors communicate a stream of events $\mathcal{S} = \{s_i\}_{i=1}^{K}$, $s_i = [x_i, y_i, p_i, t_i]$, where $x_i, y_i$ are the spatial indices from the $M \times N$ resolution pixel array and $t_i$ is the time of the $i^{th}$ event, ordered such that $\forall i < K$, $t_i \leq t_{i+1}$ where $K$ is the total number of events. $p_i$ is the *polarity* for event $i$. Polarity denotes the sign of the change in the light intensity resulting in event $s_i$.

## 3.2  Preprocessing

Given the precise temporal resolution and asynchronous nature of a typical event-camera, it is generally the case that any instant will contain only one event. It is therefore necessary to consider past events to perform even basic computer vision tasks. Standard approaches include using time windows [17,27], batching a fixed number of events together [15], or using "time surfaces", which are monotonically decreasing functions applied to the elapsed time since the last event at each spatial pixel [18,28,29].

Our approach is to smoothly integrate the past with multiple time scales which avoids explicitly counting events and allows for event-based processing. Consider a single pixel with coordinate $(x, y)$ detecting polarity $p$ events. Let us define a *leaky integrating pixel* with a voltage variable $v(t)$, similar to membrane potentials in spiking neural networks (SNN) [30], as the first-order filtering of input events represented as a sequence of Dirac delta functions $I(t) = \sum_i \delta(t-t_i)$ for all events:

$$v(t) = \int_{-\infty}^{t} I(s) \cdot e^{-(t-s)/\tau} \mathrm{d}s = \sum_{t_i \leq t} e^{-(t-t_i)/\tau} \tag{1}$$

where $\tau > 0$ is the time constant.

We refer to the voltage of any single pixel as $v_{xy}^{\tau p}(t)$ where the superscript $\tau$ indicates the time constant of that neuron and $p \in \{+, -\}$ separates events of different polarity into different images. Subscripts $x, y$ are the spatial indices of the corresponding dynamic vision sensor (DVS) pixel. We refer to the image of all leaky integrating pixels with the same $\tau$ and polarity at a time $t$ as $\mathcal{V}^{\tau p}(t)$. In the supplementary material, we show an example of these images for two different $\tau$ and both polarities.

Intuitively, an image of leaky integrating pixels accumulates signal in pixels with recent events. The voltage at any given pixel is bounded below by 0 and unbounded from above. The choice of $\tau$ then controls the depth of the memory of past events, with large $\tau$ approximating an event counter, and small $\tau$ providing timing information of events occurring within a short past.

We use two time constants, motivated by delay lines utilized in biological motion detectors [10–14]. We will refer to these decay time constants as $\tau_{\text{slow}}$ and $\tau_{\text{fast}}$. In the supplementary material, we provide an argument for the selection of these time constants in order to predict velocities in a specified range. For the rest of the paper, we use $\tau_{\text{slow}} = 20$ ms and $\tau_{\text{fast}} = 10$ ms.

## 3.3  Visual Motion Model and Assumptions

Visual motion in traditional vision can be defined as a vector field of pixel translations between two image frames. As event-based cameras do not have temporal frames, we will define visual motion for events. Let $[u_{x_i y_i}(t_i), v_{x_i y_i}(t_i)]$ be the visual motion at $(x_i, y_i)$ at time $t_i$. Assuming nonzero $[u_{x_i y_i}(t_i), v_{x_i y_i}(t_i)]$, noiseless observation, and constant motion, an event $s_i = [x_i, y_i, p_i, t_i]$ will produce an event $s_j$ at time $t_j > t_i$ at location $x_j = x_i + (t_j - t_i) u_{x_i y_i}(t_i)$ and $y_j = y_i + (t_j - t_i) v_{x_i y_i}(t_i)$.

Instead of just considering flows $[u_{xy}, v_{xy}]$ corresponding to camera axes $x$ and $y$, we will consider $[u_{xy}^p, v_{xy}^p]$ where $p$ enumerates $\theta_p \in \{0, \frac{\pi}{8}, \frac{\pi}{4}, \frac{3\pi}{8}\}$:

$$\begin{bmatrix} x_j \\ y_j \end{bmatrix} = \begin{bmatrix} x_i \\ y_i \end{bmatrix} + (t_j - t_i) \begin{bmatrix} \cos(\theta_p) & -\sin(\theta_p) \\ \sin(\theta_p) & \cos(\theta_p) \end{bmatrix}^T \begin{bmatrix} u_{x_i y_i}^p \\ v_{x_i y_i}^p \end{bmatrix} \quad (2)$$

Our approach will assume events within small spatial neighborhoods experience uniform visual motion [31]. Furthermore, we assume that pure pan-tilt egomotion generates uniform visual motion over the image. Such an assumption is justified in a camera with a moderate viewing angle, such as our Samsung Gen 3 DVS's 45 degree view, and pan/tilt egomotions constrained within a 20 degree cap. Under this assumption, the visual motion at any location in the image is equal to the pan-tilt of the camera.

### 3.4   Network Architecture

Our approach uses two convolutional networks, one for predicting visual motion, and the other for predicting confidence (Fig. 1). We design both convolutional networks such that each is equivalent to a fully connected subnetwork applied at each small spatial window. This is achieved in both networks by one $15 \times 15$ convolution followed by $1 \times 1$ convolutions. This subnetwork design is relevant for our training approach, and we will refer to the fully connected subnetworks as $f$ and $g$ for the visual motion and confident networks respectively (Fig. 1).

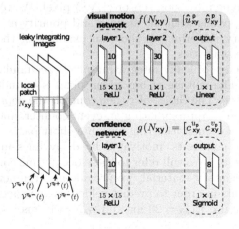

**Fig. 1.** Convolutional architecture implementing many parallel fully connected networks. Computation path for a local patch $N_{xy}$ is highlighted. The convolutions applied to this patch are mathematically equivalent to the fully connected network $f$ (in red), and $g$ (in blue). (Color figure online)

**Local, Fully Connected Visual Motion Network $f$.** The input to our visual motion subnetwork $f$ is the neighborhood of a point $(x, y)$ in the four leaky integrating images (described in Sect. 3.2):

$$N_{xy}(t) = \left\{ v^{\tau_{slow}-}_{(x+a)(y+b)}(t), v^{\tau_{fast}-}_{(x+a)(y+b)}(t), \quad v^{\tau_{slow}+}_{(x+a)(y+b)}(t), v^{\tau_{fast}+}_{(x+a)(y+b)}(t) \right\}^{7}_{a,b=-7}$$

The subnetwork is then a function $f: \mathbb{R}^{4 \times 15^2} \to \mathbb{R}^9$,

$$f\left(N_{xy}(t)\right) = [\hat{u}^p_{xy}(t), \hat{v}^p_{xy}(t)]_p,$$

that estimates the visual motion for projection $p$, i.e $[\hat{u}^p_{xy}(t), \hat{v}^p_{xy}(t)]_p$, from the information accumulated in the input images around $(x, y)$. This prediction is ill-posed due to the aperture problem [32], observation noise [1], as well as the unknown correspondence and the typical sparseness of events. For this reason, we expect that $f$ will typically only be able to read out velocity in a subset of $N_{xy}$'s from the full leaky integrating image. On this subset, however, a shallow network may be sufficient to accurately predict visual motion. We anticipate this and propose a neural network architecture with three fully connected layers (two ReLU layers followed by a linear readout; Fig. 1).

**Confidence Network $g$.** Subnetwork $g$ will be trained to identify whether the prediction from $f$ on the same window can be expected to be accurate. As with $f$, we can summarize this network as a function:

$$g(N_{xy}(t)) = [c^{u_p}_{xy}(t), c^{v_p}_{xy}(t)],$$

where $c^{u_p}_{xy}(t), c^{v_p}_{xy}(t) \in [0, 1]$ are the confidences for visual motion predictions $\hat{u}^p_{xy}(t)$ and $\hat{v}^p_{xy}(t)$ respectively. Importantly, this means confidence is considered for each projection separately.

$g$ is a two layer fully connected network, with the first nonlinearity being a ReLU and the second a sigmoid. The sigmoid function enables a binary interpretation of the output of this network while maintaining differentiability. The schematic of this network is shown in Fig. 1.

## 3.5 Supervised Training Local Networks from Global Signal

**The DVS-COCO Dataset.** To train the aforementioned pair of networks, we use the DVS-COCO pan-tilt dataset. In this dataset, the Samsung Gen 3 HVGA ($320 \times 480$ resolution) dynamic vision sensor (DVS) has been mounted on a motorized pan-tilt stage and set in front of a computer monitor (see supplement for schematic). Random saccade-like velocities move the stage up to 75 degrees/second while the images of the Microsoft COCO dataset are presented on the screen. [33] Each one of the 10,000 selected images are presented for 15 s and for an average of 30 saccades. For a full description of the DVS-COCO dataset, please see the supplementary material.

We will refer to the angular velocity of the camera as $[\omega_{\text{pan}}, \omega_{\text{tilt}}]$. With our approximation that pure pan/tilt motion produces globally uniform visual motion, it follows that our goal is to train $f$ to accurately predict $[\omega_{\text{pan}}, \omega_{\text{tilt}}]$.

**Mixture of Inputs Training.** Even with ground truth visual motion, we do not know a priori which spatial neighborhoods contain sufficient information to predict that visual motion. For example, regions without events cannot predict flow. In traditional computer vision, this is analogous to training a Region Proposal Network (RPN) without ground truth bounding boxes. Without labelled data, we can't use approaches like Faster RCNN [24–26]. We therefore developed a novel approach, which we will call Mixture of Inputs training.

We define the loss function $\mathcal{L}_f$ of the network $f$ at time $t$ on spatial region $N_{xy}(t)$ to be the squared error of predictions weighted by confidence $g$:

$$\mathcal{L}_f\left(f(N_{xy}(t)), g(N_{xy}(t)), \omega_{\text{pan}}(t), \omega_{\text{tilt}}(t)\right) = \tag{3}$$

$$\sum_p \left( \begin{bmatrix} c_{xy}^{u_p}(t) \\ c_{xy}^{v_p}(t) \end{bmatrix}^T \left( \begin{bmatrix} \hat{u}_{xy}^p(t) \\ \hat{v}_{xy(t)}^p \end{bmatrix} - R_{\theta_p} \begin{bmatrix} \omega_{\text{pan}}(t) \\ \omega_{\text{tilt}}(t) \end{bmatrix} \right) \right)^2$$

where $R_{\theta_p}$ is the Euclidean rotational matrix for angle $\theta_p$.

Our convolutional architecture then batches all spatial neighborhoods in an image, and thus the local loss over a single image, $\mathcal{L}_{\text{local}}$ can be computed:

$$\mathcal{L}_{\text{local}} = \sum_{x,y} \mathcal{L}_f\left(f(N_{xy}(t)), g(N_{xy}(t)), \omega_{\text{pan}}(t), \omega_{\text{tilt}}(t)\right)$$

Note that $\mathcal{L}_{\text{local}}$ cannot be used to train $g$. This is because $\mathcal{L}_f$ has a trivial global minimum for where $g(N_{xy}(t)) = 0$. Therefore, to train $g$ we use a separate loss function which takes global information into account. We define confidence normalization terms $Z_{u_p}(t) = \sum_{x,y} c_{xy}^{u_p}(t)$ and $Z_{v_p}(t) = \sum_{x,y} c_{xy}^{v_p}(t)$. We will refer to the weighted average of optical flow projection predictions as the global prediction of the camera angular velocity in reference frame $p$, $[\hat{\omega}_{\text{pan}}^p(t), \hat{\omega}_{\text{tilt}}^p(t)]$:

$$\begin{bmatrix} \hat{\omega}_{\text{pan}}^p(t) \\ \hat{\omega}_{\text{tilt}}^p(t) \end{bmatrix} = \sum_{x,y} R_{\theta_p}^T \begin{bmatrix} \dfrac{c_{xy}^{u_p} \hat{u}_{xy}^p}{Z_{u_p}}(t) \\ \dfrac{c_{xy}^{u_p} \hat{v}_{xy}^p}{Z_{v_p}}(t) \end{bmatrix}$$

Now we define the loss function for $g$, $\mathcal{L}_g$, to be the squared error between this global optical flow prediction and the rotational velocity:

$$\mathcal{L}_g = \sum_p \left( \left(\hat{\omega}_{\text{pan}}^p(t) - \omega_{\text{pan}}(t)\right)^2 + \left(\hat{\omega}_{\text{tilt}}^p(t) - \omega_{\text{tilt}}(t)\right)^2 \right)$$

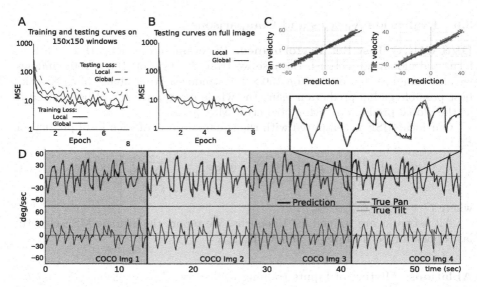

**Fig. 2.** Training and Testing on the DVS-COCO Benchmark. (A) Global, $\mathcal{L}_g$, and local, $\mathcal{L}_f$, loss functions over the course of training using 150×150 windows. (B) Test set mean squared error (MSE) of global predictions (red), local predictions (blue) using the full 320×480 image (C) Scatter plots between predicted and true velocities over the whole test set. (D) Continuous predictions on four testing videos.

Mathematically, $\mathcal{L}_g$ is similar to the gating network in Mixture of Expert (MoE) models [22]. In MoE, many networks compete to make predictions and the gating function selects the best predictors. Here, however, we have the same network and many different samples. Our "gating" network (the confidence network $g$), selects the best inputs, not the most suitable expert. We therefore call this approach *Mixture of Inputs*. Another distinction is that we do not have any explicit competition between inputs, although there is implicit competition for the training error signal through $\mathcal{L}_g$.

**Training Protocol.** We subsample each image by taking a randomly located 150 × 150 window from the full 320 × 480 Samsung Gen3 HVGA DVS image. We randomly select a batch of 80 time points from our training set (full description of training and testing set in supplementary material). For each time and corresponding 150×150 window, the four leaky integrated images $\mathcal{V}^{\tau p}$ are calculated with events histories of $3\tau$. Parameters of $f$ are updated according to $\mathcal{L}_f$, and the parameters of $g$ according to $\mathcal{L}_g$. We schedule our training rate with ADAM [34], using parameters $\beta_1 = 0.9$, $\beta_2 = 0.999$, $\eta = .01$.

## 3.6   Evaluation Metrics and Comparisons

**DVS COCO Test Set Performance.** We evaluate our network by both its local and global predictions. Because we train $f$ and $g$ on $150 \times 150$ windows, we also compute the test loss on $150 \times 150$ windows. We evaluate our network's best possible global prediction using the whole image, which will be referred to as the global prediction with global error $\text{MSE}_{\text{global}}$.

Our local MSE is computed with the squared errors of each local prediction, $\mathcal{E}_{xy}^p$:

$$\mathcal{E}_{xy}^p = \left( \begin{bmatrix} \hat{u}_{xy}^p \\ \hat{v}_{xy}^p \end{bmatrix} - R_{\theta_p} \begin{bmatrix} \omega_{\text{pan}} \\ \omega_{\text{tilt}} \end{bmatrix} \right)^2, \ \text{MSE}_{\text{local}} = \sum_{x,y,p} \frac{1}{C} \begin{bmatrix} c_{xy}^{u_p} \\ c_{xy}^{v_p} \end{bmatrix}^T \mathcal{E}_{xy}^p \qquad (4)$$

where $C = \sum_{x,y,p} (c_{xy}^{u_p} + c_{xy}^{v_p})$

All networks are trained for 10 epochs. We report the average MSE over the last epoch for both $\text{MSE}_{\text{local}}$ and $\text{MSE}_{\text{global}}$.

**Ablations.** Mixture of Inputs training utilizes two loss functions, $\mathcal{L}_g$ and $\mathcal{L}_f$. While the confident local loss $\mathcal{L}_f$ has a trivial global minimum for $g$, $\mathcal{L}_g$ can be used to train $f$. To understand the contribution of $\mathcal{L}_f$ we train a network this way and refer to it as the "$\mathcal{L}_g$ only" network.

To evaluate the contribution of our confidence network, we train a network using a heuristic confidence instead. This heuristic provides a binary confidence measure, 1 for predictions with above average number of events in the last $3\tau$ and 0 for those below. Intuitively, this heuristic will identify neighborhoods that contain more than just events from noise. Visual motion networks trained with this confidence signal will be referred to as "Mean confidence network".

**Contrast Maximization (CM).** We also compare our network's performance with that of an optimization approach called Contrast Maximization (CM) [19, 20]. We briefly describe this in the supplementary material for completeness. CM is expected to provide strong results for pan/tilt conditions. We performed a brute force search to optimize the time window size for CM on the DVS-COCO dataset and found 60 ms.

To compare local predictions, we use CM with a $15 \times 15$ spatial window size. We also extend their method to use both our network's confidence scores as well as heuristic confidence metrics designed to utilize the information available to their optimization. In particular, we use the mean and variance of the $15 \times 15$ windows. We include a full description of these confidence models in the supplementary material.

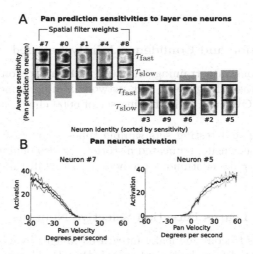

**Fig. 3.** Analysis of the visual motion network $f$. Panel A shows the sensitivity of pan predictions to the activity of all ten neurons in layer 1. Accompanying each sensitivity is a heatmap of the spatial weights of that neuron. There are two spatial filters for each neuron, one for each time constant. Panel B shows the activation of individual neurons to pan velocity (see supplementary material for tilt) in regions which have confidence greater than 0.1. Mean activation across the DVS-COCO testing set is shown in black, with colored lines to show one standard deviation above and below the mean. Color indicates neurons which are selective for negative velocity (blue) or positive velocity (red). (Color figure online)

**Extreme Event Dataset and Motion Segmentation.** We use a set of public test sequences called the Extreme Event Dataset (EED) [6]. The EED features independently moving objects and 6DOF motion in challenging lighting scenarios, including a strobe light. This dataset serves as a benchmark for event-based motion segmentation algorithms. It comes with hand labeled ground truth bounding boxes of independently moving objects in the scene.

To segment a scene, we cluster the confident flows output from our network. We compute a distance between each confident flow, e.g. $u_{x_i y_i}$ and $u_{x_j y_j}$:

$$d_{ij} = \sqrt{(u_{x_i y_i} - u_{x_j y_j})^2 + (x_i - x_j)^2 + (y_i + y_j)^2} \tag{5}$$

We threshold $d_{ij}$ at 10, and cluster all graph connected flows together. This parameter is flexible, and was selected to be on the order of one of our kernel filters. To compare with [6,21,35] we use the success rate defined in [6], which is the percentage of bounding boxes in a sequence overlapping 50% or more with a proposed segmentation.

# 4  Results

## 4.1  Visual Motion and Confidence Jointly Learned

In Fig. 2, we demonstrate training and test performance on the DVS-COCO velocity recovery task. In general, our network is able to accurately recovers test set velocities. Over the entire testing set of 6000 clips, our $MSE_{global}$ is 4.5 $(degrees/sec)^2$.

As our training and testing sets sample times sparsely from 1000 training and 300 testing videos using truncated histories, we also demonstrate the ability of our network to make continuous predictions with full time histories on four testing videos (Fig. 2).

## 4.2  Network $f$ Learns Direction Selective Neurons

Our network learns to combine leaky integrated images by computing their difference, as is expected from biological models [10,11]. This can be seen qualitatively in Fig. 3, which shows learned filters for the two $\tau$ are opposite in sign. The median correlation between $\tau_{fast}$ weights and $\tau_{slow}$ is $-.83$.

The high sensitivity learned kernels for pan prediction shown in Fig. 3A are polarized horizontally. This suggests that diagonal edges are being ignored for pan predictions in the unrotated reference frame, which is consistent with a solution to the aperture problem. In Fig. 3B, we see those neurons are direction selective, with an approximately linear relationship with speed in their selected direction.

## 4.3  Confidence Network Identifies Edges and Phase

The behavior of our confidence network is shown in Fig. 4. For predictions in the unrotated reference frame, our confidence network outputs vertical and horizontal lines. In general, this strategy enables identifying regions $x, y$ in which either $\hat{u}_{xy}$ or $\hat{v}_{xy}$ are confident, but not both. This is unlike corner detectors, such as the Harris detector [36], which can be used for both components of optical flow. That our network does not look for corners could be due to the relative sparsity of corners compared to edges. Our network is trained on $150 \times 150$ windows, and such corners might not always be present.

In Fig. 4(right), we show the optical flow predictions with confidence greater than zero. Only optical flow predictions with the proper phase, i.e. the phase corresponding to predictions with the same sign as the ground truth, are selected. Thus our optical flow network need only make accurate predictions given a single phase.

## 4.4  Ablation Results

**Two $\tau$ leaky Integrating Image Ablation.** Networks trained with a single $\tau$ leaky integrating image are unable to learn velocity. Such networks output only zero, and therefore have a MSE of about 700 $(degrees/s)^2$.

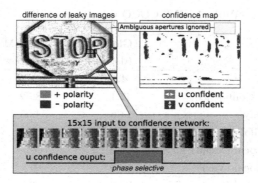

**Fig. 4.** Confidence network in action. Top left: difference of leaky integrated images is shown for a scene from the DVS-COCO dataset. Top right: the confidence output from the corresponding input. No confidence is shown in white. Bottom: sequential 15 × 15 windows of the input are shown above the confidence output of that region. The confidence network is selective to the phase of the edge orthogonal to the direction of visual motion.

**Learned Confidence Ablation.** Using the heuristic confidence described in Sect. 3.6 learns to predict pan/tilt with significantly higher MSE (47.6 $(\text{degree/s})^2$). This filter is agnostic to the orientation of edges, and thus suffers due to the aperture problem.

**Mixture of Input Ablation.** Networks trained using only the loss function $\mathcal{L}_g$ learn accurate global optical flow (MSE 9.61), but local predictions are often inaccurate (MSE 54.02). This is because, although the weighted average is constrained by the loss $\mathcal{L}_g$, the variance of that distribution of predictions is not. More surprisingly, constrained global predictions are worse than those trained with the local loss $\mathcal{L}_f$. Together, this suggests Mixture of Inputs training helps in both the identification and learning of accurate predictions.

## 4.5    Comparison Results

**Global Contrast Maximization.** Global contrast maximization [20], iterating over all possible optical flow vectors and taking as evidence all events in the image over a time window, can be expected to very accurately recover velocity in our pan-tilt setup. Indeed on the DVS-COCO testing set, this method recovers velocities with a low MSE of 6.0. While our network's globally weighted average prediction made better predictions overall (4.5), our local predictions, each made using only a single 15 × 15 window, are on average as accurate as the global CM predictions (6.1 vs 6.0) (Table 1).

**Table 1.** DVS-COCO velocity prediction

|  | Global MSE (degrees/sec)$^2$ | Local MSE (degrees/sec)$^2$ |
|---|---|---|
| Ours | **4.5** | **6.1** |
| Mean Confidence | 47.1 | 48.52 |
| $\mathcal{L}_g$ Only | 11.6 | 54.05 |
| CM Global | 6.0 | N/A |
| CM Local (Mean) | 14.9 | (69.7) |
| CM Local (Var) | 10.4 | (129.7) |
| CM Local (Our confidence) | 28.6 | 193.7 |

**Local Contrast Maximization.** Local contrast maximization, using the same $15 \times 15$ windows as our network, provides comparisons to our local predictions. Without any kind of confidence metric, the average of all such local predictions are, as one would expect, not very accurate. Therefore we extend their method to include heuristic confidences which aim to cover the information available to the CM calculation (see supplementary material for more detail).

Using global averages of local CM weighted by the mean, variance, and our network's own confidence, improves CM prediction accuracy (10.4 MSE for variance weighting, 14.9 for mean, and 28.6 using our confidence weights). Identifying accurate local CM predictions is difficult, resulting in higher local predictions errors (ours: 6.1, contrast maximization with mean: 69.7, variance: 129.7, our confidence: 193.7). The challenge of identifying accurate local predictions in other approaches demonstrates the importance of joint training in our network.

**Motion Segmentation of Extreme Event Dataset.** The Extreme Event Dataset [6] is comprised of several scenarios designed to be challenging for traditional cameras. In particular, it features a moving DAVIS240B with independently moving, small objects with speeds around 600 pixels/s in dark, uneven, and in stobe lighting. The task for this dataset is to segment these moving objects, despite possible occlusion from netting or other objects.

Our network relies on identifying regions for which cheap visual motion calculations can be reliable. There is no guarantee that every object will contain these confident regions, and the purpose of evaluating on the EED is that it contains small, fast moving drones and occluded objects which will challenge our confidence network. Furthermore, as there is no accompanying training data for this task, our network must generalize from training on a static, well-lit computer screen using a different DVS with pan/tilt motions. The EED, by contrast, contains 3D translational camera motions and Z-axis rotions and challenging lighting.

From Fig. 5 and our segmentation results in Table 2, we demonstrate that our network generalizes to these challenging conditions. Our network is able to

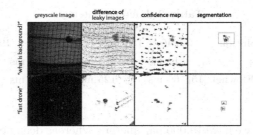

**Fig. 5.** Motion segmentation examples from the extreme event dataset [6].

**Table 2.** EED success percentage

| Sequence | SOFAS [35] | Mitrokhin [6] | Stoffregen [21] | Ours |
|---|---|---|---|---|
| Fast moving drone | 87.89 | 92.78 | 96.30 | **100.00** |
| Multiple objects | 46.15 | 87.32 | **96.77** | 93.3 |
| Lighting variation | 0.0 | 84.52 | 80.51 | **97.40** |
| What is background? | 22.08 | 89.21 | **100.00** | **100.00** |
| Occluded sequence | 80.00 | 90.83 | 92.31 | **100.00** |

reliably produce confident flows on the background as well as the often small and quick independently moving objects in the scene. Furthermore, these confident flows are accurate enough to separate the flows of these objects from the flows due to camera motion. Our performance is strong particularly on the strobe light sequence. This is perhaps due to our confidence network rejecting regions and times which are greatly affected by the sudden changes in lighting. We show relatively weak performance on the multiple drones sequences, showing the limitations of our confidence network.

**Computational Comparisons.** In Table 3, we show the inference latency using a GeForce GTX 1080 of our network and EV-Flownet, a deep network which produces dense optical flow [15]. From this comparison we see that our network performs significantly faster on low resolutions (5 times speed on 240 × 180) and saturates with increasing number of pixels to 3.5 times faster on HD resolution.

From [21] the processing latency of Contrast Maximization's image warp is 1ms for 4000events on a scene with egomotion and one independently moving object using a 240 × 180 DVS. [21] does not mention the number of events used for a calculation, only that the set of events span the order of milliseconds. If we assume a motion generating events in three percent DVS pixels per millisecond, then a 240 × 180 DVS will generate on the order of 10000 events and we approximate the latency of [21] on the order of 10ms. Importantly, the latency increases linearly with number of objects moving and with the resolution of the camera. Our approach does not use a motion model and is invariant to the number of objects in the scene. Thus, in the absence of moving objects and with low resolution cameras, [21] will have a lower latency than our approach.

**Table 3.** Inference latency

| Resolution | 240 × 180 | 320 × 480 | 1080 × 1920 |
|---|---|---|---|
| Ours | 12 ms | 25 ms | 500 ms |
| EV-Flownet [15] | 65 ms | 125 ms | 1800 ms |

In our network, we have 19,000 parameters, whereas deep networks producing dense optical flow predictions in [17] and [15] use 2 million and 14 million respectively. In memory limited systems, high parameter networks may require slow, sequential loading of subnetworks from external memory. Deep networks such as [17] and [15] also use skip connections, requiring storage of past activations. In our approach, only one layer's activations are used in any calculation, meaning previous layer's activation can be forgotten. Contrast Maximization based approaches, however, need only store events and are therefore are the lowest memory approach.

## 5  Discussion

In this work we proposed a low-parameter network which makes accurate motion predictions with low latency for event cameras. Our novel training approach enables the joint learning of a spatially local prediction network and its confidence using a global signal. We show that local predictions generalize well to untrained conditions such as challenging lighting and scenes with ego-motion and independently moving objects for motion segmentation. We suggest our approach is valuable in resource limited systems where accurate motion information is necessary, such as those arising in robotics.

Future work will investigate furthering the computational efficiency of our network, such as using multiple smaller convolutions, or dilation, as our large convolution size is the current computational bottleneck of our approach. The fully-local nature of our predictions also enables the network's stride to be adjusted without compromising predictions. This suggests that not only could the resolution of our predictions be adjusted to meet a systems resources, one could also dynamically adjust the stride to use more or less computation in response to environmental conditions.

While our network was trained on a simple motion task, our global training signal could come from an IMU, where local predictions and depth information are combined in an ego-motion model for training.

## References

1. Gallego, G., et al.: Event-based vision: a survey. arXiv preprint arXiv:1904.08405 (2019)
2. Drazen, D., Lichtsteiner, P., Häfliger, P., Delbrück, T., Jensen, A.: Toward real-time particle tracking using an event-based dynamic vision sensor. Exp. Fluids **51**(5), 1465 (2011)

3. Lichtsteiner, P., Posch, C., Delbruck, T.: A $128\times 128$ 120 db 15 $\mu s$ latency asynchronous temporal contrast vision sensor. IEEE J.JSSC, **43**(2), 566–576 (2008)
4. Rebecq, H., Ranftl, R., Koltun, V., Scaramuzza, D.: High speed and high dynamic range video with an event camera. IEEE Trans. Pattern Anal. Mach. Intell. (2019)
5. Delmerico, J., Cieslewski, T., Rebecq, H., Faessler, M., Scaramuzza, D.: Are we ready for autonomous drone racing? the UZH-FPV drone racing dataset. In: 2019 International Conference on Robotics and Automation (ICRA), pp. 6713–6719. IEEE (2019)
6. Mitrokhin, A., Fermuller, C., Parameshwara, C., Aloimonos, Y.: Event-based moving object detection and tracking. In: 2018 IEEE/RSJ International Conference on Intelligent Robots and Systems (IROS), October 2018. http://dx.doi.org/10.1109/IROS.2018.8593805
7. Zhu, A.Z., Thakur, D., Özaslan, T., Pfrommer, B., Kumar, V., Daniilidis, K.: The multivehicle stereo event camera dataset: an event camera dataset for 3D perception. IEEE Robot. Autom. Lett. **3**(3), 2032–2039 (2018)
8. Amir, A., et al.: A low power, fully Event-Based gesture recognition system. In: 2017 IEEE Conference on Computer Vision and Pattern Recognition (CVPR), pp. 7388–7397, July 2017
9. Barranco, F., Fermuller, C., Aloimonos, Y., Delbruck, T.: A dataset for visual navigation with neuromorphic methods. Front. Neurosci. **10**, 49 (2016)
10. Reichrdt, W.E.: Autocorrelation, a principle for the evaluation of sensory information by the central nervous system. Sens. Commun. 303–317 (1961)
11. Adelson, E.H., Bergen, J.R.: Spatiotemporal energy models for the perception of motion. J. Opt. Soc. Am. A. **2**(2), 284–299 (1985)
12. Britten, K.H., Shadlen, M.N., Newsome, W.T., Movshon, J.A.: Responses of neurons in macaque MT to stochastic motion signals. Vis. Neurosci. **10**(6), 1157–1169 (1993)
13. Simoncelli, E.P., Heeger, D.J.: A model of neuronal responses in visual area MT. Vis. Res. **38**(5), 743–761 (1998)
14. Borst, A., Haag, J., Reiff, D.F.: Fly motion vision. Annu. Rev. Neurosci. **33**, 49–70 (2010)
15. Zhu, A.Z., Yuan, L., Chaney, K., Daniilidis, K.: EV-FlowNet: self-supervised optical flow estimation for event-based cameras, February 2018
16. Ye, C., Mitrokhin, A., Parameshwara, C., Fermüller, C., Yorke, J.A., Aloimonos, Y.: Unsupervised learning of dense optical flow and depth from sparse event data. CoRR, vol. abs/1809.08625 (2018). http://arxiv.org/abs/1809.08625
17. Mitrokhin, A., Ye, C., Fermuller, C., Aloimonos, Y., Delbruck, T.: EV-IMO: motion segmentation dataset and learning pipeline for event cameras, March 2019
18. Benosman, R., Clercq, C., Lagorce, X., Ieng, S.-H., Bartolozzi, C.: Event-based visual flow. IEEE Trans. Neural Netw. Learn. Syst. **25**(2), 407–417 (2014)
19. Gallego, G., Rebecq, H., Scaramuzza, D.: A unifying contrast maximization framework for event cameras, with applications to motion, depth, and optical flow estimation. CoRR, vol. abs/1804.01306, 2018. http://arxiv.org/abs/1804.01306
20. Gallego, G., Scaramuzza, D.: Accurate angular velocity estimation with an event camera. IEEE Robot. Autom. Lett. **2**(2), 632–639 (2017)
21. Stoffregen, T., Gallego, G., Drummond, T., Kleeman, L., Scaramuzza, D.: Event-based motion segmentation by motion compensation (2019)
22. Jacobs, R.A., et al.: Adaptive mixtures of local experts. Neural Comput. **3**(1), 79–87 (1991)
23. Vaswani, A., et al.: Attention is all you need. In: Advances in neural information processing systems, pp. 5998–6008 (2017)

24. Girshick, R.: Fast r-cnn. In: Proceedings of the IEEE International Conference on Computer Vision, pp. 1440–1448 (2015)
25. Redmon, J., Divvala, S., Girshick, R., Farhadi, A.: You only look once: unified, real-time object detection. In: Proceedings of the IEEE Conference on Computer Vision and Pattern Recognition (CVPR), June 2016
26. Liu, W., et al.: SSD: single shot multibox detector. In: Leibe, B., Matas, J., Sebe, N., Welling, M. (eds.) ECCV 2016. LNCS, vol. 9905, pp. 21–37. Springer, Cham (2016). https://doi.org/10.1007/978-3-319-46448-0_2
27. Mueggler, E., Rebecq, H., Gallego, G., Delbruck, T., Scaramuzza, D.: The event-camera dataset and simulator: event-based data for pose estimation, visual odometry, and SLAM. Int. J. Rob. Res. **36**(2), 142–149 (2017)
28. Sironi, A., Brambilla, M., Bourdis, N., Lagorce, X., Benosman, R.: HATS: histograms of averaged time surfaces for robust event-based object classification. In: Proceedings of the IEEE Conference on Computer Vision and Pattern Recognition, pp. 1731–1740 (2018)
29. Lagorce, X., Orchard, G., Galluppi, F., Shi, B.E., Benosman, R.B.: HOTS: a hierarchy of event-based time-surfaces for pattern recognition. IEEE Trans. Pattern Anal. Mach. Intell. **39**(7), 1346–1359 (2017)
30. Gerstner, W., Kistler, W.M.: Spiking Neuron Models: Single Neurons, Populations, Plasticity. Cambridge University Press, Cambridge (2002)
31. Baker, S., Matthews, I.: Lucas-Kanade 20 years on: a unifying framework. Int. J. Comput. Vis. **56**(3), 221–255 (2004)
32. Wallach, H.: Über visuell wahrgenommene bewegungsrichtung. Psychologische Forschung **20**(1), 325–380 (1935)
33. Lin, T.-Y., et al.: Microsoft COCO: common objects in context. In: Fleet, D., Pajdla, T., Schiele, B., Tuytelaars, T. (eds.) ECCV 2014. LNCS, vol. 8693, pp. 740–755. Springer, Cham (2014). https://doi.org/10.1007/978-3-319-10602-1_48
34. Kingma, D.P., Ba, J.: Adam: a method for stochastic optimization, December 2014
35. Stoffregen, T., Kleeman, L.: Simultaneous optical flow and segmentation (sofas) using dynamic vision sensor (2018)
36. Harris, C., Stephens, M.: A combined corner and edge detector. In: Proceeding of Fourth Alvey Vision Conference, pp. 147–151 (1988)

# SODA: Story Oriented Dense Video Captioning Evaluation Framework

Soichiro Fujita[1]([✉]), Tsutomu Hirao[2], Hidetaka Kamigaito[1],
Manabu Okumura[1], and Masaaki Nagata[2]

[1] Institute of Innovative Research, Tokyo Institute of Technology, Kanagawa, Japan
{fujiso,kamigaito,oku}@lr.pi.titech.ac.jp
[2] NTT Communication Science Laboratories, NTT Corporation, Kyoto, Japan
{tsutomu.hirao.kp,masaaki.nagata.et}@hco.ntt.co.jp

**Abstract.** Dense Video Captioning (DVC) is a challenging task that localizes all events in a short video and describes them with natural language sentences. The main goal of DVC is video story description, that is, to generate a concise video story that supports human video comprehension without watching it. In recent years, DVC has attracted increasing attention in the vision and language research community, and has been employed as a task of the workshop, ActivityNet Challenge. In the current research community, the official scorer provided by ActivityNet Challenge is the de-facto standard evaluation framework for DVC systems. It computes averaged METEOR scores for matched pairs between generated and reference captions whose Intersection over Union (IoU) exceeds a specific threshold value. However, the current framework does not take into account the story of the video or the ordering of captions. It also tends to give high scores to systems that generate several hundred redundant captions, that humans cannot read. This paper proposes a new evaluation framework, Story Oriented Dense video cAptioning evaluation framework (SODA), for measuring the performance of video story description systems. SODA first tries to find temporally optimal matching between generated and reference captions to capture the story of a video. Then, it computes METEOR scores for the matching and derives F-measure scores from the METEOR scores to penalize redundant captions. To demonstrate that SODA gives low scores for inadequate captions in terms of video story description, we evaluate two state-of-the-art systems with it, varying the number of captions. The results show that SODA gives low scores against too many or too few captions and high scores against captions whose number equals to that of a reference, while the current framework gives good scores for all the cases. Furthermore, we show that SODA tends to give lower scores than the current evaluation framework in evaluating captions in the incorrect order.

**Keywords:** Automatic evaluation · Dense Video Captioning · Video story description

**Electronic supplementary material** The online version of this chapter (https://doi.org/10.1007/978-3-030-58539-6_31) contains supplementary material, which is available to authorized users.

© Springer Nature Switzerland AG 2020
A. Vedaldi et al. (Eds.): ECCV 2020, LNCS 12351, pp. 517–531, 2020.
https://doi.org/10.1007/978-3-030-58539-6_31

# 1  Introduction

Dense Video Captioning (DVC) [6] mainly involves two tasks: event detection to identify all events in a short video, and caption generation to describe the event proposals using natural language sentences. DVC is one of the major tasks in vision and language research and has attracted more attention in recent years. In fact, it has been adopted as a task of ActivityNet Challenge[1] since 2017. Its main goal is to generate concise captions that describe the story of a video to help humans understand it. Actually, humans describe the story of a video using 3–4 captions on average. Thus, the generated captions are utilized for grasping an overview of the video without having to watch the entire video [3].

However, the current de-facto standard evaluation framework for DVC systems, which is the official evaluation framework in ActivityNet Challenge, is inappropriate for measuring the performance of a video story description since it disregards the story of the video and the ordering of captions[2]. The framework first matches generated and reference captions when the Intersection over Union (IoU) between them exceeds a specific threshold value. Then, it computes METEOR [2] scores for all matched pairs between the generated and reference captions, and averages them by the number of the pairs. That is, the framework evaluates captions for events without considering the order of their proposals.

In addition, another problem with the current framework is that it often obtains a high score by producing several hundred captions that are inadequate as video story descriptions since the scores rely only on the number of matched pairs. As the result, as we will point out in Sect. 4.2, systems that produce more redundant captions are more advantageous. Most current DVC systems generate several hundred captions for a video, while the number of reference captions is only 3–4.

To appropriately and correctly evaluate video story description systems, we need a framework that can consider a video story, the ordering of captions, and can penalize redundant captions. This paper proposes a new evaluation framework, Story Oriented Dense video cAptioning evaluation framework (SODA), for measuring the performance of video story description systems. SODA first applies dynamic programming, that finds the optimal matching between generated and reference captions that maximizes the sum of the IoU by considering the temporal ordering of captions. Thus, it finds the best sequence of generated proposals that maximizes the sum of the IoU against reference proposals. Then, it computes METEOR scores for the matched pairs and derives precision and recall scores on the basis of the calculated METEOR scores. Finally, our framework evaluates generated captions with F-measure scores to consider both the numbers of generated and reference captions.

To demonstrate the effectiveness of our framework, we evaluate two state-of-the-art systems with it, varying the number of captions. Experimental results

---

[1] http://activity-net.org/.

[2] In this paper, we follow the concept in [3] that the correct order of captions represents a story.

on the ActivityNet Captions dataset [6] show that our framework gives low scores to too many or too few captions, inadequate captions as video story description, and gives high scores to captions whose number equals to that of a reference, while the current framework gives almost the same scores to all the cases. Furthermore, we demonstrate that SODA gives lower scores to captions with incorrect order, inconsistent story description, than the current evaluation framework. In addition to the above automatic evaluation, our simple manual evaluation also shows that SODA is superior to the current framework.

Our main contributions are as follows:

- We demonstrate that the current evaluation framework, utilized in ActivityNet Challenge, is insufficient for evaluating video story descriptions.
- We propose a new evaluation framework, Story Oriented Dense video cAptioning evaluation framework (SODA), for measuring the performance of video story description systems by considering the ordering of captions.
- We introduce F-measure into the evaluation metric to prevent redundant captions from obtaining good scores.
- Our source code will be available on https://github.com/fujiso/SODA.

## 2 Related Work

### 2.1 Dense Video Captioning

The goal of DVC is to obtain concise and coherent description of all events in a video. It requires understanding the entire video contents and contextual reasoning of individual events. Recent researches [6,8,17,20] handled this challenge by dividing it into two subtasks: event proposal detection and caption generation for the events. For example, Wang et al. [17] proposed a bidirectional LSTM-based encoder-decoder model with a context gating mechanism. The mechanism reflects both past and future contexts to the event proposals and the captions. Zhou et al. [20] proposed a self-attention [14] based end-to-end model. The end-to-end architecture could bridge the event detection and the captioning modules, hence it tended to generate a consistent caption for each individual event. However, these models did not explicitly consider the dependency or relationship among the individual events. Mun et al. [10] challenged to generate brief and consistent captions by reducing the number of event proposals with pointer networks [16].

There are several existing datasets for video-to-text generation other than ActivityNet Captions [6]: Youcook II [19], VideoStory [3], TACoS [12], and TACoS Multi-Sentence [13]. Youcook II, TACoS, and TACoS Multi-Sentence datasets were constructed to evaluate the captioning of cooking videos. As these types of captions temporally depend on each other, their order is an important factor to evaluate the systems. However, since Youcook II employed the same evaluation framework as ActivityNet Challenge, and TaCoS and TaCoS Multi-Sentence employed BLEU, the systems might not be evaluated correctly on the datasets. The VideoStory dataset was constructed to evaluate video story description systems for short videos on an social networking service. However, the systems are also evaluated on the dataset with the same framework as ActivityNet Challenge, which is insufficient to evaluate the story of a video. We believe that SODA is useful not only for the ActivityNet Captions dataset but also for the other datasets constructed to evaluate system captions that convey the story.

## 2.2  Dense Caption Evaluation

The automatic evaluation of video description/captioning is a long term and unsolved problem. The evaluation of DVC is required to measure two aspects: 1) the accuracy of localized events, and 2) that of generated captions for each event. The current evaluation framework of DVC is inspired by that of dense image captioning (DIC) [4], which generates captions that describe localized objects in an image comprehensively. In this evaluation framework, each generated caption is separately evaluated using some metrics (See Sect. 3 for details.) because the captions independently describe each localized object.

Thus, there is a significant difference between DVC and DIC in whether generated captions should consist of a story or not. However, the current evaluation framework of DVC, which is a simple extension of that of DIC, does not consider the temporal dependency between captions explicitly, which causes the potential risk of overestimation (See Sect. 4.2 for details.).

In contrast, SODA solves this problem through optimal matching with ground-truth events and penalizing redundant events, as we will explain in Sect. 5. It would be more difficult to obtain a factitiously high score with SODA compared with the current evaluation framework because SODA requires systems to detect the exact number of events and captions, that we believe will lead to further progress of DVC tasks.

The research community of DVC has mainly used the following six different evaluation metrics for caption sentences: ROUGE-L [9], METEOR [2], BLEU [11], CIDEr [15], SPICE [1], and WMD [7]. These metrics were originated from text generation tasks in natural language processing such as machine translation, text summarization, and image captioning. There have been several experiments to make clear which metrics are better for caption evaluation [5, 18] because of too many metrics. They showed that evaluation metrics being relatively less sensitive to word order and synonym changes in a sentence, like CIDEr and METEOR, can provide a high correlation with human judgments. Therefore, METEOR was adopted as the main evaluation metric in DVC.

## 3  Current Evaluation Framework

The automatic evaluation framework proposed for ActivityNet Captions [6] has been widely utilized for the DVC task. Let $\mathcal{G}$ be a set of manually-generated reference captions for a video and $\mathcal{P}$ be a set of captions generated by a system. We denote $g$ as a reference caption and $p$ as a caption generated by the system.

|       | $p_1$ | $p_2$ | $p_3$ | $p_4$ | $p_5$ |
|-------|-------|-------|-------|-------|-------|
| $g_1$ | 0.7   | 0.1   | 0.4   | 0.9   | 0.1   |
| $g_2$ | 0.2   | 0.3   | 0.5   | 0.4   | 0.5   |
| $g_3$ | 0.4   | 1.0   | 0.3   | 0.7   | 0.8   |
| $g_4$ | 0.8   | 0.7   | 0.6   | 1.0   | 0.1   |

**Fig. 1.** An example of IoUs between generated and reference captions.

Each caption has a proposal that indicates a time span of an event that appears in a video. Here, the IoU between $g$ and $p$ is defined as follows:

$$\text{IoU}(g, p) = \max\left( 0, \frac{\min(e(g), e(p)) - \max(s(g), s(p))}{\max(e(g), e(p)) - \min(s(g), s(p))} \right), \tag{1}$$

where functions $s(\cdot)$ and $e(\cdot)$ return the start and end time of the proposal, respectively. Here, a set of reference captions whose IoU exceeds a specific threshold, $\tau$, for $p$ is defined as follows:

$$G_{p,\tau} = \{g \in \mathcal{G} | \text{IoU}(g, p) \geq \tau\}. \tag{2}$$

When $G_{p,\tau} = \phi$, i.e., $p$ does not have any $g$ that exceeds a specific threshold, we add a random string to $G_{p,\tau}$ as a member instead of the caption as a penalty. Finally, a set of generated captions, $\mathcal{P}$, is evaluated on the basis of a set of reference captions, $\mathcal{G}$, by the following equation:

$$E(\mathcal{G}, \mathcal{P}, \tau) = \frac{\sum_{p \in \mathcal{P}} \sum_{g \in G_{p,\tau}} f(g, p)}{\sum_{p \in \mathcal{P}} |G_{p,\tau}|}, \tag{3}$$

where function $f(\cdot, \cdot)$ denotes an evaluation metric such as METEOR [2], BLEU [11], or CIDEr [15]. In this paper, we use METEOR as $f(\cdot, \cdot)$ since ActivityNet Challenge use it as its official metric. In most cases, the final evaluation score was computed as the average for $\tau = 0.9, 0.7, 0.5, 0.3$.

Consider, for example, that IoUs between $\mathcal{G}$ and $\mathcal{P}$ are given as in Fig. 1. When we set $\tau$ to 0.5, we obtain the following: $G_{p_1,0.5} = \{g_1, g_4\}$, $G_{p_2,0.5} = \{g_3, g_4\}$, $G_{p_3,0.5} = \{g_2, g_4\}$, $G_{p_4,0.5} = \{g_1, g_3, g_4\}$, $G_{p_5,0.5} = \{g_2, g_3\}$.

Then, we compute METEOR scores for the eleven matched pairs between $g$ and $p$, $(p_1, g_1)$, $(p_1, g_4)$, $(p_2, g_3)$, $(p_2, g_4)$, $(p_3, g_2)$, $(p_3, g_4)$, $(p_4, g_1)$, $(p_4, g_3)$, $(p_4, g_4)$, $(p_5, g_2)$, and $(p_5, g_3)$, and average the scores.

## 4   Problems of Current Framework

### 4.1   Loose Matching

As we explained in the previous section, the current evaluation framework determines the correspondence between $g$ and $p$ only with the IoU threshold, $\tau$. Thus,

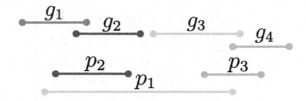

**Fig. 2.** Example of system and reference proposals that produce loose matching.

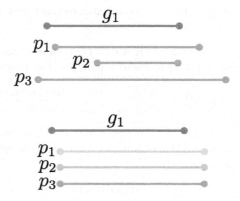

**Fig. 3.** Examples of system and reference proposals that produce redundant captions.

it causes loose matching; a generated caption is matched with many reference captions or a reference caption is matched with many generated captions. The order of generated captions produced by the matching does not correspond to the order of reference captions, i.e., the loose matching disregards the story of the video. For example, when reference and generated captions are given as shown in Fig. 2, the current evaluation framework produces the following matches, $(g_1, p_1)$, $(g_1, p_2)$, $(g_2, p_1)$, $(g_2, p_2)$, $(g_3, p_1)$, $(g_3, p_3)$, and $(g_4, p_3)$ for small $\tau$. Thus, the order of the generated captions corresponding to the reference captions is $p_1, p_2, p_1, p_2, p_1, p_3, p_3$, which is invalid because it contains many duplicates, i.e., the captions do not represent the story of the video. The best order of the generated captions that represents the story can be $p_2, p_1, p_3$.

Furthermore, loose matching produces overestimations of METEOR scores. When we have the same sentences with different length proposals, any of them would match with a reference caption for any $\tau$, even though the redundant captions make no sense. Consider IoUs and METEOR scores are given as follows: $\text{IoU}(g_1, p_1) = 0.9$, $\text{IoU}(g_1, p_2) = 0.4$, $\text{IoU}(g_1, p_3) = 0.6$, and $\text{METEOR}(g_1, p_*) = 0.6$, as shown in the top of Fig. 3. When we set $\tau$ to 0.9, only $g_1$ matches to $p_1$, and the average METEOR score is 0.2, while $p_2$ and $p_3$ are eliminated in the matching. However, when we have only $p_2$, $g_1$ is not matched, and the average METEOR score is 0.0. It indicates that the current evaluation sometimes gives higher scores for low-confidence proposals than a single high-confidence proposal.

Thus, redundant caption sentences, such as identical sentences with proposals of different lengths, may obtain good METEOR scores.

Another problematic case is when we generate multiple different sentences for a proposal, the average METEOR score tends to be good. Consider, for example, METEOR scores are given as follows: $\text{METEOR}(g_1, p_1) = 0$, $\text{METEOR}(g_1, p_2) = 0.3$, and $\text{METEOR}(g_1, p_3) = 0.6$, as shown in the bottom of Fig. 3. In this example, the average METEOR score is 0.3, while it is 0 when generating only $p_1$. Thus, generating multiple different caption sentences for a proposal tends to prevent a zero Meteor score.

### 4.2  Averaging METEOR Scores

As shown in Equation (3), the sum of METEOR scores is averaged based on the number of matched pairs between $g$ and $p$. That is, the number of captions generated by a system, $|\mathcal{P}|$, and the number of reference captions, $|\mathcal{G}|$, are disregarded in calculating the evaluation metric. Thus, it cannot take into account the coverage of generated captions (recall) and the accuracy of the captions (precision) either.

As we mentioned above, a better score is obtained by generating more different sentences for a proposal and more identical sentences for different proposals. Most of current DVC systems generate many and redundant caption sentences for a video. The average number of generated caption sentences is around several hundred. Thus, the current evaluation framework is inadequate since we cannot read several hundred sentences in a short time, while, of course, it may be reasonable to assess DVC systems in terms of video indexing, which does not require human reading. This is a critical problem of the current evaluation framework for video story description systems.

Furthermore, too few caption sentences are also inappropriate because such captions cannot represent the whole story of a video. To penalize such inappropriate captions, we can derive precision and recall by replacing the denominator of Equation (3) with $|\mathcal{P}|$ and $|\mathcal{G}|$, respectively. However, they are invalid since the scores might exceed 1.0.

## 5  Story Oriented Dense Video cAptioning Evaluation Framework (SODA)

### 5.1  Optimal Matching Using Dynamic Programming

To determine the matching between generated and reference captions, we regard the matching as a combinatorial optimization problem: finding one-to-one matching between the captions that maximizes the sum of the IoU by considering temporal ordering. Following the current evaluation framework, we also use the threshold $\tau$ for the matching; we define cost $C_{i,j}$ between a reference caption $g_i$ and a generated caption $p_j$ based on the IoU as follows:

$$C_{i,j} = \begin{cases} \text{IoU}(g_i, p_j) & \text{if } \text{IoU}(g_i, p_j) \geq \tau, \\ 0 & \text{otherwise.} \end{cases} \tag{4}$$

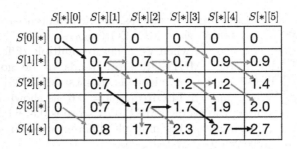

**Fig. 4.** Illustration of a dynamic programming table.

Then, we sort the captions based on temporal ordering, that is, in the order of the beginning time of their proposals, by utilizing function $s(\cdot)$, and define $S[i][j]$, which stores the maximum score of optimal matching between 1st to $i$-th generated captions and the 1st to $j$-th reference truth captions, as follows:

- Initialization

$$S[i][0] = 0 \ (0 \le i \le |\mathcal{P}|), S[0][j] = 0 \ (0 \le j \le |\mathcal{G}|), \tag{5}$$

- Recurrence $(1 \le i \le |\mathcal{P}|, 1 \le k \le |\mathcal{G}|)$

$$S[i][j] = \max \begin{cases} S[i-1][j], \\ S[i-1][j-1] + C_{i,j}, \\ S[i][j-1]. \end{cases} \tag{6}$$

Figure 4 shows an example process to obtain the optimal matching for the example given in Fig. 1, with $\tau = 0$. After filling out table $S$ by dynamic programming, $S[4][5]$ stores the optimal matching score, 2.7. Thus, we can obtain the optimal matching between $g_k$ and $p_\ell$ by tracing the path, from [4,5] to [0,0]. In the example, the optimal matching is $(g_1, p_1)$, $(g_3, p_2)$, $(g_4, p_4)$. The pseudo code of the algorithm is shown in the supplementary material.

## 5.2 F-Measure for Evaluating Video Story Description

To give a low score for too many or too few captions, the sum of METEOR scores should be normalized by considering the number of generated and reference captions. Thus, we propose an evaluation metric based on F-measure as follows:

$$\text{F-measure}(\mathcal{G}, \mathcal{P}) = \frac{2 \times \text{Precision}(\mathcal{G}, \mathcal{P}) \times \text{Recall}(\mathcal{G}, \mathcal{P})}{\text{Precision}(\mathcal{G}, \mathcal{P}) + \text{Recall}(\mathcal{G}, \mathcal{P})}. \tag{7}$$

Here, $\text{Precision}(\mathcal{G}, \mathcal{P})$ and $\text{Recall}(\mathcal{G}, \mathcal{P})$ are defined on the basis of the optimal matching as follows:

$$\text{Precision}(\mathcal{G}, \mathcal{P}) = \frac{\sum_{g \in \mathcal{G}} f(g, p_{a(g)})}{|\mathcal{P}|}, \tag{8}$$

$$\text{Recall}(\mathcal{G}, \mathcal{P}) = \frac{\sum_{g \in \mathcal{G}} f(g, p_{a(g)})}{|\mathcal{G}|}. \tag{9}$$

When systems generate too many captions, Precision scores tend to be low, while Recall scores tend to be high. Thus, the systems cannot obtain good F-measure scores. When systems generate too few captions, they also cannot obtain good F-measure scores since they tend to receive good Precision scores but poor Recall scores.

### 5.3   Evaluation Scores Directly Dependent on IoU

In evaluating video story descriptions, the IoU plays an important role. Even if METEOR scores between generated and reference captions are perfect, they make no sense if the IoU between the captions is zero. However, in the current evaluation framework, the IoU is utilized only for determining the matching between the captions. Thus, the IoU does not directly affect the sum of METEOR scores. In fact, METEOR scores with larger IoUs and those with smaller ones cannot be distinguished when computing them. To reflect the IoU more directly to evaluation scores, we propose an alternative of the cost in Equation (4), which is utilized to solve dynamic programming as follows:

$$C_{i,j} = \text{IoU}(g_i, p_j) f(g_i, p_j). \tag{10}$$

By utilizing this cost, even if the METEOR score is high, the evaluation score can be lowered when the IoU score is low.

## 6   Experiments

### 6.1   Experimental Settings

We used the ActivityNet Captions dataset [6][3], which contains 20k YouTube videos. The dataset consists of 10,024, 4,915 and 5,044 videos for training, validation and test data, respectively. We evaluated our evaluation framework only on the validation data because the test data is not publicly available[4]. Each video in the validation data has on average 3.52 human-written captions with start/end time annotations. The average number of words in a caption is 13.54.

Because it is known that METEOR has sufficient correlation against human evaluation, we did not evaluate our framework by calculating the correlation against manual evaluation. To demonstrate the effectiveness of the optimal proposal detection and F-measure, we simply examined whether our framework could give low scores for inadequate captions and high scores for adequate captions in terms of video story description. Thus, we evaluated the following two state-of-the-art DVC systems with two settings below:

---

[3] Using the VideoStory dataset [3] would have been more effective as it was constructed to evaluate video story description systems. However, unfortunately, it has not been publicly available.

[4] The test data is only available on the ActivityNet evaluation server.

- End-to-end transformer-based system [20]: The end-to-end transformer-based models could detect events by considering the whole video information and generate consistent captions for the events simultaneously. The number of output captions per video is 228.21 on average.
- LSTM-based system [17]: The bidirectional LSTM-based encoder-decoder models with a context gating mechanism. The context gating mechanism makes it possible to generate captions by filtering both past and future contexts. The number of output captions per video is 97.10 on average.

Note that we obtained captions generated by the end-to-end transformer-based model by running their code, available at the github repository[5], and those by the LSTM-based model were provided by the authors of the paper.

**Detecting Inappropriate Captions:** To demonstrate whether SODA gives low scores to inadequate captions, we first performed experiments by varying the number of captions. Since both systems generate around hundred or more captions for each video, we randomly selected $\text{int}(m \times |\mathcal{G}|)$ captions[6] without duplication and evaluated the captions by the current evaluation framework[7], and the following metrics in our framework:

- SODA (a): averaging F-measure scores with $\tau = 0.9, 0.7, 0.5, 0.3$,
- SODA (b): F-measure, where $\tau$ is set to 0,
- SODA (c): F-measure, utilizing the cost in Equation (11).

We examined $m = 0.1, 0.5, 1.0, 2.0, 10$, and "all", where $m = 1.0$ indicates a case of outputting the same number of captions as a reference. We report the average scores with five times of the randomized procedure.

**Detecting Incorrect Ordering:** To demonstrate whether SODA gives low scores to captions with incorrect ordering, we evaluated original captions with correct ordering and two types of captions with incorrect ordering: (a) Swap, swapping the order of two adjacent captions for a randomly selected pair in the original, and (b) Shuffle, randomly shuffling the order of captions in the original. Since systems generate a huge number of captions, we cannot evaluate them as they are, and we need to perform the experiments with a reasonable number of captions. Therefore, we assessed the systems by their potential, the upper bound performances; we examined captions that were the closest to the corresponding references. That is, we used oracle captions as the original captions with correct ordering. Here, an oracle caption indicates a caption of the same length as a reference caption that receives the maximum METEOR score. We

---

[5] https://github.com/salesforce/densecap.

[6] $m$ is a parameter for controlling the number of captions in the experiments.

[7] We utilized the official scorer provided by ActivityNet Challenge. The code is available at https://github.com/ranjaykrishna/densevid_eval. We used the revised version from November 2017 that fixed an overestimation bug; the number of pairs (the denominator in Equation (3)) was not counted correctly.

created the oracles by selecting those generated captions that receive the maximum METEOR score for each reference caption. Then, we created the Swap and Shuffle captions from the oracle captions by randomly varying their proposals so that keeping IoUs exceed 0.7.

## 6.2  Results

**Detecting Inappropriate Captions:** Table 1 shows the results. From the results, the scores of the current evaluation framework do not change significantly even when the number of captions changes. We observe a similar tendency in both results obtained from the two different systems. In particular, there is only a slight difference between $m = 1$, the appropriate number of captions, and "all", the inappropriate number of captions for humans to read. As long as DVC systems are evaluated with the current evaluation framework, they would continue to generate many and redundant captions. As we mentioned before, the results are caused by (1) loose matching between generated and reference captions, and (2) averaging METEOR scores by the number of the matched pairs. The results reveal that the framework has a critical problem, i.e., it cannot distinguish good captions from bad captions in terms of video story description. In contrast, SODA gave low scores for too many and too few captions. When we utilized a small $m$, precision became high, while recall became low. Precision became low and recall became high when we utilized a large $m$. Thus, SODA can penalize inadequate captions.

Before we compare the performance of the two systems, we need to address the question: "Which is better: E2E Transformer or LSTM in terms of video story description?". Therefore, we compared their oracle performances and their diversities. We created the oracles as above and averaged their METEOR scores. Then, we computed Self-BLEU [21][8] as a measure to assess the quality of oracle captions in terms of diversity. The results shown in Table 2 demonstrate that E2E Transformer outperformed LSTM in terms of both METEOR and Self-BLEU scores with significant differences. Thus, we can conclude that the potential of E2E Transformer to describe the video story is superior to that of LSTM. Although LSTM outperformed E2E Transformer with the current evaluation framework in Table 1, the result does not agree with Table 2. However, the evaluation results with SODAs in Table 1 can agree with Table 2 in that E2E Transformer outperformed LTSM.

Comparing the variants of SODA, the fluctuation of SODA (a) is smaller than that of the other metrics since it received low scores when utilizing a big $\tau$. On the other hand, the scores of SODA (b) and (c) sensitively change with $m$, and the fluctuation is large. To assess the performance of video story description, the metric should be sensitive to the number of captions to be evaluated. Thus, SODA (b) and (c) are more appropriate for measuring the performance of video story description systems. Since SODA (c) involves the IoU in the evaluation

---

[8] Self-BLEU has been used to assess the diversity of a set of generated sentences in text generation tasks. A lower score indicates a higher diversity.

**Table 1.** Changes of scores (%) obtained from the current evaluation framework and SODA when varying the number of captions. Prec., Rec., and $F_1$ indicate precision, recall, and F-measure, respectively.

| | $m$ | E2E Transformer [20] | | | | | | LSTM [17] | | | | | |
|---|---|---|---|---|---|---|---|---|---|---|---|---|---|
| | | 0.1 | 0.5 | 1.0 | 2.0 | 10 | All | 0.1 | 0.5 | 1.0 | 2.0 | 10 | All |
| | Current | 3.78 | 4.04 | 4.10 | 4.14 | 4.18 | 4.19 | 4.72 | 4.88 | 4.92 | 4.94 | 4.96 | 4.97 |
| SODA (a) | Prec. | 10.06 | 5.22 | 3.86 | 2.59 | 0.77 | 0.27 | 9.97 | 4.77 | 3.14 | 1.85 | 0.47 | 0.37 |
| | Rec. | 1.43 | 2.79 | 3.86 | 5.18 | 7.65 | 8.76 | 1.42 | 2.54 | 3.14 | 3.70 | 4.53 | 4.66 |
| | $F_1$ | 2.51 | 3.63 | 3.86 | 3.45 | 1.40 | 0.52 | 2.44 | 3.32 | 3.14 | 2.46 | 0.86 | 0.63 |
| SODA (b) | Prec. | 10.50 | 9.32 | 7.55 | 4.68 | 1.06 | 0.34 | 9.94 | 8.05 | 6.07 | 3.50 | 0.81 | 0.57 |
| | Rec. | 1.50 | 4.97 | 7.55 | 9.36 | 10.52 | 11.1 | 1.42 | 4.29 | 6.07 | 7.00 | 7.75 | 7.82 |
| | $F_1$ | 2.62 | 6.48 | 7.55 | 6.24 | 1.92 | 0.66 | 2.43 | 5.60 | 6.07 | 4.67 | 1.47 | 1.05 |
| SODA (c) | Prec. | 5.93 | 4.89 | 4.02 | 2.87 | 0.94 | 0.33 | 7.01 | 4.49 | 3.15 | 1.94 | 0.53 | 0.37 |
| | Rec. | 0.84 | 2.61 | 4.02 | 5.74 | 9.30 | 10.62 | 1.00 | 2.40 | 3.15 | 3.87 | 5.06 | 5.25 |
| | $F_1$ | 1.47 | 3.41 | 4.02 | 3.83 | 1.70 | 0.63 | 1.75 | 3.12 | 3.15 | 2.58 | 0.96 | 0.71 |

**Table 2.** Average METEOR and Self-BLEU scores (%) for oracle captions.

| | E2E Transformer | LSTM |
|---|---|---|
| METEOR | 21.3 | 13.43 |
| Self-BLEU | 79.5 | 90.6 |

score, that is, the score depends both on METEOR and IoU, we believe that SODA (c) is the most appropriate.

**Detecting Incorrect Ordering:** Table 3 shows the scores obtained with the current evaluation framework and SODA (c) (F-measure) for correctly- and incorrectly-ordered captions. With both metrics, the scores for captions with incorrect ordering degraded properly. The percentage decreases for Shuffle are larger than those for Swap because Shuffle tends to be worse in the ordering. In comparing SODA with the current evaluation framework, the percentage decreases for Shuffle with SODA (c) are in range of 47–57%, while those with Current are in range of 18–33%. Therefore, SODA (c) can evaluate the incorrectly-ordered captions more severely than the current framework. While the percentage decreases for Swap are smaller than those for Shuffle, we can find a similar tendency as Shuffle that SODA (c) can evaluate the incorrectly ordered captions more severely. These results indicate that SODA is more sensitive to the incorrect ordering of captions than Current, i.e., SODA is more suitable to evaluate the story of a video than the current evaluation framework.

**Table 3.** Evaluation scores (%) for captions with correct and incorrect order. The number in parentheses indicates the percentage decrease from the score for Correct.

| | E2E Transformer | | | LSTM | | |
|---|---|---|---|---|---|---|
| | Correct | Swap | Shuffle | Correct | Swap | Shuffle |
| Current | 16.1 | 14.5 (−10.2) | 10.8 (−33.1) | 10.5 | 9.92 (−5.6) | 8.58 (−18.4) |
| SODA (c) | 17.8 | 14.5 (−18.9) | 7.66 (−57.0) | 10.7 | 8.89 (−17.0) | 5.60 (−47.7) |

In summary, our experiments revealed that SODA finds inappropriate captions in terms of video story description. That is, SODA gives low scores to too many or too few captions and incorrectly ordered captions. These are significant advantages of SODA against the current evaluation framework.

### 6.3 Manual Evaluation

To investigate whether SODA agrees with human judgment, we computed the accuracies of SODA (c) and the current evaluation framework against the results obtained from human judgment, (1) that compared E2E Transformer with LSTM oracles, and (2) that compared Shuffle with Swap for gold standard captions[9]. We randomly selected 50 videos with less than 6 captions, whose length is from 90 to 180 s, from the validation data. Then, we showed the video and the two captions to 12 crowdsourced workers and asked them to compare the captions A and B and to select an integer score from −2 to 2, where the score −2 indicates A is better and the score 2 indicates B is better. We asked them to judge whether the captions correctly describe the entire video, and the events are described in the correct order. We employed only faithful workers who correctly answered test questions, which cannot be answered without watching the video.

In the former human judgment, E2E Transformer obtained better results for 80% of the 50 videos. Thus, the results demonstrate that the potential of E2E Transformer is superior to LSTM. The results agree with those in Table 2. The accuracies of SODA and the current evaluation framework against the human judgment are 0.76 and 0.66, respectively. The results imply that SODA is superior to the current evaluation framework.

In the latter human judgment, Swap obtained better results for 94% of the 50 videos. The results are reasonable and agree with our intuition since Swap keeps better temporal ordering than Shuffle. The results indicate that humans give higher scores when captions meet correct ordering. The accuracies of SODA and the current evaluation framework are 0.94 and 0.72, respectively. The results also show that SODA is superior to the current evaluation framework.

---

[9] In order to prevent Shuffle from being the same as Swap, we employed only captions with reverse ordering of the gold standard as Shuffle in the human judgment.

# 7    Conclusion

In this paper, we demonstrated that the current evaluation framework, which is the official evaluation framework utilized in ActivityNet Challenge, is inadequate for evaluating the performance of video story description systems. Then, we proposed a new evaluation framework, Story Oriented Dense video cAptioning evaluation framework (SODA), to perform better evaluations. To match generated and reference captions considering temporal ordering, SODA first finds the optimal matching that maximizes the sum of the IoU by using dynamic programming. Then, it computes F-measure based on the METEOR scores for the matched pairs.

Evaluation results obtained on the ActivityNet Captions dataset showed that we can detect inadequate captions and too many or too few captions by utilizing SODA, which cannot be detected by using the current evaluation framework. Furthermore, we demonstrated that SODA gives lower scores to captions with incorrect ordering and inconsistent story descriptions, than the current evaluation framework. We also showed that SODA is superior to the current framework in detecting appropriate captions and in detecting captions with incorrect temporal order via manual evaluation.

# References

1. Anderson, P., Fernando, B., Johnson, M., Gould, S.: SPICE: semantic propositional image caption evaluation. In: Leibe, B., Matas, J., Sebe, N., Welling, M. (eds.) ECCV 2016. LNCS, vol. 9909, pp. 382–398. Springer, Cham (2016). https://doi.org/10.1007/978-3-319-46454-1_24
2. Banerjee, S., Lavie, A.: METEOR: an automatic metric for MT evaluation with improved correlation with human judgments. In: Proceedings of the ACL Workshop on Intrinsic and Extrinsic Evaluation Measures for Machine Translation and/or Summarization, pp. 65–72 (2005)
3. Gella, S., Lewis, M., Rohrbach, M.: A dataset for telling the stories of social media videos. In: Proceedings of the 2018 Conference on Empirical Methods in Natural Language Processing, pp. 968–974 (2018). https://www.aclweb.org/anthology/D18-1117.pdf
4. Johnson, J., Karpathy, A., Fei-Fei, L.: Densecap: fully convolutional localization networks for dense captioning. In: Proceedings of the IEEE Conference on Computer Vision and Pattern Recognition (2016)
5. Kilickaya, M., Erdem, A., Ikizler-Cinbis, N., Erdem, E.: Re-evaluating automatic metrics for image captioning. In: Proceedings of the 15th Conference of the European Chapter of the Association for Computational Linguistics: Volume 1, Long Papers, pp. 199–209. Association for Computational Linguistics, Valencia, Spain, April 2017. https://www.aclweb.org/anthology/E17-1019
6. Krishna, R., Hata, K., Ren, F., Fei-Fei, L., Carlos Niebles, J.: Dense-captioning events in videos. In: Proceedings of the IEEE International Conference on Computer Vision, pp. 706–715 (2017). http://openaccess.thecvf.com/content_ICCV_2017/papers/Krishna_Dense-Captioning_Events_in_ICCV_2017_paper.pdf

7. Kusner, M., Sun, Y., Kolkin, N., Weinberger, K.: From word embeddings to document distances. In: International Conference on Machine Learning, pp. 957–966 (2015)
8. Li, Y., Yao, T., Pan, Y., Chao, H., Mei, T.: Jointly localizing and describing events for dense video captioning. In: Proceedings of the IEEE Conference on Computer Vision and Pattern Recognition, pp. 7492–7500 (2018). http://openaccess.thecvf.com/content_cvpr_2018/papers/Li_Jointly_Localizing_and_CVPR_2018_paper.pdf
9. Lin, C.Y.: ROUGE: a package for automatic evaluation of summaries. In: Text Summarization Branches Out, pp. 74–81. Association for Computational Linguistics, Barcelona, Spain, July 2004. https://www.aclweb.org/anthology/W04-1013
10. Mun, J., Yang, L., Ren, Z., Xu, N., Han, B.: Streamlined dense video captioning. In: Proceedings of the IEEE Conference on Computer Vision and Pattern Recognition, pp. 6588–6597 (2019). http://openaccess.thecvf.com/content_CVPR_2019/papers/Mun_Streamlined_Dense_Video_Captioning_CVPR_2019_paper.pdf
11. Papineni, K., Roukos, S., Ward, T., Zhu, W.J.: Bleu: a method for automatic evaluation of machine translation. In: Proceedings of the 40th Annual Meeting on Association for Computational Linguistics, pp. 311–318 (2002)
12. Regneri, M., Rohrbach, M., Wetzel, D., Thater, S., Schiele, B., Pinkal, M.: Grounding action descriptions in videos. Trans. Assoc. Comput. Linguist. 1, 25–36 (2013). https://www.aclweb.org/anthology/Q13-1003.pdf
13. Rohrbach, A., Rohrbach, M., Qiu, W., Friedrich, A., Pinkal, M., Schiele, B.: Coherent multi-sentence video description with variable level of detail. In: Jiang, X., Hornegger, J., Koch, R. (eds.) GCPR 2014. LNCS, vol. 8753, pp. 184–195. Springer, Cham (2014). https://doi.org/10.1007/978-3-319-11752-2_15
14. Vaswani, A., et al.: Attention is all you need. In: Advances in Neural Information Processing Systems, pp. 5998–6008 (2017)
15. Vedantam, R., Zitnick, C.L., Parikh, D.: Cider: consensus-based image description evaluation. In: Proceedings of the IEEE Conference on Computer Vision and Pattern Recognition, pp. 4566–4575 (2015)
16. Vinyals, O., Fortunato, M., Jaitly, N.: Pointer networks. In: Advances in Neural Information Processing Systems, pp. 2692–2700 (2015)
17. Wang, J., Jiang, W., Ma, L., Liu, W., Xu, Y.: Bidirectional attentive fusion with context gating for dense video captioning. In: Proceedings of the IEEE Conference on Computer Vision and Pattern Recognition, pp. 7190–7198 (2018)
18. Wang, J., Gaizauskas, R.: Cross-validating image description datasets and evaluation metrics. In: Proceedings of the Tenth International Conference on Language Resources and Evaluation (LREC'16), pp. 3059–3066. European Language Resources Association (ELRA), Portorož, Slovenia, May 2016. https://www.aclweb.org/anthology/L16-1489
19. Zhou, L., Xu, C., Corso, J.J.: Towards automatic learning of procedures from web instructional videos. In: Thirty-Second AAAI Conference on Artificial Intelligence (2018). https://aaai.org/ocs/index.php/AAAI/AAAI18/paper/view/17344/16367
20. Zhou, L., Zhou, Y., Corso, J.J., Socher, R., Xiong, C.: End-to-end dense video captioning with masked transformer. In: Proceedings of the IEEE Conference on Computer Vision and Pattern Recognition, pp. 8739–8748 (2018). http://openaccess.thecvf.com/content_cvpr_2018/papers/Zhou_End-to-End_Dense_Video_CVPR_2018_paper.pdf
21. Zhu, Y., et al.: Texygen: a benchmarking platform for text generation models. In: Proceedings of SIGIR 18: The 41st International ACM SIGIR Conference on Research & Development in Information Retrieval, pp. 1097–1100 (2018)

# Sketch-Guided Object Localization in Natural Images

Aditay Tripathi[1], Rajath R. Dani[1], Anand Mishra[2],
and Anirban Chakraborty[1(✉)]

[1] Indian Institute of Science, Bengaluru, India
[2] Indian Institute of Technology, Jodhpur, Jodhpur, India
anirban@iisc.ac.in
http://visual-computing.in/sketch-guided-object-localization/

**Abstract.** We introduce a novel problem of localizing all the instances of an object (seen or unseen during training) in a natural image via sketch query. We refer to this problem as sketch-guided object localization. This problem is distinctively different from the traditional sketch-based image retrieval task where the gallery set often contains images with only one object. The sketch-guided object localization proves to be more challenging when we consider the following: (i) the sketches used as queries are abstract representations with little information on the shape and salient attributes of the object, (ii) the sketches have significant variability as they are hand-drawn by a diverse set of untrained human subjects, and (iii) there exists a domain gap between sketch queries and target natural images as these are sampled from very different data distributions. To address the problem of sketch-guided object localization, we propose a novel *cross-modal attention* scheme that guides the region proposal network (RPN) to generate object proposals relevant to the sketch query. These object proposals are later scored against the query to obtain final localization. Our method is effective with as little as a single sketch query. Moreover, it also generalizes well to object categories not seen during training and is effective in localizing multiple object instances present in the image. Furthermore, we extend our framework to a multi-query setting using novel feature fusion and attention fusion strategies introduced in this paper. The localization performance is evaluated on publicly available object detection benchmarks, viz. MS-COCO and PASCAL-VOC, with sketch queries obtained from 'Quick, Draw!'. The proposed method significantly outperforms related baselines on both single-query and multi-query localization tasks.

**Keywords:** Sketch · Cross-modal retrieval · Object localization · One-shot learning · Attention

**Electronic supplementary material** The online version of this chapter (https:// doi.org/10.1007/978-3-030-58539-6_32) contains supplementary material, which is available to authorized users.

A. Vedaldi et al. (Eds.): ECCV 2020, LNCS 12351, pp. 532–547, 2020.
https://doi.org/10.1007/978-3-030-58539-6_32

# 1    Introduction

Localizing objects in a scene via an image query has been a long-sought pursuit in computer vision literature. The seminal paper Video Google [29] addresses object localization in videos using a text retrieval approach. More recent works on this problem focus on localizing seen as well as unseen object categories with as little as one image query during test time [12,17]. There are several applications associated with object localization in an image via image query - examples include object tracking [17] and content-based image retrieval [27,33]. However, the image of an object may not always be preferred as a query due to many practical reasons. These include (i) copyright issues, (ii) privacy concerns, or (iii) significant overhead to collect and annotate images of a rapidly expanding object category set, e.g., in industrial applications where images of each part of the equipment may not be available during the training. Further, it is also not practical to assume that the object names are always available for localization. In such situations, where stronger visual or semantic cues are unavailable, it would be worth exploring if a hand-drawn sketch of an object can be utilized for localizing the object in a natural image. In other words, given hand-drawn sketches of objects (for example, cake, pizza, and bird as shown in the top row of Fig. 1) can we design a framework that learns to localize all instances of these objects present in natural images? In this work, we explore this problem for the first time in the literature and propose a solution to it.

Despite the problem of sketch-guided object localization has a relation to the well-studied sketch-based image retrieval (SBIR) problem [5,14,20,25,28,30,38, 40], these are distinctively different in terms of objectives. It is important to note that SBIR aims to retrieve images from a gallery of localized objects for a given sketch query. Contrary to this, our objective is to precisely localize all instances of an object of interest in a natural scene in presence of many other distracting objects. Furthermore, sketch-guided object localization poses several additional challenges compared to image query-guided object localization, notably - (i) the sketches used as queries are abstract drawings with little information on shape and salient attributes of the object, (ii) the sketches have significant variability as they are drawn by a diverse set of untrained human subjects, and (iii) a large domain gap exists between the sketch queries and the target gallery images.

**Plausible Baseline Approaches vs. Proposed Solution:** Despite its practical utility, sketch-guided object localization has never been explored in the literature. In this work, we consider a state-of-the-art image query-guided localization method [12] and a modified Faster R-CNN [24] as probable baseline approaches. We empirically show that these methods are insufficient due to their sensitivity to the domain gap present between sketches and natural images, and their ineffective attention mechanisms in this context. To mitigate these issues, we develop a *cross-modal attention* scheme to guide proposal generation, which is a crucial step in the localization framework. The proposed *cross-modal attention* scheme generates a spatial compatibility matrix by comparing the global sketch representation with the local image representations obtained from each location

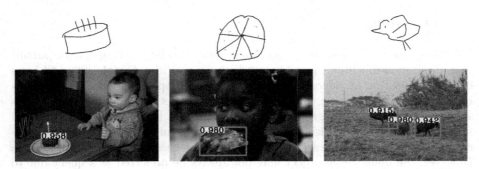

**Fig. 1. Sketch-guided object localization.** Can we localize a cake, a pizza and birds in these images by just drawing their sketches? In this paper, we introduce the problem of sketch-guided object localization, and propose a novel *cross-modal attention* scheme to address this problem. [**Best viewed in color**]. (Color figure online)

of the image feature map. This spatial compatibility matrix creates an attention feature map that is fused with the original feature map of the image. The result of this fusion is subsequently fed to a region proposal network (RPN) to generate proposals relevant to the sketch query. Finally, the proposals are pooled and compared against the query to precisely localize the object of interest.

Our proposed model, by virtue of the aforementioned *cross-modal attention*, embeds query information in the image feature representation before generating region proposals. Therefore, it is inherently able to generate relevant object proposals even for object categories unseen during the training time. This enables the proposed method to achieve superior performance to baseline methods for unseen categories while achieving reasonably high performance for seen categories as well. We also explore the possibility of using multiple sketch queries towards the localization task. To generalize our proposed model to the multi-query setting, we propose novel feature and attention pooling mechanisms.

**Contributions:** In summary, we make the following contributions:

(i) We introduce an important but unexplored problem – *sketch-guided object localization in natural images*. This novel problem is well motivated from scenarios where a query image corresponding to the object of interest or the object category names are not available, but a sketch can be hand-drawn to provide a minimal visual description of the object.

(ii) We propose a novel *cross-modal attention* scheme to guide the region proposal network to generate object proposals relevant to the sketch query. Our method is effective with as little as one sketch used as a query. Moreover, it generalizes well to unseen object categories with $\approx 3\%$ improvement over a one-shot detection method used as baseline [12] and is also effective in localizing multiple object instances present in the image.

(iii) To support multiple sketch-query based object localization, we propose feature and attention pooling in our architecture and demonstrate promising performance.

(iv) We have performed extensive experimentation and ablation studies on two public benchmarks. We firmly believe that our work will open-up novel future research directions under sketch-guided computer vision tasks.

## 2    Related Work

**Sketch-Based Image Retrieval:** Given a sketch query, sketch-based image retrieval (SBIR) aims to retrieve from a gallery of images containing a single object. Methods in SBIR can be grouped into two broad categories- (a) *classical methods* which use hand-crafted features, for example, SIFT or gradient-field histogram of gradients along with a bag-of-words representation of sketches as shown in [5, 14], (b) *deep methods* which utilize cross-modal deep learning techniques by incorporating ranking loss such as the contrastive loss [25] or the triplet loss [38] to learn a ranking function between candidate images and sketch queries which are then subsequently used to score the candidate images, and the top-scoring image is retrieved. In [30], researchers have utilized an attention model to solve fine-grained SBIR, and have introduced HOLEF loss to bridge the domain gap between the sketches and images. Since the time complexity of such methods for large-scale SBIR problem is significantly high, researchers have proposed hashing models, such as [20, 28, 35, 40], which significantly reduces the retrieval time. Contrary to these works, our goal is to use a sketch query to *localize* all instances of an object in an image that usually contains many objects of different categories.

**Object Detection:** Object detection involves localizing and classifying an object in a given image. State-of-the-art object localization methods can be primarily grouped into two categories: *proposal-free* [16, 18, 21–23, 26] and *proposal-based* [1, 7, 8, 10, 11, 24]. *Proposal-free* methods are single-stage detectors, and are faster during inference. However, they often fall short in performance as compared to *proposal-based* methods. *Proposal-based* methods first generate object proposals and then refine them by classifying each of them into one of the object categories. In [8], one such method, selective search [32] was utilized to generate proposals in the first stage, and then use these generated proposals to classify the object. However, the two-stages in this model were trained independently. Faster R-CNN [24] introduced a region proposal network (RPN) that made the detection pipeline end-to-end trainable. Note that, both these types of object detectors are query-free. More recently, Hsieh et al. [12] have introduced one-shot object detection via an image query, where the goal is to localize all the instances of an unseen object in the target image via an image query of the same object. Unlike their work, where query and target images are from the same distribution, our queries, i.e., hand-drawn sketches, are from a significantly different domain as compared to that of the target images.

**Attention in Deep Neural Networks:** The attention model in deep neural networks helps the salient features of the input image to become more critical when required. In [3,31], the authors proposed attention networks to generate attention scores on each of the object proposals, and an attention-based dropout layer for weakly supervised object localization. In [2] a dynamic attention-action strategy using deep reinforcement learning was proposed to localize objects in an image. Hsieh et al. [12] adapted the self-attention mechanism proposed in [34] and applied it to image query-guided object detection. In this method, each pixel in an image was represented as a weighted combination of the pixels in the query image. The weights depend on the similarity between each image pixel and query pixel pairs for all pixels in the query. Conversely, our proposed *cross-modal attention* computes the spatial compatibility between global query representation and localized representations of image regions. This enables it to mitigate the domain misalignment problem prevalent in sketch-guided object localization. Yan et al. [37] used class-specific attentive vectors inferred from images of objects in a meta-set for applying channel-wise soft attention to feature maps of the proposals. However, the channel-wise soft attention may not be trivially utilized in our case due to the domain gap between query sketch and target natural images.

**Sketch Representation:** Besides the traditionally used convolutional neural networks [39], there have been some recent advancements towards robust representation learning for sketches, e.g., SketchRNN [9], transformer-based architecture [36]. Although we have chosen to utilize CNN (ResNet)-based feature encoders in this work, our proposed localization framework can seamlessly integrate more advanced sketch representation learning methods in the feature extraction modules.

## 3   Proposed Methodology

In this section, we first formally introduce the novel problem of sketch-guided object localization in natural images. Then, we present a solution framework built around our novel *cross-modal attention* scheme and discuss its utility for one-shot object detection using a sketch query. Further, we extend our proposed scheme to a multi-query setting, i.e., *multiple sketch query-based object localization* task by introducing principled fusion strategies.

### 3.1   Problem Formulation

Let $I = \{I_{train}, I_{test}\}$ be a set of all natural images, each containing variable number of object instances and categories, in a dataset $\mathcal{D}_I$. Here $I_{train}$ and $I_{test}$ are sets of train and test images respectively. Like any other machine learning task these two sets are mutually exclusive and only $I_{train}$ is available during training time. Further, let $S = \{S_{train}, S_{test}\}$ be a set of all sketches, each containing one object, and $C = \{C_{train}, C_{test}\}$ be a set of all object categories. During training time, each training sample contains an image $i \in I_{train}$, a query sketch $s_c \in S_{train}$, where $c \in C_{train}$, and all the bounding boxes corresponding to object category $c$ in the image $i$. During test time, given an image $i' \in I_{test}$

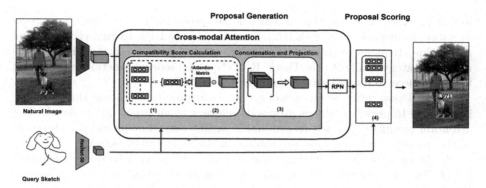

**Fig. 2.** Given an image and a query sketch, our end-to-end trainable sketch-guided localization framework works in the following two stages: (i) **query-guided proposal generation:** in this stage, feature vectors corresponding to different regions in the image feature map (shown using pink) are scored with the global sketch representation (shown using blue) to identify the compatibility (Block-1). Then, these compatibility scores (shown using violet) are multiplied with image feature maps (shown using pink) to get attention feature (Block-2). Further, these attention feature maps are concatenated with the original feature maps and projected to lower-dimensional space which is then passed through region proposal network to generate relevant object proposals (Block-3), (ii) **proposal scoring:** the pooled object proposals (shown using indigo) are scored with sketch feature vector (shown using blue) to generate localization for the object of interest (Block-4). [**Best viewed in color**]. (Color figure online)

and sketch query $s_c \in S_{test}$, where $c \in C_{test}$, the problem is to localize all the instances of the object category $c$ in the image $i'$. Note that we show experimental results in cases where $C_{train} = C_{test}$ i.e., categories in $C_{test}$ are seen during training time (common train-test categories), as well as $C_{train} \cap C_{test} = \phi$, i.e., categories in $C_{test}$ are not seen during training (disjoint train-test categories).

The proposed sketch-guided object localization is an end-to-end trainable framework which works in the following two stages: (i) query-guided object proposal generation (Sect. 3.2), (ii) proposal scoring (Sect. 3.3). Figure 2 illustrates the overall architecture of the proposed framework.

## 3.2   Cross-Modal Attention for Query-Guided Object Proposal Generation

A popular object detection framework, viz. Faster R-CNN [24] uses a region proposal network (RPN) module to generate object proposals. We can use the same module for generating object proposals in our task. However, the RPN is not designed to utilize any information on object appearance available in the query images. Hence, the object proposals that are relevant to the sketch query may not even be generated, especially when the object of interest is of low resolution, occluded or hidden among objects that are better represented in the input images. Therefore, using a RPN in its vanilla form may not be useful in our pipeline. To solve the aforementioned problem, we propose *cross-modal attention* to incorporate the sketch information in the RPN to guide the proposal generation. Regions of interest (ROIs) are pooled from these region proposals using a strategy similar to the Faster R-CNN, and a scoring function $\Theta$ is learned between these ROIs and sketch queries.

We will now describe our novel *cross-modal attention* scheme that we have introduced to generate object proposals relevant to an input query sketch. The attention module is trained to produce a weight map that provides high scores to the areas in an image that are similar to the given query sketch.

A sketch $s_c \in S$ of an object category $c \in C$ is used to query an image $i \in I$. To generate the feature representation of sketches and images, we use ResNet-50 models pretrained on Imagenet [4] and Quick-Draw [15] datasets for images and sketches respectively as a backbone. Suppose $\phi_I$ and $\phi_S$ represent these backbone models, then image and sketch feature maps are computed as:

$$i^{\phi_I} = \phi_I(i) \quad \text{and} \quad s_c^{\phi_S} = \phi_S(s_c), \tag{1}$$

where, $i^{\phi_I} \in \mathbb{R}^{w \times h \times d}$ and $s_c^{\phi_S} \in \mathbb{R}^{w' \times h' \times d}$ are the extracted image and sketch feature maps respectively. From these feature maps, the compatibility score is learned between the sketch and the image feature maps by first applying non-linear transformations as below:

$$i^{\psi_I} = \psi_I(i^{\phi_I}) \quad \text{and} \quad s_c^{\psi_S} = \psi_S(s_c^{\phi_S}). \tag{2}$$

A set of local feature vectors is formed by obtaining one vector at each location $(m, n)$ in the image feature map $i^{\psi_I}$, where $m \in \{1, 2, \ldots, w\}$ and $n \in \{1, 2, \ldots, h\}$. Each vector represents a spatial region on the target image and the set gives us spatial distribution of the features. Subsequently, this is compared against a global representation of the sketch features. For image feature map i.e. $i^{\psi_I} \in \mathbb{R}^{w \times h \times d}$, the extracted set of feature vectors is represented as $L^i = \{\mathbf{L}_1^i, \mathbf{L}_2^i, ..., \mathbf{L}_{w \times h}^i\}$ where $\mathbf{L}_j^i \in \mathbb{R}^{1 \times 1 \times d} \ \forall \ j \in \{1, 2, \cdots w \times h\}$.

In the case of sketches, a global representation of sketch feature maps is obtained via the global max pool ($\mathcal{GMP}$) operation, i.e.,

$$\mathbf{L}_g^{s_c} = \mathcal{GMP}(s_c^{\psi_S}), \tag{3}$$

where, $\mathbf{L}_g^{s_c} \in \mathbb{R}^{1 \times 1 \times d}$. A spatial compatibility score between $\mathbf{L}_j^i \in L^i$ and $\mathbf{L}_g^{s_c}$, is evaluated as follows:

$$\lambda(\mathbf{L}_j^i, \mathbf{L}_g^{s_c}) = \frac{\left(\mathbf{L}_j^i\right)^T \left(\mathbf{L}_g^{s_c}\right)}{\mathcal{K}}, \tag{4}$$

where $\mathcal{K}$ is a constant. For simplicity of notation, we will refer to the left hand side of Eq. (4) as $\lambda_{jg}$ from here onwards.

Note that these compatibility scores are generated as a spatial map, which can be understood as a weight map representing attention weights. Therefore, in order to obtain attended feature maps, we perform element-wise multiplication of these compatibility scores and the original image feature map at each spatial location, i.e.,

$$i_j^{a_I} = i_j^{\phi_I} \odot \lambda_{jg}, \forall j \in \{1, 2, \cdots, w \times h\}. \tag{5}$$

This attention feature map aims to capture information about the location of objects in an image that shares high compatibility score with the sketch query. Therefore, to incorporate this information, attention feature maps are concatenated along the depth with the original feature maps, i.e., $i_f^{\phi_I} = [(i^{a_I})^T; (i^{\phi_I})^T]^T$, where $i_f^{\phi_I} \in \mathbb{R}^{w \times h \times 2d}$. These concatenated feature maps are projected to a lower dimensional space to obtain the final feature maps, which are subsequently passed through the RPN to generate object proposals relevant to the sketch query.

### 3.3 Proposal Scoring

Once a small set of proposals, represented as $R_i$ for $i \in I$, are pooled from all query-guided region proposals generated by RPN, a scoring function $\Theta$ is learned to rank these proposals with respect to the sketch query. To this end, during the training phase, each of these region proposals are labeled as foreground (1) if it has $\geq 0.5$ intersection over union (IoU) with any of the ground-truth bounding boxes and the object in the ground-truth bounding box is the same class as sketch query, and background (0) otherwise. Then, we minimize a margin rank loss between the generated object proposals and the sketch query such that object proposals similar to the query sketch are ranked higher.

To learn the scoring function $\Theta$, firstly, we generate feature vectors for the sketch query and the object proposals by taking a global mean pool operation on the sketch feature maps and object proposal feature maps, respectively. Each of the proposal feature vectors is concatenated with the sketch feature vector. These concatenated feature vectors are passed through a scoring function and the foreground probabilities of the proposals in context with the sketch query are predicted. Let $a_k$ be the predicted foreground probability for proposal $r_k \in R_i$, and it is given by:

$$a_k = \Theta([g_m(r_k^{\phi_I'})^T; g_m(s_c^{\phi_S'})^T]^T), \tag{6}$$

where, $r_k^{\phi_I'}$ is the feature map for $r_k \in R_i$ generated using standard Faster R-CNN protocols and $g_m : \mathbb{R}^{W \times H \times D} \to \mathbb{R}^{1 \times 1 \times D}$ is the global mean pool operation. Now, towards training the scoring function, a label $y_k = 1$ is assigned to $r_k$ if it is part of any foreground bounding box and $y_k = 0$, otherwise. Motivated from [12] the loss function used in training is defined as:

$$L(R_i, s_c) = \sum_k \left\{ y_k \max(m^+ - a_k, 0) + (1 - y_k) \max(a_k - m^-, 0) + L_{MR}^k \right\} \tag{7}$$

$$L_{MR}^k = \sum_{l=k+1} \left\{ \mathbb{1}_{[y_l = y_k]} \max(|a_k - a_l| - m^-, 0) \right.$$

$$\left. + \mathbb{1}_{[y_l \neq y_k]} \max(m^+ - |a_k - a_l|, 0) \right\}, \tag{8}$$

where $m^+$ and $m^-$ are positive and negative margins, respectively. The above loss function consists of two parts: (i) The first part of the loss (see Eq. (7)) ensures that the proposals overlapping with the ground truth object locations are predicted as foreground with high confidence. (ii) The second part of the loss function (see Eq. (8)) is a margin-ranking loss that considers pairs of the proposals as input. It helps to further enforce a wider separation between foreground and background proposals in terms of the prediction probabilities, thereby improving the ranking of all the foreground proposals overlapping with the true location(s) of the object of interest. In addition to this loss, cross-entropy loss on the labeled (background or foreground) feature vectors of the region proposals and a regression loss on the predicted bounding box locations with respect to the ground truth bounding box are also used for training.

### 3.4    Multi-query Object Localization Setup

The quality of the sketches can hinder the object localization performance. In many cases, sketches can be abstract and may not often contain the structural attributes that differentiate one object from another. The noise present in such sketches, along with their abstract nature, makes the task of sketch-guided object localization extremely challenging. However, we observe that the sketches are diverse in quality and when produced by different creators, they often tend to capture complementary information on an object's shape, attributes and appearance. This quality of complementarity can be leveraged towards improving the overall localization performance if information across these sketches is judiciously combined. With these motivations, we introduce the task of multi sketch query-guided object localization and present the following fusion strategies:

**Feature Fusion:** We observed complementarity across filter responses for different input sketches containing the same object. Such complementarity can be leveraged by a suitable feature fusion strategy to obtain less noisy and more holistic representation of the sketched object. In this paper, we used the global max pool operation to fuse feature maps of different sketch queries. Let $\{s_c^1, \ldots, s_c^N\}$ be the set of $N$ sketches for the same object category $c \in C$ and the representation learned by the backbone network for the $n^{th}$ sketch in this set is ${}^n s_c^{\phi_s}$. These feature maps are concatenated together to yield a composite feature map $R^{w \times h \times d \times N}$. A global max pool operation across all $N$ channels is subsequently performed to obtain a fused feature map for all the $N$ queries and the same is fed as input to the *cross-modal attention* model.

**Attention Fusion:** In an alternative strategy, to attenuate noise in the attention maps produced by individual sketches, we concatenate these maps as generated by multiple queries and subsequently perform a depth-wise average pooling operation to obtain the final attention map. The fused attention map, thus generated, is used as input to the object localization pipeline (Sect. 3.3).

# 4    Experiments and Results

## 4.1    Datasets

We use the following datasets for evaluating the performance of the proposed sketch-guided object localization framework.

**QuickDraw** [15] is a large-scale sketch dataset containing 50 million sketches across 345 categories. Sketches drawn from a subset of this dataset (please refer to the next paragraphs) are used as query. QuickDraw sketches are stored as vector graphics and are rasterized before feeding into ResNet.

**MS-COCO** [19] is a large-scale image dataset which has been extensively used in object detection research. It has a total of 81 classes, including background class, with dense object bounding box annotations. There are a total of 56 classes which are common between MS-COCO and QuickDraw datasets. Therefore, in our object localization experiments, we randomly selected a total of $800K$ sketches across these common classes. We trained our model on COCO *train2017* and evaluated on COCO *val2017* dataset.

**PASCAL VOC** [6] is a popular object detection dataset with a total of 20 classes. Among these, nine classes common with the QuickDraw dataset are selected for our experiments. Our model is trained on the union of VOC2007 *train-val* and VOC2012 *train-val* sets and evaluated on VOC *test2007* set.

## 4.2    Baselines

We adapt the following popular models from the object detection and image-guided localization communities as baselines towards evaluating sketch-guided object localization performance and compare them with our proposed method.

**Faster R-CNN** [24] We adapt this object detector for query-guided object localization task. To this end, during training, we assign a 1 (or 0) class label to the object instance in the image if it belongs to the same (or different) class as the sketch query, and generate object proposals. Then, a binary classifier is used to classify each proposal as background or foreground. The query features are first concatenated with the region of interests(ROIs) features (pooled from region proposals) before passing it through the binary classifier. Additionally, we used a triplet loss to rank the object region proposal with respect to the sketch query. We refer to this baseline as *modified Faster R-CNN*.

**Matchnet** [12] is a one-shot object localization method via image query. Here, non-local neural networks [34] and channel co-excitation [13] were used to incorporate the query information in the image feature maps. We adapt this recent method to directly work with a sketch query and treat it as a second baseline.

For both these baseline methods, the feature extractors for sketches and images are ResNet-50 models pretrained on Imagenet and QuickDraw respectively.

**Table 1. Results in one-shot common train-test categories setting on COCO val2017 dataset.** Comparison of various object localization baseline methods with the proposed *cross-modal attention* model for sketch-guided object localization. We clearly outperform both the baselines based on mean average precision as well as % AP@50. For more details please refer to Sect. 4.4.

| Model | mAP | %AP@50 |
|---|---|---|
| Modified Faster R-CNN | 0.18 | 31.5 |
| Matchnet [12] | 0.28 | 48.5 |
| Cross-modal attention (this work) | **0.30** | **50.0** |

## 4.3  Experimental Setup

We used two ResNet-50 models pre-trained on Imagenet [4] and 5 million images of QuickDraw [15] to get the feature representation for images and sketches respectively. The images from MS-COCO and PASCAL VOC datasets are used as target images, and the sketches randomly-drawn from the common classes of QuickDraw are used as queries. We evaluate performance of our model under the following four settings: (i) one-shot common train-test categories, (ii) one-shot disjoint train-test categories, (iii) multi-query common train-test categories, and (iv) multi-query disjoint train-test categories.

**Disjoint Train-Test Experimental Setting:** Out of the 56 classes common across COCO and QuickDraw datasets, 42 and 14 classes are arbitrarily picked as 'seen' and 'unseen' categories, respectively. To ensure a one-shot disjoint train-test setting, the 'seen' and 'unseen' splits are mutually exclusive in terms of object classes as well as labeled bounding boxes present. Our model is trained solely on the 'seen' classes and only the 'unseen' classes are used for one-shot evaluation. Similarly for PASCAL VOC dataset, out of 9 classes common with QuickDraw, 3 and 6 are arbitrarily picked as 'unseen' and 'seen' categories respectively. The image encoder is pre-trained using Imagenet dataset excluding 14 'unseen' as well as all related classes to these 14 classes obtained by matching their WordNet synsets. Similarly, the sketch encoder is pre-trained using all the QuickDraw classes except the 14 categories in the unseen set.

## 4.4  Results and Discussion

In this section, we report results on the four experimental settings discussed in Sect. 4.3. We then provide extensive discussions around merits and limitations of our proposed method in comparison to the chosen baselines.

**One-Shot Common Train-Test Categories:** The results for the proposed method in this setting are shown in Table 1 for MS-COCO dataset. As shown, the proposed method outperforms both the baselines significantly. When compared to the modified Faster R-CNN baseline, our method performs significantly

**Table 2. Results in one-shot common train-test categories setting on VOC test2007 dataset.** Comparison of various object localization baseline methods with the proposed *Cross-modal attention* model for sketch-guided object localization. We clearly outperform the state-of-the-art object localization method [12] and the results are comparable to Faster R-CNN based baseline. Please refer to Sect. 4.4 for more details.

| Model | mAP |
|---|---|
| Modified Faster R-CNN | **0.65** |
| Matchnet [12] | 0.61 |
| Cross-modal attention (this work) | **0.65** |

better. This is primarily because, unlike Faster R-CNN, our *cross-modal attention* framework effectively incorporates information from the query using spatial compatibility (attention) map to generate relevant region proposals. Moreover, our method also outperforms the Matchnet baseline because the non-local feature maps and channel co-excitation module in Matchnet are sensitive towards the domain gap present between query and image feature maps in our task. On the contrary, our *cross-modal attention* framework addresses this by explicitly computing a spatial compatibility map (attention map).

The results on the PASCAL VOC dataset are reported in Table 2. PASCAL VOC contains less number of training images ($\approx$ 9K) with small variability across training classes in our setting (only 9 classes in the training set). The Faster R-CNN baseline is comparable to the proposed method indicating that sketch query-guided object localization is challenging without sufficient data. The Matchnet baseline model degrades in performance, indicating its inability to incorporate sketch information during proposal generation in the case of small data size and large domain gap.

**One-Shot Disjoint Train-Test Categories:** In this setting, models are evaluated on the object categories which are not seen during training. The results are provided in Table 3 for MS-COCO dataset. We have selected model checkpoints that perform the best on *unseen* categories for each model. It is evident that one-shot object localization under disjoint train-test object categories is a hard problem as it leads to degradation in performance for all three models. Faster R-CNN baseline suffers most degradation because it does not incorporate sketch information during proposal generation and perform poorly in proposal generation for unseen categories. While Matchnet outperforms the modified Faster R-CNN baseline, it still performs significantly worse than the proposed method. Contrary to baseline methods, our model, by virtue of *cross-modal attention*, embeds query information in the image feature representation before generating region proposals. Therefore, it is inherently capable of generating relevant object proposals even when attempting to localize unseen object classes. As a result, our method reports superior performance on unseen categories while achieving reasonably high performance for seen categories as well.

**Table 3. Results in one-shot disjoint train-test categories setting on MS-COCO *val2017* dataset.** We report % AP@50 scores in this table. Here, *unseen classes* contain the evaluation images and sketches of object categories that are not seen during training. Our proposed method significantly outperforms other baselines on unseen classes while achieving reasonably high performance for seen categories as well. Please refer to Sect. 4.4 for more details.

| Model | Unseen Classes | Seen Classes |
|---|---|---|
| Modified Faster R-CNN | 7.4 | 34.5 |
| Matchnet [12] | 12.4 | **49.1** |
| Cross-modal attention (this work) | **15.0** | 48.8 |

**Multi-Query Common and Disjoint Train-Test Categories:** Here we discuss the effect of utilizing multiple sketch queries on the object localization performance. We evaluated our model using two fusion strategies presented in Sect. 3.4 under the following two settings: (a) common train and test categories, (b) completely disjoint train and test object classes. The evaluation results of these fusion strategies are provided in Table 4. Both these fusion strategies provide consistent improvement in performance over the proposed cross-modal attention based baseline model, which just uses a single sketch query as input. This suggests that the fusion strategies are able to capture the complementary information present across the multiple sketches of the same object. Moreover, we also evaluated the proposed fusion strategies for sketch-guided object localization on *unseen* categories and observe that even in such cases, these fusion strategies are able to aid the proposed localization framework.

**Utility of Margin-Based Ranking Loss:** We analyze the effect of different components of loss function defined in Eq. (7) and Eq. (8) on the model's performance using MS-COCO *val2017* dataset. The model which is trained with only foreground-background classification loss (first part of Eq. (7)) gives %AP@50 of 40.0% as compared to 41.4%, achieved by the model trained on only the margin-ranking loss ($L_{MR}$) (Eq. (8)). However, training the model on both these losses significantly improves the performance (50.0 %AP@50).

**Visualizing the Attention Map and Localization:** In order to visualize the effect of sketch queries on the generated attention maps and the resulting localizations, we query an image with sketches of different object categories. As shown in Fig. 3, our novel *cross-modal attention* scheme is able to assign high compatibility scores to the ground-truth object locations in the natural image while at the same time ignoring instances of other object categories, thereby producing precise localizations.

**Table 4. Results in multi-query common and disjoint train-test categories setting on MS-COCO** *val2017* **dataset.** Comparison of the proposed fusion strategies for 5 sketch queries. Here, 5*Q*, (C) and (D) represents 5 sketch queries, common train and test categories, and disjoint train and test categories respectively. % AP@50 is reported except the last column which reports mAP.

| Our models | Unseen (D) | Seen (D) | All (C) | mAP (C) |
|---|---|---|---|---|
| Cross-modal attention | 15.0 | 48.8 | 50.0 | 0.30 |
| +Query Fusion(5Q) | 16.3 | **52.2** | 52.6 | **0.32** |
| +Attention Fusion(5Q) | **17.1** | 51.9 | **53.1** | **0.32** |

**Fig. 3.** Sketch queries and object localization results are shown along with the corresponding attention maps. The attention map produces high compatibility scores (shown in red color) for the regions on the natural image that contains object same as that in the sketch query. This leads to the localization (shown using a red bounding box on input image) of the relevant object. Please note that sketches have been enhanced for better visualization. [**Best viewed in color**]. (Color figure online)

## 5    Conclusion

In this paper, we have introduced a novel problem of sketch-guided object localization in natural images and presented an end-to-end trainable framework using novel *cross-modal attention* for this task. The effectiveness of the proposed attention scheme is substantiated by the significant performance improvement achieved over the baseline methods on two public benchmarks. We have extended the framework to a multi-query setup and proposed two fusion strategies towards the same. The superior performance of our framework over the baseline in this setting corroborates that the proposed fusion strategies are able to leverage the complementarity present across multiple sketches of the same object. We look forward to exciting future research in sketch-guided computer vision tasks inspired by the problem that we have introduced.

**Acknowledgements.** The authors would like to thank the Advanced Data Management Research Group, Corporate Technologies, Siemens Technology and Services Pvt. Ltd., and Pratiksha Trust, Bengaluru, India for partly supporting this research.

# References

1. Cai, Z., Vasconcelos, N.: Cascade R-CNN: delving into high quality object detection. In: CVPR (2018)
2. Caicedo, J.C., Lazebnik, S.: Active object localization with deep reinforcement learning. In: ICCV (2015)
3. Choe, J., Shim, H.: Attention-based dropout layer for weakly supervised object localization. In: CVPR (2019)
4. Deng, J., Dong, W., Socher, R., Li, L.J., Li, K., Fei-Fei, L.: Imagenet: a large-scale hierarchical image database. In: CVPR (2009)
5. Eitz, M., Hildebrand, K., Boubekeur, T., Alexa, M.: Sketch-based image retrieval: benchmark and bag-of-features descriptors. IEEE Trans. Vis. Comput. Graph. **17**(11), 1624–1636 (2010)
6. Everingham, M., Van Gool, L., Williams, C.K.I., Winn, J., Zisserman, A.: The pascal Visual Object Classes (VOC) challenge. Int. J. Comput. Vis. **88**(2), 303–338 (2010). https://doi.org/10.1007/s11263-009-0275-4
7. Girshick, R.: Fast R-CNN. In: ICCV (2015)
8. Girshick, R., Donahue, J., Darrell, T., Malik, J.: Rich feature hierarchies for accurate object detection and semantic segmentation. In: CVPR (2014)
9. Ha, D., Eck, D.: A neural representation of sketch drawings. arXiv preprint arXiv:1704.03477 (2017)
10. He, K., Gkioxari, G., Dollár, P., Girshick, R.: Mask R-CNN. In: ICCV (2017)
11. He, K., Zhang, X., Ren, S., Sun, J.: Spatial pyramid pooling in deep convolutional networks for visual recognition. IEEE Trans. Pattern Anal. Mach. Intell. **37**(9), 1904–1916 (2015)
12. Hsieh, T.I., Lo, Y.C., Chen, H.T., Liu, T.L.: One-shot object detection with co-attention and co-excitation. In: NeurIPS (2019)
13. Hu, J., Shen, L., Sun, G.: Squeeze-and-excitation networks. In: CVPR (2018)
14. Hu, R., Collomosse, J.: A performance evaluation of gradient field hog descriptor for sketch based image retrieval. Comput. Vis. Image Underst. **117**(7), 790–806 (2013)
15. Jongejan, J., Rowley, H., Kawashima, T., Kim, J., Fox-Gieg, N.: The quick, draw!-ai experiment (2016). https://quickdraw.withgoogle.com
16. Kong, T., Sun, F., Liu, H., Jiang, Y., Shi, J.: Foveabox: beyond anchor-based object detector (2019). arXiv preprint arXiv:1904.03797
17. Li, B., Yan, J., Wu, W., Zhu, Z., Hu, X.: High performance visual tracking with siamese region proposal network. In: CVPR (2018)
18. Lin, T.Y., Goyal, P., Girshick, R., He, K., Dollár, P.: Focal loss for dense object detection. In: ICCV (2017)
19. Lin, T.Y., et al.: Microsoft COCO: common objects in context. In: ECCV (2014)
20. Liu, L., Shen, F., Shen, Y., Liu, X., Shao, L.: Deep sketch hashing: fast free-hand sketch-based image retrieval. In: CVPR (2017)
21. Liu, W., et al.: SSD: single shot multibox detector. In: Leibe, B., Matas, J., Sebe, N., Welling, M. (eds.) ECCV 2016. LNCS, vol. 9905, pp. 21–37. Springer, Cham (2016). https://doi.org/10.1007/978-3-319-46448-0_2
22. Redmon, J., Divvala, S., Girshick, R., Farhadi, A.: You only look once: unified, real-time object detection. In: CVPR (2016)
23. Redmon, J., Farhadi, A.: Yolov3: an incremental improvement (2018). arXiv preprint arXiv:1804.02767

24. Ren, S., He, K., Girshick, R., Sun, J.: Faster R-CNN: towards real-time object detection with region proposal networks. In: NeurIPS (2015)
25. Sangkloy, P., Burnell, N., Ham, C., Hays, J.: The sketchy database: learning to retrieve badly drawn bunnies. ACM Trans. Graph. (TOG) **35**(4), 1–12 (2016)
26. Sermanet, P., Eigen, D., Zhang, X., Mathieu, M., Fergus, R., LeCun, Y.: Overfeat: integrated recognition, localization and detection using convolutional networks (2013). arXiv preprint arXiv:1312.6229
27. Sharif Razavian, A., Azizpour, H., Sullivan, J., Carlsson, S.: CNN features off-the-shelf: an astounding baseline for recognition. In: CVPRW (2014)
28. Shen, Y., Liu, L., Shen, F., Shao, L.: Zero-shot sketch-image hashing. In: CVPR (2018)
29. Sivic, J., Zisserman, A.: Video Google: a text retrieval approach to object matching in videos. In: ICCV (2003)
30. Song, J., Yu, Q., Song, Y.Z., Xiang, T., Hospedales, T.M.: Deep spatial-semantic attention for fine-grained sketch-based image retrieval. In: ICCV (2017)
31. Teh, E.W., Rochan, M., Wang, Y.: Attention networks for weakly supervised object localization. In: BMVC (2016)
32. Uijlings, J.R., Van De Sande, K.E., Gevers, T., Smeulders, A.W.: Selective search for object recognition. Int. J. Comput. Vis. **104**(2), 154–171 (2013). https://doi. org/10.1007/s11263-013-0620-5
33. Wan, J., et al.: Deep learning for content-based image retrieval: a comprehensive study. In: ACM MM (2014)
34. Wang, X., Girshick, R., Gupta, A., He, K.: Non-local neural networks. In: CVPR (2018)
35. Xu, P., et al.: Sketchmate: deep hashing for million-scale human sketch retrieval. In: CVPR (2018)
36. Xu, P., Joshi, C.K., Bresson, X.: Multi-graph transformer for free-hand sketch recognition (2019). arXiv preprint arXiv:1912.11258
37. Yan, X., Chen, Z., Xu, A., Wang, X., Liang, X., Lin, L.: Meta R-CNN: towards general solver for instance-level low-shot learning. In: ICCV (2019)
38. Yu, Q., Liu, F., Song, Y.Z., Xiang, T., Hospedales, T.M., Loy, C.C.: Sketch me that shoe. In: CVPR (2016)
39. Yu, Q., Yang, Y., Liu, F., Song, Y.Z., Xiang, T., Hospedales, T.M.: Sketch-a-net: a deep neural network that beats humans. Int. J. Comput. Vis. **122**(3), 411–425 (2017). https://doi.org/10.1007/s11263-016-0932-3
40. Zhang, J., et al.: Generative domain-migration hashing for sketch-to-image retrieval. In: ECCV (2018)

# A Unifying Mutual Information View of Metric Learning: Cross-Entropy vs. Pairwise Losses

Malik Boudiaf[1][(✉)] ⓘ, Jérôme Rony[1] ⓘ, Imtiaz Masud Ziko[1] ⓘ, Eric Granger[1] ⓘ, Marco Pedersoli[1] ⓘ, Pablo Piantanida[2] ⓘ, and Ismail Ben Ayed[1] ⓘ

[1] Laboratoire d'Imagerie, de Vision et d'Intelligence Artificielle (LIVIA), ÉTS Montreal, Montreal, Canada
{malik.boudiaf.1,jerome.rony.1,imtiaz-masud.ziko.1}@etsmtl.net
[2] Laboratoire des Signaux et Systèmes (L2S), CentraleSupelec-CNRS-Université Paris-Saclay, Paris, France

**Abstract.** Recently, substantial research efforts in Deep Metric Learning (DML) focused on designing complex pairwise-distance losses, which require convoluted schemes to ease optimization, such as sample mining or pair weighting. The standard cross-entropy loss for classification has been largely overlooked in DML. On the surface, the cross-entropy may seem unrelated and irrelevant to metric learning as it does not explicitly involve pairwise distances. However, we provide a theoretical analysis that links the cross-entropy to several well-known and recent pairwise losses. Our connections are drawn from two different perspectives: one based on an explicit optimization insight; the other on discriminative and generative views of the mutual information between the labels and the learned features. First, we explicitly demonstrate that the cross-entropy is an upper bound on a new pairwise loss, which has a structure similar to various pairwise losses: it minimizes intra-class distances while maximizing inter-class distances. As a result, minimizing the cross-entropy can be seen as an approximate *bound-optimization* (or *Majorize-Minimize*) algorithm for minimizing this pairwise loss. Second, we show that, more generally, minimizing the cross-entropy is actually equivalent to maximizing the mutual information, to which we connect several well-known pairwise losses. Furthermore, we show that various standard pairwise losses can be explicitly related to one another via bound relationships. Our findings indicate that the cross-entropy represents a proxy for maximizing the mutual information – as pairwise losses do – without the need for convoluted sample-mining heuristics. Our experiments (Code available at: https://github.com/jeromerony/dml_cross_entropy) over four standard DML benchmarks strongly support our findings. We obtain state-of-the-art results, outperforming recent and complex DML methods.

---

M. Boudiaf, J. Rony, I. M. Ziko—Equal contributions.

---

**Electronic supplementary material** The online version of this chapter (https://doi.org/10.1007/978-3-030-58539-6_33) contains supplementary material, which is available to authorized users.

A. Vedaldi et al. (Eds.): ECCV 2020, LNCS 12351, pp. 548–564, 2020.
https://doi.org/10.1007/978-3-030-58539-6_33

**Keywords:** Metric learning · Deep learning · Information theory

# 1   Introduction

The core task of metric learning consists in learning a metric from high-dimensional data, such that the distance between two points, as measured by this metric, reflects their semantic similarity. Applications of metric learning include image retrieval, zero-shot learning or person re-identification, among others. Initial attempts to tackle this problem tried to learn metrics directly on the input space [15]. Later, the idea of learning suitable embedding was introduced, with the goal of learning Mahalanobis distances [2,5,25,38,41], which corresponds to learning the best linear projection of the input space onto a lower-dimensional manifold, and using the Euclidean distance as a metric. Building on the embedding-learning ideas, several papers proposed to learn more complex mappings, either by kernelization of already existing linear algorithms [2], or by using a more complex hypothesis such as linear combinations of gradient boosted regressions trees [10].

The recent success of deep neural networks at learning complex, nonlinear mappings of high-dimensional data aligns with the problem of learning a suitable embedding. Following works on Mahalanobis distance learning, most Deep Metric Learning (DML) approaches are based on pairwise distances. Specifically, the current paradigm is to learn a deep encoder that maps points with high semantic similarity close to each other in the embedded space (w.r.t. pairwise Euclidean or cosine distances). This paradigm concretely translates into *pairwise losses* that encourage small distances for pairs of samples from the same class and large distances for pairs of samples from different classes. While such formulations seem intuitive, the practical implementations and optimization schemes for pairwise losses may become cumbersome, and randomly assembling pairs of samples typically results in slow convergence or degenerate solutions [8]. Hence, research in DML focused on finding efficient ways to reformulate, generalize and/or improve sample mining and/or sample weighting strategies over the existing pairwise losses. Popular pairwise losses include triplet loss and its derivatives [4,8,26,27,47], contrastive loss and its derivatives [6,37], Neighborhood Component Analysis and its derivatives [5,16,40], among others. However, such modifications are often heuristic-based, and come at the price of increased complexity and additional hyper-parameters, reducing the potential of these methods in real-world applications. Furthermore, the recent experimental study in [17] showed that the improvement brought by an abundant metric learning literature in the last 15 years is at best marginal when the methods are compared fairly.

Admittedly, the objective of learning a useful embedding of data points intuitively aligns with the idea of directly acting on the distances between pairs of points in the embedded space. Therefore, the standard cross-entropy loss, widely used in classification tasks, has been largely overlooked by the DML community, most likely due to its apparent irrelevance for Metric Learning [39]. As a matter of fact, why would anyone use a point-wise prediction loss to enforce pairwise-distance properties on the embedding space? Even though the cross-entropy was shown to be competitive for face recognition applications [13,33,34], to the best of our knowledge, only one paper empirically observed competitive results of a normalized, temperature-weighted version of the cross-entropy in the context of deep metric learning [46]. However, the authors did not provide any theoretical insights for these results.

On the surface, the standard cross-entropy loss may seem unrelated to the pairwise losses used in DML. Here, we provide theoretical justifications that connect directly the cross-entropy to several well-known and recent pairwise losses. Our connections are drawn from two different perspectives; one based on an explicit optimization insight and the other on mutual-information arguments. We show that four of the most prominent pairwise metric-learning losses, as well as the standard cross-entropy, are maximizing a common underlying objective: the Mutual Information (MI) between the learned embeddings and the corresponding samples' labels. As sketched in Sect. 2, this connection can be intuitively understood by writing this MI in two different, but equivalent ways. Specifically, we establish tight links between pairwise losses and the *generative* view of this MI. We study the particular case of contrastive loss [6], explicitly showing its relation to this MI. We further generalize this reasoning to other DML losses by uncovering tight relations with contrastive loss. As for the cross-entropy, we demonstrate that the cross-entropy is an upper bound on an underlying pairwise loss – on which the previous reasoning can be applied – which has a structure similar to various existing pairwise losses. As a result, minimizing the cross-entropy can be seen as an approximate *bound-optimization* (or *Majorize-Minimize*) algorithm for minimizing this pairwise loss, implicitly minimizing intra-class distances and maximizing inter-class distances. We also show that, more generally, minimizing the cross-entropy is equivalent to maximizing the *discriminative* view of the mutual information. Our findings indicate that the cross-entropy represents a proxy for maximizing the mutual information, as pairwise losses do, without the need for complex sample-mining and optimization schemes. Our comprehensive experiments over four standard DML benchmarks (CUB200, Cars-196, Stanford Online Product and In-Shop) strongly support our findings. We consistently obtained state-of-the-art results, outperforming many recent and complex DML methods.

## Summary of Contributions

1. Establishing relations between several pairwise DML losses and a generative view of the mutual information between the learned features and labels;
2. Proving explicitly that optimizing the standard cross-entropy corresponds to an approximate bound-optimizer of an underlying pairwise loss;
3. More generally, showing that minimizing the standard cross-entropy loss is equivalent to maximizing a discriminative view of the mutual information between the features and labels.
4. Demonstrating state-of-the-art results with cross-entropy on several DML benchmark datasets.

**Table 1.** Definition of the random variables and information measures used in this paper.

| General | | Model | |
| --- | --- | --- | --- |
| Labeled dataset | $\mathcal{D} = \{(\boldsymbol{x}_i, y_i)\}_{i=1}^n$ | Encoder | $\phi_{\mathcal{W}} : \mathcal{X} \to \mathcal{Z}$ |
| Input feature space | $\mathcal{X}$ | Soft-classifier | $f_\theta : \mathcal{Z} \to [0,1]^K$ |
| Embedded feature space | $\mathcal{Z} \subset \mathbb{R}^d$ | | |
| Label/Prediction space | $\mathcal{Y} \subset \mathbb{R}^K$ | **Random variables (RVs)** | |
| | | Data | $X, Y$ |
| Euclidean distance | $D_{ij} = \|\boldsymbol{z}_i - \boldsymbol{z}_j\|_2$ | Embedding | $\widehat{Z}\|X \sim \phi_{\mathcal{W}}(X)$ |
| Cosine distance | $D_{ij}^{\cos} = \frac{z_i^\mathsf{T} z_j}{\|z_i\|\|z_j\|}$ | Prediction | $\widehat{Y}\|\widehat{Z} \sim f_\theta(\widehat{Z})$ |
| **Information measures** | | | |
| Entropy of $Y$ | $\mathcal{H}(Y) := \mathbb{E}_{p_Y}\left[-\log p_Y(Y)\right]$ | | |
| Conditional entropy of $Y$ given $Z$ | $\mathcal{H}(Y\|\widehat{Z}) := \mathbb{E}_{p_{Y\widehat{Z}}}\left[-\log p_{Y\|\widehat{Z}}(Y\|\widehat{Z})\right]$ | | |
| Cross entropy (CE) between $Y$ and $\widehat{Y}$ | $\mathcal{H}(Y;\widehat{Y}) := \mathbb{E}_{p_Y}\left[-\log p_{\widehat{Y}}(Y)\right]$ | | |
| Conditional CE given $\widehat{Z}$ | $\mathcal{H}(Y;\widehat{Y}\|\widehat{Z}) := \mathbb{E}_{p_{\widehat{Z}Y}}\left[-\log p_{\widehat{Y}\|\widehat{Z}}(Y\|\widehat{Z})\right]$ | | |
| Mutual information between $\widehat{Z}$ and $Y$ | $\mathcal{I}(\widehat{Z};Y) := \mathcal{H}(Y) - \mathcal{H}(Y\|\widehat{Z})$ | | |

## 2   On the Two Views of the Mutual Information

The Mutual Information (MI) is a well known-measure designed to quantify the amount of information shared by two random variables. Its formal definition is presented in Table 1. Throughout this work, we will be particularly interested in $\mathcal{I}(\widehat{Z};Y)$ which represents the MI between learned features $\widehat{Z}$ and labels $Y$. Due to its symmetry property, the MI can be written in two ways, which we will refer to as the *discriminative view* and *generative view* of MI:

$$\mathcal{I}(\widehat{Z};Y) = \underbrace{\mathcal{H}(Y) - \mathcal{H}(Y|\widehat{Z})}_{\text{discriminative view}} = \underbrace{\mathcal{H}(\widehat{Z}) - \mathcal{H}(\widehat{Z}|Y)}_{\text{generative view}} \qquad (1)$$

While being analytically equivalent, these two views present two different, complementary interpretations. In order to maximize $\mathcal{I}(\widehat{Z};Y)$, the discriminative view conveys that the labels should be balanced (out of our control) and easily identified from the features. On the other hand, the generative view conveys that the features learned should spread as much as possible in the feature space, while keeping samples sharing the same class close to each other. Hence, the discriminative view is more focused on label identification, while the generative view focuses on more explicitly shaping the distribution of the features learned by the model. Therefore, the MI enables us to draw links between classification losses (*e.g.* cross-entropy) and feature-shaping losses (including all the well-known pairwise metric learning losses).

# 3 Pairwise Losses and the Generative View of the MI

In this section, we study four pairwise losses used in the DML community: center loss [39], contrastive loss [6], Scalable Neighbor Component Analysis (SNCA) loss [40] and Multi-Similarity (MS) loss [37]. We show that these losses can be interpreted as proxies for maximizing the generative view of mutual information $\mathcal{I}(\widehat{Z}; Y)$. We begin by analyzing the specific example of contrastive loss, establishing its tight link to the MI, and further generalize our analysis to the other pairwise losses (see Table 2). Furthermore, we show that these pairwise metric-learning losses can be explicitly linked to one another via bound relationships.

## 3.1 The Example of Contrastive Loss

We start by analyzing the representative example of contrastive loss [6]. For a given margin $m \in \mathbb{R}^+$, this loss is formulated as:

$$\mathcal{L}_{\text{contrast}} = \underbrace{\frac{1}{n}\sum_{i=1}^{n}\sum_{j:y_j=y_i}D_{ij}^2}_{T_{\text{contrast}}} + \underbrace{\frac{1}{n}\sum_{i=1}^{n}\sum_{j:y_j\neq y_i}[m - D_{ij}]_+^2}_{C_{\text{contrast}}} \qquad (2)$$

where $[x]_+ = \max(0, x)$. This loss naturally breaks down into two terms: a *tightness* part $T_{\text{contrast}}$ and a *contrastive* part $C_{\text{contrast}}$. The tightness part encourages samples from the same class to be close to each other and form *tight* clusters. As for the *contrastive* part, it forces samples from different classes to stand far apart from one another in the embedded feature space. Let us analyze these two terms from a mutual-information perspective.

As shown in the next subsection, the tightness part of contrastive loss is equivalent to the tightness part of the center loss [39]: $T_{\text{contrast}} \overset{c}{=} T_{\text{center}} = \frac{1}{2}\sum_{i=1}^{n}\|z_i - c_{y_i}\|^2$, where $c_k = \frac{1}{|\mathcal{Z}_k|}\sum_{z\in\mathcal{Z}_k} z$ denotes the mean of feature points from class $k$ in embedding space $\mathcal{Z}$ and symbol $\overset{c}{=}$ denotes equality up to a multiplicative and/or additive constant. Written in this way, we can interpret $T_{\text{contrast}}$ as a conditional cross entropy between $\widehat{Z}$ and another random variable $\bar{Z}$, whose conditional distribution given $Y$ is a standard Gaussian centered around $c_Y$: $\bar{Z}|Y \sim \mathcal{N}(c_Y, I)$:

$$T_{\text{contrast}} \overset{c}{=} \mathcal{H}(\widehat{Z}; \bar{Z}|Y) = \mathcal{H}(\widehat{Z}|Y) + \mathcal{D}_{KL}(\widehat{Z}||\bar{Z}|Y) \qquad (3)$$

As such, $T_{\text{contrast}}$ is an upper bound on the conditional entropy that appears in the mutual information:

$$T_{\text{contrast}} \geq \mathcal{H}(\widehat{Z}|Y) \qquad (4)$$

This bound is tight when $\widehat{Z}|Y \sim \mathcal{N}(c_Y, I)$. Hence, minimizing $T_{\text{contrast}}$ can be seen as minimizing $\mathcal{H}(\widehat{Z}|Y)$, which exactly encourages the encoder $\phi_{\mathcal{W}}$ to produce low-entropy (=compact) clusters in the feature space for each given class. Notice that using this term only will inevitably lead to a trivial encoder that maps all data points in $\mathcal{X}$ to a single point in the embedded space $\mathcal{Z}$, hence achieving a global optimum.

To prevent such a trivial solution, a second term needs to be added. This second term – that we refer to as the *contrastive* term – is designed to push each point away from points that have a different label. In this term, only pairs such that $D_{ij} \leq m$ produce a cost. Given a pair $(i, j)$, let us define $x = D_{ij}/m$. Given that $x \in [0, 1]$, one can show the following: $1 - 2x \leq (1 - x)^2 \leq 1 - x$. Using linear approximation $(1 - x)^2 \approx 1 - 2x$ (with error at most $x$), we obtain:

$$C_{\text{contrast}} \overset{c}{\approx} -\frac{2m}{n} \sum_{i=1}^{n} \sum_{j:y_j \neq y_i} D_{ij} = -\frac{2m}{n} \sum_{i=1}^{n} \sum_{j=1}^{n} D_{ij} + \frac{2m}{n} \sum_{i=1}^{n} \sum_{j:y_j=y_i} D_{ij} \quad (5)$$

While the second term in Eq. 5 is redundant with the tightness objective, the first term is close to the differential entropy estimator proposed in [36]:

$$\widehat{\mathcal{H}}(\widehat{Z}) = \frac{d}{n(n-1)} \sum_{i=1}^{n} \sum_{j=1}^{n} \log D_{ij}^2 \overset{c}{=} \sum_{i=1}^{n} \sum_{j=1}^{n} \log D_{ij} \quad (6)$$

Both terms measure the spread of $\widehat{Z}$, even though they present different gradient dynamics. All in all, minimizing the whole contrastive loss can be seen as a proxy for maximizing the MI between the labels $Y$ and the embedded features $\widehat{Z}$:

$$\mathcal{L}_{\text{contrast}} = \underbrace{\frac{1}{n} \sum_{i=1}^{n} \sum_{j:y_j=y_i} (D_{ij}^2 + 2mD_{ij})}_{\propto \mathcal{H}(\widehat{Z}|Y)} - \underbrace{\frac{2m}{n} \sum_{i=1}^{n} \sum_{j=1}^{n} D_{ij}}_{\propto \mathcal{H}(\widehat{Z})} \quad \propto \ -\mathcal{I}(\widehat{Z}; Y) \quad (7)$$

## 3.2   Generalizing to Other Pairwise Losses

A similar analysis can be carried out on other, more recent metric learning losses. More specifically, they can also be broken down into two parts: a *tightness* part that minimizes intra-class distances to form compact clusters, which is related to the *conditional entropy* $\mathcal{H}(\widehat{Z}|Y)$, and a second *contrastive* part that prevents trivial solutions by maximizing inter-class distances, which is related to the *entropy* of features $\mathcal{H}(\widehat{Z})$. Note that, in some pairwise losses, there might be some redundancy between the two terms, *i.e.*, the tightness term also contains some contrastive subterm, and vice-versa. For instance, the cross-entropy loss is used as the contrastive part of the center-loss but, as we show in Sect. 4.2, the cross-entropy, used alone, already contains both tightness (conditional entropy) and contrastive (entropy) parts. Table 2 presents the split for four DML losses. The rest of the section is devoted to exhibiting the close relationships between several pairwise losses and the tightness and contrastive terms (*i.e.*, $T$ and $C$).

**Links Between Losses:** In this section, we show that the tightness and contrastive parts of the pairwise losses in Table 2, even though different at first sight, can actually be related to one another.

**Table 2.** Several well-known and/or recent DML losses broken into a *tightness* term and a *contrastive* term. Minimizing the cross-entropy corresponds to an approximate bound optimization of PCE.

| Loss | Tightness part $\propto \mathcal{H}(\widehat{Z}|Y)$ | Contrastive part $\propto \mathcal{H}(\widehat{Z})$ |
|---|---|---|
| Center [39] | $\dfrac{1}{2}\sum\limits_{i=1}^{n}\left\|z_i - c_{y_i}\right\|^2$ | $-\dfrac{1}{n}\sum\limits_{i=1}^{n}\log p_{iy_i}$ |
| Contrast [6] | $\dfrac{1}{n}\sum\limits_{i=1}^{n}\sum\limits_{j:y_j=y_i} D_{ij}^2$ | $\dfrac{1}{n}\sum\limits_{i=1}^{n}\sum\limits_{j:y_j\neq y_i}[m - D_{ij}]_+^2$ |
| SNCA [40] | $-\dfrac{1}{n}\sum\limits_{i=1}^{n}\log\left[\sum\limits_{j:y_j=y_i}\exp\dfrac{D_{ij}^{\cos}}{\sigma}\right]$ | $\dfrac{1}{n}\sum\limits_{i=1}^{n}\log\left[\sum\limits_{k\neq i}\exp\dfrac{D_{ik}^{\cos}}{\sigma}\right]$ |
| MS [37] | $\dfrac{1}{n}\sum\limits_{i=1}^{n}\dfrac{1}{\alpha}\log\left[1+\sum\limits_{j:y_j=y_i}e^{-\alpha(D_{ij}^{\cos}-m)}\right]$ | $\dfrac{1}{n}\sum\limits_{i=1}^{n}\dfrac{1}{\beta}\log\left[1+\sum\limits_{j:y_j\neq y_i}e^{\beta(D_{ij}^{\cos}-m)}\right]$ |
| PCE Proposition 1 | $-\dfrac{1}{2\lambda n^2}\sum\limits_{i=1}^{n}\sum\limits_{j:y_j=y_i} z_i^\mathsf{T} z_j$ | $\dfrac{1}{n}\sum\limits_{i=1}^{n}\log\left[\sum\limits_{k=1}^{K}\exp\left[\dfrac{1}{\lambda n}\sum\limits_{j=1}^{n} p_{jk} z_i^\mathsf{T} z_j\right]\right]$ $-\dfrac{1}{2K^2\lambda^2}\sum\limits_{k=1}^{K}\left\|c_k^s\right\|^2$ |

**Lemma 1.** *Let $T_A$ denote the tightness part of the loss from method A. Assuming that features are $\ell_2$-normalized, and that classes are balanced, the following relations between Center [39], Contrastive [6], SNCA [40] and MS [37] losses hold:*

$$T_{SNCA} \overset{\mathrm{c}}{\leq} T_{Center} \overset{\mathrm{c}}{=} T_{Contrastive} \overset{\mathrm{c}}{\leq} T_{MS} \tag{8}$$

*where $\overset{\mathrm{c}}{\leq}$ stands for lower than, up to a multiplicative and an additive constant, and $\overset{\mathrm{c}}{=}$ stands for equal to, up to a multiplicative and an additive constant.*

The detailed proof of Lemma 1 is deferred to the supplemental material. As for the contrastive parts, we show in the supplemental material that both $C_{SNCA}$ and $C_{MS}$ are lower bounded by a common contrastive term that is directly related to $\mathcal{H}(\widehat{Z})$. We do not mention the *contrastive* term of center-loss, as it represents the cross-entropy loss, which is exhaustively studied in Sect. 4.

## 4    Cross-Entropy Does It All

We now completely change gear to focus on the widely used *unary* classification loss: cross-entropy. On the surface, the cross-entropy may seem unrelated to metric-learning losses as it does not involve pairwise distances. We show that a close relationship exists between these pairwise losses widely used in deep metric learning and the cross-entropy classification loss. This link can be drawn from two different perspectives, one is based on an explicit optimization insight and the other is based on a discriminative view of the mutual information. First, we explicitly demonstrate that the cross-entropy is an upper bound on a new pairwise loss, which has a structure similar to all the metric-learning losses listed in Table 2, *i.e.*, it contains a tightness term and a contrastive term. Hence, minimizing the cross-entropy can be seen as an approximate *bound-optimization (or Majorize-Minimize)* algorithm for minimizing this pairwise loss. Second, we show that, more generally, minimization of the cross-entropy is actually equivalent to maximization of the mutual information, to which we connected various DML losses. These findings indicate that the cross-entropy represents a proxy for maximizing $\mathcal{I}(\widehat{Z}, Y)$, just like pairwise losses, without the need for dealing with the complex sample mining and optimization schemes associated to the latter.

## 4.1   The Pairwise Loss Behind Unary Cross-Entropy

**Bound Optimization:** Given a function $f(\mathcal{W})$ that is either intractable or hard to optimize, bound optimizers are iterative algorithms that instead optimize auxiliary functions (upper bounds on $f$). These auxiliary functions are usually more tractable than the original function $f$. Let $t$ be the current iteration index, then $a_t$ is an auxiliary function if:

$$f(\mathcal{W}) \leq a_t(\mathcal{W}) \quad , \forall \; \mathcal{W}$$
$$f(\mathcal{W}_t) = a_t(\mathcal{W}_t) \tag{9}$$

A bound optimizer follows a two-step procedure: first an auxiliary function $a_t$ is computed, then $a_t$ is minimized, such that:

$$\mathcal{W}_{t+1} = \arg\min_{\mathcal{W}} a_t(\mathcal{W}) \tag{10}$$

This iterative procedure is guaranteed to decrease the original function $f$:

$$f(\mathcal{W}_{t+1}) \leq a_t(\mathcal{W}_{t+1}) \leq a_t(\mathcal{W}_t) = f(\mathcal{W}_t) \tag{11}$$

Note that bound optimizers are widely used in machine learning. Examples of well-known bound optimizers include the concave-convex procedure (CCCP) [45], expectation maximization (EM) algorithms or submodular-supermodular procedures (SSP) [18]. Such optimizers are particularly used in clustering [30] and, more generally, in problems involving latent-variable optimization.

**Pairwise Cross-Entropy:** We now prove that minimizing cross-entropy can be viewed as an approximate bound optimization of a more complex pairwise loss.

**Proposition 1.** *Alternately minimizing the cross-entropy loss $\mathcal{L}_{CE}$ with respect to the encoder's parameters $\mathcal{W}$ and the classifier's weights $\boldsymbol{\theta}$ can be viewed as an approximate bound-optimization of a Pairwise Cross-Entropy (PCE) loss, which we define as follows:*

$$\mathcal{L}_{PCE} = \underbrace{-\frac{1}{2\lambda n^2} \sum_{i=1}^{n} \sum_{j:y_j=y_i} z_i^\mathsf{T} z_j}_{\text{TIGHTNESS PART}} + \underbrace{\frac{1}{n} \sum_{i=1}^{n} \log \sum_{k=1}^{K} e^{\frac{1}{\lambda n} \sum_{j=1}^{n} p_{jk} z_i^\mathsf{T} z_j} - \frac{1}{2\lambda} \sum_{k=1}^{K} \|c_k^s\|^2}_{\text{CONTRASTIVE PART}}$$

$$\tag{12}$$

where $c_k^s = \frac{1}{n}\sum_{i=1}^n p_{ik}z_i$ represents the soft-mean of class $k$, $p_{ik}$ represents the softmax probability of point $z_i$ belonging to class $k$, and $\lambda \in \mathbb{R}, \lambda > 0$ depends on the encoder $\phi_\mathcal{W}$.

The full proof of Proposition 1 is provided in the supplemental material. We hereby provide a quick sketch. Considering the usual softmax parametrization for our model's predictions $\widehat{Y}$, the idea is to break the cross-entropy loss in two terms, and artificially add and remove the regularization term $\frac{\lambda}{2}\sum_{k=1}^K \theta_k^\mathsf{T}\theta_k$:

$$\mathcal{L}_{\mathrm{CE}} = \underbrace{-\frac{1}{n}\sum_{i=1}^n \theta_{y_i}^\mathsf{T} z_i + \frac{\lambda}{2}\sum_k \theta_k^\mathsf{T}\theta_k}_{f_1(\theta)} + \underbrace{\frac{1}{n}\sum_{i=1}^n \log \sum_{k=1}^K e^{\theta_k^\mathsf{T} z_i} - \frac{\lambda}{2}\sum_{k=1}^K \theta_k^\mathsf{T}\theta_k}_{f_2(\theta)} \qquad (13)$$

By properly choosing $\lambda \in \mathbb{R}$ in Eq. (13), both $f_1$ and $f_2$ become convex functions of $\theta$. For any class $k$, we then show that the optimal values of $\theta_k$ for $f_1$ and $f_2$ are proportional to, respectively, the hard mean $c_k = \frac{1}{|\mathcal{Z}_k|}\sum_{i:y_i=k} z_i$ and the soft mean $c_k^s = \frac{1}{n}\sum_{i=1}^n p_{ik}z_i$ of class $k$. By plugging-in those optimal values, we can lower bound $f_1$ and $f_2$ individually in Eq. 13 and get the result.

Proposition 1 casts a new light on the cross-entropy loss by explicitly relating it to a new pairwise loss (PCE), following the intuition that the optimal weights $\theta^*$ of the final layer, i.e., the linear classifier, are related to the centroids of each class in the embedded feature space $\mathcal{Z}$. Specifically, finding the optimal classifier's weight $\theta^*$ for cross-entropy can be interpreted as building an auxiliary function $a_t(\mathcal{W}) = \mathcal{L}_{CE}(\mathcal{W}, \theta^*)$ on $\mathcal{L}_{PCE}(\mathcal{W})$. Subsequently minimizing cross-entropy w.r.t. the encoder's weights $\mathcal{W}$ can be interpreted as the second step of bound optimization on $\mathcal{L}_{PCE}(\mathcal{W})$. Similarly to other metric learning losses, PCE contains a *tightness* part that encourages samples from the same classes to align with one another. In echo to Lemma 1, this tightness term, noted $T_{\mathrm{PCE}}$, is equivalent, up to multiplicative and additive constants, to $T_{\mathrm{center}}$ and $T_{\mathrm{contrast}}$, when the features are assumed to be normalized:

$$T_{\mathrm{PCE}} \overset{\mathrm{c}}{=} T_{\mathrm{center}} \overset{\mathrm{c}}{=} T_{\mathrm{contrast}} \qquad (14)$$

PCE also contains a *contrastive* part, divided into two terms. The first pushes all samples away from one another, while the second term forces soft means $c_k^s$ far from the origin. Hence, minimizing the cross-entropy can be interpreted as implicitly minimizing a pairwise loss whose structure appears similar to the well-established metric-learning losses in Table 2.

**Simplified Pairwise Cross-Entropy:** While PCE brings interesting theoretical insights, the computation of the parameter $\lambda$ at every iteration requires computating the eigenvalues of a $d \times d$ matrix at every iteration (cf. full proof in supplemental material), which makes the implementation of PCE difficult in practice. In order to remove the dependence upon $\lambda$, one can plug in the same $\theta$

for both $f_1$ and $f_2$ in Eq. 13. We choose to use $\boldsymbol{\theta}_1^* = \arg\min_{\theta} f_1(\boldsymbol{\theta}) \propto [\boldsymbol{c}_1, ..., \boldsymbol{c}_K]^{\mathsf{T}}$. This yields a simplified version of PCE, that we call SPCE:

$$\mathcal{L}_{SPCE} = \underbrace{-\frac{1}{n^2} \sum_{i=1}^{n} \sum_{j:y_j=y_i} \boldsymbol{z}_i^{\mathsf{T}} \boldsymbol{z}_j}_{\text{TIGHTNESS}} + \underbrace{\frac{1}{n} \sum_{i=1}^{n} \log \sum_{k=1}^{K} \exp\left(\frac{1}{n} \sum_{j:y_j=k} \boldsymbol{z}_i^{\mathsf{T}} \boldsymbol{z}_j\right)}_{\text{CONTRASTIVE}} \quad (15)$$

SPCE and PCE are similar (the difference is that PCE was derived after plugging in the soft means instead of hard means in $f_2$). Contrary to PCE, however, SPCE is easily computable, and the preliminary experiments we provide in the supplementary material indicate that CE and SPCE exhibit similar behaviors at training time. Interestingly, our derived SPCE loss has a form similar to contrastive learning losses in unsupervised representation learning [1,20,31].

## 4.2 A Discriminative View of Mutual Information

**Lemma 2.** *Minimizing the conditional cross-entropy loss, denoted by $\mathcal{H}(Y; \widehat{Y}|\widehat{Z})$, is equivalent to maximizing the mutual information $\mathcal{I}(\widehat{Z}; Y)$.*

The proof of Lemma 2 is provided in the supplementary material. Such result is compelling. Using the discriminative view of mutual information allows to show that minimizing cross-entropy loss is equivalent to maximizing the mutual information $\mathcal{I}(\widehat{Z}; Y)$. This information theoretic argument reinforces our conclusion from Proposition 1 that cross-entropy and the previously described metric learning losses are essentially doing the same job.

## 4.3 Then Why Would Cross-Entropy Work Better?

We showed that cross-entropy essentially optimizes the same underlying mutual information $\mathcal{I}(\widehat{Z}; Y)$ as other DML losses. This fact alone is not enough to explain why the cross-entropy is able to consistently achieve better results than DML losses as shown in Sect. 5. We argue that the difference is in the optimization process. On the one hand, pairwise losses require careful sample mining and weighting strategies to obtain the most informative pairs, especially when considering mini-batches, in order to achieve convergence in a reasonable amount of time, using a reasonable amount of memory. On the other hand, optimizing cross-entropy is substantially easier as it only implies minimization of unary terms. Essentially, cross-entropy does it all without dealing with the difficulties of pairwise terms. Not only it makes optimization easier, but also it simplifies the implementation, thus increasing its potential applicability in real-world problems.

**Table 3.** Summary of the datasets used for evaluation in metric learning.

| Name | Objects | Categories | Images |
|---|---|---|---|
| Caltech-UCSD Birds-200-2011 (CUB)[32] | Birds | 200 | 11 788 |
| Cars Dataset [12] | Cars | 196 | 16 185 |
| Stanford Online Products (SOP) [27] | House furniture | 22 634 | 120 053 |
| In-shop Clothes Retrieval [14] | Clothes | 7 982 | 52 712 |

# 5    Experiments

## 5.1    Metric

The most common metric used in DML is the recall. Most methods, especially recent ones, use the cosine distance to compute the recall for the evaluation. They include $\ell_2$ normalization of the features in the model [4, 16, 19, 21, 23, 35, 37, 42–44, 46], which makes cosine and Euclidean distances equivalent. Computing cosine similarity is also more memory efficient and typically leads to better results [24]. For these reasons, the Euclidean distance on non normalized features has rarely been used for both training and evaluation. In our experiments, $\ell_2$-normalization of the features during training actually hindered the final performance, which might be explained by the fact that we add a classification layer on top of the feature extractor. Thus, we did not $\ell_2$-normalize the features during training and reported the recall with both Euclidean and cosine distances.

## 5.2    Datasets

Four datasets are commonly used in metric learning to evaluate the performances. These datasets are summarized in Table 3. CUB [32], Cars [12] and SOP [27] datasets are divided into train and evaluation splits. For the evaluation, the recall is computed between each sample of the evaluation set and the rest of the set. In-Shop [14] is divided into a query and a gallery set. The recall is computed between each sample of the query set and the whole gallery set.

## 5.3    Training Specifics

**Model Architecture and Pre-training:** In the metric learning literature, several architectures have been used, which historically correspond to the state-of-the-art image classification architectures on ImageNet [3], with an additional constraint on model size (*i.e.*, the ability to train on one or two GPUs in a reasonable time). These include GoogLeNet [28] as in [11], BatchNorm-Inception [29] as in [37] and ResNet-50 [7] as in [43]. They have large differences in classification performances on ImageNet, but the impact on performances over DML benchmarks has rarely been studied in controlled experiments. As this is not the focus of our paper, we use ResNet-50 for our experiments. We concede that one may obtain better performances by modifying the architecture (*e.g.*, reducing model stride and performing multi-level fusion of features). Here, we limit our comparison to standard architectures. Our implementation uses the PyTorch [22] library, and initializes the ResNet-50 model with weights pre-trained on ImageNet.

**Sampling:** To the best of our knowledge, all DML papers – including [46] – use a form of pairwise sampling to ensure that, during training, each mini-batch contains a fixed number of classes and samples per class (*e.g.* mini-batch size of 75 with 3 classes and 25 samples per class in [46]). Deviating from that, we use the common random sampling among all samples (as in most classification training schemes) and set the mini-batch size to 128 in all experiments (contrary to [37] in which the authors use a mini-batch size of 80 for CUB, 1 000 for SOP and did not report for Cars and In-Shop).

**Data Augmentation:** As is common in training deep learning models, data augmentation improves the final performances of the methods. For CUB, the images are first resized so that their smallest side has a length of 256 (*i.e.*, keeping the aspect ratio) while for Cars, SOP and In-Shop, the images are resized to $256 \times 256$. Then a patch is extracted at a random location and size, and resized to $224 \times 224$. For CUB and Cars, we found that random jittering of the brightness, contrast and saturation slightly improves the results. All of the implementation details can be found in the publicly available code.

**Cross-entropy:** The focus of our experiments is to show that, with careful tuning, it is possible to obtain similar or better performance than most recent DML methods, while using only the cross-entropy loss. To train with the cross-entropy loss, we add a linear classification layer (with bias) on top of the feature extraction – similar to many classification models – which produces logits for all the classes present in the training set. Both the weights and biases of this classification layer are initialized to $\mathbf{0}$. We also add dropout with a probability of 0.5 before this classification layer. To further reduce overfitting, we use label smoothing for the target probabilities of the cross-entropy. We set the probability of the true class to $1 - \epsilon$ and the probabilities of the other classes to $\frac{\epsilon}{K-1}$ with $\epsilon = 0.1$ in all our experiments.

**Optimizer:** In most DML papers, the hyper-parameters of the optimizer are the same for Cars, SOP and In-Shop whereas, for CUB, the methods typically use a smaller learning rate. In our experiments, we found that the best results were obtained by tuning the learning rate on a per dataset basis. In all experiments, the models are trained with SGD with Nesterov acceleration and a weight decay of 0.0005, which is applied to convolution and fully-connected layers' weights (but not to biases) as in [9]. For CUB and Cars, the learning rate is set to 0.02 and 0.05 respectively, with 0 momentum. For both SOP and In-Shop, the learning rate is set to 0.003 with a momentum of 0.99.

**Batch Normalization:** Following [37], we freeze all the batch normalization layers in the feature extractor. For Cars, SOP and In-Shop, we found that adding

**Table 4.** Performance on CUB200, Cars-196, SOP and In-Shop datasets. $d$ refers to the distance used to compute the recall when evaluating.

| | Method | $d$ | Architecture | Recall at | | | | | |
|---|---|---|---|---|---|---|---|---|---|
| Caltech-UCSD Birds-200-2011 | | | | 1 | 2 | 4 | 8 | 16 | 32 |
| | Lifted Structure [27] | $\ell_2$ | GoogLeNet | 47.2 | 58.9 | 70.2 | 80.2 | 89.3 | 93.2 |
| | Proxy-NCA [16] | cos | BN-Inception | 49.2 | 61.9 | 67.9 | 81.9 | – | – |
| | HTL [4] | cos | GoogLeNet | 57.1 | 68.8 | 78.7 | 86.5 | 92.5 | 95.5 |
| | ABE [11] | cos | GoogLeNet | 60.6 | 71.5 | 79.8 | 87.4 | – | – |
| | HDC [44] | cos | GoogLeNet | 60.7 | 72.4 | 81.9 | 89.2 | 93.7 | 96.8 |
| | DREML [42] | cos | ResNet-18 | 63.9 | 75.0 | 83.1 | 89.7 | – | – |
| | EPSHN [43] | cos | ResNet-50 | 64.9 | 75.3 | 83.5 | – | – | – |
| | NormSoftmax [46] | cos | ResNet-50 | 65.3 | 76.7 | 85.4 | 91.8 | – | – |
| | Multi-Similarity [37] | cos | BN-Inception | 65.7 | 77.0 | 86.6 | 91.2 | 95.0 | 97.3 |
| | D&C [23] | cos | ResNet-50 | 65.9 | 76.6 | 84.4 | 90.6 | – | – |
| | Cross-Entropy | $\ell_2$ | ResNet-50 | 67.6 | 78.1 | 85.6 | 91.1 | 94.7 | 97.2 |
| | | cos | | 69.2 | 79.2 | 86.9 | 91.6 | 95.0 | 97.3 |
| Stanford Cars | | | | 1 | 2 | 4 | 8 | 16 | 32 |
| | Lifted Structure [27] | $\ell_2$ | GoogLeNet | 49.0 | 60.3 | 72.1 | 81.5 | 89.2 | 92.8 |
| | Proxy-NCA [16] | cos | BN-Inception | 73.2 | 82.4 | 86.4 | 88.7 | – | – |
| | HTL [44] | cos | GoogLeNet | 81.4 | 88.0 | 92.7 | 95.7 | 97.4 | 99.0 |
| | EPSHN [43] | cos | ResNet-50 | 82.7 | 89.3 | 93.0 | – | – | – |
| | HDC [44] | cos | GoogLeNet | 83.8 | 89.8 | 93.6 | 96.2 | 97.8 | 98.9 |
| | Multi-Similarity [37] | cos | BN-Inception | 84.1 | 90.4 | 94.0 | 96.5 | 98.0 | 98.9 |
| | D&C [23] | cos | ResNet-50 | 84.6 | 90.7 | 94.1 | 96.5 | – | – |
| | ABE [11] | cos | GoogLeNet | 85.2 | 90.5 | 94.0 | 96.1 | – | – |
| | DREML [42] | cos | ResNet-18 | 86.0 | 91.7 | 95.0 | 97.2 | – | – |
| | NormSoftmax [46] | cos | ResNet-50 | 89.3 | 94.1 | 96.4 | 98.0 | – | – |
| | Cross-Entropy | $\ell_2$ | ResNet-50 | 89.1 | 93.7 | 96.5 | 98.1 | 99.0 | 99.4 |
| | | cos | | 89.3 | 93.9 | 96.6 | 98.4 | 99.3 | 99.7 |
| Stanford Online Product | | | | 1 | 10 | 100 | 1000 | | |
| | Lifted Structure [27] | $\ell_2$ | GoogLeNet | 62.1 | 79.8 | 91.3 | 97.4 | | |
| | HDC [44] | cos | GoogLeNet | 70.1 | 84.9 | 93.2 | 97.8 | | |
| | HTL [4] | cos | GoogLeNet | 74.8 | 88.3 | 94.8 | 98.4 | | |
| | D&C [23] | cos | ResNet-50 | 75.9 | 88.4 | 94.9 | 98.1 | | |
| | ABE [11] | cos | GoogLeNet | 76.3 | 88.4 | 94.8 | 98.2 | | |
| | Multi-Similarity [37] | cos | BN-Inception | 78.2 | 90.5 | 96.0 | 98.7 | | |
| | EPSHN [43] | cos | ResNet-50 | 78.3 | 90.7 | 96.3 | – | | |
| | NormSoftmax [46] | cos | ResNet-50 | 79.5 | 91.5 | 96.7 | – | | |
| | Cross-Entropy | $\ell_2$ | ResNet-50 | 80.8 | 91.2 | 95.7 | 98.1 | | |
| | | cos | | 81.1 | 91.7 | 96.3 | 98.8 | | |
| In-Shop Clothes Retrieval | | | | 1 | 10 | 20 | 30 | 40 | 50 |
| | HDC [44] | cos | GoogLeNet | 62.1 | 84.9 | 89.0 | 91.2 | 92.3 | 93.1 |
| | DREML [42] | cos | ResNet-18 | 78.4 | 93.7 | 95.8 | 96.7 | – | – |
| | HTL [4] | cos | GoogLeNet | 80.9 | 94.3 | 95.8 | 97.2 | 97.4 | 97.8 |
| | D&C [23] | cos | ResNet-50 | 85.7 | 95.5 | 96.9 | 97.5 | – | 98.0 |
| | ABE [11] | cos | GoogLeNet | 87.3 | 96.7 | 97.9 | 98.2 | 98.5 | 98.7 |
| | EPSHN [43] | cos | ResNet-50 | 87.8 | 95.7 | 96.8 | – | – | – |
| | NormSoftmax [46] | cos | ResNet-50 | 89.4 | 97.8 | 98.7 | 99.0 | – | – |
| | Multi-Similarity [37] | cos | BN-Inception | 89.7 | 97.9 | 98.5 | 98.8 | 99.1 | 99.2 |
| | Cross-Entropy | $\ell_2$ | ResNet-50 | 90.6 | 97.8 | 98.5 | 98.8 | 98.9 | 99.0 |
| | | cos | | 90.6 | 98.0 | 98.6 | 98.9 | 99.1 | 99.2 |

batch normalization – without scaling and bias – on top of the feature extractor improves our final performance and reduces the gap between $\ell_2$ and cosine distances when computing the recall. On CUB, however, we obtained the best recall without this batch normalization.

## 5.4 Results

Results for the experiments are reported in Table 4. We also report the architecture used in the experiments as well as the distance used in the evaluation to compute the recall. $\ell_2$ refers to the Euclidean distance on non normalized features while *cos* refers to either the cosine distance or the Euclidean distance on $\ell_2$-normalized features, both of which are equivalent.

On all datasets, we report state-of-the-art results except on Cars, where the only method achieving similar recall uses cross-entropy for training. We also notice that, contrary to common beliefs, using Euclidean distance can actually be competitive as it also achieves near state-of-the-art results on all four datasets. These results clearly highlight the potential of cross-entropy for metric learning, and confirm that this loss can achieve the same objective as pairwise losses.

## 6   Conclusion

Throughout this paper, we revealed non-obvious relations between the cross-entropy loss, widely adopted in classification tasks, and pairwise losses commonly used in DML. These relations were drawn under two different perspectives. First, cross-entropy minimization was shown equivalent to an approximate bound-optimization of a pairwise loss, introduced as Pairwise Cross-Entropy (PCE), which appears similar in structure to already existing DML losses. Second, adopting a more general information theoretic view of DML, we showed that both pairwise losses and cross-entropy were, in essence, maximizing a common mutual information $\mathcal{I}(\hat{Z}, Y)$ between the embedded features and the labels. This connection becomes particularly apparent when writing mutual information in both its *generative* and *discriminative* views. Hence, we argue that most of the differences in performance observed in previous works come from the optimization process during training. Cross-entropy only contains unary terms, while traditional DML losses are based on pairwise terms optimization, which requires substantially more tuning (*e.g.* mini-batch size, sampling strategy, pair weighting). And while we acknowledge that some losses have better properties than others regarding optimization, we empirically showed that the cross-entropy loss was also able to achieve state-of-the-art results when fairly tuned, highlighting the fact that most improvements have come from enhanced training schemes (*e.g.* data augmentation, learning rate policies, batch normalization freeze) rather than intrinsic properties of pairwise losses. We strongly advocate that cross-entropy should be carefully tuned to be compared against as a baseline in future works.

# References

1. Chen, T., Kornblith, S., Norouzi, M., Hinton, G.: A simple framework for contrastive learning of visual representations. In: Proceedings of the International Conference on Machine Learning (ICML) (2020)
2. Davis, J.V., Kulis, B., Jain, P., Sra, S., Dhillon, I.S.: Information-theoretic metric learning. In: Proceedings of the International Conference on Machine Learning (ICML) (2007)
3. Deng, J., Dong, W., Socher, R., Li, L.J., Li, K., Fei-Fei, L.: Imagenet: a large-scale hierarchical image database. In: Proceedings of the IEEE/CVF Conference on Computer Vision and Pattern Recognition (CVPR) (2009)
4. Ge, W., Huang, W., Dong, D., Scott, M.R.: Deep metric learning with hierarchical triplet loss. In: Ferrari, V., Hebert, M., Sminchisescu, C., Weiss, Y. (eds.) ECCV 2018. LNCS, vol. 11210, pp. 272–288. Springer, Cham (2018). https://doi.org/10.1007/978-3-030-01231-1_17
5. Goldberger, J., Hinton, G.E., Roweis, S.T., Salakhutdinov, R.R.: Neighbourhood components analysis. In: Advances in Neural Information Processing Systems (NeurIPS) (2005)
6. Hadsell, R., Chopra, S., LeCun, Y.: Dimensionality reduction by learning an invariant mapping. In: Proceedings of the IEEE/CVF Conference on Computer Vision and Pattern Recognition (CVPR) (2006)
7. He, K., Zhang, X., Ren, S., Sun, J.: Identity mappings in deep residual networks. In: Leibe, B., Matas, J., Sebe, N., Welling, M. (eds.) ECCV 2016. LNCS, vol. 9908, pp. 630–645. Springer, Cham (2016). https://doi.org/10.1007/978-3-319-46493-0_38
8. Hermans, A., Beyer, L., Leibe, B.: In defense of the triplet loss for person re-identification. arXiv preprint arXiv:1703.07737 (2017)
9. Jia, X., et al.: Highly scalable deep learning training system with mixed-precision: training ImageNet in four minutes. arXiv preprint arXiv:1807.11205 (2018)
10. Kedem, D., Tyree, S., Sha, F., Lanckriet, G.R., Weinberger, K.Q.: Non-linear metric learning. In: Advances in Neural Information Processing Systems (NeurIPS) (2012)
11. Kim, W., Goyal, B., Chawla, K., Lee, J., Kwon, K.: Attention-based ensemble for deep metric learning. In: Ferrari, V., Hebert, M., Sminchisescu, C., Weiss, Y. (eds.) ECCV 2018. LNCS, vol. 11205, pp. 760–777. Springer, Cham (2018). https://doi.org/10.1007/978-3-030-01246-5_45
12. Krause, J., Stark, M., Deng, J., Fei-Fei, L.: 3D object representations for fine-grained categorization. In: Proceedings of the IEEE International Conference on Computer Vision (ICCV) Workshops (2013)
13. Liu, W., Wen, Y., Yu, Z., Li, M., Raj, B., Song, L.: SphereFace: deep hypersphere embedding for face recognition. In: Proceedings of the IEEE/CVF Conference on Computer Vision and Pattern Recognition (CVPR) (2017)
14. Liu, Z., Luo, P., Qiu, S., Wang, X., Tang, X.: DeepFashion: powering robust clothes recognition and retrieval with rich annotations. In: Proceedings of the IEEE/CVF Conference on Computer Vision and Pattern Recognition (CVPR) (2016)
15. Lowe, D.G.: Similarity metric learning for a variable-kernel classifier. Neural Comput. 7, 72–85 (1995)
16. Movshovitz-Attias, Y., Toshev, A., Leung, T.K., Ioffe, S., Singh, S.: No fuss distance metric learning using proxies. In: Proceedings of the IEEE International Conference on Computer Vision (ICCV) (2017)

17. Musgrave, K., Belongie, S., Lim, S.N.: A metric learning reality check. arXiv preprint arXiv:2003.08505 (2020)
18. Narasimhan, M., Bilmes, J.: A submodular-supermodular procedure with applications to discriminative structure learning. In: Proceedings of the Twenty-First Conference on Uncertainty in Artificial Intelligence (UAI) (2005)
19. Oh Song, H., Jegelka, S., Rathod, V., Murphy, K.: Deep metric learning via facility location. In: Proceedings of the IEEE/CVF Conference on Computer Vision and Pattern Recognition (CVPR) (2017)
20. Oord, A.V.d., Li, Y., Vinyals, O.: Representation learning with contrastive predictive coding. arXiv preprint arXiv:1807.03748 (2018)
21. Opitz, M., Waltner, G., Possegger, H., Bischof, H.: Bier-boosting independent embeddings robustly. In: Proceedings of the IEEE International Conference on Computer Vision (ICCV) (2017)
22. Paszke, A., et al.: Pytorch: an imperative style, high-performance deep learning library. In: Advances in Neural Information Processing Systems (NeurIPS). Curran Associates, Inc. (2019)
23. Sanakoyeu, A., Tschernezki, V., Buchler, U., Ommer, B.: Divide and conquer the embedding space for metric learning. In: Proceedings of the IEEE/CVF Conference on Computer Vision and Pattern Recognition (CVPR) (2019)
24. Schroff, F., Kalenichenko, D., Philbin, J.: Facenet: a unified embedding for face recognition and clustering. In: Proceedings of the IEEE/CVF Conference on Computer Vision and Pattern Recognition (CVPR) (2015)
25. Schultz, M., Joachims, T.: Learning a distance metric from relative comparisons. In: Advances in Neural Information Processing Systems (NeurIPS) (2004)
26. Sohn, K.: Improved deep metric learning with multi-class n-pair loss objective. In: Advances in Neural Information Processing Systems (NeurIPS) (2016)
27. Song, H.O., Xiang, Y., Jegelka, S., Savarese, S.: Deep metric learning via lifted structured feature embedding. In: Proceedings of the IEEE/CVF Conference on Computer Vision and Pattern Recognition (CVPR) (2016)
28. Szegedy, C., et al.: Going deeper with convolutions. In: Proceedings of the IEEE/CVF Conference on Computer Vision and Pattern Recognition (CVPR) (2015)
29. Szegedy, C., Vanhoucke, V., Ioffe, S., Shlens, J., Wojna, Z.: Rethinking the inception architecture for computer vision. In: Proceedings of the IEEE/CVF Conference on Computer Vision and Pattern Recognition (CVPR) (2016)
30. Tang, M., Marin, D., Ben Ayed, I., Boykov, Y.: Kernel cuts: kernel and spectral clustering meet regularization. Int. J. Comput. Vision 127, 477–511 (2019). https://doi.org/10.1007/s11263-018-1115-1
31. Tschannen, M., Djolonga, J., Rubenstein, P.K., Gelly, S., Lucic, M.: On mutual information maximization for representation learning. In: International Conference on Learning Representations (2020)
32. Wah, C., Branson, S., Welinder, P., Perona, P., Belongie, S.: The Caltech-UCSD Birds-200-2011 Dataset. Technical report, CNS-TR-2011-001, California Institute of Technology (2011)
33. Wang, F., Cheng, J., Liu, W., Liu, H.: Additive margin softmax for face verification. IEEE Sig. Process. Lett. 25, 926–930 (2018)
34. Wang, H., et al.: CosFace: large margin cosine loss for deep face recognition. In: Proceedings of the IEEE/CVF Conference on Computer Vision and Pattern Recognition (CVPR) (2018)

35. Wang, J., Zhou, F., Wen, S., Liu, X., Lin, Y.: Deep metric learning with angular loss. In: Proceedings of the IEEE International Conference on Computer Vision (ICCV) (2017)
36. Wang, M., Sha, F.: Information theoretical clustering via semidefinite programming. In: Proceedings of the Fourteenth International Conference on Artificial Intelligence and Statistics (AIStats) (2011)
37. Wang, X., Han, X., Huang, W., Dong, D., Scott, M.R.: Multi-similarity loss with general pair weighting for deep metric learning. In: Proceedings of the IEEE/CVF Conference on Computer Vision and Pattern Recognition (CVPR) (2019)
38. Weinberger, K.Q., Saul, L.K.: Distance metric learning for large margin nearest neighbor classification. J. Mach. Learn. Res. (JMLR) (2009)
39. Wen, Y., Zhang, K., Li, Z., Qiao, Yu.: A discriminative feature learning approach for deep face recognition. In: Leibe, B., Matas, J., Sebe, N., Welling, M. (eds.) ECCV 2016. LNCS, vol. 9911, pp. 499–515. Springer, Cham (2016). https://doi.org/10.1007/978-3-319-46478-7_31
40. Wu, Z., Efros, A.A., Yu, S.X.: Improving generalization via scalable neighborhood component analysis. In: Ferrari, V., Hebert, M., Sminchisescu, C., Weiss, Y. (eds.) ECCV 2018. LNCS, vol. 11211, pp. 712–728. Springer, Cham (2018). https://doi.org/10.1007/978-3-030-01234-2_42
41. Xing, E.P., Jordan, M.I., Russell, S.J., Ng, A.Y.: Distance metric learning with application to clustering with side-information. In: Advances in Neural Information Processing Systems (NeurIPS) (2003)
42. Xuan, H., Souvenir, R., Pless, R.: Deep randomized ensembles for metric learning. In: Ferrari, V., Hebert, M., Sminchisescu, C., Weiss, Y. (eds.) ECCV 2018. LNCS, vol. 11220, pp. 751–762. Springer, Cham (2018). https://doi.org/10.1007/978-3-030-01270-0_44
43. Xuan, H., Stylianou, A., Pless, R.: Improved embeddings with easy positive triplet mining. In: The IEEE Winter Conference on Applications of Computer Vision (WACV) (2020)
44. Yuan, Y., Yang, K., Zhang, C.: Hard-aware deeply cascaded embedding. In: Proceedings of the IEEE/CVF Conference on Computer Vision and Pattern Recognition (CVPR) (2017)
45. Yuille, A.L., Rangarajan, A.: The concave-convex procedure (CCCP). In: Advances in Neural Information Processing Systems (NeurIPS) (2002)
46. Zhai, A., Wu, H.Y.: Classification is a strong baseline for deep metric learning. In: British Machine Vision Conference (BMVC) (2019)
47. Zheng, W., Chen, Z., Lu, J., Zhou, J.: Hardness-aware deep metric learning. In: Proceedings of the IEEE/CVF Conference on Computer Vision and Pattern Recognition (CVPR) (2019)

# Behind the Scene: Revealing the Secrets of Pre-trained Vision-and-Language Models

Jize Cao[1]($\boxtimes$), Zhe Gan[2], Yu Cheng[2], Licheng Yu[3], Yen-Chun Chen[2], and Jingjing Liu[2]

[1] University of Washington, Seattle, USA
caojize@cs.washington.edu
[2] Microsoft Dynamics 365 AI Research, Redmond, USA
{zhe.gan,yu.cheng,yen-chun.chen,jingjl}@microsoft.com
[3] Facebook AI, Menlo Park, USA
lichengyu@fb.com

**Abstract.** Recent Transformer-based large-scale pre-trained models have revolutionized vision-and-language (V+L) research. Models such as ViLBERT, LXMERT and UNITER have significantly lifted state of the art across a wide range of V+L benchmarks. However, little is known about the inner mechanisms that destine their impressive success. To reveal the secrets behind the scene, we present VALUE (**V**ision-**A**nd-**L**anguage **U**nderstanding **E**valuation), a set of meticulously designed probing tasks (*e.g.*, Visual Coreference Resolution, Visual Relation Detection) generalizable to standard pre-trained V+L models, to decipher the inner workings of multimodal pre-training (*e.g.*, implicit knowledge garnered in individual attention heads, inherent cross-modal alignment learned through contextualized multimodal embeddings). Through extensive analysis of each archetypal model architecture via these probing tasks, our key observations are: (*i*) Pre-trained models exhibit a propensity for attending over text rather than images during inference. (*ii*) There exists a subset of attention heads that are tailored for capturing cross-modal interactions. (*iii*) Learned attention matrix in pre-trained models demonstrates patterns coherent with the latent alignment between image regions and textual words. (*iv*) Plotted attention patterns reveal visually-interpretable relations among image regions. (*v*) Pure linguistic knowledge is also effectively encoded in the attention heads. These are valuable insights serving to guide future work towards designing better model architecture and objectives for multimodal pre-training. (Code is available at https://github.com/JizeCao/VALUE).

---

J. Cao and L. Yu—This work was done when Jize and Licheng worked at Microsoft.

---

**Electronic supplementary material** The online version of this chapter (https://doi.org/10.1007/978-3-030-58539-6_34) contains supplementary material, which is available to authorized users.

A. Vedaldi et al. (Eds.): ECCV 2020, LNCS 12351, pp. 565–580, 2020.
https://doi.org/10.1007/978-3-030-58539-6_34

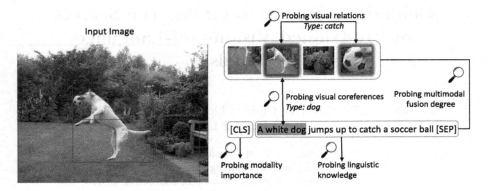

**Fig. 1.** Illustration of the proposed VALUE framework for investigating pre-trained vision-and-language models. VALUE consists of a set of well-designed probing tasks that unveil the inner mechanisms of V+L pre-trained models across: (*i*) Multimodal Fusion Degree; (*ii*) Modality Importance; (*iii*) Cross-modal Interaction via probing visual coreferences; (*iv*) Image-to-image Interaction via probing visual relations; and (*v*) Text-to-text Interaction via probing learned linguistic knowledge.

## 1  Introduction

Recently, Transformer-based [35] large-scale pre-trained models [6, 19, 21, 22, 27, 32] have prevailed in Vision-and-Language (V+L) research, an important area that sits at the nexus of computer vision and natural language processing (NLP). Inspired by BERT [9], a common practice for pre-training V+L models is to first encode image regions and sentence words into a common embedding space, then use multiple Transformer layers to learn image-text contextualized joint embeddings through well-designed pre-training tasks. There are two main schools of model design: (*i*) single-stream architecture, such as VLBERT [27] and UNITER [27], where a single Transformer is applied to both image and text modalities; and (*ii*) two-stream architecture, such as LXMERT [32] and ViLBERT [22], in which two Transformers are applied to images and text independently, and a third Transformer is stacked on top for later fusion. When finetuned on downstream tasks, these pre-trained models have achieved new state of the art on image-text retrieval [18], visual question answering [4,11], referring expression comprehension [37], and visual reasoning [13,28,38]. This suggests that substantial amount of visual and linguistic knowledge has been encoded in the pre-trained models.

There has been several studies that investigate latent knowledge encoded in pre-trained language models [7,16,25,33]. However, analyzing multimodal pre-trained models is still an unexplored territory. It remains unclear how the inner mechanisms of cross-modal pre-trained models induce their empirical success on downstream tasks. Motivated by this, we present VALUE (**V**ision-**A**nd-**L**anguage **U**nderstanding **E**valuation), a set of well-designed probing tasks that aims to reveal the secrets of these pre-trained V+L models. To investigate both single-

and two-stream model architectures, we select one model from each category (LXMERT for two-stream and UNITER for single-stream, because of their superb performance across many V+L tasks). As illustrated in Fig. 1, VALUE is designed to provide insights on: (a) Multimodal Fusion Degree; (b) Modality Importance; (c) Cross-modal Interaction (Image-to-text/Text-to-image); (d) Image-to-image Interaction; and (e) Text-to-text Interaction.

For (a) Multimodal Fusion Degree, clustering analysis between image and text representations shows that in single-stream models like UNITER, as the network layers go deeper, the fusion between two modalities becomes more intertwined. However, the opposite phenomenon is observed in two-stream models like LXMERT. For (b) Modality Importance, by analyzing the attention trace of the [CLS] token, which is commonly considered as containing the intended fused multimodal information and often used as the input signal for downstream tasks, we find that the final predictions tend to depend more on textual input rather than visual input.

To gain deeper insights into how pre-trained models drive success in downstream tasks, we look into three types of interactions between modalities. For (c) Cross-modal Interaction, we propose a Visual Coreference Resolution task to probe its encoded knowledge. For (d) Image-to-image Interaction, we conduct analysis via Visual Relation Detection between two image regions. For (e) Text-to-text Interaction, we evaluate the linguistic knowledge encoded in each layer of the tested model with SentEval tookit [8], and compare with the original BERT [9]. Experiments show that both single- and two-stream models, especially the former, can well capture cross-modal alignment, visual relations, and linguistic knowledge.

To the best of our knowledge, this is the first known effort on thorough analysis of pre-trained V+L models, to gain insights from different perspectives about the latent knowledge encoded in self-attention weights, and to distill the secret ingredients that drive the empirical success of prevailing V+L models.

## 2   Related Work

For image-text representation learning, ViLBERT [22] and LXMERT [32] used two-stream architecture for pre-training, while B2T2 [2], VisualBERT [21], Unicoder-VL [19], VL-BERT [27] and UNITER [6] adopted single-stream architecture. VLP [39] proposed a unified pre-trained model for both image captioning and VQA. Multi-task learning [23] and adversarial training in VILLA [10] have been studied to boost performance. On video+language side, VideoBERT [30] applied BERT to learn joint embeddings of video frame tokens and linguistic tokens from video-text pairs. CBT [29] introduced contrastive learning to handle real-valued video frame features, and HERO [20] proposed hierarchical Transformer architectures to leverage both global and local temporal visual-textual alignments. However, except for some simple visualization of the learned attention maps [32], no existing work has systematically analyzed these pre-trained models.

There has been some recent studies on assessing the capability of BERT in capturing structural properties of language [15,31,34]. Multi-head self-attention has been analyzed for machine translation in [24,36], which observed that only a small subset of heads is important, and the other heads can be pruned without affecting model performance. [33] reported that BERT can rediscover the classical NLP pipeline, where basic syntactic information appears in lower layers, while high-level semantic information appears in higher layers. Analysis on BERT self-attention [7,12,16] showed that BERT can learn syntactic relations, and a limited set of attention patterns are repeated across different heads. [5,25] and [40] demonstrated that BERT has surprisingly strong ability to recall factual relational knowledge and perform commonsense reasoning. A layer-wise analysis of Transformer representations in [1] provided insights to the reasoning process of how BERT answers questions. All these studies have focused on the analysis of BERT, while investigating pre-trained V+L models is still an uncharted territory. Given their empirical success and unique multimodal nature, we believe it is instrumental to conduct an in-depth analysis to understand these models, to provide useful insights and guidelines for future studies. New probing tasks such as visual coreference resolution and visual relation detection are proposed for this purpose, which can lend insights to other evaluation tasks as well.

## 3   VALUE: Probing Pre-trained V+L Models

Key curiosities this study aims to unveil include:

 (i) What is the correlation between multimodal fusion and the number of layers in pre-trained models? (Sect. 3.1)
 (ii) Which modality plays a more important role that drives the pre-trained model to make final predictions? (Sect. 3.2)
(iii) What knowledge is encoded in pre-trained models that supports cross-modal interaction and alignment? (Sect. 3.3)
(iv) What knowledge has been learned for image-to-image (intra-modal) interaction (*i.e.*, visual relations)? (Sect. 3.4)
 (v) Compared with BERT, do pre-trained V+L models effectively encode linguistic knowledge for text-to-text (intra-modal) interaction? (Sect. 3.5)

To answer these questions, we select one model from each archetypal model architecture for dissection: UNITER-base [6] (12 layers, 768 hidden units per layer, 12 attention heads) for single-stream model, and LXMERT [32] for two-stream model.[1] Single-stream model (UNITER) shares the same structure as BERT [9], except that the input now becomes a mixed sequence of two modalities. Two-stream model (LXMERT) first performs self-attention through several layers on each modality independently, then fuses the inputs through a stack of cross-self-attention layers (first cross-attention, then self-attention). Therefore, the attention pattern in two-stream models is fixed, as one modality is only

---

[1] Our probing analysis can be readily extended to other pre-trained models as well.

allowed to attend over either itself or the other modality at any time (there is no such constraint in single-stream models). A more detailed model description is provided in the Appendix.

Two datasets are selected for our probing experiments:

(i) **Visual Genome (VG)** [17]: image-text dataset with annotated dense captions and scene graphs.
(ii) **Flickr30k Entities** [26]: image-text dataset with annotated visual co-reference links between image regions and noun phrases in the captions.

Each data sample consists of three components: ($i$) an input image; ($ii$) a set of detected image regions;[2] and ($iii$) a caption. In Flickr30k Entities, the caption is relatively long, describing the whole image; while in VG, a few short captions are provided (called dense captions), each describing an image region.

The number of annotated image regions in an image is relatively small (5–6 for Flick30k Entities, and 2–4 for VG dense annotated graph); while in pre-trained V+L models, the number of image regions fed to the model is typically 36 [3]. Therefore, we extract an additional set of image regions from a Faster R-CNN pre-trained on the VG dataset [3], and combine them with the original image regions provided in the dataset. The initial image representation is obtained from the Faster R-CNN as well. Finally, we feed both image regions and textual tokens into the pre-trained model for probing analysis. The following sub-sections describe analysis results and key observations from each proposed probing task.

## 3.1 Deep to Profound: Deeper Layers Lead to More Intertwined Multimodal Fusion

By nature, visual features in images and linguistic clues in text have distinctive characteristics. However, it is unknown whether the semantic gap between their corresponding representations narrows (*i.e.*, the contextualized representations of the two modalities become less differentiable) through the cross-modal fusion between intermediate layers.

### 3.1.1 Probing Task
To answer this question, we design a probing task to test the multimodal fusion degree of a model. First, we extract all the embedding features of both image regions and textual tokens from aforementioned two datasets (VG and Flickr30k Entities). For single-stream model (UNITER-base), we extract the output representation from each layer, as multimodal fusion is performed through all the layers. For two-stream model (LXMERT), we only consider the output embeddings from the last 5 layers (*i.e.*, the layers constituting the cross-modality encoder), because the two modalities do not have any interaction prior to that. To gain

---

[2] An image region is also called a visual token in this paper; these two terms will be used interchangeable throughout the paper.

**Table 1.** NMI scores on multimodal fusion probing. A smaller NMI value indicates a higher fusion degree. Note that the two-stream model (LXMERT) only has 5 layers in its cross-modality encoder. A larger layer number corresponds to an upper layer.

| Layer | 0 | 1 | 2 | 3 | 4 | 5 | 6 | 7 | 8 | 9 | 10 | 11 |
|---|---|---|---|---|---|---|---|---|---|---|---|---|
| *single-stream* | | | | | | | | | | | | |
| Flickr30k | 0.36 | 0.38 | 0.39 | 0.41 | 0.38 | 0.38 | 0.38 | 0.38 | 0.32 | **0.20** | 0.26 | **0.20** |
| Visual Genome | 0.25 | 0.25 | 0.24 | 0.24 | 0.22 | 0.22 | 0.21 | 0.21 | 0.20 | 0.17 | **0.16** | **0.16** |
| *two-stream (cross)* | | | | | | | | | | | | |
| Flickr30k | **0.42** | 0.48 | 0.67 | 0.75 | 0.43 | – | – | – | – | – | – | – |
| Visual Genome | **0.43** | 0.56 | 0.68 | 0.78 | 0.57 | – | – | – | – | – | – | – |

quantitative measurement, for each data sample, we apply the $k$-means algorithm (with $k = 2$) on the representations from each layer to partition them into two clusters, and measure the difference between the formed clusters and ground-truth visual/textual clusters via Normalized Mutual Information (NMI), an unsupervised metric for evaluating differences between clusters. A larger NMI value implies that the distinction between two clusters is more significant, indicating a lower fusion degree [14]. For example, when NMI is equal to 1.0, the two clusters represent the original visual tokens and textual tokens, respectively. We use the mean value of NMI for all the data samples to measure the level of multimodal fusion.

### 3.1.2 Results
Table 1 summarizes the probing results on multimodal fusion degree. For single-stream model (UNITER-base), the NMI scores gradually decrease, indicating that the representations from the two modalities fuse together deeper and deeper from lower to higher layers. This observation matches our intuition that the embedding of a modality from a higher layer better attends over the other modality than a lower layer. However, in two-stream model (LXMERT), as the layers go deeper (except for the last layer), the representations deviate from each other. One possible explanation is that single-stream model applies the same set of parameters to both image and text modalities, while two-stream model uses two separate sets of parameters (as part of its network design) to model the attention on the image and text modality independently. The latter makes it relatively easier to distinguish the two representations, leading to a higher NMI score. An t-SNE visualization is provided in the Appendix.

### 3.2 Who Pulls More Strings: Textual Modality Is More Dominant Than Image

Following BERT [9], pre-trained V+L models add a special [CLS] token at the beginning of a sequence, and a special [SEP] token at the end. In practice, the [CLS] token representation from the last layer is used as the fused representation

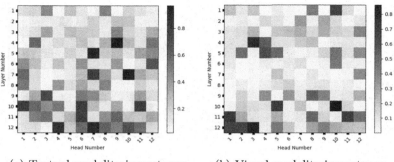

(a) Textual modality importance        (b) Visual modality importance

**Fig. 2.** Visualization of the modality importance score for all the 144 attention heads.

for both modalities in downstream tasks. Since the [CLS] token absorbs information from both modalities through self-attention, the degree of attention of the [CLS] token over each modality could be regarded as evidence to answer the following question: *which modality is more dominant during inference?* Note that in the two-stream model design, the [CLS] token is not allowed to attend to both image and textual modality simultaneously. Therefore, the probing experiments for modality importance is focused on single-stream model.

### 3.2.1 Probing Task

Formally, to quantitatively analyze the [CLS] attention trace, the *Modality Importance* (MI) of a head $j$ is defined as the sum of the attention values that the [CLS] token spent on the modality $M$ (visual or textual) at $j$ for the whole sequence $S = ([CLS], t_1, \ldots, t_m, [SEP], v_1, \ldots, v_n)$, where $t_1, \ldots, t_m$ and $v_1, \ldots, v_n$ are textual and visual tokens, respectively. That is,

$$I_{M,j} = \sum_{i \in S} \mathbb{1}(i \in M) \cdot \alpha_{ij}, \qquad (1)$$

where $\alpha_{ij}$ represents the attention weight that the [CLS] token attends on token $i$ at head $j$, and $\mathbb{1}(\cdot)$ is the indicator function.

Since the attention heads in the same layer perform attention on the same representation, it is natural to expand the above head-level analysis to a layer-level analysis, by considering the mean of MI scores of all the 12 heads as the MI measurement of that layer. In addition, we calculate an overall MI score via summing up the MI scores of all the 144 heads. The mean MI value of all the data samples is reported as the score for probing modality importance. Note that the MI score for visual/textual modality is calculated based on the attention weights on the visual/textual tokens; while the attention weights on the special [CLS] and [SEP] tokens are not considered. Therefore, the two mean MI scores from the two modalities do not sum to one.

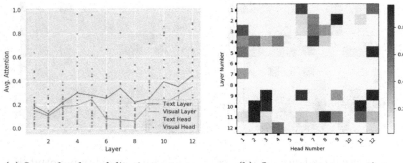

(a) Layer-level modality importance    (b)  Image-to-text attention

**Fig. 3.** Layer-level modality importance scores and visualization of the image-to-text attention for all the 144 attention heads.

### 3.2.2    Results

Experiments are conducted on the Flickr30k Entity dataset. Fig. 2 provides the MI scores for all the 144 attention heads of UNITER-base. The heatmap on the textual MI is denser than that of the visual MI, showing that more attention heads are learning useful knowledge from the textual modality than the image modality. Figure 3a further shows the layer-level MI scores for each modality. The average MI score on the text modality is higher than that on the image modality, especially for intermediate layers, suggesting that the pre-trained model relies more on the textual modality for making decisions during inference time.

### 3.3    Winner Takes All: A Subset of Heads Is Specialized for Cross-Modal Interaction

The key difference between single-modal Transformer (such as BERT) and two-modal Transformer (such as UNITER and LXMERT) is that two-modal Transformer requires extra cross-modal interaction. To gain an in-depth understanding of cross-modal attention heads, which is instructive to prompt better model design and enhance model interpretability, we look into two special types of head: ($i$) image-to-text head; and ($ii$) visual-coreference head.

### 3.3.1    Probing Image-to-Text Head

We first analyze whether there exists any head specialized in learning cross-modal interaction. Formally, for a given image-text pair, visual and textual tokens are denoted as $V$ and $T$, respectively. We define a head as *image-to-text head* if:

$$\exists v \in V \sum_{t \in T} \alpha_{v \to t} > 0.5 , \qquad (2)$$

where $\alpha_{v \to t}$ denotes the attention weight from a visual token to a textual token. This defines whether a visual token pays more attention to the text modality. Specifically, if there exists one visual token that has higher attention weight on

**Table 2.** Results on visual coreference resolution. Each number represents the maximum attention weights between two linked tokens, averaged across all data samples. $V \rightarrow T$ records the attention trace where a visual token attends to the linked noun phrase; $T \rightarrow V$ records the attention trace on the other direction. The head that achieves the maximum attention weight is shown in the bracket.

| *Results on single-stream model* | | | | |
|---|---|---|---|---|
| Coref Type | $V \rightarrow T$ | $T \rightarrow V$ | $V \rightarrow T$ (Rand.) | $T \rightarrow V$ (Rand.) |
| people | **0.165 (9–12)** | 0.060 (3–1) | 0.106 (9–12) | 0.035 (11–8) |
| bodyparts | **0.108 (9–3)** | 0.051 (11–8) | 0.084 (9–12) | 0.038 (11–8) |
| scene | **0.151 (9–12)** | 0.048 (3–1) | 0.111 (9–12) | 0.035 (11–8) |
| clothing | **0.157 (9–3)** | 0.040 (3–1) | 0.092 (9–12) | 0.040 (10–2) |
| animals | **0.285 (9–12)** | 0.137 (3–1) | 0.139 (9–12) | 0.047 (9–12) |
| instruments | **0.244 (11–8)** | 0.042 (9–12) | 0.091 (9–12) | 0.031 (9–12) |
| vehicles | **0.194 (9–12)** | 0.065 (3–1) | 0.112 (9–12) | 0.039 (9–12) |
| *Results on two-stream model* | | | | |
| people | **0.145 (2–8)** | 0.063 (2–6) | 0.056 (1–7) | 0.057 (3–9) |
| bodyparts | **0.079 (5–7)** | 0.059 (1–7) | 0.041 (1–2) | 0.060 (3–9) |
| scene | **0.076 (5–7)** | 0.059 (1–7) | 0.038 (1–7) | 0.060 (3–9) |
| clothing | **0.062 (5–7)** | 0.062 (2–6) | 0.040 (1–7) | 0.061 (3–9) |
| animals | **0.235 (3–4)** | 0.106 (4–7) | 0.075 (1–7) | 0.072 (3–9) |
| instruments | **0.144 (5–7)** | 0.040 (1–7) | 0.055 (1–11) | 0.058 (3–9) |
| vehicles | **0.097 (1–1)** | 0.046 (2–6) | 0.097 (1–7) | 0.062 (3–9) |

text than other tokens, we regard the corresponding head as performing cross-modal attention from image to text.

Based on the above definition, we count the number of occurrences of head as an *image-to-text head* for all data samples in the Flickr30k Entities dataset, and report the empirical probability of each head being an *image-to-text head*. Note that in the two-stream model, the image-to-text head is by design, therefore, we only conduct this analysis on single-stream model.

Figure 3b shows there is a specific set of heads in UNITER-base that perform cross-modal interaction. The maximum probability of a head performing image-to-text attention is 0.92, the minimum probability is 0, and only 15% heads have more than 0.5 probability to pay the majority attention weight on the image-to-text part. Interestingly, by training single-stream model, the attention heads are automatically learned to exhibit a "two-stream" pattern, where some heads control the message sharing from the visual modality to the textual modality.

### 3.3.2 Visual Coreference Resolution

One straightforward way to investigate the visual-linguistic knowledge encoded in the model is to evaluate whether the model is able to match an image region to its corresponding textual phrase in the sentence. Thus, we design a

*Visual Coreference Resolution* task (similar to coreference resolution) to predict whether there is a link between an image region and a noun phrase in the sentence that describes the image. In addition, each coreference link in the dataset is annotated with a label (8 in total).

Through this task, we can find out whether the coreference knowledge can be captured by the attention trace. To achieve this goal, for each data sample in the Flickr30k Entity dataset, we extract the encoder's attention weights for all the 144 heads. Note that noun phrases typically consist of two or more tokens in the sequence. Thus, we extract the maximum attention weight between the image region and each word of the noun phrase for each head. The maximum weight is then used to evaluate which head identifies visual coreference (*i.e.*, performing multimodal alignment).

Results are summarized in Table 2. The columns labeled with "(Rand.)" are considered as ablation groups to identify whether the high attention weight of a certain coreference relationship is triggered by the relation between the image-text pair rather than the effect of one specific image/text token. For a link $V \rightarrow T$, we measure the maximum attention weight of the visual token $V$ to a random noun phrase, to obtain the results for $V \rightarrow T$ (Rand.). Similarly, we use the maximum attention weight of a noun phrase $T$ to a random visual token to obtain the results for $T \rightarrow V$ (Rand.).

Results show that the relation between a noun phase and its linked visual token is encoded in the attention pattern, especially for $V \rightarrow T$. The heads $(9\text{-}3)^3$, $(9\text{-}12)$ and $(3\text{-}1)$ have captured richer coreference knowledge than other heads, indicating that there exists a subset of heads in the pre-trained model that is specialized in coreference linking between the two modalities. Furthermore, for single-stream model, we observe that some heads encode the coreference information in both directions, serving as additional evidence that these heads perform cross-modal alignment specifically. On the other hand, the amount of learned coreference knowledge is limited in the text modality attention trace $(T \rightarrow V)$, which provides indirect evidence that the text modality does not incorporate much visual information, even with the forced cross-attention design in the two-stream model.

### 3.3.3   Probing Combinations of Heads

Previous analysis mainly investigates whether cross-modal knowledge can be captured through individual attention head. It is also possible that such knowledge can be induced via the cooperation of multiple heads. To quantitatively analyze this, we further examine visual coreference through probing over combinations of heads.

**1) Attention Prober** To reveal the learned knowledge across different attention heads, we use a linear classifier based on the combination of attention weights, following [7]. Specifically,

$$p(c|i,j) \propto \sum_{k=1}^{N}(w_k \alpha_{ij}^k + \mu_k \alpha_{ji}^k),  \tag{3}$$

---

[3] Head $(i\text{-}j)$ means the $j$-th head at the $i$-th layer.

**Table 3.** Results of attention and layer-wise embedding probers on Visual Coreference Detection and Classification (VCD and VCC). SS: single-stream; TS: two-stream.

| Classifier Input | VCD (SS) | VCD (TS) | VCC (SS) | VCC (TS) |
|---|---|---|---|---|
| 144 Attention Heads | 52.04 | **53.68** | 75.10 | 54.47 |
| Random Guess | 50.00 | 50.00 | 12.50 | 12.50 |
| Layer 1 | 56.86 | **53.68** | 93.51 | **93.35** |
| Layer 5 | **59.12** | 52.59 | **94.05** | 92.62 |
| Layer 12 | 58.40 | / | 93.44 | / |

where given tokens $i$ and $j$ in the sequence, $p(c|i,j)$ is the probability of the link label between these two tokens being $c$. $\alpha_{ij}^k$ is the attention weight for token $i$ attending to token $j$ at head $k$, $w_k$ and $\mu_k$ are two learnable scalars, and $N$ is the number of attention heads.

**2) Layer-wise Embedding Prober** Similarly, to further examine the knowledge encoded in the model, we can naturally extend the above attention-based prober into an embedding-based prober:

$$p_k(c|i,j) \propto w_{cls}^{k\top}(W_w^k e_i^k \odot W_\mu^k e_j^k), \qquad (4)$$

where $p_k(c|i,j)$ is the same as defined in (3), $e_i^k$ and $e_j^k$ are the embeddings of token $i$ and $j$ at the $k$-th layer, and $W_w^k$, $W_\mu^k \in \mathbb{R}^{768 \times 768}$, $w_{cls}^k \in \mathbb{R}^{768 \times 1}$. By training a linear classifier on top of extracted embeddings, this prober provides a way to probe the encoded knowledge between each pair of tokens on each layer.

For visual coreference resolution, we probe the model on two sub-tasks: ($i$) `Visual Coref Detection` (VCD): determine whether a noun phrase is coreferenced to a specific visual token (binary classification); and ($ii$) `Visual Coref Classification` (VCC): classify the label of the coreference relation between a noun phrase and a visual token (multi-class classification). With these tasks, we can examine whether certain type of knowledge is encoded, as well as the granularity of the knowledge encoded in the probed feature space[4].

Results are shown in Table 3. Neither model performs well on the VCD task, suggesting that there is no attention pattern or embedding feature that can handle all the coreference relations. However, the results on VCC are encouraging. This aligns with our observation from Table 2 that some attention heads of the two models are significantly effective in certain coreference relations.[5]

---

[4] Since noun phrase may contain several tokens, we use the maximum attention weight among the tokens in that phrase over an image region as the attention weight between the noun phase and the image region. The embedding of the noun phrase is the mean of all the representations of its textual tokens.

[5] Though both models' embedding probers achieve higher than 94% accuracy on the VCC task, it is worth noting that text embedding input can potentially leak the link information. For instance, the phrase "A guard with a white hat" may already provide coreference information between `person` and the corresponding image region.

**Table 4.** Results on Visual Relation Identification/Classification using maximum attention weight between two visual tokens. SS: single stream; TS: two stream.

| Relation Type | SS | SS (Rand.) | TS | TS (Rand.) |
|---|---|---|---|---|
| on | **0.154 (10–1)** | 0.055 (1–8) | **0.157 (3–12)** | 0.063 (5–9) |
| standing in | **0.107 (2–8)** | 0.051 (1–8) | **0.173 (7–4)** | 0.064 (3–1) |
| wearing | **0.311 (10–1)** | 0.049 (1–8) | **0.230 (7–4)** | 0.055 (3–1) |
| playing | **0.135 (4–1)** | 0.050 (1–8) | **0.103 (7–10)** | 0.062 (3–1) |
| eating | **0.138 (10–1)** | 0.056 (1–8) | **0.142 (7–4)** | 0.067 (3–1) |
| holds | **0.200 (10–1)** | 0.055 (1–8) | **0.173 (7–4)** | 0.066 (3–1) |
| covering | **0.151 (7–2)** | 0.053 (1–8) | **0.173 (3–1)** | 0.061 (3–6) |

### 3.4  Secret Liaison Revealed: Cross-Modality Fusion Registers Visual Relations

To evaluate the encoded knowledge learned from the image modality, we adopt the visual relation detection task, which requires a model to identify and classify the relation between two image regions. This task can be viewed as examining whether the model captures visual relations between image regions.

The VG dataset is used for this task, which contains 1,531,448 first-order object-object relations. First-order object-object relation can be determined simply by the visual representations of two objects, independent to other objects in the image or text annotation. To reduce the imbalance in the number of relations per relation type, we randomly select at most 15,000 subject-object relation pairs $(s, o)$ per relation type. Furthermore, to de-duplicate cases where the same type of relation comes from the same text annotation, we select at most 5 same relation types $(s, o)$ from the same annotation. This probing task is performed on 32 most frequent relation pairs in the dataset.

**1) Probing Individual Attention Head** We apply the same analysis here similar to the visual coreference resolution task. The only difference is that we do not consider the directions of attention (*i.e.*, $s \rightarrow o$, or $o \rightarrow s$), as both directions correspond to the same visual modality. The average of maximum attention value in both $s \rightarrow o$ and $o \rightarrow s$ directions is reported for visual relation analysis.

Results are summarized in Table 4. We report the maximum attention weights of 7 of 30 relations. The columns with "(Rand.)" are ablation groups. As shown in the comparison, the learned attention heads encode rich knowledge about the relations between visual tokens with much higher attention weights. Moreover, similar to the observation in visual coreference resolution task, specific heads (10–1 head in the single-stream model, 7–4 head in the two-stream model) have captured richer visual relations than others.

**2) Probing Combinations of Attention Heads** The above analysis only reveals the behavior of individual attention heads. Similar to Sect. 3.3, we further examine visual relations by training a linear classifier on top of a combination of attention heads over two sub-tasks: (*i*) Relation Identification:

| Classifier Input | VRI (SS) | VRC (SS) | VRI (TS) | VRC (TS) |
|---|---|---|---|---|
| 144 Attention Heads | **69.81** | **24.67** | **67.53** | **18.89** |
| 144 Attention Heads (mismatch) | 64.66 | 23.64 | 64.72 | 18.42 |
| Random Guess | 50.00 | 3.33 | 50.00 | 3.33 |

(a) Accuracies (%) of the attention probers on VRI and VRC

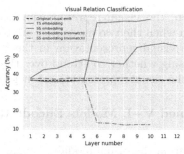

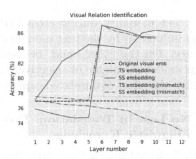

(b) Layer-wise emb. prober on VRC    (c) Layer-wise emb. prober on VRI

**Fig. 4.** Results of attention and layer-wise embedding probers on Visual Relation Identification and Classification (VRI and VRC)

determine whether two image regions have a relationship; and (*ii*) **Relation Classification**: classify the relation label between two image regions.

Results on probing a combination of heads are summarized in Fig. 4. Two baselines are considered in this task. (*i*) Original visual embeddings from Faster R-CNN [3]. This setup evaluates how much correlation between two related visual representations has elevated or diluted by the V+L models. (*ii*) Mismatched image-text representation. In this baseline, we construct a dataset where an image is associated with an unrelated dense annotation instead of a related one. This baseline evaluates how the correlation between the image regions changes based on the text modality. Note that for the two-stream model, there are 10 layers involved in visual relation reasoning. The first five layers perform self-attention across the visual modality only, and in the last five layers the visual representation interacts with the text modality.

As shown, both models perform much better than the baseline with related annotations (the dashed balck line in Fig. 4), indicating there is a substantial amount of visual-relation knowledge encoded in these representations. On the other hand, the specific visual relation knowledge degrades a lot with mismatched image regions and dense annotations (the solid red and blue lines vs. the dashed lines in Fig. 4). For single-stream model, the visual-relation knowledge decayed to that of the original visual embedding. This makes sense because no visual relation information can be obtained from the mismatched caption.

The visual relation knowledge of the two-stream model is greatly influenced by the unpaired caption, leading to a huge performance drop after Layer 5 in the VRC task. This result may contribute to different inductive bias between the two models. For two-stream model, since the visual modality has to attend

**Table 5.** Results on the linguistic probing tasks. L*n*: Layer *n*.

| Model | SentLen (Surface) | TreeDepth (Syntactic) | TopConst (Syntactic) | BShift (Syntactic) | Tense (Semantic) | SubjNum (Semantic) | ObjNum (Semantic) | SOMO (Semantic) | CoordInv (Semantic) |
|---|---|---|---|---|---|---|---|---|---|
| SS | 88.8 (L2) | 36.4 (L5) | 79.0 (L7) | 81.6 (L10) | 86.6 (L11) | 83.4 (L7) | 78.8 (L9) | 57.1 (L12) | 62.1 (L11) |
| TS | 83.8 (L7) | 34.0 (L8) | 67.2 (L8) | 64.9 (L8) | 75.6 (L6) | 78.8 (L9) | 76.8 (L8) | 51.4 (L8) | 58.7 (L8) |
| BERT | **96.2 (L3)** | **41.3 (L6)** | **84.1 (L7)** | **87.0 (L9)** | **90.0 (L9)** | **88.1 (L6)** | **82.2 (L7)** | **65.2 (L12)** | **78.7 (L9)** |

to the text modality during cross attention, the visual representation will be greatly influenced by the text modality even when the two modalities are totally unrelated. On the other hand, because the visual representation in the single-stream model is capable of selectively choosing whether to attend over the text modality, the effect of unrelated caption on the visual representation is negligible.

### 3.5 No Lost in Translation: Pre-trained V+L Models Encode Rich Linguistic Knowledge

Besides looking into the knowledge learned from the visual modality, we are also interested in the encoded knowledge learned from the text modality. To achieve this goal, we probe the pre-trained models over nine tasks defined in the SentEval toolkit [8]. Descriptions about the tasks are provided in the Appendix.

First, we extract contextualized word representations from the pre-trained models. For single-stream model, the input is the sequence of tokens with text only. For two-stream model, since the last 5 cross-attention layers require visual input, which is not covered by these linguistic benchmarks, we only evaluate the first 9 layers that are performing self-attention over pure text input.

We use the Google-pretrained BERT-base model as the baseline. For each task, we obtain the results from all the layers and report the best number. The results in Table 5 show that pre-trained V+L model generally performs worse than the original BERT-base model on these linguistic benchmarks, which is as expected. A full table with results from all the layers is provided in the Appendix. As shown in the table, the single-stream model performs better than the two-stream model across all the tasks. One possible reason is that LXMERT does not initialize the parameters of the language Transformer encoder from BERT-base, whereas UNITER does. Thus, using the parameters of BERT as initialization is potentially useful for the model to acquire rich linguistic knowledge, and helpful for tasks involving complex text-based reasoning.

To measure the gains due to learning, we have conducted all the above experiments (Sects. 3.1–3.5) on untrained baselines with random weights. These additional results are provided in the Appendix.

## 4   Conclusion and Key Takeaways

Intrigued by the five questions presented at the beginning of Sect. 3, we have provided a thorough analysis of UNITER-base and LXMERT models as a deep dive into Vision+Language pre-training. To summarize our key findings:

(i) In single-stream model, deeper layers lead to more intertwined multimodal fusion; while the opposite trend is observed in two-stream model.

(ii) Textual modality plays a more important role than image in making final decisions, consistent across both single- and two-stream models.
(iii) In single-stream model, a subset of heads organically evolves to pivot on cross-modal interaction and alignment, which on the other hand is enforced by model design in two-stream model.
(iv) Visual relations are inherently registered in both single- and two-stream pre-trained models.
(v) Rich linguistic knowledge is naturally encoded, even though the models are specifically designed for multimodal pre-training.

We provide additional guidelines in the Appendix. For future work, we plan to perform model compression via pruning attention heads based on the analysis and observations in this work.

# References

1. van Aken, B., Winter, B., Löser, A., Gers, F.A.: How does bert answer questions? A layer-wise analysis of transformer representations. In: CIKM (2019)
2. Alberti, C., Ling, J., Collins, M., Reitter, D.: Fusion of detected objects in text for visual question answering. In: EMNLP (2019)
3. Anderson, P., et al.: Bottom-up and top-down attention for image captioning and visual question answering. In: CVPR (2018)
4. Antol, S., et al.: VQA: visual question answering. In: ICCV (2015)
5. Bouraoui, Z., Camacho-Collados, J., Schockaert, S.: Inducing relational knowledge from BERT. In: AAAI (2020)
6. Chen, Y.C., et al.: Uniter: Learning universal image-text representations. arXiv preprint arXiv:1909.11740 (2019)
7. Clark, K., Khandelwal, U., Levy, O., Manning, C.D.: What does bert look at? an analysis of bert's attention. arXiv preprint arXiv:1906.04341 (2019)
8. Conneau, A., Kiela, D.: Senteval: An evaluation toolkit for universal sentence representations. arXiv preprint arXiv:1803.05449 (2018)
9. Devlin, J., Chang, M.W., Lee, K., Toutanova, K.: BERT: pre-training of deep bidirectional transformers for language understanding. In: NAACL (2019)
10. Gan, Z., Chen, Y.C., Li, L., Zhu, C., Cheng, Y., Liu, J.: Large-scale adversarial training for vision-and-language representation learning. arXiv preprint arXiv:2006.06195 (2020)
11. Goyal, Y., Khot, T., Agrawal, A., Summers-Stay, D., Batra, D., Parikh, D.: Making the V in VQA matter: elevating the role of image understanding in visual question answering. Int. J. Comput. Vis. **127**(4), 398–414 (2018). https://doi.org/10.1007/s11263-018-1116-0
12. Htut, P.M., Phang, J., Bordia, S., Bowman, S.R.: Do attention heads in bert track syntactic dependencies? arXiv preprint arXiv:1911.12246 (2019)
13. Hudson, D.A., Manning, C.D.: GQA: a new dataset for compositional question answering over real-world images. In: CVPR (2019)
14. Jawahar, G., Sagot, B., Seddah, D.: What does BERT learn about the structure of language? In: ACL (2019)
15. Jiang, Z., Xu, F.F., Araki, J., Neubig, G.: How can we know what language models know? arXiv preprint arXiv:1911.12543 (2019)
16. Kovaleva, O., Romanov, A., Rogers, A., Rumshisky, A.: Revealing the dark secrets of BERT. In: EMNLP (2019)

17. Krishna, R., et al.: Visual genome: connecting language and vision using crowd-sourced dense image annotations. Int. J. Comput. Vis. **123**(1), 32–73 (2017). https://doi.org/10.1007/s11263-016-0981-7
18. Lee, K.H., Chen, X., Hua, G., Hu, H., He, X.: Stacked cross attention for image-text matching. In: ECCV (2018)
19. Li, G., Duan, N., Fang, Y., Jiang, D., Zhou, M.: Unicoder-VL: a universal encoder for vision and language by cross-modal pre-training. In: AAAI (2020)
20. Li, L., Chen, Y.C., Cheng, Y., Gan, Z., Yu, L., Liu, J.: Hero: Hierarchical encoder for video+ language omni-representation pre-training. arXiv preprint arXiv:2005.00200 (2020)
21. Li, L.H., Yatskar, M., Yin, D., Hsieh, C.J., Chang, K.W.: Visualbert: A simple and performant baseline for vision and language. arXiv preprint arXiv:1908.03557 (2019)
22. Lu, J., Batra, D., Parikh, D., Lee, S.: ViLBERT: pretraining task-agnostic visiolinguistic representations for vision-and-language tasks. In: NeurIPS (2019)
23. Lu, J., Goswami, V., Rohrbach, M., Parikh, D., Lee, S.: 12-in-1: multi-task vision and language representation learning. In: CVPR (2020)
24. Michel, P., Levy, O., Neubig, G.: Are sixteen heads really better than one? In: NeurIPS (2019)
25. Petroni, F., et al.: Language models as knowledge bases? In: EMNLP (2019)
26. Plummer, B.A., et al.: Flickr30k entities: collecting region-to-phrase correspondences for richer image-to-sentence models. Int. J. Comput. Vis. **123**(1), 74–93 (2016). https://doi.org/10.1007/s11263-016-0965-7
27. Su, W., et al.: VL-BERT: pre-training of generic visual-linguistic representations. In: ICLR (2020)
28. Suhr, A., Zhou, S., Zhang, A., Zhang, I., Bai, H., Artzi, Y.: A corpus for reasoning about natural language grounded in photographs. In: ACL (2019)
29. Sun, C., Baradel, F., Murphy, K., Schmid, C.: Contrastive bidirectional transformer for temporal representation learning. arXiv preprint arXiv:1906.05743 (2019)
30. Sun, C., Myers, A., Vondrick, C., Murphy, K., Schmid, C.: VideoBERT: a joint model for video and language representation learning. In: ICCV (2019)
31. Talmor, A., Elazar, Y., Goldberg, Y., Berant, J.: olmpics-on what language model pre-training captures. arXiv preprint arXiv:1912.13283 (2019)
32. Tan, H., Bansal, M.: LXMERT: learning cross-modality encoder representations from transformers. In: EMNLP (2019)
33. Tenney, I., Das, D., Pavlick, E.: BERT rediscovers the classical NLP pipeline. In: ACL (2019)
34. Tenney, I., et al.: What do you learn from context? Probing for sentence structure in contextualized word representations. In: ICLR (2019)
35. Vaswani, A., et al.: Attention is all you need. In: NeurIPS (2017)
36. Voita, E., Talbot, D., Moiseev, F., Sennrich, R., Titov, I.: Analyzing multi-head self-attention: specialized heads do the heavy lifting, the rest can be pruned. In: ACL (2019)
37. Yu, L., Poirson, P., Yang, S., Berg, A.C., Berg, T.L.: Modeling context in referring expressions. In: ECCV (2016)
38. Zellers, R., Bisk, Y., Farhadi, A., Choi, Y.: From recognition to cognition: visual commonsense reasoning. In: CVPR (2019)
39. Zhou, L., Palangi, H., Zhang, L., Hu, H., Corso, J.J., Gao, J.: Unified vision-language pre-training for image captioning and VQA. In: AAAI (2020)
40. Zhou, X., Zhang, Y., Cui, L., Huang, D.: Evaluating commonsense in pre-trained language models. In: AAAI (2020)

# The Hessian Penalty: A Weak Prior
# for Unsupervised Disentanglement

William Peebles[1]([✉]), John Peebles[2], Jun-Yan Zhu[3], Alexei Efros[1],
and Antonio Torralba[4]

[1] University of California, Berkeley, Berkeley, USA
peebles@berkeley.edu
[2] Yale University, New Haven, USA
[3] Adobe Research, San Jose, USA
[4] MIT CSAIL, Cambridge, USA

**Abstract.** Existing disentanglement methods for deep generative models rely on hand-picked priors and complex encoder-based architectures. In this paper, we propose the *Hessian Penalty*, a simple regularization term that encourages the Hessian of a generative model with respect to its input to be diagonal. We introduce a model-agnostic, unbiased stochastic approximation of this term based on Hutchinson's estimator to compute it efficiently during training. Our method can be applied to a wide range of deep generators with just a few lines of code. We show that training with the Hessian Penalty often causes axis-aligned disentanglement to emerge in latent space when applied to ProGAN on several datasets. Additionally, we use our regularization term to identify interpretable directions in BigGAN's latent space in an unsupervised fashion. Finally, we provide empirical evidence that the Hessian Penalty encourages substantial shrinkage when applied to over-parameterized latent spaces. We encourage readers to view videos of our disentanglement results at www.wpeebles.com/hessian-penalty, and code at https://github.com/wpeebles/hessian_penalty.

## 1 Introduction

What does it mean to disentangle a function? While Yoshua Bengio has advocated for using "broad generic priors" to design disentanglement algorithms [4], most recent disentanglement efforts end up being specific to the network architecture used [12,27,29,47] and the types of variation present in datasets [6,35].

In this paper, we propose a notion of disentanglement that is simple and general, and can be implemented in a few lines of code (Fig. 1). Our method is based on the following observation: if we perturb a single component of a network's input, then we would like the *change* in the output to be independent of the other input components. As discussed later, this information is present

**Electronic supplementary material** The online version of this chapter (https://doi.org/10.1007/978-3-030-58539-6_35) contains supplementary material, which is available to authorized users.

© Springer Nature Switzerland AG 2020
A. Vedaldi et al. (Eds.): ECCV 2020, LNCS 12351, pp. 581–597, 2020.
https://doi.org/10.1007/978-3-030-58539-6_35

in the function's Hessian matrix. To encourage a deep neural network to be disentangled, we propose minimizing the off-diagonal entries of the function's Hessian matrix. We call this regularization term a *Hessian Penalty*. Since we can always obtain an estimate of a function's Hessian via finite differences, our method is model-agnostic and requires no auxiliary networks such as encoders.

We present experiments spanning several architectures and datasets that show applying our Hessian Penalty to generative image models causes the generator's output to become smoother and more disentangled in latent space. We also show that the Hessian Penalty has a tendency to "turn-off" latent components, introducing sometimes significant shrinkage in the latent space. We apply our regularization term to BigGAN [5] and ProGAN [22] on ImageNet [8], Zappos50K [43] and CLEVR [20]. We provide quantitative metrics that demonstrate our method induces disentanglement, latent space shrinkage and smoothness compared to baseline models.

## 2 Related Work

**Derivative-Based Regularization.** Recently, researchers have proposed regularizing derivatives of various orders to enhance the performance of deep networks. Most notably, Moosavi et al. [34] regularized the eigenvalues of classifiers' Hessian matrices to improve adversarial robustness. Several works have also explored regularizing derivatives in generative models. StyleGAN-v2 [24] presented a regularization function to encourage the Jacobian matrix of the generator in generative adversarial networks (GANs) [9] to be orthogonal. Odena et al. [36] introduced a regularization term for clamping the generator's Jacobian's singular values to a target range. To combat mode collapse in image-to-image translation [17,45], Yang et al. [42] proposed a regularization term that encourages changes in the output of the generator to be proportional to changes in latent space; this effectively amounts to preventing the generator's average gradient norm from being degenerate. The gradient penalty [10] was proposed to regularize the input gradient of discriminators in GANs.

**Disentanglement in Generative Models.** A plethora of prior work on disentangling deep networks focuses on variational autoencoders (VAEs) [29] with various extensions to the original VAE formulation [12,19,21,27,30,32]. Several methods have been proposed to induce disentangled representations in GANs. InfoGAN [6] proposed maximizing the mutual information between an auxiliary latent code and the generator's output. Recent methods have used latent code swapping and mixing for learning disentangled models, coupled with adversarial training [13,33,39]. StyleGAN [23] introduced a generator architecture that enables control of aspects such as object pose and color. Disentanglement of 3D factors of variation has been learned by introducing implicit 3D convolutional priors into the generator [35] or by using explicit differentiable rendering pipelines [47]. Recently, it has been shown that GANs automatically learn to disentangle certain object categories in the channels of their intermediate activations [3]; this innate disentanglement can then be leveraged to perform semantic edits on inversions of natural images in the generator's latent space [2,7,38].

A line of work has also explored using vector arithmetic in latent space to control factors of variation. For example, DCGAN [37] showed that latent vectors corresponding to specific semantic attributes could be added or subtracted in latent space to change synthesized images in a consistent way. Jahanian et al. [18] learned directions in GANs corresponding to user-provided image transformations. Recently, an unsupervised approach [40] learns to discover interpretable directions by learning both latent space directions and a classifier to distinguish between those directions simultaneously.

**Independent Component Analysis.** The Hessian Penalty is somewhat reminiscent of Independent Component Analysis (ICA) [16], a class of algorithms that tries to "unmix" real data into its underlying independent latent factors. Recent work has extended nonlinear ICA to modern generative models [25,26], including VAEs and energy-based models [31]. These papers have shown that, under certain conditions, the independent latent factors can be identified up to simple transformations. A simple way to connect our work to ICA is by considering the Hessian Penalty as imposing a prior on the space of possible mixing functions. This prior biases the mixing function to have a diagonal Hessian.

## 3   Method

### 3.1   Formulation

Consider any scalar-valued function $G : \mathbb{R}^{|z|} \to \mathbb{R}$, where $z$ denotes the input vector to $G$ and $|z|$ denotes the dimensionality of $z$. To disentangle $G$ with respect to $z$, we need each component of $z$ to control just a single aspect of variation in $G$; in other words, varying $z_i$ should produce a change in the output of $G$, mostly independently of the other components $z_{j \neq i}$.

Let's consider what this means mathematically. We refer to the Hessian matrix of $G$ with respect to $z$ as $H$. Let's consider an arbitrary off-diagonal term $H_{ij}$ of this Hessian and contemplate what it means if it is equal to zero:

$$H_{ij} = \frac{\partial^2 G}{\partial z_i \partial z_j} = \frac{\partial}{\partial z_j}\left(\frac{\partial G}{\partial z_i}\right) = 0. \tag{1}$$

Consider the inner derivative with respect to $z_i$ in Eq. 1. Intuitively, that derivative measures how much $G$'s output changes as $z_i$ is perturbed. If the outer derivative with respect to $z_j$ of the inner derivative is zero, it means that $\frac{\partial G}{\partial z_i}$ is not a function of $z_j$. In other words, as we change $z_i$, $z_j$ has no effect on how $G$'s output changes.

The above observation gives rise to our main idea. We propose adding a simple regularizer to any function/ deep neural network $G$ to encourage its Hessian with respect to an input to be diagonal; we simply minimize the sum of squared

```
def hessian_penalty(G, z, k, epsilon):
    # Input G: Function to compute the Hessian Penalty of
    # Input z: Input to G that the Hessian Penalty is taken w.r.t.
    # Input k: Number of Hessian directions to sample
    # Input epsilon: Finite differences hyperparameter
    # Output: Hessian Penalty loss
    G_z = G(z)
    vs = epsilon * random_rademacher(shape=[k, *z.size()])
    finite_diffs = [G(z + v) - 2 * G_z + G(z - v) for v in vs]
    finite_diffs = stack(finite_diffs) / (epsilon ** 2)
    penalty = var(finite_diffs, dim=0).max()
    return penalty
```

**Fig. 1.** PyTorch-style pseudo-code for the Hessian Penalty.

off-diagonal terms. We call this regularization function a *Hessian Penalty*:

$$\mathcal{L}_H(G) = \sum_{i=1}^{|z|} \sum_{j \neq i}^{|z|} H_{ij}^2. \tag{2}$$

### 3.2    Generalization to Vector-Valued Functions

Of course, most deep networks are *not* scalar-valued functions, such as generative networks that synthesize realistic images, video, or text. A simple way to extend the above formulation to these vector-valued functions is to instead penalize the Hessian matrix of each scalar component in the output of $x = G(z)$ individually, where $x$ denotes the vector of outputs. For brevity, we refer to the length-$|x|$ collection of each $|z| \times |z|$ Hessian matrix as $\mathbf{H}$, where $\mathbf{H}_i$ is the Hessian matrix of $x_i$. Then Eq. 2 can be slightly modified to:

$$\mathcal{L}_{\mathbf{H}}(G) = \max_i \mathcal{L}_{\mathbf{H}_i}(G), \tag{3}$$

where $\mathcal{L}_{\mathbf{H}_i}$ refers to computing Eq. 2 with $H = \mathbf{H}_i$. This is a general way to extend the Hessian Penalty to vector-valued functions without leveraging any domain knowledge. In place of the max, we also experimented with taking a mean. We have found that the formulation above imposes a stronger regularization in certain instances, but we have not thoroughly explored alternatives.

### 3.3    The Hessian Penalty in Practice

Computing the Hessian matrices in Eq. 2 and Eq. 3 during training is slow when $|z|$ is large. Luckily, it turns out that we can express Eq. 2 in a different form which admits an unbiased stochastic approximator:

$$\mathcal{L}_H(G) = \mathrm{Var}_v \left( v^T H v \right) \tag{4}$$

Where $v$ are Rademacher vectors (each entry has equal probability of being $-1$ or $+1$), and $v^T H v$ is the second directional derivative of $G$ in the direction $v$ times $|v|$. Eq. 4 can be estimated using the unbiased empirical variance. In practice, we sample a small number of $v$ vectors, typically just two, to compute this empirical variance. If Eq. 2 and Eq. 4 are equal to each other, then minimizing Eq. 4 is equivalent to minimizing the sum of squared off-diagonal elements in $H$. This result was previously shown by Hutchinson [1,15], but we include a simple proof in Appendix B (see Supplementary Material).

**Theorem 1.** $Var_v \left( v^T H v \right) = 2 \sum_{i=1}^{|z|} \sum_{j \neq i}^{|z|} H_{ij}^2$.

*Proof.* See Appendix B (see Supplementary Material). $\qquad\qquad\qquad\qquad\square$

One problem still remains: we need to be able to quickly compute the second directional derivative term in Eq. 4. We can do this via a second-order central finite difference approximation:

$$v^T H v \approx \frac{1}{\epsilon^2} \left[ G(z + \epsilon v) - 2G(z) + G(z - \epsilon v) \right], \tag{5}$$

where $\epsilon > 0$ is a hyperparameter that controls the granularity of the second directional derivative estimate. In practice, we use $\epsilon = 0.1$. This approximation enables the Hessian Penalty to work for functions whose analytic Hessians are zero, such as piece-wise linear neural networks.

Figure 1 shows an implementation of Eq. 4 in PyTorch using the finite difference approximation described in Eq. 5; it is only about seven lines of code and can be easily inserted into most code bases.

**Generalization to Arbitrary Feature Spaces.** In the above description of the Hessian Penalty, $z$ has referred to the input to the function $G$. In general, though, $z$ could be any intermediate feature space of $G$. Similarly, $G$ could refer to any downstream intermediate activation in a generator. In most experiments, we tend to optimize the Hessian Penalty of several intermediate activations with respect to the initial input $z$ vector to achieve a stronger regularization effect.

### 3.4 Applications in Deep Generative Models

The above formulation of the Hessian Penalty is model-agnostic; it can be applied to any function without modification. But, here we focus on applying it to generative models. Specifically, we will investigate its applications with generative adversarial networks (GANs) [9]. For the remainder of this paper, $G$ will now refer to the generator and $D$ will refer to the discriminator. GANs are commonly trained with the following adversarial objective, where $x$ now refers to a sample from the real distribution being learned, and $f$ specifies the GAN loss used:

$$\mathcal{L}_{\text{adv}} = \underset{x \sim p_{\text{data}}(x)}{\mathbb{E}} \left[ f(D(x)) \right] + \underset{z \sim p_z(z)}{\mathbb{E}} \left[ f(1 - D(G(z))) \right]. \tag{6}$$

When we apply a Hessian Penalty, the discriminator's objective remains unchanged. The generator's loss becomes:

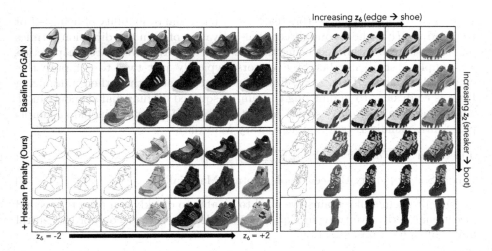

**Fig. 2.** The effect of the Hessian Penalty on disentangling the edge → shoe factor of variation in unconditional ProGAN trained on Edges+Shoes. We sample three 12-dimensional $z$ vectors from a standard Gaussian. Each row corresponds to one of these three vectors. Moving across a row, we interpolate the scalar component $z_6$ from $-2$ to $+2$, leaving the other 11 components fixed. **Top:** A ProGAN prior to fine-tuning. It fails to uncover a disentangled $z$ component that controls edge → shoe; sometimes the shoe never becomes an edge (first row), and the value of $z_6$ where an edge becomes a shoe is inconsistent. Even when the edge does transform, the resulting shoe barely resembles the edge. **Bottom:** Fine-tuning the same ProGAN with our Hessian Penalty. After fine-tuning, edge → shoe is cleanly disentangled by $z_6$; edges consistently become shoes right at $z_6 = 0$. For $z_6 > 0$, the component changes the style of the shoe while preserving the structure. **Right:** Manipulating two components simultaneously; we sample $z_6$ at $-1$, 0.3, 0.6, 0.9 and 1.2, and $z_2$ regularly between $-2$ and 2.

$$\mathcal{L}_{\mathrm{G}} = \underbrace{\mathop{\mathbb{E}}_{z \sim p_z(z)} \left[ f\left(1 - D(G(z))\right)\right]}_{\text{Standard Adversarial Loss}} + \lambda \underbrace{\mathop{\mathbb{E}}_{z \sim p_z(z)} \left[\mathcal{L}_{\mathbf{H}}(G)\right]}_{\text{The Hessian Penalty}}, \qquad (7)$$

where the weight $\lambda$ balances the two terms. Interestingly, we find that fine-tuning a pre-trained GAN with Eq. 7 in many cases tends to work as well as or better than training from scratch with the Hessian Penalty. This feature makes our method more practical since it can be used to quickly adapt pre-trained GANs.

## 4   Experiments

### 4.1   ProGAN with Hessian Penalty

We first qualitatively assess how well our Hessian Penalty performs when disentangling an unconditional ProGAN [22] trained on various datasets. In these

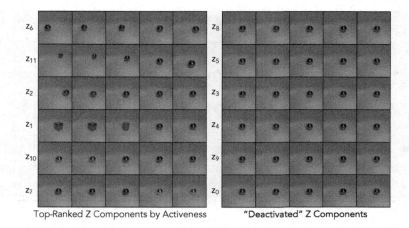

**Fig. 3.** All 12 $z$ components learned by our method on CLEVR-Simple, sorted by their activeness scores (see Sect. 4.2). **Left:** The top six scoring components which uncover color, position, and shape factors of variation. **Right:** The bottom six scoring components; note that they barely affect the image.

experiments, we apply the Hessian Penalty to the first ten out of thirteen convolutions, immediately following pixel normalization layers.

**Edges+Shoes.** A commonly-used dataset for the problem of image-to-image translation [17,45] is Edges→Shoes [43]. To see if our method can automatically uncover a $z$ component that performs image-to-image translation without domain supervision, we train an unconditional ProGAN on Edges+Shoes, created by mixing all 50,000 edges and 50,000 shoes into a single image dataset. We then train ProGAN on this mixture of images.

As seen in Fig. 2, the baseline ProGAN is unable to uncover a component that controls edges↔shoes. However, once we fine-tune the ProGAN with the Hessian Penalty, we uncover such a component—$z_6$. When this component is set greater than zero, it produces shoes; when set less than zero, it produces edges. Interestingly, this component is akin to recent multimodal image-to-image translation methods [14,46]. As one increases $z_6$ beyond zero, it changes the style and colors of the shoe while preserving the underlying structure. Figure 2 also shows how we can leverage this disentanglement to easily manipulate the height of a shoe without inadvertently switching from the edge domain to the shoe domain, or vice versa. The baseline model fails to perform such clean edits.

**CLEVR.** It is difficult to determine if a disentanglement algorithm "works" by only testing on real data since the ground truth factors of variation in such datasets are usually unknown and sometimes subjective. As a result, we create three synthetic datasets based on CLEVR [20]. The first dataset, CLEVR-Simple, has four factors of variation: object color, shape, and location (both horizontal and vertical). The second, CLEVR-1FOV, features a red cube with just a single

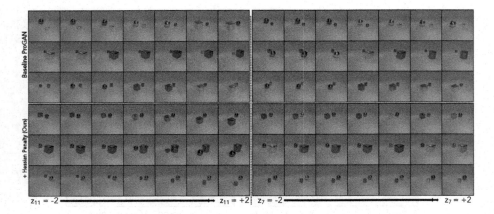

$z_{11} = -2$ ⟶ $z_{11} = +2$  $z_7 = -2$ ⟶ $z_7 = +2$

**Fig. 4.** We compare the disentanglement quality of a ProGAN with and without our regularization term on CLEVR-Complex. **Top-Left:** In the baseline ProGAN, the latent component $z_{11}$ somewhat controls the vertical position of the left-most object in the scene. However, it significantly alters the appearance of the right-most object. **Bottom-Left:** After fine-tuning with our Hessian Penalty, $z_{11}$ more cleanly controls vertical movement of the left-most object, although the color of the object still slightly changes sometimes. However, the right-most object barely changes. **Top-Right:** The baseline ProGAN's $z_7$ component does not appear to control a disentangled, interpretable factor of variation. **Bottom-Right:** After fine-tuning, $z_7$ controls the color of both objects in the scene. Although the component is interpretable, it is not truly disentangled since the color of the objects are two independent factors of variation.

factor of variation (FOV): object location along a single axis. The third, CLEVR-Complex, retains all factors of variation from CLEVR-Simple but adds a second object and multiple sizes for a total of ten factors of variation (five per object). Each dataset consists of approximately 10,000 images.

Figure 3 shows all 12 $z$ components learned by our method when trained on CLEVR-Simple; we are able to uncover all major factors of variation in the dataset. Figure 4 compares the performance of our method on CLEVR-Complex. Our method does a better job of separating object control into distinct $z$ components. For example, changing $z_{11}$ in the baseline model leads to significant changes in both objects. After fine-tuning with the Hessian Penalty, it mostly—but not entirely—controls the vertical position of the left-most object.

## 4.2   Overparameterized Latent Spaces

In most circumstances, we do not know a-priori how many factors of variation are in a dataset. Therefore, an ideal disentanglement algorithm would be able to learn a *sparse* representation where it only has $c$ active $z$ components if there are $c$ factors of variation in the dataset. Qualitatively, we observe in several instances that our method "turns-off" extra components when its latent space is overparameterized. Figure 3 illustrates this. For CLEVR-Simple, only half of

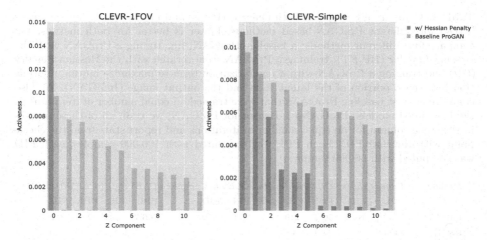

**Fig. 5.** Latent space shrinkage. We sort the 12 $z$ components of different generators by their "activeness" (how much they control $G$'s output). In baseline ProGAN, $z$ components have somewhat uniform activeness, regardless of the number of factors of variation in the data. When training with the Hessian Penalty on CLEVR-1FOV (one true factor of variation), all $z$ components except one are effectively turned-off. We observe a similar effect in CLEVR-Simple (four factors of variation), where six $z$ components have virtually no control of $G$'s output after being trained with the Hessian Penalty.

the components produce significant changes in $G(z)$; $G$ effectively collapses on the remaining six components. Is there a way to quantitatively assess the extent to which components get deactivated?

We propose defining the *activeness* of a component $z_i$ as the mean variance of $G(z)$ as we change $z_i$, but leave the other components fixed (where the variance is over $z_i$ and the mean is over all pixels in $G(z)$). We compare the activeness of all 12 components in models trained with and without the Hessian Penalty in Fig. 5. Indeed, in several instances, training with the Hessian Penalty substantially reduces the activeness of a subset of $z$ components. In particular, our model trained on CLEVR-1FOV effectively deactivates all but one of its $z$ components.

An informal yet intuitive reason to expect that the Hessian Penalty encourages such behavior is by observing that a degenerate solution to the regularization term is for $G$ to completely mode collapse on $z$; if $G$ is no longer a function of $z$, then by definition, its Hessian (including its off-diagonal terms) has all zeros. Similarly, if $G$ collapses on just a subset of $z$ components, then any off-diagonal terms in the Hessian involving those collapsed components will be zero as well.

We also explore what happens when we *underparameterize* the latent space. We train a ProGAN component with $|z| = 3$ on CLEVR-Simple, which has four factors of variation (we refer to this experiment as CLEVR-U). Although it is impossible to fully disentangle CLEVR in this case, we observe that each

**Table 1.** Comparing Perceptual Path Lengths (PPLs) and Fréchet Inception Distances (FIDs) for different ProGAN-based methods. Lower is better for both metrics. We compare four different methods: a baseline ProGAN, fine-tuning a ProGAN with the Hessian Penalty (HP FT), training a ProGAN from scratch with the Hessian Penalty (HP) and training a ProGAN with a regularization term to maximize mutual information between a portion of the latent code and the output image (InfoGAN). We also compare against baseline ProGANs that were trained an equal number of iterations as the fine-tuned models (ProGAN+). Except for ProGAN, we train all of these models in the same column for an equal number of iterations and report stats from the checkpoint with the best FID. Each PPL was computed with 100,000 samples; each FID was computed with 50,000 samples.

| Method | *Edges+Shoes* | | *CLEVR-Simple* | | *CLEVR-Complex* | | *CLEVR-U* | | *CLEVR-1FOV* | |
|--------|------|------|------|------|------|------|------|------|------|------|
|        | PPL | FID | PPL | FID | PPL | FID | PPL | FID | PPL | FID |
| InfoGAN | 2952.2 | **10.4** | 56.2 | **2.9** | 83.9 | **4.2** | 766.7 | 3.6 | 22.1 | 6.2 |
| ProGAN+ | 3154.1 | 10.8 | 64.5 | 3.8 | 92.8 | 5.8 | 697.7 | 3.4 | 30.3 | 9.0 |
| ProGAN | 1809.7 | 14.0 | 61.5 | 3.5 | 92.8 | 5.8 | 720.2 | **3.2** | 35.5 | 11.5 |
| w/ HP | 1301.3 | 21.2 | 45.7 | 25.0 | **73.1** | 21.1 | 68.7 | 26.6 | 20.8 | **2.3** |
| w/ HP FT | **554.1** | 17.3 | **39.7** | 6.1 | 74.7 | 7.1 | **61.6** | 26.8 | **10.0** | 4.5 |

$z$ component controls $G(z)$ substantially more smoothly after fine-tuning with the Hessian Penalty; we quantitatively assess this in the next section.

### 4.3   Quantitative Evaluation of Disentanglement

Evaluating disentanglement remains a significant challenge [32]. Moreover, most existing metrics are designed for methods that have access to an encoder to approximately invert $G$ [23]. As a result, we report Perceptual Path Length (PPL) [23], a disentanglement metric proposed for methods without encoders:

$$\text{PPL}(G) = \mathop{\mathbb{E}}_{z^{(1)}, z^{(2)} \sim p_z(z)} \left[ \frac{1}{\alpha^2} d\left( G(z^{(1)}), G(\text{slerp}(z^{(1)}, z^{(2)}; \alpha)) \right) \right], \qquad (8)$$

where $z^{(1)}$ and $z^{(2)}$ are two randomly sampled latent vectors, $d(\cdot, \cdot)$ denotes a distance metric, such as LPIPS [44], and slerp refers to spherical linear interpolation [41]. Intuitively, PPL measures how much $G(z)$ changes under perturbations to $z$; it is a measure of smoothness. Given that we are regularizing the Hessian, which controls smoothness, a reasonable question is: "are we just optimizing PPL?" The answer is no; since our method only explicitly penalizes off-diagonal components of the Hessian, we are not optimizing the smoothness of $G$ (which is usually defined as being proportional to the maximum eigenvalue of $G$'s Hessian). As a simple counter-example, the one-to-one function $G(z) = \beta z^3$ would trivially satisfy $\mathcal{L}_\mathbf{H} = 0$ but could be arbitrarily "unsmooth"—and thus have large (bad) PPL—for large $\beta$. Empirically, we find that smaller Hessian Penalties do not imply lower PPLs in general.

Table 1 reports PPLs as well as Fréchet Inception Distances (FIDs) [11], a coarse measure of image quality. We also compare against a ProGAN trained

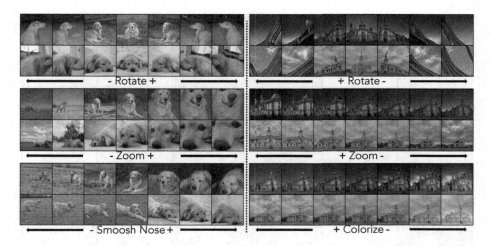

**Fig. 6.** Examples of orthonormal directions learned by our method in BigGAN conditioned to synthesize ImageNet Golden Retrievers or Churches. Each factor of variation is a single linear direction in $z$-space. For each direction $Aw_i$ shown, we show $z + \eta Aw_i$, where we linearly interpolate $\eta$. We move from $\eta = -5$ to $5$ for all directions except rotation and "smoosh nose" for dogs, where we move from $\eta = -3$ to $3$ instead. We note that the directions are not completely disentangled; for example, undergoing extreme zooms in Golden Retrievers can sometimes cause substantial changes to the background.

to maximize the mutual information between a subset of the inputs $z$ vector and the output image, as in InfoGAN [6]. In general, our method attains substantially better PPLs compared to other methods across datasets. However, we do sometimes observe a degradation of image quality, especially early in training/fine-tuning. This trait is somewhat shared with $\beta$-VAE-based methods, which essentially trade disentanglement for reconstruction accuracy [12].

### 4.4  Unsupervised Learning of Directions in BigGAN

So far, we have only explored training $G$ with the Hessian Penalty. We can also use the Hessian Penalty to identify interesting directions in $z$-space while leaving $G$'s weights fixed. Recent works have explored learning directions of meaningful variation in $z$-space of pre-trained generators [18,40]. Most notably, Voynov and Babenko [40] proposed an unsupervised method for learning directions.

We propose a simple way to learn interesting directions in an unsupervised fashion. Our method begins similarly to prior work [40]. We instantiate a random orthogonal matrix $A \in \mathbb{R}^{|z| \times N}$, where $N$ refers to the number of directions we wish to learn; the columns of $A$ store the directions we are learning. We then generate images by computing $G(z + \eta Aw_i)$, where $w_i \in \{0,1\}^N$ is a one-hot vector which indexes the columns of $A$ and $\eta$ is a scalar which controls how far $z$ should move in the direction $Aw_i$. $\eta$ is sampled from a uniform distribution

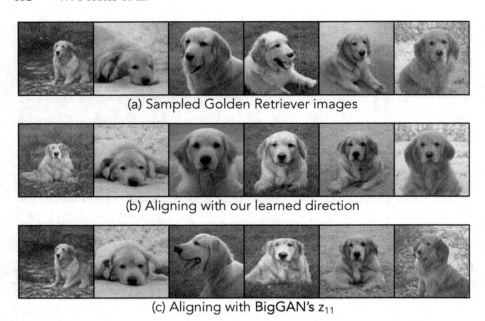

(a) Sampled Golden Retriever images

(b) Aligning with our learned direction

(c) Aligning with BigGAN's $z_{11}$

**Fig. 7.** Comparing the quality of latent space edits with our learned directions to BigGAN's coordinate axes. (a) We sample six images of golden retrievers from BigGAN. (b) We can simultaneously align all the dogs by orthogonalizing their $z$ vectors against our learned rotation direction. (c) BigGAN's $z_{11}$ component somewhat controls—but does not fully disentangle—rotation; no one value of $z_{11}$ aligns all six dogs.

$[-5, 5]$. Our methods diverge at this point. While Voynov and Babenko [40] simultaneously learn a randomly-initialized regression and classification network to reconstruct $Aw_i$ and $\eta$ from $G(z)$ and $G(z + \eta Aw_i)$, we directly optimize $A^* = \arg\min_A \mathbb{E}_{z, w_i, \eta} \mathcal{L}_{\mathbf{H}}(G(z + \eta Aw_i))$, where the Hessian Penalty is now taken w.r.t. $w_i$ instead of $z$. Intuitively, this amounts to trying to disentangle the columns of $A$. Importantly, we *only* backprop the gradients into $A$, while $G$ is frozen throughout learning. There are no additional loss terms beyond the Hessian Penalty. We set $N = |z|$ in our experiments and restrict $A$ to be orthogonal by applying Gram-Schmidt during each forward pass.

We apply our discovery method to class-conditional BigGAN [5] trained on ImageNet [8]. We perform two experiments; learning directions when BigGAN is restricted to producing (1) golden retrievers and (2) churches. Figure 6 shows our results. We are able to uncover several interesting directions, such as rotation, zooming, and grayscale. In Fig. 7, we compare one of our learned directions that performs rotations to a similar axis-aligned direction $z_{11}$ in BigGAN. Our direction better disentangles rotation than $z_{11}$. Empirically, we found that some of BigGAN's $z$ components, which are injected directly into deeper layers in $G$, already achieve a reasonable amount of axis-aligned disentanglement; they control aspects such as lighting, color filtering, and background removal. As a

**Table 2.** The empirical effect of the Hessian Penalty to strengthen the Hessian's diagonal. We compute the percentage of Hessian matrices whose max elements lies on the diagonal $(D_\%)$. We also measure the ratio between the average magnitude of diagonal elements versus off-diagonal elements $(D_R)$.

| Method | Edges+Shoes | | CLEVR-Simple | | CLEVR-Complex | | CLEVR-U | | CLEVR-1FOV | |
|---|---|---|---|---|---|---|---|---|---|---|
| | $D_\%$ | $D_R$ | $D_\%$ | $D_R$ | $D_\%$ | $D_R$ | $D_\%$ | $D_R$ | $D_\%$ | $D_R$ |
| InfoGAN | 63.2% | 1.6 | 74.7% | 2.2 | 66.0% | 1.6 | 74.9% | 2.2 | 89.9% | 5.8 |
| ProGAN- | 64.9% | 1.6 | 69.3% | 1.5 | 63.8% | 1.5 | 75.4% | 2.2 | 78.7% | 1.5 |
| w/ HP | 80.8% | **7.3** | 79.3% | **6.0** | 82.7% | 2.5 | 76.3% | 2.0 | **92.8%** | 61.3 |
| w/ HP FT | **81.0%** | 4.5 | **85.7%** | 5.6 | **85.4%** | **3.0** | **79.7%** | 2.2 | 87.9% | 14.6 |

negative, we did not observe that our learned directions control finer-grained details as well as these $z$ components.

One surprising trend we observed was that some of our more interesting and effective components—such as the rotation one—consistently emerged within the first several columns of $A$ across different initializations of $A$.

### 4.5   What Is the Hessian Penalty Actually Doing?

The story of this paper is that our regularization term *encourages* the Hessian matrix of the generative model to be diagonal. Does this hold up in practice?

If the Hessian Penalty is working as expected, then the relative weight of the diagonal to the off-diagonal components of the Hessian should increase when we apply our method. We propose two ways to measure this. First, we generate 100 fake images and compute the Hessian matrix for each pixel in all of these images (estimated via second-order finite differences). For each of these Hessians, we measure two quantities: (1) if the largest element in that Hessian lies on the diagonal; (2) the relative magnitude between elements on the diagonal versus off-diagonal. For each quantity, we average results over all $100 \cdot 128 \cdot 128 \cdot 3 = 4,915,200$ Hessian matrices; see Table 2. Under these two metrics, we find that the Hessian Penalty always strengthens the diagonal, with the exception of CLEVR-U which has an underparameterized latent space and small $3 \times 3$ Hessians. As an aside, this is somewhat interesting since in all ProGAN experiments, we never explicitly regularize the Hessian of the pixels directly. We only regularize the Hessian of intermediate activations, three or more convolutions before pixels. We also present visualizations of the Hessian matrices themselves; see Appendix C (see Supplementary Material).

## 5   Discussion

In this paper, we presented the Hessian Penalty, a simple regularization function that encourages the Hessian matrix of deep generators to be diagonal. When applied to ProGAN trained on Edges+Shoes, our method is capable of disentangling several significant factors of variation, such as edges↔shoes, a component reminiscent of multimodal image-to-image translation [14,46]. When trained on synthetic CLEVR datasets, our method can also uncover the known factors of variation while shrinking the overparameterized latent space. We also showed that our method can discover interesting factors such as rotation, colorization, and zooming, in the latent space of BigGAN.

**Limitations.** Although the Hessian Penalty works well for several datasets discussed above, our method does exhibit several notable failure modes. First, given that the Hessian Penalty is such a weak prior, we cannot expect to obtain perfect disentanglement results. For example, on CLEVR-Complex, our method learns to control the color of both objects—which are independent in the dataset—with a single component. Second, when fine-tuning a generator's weights with our method, image quality can sometimes degrade. Third, computing the Hessian Penalty only at early layers in the network can lead to a degenerate solution where the generator substantially reduces the Hessian Penalty seemingly without any effects on disentanglement or latent space shrinkage. We found that this degeneracy can be mitigated by also applying the Hessian Penalty to deeper intermediate layers and immediately after normalization layers. Nonetheless, given the simplicity of our method, the Hessian Penalty could be a small step towards the grand goals outlined by Yoshua Bengio.

**Acknowledgments.** We thank Pieter Abbeel, Taesung Park, Richard Zhang, Mathieu Aubry, Ilija Radosavovic, Tim Brooks, Karttikeya Mangalam, and all of BAIR for valuable discussions and encouragement. This work was supported, in part, by grants from SAP, Adobe, and Berkeley DeepDrive.

# References

1. Avron, H., Toledo, S.: Randomized algorithms for estimating the trace of an implicit symmetric positive semi-definite matrix. J. ACM (JACM) **58**(2), 1–34 (2011)
2. Bau, D., et al.: Semantic photo manipulation with a generative image prior. In: SIGGRAPH (2019)
3. Bau, D., et al.: Gan dissection: visualizing and understanding generative adversarial networks. In: International Conference on Learning Representations (ICLR) (2019)
4. Bengio, Y.: Deep learning of representations: looking forward. In: Dediu, A.-H., Martín-Vide, C., Mitkov, R., Truthe, B. (eds.) SLSP 2013. LNCS (LNAI), vol. 7978, pp. 1–37. Springer, Heidelberg (2013). https://doi.org/10.1007/978-3-642-39593-2_1
5. Brock, A., Donahue, J., Simonyan, K.: Large scale GAN training for high fidelity natural image synthesis. In: International Conference on Learning Representations (ICLR) (2019)
6. Chen, X., Duan, Y., Houthooft, R., Schulman, J., Sutskever, I., Abbeel, P.: Info-GAN: interpretable representation learning by information maximizing generative adversarial nets. In: Advances in Neural Information Processing Systems, pp. 2172–2180 (2016)

7. Collins, E., Bala, R., Price, B., Susstrunk, S.: Editing in style: uncovering the local semantics of GANs. In: IEEE Conference on Computer Vision and Pattern Recognition (CVPR) (2020)
8. Deng, J., Dong, W., Socher, R., Li, L.J., Li, K., Fei-Fei, L.: ImageNet: a large-scale hierarchical image database. In: IEEE Conference on Computer Vision and Pattern Recognition (CVPR) (2009)
9. Goodfellow, I., et al.: Generative adversarial nets. In: NIPS (2014)
10. Gulrajani, I., Ahmed, F., Arjovsky, M., Dumoulin, V., Courville, A.C.: Improved training of Wasserstein GANs. In: Advances in Neural Information Processing Systems (2017)
11. Heusel, M., Ramsauer, H., Unterthiner, T., Nessler, B., Hochreiter, S.: GANs trained by a two time-scale update rule converge to a local Nash equilibrium. In: Advances in Neural Information Processing Systems (2017)
12. Higgins, I., et al.: beta-VAE: learning basic visual concepts with a constrained variational framework. In: 5th International Conference on Learning Representations, ICLR 2017, Toulon, France, 24–26 April 2017, Conference Track Proceedings. OpenReview.net (2017). https://openreview.net/forum?id=Sy2fzU9gl
13. Hu, Q., Szabó, A., Portenier, T., Favaro, P., Zwicker, M.: Disentangling factors of variation by mixing them. In: IEEE Conference on Computer Vision and Pattern Recognition (CVPR) (2018)
14. Huang, X., Liu, M.-Y., Belongie, S., Kautz, J.: Multimodal unsupervised image-to-image translation. In: Ferrari, V., Hebert, M., Sminchisescu, C., Weiss, Y. (eds.) ECCV 2018. LNCS, vol. 11207, pp. 179–196. Springer, Cham (2018). https://doi.org/10.1007/978-3-030-01219-9_11
15. Hutchinson, M.F.: A stochastic estimator of the trace of the influence matrix for Laplacian smoothing splines. Commun. Stat.-Simul. Comput. **18**(3), 1059–1076 (1989)
16. Hyvärinen, A., Oja, E.: Independent component analysis: algorithms and applications. Neural Netw. **13**(4–5), 411–430 (2000)
17. Isola, P., Zhu, J.Y., Zhou, T., Efros, A.A.: Image-to-image translation with conditional adversarial networks. In: IEEE Conference on Computer Vision and Pattern Recognition (CVPR) (2017)
18. Jahanian, A., Chai, L., Isola, P.: On the "steerability" of generative adversarial networks. arXiv preprint arXiv:1907.07171 (2019)
19. Jha, A.H., Anand, S., Singh, M., Veeravasarapu, V.S.R.: Disentangling factors of variation with cycle-consistent variational auto-encoders. In: Ferrari, V., Hebert, M., Sminchisescu, C., Weiss, Y. (eds.) ECCV 2018. LNCS, vol. 11207, pp. 829–845. Springer, Cham (2018). https://doi.org/10.1007/978-3-030-01219-9_49
20. Johnson, J., Hariharan, B., van der Maaten, L., Fei-Fei, L., Lawrence Zitnick, C., Girshick, R.: CLEVR: a diagnostic dataset for compositional language and elementary visual reasoning. In: Proceedings of the IEEE Conference on Computer Vision and Pattern Recognition, pp. 2901–2910 (2017)
21. Karaletsos, T., Belongie, S., Rätsch, G.: Bayesian representation learning with oracle constraints. arXiv preprint arXiv:1506.05011 (2015)
22. Karras, T., Aila, T., Laine, S., Lehtinen, J.: Progressive growing of GANs for improved quality, stability, and variation. In: International Conference on Learning Representations (ICLR) (2018)
23. Karras, T., Laine, S., Aila, T.: A style-based generator architecture for generative adversarial networks. In: IEEE Conference on Computer Vision and Pattern Recognition (CVPR) (2019)

24. Karras, T., Laine, S., Aittala, M., Hellsten, J., Lehtinen, J., Aila, T.: Analyzing and improving the image quality of StyleGAN. CoRR abs/1912.04958 (2019)
25. Khemakhem, I., Kingma, D., Monti, R., Hyvarinen, A.: Variational autoencoders and nonlinear ICA: a unifying framework. In: International Conference on Artificial Intelligence and Statistics, pp. 2207–2217 (2020)
26. Khemakhem, I., Monti, R.P., Kingma, D.P., Hyvärinen, A.: ICE-Beem: identifiable conditional energy-based deep models. arXiv preprint arXiv:2002.11537 (2020)
27. Kim, H., Mnih, A.: Disentangling by factorising. arXiv preprint arXiv:1802.05983 (2018)
28. Kingma, D., Ba, J.: Adam: a method for stochastic optimization. In: International Conference on Learning Representations (ICLR) (2015)
29. Kingma, D.P., Welling, M.: Auto-encoding variational bayes. In: International Conference on Learning Representations (ICLR) (2014)
30. Kulkarni, T.D., Whitney, W.F., Kohli, P., Tenenbaum, J.: Deep convolutional inverse graphics network. In: Advances in Neural Information Processing Systems, pp. 2539–2547 (2015)
31. LeCun, Y., Chopra, S., Hadsell, R., Ranzato, M., Huang, F.: A tutorial on energy-based learning. Predicting Struct. Data 1 (2006)
32. Locatello, F., et al.: Challenging common assumptions in the unsupervised learning of disentangled representations. In: International Conference on Machine Learning, pp. 4114–4124 (2019)
33. Mathieu, M.F., Zhao, J., Ramesh, A., Sprechmann, P., LeCun, Y.: Disentangling factors of variation in deep representation using adversarial training. In: Advances in Neural Information Processing Systems (2016)
34. Moosavi-Dezfooli, S.M., Fawzi, A., Uesato, J., Frossard, P.: Robustness via curvature regularization, and vice versa. In: Proceedings of the IEEE Conference on Computer Vision and Pattern Recognition, pp. 9078–9086 (2019)
35. Nguyen-Phuoc, T., Li, C., Theis, L., Richardt, C., Yang, Y.L.: HoloGAN: unsupervised learning of 3D representations from natural images. In: Proceedings of the IEEE International Conference on Computer Vision, pp. 7588–7597 (2019)
36. Odena, A., et al.: Is generator conditioning causally related to GAN performance? arXiv preprint arXiv:1802.08768 (2018)
37. Radford, A., Metz, L., Chintala, S.: Unsupervised representation learning with deep convolutional generative adversarial networks. In: International Conference on Learning Representations (ICLR) (2016)
38. Shen, Y., Gu, J., Tang, X., Zhou, B.: Interpreting the latent space of GANs for semantic face editing. In: IEEE Conference on Computer Vision and Pattern Recognition (CVPR) (2020)
39. Singh, K.K., Ojha, U., Lee, Y.J.: FineGAN: unsupervised hierarchical disentanglement for fine-grained object generation and discovery. In: IEEE Conference on Computer Vision and Pattern Recognition (CVPR) (2019)
40. Voynov, A., Babenko, A.: Unsupervised discovery of interpretable directions in the GAN latent space (2020)
41. White, T.: Sampling generative networks. arXiv preprint arXiv:1609.04468 (2016)
42. Yang, D., Hong, S., Jang, Y., Zhao, T., Lee, H.: Diversity-sensitive conditional generative adversarial networks. arXiv preprint arXiv:1901.09024 (2019)
43. Yu, A., Grauman, K.: Fine-grained visual comparisons with local learning. In: CVPR (2014)
44. Zhang, R., Isola, P., Efros, A.A., Shechtman, E., Wang, O.: The unreasonable effectiveness of deep features as a perceptual metric. In: CVPR (2018)

45. Zhu, J.Y., Park, T., Isola, P., Efros, A.A.: Unpaired image-to-image translation using cycle-consistent adversarial networks. In: IEEE International Conference on Computer Vision (ICCV) (2017)

46. Zhu, J.Y., et al.: Toward multimodal image-to-image translation. In: Advances in Neural Information Processing Systems (2017)

47. Zhu, J.Y., et al.: Visual object networks: image generation with disentangled 3D representations. In: Advances in Neural Information Processing Systems, pp. 118–129 (2018)

# STAR: Sparse Trained Articulated Human Body Regressor

Ahmed A. A. Osman[✉], Timo Bolkart, and Michael J. Black

Max Planck Institute for Intelligent Systems, Tübingen, Germany
{aosman,tbolkart,black}@tuebingen.mpg.de

**Abstract.** The SMPL body model is widely used for the estimation, synthesis, and analysis of 3D human pose and shape. While popular, we show that SMPL has several limitations and introduce STAR, which is quantitatively and qualitatively superior to SMPL. First, SMPL has a huge number of parameters resulting from its use of global blend shapes. These dense pose-corrective offsets relate every vertex on the mesh to all the joints in the kinematic tree, capturing spurious long-range correlations. To address this, we define per-joint pose correctives and learn the subset of mesh vertices that are influenced by each joint movement. This sparse formulation results in more realistic deformations and significantly reduces the number of model parameters to 20% of SMPL. When trained on the same data as SMPL, STAR generalizes better despite having many fewer parameters. Second, SMPL factors pose-dependent deformations from body shape while, in reality, people with different shapes deform differently. Consequently, we learn shape-dependent pose-corrective blend shapes that depend on both body pose and BMI. Third, we show that the shape space of SMPL is not rich enough to capture the variation in the human population. We address this by training STAR with an additional 10,000 scans of male and female subjects, and show that this results in better model generalization. STAR is compact, generalizes better to new bodies and is a drop-in replacement for SMPL. STAR is publicly available for research purposes at http://star.is.tue.mpg.de.

## 1 Introduction

Human body models are widely used to reason about 3D body pose and shape in images and videos. While several models have been proposed [5–10, 30, 35, 37], SMPL [21] is currently the most widely use in academia and industry. SMPL is trained from thousands of 3D scans of people and captures the statistics of human body shape and pose. Key to SMPL's success is its compact and intuitive parametrization, decomposing the 3D body into pose parameters $\theta \in \mathbb{R}^{72}$

**Electronic supplementary material** The online version of this chapter (https://doi.org/10.1007/978-3-030-58539-6_36) contains supplementary material, which is available to authorized users.

© Springer Nature Switzerland AG 2020
A. Vedaldi et al. (Eds.): ECCV 2020, LNCS 12351, pp. 598–613, 2020.
https://doi.org/10.1007/978-3-030-58539-6_36

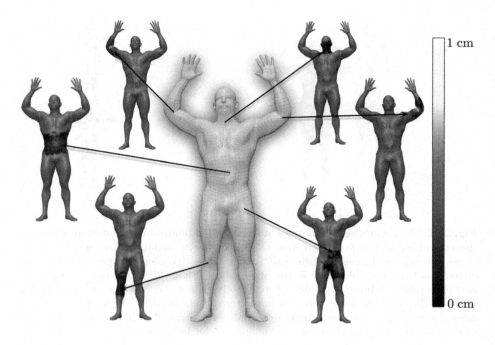

**Fig. 1.** Sparse Local Pose Correctives: STAR factorizes pose-dependent deformation into a set of sparse and spatially local pose-corrective blendshape functions, where each joint influences only a sparse subset of mesh vertices. The white mesh is STAR fit to a 3D scan of a professional body builder. The arrows point to joints in the STAR kinematic tree and the corresponding predicted corrective offset for the joint. The heat map encodes the magnitude of the corrective offsets. The joints have no influence on the gray mesh vertices.

corresponding to axis angle rotations of 24 joints and shape $\beta \in \mathbb{R}^{10}$ capturing subject identity (the number of shape parameters can be as high as 300 but most research uses only 10). This makes it useful to reason about 3D human body pose and shape given sparse measurements, such as IMU accelerations [11,12,26], sparse mocap markers [22,25] or 2D key points in images and videos [3,14–16,28,33,36,38].

While SMPL is widely used it suffers from several drawbacks. SMPL augments traditional linear blend skinning (LBS) with pose-dependent corrective offsets that are learned from 3D scans. Specifically, SMPL uses a pose-corrective blendshape function $\mathcal{P}(\boldsymbol{\theta}) : \mathbb{R}^{|\theta|} \rightarrow \mathbb{R}^{3N}$, where $N$ is the number of mesh vertices. The function $\mathcal{P}$ predicts corrective offsets for every mesh vertex such that, when the model is posed, the output mesh looks realistic. The function $\mathcal{P}$ can be viewed as a fully connected layer (FC), that relates the corrective offsets of every mesh vertex to the elements of the part rotation matrices of all the body joints. This dense blendshape formulation has several drawbacks. First, it significantly inflates the number of model parameters to > 4.2 million, making SMPL

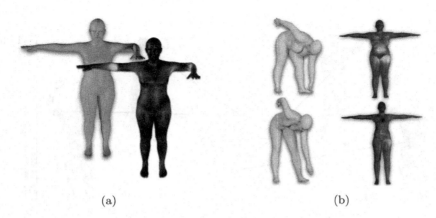

(a)                                                    (b)

**Fig. 2.** SMPL Limitations: Examples of some SMPL limitations. Heat maps illustrate the magnitude of the pose-corrective offsets. Figure 2a highlights the spurious long-range correlations learned by the SMPL pose corrective blend shapes. Bending one elbow results in a visible bulge in the other elbow. Figure 2b shows two subjects registrations (show in blue) with two different body shapes (High BMI) and (Low BMI). While both are in the same pose, the corrective offsets are different since body deformation are influenced by both body pose and body shape. The SMPL pose corrective offsets are the same regardless of body shape. (Color figure online)

prone to overfitting during training. Even with numerous regularization terms, the model learns spurious correlations in the training set, as shown in Fig. 2a; moving one elbow causes a bulge in the other elbow.

This is problematic for graphics, model fitting, and deep learning. The dense formulation causes dense spurious gradients to be propagated through the model. A loss on the mesh surface back propagates spurious gradients to geodesically distant joints. The existing formulation of the pose corrective blend shapes limits the model compactness and visual realism.

To address this, we create a new compact human body model, called **STAR** (Sparse Trained Articulated Regressor), that is more accurate than SMPL yet has sparse and spatially local blend shapes, such that a joint only influences a sparse set of vertices that are geodesically close to it. The original SMPL paper acknowledges the problem and proposes a model called SMPL-LBS-Sparse that restricts the pose corrective blend shapes such that a vertex is only influenced by joints with the highest skinning weights. SMPL-LBS-Sparse, however, is less accurate than SMPL.

Our key insight is that the influence of a body joint should be inferred from the training data. The main challenge is formalizing a model and training objective such that we learn meaningful joint support regions that are sparse and spatially local as shown in Fig. 1. To this end we formalize a differentiable thresholding function based on the Rectified Linear Unit operator, **ReLU**, that learns to predict 0 activations for irrelevant vertices in the model. The output activations are used to mask the output of the joint blendshape regressor to only influence vertices with non-zero activations. This results in a sparse model of pose-dependent deformation.

We go further in improving the model compactness. SMPL uses a Rodrigues representation of the joints angles and has a separate pose-corrective regressor for each element of the matrix, resulting in 9 regressors per joint. We switch to a quaternion representation with only 4 numbers per joint, with no loss in performance. This, in combination with the sparsity, means that STAR has 20% of the parameters of SMPL. We evaluate STAR by training it on different datasets. When we train STAR on the same data as SMPL, we find that it is more accurate on held-out test data. Note that the use of quaternions is an internal representation change from SMPL and transparent to users who can continue to use the SMPL pose parameters.

SMPL disentangles shape due to identity from shape due to pose. This is a strength because it results in a simple model with additive shape functions. It is also a weakness, however, because it cannot capture correlations between body shape and how soft tissue deforms with pose. To address this we extend the existing pose corrective formulation by regressing the correctives using both body pose $\theta$ and body shape $\beta$. Here we use the second principal component of the of the body shape space, which correlates highly with Body Mass Index (BMI). This change results in more realistic pose-based deformations.

SMPL is used in many fields such as apparel and healthcare because it captures the statistics of human body shape. The SMPL shape space was trained using the CAESAR database, which contains 1700 male and 2107 female subjects. CAESAR bodies, however, are distributed according to the US population in 1990 [32] and do not reflect global body shape statistics today. Additionally, CAESAR's capture protocol dressed all women in the same sports-bra-type top, resulting in a female chest shape that does not reflect the diversity of shapes found in real applications. We show that SMPL trained on CAESAR is not able to capture the variation in the more recent, and more diverse, SizeUSA dataset of 10,000 subjects (2845 male and 6436 female) [2], and vice versa. To address these problems, we train STAR from the combination of CAESAR and SizeUSA scans and show that the complementary information contained in both datasets enables STAR to generalize better to unseen body shapes.

We summarize our contributions by organizing them around impact areas where SMPL is currently used:

1. **Computer vision:** We propose a compact model that is 80% smaller than SMPL. We achieve compactness in two ways: First, we formalize sparse corrective blend shapes and learn the set of vertices influenced by each joint. Second, we use quaternion features for offset regression. While STAR is more compact than SMPL, it generalizes better on held-out test data.
2. **Graphics:** Non-local deformations make animation difficult because changing the pose of one body part affects other parts. Our local model fixes this problem with SMPL.

3. **Health:** Realistic avatars are important in health research. We increase realism by conditioning the pose corrective blend shapes on body shape. Bodies with different BMI produce different pose corrective blend shapes.
4. **Clothing Industry:** Accurate body shape matters for clothing. We use the largest training set to date to learn body shape and show that previous models were insufficient to capture the diversity of human shape.

The model is a drop-in replacement for SMPL, with the same pose and shape parametrization. We make the model with a 300 principal component shape space publicly available for research purposes at http://star.is.tue.mpg.de.

## 2   Related Work

There is a long literature on 3D modelling of the human body, either manually or using data-driven methods. We review the most related literature here with a focus on methods that learn bodies from data, pioneered by [4,6].

*Linear Blend Skinning.* Linear Blend Skinning (LBS), also known as Skeletal-Subspace Deformation (SSD) [23,24], is the foundation for many existing body models because of its simplicity. With LBS, the mesh is rigged with an underling set of joints forming a kinematic tree where each mesh vertex $v_i$ is associated with $n$ body joints and corresponding skinning weights $w_i$. The transformations applied to each mesh vertex are a weighted function of the transformations of the associated $n$ joints. The skinning weights are typically defined by an artist or learned from data. In SMPL [21] the skinning weights are initialized by an artist and fine tuned as part of the training process. Numerous works attempt to predict the skinning weights for arbitrary body meshes, e.g. [13,20].

*Pose Corrective Blend Shapes.* Although LBS is widely used, it suffers from well known shortcomings, which several method have been proposed to address. Lewis [19] introduces the pose space deformation model (PSD) where LBS is complemented with corrective deformations. The deformations are in the form of corrective offsets added to the mesh vertices posed with LBS. The corrective deformations are related to the underlying kinematic tree pose. Weighted pose deformation (WPD) [18,31] adds pose corrective offsets to the base template mesh in the canonical (rest) pose before posing it with LBS, such that final posed mesh is plausible. Typically, such correctives are artist defined in key poses. Given a new pose, a weighted combination of correctives from nearby key poses is applied. Allen et al. [4] are the first to learn such corrective offsets from 3D scans of human bodies.

*Learned Models.* The release of the CAESAR dataset of 3D scans [32] enabled researchers to begin training statistical models of body shape [5,35]. SCAPE [6] is the first model to learn a factored representation of body shape and pose. SCAPE models body deformations due pose and shape as triangle deformations and has been extended in many ways [7–10,29,30]. SCAPE has several downsides, however. It requires a least-squares solver to create a valid mesh, has no explicit joints or skeletal structure, may not maintain limb lengths when posed, and is not compatible with graphics pipelines and game engines.

To address these issues, Loper et al. [21] introduced SMPL, which uses vertex-based corrective offsets. Like SCAPE, SMPL factors the body into shape dependent deformations and pose dependent deformations. SMPL is more accurate than SCAPE when trained on the same data and is based on LBS, making it easier to use. SMPL is also the first model trained using the full CAESAR dataset [32], giving it a realistic shape space; previous methods used a subset of CAESAR or even smaller datasets.

SMPL models pose correctives as a linear function of the elements of the part rotation matrices. This results in 207 pose blend shapes with each one having a global effect. Instead, we train a non-linear model that is linear in the pose (for good generalization) but non-linear in the spatial extent (to make it local). We adopt a unit quaternion representation and reduce that number of blend shapes from 207 to 23. These functions are not based on a single joint but rather on groups of joints, giving more expressive power. We train the correctives using a non-linear function that encourages spatial sparsity in the blend shapes. This results in a model that is 80% smaller than SMPL and reduces long-range spurious deformations. Loper et al. [21] also proposed a sparse version of SMPL but found that it reduced accuracy. In contrast, when trained on the same data, STAR is more accurate than SMPL. Additionally, we show that CAESAR is not sufficient and we train on more body shape data (14,000 scans in total) than any previous model.

SMPL and SCAPE factor body shape and pose-dependent shape change, but ignore correlations between them. Several methods model this with a tensor representation [7,9]. This allows them to vary muscle deformation with pose depending on the muscularity of the subject. Here we achieve similar effects while keeping the benefits of simple models like SMPL.

*Sparse Pose Corrective Blend Shapes.* Human pose deformations are largely local in nature and, hence, the pose corrective deformations should be similarly local. Kry et al. [17] introduce EigenSkin to learn a localized model of pose deformations. STAR is similar to EigenSkin in that it models localized joint support but, unlike EigenSkin we infer the joint support region from posed scan data without requiring a dedicated routine of manually posing joints. Neumann et al. [27], use sparse PCA to learn local and sparse deformations of pose-dependent body deformations but do not learn a function mapping body pose to these deformations. In contrast, STAR learns sparse and local pose deformations that are regressed directly from the body pose. Contemporaneous with our work, GHUM [37] builds on SMPL and its Rodrigues pose representation but reduces the pose parameters (including face and hands) to a 32-dimensional latent code. Pose correctives are linearly regressed from this latent representation with L1 sparsity, giving sparse correctives.

## 3   Model

STAR is a vertex-based LBS model complemented with a learned set of shape and pose corrective functions. Similar to SMPL, we factor the body shape into the subject's intrinsic shape and pose-dependent deformations. In STAR we define a pose corrective function for each joint, $j$, in the kinematic tree. In contrast to SMPL, we condition the pose corrective deformation function on both body pose $\boldsymbol{\theta} \in \mathbb{R}^{|\theta|}$ and shape $\boldsymbol{\beta} \in \mathbb{R}^{|\beta|}$. Additionally, during training, we use a non-linear activation function, $\phi(.)$, that selects the subset of mesh vertices relevant to the joint $j$. The pose corrective blend shape function makes predictions only about a subset of the mesh vertices. We adopt the same notation used in SMPL [21]. We start with an artist defined template, $\overline{\boldsymbol{T}} \in \mathbb{R}^{3N}$ in the rest pose $\boldsymbol{\theta}^*$ (i.e. T-Pose) where $N = 6890$ is the number of mesh vertices. The model kinematic tree contains $K = 24$ joints, corresponding to 23 body joints in addition to a root joint. The template $\overline{\boldsymbol{T}}$ is then deformed by a shape corrective blend shape function $B_S$ that captures the subjects identity and a function $B_P$ that adds correctives offsets such that mesh looks realistic when posed.

*Shape Blend Shapes.* The shape blend shape function $B_S(\boldsymbol{\beta}; \mathcal{S}) : \mathbb{R}^{|\beta|} \rightarrow \mathbb{R}^{3N}$ maps the identity parameters $\boldsymbol{\beta}$ to vertex offsets from the template mesh as

$$B_S(\boldsymbol{\beta}; \mathcal{S}) = \sum_{n=1}^{|\beta|} \beta_n S_n, \tag{1}$$

where $\boldsymbol{\beta} = [\beta_1, \cdots, \beta_{|\beta|}]$ are the shape coefficients, and $\mathcal{S} = [S_1, \cdots, S_{|\beta|}] \in \mathbb{R}^{3N \times |\beta|}$ are the principal components capturing the space of human shape variability. The shape correctives are added to the template:

$$\boldsymbol{V}_{shaped} = \overline{\boldsymbol{T}} + B_S(\boldsymbol{\beta}; \mathcal{S}), \tag{2}$$

where $\boldsymbol{V}_{shaped}$ contains the vertices representing the subject's physical attributes and identity.

*Pose and Shape Corrective Blend Shapes.* The output of the shape corrective blend shape function, $\boldsymbol{V}_{shaped}$, is further deformed by a pose corrective function. The pose corrective function is conditioned on both pose and shape and adds corrective offsets such that, when the mesh is posed with LBS, it looks realistic. We denote the kinematic tree unit quaternion vector as $\boldsymbol{q} \in \mathbb{R}^{96}$ (24 joints each represented with 4 parameters). The pose corrective function is denoted as $B_P(\boldsymbol{q}, \beta_2) \in \mathbb{R}^{|q| \times 1} \rightarrow \mathbb{R}^{3N}$, where $\beta_2$ is the PCA coefficient of the second principal component, which highly correlates with the body mass index (BMI) as shown in Sup. Mat.. The STAR pose corrective function is factored into a sum of pose corrective functions:

$$B_P(\boldsymbol{q}, \beta_2; \mathcal{K}, \mathbf{A}) = \sum_{j=1}^{K-1} B_P^j(\boldsymbol{q}_{ne(j)}, \beta_2; \mathcal{K}_j, \boldsymbol{A}_j), \tag{3}$$

where a pose corrective function is defined for each joint in the kine-matic tree excluding the root joint. The per-joint pose corrective function $B_P^j(\boldsymbol{q}_{ne(j)}, \beta_2; \mathcal{K}_j, \boldsymbol{A}_j)$ predicts corrective offsets given $\boldsymbol{q}_{ne(j)} \subset \boldsymbol{q}$, where $\boldsymbol{q}_{ne(j)}$ is a set containing the joint $j$ and its direct neighbors in the kinematic tree. This formulation results in more powerful regressors compared to SMPL. $\mathcal{K}_j \in \mathbb{R}^{3N \times |\boldsymbol{q}_{ne(j)}|+1}$ is a linear regressor weight matrix and $\boldsymbol{A}_j$ are the activation weights for each vertex, both of which are learned. Each pose corrective function, $B_P^j(\boldsymbol{q}_{ne(j)}, \beta_2)$, is defined as a composition of two functions, an activation function and a pose corrective regressor.

*Activation Function.* For each joint, $j$, we define a learnable set of mesh vertex weights, $\boldsymbol{A}_j = [w_j^1, \cdots, w_j^N] \in \mathbb{R}^N$, where $w_j^i \in \mathbb{R}$ denotes the weight of the $i^{th}$ mesh vertex with respect to the $j$ joint. The weight $w_j^i$ for each vertex $i$ is initialized as the reciprocal of the minimum geodesic to the set of vertices around joint $j$, normalized to the range $[0, 1]$. The weights are thresholded by a non-linear activation function, specifically a rectified linear unit (ReLU):

$$\phi(w_j^i) = \begin{cases} 0, & \text{if } w_j^i \leq 0, \\ w_j^i, & \text{otherwise,} \end{cases} \tag{4}$$

such that during training, vertices with a $w_j^i \leq 0$ have weight 0. The remaining set of vertices with $w_j^i > 0$ defines the support region of joint $j$.

*Pose Corrective Regressor.* The per-joint pose corrective function is defined as $P_j(\boldsymbol{q}_{ne(j)}) \in \mathbb{R}^{|\boldsymbol{q}_{ne(j)}|+1} \to \mathbb{R}^{3N}$, which regresses corrective offsets given the joint and its direct neighbors' quaternion values

$$P_j(\boldsymbol{q}_{ne(j)}, \beta_2; \mathcal{K}_j) = \mathcal{K}_j((\boldsymbol{q}_{ne(j)} - \boldsymbol{q}_{ne(j)}^*)^T | \beta_2)^T, \tag{5}$$

where $\boldsymbol{q}_{ne(j)}^*$ is the vector of quaternion values for the set of joints $ne(j)$ in rest pose, and $\beta_2$ is concatenated to the quaternion difference vector. $\mathcal{K}_j \in \mathbb{R}^{3N \times |\boldsymbol{q}_{ne(j)}|+1}$ is the regression matrix for joint $j$'s pose correctives offsets. The predicted pose corrective offsets in Equation 5 are masked by the joint activation function:

$$B_P^j(\boldsymbol{q}_{ne(j)}; \boldsymbol{A}_j, \mathcal{K}_j) = \phi(\boldsymbol{A}_j) \circ P_j(\boldsymbol{q}_{ne(j)}, \beta_2; \mathcal{K}_j), \tag{6}$$

where $\boldsymbol{X} \circ \boldsymbol{Y}$ is the element wise Hadamard product between the vectors $\boldsymbol{X}$ and $\boldsymbol{Y}$. During training, vertices with zero activation with respect to joint $j$, will have no corrective offsets added to them. Therefore when summing the contribution of the individual joint pose corrective functions in Eq. 3, each joint only contributes pose correctives to the vertices for which there is support.

*Blend Skinning.* Finally, the mesh with the added pose and shape corrective offsets is transformed using a standard skinning function $W(\overline{\boldsymbol{T}}, \boldsymbol{J}, \theta, \mathcal{W})$ around the joints, $\boldsymbol{J} \in \mathbb{R}^{3K}$ and linearly smoothed by a learned set of blend weight parameters $\mathcal{W}$. The joint locations are intuitively influenced by the body shape and physical attributes. Similar to SMPL, the joints $J(\boldsymbol{\beta}; \mathcal{J}, \overline{\boldsymbol{T}}, \mathcal{S}) = \mathcal{J}(\boldsymbol{V}_{shaped})$ are regressed from $\boldsymbol{V}_{shaped}$ by a sparse function $\mathcal{J} : \mathbb{R}^{3N} \to \mathbb{R}^{3K}$.

To summarize, STAR is full defined by:

$$M(\boldsymbol{\beta}, \boldsymbol{\theta}) = W(T_p(\boldsymbol{\beta}, \boldsymbol{\theta}), J(\boldsymbol{\beta}), \boldsymbol{\theta}, \mathcal{W}), \tag{7}$$

where $T_P$ is defined as:

$$T_p(\boldsymbol{\beta}, \boldsymbol{\theta}) = \overline{\boldsymbol{T}} + B_S(\boldsymbol{\beta}) + B_P(\boldsymbol{q}, \beta_2), \tag{8}$$

where $\boldsymbol{q}$ is the quaternion representation of pose $\boldsymbol{\theta}$. The STAR model is fully parameterized by 72 (i.e. 24 * 3) pose parameters $\boldsymbol{\theta}$ in axis-angle representation, and up to 300 shape parameters $\boldsymbol{\beta}$.

### 3.1 Model Training

STAR training is similar to SMPL [22]. The key difference is the training of the pose corrective function in Eq. 3. STAR pose corrective blend shapes are trained to minimize the *vertex-to-vertex* error between the model predictions and the ground-truth registrations where, in each iteration, the model parameters $(\mathcal{A}, \mathcal{K})$ are minimized by stochastic gradient descent across a batch of B registrations, denoted as $\boldsymbol{R} \in \mathbb{R}^{3N}$. The data term is given by:

$$\mathcal{L}_D = \frac{1}{B} \sum_{i=1}^{B} ||M(\boldsymbol{\beta}_i, \boldsymbol{\theta}_i) - \boldsymbol{R}_i||_2. \tag{9}$$

In addition to the data term we regularize the pose corrective regression weights $(\mathcal{K})$ with an $L2$ norm:

$$\mathcal{L}_B = \lambda_b \sum_{i=1}^{K-1} ||\mathcal{K}_i||_2, \tag{10}$$

where $K$ is the number of joints in STAR and $\lambda_b$ is a scalar constant. In order to induce sparsity in the activation masks $\phi(.)$, we use an $L1$ penalty

$$\mathcal{L}_A = \lambda_c || \sum_{i=1}^{K-1} \phi_j(\boldsymbol{A}_j)||_1, \tag{11}$$

where $\lambda_c$ is a scalar constant. Similar to SMPL we use a sparsity regularizer term on the skinning weights $\mathcal{W}$ and regularize the skinning weights to initial artist-defined skinning weights, $\mathcal{W}_{\text{prior}} \in \mathbb{R}^{N \times K}$:

$$\mathcal{L}_W = \lambda_p ||\mathcal{W} - \mathcal{W}_{\text{prior}}||_2 + \lambda_s ||\mathcal{W}||_1, \tag{12}$$

where $\lambda_p$ and $\lambda_s$ are scalar constants. To summarize the complete training objective is given by

$$\mathcal{L} = \mathcal{L}_D + \mathcal{L}_B + \mathcal{L}_A + \mathcal{L}_W. \tag{13}$$

The objective in Eq. 13 is minimized with respect to the skinning weights $\mathcal{W}$, pose corrective regression weights $\mathcal{K}_{1:24}$, activation weights $\boldsymbol{A}_{1:24}$. We train the model iteratively. In each training iteration, we anneal the regularization parameters as described in the Sup. Mat.

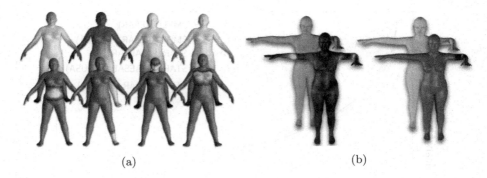

(a)                                                      (b)

**Fig. 3.** Spatially local and sparse pose corrective blend shapes. (a) The top row shows a sample of the joints activation functions output before training and the bottom row shows the output after training (gray is zero). (b) shows SMPL (brown) and STAR (white) in the rest pose except for the left elbow, which is rotated. The heat map visualizes the corrective offsets for each model caused by moving this one joint. Note that unlike STAR, SMPL has spurious long-range displacements. (Color figure online)

## 4    Experiments

### 4.1    Activation

Key to learning the sparse and spatially local pose corrective blend shapes are the joint activation functions introduced in Eq. 4. During training the output of the activation functions becomes more sparse, limiting the number of vertices a joint can influence. Figure 3a summarizes a sample of the activation functions output before and after training. As a result of the output of the activation functions becoming more sparse, the number of model parameters decreases. By the end of training, the male model pose blend shapes contained $3.37 \times 10^5$ non-zero parameters and the female model contained $3.94 \times 10^5$ non-zero parameters compared to SMPL which has a dense pose corrective blendshape formulation with $4.28 \times 10^6$ parameters. At test time only the non-zero parameters need to be stored.

Figure 3b show a SMPL model bending an elbow resulting in a bulge in the other elbow, as a result of the pose corrective blend shapes learning long range spurious correlations from the training data. In contrast, STAR correctives are spatially local and sparse, this is a result of the learned local sparse pose corrective blend shape formulation of STAR.

### 4.2    Model Generalization

While the learned activation masks are sparse and spatially local, which is good, it is equally important that the model still generalizes to unseen bodies. To this end, we evaluate the model generalization on held out test subjects. The test set we use contains the publicly available Dyna dataset [1] (the same evaluation set

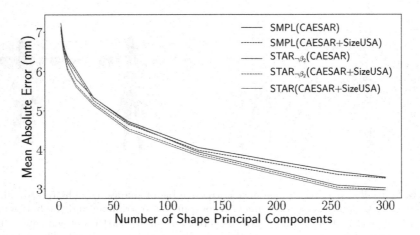

**Fig. 4.** Generalization Accuracy: Evaluating STAR and SMPL on unseen bodies. $STAR_{\neg\beta_2}(CAESAR)$ is STAR trained on CAESAR with pose correctives depending on pose only (i.e. independent of $\beta_2$), $STAR_{\neg\beta_2}(CAESAR+SizeUSA)$ is STAR trained on CAESAR and SizeUSA with pose corrective blend shapes depending on pose only, and STAR(CAEAR+SizeUSA) is STAR trained on CAEASAR and SizeUSA with pose and shape dependent pose corrective blend shapes.

used in evaluating the SMPL model), in addition to the 3DBodyTex dataset [34] which contains static scans for 100 male and 100 female subjects in a diversity of poses. The total test set contains 570 registered meshes of 102 male subjects and 104 female subjects. We fit the models by minimizing the vertex to vertex mean absolute error (v2v), where the pose $\theta$ and shape parameters $\beta$ are the free optimization variables. We report the mean absolute error in (mm) as a function of the number of used shape coefficients in Fig. 4. We first evaluate SMPL and STAR when they are both trained using the CAESAR dataset. In this evaluation both models are trained on the exact same pose and shape data. Since they both share the same topology and kinematic tree, differences in the fitting results are solely due to the different formulation of the two models. In Fig. 4, STAR uniformly generalizes better than SMPL on the unseen test subjects. A sample qualitative comparison between SMPL and STAR fits is shown in Fig. 5.

### 4.3 Extended Training Data

The CAESAR dataset is limited in its diversity, consequently limiting model generalization. Consequently, we extend the shape training database to include the SizeUSA database [2]. SizeUSA contains low quality scans of 2845 male and 6434 females with ages varying between 18 to 66+; a sample of the SizeUSA bodies compared to the CAESAR bodies are shown in Fig. 6a and Fig. 6b. We evaluate the generalization power of models trained separately on CEASER and SizeUSA. We do so by computing the percentage of explained variance of the SizeUSA subjects given a shape space trained on the CAESAR subjects, and vice

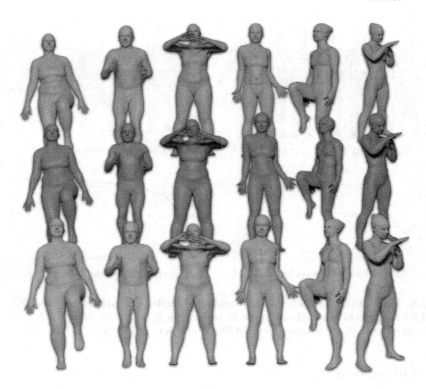

**Fig. 5.** Qualitative Evaluation: Comparison between SMPL and STAR. The ground truth registrations are shown in blue, the corresponding SMPL model fit meshes are shown in brown and STAR fits are shown in white. Here, both STAR and SMPL are trained on the CAESAR database. (Color figure online)

versa. The results are shown in Fig. 6 for the female subjects, the full analysis for both male and female subjects is shown in the Sup. Mat.. The key insight from this experiment is that a shape space trained on a single data set was not sufficient to explain the variance in the other data set. This suggests that training on both dataset should improve the model shape space expressiveness.

We retrain train both STAR and SMPL on the combined CAESAR and SizeUSA datasets an evaluate the model generalization on the held out test set as a function of the number of shape coefficient used as shown in Fig. 4. Training on both CAESAR and SizeUSA results in both SMPL and STAR generalizing better than when trained only on CAESAR. We further note that STAR still uniformly generalizes better than SMPL when both models are trained on the combined CAESAR and SizeUSA dataset. Importantly STAR is more accurate than SMPL despite the fact that uses many fewer parameters. Finally we extend the pose corrective blend shapes of STAR to be conditioned on both body pose and body shape and evaluate the model on the held out set. This results in a further improvement in the model generalization accuracy that, while modest, is consistent.

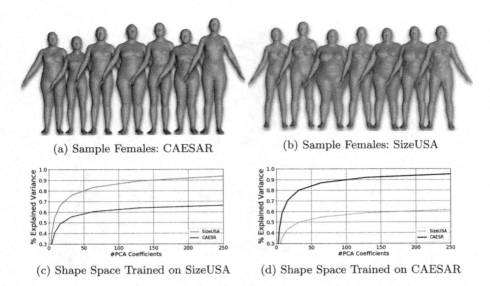

(a) Sample Females: CAESAR        (b) Sample Females: SizeUSA

(c) Shape Space Trained on SizeUSA        (d) Shape Space Trained on CAESAR

**Fig. 6.** Explained Variance: The percentage of explained variance of SizeUSA and CAESAR subjects when shape space is trained on SizeUSA is shown in Fig. 6c and when the shape space is trained on CAESAR subjects in Fig. 6d.

## 5   Discussion

STAR has 93 pose corrective blend shapes compared to 207 in SMPL and is 80% smaller than SMPL. It is surprising that it is able to uniformly perform better than SMPL when trained on the same data. This highlights the fact that the local and sparse assumptions of the pose corrective blend shapes is indeed realistic a priori knowledge that should be incorporated in any body model. Importantly, having fewer parameters means that STAR is less likely to overfit, even though our non-linear model makes training more difficult.

For SMPL, the authors report that enforcing sparsity of the pose corrective blend shapes resulted into worse results than SMPL. We take a different approach and learn the sparse set of vertices relevant to a joint from data. The key strength of our approach is that it is learned from data.

We are able to learn spatially local and sparse joint support regions due to two key implementation details: The initialization of the vertex weight $A_j$ with the normalized inverse of geodesic distance to a joint. Secondly, the pose corrective blend shapes for each joint are regressed from local pose information, corresponding to the joint and its direct neighbors in the kinematic tree; this is a richer representation than SMPL. These two factors together with the sparsity inducing $L1$ norm on the activation weights, act as an inductive bias to learn a sparse set of vertices that are geodesically local to a joint.

The sparse pose correctives formulation reduces the number of parameters and regularizes the model, preventing it from learning spurious long range correlations from the training data. Since each vertex is only influenced by a limited number of joints in the kinematic tree, the gradients propagated through the model are sparse and the derivative of a vertex with respect to a geodesically distant joint is 0, which is not the case in the SMPL.

# 6    Conclusion

We have introduced STAR, which has fewer parameters than SMPL yet is more accurate and generalizes better to unseen bodies when trained on the same data. Our key insight is that human pose deformation is local and sparse. While this observation is not new, our formulation is. We define a non-linear (ReLU) activation function for each joint and train the model from data to estimate both the linear corrective pose blend shapes and the activation region on the mesh that these joints influence. We kept what is popular with SMPL while improving on it in every sense. STAR has only 20% of the pose corrective parameters of SMPL. Our training method and localized model fixes a key problem of SMPL– the spurious, long-range, correlations that result in non-local deformations. Such artifacts make SMPL unappealing for animators. Moreover, we show that, while SMPL is trained from thousands of scans, human bodies are more varied than the CAESAR dataset. More training scans results in a better model. Finally we make pose-corrective blend shapes depend on body shape, producing more realistic deformations. We make STAR available for research with 300 shape principal components. It can be swapped in for SMPL in any existing application since the pose and shape parameterization is the same to the user. Future work should extend this approach to the SMPL-X model which includes an expressive face and hands.

**Acknowledgments.** The authors thank N. Mahmood for insightful discussions and feedback, and the International Max Planck Research School for Intelligent Systems (IMPRS-IS) for supporting A. A. A. Osman. The authors would like to thank Joachim Tesch, Muhammed Kocabas, Nikos Athanasiou, Nikos Kolotouros and Vassilis Choutas for their support and fruitful discussions.

**Disclosure:** In the last five years, MJB has received research gift funds from Intel, Nvidia, Facebook, and Amazon. He is a co-founder and investor in Meshcapade GmbH, which commercializes 3D body shape technology. While MJB is a part-time employee of Amazon, his research was performed solely at, and funded solely by, MPI.

# References

1. Dyna dataset (2015). http://dyna.is.tue.mpg.de/. Accessed 15 May 2015
2. SizeUSA dataset (2017). https://www.tc2.com/size-usa.html
3. Alldieck, T., Magnor, M., Xu, W., Theobalt, C., Pons-Moll, G.: Detailed human avatars from monocular video. In: International Conference on 3D Vision (3DV), pp. 98–109 (2018)
4. Allen, B., Curless, B., Popović, Z.: Articulated body deformation from range scan data. ACM Trans. Graph. (Proc. SIGGRAPH) **21**(3), 612–619 (2002)

5. Allen, B., Curless, B., Popović, Z.: The space of human body shapes: reconstruction and parameterization from range scans. ACM Trans. Graph. (Proc. SIGGRAPH) **22**(3), 587–594 (2003)
6. Anguelov, D., Srinivasan, P., Koller, D., Thrun, S., Rodgers, J., Davis, J.: SCAPE: shape completion and animation of PEople. ACM Trans. Graph. (Proc. SIGGRAPH) **24**(3), 408–416 (2005)
7. Chen, Y., Liu, Z., Zhang, Z.: Tensor-based human body modeling. In: Proceedings of the IEEE Conference on Computer Vision and Pattern Recognition (CVPR), pp. 105–112 (2013)
8. Freifeld, O., Black, M.J.: Lie bodies: a manifold representation of 3D human shape. In: Fitzgibbon, A., Lazebnik, S., Perona, P., Sato, Y., Schmid, C. (eds.) ECCV 2012. LNCS, vol. 7572, pp. 1–14. Springer, Heidelberg (2012). https://doi.org/10.1007/978-3-642-33718-5_1
9. Hasler, N., Stoll, C., Sunkel, M., Rosenhahn, B., Seidel, H.P.: A statistical model of human pose and body shape. Comput. Graph. Forum **28**(2), 337–346 (2009)
10. Hirshberg, D.A., Loper, M., Rachlin, E., Black, M.J.: Coregistration: simultaneous alignment and modeling of articulated 3D shape. In: Fitzgibbon, A., Lazebnik, S., Perona, P., Sato, Y., Schmid, C. (eds.) ECCV 2012. LNCS, vol. 7577, pp. 242–255. Springer, Heidelberg (2012). https://doi.org/10.1007/978-3-642-33783-3_18
11. Huang, Y., et al.: Towards accurate marker-less human shape and pose estimation over time. In: International Conference on 3D Vision (3DV), pp. 421–430 (2017)
12. Huang, Y., Kaufmann, M., Aksan, E., Black, M.J., Hilliges, O., Pons-Moll, G.: Deep inertial poser: learning to reconstruct human pose from sparse inertial measurements in real time. ACM Trans. Graph. (Proc. SIGGRAPH Asia) **37**, 185:1–185:15 (2018)
13. Jacobson, A., Baran, I., Kavan, L., Popović, J., Sorkine, O.: Fast automatic skinning transformations. ACM Trans. Graph. (TOG) **31**(4), 1–10 (2012)
14. Kanazawa, A., Black, M.J., Jacobs, D.W., Malik, J.: End-to-end recovery of human shape and pose. In: Proceedings of the IEEE Conference on Computer Vision and Pattern Recognition (CVPR), pp. 7122–7131 (2018)
15. Kocabas, M., Athanasiou, N., Black, M.J.: VIBE: video inference for human body pose and shape estimation. In: Proceedings of the IEEE Conference on Computer Vision and Pattern Recognition (CVPR), pp. 5253–5263 (2020)
16. Kolotouros, N., Pavlakos, G., Black, M.J., Daniilidis, K.: Learning to reconstruct 3D human pose and shape via model-fitting in the loop. In: Proceedings of the IEEE International Conference on Computer Vision (ICCV), pp. 2252–2261 (2019)
17. Kry, P.G., James, D.L., Pai, D.K.: Eigenskin: real time large deformation character skinning in hardware. In: Proceedings of the 2002 ACM SIGGRAPH/Eurographics Symposium on Computer Animation, pp. 153–159 (2002)
18. Kurihara, T., Miyata, N.: Modeling deformable human hands from medical images. In: Proceedings of the 2004 ACM SIGGRAPH/Eurographics Symposium on Computer Animation, pp. 355–363 (2004)
19. Lewis, J.P., Cordner, M., Fong, N.: Pose space deformation: a unified approach to shape interpolation and skeleton-driven deformation. In: Proceedings of the 27th Annual Conference on Computer Graphics and Interactive Techniques, pp. 165–172. SIGGRAPH 2000 (2000)
20. Liu, L., Zheng, Y., Tang, D., Yuan, Y., Fan, C., Zhou, K.: NeuroSkinning: automatic skin binding for production characters with deep graph networks. ACM Trans. Graph. (TOG) **38**(4), 1–12 (2019)
21. Loper, M., Mahmood, N., Romero, J., Pons-Moll, G., Black, M.J.: SMPL: a skinned multi-person linear model. ACM Trans. Graph. (Proc. SIGGRAPH Asia) **34**(6), 248:1–248:16 (2015)

22. Loper, M.M., Mahmood, N., Black, M.J.: MoSh: motion and shape capture from sparse markers. ACM Trans. Graph. (Proc. SIGGRAPH Asia) **33**(6), 220:1–220:13 (2014)
23. Magnenat-Thalmann, N., Laperrire, R., Thalmann, D.: Joint-dependent local deformations for hand animation and object grasping. In: Proceedings on Graphics Interface. Citeseer (1988)
24. Magnenat-Thalmann, N., Thalmann, D.: Human body deformations using joint-dependent local operators and finite-element theory. Technical report, EPFL (1990)
25. Mahmood, N., Ghorbani, N., Troje, N.F., Pons-Moll, G., Black, M.J.: AMASS: archive of motion capture as surface shapes. In: Proceedings of the IEEE International Conference on Computer Vision (ICCV), pp. 5442–5451 (2019)
26. von Marcard, T., Rosenhahn, B., Black, M., Pons-Moll, G.: Sparse inertial poser: automatic 3D human pose estimation from sparse IMUs. Comput. Graph. Forum **36**(2) (2017). Proceedings of the 38th Annual Conference of the European Association for Computer Graphics (Eurographics), pp. 349–360
27. Neumann, T., Varanasi, K., Wenger, S., Wacker, M., Magnor, M., Theobalt, C.: Sparse localized deformation components. ACM Trans. Graph. (TOG) **32**(6), 1–10 (2013)
28. Pavlakos, G., Zhu, L., Zhou, X., Daniilidis, K.: Learning to estimate 3D human pose and shape from a single color image. In: Proceedings of the IEEE Conference on Computer Vision and Pattern Recognition (CVPR), pp. 459–468 (2018)
29. Pishchulin, L., Wuhrer, S., Helten, T., Theobalt, C., Schiele, B.: Building statistical shape spaces for 3D human modeling. Pattern Recogn. **67**, 276–286 (2017)
30. Pons-Moll, G., Romero, J., Mahmood, N., Black, M.J.: Dyna: a model of dynamic human shape in motion. ACM Trans. Graph. (Proc. SIGGRAPH) **34**(4), 120:1–120:14 (2015)
31. Rhee, T., Lewis, J.P., Neumann, U.: Real-time weighted pose-space deformation on the GPU. Comput. Graph. Forum **25**(3), 439–448 (2006)
32. Robinette, K.M., et al.: Civilian American and European surface anthropometry resource (CAESAR) final report. Technical report AFRL-HE-WP-TR-2002-0169, US Air Force Research Laboratory (2002)
33. Rueegg, N., Lassner, C., Black, M.J., Schindler, K.: Chained representation cycling: learning to estimate 3D human pose and shape by cycling between representations. In: Conference on Artificial Intelligence (AAAI-20) (2020)
34. Saint, A., Ahmed, E., Cherenkova, K., Gusev, G., Aouada, D., Ottersten, B.: 3DBodyTex: textured 3D body dataset. In: International Conference on 3D Vision (3DV), pp. 495–504 (2018)
35. Seo, H., Cordier, F., Magnenat-Thalmann, N.: Synthesizing animatable body models with parameterized shape modifications. In: ACM SIGGRAPH/Eurographics Symposium on Computer Animation, SCA 2003, pp. 120–125 (2003)
36. Tan, J., Budvytis, I., Cipolla, R.: Indirect deep structured learning for 3D human body shape and pose prediction. In: Proceedings of the British Machine Vision Conference (BMVC), pp. 4–7 (2017)
37. Xu, H., Bazavan, E.G., Zanfir, A., Freeman, W.T., Sukthankar, R., Sminchisescu, C.: GHUM & GHUML: generative 3D human shape and articulated pose models. In: Proceedings of the IEEE Conference on Computer Vision and Pattern Recognition (CVPR), pp. 6184–6193 (2020)
38. Zanfir, A., Marinoiu, E., Sminchisescu, C.: Monocular 3D pose and shape estimation of multiple people in natural scenes-the importance of multiple scene constraints. In: Proceedings of the IEEE Conference on Computer Vision and Pattern Recognition (CVPR), pp. 2148–2157 (2018)

# Optical Flow Distillation: Towards Efficient and Stable Video Style Transfer

Xinghao Chen[1(✉)], Yiman Zhang[1], Yunhe Wang[1], Han Shu[1],
Chunjing Xu[1], and Chang Xu[2]

[1] Noah's Ark Lab, Huawei Technologies, Shenzhen, China
{xinghao.chen,zhangyiman1,yunhe.wang,
han.shu,xuchunjing}@huawei.com
[2] School of Computer Science, Faculty of Engineering, University of Sydney,
Sydney, Australia
c.xu@sydney.edu.au

**Abstract.** Video style transfer techniques inspire many exciting applications on mobile devices. However, their efficiency and stability are still far from satisfactory. To boost the transfer stability across frames, optical flow is widely adopted, despite its high computational complexity, *e.g.* occupying over 97% inference time. This paper proposes to learn a lightweight video style transfer network via knowledge distillation paradigm. We adopt two teacher networks, one of which takes optical flow during inference while the other does not. The output difference between these two teacher networks highlights the improvements made by optical flow, which is then adopted to distill the target student network. Furthermore, a low-rank distillation loss is employed to stabilize the output of student network by mimicking the rank of input videos. Extensive experiments demonstrate that our student network without an optical flow module is still able to generate stable video and runs much faster than the teacher network.

**Keywords:** Knowledge distillation · Optical flow · Video style transfer

## 1 Introduction

Artistic style transfer aims to transform the artistic style of a given painting to an image and has attracted tremendous interests since the seminal work of Gatys *et al.* [10]. Plenty of works have been dedicated to improving the performance of single image style transfer from different perspectives [3,7,22,24,25,29,30]. Meanwhile, there is growing attention for video style transfer [8,9,19,33,34,39]

---

X. Chen and Y. Zhang—Equal Contribution.

---

**Electronic supplementary material** The online version of this chapter (https://doi.org/10.1007/978-3-030-58539-6_37) contains supplementary material, which is available to authorized users.

© Springer Nature Switzerland AG 2020
A. Vedaldi et al. (Eds.): ECCV 2020, LNCS 12351, pp. 614–630, 2020.
https://doi.org/10.1007/978-3-030-58539-6_37

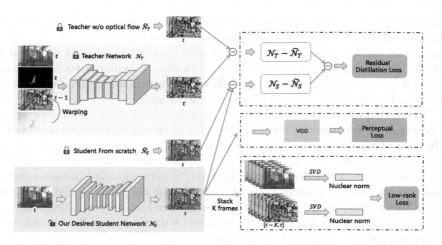

**Fig. 1.** The diagram of our proposed method. Our optical flow distillation method transfers knowledge from a stable video style transfer network $\mathcal{N}_T$ with optical flow to a lightweight network $\mathcal{N}_S$ that does not require optical flow during inference. The *residual distillation loss* encourages the student network to learn knowledge of the difference between the teacher networks with and without optical flow ($\mathcal{N}_T - \tilde{\mathcal{N}}_T$). Additionally, the *low rank distillation loss* is exploited to stabilize the output stylized videos of student network by mimicking the low rank of input videos. The basic *perceptual loss* is also used for style transfer.

due to its wider application scenarios, *e.g.*, movie synthesis and mobile applications. Compared with single image style transfer, stylizing a video is a much more challenging task. The key problem is the flickering phenomenon of the stylized videos. Due to the motion of objects and the changing of light in the video *etc.*, transferring the videos frame-by-frame independently causes the temporal inconsistency between consecutive stylized frames.

To tackle the problem discussed above, Ruder *et al.* [33,34] proposed a network that takes several inputs, including the current frame, occlusion mask and the previous stylized image warped by the optical flow. Despite producing smooth and coherent stylized videos, the inference speeds of these methods are relatively slow due to the calculation of optical flow on the fly. For example, the method of Ruder *et al.* [34] takes about $210ms$ to process a frame of $640 \times 320$ in the video, among which almost 97% of time is related to the time-consuming calculation of optical flow and warping operation.

Many methods have been proposed to alleviate the burden of on-the-fly optical flow computation and have achieved real-time speed for video style transfer [8,13,19]. These methods utilize temporal consistent loss guided by precomputed optical flow in training, which encourages the model to learn smooth and coherent stylized images in consecutive video frames. These methods are faster since they only take the current frame as input and get rid of optical flow estimation in the inference stage. Despite the fast speed, they still have less stable results when compared with methods that adopt optical flow during inference phase, as also indicated in some prior literature [8,19]. In addition, there are a number of model compression and speeding-up methods, *e.g.*, pruning [15,28,37], quantization [27,36,45], distillation [26,32,44] and neural architecture search [12,42]. Most of existing methods are explored for single image processing or recognition models. An efficient algorithm for learning efficient and stable video style transfer networks is urgently required.

In this paper, we present a novel knowledge distillation method to achieve a better trade-off between inference speed and stability of the stylized videos. The framework of our proposed method is depicted in Fig. 1. We choose a stable video style transfer network including an optical flow module in the inference phase as the teacher network, and a lightweight network only consumes current frame as the desired student network. We propose the residual distillation loss to encourage the student network to learn the residual between output stylized videos produced by teacher network with and without optical flow in inference. Moreover, motivated by the fact that consistent frames have the properties of low rank, we add additional low rank loss so that student network produces coherent stylized videos that have similar low rank with input videos. The inference speed of the student network is significantly faster than that of the teacher network after removing the optical flow module.

We then carefully design the evaluation experiments on benchmarks. The results illustrate that videos generated by student network learned using the proposed optical flow distillation paradigm have similar visualization quality to that of the teacher model but obviously lower computational costs, which can be further launched in real-time on mobile devices.

The rest of the paper is organized as follows: Sect. 2 investigates the state-of-the-art neural style transfer methods and knowledge distillation approaches. Section 3 elaborates the proposed knowledge distillation for real-time video style transfer. In Sect. 4, we provide extensive experiments to compare with state-of-the-art methods and perform ablation studies. Section 5 provides a brief conclusion of this paper and discusses future work.

## 2   Related Work

In this section, we briefly review the related work about neural style transfer and knowledge distillation.

### 2.1   Video Style Transfer

Neural style transfer is one of the most popular research hotspots in recent years. Gatys *et al.* [10,11] used CNN to iteratively reconstruct a stylized image by minimizing the difference between the target image, the content image and the style image in high-level features. These methods solve the optimization by backward propagation and are computationally expensive. To make the inference more efficient, Johnson *et al.* [22] proposed a feed-forward network to stylize images, which replaces the iterative process of optimizing pictures with the optimization of CNNs via training.

Video style transfer is attracting more and more research interests. Researchers tried to utilize the inter-frame temporal relation to improve the visual stability of stylized videos, specifically motion estimation based on optical flow. Ruder et al. [33] initialized the optimization of the current frame with stylized output of the previous frame and proposed temporal loss which uses optical flow to maintain inter-frame consistency. This image based optimization algorithm outputs a very stable video but costs about 3 min to process a frame even with precomputed optical flow. Therefore, fast video style transfer is mainly based on model optimization. Ruder et al. [34] proposed a framework to use optical flow both in the training stage and in the inference stage to improve temporal consistency of output stylized videos. This framework contains two networks. The first network obtains the first frame of the video as input and outputs the stylized result. The second network obtains three inputs, including the current frame, the previous stylized frame warped by the optical flow and the mask which indicates motion boundaries and outputs the stylized result of current frame. Similarly, the architecture in [2] utilized optical flow both in training stage and inference stage. All these methods [2, 34] got stable stylized video but can not be used for real-time video style transfer. To address this problem, another family of video style transfer methods [8, 19] utilize optical flow only in the training stage thus speed up the inference. These methods utilize similar temporal loss to train the feed-forward transform network to improve the temporal consistency of output videos. They get rid of computing optical flows on the fly but produce less stable stylized results than those networks that adopt optical flows during inference stage [19, 34]. Our method aims to mitigate the gap between optical flow based and optical flow free methods for video style transfer via knowledge distillation.

## 2.2   Knowledge Distillation

Knowledge distillation is a technique that leverages intrinsic information of teacher network to train a smaller one, which is first pioneered by Hinton et al. [18]. Since then many algorithms have been proposed to improve knowledge distillation [6, 16, 20, 32, 43]. Wang et al. [40] exploited generative adversarial network to encourage the student network to learn similar feature distribution with teacher network. Zagoruyko and Komodakis [44] proposed to utilize spatial attention for distilling intermediate latent features of the network. Heo et al. [17] proposed a novel activation transfer loss to distill knowledge of activation boundaries from the teacher network. Chen et al. [5] introduced the locality preserving loss to preserve relationships between samples in high dimensional features from teacher network and low dimensional features from student network. Knowledge distillation has also been adopted in many other applications, e.g., object detection [4, 23, 41], semantic segmentation [14, 21, 26] and pose regression [35, 38]. However, distilling knowledge from a stable video style transfer to a lightweight student network is not yet explored, which is the main purpose of this paper.

# 3   Method

Let $\mathcal{N}_T$ and $\mathcal{N}_S$ denote the teacher network and the desired student network, respectively. The teacher network [34] utilizes optical flow in both training and inference phase to increase the stability of video neural style transfer. Since the teacher network needs to calculate optical flow in inference phase, it is time-consuming and not suitable for real-time applications. Thus, the student network is expected to have no optical flow module. The lightweight student network gets rid of optical flow estimation in inference phase and thus runs much faster. We choose similar network architecture with ReCoNet [8] as our student network. The goal of the proposed optical flow knowledge distillation is to train the student network $\mathcal{N}_S$ with aid of teacher network $\mathcal{N}_T$, so that $\mathcal{N}_S$ obtains similar stability as $\mathcal{N}_T$ yet still runs fast since $\mathcal{N}_S$ does not compute optical flow on-the-fly during inference.

## 3.1   Preliminaries: Style Transfer Loss

Here we briefly revisit the perceptual loss introduced by Johnson *et al.* [22], which has been widely used for style transfer algorithms. The perceptual loss includes the content loss to encourage the output stylized image to have similar content representations with the input image, and the style loss to capture the style information. In addition, total variation regularization ($\mathcal{L}_{tv}$) is generally introduced to encourage spatial smoothness in the stylized images. Therefore, the basic style transfer perceptual loss contains three terms:

$$\mathcal{L}_{percep}(x, I_s) = \lambda_c \mathcal{L}_{content}(x, I_s) + \lambda_s \mathcal{L}_{style}(x, I_s) + \lambda_{tv} \mathcal{L}_{tv}(x, I_s), \qquad (1)$$

where $I_s$ is the given style image and $x$ is an input image. $\lambda_c$, $\lambda_s$ and $\lambda_{tv}$ are hyper parameters to balance three different losses. To simplify the notations, we omit the $I_s$ and denote the perceptual loss as $\mathcal{L}_{percep}(x)$ in the following sections.

This basic style transfer loss can be exploited to train a student network from scratch, which is denoted as $\tilde{\mathcal{N}}_S$. Since $\tilde{\mathcal{N}}_S$ is trained frame by frame, it suffers from flickering in consecutive frames and produces unstable stylized videos. Our goal is transferring the knowledge of a teacher network $\mathcal{N}_T$ to train the desired student network $\mathcal{N}_S$, so that student network produces coherent stylized videos.

## 3.2   Residual Distillation Loss

A straightforward way to train the desired student network $\mathcal{N}_S$ via knowledge distillation is directly using the output stylized image of teacher network to teach the student network, as shown in the following loss function:

$$\mathcal{L}_{vanilla}(x) = ||\mathcal{N}_T(x, f) - \mathcal{N}_S(x)||_2^2, \qquad (2)$$

where $\mathcal{N}_T(x, f)$ and $\mathcal{N}_S(x)$ are the output stylized images for input image $x$ of teacher network and student network respectively, $f$ is the corresponding optical flow.

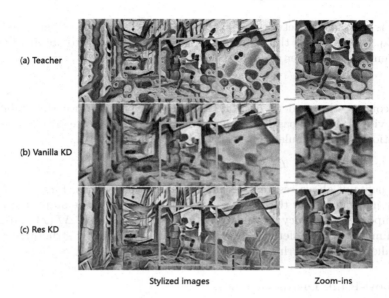

(a) Teacher

(b) Vanilla KD

(c) Res KD

Stylized images                    Zoom-ins

**Fig. 2.** (a) Output stylized frames from teacher network, (b) Results of student network with vanilla distillation loss and (c) Results of student network with residual distillation loss.

However, this strategy produces blurred stylized images, as shown in Fig. 2. The reasons behind are two folds. Firstly, it is a challenging optimization problem to force the output of student network to align with that of the teacher network at pixel level. More importantly, due to the difference of network architectures between student network and teacher network, the style of the output images from student network may slightly differ from those produced by teacher network. Therefore, directly distilling knowledge from the output stylized images of teacher network is hard to train a good student network.

To address the above problem, we propose the residual distillation loss for better knowledge distillation. Our goal is to train an optical flow free student network from the knowledge of an optical flow based teacher network. Therefore, the knowledge of the difference between teacher networks with and without optical flow is the key information to train a stable student network. Let $\tilde{\mathcal{N}}_T$ denotes the model similar to teacher model $\mathcal{N}_T$ but does not adopt optical flow for video style transfer and $\tilde{\mathcal{N}}_T(x)$ is the output of $\tilde{\mathcal{N}}_T$ for input image $x$. Obviously the output stylized video flickers since basically $\tilde{\mathcal{N}}_T$ just predicts stylized images frame by frame. The difference between the output of $\mathcal{N}_T$ and $\tilde{\mathcal{N}}_T$ is:

$$\Delta \mathcal{T}(x) = \mathcal{N}_T(x, f) - \tilde{\mathcal{N}}_T(x). \tag{3}$$

$\Delta \mathcal{T}(x)$ is attributed to additional temporal consistency that is brought by optical flows to the output stylized videos, which is the key information for student network to improve the stability.

$\tilde{\mathcal{N}}_S$ is the student network that is trained only using basic style transfer loss as in Eq. (1) and $\mathcal{N}_S$ is the stable student network we want to obtain. Thus the improvement of $\mathcal{N}_S$ over a vanilla baseline is:

$$\Delta \mathcal{S}(x) = \mathcal{N}_S(x) - \tilde{\mathcal{N}}_S(x). \tag{4}$$

We encourage the student network to learn how to improve the stability of output videos over the baseline model by forcing $\Delta \mathcal{S}$ to imitate $\Delta \mathcal{T}$. The residual distillation loss is formulated as follow:

$$\mathcal{L}_{res}(x) = ||\Delta \mathcal{T}(x) - \Delta \mathcal{S}(x)||_2^2. \tag{5}$$

The benefits of above residual distillation loss are two folds. Firstly, $\Delta \mathcal{T}(x)$ is the key information for the teacher network to become stable and could benefit the temporal consistency of student network. What's more, $\Delta \mathcal{T}(x)$ and $\Delta \mathcal{S}(x)$ have eliminated the difference of stylized images brought by structures, thus it could alleviate the blurring effect as shown in Fig. 2.

### 3.3   Low-Rank Distillation Loss

In the above section, Eq. (5) is proposed for distilling knowledge from teacher network for one frame. We further develop a distillation loss by exploiting the temporal property of the video.

For a stylized video that is temporally consistent and stable, the same regions that are not located at the occluded regions or motion boundaries are supposed to have similar stylized patterns and strokes. Therefore, a basic assumption for a stable stylized video is that the non-occluded regions should be low rank representations.

Suppose we have $K$ consecutive frames $\{x_t\}_{t=1}^K$ and the corresponding optical flows $\{f_t\}_{t=1}^K$, the output stylized frames from the student network are calculated as $\{\mathcal{N}_S(x_t)\}_{t=1}^K$. We warp all stylized frames to a specific frame $\mathcal{N}_S(x_\tau)$ using the optical flows, where $x_\tau$ is often chosen as the middle frame, i.e., $\tau = \lfloor K/2 \rfloor$. We denote the warped frames as $\mathcal{W}_{t \to \tau}(\mathcal{N}_S(x_t), f_t)$, where $\mathcal{W}_{t \to \tau}(\cdot)$ means warping the $t^{th}$ frame to $\tau^{th}$ frame. $\mathcal{M}_t$ is the occlusion mask for $x_t$, where 0 indicates the motion regions or boundaries and 1 indicates the traceable regions. In this way, if we put all traceable regions $\mathcal{R}_t = \mathcal{M}_t \odot \mathcal{W}_{t \to \tau}(\mathcal{N}_S(x_t), f_t)$ into a matrix $\mathcal{X}$, then $\mathcal{X}$ is low rank, i.e.,

$$\mathcal{X} = [vec(\mathcal{R}_0), \dots, vec(\mathcal{R}_K)]^T \in \mathbb{R}^{K \times L}, \tag{6}$$

where $L = H \times W$ is the number of pixels in the images and $vec(\cdot)$ means transforming a two dimensional image into a one-dimensional vector.

We can get the Singular Value Decomposition (SVD) of $\mathcal{X}$ by:

$$\mathcal{X} := \mathcal{U}\Sigma\mathcal{V}^T, \tag{7}$$

where $\mathcal{U} \in \mathbb{R}^{K \times K}$ and $\mathcal{V} \in \mathbb{R}^{L \times L}$ are orthogonal matrices and $\Sigma \in \mathbb{R}^{K \times L}$ is the singular value matrix. The diagonal elements in $\Sigma$ are singular values $\Gamma = \{\gamma_0, \dots, \gamma_K\}$ of the matrix $\mathcal{X}$. The rank of $\mathcal{X}$ is calculated as:

$$\text{rank}(\mathcal{X}) = \sum_i^K \mathbb{I}(\gamma_i > 0), \tag{8}$$

where $\mathbb{I}(\cdot)$ is the indicator function.

However, the rank of a matrix is a non-differentiable function and can not directly be optimized via CNNs. Therefore, we instead adopt nuclear norm of $\mathcal{X}$, which is a convex relaxation of the rank function. The nuclear norm $||\cdot||_*$ is given by:

$$||\mathcal{X}||_* = \sum_i^K \gamma_i. \tag{9}$$

where $\gamma_i$ is the $i^{th}$ singular value of $\mathcal{X}$.

We expect that the rank of output stylized videos from student network should be similar with the stable videos. Intuitively, a straightforward way is to encourage the student network to imitate the nuclear norm of teacher network by the following low-rank distillation loss:

$$\mathcal{L}_{rank}^T = (||\mathcal{X}_T||_* - ||\mathcal{X}_S||_*)^2, \tag{10}$$

where $||\mathcal{X}_T||_*$ and $||\mathcal{X}_S||_*$ are nuclear norms of output stylized videos from teacher network and student network, respectively. Distilling knowledge of low rank from teacher network may help to improve the results of student network. However, the stability of output videos from the teacher network is still worse than the input videos. The stability of input video is a better teacher for the student network. To this end, we propose to distill the rank of input videos to train the student network by the following distillation loss:

$$\mathcal{L}_{rank}^{input} = (||\mathcal{X}_{input}||_* - ||\mathcal{X}_S||_*)^2, \tag{11}$$

where $||\mathcal{X}_{input}||_*$ is the nuclear norm of the input video. We utilize $\mathcal{L}_{rank}^{input}$ to train the student network and will further discuss the different low rank losses in experiments.

### 3.4  Optimization

Temporal consistency loss imposes constraints on consecutive output frames and is widely used in prior methods [2,8,19], which is formulated as follows:

$$\mathcal{L}_{temp}(x_t, x_{t-1}, f_t) = ||\mathcal{M}_t \odot (\mathcal{N}_S(x_t) - \mathcal{W}_{t-1 \to t}(\mathcal{N}_S(x_{t-1}), f_t))||_2^2. \tag{12}$$

Using temporal loss improves the temporal consistency of student network and thus serves as a stronger baseline than vanilla perceptual loss. We will demonstrate the effectiveness of our proposed method on both two baselines in experiments.

To train student network with perceptual loss or residual distillation loss, the network only needs the current input frame. However, calculating low rank loss and temporal loss needs $K$ consecutive frames. Suppose the input video

---

**Algorithm 1.** Optical Flow Knowledge Distillation.

---

**Input:** A given teacher network $\mathcal{N}_T$, a given vanilla teacher network $\tilde{\mathcal{N}}_T$ that is similar with $\mathcal{N}_T$ but does not use optical flow, a student network that is trained from scratch $\tilde{\mathcal{N}}_S$, a style image $I_{style}$, the training set $\{x^i, f^i\}_{i=1}^N$ where $x^i = \{x_t^i\}_{t=1}^K$ and $f^i = \{f_t^i\}_{t=1}^K$ are input images and optical flows, respectively.

1: Initialize a neural network $\mathcal{N}_S$, which does not need to compute optical flows during inference.

2: **repeat**

3:   Randomly select a batch of training data $\{x^i, f^i\}_{i=1}^m$.

4:   **Residual Distillation Loss**

5:   Employ teacher network $\mathcal{N}_T$ and $\tilde{\mathcal{N}}_T$ on the mini-batch and calculate Eq. (3).
$$\Delta T(x) \leftarrow \mathcal{N}_T(x, f) - \tilde{\mathcal{N}}_T(x)$$

6:   Employ student network $\mathcal{N}_S$ and $\tilde{\mathcal{N}}_S$ on the mini-batch and calculate Eq. (4).
$$\Delta S(x) \leftarrow \mathcal{N}_S(x) - \tilde{\mathcal{N}}_S(x)$$

7:   Calculate the loss function $\mathcal{L}_{res}$ according to Eq. (5).

8:   **Baseline Loss**

9:   Calculate perceptual loss $\mathcal{L}_{percrp}$ according to Eq. (1).

10:  Calculate the temporal loss function $\mathcal{L}_{temp}$ according to Eq. (12).

11:  **Low-Rank Distillation Loss**

12:  Calculate the nuclear norm $\|\mathcal{X}_{input}\|_*$ of input videos.

13:  Calculate the nuclear norm $\|\mathcal{X}_S\|_*$ of output videos from student network $\mathcal{N}_S$.

14:  Calculate low rank loss $\mathcal{L}_{rank}^{input}$ according to Eq. (11).

15:  **Total Loss and Back Propagation**

16:  Calculate the total loss function $\mathcal{L}_{total}$ according to Eq. (13).

17:  Update weights in $\mathcal{N}_S$ using gradient descent;

18: **until** convergence

**Output:** The student network $\mathcal{N}_S$.

---

segments are $x = \{x_t\}_{t=1}^K$ and the corresponding optical flows are $f = \{f_t\}_{t=1}^K$. The desired student network can be optimized using the total distillation loss as follow:

$$\mathcal{L}_{total}(x, f) = \sum_{t=1}^K (\mathcal{L}_{percep}(x_t) + \lambda_{res}\mathcal{L}_{res}(x_t))$$

$$+ \sum_{t=2}^K \lambda_{temp}\mathcal{L}_{temp}(x_t, x_{t-1}, f_t) + \lambda_{rank}\mathcal{L}_{rank}^{input}(x, f), \qquad (13)$$

where $\lambda_{res}$, $\lambda_{temp}$ and $\lambda_{rank}$ are hyper parameters to balance different terms of losses.

The $\mathcal{L}_{percep}$ and $\mathcal{L}_{temp}$ in Eq. (13) are used as our baseline for training the student network from scratch. We will explore the baseline with and without the temporal loss. The other two terms are knowledge distillation losses proposed in this paper and we will demonstrate in experiments that these distillation losses improve the stability of output stylized videos.

# 4    Experiments

In this section, we will demonstrate the effectiveness of our proposed knowledge distillation for lightweight video style transfer network. In addition, we will provide extensive ablation experiments to discuss the impact of different components in our proposed method.

## 4.1    Experimental Settings

We use the Hollywood2 video scene dataset [31] as the training data and evaluate our method on MPI Sintel dataset [1]. We follow the same data preprocessing methods as in [34] and randomly sample 2000 tuples consisting of 5 consecutive frames from Hollywood2 dataset. MPI Sintel dataset provides ground truth optical flow and occlusion masks, which is widely used for the task of optical flow estimation and is also adopted to evaluate the temporal consistency of video style transfer. Following prior work [8,19,34], we evaluate our method on five videos in the MPI Sintel dataset.

During training all frames are downscaled to $640 \times 360$ and the input size for evaluation is $1024 \times 436$. We train the student network with learning rate of $10^{-3}$ and a batch size of 1 using Adam optimizer for 10 epochs. The learning rate is decayed by 1.2 in every 500 iterations. The hyper-parameters in Eq. (13) are set to be $K = 5$, $\lambda_{res} = 4 \times 10^8$, $\lambda_{temp} = 1 \times 10^6$ and $\lambda_{rank} = 1 \times 10^2$.

Following the quantitative evaluation metric in prior methods [2,8,19], we utilize $e_{stab}$ to evaluate the temporal consistency of the output stylized videos. $e_{stab}$ is the square root of temporal errors between consecutive frames for the traceable regions of the videos:

$$e_{stab} = \sqrt{\frac{1}{N} \sum_{t=1}^{N} \frac{1}{D} ||\mathcal{M}_t \odot (y_t - \mathcal{W}(y_{t-1}))||_2}, \tag{14}$$

where $N$ is the number of frames in the testing video, $y_t$ and $y_{t-1}$ are output stylized images for frame $t$ and $t - 1$ respectively, $D$ is the number of pixels of output stylized image.

## 4.2    Experimental Resutls

***Quantitative Analysis.*** We compare our proposed methods with other video style transfer networks with style *Candy* on five scenes from MPI Sintel Dataset. The temporal error $e_{stab}$ is calculated as Eq. (14) and is used to indicate the temporal consistency of output stylized videos. Output videos with smaller values of $e_{stab}$ are more stable. All inference speeds are evaluated on NVIDIA Tesla P100 GPU with the input size of $640 \times 320$.

As shown in Table 1, our proposed method consistently outperforms student baselines that are trained from scratch. For example, when we choose student

**Table 1.** Comparisons of different methods for temporal error $e_{stab}$ and speed ($FPS$) with style *Candy* on five scenes from *MPI Sintel* Dataset. [†]Numbers are quoted from [8].

| Models | Alley_2 | Ambush_5 | Bandage_2 | Market_6 | Temple_2 | Sum | FPS |
|---|---|---|---|---|---|---|---|
| Teacher [34] | 0.0560 | 0.0751 | 0.0489 | 0.0956 | 0.0679 | 0.3435 | 4.67 |
| Student [8] | | | | | | | |
| - From scratch | 0.0746 | 0.0887 | 0.0575 | 0.0997 | 0.0815 | 0.4019 | **183** |
| - Ours | **0.0524** | **0.0676** | **0.0445** | **0.0779** | **0.0627** | **0.3050** | 183 |
| Student [8] w/ $\mathcal{L}_{temp}$ | | | | | | | |
| - From scratch | 0.0701 | 0.0844 | 0.0535 | 0.0948 | 0.0758 | 0.3787 | **183** |
| - Ours | **0.0506** | **0.0643** | **0.0423** | **0.0770** | **0.0596** | **0.2938** | 183 |
| Chen et al. [2][†] | 0.0934 | 0.1352 | 0.0715 | 0.103 | 0.1094 | 0.5125 | 17.5 |
| Ruder et al. [33][†] | 0.0252 | 0.0512 | 0.0195 | 0.0407 | 0.0361 | 0.1727 | 0.62 |

**Table 2.** Temporal error $e_{stab}$ with style *Candy* for networks with different distillation losses.

| Models | Alley_2 | Ambush_5 | Bandage_2 | Market_6 | Temple_2 | Sum |
|---|---|---|---|---|---|---|
| Student | 0.0746 | 0.0887 | 0.0575 | 0.0997 | 0.0815 | 0.4019 |
| + $\mathcal{L}_{res}$ | 0.0606 | 0.0764 | 0.0493 | 0.0870 | 0.0691 | 0.3424 |
| + $\mathcal{L}_{rank}^{input}$ | 0.0716 | 0.0862 | 0.0554 | 0.0950 | 0.0773 | 0.3855 |
| + $\mathcal{L}_{res}$ + $\mathcal{L}_{rank}^{input}$ | **0.0524** | **0.0676** | **0.0445** | **0.0779** | **0.0627** | **0.3050** |
| + $\mathcal{L}_{res}$ + $\mathcal{L}_{rank}^{T}$ | 0.0601 | 0.0755 | 0.0488 | 0.0882 | 0.0689 | 0.3415 |
| Student w/ $\mathcal{L}_{temp}$ | 0.0701 | 0.0844 | 0.0535 | 0.0948 | 0.0758 | 0.3787 |
| + $\mathcal{L}_{res}$ | 0.0574 | 0.0729 | 0.0483 | 0.0870 | 0.0661 | 0.3317 |
| + $\mathcal{L}_{res}$ + $\mathcal{L}_{rank}^{input}$ | **0.0506** | **0.0643** | **0.0423** | **0.0770** | **0.0596** | **0.2938** |

network with only perceptual loss as baseline, training it with our proposed distillation losses improves $e_{stab}$ from 0.4019 to 0.3050. To further investigate the effectiveness of our proposed method, we then switch to a strong baseline, *i.e.*, using perceptual loss and temporal loss to train the student network. Training it from scratch using additional temporal loss gets more stable results. Nevertheless, our proposed method outperforms the vanilla student by a 22.4% improvement for $e_{stab}$. When compared with the teacher network [34], our method achieves similar or better temporal consistency and runs much faster, since our method gets rid of time-consuming optical flow calculation during inference stage.

We further compare our proposed methods with state-of-the-art video style transfer methods [2,33]. Table 1 shows that our method outperforms Chen *et al.* [2] for both temporal error $e_{stab}$ and running speed. Ruder *et al.* [33] obtained smaller temporal error than our methods. However, it runs orders of magnitudes slower than our network.

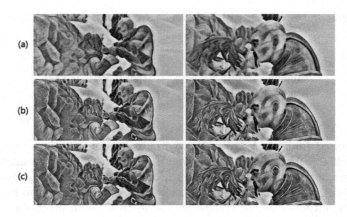

**Fig. 3.** Training the student network with (a) vanilla distillation loss $\mathcal{L}_{vanilla}$, (b) residual distillation loss $\mathcal{L}_{res}$ and (c) residual distillation loss and perceptual loss $\mathcal{L}_{percep} + \mathcal{L}_{res}$.

*Qualitative Analysis.* Qualitative results of different methods are shown in Fig. 4. The first row shows two consecutive frames from the Alley_2 scene of MPI Sintel Dataset. In this video, the viewpoint of the camera is continually changing. Meanwhile, only the person in the video moves and background regions remain unchanged. Figure 4 (b) shows the temporal consistency error of the baseline student network, *i.e.*, which is trained from scratch with perceptual loss. It shows that the student baseline produces less temporally consistent stylized frames. The results of our method are shown in Fig. 4 (c) and achieve better temporal consistency. A stronger student baseline, *i.e.*, trained with additional temporal loss, performs slightly better than the counterpart without temporal loss. Nevertheless, our method still obtains higher temporal consistency, which demonstrates the effectiveness of our proposed method.

### 4.3 Ablation Studies

*Impacts of Distillation Loss.* We first examine the impact of our proposed distillation losses, *i.e.*, residual distillation loss $\mathcal{L}_{res}$ and low rank loss $\mathcal{L}_{rank}^{input}$. As shown in Table 2, residual distillation loss reduces $e_{stab}$ by 15%. Adding low-rank distillation loss to the baseline network improve $e_{stab}$ from 0.4019 to 0.3855. Furthermore, utilizing low rank loss along with residual distillation loss reduces $e_{stab}$ by 24%. For a stronger baseline student network that adopts temporal loss, residual distillation loss and low rank loss harvest consistent improvements. These experimental results demonstrate that our proposed distillation losses effectively improve the stability of output stylized videos.

**Table 3.** Temporal error $e_{stab}$ with style *Candy* for different $K$ frames to calculate low rank loss.

| K | 3 | 4 | 5 |
|---|---|---|---|
| Student (Ours) | 0.3158 | 0.3061 | 0.3050 |
| Student w/ $\mathcal{L}_{temp}$ (Ours) | 0.2986 | 0.2950 | 0.2938 |

*Discussion of Low-rank Loss.* As we discuss in Sect. 3.3, there are two different design choices for low-rank distillation loss, *i.e.*, distilling low-rank knowledge from teacher network ($\mathcal{L}_{rank}^{T}$) and from input videos ($\mathcal{L}_{rank}^{input}$). As shown in the fifth and sixth row in Table 2, learning low-rank information from input videos significantly outperforms the counterpart of learning from teacher network. It's not surprising since the stability of input videos is better than output videos of teacher network. Therefore, distilling low-rank information from input videos helps to improve the temporal consistency of student network.

*Residual KD vs. Vanilla KD.* As we have discussed in Sect. 3.2, it's difficult to learn directly from the output of teacher network and thus produces blurry stylized images. As shown in Fig. 3 (a) and (b), and also in Fig. 2, training student network with $\mathcal{L}_{res}$ in Eq. (5) significantly improves the quality of stylized images compared with $\mathcal{L}_{vanilla}$ in Eq. (2).

*The Impact of Perceptual Loss.* An intuitive question is that, can we simply train the student network with only the information of teacher network? Figure 3 shows that even if residual distillation loss alleviates the blurring problem, it is still not satisfying without the perceptual loss. Combining residual distillation loss and perceptual loss obtains better results with sharp edges and good style patterns. It is a reasonable observation since the task of style transfer has no groundtruth labels and it is difficult to force the student network to produce aligned outputs with teacher network in pixel-level. Therefore, the perceptual loss is still critical for the task of video style transfer knowledge distillation.

*Impact of $K$.* Here we discuss the impact of hyper parameter $K$, *i.e.*, the number of frames to calculate low rank loss. As shown in Table 3, increasing $K$ from 3 to 4 slightly improves the temporal consistency of the output stylized videos. Further increasing $K$ to 5 obtains nearly saturated improvement. To balance the performance and training cost, we choose $K = 5$ in our experiments.

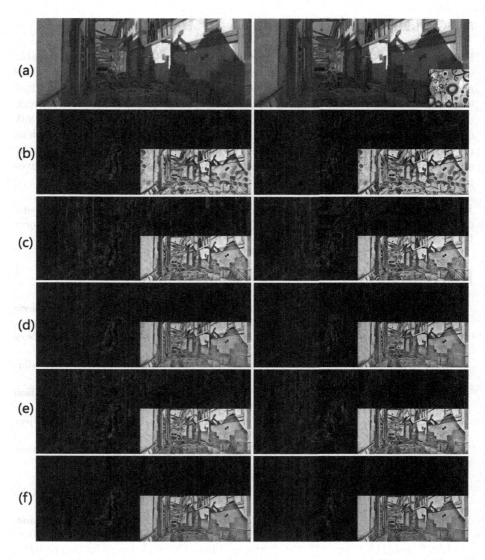

**Fig. 4.** Qualitative results of different methods. (a) Two consecutive input video frames from MPI Sintel Alley_2 scene. The following rows show the temporal consistency errors of (b) Teacher network, (c) Student network trained from scratch, (d) Student network by our method, (e) Student network trained from scratch with additional $\mathcal{L}_{temp}$ and (f) Student network by our method with additional $\mathcal{L}_{temp}$. The temporal errors increase as shown from black to white in gray scale. Best viewed on screen.

## 5  Conclusion

In this paper, we propose a novel method to distill knowledge from a stable video style transfer network with optical flow to a lightweight network that does not require optical flow during inference. In particular, we propose the residual loss to encourage student network to learn knowledge of the difference between the teacher networks with and without optical flow. Additionally, the low rank distillation loss is exploited to constrain the output stylized videos of student network to mimic the low rank of input videos, thus to further improve the stability. Extensive experiments demonstrate that our proposed method achieves pleasing and stable stylized videos in high inference speed.

**Acknowledgments.** We thank anonymous reviewers for their helpful comments. Chang Xu was supported by the Australian Research Council under Project DE180101438.

## References

1. Butler, D.J., Wulff, J., Stanley, G.B., Black, M.J.: A naturalistic open source movie for optical flow evaluation. In: Fitzgibbon, A., Lazebnik, S., Perona, P., Sato, Y., Schmid, C. (eds.) ECCV 2012. LNCS, vol. 7577, pp. 611–625. Springer, Heidelberg (2012). https://doi.org/10.1007/978-3-642-33783-3_44
2. Chen, D., Liao, J., Yuan, L., Yu, N., Hua, G.: Coherent online video style transfer. In: ICCV, pp. 1105–1114 (2017)
3. Chen, D., Yuan, L., Liao, J., Yu, N., Hua, G.: Stylebank: an explicit representation for neural image style transfer. In: CVPR, pp. 1897–1906 (2017)
4. Chen, G., Choi, W., Yu, X., Han, T., Chandraker, M.: Learning efficient object detection models with knowledge distillation. In: NIPS, pp. 742–751 (2017)
5. Chen, H., Wang, Y., Xu, C., Xu, C., Tao, D.: Learning student networks via feature embedding. TNNLS (2020)
6. Chen, H., et al.: Data-free learning of student networks. In: ICCV (2019)
7. Dumoulin, V., Shlens, J., Kudlur, M.: A learned representation for artistic style. In: ICLR (2017)
8. Gao, C., Gu, D., Zhang, F., Yu, Y.: ReCoNet: real-time coherent video style transfer network. In: Jawahar, C.V., Li, H., Mori, G., Schindler, K. (eds.) ACCV 2018. LNCS, vol. 11366, pp. 637–653. Springer, Cham (2019). https://doi.org/10.1007/978-3-030-20876-9_40
9. Gao, W., Li, Y., Yin, Y., Yang, M.H.: Fast video multi-style transfer. In: WACV, pp. 3222–3230 (2020)
10. Gatys, L.A., Ecker, A.S., Bethge, M.: A neural algorithm of artistic style. arXiv preprint arXiv:1508.06576 (2015)
11. Gatys, L.A., Ecker, A.S., Bethge, M.: Image style transfer using convolutional neural networks. In: CVPR, pp. 2414–2423 (2016)
12. Gong, X., Chang, S., Jiang, Y., Wang, Z.: Autogan: neural architecture search for generative adversarial networks. In: ICCV, pp. 3224–3234 (2019)
13. Gupta, A., Johnson, J., Alahi, A., Fei-Fei, L.: Characterizing and improving stability in neural style transfer. In: ICCV, pp. 4067–4076 (2017)

14. He, T., Shen, C., Tian, Z., Gong, D., Sun, C., Yan, Y.: Knowledge adaptation for efficient semantic segmentation. In: CVPR, pp. 578–587 (2019)
15. He, Y., Zhang, X., Sun, J.: Channel pruning for accelerating very deep neural networks. In: ICCV (2017)
16. Heo, B., Kim, J., Yun, S., Park, H., Kwak, N., Choi, J.Y.: A comprehensive overhaul of feature distillation. In: ICCV, pp. 1921–1930 (2019)
17. Heo, B., Lee, M., Yun, S., Choi, J.Y.: Knowledge transfer via distillation of activation boundaries formed by hidden neurons. In: AAAI, vol. 33, pp. 3779–3787 (2019)
18. Hinton, G., Vinyals, O., Dean, J.: Distilling the knowledge in a neural network. arXiv preprint arXiv:1503.02531 (2015)
19. Huang, H., et al.: Real-time neural style transfer for videos. In: CVPR, pp. 783–791 (2017)
20. Huang, Z., Wang, N.: Like what you like: Knowledge distill via neuron selectivity transfer. arXiv preprint arXiv:1707.01219 (2017)
21. Jiao, J., Wei, Y., Jie, Z., Shi, H., Lau, R.W., Huang, T.S.: Geometry-aware distillation for indoor semantic segmentation. In: CVPR, pp. 2869–2878 (2019)
22. Johnson, J., Alahi, A., Fei-Fei, L.: Perceptual losses for real-time style transfer and super-resolution. In: Leibe, B., Matas, J., Sebe, N., Welling, M. (eds.) ECCV 2016. LNCS, vol. 9906, pp. 694–711. Springer, Cham (2016). https://doi.org/10.1007/978-3-319-46475-6_43
23. Li, Q., Jin, S., Yan, J.: Mimicking very efficient network for object detection. In: CVPR, pp. 6356–6364 (2017)
24. Li, Y., Fang, C., Yang, J., Wang, Z., Lu, X., Yang, M.H.: Universal style transfer via feature transforms. In: NIPS, pp. 386–396 (2017)
25. Liao, J., Yao, Y., Yuan, L., Hua, G., Kang, S.B.: Visual attribute transfer through deep image analogy. ACM Trans. Graph. (TOG) **36**(4), 1–15 (2017)
26. Liu, Y., Chen, K., Liu, C., Qin, Z., Luo, Z., Wang, J.: Structured knowledge distillation for semantic segmentation. In: CVPR, pp. 2604–2613 (2019)
27. Liu, Z., Wu, B., Luo, W., Yang, X., Liu, W., Cheng, K.-T.: Bi-real net: enhancing the performance of 1-Bit CNNs with improved representational capability and advanced training algorithm. In: Ferrari, V., Hebert, M., Sminchisescu, C., Weiss, Y. (eds.) ECCV 2018. LNCS, vol. 11219, pp. 747–763. Springer, Cham (2018). https://doi.org/10.1007/978-3-030-01267-0_44
28. Liu, Z., Sun, M., Zhou, T., Huang, G., Darrell, T.: Rethinking the value of network pruning. In: ICLR (2019)
29. Lu, M., Zhao, H., Yao, A., Chen, Y., Xu, F., Zhang, L.: A closed-form solution to universal style transfer. In: ICCV, October 2019
30. Lu, M., Zhao, H., Yao, A., Xu, F., Chen, Y., Zhang, L.: Decoder network over lightweight reconstructed feature for fast semantic style transfer. In: ICCV, pp. 2469–2477 (2017)
31. Marszałek, M., Laptev, I., Schmid, C.: Actions in context. In: CVPR, pp. 2929–2936. IEEE Computer Society (2009)
32. Romero, A., Ballas, N., Kahou, S.E., Chassang, A., Gatta, C., Bengio, Y.: Fitnets: hints for thin deep nets. In: ICLR (2015)
33. Ruder, M., Dosovitskiy, A., Brox, T.: Artistic style transfer for videos. In: Rosenhahn, B., Andres, B. (eds.) GCPR 2016. LNCS, vol. 9796, pp. 26–36. Springer, Cham (2016). https://doi.org/10.1007/978-3-319-45886-1_3
34. Ruder, M., Dosovitskiy, A., Brox, T.: Artistic style transfer for videos and spherical images. IJCV **126**(11), 1199–1219 (2018)

35. Saputra, M.R.U., de Gusmao, P.P., Almalioglu, Y., Markham, A., Trigoni, N.: Distilling knowledge from a deep pose regressor network. In: ICCV (2019)
36. Shen, M., Han, K., Xu, C., Wang, Y.: Searching for accurate binary neural architectures. In: ICCV Neural Architects Workshop (2019)
37. Shu, H., et al.: Co-evolutionary compression for unpaired image translation. In: ICCV, pp. 3235–3244 (2019)
38. Wang, C., Kong, C., Lucey, S.: Distill knowledge from NRSfM for weakly supervised 3D pose learning. In: ICCV, pp. 743–752 (2019)
39. Wang, W., Xu, J., Zhang, L., Wang, Y., Liu, J.: Consistent video style transfer via compound regularization. In: AAAI, pp. 12233–12240 (2020)
40. Wang, Y., Xu, C., Xu, C., Tao, D.: Adversarial learning of portable student networks. In: AAAI (2018)
41. Wei, Y., Pan, X., Qin, H., Ouyang, W., Yan, J.: Quantization mimic: towards very tiny CNN for object detection. In: Ferrari, V., Hebert, M., Sminchisescu, C., Weiss, Y. (eds.) ECCV 2018. LNCS, vol. 11212, pp. 274–290. Springer, Cham (2018). https://doi.org/10.1007/978-3-030-01237-3_17
42. Yang, Z., et al.: Cars: continuous evolution for efficient neural architecture search. In: CVPR, pp. 1829–1838 (2020)
43. Yim, J., Joo, D., Bae, J., Kim, J.: A gift from knowledge distillation: fast optimization, network minimization and transfer learning. In: CVPR, pp. 4133–4141 (2017)
44. Zagoruyko, S., Komodakis, N.: Paying more attention to attention: improving the performance of convolutional neural networks via attention transfer. In: ICLR (2017)
45. Zhou, S., Wu, Y., Ni, Z., Zhou, X., Wen, H., Zou, Y.: DoReFa-Net: Training low bitwidth convolutional neural networks with low bitwidth gradients. arXiv preprint arXiv:1606.06160 (2016)

# Collaboration by Competition: Self-coordinated Knowledge Amalgamation for Multi-talent Student Learning

Sihui Luo[1], Wenwen Pan[1], Xinchao Wang[2], Dazhou Wang[3], Haihong Tang[3], and Mingli Song[1(✉)]

[1] Zhejiang University, Hangzhou, China
{sihuiluo829,wenwenpan,brooksong}@zju.edu.cn
[2] Stevens Institute of Technology, Hoboken, NJ, USA
xinchao.wang@stevens.edu
[3] Alibaba Group, Hangzhou, China
{dazhou.wangdz,piaoxue}@alibaba-inc.com

**Abstract.** A vast number of well-trained deep networks have been released by developers online for plug-and-play use. These networks specialize in different tasks and in many cases, the data and annotations used to train them are not publicly available. In this paper, we study how to reuse such heterogeneous pre-trained models as teachers, and build a versatile and compact student model, without accessing human annotations. To this end, we propose a self-coordinate knowledge amalgamation network (SOKA-Net) for learning the multi-talent student model. This is achieved via a dual-step adaptive competitive-cooperation training approach, where the knowledge of the heterogeneous teachers are in the first step amalgamated to guide the shared parameter learning of the student network, and followed by a gradient-based competition-balancing strategy to learn the multi-head prediction network as well as the loss weightings of the distinct tasks in the second step. The two steps, which we term as the collaboration and competition step respectively, are performed alternatively until the balance of the competition is reached for the ultimate collaboration. Experimental results demonstrate that, the learned student not only comes with a smaller size but achieves performances on par with or even superior to those of the teachers.

**Keywords:** Knowledge amalgamation · Competitive collaboration

**Electronic supplementary material** The online version of this chapter (https://doi.org/10.1007/978-3-030-58539-6_38) contains supplementary material, which is available to authorized users.

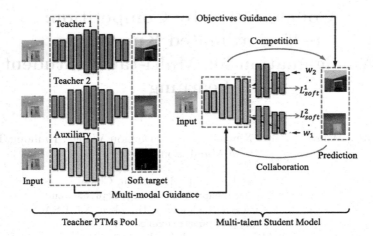

**Fig. 1.** Illustration of self-coordinated knowledge amalgamation pipeline.

# 1   Introduction

Driven by the recent advances of deep learning, remarkable progress has been made in almost all the research areas of computer vision. The unprecedentedly prominent results, nevertheless, are made possible by the immense number of annotations and hundreds or even thousands of GPU hours spent to train the deep models. To save the reproducing effort, many researchers have, therefore, generously published their pre-trained models (PTMs) online. Yet in many cases, such publicly available PTMs come without the training annotations, due to for example the data privacy issues.

In this paper, we study how to exploit PTMs that handle distinct tasks, to learn a multi-talent and compact student model, without accessing human annotations. Specifically, given a pool of heterogeneous PTMs, such as Taskonomy [34], we allow the user to pick any combination of the models from the same family, in our case autoencoder networks, and then customize a student that simultaneously tackles the distinct tasks of the selected teachers. The student training process is, again, free of human annotations. Once trained, the student not only comes with a size considerably smaller than the sum of the teachers, but also preserves and even at times surpasses performances of the teachers.

To this end, we introduce a novel strategy that treats the distinct tasks handled by the teachers as competing counterparts, and devise a *collaboration-by-competition* approach to amalgamating their heterogeneous knowledge and building the multi-talent student. In other words, different tasks compete for the student network resources to be allocated for themselves, in which process they also share features, collaborate with and benefit each other. Such collaboration-by-competition scheme leads to an adaptive loss function, of which the balance between the multiple tasks of interest is *learned* rather than handcrafted.

The proposed approach is therefore named as self-coordinated knowledge amalgamation (SOKA). The student training is achieved via a dual-step competitive-cooperation approach, where the correlated multi-modal information of the teacher models are in the first step amalgamated to guide the shared parameter learning of the student network, and followed by a competition balancing strategy to learn the multi-head prediction sub-network in the second step. The overall pipeline of the proposed SOKA is illustrated in Fig. 1.

Specifically, we adopt as teacher models some pixel-to-pixel task-specific PTMs, in our case the public available ones from Taskonomy. The intermediate representations of PTMs are utilized to guide the training of the features of the student, which are to be shared by the different tasks. The shared features are then used to train the final target task through a multi-head prediction sub-network, in which the gradient based loss balancing method is used to balance the competition of the terminal target tasks. Both the network and the weight of the target task are learnable in the alternative learning process, until the final collaboration of the task involved are reached.

As aforementioned, the customized network can be amalgamated from any combination of the models selected by the user from the same family, and thus the tasks involved may not be in strong interconnection. To this end, we seek for additional intermediate supervising information to guide the training of the student. We found that, as will be demonstrated in our experiments, cross modal information can serve as extra guidance in supervising the training of unlabeled data for learning more robust representation. Therefore, we introduce an auxiliary PTM, which specializes in an intermediate task close to both teachers, to providing extra-modal supervision for learning a robust shared representation of the student network. In the case of Fig. 1, for example, we take the edge 3D (occlusion edges) extracting task to be the auxiliary task to facilitate the training of surface normal and depth estimation.

Our contribution is thus summarized as follows.

- We propose a self-coordinate knowledge amalgamation method for generating a customized multi-talent student network, by reusing heterogeneous pretrained models without accessing the human annotations. This is achieved, specifically, via a novel competitive-collaboration strategy, in which both the parameters of the student network and the task-wise loss weightings are learnable.
- To bridge the potential semantic gaps between the heterogeneous tasks, we introduce an auxiliary model, which are inter-correlated to both target tasks of interest, to provide extra-modal supervision.
- We conduct a series of experiments on various combinations of PTMs set, from which we train multi-talent student models. Our results demonstrate that, the student model, which comes with a compact size, achieves results on par and at times even superior to those of the teachers.

## 2   Related Work

**Multi-task Learning.** Deep multi-task learning (MTL) [4,10,13,17,18] has been widely used in various computer vision problems, such as joint inference scene geometric and semantic [15], simultaneous depth estimation, surface normals and semantic segmentation [6]. It is typically conducted via hard or soft parameter sharing. In hard parameter sharing, a subset of the parameters is shared between tasks while other parameters are task-specific. In soft parameter sharing, all parameters are task-specific but they are jointly constrained via Bayesian priors. However, most multi-task methods requires ground truth data which are either impractical or expensive to gather. Some researchers [15] have recently introduced competitive collaboration mechanism to unsupervised multi task learning for some complex geometric coupled vision tasks. Though the authors have demonstrated promising results, the balance of the task are driven by massive hand-crafted hyper-parameters. In contrast, our approach, which assume no manually labelled annotation are available, adopts gradient based loss balancing scheme in competition-collaboration training cycle, which is adaptive and requires much fewer hyperparameter.

**Knowledge Distillation.** Knowledge distillation (KD) [8,9,29,35] adopts a teacher-guiding student strategy where a small student network learns to imitate the output of a large and deeper teacher network. In this way, the large teacher can transfer knowledge to the student with smaller model size, which is widely applied to model compression [32]. Following [8], some works are proposed to exploit the intermediate representation to optimize the learning of student network, such as FitNet [16], DK2PNet [27], AT [33] and NST [26]. Albeit many heuristics are found by these works, most knowledge distillation methods fall into single-teacher single-student manner, where the teacher and the student handles the same task. Recently, some researches [12,20,30,31] started to investigate how to transfer knowledge from multiple trained models into a single one with unlabeled dataset. They generally adopted an auto-encoder architecture to amalgamate features from multiple single-task teachers in a layerwise manner. [21] customized the student network by generating component nets as byproducts for attribute learning tasks. [12] proposed a common feature learning approach for learning the student from heterogeneous-architecture teachers. These methods generally focus on designing better teacher-student learning architecture. In contrast, the proposed method aims at adaptive balancing of the target task learning and seek the collaboration of the target tasks by self-coordinated training strategy.

**Model Transferability.** Transfer learning [3,14], is similar to multi-task learning in that solutions are learned for multiple tasks. Unlike multi-task learning, however, transfer learning methods first learn a model for a source task and then adapt that model to a target task. Razavian et al. [19] demonstrated that features extracted from deep neural networks could be used as generic image representations to tackle the diverse range of visual tasks. Azizpour et al. [2] studied several factors affecting the transferability of deep features. Albeit many heuristics are found by these works, none of them explicitly quantify the transferability among different tasks and layers to provide a principled way for model selection. Recently, Taskonomy [34] aimed to find the underlying task relatedness by computing the transfer performance among tasks. This was followed by

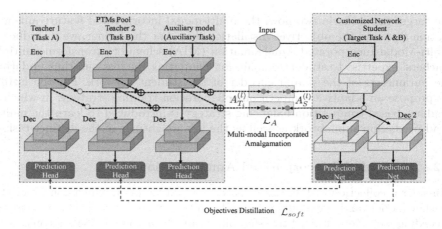

**Fig. 2.** Illustration of the proposed SOKA for customizing pixel2pixel multi-task network with unlabeled data. The student learns both the predictions and the intermediate representation from multiple teacher models in the PTMs pool. Auxiliary PTM, which is specialized at task strongly correlated to the target ones, is utilized to incorporate the teacher PTMs for providing multi-modal information in training more robust representation of the student network. Losses of representation transfer and objectives distillation are penalized to train the parameter of the student network.

a number of recent works, which further analyzed task relationships [1,5,17,22–24] for transfer learning. RSA [5] adopted representation similarity analysis to find relationship between visual tasks for efficient task taxonomy. [13] utilizes the mid-level representations from the labeled modality to supervise learning representations on the paired unlabeled modality. Model transferability provides the quantified evaluation of how connected the vision task are and it inspires us at introducing such evaluation to decide which auxiliary model can reinforce the target tasks via joint learning.

## 3    Self-coordinated Knowledge Amalgamation

In this section, we describe the proposed approach of Self-coordinated Knowledge Amalgamation (SOKA), which enables customizing a student network from coupled PTMs without accessing annotations. Specifically, we build SOKA by a multi-head encoder-decoder network, allowing for dense pixel-level prediction tasks, such as depth and surface-normal prediction. Our training, as will be demonstrated in the following section, is achieved via a novel strategy that learns the parameters of the student intertwined with those of the pre-trained teachers.

### 3.1    Architecture Design

As depicted in Fig. 2, the SOKA mainly consists of two parts, the PTMs pool and the customized network. The knowledge are transferred from the PTMs to the target network via two flow, the multi-modal incorporated feature amalgamation flow and the objectives distillation flow. For the former, we introduce a Multi-Modal Incorporated Amalgamation (MIA) scheme to transform multiple teachers' expertise to student domain for computing the loss and thus updating the parameters of the shared encoder of the student network. For the latter, we propose an adaptive competition-collaboration training strategy, in which a gradient-based competition-balancing strategy is introduced to learn the multi-head prediction subnetwork as well as the loss weightings of the distinct tasks.

## 3.2   Multi Modal Incorporated Amalgamation

Consider a collection of PTM models term as PTMs pool, which consist of the teacher models and some auxiliary model. The auxiliary PTM, which is chosen according to the quantilized transferability of task taskonomy [34], is considered beneficial for providing multi-modal information for supervising the student network. To PTMs with the same CNN backbone, the regions with high activation from a neuron at the same depth may share some task related similarities, even though these similarities may not be intuitive for human interpretation.

**Auxiliary PTM Selection.** We set a gate condition on basis of RDM correlation [25] to determine whether it is necessary to introduce an auxiliary PTM before training to guide the training of their student network. Representation dissimilarity matrices (RDMs) are generated by computing the pairwise dissimilarity (1 - Pearson's correlation) of each image pair in a subset of selected images. The similarity score $S(i,j)$ of task $i$ and $j$ are computed by Spearman's correlation of the low triangular RDMs of the two models.

Assume we have a set of PTM models $\{T_k\}_{k=1,...,m}$, denote $T_i$ and $T_j$ as the teacher PTMs of target task $i$ and $j$ respectively, and the pairwise similarity score [25] of them is $S_{(i,j)}$. Denote $\delta$ as the similarity score threshold that determines whether the two task are considered as correlated. If $S_{(i,j)} < \delta$, we search for a PTM term as $T_x$, which satisfy $\frac{(S_{(i,x)} - S_{(i,j)})^2}{S_{(i,x)} - S_{(i,j)}} + \frac{(S_{(i,x)} - S_{(i,j)})^2}{S_{(i,x)} - S_{(i,j)}} > 0$.

In our implementation, $\{T_k\}_{k=1,...,m}$ are the 21 single-task taskonomy models. The code of computing RDMs and similarity scores is available on the Internet[1]. More details are available in the supplementary document.

**Feature Amalgamation with Multi-modal Knowledge.** In iteration $t$, denote the activation map produced by the teacher network $T_i$ at a particular layer $l$ by $A_{T_i}^{(l)} \in \mathbb{R}^{c \times h \times w}$, where $c$ is the number of output channels, and $h$ and $w$ are spatial dimensions. Let the activation map produced by the student network $S$ at layer $l$ be given by $A_S^{(l)} \in \mathbb{R}^{c \times h \times w}$. We note that as our student and its teachers share the same depth such that we compare the representation of them at the same depth. $l$ can be a intermediate layer and the encoder output.

---

[1] https://github.com/kshitijd20/RSA-CVPR19-release.

Student mimic the target representation filtered from heterogeneous teachers by the Multi-modal Incorporated Amalgamation (MIA) module, we write

$$\sigma^{(l)}(t) = MIA\left(A_{T_1}^{(l)}(t), \cdots, A_{T_m}^{(l)}(t)\right). \tag{1}$$

The MIA takes as input the stacked representation of the teacher network and generate the target representation $\sigma^{(l)}(t)$ via passing message from the feature maps of other tasks as follows,

$$MIA\left(A_{T_1}^{(l)}(t), \cdots, A_{T_m}^{(l)}(t)\right) = C \odot \sum_i^m W_i^{(l)}(t) \otimes A_{T_i}^{(l)}(t), \tag{2}$$

where $\otimes$ denotes matrix multiplication operation, $\odot$ denotes the elementary multiplication and $W_i^{(l)}(t)$ denotes the parameters of the weight. Both $C$ and $W_i^{(l)}(t)$ are learnable in the representation learning process.

To guide the student towards the activation correlations induced in the amalgamated activation of the multiple teachers, we define a representation transfer loss that penalizes differences in the L2-normalized outer products of the student's activation and the corresponding target activation $\sigma^{(l)}(t)$:

$$\mathcal{L}_A^{(l)}(t) = \|A_S^{(l)}(t) - \sigma^{(l)}(t)\|_2^2 \tag{3}$$

To this end, we define the total loss for transferring the knowledge induced in representation of the selected group of teachers to the student network as:

$$\mathcal{L}_A(t) = \sum_l^L \mathcal{L}_A^{(l)}(t), \tag{4}$$

where $L$ is the number of layers, whose knowledge needs to be transferred from the teacher to the student network. In our implementation, we tile the representation similarity comparison in the 3rd block of convolution layer and the encoder output of the PTMs set and the student.

### 3.3    Objectives Distillation

To imitate the predictions of teachers, we introduce a soft target loss between the predictions of teacher networks and that of the student. We write,

$$\mathcal{L}_{soft}^i(t) = \|\mathcal{F}_S^{score}(t) - \mathcal{F}_{T_i}^{score}(t)\|^2, \tag{5}$$

where $\mathcal{F}_S^{score}$ and $\mathcal{F}_{T_i}^{score}$ denote the prediction of the student and teachers. Our multi-task loss function is thus defined as:

$$\mathcal{L}_{soft}(t) = \sum_i^n \omega_g^i(t)\mathcal{L}_{soft}^i(t), \tag{6}$$

where $\omega_g^i(t)$ is the gradient based weighting function for balancing the target tasks. Let $G_W^{(i)}(t) = \|\nabla_W \omega^i(t)\mathcal{L}^i(t)\|_2^2$ be the L2 norm of the gradient of the

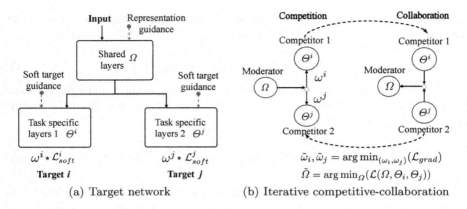

(a) Target network          (b) Iterative competitive-collaboration

**Fig. 3.** The illustrative diagram of the adaptive competitive-collaboration training (ACCT) process. (a) is the parameterized target network. (b) demonstrate the training cycle of competition-collaboration. Task specific layers are considered as two competitor that are moderated by the moderator. The shared layers are considered as the moderator who controls the resource, which is the shared representation utilized for inference of task $i$ and $j$. The task balance weight $\omega^i$ and $\omega^j$ are adaptively determined by the function of $\Omega$.

weighted single-task loss $\omega^i(t)\mathcal{L}^i(t)$ with respect to the chosen weights $\omega$. As in GradNorm [4], we use the relative inverse training rate of task $i$, $r_i(t)$, to balance our gradients of objectives distillation. $w_i^g(t)$ is designed to move gradient norms towards the target for each task, $\bar{G}(t) \times [r^i(t)]^\alpha$. GradNorm is then implemented as an L1 loss function $\mathcal{L}_{grad}$ between the actual and target gradient norms at each time step for each target task, summed over all tasks:

$$\mathcal{L}_{grad}(t; w_g^i(t)) = \sum_i \|G_W^i(t) - \bar{G}(t) \times [r^i(t)]^\alpha\|_1, \qquad (7)$$

where the summation runs through all $T$ tasks. When differentiating this loss $\mathcal{L}_{grad}$, we treat the target gradient norm $\bar{G}(t) \times [r^i(t)]^\alpha$ as a fixed constant to prevent loss weights $w_g^i(t)$ from spuriously drifting towards zero. $\mathcal{L}_{grad}$ is then differentiated only with respect to $w_g^i$, as it directly control gradient magnitudes per task.

### 3.4   Adaptive Competitive-Collaboration Training Strategy

Competitive collaboration is typically formulated as a three-player game consisting of two counterparts competing for a resource that is regulated by a moderator. In the context of knowledge amalgamation for customizing a multi-task model, the moderator is the shared layers (the encoder) who map the input to some shared activation for inference. The two counterparts thus are the prediction subnetworks of the target tasks and compete for more inference-beneficial information in the shared representation to minimize their individual loss.

As depicted in Fig. 3, we use $\Omega$, $\Theta_i$, and $\Theta_j$ to denote the parameter of the shared encoder, and that of the two task specific prediction subnetwork respectively. The competing players $\Theta_i$ and $\Theta_j$ minimize their loss function $\mathcal{L}_{soft}^i$ and $\mathcal{L}_{soft}^j$ respectively such that each player optimizes for itself but not for the group. To resolve this problem, our training cycle consists of three phases. In the first phase which we term as competition step, we train the competitors by fixing the moderator network parameter $\Omega$ and minimizing Eq. 5. In the second phase which we term as collaboration phase, the competitors($\Theta_i$, $\Theta_j$) form a consensus and train the moderator $\Omega$ such that it correctly distributes the data in the next phase of the training cycle. In the third phase, task weights $\omega^i$ and $\omega^j$ are learnt adaptively by minimizing the gradient loss $\mathcal{L}_{grad}$. We note that the moderator and the competitors are initialized jointly before the training cycle to set the whole network to a good start point.

To summarize, $\Omega$, $\Theta_i$, and $\Theta_j$ are learnt through a multi-stage alternate training process as follows:

- **Step 1**: Randomly initialize the parameters of the student network.
- **Step 2**: Jointly initialize $\Omega$, $\Theta_i$ and $\Theta_j$ with the input and the prediction of the teacher PTMs for 1000 steps. $\omega^i$ and $\omega^j$ are fixed to an initial value of 0.5 in this step.
- **Step 3**: Competition step. Freeze $\Omega$, updating $\Theta_i$ and $\Theta_j$ by minimizing the soft target distilling loss $\mathcal{L}_{soft}$ with the weight $w_i$ and $w_j$.
- **Step 4**: Collaborative step. Freeze $\Theta_i$ and $\Theta_j$, training the shared layers $\Omega$ by Eq. 8 with representation transfer loss defined in Eq. 4 and the inference loss of the two competitors. The $\alpha$ in Eq. 8 is a hyperparameter to balance the magnitude level of $\mathcal{L}_A$ and $\mathcal{L}_{soft}$ and is set to be 0.05.

$$\tilde{\Omega} = \arg\min_{\Omega}(\alpha(\mathcal{L}_{soft}^i(x;\Omega,\Theta_i) + \mathcal{L}_{soft}^j(x;\Omega,\Theta_j)) + \mathcal{L}_A(x;\Omega)) \qquad (8)$$

- **Step 5**: Adaptive weighting step. Update $w_i^g(t)$ with the task specific weight function by minimizing the gradient loss $\mathcal{L}_{grad}$ defined in Eq. 7:

$$\tilde{\omega}_i, \tilde{\omega}_j = \arg\min_{(\omega_i,\omega_j)}(\mathcal{L}_{grad}). \qquad (9)$$

After every update step, we renormalize the weights $\omega^i$ so that $\sum_i \omega_g^i(t) = 1$ in order to decouple gradient normalization from the global learning rate.
- **Step 6**: If the maximum training step is not reached, go to step 3 and continue the training loop. The maximum step in our case is set to be $6 \times 10^5$.

## 4    Experiment

We now describe a number of diagnostic experiments of the proposed approach carried out using taskonomy dataset [34] which provide various pre-trained vision models as well as extensive data. In the following the detailed description of our experimental evaluation is given. Besides, detailed experimental settings and more experimental results refer to our supplementary document.

### 4.1  Experimental Setup

**Dataset.** Taskonomy dataset includes over 4 million indoor images from 500 buildings with annotations available for 26 image tasks. 21 of these tasks are single image tasks, and 5 tasks are multi-image tasks. For this work, we select one building (wiconisco) from taskonomy dataset, which contains 16749 images, to evaluate the proposed method. We divide them into 13749 training and 3000 validation images. For training, only RGB images are feed as the input to the student and teacher network. The student take the prediction of the task specific teacher network as supervision without accessing the annotations.

**Pre-trained Teacher Models.** We adopt the taskonomy models[2], which consist of an encoder and decoder, as our pre-trained teacher models. The encoder for all the tasks is a ResNet-50 [7] model followed by convolution layer that compresses the channel dimension of the encoder output from 2048 to 8. The decoder is task-specific and varies according to the task. Among these models, we mainly select ones specialized for pixel prediction tasks. The decoder of these pixel prediction models consists of 15 layers (except colorization with 12 layers) consisting of convolution and deconvolution layers. The compressed output as long as representation of earlier layers of the teachers' encoder is also used as guidance to train the target network.

In addition to the representation of the target task specific PTMs, we also explore the representation of highly correlated tasks as auxiliary guidance for training the target ones. We perform this analysis to investigate how the features of models of interconnected tasks cooperate to reinforce the target network especially for loosely related target tasks.

**Evaluation Metric.** For evaluating the performance of the vision tasks involved in this paper, we use several quantitative metrics following previous works [28]. For the pixel-wise prediction tasks involved in this paper, we adopt several metric including mean relative error (rel), root mean squared error (rmse) and the percentage of relative errors inside three thresholds $(1.25, 1.25^2, 1.25^3)$.

**Implementation Details.** The proposed method is implemented using TensorFlow with a NVIDIA M6000 with 24GB memory. We use the poly learning rate policy as done in [11], and set the base learning rate to 0.001, the power to 0.9, and the weight decay to $10^{-6}$. The student take the prediction of the task specific teacher network as supervision without accessing the annotations.

### 4.2  Qualitative Evaluation

Given some sample queries, the results of student network built by proposed SOKA and the teacher PTMs are shown in Fig. 4 for visual perception. Synchronous depth estimation and surface normal, as well as synchronous edge prediction and depth estimation are compared in Fig. 4. It can be observed that

---

[2] Publicly available at https://github.com/StanfordVL/taskonomy.

Input            Ours            Teacher PTMs            Ground Truth

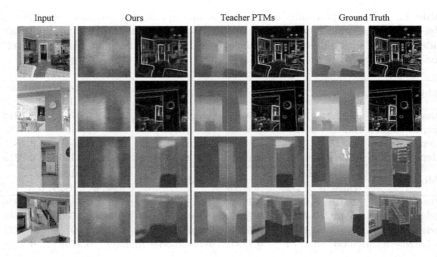

**Fig. 4.** Qualitative illustration of task specific outputs for the query (first column). Here, prediction of teacher PTMs, and proposed SOKA are compared. The first two rows are results of our synchronous depth and edge2d prediction in contrast with the task-specific teacher PTMs. The bottom two rows are results of our synchronous depth and surface normal prediction and that of the task-specific teacher PTMs.

though smaller in model size, the multi-talent student network, which are built via the proposed SOKA with limited unlabeled training data, achieves comparable visual performance with the teacher PTMs which are trained on the million-level training data with ground truth.

### 4.3  Quantitative Evaluation

**Performance of Student Network Learnt by SOKA.** We show in Table 1 the quantitative results of the teacher network and those of the student network that specialized in five group of target tasks. We performed tests on five group of pixel2pixel prediction tasks to evaluate the performance of SOKA. The five group are (Edge 2D, Depth estimation), (Edge 2D, Surface Norm), (Depth estimation, Surface Norm), (Depth estimation, Edge 3D), (Edge 2D, Edge 3D) and (Edge 3D, Surface Norm) respectively. Additionally, we collect the parameters of student network, teacher PTMs and a direct multi-task learning method with the same architecture as the student do. The number of their parameters are shown in Table. 2. It can be observed from Table 1 and Table 2 that the performance of multi-talent student networks learnt via proposed SOKA under different target task groups are generally on par or sometimes even better than the teacher PTMs and yet compact in model size.

**Robustness of the Task Weightings Learning.** As $\omega^i$ and $\omega^j$ are changing over time due to the alternative competition-collaboration training, we study

**Table 1.** Comparative results on Depth Estimation, Surface Normal, Edge 2D, and Edge 3D task specific prediction of the single-task teacher PTMs and multi-talent student trained with different task groups. ($\sigma < 1.25, 1.25^2, 1.25^3$: *the higher the better*, rmse and rel: *the lower the better*)

| Model | Depth | | | Model | Surface Normals | | |
|---|---|---|---|---|---|---|---|
| | rmse | rel | $\sigma < 1.25$ | | rmse | $\sigma < 1.25$ | $\sigma < 1.25^2$ |
| teacher | 10.22 | 1.57 | 0.6687 | teacher | 7.52 | 0.6767 | 0.7943 |
| depth-edge2d | 10.21 | 1.22 | 0.6581 | sfnorm-depth | 7.56 | 0.6400 | 0.7283 |
| depth-sfnorm | 10.32 | 1.32 | 0.4656 | sfnorm-edge2d | 7.51 | 0.6587 | 0.7845 |
| depth-edge3d | 10.21 | 1.25 | 0.5841 | sfnorm-edge3d | 7.57 | 0.6323 | 0.7215 |
| Model | Edge 2D | | | Model | Edge 3D | | |
| | rmse | $\sigma < 1.25$ | $\sigma < 1.25^2$ | | rmse | $\sigma < 1.25$ | $\sigma < 1.25^2$ |
| teacher | 6.07 | 0.4841 | 0.7256 | teacher | 6.11 | 0.4840 | 0.7056 |
| edge2d-depth | 6.40 | 0.4586 | 0.7112 | edge3d-depth | 6.12 | 0.4706 | 0.6988 |
| edge2d-sfnorm | 6.51 | 0.4508 | 0.6997 | edge3d-sfnorm | 6.43 | 0.3913 | 0.6731 |
| edge2d-edge3d | 6.06 | 0.4774 | 0.7231 | edge3d-edge2d | 6.09 | 0.4763 | 0.7159 |

**Table 2.** Parameters of the teachers, student and MTL network. M is short for million.

| Model | Teacher PTM | Student | MTL |
|---|---|---|---|
| #params | ~246.46 M | ~175.75 M | ~175.73 M |

the effect of $\omega^i$ and $\omega^j$ on performance of the target tasks of the learned student network when their value varies in a rather wide range, and show the results in Fig. 5. Under the initial learning rate of 0.001 in Fig. 5(a), the ratio $\omega^i/\omega^j$ of the final $\omega^i$ and $\omega^j$ have eventually grown to hundreds while that under an initial learning rate of 0.0001 grew to about 2 times (Fig. 5(b)). It can be observed that no matter the weighting ratios is small to 2 or big to hundreds, parameter training of the whole network seem still goes the right way.

**Comparative Results of SOKA Against Supervised Method.** Though we assume no manually labeled annotations but only some pre-trained PTMs are available in training the student network, we compare our method with supervised multi-task learning method. In particular, two alternative methods are compared. The first is direct multi-task learning (dMTL) that intuitively train the two target task together under the same student network architecture but with labeled data as ground truth. The second is similar to the first one but with GradNorm [4] method to balance the task weight during learning. The results of these methods on synchronous depth and edge2d prediction tasks are shown in Table 3. As demonstrated in Table 3, The performance of student network generated by SOKA generally outperforms the two multi-task learning methods on these two target tasks.

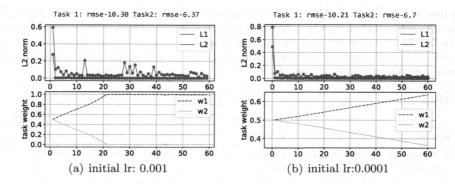

**Fig. 5.** Illustration of task training loss decay of the proposed SOKA method with different learning rate in the steps of task weightings learning. The corresponding rmse results of the final model on both tasks are also shown on the top of each subfigure.

**Table 3.** Comparative results of student generated by SOKA against supervised multi-task learning method under the task of synchronous depth and edge2d prediction.

| Methods | Depth | | | Edge2D | | | |
|---------|-------|-----|-------------|--------|-------------|----------------|----------------|
|         | rmse  | rel | $\sigma < 1.25$ | rmse   | $\sigma < 1.25$ | $\sigma < 1.25^2$ | $\sigma < 1.25^3$ |
| dMTL    | 10.26 | 1.23 | 0.4953     | 8.84   | 0.2002      | 0.3763         | 0.5037         |
| GradNorm [4] | 10.23 | 1.22 | 0.5581 | 7.48   | 0.4191      | 0.5270         | 0.6402         |
| Ours    | 10.21 | 1.22 | 0.6176     | 6.40   | 0.4586      | 0.7112         | 0.7855         |

**Ablation Studies.** In the basic mode, proposed SOKA takes unlabeled training image as input, and adopts knowledge distillation (KD) [8] method to impel the student to mimic the prediction of the teacher PTM. Due to the possible weak-interconnection of the customized task, we add multi-modal incorporated amalgamation (MIA) to the basic KD mode. Besides, to further achieve the collaboration of the tasks by balancing the competition, we introduce the adaptive competitive-collaboration training on basis of the KD and MIA.

In this section, ablation studies are conducted to investigate the effectiveness of the modules adopted in SOKA. We verify the effectiveness of each module by comparing the whole model to the model without the corresponding module. The additional compared method is KD, and KD with MIA. The results are shown in Table 5. Besides, we also analyze if correlated auxiliary model can enhance the performance of target task in Table 4. It can be observed from the two tables that both MIA and ACCT are beneficial for alleviating errors and enhancing the inference performance.

**Table 4.** Comparative results of the teacher PTMs and the student of synchronous Depth estimation and Surface Normals with/without supervision of auxiliary PTM. For auxiliary supervision in multi-modal incorporated representation amalgamation, a weak connected auxiliary task, Vanishing Point, is compared against the strong connected auxiliary task Keypoint 3D.

| Methods | Depth | | | Edge2D | | | |
|---|---|---|---|---|---|---|---|
| | rmse | rel | $\sigma < 1.25$ | rmse | $\sigma < 1.25$ | $\sigma < 1.25^2$ | $\sigma < 1.25^3$ |
| teacher | 10.22 | 1.57 | **0.6687** | **6.07** | **0.4841** | **0.7256** | **0.8148** |
| w/o auxiliary | 10.26 | 1.23 | 0.4953 | 7.83 | 0.4002 | 0.5295 | 0.6132 |
| vanishing Point | 10.42 | 1.23 | 0.4737 | 8.86 | 0.2144 | 0.3227 | 0.5159 |
| keypoint3d | **10.21** | **1.22** | 0.6176 | 6.70 | 0.4586 | 0.7112 | 0.7981 |

**Table 5.** Ablation study of each component of the proposed SOKA under the task of synchronous depth and edge2d prediction.

| Methods | Depth | | Edge2D | | | |
|---|---|---|---|---|---|---|
| | rmse | rel | rmse | $\sigma < 1.25$ | $\sigma < 1.25^2$ | $\sigma < 1.25^3$ |
| KD | 10.26 | 1.23 | 7.83 | 0.2002 | 0.3905 | 0.5295 |
| KD + MIA | 10.22 | 1.25 | 6.91 | 0.3102 | 0.5216 | 0.7690 |
| KD + MIA + ACCT | 10.21 | 1.22 | 6.40 | 0.4586 | 0.7112 | 0.7855 |

# 5   Conclusions

In this paper, we study how to reuse heterogeneous pre-trained models as teachers, and build a versatile and compact student model, without accessing human annotations. To this end, we introduce a novel strategy that treats the multiple tasks handled by the distinct teachers as competing counterparts, and devise a collaboration-by-competition approach to amalgamating their heterogeneous knowledge and building the multi-talent student. This collaboration-by-competition approach, which we call as SOKA, is achieved via a dual-step adaptive competitive-cooperation training approach, where the knowledge of the heterogeneous teachers are in the first step amalgamated to guide the shared parameter learning of the student network, and followed by a gradient-based competition-balancing strategy to learn the multi-head prediction subnetwork as well as the loss weightings of the distinct tasks in the second step. Experimental results demonstrate that, the learned student not only comes with a smaller size but all achieves performances on par with or even superior to those of the teachers.

**Acknowledgments.** This work is supported by National Key Research and Development Program (2018AAA0101503), National Natural Science Foundation of China (61976186), Key Research and Development Program of Zhejiang Province (2018C01004), and the Major Scientific Research Project of Zhejiang Lab (No. 2019KD0AC01).

# References

1. Achille, A., et al.: Task2vec: task embedding for meta-learning. In: IEEE International Conference on Computer Vision (ICCV), pp. 6430–6439 (2019)
2. Azizpour, H., Razavian, A.S., Sullivan, J., Maki, A., Carlsson, S.: Factors of transferability for a generic convnet representation. IEEE Trans. Pattern Anal. Mach. Intell. (TPAMI) **38**(9), 1790–1802 (2015)
3. Ben-David, S., Blitzer, J., Crammer, K., Kulesza, A., Pereira, F., Vaughan, J.W.: A theory of learning from different domains. Mach. Learn. **79**(1–2), 151–175 (2010)
4. Chen, Z., Badrinarayanan, V., Lee, C.Y., Rabinovich, A.: Gradnorm: gradient normalization for adaptive loss balancing in deep multitask networks. In: International Conference on Machine Learning (ICML), pp. 794–803 (2018)
5. Dwivedi, K., Roig, G.: Representation similarity analysis for efficient task taxonomy & transfer learning. In: IEEE Conference on Computer Vision and Pattern Recognition (CVPR), pp. 12387–12396 (2019)
6. Eigen, D., Fergus, R.: Predicting depth, surface normals and semantic labels with a common multi-scale convolutional architecture. In: IEEE International Conference on Computer Vision (ICCV) (2015)
7. He, K., Zhang, X., Ren, S., Sun, J.: Deep residual learning for image recognition. In: IEEE Conference on Computer Vision and Pattern Recognition (CVPR), pp. 770–778 (2016)
8. Hinton, G., Vinyals, O., Dean, J.: Distilling the knowledge in a neural network. arXiv preprint arXiv:1503.02531 (2015)
9. Huang, Z., Wang, N.: Like what you like: Knowledge distill via neuron selectivity transfer. arXiv preprint arXiv:1707.01219 (2017)
10. Liu, S., Johns, E., Davison, A.J.: End-to-end multi-task learning with attention. In: IEEE Conference on Computer Vision and Pattern Recognition (CVPR), pp. 1871–1880 (2019)
11. Liu, W., Rabinovich, A., Berg, A.C.: Parsenet: Looking wider to see better. arXiv preprint arXiv:1506.04579 (2015)
12. Luo, S., Wang, X., Fang, G., Hu, Y., Tao, D., Song, M.: Knowledge amalgamation from heterogeneous networks by common feature learning. In: International Joint Conference on Artificial Intelligence (IJCAI) (2019)
13. Misra, I., Shrivastava, A., Gupta, A., Hebert, M.: Cross-stitch networks for multitask learning. In: IEEE Conference on Computer Vision and Pattern Recognition (CVPR), pp. 3994–4003 (2016)
14. Pan, S.J., Yang, Q.: A survey on transfer learning. IEEE Trans. Knowl. Data Eng. **22**(10), 1345–1359 (2009)
15. Ranjan, A., et al.: Competitive collaboration: joint unsupervised learning of depth, camera motion, optical flow and motion segmentation. In: IEEE Conference on Computer Vision and Pattern Recognition (CVPR), pp. 12240–12249 (2019)
16. Romero, A., Ballas, N., Kahou, S.E., Chassang, A., Gatta, C., Bengio, Y.: Fitnets: hints for thin deep nets. In: International Conference on Learning Representations (ICLR) (2015)
17. Ruder, S., Bingel, J., Augenstein, I., Søgaard, A.: Latent multi-task architecture learning. In: AAAI Conference on Artificial Intelligence (AAAI), vol. 33, pp. 4822–4829 (2019)
18. Sener, O., Koltun, V.: Multi-task learning as multi-objective optimization. In: Neural Information Processing Systems (NeurIPS), pp. 527–538 (2018)
19. Sharif Razavian, A., Azizpour, H., Sullivan, J., Carlsson, S.: CNN features off-the-shelf: an astounding baseline for recognition. In: CVPR Workshops, pp. 806–813 (2014)

20. Shen, C., Wang, X., Song, J., Sun, L., Song, M.: Amalgamating knowledge towards comprehensive classification. In: AAAI Conference on Artificial Intelligence (AAAI) (2019)
21. Shen, C., Xue, M., Wang, X., Song, J., Sun, L., Song, M.: Customizing student networks from heterogeneous teachers via adaptive knowledge amalgamation. In: IEEE International Conference on Computer Vision (ICCV), pp. 3504–3513 (2019)
22. Song, J., Chen, Y., Wang, X., Shen, C., Song, M.: Deep model transferability from attribution maps. In: Advances in Neural Information Processing Systems (NeurIPS) (2019)
23. Song, J., et al.: Depara: deep attribution graph for deep knowledge transferability. In: Proceedings of the IEEE Conference on Computer Vision and Pattern Recognition (CVPR) (2020)
24. Standley, T., Zamir, A.R., Chen, D., Guibas, L., Malik, J., Savarese, S.: Which tasks should be learned together in multi-task learning? arXiv preprint arXiv:1905.07553 (2019)
25. Tung, F., Mori, G.: Similarity-preserving knowledge distillation. In: IEEE International Conference on Computer Vision (ICCV), pp. 1365–1374 (2019)
26. Wang, H., Zhao, H., Li, X., Tan, X.: Progressive blockwise knowledge distillation for neural network acceleration. In: International Joint Conference on Artificial Intelligence (IJCAI), pp. 2769–2775 (2018)
27. Wang, Z., Deng, Z., Wang, S.: Accelerating convolutional neural networks with dominant convolutional kernel and knowledge pre-regression. In: Leibe, B., Matas, J., Sebe, N., Welling, M. (eds.) ECCV 2016. LNCS, vol. 9912, pp. 533–548. Springer, Cham (2016). https://doi.org/10.1007/978-3-319-46484-8_32
28. Xu, D., Ouyang, W., Wang, X., Sebe, N.: PAD-Net: multi-tasks guided prediction-and-distillation network for simultaneous depth estimation and scene parsing. In: IEEE Conference on Computer Vision and Pattern Recognition (CVPR), pp. 675–684 (2018)
29. Yang, Y., Qiu, J., Song, M., Tao, D., Wang, X.: Distilling knowledge from graph convolutional networks. In: Proceedings of the IEEE Conference on Computer Vision and Pattern Recognition (CVPR) (2020)
30. Ye, J., Ji, Y., Wang, X., Gao, X., Song, M.: Data-free knowledge amalgamation via group-stack dual-GAN. In: Proceedings of the IEEE Conference on Computer Vision and Pattern Recognition (CVPR) (2020)
31. Ye, J., Ji, Y., Wang, X., Ou, K., Tao, D., Song, M.: Student becoming the master: knowledge amalgamation for joint scene parsing, depth estimation, and more. In: IEEE Conference on Computer Vision and Pattern Recognition (CVPR) (2019)
32. Yu, X., Liu, T., Wang, X., Tao, D.: On compressing deep models by low rank and sparse decomposition. In: Proceedings of the IEEE Conference on Computer Vision and Pattern Recognition (CVPR) (2017)
33. Zagoruyko, S., Komodakis, N.: Paying more attention to attention: improving the performance of convolutional neural networks via attention transfer. In: International Conference on Learning Representations (ICLR) (2017)
34. Zamir, A.R., Sax, A., Shen, W., Guibas, L.J., Malik, J., Savarese, S.: Taskonomy: disentangling task transfer learning. In: IEEE Conference on Computer Vision and Pattern Recognition (CVPR), pp. 3712–3722 (2018)
35. Zhao, Y., Xu, R., Wang, X., Hou, P., Tang, H., Song, M.: Hearing lips: improving lip reading by distilling speech recognizers. In: AAAI Conference on Artificial Intelligence, (AAAI) (2020)

# Do Not Disturb Me: Person Re-identification Under the Interference of Other Pedestrians

Shizhen Zhao[1], Changxin Gao[1(✉)], Jun Zhang[2], Hao Cheng[2], Chuchu Han[1], Xinyang Jiang[2], Xiaowei Guo[2], Wei-Shi Zheng[3], Nong Sang[1], and Xing Sun[2]

[1] Key Laboratory of Image Processing and Intelligent Control, School of Artificial Intelligence and Automation, Huazhong University of Science and Technology, Wuhan, China
{zhaosz,cgao}@hust.edu.cn
[2] Tencent Youtu Lab, Shanghai, China
[3] Sun Yat-sen University, Guangzhou, China

**Abstract.** In the conventional person Re-ID setting, it is assumed that cropped images are the person images within the bounding box for each individual. However, in a crowded scene, off-shelf-detectors may generate bounding boxes involving multiple people, where the large proportion of background pedestrians or human occlusion exists. The representation extracted from such cropped images, which contain both the target and the interference pedestrians, might include distractive information. This will lead to wrong retrieval results. To address this problem, this paper presents a novel deep network termed Pedestrian-Interference Suppression Network (PISNet). PISNet leverages a Query-Guided Attention Block (QGAB) to enhance the feature of the target in the gallery, under the guidance of the query. Furthermore, the involving Guidance Reversed Attention Module and the Multi-Person Separation Loss promote QGAB to suppress the interference of other pedestrians. Our method is evaluated on two new pedestrian-interference datasets and the results show that the proposed method performs favorably against existing Re-ID methods.

**Keywords:** Person re-identification · Pedestrian-Interference · Location accuracy · Feature distinctiveness · Query-guided attention

## 1 Introduction

Re-IDentification (Re-ID) aims to identify the same person across a set of images from nonoverlapping camera views, facilitating cross-camera tracking techniques

---

S. Zhao—This work was done when Shizhen Zhao was an intern at Tencent Youtu Lab.

---

**Electronic supplementary material** The online version of this chapter (https://doi.org/10.1007/978-3-030-58539-6_39) contains supplementary material, which is available to authorized users.

A. Vedaldi et al. (Eds.): ECCV 2020, LNCS 12351, pp. 647–663, 2020.
https://doi.org/10.1007/978-3-030-58539-6_39

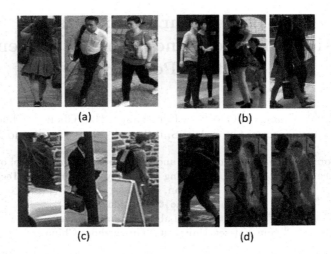

**Fig. 1.** Typical samples in the (a) traditional Re-ID, (b) Pedestrian-Interference Re-ID, and (c) Occluded Re-ID from Market-1501 [49], our constructed PI-CUHK-SYSU, and Occluded-DukeMTMC [27,53], respectively. (d) shows the query image (the first sample) and, the comparison of visualization results between the Occluded Re-ID method Foreground-aware Pyramid Reconstruction [7] (the second one) and our PISNet (the third one)

used in video surveillance for public security and safety. In general, person Re-ID is considered to be the next high-level task after a pedestrian detection system. Therefore, as shown in Fig. 1(a), the basic assumption of Re-ID is that the detection model can provide a precise and highly-aligned bounding box for each individual. However, in a crowed scene, off-shelf-detectors may draw a bounding box containing multiple people, as shown in Fig. 1(b). This means the cropped images contain both the target and the interference pedestrians. The interference pedestrian makes the feature ambiguous to identify the target person, which might lead to wrong retrieval results. We call this the Pedestrian-Interference person Re-IDentification (PI Re-ID) problem.

We observe that mutual occlusion of pedestrians often occurs in PI Re-ID. Recent works [3,7,23,41] have well studied the Occluded Re-ID problem. However, in their setting of Occluded Re-ID, the person images are mainly occluded by obstructions like cars, trees, or shelves. This is also reflected in the existing benchmarking Occluded Re-ID datasets, most of which consist of non-pedestrian occlusion, as shown in Fig. 1(c). The performance of their approaches degrades if directly applied to PI Re-ID, as shown in the second sample of Fig. 1(d). Because they only focus on reducing the influence caused by obstructions and do not specifically consider the interference between pedestrians in a cropped image. Moreover, they do not explicitly learn to draw a precise boundary between two overlapping people so that the extract features are corrupted by each other. As for PI Re-ID, it is different from Occluded Re-ID in two aspects: 1) PI Re-ID focuses on the pedestrian interference, which is more confusing than the non-pedestrian obstructions. 2) PI Re-ID aims to re-identify all the pedestrians appearing in a cropped image, which might be interfered with the background pedestrians or the pedestrian occlusion. Therefore, our setting is more challenging than Occluded Re-ID. Moreover, our setting is more practical in the crowed situation (*e.g.*, airports, railway stations, malls, and hospitals), where people always share overlapping regions under cameras.

To retrieve a person in the PI Re-ID setting, the extracted features should ensure 1) **location accuracy**: the strong activation on all the regions of targets, 2) **feature distinctiveness**: the trivial feature corruption by other pedestrians. To achieve this goal, we propose a novel deep network termed Pedestrian-Interference Suppression Network (PISNet), which consists of a backbone Fully Convolutional Network (FCN), a Query-Guided Attention Block (QGAB) and a Guidance Reversed Attention Module (GRAM). First, FCN is utilized to extract features for person images. Since the target feature, in a gallery image containing multi-person information, differs on the query, QGAB is designed to enhance the feature of the target in the gallery and suppress that of interference pedestrians, under the guidance of the query. On the one hand, as shown Fig. 2(a), for encouraging the **location accuracy** of the attention, our motivation is that, if the attention well covers the regions of the target, the attention feature can be further utilized as the guidance to search the target in other multi-person images. Therefore, GRAM leverages the refined gallery features to guide other multi-person features to formulate attention for targets. On the other hand, as shown in Fig. 2(b), to facilitate the **feature distinctiveness** of the attention learning, PISNet utilizes the Multi-Person Separation Loss (MPSL) to maximize the distance between the features, which are extracted from the same gallery but guided by different queries. In addition, as shown in the third sample of Fig. 1(d),

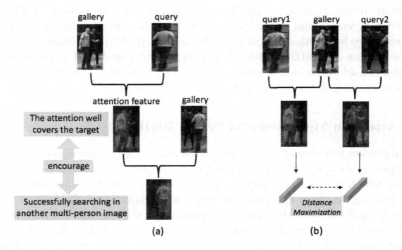

**Fig. 2.** (a) Enhance the location accuracy of the attention by GRAM. (b) Facilitate the feature distinctiveness of the attention by MPSL

our PISNet is more capable of depressing the pedestrian interference than the Occluded Re-ID method.

Our **contributions** are listed as follows: 1) To the best of our knowledge, it is the first work that particularly addresses the problem of PI Re-ID. 2) We propose a Pedestrian-Interference Suppression Network (PISNet), which utilizes a query-guided approach to extract the target feature. The involving GRAM and MPSL further promote the location accuracy and the feature distinctiveness of the attention learning, respectively. 3) Since the existing benchmarks largely ignored this problem, we contribute two new datasets, which are specifically designed for this problem with a great deal more pedestrian-interference instances. Our experimental results on these two datasets show that the proposed model is effective in addressing the PI Re-ID problem, yielding significant improvement over representative Re-ID methods applied to the same problem. The experimental results also demonstrate the generalization ability of our method on the general Re-ID datasets (Market-1501 and DukeMTMC-ReID).

## 2 Related Work

### 2.1 Person Re-ID

Generally, Person Re-ID can be divided into two steps: calculating a feature embedding and performing feature matching under some distance metric [10, 16, 35]. We mainly review the former including both handcrafted feature [10, 11, 13, 22] and learned feature [2, 8, 14, 19, 45, 47] approaches.

In recent years, Re-ID has witnessed great progress owing to the prevailing success of convolutional neural networks (CNNs) in computer vision. However, simply applying CNNs to feature extraction may not yield ideal Re-ID performance due to many problem-specific challenges such as partial body, background perturbance, view point variation, as well as occlusion/misalignment. Combining the image-level information with the human-part information can enhance the robustness of Re-ID models. Moreover, many part-based approaches have achieved considerable improvement [2, 4, 17, 21, 24, 29, 30, 34, 43, 44, 48, 52, 54]. We refer readers to [50] for a more comprehensive review.

### 2.2 Attention Mechanisms in Person Re-ID

Several studies leverage attention mechanisms to address the misalignment problem in person Re-ID. For example, Chen et al. [1] propose an attentive but diverse network which consists of a pair of complementary attention modules, focusing on channel aggregation and position awareness, respectively. Si et al. [28] use an inter-class and an intra-class attention module to capture the context information for person Re-ID in video sequences. Li et al. [15] leverage hard region-level and soft pixel-level attention, which can jointly produce more discriminative feature representations. Xu et al. [39] utilize pose information to learn attention masks and then combine the global with the part features as feature embeddings.

Previous methods [1,37,39] leverage attention mechanisms to enhance the feature of human bodies. In contrast, in our proposed setting, images contain other pedestrians, which severely corrupt the feature of a target. Since they cannot distinguish between the target and interference pedestrians, directly applying their approaches will cause the severe corruption of the target feature.

### 2.3  Occluded Re-ID

Some related works for the Occluded Re-ID have been well studied. Zheng et al. [36] propose an Ambiguity sensitive Matching Classifier (AMC) and a Sliding Window Matching (SWM) model for the local patch-level matching and the part-level matching, respectively. He et al. [6] propose a Deep Spatial Feature Reconstruction (DSR) model for the alignment-free matching, which can sparsely reconstruct the spatial probe maps from spatial maps of gallery images. He et al. [7] further present a Spatial Feature Reconstruction (SFR) method to match different sized feature maps for the Partial Re-ID. Miao et al. [23] propose the Pose-Guided Feature Alignment (PGFA), which introduces the pose estimation algorithm to enhance the human part feature in an occlusion image. Sun et al. [41] propose a self-supervision model called Visibility-aware Part Model (VPM), which can perceive the visibility of regions. Fan et al. [3] propose a spatial-channel parallelism network (SCPNet), which enhances the feature of a given spatial part of the body in each channel of the feature map.

These methods ignore the interference between pedestrians within a cropped image. Therefore, they cannot well address the PI Re-ID problem, where the large proportion of the pedestrian interference exists. In contrast, in this paper, we focus on suppressing the pedestrian interference, by learning the query-guided attention with the location accuracy and the feature distinctiveness.

## 3  Pedestrian-Interference Suppression Network

In this work, we assume that in PI Re-ID a query image contains only a single person and the task is to match this query with a gallery consisting of the pedestrian interference. This is based on a practical scenario where a human operator has manually cropped the human body and sent a query to a Re-ID system to search for the same person in another camera view. In this section, we first give an overview of our framework, and then describe more details for each component individually.

### 3.1  Overview

As shown in Fig. 3, PISNet consists of (1) a backbone Fully Convolutional Network (FCN), (2) a Query-Guided Attention Block (QGAB), and (3) a Guidance Reversed Attention Module (GRAM). For each forward propagation in the training stage, we pair a gallery image with a query image. FCN can extract features for the query and the gallery. QGAB finds the common regions between the

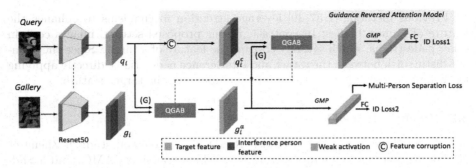

**Fig. 3.** Illustration of our Pedestrian-Interference Suppression Network (PISNet). For further clarity, the target feature represents the same ID information to the query. PISNet consists of (1) a backbone Fully Convolutional Network (FCN), (2) a Query-Guided Attention Block (QGAB), and (3) a Guidance Reversed Attention Module (GRAM). FCN can extract features for the query and the gallery. QGAB leverages the query feature as the guiding feature (single-person) to formulate attention on the gallery feature (with pedestrian interference). GRAM plays a role in encouraging QGAB to enhance the feature on the regions of a target. The Multi-person Separation Loss promotes the attention to draw a more precise boundary for overlapping instances. $g_i$ and $q_i$ denote the feature map of a gallery and a query, respectively. $g_i^a$ and $q_i^c$ are the refined gallery feature and the corrupted query feature, respectively. GMP denotes the Global Max Pooling. QGABs share the same parameters. (G) denotes the feature as the guidance to QGAB. GRAM is only used in the training stage

query and gallery feature maps, and then enhances the common feature in the gallery feature. For encouraging the location accuracy of the attention, GRAM aims to guarantee that the refined gallery feature has strong attention on all the regions of the target. For the feature distinctiveness of the attention, the Multi-person Separation Loss (MPSL) magnifies distance of the features from the same gallery but guided by different queries. In addition, GRAM is ignored in the testing stage.

## 3.2 Query-Guided Attention Block

QGAB is depicted in Fig. 4. The main goal of this block is to search for spatial similarity between the query and the multi-person gallery. The inputs of QGAB are the query and gallery feature maps. The query is used as the guidance. The output is the spatially enhanced gallery feature. The spatial similarity calculates the inner product of the features from gallery and query branch first, after which Global Max Pooling (GMP) in the channel dimension is applied to formulate a pixel-wise attention matrix. This matrix then is multiplied with the gallery feature in order to enforce a spatial similarity search between the query and gallery feature maps. The overall process of this feature enhancement is formulated as:

$$QGAB(g_i, q_i) = GMP\big(Softmax(c_1(g_i)^T \times c_2(q_i))\big) \times g_i + g_i, \tag{1}$$

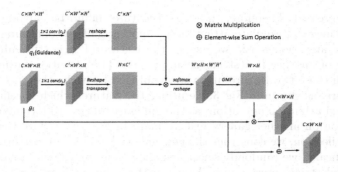

**Fig. 4.** Illustration of our proposed Query-Guided Attention Block (QGAB). $g_i$ denotes the feature map of a gallery. $q_i$ is the feature map of a query. The feature maps are shown as the shape of their tensors. $W$ and $H$ are the width and height of the gallery feature map. $W'$ and $H'$ are the width and height of the query feature map. $C$ is the number of channels after the backbone. GMP denotes the Global Max Pooling

where $g_i$ is the multi-person feature (gallery), $q_i$ is the single-person feature (query), $c_1$ and $c_2$ are convolutional layers, $GMP$ is the Global Max Pooling in the channel dimension and $\times$ denotes matrix multiplication.

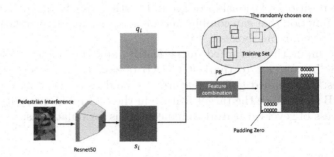

**Fig. 5.** Illustration of the feature corruption. $q_i$ denotes the query feature map. $s_i$ denotes the feature map of the sampled single-person image. $PR$ denotes the function that extracts the relative position relationship of ground-truth boxes from a multi-person image. Two features are combined following the relative position relationship

### 3.3 Guidance Reversed Attention Module

GRAM aims to guarantee that the refined gallery feature has the strong attention on all the regions of the target. As shown in Fig. 2(a), our motivation is that a well-refined gallery feature can be used as the guidance to formulate the attention for another gallery feature containing the pedestrian interference. For example, if a gallery contains IDs of A and B. Using the query image of A, the well-refined gallery feature will have the strong activation on regions of A while the feature of B is suppressed. Therefore, the refined feature should be capable of serving as the guidance to formulate attention for another gallery containing person A. In this new attention mask, we expect the feature of A is still enhanced and the feature of another pedestrian is suppressed. The attention formulation for person A in these two feature maps is encouraged by each other.

Therefore, as shown in Fig. 3, we utilize the feature, which is refined by our query-guided attention operation, as the guidance feature to formulate the spatial attention on another gallery feature map. In order to reduce the labour of the data collection, we construct the new gallery by a feature corruption operation. Specifically, we randomly select a single-person image and a gallery image with the pedestrian interference. We can extract the single-person feature from the former and the relative position relationship of the involving ground-truth bounding boxes from the latter. Then we corrupt the query feature by combining it with the single-person feature. Specifically, as shown in Fig. 5, following the relative position relationship, we put two feature maps on the corresponding positions to generate a multi-person feature map and we pad the remaining regions with zero. The process of this feature corruption is formulated as:

$$FC(q_i, s_i, m) = Combine(q_i, s_i, PR(m)),  \tag{2}$$

where $s_i$ is the feature map of the sampled single person image, $m$ denotes the image with pedestrian interference, $PR$ denotes the function that extracts the relative position relationship of ground-truth boxes from $m$, and $Combine$ denotes the function that can combine features depending on the relative position relationship of bounding boxes.

Then we input the corrupted query feature and the refined gallery feature into QGAB. In contrast to the last QGAB operation, we reverse the roles of two features. The refined gallery feature is served as a query feature that can guide QGAB to enhance the target feature in the corrupted query features. The overall process of reversed feature enhancement is formulated as:

$$QGAB^r(g_i^a, q_i^c) = GMP\big(Softmax(c_1(q_i^c)^T \times c_2(g_i^a))\big) \times q_i^c + q_i^c,  \tag{3}$$

where $g_i^a$ is the refined gallery feature, $q_i^c$ is the corrupted query feature, and $c_1$ and $c_2$ share parameters with the last QGAB.

### 3.4   Multi-person Separation Loss

In a pedestrian-interference image, people always share an overlapping area of their body. This is the key reason that causes the failure detection. Moreover, it also improves the difficulty of the attention learning. Therefore, we conduct the feature distinctiveness enhancement by the Multi-Person Separation Loss for further guaranteeing the purity of refined features.

As shown in Fig. 2(b), we expect that the refined feature should have a large distance to the feature guided by another query image with a different person

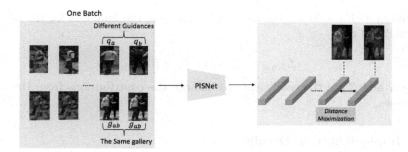

**Fig. 6.** The computation process of the Multi-Person Separation Loss. $q_a$ and $q_b$ denote the queries. $g_{ab}$ is the gallery. The subscripts represent the IDs that appear in the image. In one batch, we pair a multi-person gallery image with different query images as the guidances. To promote the feature distinctiveness of the attention, the distance between the refined features guided by different query images should be maximized

ID. For example, if a gallery image contains A and B, given the query image of A, we expect to extract the pure feature of A while suppressing the feature of B. In contrast, given the query image of person B, the pure feature of B should be extracted. In order to achieve this goal, as shown in Fig. 6, we first construct the image batch for training, where a multi-person gallery image is paired with different query images as the guidances. Then, the distances can be minimized and maximized, respectively, by the Multi-Person Separation Loss, which is given by,

$$L_m = max(0, c + dist(QGAB(g_{ab}, q_a), QGAB(g_{ab}, q_b)) - dist(QGAB(g_{ab}, q_a), q_a)), \tag{4}$$

where $dist$ is the cosine distance and $c$ denotes the margin coefficient. We should maximize the distance between $QGAB(g_{ab}, q_a)$ and $QGAB(g_{ab}, q_b)$ and meanwhile minimize the distance between $QGAB(g_{ab}, q_a)$ and $q_a$, where the subscripts represent the IDs that appear in the image.

### 3.5 Overall Objective Function

We utilize the cross entropy loss for both the gallery branch and GRAM, which is denoted as $L_g$ and $L_q$, which is corresponding to $ID\ Loss_1$ and $ID\ Loss_2$, respectively, in Fig. 3.

$$L_g = CE(\hat{y}, y), \tag{5}$$

$$L_q = CE(\bar{y}, y), \tag{6}$$

where $CE$ denotes the cross-entropy loss, $\hat{y}$ and $\bar{y}$ denote the prediction ID in the gallery branch and GRAM, respectively, and $y$ is the ground-truth ID. By combining with the Multi-Person Separation Loss, the final loss for the network is formulated as

$$L_{final} = L_g + \alpha * L_q + \beta * L_m,  \tag{7}$$

where $\alpha$ and $\beta$ are the coefficients to balance the contributions from the latter two losses.

### 3.6   Implementation Details

To implement our proposed model, we adopt Resnet-50 [5] as our basic CNN for feature extraction, which is pretrained on ImageNet. We first train the backbone on the single-person images using all training tricks in the strong baseline [20]. Then we add QGAB on the top of the Siamese Network. Both $c_1$ and $c_2$ are $1 \times 1$ convolutional layers with 1024 channels. Then we freeze the backbone network and train QGAB by pairing the multi-person images with single person ones. The batch size of samples for training is 64. The SGD optimizer is applied, with a learning rate of 0.00035. They are decayed by 0.1 after 20 epochs, and the training stops at 60 epochs. Parameters for the final loss function are $\alpha = 1.0$ and $\beta = 0.5$.

## 4   Experiments

### 4.1   Datasets and Evaluation Metrics

To demonstrate the effectiveness of our model on the Person-Interference Re-ID problem, we carry out the experiment on our constructed PI-PRW and PI-CUHK-SYSU dataset. Besides, in order to prove the generalization ability of our method on single-person images, we also evaluate the proposed PISNet on the another two datasets: Market-1501 [49] and DukeMTMC-ReID [27,53].

**PI-PRW** is derived from the PRW [51] dataset. We use the off-the-shelf detector Faster R-CNN [26] to perform pedestrian detection. Then we select the bounding boxes with multiple pedestrians. The selection criterion is: 1) At least 70% area of each ground-truth bounding box should be contained in the multi-person boxes. 2) The contained part of bounding boxes is at least 0.3 times the size of multi-person boxes in order to ensure the degree of the person interference. 3) Each bounding box has the overlapping area with any other ones. We get 1792 multi-person images with 273 IDs for training and 1258 multi-person gallery images and 211 single person query images with 211 person IDs for testing. Besides, in order to get closer to the actual scene, we add another 10000 single-person images in the test set as gallery images.

**PI-CUHK-SYSU** is derived from the CUHK-SYSU [38] dataset. We get multi-person cropped images following the same procedure in PI-PRW, resulting 3600 multi-person images for training with 1485 IDs and 3018 multi-person gallery images and 1479 single person query images with 1479 person IDs for testing. We also add another 10000 single-person images in the test set as gallery images. More details of PI-PRW and PI-CUHK-SYSU can be referred to our supplementary material.

**Evaluation Metrics.** We use Cumulative Matching Characteristic (CMC) curves and mean average precision (mAP) to evaluate the quality of different Re-ID models. All the experiments are performed in a single query setting.

**Table 1.** Comparison results (%) on PI-PRW and PI-CUHK-SYSU dataset at 4 evaluation metrics: *rank 1, rank 5, rank 10, mAP* where the bold font denotes the best method. The methods in the 1st group are proposed for the traditional Re-ID problem. The methods in the 2nd group are proposed for the multi-label learning. The 3rd group is the methods of Occluded Re-ID. The 4th group is our method

| Method | PI-PRW | | | | PI-CUHK-SYSU | | | |
|---|---|---|---|---|---|---|---|---|
| | *rank1* | *rank 5* | *rank 10* | *mAP* | *rank1* | *rank 5* | *rank 10* | *mAP* |
| HA-CNN [15] | 32.4 | 56.9 | 68.0 | 32.0 | 71.3 | 82.0 | 87.5 | 65.3 |
| PCB [32] | 31.3 | 55.1 | 67.5 | 30.2 | 70.1 | 80.4 | 86.9 | 63.1 |
| Strong Baseline [20] | 34.7 | 59.4 | 70.3 | 36.0 | 72.5 | 83.9 | 88.2 | 70.1 |
| PyramidNet [47] | 35.9 | 60.2 | 70.1 | 37.0 | 73.1 | 83.5 | 87.9 | 70.5 |
| ABD-Net [1] | 35.4 | 59.9 | 69.7 | 36.3 | 72.9 | 82.6 | 87.5 | 70.4 |
| QAConv [18] | 36.0 | 61.2 | 70.9 | 38.2 | 73.2 | 84.7 | 88.3 | 70.9 |
| HCP [42] | 30.2 | 49.7 | 61.2 | 29.6 | 67.2 | 75.3 | 83.5 | 61.9 |
| LIMOC [40] | 32.9 | 52.4 | 63.3 | 32.6 | 69.1 | 78.2 | 85.3 | 65.2 |
| FPR [7] | 36.3 | 60.7 | 70.4 | 37.9 | 73.7 | 85.0 | 89.1 | 71.2 |
| AFPB [56] | 34.1 | 58.2 | 67.2 | 35.1 | 70.7 | 83.2 | 87.3 | 68.3 |
| Ours | **42.7** | **67.4** | **76.2** | **43.2** | **79.1** | **88.4** | **91.9** | **76.5** |

## 4.2 Results Comparison

**Results on PI-PRW and PI-CUHK-SYSU.** We first compare the proposed approach with the existing methods on the two proposed PI Re-ID datasets. Table 1 shows the result of our method and previous works. The compared methods (including six existing representative Re-ID models, two multi-label learning approaches, and two Occluded Re-ID methods) are listed in the table. These results show: (1) Among existing methods, the Occluded Re-ID model FPR is superior. For example, FPR achieves 36.3% Rank-1 accuracy and 37.9% mAP on PI-PRW, which outperforms all the previous Re-ID methods. This is because, similar to our method, FPR [7] leverage query feature maps as multi-kernels to calculate the spatial affinity with the gallery feature maps, and then enhance the common features in the gallery features. (2) The performance of LIMOC [40] and HCP [42] proposed for the multi-label learning is ordinary. For example, compared to the strong baseline [20], HCP [42] is less by −4.5% Rank-1 accuracy and -3.5% mAP on PI-PRW. (3) Our new model PISNet outperforms all competitors by significant margins. For example, PISNet achieves

42.7% Rank-1 accuracy and 43.2% mAP on PI-PRW and 79.1% Rank-1 accuracy and 76.5% mAP on PI-CUHK-SYSU. This is because our proposed method explicitly utilizes query information and learn a more precise boundary between pedestrians by GRAM and MPSL.

**Table 2.** Component analysis of the proposed method on the PI-PRW and PI-CUHK-SYSU datasets (%)

| Method | PI-PRW | | | | PI-CUHK-SYSU | | | |
|---|---|---|---|---|---|---|---|---|
| | rank1 | rank 5 | rank 10 | mAP | rank1 | rank 5 | rank 10 | mAP |
| Baseline | 34.7 | 59.4 | 70.3 | 36.0 | 72.5 | 83.9 | 88.2 | 70.1 |
| Baseline + QGAB | 38.9 | 61.5 | 72.4 | 38.0 | 73.9 | 85.0 | 89.1 | 72.3 |
| Baseline + QGAB + MPSL | 39.7 | 63.2 | 74.1 | 40.1 | 76.2 | 87.1 | 91.4 | 74.2 |
| Baseline + QGAB + GRAM | 41.8 | 66.1 | 75.2 | 42.4 | 77.9 | 87.5 | 91.0 | 75.0 |
| Baseline + QGAB + GRAM + MPSL | 42.7 | 67.4 | 76.2 | 43.2 | 79.1 | 88.4 | 91.9 | 76.5 |

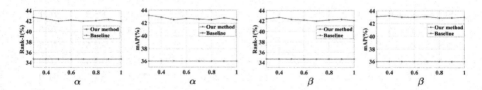

**Fig. 7.** Evaluation of different parameters of PISNet using Rank-1 and mAP accuracy on the PI-PRW dataset (%)

### 4.3 Further Analysis

**Contributions of Individual Components.** In Table 2, we evaluate the three components on how they contribute to the full model. The results show that all of them are effective on their own (each outperforms all the compared methods). Moreover, when combined, the best performance is achieved. This validates our design consideration in that they are complementary and should be combined.

**Does PISNet Perform well on the General Re-ID Dataset?** We also apply our method on the general Re-ID datasets, Market-1501 and DukeMTMC-ReID. The compared methods (including fifteen existing representative Re-ID models, and two state-of-the-art Occluded Re-ID methods) are listed in Table 3. The results show that: 1) Compared to existing representative Re-ID models, our method achieves comparable performances with state-of-the-art on both datasets. These models leverage complicated attention mechanisms or local-based methods to achieve the results, while our PISNet is specifically designed for PI Re-ID. 2) Our method outperforms the existing Occluded Re-ID models on both general Re-ID datasets. Specifically, our method can reach 95.6% rank-1 accuracy and 87.1% mAP on Market1501, and 88.8% rank-1 accuracy and

**Table 3.** Comparison results (%) on the Market-1501 and DukeMTMC-ReID datasets. $N_f$ is the number of features used in the inference stage. The methods in the 1st group are proposed for the traditional Re-ID problem. The 2nd group is the state-of-the-art methods of Occluded Re-ID. The 3rd group is our method

| Method | $N_f$ | Market1501 | | DukeMTMC-ReID | |
| --- | --- | --- | --- | --- | --- |
| | | r = 1 | mAP | r = 1 | mAP |
| PIE [48] | 3 | 87.7 | 69.0 | 79.8 | 62.0 |
| SPReID [9] | 5 | 92.5 | 81.3 | 84.4 | 71.0 |
| MaskReID [12] | 3 | 90.0 | 75.3 | 78.8 | 61.9 |
| MGN [33] | 1 | 95.7 | 86.9 | 88.7 | 78.4 |
| SCPNet [3] | 1 | 91.2 | 75.2 | 80.3 | 62.6 |
| PCB [32] | 6 | 93.8 | 81.6 | 83.3 | 69.2 |
| Pyramid [47] | 1 | 92.8 | 82.1 | – | – |
| Pyramid [47] | 21 | 95.7 | 88.2 | 89.0 | 79.0 |
| HA-CNN [15] | 4 | 91.2 | 75.7 | 80.5 | 63.8 |
| ABD-Net [1] | 1 | 95.6 | 88.3 | 89.0 | 78.6 |
| Camstyle [55] | 1 | 88.1 | 68.7 | 75.3 | 53.5 |
| PN-GAN [25] | 9 | 89.4 | 72.6 | 73.6 | 53.2 |
| IDE [46] | 1 | 79.5 | 59.9 | – | – |
| SVDNet [31] | 1 | 82.3 | 62.1 | 76.7 | 56.8 |
| TriNet [8] | 1 | 84.9 | 69.1 | – | – |
| SONA [37] | 1 | 95.6 | 88.8 | 89.6 | 78.2 |
| FPR [7] | 1 | 95.4 | 86.5 | 88.6 | 78.2 |
| PGFA [23] | 1 | 91.2 | 76.8 | 82.6 | 65.5 |
| Baseline | 1 | 94.5 | 85.9 | 86.4 | 76.4 |
| **Ours** | 1 | 95.6 | 87.1 | 88.8 | 78.7 |

78.7% mAP on DukeMTMC-ReID. The results prove the generalization ability of PISNet on the general Re-ID datasets.

**Influence of Parameters.** We evaluate two key parameters in our modelling, the loss weights $\alpha$ and $\beta$ in Eq.(7). The two parameters would influence the performance of the proposed method. As shown in Fig. 7, when $\alpha$ and $\beta$ are set between 0.3 and 1.0, and 0.4 and 1.0, respectively, the performance does not change dramatically, which indicates that PISNet is not sensitive to the $\alpha$ and $\beta$ in the value ranges.

## 4.4   Attention Visualisation

We visualise our query-guided attention for multi-person images in the PI-CUHK-SYSU dataset. Figure 8 shows that: (1) The attention mask filters out other pedestrians in multi-person images, (2) When the multi-person gallery does not include the query, the attention is weak for the whole image (the third group in the second rows). The visualisation results further prove that our method can suppress the pedestrian interference effectively.

**Fig. 8.** Visualisation of our query-guided attention for multi-person images in PI-CUHK-SYSU. In each group, from left to right, (1) the single-person query, (2) the multi-person gallery and (3) the masked feature map. In the heat map, the response increases from blue to red. Best viewed in color (Color figure online)

## 5   Conclusions

We have considered a new and more realistic person Re-ID challenge: pedestrian-interference person re-identification problem. To address the particular challenges associated with this new Re-ID problem, we propose a novel query-guided framework PISNet with a Guidance Reversed Attention Module and the Multi-Person Separation Loss. Both are specifically designed to address the person interference problem. The effectiveness of our model has been demonstrated by extensive experiments on two new pedestrian-interference Re-ID datasets introduced in this paper. In our future work, we will extend this work to handle more kinds of hard cases caused by a non-perfect detector.

**Acknowledgment.** This work was supported by the National Key R&D Program of China No. 2018YFB1004602 and the Project of the National Natural Science Foundation of China No. 61876210.

## References

1. Chen, T., et al.: ABD-Net: attentive but diverse person re-identification. In: The IEEE International Conference on Computer Vision (ICCV) (2019)
2. Cheng, D., Gong, Y., Zhou, S., Wang, J., Zheng, N.: Person re-identification by multi-channel parts-based CNN with improved triplet loss function. In: The IEEE Conference on Computer Vision and Pattern Recognition (CVPR) (2016)
3. Fan, X., Luo, H., Zhang, X., He, L., Zhang, C., Jiang, W.: SCPNet: spatial-channel parallelism network for joint holistic and partial person re-identification. In: Jawahar, C.V., Li, H., Mori, G., Schindler, K. (eds.) ACCV 2018. LNCS, vol. 11362, pp. 19–34. Springer, Cham (2019). https://doi.org/10.1007/978-3-030-20890-5_2

4. Gray, D., Tao, H.: Viewpoint invariant pedestrian recognition with an ensemble of localized features. In: Forsyth, D., Torr, P., Zisserman, A. (eds.) ECCV 2008. LNCS, vol. 5302, pp. 262–275. Springer, Heidelberg (2008). https://doi.org/10.1007/978-3-540-88682-2_21
5. He, K., Zhang, X., Ren, S., Sun, J.: Deep residual learning for image recognition. In: The IEEE Conference on Computer Vision and Pattern Recognition (CVPR) (2016)
6. He, L., Liang, J., Li, H., Sun, Z.: Deep spatial feature reconstruction for partial person re-identification: alignment-free approach. In: The IEEE Conference on Computer Vision and Pattern Recognition (CVPR) (2018)
7. He, L., Wang, Y., Liu, W., Zhao, H., Sun, Z., Feng, J.: Foreground-aware pyramid reconstruction for alignment-free occluded person re-identification. In: The IEEE International Conference on Computer Vision (ICCV) (2019)
8. Hermans, A., Beyer, L., Leibe, B.: In defense of the triplet loss for person re-identification. arXiv preprint arXiv:1703.07737 (2017)
9. Kalayeh, M.M., Basaran, E., Gökmen, M., Kamasak, M.E., Shah, M.: Human semantic parsing for person re-identification. In: The IEEE Conference on Computer Vision and Pattern Recognition (CVPR) (2018)
10. Khamis, S., Kuo, C.-H., Singh, V.K., Shet, V.D., Davis, L.S.: Joint learning for attribute-consistent person re-identification. In: Agapito, L., Bronstein, M.M., Rother, C. (eds.) ECCV 2014. LNCS, vol. 8927, pp. 134–146. Springer, Cham (2015). https://doi.org/10.1007/978-3-319-16199-0_10
11. Koestinger, M., Hirzer, M., Wohlhart, P., Roth, P.M., Bischof, H.: Large scale metric learning from equivalence constraints. In: The IEEE Conference on Computer Vision and Pattern Recognition (CVPR) (2012)
12. Lei, Q., Jing, H., Lei, W., Yinghuan, S., Yang, G.: MaskReID: a mask based deep ranking neural network for person re-identification (2019)
13. Li, W., Wang, X.: Locally aligned feature transforms across views. In: The IEEE Conference on Computer Vision and Pattern Recognition (CVPR) (2013)
14. Li, W., Zhao, R., Xiao, T., Wang, X.: DeepReID: deep filter pairing neural network for person re-identification. In: Proceedings of the IEEE Conference on Computer Vision and Pattern Recognition (CVPR) (2014)
15. Li, W., Zhu, X., Gong, S.: Harmonious attention network for person re-identification. In: The IEEE Conference on Computer Vision and Pattern Recognition (CVPR) (2018)
16. Li, Z., Chang, S., Liang, F., Huang, T.S., Cao, L., Smith, J.R.: Learning locally-adaptive decision functions for person verification. In: The IEEE Conference on Computer Vision and Pattern Recognition (CVPR) (2013)
17. Liao, S., Hu, Y., Zhu, X., Li, S.Z.: Person re-identification by local maximal occurrence representation and metric learning. In: The IEEE Conference on Computer Vision and Pattern Recognition (CVPR) (2015)
18. Liao, S., Shao, L.: Interpretable and generalizable deep image matching with adaptive convolutions (2019)
19. Liao, W., Yang, M.Y., Zhan, N., Rosenhahn, B.: Triplet-based deep similarity learning for person re-identification. In: The 2017 IEEE International Conference on Computer Vision Workshop (ICCVW) (2017)
20. Luo, H., Gu, Y., Liao, X., Lai, S., Jiang, W.: Bag of tricks and a strong baseline for deep person re-identification (2019)
21. Ma, A.J., Yuen, P.C., Li, J.: Domain transfer support vector ranking for person re-identification without target camera label information. In: The IEEE International Conference on Computer Vision (CVPR) (2013)

22. Ma, B., Su, Y., Jurie, F.: BiCov: a novel image representation for person re-identification and face verification. In: British Machive Vision Conference (BMVC) (2012)
23. Miao, J., Wu, Y., Liu, P., Ding, Y., Yang, Y.: Pose-guided feature alignment for occluded person re-identification. In: The IEEE International Conference on Computer Vision (ICCV) (2019)
24. Prosser, B.J., Zheng, W.S., Gong, S., Xiang, T., Mary, Q.: Person re-identification by support vector ranking. In: British Machive Vision Conference (BMVC) (2010)
25. Qian, X., et al.: Pose-normalized image generation for person re-identification. In: Ferrari, V., Hebert, M., Sminchisescu, C., Weiss, Y. (eds.) ECCV 2018. LNCS, vol. 11213, pp. 661–678. Springer, Cham (2018). https://doi.org/10.1007/978-3-030-01240-3_40
26. Ren, S., He, K., Girshick, R., Sun, J.: Faster R-CNN: towards real-time object detection with region proposal networks (2015)
27. Ristani, E., Solera, F., Zou, R., Cucchiara, R., Tomasi, C.: Performance measures and a data set for multi-target, multi-camera tracking. In: Hua, G., Jégou, H. (eds.) ECCV 2016. LNCS, vol. 9914, pp. 17–35. Springer, Cham (2016). https://doi.org/10.1007/978-3-319-48881-3_2
28. Si, J., et al.: Dual attention matching network for context-aware feature sequence based person re-identification. arXiv preprint arXiv:1803.09937 (2018)
29. Su, C., Li, J., Zhang, S., Xing, J., Gao, W., Tian, Q.: Pose-driven deep convolutional model for person re-identification. In: The IEEE International Conference on Computer Vision (ICCV) (2017)
30. Suh, Y., Wang, J., Tang, S., Mei, T., Lee, K.M.: Part-aligned bilinear representations for person re-identification. arXiv preprint arXiv:1804.07094 (2018)
31. Sun, Y., Zheng, L., Deng, W., Wang, S.: SVDNet for pedestrian retrieval. In: The IEEE International Conference on Computer Vision (ICCV), October 2017
32. Sun, Y., Zheng, L., Yang, Y., Tian, Q., Wang, S.: Beyond part models: person retrieval with refined part pooling (and a strong convolutional baseline). In: Ferrari, V., Hebert, M., Sminchisescu, C., Weiss, Y. (eds.) ECCV 2018. LNCS, vol. 11208, pp. 501–518. Springer, Cham (2018). https://doi.org/10.1007/978-3-030-01225-0_30
33. Wang, G., Yuan, Y., Chen, X., Li, J., Zhou, X.: Learning discriminative features with multiple granularities for person re-identification. In: ACM Multimedia Conference on Multimedia Conference (ACM MM) (2018)
34. Wei, L., Zhang, S., Yao, H., Gao, W., Tian, Q.: Glad: global-local-alignment descriptor for pedestrian retrieval. In: ACM on Multimedia Conference (ACM MM) (2017)
35. Weinberger, K.Q., Blitzer, J., Saul, L.K.: Distance metric learning for large margin nearest neighbor classification. In: Advances in Neural Information Processing Systems (NIPS) (2006)
36. Weishi, Z., Xiang, L., Tao, X., Shengcai, L., Jianhuang, L., Shaogang, G.: Partial person re-identification. In: The IEEE International Conference on Computer Vision, ICCV (2015)
37. Xia, B.N., Gong, Y., Zhang, Y., Poellabauer, C.: Second-order non-local attention networks for person re-identification. In: The IEEE International Conference on Computer Vision (ICCV) (2019)
38. Xiao, T., Li, S., Wang, B., Lin, L., Wang, X.: Joint detection and identification feature learning for person search. In: The IEEE Conference on Computer Vision and Pattern Recognition (CVPR) (2017)

39. Xu, J., Zhao, R., Zhu, F., Wang, H., Ouyang, W.: Attention-aware compositional network for person re-identification. arXiv preprint arXiv:1805.03344 (2018)
40. Yang, H., Tianyi Zhou, J., Zhang, Y., Gao, B.B., Wu, J., Cai, J.: Exploit bounding box annotations for multi-label object recognition. In: The IEEE Conference on Computer Vision and Pattern Recognition (CVPR) (2016)
41. Yifan, S., et al.: Perceive where to focus: learning visibility-aware part-level features for partial person re-identification. In: The IEEE Conference on Computer Vision and Pattern Recognition (CVPR) (2019)
42. Yunchao, W., et al.: HCP: a flexible CNN framework for multi-label image classification. IEEE Trans. Pattern Anal. Mach. Intell. (PAMI) **28**, 1901–1907 (2016)
43. Zhao, H., et al.: Spindle net: person re-identification with human body region guided feature decomposition and fusion. In: The IEEE Conference on Computer Vision and Pattern Recognition (CVPR) (2017)
44. Zhao, L., Li, X., Zhuang, Y., Wang, J.: Deeply-learned part-aligned representations for person re-identification. In: The IEEE International Conference on Computer Vision (ICCV) (2017)
45. Zhao, R., Ouyang, W., Wang, X.: Learning mid-level filters for person re-identification. In: The IEEE Conference on Computer Vision and Pattern Recognition (CVPR) (2014)
46. Zhedong, Z., Liang, Z., Yi, Y.: A discriminatively learned CNN embedding for person reidentification. ACM Trans. Multimed. Comput. Commun. Appl. (TOMM) **14**, 1–20 (2018)
47. Zheng, F., et al.: Pyramidal person re-identification via multi-loss dynamic training. In: The IEEE Conference on Computer Vision and Pattern Recognition (CVPR), June 2019
48. Zheng, L., Huang, Y., Lu, H., Yang, Y.: Pose invariant embedding for deep person re-identification. arXiv preprint arXiv:1701.07732 (2017)
49. Zheng, L., Shen, L., Tian, L., Wang, S., Wang, J., Tian, Q.: Scalable person re-identification: a benchmark. In: The IEEE International Conference on Computer Vision (ICCV) (2015)
50. Zheng, L., Yang, Y., Hauptmann, A.G.: Person re-identification: past, present and future. arXiv preprint arXiv:1610.02984 (2016)
51. Zheng, L., Zhang, H., Sun, S., Chandraker, M., Yang, Y., Tian, Q.: Person re-identification in the wild. In: The IEEE Conference on Computer Vision and Pattern Recognition (CVPR) (2017)
52. Zheng, W.S., Gong, S., Xiang, T.: Reidentification by relative distance comparison. IEEE Trans. Pattern Analysis Mach. Intell. (PAMI) **35**, 653–668 (2013)
53. Zheng, Z., Zheng, L., Yang, Y.: Unlabeled samples generated by GAN improve the person re-identification baseline in vitro. arXiv preprint arXiv:1701.07717 (2017)
54. Zhu, F., Kong, X., Zheng, L., Fu, H., Tian, Q.: Part-based deep hashing for large-scale person re-identification. IEEE Trans. Image Process. (TIP) **26**, 4806–4817 (2017)
55. Zhun, Z., Liang, Z., Zhedong, Z., Shaozi, L., Yi, Y.: CamStyle: a novel data augmentation method for person re-identification. IEEE Trans. Image Process. (TIP) **28**, 1176–1190 (2019)
56. Zhuo, J., Chen, Z., Lai, J., Wang, G.: Occluded person re-identification. In: 2018 IEEE International Conference on Multimedia and Expo (ICME) (2018)

# Learning 3D Part Assembly from a Single Image

Yichen Li[1(✉)], Kaichun Mo[1], Lin Shao[1], Minhyuk Sung[2],
and Leonidas Guibas[1]

[1] Stanford University, Stanford, USA
liyichen@stanford.edu
[2] Adobe Research, San Jose, USA

**Abstract.** Autonomous assembly is a crucial capability for robots in many applications. For this task, several problems such as obstacle avoidance, motion planning, and actuator control have been extensively studied in robotics. However, when it comes to task specification, the space of possibilities remains underexplored. Towards this end, we introduce a novel problem, *single-image-guided 3D part assembly*, along with a learning-based solution. We study this problem in the setting of *furniture assembly* from a given complete set of parts and a single image depicting the entire assembled object. Multiple challenges exist in this setting, including handling ambiguity among parts (*e.g.*, slats in a chair back and leg stretchers) and 3D pose prediction for parts and part subassemblies, whether visible or occluded. We address these issues by proposing a two-module pipeline that leverages strong 2D-3D correspondences and assembly-oriented graph message-passing to infer part relationships. In experiments with a PartNet-based synthetic benchmark, we demonstrate the effectiveness of our framework as compared with three baseline approaches (code and data available at https://github.com/AntheaLi/3DPartAssembly).

**Keywords:** Single-image 3D part assembly · Vision for robotic assembly

## 1 Introduction

The important and seemingly straightforward task of furniture assembly presents serious difficulties for autonomous robots. A general robotic assembly task consists of action sequences incorporating the following stages: (1) picking up a particular part, (2) moving it to a desired 6D pose, (3) mating it precisely with

---

Y. Li and K. Mo—Equal contributions.

---

**Electronic supplementary material** The online version of this chapter (https://doi.org/10.1007/978-3-030-58539-6_40) contains supplementary material, which is available to authorized users.

© Springer Nature Switzerland AG 2020
A. Vedaldi et al. (Eds.): ECCV 2020, LNCS 12351, pp. 664–682, 2020.
https://doi.org/10.1007/978-3-030-58539-6_40

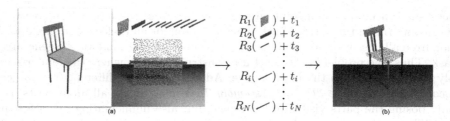

$$R_1(\ \blacksquare\ ) + t_1$$
$$R_2(\ \diagup\ ) + t_2$$
$$R_3(\ \diagup\ ) + t_3$$
$$\vdots$$
$$R_i(\ \diagup\ ) + t_i$$
$$\vdots$$
$$R_N(\ \diagup\ ) + t_N$$

**Fig. 1.** Single-Image-Based 3D Part Assembly Task. Given as inputs an image and a set of part point clouds depicted in (a), the task is to predict 6D part poses in camera coordinates that assemble the parts to a 3D shape in the given image as shown in (b).

the other parts, (4) returning the manipulator to a pose appropriate for the next pick-up movement. Solving such a complicated high-dimensional motion planning problem [21,25] requires considerable time and engineering effort. Current robotic assembly solutions first determine the desired 6D pose of parts [9] and then hard-code the motion trajectories for each specific object [55]. Such limited generalizability and painstaking process planning fail to meet demands for fast and flexible industrial manufacturing and household assembly tasks [31] (Fig. 1).

To generate smooth and collision-free motion planning and control solutions, it is required to accurately predict 6D poses of parts in 3D space [27,55]. We propose a *3D part assembly task* whose output can reduce the complexity of the high-dimensional motion planning problem. We aim to learn generalizable skills that allow robots to autonomously assemble unseen objects from parts [16]. Instead of hand-crafting a fixed set of rules to assemble one specific chair, for example, we explore category-wise structural priors that helps robots to assemble all kinds of chairs. The shared part relationships across instances in a category not only suggest potential pose estimation solutions for unseen objects but also lead to possible generalization ability for robotic control policies [43,54,61,65].

We introduce the task of *single-image-guided 3D part assembly*: inducing 6D poses of the parts in 3D space [30] from a set of 3D parts and an image depicting the complete object. Robots can acquire geometry information for each part using 3D sensing, but the only information provided for the entire object shape is the instruction image. Different from many structure-aware shape modeling works [17,32,40,53,63,71,72], we do not assume any specific granularity or semantics of the input parts, since the given furniture parts may not belong to any known part semantics and some of the parts may be provided pre-assembled into bigger units. We also step away from instruction manuals illustrating the step-by-step assembling process, as teaching machines to read sequential instructions depicted with natural languages and figures is still a hard problem.

At the core of the task lie several challenges. First, some parts may have similar geometry. For example, distinguishing the geometric subtlety of chair leg bars, stretcher bars, and back bars is a difficult problem. Second, 3D geometric reasoning is essential in finding a joint global solution, where every piece fits perfectly in the puzzle. Parts follow a more rigid relationship graph which determines a unique final solution that emerges from the interactions between the geometries of the parts. Third, the image grounds and selects one single solution from all possible part combinations that might all be valid for the generative task. Thus, the problem is at heart a reconstruction task where the final assembly needs to agree to the input image. Additionally, and different from object localization tasks, *the 3D Part Assembly Task* must locate all input parts, not only posing the parts visible in the image, but also hallucinating poses for the invisible ones by leveraging learned data priors. One can think of having multiple images to expose all parts to the robot, but this reduces the generalizability to real-world scenarios, and might not be easy to achieve. Thus, we focus on solving the task of single-image and category-prior-guided pose prediction.

In this paper, we introduce a learning-based method to tackle the proposed *single-image-guided 3D part assembly* problem. Given the input image and a set of 3D parts, we first focus on 2D structural guidance by predicting an part-instance image segmentation to serve as a 2D-3D grounding for the downstream pose prediction. To enforce reasoning involving fine geometric subtleties, we design a context-aware 3D geometric feature to help the network reason about each part pose, conditioned on the existence of other parts, which might be of similar geometry. Building on the 2D structural guidance, we generate a pose proposal for each visible part and leverage these predictions to help hallucinate poses for invisible parts. We use a part graph network, using edges to encode different relationships among parts, and design a two-phase message-passing mechanism to take part relationship constraints into consideration in the assembly.

To best of our knowledge, we are the first to assemble *unlabeled* 3D parts with a *single image* input. We set up a testbed of the problem on the recently released PartNet [42] dataset. We compare our method with several baseline methods to demonstrate the effectiveness of our approach. We evaluate all model performances on the unseen test shapes. Extensive ablation experiments also demonstrate the effectiveness and necessity of the proposed method.

In summary, our contributions are:

- we formulate the task of *single-image-guided 3D part assembly*;
- we propose a two-module method, consisting of a part-instance image segmentation network and an assembly-aware part graph convolution network;
- we compare with three baseline methods and conduct ablation studies demonstrating the effectiveness of our proposed method.

## 2   Related Work

We review previous works on 3D pose estimation, single-image 3D reconstruction, as well as part-based shape modeling, and discuss how they relate to our task.

*3D Pose Estimation.* Estimating the pose of objects or object parts is a long-standing problem with a rich literature. Early in 2001, Langley *et al.* [76] attempted to utilize visual sensors and neural networks to predict the pose for robotic assembly tasks. Zeng *et al.* [78] built an robotic system taking multi-view RGB-D images as the input and predicting 6D pose of objects for Amazon Picking Challenge. Recently, Litvak *et al.* [37] proposed a two-stage pose estimation procedure taking depth images as input. In the vision community, there is also a line of works studying instance-level object pose estimation for known instances [1,2,28,49,59,60,73] and category-level pose estimation [3,7,19,45,64] that can possibly deal with unseen objects from known categories. There are also works on object re-localization from scenes [23,62,77]. Different from these works, our task takes as inputs unseen parts without any semantic labels at the test time, and requires certain part relationships and constraints to be held in order to assemble a plausible and physically stable 3D shape.

*Single-Image 3D Reconstruction.* There are previous works of reconstructing 3D shape from a single image with the representations of voxel grids [10,50, 58,68], point clouds [14,22,34], meshes [66,70], parametric surfaces [18], and implicit functions [8,39,46,52,75]. While one can consider employing such 2D-to-3D lifting techniques as a prior step in our assembly process so that the given parts can be matched to the predicted 3D shape, it can misguide the assembly in multiple ways. For instance, the 3D prediction can be inaccurate, and even some small geometric differences can be crucial for part pose prediction. Also, the occluded area can be hallucinated in different ways. In our case, the set of parts that should compose the object is given, and thus the poses of occluded parts can be more precisely specified.

*Part-Based Shape Modeling.* 3D shapes have compositional part structures. Chaudhuri *et al.* [5], Kalogerakis *et al.* [26] and Jaiswal *et al.* [24] introduced frameworks learning probabilistic graphical models that describe pairwise relationships of parts. Chaudhuri and Koltun [6], Sung *et al.* [57] and Sung *et al.* [56] predict the compatibility between a part and a *partial* object for sequential shape synthesis by parts. Dubrovina *et al.* [13], PAGENet [32] and CompoNet [53] take the set of parts as the input and generates the shape of assembled parts. Different from these works that usually assume known part semantics or a part database, our task takes a set of unseen parts during the test time and we do not assume any provided part semantic labels.

GRASS [33], Im2Struct [44] and StructureNet [40,41] learns to generate box-abstracted shape hierarchical structures. SAGNet [72] and SDM-Net [17] learn the pairwise relationship among parts that are subsequently integrated into a latent representation of the global shape. G2LGAN [63] autoencodes the shape of an entire object with per-point part labels, and a subsequent network in the decoding refines the geometry of each part. PQ-Net [71] represents a shape as a sequence of parts and generates each part at every step of the iterative decoding process. All of these works are relevant but different from ours in that we obtain the final geometry of the object not by directly decoding the latent code into part geometry but by predicting the poses of the given parts and explicitly assembling them. There are also works studying partial-to-full shape matching [12,35,36]. Unlike these works, we use a single image as the guidance, instead of a 3D model.

## 3   Problem Formulation

We define the task of *single-image-guided 3D part assembly*: given a single RGB image $I$ of size $m \times m$ depicting a 3D object $S$ and a set of $N$ 3D part point clouds $\mathcal{P} = \{p_1, p_2, \cdots, p_N\}$ ($\forall i, p_i \in \mathbb{R}^{d_{pc} \times 3}$), we predict a set of part poses $\{(R_i, t_i) \mid R_i \in \mathbb{R}^{3 \times 3}, t_i \in \mathbb{R}^3, i = 1, 2, \cdots, N\}$ in $SE(3)$ space. After applying the predicted rigid transformation to all the input parts $p_i$'s, the union of them reconstructs the 3D object $S$. We predict output part poses $\{(R_i, t_i) \mid i = 1, 2, \cdots, N\}$ in the camera space, following previous works [15,67]. In our paper, we use Quaternion to represent rotation and use $q_i$ and $R_i$ interchangeably.

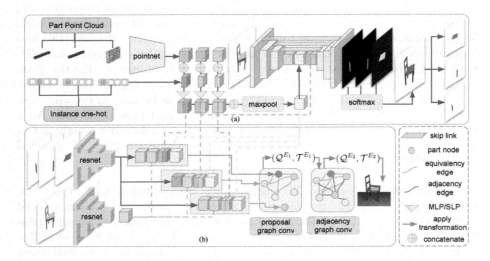

**Fig. 2.** Network Architecture. Our approach contains two network modules: (a) the part-instance image segmentation module, in which we predict 2D instance-level part masks on the image, and (b) the part pose prediction module, where we combine 2D mask information and 3D geometry feature for each part, push them through two phases of graph convolution, and finally predict 6D part poses.

We conduct a series of pose and scale normalization on the input part point clouds to ensure *synthetic-to-real* generalizability. We normalize each part point cloud pose $p_i \in \mathcal{P}$ to have a zero-mean center and use a local part coordinate system computed using PCA [47]. To normalize the global scale of all training and testing data, we compute Axis-Aligned-Bounding-Boxes (AABB) for all the parts and normalize them so that the longest box diagonal across all $p_i$'s of a shape has a unit length while preserving their relative scales. We cluster the normalized part point clouds $p_i$'s into sets of geometrically equivalent part classes $\mathcal{C} = \{C_1, C_2, \cdots, C_K\}$, where $C_1 = \{p_i\}_{i=1}^{N_1}$, $C_2 = \{p_i\}_{i=N_1+1}^{N_1+N_2}$, etc. For example, four legs of a chair are clustered together if their geometry is identical. This process of grouping indiscernible parts is essential to resolve the ambiguity among them in our framework. $\mathcal{C}$ is a disjoint complete set such that $C_k \cap C_l = \phi$ for every $C_k, C_l \in \mathcal{C}, k \neq l$ and $\cup_{k=1}^{K} C_k = \mathcal{P}$. We denote the representative point cloud $p_j$ for each class $C_j \in \mathcal{C}$.

# 4    Method

We propose a method for the task of *single-image-guided 3D part assembly*, which is composed of two network modules: 1) part-instance image segmentation and 2) part pose prediction. Figure 2 illustrates the overall architecture. We first extract a geometry feature of each part from the input point cloud $p_j \in \mathcal{C}$ and generates $N$ instance-level 2D segmentation masks $\{M_i \in \{0,1\}^{m \times m} | i = 1, 2, \cdots, N\}$ on the input image ($m = 224$). Conditioned on the predicted segmentation masks, our model then leverages both the 2D mask features and the 3D geometry features to propose 6D part poses $\{(q_i, t_i) | i = 1, 2, \cdots, N\}$. Below, we explain the two network module designs and refer to supplementary for implementation details.

## 4.1    Part-Instance Image Segmentation

To induce a faithful reconstruction of the object represented in the image, we need to learn a structural layout of the input parts from the 2D input. We predict a part instance mask $M_i \in \{0,1\}^{m \times m}$ for each part $p_i$. All part masks subject to the disjoint constraint, *i.e.*, $M_{bg} + \sum_{i=1}^{N} M_i = \mathbf{1}$, where $M_{bg}$ denotes a background mask. If a part is invisible, we simply predict an empty mask and let the second network to hallucinate a pose leveraging contextual information and learned data priors. The task difficulties are two folds. First, the network needs to distinguish between the geometric subtlety of the input part point clouds to establish a valid 2D-3D correspondence. Second, for the identical parts within each geometrically equivalent class, we need to identify separate 2D mask regions to pinpoint their exact locations.

*Context-Aware 3D Part Features.* To enable the network to reason the delicate differences between parts, we construct the context-aware 3D conditional feature $f_{3d} \in \mathbb{R}^{2F_2}$ ($F_2 = 256$), which is computed from three components: part geometry feature $f_{geo} \in \mathbb{R}^{F_2}$, instance one-hot vector $f_{ins} \in \mathbb{R}^{P_{max}}$ ($P_{max} = 20$), and a global part contextual feature $f_{global} \in \mathbb{R}^{F_2}$. We use PointNet [48] to extract a global geometry feature $f_{geo}$ for each part point cloud $p_i$. If a part $p_j$ has multiple instances $k_j > 1$ within a geometrically equivalent class $C_j$ (*e.g.*, four chair legs), we introduce an additional instance one-hot vector $f_{ins}$ to tell them apart. For part which has only one instance, we use an one-hot vector with the first element to be 1. For contextual awareness, we extract a global feature $f_{global}$ over all the input part point clouds, to facilitate the network to distinguish between similar but not equivalent part geometries (*e.g.*, a short bar or a long bar).

Precisely, we first compute $f_{geo}$ and $f_{ins}$ for every part, then compute $f_{local} = SLP_1([f_{geo}; f_{ins}]) \in \mathbb{R}^{F_2}$ to obtain per-part local feature, where SLP is short for Single-Layer Perception. We aggregate over all part local features via a max-pooling symmetric function to compute the global contextual feature $f_{global} = SLP_2(MAX_{i=1,2,\cdots,N}(f_{i,local}))$. Finally, we define $f_{3d} = [f_{local}; f_{global}] \in \mathbb{R}^{2F_2}$ to be the context-aware 3D per-part feature.

*Conditional U-Net Segmentation.* We use a conditional U-Net [51] for the part-instance segmentation task. Preserving the standard U-Net CNN architecture, our encoder takes an 3-channel RGB image as input and produce a bottleneck feature map $f_{2d} \in \mathbb{R}^{F_1 \times 7 \times 7}$ ($F_1 = 512$). Concatenating the image feature $f_{2d}$ with our context-aware 3D part conditional feature $f_{3d}$, we obtain $f_{2d+3d} = [f_{2d}, f_{3d}] \in \mathbb{R}^{(F_1+2F_2) \times 7 \times 7}$, where we duplicate $f_{3d}$ along the spatial dimensions for $7 \times 7$ times. The decoder takes the conditional bottleneck feature $f_{2d+3d}$ and decodes a part mask $M_i$ for evert input part $p_i$. We keep skip links as introduced in the original U-Net paper between encoder and decoder layers. To satisfy the non-overlapping constraint, we add a SoftMax layer across all predicted masks, augmented with a background mask $M_{bg} \in \{0,1\}^{(m \times m)}$.

## 4.2   Part Pose Prediction

With the 2D grounding masks produced by the part-instance image segmentation module, we predict a 6D part pose $(R_i, t_i)$ for every input part $p_i \in \mathcal{P}$ using the part pose prediction module. We predict a unit Quaternion vector $q_i$ that corresponds to a 3D rotation $R_i$ and a translation vector $t_i$ denoting the part center position in the camera space.

Different from object pose estimation, the task of part assembly requires a joint prediction of all part poses. Part pose predictions should not be independent with each other, as part poses follow a set of more rigid relationships, such as symmetry and parallelism. For a valid assembly, parts must be in contact with adjacent parts. The rich part relationships restrict the solution space for each part pose. We leverage a two-phase graph convolutional neural network to address the joint communication of part poses for the task of part assembly.

*Mask-Conditioned Part Features.* We consider three sources of features for each part: 2D image feature $f_{img} \in \mathbb{R}^{F_3}$, 2D mask feature $f_{mask} \in \mathbb{R}^{F_3}$ ($F_3 = 512$), context-aware 3D part feature $f_{3d} \in \mathbb{R}^{2F_2}$. We use a ResNet-18 [20] pretrained on ImageNet [11] to extract 2D image feature $f_{img}$. We use a separate ResNet-18 that takes the 1-channel binary mask as input and extracts a 2D mask feature $f_{mask}$, where masks for invisible parts are predicted as empty. Then, finally, we propagate the 3D context-aware part feature $f_{3d}$ introduced in the Sect. 4.1 that encodes 3D part geometry information along with its global context.

*Two-Phase Graph Convolution.* We create a part graph $\mathcal{G} = (V, E)$, treating every part as a node and propose a two-phase of graph convolution to predict the pose of each part.

During the first phase, we draw pairwise edges among all parts $p_i$ in every geometrically equivalent part classes $C_j$ and perform graph convolution over $\mathcal{G}^1 = (V, E^1)$, where

$$E^1 = \{(p_{i_1}, p_{i_2}) | \forall p_{i_1}, p_{i_2} \in C_j, i_1 \neq i_2, \forall C_j \in \mathcal{C}\}. \tag{1}$$

Edges in $E^1$ allow message passing among geometrically identical parts that are likely to have certain spatial relationships or constraints (*e.g.*, four legs of a chair have two orthogonal reflection planes). After the first-phase graph convolution, each node $p_i$ has an updated node feature. The updated node feature is then decoded as an 6D pose $(R_i, t_i)$ for each part. The predicted part poses produce an initial assembled shape.

We leverage a second phase of graph convolution to refine the predicted part poses. Besides the edges in $E^1$, we draw a new set of edges $E^2$ by finding top-5 nearest neighbors for each part based upon the initial assembly and define $\mathcal{G}^2 = (V, E^1 \cup E^2)$. The intuition is that once we have an initial part assembly, we are able to connect the adjacent parts so that they learn to attach to each other with certain joint constraints.

We implement the graph convolution as two iterations of message passing [40, 69,74]. Given a part graph $\mathcal{G} = (V, E)$ with initial node features $f^0$ and edge features $e^0$, each iteration of message passing starts from computing edge features

$$e_{(p_{i_1}, p_{i_2})}^{t+1} = SLP_g \left( [f_{i_1}^t; f_{i_2}^t; e_{(p_{i_1}, p_{i_2})}^t] \right), t \in \{0, 1\}. \tag{2}$$

where we do not use $e^0$ during the first phase of graph convolution, and define $e_{(p_{i_1}, p_{i_2})}^0 = 0$ if $(p_{i_1}, p_{i_2}) \in E^1$ and $e_{(p_{i_1}, p_{i_2})}^0 = 1$ if $(p_{i_1}, p_{i_2}) \in E^2$ for the second phase. Then, we perform average-pooling over all edge features that are connected to a node and obtain the updated node feature

$$f_i^{t+1} = \frac{1}{|\{u \mid (p_i, p_u) \in E\}|} \sum_{(p_i, p_u) \in E} e_{(p_i, p_u)}^{t+1}, t \in \{0, 1\}. \tag{3}$$

We define $f_i^{t+1} = f_i^t$ if there is no edge drawn from node $i$. We define the final node features to be $f_i = [f_i^0; f_i^1; f_i^2]$ for each phase of graph convolution.

Respectively, we denote the final node feature of first phase and second phase graph convolution to be ${}^1f_i$ and ${}^2f_i$ for a part $p_i$.

*Part Pose Decoding.* After gathering the node features after conducting the two-phase graph convolution operations as ${}^1f_i$ and ${}^2f_i, i \in \{1, 2, \cdots, N\}$, we use a Multiple-Layer Perception (MLP) to decode part poses at each phase.

$${}^sq_i, {}^st_i = MLP_{PoseDec} ({}^sf_i), s \in \{1, 2\}, i \in \{1, 2, \cdots, N\}. \tag{4}$$

To ensure the output of unit Quaternion prediction, we normalize the output vector length so that $\|{}^sq_i\|_2 = 1$.

### 4.3   Training and Losses

We first train the part-instance image segmentation module until convergence and then train the part pose prediction module. Empirically, we find that having a good mask prediction is necessary before training for the part poses.

*Loss for Part-Instance Image Segmentation.* We adapt the negative *soft-iou* loss from [38] to supervise the training of the part-instance image segmentation module. We perform Hungarian matching [29] within each geometrically equivalent class to guarantee that the loss is invariant to the order of part poses in ground-truth and prediction. The loss is defined as

$$\mathcal{L}_{mask_i} = -\frac{\sum_{u,v \in [m,m]} \hat{M}_i^{(u,v)} \cdot M_{\mathcal{M}(i)}^{(u,v)}}{\sum_{u,v \in [m,m]} \left( \hat{M}_{\mathcal{M}(i)}^{(u,v)} + M_i^{(u,v)} - \hat{M}_{\mathcal{M}(i)}^{(u,v)} \cdot M_i^{(u,v)} \right)}. \tag{5}$$

where $M_i \in \{0,1\}^{[m,m]}$ and $\hat{M}_{\mathcal{M}(i)} \in [0,1]^{[m,m]}$ denote the ground truth and the matched predicted mask. $\mathcal{M}$ refers to the matching results that match ground-truth part indices to the predicted ones. $[m,m]$ includes all 2D index $(u,v)$'s on a $224 \times 224$ image plane.

*Losses for Part Pose Prediction.* For the pose prediction module, we design an order-invariant loss by conducting Hungarian matching within each geometry-equivalent classes $C_i \in \mathcal{C}$. Additionally, we observe that separating supervision loss for translation and rotation helps stabilize training. We use the following training loss for the pose prediction module.

$$\mathcal{L}_{pose} = \sum_{i=1}^{N} (\lambda_1 \times \mathcal{L}_T + \lambda_2 \times \mathcal{L}_C + \lambda_3 \times \mathcal{L}_E) + \lambda_4 \times \mathcal{L}_W \tag{6}$$

We use the $L_2$ Euclidean distance to measure the difference between the 3D translation prediction and ground truth translation for each part. We denote $\mathcal{M}$ as the matching results.

$$\mathcal{L}_{T_i} = \|\hat{t}_{\mathcal{M}(i)} - t_i\|_2, \forall i \in \{1, 2, \cdots, N\}. \tag{7}$$

where $\hat{t}_{\mathcal{M}(i)}$ and $t_i$ denote the matched predicted translation and the ground truth 3D translation. We use weight parameter of $\lambda_1 = 1$ in training.

We use two losses for rotation prediction: Chamfer distance [15] $\mathcal{L}_C$ and $L2$ distance $\mathcal{L}_E$. Because many parts have symmetric geometry (*e.g.*, bars and boards) which results in multiple rotation solutions, we use Chamfer distance as the primary supervising loss to address such pose ambiguity. Given the point cloud of part $p_i$, the ground truth rotation $R_i$, and the matched predicted rotation $\hat{R}_{\mathcal{M}(i)}$, the Chamfer distance loss is defined as

$$\mathcal{L}_{C_i} = \frac{1}{d_{pc}} \sum_{x \in \hat{R}_{\mathcal{M}(i)}(p_i)} \min_{y \in R_i(p_i)} \|x - y\|_2^2 + \frac{1}{d_{pc}} \sum_{y \in R_i(p_i)} \min_{x \in \hat{R}_{\mathcal{M}(i)}(p_i)} \|x - y\|_2^2, \tag{8}$$

where $R_i(p_i)$ and $\hat{R}_{\mathcal{M}(i)}(p_i)$ denote the rotated part point clouds using $R_i$ and $\hat{R}_{\mathcal{M}(i)}$ respectively. We use $\lambda_2 = 20$ for the Chamfer loss. Some parts may be not *perfectly* symmetric (*e.g.*, one bar that has small but noticeable different geometry at two ends), using Chamfer distance by itself in this case would make the network fall into local minima. We encourage the network to correct this situation by penalizing the $L_2$ distance between the matched predicted rotated point cloud and the ground truth rotated point cloud in Euclidean distance.

$$\mathcal{L}_{E_i} = \frac{1}{d_{pc}} \left\| \hat{R}_{\mathcal{M}(i)}(p_i) - R_i(p_i) \right\|_F^2, \tag{9}$$

where $\|\cdot\|_F$ denotes the Frobenius norm, $d_{pc} = 1000$ is the number of points per part. Note that $\mathcal{L}_{E_i}$ on its own is not sufficient in cases when the parts are completely symmetric. Thus, we add the $\mathcal{L}_E$ loss as a regularizing term with a smaller weight of $\lambda_3 = 1$. We conducted an ablation experiment demonstrating the $\mathcal{L}_E$ loss contributes to correcting rotation for some parts.

Finally, we compute a shape holistic Chamfer distance as the predicted assembly should be close to the ground truth Chamfer distance.

$$\mathcal{L}_W = \frac{1}{N \cdot d_{pc}} \sum_{x \in \hat{S}} \min_{y \in S} \|x - y\|_2^2 + \frac{1}{N \cdot d_{pc}} \sum_{y \in S} \min_{x \in \hat{S}} \|x - y\|_2^2, \tag{10}$$

where $\hat{S} = \cup_{i=1}^N (\hat{R}_{\mathcal{M}(i)}(p_i) + \hat{t}_i)$ denotes the predicted assembled shape point cloud and $S = \cup_{i=1}^N (R_i(p_i) + t_i)$ denotes the ground truth shape point cloud. This loss encourages the holistic shape appearance and the part relationships to be close to the ground-truth. We use $\lambda_4 = 1$.

## 5    Experiments

In this section, we set up the testbed for the proposed *single-image 3D part assembly* problem on the PartNet [42] dataset. To validate the proposed approach, we compare against three baseline methods. Both qualitative and quantitative results demonstrate the effectiveness of our method.

### 5.1    Dataset

Recently, Mo et al. [42] proposed the PartNet dataset, which is the largest 3D object dataset with fine-grained and hierarchical part annotation. In our work, we use the three largest furniture categories that requires assembly: Chair, Table and Cabinet. We follow the official PartNet train/val/test split (70% : 10% : 20%) and filter out the shapes with more than 20 parts.

For each object category, we create two data modalities: *Level-3* and *Level-mixed*. The *Level-3* corresponds to the most fine-grained PartNet segmentation. Since an algorithm can implicitly learn the semantic priors dealing with the only *Level-3* data, which impedes generalization, as IKEA furnitures might not follow

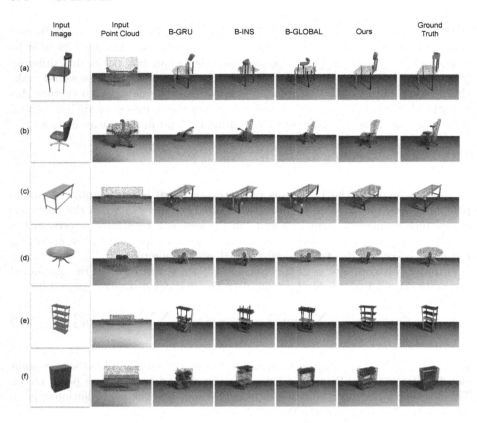

**Fig. 3.** Qualitative Results. We show six examples of each category in the two modalities. The upper and lower rows are Level-3 and Level-mixed respectively.

the PartNet semantics, we created an additional category modality, *Level-mixed*, which contains part segmentation at all levels in the hierarchy. Specifically, for each shape, we traverse every path of the ground-truth part hierarchy and stop randomly. We have 3736 chairs, 2431 tables, 704 cabinets in *Level-3* and 4664 chairs, 5987 tables, 888 cabinets in *Level-mixed*.

For the input image, we render a set of $224 \times 224$ images the PartNet models with ShapeNet textures [4]. We randomize the viewpoints by azimuth $[0°, 360°)$, elevation $[25°, 30°]$ and distance $[0.6, 1.0]$. We then compute the world-to-camera matrix and obtain the 3D object position in the camera space used for supervising segmentation module. For the input point cloud, we use Furthest Point Sampling (FPS) to sample $d_{pc} = 1000$ points over the each part mesh. We then normalize them following the descriptions in Sect. 3. With normalized parts, we detect geometrically equivalent parts by first filtering out parts comparing dimensions of AABB under a threshold of 0.1. We further process the remaining parts computing all possible pairwise part Chamfer distance normalized by their average diagonal length under a hand-picked threshold of 0.02.

## 5.2  Evaluation Metric

To evaluate the part assembly performance, we use two metrics: *part accuracy* and *shape Chamfer distance*. The *part accuracy* metric that leverages Chamfer distance between the part point clouds after applying the predicted part pose and the ground truth pose to address such ambiguity. Following previously defined notation in Sect. 4.3, we define the Part Accuracy Score (PA) as follows and set a threshold of $\tau = 0.1$.

$$PA = \frac{1}{N} \sum_{i=1}^{N} \mathbb{1} \left( \left\| (\hat{R}_{\mathcal{M}(i)}(p_i) + \hat{t}_i) - (R_i(p_i) + t_i) \right\|_{chamfer} < \tau \right) \qquad (11)$$

Borrowing the evaluation metric heavily used in the community of 3D object reconstruction, we also measure the *shape Chamfer distance* from the predicted assembled shape to the ground-truth assembly. Formally, we define the *shape Chamfer distance* metric $SC$ borrowing notations defined in Sect. 4.3 as follows.

$$SC(S, \hat{S}) = \frac{1}{N \cdot d_{pc}} \sum_{x \in \hat{S}} \min_{y \in S} \|x - y\|_2 + \frac{1}{N \cdot d_{pc}} \sum_{y \in S} \min_{x \in \hat{S}} \|x - y\|_2 \qquad (12)$$

## 5.3  Baseline Methods

We compare to three baseline methods. Since there is no direct comparison from previous works that address the exactly same task, we try to adapt previous works on part-based shape generative modeling [40,44,57,71] to our setting and compare with them. Most of these works require known part semantics. However, in our task, there is no assumption for part semantics or part priors, and thus all methods must explicitly take the part input point clouds as is. We train all three baselines with the same pose loss used in our method defined in Sect. 4.3.

*Sequential Pose Proposal (B-GRU).* The first baseline is a sequential model, similar to the method proposed by [57,71], instead of sequentially generating parts, we sequentially decode $k$ candidate possible poses for a given part geometry, conditioned on an image. For each input part, if there is $n$ geometrically equivalent parts, where $n \leq k$, we take the first n pose proposal generated using GRU, and conduct Hungarian matching to match with the $n$ ground truth part poses.

*Instance One-hot Pose Proposal (B-InsOneHot).* The second baseline uses MLP to directly infer pose for a given part from its geometry and the input image, similar to previous works [40,44] that output box abstraction for shapes. Here, instead of predicting a box for each part, we predict a 6D part pose $(R_j, t_j)$. We use instance one-hot features to differentiate between the equivalent part point clouds, and conduct Hungarian matching to match with the ground truth part poses regardless of the onehot encoding.

*Global Feature Model (B-Global).* The third baseline is proposed by improving upon the second baseline by adding our context-aware 3D part feature defined in Sect. 4.1. Each part pose proposal not only considers the part-specific 3D feature and the 2D image feature, but also a 3D global feature obtained by aggregating the all 3D part feature then max-pool to a global 3D feature containing information of all parts. This baseline shares similar ideas to PAGENet [32] and CompoNet [53] that also compute global features to assemble each of the generated parts.

**Table 1.** Part Accuracy and Assembly Chamfer Distance (CD)

| Modality | Method | Part Accuracy ↑ | | | Assembly CD ↓ | | |
|---|---|---|---|---|---|---|---|
| | | Chair | Table | Cabinet | Chair | Table | Cabinet |
| Level-3 | B-GRU | 0.310 | 0.574 | 0.334 | 0.107 | 0.057 | 0.062 |
| | B-InsOnehot | 0.173 | 0.507 | 0.295 | 0.130 | 0.064 | 0.065 |
| | B-Global | 0.170 | 0.530 | 0.339 | 0.125 | 0.061 | 0.065 |
| | Ours | **0.454** | **0.716** | **0.402** | **0.067** | **0.037** | **0.050** |
| Mixed | B-GRU | 0.326 | 0.567 | 0.283 | 0.101 | 0.070 | 0.066 |
| | B-InsOnehot | 0.286 | 0.572 | 0.320 | 0.108 | 0.067 | 0.061 |
| | B-Global | 0.337 | 0.619 | 0.290 | 0.093 | 0.062 | 0.0677 |
| | Ours | **0.491** | **0.778** | **0.483** | **0.065** | **0.037** | **0.043** |

## 5.4   Results and Analysis

We compare with the three baselines and observe that our method outperforms the baseline methods both qualitatively and quantitatively using the two evaluation metrics, PA and SC. We show significant improvement for occluded part pose hallucination as Table 2 demonstrates. Qualitatively, we observe that our method can learn to infer part poses for invisible parts by (1) learning a category prior and (2) leveraging visible parts of the same geometric equivalent class. Our network can reason the stacked placement structure of cabinets as shown in the last row in Fig. 3. The input image does not reveal the inner structure of the cabinet and our proposed approach learns to vertically distribute the geometrically equivalent boards to fit inside the cabinet walls, similar to the ground truth shape instance. The top row of Fig. 3 demonstrates how our network learns to place the occluded back bar along the visible ones. This could be contributed to our first stage of graph convolution where we leverage visible parts to infer the pose for occluded parts in the same geometrically equivalent class.

**Table 2.** Visible and Invisible Part Accuracies

| Modality | Method | Part Accuracy (Visible) ↑ | | | Part Accuracy (Invisible) ↑ | | |
|---|---|---|---|---|---|---|---|
| | | Chair | Table | Cabinet | Chair | Table | Cabinet |
| Level-3 | B-GRU | 0.3182 | 0.598 | 0.353 | 0.206 | 0.481 | 0.304 |
| | B-InsOnehot | 0.178 | 0.572 | 0.291 | 0.104 | 0.369 | 0.289 |
| | B-Global | 0.174 | 0.563 | 0.354 | 0.120 | 0.427 | 0.269 |
| | Ours | **0.471** | **0.753** | **0.455** | **0.270** | **0.557** | **0.358** |
| Mixed | B-GRU | 0.335 | 0.593 | 0.302 | 0.180 | 0.267 | 0.258 |
| | B-InsOnehot | 0.295 | 0.592 | 0.346 | 0.133 | 0.275 | 0.279 |
| | B-Global | 0.334 | 0.638 | 0.320 | 0.184 | 0.349 | 0.227 |
| | Ours | **0.505** | **0.803** | **0.537** | **0.262** | **0.515** | **0.360** |

Our method demonstrates the most faithful part pose prediction for the shape instance depicted by the input image. As shown in Fig. 3 row (e), our method equally spaces the board parts vertically, which is consistent with the shape structure revealed by the input image. This is likely resulted from our part-instance image segmentation module where we explicitly predict a 2D-3D grounding, whereas the baseline methods lack such components.

However, our proposed method has its limitations in dealing with unusual image views, exotic shape instance, and single-modal part geometry, which result in noisy mask prediction. The 2D-3D grounding error cascades to later network modules resulting in poor pose predictions. As shown in Fig. 4 row (a), the image view is not very informative of the shape structure, making it difficult to leverage 3D geometric cues to find 2D-3D grounding. Additionally, this chair instance itself is foreign to Chair category. We avoided employing differentiable rendering because it does not help address such failure cases. Figure 4 row (b) reflects a case where a shape instance is composed of a single modality of part geometry. Geometric affinity of the board parts makes it difficult for the network to come to a determinant answer for the segmentation prediction, resulting in a sub-optimal part pose prediction. These obstacles arise from the task itself that all baselines also suffer from the same difficulties.

*Ablation Experiments.* We conduct several ablation experiments on our proposed method and losses trained on PartNet Chair Level-3. Table 1 in Appendix demonstrates the effectiveness of each ablated component. The part-instance image segmentation module plays the most important role in our pipeline. Removing it results in the most significant performance decrease.

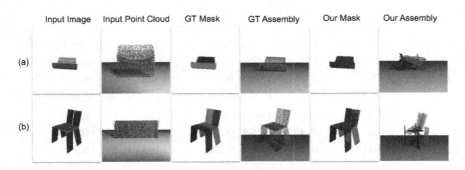

**Fig. 4.** Failure Cases. We show two examples of failure cases. In (a), the input image is not geometrically informative. In (b), the chair has only one type of part geometry.

## 6    Conclusion and Future Works

We formulated a novel problem of *single-image-guided 3D part assembly* and proposed a neural-net-based pipeline for the task that leverages information from both 2D grounding and 3D geometric reasoning. We established a test bed on the PartNet dataset. Quantitative evaluation demonstrates that the proposed method achieves a significant improvement upon three baseline methods. For the future works, one can study how to leverage multiple images or 3D partial scans as inputs to achieve better results. We also do not explicitly consider the connecting junctions between parts in our framework, which are strong constraints for real-world robotic assembly.

**Acknowledgements.** We thank the anonymous reviewers for their comments and suggestions. This work was supported by a Vannevar Bush Faculty Fellowship, the grants from the Samsung GRO program, the SAIL Toyota Research Center, and gifts from Autodesk and Adobe.

## References

1. Brachmann, E., Krull, A., Michel, F., Gumhold, S., Shotton, J., Rother, C.: Learning 6D object pose estimation using 3D object coordinates. In: Fleet, D., Pajdla, T., Schiele, B., Tuytelaars, T. (eds.) ECCV 2014. LNCS, vol. 8690, pp. 536–551. Springer, Cham (2014). https://doi.org/10.1007/978-3-319-10605-2_35
2. Brachmann, E., Michel, F., Krull, A., Ying Yang, M., Gumhold, S., et al.: Uncertainty-driven 6D pose estimation of objects and scenes from a single RGB image. In: Proceedings of the IEEE Conference on Computer Vision and Pattern Recognition, pp. 3364–3372 (2016)
3. Braun, M., Rao, Q., Wang, Y., Flohr, F.: Pose-RCNN: joint object detection and pose estimation using 3D object proposals. In: 2016 IEEE 19th International Conference on Intelligent Transportation Systems (ITSC), pp. 1546–1551. IEEE (2016)
4. Chang, A.X., et al.: ShapeNet: an information-rich 3D model repository (2015)

5. Chaudhuri, S., Kalogerakis, E., Guibas, L.J., Koltun, V.: Probabilistic reasoning for assembly-based 3D modeling. In: ACM SIGGRAPH (2011)

6. Chaudhuri, S., Koltun, V.: Data-driven suggestions for creativity support in 3D modeling. In: ACM SIGGRAPH Asia (2010)

7. Chen, D., Li, J., Wang, Z., Xu, K.: Learning canonical shape space for category-level 6D object pose and size estimation. In: Proceedings of the IEEE/CVF Conference on Computer Vision and Pattern Recognition, pp. 11973–11982 (2020)

8. Chen, Z., Zhang, H.: Learning implicit fields for generative shape modeling. In: CVPR (2019)

9. Choi, C., Taguchi, Y., Tuzel, O., Liu, M., Ramalingam, S.: Voting-based pose estimation for robotic assembly using a 3D sensor. In: 2012 IEEE International Conference on Robotics and Automation, pp. 1724–1731, May 2012

10. Choy, C.B., Xu, D., Gwak, J.Y., Chen, K., Savarese, S.: 3D-R2N2: a unified approach for single and multi-view 3D object reconstruction. In: Leibe, B., Matas, J., Sebe, N., Welling, M. (eds.) ECCV 2016. LNCS, vol. 9912, pp. 628–644. Springer, Cham (2016). https://doi.org/10.1007/978-3-319-46484-8_38

11. Deng, J., Dong, W., Socher, R., Li, L.J., Li, K., Fei-Fei, L.: ImageNet: a large-scale hierarchical image database. In: 2009 IEEE Conference on Computer Vision and Pattern Recognition, pp. 248–255. IEEE (2009)

12. Domokos, C., Kato, Z.: Realigning 2D and 3D object fragments without correspondences. IEEE Trans. Pattern Anal. Mach. Intell. **38**(1), 195–202 (2015)

13. Dubrovina, A., Xia, F., Achlioptas, P., Shalah, M., Groscot, R., Guibas, L.J.: Composite shape modeling via latent space factorization. In: Proceedings of the IEEE International Conference on Computer Vision, pp. 8140–8149 (2019)

14. Fan, H., Su, H., Guibas, L.: A point set generation network for 3D object reconstruction from a single image. In: CVPR (2017)

15. Fan, H., Su, H., Guibas, L.J.: A point set generation network for 3D object reconstruction from a single image. In: Proceedings of the IEEE Conference on Computer Vision and Pattern Recognition, pp. 605–613 (2017)

16. Feng, C., Xiao, Y., Willette, A., McGee, W., Kamat, V.R.: Vision guided autonomous robotic assembly and as-built scanning on unstructured construction sites. Autom. Constr. **59**, 128–138 (2015)

17. Gao, L., et al.: SDM-NET: deep generative network for structured deformable mesh. In: ACM SIGGRAPH Asia (2019)

18. Groueix, T., Fisher, M., Kim, V.G., Russell, B.C., Aubry, M.: AtlasNet: a papier-mâché approach to learning 3D surface generation. In: CVPR (2019)

19. Gupta, S., Arbeláez, P., Girshick, R., Malik, J.: Aligning 3D models to RGB-D images of cluttered scenes. In: Proceedings of the IEEE Conference on Computer Vision and Pattern Recognition, pp. 4731–4740 (2015)

20. He, K., Zhang, X., Ren, S., Sun, J.: Deep residual learning for image recognition. In: CVPR (2015)

21. Hutchinson, S.A., Kak, A.C.: Extending the classical AI planning paradigm to robotic assembly planning. In: Proceedings of the IEEE International Conference on Robotics and Automation, pp. 182–189. IEEE (1990)

22. Insafutdinov, E., Dosovitskiy, A.: Unsupervised learning of shape and pose with differentiable point clouds. In: NeurIPS (2018)

23. Izadinia, H., Shan, Q., Seitz, S.M.: IM2CAD. In: Proceedings of the IEEE Conference on Computer Vision and Pattern Recognition, pp. 5134–5143 (2017)

24. Jaiswal, P., Huang, J., Rai, R.: Assembly-based conceptual 3D modeling with unlabeled components using probabilistic factor graph. Comput.-Aided Des. **74**, 45–54 (2016)

25. Jiménez, P.: Survey on assembly sequencing: a combinatorial and geometrical perspective. J. Intell. Manuf. **24**(2), 235–250 (2013)
26. Kalogerakis, E., Chaudhuri, S., Koller, D., Koltun, V.: A probabilistic model of component-based shape synthesis. In: ACM SIGGRAPH (2012)
27. Kaufman, S.G., Wilson, R.H., Jones, R.E., Calton, T.L., Ames, A.L.: The Archimedes 2 mechanical assembly planning system. In: Proceedings of IEEE International Conference on Robotics and Automation, vol. 4, pp. 3361–3368. IEEE (1996)
28. Kehl, W., Manhardt, F., Tombari, F., Ilic, S., Navab, N.: SSD-6D: Making RGB-based 3D detection and 6D pose estimation great again. In: Proceedings of the IEEE International Conference on Computer Vision, pp. 1521–1529 (2017)
29. Kuhn, H.W.: The Hungarian method for the assignment problem. Nav. Res. Logist. Q. **2**, 83–97 (1955)
30. Langley, C.S., D'Eleuterio, G.M.T.: Neural network-based pose estimation for fixtureless assembly. In: Proceedings 2001 IEEE International Symposium on Computational Intelligence in Robotics and Automation (Cat. No.01EX515), pp. 248–253, July 2001
31. Levitin, G., Rubinovitz, J., Shnits, B.: A genetic algorithm for robotic assembly line balancing. Eur. J. Oper. Res. **168**(3), 811–825 (2006)
32. Li, J., Niu, C., Xu, K.: Learning part generation and assembly for structure-aware shape synthesis. In: AAAI (2020)
33. Li, J., Xu, K., Chaudhuri, S., Yumer, E., Zhang, H., Guibas, L.: GRASS: generative recursive autoencoders for shape structures. In: ACM SIGGRAPH (2019)
34. Lin, C.H., Kong, C., Lucey, S.: Learning efficient point cloud generation for dense 3D object reconstruction. In: AAAI (2018)
35. Litany, O., Bronstein, A.M., Bronstein, M.M.: Putting the pieces together: regularized multi-part shape matching. In: Fusiello, A., Murino, V., Cucchiara, R. (eds.) ECCV 2012. LNCS, vol. 7583, pp. 1–11. Springer, Heidelberg (2012). https://doi.org/10.1007/978-3-642-33863-2_1
36. Litany, O., Rodolà, E., Bronstein, A.M., Bronstein, M.M., Cremers, D.: Non-rigid puzzles. In: Computer Graphics Forum, vol. 35, pp. 135–143. Wiley Online Library (2016)
37. Litvak, Y., Biess, A., Bar-Hillel, A.: Learning pose estimation for high-precision robotic assembly using simulated depth images. In: 2019 International Conference on Robotics and Automation (ICRA), pp. 3521–3527, May 2019
38. Máttyus, G., Luo, W., Urtasun, R.: DeepRoadMapper: extracting road topology from aerial images. In: 2017 IEEE International Conference on Computer Vision (ICCV), pp. 3458–3466 (2017)
39. Mescheder, L., Oechsle, M., Niemeyer, M., Nowozin, S., Geiger, A.: Occupancy networks: learning 3D reconstruction in function space. In: CVPR (2019)
40. Mo, K., et al.: StructureNet: hierarchical graph networks for 3D shape generation. In: ACM SIGGRAPH Asia (2019)
41. Mo, K., et al.: StructEdit: learning structural shape variations. In: Proceedings of the IEEE Conference on Computer Vision and Pattern Recognition (2020)
42. Mo, K., et al.: PartNet: a large-scale benchmark for fine-grained and hierarchical part-level 3D object understanding. In: CVPR (2019)
43. Nelson, B., Papanikolopoulos, N., Khosla, P.: Visual servoing for robotic assembly. In: Visual Servoing: Real-Time Control of Robot Manipulators Based on Visual Sensory Feedback, pp. 139–164. World Scientific (1993)
44. Niu, C., Li, J., Xu, K.: Im2Struct: recovering 3D shape structure from a single RGB image. In: CVPR (2018)

45. Papon, J., Schoeler, M.: Semantic pose using deep networks trained on synthetic RGB-D. In: Proceedings of the IEEE International Conference on Computer Vision, pp. 774–782 (2015)
46. Park, J.J., Florence, P., Straub, J., Newcombe, R., Lovegrove, S.: DeepSDF: Learning continuous signed distance functions for shape representation. In: CVPR (2019)
47. Pearson, K.: On lines and planes of closest fit to systems of points in space. Phil. Mag. **2**, 559–572 (1901)
48. Qi, C.R., Su, H., Mo, K., Guibas, L.J.: PointNet: deep learning on point sets for 3D classification and segmentation. In: CVPR (2017)
49. Rad, M., Lepetit, V.: Bb8: a scalable, accurate, robust to partial occlusion method for predicting the 3D poses of challenging objects without using depth. In: Proceedings of the IEEE International Conference on Computer Vision, pp. 3828–3836 (2017)
50. Richter, S.R., Roth, S.: Matryoshka networks: predicting 3D geometry via nested shape layers. In: CVPR (2018)
51. Ronneberger, O., Fischer, P., Brox, T.: U-Net: convolutional networks for biomedical image segmentation. In: Navab, N., Hornegger, J., Wells, W.M., Frangi, A.F. (eds.) MICCAI 2015. LNCS, vol. 9351, pp. 234–241. Springer, Cham (2015). https://doi.org/10.1007/978-3-319-24574-4_28
52. Saito, S., Huang, Z., Natsume, R., Morishima, S., Kanazawa, A., Li, H.: PIFu: pixel-aligned implicit function for high-resolution clothed human digitization. In: ICCV (2019)
53. Schor, N., Katzir, O., Zhang, H., Cohen-Or, D.: CompoNet: learning to generate the unseen by part synthesis and composition. In: ICCV (2019)
54. Shao, L., Migimatsu, T., Bohg, J.: Learning to scaffold the development of robotic manipulation skills. In: 2020 International Conference on Robotics and Automation (ICRA). IEEE (2020)
55. Suárez-Ruiz, F., Zhou, X., Pham, Q.C.: Can robots assemble an IKEA chair?Sci. Robot. **3**(17) (2018)
56. Sung, M., Dubrovina, A., Kim, V.G., Guibas, L.: Learning fuzzy set representations of partial shapes on dual embedding spaces. In: Eurographics Symposium on Geometry Processing (2018)
57. Sung, M., Su, H., Kim, V.G., Chaudhuri, S., Guibas, L.: ComplementMe: weakly-supervised component suggestions for 3D modeling. In: ACM SIGGRAPH Asia (2017)
58. Tatarchenko, M., Dosovitskiy, A., Brox, T.: Octree generating networks: efficient convolutional architectures for high-resolution 3d outputs. In: ICCV (2017)
59. Tejani, A., Kouskouridas, R., Doumanoglou, A., Tang, D., Kim, T.K.: Latent-class Hough forests for 6 DoF object pose estimation. IEEE Trans. Pattern Anal. Mach. Intell. **40**(1), 119–132 (2017)
60. Tekin, B., Sinha, S.N., Fua, P.: Real-time seamless single shot 6D object pose prediction. In: Proceedings of the IEEE Conference on Computer Vision and Pattern Recognition, pp. 292–301 (2018)
61. Thorsley, M., Okouneva, G., Karpynczyk, J.: Stereo vision algorithm for robotic assembly operations. In: Proceedings of the First Canadian Conference on Computer and Robot Vision, pp. 361–366. IEEE (2004)
62. Wald, J., Avetisyan, A., Navab, N., Tombari, F., Nießner, M.: Rio: 3D object instance re-localization in changing indoor environments. In: Proceedings of the IEEE International Conference on Computer Vision, pp. 7658–7667 (2019)
63. Wang, H., Schor, N., Hu, R., Huang, H., Cohen-Or, D., Huang, H.: Global-to-local generative model for 3D shapes. In: ACM SIGGRAPH Asia (2018)

64. Wang, H., Sridhar, S., Huang, J., Valentin, J., Song, S., Guibas, L.J.: Normalized object coordinate space for category-level 6D object pose and size estimation. In: Proceedings of the IEEE Conference on Computer Vision and Pattern Recognition, pp. 2642–2651 (2019)
65. Wang, L., Schmidt, B., Givehchi, M., Adamson, G.: Robotic assembly planning and control with enhanced adaptability through function blocks. Int. J. Adv. Manuf. Technol. **77**(1), 705–715 (2015)
66. Wang, N., Zhang, Y., Li, Z., Fu, Y., Liu, W., Jiang, Y.G.: Pixel2Mesh: generating 3D mesh models from single RGB images. In: Ferrari, V., Hebert, M., Sminchisescu, C., Weiss, Y. (eds.) ECCV 2018. LNCS, vol. 11215, pp. 55–71. Springer, Cham (2018). https://doi.org/10.1007/978-3-030-01252-6_4
67. Wang, N., Zhang, Y., Li, Z., Fu, Y., Liu, W., Jiang, Y.G.: Pixel2mesh: generating 3D mesh models from single RGB images. In: Proceedings of the European Conference on Computer Vision (ECCV), pp. 52–67 (2018)
68. Wang, P.S., Liu, Y., Guo, Y.X., Sun, C.Y., Tong, X.: Adaptive O-CNN: a patch-based deep representation of 3D shapes. In: ACM SIGGRAPH Asia (2018)
69. Wang, Y., Sun, Y., Liu, Z., Sarma, S.E., Bronstein, M.M., Solomon, J.M.: Dynamic graph CNN for learning on point clouds. ACM Trans. Graph. (TOG) **38**(5), 1–12 (2019)
70. Wen, C., Zhang, Y., Li, Z., Fu, Y.: Pixel2Mesh++: multi-view 3D mesh generation via deformation. In: ICCV (2019)
71. Wu, R., Zhuang, Y., Xu, K., Zhang, H., Chen, B.: PQ-NET: a generative part seq2seq network for 3D shapes (2019)
72. Wu, Z., Wang, X., Lin, D., Lischinski, D., Cohen-Or, D., Huang, H.: SAGNet: structure-aware generative network for 3D-shape modeling. In: ACM SIGGRAPH Asia (2019)
73. Xiang, Y., Schmidt, T., Narayanan, V., Fox, D.: PoseCNN: a convolutional neural network for 6D object pose estimation in cluttered scenes. Robot.: Sci. Syst. (RSS) (2018)
74. Xu, K., Hu, W., Leskovec, J., Jegelka, S.: How powerful are graph neural networks? In: International Conference on Learning Representations (2019)
75. Xu, Q., Wang, W., Ceylan, D., Mech, R., Neumann, U.: DISN: deep implicit surface network for high-quality single-view 3D reconstruction. In: NeurIPS (2019)
76. Yoon, Y., DeSouza, G.N., Kak, A.C.: Real-time tracking and pose estimation for industrial objects using geometric features. In: 2003 IEEE International Conference on Robotics and Automation (Cat. No. 03CH37422), vol. 3, pp. 3473–3478. IEEE (2003)
77. Zeng, A., Song, S., Nießner, M., Fisher, M., Xiao, J., Funkhouser, T.: 3DMatch: learning local geometric descriptors from RGB-D reconstructions. In: Proceedings of the IEEE Conference on Computer Vision and Pattern Recognition, pp. 1802–1811 (2017)
78. Zeng, A., et al.: Multi-view self-supervised deep learning for 6d pose estimation in the amazon picking challenge. In: 2017 IEEE International Conference on Robotics and Automation (ICRA), pp. 1386–1383. IEEE (2017)

# PT2PC: Learning to Generate 3D Point Cloud Shapes from Part Tree Conditions

Kaichun Mo[1]($\boxtimes$), He Wang[1], Xinchen Yan[2], and Leonidas Guibas[1]

[1] Stanford University, Stanford, USA
`kaichun@cs.stanford.edu`
[2] Uber ATG, Pittsburgh, USA

**Abstract.** Generative 3D shape modeling is a fundamental research area in computer vision and interactive computer graphics, with many real-world applications. This paper investigates the novel problem of generating a 3D point cloud geometry for a shape from a symbolic part tree representation. In order to learn such a conditional shape generation procedure in an end-to-end fashion, we propose a conditional GAN "part tree"-to-"point cloud" model ($PT2PC$) that disentangles the *structural* and *geometric* factors. The proposed model incorporates the part tree condition into the architecture design by passing messages *top-down* and *bottom-up* along the part tree hierarchy. Experimental results and user study demonstrate the strengths of our method in generating perceptually plausible and diverse 3D point clouds, given the part tree condition. We also propose a novel structural measure for evaluating if the generated shape point clouds satisfy the part tree conditions. Code and data can be accessed on the webpage: https://cs.stanford.edu/~kaichun/pt2pc.

**Keywords:** Part-tree to point-cloud · Conditional generative adversarial network · Part-based and structure-aware point cloud generation

## 1 Introduction

Generating 3D shape is a central topic in computer vision and graphics. Recent works (*e.g.* [9,11,19]) have been focusing on generating the entire shape geometry without explicitly modeling part semantics and shape structures. Although these works have demonstrated the ability to generate simple 3D object shapes to some extent, such holistic shape generation methods usually have difficulties in modeling complicated shape structures and delicate shape parts. In computer-aided design (CAD), constructing a whole shape geometry from scratch is an extremely laborious and time-consuming task. It can save a good amount of time for graphics designers with such a system to generate multiple shape candidates

**Electronic supplementary material** The online version of this chapter (https://doi.org/10.1007/978-3-030-58539-6_41) contains supplementary material, which is available to authorized users.

A. Vedaldi et al. (Eds.): ECCV 2020, LNCS 12351, pp. 683–701, 2020.
https://doi.org/10.1007/978-3-030-58539-6_41

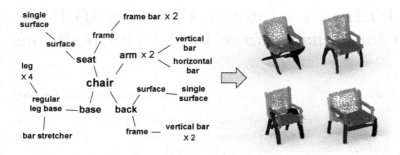

**Fig. 1.** We formulate the problem of "part tree"-to-"point cloud" (*PT2PC*) synthesis as a conditional generation task which takes in a symbolic part tree as condition and generates multiple diverse point clouds satisfying the structure defined by the part tree.

to select and edit from, given a sentence description such as "A chair with 1 seat, 4 legs and a back with 3 bars". Disentangling shape structure and geometry factors also encourages more fine-grained and controllable 3D shape generation – thus supporting many real-world applications, including structure-conditioned shape design [38,40] and structure-aware shape re-synthesis [13].

In this paper, we formulate a new task of generating 3D point cloud shapes with *geometric* variations conditioned on *structural* shape descriptions. Figure 1 illustrates our task input and output with an example. More specifically, we represent each 3D shape as a hierarchy of parts, following PartNet [40], where each part node has an associated semantic label and the part hierarchy includes parts at different segmentation granularities. Abstracting away the concrete part geometry, the shape structure can be defined by a symbolic part tree with only part semantics and their relationships (Fig. 1, left). Given such symbolic part tree conditions, we propose a conditional-GAN *PT2PC* to generate diverse 3D point cloud shapes that satisfy the structural conditions (Fig. 1, right).

The symbolic part tree conditions are central to the architecture designs for both *PT2PC* generator and discriminator. Our generator first encodes the part tree template feature using semantic and structural information for each part node in a *bottom-up* fashion along the tree hierarchy. Then, given a random noise vector capturing the global geometry information at the root node, we recursively propagate such geometric information to each part node in a *top-down* fashion along the part tree. The final point clouds are generated by aggregating the point clouds decoded at each leaf node representing its corresponding fine-grained semantic part. Our discriminator first computes per-part features at the leaf level, propagates the information in a *bottom-up* fashion along the tree hierarchy until the root node and finally produces a score judging if the generated shape *geometry* looks realistic and the shape *structure* satisfies the input condition.

We evaluate the proposed model on four major semantic classes from the PartNet dataset. To justify the merits of our tree-structure architecture for both the generator and discriminator, we compare with two conditional GAN baselines. Both quantitative and qualitative results demonstrate clear advantages of our design in terms of global shape quality, part shape quality, and shape diversity, under both seen and unseen templates as the condition. Results on human evaluation agree with our observations in the experiments and further strengthen our claims. Additionally, we propose a novel hierarchical part instance segmentation method that is able to segment an input point cloud without any part labels into a symbolic part tree. This provides us a metric to evaluate how well our generated shape geometry satisfies the part tree conditions.

In summary, our contributions are:

- we formulate the novel task of part-tree conditioned point cloud generation;
- we propose a conditional GAN method, *PT2PC*, that generates realistic and diverse point cloud shapes given symbolic part tree conditions;
- we demonstrate superior performance both quantitatively and qualitatively under standard GAN metrics and a user study, comparing against two baseline conditional-GAN methods;
- we propose a novel point cloud structural evaluation metric for evaluating if the generated point clouds satisfy the part tree conditions.

## 2    Related Works

We review related works on 3D generative shape modeling, part-based shape modeling and structure-conditioned content generation.

*3D Generative Shape Modeling.* Reconstructing and synthesizing 3D shapes is a popular research topic in computer vision and graphics. Recently, tremendous progresses have been made in generating 3D voxel grids [9,18,47,63,64,67,71], point clouds [1,11,14,72,73], and surface meshes [19,21,36,50] using deep neural networks. Point clouds representation is a collection of unordered points irregularly distributed in the 3D space, which makes the minimax optimization very challenging [1,32]. Achlioptas *et al.* [1] proposed a latent-GAN approach that conducts minimax optimization on the shape feature space which outperforms the raw-GAN operating on the raw point clouds. To better capture the local geometric structure of point clouds, Valsesia *et al.* [57] proposed a graph-based generator that dynamically builds the graph based on distance in feature space. Shu *et al.* [49] proposed Tree-GAN with a tree-structured graph convolutional neural network as the generator. Recently, Wang *et al.* [60] proposed a new discriminator, PointNet-Mix, that improves the sampling uniformity of the generated point clouds. Unlike these shape point cloud GAN works that generate shapes without explicit part semantic and structural constraints, we learn to generate diverse point cloud shapes satisfying symbolic part tree conditions.

*Part-Based Shape Modeling.* There is a line of research on understanding shapes by their semantic parts and structures. Previous works study part segmentation [7,10,27,29,40,44,61,75,76], box abstraction [42,51,56,82], shape template fitting [15,17,31,43], generating shapes by parts [16,28,33,34,38,48,52,54,59,65,66], or editing shape by parts [12,39,79]. We refer to the survey papers [37,69] for more related works. Shape parts have hierarchical structures [40,58,62].

Yi *et al.* [74] learns consistent part hierarchy from noisy online tagged shape parts. GRASS [34] propose binary part trees to generate novel shapes. A follow-up work [78] learns to segment shapes into the binary part hierarchy. PartNet [40] proposes a large-scale 3D model dataset with hierarchical part segmentation. Using PartNet, recent works such as StructureNet [38] and StructEdit [39] learns to generate and edit shapes explicitly following the pre-defined part hierarchy. We use the tree hierarchy defined in PartNet [40] and propose a new task *PT2PC* that learns to generate point cloud shapes given symbolic part tree conditions.

*Conditional Content Generation.* Understanding the 3D visual world, parsing the geometric and structural properties of 3D primitives (*e.g.* objects in the scene or parts of an object) and their relationships is at the core of computer vision [23,26,55,68]. Many works learn to synthesize high-quality images from text descriptions [30,35,45,46,53,77,80], semantic attributes [8,70], scene-graph representations [3,26], and rough object layouts [24,25,41,81]. There are also works to generate 3D content with certain input conditions. Chang *et al.* [4,5] learns to generate 3D scenes from text. Chen *et al.* [6] studied how to generate 3D voxel shapes from a sentence condition. StructEdit [39] learns to generate structural shape variations conditioned on an input source shape. Our work introduces a conditional Generative Adversarial Network that generates shape point clouds conditioned on an input symbolic part tree structure.

# 3    Method

In this work, we propose *PT2PC*, a conditional GAN (c-GAN) that learns a mapping from a given *symbolic part tree* $\mathcal{T}$ and a random noise vector $\mathbf{z}$ to a 3D shape point cloud $\mathbf{X}$ composed of part point clouds for the leaf nodes of the conditional part tree. We propose novel part-based conditional point cloud generator $G(\mathbf{z}, \mathcal{T})$ and discriminator $D(\mathbf{X}, \mathcal{T})$ conditioned on the symbolic part tree input $\mathcal{T}$. Different from holistic point cloud GANs [1,49,57] that produce a shape point cloud as a whole, our proposed *PT2PC* generate a hierarchy of part point clouds along with part semantics and shape structures.

## 3.1    Symbolic Part Tree Representation

We follow the semantic part hierarchy defined in PartNet [40]. Every PartNet shape instance (*e.g.* a chair) is annotated with a hierarchical part segmentation that provides both coarse-level parts (*e.g.* chair base, chair back) and parts at fine-grained levels (*e.g.* chair leg, chair back bar). Figure 2 shows the ground-truth part hierarchy of an exemplar chair.

A symbolic part tree $\mathcal{T}$ is defined as $\mathcal{T} = (\mathcal{T}_V, \mathcal{T}_E)$, where $\mathcal{T}_V = \{P^j | P^j = (\mathbf{s}^j, \mathbf{d}^j)\}_j$

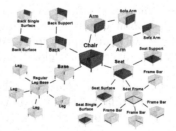

**Fig. 2.** An example PartNet hierarchical part segmentation.

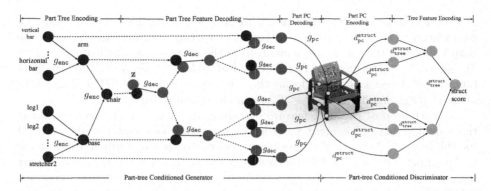

**Fig. 3.** Our c-GAN *PT2PC* architecture. Our part-tree conditioned generator first extracts the subtree features by traversing the input symbolic part tree in a *bottom-up* fashion, and then recursively decodes part features in a *top-down* way until leaf nodes, where part point clouds are finally generated. Our part-tree conditioned geometry discriminator recursively consumes the generated part tree with leaf node geometry in a *bottom-up* fashion to generate the final score. The solid arrow indicates a network module while a dashed arrow means to copy the content. As defined in Sect. 3, the brown, red and orange nodes represent the encoded symbolic part feature $\mathbf{t}$, the decoded part geometry feature $\mathbf{f}$ and the encoded part geometry feature $\mathbf{h}$ respectively. (Color figure online)

represents a set of part instances and $\mathcal{T}_E$ represents an directed edge set of the part parent-children relationships $\mathcal{T}_E = \{(j,k)\}$. In $\mathcal{T}_V$, each part instance $P^j$ is composed of two components: a semantic label $\mathbf{s}^j$ (*e.g.* chair seat, chair back), and a part instance identifier $\mathbf{d}^j$ (*e.g.* the first leg, the second leg), both of which are represented as one-hot vectors. The set of part semantic labels are pre-defined in PartNet and consistent within one object category. In $\mathcal{T}_E$, each edge $(j,k)$ indicates $P^j$ is the parent node of $P^k$. The set $C^j = \{k|(j,k) \in \mathcal{T}_E\}$ defines all children part instances of a node $P^j$. We denote a special part node $P^{\text{root}}$ to be the root node of the part tree $\mathcal{T}$, with the semantic label $\mathbf{s}^{\text{root}}$ and the instance identifier $\mathbf{d}^{\text{root}}$. The leaf node of the symbolic part tree has no children, namely, $\mathcal{T}_{\text{leaf}} = \{P^j \mid |C^j| = 0\} \subsetneq \mathcal{T}_V$ (Fig. 3).

### 3.2 Part-Tree Conditioned Generator

Our conditional generator $G(\mathbf{z}, \mathcal{T})$ takes a random Gaussian variable $\mathbf{z} \sim \mathcal{N}(\cdot|\mu = 0, \sigma = 1)$ and a symbolic part tree condition $\mathcal{T} = (\mathcal{T}_V, \mathcal{T}_E)$ as inputs and outputs a set of part point clouds $\mathbf{X} = \{\mathbf{x}^j \mid P^j \in \mathcal{T}_{\text{leaf}}\}$ where $\mathbf{x}^j \in \mathbb{R}^{M \times 3}$ is a part point cloud in the shape space representing the leaf node part $P^j$. Namely,

$$\mathbf{X} = G(\mathbf{z}, \mathcal{T}) \tag{1}$$

The generator is composed of three network modules: a symbolic part tree encoder $G_{\text{enc}}$, a part tree feature decoder $G_{\text{dec}}$ and a part point cloud decoder $G_{\text{pc}}$. First, the symbolic part tree encoder $G_{\text{enc}}$ embeds the nodes of $\mathcal{T}$ into compact features $\mathbf{t}^j$ hierarchically from the leaf nodes to the root node for every node

$P^j$. Then, taking in both the random variable $\mathbf{z}$ and the hierarchy of symbolic part features $\{\mathbf{t}^j\}_j$, the part tree feature decoder $G_{\text{dec}}$ hierarchically decodes the part features in the top-down manner, from the root node to the leaf nodes, and finally produces part feature $\mathbf{f}^j$ for every leaf node $P^j \in \mathcal{T}_{\text{leaf}}$. Finally, the part point cloud decoder $G_{\text{pc}}$ transforms the leaf node features $\{\mathbf{f}^j \mid P^j \in \mathcal{T}_{\text{leaf}}\}$ into 3D part point clouds $\{\mathbf{x}^j \mid P^j \in \mathcal{T}_{\text{leaf}}\}$ in the shape space.

At each step of the part feature decoding, the parent node needs to know the global structural context in order to propagate coherent signals to all of its children so that the generated part point clouds can form a valid shape in a compatible way. This is the reason why we introduce the symbolic part tree encoder $G_{\text{enc}}$ as a *bottom-up* module to summarize the part tree structural context for each decoding step. Our part tree decoder $G_{\text{dec}}$ is then conditioned on the symbolic structural context and recursively propagates the random noise $\mathbf{z}$ from the root node to the leaf nodes in a *top-down* fashion.

*Symbolic Part Tree Encoder* $G_{\text{enc}}$. For a given symbolic part tree $\mathcal{T}$, we encode the nodes of the part tree starting from the leaf nodes and propagate the messages to the parent node of the encoded nodes until the root node gets encoded. The message propagation is performed in a *bottom-up* fashion. As shown in Eq. 2, each node $P^j$ takes the node feature $\mathbf{t}^k$, the semantic label $\mathbf{s}^k$ and the part instance identifier $\mathbf{d}^k$ from all its children $\{P^k | k \in C^j\}$, aggregates the information and computes its node feature $\mathbf{t}^j$ using a learned function $g_{enc}$. Then, it further propagates a message to its parent node. We initialize $\mathbf{t}^j = 0$ for every leaf node $P^j \in \mathcal{T}_{\text{leaf}}$.

$$\mathbf{t}^j = \mathbf{0}, \qquad\qquad\qquad\qquad\quad \forall P^j \in \mathcal{T}_{\text{leaf}}$$
$$\mathbf{t}^j = g_{\text{enc}} \left( \left\{ [\mathbf{t}^k; \mathbf{s}^k; \mathbf{d}^k] \mid k \in C^j \right\} \right), \qquad \forall P^j \in \mathcal{T}_V - \mathcal{T}_{\text{leaf}} \qquad (2)$$

where $[\cdot; \cdot]$ means a concatenation of the inputs. $g_{\text{enc}}$ is implemented as a small PointNet [44], treating each children-node feature as a high dimensional point, to enforce the permutation invariance between children nodes. We first use a fully-connected layer to embed each $[\mathbf{t}^k; \mathbf{s}^k; \mathbf{d}^k]$ into a 256-dim feature, then perform a max-pooling over $K = |C^j|$ features over all children nodes to obtain an aggregated feature, and finally push the aggregated feature through another fully-connected layer to obtain the final parent node feature $\mathbf{t}^j$. We use leaky ReLU as the activation functions in our fully-connected layers.

*Part Tree Feature Decoder* $G_{\text{dec}}$. Taking in the random variable $\mathbf{z}$ and encoded node features $\{\mathbf{t}^j\}_j$, we hierarchically decode the part features $\{\mathbf{f}^j\}_j$ from the root node to the leaf nodes in a *top-down* fashion along the given part tree structure $\mathcal{T}$. As shown in Eq. 3, for every part $P^j$, we learn a shared function $g_{dec}$ transforming the concatenation of its own features $(\mathbf{t}^j, \mathbf{s}^j, \mathbf{d}^j)$ and the decoded feature $\mathbf{f}^p$ from its parent node $P^p$ into part feature $\mathbf{f}^j$. For the root node, we use random noise $\mathbf{z}$ to replace parent node feature.

$$\mathbf{f}^{\text{root}} = g_{\text{dec}} \left( [\mathbf{z}; \mathbf{t}^{\text{root}}; \mathbf{s}^{\text{root}}; \mathbf{d}^{\text{root}}] \right),$$
$$\mathbf{f}^j = g_{\text{dec}} \left( [\mathbf{f}^p; \mathbf{t}^j; \mathbf{s}^j; \mathbf{d}^j] \right), \qquad\qquad \forall (p, j) \in \mathcal{T}_E \qquad (3)$$

We implement $g_{\tt dec}$ as a two-layer MLP with leaky $\tt ReLU$ as the activation functions. The output feature size is 256.

*Part Point Cloud Decoder* $G_{\tt pc}$. Given the part features of all the leaf nodes $\{\mathbf{f}^j \mid P^j \in \mathcal{T}_{\tt leaf}\}$, our point cloud decoder $G_{\tt pc}$ transforms each individual feature $\mathbf{f}^j$ into a 3D part point cloud $\mathbf{x}^j$ in the shape space for every $P^j \in \mathcal{T}_{\tt leaf}$, as shown in Eq. 4. To get the final shape point cloud, we down-sample the union of all part point clouds $\{\mathbf{x}^j \mid P^j \in \mathcal{T}_{\tt leaf}\}$. We generate the same number $M$ points for all the parts.

$$\mathbf{x}^j = g_{\tt pc}(\mathbf{f}^j), \forall P^j \in \mathcal{T}_{\tt leaf}$$
$$\mathbf{x} = \texttt{DownSample}\left(\cup\left\{\mathbf{x}^j \mid P^j \in \mathcal{T}_{\tt leaf}\right\}\right) \qquad (4)$$

$g_{\tt pc}$ is designed to deform a fixed surface point cloud of a unit cube $\mathbf{x}_{\tt cube}$ into our target part point cloud based on its input $\mathbf{f}$, inspired by the shape decoder introduced in Groueix *et al.* [20]. We uniformly sample a 1000-size point cloud from the surface of a unit cube to form $\mathbf{x}_{\tt cube} \in \mathbb{R}^{1000 \times 3}$. Then, for each point in $\mathbf{x}_{\tt cube}$, we concatenate its XYZ coordinate with the feature $\mathbf{f}$, push it through a $MLP(256 + 3, 1024, 1024, 3)$ using leaky $\tt ReLU$, and finally obtain an XYZ coordinate for a point on our target point cloud. Finally, we use Furthest Point Sampling (FPS) for our $\tt Downsample$ operation to obtain shape point cloud $\mathbf{x}$.

Compared to existing works [1,49,57] that generate shape point clouds as a whole, the key difference here is that our point cloud decoder generates part point clouds for every leaf node in the part tree $\mathcal{T}$ separately, but in a manner aware of the inter-part structure and relationships. Another big advantage is that we get the semantic label of each generated part point cloud. Furthermore, we observe that the holistic point cloud generators usually suffer from non-uniform point distribution. The generators tend to allocate way more points to bulky parts (*e.g.*, chair back and chair seat) while only generating sparse points for small parts with thin geometry (*e.g.*, chair wheel, chair back bar). Since our $G_{\tt pc}$ generates the same number of points for each part and then performs global down-sampling, we can generate shape point clouds with fine structures and appropriate point density for all the parts.

### 3.3  Part-Tree Conditioned Discriminator

Our conditional discriminator $D(\mathbf{X}, \mathcal{T})$ receives a generated sample or a true data sample, composed of a set of part point clouds $\mathbf{X} = \{\mathbf{x}^j \in \mathbb{R}^{M \times 3} | P^j \in \mathcal{T}_{\tt leaf}\}$, and outputs a scalar $y \in \mathbb{R}$ based on the tree condition $\mathcal{T}$. Following the WGAN-gp [2,22], $D$ is learned to be a 1-Lipschitz function of $\mathbf{X}$ and its output $y$ depicts the realness of the sample.

Since the input $\mathbf{X}$ always contains part point clouds for every leaf node part instances in the symbolic part tree $\mathcal{T}$, our discriminator mainly focus on judging the geometry of each part point clouds along with the whole shape point clouds assembled from the parts. This is to say, the discriminator should tell if each part point cloud is realistic and plausible regarding its part semantics; in addition, the discriminator needs to look at the spatial arrangement of the part point clouds, judge whether it follows a realistic structure specified by the part tree $\mathcal{T}$, *e.g.* connected parts need to contact each other and some parts may exhibit certain kind of symmetry; finally, the discriminator should judge whether the generated part point clouds form a realistic shape point cloud.

To address the requirements above, our discriminator leverages two modules: a structure-aware part point cloud discriminator $D^{\texttt{struct}}(\mathbf{X}, \mathcal{T})$, and a holistic shape point cloud discriminator $D^{\texttt{whole}}(\mathbf{x})$, where $\mathbf{x} = \texttt{DownSample}(\cup\mathbf{X})$. $D^{\texttt{struct}}(\mathbf{X}, \mathcal{T})$ takes as input the part tree condition $\mathcal{T}$ and the generated set of part point clouds $\mathbf{X}$ and outputs a scalar $y^{\texttt{struct}} \in \mathbb{R}$ regarding the tree-conditioned generation quality. $D^{\texttt{whole}}(\mathbf{x}) \in \mathbb{R}$ only takes the down-sampled shape point cloud $\mathbf{x}$ as input and outputs a scalar $y^{\texttt{whole}}$ regarding the unconditioned shape quality. As shown in Eq. 5, the final output of our discriminator $D$ is the sum of the two discriminators.

$$
\begin{aligned}
y &= y^{\texttt{struct}} + y^{\texttt{whole}} \\
y^{\texttt{struct}} &= D^{\texttt{struct}}(\mathbf{X}, \mathcal{T}) \\
y^{\texttt{whole}} &= D^{\texttt{whole}}(\mathbf{x})
\end{aligned}
\tag{5}
$$

For the structure-aware part point cloud discriminator $D^{\texttt{struct}}(\mathbf{X}, \mathcal{T})$, we constitute it using three network components: a part point cloud encoder $D^{\texttt{struct}}_{\texttt{pc}}$, a tree-based feature encoder $D^{\texttt{struct}}_{\texttt{tree}}$, and a scoring network $D^{\texttt{struct}}_{\texttt{score}}$. First, the point cloud encoder $D^{\texttt{struct}}_{\texttt{pc}}$ encodes the part point cloud $\mathbf{x}^j$ into a part feature $\mathbf{h}^j$ for each leaf node $P^j \in \mathcal{T}_{\texttt{leaf}}$. Then, taking in the part features at leaf level $\{\mathbf{h}^j \mid P^j \in \mathcal{T}_{\texttt{leaf}}\}$, the tree-based feature encoder $D^{\texttt{struct}}_{\texttt{tree}}$ recursively propagates the part features $\mathbf{h}$ along with the part semantics $\mathbf{s}$ to the parent nodes starting from the leaf nodes and finally reaching the root node, in a *bottom-up* fashion. Finally, a scoring function $D^{\texttt{struct}}_{\texttt{score}}$ outputs a score $y^{\texttt{struct}} \in \mathbb{R}$ for the shape generation quality. For the holistic shape point cloud discriminator $D^{\texttt{whole}}$, it is simply composed of a PointNet encoder $D^{\texttt{whole}}_{\texttt{pc}}$ and a scoring network $D^{\texttt{whole}}_{\texttt{score}}$ which outputs a scalar $y^{\texttt{whole}} \in \mathbb{R}$.

*Point Cloud Encoder* $D^{\texttt{struct}}_{\texttt{pc}}$ *and* $D^{\texttt{whole}}_{\texttt{pc}}$. Both $D^{\texttt{struct}}_{\texttt{pc}}$ and $D^{\texttt{whole}}_{\texttt{pc}}$ use vanilla PointNet [44] architecture without spatial transformer layers or batch normalization layers. For $D^{\texttt{struct}}_{\texttt{pc}}$, we learn a function $d^{\texttt{struct}}_{\texttt{pc}}$ to extract a part geometry feature $\mathbf{h}^j$ for each part point cloud $\mathbf{x}^j$.

$$
\mathbf{h}^j = d^{\texttt{struct}}_{\texttt{pc}}(\mathbf{x}^j), \forall P^j \in \mathcal{T}_{\texttt{leaf}}
\tag{6}
$$

$d^{\texttt{struct}}_{\texttt{pc}}$ is implemented as a four-layer $MLP(3, 64, 128, 128, 1024)$ to process each point individually followed by a max-pooling. Similarly, $D^{\texttt{whole}}_{\texttt{pc}}$ takes a shape point cloud $\mathbf{x}$ as input and outputs a global shape feature $\mathbf{h}^{\texttt{shape}}$.

$$
\mathbf{h}^{\texttt{shape}} = D^{\texttt{whole}}_{\texttt{pc}}(\mathbf{x})
\tag{7}
$$

*Tree Feature Encoder* $D^{\texttt{struct}}_{\texttt{tree}}$. Similar to the symbolic part tree encoder $G_{\texttt{dec}}$ in the generator, $D^{\texttt{struct}}_{\texttt{tree}}$ learns an aggregation function $d^{\texttt{struct}}_{\texttt{tree}}$ that transforms features from children nodes into parent node features, as shown in Eq. 8. By leveraging the tree structure specified by $\mathcal{T}$ in its architecture, the module enforces the structure-awareness of $D^{\text{struct}}$. In a *bottom-up* fashion, the features propagate from the leaf level finally to the root yielding $\mathbf{h}^{\text{root}}$, according to Eq. 8.

$$\mathbf{h}^j = d^{\text{struct}}_{\text{tree}} \left( \left\{ [\mathbf{h}^k; \mathbf{s}^k] \mid k \in C^j \right\} \right), \forall P^j \in \mathcal{T}_V - \mathcal{T}_{\text{leaf}} \tag{8}$$

To implement $D^{\text{struct}}_{\text{tree}}$, we extract a latent 256-dim feature after applying a fully-connected layer over each input $[\mathbf{h}^k; \mathbf{s}^k]$, perform max-pooling over all children nodes and finally push it through another fully-connected layer to obtain $\mathbf{h}^j$. We use the leaky ReLU activation functions for both layers.

Note that the key difference between $D^{\text{struct}}_{\text{tree}}$ and $G_{\text{enc}}$ is that $D^{\text{struct}}_{\text{tree}}$ no longer requires the part instance identifiers $\mathbf{d}^k$ since the children part features $\{\mathbf{h}^k\}_k$ for each parent node $P^j$ already encode the part geometry information that are naturally different even for part instances of the same part semantics.

*Scoring Functions $D^{\text{part}}_{\text{score}}$ and $D^{\text{whole}}_{\text{score}}$.* After obtaining the structure-aware root feature $\mathbf{h}^{\text{root}}$ and the holistic PointNet feature $\mathbf{h}^{\text{shape}}$, we compute

$$y^{\text{struct}} = D^{\text{struct}}_{\text{score}} \left( \mathbf{h}^{\text{root}} \right)$$
$$y^{\text{whole}} = D^{\text{whole}}_{\text{score}} \left( \mathbf{h}^{\text{shape}} \right) \tag{9}$$

Both scoring functions are implemented as a simple fully-connected layer with no activation function.

### 3.4  Training

We follow WGAN-gp [2,22] for training our *PT2PC* conditional generator $G(\cdot, \mathcal{T})$ and discriminator $D(\cdot, \mathcal{T})$. The objective function is defined in Eq. 10.

$$\mathcal{L} = \mathbb{E}_{\mathbf{z} \sim \mathcal{Z}}[D(G(\mathbf{z}, \mathcal{T}), \mathcal{T})] - \mathbb{E}_{\mathbf{X} \sim \mathcal{R}}[D(\mathbf{X}, \mathcal{T})] + \lambda_{gp}\mathbb{E}_{\hat{\mathbf{X}}} \left[ (\|\nabla_{\hat{\mathbf{X}}} D(\hat{\mathbf{X}}, \mathcal{T})\|_2 - 1)^2 \right] \tag{10}$$

where we interpolate each pair of corresponding part point clouds from a real set $\mathbf{X}_{\text{real}} = \left\{ \mathbf{x}^j_{\text{real}} | P^j \in \mathcal{T}_{\text{leaf}} \right\}$ and a fake set $\mathbf{X}_{\text{fake}} = \left\{ \mathbf{x}^j_{\text{fake}} | P^j \in \mathcal{T}_{\text{leaf}} \right\}$ to get $\hat{\mathbf{X}} = \left\{ \hat{\mathbf{x}}^j | P^j \in \mathcal{T}_{\text{leaf}} \right\}$, as shown in below:

$$\hat{\mathbf{x}}^j = \alpha \cdot \mathbf{x}^j_{\text{real}} + (1 - \alpha) \cdot \mathbf{x}^j_{\text{fake}}, \forall P^j \in \mathcal{T}_{\text{leaf}}, \tag{11}$$

where $\alpha \in (0, 1)$ is a random interpolation coefficient always remaining same for all parts. We iteratively train the generator and discriminator with $n_{critic} = 10$. We choose $\lambda_{gp} = 1$, $N = 2,048$ and $M = 1,000$ in our experiments.

## 4  Experiments

We evaluate our proposed *PT2PC* on the PartNet [40] dataset and compare to two baseline c-GAN methods. We show superior performance on all standard point cloud GAN metrics. Besides, we propose a new structural metric evaluating how well the generated point clouds satisfy the input part tree conditions, based on a novel hierarchical instance-level shape part segmentation algorithm. We also conduct a user study which confirms our strengths over baseline methods.

## 4.1   Dataset

We use the PartNet [40] dataset as our main testbed. PartNet contains fine-grained and hierarchical instance-level semantic part annotations including 573,585 part instances over 26,671 3D models covering 24 categories. In this paper, we use the four largest categories that contain diverse part structures: chairs, tables, cabinets and lamps. Following StructureNet [38], we assume there are at

**Table 1.** Dataset Statistics. We summarize the number of shapes and symbolic part trees in the train and test splits for each object category.

| Category | #Shapes | | | #Part Trees | | |
|---|---|---|---|---|---|---|
| | Total | Train | Test | Total | Train | Test |
| Chair | 4871 | 3848 | 1023 | 2197 | 1648 | 549 |
| Table | 5099 | 4146 | 953 | 1267 | 925 | 342 |
| Cabinet | 846 | 606 | 240 | 619 | 470 | 149 |
| Lamp | 802 | 569 | 233 | 302 | 224 | 78 |

maximum 10 children for every parent node and remove the shapes containing unlabeled parts for the canonical sets of part semantics in PartNet [40]. Table 1 summarizes data statistics and the train/test splits. We split by part trees with a ratio 75%:25%. See Table 1 for more details. We observe that most part trees (*e.g.* 1,787 out of 2,197 for chairs) have only one real data point in PartNet, which posts challenges to generate shapes with geometry variations.

## 4.2   Baselines

We compare to two vanilla versions of conditional GAN methods as baselines.

- **Whole-shape Vanilla c-GAN (B-Whole):** the method uses a Multiple-layer Perception (MLP) $G_{\texttt{baseline}}(\mathbf{z}, \mathcal{T})$ as the generator and the holistic shape point cloud discriminator $D_{\texttt{baseline}}^{\texttt{whole}}(\mathbf{x}, \mathcal{T})$;
- **Part-based Vanilla c-GAN (B-Part):** the method uses exactly the same proposed generator $G(\mathbf{z}, \mathcal{T})$ as in our method and a holistic shape point cloud discriminator $D_{\texttt{baseline}}^{\texttt{whole}}(\mathbf{x}, \mathcal{T})$.

One can think B-Part as an ablated version of our proposed method, without the structural discriminator $D^{\texttt{struct}}(\mathbf{X})$. The B-Whole method further removes our part-based generator and generates whole shape point clouds in one shot, similar to previous works [1,49,57]. We implement $D_{\texttt{baseline}}^{\texttt{whole}}(\mathbf{x}, \mathcal{T})$ similar to $D^{\texttt{whole}}(\mathbf{x})$ used as part of our discriminator. It uses a vanilla PointNet [44] to extract global geometry features for input point clouds. Additionally, to make it be aware of the input part tree condition $\mathcal{T}$, we re-purpose the proposed part tree feature encoder network $G_{\texttt{enc}}$ in our generator to recursively compute

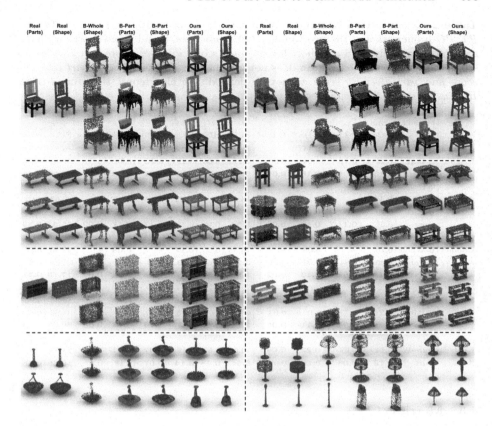

**Fig. 4.** Qualitative Comparisons. We show two examples for each of the four categories: chair, table, cabinet and lamp. The leftmost two columns show the real examples illustrating the conditional part tree input (see supplementary for part tree visualization). We show three random real examples unless there are only one or two in the dataset. For our method and **B-Part** we show both the generated part point clouds with colors and the down-sampled shape point clouds, to fairly compare with **B-Whole** that only produces shape point clouds.

a root node feature summarizing the entire part tree structural information. We make $D_{\text{baseline}}^{\text{whole}}(\mathbf{x}, \mathcal{T})$ conditional on the extracted root node feature. For $G_{\text{baseline}}(\mathbf{z}, \mathcal{T})$, we follow Achlioptas *et al.* [1] and design a five-layer MLP with sizes 512, 512, 512, 1024, 2048 × 3 that finally produces a point cloud of size 2048 × 3. We use leaky **ReLU** as activation functions except for the final output layer. We also condition $G_{\text{baseline}}(\mathbf{z}, \mathcal{T})$ on the root feature extracted from the template feature encoder.

**Table 2.** Quantitative Evaluations. We report the quantitative metric scores for our *PT2PC* framework and the two vanilla c-GAN baselines. S and P are short for Shape and Part. Cov, Div, HIS are short for *coverage* score, *diversity* score and *HierInsSeg* score. Since the baseline `B-Whole` does not predict part point clouds, so *part coverage score* and *part diversity score* cannot be defined. We also report the ground-truth *HierInsSeg* scores for each category.

| | Method | Train | | | | | | Test | | | | | |
|---|---|---|---|---|---|---|---|---|---|---|---|---|---|
| | | S-Cov↓ | P-Cov↓ | S-Div↑ | P-Div↑ | FPD↓ | HIS↓ | S-Cov | P-Cov | S-Div | P-Div | FPD | HIS |
| Chair | B-Whole | **0.13** | – | 0.14 | – | 7.32 | 0.57 | **0.13** | – | 0.13 | – | 10.88 | 0.57 |
| | B-Part | 0.14 | 0.41 | 0.14 | 0.06 | 7.17 | 0.58 | 0.15 | 0.41 | 0.14 | 0.06 | 11.10 | 0.58 |
| | Ours | **0.13** | **0.06** | **0.18** | **0.07** | **6.64** | **0.48** | 0.14 | **0.07** | **0.18** | **0.07** | **10.69** | **0.48** |
| | GT | | | | | | 0.30 | | | | | | 0.31 |
| Table | B-Whole | **0.19** | – | 0.14 | – | 13.02 | 1.04 | **0.21** | – | 0.14 | – | 20.63 | 1.02 |
| | B-Part | 0.20 | 0.60 | 0.15 | **0.09** | 6.45 | 1.02 | **0.21** | 0.60 | 0.15 | **0.09** | 16.92 | 0.99 |
| | Ours | 0.21 | **0.11** | **0.18** | **0.09** | **5.58** | **0.93** | 0.23 | **0.17** | **0.17** | 0.09 | **15.33** | **0.89** |
| | GT | | | | | | 0.62 | | | | | | 0.64 |
| Cabinet | B-Whole | 0.15 | – | 0.09 | – | 16.38 | 0.90 | **0.17** | – | **0.08** | – | 22.90 | 0.86 |
| | B-Part | 0.30 | 0.84 | 0.03 | 0.01 | **3.25** | 0.64 | 0.43 | 0.84 | 0.03 | 0.01 | 24.29 | 0.81 |
| | Ours | **0.13** | **0.08** | **0.13** | **0.02** | 4.13 | **0.52** | 0.24 | **0.18** | 0.05 | **0.02** | **17.73** | **0.57** |
| | GT | | | | | | 0.32 | | | | | | 0.35 |
| Lamp | B-Whole | 0.38 | – | 0.08 | – | 17.87 | 1.00 | **0.38** | – | 0.09 | – | 86.96 | 0.96 |
| | B-Part | **0.28** | 0.73 | 0.09 | 0.03 | 6.52 | 0.78 | 0.43 | 0.70 | 0.09 | 0.03 | 94.66 | 0.88 |
| | Ours | 0.32 | **0.04** | **0.11** | **0.05** | **5.71** | **0.68** | 0.41 | **0.19** | **0.12** | **0.05** | **80.55** | **0.83** |
| | GT | | | | | | 0.51 | | | | | | 0.57 |
| Chair | Ours-W | 0.14 | 0.07 | **0.22** | **0.08** | 10.60 | 0.51 | 0.15 | **0.07** | **0.21** | **0.08** | 13.52 | 0.49 |
| Abla. | Ours | **0.13** | **0.06** | 0.18 | 0.07 | **6.64** | **0.48** | **0.14** | **0.07** | 0.18 | 0.07 | **10.69** | **0.48** |

## 4.3   Metrics

We report standard point cloud GAN metrics, including coverage, diversity [1], and Frechét Point-cloud Distance (FPD) [49]. Note that coverage and diversity originally measure the distance between shape point clouds, which is, more or less, structure-unaware. We introduce two structure-aware metrics, *part coverage* and *part diversity* adopting the original ones by evaluating the average distance between corresponding parts of the two shapes. See supplementary for more details. In addition, we devise a novel perceptual structure-aware metric *HierInsSeg* that measures the part tree edit distance leveraging deep neural networks.

*HierInsSeg Score.* The *HierInsSeg* algorithm performs hierarchical part instance segmentation on the input shape point cloud $\mathbf{x}$ and outputs a symbolic part tree depicting its part structure. Then we compute a tree-editing distance between this part tree prediction and the part tree used as the generation condition. For each part tree, we conditionally generate 100 shape point clouds and compute the mean tree-editing distance. To get the *HierInsSeg* score, we simply average the mean tree-editing distances from all part trees. In Table 2 (the `GT` rows), we present *HierInsSeg* scores operating on the real point clouds to provide a upper bound for the performance. Qualitative and quantitative results show that the

**Table 3.** User Study Results on Chair Generation. Here we show the average ranking of the three methods. The ranking ranges from 1 (the best) to 3 (the worst). The results on train templates are calculated based on 267 trials while the results on test templates are from the rest 269 trials.

|         | Train | | | Test | | |
|---------|-----------|----------|---------|-----------|----------|---------|
|         | Structure | Geometry | Overall | Structure | Geometry | Overall |
| B-Whole | 2.39 | 2.07 | 2.22 | 2.40 | 2.10 | 2.21 |
| B-Part  | 2.33 | 2.41 | 2.38 | 2.36 | 2.47 | 2.46 |
| Ours    | **1.29** | **1.51** | **1.40** | **1.24** | **1.43** | **1.33** |

proposed *HierInsSeg* algorithm is effective on judging if the generated shape point cloud satisfies the part tree condition. See supplementary for more details.

### 4.4 Results and Analysis

We train our proposed *PT2PC* method and the two vanilla c-GAN baselines on the training splits of the four PartNet categories. The part trees in the test splits are unseen during the training time. Table 2 summarizes the quantitative evaluations. Our *HierInsSeg* scores are always the best as we explicitly generate part point clouds and hence render clearer part structures. Moreover, we win most of the FPD scores, showing that our method can generate realistic point cloud shapes. Finally, we find that our part-based generative model usually provides higher shape diversity as a result of part compositionality.

Figure 4 shows qualitative comparisons of our method to the two baseline methods. One can clearly observe that B-Whole produces holistically reasonable shape geometry but with unclear part structures, which explains why it achieves decent shape coverage scores but fails to match our method under FPD and HIS. For B-Part, it fails severely for chair, table and cabinet examples that it does not assign clear roles for the parts and the generated part point clouds are overlaid with each other, which explains the high part coverage scores in Table 2. Obviously, our method generates shapes with clearer part structures and boundaries. We also see a reasonable amount of generation diversity even for part trees with only one real data in PartNet, thanks to the knowledge sharing among similar part tree and sub-tree structures when training a unified and conditional network. We also conduct an ablation study on chairs where we remove the holistic discriminator $D^{\text{whole}}$.

### 4.5 User Study

Although we provide both Euclidean metrics (*i.e.* coverage and diversity scores) and perceptual metrics (*i.e.* FPD and the proposed *HierInsSeg* scores) for evaluating generation quality in Table 2, the true measure of success is human judgement of the generated shapes. For this reason we perform a user study to evaluate the generation quality on chair class. For each trial, we show users a part tree as the condition, 5 ground truth shapes as references, and 5 randomly generated shape point clouds for each of the three methods. We ask users to rank the methods regarding the following three aspects: 1) structure similarity to the given part tree; 2) geometry plausibility; 3) overall generation quality. For fair comparison, we randomize the order between the methods in all trials and only show the shape point clouds without part labels. In total, we collected 536 valid records from 54 users. In Table 3, we report the average ranking of the three methods. Our method significantly outperforms the other two baseline methods on all of the three aspects and on both train and test templates. Please refer to supplementary material for the user interface and more details.

### 4.6  Decoupling Geometry and Structure for PC-GAN

Our proposed *PT2PC* framework enables disentanglement of shape *structure* and *geometry* generation factors. We demonstrate the capability of exploring structure-preserving geometry variation and geometry-preserving structure variation using our method. Conditioned on the same symbolic part tree, our network is able to generate shape point clouds with *geometric* variations by simply changing the Gaussian random noise **z**. On the other hand, if we fix the same noise **z**, conditioned on different input part trees, we observe that *PT2PC* is able to produce *geometrically* similar but *structurally* different shapes. Figure 5 shows the generated shape point clouds $\{\mathbf{x}_{i,j} = G(\mathbf{z}_i, \mathcal{T}_j)\}$ from a set of Gaussian noises $\{\mathbf{z}_i\}_i$ and a set of part trees $\{\mathcal{T}_j\}_j$. Each row shows shape structural interpolation results while sharing similar shape geometry, and every column presents geometric interpolation results conditioned on the same part tree structure.

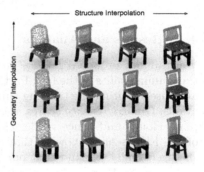

**Fig. 5.** Our approach enables disentanglement of *geometry* and *structure* factors in point cloud generation. Each row shares the same Gaussian noise **z** and every column is conditioned on the same part tree input.

## 5   Conclusion

We have proposed *PT2PC*, a conditional generative adversarial network (c-GAN) that generates point cloud shapes given a symbolic part-tree condition. The part tree input specifies a hierarchy of semantic part instances with their parent-children relationships. Extensive experiments and user study show our superior performance compared to two baseline c-GAN methods. We also propose a novel metric *HierInsSeg* to evaluate if the generated shape point clouds satisfy the part tree conditions. Future works may study incorporating more part relationships and extrapolating our method to unseen categories.

**Acknowledgments.** This research was supported by a Vannevar Bush Faculty Fellowship, grants from the Samsung GRO program and the Stanford SAIL Toyota Research Center, and gifts from Autodesk and Adobe.

# References

1. Achlioptas, P., Diamanti, O., Mitliagkas, I., Guibas, L.: Learning representations and generative models for 3D point clouds. In: ICML, pp. 40–49 (2018)
2. Arjovsky, M., Chintala, S., Bottou, L.: Wasserstein GAN. arXiv preprint arXiv:1701.07875 (2017)
3. Ashual, O., Wolf, L.: Specifying object attributes and relations in interactive scene generation. In: Proceedings of the IEEE International Conference on Computer Vision, pp. 4561–4569 (2019)
4. Chang, A., Monroe, W., Savva, M., Potts, C., Manning, C.D.: Text to 3D scene generation with rich lexical grounding. arXiv preprint arXiv:1505.06289 (2015)
5. Chang, A., Savva, M., Manning, C.D.: Learning spatial knowledge for text to 3D scene generation. In: Proceedings of the 2014 Conference on Empirical Methods in Natural Language Processing (EMNLP), pp. 2028–2038 (2014)
6. Chen, K., Choy, C.B., Savva, M., Chang, A.X., Funkhouser, T., Savarese, S.: Text2Shape: generating shapes from natural language by learning joint embeddings. In: Jawahar, C.V., Li, H., Mori, G., Schindler, K. (eds.) ACCV 2018. LNCS, vol. 11363, pp. 100–116. Springer, Cham (2019). https://doi.org/10.1007/978-3-030-20893-6_7
7. Chen, X., Golovinskiy, A., Funkhouser, T.: A benchmark for 3D mesh segmentation. ACM Trans. Graph. (TOG) **28**(3), 1–12 (2009)
8. Choi, Y., Choi, M., Kim, M., Ha, J.W., Kim, S., Choo, J.: StarGAN: unified generative adversarial networks for multi-domain image-to-image translation. In: Proceedings of the IEEE Conference on Computer Vision and Pattern Recognition, pp. 8789–8797 (2018)
9. Choy, C.B., Xu, D., Gwak, J.Y., Chen, K., Savarese, S.: 3D-R2N2: a unified approach for single and multi-view 3D object reconstruction. In: Leibe, B., Matas, J., Sebe, N., Welling, M. (eds.) ECCV 2016. LNCS, vol. 9912, pp. 628–644. Springer, Cham (2016). https://doi.org/10.1007/978-3-319-46484-8_38
10. Deng, B., Genova, K., Yazdani, S., Bouaziz, S., Hinton, G., Tagliasacchi, A.: CvxNets: learnable convex decomposition. arXiv preprint arXiv:1909.05736 (2019)
11. Fan, H., Su, H., Guibas, L.J.: A point set generation network for 3D object reconstruction from a single image. In: Proceedings of the IEEE Conference on Computer Vision and Pattern Recognition, pp. 605–613 (2017)
12. Fish, N., Averkiou, M., Van Kaick, O., Sorkine-Hornung, O., Cohen-Or, D., Mitra, N.J.: Meta-representation of shape families. ACM Trans. Graph. (TOG) **33**(4), 1–11 (2014)
13. Funkhouser, T., et al.: Modeling by example. ACM Trans. Graph. (TOG) **23**(3), 652–663 (2004)
14. Gadelha, M., Wang, R., Maji, S.: Multiresolution tree networks for 3D point cloud processing. In: Proceedings of the European Conference on Computer Vision (ECCV), pp. 103–118 (2018)

15. Ganapathi-Subramanian, V., Diamanti, O., Pirk, S., Tang, C., Niessner, M., Guibas, L.: Parsing geometry using structure-aware shape templates. In: 2018 International Conference on 3D Vision (3DV), pp. 672–681. IEEE (2018)

16. Gao, L., et al.: SDM-Net: deep generative network for structured deformable mesh. ACM Trans. Graph. (TOG) **38**(6), 1–15 (2019)

17. Genova, K., Cole, F., Vlasic, D., Sarna, A., Freeman, W.T., Funkhouser, T.: Learning shape templates with structured implicit functions. In: Proceedings of the IEEE International Conference on Computer Vision, pp. 7154–7164 (2019)

18. Girdhar, R., Fouhey, D.F., Rodriguez, M., Gupta, A.: Learning a predictable and generative vector representation for objects. In: Leibe, B., Matas, J., Sebe, N., Welling, M. (eds.) ECCV 2016. LNCS, vol. 9910, pp. 484–499. Springer, Cham (2016). https://doi.org/10.1007/978-3-319-46466-4_29

19. Gkioxari, G., Malik, J., Johnson, J.: Mesh R-CNN. In: Proceedings of the IEEE International Conference on Computer Vision, pp. 9785–9795 (2019)

20. Groueix, T., Fisher, M., Kim, V.G., Russell, B.C., Aubry, M.: AtlasNet: a papier-mâché approach to learning 3D surface generation. In: CVPR (2018)

21. Groueix, T., Fisher, M., Kim, V.G., Russell, B.C., Aubry, M.: A papier-mâché approach to learning 3D surface generation. In: Proceedings of the IEEE Conference on Computer Vision and Pattern Recognition, pp. 216–224 (2018)

22. Gulrajani, I., Ahmed, F., Arjovsky, M., Dumoulin, V., Courville, A.C.: Improved training of Wasserstein GANs. In: Advances in Neural Information Processing Systems, pp. 5767–5777 (2017)

23. Gupta, A., Efros, A.A., Hebert, M.: Blocks world revisited: image understanding using qualitative geometry and mechanics. In: Daniilidis, K., Maragos, P., Paragios, N. (eds.) ECCV 2010. LNCS, vol. 6314, pp. 482–496. Springer, Heidelberg (2010). https://doi.org/10.1007/978-3-642-15561-1_35

24. Hong, S., Yan, X., Huang, T.S., Lee, H.: Learning hierarchical semantic image manipulation through structured representations. In: Advances in Neural Information Processing Systems, pp. 2708–2718 (2018)

25. Hong, S., Yang, D., Choi, J., Lee, H.: Inferring semantic layout for hierarchical text-to-image synthesis. In: Proceedings of the IEEE Conference on Computer Vision and Pattern Recognition, pp. 7986–7994 (2018)

26. Johnson, J., Gupta, A., Fei-Fei, L.: Image generation from scene graphs. In: Proceedings of the IEEE Conference on Computer Vision and Pattern Recognition, pp. 1219–1228 (2018)

27. Kalogerakis, E., Averkiou, M., Maji, S., Chaudhuri, S.: 3D shape segmentation with projective convolutional networks. In: Proceedings of the IEEE Conference on Computer Vision and Pattern Recognition, pp. 3779–3788 (2017)

28. Kalogerakis, E., Chaudhuri, S., Koller, D., Koltun, V.: A probabilistic model for component-based shape synthesis. ACM Trans. Graph. (TOG) **31**(4), 1–11 (2012)

29. Kalogerakis, E., Hertzmann, A., Singh, K.: Learning 3D mesh segmentation and labeling (2010)

30. Karacan, L., Akata, Z., Erdem, A., Erdem, E.: Learning to generate images of outdoor scenes from attributes and semantic layouts. arXiv preprint arXiv:1612.00215 (2016)

31. Kim, V.G., Li, W., Mitra, N.J., Chaudhuri, S., DiVerdi, S., Funkhouser, T.: Learning part-based templates from large collections of 3D shapes. ACM Trans. Graph. (TOG) **32**(4), 1–12 (2013)

32. Li, C.L., Zaheer, M., Zhang, Y., Poczos, B., Salakhutdinov, R.: Point cloud GAN. arXiv preprint arXiv:1810.05795 (2018)

33. Li, J., Niu, C., Xu, K.: Learning part generation and assembly for structure-aware shape synthesis. In: AAAI (2020)
34. Li, J., Xu, K., Chaudhuri, S., Yumer, E., Zhang, H., Guibas, L.: Grass: generative recursive autoencoders for shape structures. ACM Trans. Graph. (TOG) **36**(4), 1–14 (2017)
35. Li, W., et al.: Object-driven text-to-image synthesis via adversarial training. In: Proceedings of the IEEE Conference on Computer Vision and Pattern Recognition, pp. 12174–12182 (2019)
36. Liao, Y., Donne, S., Geiger, A.: Deep marching cubes: learning explicit surface representations. In: Proceedings of the IEEE Conference on Computer Vision and Pattern Recognition, pp. 2916–2925 (2018)
37. Mitra, N.J., Wand, M., Zhang, H., Cohen-Or, D., Kim, V., Huang, Q.X.: Structure-aware shape processing. In: ACM SIGGRAPH 2014 Courses, pp. 1–21 (2014)
38. Mo, K., et al.: StructureNet: hierarchical graph networks for 3D shape generation. ACM Trans. Graph. (TOG), Siggraph Asia 2019 **38**(6), Article 242 (2019)
39. Mo, K., et al.: StructEdit: learning structural shape variations. In: Proceedings of the IEEE Conference on Computer Vision and Pattern Recognition (2020)
40. Mo, K., et al.: PartNet: a large-scale benchmark for fine-grained and hierarchical part-level 3D object understanding. In: The IEEE Conference on Computer Vision and Pattern Recognition (CVPR), June 2019
41. Mo, S., Cho, M., Shin, J.: InstaGAN: instance-aware image-to-image translation. arXiv preprint arXiv:1812.10889 (2018)
42. Niu, C., Li, J., Xu, K.: Im2struct: recovering 3D shape structure from a single RGB image. In: Proceedings of the IEEE Conference on Computer Vision and Pattern Recognition, pp. 4521–4529 (2018)
43. Paschalidou, D., Ulusoy, A.O., Geiger, A.: Superquadrics revisited: learning 3D shape parsing beyond cuboids. In: Proceedings of the IEEE Conference on Computer Vision and Pattern Recognition, pp. 10344–10353 (2019)
44. Qi, C.R., Su, H., Mo, K., Guibas, L.J.: PointNet: deep learning on point sets for 3D classification and segmentation. In: Proceedings of the IEEE Conference on Computer Vision and Pattern Recognition, pp. 652–660 (2017)
45. Reed, S., Akata, Z., Yan, X., Logeswaran, L., Schiele, B., Lee, H.: Generative adversarial text to image synthesis. arXiv preprint arXiv:1605.05396 (2016)
46. Reed, S.E., Akata, Z., Mohan, S., Tenka, S., Schiele, B., Lee, H.: Learning what and where to draw. In: Advances in Neural Information Processing Systems, pp. 217–225 (2016)
47. Riegler, G., Osman Ulusoy, A., Geiger, A.: OctNet: learning deep 3D representations at high resolutions. In: Proceedings of the IEEE Conference on Computer Vision and Pattern Recognition, pp. 3577–3586 (2017)
48. Schor, N., Katzir, O., Zhang, H., Cohen-Or, D.: CompoNet: learning to generate the unseen by part synthesis and composition. In: Proceedings of the IEEE International Conference on Computer Vision, pp. 8759–8768 (2019)
49. Shu, D.W., Park, S.W., Kwon, J.: 3D point cloud generative adversarial network based on tree structured graph convolutions. In: Proceedings of the IEEE International Conference on Computer Vision, pp. 3859–3868 (2019)
50. Sinha, A., Unmesh, A., Huang, Q., Ramani, K.: SurfNet: generating 3D shape surfaces using deep residual networks. In: Proceedings of the IEEE Conference on Computer Vision and Pattern Recognition, pp. 6040–6049 (2017)
51. Sun, C.Y., Zou, Q.F., Tong, X., Liu, Y.: Learning adaptive hierarchical cuboid abstractions of 3D shape collections. ACM Trans. Graph. (TOG) **38**(6), 1–13 (2019)

52. Sung, M., Su, H., Kim, V.G., Chaudhuri, S., Guibas, L.: ComplementMe: weakly-supervised component suggestions for 3D modeling. ACM Trans. Graph. (TOG) **36**(6), 1–12 (2017)
53. Tan, F., Feng, S., Ordonez, V.: Text2scene: generating compositional scenes from textual descriptions. In: Proceedings of the IEEE Conference on Computer Vision and Pattern Recognition, pp. 6710–6719 (2019)
54. Tian, Y., et al.: Learning to infer and execute 3D shape programs. arXiv preprint arXiv:1901.02875 (2019)
55. Tulsiani, S., Gupta, S., Fouhey, D.F., Efros, A.A., Malik, J.: Factoring shape, pose, and layout from the 2D image of a 3D scene. In: Proceedings of the IEEE Conference on Computer Vision and Pattern Recognition, pp. 302–310 (2018)
56. Tulsiani, S., Su, H., Guibas, L.J., Efros, A.A., Malik, J.: Learning shape abstractions by assembling volumetric primitives. In: Proceedings of the IEEE Conference on Computer Vision and Pattern Recognition, pp. 2635–2643 (2017)
57. Valsesia, D., Fracastoro, G., Magli, E.: Learning localized generative models for 3D point clouds via graph convolution (2018)
58. Van Kaick, O., et al.: Co-hierarchical analysis of shape structures. ACM Trans. Graph. (TOG) **32**(4), 1–10 (2013)
59. Wang, H., Schor, N., Hu, R., Huang, H., Cohen-Or, D., Huang, H.: Global-to-local generative model for 3D shapes. ACM Trans. Graph. (TOG) **37**(6), 1–10 (2018)
60. Wang, H., Jiang, Z., Yi, L., Mo, K., Su, H., Guibas, L.J.: Rethinking sampling in 3D point cloud generative adversarial networks. arXiv preprint arXiv:2006.07029 (2020)
61. Wang, P., et al.: 3D shape segmentation via shape fully convolutional networks. Comput. Graph. **70**, 128–139 (2018)
62. Wang, Y., et al.: Symmetry hierarchy of man-made objects. In: Computer Graphics Forum, pp. 287–296. no. 2. Wiley Online Library (2011)
63. Wu, J., Wang, Y., Xue, T., Sun, X., Freeman, B., Tenenbaum, J.: MarrNet: 3D shape reconstruction via 2.5 d sketches. In: NIPS, pp. 540–550 (2017)
64. Wu, J., Zhang, C., Xue, T., Freeman, B., Tenenbaum, J.: Learning a probabilistic latent space of object shapes via 3D generative-adversarial modeling. In: NIPS, pp. 82–90 (2016)
65. Wu, R., Zhuang, Y., Xu, K., Zhang, H., Chen, B.: PQ-Net: a generative part seq2seq network for 3D shapes. arXiv preprint arXiv:1911.10949 (2019)
66. Wu, Z., Wang, X., Lin, D., Lischinski, D., Cohen-Or, D., Huang, H.: SagNet: structure-aware generative network for 3D-shape modeling. ACM Trans. Graph. (TOG) **38**(4), 1–14 (2019)
67. Wu, Z., et al.: 3D shapenets: a deep representation for volumetric shapes. In: CVPR, pp. 1912–1920 (2015)
68. Xu, D., Zhu, Y., Choy, C.B., Fei-Fei, L.: Scene graph generation by iterative message passing. In: Proceedings of the IEEE Conference on Computer Vision and Pattern Recognition, pp. 5410–5419 (2017)
69. Xu, K., Kim, V.G., Huang, Q., Mitra, N., Kalogerakis, E.: Data-driven shape analysis and processing. In: SIGGRAPH ASIA 2016 Courses, pp. 1–38 (2016)
70. Yan, X., Yang, J., Sohn, K., Lee, H.: Attribute2Image: conditional image generation from visual attributes. In: Leibe, B., Matas, J., Sebe, N., Welling, M. (eds.) ECCV 2016. LNCS, vol. 9908, pp. 776–791. Springer, Cham (2016). https://doi.org/10.1007/978-3-319-46493-0_47
71. Yan, X., Yang, J., Yumer, E., Guo, Y., Lee, H.: Perspective transformer nets: learning single-view 3D object reconstruction without 3D supervision. In: NIPS, pp. 1696–1704 (2016)

72. Yang, G., Huang, X., Hao, Z., Liu, M.Y., Belongie, S., Hariharan, B.: Pointflow: 3D point cloud generation with continuous normalizing flows. In: Proceedings of the IEEE International Conference on Computer Vision, pp. 4541–4550 (2019)

73. Yang, Y., Feng, C., Shen, Y., Tian, D.: FoldingNet: point cloud auto-encoder via deep grid deformation. In: Proceedings of the IEEE Conference on Computer Vision and Pattern Recognition, pp. 206–215 (2018)

74. Yi, L., Guibas, L., Hertzmann, A., Kim, V.G., Su, H., Yumer, E.: Learning hierarchical shape segmentation and labeling from online repositories. arXiv preprint arXiv:1705.01661 (2017)

75. Yi, L., et al.: A scalable active framework for region annotation in 3D shape collections. ACM Trans. Graph. (TOG) $35$(6), 1–12 (2016)

76. Yi, L., Su, H., Guo, X., Guibas, L.J.: SyncSpecCNN: synchronized spectral CNN for 3D shape segmentation. In: Proceedings of the IEEE Conference on Computer Vision and Pattern Recognition, pp. 2282–2290 (2017)

77. Yin, G., Liu, B., Sheng, L., Yu, N., Wang, X., Shao, J.: Semantics disentangling for text-to-image generation. In: Proceedings of the IEEE Conference on Computer Vision and Pattern Recognition, pp. 2327–2336 (2019)

78. Yu, F., Liu, K., Zhang, Y., Zhu, C., Xu, K.: PartNet: a recursive part decomposition network for fine-grained and hierarchical shape segmentation. In: Proceedings of the IEEE Conference on Computer Vision and Pattern Recognition, pp. 9491–9500 (2019)

79. Yumer, M.E., Chaudhuri, S., Hodgins, J.K., Kara, L.B.: Semantic shape editing using deformation handles. ACM Trans. Graph. (TOG) $34$(4), 1–12 (2015)

80. Zhang, H., et al.: StackGAN: text to photo-realistic image synthesis with stacked generative adversarial networks. In: Proceedings of the IEEE International Conference on Computer Vision, pp. 5907–5915 (2017)

81. Zhao, B., Meng, L., Yin, W., Sigal, L.: Image generation from layout. In: Proceedings of the IEEE Conference on Computer Vision and Pattern Recognition, pp. 8584–8593 (2019)

82. Zou, C., Yumer, E., Yang, J., Ceylan, D., Hoiem, D.: 3D-PRNN: generating shape primitives with recurrent neural networks. In: Proceedings of the IEEE International Conference on Computer Vision, pp. 900–909 (2017)

# Highly Efficient Salient Object Detection with 100K Parameters

Shang-Hua Gao[1], Yong-Qiang Tan[1], Ming-Ming Cheng[1(✉)],
Chengze Lu[1], Yunpeng Chen[2], and Shuicheng Yan[2]

[1] College of Computer Science, Nankai University, Tianjin, China
shgao@mail.nankai.edu.cn, cmm@nankai.edu.cn
[2] Yitu Technology, Shanghai, China

**Abstract.** Salient object detection models often demand a considerable amount of computation cost to make precise prediction for each pixel, making them hardly applicable on low-power devices. In this paper, we aim to relieve the contradiction between computation cost and model performance by improving the network efficiency to a higher degree. We propose a flexible convolutional module, namely generalized Oct-Conv (gOctConv), to efficiently utilize both in-stage and cross-stages multi-scale features, while reducing the representation redundancy by a novel dynamic weight decay scheme. The effective dynamic weight decay scheme stably boosts the sparsity of parameters during training, supports learnable number of channels for each scale in gOctConv, allowing 80% of parameters reduce with negligible performance drop. Utilizing gOctConv, we build an extremely light-weighted model, namely CSNet, which achieves comparable performance with ∼0.2% parameters (100k) of large models on popular salient object detection benchmarks. The source code is publicly available at https://mmcheng.net/sod100k/.

**Keywords:** Salient object detection · Highly efficient

## 1 Introduction

Salient object detection (SOD) is an important computer vision task with various applications in image retrieval [5,17], visual tracking [23], photographic composition [15], image quality assessment [69], and weakly supervised semantic segmentation [25]. While convolutional neural networks (CNNs) based SOD methods have made significant progress, most of these methods focus on improving the state-of-the-art (SOTA) performance, by utilizing both fine details and global semantics [11,64,76,80,83], attention [2,3], as well as edge cues [12,61,68,85] *etc.* Despite the great performance, these models are usually resource-hungry, which are hardly applicable on low-power devices with limited storage/computational capability. How to build an extremely light-weighted SOD model with SOTA performance is an important but less explored area (Fig. 1).

**Electronic supplementary material** The online version of this chapter (https://doi.org/10.1007/978-3-030-58539-6_42) contains supplementary material, which is available to authorized users.

© Springer Nature Switzerland AG 2020
A. Vedaldi et al. (Eds.): ECCV 2020, LNCS 12351, pp. 702–721, 2020.
https://doi.org/10.1007/978-3-030-58539-6_42

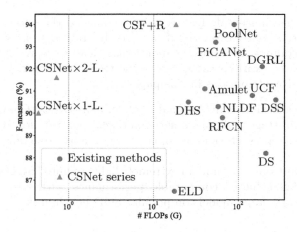

**Fig. 1.** FLOPs and performance of models on salient object detection task.

The SOD task requires generating accurate prediction scores for every image pixel, thus requires both large scale high level feature representations for correctly locating the salient objects, as well as fine detailed low level representations for precise boundary refinement [12,24,67]. There are two major challenges towards building an extremely light-weighted SOD models. **Firstly**, serious redundancy could appear when the low frequency nature of high level feature meets the high output resolution of saliency maps. **Secondly**, SOTA SOD models [10,12,44,46,72,84] usually rely on ImageNet pre-trained backbone architectures [13,19] to extract features, which by itself is resource-hungry.

Very recently, the spatial redundancy issue of low frequency features has also been noticed by Chen *et al.* [4] in the context of image and video classification. As a replacement of vanilla convolution, they design an OctConv operation to process feature maps that vary spatially slower at a lower spatial resolution to reduce computational cost. However, directly using OctConv [4] to reduce redundancy issue in the SOD task still faces two major challenges. 1) Only utilizing two scales, *i.e.,* low and high resolutions as in OctConv, is not sufficient to fully reduce redundancy issues in the SOD task, which needs much stronger multi-scale representation ability than classification tasks. 2) The number of channels for each scale in OctConv is manually selected, requiring lots of efforts to re-adjust for saliency model as SOD task requires less category information.

In this paper, we propose a generalized OctConv (gOctConv) for building an extremely light-weighted SOD model, by extending the OctConv in the following aspects: 1). The flexibility to take inputs from arbitrary number of scales, from both in-stage features as well as cross-stages features, allows a much larger range of multi-scale representations. 2). We propose a dynamic weight decay scheme to support learnable number of channels for each scale, allowing 80% of parameters reduce with negligible performance drop.

Benefiting from the flexibility and efficiency of gOctConv, we propose a highly light-weighted model, namely CSNet, that fully explores both in-stage and **Cross-Stages** multi-scale features. As a bonus to the extremely low number of parameters, our CSNet could be directly trained from scratch without ImageNet pre-training, avoiding the unnecessary feature representations for distinguishing between various categories in the recognition task. In summary, we make two major contributions in this paper:

- We propose a flexible convolutional module, namely gOctConv, to efficiently utilize both in-stage and cross-stages multi-scale features for SOD task, while reducing the representation redundancy by a novel dynamic weight decay scheme.
- Utilizing gOctConv, we build an extremely light-weighted SOD model, namely CSNet, which achieves comparable performance with ∼0.2% parameters (100k) of SOTA large models on popular SOD benchmarks.

## 2   Related Works

### 2.1   Salient Object Detection

Early works [6,31,62,74,87] mainly rely on hand-craft features to detect salient objects. [37,45,65] utilize CNNs to extract more informative features from image patches to improve the quality of saliency maps. Inspired by the fully convolutional networks (FCNs) [49], recent works [9,35,46,67,78,80] formulate the salient object detection as a pixel-level prediction task and predict the saliency map in an end-to-end manner using FCN based models. [24,57,66,80,83] capture both fine details and global semantics from different stages of the backbone network. [40,51,68,85] introduce edge cues to further refine the boundary of saliency maps. [70,80,86] improve the saliency detection from the perspective of network optimization. Despite the impressive performance, all these CNN based methods require ImageNet pre-trained powerful backbone networks as the feature extractor, which usually results in high computational cost.

### 2.2   Light-Weighted Models

Currently, most light-weighted models that are initially designed for classification tasks utilize modules such as inverted block [27,28], channel shuffling [52,82], and SE attention module [27,60] to improve network efficiency. Classification tasks [58] predict semantic labels for an image, requiring more global information but fewer details. Thus, light-weighted models [27,28,52,81,82] designed for classification use aggressive downsampling strategies at earlier stages to save FLOPs, which are not applicable to be the feature extractor for SOD task that requires multi-scale information with both coarse and fine features. Also, SOD task focuses on determine the salient region while classification tasks predicts category information. To improve performance under limited computing budget, the allocation of computational resources, *i.e.,* feature resolution, channels, for saliency models should be reconsidered.

## 2.3   Network Pruning

Many network pruning methods [21,22,38,47,48,50] have been proposed to prune unimportant filters especially on channel level. [20,38] use the norm criterion to estimate redundant filters. [50] prunes filters based on statistics information of the next layer. [48] reuses the scaling factor of BatchNorm layer as the indicator of filter importance. [21] computes the geometric median of weights to select filters. [47] utilizes generated weights to estimate the performance of remaining filters. Mostly pruning approaches rely on regularization tricks such as weight decay to introduce sparsity to filters. Our proposed dynamic weight decay stably introduces sparsity for assisting pruning algorithms to prune redundant filters, resulting in learnable channels for each scale in our proposed gOctConv.

# 3   Light-Weighted Network with Generalized OctConv

## 3.1   Overview of Generalized OctConv

Originally designed to be a replacement of traditional convolution unit, the vanilla OctConv [4] shown in Fig. 2 (a) conducts the convolution operation across high/low scales within a stage. However, only two-scales within a stage can not introduce enough multi-scale information required for SOD task. The channels for each scale in vanilla OctConv is manually set, requires lots of efforts to readjust for saliency model as SOD task requires less category information. Therefore, we propose a generalized OctConv (gOctConv) allows arbitrary number of input resolutions from both in-stage and cross-stages conv features with learnable number of channels as shown in Fig. 2 (b). As a generalized version of vanilla OctConv, gOctConv improves the vanilla OctConv for SOD task in following aspects: 1). Arbitrary numbers of input and output scales is available to support a larger range of multi-scale representation. 2). Except for in-stage features, the gOctConv can also process cross-stages features with arbitrary scales from the feature extractor. 3). The gOctConv supports learnable channels for each

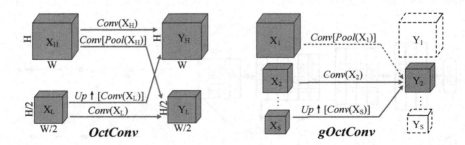

**Fig. 2.** While originally designed to be a replacement of traditional convolution unit, the OctConv [4] takes two high/low resolution inputs from the same stage with fixed number of feature channels. Our gOctConv allows arbitrary number of input resolutions from both in-stage and cross-stages conv features with learnable number of channels.

scale through our proposed dynamic weight decay assisting pruning scheme. 4). Cross-scales feature interaction can be turned off to support a large complexity flexibility. The flexible gOctConv allows many instances under different designing requirements. We will give a detailed introduction of different instances of gOctConvs in following light-weighted model designing.

## 3.2  Light-Weighted Model Composed of gOctConvs

**Overview.** As shown in Fig. 3, our proposed light-weighted network, consisting of a feature extractor and a cross-stages fusion part, synchronously processes features with multiple scales. The feature extractor is stacked with our proposed in-layer multi-scale block, namely ILBlocks, and is split into 4 stages according to the resolution of feature maps, where each stage has 3, 4, 6, and 4 ILBlocks, respectively. The cross-stages fusion part, composed of gOctConvs, processes features from stages of the feature extractor to get a high-resolution output.

**In-layer Multi-scale Block.** ILBlock enhances the multi-scale representation of features within a stage. gOctConvs are utilized to introduce multi-scale within ILBlock. Vanilla OctConv requires about 60% FLOPs [4] to achieves the similar performance to standard convolution, which is not enough for our objective of designing a highly light-weighted model. To save computational cost, interacting features with different scales in every layer is unnecessary. Therefore, we apply an instance of gOctConv that each input channel corresponds to an output channel with the same resolution through eliminating the cross scale operations. A depthwise operation within each scale in utilized to further save computational cost. This instance of gOctConv only requires about $1/channel$ FLOPs compared with vanilla OctConv. ILBlock is composed of a vanilla OctConv and two $3 \times 3$ gOctConvs as shown in Fig. 3. Vanilla OctConv interacts features with two scales and gOctConvs extract features within each scale. Multi-scale features within a block are separately processed and interacted alternately. Each convolution is followed by the BatchNorm [30] and PRelu [18]. Initially, we roughly double the channels of ILBlocks as the resolution decreases, except for the last two stages that have the same channel number. Unless otherwise stated, the channels for

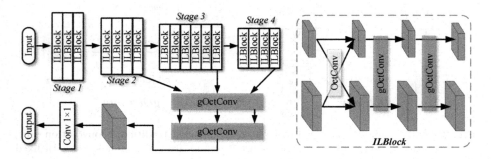

**Fig. 3.** Illustration of our salient object detection pipeline, which uses gOctConv to extract both in-stage and cross-stages multi-scale features in a highly efficient way.

different scales in ILBlocks are set evenly. Learnable channels of OctConvs then are obtained through the scheme as described in Sect. 3.3.

**Cross-Stages Fusion.** To retain a high output resolution, common methods retain high feature resolution on high-level of the feature extractor and construct complex multi-level aggregation module, inevitably increase the computational redundancy. While the value of multi-level aggregation is widely recognized [16,43], how to efficiently and concisely achieve it remains challenging. Instead, we simply use gOctConvs to fuse multi-scale features from stages of the feature extractor and generate the high-resolution output. As a trade-off between efficiency and performance, features from last three stages are used. A gOctConv $1 \times 1$ takes features with different scales from the last conv of each stage as input and conducts a cross-stages convolution to output features with different scales. To extract multi-scale features at a granular level, each scale of features is processed by a group of parallel convolutions with different dilation rates. Features are then sent to another gOctConv $1 \times 1$ to generate features with the highest resolution. Another standard conv $1 \times 1$ outputs the prediction result of saliency map. Learnable channels of gOctConvs in this part are also obtained.

### 3.3 Learnable Channels for gOctConv

We propose to get learnable channels for each scale in gOctConv by utilizing our proposed dynamic weight decay assisted pruning during training. Dynamic weight decay maintains a stable weights distribution among channels while introducing sparsity, helping pruning algorithms to eliminate redundant channels with negligible performance drop.

**Dynamic Weight Decay.** The commonly used regularization trick weight decay [33,77] endows CNNs with better generalization performance. Mehta *et al.* [53] shows that weight decay introduces sparsity into CNNs, which helps to prune unimportant weights. Training with weight decay makes unimportant weights in CNN have values close to zero. Thus, weight decay has been widely used in pruning algorithms to introduce sparsity [21,22,38,47,48,50]. The common implementation of weight decay is by adding the L2 regularization to the loss function, which can be written as follows:

$$L = L_0 + \lambda \sum \frac{1}{2} {w_i}^2, \tag{1}$$

where $L_0$ is the loss for the specific task, $w_i$ is the weight of $i$th layer, and $\lambda$ is the weight for weight decay. During back propagation, the weight $w_i$ is updated as

$$w_i \leftarrow w_i - \nabla f_i(w_i) - \lambda w_i, \tag{2}$$

where $\nabla f_i(w_i)$ is the gradient to be updated, and $\lambda w_i$ is the decay term, which is only associated with the weight itself. Applying a large decay term enhances

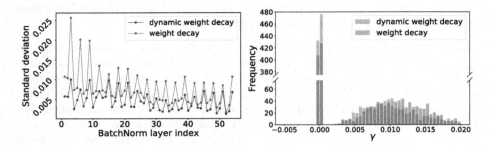

**Fig. 4.** a) Left: The averaged standard deviation of outputs among channels from BatchNorm layer in models trained with/without dynamic weight decay. b) Right: Distribution of $\gamma$ in Eq. (5) of models trained with/without dynamic weight decay.

sparsity, and meanwhile inevitably enlarges the diversity of weights among channels. Figure 4 (a) shows that diverse weights cause unstable distribution of outputs among channels. Ruan *et al.* [8] reveals that channels with diverse outputs are more likely to contain noise, leading to biased representation for subsequent filters. Attention mechanisms have been widely used to re-calibrate the diverse outputs with extra blocks and computational cost [8,29]. We propose to relieve diverse outputs among channels with no extra cost during inference. We argue that the diverse outputs are mainly caused by the indiscriminate suppression of decay terms to weights. Therefore, we propose to adjust the weight decay based on specific features of certain channels. Specifically, during back propagation, decay terms are dynamically changed according to features of certain channels. The weight update of the proposed dynamic weight decay is written as

$$w_i \leftarrow w_i - \nabla f_i(w_i) - \lambda_d \, \mathrm{S}(x_i) \, w_i, \tag{3}$$

where $\lambda_d$ is the weight of dynamic weight decay, $x_i$ denotes the features calculated by $w_i$, and $\mathrm{S}(x_i)$ is the metric of the feature, which can have multiple definitions depending on the task. In this paper, our goal is to stabilize the weight distribution among channels according to features. Thus, we simply use the global average pooling (GAP) [42] as the metric for a certain channel:

$$\mathrm{S}(x_i) = \frac{1}{HW} \sum_{h=0}^{H} \sum_{w=0}^{W} x_{i\,h,w}, \tag{4}$$

where $H$ and $W$ are the height and width of the feature map $x_i$. The dynamic weight decay with the GAP metric ensures that the weights producing large value features are suppressed, giving a compact and stable weights and outputs distribution as revealed in Fig. 4. Also, the metric can be defined as other forms to suit certain tasks as we will study in our future work. Please refer to Sect. 4.3 for a more detailed interpretation of dynamic weight decay.

**Learnable Channels with Model Compression.** Now, we incorporate dynamic weight decay with pruning algorithms to remove redundant weights, so as to get learnable channels of each scale in gOctConvs. In this paper, we follow [48] to use the weight of BatchNorm layer as the indicator of the channel importance. The BatchNorm operation [30] is written as follows:

$$y = \frac{x - \mathrm{E}(x)}{\sqrt{\mathrm{Var}(x) + \epsilon}} \gamma + \beta, \tag{5}$$

where $x$ and $y$ are input and output features, $\mathrm{E}(x)$ and $\mathrm{Var}(x)$ are the mean and variance, respectively, and $\epsilon$ is a small factor to avoid zero variance. $\gamma$ and $\beta$ are learned factors. We apply the dynamic weight decay to $\gamma$ during training. Figure 4 (b) reveals that there is a clear gap between important and redundant weights, and unimportant weights are suppressed to nearly zero ($w_i < 1e{-}20$). Thus, we can easily remove channels whose $\gamma$ is less than a small threshold. The learnable channels of each resolution features in gOctConv are obtained. The algorithm of getting learnbale channels of gOctConvs is illustrated in Algorithm 1.

---

**Algorithm 1.** Learnable Channels for gOctConv with Dynamic Weight Decay

---

**Require:** The initial CSNet in which channels for all scales in gOctConvs are set. Input images $X$ and corresponding label $Y$.

1: **for** each iteration $i \in [1, MaxIteration]$ **do**
2:     Feed input $X$ into the network to get the result $\hat{Y}$;
3:     Compute $Loss = criterion(\hat{Y}, Y)$;
4:     Compute metric for each channel using Eqn. (4);
5:     Backward with dynamic weight decay using Eqn. (3).
6: **end for**
7: Eliminate redundant channels to get learnable channels for each scale in gOctConv.

8: Train for several iterations to fine-tune remaining weights.

---

## 4    Experiments

### 4.1    Implementation

**Settings.** The implementation of the proposed method is based on the PyTorch framework. For light-weighted models, we train models using the Adam optimizer [32] with a batch-size of 24 for 300 epochs from scratch. Even with no ImageNet pre-training, the proposed CSNet still achieves comparable performance to large models based on pre-trained backbones [19,59]. The learning rate is set to $1e{-}4$ initially, and divided by 10 at the epochs of 200, and 250. We eliminate redundant weights and fine-tune the model for the last 20 epochs to compress models and get gOctConvs with the learnable channels of different

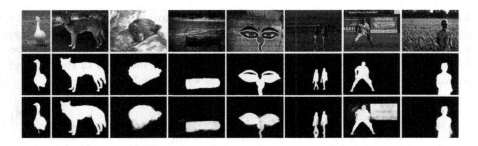

**Fig. 5.** Visualisation of predicted results on salient object detection. Each row gives the image, GT, and predicted result, respectively.

resolutions. We only use the data augmentation of random flip and crop. The weight decay of BatchNorms following gOctConvs is replaced with our proposed dynamic weight decay with the weight of 3 by default while the weight decay for other weights is set to 5e−3 by default. For large models based on the pre-trained backbones, we train our models following the implementation of [44]. The commonly used evaluation metrics maximum F-measure $(F_\beta)$ [1] and MAE $(M)$ [7] are used for evaluation. FLOPs of light-weighted models are computed with an image size of 224 × 224.

**Datasets.** We following common settings of recent methods [44,46,66,67,83,85] to train our models using the DUTS-TR [63] dataset, and evaluate the performance on several commonly used datasets, including ECSSD [73], PASCAL-S [41], DUT-O [74], HKU-IS [36], SOD [55], and DUTS-TE [63]. On ablation studies, the performance on the ECSSD dataset is reported if not mentioned otherwise.

### 4.2 Performance Analysis

In this section, we firstly evaluate the performance of our proposed light-weighted model CSNet with fixed channels. Then, the performance of CSNet with learn-able channels using dynamic weight decay is also evaluated. Figure 5 shows the visualized results of salient object detection using our proposed light-weighted CSNet. Also, we transfer the proposed cross-stages fusion part to commonly used large backbones [19] to verify the cross-stages feature extraction ability.

**Performance of CSNet with Fixed Channels in gOctConv.** The extractor model only composed of ILBlocks. With fixed parameters, we adjust the split-ratio of channels for high/low resolution features in gOctConvs of ILBlocks to construct models with different FLOPs, denoted by $C_H/C_L$. Table 1 shows feature extraction models with different split-ratios of high/low resolution features. Extractors achieve an low complexity thanks to the simplified instance of gOctConvs. Benefiting from the in-stage multi-scale representation and the low scale features in ILBlock, the extractor-3/1 achieves performance gain of 0.4% in terms of F-measure with 80% FLOPs over the extractor-1/0. The gOctConvs

**Table 1.** Performance of CSNet with the fixed split-ratio of channels in gOctConvs, and CSNet with learnable channels. CSNet denotes the CSNet with the fixed split-ratio in gOctConvs. Extractor denotes the network only composed of ILBlocks. CSNet-L denotes the model with learnable channels using Algorithm 1.

| Method | | PARM. | FLOPs | $F_\beta \uparrow$ | $M \downarrow$ |
|---|---|---|---|---|---|
| Extractor | 1/0 | 180K | 0.80G | 88.2 | 0.088 |
| | 3/1 | 180K | 0.64G | **88.6** | **0.085** |
| | 5/5 | 180K | 0.45G | 88.1 | 0.086 |
| | 1/3 | 180K | 0.30G | 87.4 | 0.090 |
| | 0/1 | 180K | 0.20G | 86.4 | 0.095 |
| CSNet | 1/0 | 211K | 0.91G | 90.0 | **0.076** |
| | 3/1 | 211K | 0.78G | 89.9 | 0.077 |
| | 5/5 | 211K | 0.61G | **90.0** | 0.077 |
| | 1/3 | 211K | 0.47G | 89.2 | 0.082 |
| | 0/1 | 211K | 0.35G | 88.2 | 0.089 |
| CSNet-L | ×2 | 140K | 0.72G | **91.6** | **0.066** |
| | ×1 | 94K | 0.43G | 90.0 | 0.075 |

in cross-stages fusion part enhance the cross-stages multi-scale ability of the network while maintaining the high output resolution by utilizing features from different stages. As shown in Table 1, the CSNet-5/5 surpasses the extractor-3/1 by 1.4% in terms of F-measure with fewer FLOPs. Even in extreme case that the CSNet-0/1 with only low resolution features in extractor has comparable performance with 44% FLOPs over extractor-1/0 with all high resolution features. However, manually tune the overall split-ratio of feature channels of different resolution may achieves sub-optimal balance between performance and computational cost.

To further verify the effectiveness of the cross-stage fusion (CSF) part on large models, we implement this part into commonly used backbone network ResNet [19] and Res2Net [13]. As shown in Table 2, the ResNet+CSF achieves similar performance to the ResNet+PoolNet with 53% parameters and 21% FLOPs. Unlike other models such as PoolNet that eliminates downsampling operations to maintain a high feature resolution on high-levels of the backbone, the gOctConvs obtains both high and low resolution features across different stages of the backbone, getting a high-resolution output while saving a large amount of computational cost. When utilizing the recently proposed Res2Net as the backbone network, the performance is further boosted.

**Performance of CSNet with Learnable Channels in gOctConv.** We further train the model with our proposed dynamic weight decay and get the learnable channels for gOctConv as described in Algorithm 1, named CSNet-L. The channel for each gOctConv is expanded to enlarge the available space for compression. Models with channels expanded to $k$ times are denoted by

**Table 2.** Performance and complexity comparison with state-of-the-art methods. +R, R2 denotes using the ImageNet pre-trained ResNet50 [19] and Res2Net50 [13] backbone network. Unlike previous methods that require the ImageNet pre-trained backbone, our proposed light-weighted CSNet is trained from scratch without ImageNet pre-training.

| Model | Complexity | | ECSSD | | PASCAL-S | | DUT-O | | HKU-IS | | SOD | | DUTS-TE | |
|---|---|---|---|---|---|---|---|---|---|---|---|---|---|---|
| | #PARM. | FLOPs | $F_\beta$ | $M$ | $F_\beta$ | $M$ | $F_\beta$ | $M$ | $F_\beta$ | $M$ | $F_\beta$ | $M$ | $F_\beta$ | $M$ |
| ELD [14] | 43.15M | 17.63G | .865 | .981 | .767 | .121 | .719 | .091 | .844 | .071 | .760 | .154 | – | – |
| DS [39] | 134.27M | 211.28G | .882 | .122 | .765 | .176 | .745 | .120 | .865 | .080 | .784 | .190 | .777 | .090 |
| DCL [37] | – | – | .896 | .080 | .805 | .115 | .733 | .094 | .893 | .063 | .831 | .131 | .786 | .081 |
| RFCN [65] | 19.08M | 64.95G | .898 | .097 | .827 | .118 | .747 | .094 | .895 | .079 | .805 | .161 | .786 | .090 |
| DHS [45] | 93.76M | 25.82G | .905 | .062 | .825 | .092 | – | – | .892 | .052 | .823 | .128 | .815 | .065 |
| MSR [35] | – | – | .903 | .059 | .839 | .083 | .790 | .073 | .907 | .043 | .841 | .111 | .824 | .062 |
| DSS [24] | 62.23M | 276.37G | .906 | .064 | .821 | .101 | .760 | .074 | .900 | .050 | .834 | .125 | .813 | .065 |
| NLDF [51] | 35.48M | 57.73G | .903 | .065 | .822 | .098 | .753 | .079 | .902 | .048 | .837 | .123 | .816 | .065 |
| UCF [80] | 29.47M | 146.42G | .908 | .080 | .820 | .127 | .735 | .131 | .888 | .073 | .798 | .164 | .771 | .116 |
| Amulet [79] | 33.15M | 40.22G | .911 | .062 | .826 | .092 | .737 | .083 | .889 | .052 | .799 | .146 | .773 | .075 |
| GearNet [26] | – | – | .923 | .055 | – | – | .790 | .068 | .934 | .034 | .853 | .117 | – | – |
| PAGR [83] | – | – | .924 | .064 | .847 | .089 | .771 | .071 | .919 | .047 | – | – | .854 | .055 |
| SRM [66] | 53.14M | 36.82G | .916 | .056 | .838 | .084 | .769 | .069 | .906 | .046 | .840 | .126 | .826 | .058 |
| DGRL [67] | 161.74M | 191.28G | .921 | .043 | .844 | .072 | .774 | .062 | .910 | .036 | .843 | .103 | .828 | .049 |
| PiCANet [46] | 47.22M | 54.05G | .932 | .048 | .864 | .075 | .820 | .064 | .920 | .044 | .861 | .103 | .863 | .050 |
| PoolNet [44] | 68.26M | 88.89G | .940 | .042 | .863 | .075 | .830 | .055 | .934 | .032 | .867 | .100 | .886 | .040 |
| Light-weighted models designed for other tasks: | | | | | | | | | | | | | | |
| Eff.Net [60] | 8.64M | 2.62G | .828 | .129 | .739 | .158 | .696 | .129 | .807 | .116 | .712 | .199 | .687 | .135 |
| Sf.Netv2 [52] | 9.54M | 4.35G | .870 | .092 | .781 | .127 | .720 | .100 | .853 | .078 | .779 | .163 | .743 | .096 |
| ENet [56] | 0.36M | 0.40G | .857 | .107 | .770 | .138 | .730 | .109 | .839 | .094 | .741 | .183 | .730 | .111 |
| CGNet [71] | 0.49M | 0.69G | .868 | .099 | .784 | .130 | .727 | .108 | .849 | .088 | .772 | .168 | .742 | .106 |
| DABNet [34] | 0.75M | 1.03G | .877 | .091 | .790 | .123 | .747 | .094 | .862 | .078 | .778 | .157 | .759 | .093 |
| ESPNetv2 [54] | 0.79M | 0.31G | .889 | .081 | .795 | .119 | .760 | .088 | .872 | .069 | .780 | .157 | .765 | .089 |
| BiseNet [75] | 12.80M | 2.50G | .894 | .078 | .817 | .115 | .762 | .087 | .872 | .071 | .796 | .148 | .778 | .084 |
| Ours: | | | | | | | | | | | | | | |
| CSF+R | 36.37M | 18.40G | .940 | .041 | .866 | .073 | .821 | .055 | .930 | .033 | .866 | .106 | .881 | .039 |
| CSF+R2 | 36.53M | 18.96G | .947 | .036 | .876 | .068 | .833 | .055 | .936 | .030 | .870 | .098 | .893 | .037 |
| CSNet×1-L | 94K | 0.43G | .900 | .075 | .819 | .110 | .777 | .087 | .889 | .065 | .809 | .149 | .799 | .082 |
| CSNet×2-L | 140K | 0.72G | .916 | .066 | .835 | .102 | .792 | .080 | .899 | .059 | .825 | .137 | .819 | .074 |

CSNet-$\times k$. Table 4 shows that our proposed dynamic weight decay assisted pruning scheme can compress the model up to 18% of the original model size with negligible performance drop. Compared with manually tuned split-ratio of feature resolution, the learnable channels of gOctConvs obtained by model compression achieves much better efficiency. As shown in Table 1, the compressed CSNet×2-L outperforms the CSNet-5/5 by 1.6% with fewer parameters and 18%

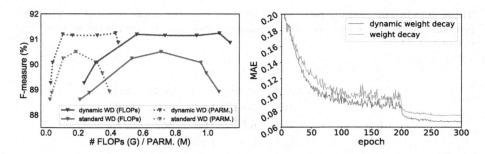

**Fig. 6.** a) Left: Performance and complexity of compressed model using dynamic/standard weight decay under different $\lambda$ as shown in Eq. (1). b) Right: The test MAE of models with/without dynamic weight decay.

**Table 3.** Integrating dynamic weight decay into pruning methods. Standard/Dynamic denote the standard/dynamic weight decay, respectively.

| Pruning Filters [38] | | | | | Geometric-Median [21] | | | | |
|---|---|---|---|---|---|---|---|---|---|
| | PARM. | FLOPs | $F_\beta$ | $M$ | | PARM. | FLOPs | $F_\beta$ | $M$ |
| Standard | 227K | 0.69G | 88.7 | 0.080 | Standard | 227K | 0.70G | 88.7 | 0.083 |
| Dynamic | 226K | 0.69G | 89.4 | 0.078 | Dynamic | 226K | 0.68G | 89.6 | 0.082 |

additional FLOPs. The CSNet×1-L achieves comparable performance compared with CSNet-5/5 with 45% parameters and 70% FLOPs. Table 2 shows that CSNet-L series achieve comparable performance compared with some models with extensive parameters such as SRM [66], and Amulet [80] with ∼0.2% parameters. Note that our light-weighted models are trained from scratch while those large models are pre-trained with ImageNet. The performance gap between the proposed CSNet and the SOTA models with extensive parameters and FLOPs is only ∼3%, considering that CSNet has the limited capacity with about 0.2% parameters of large models. We believe that more techniques such as ImageNet pre-training will bring more performance gain.

**Comparison with Light-Weighted Models.** To the best of our knowledge, we are the first work that aims to design an extremely light-weighted model for SOD task. Therefore, we port several SOTA light-weighted models designed for other tasks such as classification and semantic segmentation for comparison. All models share the same training configuration with our training strategy. Table 2 shows that our proposed models have considerable improvements compared with those light-weighted models.

## 4.3 Dynamic Weight Decay

In this section, we verify the effectiveness of our proposed dynamic weight decay. We apply different degrees of standard weight decay to achieve the trade-off

**Table 4.** The compression ratio of CSNet with different initial channel widths. The pruning rate is defined as the ratio of model complexity between pruned parts and complete CSNet.

| Width | Prune | ×1 | ×1.2 | ×1.5 | ×1.8 | ×2.0 |
|-------|-------|------|------|------|------|------|
| Parms | N | 211K | 298K | 455K | 645K | 788K |
|       | Y | 94K | 109K | 118K | 134K | 140K |
| Ratio |   | 55% | 63% | 74% | 79% | 82% |
| FLOPs | N | 0.61G | 0.82G | 1.17G | 1.58G | 1.87G |
|       | Y | 0.43G | 0.52G | 0.63G | 0.71G | 0.72G |
| Ratio |   | 30% | 37% | 46% | 55% | 61% |
| $F_\beta$ | N | 90.0 | 90.7 | 91.1 | 91.2 | 91.5 |
|       | Y | 90.0 | 90.7 | 91.2 | 91.3 | 91.6 |

between model performance and sparsity, while keeping the weights for dynamic weight decay unchanged. We insert our proposed dynamic weight decay to the weights of BatchNorm layers while using the standard weight decay on remaining weights for a fair comparison. Figure 6 (a) shows the performance and complexity of the compressed model using dynamic/standard weight decay under different $\lambda$ in Eq. (1). Models trained with dynamic weight decay have better performance under the same complexity. Also, the performance of dynamic weight decay based models is less sensitive to the model complexity. We eliminate redundant channels according to the absolute value of $\gamma$ in Eq. (5) as described in Sect. 3.3. Figure 4 (b) shows the distribution of $\gamma$ for models trained with/without dynamic weight decay. By suppressing weights according to features, dynamic weight decay enforces the model with more sparsity. Figure 4 (a) reveals the average standard deviation of outputs among channels from the BatchNorm layer of models trained with/without dynamic weight decay. Features of dynamic weight decay based model are more stabilized due to the stable weight distribution. Figure 6 (b) shows the testing MAE of each epoch with/without dynamic weight decay. Training with dynamic weight decay brings better performance in terms of MAE and faster convergence. The dynamic weight decay generalizes well on other tasks such as classification, and semantic segmentation.

**Cooperating with Pruning Methods.** By default, we use the pruning method in [48] to eliminate redundant weights. Since our proposed dynamic weight decay focuses on introducing sparsity while maintaining a stable and compact distribution of weights among channels, it is orthogonal to commonly use pruning methods that focus on identify unnecessarily weights. Therefore, we integrate the dynamic weight decay into several pruning methods as shown in Table 3. All configurations remain the same except for replacing the standard weight decay to our proposed dynamic weight decay. Pruning methods [21,38] equipped with dynamic weight decay achieve better performance under the similar parameters.

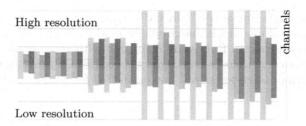

**Fig. 7.** Visualization of the feature extractor of CSNet. Gray is CSNet with fixed channel, Yellow and Green are the CSNet-L trained with standard/dynamic weight decay, respectively. (Color figure online)

**Table 5.** Run-time using 224 × 224 input on a single core of i7-8700K CPU.

| Method | FLOPs | Run-time | Method | FLOPs | Run-time |
|---|---|---|---|---|---|
| PiCANet [45] | 54.06G | 2850.2 ms | PoolNet [44] | 88.89G | 997.3 ms |
| ENet [56] | 0.40G | 89.9 ms | ESPNetv2 [54] | 0.31G | 186.3 ms |
| CSNet×1 | 0.61G | 135.9 ms | CSNet×1-L | 0.43G | 95.3 ms |

### 4.4 CSNet with Learned Channels in gOctConv

**Pruning Rate & Channel Width.** An initial training space with a large channel width is required for learning more useful features. To enlarge the available training space, we linearly expand the channel number of gOctConvs. A pruning rate is defined as the ratio of model complexity between pruned parts and complete CSNet. Table 4 shows the pruning rate of CSNet with different initial channel widths. The split-ratio of gOctConvs for the initial model is set to 5/5. Larger initial width results in better performance as expected. As the initial width rises, the complexity of pruned models only has a limited increment. The quality of the pruned model is dependant on the available training space. With a large enough training space, results are closing to the optimal. Also, benefited from the stable distribution introduced by dynamic weight decay, compressed models have similar or even better performance compared with the initial model.

**Visualization of Channels of gOctConvs.** We visualize the learned channel number of gOctConvs in Fig. 7. It can be seen that as the network goes deeper, the feature extraction network shows a trend of utilizing more low resolution features. Within the same stage, high resolution features are urged in the middle of the stage. Also, the model trained with dynamic weight decay has a stabler channel number variation among different layers. Deeper layers contain more redundant channels compared with shallow layers.

### 4.5 Run-Time

We compare the run-time of our proposed CSNet with existing models from Table 2 as shown in Table 5. The run-time is tested with an image of

$224 \times 224$ on a single core of i7-8700K CPU. Our proposed CSNet has more than x10 acceleration compared with large-weight models. With similar speed, CSNet achieves up to 6% gain in F-measure compared with those models designed for other tasks. However, there is still a gap between FLOPs and run-time, as current deep learning frameworks are not optimized for vanilla and our proposed gOctConvs.

## 5   Conclusion

In this paper, we propose the generalized OctConv with more flexibility to efficiently utilize both in-stage and cross-stages multi-scale features, while reducing the representation redundancy by a novel dynamic weight decay scheme. The dynamic weight decay scheme maintains a stable weights distribution among channels and stably boosts the sparsity of parameters during training. Dynamic weight decay supports learnable number of channels for each scale in gOctConvs, allowing 80% of parameters reduce with negligible performance drop. Utilizing different instances of gOctConvs, we build an extremely light-weighted model, namely CSNet, which achieves comparable performance with ∼0.2% parameters (100k) of large models on popular salient object detection benchmarks.

**Acknowledgements.** Ming-Ming Cheng is the corresponding author. This research was supported by Major Project for New Generation of AI under Grant No. 2018AAA0100400, NSFC (61922046), Tianjin Natural Science Foundation (18ZXZNGX00110), and the Fundamental Research Funds for the Central Universities, Nankai University (63201169).

## References

1. Achanta, R., Hemami, S., Estrada, F., Süsstrunk, S.: Frequency-tuned salient region detection. In: IEEE Conference on Computer Vision and Pattern Recognition (CVPR), pp. 1597–1604 (2009)
2. Borji, A., Cheng, M.M., Hou, Q., Jiang, H., Li, J.: Salient object detection: a survey. Comput. Vis. Media **5**(2), 117–150 (2019). https://doi.org/10.1007/s41095-019-0149-9
3. Chen, S., Tan, X., Wang, B., Hu, X.: Reverse attention for salient object detection. In: Ferrari, V., Hebert, M., Sminchisescu, C., Weiss, Y. (eds.) ECCV 2018. LNCS, vol. 11213, pp. 236–252. Springer, Cham (2018). https://doi.org/10.1007/978-3-030-01240-3_15
4. Chen, Y., et al.: Drop an octave: reducing spatial redundancy in convolutional neural networks with octave convolution. In: IEEE International Conference on Computer Vision (ICCV) (2019)
5. Cheng, M.M., Hou, Q.B., Zhang, S.H., Rosin, P.L.: Intelligent visual media processing: when graphics meets vision. J. Comput. Sci. Technol. **32**(1), 110–121 (2017). https://doi.org/10.1007/s11390-017-1681-7
6. Cheng, M.M., Mitra, N.J., Huang, X., Torr, P.H., Hu, S.M.: Global contrast based salient region detection. IEEE Trans. Pattern Anal. Mach. Intell. **37**(3), 569–582 (2015)

7. Cheng, M.M., Warrell, J., Lin, W.Y., Zheng, S., Vineet, V., Crook, N.: Efficient salient region detection with soft image abstraction. In: IEEE International Conference on Computer Vision (ICCV), pp. 1529–1536 (2013)
8. Dongsheng, R., Jun, W., Nenggan, Z.: Linear context transform block. arXiv preprint arXiv:1909.03834 (2019)
9. Fan, D.-P., Cheng, M.-M., Liu, J.-J., Gao, S.-H., Hou, Q., Borji, A.: Salient objects in clutter: bringing salient object detection to the foreground. In: Ferrari, V., Hebert, M., Sminchisescu, C., Weiss, Y. (eds.) ECCV 2018. LNCS, vol. 11219, pp. 196–212. Springer, Cham (2018). https://doi.org/10.1007/978-3-030-01267-0_12
10. Fan, D.-P., Zhai, Y., Borji, A., Yang, J., Shao, L.: BBS-Net: RGB-D salient object detection with a bifurcated backbone strategy network. In: Vedaldi, A., Bischof, H., Brox, T., Frahm, J.-M. (eds.) ECCV 2020. LNCS, vol. 12357, pp. 275–292. Springer, Cham (2020). https://doi.org/10.1007/978-3-030-58610-2_17
11. Fan, R., Cheng, M.M., Hou, Q., Mu, T.J., Wang, J., Hu, S.M.: S4Net: single stage salient-instance segmentation. Comput. Vis. Media 6(2), 191–204 (2020). https://doi.org/10.1007/s41095-020-0173-9
12. Feng, M., Lu, H., Ding, E.: Attentive feedback network for boundary-aware salient object detection. In: IEEE Conference on Computer Vision and Pattern Recognition (CVPR) (2019)
13. Gao, S.H., Cheng, M.M., Zhao, K., Zhang, X.Y., Yang, M.H., Torr, P.: Res2Net: a new multi-scale backbone architecture. IEEE Trans. Pattern Anal. Mach. Intell. (2020)
14. Gayoung, L., Yu-Wing, T., Junmo, K.: Deep saliency with encoded low level distance map and high level features. In: IEEE Conference on Computer Vision and Pattern Recognition (CVPR) (2016)
15. Han, Q., Zhao, K., Xu, J., Cheng, M.M.: Deep Hough transform for semantic line detection. In: Vedaldi, A., et al. (eds.) ECCV 2020. LNCS, vol. 12354, pp. 249–265. Springer, Cham (2020)
16. Hariharan, B., Arbeláez, P., Girshick, R., Malik, J.: Hypercolumns for object segmentation and fine-grained localization. In: Proceedings of the IEEE Conference on Computer Vision and Pattern Recognition, pp. 447–456 (2015)
17. He, J., Feng, J., Liu, X., Tao, C., Chang, S.F.: Mobile product search with bag of hash bits and boundary reranking. In: IEEE Conference on Computer Vision and Pattern Recognition (CVPR) (2012)
18. He, K., Zhang, X., Ren, S., Sun, J.: Delving deep into rectifiers: surpassing human-level performance on imagenet classification. In: IEEE International Conference on Computer Vision (ICCV), pp. 1026–1034 (2015)
19. He, K., Zhang, X., Ren, S., Sun, J.: Deep residual learning for image recognition. In: IEEE Conference on Computer Vision and Pattern Recognition (CVPR), pp. 770–778 (2016)
20. He, Y., Kang, G., Dong, X., Fu, Y., Yang, Y.: Soft filter pruning for accelerating deep convolutional neural networks. In: International Joint Conference on Artificial Intelligence (IJCAI) (2018)
21. He, Y., Liu, P., Wang, Z., Hu, Z., Yang, Y.: Filter pruning via geometric median for deep convolutional neural networks acceleration. In: IEEE Conference on Computer Vision and Pattern Recognition (CVPR), pp. 4340–4349 (2019)
22. He, Y., Zhang, X., Sun, J.: Channel pruning for accelerating very deep neural networks. In: IEEE International Conference on Computer Vision (ICCV), pp. 1389–1397 (2017)

23. Hong, S., You, T., Kwak, S., Han, B.: Online tracking by learning discriminative saliency map with convolutional neural network. In: International Conference on Machine Learning (ICML) (2015)
24. Hou, Q., Cheng, M.M., Hu, X., Borji, A., Tu, Z., Torr, P.: Deeply supervised salient object detection with short connections. IEEE Trans. Pattern Anal. Mach. Intell. **41**(4), 815–828 (2019). https://doi.org/10.1109/TPAMI.2018.2815688
25. Hou, Q., Jiang, P.T., Wei, Y., Cheng, M.M.: Self-erasing network for integral object attention. In: NeurIPS (2018)
26. Hou, Q., Liu, J., Cheng, M.M., Borji, A., Torr, P.H.: Three birds one stone: a unified framework for salient object segmentation, edge detection and skeleton extraction. arXiv preprint arXiv:1803.09860 (2018)
27. Howard, A., et al.: Searching for mobilenetv3. arXiv preprint arXiv:1905.02244 (2019)
28. Howard, A.G., et al.: MobileNets: efficient convolutional neural networks for mobile vision applications. arXiv preprint arXiv:1704.04861 (2017)
29. Hu, J., Shen, L., Sun, G.: Squeeze-and-excitation networks. In: IEEE Conference on Computer Vision and Pattern Recognition (CVPR) (2018)
30. Ioffe, S., Szegedy, C.: Batch normalization: accelerating deep network training by reducing internal covariate shift. In: International Conference on Machine Learning (ICML) (2015)
31. Itti, L., Koch, C., Niebur, E.: A model of saliency-based visual attention for rapid scene analysis. IEEE Trans. Pattern Anal. Mach. Intell. **20**(11), 1254–1259 (1998)
32. Kingma, D.P., Ba, J.: Adam: a method for stochastic optimization. In: International Conference on Learning Representations (ICLR) (2014)
33. Krogh, A., Hertz, J.A.: A simple weight decay can improve generalization. In: Advances in Neural Information Processing Systems (NIPS), pp. 950–957 (1992)
34. Li, G., Kim, J.: DABNet: depth-wise asymmetric bottleneck for real-time semantic segmentation. In: British Machine Vision Conference (BMVC) (2019)
35. Li, G., Xie, Y., Lin, L., Yu, Y.: Instance-level salient object segmentation. In: IEEE Conference on Computer Vision and Pattern Recognition (CVPR), July 2017
36. Li, G., Yu, Y.: Visual saliency based on multiscale deep features. In: IEEE Conference on Computer Vision and Pattern Recognition (CVPR), June 2015
37. Li, G., Yu, Y.: Deep contrast learning for salient object detection. In: IEEE Conference on Computer Vision and Pattern Recognition (CVPR), June 2016
38. Li, H., Kadav, A., Durdanovic, I., Samet, H., Graf, H.P.: Pruning filters for efficient convnets. In: International Conference on Learning Representations (ICLR) (2016)
39. Li, X., et al.: Deepsaliency: multi-task deep neural network model for salient object detection. IEEE Trans. Image Process. **25**(8), 3919–3930 (2016). https://doi.org/10.1109/TIP.2016.2579306
40. Li, X., Yang, F., Cheng, H., Liu, W., Shen, D.: Contour knowledge transfer for salient object detection. In: European Conference on Computer Vision (ECCV), pp. 355–370 (2018)
41. Li, Y., Hou, X., Koch, C., Rehg, J.M., Yuille, A.L.: The secrets of salient object segmentation. In: IEEE Conference on Computer Vision and Pattern Recognition (CVPR), June 2014
42. Lin, M., Chen, Q., Yan, S.: Network in network. In: International Conference on Learning Representations (ICLR) (2013)
43. Lin, T.Y., Dollár, P., Girshick, R., He, K., Hariharan, B., Belongie, S.: Feature pyramid networks for object detection. In: IEEE Conference on Computer Vision and Pattern Recognition (CVPR), pp. 2117–2125 (2017)

44. Liu, J.J., Hou, Q., Cheng, M.M., Feng, J., Jiang, J.: A simple pooling-based design for real-time salient object detection. In: IEEE Conference on Computer Vision and Pattern Recognition (CVPR) (2019)
45. Liu, N., Han, J.: DHSNet: deep hierarchical saliency network for salient object detection. In: IEEE Conference on Computer Vision and Pattern Recognition (CVPR), June 2016
46. Liu, N., Han, J., Yang, M.H.: PiCANet: learning pixel-wise contextual attention for saliency detection. In: IEEE Conference on Computer Vision and Pattern Recognition (CVPR), June 2018
47. Liu, Z., et al.: MetaPruning: meta learning for automatic neural network channel pruning. In: IEEE International Conference on Computer Vision (ICCV) (2019)
48. Liu, Z., Li, J., Shen, Z., Huang, G., Yan, S., Zhang, C.: Learning efficient convolutional networks through network slimming. In: IEEE International Conference on Computer Vision (ICCV), pp. 2736–2744 (2017)
49. Long, J., Shelhamer, E., Darrell, T.: Fully convolutional networks for semantic segmentation. In: IEEE Conference on Computer Vision and Pattern Recognition (CVPR), pp. 3431–3440 (2015)
50. Luo, J.H., Wu, J., Lin, W.: ThiNet: a filter level pruning method for deep neural network compression. In: IEEE International Conference on Computer Vision (ICCV), pp. 5058–5066 (2017)
51. Luo, Z., Mishra, A., Achkar, A., Eichel, J., Li, S., Jodoin, P.M.: Non-local deep features for salient object detection. In: IEEE Conference on Computer Vision and Pattern Recognition (CVPR), July 2017
52. Ma, N., Zhang, X., Zheng, H.T., Sun, J.: ShuffleNet V2: practical guidelines for efficient CNN architecture design. In: European Conference on Computer Vision (ECCV), pp. 116–131 (2018)
53. Mehta, D., Kim, K.I., Theobalt, C.: On implicit filter level sparsity in convolutional neural networks. In: IEEE Conference on Computer Vision and Pattern Recognition (CVPR), pp. 520–528 (2019)
54. Mehta, S., Rastegari, M., Shapiro, L., Hajishirzi, H.: ESPNetv2: a light-weight, power efficient, and general purpose convolutional neural network. In: IEEE Conference on Computer Vision and Pattern Recognition (CVPR), pp. 9190–9200 (2019)
55. Movahedi, V., Elder, J.H.: Design and perceptual validation of performance measures for salient object segmentation. In: IEEE Conference on Computer Vision and Pattern Recognition Workshop (CVPRW). pp. 49–56, June 2010
56. Paszke, A., Chaurasia, A., Kim, S., Culurciello, E.: ENet: a deep neural network architecture for real-time semantic segmentation. arXiv preprint arXiv:1606.02147 (2016)
57. Piao, Y., Ji, W., Li, J., Zhang, M., Lu, H.: Depth-induced multi-scale recurrent attention network for saliency detection. In: IEEE International Conference on Computer Vision (ICCV), October 2019
58. Russakovsky, O., et al.: ImageNet large scale visual recognition challenge. Int. J. Comput. Vis. **115**(3), 211–252 (2015)
59. Simonyan, K., Zisserman, A.: Very deep convolutional networks for large-scale image recognition. In: International Conference on Learning Representations (ICLR) (2014)
60. Tan, M., Le, Q.V.: EfficientNet: rethinking model scaling for convolutional neural networks. arXiv preprint arXiv:1905.11946 (2019)

61. Tan, Y.Q., Gao, S.H., Li, X.Y., Cheng, M.M., Ren, B.: VecRoad: point-based iterative graph exploration for road graphs extraction. In: IEEE Conference on Computer Vision and Pattern Recognition (CVPR) (2020)
62. Wang, J., Jiang, H., Yuan, Z., Cheng, M.M., Hu, X., Zheng, N.: Salient object detection: a discriminative regional feature integration approach. Int. J. Comput. Vis. **123**(2), 251–268 (2017). https://doi.org/10.1007/s11263-016-0977-3
63. Wang, L., et al.: Learning to detect salient objects with image-level supervision. In: IEEE Conference on Computer Vision and Pattern Recognition (CVPR) (2017)
64. Wang, L., Lu, H., Xiang, R., Yang, M.H.: Deep networks for saliency detection via local estimation and global search. In: 2015 IEEE Conference on Computer Vision and Pattern Recognition (CVPR) (2015)
65. Wang, L., Wang, L., Lu, H., Zhang, P., Ruan, X.: Saliency detection with recurrent fully convolutional networks. In: Leibe, B., Matas, J., Sebe, N., Welling, M. (eds.) ECCV 2016. LNCS, vol. 9908, pp. 825–841. Springer, Cham (2016). https://doi.org/10.1007/978-3-319-46493-0_50
66. Wang, T., Borji, A., Zhang, L., Zhang, P., Lu, H.: A stagewise refinement model for detecting salient objects in images. In: IEEE International Conference on Computer Vision (ICCV), October 2017
67. Wang, T., et al.: Detect globally, refine locally: a novel approach to saliency detection. In: IEEE Conference on Computer Vision and Pattern Recognition (CVPR), June 2018
68. Wang, W., Zhao, S., Shen, J., Hoi, S.C.H., Borji, A.: Salient object detection with pyramid attention and salient edges. In: The IEEE Conference on Computer Vision and Pattern Recognition (2019)
69. Wang, X., Liang, X., Yang, B., Li, F.W.: No-reference synthetic image quality assessment with convolutional neural network and local image saliency. Comput. Vis. Media **5**(2), 193–208 (2019)
70. Wu, R., Feng, M., Guan, W., Wang, D., Lu, H., Ding, E.: A mutual learning method for salient object detection with intertwined multi-supervision. In: The IEEE Conference on Computer Vision and Pattern Recognition (CVPR), June 2019
71. Wu, T., Tang, S., Zhang, R., Zhang, Y.: CGNet: a light-weight context guided network for semantic segmentation. arXiv preprint arXiv:1811.08201 (2018)
72. Wu, Z., Su, L., Huang, Q.: Cascaded partial decoder for fast and accurate salient object detection. In: IEEE Conference on Computer Vision and Pattern Recognition (CVPR), June 2019
73. Yan, Q., Xu, L., Shi, J., Jia, J.: Hierarchical saliency detection. In: IEEE Conference on Computer Vision and Pattern Recognition (CVPR), June 2013
74. Yang, C., Zhang, L., Lu, H., Ruan, X., Yang, M.H.: Saliency detection via graph-based manifold ranking. In: IEEE Conference on Computer Vision and Pattern Recognition (CVPR), pp. 3166–3173 (2013)
75. Yu, C., Wang, J., Peng, C., Gao, C., Yu, G., Sang, N.: BiseNet: bilateral segmentation network for real-time semantic segmentation. In: European Conference on Computer Vision (ECCV), pp. 325–341 (2018)
76. Zeng, Y., Zhang, P., Zhang, J., Lin, Z., Lu, H.: Towards high-resolution salient object detection. In: The IEEE International Conference on Computer Vision (ICCV), October 2019
77. Zhang, G., Wang, C., Xu, B., Grosse, R.: Three mechanisms of weight decay regularization. In: International Conference on Learning Representations (ICLR) (2019)

78. Zhang, L., Dai, J., Lu, H., He, Y., Wang, G.: A bi-directional message passing model for salient object detection. In: The IEEE Conference on Computer Vision and Pattern Recognition (CVPR), June 2018
79. Zhang, P., Wang, D., Lu, H., Wang, H., Ruan, X.: Amulet: aggregating multi-level convolutional features for salient object detection. In: IEEE International Conference on Computer Vision (ICCV), October 2017
80. Zhang, P., Wang, D., Lu, H., Wang, H., Yin, B.: Learning uncertain convolutional features for accurate saliency detection. In: IEEE International Conference on Computer Vision (ICCV), pp. 212–221. IEEE (2017)
81. Zhang, Q., et al.: Split to be slim: an overlooked redundancy in vanilla convolution. In: International Joint Conference on Artificial Intelligence (IJCAI) (2020)
82. Zhang, X., Zhou, X., Lin, M., Sun, J.: ShuffleNet: an extremely efficient convolutional neural network for mobile devices. In: IEEE Conference on Computer Vision and Pattern Recognition (CVPR), pp. 6848–6856 (2018)
83. Zhang, X., Wang, T., Qi, J., Lu, H., Wang, G.: Progressive attention guided recurrent network for salient object detection. In: IEEE Conference on Computer Vision and Pattern Recognition (CVPR), June 2018
84. Zhang, Z., Jin, W., Xu, J., Cheng, M.-M.: Gradient-induced co-saliency detection. In: Vedaldi, A., Bischof, H., Brox, T., Frahm, J.-M. (eds.) ECCV 2020. LNCS, vol. 12357, pp. 455–472. Springer, Cham (2020). https://doi.org/10.1007/978-3-030-58610-2_27
85. Zhao, J.X., Liu, J.J., Fan, D.P., Cao, Y., Yang, J., Cheng, M.M.: EGNet: edge guidance network for salient object detection. In: IEEE International Conference on Computer Vision (ICCV), October 2019
86. Zhao, K., Gao, S.H., Wang, W., Cheng, M.M.: Optimizing the f-measure for threshold-free salient object detection. In: IEEE International Conference on Computer Vision (ICCV), October 2019
87. Zhu, W., Liang, S., Wei, Y., Sun, J.: Saliency optimization from robust background detection. In: IEEE Conference on Computer Vision and Pattern Recognition (CVPR), pp. 2814–2821 (2014)

# HardGAN: A Haze-Aware Representation Distillation GAN for Single Image Dehazing

Qili Deng[2], Ziling Huang[1(✉)] ⓘ, Chung-Chi Tsai[3]ⓘ, and Chia-Wen Lin[1]ⓘ

[1] National Tsing Hua University, Hsinchu 30013, Taiwan
`huangziling@gapp.nthu.edu.tw`, `cwlin@ee.nthu.edu.tw`
[2] ByteDance AI Lab, Beijing, China
`dengqili@bytedance.com`
[3] Qualcomm Technologies, Inc., San Diego, USA
`chuntsai@qti.qualcomm.com`

**Abstract.** In this paper, we present a Haze-Aware Representation Distillation Generative Adversarial Network (HardGAN) for single-image dehazing. Unlike previous studies that intend to model the transmission map and global atmospheric light jointly to restore a clear image, we approach this restoration problem by using a multi-scale structure neural network composed of our proposed haze-aware representation distillation layers. Moreover, we re-introduce to utilize the normalization layer skillfully instead of stacking with the convolutional layers directly as before to avoid useful information wash away, as claimed in many image quality enhancement studies. Extensive experiments on several synthetic benchmark datasets as well as the NTIRE 2020 real-world images show our proposed HardGAN performs favorably against the state-of-the-art methods in terms of PSNR, SSIM, LPIPS, and individual subjective evaluation.

**Keywords:** Image dehazing · Generative Adversarial Network (GAN) · Image restoration · Deep learning

## 1 Introduction

Haze often occurs when dusk and smoke particles accumulate in the air that absorbs and scatters the sunlight, resulting in noticeable visual quality degradation in object appearance and contrast. Thus, taking those low contrast input for many computer vision systems designed under the assumption of an ideal capture environment will impede its real performance. Hence, image dehazing becomes a prerequisite task for several important visual analysis tasks.

---

Q. Deng and Z. Huang are equal contribution.

© Springer Nature Switzerland AG 2020
A. Vedaldi et al. (Eds.): ECCV 2020, LNCS 12351, pp. 722–738, 2020.
https://doi.org/10.1007/978-3-030-58539-6_43

Image dehazing has been explored for many years. Many previous approaches [10,11,21,35] depend on the formation of haze images by the following mathematical formulation [20]:

$$I(z) = J(z)t(z) + A(z)(1 - t(z)), \tag{1}$$

where $I(z)$ is an observed hazy image, $J(z)$ is its haze-free version, $A(z)$ is the global atmospheric light intensity that depends on the unknown depth map, $t(z)$ is the transmission map, and $z$ is the pixel location. Thereby, the solution for haze-free image restoration is by estimating the transmission map and global atmospheric light intensity and then calculate the final result by Eq. (1). Though the approaches [10,11,21,35] mentioned above show its effectiveness, many drawbacks remain. As we know, fitting the estimated transmission and the global atmospheric light intensity maps into Eq. (1) to obtain haze-free images might become problematic, since the formation of haze depends on several factors, e.g. temperature, humidity, altitude. Therefore, the transmission map can hardly be described by a simple function, nonetheless to say, trying to approximate it in a complex natural environment.

With the success of data-driven approaches, many researchers proposed end-to-end CNN models [5,19] for single image dehazing. To avoid washing away the essential spatial information, they discarded the normalization layer from the convolution layers [13,30,32]. However, lacking the normalization layer implies the networks will be shallower and hard to fit large-scale arbitrariness caused by haze. Furthermore, the gradient could vanish during training without the normalization layer even if skip-connection is implemented.

To address these two issues jointly, we propose a Haze-Aware Representation Distillation GAN (HardGAN) to learn the mapping function between haze images and haze-free images directly. Different from previous works, we design a Haze-Aware Representation Distillation (HARD) module to incorporate the normalization layer into our work. The spatial information and atmospheric brightness are fused based on the haze-aware map due to different levels of haze concentration. The contribution of this paper is fourfold. First, We proposed a multi-scale network named HardGAN to learn style transfer mapping directly. Second, the instance normalization is introduced to image dehazing task skillfully, and we create Haze-Aware Representation Distillation (HARD) module to fuse global atmospheric brightness and local spatial structures attentively. Third, extensive experiments on existing datasets show more favorable results over state-of-the-art methods. We also provide comprehensive ablation studies to validate the importance and necessity of each Module. Lastly, we further apply our algorithm to nature dense non-homogeneous haze dataset. Our proposed Generative Adversarial Network can still accurately recover the unseen objects in those problematic cases.

## 2   Related Work

**Single Image Dehazing.** Single image dehazing with unknown transmission map and global atmospheric light is a challenging problem. In the past two decades, several methods are proposed to address this issue, and we categorize them into two types: prior-based method and learning-based method.

Previously, researchers utilized image statistics prior to compensate for information loss. For example, the albedo of the scene could be estimated as prior knowledge based on [6]. Assuming local contrast of haze images were low, [29] proposed Markov Random Field to maximize color contrast. To calculate the transmission map more reliably, [11] discovered the dark channel to improve the quality of the dehaze image. More improvements for the dark channel were made on [33,34]. [3,7] introduced their algorithm separately based on the observation that small image patches typically exhibited a one-dimensional distribution in the RGB color space. In traditional prior-based methods, the assumption could hold only in some cases, not all which was restricted.

Unlike prior-based work, learning-based methods can learn the image prior automatically by large-scale datasets. [4,24] proposed trainable end-to-end systems for transmission map estimation. However, in dehazing task, both transmission map and global atmospheric light should be considered. [16] leveraged a linear transformation to encode the transmission map and the atmospheric light into one variable. [35] introduced a new edge-preserving densely connected encoder-decoder structure with multi-level pyramid pooling module for estimating the transmission map. [5] adopted a multi-level gated network and smoothed dilation technique to restore high-quality haze-free images.

**Generative Adversarial Network (GAN).** Recently, we had witnessed the power of generative adversarial learning network in image-to-image translation field. [37] defined a class of image editing operations, and constrained their output image to lie on that learned manifold at all time. [31] could generate $2048 \times 1024$ visually appealing results with a unique adversarial loss, as well as multi-scale generator and discriminator architectures. [22] made a huge success in semantic image synthesis by proposing a spatially-adaptive normalization for modulating the activations in normalization layers through a spatially-adaptive, learned affine transformation. [27] attracted much haze-aware last year by constructing a pyramid of fully convolutional GANs, each responsible for determining the patch distribution at a different scale of the image.

## 3    Haze-Aware Representation Distillation GAN

Traditional dehazing methods resort to estimating the transmission map and global atmospheric light density in Eq. (1) based on certain prior information. However, the density of haze can be influenced by various factors, such as temperature, altitude, and humidity, making the formation of haze at individual spatial locations space-variant and non-homogeneous. As a result, haze usually cannot be accurately characterized by just a single transmission map. Therefore, to effectively tackle the spatial variance of haze, instead of learning the transmission map and atmospheric light density, our work focus on learning and distilling the global and spatial features for representing the underlying haze-free image using a GAN guided by non-homogeneous haze conditions. Given an input hazy

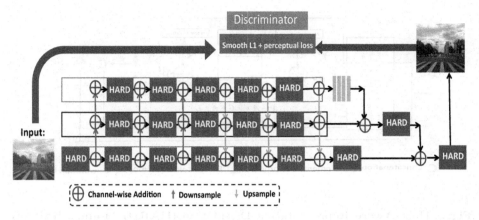

**Fig. 1.** Total framework of our HardGAN. The images are feed into the generator. We downsample the feature map at first to learn spatial information and upsample feature maps so as to learn details from different scales. The whole procedure is similar to climbing a stair. After obtaining haze-free images, we feed them into discriminator with full-scale haze images to discriminate our generated haze-free images real or fake.

image $X$, our goal is to restore a haze-free image from $X$. To capture the global properties (e.g. atmospheric light) of each object and the local structures), we propose a generator to capture useful information at different scales. We then propose a Haze-Aware Representation Distillation (HARD) module to distill and combine the spatial features and atmospheric brightness adaptively. To ensure the visual realisticness of dehazed images, multi-scale patch-GAN discriminators [14] are utilized to discriminate real images from fake ones. Our framework is shown in Fig. 1.

### 3.1 Haze-Aware Representation Distillation GAN (HardGAN)

As illustrated in Fig. 1, the generator of HardGAN consists of three layers from coarse to fine: the first (coarsest) layer involving five Haze-Aware Representation Distillation (HARD) modules, the second (medium) with six HARDs, and the third (finest) with eight HARDs. Given an input hazy image $X$ and its target haze-free image $Y$, let $x_m^n$ and $y_m^n$ denote the input and output of the $n$-th HARD in the $m$-th layer (denoted $G_m^n$). The inputs of the second and first layers are $X \downarrow$ and $X \downarrow\downarrow$, respectively, where $\downarrow$ represents downsampling.

The generator at each scale starts from the finest scale and sequentially passes the extracted features up to the coarsest (1/4) scale, as formulated in Eq. (2) and Eq. (3):

$$x_2^n = ADD(y_3^{n-1} \downarrow, y_2^{n-1}) \tag{2}$$

$$x_1^n = ADD((y_3^{n-1} \downarrow) \downarrow, y_2^{n-1} \downarrow, y_1^{n-1}) \tag{3}$$

Subsequently, the multi-scale features are passed backward from the coarsest to the finest scale and finally fused at the finest scale to reconstruct the haze-free image as expressed by Eq. (4) and Eq. (5) for layers 2 and 1 respectively.

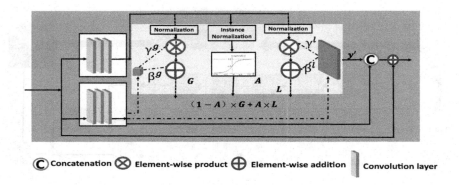

C) Concatenation ⊗ Element-wise product ⊕ Element-wise addition ▮ Convolution layer

**Fig. 2. Haze-Aware Representation Distillation (HARD) Module.** HARD is composed of two branches. The second branch is used to learn spatial information $\gamma_g$, $\beta_g$ and global atmospheric light information $\gamma_l$, $\beta_l$, then feed them into the first branch to form intermediate results $y'$. After channel attention, the final result of HARD is produced.

$$x_2^n = ADD(y_1^{n-1} \uparrow, y_2^{n-1}) \tag{4}$$

$$x_3^n = ADD((y_1^{n-1} \uparrow) \uparrow, y_2^{n-1} \uparrow, y_3^{n-1}) \tag{5}$$

where $ADD(\cdot)$ denote channel-wise addition, and $\uparrow$ represents upsampling.

### 3.2   Haze-Aware Feature Distillation (HARD) Module

Existing dehazing networks usually discard normalization layers and introduce skip connections in convolutional layers to avoid losing local spatial structures in representation learning. However, the normalization layer is helpful as it can avoid gradient vanishing so that the number of layers can be increased, thereby increasing the network capacity of representation learning as well. Therefore, in this work we propose adding normalization layers back again. Furthermore, since haze can be space-variant when the density of haze is high, distilling features that can well capture local structures becomes crucial. We therefore propose using two instance normalization layers to distill global atmospheric light intensity and local spatial structures and then adaptively fuse them together. To this end, we introduce a haze-aware attention map to estimate the density of haze at individual locations and propose a haze-guided adaptive feature distillation and fusion approach.

Previous works [5, 19] feed input haze images into a deep network to learn spatial information by stacking a number of convolutional layers simply. Nevertheless, the more the number of stacked convolutional layers, the higher the possibility of gradient vanishing, thereby significantly limiting the representing power of learned features. To tackle this problem, we introduce the Haze-Aware Representation Distillation (HARD) modules each having the same structure.

Let $x_i$ denote the $i$-th feature map of the input, where $C_i$, $H_i$ and $W_i$ stand for the image channel, height, and width, respectively. We aim to fuse the spatial information and atmospheric brightness together based on a learned haze-aware map. To this end, we combine SPADE [22] that can well preserve spatial information and adaIN [12] that can restore targeted atmospheric brightness together to produce haze-free images.

Each HARD module contains two branches, as shown in Fig. 2. Instead of computing atmospheric brightness such as the mean and standard deviation from training samples directly like [30], we learn it automatically. The second branch is used to combine the spatial information and atmospheric brightness together. It contains three sub-branches for haze-aware map generation, global atmospheric brightness estimation, and spatial information insertion.

Because haze in the real world is always in an irregular pattern and it obscures objects resulting in low contrast images, restoring image contrast selectively is a key task in image dehazing. To this end, we encode the atmospheric brightness as a linear model of the input in a $1 \times 1 \times 2$ matrix for each channel, represented as $\gamma_i^g$ and $\beta_i^g$. The atmospheric brightness control function is defined as follows:

$$G_i = \gamma_i^g \frac{x - \mu}{\sigma} + \beta_i^g \tag{6}$$

where $\mu$ and $\sigma$ are the mean and standard deviation of input $x$.

Similarly, we use an $H \times W \times 2$ matrix to encode the pixel-wise spatial information for each channel, represented as $\gamma_i^l$ and $\beta_i^l$. The spatial information preserving function is defined in Eq. (7).

$$L_i = \gamma_i^l \frac{x - \mu}{\sigma} + \beta_i^l \tag{7}$$

To fuse atmospheric brightness and spatial information adaptively, the output feature maps are fed into an Instance Normalization followed by a Sigmoid layer to produce the haze-aware map $A$ for each channel, where $A_i$ represents haze-aware map for the $i$-th channel. This approach ensures our model changes their focus when encountering irregular type haze.

After obtaining these three features, we consider to fuse them together to produce the output by

$$y_i = (1 - A_i) \otimes G_i + A_i \otimes L_i \tag{8}$$

where $\otimes$ denotes element-wise product.

### 3.3 Network Training

We train our proposed architecture step by step in a coarse-to-fine manner. The training loss for HardGAN is comprised of an adversarial loss term, a smooth L1 loss term, and a perceptual loss term [15], as formulated below:

$$\mathcal{L} = \lambda_{adv}\mathcal{L}_{adv} + \lambda_{L_1}\mathcal{L}_1 + \lambda_{per}\mathcal{L}_{per} \tag{9}$$

**Adversarial Loss.** We use the WGAN-GP loss [9] to increase the training stability coupled with a patch Discriminator to classify each of the overlapping patches of its input as real or fake, so we define adversarial loss in Eq. (10):

$$\mathcal{L}_{adv}(G,D) = E[D(y)] - E[D(G(x))] + \lambda E[(|\nabla D(\alpha x - (1-\alpha G(x)))| - 1)^2] \quad (10)$$

**Smooth L1 Loss.** We employ the smooth L1 loss to measure the difference between a dehazed image and its ground-truth image quantitatively. Compared with L2 loss, the smooth L1 loss, as expressed in Eq. (11), can prevent potential gradient explosion [8].

$$\mathcal{L}_1 = \frac{1}{N} \sum_{y=1}^{N} \sum_{i=1}^{3} \alpha(\hat{Y}_i(z) - Y_i(z)) \quad (11)$$

where $\hat{Y}_i(z)$ and $Y_i(z)$ denote the intensity of the $i$-th channel of pixel $z$ in the reconstructed haze-free image and in the ground truth, respectively, $N$ denote the total number of pixels. and $\alpha$ is specified in Eq. (12).

$$\alpha(e) = \begin{cases} 0.5e^2, & \text{if } |e| < 1 \\ |e| - 0.5, & \text{otherwise} \end{cases} \quad (12)$$

**Perceptual Loss.** Instead of encouraging an output dehazed image $y$ to be exactly the same as its ground-truth $y_t$ in the pixel domain, the perceptual loss aims to encourage it to have similar a feature representation in the backbone network (e.g., VGG19 pre-trained on imagenet [25] in this work). The perceptual loss is defined as follows:

$$\mathcal{L}_{per} = \sum_{j=1}^{3} \frac{1}{C_j H_j W_j} ||\phi_j(y) - \phi_j(y_t)|| \quad (13)$$

where $H_j$, $W_j$, and $C_j$ denote the height, width, and image channel of the feature map in the $j$-th layer of the backbone network, $\phi_j$ is the activation of the $j$-th layer.

## 4   Experiments

We first conduct our experiments on two public synthetic datasets to validate the effectiveness of the proposed HardGAN. Furthermore, we apply our algorithm to a dense non-homogeneous haze image dataset to demonstrate its generality. We also conduct an ablation study to justify the use of the core modules of HardGAN. The source code cab be found in our Github site. https://github.com/huangzilingcv/HardGAN.

## 4.1   Datasets

It is time-consuming to collect real-world hazy images and their haze-free counterparts at various locations, which poses a challenge to collect a large-scale useful dataset for data-driven dehazing methods. To address this problem, a few synthetic datasets have been proposed, in which haze images are generated from haze-free images based on the atmosphere scattering model in Eq. (1) via a random and proper choice of the scattering coefficient and the atmospheric light intensity. In this work, we utilize the synthetic RESIDE dataset proposed in [17] to train and test HardGAN. RESIDE contains synthetic hazy images in both indoor and outdoor scenarios. In its Indoor Training Set (ITS), 13,990 hazy indoor images are generated from 1,399 haze-free images with $\beta \in [0.6, 1.8]$ based on Eq. (1) with $t(z) = e^{-\beta d(z)}$ and $A \in [0.7, 1.0]$, where the depth maps $d(z)$ of images are obtained from the NYU Depth V2 [28] and Middlebury Stereo [26] datasets. The Synthetic Objective Testing Set (SOTS) with 500 indoor and 500 outdoor hazy images are produced in the same way. For Outdoor Training Set (OTS), 296,695 hazy outdoor images are generated from 8,477 haze-free images with $\beta \in [0.04, 0.2]$ and $A \in [0.8, 1.0]$, for which the depth maps of outdoor images are obtained based on [18]. Moreover, for evaluations on real-world images, we use the SOTS real-world dataset containing Internet-collected indoor and outdoor hazy images without haze-free ground-truths.

## 4.2   Experiment Settings

To train HardGAN, we follow the training manner in [27] from coarse to fine: training the 1/4-scale generator at first, then the 1/2-scale generator, and finally the full-scale generator. The full-scale RGB input images are with a resolution of $240 \times 240$. For the indoor dataset, each scale is trained for 120 epochs using the Adam optimizer with an initial learning rate of 0.001, which is then halved every 3 epochs. For the outdoor dataset, since the synthetic haze is lighter, the number of epochs for each scale is reduced to 18, while the setting for Adam optimizer is the same as above. Our experiments are carried out on two NVIDIA GeForce GTX 1080Ti with a batch size of 24 separately. In the following experiments, we set $\lambda_1 = 1.2$, $\lambda_{per} = 0.04$, and $\lambda_{adv} = 0.05$, respectively.

## 4.3   Synthetic Hazy Images

[1]We compare the performance of HardGAN with several state-of-the-art data-driven methods including AODNet [16], DehazeNet [4], GCANet [5], GridDehazeNet [19], and FFANet [23] on synthetic hazy images qualitatively and quantitatively. For a fair comparison, all methods are trained in the same way with HardGAN and then evaluated on RESIDE and SOTS. For the quantitative comparison, we use three objective quality metrics: Peak Signal to Noise Ratio (PSNR), Structural SIMilarity index (SSIM), and Learned Perceptual Image Patch Similarity (LPIPS) [36]. Given a dehazed image and its

---

[1] The authors from Taiwan universities and ByteDance completed the experiments.

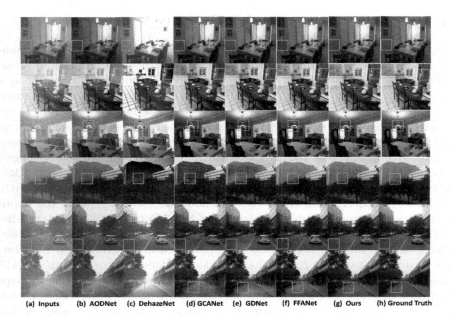

(a) Inputs  (b) AODNet  (c) DehazeNet  (d) GCANet  (e) GDNet  (f) FFANet  (g) Ours  (h) Ground Truth

**Fig. 3.** Qualitative comparison of various dehazing methods on some indoor (the first three rows) and outdoor (the last three rows) synthetic hazy images of SOTS. Compared with the ground-truths in (h), we can observe a significant amount of haze and severe color distortions in the dehazed outputs of AODNet, DehazeNet and GCANet. In contrast, GridDehazeNet and FFANet effectively mitigate color distortions but still cannot fully clean the haze in their outputs (see the roads and buildings in (e) and (f)). Besides, both GridDehazeNet and FFANet also introduce unexpected noisy artifacts (see the wall and ceiling in (e) and (f)). (Color figure online)

ground-truth, PSNR and SSIM measure their average pixel-wise and structural fidelity/similarity (i.e., the higher, the better), whereas LPIPS measures their perceptual discrepancy (the lower, the better).

Figure 3 shows the qualitative comparisons on some synthetic indoor and outdoor images of SOTS. Compared with the ground-truths, the dehazed outputs of AODNet, DehazeNet, and GCANet still contain a significant amount of haze. Moreover, we can observe severe color distortions in all of their outputs. In contrast, although GridDehazeNet and FFANet effectively mitigate the color distortion problem effectively, they cannot completely clean the haze in their outputs (see the roads and buildings in Fig. 3(e) and Fig. 3(f)). Besides, both GridDehazeNet and FFANet introduce unexpected noisy artifacts (see the wall and ceiling in Fig. 3(e) and Fig. 3(f)). Compared with these state-of-the-art data-driven methods, **HardGAN** produces the highest-fidelity dehazed results that also look perceptually close to the reference ground-truths.

Furthermore, Table 1 compares the quantitative dehazing results on the SOTA test dataset, showing that **HardGAN** outperforms all the previous dehazing methods in terms of PSNR, SSIM, and LPIPS.

**Table 1.** Quantitative comparison of various dehazing methods on SOTS. HardGAN outperforms all previous dehazing methods in all metrics, where ↑ means the higher the better, and ↓ means the lower the better

| Method | Indoor | | | Outdoor | | |
|---|---|---|---|---|---|---|
| | PSNR↑ | SSIM↑ | LPIPS↓ | PSNR↑ | SSIM↑ | LPIPS↓ |
| AODNet [16] | 20.5 | 0.8162 | 0.247 | 24.14 | 0.9198 | 0.085 |
| DehazeNet [4] | 19.82 | 0.8209 | 0.334 | 24.75 | 0.9296 | 0.127 |
| GCANet [5] | 30.23 | 0.9800 | 0.217 | - | - | 0.048 |
| GridDehazeNet [19] | 32.16 | 0.9836 | 0.209 | 30.86 | 0.9819 | 0.012 |
| FFANet [23] | 36.39 | 0.9556 | 0.209 | 33.57 | 0.9840 | 0.021 |
| HardGAN (Ours) | **36.56** | **0.9905** | **0.201** | **34.34** | **0.9871** | **0.010** |

## 4.4  Real-World Hazy Images

In this section, we test our methods on real-world datasets. For a fair comparison, all the compared models are trained on the SOTS outdoor training dataset. Because there is no ground-truth for real-world dataset, we conduct a user study to evaluate the subjective perceptual quality quantitatively.

Figure 6 shows the qualitative comparisons on real-world images. Similar to Fig. 3, the outputs of AODNet, DehazeNet and GCANet again lead to severe color distortions (see the electric line, buildings and heaven in Fig. 6(c) and Fig. 6(e)). Although GridDehazeNet and FFANet effectively solve the color-distortion problem, they cannot fully clean the haze (see the trees and buildings in Fig. 6(e) and Fig. 6(f)). Besides, both GridDehazeNet and FFANet would introduce unexpected noisy(see building and heaven in Fig. 6(e) and Fig. 6(f)). Compared with previous state-of-the-art methods, we produce high quality results with the best perceptual quality.

**Table 2.** Quantitative comparison of various dehazing methods on NH-HAZE, where ↑ means the higher the better, and ↓ means the lower the better.

| Team name | NH-HAZE | |
|---|---|---|
| | PSNR↑ | SSIM↑ |
| ECNU-Trident | 21.41 | **0.71**$_{(1)}$ |
| ECNU-KT | 20.85 | 0.69 |
| NTU-Dehazing | 20.11 | 0.66 |
| VICLAB-DoNET | 19.70 | 0.68 |
| iPAL-NonLocal | 21.10 | 0.69 |
| VIP_UNIST | 18.77 | 0.54 |
| Team JJ | 19.49 | 0.66 |
| iPAL-END | 19.22 | 0.66 |
| Ours | **21.70** | 0.70$_{(2)}$ |

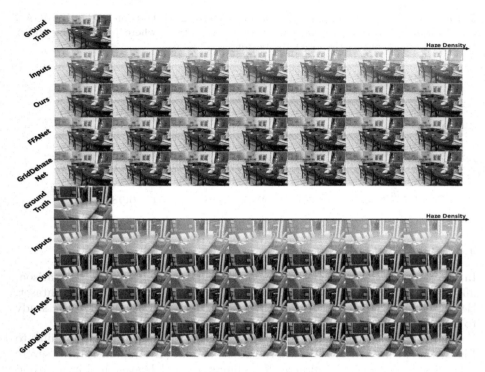

**Fig. 4.** Performance evaluation of HardGAN, FFANet, and GridDehazeNet on synthetic hazy images with different haze patterns from SOTS. In the first set of data in rows 1–5, HardGAN produces high-fidelity outcomes close to the ground-truth, regardless of the haze patterns. In contrast, the results produced by FFANet and GridDehazeNet are unstable (e.g., the wall in row 1–5), especially for heavy haze. Similar results can also be observed in the second set of data in rows 6–10 (see the red wall). (Color figure online)

**Fig. 5.** Dehazed results of five images with dense non-homogeneous haze from the validation dataset of NTIRE2020 [1,2]. The results show that HardGAN effectively removes most of the haze while uncovering clear scenes.

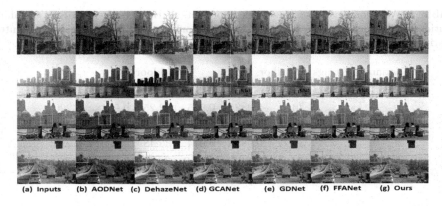

(a) Inputs    (b) AODNet  (c) DehazeNet   (d) GCANet        (e) GDNet      (f) FFANet     (g) Ours

**Fig. 6.** Qualitative comparison of various dehazing methods on the SOTS Real-World dataset. of AODNet, DehazeNet and GCANet lead to unnatural colors (see the electric line, buildings and heaven in (c) and (e)). Although GridDehazeNet and FFANet avoid such color distortions, there is still light haze that remains unremoved in their outputs (see the trees and buildings in (e) and (f)). Besides, both GridDehazeNet and FFANet introduce undesired noise (see the building and heaven in (e) and (f) (Color figure online)

**Fig. 7.** Qualitative comparison for ablation study. Compared with the baseline (Variant ①), Variant ② better preserves local details, thanks to its local spatial structures preservation. Besides, the atmospheric brightness with Variant ③ is more consistent with the corresponding ground-truth than the baseline. Considering both local and global terms together, Variant ④ preserves more details and leads to more consistent atmospheric brightness with the ground-truth.

## 4.5    Results on Dense Non-homogeneous Hazy Images

Figure 5 illustrates the results for five real-world test images with dense non-homogeneous haze from the validation dataset of NTIRE2020 Challenge [1,2].

**Table 3.** Ablation study for the core components of HardGAN. Both Spatial Information Preserving and Atmospheric Brightness Control contribute to final result. Integrating them together can produce haze-free images with highest score.

| Variant | Settings | | Outdoor | | | Indoor | | |
|---------|---|---|------|------|-------|------|------|-------|
| | $L$ | $G$ | PSNR | SSIM | LPIPS | PSNR | SSIM | LPIPS |
| ① | × | × | 30.78 | 0.9821 | 0.025 | 32.25 | 0.9838 | 0.220 |
| ② | ✓ | × | 33.54 | 0.9857 | 0.018 | 35.20 | 0.9878 | 0.222 |
| ③ | × | ✓ | 33.77 | 0.9858 | 0.014 | 35.48 | 0.9892 | 0.210 |
| ④ | ✓ | ✓ | **34.34** | **0.9871** | **0.010** | **36.56** | **0.9905** | **0.201** |

The results show that HardGAN successfully removes most haze while uncovering clear scenes. Specifically, since the training samples in [1] contain real-world scenes with similar objects (e.g., trees, grass, sculptures) to that in the test samples, the dehazed images in Fig. 5 present more natural scenes than that of real-world hazy images for which HardGAN is trained on SOTS synthetic outdoor dataset and there exist large differences between the training and testing samples. Following the protocol in [1,2], Table 2 shows HardGAN outperforms the others by a large margin in PSNR and achieves the second best SSIM.

## 4.6  Ablation Study

Table 3 shows our ablation study on the SOTS Indoor and Outdoor datasets, where $L$ stands for preserving local spatial structure and $G$ stands for controlling the global atmospheric brightness, respectively. Comparing Variant ② with Variant ①, we can find that adding the preservation of local spatial information is more effective than the baseline, since the spatial information is vital for single image dehazing. Similarly, global atmospheric light control (i.e., Variant ③) also effectively improve the performance. taking into account both the local spatial information and global atmospheric brightness (i.e., Variant ④) achieves the best performance. Figure 7 shows the qualitative comparison for the ablation study. Variant ② better preserves local details than Variant ①, thanks to the local spatial information preservation. Besides, the atmospheric brightness with Variant ③ is more consistent with the corresponding ground-truth. Again, considering both local and global terms together ④ preserves more details and leads to more consistent atmospheric brightness with the ground-truth.

## 4.7  Network Stability

To further demonstrate the effectiveness of our method, we also conduct a network stability experiment. HardGAN dehazes the hazy versions of an image synthesized with different haze patterns, as shown in Fig. 4 **Inputs**. In the first set of data in rows 1–5, HardGAN produces high-fidelity outcomes close to ground truth, regardless of the haze patterns. In contrast, In contrast, the results produced by FFANet and GridDehazeNet, however, are unstable (e.g., the wall in row 1–5 of Fig. 4), especially for heavy haze. Similar results can also be observed in the second set of data in rows 6–10 (see the red wall in Fig. 4), so our method is more robust than those methods.

## 4.8  Network Convergence Analysis

Figure 8 shows loss curves to verify the necessity of HARD module. We train generator only (without discriminator). The experiment is performed on the dataset of NTIRE2020 [1, 2] Fig. 8(a) shows that the training loss curve decreases steadily and Fig. 8(b) shows the PSNR value with adaptive and instance normalization. increases with time. Note, the training loss value shown in Fig. 8(c) drops initially then stays at 0.15 afterwards, whereas, as shown in Fig. 8(d), the PSNR value without adaptive instance normalization and SPADE increases to 8.0 but stays stable after that. These phenomenons illustrates Instance normalization can help model converge while ensures good dehazing results.

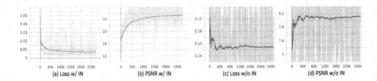

**Fig. 8.** Loss curves to verify the necessity of normalization layers (without discriminator). Here, (a) is the training loss curve with adaptive instance normalization and SPADE while (c) is the training loss curve without adaptive instance normalization and SPADE. It is clear instance normalization can help model converge.

## 5  Conclusion

We proposed a novel multi-scale image dehazing network. Instead of explicitly estimating the transmission map and atmospheric light intensity, our method adaptively fuses local spatial information and global atmospheric brightness together guided by the learned haze-aware maps for individual channels. Extensive experiments on synthetic and real-world hazy images demonstrate the effectiveness of our method. Besides images with homogeneous haze, our method can also do a good job for removing dense non-homogeneous haze in an image.

**Acknowledgments.** This work was funded in part by Qualcomm through a Taiwan University Research Collaboration Project and in part by the Ministry of Science and Technology, Taiwan, under grant MOST 109-2634-F-007-013.

# References

1. Ancuti, C.O., Ancuti, C., Timofte, R.: NH-HAZE: an image dehazing benchmark with non-homogeneous hazy and haze-free images. In: Proceedings of the IEEE/CVF Conference on Computer Vision and Pattern Recognition Workshops, pp. 444–445 (2020)
2. Ancuti, C.O., Ancuti, C., Vasluianu, F.A., Timofte, R.: NTIRE 2020 challenge on nonhomogeneous dehazing. In: Proceedings of the IEEE/CVF Conference on Computer Vision and Pattern Recognition Workshops, pp. 490–491 (2020)
3. Berman, D., Avidan, S., et al.: Non-local image dehazing. In: Proceedings of the IEEE Conference on Computer Vision and Pattern Recognition, pp. 1674–1682 (2016)
4. Cai, B., Xu, X., Jia, K., Qing, C., Tao, D.: DehazeNet: an end-to-end system for single image haze removal. IEEE Trans. Image Process. $25$(11), 5187–5198 (2016)
5. Chen, D., et al.: Gated context aggregation network for image dehazing and deraining. In: 2019 IEEE Winter Conference on Applications of Computer Vision (WACV), pp. 1375–1383. IEEE (2019)
6. Fattal, R.: Single image dehazing. ACM Trans. Graph. (TOG) $27$(3), 1–9 (2008)
7. Fattal, R.: Dehazing using color-lines. ACM Trans. Graph. (TOG) $34$(1), 1–14 (2014)
8. Girshick, R.: Fast R-CNN. In: Proceedings of the IEEE International Conference on Computer Vision, pp. 1440–1448 (2015)
9. Gulrajani, I., Ahmed, F., Arjovsky, M., Dumoulin, V., Courville, A.C.: Improved training of Wasserstein GANs. In: Advances in Neural Information Processing Systems, pp. 5767–5777 (2017)
10. Hautière, N., Tarel, J.P., Aubert, D.: Towards fog-free in-vehicle vision systems through contrast restoration. In: 2007 IEEE Conference on Computer Vision and Pattern Recognition, pp. 1–8. IEEE (2007)
11. He, K., Sun, J., Tang, X.: Single image haze removal using dark channel prior. IEEE Trans. Pattern Anal. Mach. Intell. $33$(12), 2341–2353 (2010)
12. Huang, X., Belongie, S.: Arbitrary style transfer in real-time with adaptive instance normalization. In: Proceedings of the IEEE International Conference on Computer Vision, pp. 1501–1510 (2017)
13. Ioffe, S., Szegedy, C.: Batch normalization: accelerating deep network training by reducing internal covariate shift. arXiv preprint arXiv:1502.03167 (2015)
14. Isola, P., Zhu, J.Y., Zhou, T., Efros, A.A.: Image-to-image translation with conditional adversarial networks. In: Proceedings of the IEEE Conference on Computer Vision and Pattern Recognition, pp. 1125–1134 (2017)
15. Johnson, J., Alahi, A., Fei-Fei, L.: Perceptual losses for real-time style transfer and super-resolution. In: Leibe, B., Matas, J., Sebe, N., Welling, M. (eds.) ECCV 2016. LNCS, vol. 9906, pp. 694–711. Springer, Cham (2016). https://doi.org/10.1007/978-3-319-46475-6_43
16. Li, B., Peng, X., Wang, Z., Xu, J., Feng, D.: An all-in-one network for dehazing and beyond. arXiv preprint arXiv:1707.06543 (2017)
17. Li, B., et al.: Benchmarking single-image dehazing and beyond. IEEE Trans. Image Process. $28$(1), 492–505 (2018)
18. Liu, F., Shen, C., Lin, G., Reid, I.: Learning depth from single monocular images using deep convolutional neural fields. IEEE Trans. Pattern Anal. Mach. Intell. $38$(10), 2024–2039 (2015)

19. Liu, X., Ma, Y., Shi, Z., Chen, J.: GridDehazeNet: attention-based multi-scale network for image dehazing. In: Proceedings of the IEEE International Conference on Computer Vision, pp. 7314–7323 (2019)
20. McCartney, E.J.: Optics of the Atmosphere: Scattering by Molecules and Particles, 421 p. Wiley, New York (1976)
21. Meng, G., Wang, Y., Duan, J., Xiang, S., Pan, C.: Efficient image dehazing with boundary constraint and contextual regularization. In: Proceedings of the IEEE International Conference on Computer Vision, pp. 617–624 (2013)
22. Park, T., Liu, M.Y., Wang, T.C., Zhu, J.Y.: Semantic image synthesis with spatially-adaptive normalization. In: Proceedings of the IEEE Conference on Computer Vision and Pattern Recognition, pp. 2337–2346 (2019)
23. Qin, X., Wang, Z., Bai, Y., Xie, X., Jia, H.: FFA-Net: feature fusion attention network for single image dehazing. arXiv preprint arXiv:1911.07559 (2019)
24. Ren, W., Liu, S., Zhang, H., Pan, J., Cao, X., Yang, M.-H.: Single image dehazing via multi-scale convolutional neural networks. In: Leibe, B., Matas, J., Sebe, N., Welling, M. (eds.) ECCV 2016. LNCS, vol. 9906, pp. 154–169. Springer, Cham (2016). https://doi.org/10.1007/978-3-319-46475-6_10
25. Russakovsky, O., et al.: ImageNet large scale visual recognition challenge. Int. J. Comput. Vis. **115**(3), 211–252 (2015)
26. Scharstein, D., Szeliski, R.: High-accuracy stereo depth maps using structured light. In: Proceedings of the 2003 IEEE Computer Society Conference on Computer Vision and Pattern Recognition 2003, vol. 1, p. I. IEEE (2003)
27. Shaham, T.R., Dekel, T., Michaeli, T.: SinGAN: learning a generative model from a single natural image. In: Proceedings of the IEEE International Conference on Computer Vision, pp. 4570–4580 (2019)
28. Silberman, N., Hoiem, D., Kohli, P., Fergus, R.: Indoor segmentation and support inference from RGBD images. In: Fitzgibbon, A., Lazebnik, S., Perona, P., Sato, Y., Schmid, C. (eds.) ECCV 2012. LNCS, vol. 7576, pp. 746–760. Springer, Heidelberg (2012). https://doi.org/10.1007/978-3-642-33715-4_54
29. Tan, R.T.: Visibility in bad weather from a single image. In: 2008 IEEE Conference on Computer Vision and Pattern Recognition, pp. 1–8. IEEE (2008)
30. Ulyanov, D., Vedaldi, A., Lempitsky, V.: Instance normalization: the missing ingredient for fast stylization. arXiv preprint arXiv:1607.08022 (2016)
31. Wang, T.C., Liu, M.Y., Zhu, J.Y., Tao, A., Kautz, J., Catanzaro, B.: High-resolution image synthesis and semantic manipulation with conditional gans. In: Proceedings of the IEEE Conference on Computer Vision and Pattern Recognition, pp. 8798–8807 (2018)
32. Wang, X., et al.: ESRGAN: enhanced super-resolution generative adversarial networks. In: Proceedings of the European Conference on Computer Vision (ECCV) (2018)
33. Xie, B., Guo, F., Cai, Z.: Improved single image dehazing using dark channel prior and multi-scale retinex. In: 2010 International Conference on Intelligent System Design and Engineering Application, vol. 1, pp. 848–851. IEEE (2010)
34. Xu, H., Guo, J., Liu, Q., Ye, L.: Fast image dehazing using improved dark channel prior. In: 2012 IEEE International Conference on Information Science and Technology, pp. 663–667. IEEE (2012)
35. Zhang, H., Patel, V.M.: Densely connected pyramid dehazing network. In: Proceedings of the IEEE Conference on Computer Vision and Pattern Recognition, pp. 3194–3203 (2018)

36. Zhang, R., Isola, P., Efros, A.A., Shechtman, E., Wang, O.: The unreasonable effectiveness of deep features as a perceptual metric. In: Proceedings of the IEEE Conference on Computer Vision and Pattern Recognition, pp. 586–595 (2018)
37. Zhu, J.-Y., Krähenbühl, P., Shechtman, E., Efros, A.A.: Generative visual manipulation on the natural image manifold. In: Leibe, B., Matas, J., Sebe, N., Welling, M. (eds.) ECCV 2016. LNCS, vol. 9909, pp. 597–613. Springer, Cham (2016). https://doi.org/10.1007/978-3-319-46454-1_36

# Lifespan Age Transformation Synthesis

Roy Or-El[1]([✉]), Soumyadip Sengupta[1], Ohad Fried[2], Eli Shechtman[3],
and Ira Kemelmacher-Shlizerman[1]

[1] University of Washington, Seattle, USA
royorel@cs.washington.edu
[2] Stanford University, Stanford, USA
[3] Adobe Research, Seattle, USA

**Abstract.** We address the problem of single photo age progression and
regression—the prediction of how a person might look in the future, or
how they looked in the past. Most existing aging methods are limited
to changing the texture, overlooking transformations in head shape that
occur during the human aging and growth process. This limits the applicability of previous methods to aging of adults to slightly older adults,
and application of those methods to photos of children does not produce
quality results. We propose a novel *multi-domain image-to-image generative adversarial network* architecture, whose learned latent space models
a continuous bi-directional aging process. The network is trained on the
FFHQ dataset, which we labeled for ages, gender, and semantic segmentation. Fixed age classes are used as anchors to approximate continuous
age transformation. Our framework can predict a full head portrait for
ages 0–70 from a single photo, modifying both texture and shape of the
head. We demonstrate results on a wide variety of photos and datasets,
and show significant improvement over the state of the art.

## 1 Introduction

Age transformation is a problem of synthesizing a person's appearance in a
different age while preserving their identity. Once the age gap between the input
and the desired output is significant, e.g., going from 1 to 15 year old, the problem
becomes highly challenging due to pronounced changes in head shape as well as
facial texture. Solving for shape and texture together remains an open problem.
Particularly, if the method is required to create a *lifespan* of transformations,
i.e., for any given input age, the method should synthesize a full span of 0–70
ages (rather than binary young-to-old transformations). In this paper, we aim
to enable exactly that—lifespan of transformations from a single portrait.

State of the art methods [1,13,31,43,44,46,48] focus on either minor age
gaps, or mostly on adults to elderly progression, as a large part of the aging
transformation for adults lies in the texture (rather than shape), e.g., adding

---

**Electronic supplementary material** The online version of this chapter (https://
doi.org/10.1007/978-3-030-58539-6_44) contains supplementary material, which is
available to authorized users.

© Springer Nature Switzerland AG 2020
A. Vedaldi et al. (Eds.): ECCV 2020, LNCS 12351, pp. 739–755, 2020.
https://doi.org/10.1007/978-3-030-58539-6_44

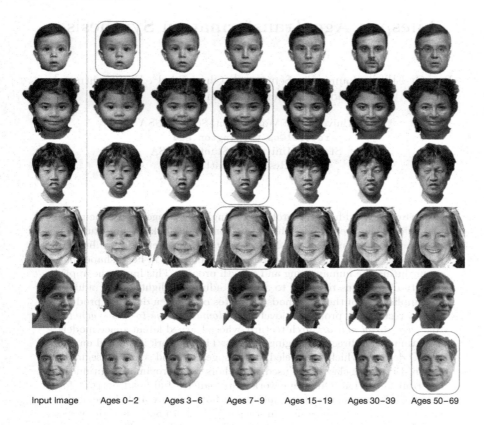

**Fig. 1.** Given a single portrait photo (left), our generative adversarial network predicts full head bi-directional age transformation. Note the diversity of the input photos spanning ethnicity, age (baby, young, adult, senior), gender, and facial expression. Gray border marks the input class, columns 2–7 are all synthesized by our method.

wrinkles. The method of Kemelmacher-Shlizerman et al. [20] allows substantial age transformations but it can be applied only on a cropped face area, rather than a full head, and cannot be modified to allow backward age prediction (adult to child) due to optical-flow-based nature of the method. Apps like FaceApp allow considerable transitions from adult to child and vice versa, but similar to state of the art methods they focus on texture, not shape, and thus produce sub-par results, in addition to focusing only on the binary case of two ambiguous age classes ("young", "old").

Theoretically, since time is a continuous variable, lifespan age transformation, e.g., 0–70 synthesis, should be modeled as a continuous process. However, it can be very difficult to learn without large datasets of identity-specific ground truth (same person captured over their lifespan). Therefore, we approximate this continuous transformation by representing age with a fixed number of anchor classes in a multi-domain transfer setting. We represent age with six anchor classes: three for children ages 0–2, 3–6, 7–9, one for young people 15–19, one for adults 30–39, and one for 50–69. Those classes are designed to learn geometric transformation in ages where most prominent shape changes occur, while covering the full span of ages in the latent space (Fig. 1).

To that end, we propose a new multi-domain image-to-image conditional GAN architecture (Fig. 2). Our main encoder—the identity encoder—encodes the input image to extract features associated with the person's identity. Next, unlike other multi-domain approaches, the various age domains are each represented by a unique distribution. Given a target age, it is assigned an age vector code sampled from the appropriate distribution. The age code is sent to a mapping network, that maps age codes into a unified, learned latent space. The resulting latent space approximates continuous age transformations. Our decoder then fuses the learned latent age representation with the identity features via StyleGAN2's [19] modulated convolutions.

Disentanglement based domain transfer approaches such as MUNIT [15] and FUNIT [27] can learn shape and texture deformation, e.g., transform cats to dogs. However, these methods cannot be directly applied to transform age, in a multi-domain setting, due to key limiting assumptions: MUNIT requires two generators per domain pair, thus training it for even 6 age classes will require 30 generators, trumping scalability. FUNIT requires an exemplar image of the target class and is not guaranteed to apply only age features from the exemplar, as other attributes like skin color, gender and ethnicity may also be transferred.

On the other hand, multi-domain transfer algorithms such as StarGAN [7] and STGAN [26] assume the domains to be distinct and encompassing contrasting facial attributes. Age domains are highly correlated however, and thus those algorithms struggle with the age transformation task. Methods like InterFace-GAN [37] aim to address that via latent space traversal of an unconditionally trained GAN. However, navigating these paths to transform a person into a specific age is difficult, as the computed traversal path does not always preserve identity characteristics. In contrast, our proposed algorithm can transform shape and texture across a wide range of ages while still maintaining the person's identity and attributes.

Another limiting factor in modeling full lifespan age transformations is that existing face aging datasets contain a very limited amount of babies and children. To compensate for that, we labeled the FFHQ dataset [18] for gender and age via crowd-sourcing. In addition, for each image we extracted face semantic maps as well as head pose angles, glasses type and eye occlusion score.

Qualitative and quantitative evaluations show that our method outperforms state-of-the-art aging algorithms as well as multi-domain transfer and latent space traversal methods applied on the face aging task. The key contributions of this paper are: 1) enabling both shape and texture transformations for lifespan age synthesis, 2) novel multi-domain image-to-image translation GAN architecture, 3) labelled FFHQ [18] dataset which we will share with the community.

We are aware of the potential ethical issues and potential bias such method can present. These issues are addressed in our Ethics and Bias statement in the supplementary material.

## 2    Related Work

Early works in age progression have focused on building separate models for specific sub-effects of aging, e.g., wrinkles [2,3,45], cranio-facial growth [33,34], and face sub-regions [39,40]. Complete face transformation was explored via calculating average faces of age clusters and transitioning between them [4,36], wavelet transformation [42], dictionary learning [38], factor analysis [47] and AAM face parameter fitting [22]. Age progression of children was specifically the focus in [20], where the aging process was modelled as cascaded flows between mean faces of pre-computed age clusters of eigenfaces.

Recently, deep learning has become the predominant approach for facial aging. Wang *et al.* [43] replaced the cascaded flows from [20] with a series of RNN forward passes. Zhang *et al.* [48] and Antipov *et al.* [1] proposed autoencoder GAN architecture where aging was performed by adding an age condition to the latent space. Duong *et al.* [31,32] introduced a cascade of restricted Boltzmann machines and ResNet based probabilistic generative models (respectively) to carry out the aging process between age groups. Yang *et al.* [46] proposed a GAN based architecture with a pyramidal discriminator over age detection features of the generated aged image. Liu *et al.* [28] introduced additional age transition discriminator to supervise the aging transitions between the age clusters. Li *et al.* [25] fused the outputs from global and local patch generators to synthesize the aged face. Wang *et al.* [44] added facial feature loss as well as age classification loss to enforce the output image to have the same identity while still progressing the age. Liu *et al.* [29] added gender and race attributes to their GAN architecture to help avoid biases in the training data, they also propose a new wavelet based discriminator to improve image quality. He *et al.* [13] encoded personalized aging basis and apply specific age transforms to create an age representation used to decode the aged face. The focus of most of those approaches was on aging adults to elderly (mostly texture changes). Our method is the first to propose a full lifespan aging, 0–70 years old. We refer the reader to these excellent surveys [9,10,35] for a broader overview of the advances in age progression over the years.

Recent success with generative adversarial networks [11] significantly improved image-to-image translations between two domains, with both paired [16] (Pix2Pix) and unpaired [50] (CycleGAN) training data. More recent methods disentangled the image into style and content latent spaces, e.g., MUNIT [15], DRIT [24], share the content space but create multiple disjoint style latent spaces. These methods are hard to scale to a large number of domains as they require training two generators per pair of domains. FUNIT [27] used a single generator that disentangled the image into shared content and style latent spaces, however, it required an additional target image to explicitly encode the style. One may consider aging effects as "style". However when transferring style between two age domains, non-age related styles, like skin color, gender and ethnicity, might be transferred as well. Multi-domain transfer algorithms like StarGAN [8] and STGAN [26] can edit multiple facial attributes, but those are assumed to be distinct and contrasting. StarGAN generalizes CycleGAN to map an input image into multiple domains using a single generator. STGAN uses a selective transfer units with encoder-decoder architecture to select and modify encoded features for attribute editing. These methods however are not designed to work on the age translation task, as aging domains are highly correlated and not distinct. Our proposed architecture enables translations between highly correlated domains, and obtains a continuous traversable age latent space while maintaining identity and image quality.

## 3   Algorithm

### 3.1   Overview

Our main goal is to design an algorithm that can learn the head shape deformation as well as appearance changes across a wide range of ages. Ideally, one would turn to supervised learning to tackle this problem. However, since this process is continuous in nature, it requires a large amount of aligned image pairs of the same person at different ages that will span all possible transitions. Unfortunately, there are no existing large-scale datasets that capture aging changes over more than several years, let alone an entire life span. Furthermore, small scale datasets like FGNET [22] capture subjects in different poses, environments and lighting conditions, making supervised training very challenging. To this end, we turn to adversarial learning and leverage the recent progress in unpaired image-to-image translation GAN architectures [7,15,24,27,41,50]. We propose to approximate the continuous aging process with six anchor age classes which results in a multi-domain transfer problem.

We propose a novel generative adversarial network architecture that consists of a single conditional generator and a single discriminator. The conditional generator is responsible for transitions across age groups, and consists of three parts: identity encoder, a mapping network, and a decoder. We assume that while a person's appearance changes with age their identity remains fixed. Therefore, we encode age and identity in separate paths.

Each age group is represented by a unique pre-defined distribution. When given a target age, we sample from the respective age group distribution and assign it a vector age code. The age code is sent to a mapping network, that maps it into a learned unified age latent space. The resulting latent space approximates continuous age transformations. The input image is processed separately by the identity encoder to extract identity features. The decoder takes the mapping network output, a target age latent vector, and injects it to the identity features using modulated convolutions, originally proposed in StyleGAN2 [19]. During training, we use an additional age encoder to relate between real and generated images to the pre-defined distributions of their respective age class.

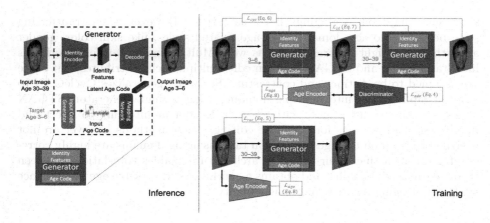

**Fig. 2.** Algorithm overview.

For transformation to an age not represented in our anchor classes, we calculate age latent codes for its two neighboring anchor classes and perform linear interpolation to get the desired age code as input to the decoder.

## 3.2  Framework

Our algorithm takes a facial image $x$ and a target age cluster as inputs. It then generates an output image of the same person at the desired age cluster. Figure 2 shows the model architecture as well as the training scheme.

As a pre-processing step, background and clothing items are removed from the image using its corresponding semantic mask, which is part of our dataset (see Sect. 4 for details). Our age input space, $\mathcal{Z}$, is represented by a $50 \times n$ element vector where $n$ is the number of age classes. When the input age class is $i$, we generate a vector $z_i \in \mathcal{Z}$ as

$$z_i = \mathbf{1}_i + v, \quad v \sim \mathcal{N}(0, 0.2^2 \cdot \mathbf{I}) \tag{1}$$

where $\mathbf{1}_i$ is a $50 \cdot n$ element vector that contains ones on elements $50 \cdot i$ through $50 \cdot (i+1) - 1$ and zeros elsewhere, and $\mathbf{I}$ is the identity matrix. A single generator is used to generate all target ages. Our generator consists of an identity encoder, a latent mapping network and a decoder. During training we also use an age encoder to embed both real and generated images into the age latent space.

**Identity Encoder.** The identity encoder $E_{id}$ takes an input image $x$ and extracts an identity features tensor $w_{id}$, where $w_{id} = E_{id}(x)$. these features contain information about the image local structures and the general shape of the face which play a key role in generating the same identity. The identity encoder contains two downsampling layers followed by four residual blocks [12].

**Mapping Network.** The mapping network $M : \mathcal{Z} \rightarrow \mathcal{W}_{age}$ embeds an age input vector $z$ to the unified age latent space $\mathcal{W}_{age}$, $w_{age} = M(z)$, where $M$ is an 8 layer MLP network and $w_{age}$ is a 256 element latent vector. The mapping network learns an optimal age latent space that enables a smooth transition and interpolation between age clusters, needed for continuous age transformations.

**Decoder.** Our decoder takes an age latent code along with identity features and produces an output image $y = F(w_{id}, w_{age})$. The identity features $w_{id}$ are processed by styled convolution blocks [18]. To reduce water droplet [19] artifacts, we replace the AdaIN normalization layers [14] with modulated convolution layers proposed in StyleGAN2 [19]. In addition, each modulated convolution layer is followed by a pixel norm layer [17] as we observed it further helps reducing these artifacts. We omit the noise injection in our implementation. Overall, we use four styled convolution layers to manipulate the identity code and two upsampling styled convolution layers to produce an image at the original size.

The overall generator mapping from an input image $x$ and an input target age vector $z_t$ to an output image $y$ is:

$$y = G(x, z_t) = F(E_{id}(x), M(z_t)). \qquad (2)$$

**Age Encoder.** The age encoder enforces a mapping of the input image $x$ into its correct location in the age vector space $\mathcal{Z}$. It produces an age vector $z_s = E_{age}(x)$ that corresponds to the source age cluster $s$ of the image $x$. The age encoder needs to capture more global data in order to encode the general appearance, regardless of the identity. To this end, we follow the architecture of MUNIT [15]'s style encoder with four downsampling layers, followed by global averaging and a fully connected layer to produce an age vector. Note that the age encoder is not used for inference.

**Discriminator.** We use the StyleGAN discriminator [18] with minibatch standard deviation. We modify the last fully connected layer to have $n$ outputs in order to discriminate multiple classes as suggested by Liu *et al.* [27]. For a real image from class $i$, we only penalize the $i$-th output. Respectively, only the $j$-th output is penalized for a generated image of class $j$.

### 3.3   Training Scheme

An overview of the training scheme can be seen in Fig. 2. To compensate for imbalances between age clusters, in each training iteration, we first sample a source cluster $s$ and a target cluster $t$ ($t \neq s$). Then we sample an image from each class. We then perform three forward passes:

$$y_{gen} = G(x, z_t), \quad y_{rec} = G(x, z_s), \quad y_{cyc} = G(y_{gen}, z_s). \qquad (3)$$

Here, $y_{gen}$ is the generated image at target age $t$ and $y_{rec}$ is the reconstructed image at source age $s$. We also apply a cycle to reconstruct $y_{cyc}$ at source age $s$ from generated image $y_{gen}$ at age $t$. These passes provide us with all the necessary signals to minimize the following loss functions.

**Adversarial Loss.** We use an adversarial loss conditioned on the source and target age cluster of the real and fake images respectively,

$$\mathcal{L}_{adv}(G, D) = E_{x,s}[\log D_s(x)] + E_{x,t}[\log(1 - D_t(y_{gen})], \tag{4}$$

where $D_i$ is the $i$-th output of the discriminator, $s$ is the source age cluster of the real image and $t$ is the target cluster for the generated image.

**Self Reconstruction Loss.** This loss is used to force the generator to learn the identity translation. When the given target age cluster is the same as the source cluster, we minimize

$$\mathcal{L}_{rec}(G) = \|x - y_{rec}\|_1. \tag{5}$$

**Cycle Loss.** To help identity preservation as well as a consistent skin tone we employ the cycle consistency loss [50],

$$\mathcal{L}_{cyc}(G) = \|x - y_{cyc}\|_1. \tag{6}$$

**Identity Feature Loss.** To make sure the generator keeps the identity of the person throughout the aging process, we minimize the $L1$ distance between the identity features of the original image and those of the generated image,

$$\mathcal{L}_{id}(G) = \|E_{id}(x) - E_{id}(y_{gen})\|_1. \tag{7}$$

**Age Vector Loss.** We enforce a correct embedding of real and generated images to the input age space by penalizing the distance between the age encoder outputs and the age vectors $z_s, z_t$ that were sampled to generate outputs at the source and target age clusters respectively. The loss is defined as

$$\mathcal{L}_{age}(G) = \|E_{age}(x) - z_s\|_1 + \|E_{age}(y_{gen}) - z_t\|_1. \tag{8}$$

The overall optimization function is

$$\min_G \max_D \mathcal{L}_{adv}(G, D) + \lambda_{rec}\mathcal{L}_{rec}(G) + \\ \lambda_{cyc}\mathcal{L}_{cyc}(G) + \lambda_{id}\mathcal{L}_{id}(G) + \lambda_{age}\mathcal{L}_{age}(G). \tag{9}$$

### 3.4    Implementation Details

We train 2 separate models, one for males and one for females. Each model was trained with a batch size of 12 for 400 epochs on 4 GeForce RTX 2080 Ti GPUs. We use the Adam optimizer [21] with $\beta_1 = 0$, $\beta_2 = 0.999$ and a learning rate of $10^{-3}$. The learning rate is decayed by 0.5 after 50 and 100 epochs. Similar to StyleGAN [18], we apply the non-saturating adversarial loss [11] with $R1$ regularization [30]. In addition, we also reduce the learning rate of the mapping network $M$ by a factor of 0.01 and employ exponential moving average for the generator weights. We set $\lambda_{rec} = 10$, $\lambda_{cyc} = 10$, $\lambda_{id} = 1$, $\lambda_{age} = 1$. We refer the readers to the supplementary material for architecture details of each component in our framework. The code and pre-trained models are publicly available.

**Fig. 3.** FFHQ-Aging dataset. We label 70k images from FFHQ dataset [18] for gender and age via crowd-sourcing. In addition, for each image we extracted face semantic maps as well as head pose angles, glasses type and eye occlusion score.

## 4   Dataset

We introduce a new facial aging dataset based on images from FFHQ [18], 'FFHQ-Aging'. We used the Appen[1] crowd-sourcing platform to annotate gender and age cluster for all 70,000 images on FFHQ, collecting 3 judgements for each image. We defined 10 age clusters that capture both geometric and appearance changes throughout a person's life: 0–2, 3–6, 7–9, 10–14, 15–19, 20–29, 30–39, 40–49, 50–69 and 70+. We trained a DeepLabV3 [6] network on the CelebAMask-HQ [23] dataset and used the trained model to extract a 19 label face semantic maps for all 70 K images. Finally, we used the Face++[2] platform to get the head pose angles, glasses type (none, normal, or dark) and left and right eye occlusion scores. We use the same alignment procedure as [17] with a slightly larger crop size (see supplementary for details). We generated our images and semantic maps at a resolution of $256 \times 256$ but the procedure is applicable to higher resolutions too. Figure 3 shows sample image & face semantics pairs from the dataset. There are 32,170 males and 37,830 females in the dataset, the age distribution per gender can be seen in the supplementary material. The dataset is publicly available to the community.

For the purpose of training our network, we assigned images 0–68,999, for training and images 69,000–69,999 for testing. Then, we pruned images with: gender confidence below 0.66, age confidence below 0.6, head yaw angle greater than 40°, head pitch angle greater than 30°, dark glasses label, and eye occlusion score greater than 90 and 50 for eye pair. After pruning, we selected 6 age clusters to train on: 0–2, 3–6, 7–9, 15–19, 30–39, 50–69. This process resulted in 14,232 male and 14,066 female training images along with 198 male and 205 female images for testing. The pruned training set age distribution per gender is presented in the supplementary material.

## 5   Evaluation

### 5.1   Comparison with Commercial Apps

We perform a qualitative comparison with the outputs of FaceApp[3]. FaceApp provides binary facial aging filters to make people appear younger or older.

---

[1] https://www.appen.com/.
[2] https://www.faceplusplus.com/.
[3] https://www.faceapp.com/.

| Input | FaceApp Old | FaceApp Cool Old | Ours 50–69 | Input | FaceApp Young2 | Ours 15–19 | Ours 0–2 |

**Fig. 4.** Comparison with FaceApp filters. Note that FaceApp cannot deform the shape of the head or generate extreme ages, e.g. 0–2.

Figure 4 shows that although the FaceApp output image quality is high, it cannot perform shape transformation and is mostly limited to skin texture. For transformations to an older age, we applied both "old" and "cool old" filters available in FaceApp and compared against our output for 50–69 age range. For transformations to a younger age, we applied the "young2" filter which is roughly equivalent to our 15–19 class. We also show our outputs for the 0–2 class to demonstrate our algorithm's ability to learn head deformation. Even though FaceApp applies a dedicated filter for each transition, in contrast with our multi-domain generator, its age filters are still not transforming the shape of the head.

## 5.2  Comparison with Age Transformation Methods

We compare our algorithm to three state-of-the-art age transformation methods: IPCGAN [44], Yang *et al.* [46], referred as PyGAN, and S2GAN [13].

**Qualitative Evaluation.** We compare with PyGAN and S2GAN on CACD dataset [5] on the images showcased by the authors in their papers. We train on FFHQ and test on CACD, while both PyGAN and S2GAN train on CACD dataset. Due to copyright issues with CACD images, we cannot present the comparison figures in this manuscript. We encourage the reader to review these images in the project's website. Even though PyGAN is trained with a different generator to produce each age cluster, our network is still able to achieve better photorealism for multiple output classes with a single generator. In comparison to S2GAN, our algorithm is able to create more pronounced wrinkles and facial features as the age progresses, all while spanning wider range of age transformations.

We also evaluate our performance w.r.t IPCGAN trained on both CACD & FFHQ-Aging datasets in Fig. 5. Here, we use IPCGAN's publically available code and retrain their framework on FFHQ-Aging dataset for fair comparison (termed as 'IPCGAN-retrained'). Our method outperforms both IPCGAN models in terms of image quality and shape deformation.

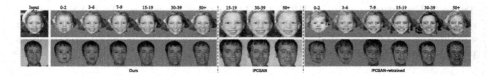

**Fig. 5.** Comparison w.r.t. IPCGAN [44] on the FFHQ-Aging dataset. Left: our method. Middle: IPCGAN trained on CACD. Right: IPCGAN trained on FFHQ-Aging. The proposed framework outperforms IPCGAN, producing sharper, more detailed and more realistic outputs across all age classes.

**Table 1.** User study results vs. PyGAN [46]. PyGAN is expectedly better at identity preservation, at the cost of not generating the target age (mean age difference 23.1, compared to our 6.9). When asked which is better overall, users prefered our results in 16 out of 20 cases.

| Age range | 50–69 | |
|---|---|---|
| | PyGAN [46] | Ours |
| Same identity | **19** | 13 |
| Age difference | 23.1 | **6.9** |
| Overall better | 4 | **16** |

**User Study.** In addition, we performed a user study to evaluate PyGAN results vs. our results. In the study we measure: (a) how well does the method preserve the identity of the person in the photo, (b) how close is the perceived age to the target age, and (c) overall which result is better. Our hypothesis was that PyGAN will excel in identity preservation but not on the other metrics, since PyGAN tends to keep the results close to the input photo (and thus cannot perform large age changes).

To measure identity preservation, we show the input and output photos and ask if the two contain the same person. To measure age accuracy, we show the output photo and ask the age of the person, selected from a list of age ranges. To measure overall quality, we show an input photo, and below it a PyGAN result and our result side-by-side in a randomized order, and ask which result is a better version of the input person in the target age range. We used Amazon Mechanical Turk to collect answers for 20 randomly selected images from FFHQ-Aging dataset, repeating each question 5 times, for a total of 500 unique answers. We show the user study interface in supplemental material.

User study results are presented in Table 1. As expected, PyGAN preserves subject identity more often (in 19 out of 20 cases, compared to 13 for our method). This comes at a cost of much larger age gaps: the perceived age of PyGAN results is on average 23.1 years away from the target age, compared to 6.9 years for our results. Since identity preservation and age preservation may conflict, we also asked participants to evaluate which result is better overall. For 16 out of 20 test photos, our results were rated as better than PyGAN.

**Table 2.** User study results vs. IPCGAN [44] for three age groups. IPCGAN is expectedly better at identity preservation, at the cost of not generating the target age (mean age difference 22.6, compared to our 11.3). When asked which is better overall, users prefered our results in 120 out of 150 cases.

| Age range | 15–19 | | 30–39 | | 50–69 | | All | |
|---|---|---|---|---|---|---|---|---|
| | IPCGAN | Ours | IPCGAN | Ours | IPCGAN | Ours | IPCGAN | Ours |
| Same identity | 50 | 50 | **50** | 45 | **50** | 41 | **150** | 136 |
| Age difference | 19.3 | **12.7** | 20.0 | **11.6** | 28.4 | **9.8** | 22.6 | **11.3** |
| Overall better | 9 | **40** | 8 | **42** | 10 | **38** | 27 | **120** |

In a second user study, we compare our results to those of IPCGAN trained on CACD dataset. We report results per age range, as well as overall results (Table 2). We collected answers for 3 age ranges, 50 randomly selected images per range, repeating each question 3 times, for a total of 2250 unique answers. Similarly to PyGAN, IPCGAN better preserves identity (in 100% of the cases) at the cost of age inaccuracies (results are on average 22.6 years away from the target age). When asked which result is better overall, participants picked our results in 120 cases, compared to 27 for IPCGAN.

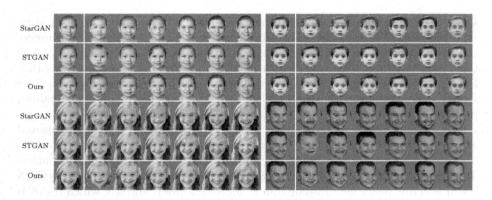

**Fig. 6.** Comparison with multi domain transfer methods. The leftmost column is the input, followed by transformations to age classes 0–2, 3–6, 7–9, 15–19, 30–39 and 50–69 respectively. Multi domain transfer methods struggle to model the gradual head deformation associated with age progression. Our method also produces better images in terms of quality and photorealism, while correctly modeling the growth of the head compared to StarGAN [7] and STGAN [26].

**Comparison with Multi-class Domain Transfer Methods.** To validate our claim that multi-domain transfer methods struggle with shape deformations, we compare our algorithm against 2 state-of-the-art baselines, StarGAN [7] and

**Fig. 7.** Comparison with InterFaceGAN [37]. **Age cluster legend only applies to our method**. Rows 1, 3, 5: results on StyleGAN generated images. Row 7: result on a real image, embedded into the StyleGAN latent space using LIA [49]. Rows 2,4,6: Our result on StyleGAN generated images. Bottom row: Our result on a real image. Existing state-of-the-art interpolation methods cannot maintain the identity (rows 1, 3, 5, 7), gender (row 5) and ethnicity (rows 3, 5) of the input image. In addition, as seen in rows 1 & 3, using the same $\lambda$ values on different photos produces different age ranges.

STGAN [26]. We retrain both algorithms on our FFHQ-Aging dataset using the same pre-processing procedure (see Sect. 3.2) to mask background and clothes and the same sampling technique to compensate for dataset imbalances (see Sect. 3.3). Figure 6 shows that although STGAN occasionally deforms the shape for the 0–2 class, both StarGAN and STGAN cannot produce a consistent shape transformation across age classes.

**Latent Space Interpolation.** We show our method's ability to generalize and produce continuous age transformations by interpolation in the $\mathcal{W}_{age}$ latent space. Interpolation between two neighboring age classes is done by generating two age latent codes $w_{age}^{t}, w_{age}^{t+1}$, where $t, t + 1$ are adjacent age classes, and then generating the desired interpolated code $w_{age} = (1 - \alpha) \cdot w_{age}^{t} + \alpha \cdot w_{age}^{t+1}$. The rest of the process is identical to Sect. 3. We compare our results on two possible setups. In the first case, we demonstrate that the StyleGAN [18] latent space paths found by InterFaceGAN [37] cannot maintain identity, gender and race. We sample a latent code in $z$ space of StyleGAN, which generates a realistic face image. We use the latent space boundary from InterFaceGAN, which can

**Fig. 8.** Limitations. Our network struggles to generalize extreme poses (top row), removing glasses (left column), removing thick beards (bottom right) and occlusions (top left).

change age by preserving gender, and edit the sampled latent code to produce both younger and older versions of the face using $\lambda \in [-3, +3]$ in $z$ space. In the second setup, we compare against real images embedded into StyleGAN's $w$ latent space using the LIA [49] framework. We then change the age of the embedded face by traversing on the latent space across the age boundary learnt with InterFaceGAN on $w$ space (this boundary was not gender conditioned). We use $\lambda \in [-20, +20]$ in $w$ space to generate younger and older versions. In Fig. 7 we can see that despite the excellent photorealism of InterFaceGAN on generated faces, the person's identity is lost, and in some occasions the gender is lost too. In addition, note how InterFaceGAN requires different $\lambda$ values for each input in order to achieve full lifespan transformation, as opposed to our consistent age outputs in the traversal paths.

### 5.3 Limitations

While our network can generalize age transformations, it has limitations in generalizing for other potential cases such as extreme poses, removing glasses and thick beards when rejuvenating a person, and handling occluded faces. Figure 8 shows a representative example for each such case. We suspect that these issues stem from a combination of using just two downsampling layers in the identity encoder and the latent identity loss. The former creates relatively local feature maps, while the latter enforces the latent identity spatial representations of two difference age classes to be the same, which in turn, limits the network's ability to generalize for these cases.

## 6  Conclusions

We presented an algorithm that produces reliable age transformations for ages 0–70. Unlike previous approaches, our framework learns to change both shape and texture as part of the aging process. The proposed architecture and training scheme accurately generalize age, and thus, we can produce results for ages never seen during training via latent space interpolation. In addition, we also introduced a new facial dataset that can be used by the vision community for various tasks. As demonstrated in our experiments, our method produces state-of-the-art results.

**Acknowledgements.** We wish to thank Xuan Luo and Aaron Wetzler for their valuable discussions and advice, and Thevina Dokka for her help in building the FFHQ-Aging dataset. This work was supported in part by Futurewei Technologies. O.F. was supported by the Brown Institute for Media Innovation. All images in this manuscript are licensed under creative commons license and were taken from the FFHQ dataset.

# References

1. Antipov, G., Baccouche, M., Dugelay, J.L.: Face aging with conditional generative adversarial networks. arXiv preprint arXiv:1702.01983 (2017)
2. Bando, Y., Kuratate, T., Nishita, T.: A simple method for modeling wrinkles on human skin. In: 10th Pacific Conference on Computer Graphics and Applications, Proceedings, pp. 166–175. IEEE (2002)
3. Boissieux, L., Kiss, G., Thalmann, N.M., Kalra, P.: Simulation of skin aging and wrinkles with cosmetics insight. In: Magnenat-Thalmann, N., Thalmann, D., Arnaldi, B. (eds.) Computer Animation and Simulation 2000. Eurographics, pp. 15–27. Springer, Heidelberg (2000). https://doi.org/10.1007/978-3-7091-6344-3_2
4. Burt, D.M., Perrett, D.I.: Perception of age in adult Caucasian male faces: computer graphic manipulation of shape and colour information. Proc. R. Soc. Lond. Ser. B: Biol. Sci. **259**(1355), 137–143 (1995)
5. Chen, B.-C., Chen, C.-S., Hsu, W.H.: Cross-age reference coding for age-invariant face recognition and retrieval. In: Fleet, D., Pajdla, T., Schiele, B., Tuytelaars, T. (eds.) ECCV 2014. LNCS, vol. 8694, pp. 768–783. Springer, Cham (2014). https://doi.org/10.1007/978-3-319-10599-4_49
6. Chen, L.C., Papandreou, G., Schroff, F., Adam, H.: Rethinking atrous convolution for semantic image segmentation. arXiv preprint arXiv:1706.05587 (2017)
7. Choi, Y., Choi, M., Kim, M., Ha, J.W., Kim, S., Choo, J.: Stargan: unified generative adversarial networks for multi-domain image-to-image translation. In: The IEEE Conference on Computer Vision and Pattern Recognition (CVPR) (2018)
8. Choi, Y., Uh, Y., Yoo, J., Ha, J.W.: Stargan v2: diverse image synthesis for multiple domains. arXiv preprint arXiv:1912.01865 (2019)
9. Duong, C.N., Luu, K., Quach, K.G., Bui, T.D.: Longitudinal face aging in the wild-recent deep learning approaches. arXiv preprint arXiv:1802.08726 (2018)
10. Fu, Y., Guo, G., Huang, T.S.: Age synthesis and estimation via faces: a survey. IEEE Trans. Pattern Anal. Mach. Intell. **32**(11), 1955–1976 (2010)
11. Goodfellow, I., et al.: Generative adversarial nets. In: Advances in Neural Information Processing Systems, pp. 2672–2680 (2014)
12. He, K., Zhang, X., Ren, S., Sun, J.: Deep residual learning for image recognition. In: Proceedings of the IEEE Conference on Computer Vision and Pattern Recognition, pp. 770–778 (2016)
13. He, Z., Kan, M., Shan, S., Chen, X.: S2gan: share aging factors across ages and share aging trends among individuals. In: The IEEE International Conference on Computer Vision (ICCV) (2019)
14. Huang, X., Belongie, S.: Arbitrary style transfer in real-time with adaptive instance normalization. In: Proceedings of the IEEE International Conference on Computer Vision, pp. 1501–1510 (2017)
15. Huang, X., Liu, M.-Y., Belongie, S., Kautz, J.: Multimodal unsupervised image-to-image translation. In: Ferrari, V., Hebert, M., Sminchisescu, C., Weiss, Y. (eds.) ECCV 2018. LNCS, vol. 11207, pp. 179–196. Springer, Cham (2018). https://doi.org/10.1007/978-3-030-01219-9_11

16. Isola, P., Zhu, J.Y., Zhou, T., Efros, A.A.: Image-to-image translation with conditional adversarial networks. In: The IEEE Conference on Computer Vision and Pattern Recognition (CVPR) (2017)
17. Karras, T., Aila, T., Laine, S., Lehtinen, J.: Progressive growing of GANs for improved quality, stability, and variation. In: International Conference on Learning Representations (2018)
18. Karras, T., Laine, S., Aila, T.: A style-based generator architecture for generative adversarial networks. In: Proceedings of the IEEE Conference on Computer Vision and Pattern Recognition, pp. 4401–4410 (2019)
19. Karras, T., Laine, S., Aittala, M., Hellsten, J., Lehtinen, J., Aila, T.: Analyzing and improving the image quality of StyleGAN. CoRR abs/1912.04958 (2019)
20. Kemelmacher-Shlizerman, I., Suwajanakorn, S., Seitz, S.M.: Illumination-aware age progression. In: The IEEE Conference on Computer Vision and Pattern Recognition (CVPR) (2014)
21. Kingma, D.P., Ba, J.: Adam: a method for stochastic optimization. arXiv preprint arXiv:1412.6980 (2014)
22. Lanitis, A., Taylor, C.J., Cootes, T.F.: Toward automatic simulation of aging effects on face images. IEEE Trans. Pattern Anal. Mach. Intell. **24**(4), 442–455 (2002)
23. Lee, C.H., Liu, Z., Wu, L., Luo, P.: MaskGan: towards diverse and interactive facial image manipulation. arXiv preprint arXiv:1907.11922 (2019)
24. Lee, H.-Y., Tseng, H.-Y., Huang, J.-B., Singh, M., Yang, M.-H.: Diverse image-to-image translation via disentangled representations. In: Ferrari, V., Hebert, M., Sminchisescu, C., Weiss, Y. (eds.) ECCV 2018. LNCS, vol. 11205, pp. 36–52. Springer, Cham (2018). https://doi.org/10.1007/978-3-030-01246-5_3
25. Li, P., Hu, Y., Li, Q., He, R., Sun, Z.: Global and local consistent age generative adversarial networks. arXiv preprint arXiv:1801.08390 (2018)
26. Liu, M., et al.: STGAN: a unified selective transfer network for arbitrary image attribute editing. In: Proceedings of the IEEE Conference on Computer Vision and Pattern Recognition, pp. 3673–3682 (2019)
27. Liu, M.Y., et al.: Few-shot unsupervised image-to-image translation. arXiv preprint arXiv:1905.01723 (2019)
28. Liu, S., Shi, J., Liang, J., Yang, M.H.: Face parsing via recurrent propagation. arXiv preprint arXiv:1708.01936 (2017)
29. Liu, Y., Li, Q., Sun, Z.: Attribute-aware face aging with wavelet-based generative adversarial networks. In: The IEEE Conference on Computer Vision and Pattern Recognition (CVPR) (2019)
30. Mescheder, L., Geiger, A., Nowozin, S.: Which training methods for GANs do actually converge? In: International Conference on Machine Learning (ICML) (2018)
31. Nhan Duong, C., Gia Quach, K., Luu, K., Le, N., Savvides, M.: Temporal non-volume preserving approach to facial age-progression and age-invariant face recognition. In: The IEEE International Conference on Computer Vision (ICCV) (2017)
32. Nhan Duong, C., Luu, K., Gia Quach, K., Bui, T.D.: Longitudinal face modeling via temporal deep restricted Boltzmann machines. In: Proceedings of the IEEE Conference on Computer Vision and Pattern Recognition, pp. 5772–5780 (2016)
33. Ramanathan, N., Chellappa, R.: Modeling age progression in young faces. In: 2006 IEEE Computer Society Conference on Computer Vision and Pattern Recognition, vol. 1, pp. 387–394. IEEE (2006)
34. Ramanathan, N., Chellappa, R.: Modeling shape and textural variations in aging faces. In: 8th IEEE International Conference on Automatic Face & Gesture Recognition, FG 2008, pp. 1–8. IEEE (2008)

35. Ramanathan, N., Chellappa, R., Biswas, S.: Computational methods for modeling facial aging: a survey. J. Vis. Lang. Comput. **20**(3), 131–144 (2009)
36. Rowland, D.A., Perrett, D.I.: Manipulating facial appearance through shape and color. IEEE Comput. Graph. Appl. **15**(5), 70–76 (1995)
37. Shen, Y., Gu, J., Tang, X., Zhou, B.: Interpreting the latent space of GANs for semantic face editing. arXiv preprint arXiv:1907.10786 (2019)
38. Shu, X., Tang, J., Lai, H., Liu, L., Yan, S.: Personalized age progression with aging dictionary. In: Proceedings of the IEEE International Conference on Computer Vision, pp. 3970–3978 (2015)
39. Suo, J., Chen, X., Shan, S., Gao, W., Dai, Q.: A concatenational graph evolution aging model. IEEE Trans. Pattern Anal. Mach. Intell. **34**(11), 2083–2096 (2012)
40. Suo, J., Zhu, S.C., Shan, S., Chen, X.: A compositional and dynamic model for face aging. IEEE Trans. Pattern Anal. Mach. Intell. **32**(3), 385–401 (2010)
41. Taigman, Y., Polyak, A., Wolf, L.: Unsupervised cross-domain image generation. In: ICLR (2017)
42. Tiddeman, B., Burt, M., Perrett, D.: Prototyping and transforming facial textures for perception research. IEEE Comput. Graph. Appl. **21**(5), 42–50 (2001)
43. Wang, W., et al.: Recurrent face aging. In: Proceedings of the IEEE Conference on Computer Vision and Pattern Recognition, pp. 2378–2386 (2016)
44. Wang, Z., Tang, X., Luo, W., Gao, S.: Face aging with identity-preserved conditional generative adversarial networks. In: Proceedings of the IEEE Conference on Computer Vision and Pattern Recognition, pp. 7939–7947 (2018)
45. Wu, Y., Thalmann, N.M., Thalmann, D.: A plastic-visco-elastic model for wrinkles in facial animation and skin aging. In: Fundamentals of Computer Graphics, pp. 201–213. World Scientific (1994)
46. Yang, H., Huang, D., Wang, Y., Jain, A.K.: Learning face age progression: a pyramid architecture of GANs. In: The IEEE Conference on Computer Vision and Pattern Recognition (CVPR) (2018)
47. Yang, H., Huang, D., Wang, Y., Wang, H., Tang, Y.: Face aging effect simulation using hidden factor analysis joint sparse representation. IEEE Trans. Image Process. **25**(6), 2493–2507 (2016)
48. Zhang, Z., Song, Y., Qi, H.: Age progression/regression by conditional adversarial autoencoder. In: The IEEE Conference on Computer Vision and Pattern Recognition (CVPR) (2017)
49. Zhu, J., Zhao, D., Zhang, B.: Lia: latently invertible autoencoder with adversarial learning. arXiv preprint arXiv:1906.08090 (2019)
50. Zhu, J.Y., Park, T., Isola, P., Efros, A.A.: Unpaired image-to-image translation using cycle-consistent adversarial networks. In: The IEEE International Conference on Computer Vision (ICCV) (2017)

# Domain2Vec: Domain Embedding
# for Unsupervised Domain Adaptation

Xingchao Peng[1]([✉]), Yichen Li[2], and Kate Saenko[1,3]

[1] Boston University, Boston, MA, USA
{xpeng,saenko}@bu.edu
[2] Stanford University, Stanford, CA, USA
liyichen@stanford.edu
[3] MIT-IBM Watson AI Lab, Boston, MA, USA

**Abstract.** Conventional unsupervised domain adaptation (UDA) studies the knowledge transfer between a limited number of domains. This neglects the more practical scenario where data are distributed in numerous different domains in the real world. A technique to measure domain similarity is critical for domain adaptation performance. To describe and learn relations between different domains, we propose a novel DOMAIN2VEC model to provide vectorial representations of visual domains based on joint learning of feature disentanglement and Gram matrix. To evaluate the effectiveness of our DOMAIN2VEC model, we create two large-scale cross-domain benchmarks. The first one is TINYDA, which contains 54 domains and about one million MNIST-style images. The second benchmark is DOMAINBANK, which is collected from 56 existing vision datasets. We demonstrate that our embedding is capable of predicting domain similarities that match our intuition about visual relations between different domains. Extensive experiments are conducted to demonstrate the power of our new datasets in benchmarking state-of-the-art multi-source domain adaptation methods, as well as the advantage of our proposed model (Data and code are available at https://github.com/VisionLearningGroup/Domain2Vec).

**Keywords:** Unsupervised domain adaptation · Domain vectorization

## 1 Introduction

Generalizing models learned on one visual domain to novel domains has been a major pursuit of machine learning in the quest for universal object recognition.

X. Peng and Y. Li—These authors contributed equally.

**Electronic supplementary material** The online version of this chapter (https://doi.org/10.1007/978-3-030-58539-6_45) contains supplementary material, which is available to authorized users.

© Springer Nature Switzerland AG 2020
A. Vedaldi et al. (Eds.): ECCV 2020, LNCS 12351, pp. 756–774, 2020.
https://doi.org/10.1007/978-3-030-58539-6_45

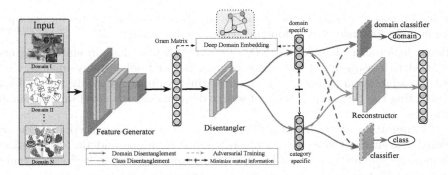

**Fig. 1.** Our DOMAIN2VEC architecture achieve deep domain embedding by joint learning of feature disentanglement and Gram matrix. We employ *domain disentanglement* (red lines) and *class disentanglement* (blue lines) to extract domain-specific features and category specific features, both trained adversarially. We further apply a mutual information minimizer to enhance the disentanglement. (Color figure online)

The performance of the learned methods degrades significantly when tested on novel domains due to the presence of *domain shift* [1].

Recently, Unsupervised Domain Adaptation (UDA) methods have been proposed to mitigate domain gap. For example, several learning-based UDA models [2–4] incorporate Maximum Mean Discrepancy loss to minimize the domain discrepancy; other models propose different learning schema to align the marginal feature distributions of the source and target domains, including aligning second-order correlation [5,6], moment matching [7], GAN-based alignment [8–10], and adversarial domain confusion [11–13]. However, most of the current UDA methods consider domain adaptation between limited number of domains (usually one source domain and one target domain). In addition, the state-of-the-art UDA models mainly focus on aligning the feature distribution of the source domain with that of the target domain, and fail to consider the natural distance and relations between different domains. In the more practical scenarios where multiple domain exists and the relations between different domains are unclear, it is critical to evaluate the natural domain distances between source and target so to be able to select one or several domains from the source domain pool such that the target domain can achieve the best performance.

In this paper, we introduce the DOMAIN2VEC embedding to represent domains as elements of a vector space. Formally, given $N$ distinct domains $\hat{\mathcal{D}} = \{\hat{\mathcal{D}}_1, \hat{\mathcal{D}}_2, ..., \hat{\mathcal{D}}_N\}^1$ domains, the aim is the learn a domain to vector mapping $\Phi : \hat{\mathcal{D}} \to V$. We would like our DOMAIN2VEC to hold the following properties: (i) given two domains $\hat{\mathcal{D}}_i$, $\hat{\mathcal{D}}_j$, the accuracy of a model trained on $\hat{\mathcal{D}}_i$ and tested on $\hat{\mathcal{D}}_j$ should be negatively correlated to the domain distance in the vector space $V$, *i.e.* smaller domain distance leads to better cross-domain performance; (ii) the

---

[1] In this literature, the calligraphic $\mathcal{G}, \mathcal{D}$ denote Gram matrix and domains, and italic $G, D$ denote feature generator and disentangler, respectively.

domain distance should match our intuition about visual relations, for example, the domain distance of two domains with building images ($\hat{\mathcal{D}}_i^{building}$, $\hat{\mathcal{D}}_j^{building}$) should be smaller than that of ($\hat{\mathcal{D}}_i^{building}$, $\hat{\mathcal{D}}_j^{car}$). Our domain embedding can be used to reason about the space of domains and solve many unsupervised domain adaptation problems. As a motivating example, we study the problem of selecting the best combination of source domains when a novel target domain emerges.

Computation of the DOMAIN2VEC embedding leverages a complementary term between the Gram matrix of deep representations and the disentangled *domain-specific* feature. Gram Matrices are commonly used to build style representations that compute the correlations between different filter activations in a deep network [14]. Since activations of a deep network trained on a visual domain are a rich representation of the domain itself, we use Gram Matrix to capture the texture information of a domain and further obtain a stationary, multi-scale representation of the input domain. Specifically, given a domain defined by $\hat{\mathcal{D}} = \{x_j, y_j\}_{j=1}^{n_i}$ with $n_i$ ($i \in [1, N]$) examples, we feed the data through a pre-train reference convolutional neural network which we call feature generator $G$, and compute the activations of the fully connected layer as the latent representation $f_G$, as shown in Fig. 1. Inspired by the feature disentanglement idea [15], we introduce a disentangler $D$ to disentangle $f_G$ into *domain-specific* feature $f_{ds}$ and *category-specific* feature $f_{cs}$. Finally, we compute the Gram matrix of the activations of the hidden convolutional layers in the feature extractor. Given a domain $\hat{\mathcal{D}} = \{x_j, y_j\}_{j=1}^{n_i}$, we average the domain-specific features of all the training examples in $\hat{\mathcal{D}}$ as the *prototype* of domain $\hat{\mathcal{D}}$. We utilize the concatenation of *prototype* and the diagonal entries of the average Gram matrix as the final embedding vector of domain $\hat{\mathcal{D}}$. We show this embedding encodes the intrinsic properties of the domains (Sect. 4).

To evaluate our DOMAIN2VEC model, a large-scale benchmark with multiple domains is required. However, state-of-the-art cross-domain datasets contain only a limited number of domains. For example, the large-scale Domain-Net [16] that contains six domains, and the Office-31 [17] benchmark that only has three domains. In this paper, we create two large-scale datasets to facilitate the research of multi-domain embedding. TINYDAdataset is by far the largest MNIST-style cross domain dataset. It contains 54 domains and about one million training examples. Following Ganin *et al.* [12], the images are generated by blending different foreground shapes over patches randomly cropped from the background images. The second benchmark is DOMAINBANK, which contains 56 domains sampled from the existing popular computer vision datasets.

Based on TINYDA dataset, we validate our DOMAIN2VEC model's property on the negative correlation between the cross-domain performance and the domain distance computed by our model. Then, we show the effectiveness of our DOMAIN2VEC on multi-source domain adaptation. In addition, comprehensive experiments on DOMAINBANK benchmark with openset domain adaptation and partial domain adaptation schema demonstrate that our model achieves significant improvements over the state-of-the-art methods.

The main contributions of this paper are highlighted as follows: (**i**) we propose a novel learning paradigm of deep domain embedding and develop a DOMAIN2VEC model to achieve the domain embedding; (**ii**) we collect two state-of-the-art benchmarks to facilitate research in multiple domain embedding and adaptation. (**iii**) we conduct extensive experiments on various domain adaptation settings to demonstrate the effectiveness of our proposed model.

## 2   Related Work

**Vectorial Representation Learning.** Discovery of effective representations that capture salient semantics for a given task is a fundamental goal for perceptual learning. The individual dimensions in the vectorial embedding have no inherent meaning. Instead, it is the overall patterns of location and distance between vectors that machine learning takes advantage of. GloVe [18] models achieve global vectorial embbedings for word by training on the nonzero elements in a word-word co-occurrence matrix, rather than on the entire sparse matrix or on individual context windows in a large corpus. DECAF [19] investigates semi-supervised multi-task learning of deep convolutional representations, where representations are learned on a set of related problems but applied to new tasks which have too few training examples to learn a full deep representation. Modern state-of-the-art deep models [20–24] learn semantic representations with supervision and are applied to various vision and language processing tasks. Another work which is very related to our work is the TASK2VEC model [25] which leverage the Fisher Information Matrix as the vectorial representation of different tasks. However, the TASK2VEC model mainly consider the similarity between different tasks. In this work, we mainly focus on the same task and introduce a DOMAIN2VEC framework to achieve deep domain embedding for multiple domains. Specifically, DOMAIN2VEC is initially proposed in the work of Deshmukh *et al.* [26]. However, their model is designed for domain generalization. Our model is developed independently for a different purpose.

**Unsupervised Domain Adaptation.** Deep neural networks have achieved remarkable success on diverse vision tasks [22,27,28] but at the expense of tedious labor work on labeling data. Given a large-scale unlabeled dataset, it is expensive to annotate enough training data such that we can train a deep model that generalizes well to that dataset. Unsupervised Domain Adaptation [4,12,13,15–17,29] provides an alternative way by transferring knowledge from a different but related domain (source domain) to the domain of interest (target domain). Specifically, unsupervised domain adaptation (UDA) aims to transfer the knowledge learned from one or more labeled source domains to an unlabeled target domain. Various methods have been proposed, including discrepancy-based UDA approaches [2,3,6,30], adversary-based approaches [11,31,32], and reconstruction-based approaches [8,9,33,34]. These models are typically designed to tackle single source to single target adaptation. Compared with single source adaptation, multi-source domain adaptation

(MSDA) assumes that training data are collected from multiple sources. Originating from the theoretical analysis in [35–37], MSDA has been applied to many practical applications [16,38,39]. Specifically, Ben-David *et al.* [35] introduce an $\mathcal{H}\Delta\mathcal{H}$-divergence between the weighted combination of source domains and a target domain. Different from the previous work, we propose a DOMAIN2VEC model to evaluate the natural distances between different domains.

**Deep Feature Disentanglement.** Deep neural networks are known to extract features where multiple hidden factors are highly entangled [40]. Learning disentangled representations can help to model the relevant factors of data variation as well as evaluate the relations between different domains by extracting the domain-specific features. To this end, recent work [32,41–43] leverages generative adversarial networks (GANs) [44] or variational autoencoders (VAEs) [45] to learn the interpretable representations. Under the multi-domain setting, Liu *et al.* [32] propose a unified feature disentanglement framework to learn domain-invariant features from data across different domains. Odena *et al.* [43] introduce an auxiliary classifier GAN (AC-GAN) to achieve representation disentanglement under supervised setting. Recent work [15,46] propose to disentangle the features into a domain-invariant content space and a domain-specific attributes space, producing diverse outputs without paired training data. In this paper, we propose a cross-disentanglement schema to disentangle the deep features into *domain-specific* and *category-specific* features.

## 3    Domain2Vec

We define the domain vectorization task as follows: given N domains $\hat{\mathcal{D}} = \{\hat{\mathcal{D}}_1, \hat{\mathcal{D}}_2, ..., \hat{\mathcal{D}}_N\}$ domains, the aim is the learn a domain to vector mapping $\Phi : \hat{\mathcal{D}} \rightarrow V$, which is capable of predicting domain similarities that match our intuition about visual relations between different domains. Our DOMAIN2VEC includes two components: we first leverage feature disentanglement to generate the *domain-specific* features, and then we achieve deep domain embedding by the joint learning of Gram Matrix of the latent representations and the *domain-specific* features.

### 3.1    Feature Disentanglement

Given an image-label pair (x,y), a deep neural network is a family of function $p_\theta(y|x)$, trained to approximate the posterior $p(y|x)$ by minimizing the cross entropy loss $H_{p_\theta,\hat{p}}(y|x) = \mathbb{E}_{x,y}[-\log p_\theta(y|x)]$, where $\hat{p}$ is the empirical distribution defined by the $i$-th domain $\hat{\mathcal{D}}_i = \{x_j, y_j\}_{j=1}^{n_i}$ with $n_i$ training examples, $i \in [1, n]$. It is beneficial, especially in domain vectorization task, to think of the deep neural network as composed of two parts: a feature generator which computes the latent representations $f_\theta = \phi_\theta(x)$ of the input data, and a classifier which encodes the distribution $p(y|x)$ given the representation $f_\theta$.

The latent representations $f_\theta = \phi_\theta(x)$ are highly entangled with multiple hidden factors. We propose to disentangle the hidden representations to *domain-specific* and *category-specific* features. Figure 1 shows the proposed model. Given $N$ domains, the feature extractor $G$ maps the input data to a latent feature vector $f_G$, which contains both the domain-specific and category-specific factors. The disentangler $D$ is trained to disentangle the feature $f_G$ to *domain-specific* feature $f_{ds}$ and *category-specific* feature $f_{cs}$ with cross-entropy loss and adversarial training loss. The feature reconstructor $R$ is responsible to recover $f_G$ from $(f_{ds}, f_{cs})$ pair, aiming to keep the information integrity in the disentanglement process. To enhance the disentanglement, we follow Peng *et al.* [15] to apply a mutual information minimizer between $f_{ds}$ and $f_{cs}$. A category classifier $C$ is trained with class labels to predict the class distributions and a domain classifier $DC$ is trained with domain labels to predict the domain distributions. In addition, the cross-adversarial training step removes domain information from $f_{cs}$ and category information from $f_{ds}$. We next describe each component in detail.

**Category Disentanglement.** Given an input image $x$, the feature generator $G$ computes the latent representation $f_G$. Our category disentanglement is achieved by two-step adversarial training. First, we train the disentangler $D$ and the $k$-way category classifier $C$ to correctly predict the class labels, supervised by the cross-entropy loss:

$$\mathcal{L}_{ce}^{class} = -\sum_{i=1}^{N} \mathbb{E}_{(x,y_c) \sim \hat{\mathcal{D}}_i} \sum_{k=1}^{K} \mathbb{1}[k = y_c] log(C(f_{cs})) \quad (1)$$

where $f_{cs} = D(G(x))$ and $y_c$ indicates the class label.

In the second step, we aim to remove the domain-specific information from $f_{cs}$. Using a well-trained domain classifier (achieved with Eq. 3), we freeze the domain classifier $DC$ and train the disentangler to generate $f_{cs}$, with the objective to fool the domain classifier. This can be achieved by minimizing the negative entropy of the predicted domain distribution:

$$\mathcal{L}_{ent}^{class} = -\sum_{i=1}^{N} \frac{1}{n_i} \sum_{j=1}^{n_i} \log DC(f_{cs}) \quad (2)$$

This adversarial training process corresponds to the blue dotted line in Fig. 1. The above adversarial training process forces the generated *category-specific* feature $f_{cs}$ contains no *domain-specific* information.

**Domain Disentanglement.** To achieve deep domain embedding, disentangling *category-specific* features is not enough, as it fails to describe the relations between different domains. We introduce domain disentanglement to disentangle the domain-specific features from the latent representations. Previous adversarial-alignment based UDA models [11,15] propose to leverage a domain classifier to classify the input feature as source or target. However, the proposed domain classifier is a binary classifier, which can not be applied to our case directly. Similar to category disentanglement, our domain disentanglement is achieved by two-step adversarial training. We first train the feature generator $G$ and disentangler $D$ to extract the domain-specific feature $f_{ds}$, supervised by domain labels and cross-entropy loss:

$$\mathcal{L}_{ce}^{domain} = -\mathbb{E}_{(x,y_d)\sim\hat{\mathcal{D}}} \sum_{k=1}^{N} \mathbb{1}[k = y_d]log(DC(f_{ds})) \tag{3}$$

where $f_{ds} = D(G(x))$ and $y_d$ denotes the domain label.

In the second step, we aim to remove the category-specific information from $f_{ds}$. With a well-trained classifier $C$, we freeze the parameter weights of $C$ and train the disentangler to generate $f_{ds}$ to confuse the category classifier $C$. Similarly, we can minimize the negative entropy of the predicted class distribution:

$$\mathcal{L}_{ent}^{domain} = -\sum_{i=1}^{N} \frac{1}{n_i} \sum_{j=1}^{n_i} \log C(f_{ds}) \tag{4}$$

This adversarial training process corresponds to the red dotted line in Fig. 1. If a well-trained category classifier $C$ is not able to predict the correct class labels, the category-specific information has been successfully removed from $f_{ds}$.

**Feature Reconstruction.** Previous literature [15] has shown that some information gets lost in the feature disentangle process, especially when the feature disentangler $D$ is composed of several fully connected and RELU layers and it cannot guarantee the information integrity in the feature disentanglement process. We therefore introduce a feature reconstructor $R$ to recover the original feature $f_G$ with the disentangled *domain-specific* feature and *category-specific* feature. The feature reconstructor $R$ has two input and will concatenate the $(f_{ds}, f_{cs})$ pair to a vector in the first layer. The feature vector is feed forward to several fully connected and RELU layers. Denoting the reconstructed feature as $\hat{f}_G$, we can train the feature reconstruction process with the following loss:

$$\mathcal{L}_{rec} = \|\hat{f}_G - f_G\|_F^2 + KL(q(z|f_G)\|p(z)) \tag{5}$$

where the first term aims at recovering the original features extracted by $G$, and the second term calculates *Kullback-Leibler divergence* which penalizes the deviation of latent features from the prior distribution $p(z_c)$ (as $z \sim \mathcal{N}(0, I)$).

**Mutual Information Minimization.** The mutual information is a pivotal measure of the mutual dependence between two variables. To enhance the disentanglement, we minimize the mutual information between *category-specific* features and *domain-specific* features. Specifically, the mutual information is defined as:

$$I(f_{ds}; f_{cs}) = \int_{\mathcal{P}\times\mathcal{Q}} \log \frac{d\mathbb{P}_{\mathcal{P}\mathcal{Q}}}{d\mathbb{P}_{\mathcal{P}} \otimes \mathbb{P}_{\mathcal{Q}}} d\mathbb{P}_{\mathcal{P}\mathcal{Q}} \tag{6}$$

where $\mathbb{P}_{\mathcal{P}\mathcal{Q}}$ is the joint probability distribution of $(f_{ds}, f_{cs})$, and $\mathbb{P}_{\mathcal{P}} = \int_{\mathcal{Q}} d\mathbb{P}_{\mathcal{P}\mathcal{Q}}$, $\mathbb{P}_{\mathcal{Q}} = \int_{\mathcal{Q}} d\mathbb{P}_{\mathcal{P}\mathcal{Q}}$ are the marginal probability of $f_{ds}$ and $f_{cs}$, respectively. The conventional mutual information is only tractable for discrete variables, for a limited family of problems where the probability distributions are unknown [47]. To address this issue, we follow [15] to adopt the Mutual Information Neural Estimator (MINE) [47] to estimate the mutual information by leveraging a neural network $T_\theta$: $I(\mathcal{P}; \mathcal{Q}) = \sup_{\theta \in \Theta} \mathbb{E}_{\mathbb{P}_{\mathcal{P}\mathcal{Q}}}[T_\theta] - \log(\mathbb{E}_{\mathbb{P}_{\mathcal{P}} \otimes \mathbb{P}_{\mathcal{Q}}}[e^{T_\theta}])$. Practically, MINE can be calculated as $I(\mathcal{P}; \mathcal{Q}) = \int \int \mathbb{P}_{\mathcal{P}\mathcal{Q}}(p, q) \, T(p, q, \theta) - \log(\int \int \mathbb{P}_{\mathcal{P}}(p)\mathbb{P}_{\mathcal{Q}}(q)e^{T(p,q,\theta)})$. To avoid computing the integrals, we leverage Monte-Carlo integration to calculate the estimation:

$$I(\mathcal{P}, \mathcal{Q}) = \frac{1}{n} \sum_{i=1}^{n} T(p, q, \theta) - \log(\frac{1}{n} \sum_{i=1}^{n} e^{T(p,q',\theta)}) \tag{7}$$

where $(p, q)$ are sampled from the joint distribution, $q'$ is sampled from the marginal distribution $\mathbb{P}_{\mathcal{Q}}$, $n$ is number of training examples, and $T(p, q, \theta)$ is the neural network parameteralized by $\theta$ to estimate the mutual information between $\mathcal{P}$ and $\mathcal{Q}$, we refer the reader to MINE [47] for more details.

### 3.2 Deep Domain Embedding

Our DOMAIN2VEC model learns a domain to vector mapping $\Phi : \hat{\mathcal{D}} \to V$ by jointly embeds the Gram matrix and *domain-specific* features. Specifically, given a domain $\hat{\mathcal{D}} = \{x_j, y_j\}_{j=1}^{n_i}$, we compute the disentangled features for all the training examples of $\hat{\mathcal{D}}$. The *prototype* of domain $\hat{\mathcal{D}}$ is defined as: $P_{\hat{\mathcal{D}}} = \frac{1}{n_i} \sum f_{ds}^j$, denoting the average of the *domain-specific* features of the examples in $\hat{\mathcal{D}}$. In addition, we compute the Gram matrix of the activations of the hidden convolutional layers in the feature extractor $G$. The Gram matrix build a style representation that computes the correlations between different filter responses. The feature correlations are given by the Gram matrix $\mathcal{G} \in \mathcal{R}^{n \times n}$, where $\mathcal{G}_{ij}$ is the inner product between the vectorised feature map between $i$ and $j$:

$$\mathcal{G}_{ij} = \sum_k F_{ik}F_{jk} \tag{8}$$

where $F$ is the vectorised feature map of the hidden convolutional layers. Since the full Gram matrix is prohibitively large for deep features we make an approximation by only leveraging the entries in the subdiagonal, main diagonal, and superdiagonal of the Gram matrix $\mathcal{G}$. We utilize the concatenation of the *prototype* $P_{\hat{\mathcal{D}}}$ and the diagonals of the $\mathcal{G}$ as the final embedding of domain $\hat{\mathcal{D}}$.

**Eliminating Sparsity.** The *domain-specific* feature and the Gram matrix are high sparsity data, which hampers the effectiveness of our DOMAIN2VEC model. To address this issue, we leverage dimensionality reduction technique to decrease the dimensionality. Empirically, we start by using PCA to reduce the dimenionality of the data to a specific length. Then we leverage Stochastic Neighbor Embedding [48] to reduce the dimensionality to our desired one.

**Optimization.** Our model is trained in an end-to-end fashion. We train the feature extractor $G$, category and domain disentanglement component $D$, MINE and the reconstructor $R$ iteratively with Stochastic Gradient Descent [49] or Adam [50] optimizer. The overall optimization objective is:

$$\mathcal{L} = w_1 \mathcal{L}^{class} + w_2 \mathcal{L}^{domain} + w_3 \mathcal{L}_{rec} + w_4 \mathcal{I}(f_{ds}, f_{cs}) \tag{9}$$

where $w_1, w_2, w_3, w_4$ are the hyper-parameters, $\mathcal{L}^{class} = \mathcal{L}_{ce}^{class} + \alpha \mathcal{L}_{ent}^{class}$, $\mathcal{L}^{domain} = \mathcal{L}_{ce}^{domain} + \alpha \mathcal{L}_{ent}^{domain}$ denote the category disentanglement loss and domain disentanglement loss.

## 4   Experiments

We test DOMAIN2VEC on two large-scale datasets we created. Our experiments aim to test both qualitative properties of the domain embedding and its performance on multi-source domain adaptation, openset domain adaptation and partial domain adaptation. In the main paper, we only report major results; more implementation details are provided in the Appendix (Table 1).

### 4.1   Dataset

To evaluate the domain-to-vector mapping ability of our DOMAIN2VEC model, a large-scale dataset with multiple domains is desired. Unfortunately, existing UDA benchmarks [16,17,51,52] only contain limited number of domains. These datasets provide limit benchmarking ability for our DOMAIN2VEC model. To address this issue, we collect two datasets for multiple domain embedding and adaptation, *i.e.*, TINYDA and DOMAINBANK.

**TinyDA.** We create our by far the largest MNIST-style cross domain dataset to data, TINYDA. This dataset contains 54 domains and about one million MNIST-style training examples. We generate our TINYDA dataset by blending different foreground shapes over patches randomly extracted from background images. This operation is formally defined for two images $I^1$, $I^2$ as $I_{ijk}^{out} = \|I_{ijk}^1 - I_{ijk}^2\|$, where $i, j$ are the coordinates of a pixel and $k$ is the channel index. The foreground shapes are from MNIST [53], USPS [54], EMNIST [55], KMNIST [56], QMNIST [57], and FashionMNIST [58]. Specifically, the MNIST, USPS, QMNIST contains digit images; EMNIST dataset includes images of MNIST-style English characters; KMNIST dataset is composed of images of Japanese characters; FashionMNIST dataset contains MNIST-style images about fashion. The background images are randomly cropped from CIFAR10 [59] or BSDS500 [60] dataset. We perform three different post-processes to our rendered images: (1) replace the background with black patch, (2) replace the background with white patch, (3) convert the images to grayscale. The three post-processes, together with the original foreground images and the generated color images, form a dataset with five different modes, *i.e.* White Background (*WB*), Black Background (*BB*), GrayScale image (*GS*), Color (*Cr*) image, Original image(*Or*).

**Table 1.** Illustration of TinyDA dataset. More images are in supplementary material.

| FG/Mode | Black BG | White BG | Color | Grayscale | Original |
|---|---|---|---|---|---|
| MNIST | | | | | |
| USPS | | | | | |
| FashionMNIST | | | | | |

**DomainBank**[2]**.** To evaluate our Domain2Vec model on state-of-the-art computer vision datasets, we collect a large-scale benchmark, named Domain-Bank. The images of DomainBank dataset are sampled from 56 existing popular computer vision datasets such as COCO [61], CALTECH-256 [62], PASCAL [63], VisDA [52], DomainNet [16], *etc.* We choose the dataset with different image modalities, illuminations, camera perspectives *etc.* to increase the diversity of the domains. In total, we collect 339,772 images with image-level and domain-level annotations. Different from TinyDA, the categories of different domains in DomainBank are not identical. This property makes DomainBank a good testbed for Openset Domain Adaptation [64,65] and Partial Domain Adaptation [66].

### 4.2 Experiments on TinyDA

**Domain Embedding Results.** We apply our devised Domain2Vec model to TinyDA dataset to achieve deep domain embedding. The results are shown in Fig. 2. Specifically, the domain knowledge graph shows the relations between different domains. The nodes in the graph show the deep domain embedding. For each domain, we connect it with five closest neighboring domains with an edge weighted by their domain distance. The size and the color of the nodes are correlated with the number of training images in that domain and the degree of that domain, respectively. To validate that the domain distance computed with our Domain2Vec is negatively correlated with the cross-domain performance, we conduct extensive experiments to calculate the cross-domain results on TinyDA dataset, as shown in Table 2. We split the cross-domain results in three sub-tables for Japanese characters (KMNIST), English characters (EMNIST) and fashion items (FashionMNIST), respectively. In each sub-table, the column-wise domains are selected as the source domain and the row-wise domains are selected as the target domain.

From the experimental results shown in Table 2, we make several interesting observations. (i) For each sub-table, the performances of training and testing on the same domain (gray background) are better than cross-domain performance, except a few outliers (pink background, mainly between MNIST, USPS,

---
[2] In this dataset, the *domain* is defined by datasets. The data from different genres or times typically have different underlying distributions.

**Table 2.** Experimental results on TINYDA. The column-wise domains are source domains, the row-wise domains are the target domain.

KMNIST

| | | BSDS | | | | CIFAR | | | |
|---|---|---|---|---|---|---|---|---|---|
| | | WB | BB | Or | Cr | GS | WB | BB | Cr | GS |
| BSDS | WB | 89.8 | 13.3 | 13.4 | 16.6 | 16.4 | 88.0 | 12.6 | 14.9 | 14.6 |
| | BB | 12.5 | 94.1 | 94.3 | 32.9 | 30.4 | 11.5 | 92.6 | 23.3 | 22.2 |
| | Or | 8.4 | 56.9 | 95.4 | 35.2 | 32.9 | 9.3 | 62.6 | 24.7 | 23.2 |
| | Cr | 73.4 | 68.6 | 89.8 | 84.2 | 69.1 | 66.2 | 66.5 | 70.9 | 56.5 |
| | GS | 72.7 | 64.0 | 87.9 | 67.4 | 74.1 | 68.7 | 66.7 | 55.1 | 59.4 |
| CIFAR | WB | 83.8 | 17.0 | 16.2 | 18.6 | 18.9 | 81.2 | 15.1 | 18.6 | 16.0 |
| | BB | 13.1 | 90.0 | 91.2 | 26.0 | 24.1 | 11.8 | 88.8 | 18.8 | 17.9 |
| | Cr | 66.5 | 65.8 | 85.3 | 81.4 | 68.8 | 61.6 | 65.7 | 76.1 | 65.7 |
| | GS | 64.5 | 60.5 | 85.8 | 58.0 | 70.7 | 60.8 | 63.4 | 56.7 | 66.8 |

EMNIST

| | | BSDS | | | | CIFAR | | | |
|---|---|---|---|---|---|---|---|---|---|
| | | WB | BB | Or | Cr | GS | WB | BB | Cr | GS |
| BSDS | WB | 86.6 | 2.9 | 2.8 | 8.1 | 8.6 | 83.2 | 5.1 | 6.9 | 7.5 |
| | BB | 3.6 | 87.3 | 88.0 | 23.4 | 18.1 | 4.2 | 82.8 | 14.9 | 13.4 |
| | Or | 12.0 | 31.1 | 91.3 | 33.4 | 32.2 | 11.1 | 33.6 | 21.1 | 21.2 |
| | Cr | 59.1 | 47.0 | 85.8 | 80.0 | 60.8 | 47.9 | 42.0 | 60.0 | 42.7 |
| | GS | 59.4 | 46.7 | 82.5 | 58.1 | 65.9 | 52.2 | 46.8 | 41.2 | 44.6 |
| CIFAR | WB | 87.8 | 13.9 | 4.5 | 15.3 | 16.7 | 86.1 | 12.2 | 13.0 | 13.6 |
| | BB | 2.1 | 85.4 | 87.1 | 16.1 | 17.1 | 1.9 | 82.7 | 12.0 | 12.5 |
| | Cr | 58.2 | 48.9 | 83.5 | 76.1 | 59.6 | 48.4 | 44.7 | 67.8 | 55.0 |
| | GS | 46.6 | 46.5 | 81.1 | 48.1 | 63.2 | 43.8 | 48.8 | 45.3 | 57.4 |

FashionMNIST

| | | BSDS | | | | CIFAR | | | |
|---|---|---|---|---|---|---|---|---|---|
| | | WB | BB | Or | Cr | GS | WB | BB | Cr | GS |
| BSDS | WB | 83.5 | 16.9 | 29.0 | 27.0 | 25.6 | 80.7 | 16.7 | 27.3 | 24.9 |
| | BB | 23.6 | 84.5 | 85.4 | 38.1 | 36.6 | 21.1 | 81.7 | 28.9 | 28.9 |
| | Or | 15.1 | 53.6 | 87.0 | 33.0 | 33.2 | 14.8 | 52.2 | 23.8 | 25.1 |
| | Cr | 75.6 | 68.6 | 85.2 | 81.6 | 74.4 | 69.9 | 54.7 | 75.6 | 71.3 |
| | GS | 72.3 | 66.3 | 83.5 | 71.5 | 77.6 | 70.2 | 61.9 | 69.5 | 73.2 |
| CIFAR | WB | 82.9 | 18.1 | 27.3 | 26.5 | 26.6 | 81.6 | 17.0 | 29.6 | 29.3 |
| | BB | 21.1 | 84.8 | 86.2 | 29.1 | 28.4 | 18.1 | 82.3 | 22.1 | 23.3 |
| | Cr | 75.1 | 67.9 | 85.1 | 82.2 | 78.6 | 72.4 | 62.4 | 78.6 | 76.6 |
| | GS | 67.9 | 61.8 | 82.2 | 65.2 | 77.0 | 66.3 | 58.0 | 68.7 | 76.3 |

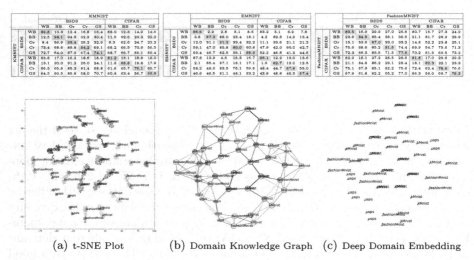

(a) t-SNE Plot     (b) Domain Knowledge Graph     (c) Deep Domain Embedding

**Fig. 2.** Deep domain embedding results of our DOMAIN2VEC model on TINYDA dataset: (**a**) t-SNE plot of the embedding result (color indicates different domain); (**b**) Domain knowledge graph. The size and color of the circles indicate the number of training examples and the degree of that domain, respectively. The width of the edge shows the domain distance between two domains. (**c**) The final deep domain embedding of our DOMAIN2VEC model. (Best viewed in color. Zoom in to see details.) (Color figure online)

and QMNIST). (**ii**) The cross-domain performance is negatively correlated with the domain distance (illustrated in Fig. 2(b)). We leverage Pearson correlation coefficient (PCC) [67] to quantitatively demonstrate the negative correlation. The PCC can be computed as $\rho_{xy} = \frac{\sum_i (x_i - \bar{x})(y_i - \bar{y})}{\sqrt{\sum_i (x_i - \bar{x})^2}\sqrt{\sum_i (y_i - \bar{y})^2}}$. We set the cross-domain performance and the domain distance as two variables. The PCC that we compute for our case is $-0.774$, which demonstrates that our DOMAIN2VEC successfully encodes the natural domain distance.

**Multi-source Domain Adaptation on TINYDA.** Our TINYDA dataset contains 54 domains. 'In our experiments, we consider the MSDA between digit datasets, *i.e.* MNIST, USPS, and QMNIST dataset, resulting in six MSDA settings. We choose the "grayscale" (*GS*) with CIFAR10 background as the target domain. For the source domains, we remove the two "grayscale" domains and leverage the remaining seven domains as the source domain.

State-of-the-art multi-source domain adaptation algorithms tackle MSDA task by adversarial alignment [38] or matching the moments of the domains [16]. However, these models neglect the effect of domain distance. We incorporate our DOMAIN2VEC model to the previous work [16,38], and devise two mod-

**Table 3.** MSDA results on the TINYDA dataset. Our model DOMAIN2VEC-$\alpha$ and DOMAIN2VEC-$\beta$ achieves **48.5%** and **49.7%** accuracy, outperforming baselines.)

| Standards | Models | MNIST→USPS | MNIST→QMNIST | USPS→MNIST | USPS→QMNIST | QMNIST→MNIST | QMNIST→USPS | Avg |
|---|---|---|---|---|---|---|---|---|
| Single best | Source Only | 17.7±0.21 | 83.4±0.55 | 16.4±0.32 | 16.3±0.25 | 83.1±0.32 | 20.2±0.31 | 39.5±0.32 |
| | DAN [4] | 21.4±0.27 | 87.1±0.64 | 19.7±0.37 | 19.9±0.34 | 85.7±0.34 | 21.8±0.37 | 42.6±0.39 |
| | RTN [68] | 18.0±0.28 | 85.0±0.58 | 18.8±0.37 | 20.0±0.26 | 84.2±0.42 | 21.3±0.34 | 41.2±0.38 |
| | JAN [2] | 21.7±0.27 | 87.6±0.64 | 19.4±0.42 | 18.0±0.29 | 87.2±0.36 | 25.1±0.33 | 43.2±0.39 |
| | DANN [12] | 21.2±0.25 | 86.1±0.55 | 20.1±0.31 | 19.4±0.24 | 86.6±0.38 | 24.0±0.34 | 42.9±0.34 |
| | ADDA [11] | 20.3±0.31 | 88.1±0.63 | 18.3±0.46 | 21.4±0.38 | 88.5±0.39 | 25.9±0.43 | 43.8±0.43 |
| | SE [29] | 13.6±0.42 | 78.1±0.87 | 10.7±0.62 | 11.8±0.50 | 80.1±0.64 | 17.0±0.55 | 35.2±0.60 |
| | MCD [13] | 23.8±0.33 | 89.0±0.61 | 22.3±0.36 | 19.6±0.26 | 86.7±0.36 | 22.6±0.41 | 44.0±0.39 |
| Source combine | Source Only | 20.2±0.23 | 85.7±0.59 | 19.2±0.42 | 20.5±0.37 | 85.1±0.25 | 19.2±0.40 | 41.6±0.38 |
| | DAN [4] | 19.8±0.30 | 85.4±0.64 | 22.4±0.43 | 21.9±0.49 | 88.0±0.33 | 19.2±0.48 | 42.8±0.45 |
| | RTN [68] | 22.9±0.27 | 88.2±0.72 | 19.9±0.54 | 23.2±0.49 | 88.1±0.29 | 20.6±0.53 | 43.8±0.47 |
| | JAN [2] | 21.8±0.29 | 88.1±0.59 | 22.2±0.50 | 23.9±0.45 | 89.5±0.36 | 22.3±0.46 | 44.6±0.44 |
| | DANN [12] | 22.3±0.31 | 87.1±0.65 | 22.1±0.47 | 21.0±0.46 | 84.7±0.35 | 19.3±0.43 | 42.8±0.45 |
| | ADDA [11] | 25.2±0.24 | 87.9±0.61 | 20.5±0.46 | 22.0±0.36 | 88.1±0.25 | 20.7±0.49 | 44.1±0.40 |
| | SE [29] | 19.4±0.28 | 82.8±0.68 | 19.3±0.45 | 19.3±0.45 | 84.3±0.34 | 18.9±0.48 | 40.7±0.45 |
| | MCD [13] | 23.20±0.31 | 91.2±0.68 | 21.6±0.46 | 25.8±0.37 | 86.9±0.33 | 23.0±0.42 | 45.3±0.43 |
| Multi-source | M³SDA [16] | 25.5±0.26 | 91.6±0.63 | 22.2±0.43 | 25.8±0.43 | 90.7±0.30 | 24.8±0.41 | 46.8±0.41 |
| | DCTN [38] | 25.5±0.28 | 93.10±0.7 | 22.9±0.41 | 29.5±0.47 | 91.2±0.29 | 26.5±0.48 | 48.1±0.44 |
| | **Domain2Vec-$\alpha$** | 27.8±0.27 | 94.3±0.64 | 24.3±0.52 | 27.1±0.39 | 89.2±0.26 | 28.1±0.41 | 48.5±0.42 |
| | **Domain2Vec-$\beta$** | 28.2±0.31 | 94.5±0.63 | 27.6±0.41 | 29.3±0.39 | 91.5±0.26 | 27.2±0.42 | 49.7±0.40 |

els, DOMAIN2VEC-$\alpha$ and DOMAIN2VEC-$\beta$. For DOMAIN2VEC-$\alpha$, we follow the implementation of Peng et al. [16], and separately align each source domain with the target by matching the moments of their feature distributions. For DOMAIN2VEC-$\beta$, we follow the framework and hyper-parameters of Xu et al. [38], and separately align each source domain with the target using adversarial learning. For both frameworks, we weight each source-target alignment pairs by the distance computed using our DOMAIN2VEC model. Following [38], we compare MSDA results with two other evaluation standards: (i) *single best*, reporting the single best-preforming source transfer result on the test set, and (ii) *source combine*, combining the source domains to a single domain and performing traditional single-source single target adaptation. The high-level motivations of these two evaluation schema are: the first metric evaluates whether MSDA can boost the best single source UDA results; the second standard measures whether MSDA can outperform the trivial baseline which combines the multiple source domains as a single domain.

For both *single best* and *source combine* experiment setting, we compare with following methods: Deep Alignment Network (**DAN**) [4], Joint Adaptation Network (**JAN**) [2], Domain Adversarial Neural Network (**DANN**) [12], Residual Transfer Network (**RTN**) [68], Adversarial Deep Domain Adaptation (**ADDA**) [11], Maximum Classifier Discrepancy (**MCD**) [13], and Self-Ensembling (**SE**) [29]. For multi-source domain adaptation, we compare to Deep Cocktail Network (**DCTN**) [38] and Moment Matching for Multi-source Domain Adaptation (**M³SDA**) [16].

The experimental results are shown in Table 3. The DOMAIN2VEC-$\alpha$ and DOMAIN2VEC-$\beta$ achieve an **48.5%** and **49.7%** average accuracy, outperforming other baselines. The results demonstrate that our models outperform the *single best* UDA results, the *combine source* results, and can boost the multi-source baselines. We argue that the performance improvement is due to the good domain embedding of our DOMAIN2VEC model.

**Table 4.** Openset domain adaption on the DOMAINBANK dataset.

| Target | VisDA | Ytb BBox | PASCAL | COCO | Average |
|---|---|---|---|---|---|
| Source only | $53.4 \pm 0.4$ | $67.2 \pm 0.4$ | $74.8 \pm 0.4$ | $80.4 \pm 0.3$ | 68.9 |
| Openset SVM [69] | $53.9 \pm 0.5$ | $68.6 \pm 0.4$ | $77.7 \pm 0.4$ | $82.1 \pm 0.4$ | 70.6 |
| AutoDIAL | $54.2 \pm 0.5$ | $68.1 \pm 0.5$ | $75.9 \pm 0.4$ | $83.4 \pm 0.4$ | 70.4 |
| AODA [70] | $56.4 \pm 0.5$ | $69.7 \pm 0.4$ | $76.7 \pm 0.4$ | $82.3 \pm 0.4$ | 71.3 |
| DOMAIN2VEC | $56.6 \pm 0.4$ | $70.6 \pm 0.4$ | $81.3 \pm 0.4$ | $86.8 \pm 0.4$ | **73.8** |

### 4.3   Experiments on DomainBank

**Domain Embedding Results.** Similar to the experiments for TINYDA dataset, we apply our devised DOMAIN2VEC model to DOMAINBANK dataset. The results are shown in Fig. 3. Since our DOMAINBANK dataset is collected from multiple existing computer vision dataset, the categories of different domains in DOMAIN-BANK are not identical. It is not feasible to compute the cross-domain performance directly like TINYDA. However, we can still make the following interesting observations: (i) Domains with similar contents tend to form a cluster. For example, the domains containing buildings ($\hat{\mathcal{D}}^{building}$) are close to each other in terms of the domain distance. The domains containing faces share the same property. (ii) The domains which contains artistic images are scattered in the exterior side of the embedding and are distinct from the domains which contains images in the wild. For example, the "cartoon", "syn", "quickdraw", "sketch", "logo" domains are distributed in the exterior side of the embedding space.

**Openset Domain Adaptation on DOMAINBANK.** Open-set domain adaptation (ODA) considers classification when the target domain contains categories unknown (unlabelled) in the source domain. Our DOMAINBANK dataset provides a good testbed for openset domain as the categories of different domains are not identical. Since DOMAINBANK contains 56 domains, it is infeasible to explore all the (source, target) domain combinations. Instead, we demo our model on the following four transfer setting: DomainNet [16] → VisDA [52], Domain-Net → Youtube BBox [71], DomainNet → PASCAL [63], DomainNet → COCO. Since DomainNet [16] contains the largest number of domains, it is best fit as a source domain for our openset adaptation setting. The experimental results are shown in Table 4. Our model achieves **73.8%** accuracy, outperforming the compared baselines.

**Partial Domain Adaptation on DOMAINBANK.** In partial domain adaptation, the source domain label space is a superset of the target domain label space. Specifically, our model utilizes the idea of PADA [66], which trains a partial adversarial alignment network to tackle the partial domain adaptation task. We compute the domain distance between the sub-domains in the source training data (DomainNet) and apply the domain distance as weight in the  partial

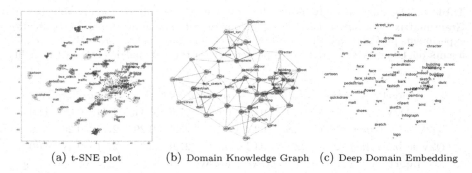

(a) t-SNE plot        (b) Domain Knowledge Graph    (c) Deep Domain Embedding

**Fig. 3.** Domain embedding results of our DOMAIN2VEC model on DOMAIN-BANK dataset.

adversarial alignment process. We consider the following four partial domain adaptation setting: DomainNet [16] → VisDA [52], DomainNet → Youtube BBox [71], DomainNet → PASCAL [63], DomainNet → COCO. The experimental results are shown in Table 5. Our model achieves **65.5%** accuracy, outperforming the compared baselines. The results demonstrate that our model can boost the performance in partial domain adaptation setting.

## 4.4 Ablation Study

Our model is composed of multiple component. To demonstrate the effectiveness of each component, we perform the ablation study analysis. Table 6 shows the ablation results on TINYDA dataset. We observe that the performance drops in most of the experiments when Mutual information minimization and Gram matrix information are **not** applied. The experimental results demonstrate the effectiveness of the mutual information minimization and Gram matrix information.

**Table 5.** Partial domain adaption on the DOMAINBANK dataset.

| Target | VisDA | Ytb BBox | PASCAL | COCO | Average |
|---|---|---|---|---|---|
| Source only | $34.5 \pm 0.5$ | $74.3 \pm 0.4$ | $68.2 \pm 0.3$ | $76.4 \pm 0.2$ | 63.3 |
| AdaBN | $35.1 \pm 0.5$ | $75.6 \pm 0.5$ | $68.2 \pm 0.4$ | $78.1 \pm 0.4$ | 64.2 |
| AutoDIAL [72] | $35.2 \pm 0.6$ | $74.0 \pm 0.4$ | $68.5 \pm 0.4$ | $77.6 \pm 0.4$ | 63.8 |
| PADA [66] | $34.2 \pm 0.6$ | $76.8 \pm 0.4$ | $69.7 \pm 0.3$ | $77.7 \pm 0.4$ | 64.6 |
| DOMAIN2VEC | $36.6 \pm 0.5$ | $76.8 \pm 0.4$ | $70.0 \pm 0.3$ | $78.8 \pm 0.4$ | **65.5** |

**Table 6.** The ablation study results show that the Mutual information minimizing and Gram matrix information is essential for our model. The above table shows ablation experiments performed on the TINYDA dataset. The table below shows ablation experiments on DOMAINBANK dataset (openset DA on the left, partial DA on the right).

| target | $MNIST \rightarrow USPS$ | $MNIST \rightarrow QMNIST$ | $USPS \rightarrow MNIST$ | $USPS \rightarrow QMNIST$ | Avg |
|---|---|---|---|---|---|
| D2V | $28.2 \pm 0.31$ | $94.5 \pm 0.63$ | $27.6 \pm 0.41$ | $29.3 \pm 0.39$ | 44.9 |
| D2V *w/o. Gram* | $28.5 \pm 0.29$ | $92.4 \pm 0.56$ | $25.5 \pm 0.29$ | $27.7 \pm 0.26$ | 43.5 |
| D2V *w/o. Mutual* | $26.7 \pm 0.27$ | $94.1 \pm 0.49$ | $27.9 \pm 0.35$ | $27.4 \pm 0.41$ | 44.0 |

| target | VisDA | Ytb BBox | PASCAL | COCO | Avg | VisDA | Ytb BBox | PASCAL | COCO | Avg |
|---|---|---|---|---|---|---|---|---|---|---|
| D2V | 56.6 | 70.6 | 81.3 | 86.8 | 73.8 | 36.6 | 76.8 | 70.0 | 78.8 | 65.5 |
| D2V *w/o. Gram* | 54.5 | 68.4 | 80.5 | 85.4 | 72.2 | 34.5 | 77.1 | 65.4 | 77.9 | 63.7 |
| D2V *w/o. Mutual* | 55.2 | 69.3 | 81.4 | 85.7 | 72.9 | 35.4 | 73.5 | 67.8 | 77.5 | 63.5 |

## 5   Conclusion

In this paper, we have proposed a novel learning paradigm to explore the natural relations between different domains. We introduced the deep domain embedding task and proposed DOMAIN2VEC to achieve domain-to-vector mapping with joint learning of Gram Matrix of the latent representations and feature disentanglement. We have collected and evaluated two state-of-the-art domain adaptation datasets, TINYDA and DOMAINBANK. These two datasets are challenging due to the presence of notable domain gaps and a large number of domains. Extensive experiments has been conducted, both qualitatively and quantitatively, on the two benchmarks we collected to demonstrate the effectiveness of our proposed model. We also show that our model can facilitate multi-source domain adaptation, openset domain adaptation and partial domain adaptation. We hope the learning schema we proposed and the benchmarks we collected will be beneficial for the future domain adaptation research.

**Acknowledgements.** We thank the anonymous reviewers for their comments and suggestions. This work was partially supported by NSF and Honda Research Institute.

## References

1. Gretton, A., Smola, A.J., Huang, J., Schmittfull, M., Borgwardt, K.M.: Covariate shift by kernel mean matching. In: Dataset Shift in Machine Learning. MIT Press (2009)
2. Long, M., Zhu, H., Wang, J., Jordan, M.I.: Deep transfer learning with joint adaptation networks. In: Proceedings of the 34th International Conference on Machine Learning, ICML 2017, Sydney, NSW, Australia, 6–11 August 2017, pp. 2208–2217 (2017)
3. Tzeng, E., Hoffman, J., Zhang, N., Saenko, K., Darrell, T.: Deep domain confusion: maximizing for domain invariance. arXiv preprint arXiv:1412.3474 (2014)

4. Long, M., Cao, Y., Wang, J., Jordan, M.: Learning transferable features with deep adaptation networks. In: Bach, F., Blei, D. (eds.) Proceedings of the 32nd International Conference on Machine Learning. Volume 37 of Proceedings of Machine Learning Research, PMLR, Lille, France, 07–09 July 2015, pp. 97–105 (2015)
5. Sun, B., Feng, J., Saenko, K.: Return of frustratingly easy domain adaptation. In: AAAI, vol. 6, p. 8 (2016)
6. Peng, X., Saenko, K.: Synthetic to real adaptation with generative correlation alignment networks. In: 2018 IEEE Winter Conference on Applications of Computer Vision, WACV 2018, Lake Tahoe, NV, USA, 12–15 March 2018, pp. 1982–1991 (2018)
7. Zellinger, W., Grubinger, T., Lughofer, E., Natschläger, T., Saminger-Platz, S.: Central moment discrepancy (CMD) for domain-invariant representation learning. CoRR abs/1702.08811 (2017)
8. Zhu, J.Y., Park, T., Isola, P., Efros, A.A.: Unpaired image-to-image translation using cycle-consistent adversarial networks. In: 2017 IEEE International Conference on Computer Vision (ICCV) (2017)
9. Hoffman, J., et al.: CyCADA: cycle-consistent adversarial domain adaptation. In: Dy, J., Krause, A. (eds.) Proceedings of the 35th International Conference on Machine Learning. Volume 80 of Proceedings of Machine Learning Research, PMLR, 10–15 July 2018, pp. 1989–1998. Stockholmsmässan, Stockholm (2018)
10. Liu, M.Y., Breuel, T., Kautz, J.: Unsupervised image-to-image translation networks. In: Advances in Neural Information Processing Systems, pp. 700–708 (2017)
11. Tzeng, E., Hoffman, J., Saenko, K., Darrell, T.: Adversarial discriminative domain adaptation. In: Computer Vision and Pattern Recognition (CVPR), vol. 1, p. 4 (2017)
12. Ganin, Y., Lempitsky, V.: Unsupervised domain adaptation by backpropagation. In: Bach, F., Blei, D. (eds.) Proceedings of the 32nd International Conference on Machine Learning. Volume 37 of Proceedings of Machine Learning Research, PMLR, Lille, France, 07–09 July 2015, pp. 1180–1189 (2015)
13. Saito, K., Watanabe, K., Ushiku, Y., Harada, T.: Maximum classifier discrepancy for unsupervised domain adaptation. In: The IEEE Conference on Computer Vision and Pattern Recognition (CVPR), June 2018
14. Gatys, L.A., Ecker, A.S., Bethge, M.: A neural algorithm of artistic style. arXiv preprint arXiv:1508.06576 (2015)
15. Peng, X., Zijun, H., Sun, X., Saenkp, K.: Domain agnostic learning with disentangled representations. arXiv preprint arXiv:1904.12347 (2019)
16. Peng, X., Bai, Q., Xia, X., Huang, Z., Saenko, K., Wang, B.: Moment matching for multi-source domain adaptation. In: Proceedings of the IEEE International Conference on Computer Vision, pp. 1406–1415 (2019)
17. Saenko, K., Kulis, B., Fritz, M., Darrell, T.: Adapting visual category models to new domains. In: Daniilidis, K., Maragos, P., Paragios, N. (eds.) ECCV 2010. LNCS, vol. 6314, pp. 213–226. Springer, Heidelberg (2010). https://doi.org/10.1007/978-3-642-15561-1_16
18. Pennington, J., Socher, R., Manning, C.: GloVe: global vectors for word representation. In: Proceedings of the 2014 Conference on Empirical Methods in Natural Language Processing (EMNLP), pp. 1532–1543 (2014)
19. Donahue, J., et al.: DeCAF: a deep convolutional activation feature for generic visual recognition. In: International Conference on Machine Learning, pp. 647–655 (2014)

20. Krizhevsky, A., Sutskever, I., Hinton, G.E.: ImageNet classification with deep convolutional neural networks. In: Advances in Neural Information Processing Systems, pp. 1097–1105 (2012)
21. Simonyan, K., Zisserman, A.: Very deep convolutional networks for large-scale image recognition. CoRR abs/1409.1556 (2014)
22. He, K., Zhang, X., Ren, S., Sun, J.: Deep residual learning for image recognition. In: Proceedings of the IEEE Conference on Computer Vision and Pattern Recognition, pp. 770–778 (2016)
23. Xie, S., Girshick, R., Dollár, P., Tu, Z., He, K.: Aggregated residual transformations for deep neural networks. In: 2017 IEEE Conference on Computer Vision and Pattern Recognition (CVPR), pp. 5987–5995. IEEE (2017)
24. Huang, G., Liu, Z., Van Der Maaten, L., Weinberger, K.Q.: Densely connected convolutional networks. In: Proceedings of the IEEE Conference on Computer Vision and Pattern Recognition, pp. 4700–4708 (2017)
25. Achille, A., et al.: Task2Vec: task embedding for meta-learning. In: Proceedings of the IEEE International Conference on Computer Vision, pp. 6430–6439 (2019)
26. Deshmukh, A.A., Bansal, A., Rastogi, A.: Domain2Vec: deep domain generalization. arXiv preprint arXiv:1807.02919 (2018)
27. Ren, S., He, K., Girshick, R., Sun, J.: Faster R-CNN: towards real-time object detection with region proposal networks. In: Advances in Neural Information Processing Systems (NIPS) (2015)
28. He, K., Gkioxari, G., Dollár, P., Girshick, R.: Mask R-CNN. In: 2017 IEEE International Conference on Computer Vision (ICCV), pp. 2980–2988. IEEE (2017)
29. French, G., Mackiewicz, M., Fisher, M.: Self-ensembling for visual domain adaptation. In: International Conference on Learning Representations (2018)
30. Ghifary, M., Kleijn, W.B., Zhang, M.: Domain adaptive neural networks for object recognition. In: Pham, D.-N., Park, S.-B. (eds.) PRICAI 2014. LNCS (LNAI), vol. 8862, pp. 898–904. Springer, Cham (2014). https://doi.org/10.1007/978-3-319-13560-1_76
31. Liu, M.Y., Tuzel, O.: Coupled generative adversarial networks. In: Advances in Neural Information Processing Systems, pp. 469–477 (2016)
32. Liu, A.H., Liu, Y., Yeh, Y., Wang, Y.F.: A unified feature disentangler for multi-domain image translation and manipulation. CoRR abs/1809.01361 (2018)
33. Yi, Z., Zhang, H.R., Tan, P., Gong, M.: DualGAN: unsupervised dual learning for image-to-image translation. In: ICCV, pp. 2868–2876 (2017)
34. Kim, T., Cha, M., Kim, H., Lee, J.K., Kim, J.: Learning to discover cross-domain relations with generative adversarial networks. In: Precup, D., Teh, Y.W. (eds.) Proceedings of the 34th International Conference on Machine Learning. Volume 70 of Proceedings of Machine Learning Research, PMLR, 06–11 August 2017, pp. 1857–1865. International Convention Centre, Sydney (2017)
35. Ben-David, S., Blitzer, J., Crammer, K., Kulesza, A., Pereira, F., Vaughan, J.W.: A theory of learning from different domains. Mach. Learn. **79**(1–2), 151–175 (2010). https://doi.org/10.1007/s10994-009-5152-4
36. Mansour, Y., Mohri, M., Rostamizadeh, A.: Domain adaptation with multiple sources. In: Koller, D., Schuurmans, D., Bengio, Y., Bottou, L. (eds.) Advances in Neural Information Processing Systems, vol. 21, pp. 1041–1048. Curran Associates, Inc. (2009)
37. Crammer, K., Kearns, M., Wortman, J.: Learning from multiple sources. J. Mach. Learn. Res. **9**(Aug), 1757–1774 (2008)

38. Xu, R., Chen, Z., Zuo, W., Yan, J., Lin, L.: Deep cocktail network: multi-source unsupervised domain adaptation with category shift. In: Proceedings of the IEEE Conference on Computer Vision and Pattern Recognition, pp. 3964–3973 (2018)
39. Duan, L., Xu, D., Chang, S.F.: Exploiting web images for event recognition in consumer videos: a multiple source domain adaptation approach. In: 2012 IEEE Conference on Computer Vision and Pattern Recognition (CVPR), pp. 1338–1345. IEEE (2012)
40. Zhuang, F., Cheng, X., Luo, P., Pan, S.J., He, Q.: Supervised representation learning: transfer learning with deep autoencoders. In: IJCAI, pp. 4119–4125 (2015)
41. Mathieu, M.F., Zhao, J.J., Zhao, J., Ramesh, A., Sprechmann, P., LeCun, Y.: Disentangling factors of variation in deep representation using adversarial training. In: Advances in Neural Information Processing Systems, pp. 5040–5048 (2016)
42. Makhzani, A., Shlens, J., Jaitly, N., Goodfellow, I., Frey, B.: Adversarial autoencoders. In: ICLR Workshop (2016)
43. Odena, A., Olah, C., Shlens, J.: Conditional image synthesis with auxiliary classifier GANs. In: Precup, D., Teh, Y.W. (eds.) Proceedings of the 34th International Conference on Machine Learning. Volume 70 of Proceedings of Machine Learning Research, PMLR, 06–11 August 2017, pp. 2642–2651. International Convention Centre, Sydney (2017)
44. Goodfellow, I., et al.: Generative adversarial nets. In: Advances in Neural Information Processing Systems, pp. 2672–2680 (2014)
45. Kingma, D.P., Welling, M.: Auto-encoding variational Bayes. arXiv preprint arXiv:1312.6114 (2013)
46. Lee, H.Y., Tseng, H.Y., Huang, J.B., Singh, M., Yang, M.H.: Diverse image-to-image translation via disentangled representations. In: Ferrari, V., Hebert, M., Sminchisescu, C., Weiss, Y. (eds.) ECCV 2018. LNCS, vol. 11205, pp. 36–52. Springer, Cham (2018). https://doi.org/10.1007/978-3-030-01246-5_3
47. Belghazi, M.I., et al.: Mutual information neural estimation. In: Dy, J., Krause, A. (eds.) Proceedings of the 35th International Conference on Machine Learning. Volume 80 of Proceedings of Machine Learning Research, PMLR, 10–15 July 2018, pp. 531–540. Stockholmsmässan, Stockholm (2018)
48. van der Maaten, L., Hinton, G.: Visualizing data using t-SNE. J. Mach. Learn. Res. 9(Nov), 2579–2605 (2008)
49. Kiefer, J., Wolfowitz, J., et al.: Stochastic estimation of the maximum of a regression function. Ann. Math. Stat. 23(3), 462–466 (1952)
50. Kingma, D.P., Ba, J.: Adam: a method for stochastic optimization. arXiv preprint arXiv:1412.6980 (2014)
51. Venkateswara, H., Eusebio, J., Chakraborty, S., Panchanathan, S.: Deep hashing network for unsupervised domain adaptation. In: IEEE Conference on Computer Vision and Pattern Recognition (CVPR) (2017)
52. Peng, X., Usman, B., Kaushik, N., Hoffman, J., Wang, D., Saenko, K.: VisDA: the visual domain adaptation challenge. arXiv preprint arXiv:1710.06924 (2017)
53. LeCun, Y., et al.: Backpropagation applied to handwritten zip code recognition. Neural Comput. 1(4), 541–551 (1989)
54. Hull, J.J.: A database for handwritten text recognition research. IEEE Trans. Pattern Anal. Mach. Intell. 16(5), 550–554 (1994)
55. Cohen, G., Afshar, S., Tapson, J., van Schaik, A.: EMNIST: an extension of MNIST to handwritten letters. arXiv preprint arXiv:1702.05373 (2017)
56. Clanuwat, T., Bober-Irizar, M., Kitamoto, A., Lamb, A., Yamamoto, K., Ha, D.: Deep learning for classical Japanese literature. arXiv preprint arXiv:1812.01718 (2018)

57. Yadav, C., Bottou, L.: Cold case: the lost MNIST digits. arXiv preprint arXiv:1905.10498 (2019)
58. Xiao, H., Rasul, K., Vollgraf, R.: Fashion-MNIST: a novel image dataset for benchmarking machine learning algorithms. arXiv preprint arXiv:1708.07747 (2017)
59. Krizhevsky, A., Hinton, G., et al.: Learning multiple layers of features from tiny images. Technical report, Citeseer (2009)
60. Arbelaez, P., Maire, M., Fowlkes, C., Malik, J.: Contour detection and hierarchical image segmentation. IEEE Trans. Pattern Anal. Mach. Intell. **33**(5), 898–916 (2011)
61. Lin, T.-Y., et al.: Microsoft COCO: common objects in context. In: Fleet, D., Pajdla, T., Schiele, B., Tuytelaars, T. (eds.) ECCV 2014. LNCS, vol. 8693, pp. 740–755. Springer, Cham (2014). https://doi.org/10.1007/978-3-319-10602-1_48
62. Griffin, G., Holub, A., Perona, P.: Caltech-256 object category dataset (2007)
63. Everingham, M., Van Gool, L., Williams, C.K.I., Winn, J., Zisserman, A.: The Pascal visual object classes (VOC) challenge. Int. J. Comput. Vis. **88**(2), 303–338 (2010). https://doi.org/10.1007/s11263-009-0275-4
64. Busto, P.P., Gall, J.: Open set domain adaptation. In: The IEEE International Conference on Computer Vision (ICCV), vol. 1 (2017)
65. Busto, P.P., Iqbal, A., Gall, J.: Open set domain adaptation for image and action recognition. IEEE Trans. Pattern Anal. Mach. Intell. **42**(2), 413–429 (2020)
66. Cao, Z., Ma, L., Long, M., Wang, J.: Partial adversarial domain adaptation. In: Proceedings of the European Conference on Computer Vision (ECCV), pp. 135–150 (2018)
67. Benesty, J., Chen, J., Huang, Y., Cohen, I.: Pearson correlation coefficient. In: Benesty, J., Chen, J., Huang, Y., Cohen, I. (eds.) Noise reduction in speech processing. STSP, vol. 2, pp. 1–4. Springer, Heidelberg (2009). https://doi.org/10.1007/978-3-642-00296-0_5
68. Long, M., Zhu, H., Wang, J., Jordan, M.I.: Unsupervised domain adaptation with residual transfer networks. In: Advances in Neural Information Processing Systems, pp. 136–144 (2016)
69. Jain, L.P., Scheirer, W.J., Boult, T.E.: Multi-class open set recognition using probability of inclusion. In: Fleet, D., Pajdla, T., Schiele, B., Tuytelaars, T. (eds.) ECCV 2014. LNCS, vol. 8691, pp. 393–409. Springer, Cham (2014). https://doi.org/10.1007/978-3-319-10578-9_26
70. Saito, K., Yamamoto, S., Ushiku, Y., Harada, T.: Open set domain adaptation by backpropagation. CoRR abs/1804.10427 (2018)
71. Real, E., Shlens, J., Mazzocchi, S., Pan, X., Vanhoucke, V.: YouTube-BoundingBoxes: a large high-precision human-annotated data set for object detection in video. In: Proceedings of the IEEE Conference on Computer Vision and Pattern Recognition, pp. 5296–5305 (2017)
72. Cariucci, F.M., Porzi, L., Caputo, B., Ricci, E., Bulo, S.R.: AutoDIAL: automatic domain alignment layers. In: 2017 IEEE International Conference on Computer Vision (ICCV), pp. 5077–5085. IEEE (2017)

# Simulating Content Consistent Vehicle Datasets with Attribute Descent

Yue Yao[1], Liang Zheng[1(✉)], Xiaodong Yang[2], Milind Naphade[2],
and Tom Gedeon[1]

[1] Australian National University, Canberra, Australia
{yue.yao,liang.zheng,tom.gedeon}@anu.edu.au
[2] NVIDIA, Santa Clara, USA
yangxd.hust@gmail.com, mnaphade@nvidia.com

**Abstract.** This paper uses a graphic engine to simulate a large amount of training data with free annotations. Between synthetic and real data, there is a two-level domain gap, *i.e.,* content level and appearance level. While the latter has been widely studied, we focus on reducing the content gap in attributes like illumination and viewpoint. To reduce the problem complexity, we choose a smaller and more controllable application, vehicle re-identification (re-ID). We introduce a large-scale synthetic dataset VehicleX. Created in Unity, it contains 1,362 vehicles of various 3D models with fully editable attributes. We propose an attribute descent approach to let VehicleX approximate the attributes in real-world datasets. Specifically, we manipulate each attribute in VehicleX, aiming to minimize the discrepancy between VehicleX and real data in terms of the Fréchet Inception Distance (FID). This attribute descent algorithm allows content domain adaptation (DA) orthogonal to existing appearance DA methods. We mix the optimized VehicleX data with real-world vehicle re-ID datasets, and observe consistent improvement. With the augmented datasets, we report competitive accuracy. We make the dataset, engine and our codes available at https://github.com/yorkeyao/VehicleX.

**Keywords:** Vehicle retrieval · Domain adaptation · Synthetic data

## 1 Introduction

Data synthesis, as can be conveniently performed in graphic engines, provides valuable convenience and flexibility for the computer vision area [25,27,28,30,35]. One can synthesize a large amount of training data under various combinations of environmental factors even from a small number of 3D object/scene models. However, there exists a huge domain gap between synthetic data and real-world data [14,27]. In order to effectively alleviate such a domain gap, it should be addressed from two levels: **content level** and **appearance level** [14]. While much existing work focuses on appearance level domain adaptation [7,11,44],

© Springer Nature Switzerland AG 2020
A. Vedaldi et al. (Eds.): ECCV 2020, LNCS 12351, pp. 775–791, 2020.
https://doi.org/10.1007/978-3-030-58539-6_46

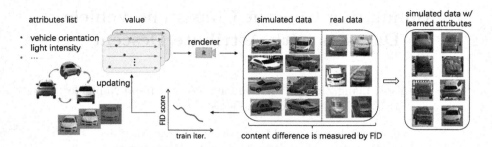

**Fig. 1.** System workflow. (**Left:**) given a list of attributes and their values, we use a renderer (*i.e.*, Unity) for vehicle simulation. We compute the Fréchet Inception Distance (FID) between the synthetic and real vehicles to indicate their distribution difference. By updating the values of attributes using the proposed attribute descent algorithm, we can minimize FID along the training iterations. (**Right:**) we use the learned attributes values that minimize FID to generate synthetic data to be used for re-ID model training.

we focus on the content level, *i.e.*, learning to synthesise data with similar content to the real data, as different computer vision tasks require different image contents.

Our system is designed based on the following considerations. It is expensive to collect large-scale real-world datasets for muti-camera system like re-ID. During annotation, one needs to associate an object across different cameras, which is a difficult and laborious process as objects might exhibit very different appearances in different cameras. In addition, there also has been an increasing concern over privacy and data security, which makes collection of large real datasets difficult [26,40]. On the other hand, we can see that datasets can be very different in their content. Here content means the object layout, illumination, and background in the image. For example, the VehicleID dataset [18] consists mostly of car rears and car fronts, while vehicle viewpoints in the VeRi-776 dataset [20] cover a very diverse range. Though the VehicleID dataset has a large number of identities which is useful for model training, this content-level domain gap might cause a model trained on VehicleID to have poor performance on VeRi. Most existing domain adaptation methods work on the pixel level or the feature level so as to allow the source and target domains to have similar appearance or feature distributions. However, these approaches are not capable of handling content differences, as can often be encountered when training on synthetic data and testing on real data.

Based on above considerations, we aim to utilize flexible 3D graphic engine to 1) scale up the real-world training data without labeling and privacy concerns, and 2) build synthetic data with *less content domain gap* to real-world data. To this end, we make contributions from two aspects. First, we introduce a large-scale synthetic dataset named VehicleX, which lays the foundation of our work. It contains 272 backbone models, with different colored textures, and creates 1,362 different vehicles. Similar to many existing 3D synthetic datasets such as

PersonX [30] and ShapeNet [5], VehicleX has editable attributes and is able to generate a large training set by varying object and environment attributes. Second, based on the VehicleX, we propose an attribute descent method which automatically configures the platform attributes, such that the synthetic data shares similar content distributions with the real data of interest. As shown in Fig. 1, specifically, we manipulate the range of five key attributes closely related to the real dataset content. To measure the distribution discrepancy between the synthetic and real data, we use the FID score and aim to minimize it. In each epoch, we optimize the values of attributes in a specific sequence.

We show the effectiveness of attribute descent by training with VehicleX only and joint training with real-world datasets. The synthetic training data with optimized attributes can improve re-ID accuracy under both settings. Furthermore, under our joint training scheme, with VehicleX data, we achieve competitive re-ID accuracy with the state-of-the-art approaches, validating the effectiveness of learning from synthetic data. A subset of VehicleX has been used in the 4th AICITY challenge [23].[1]

## 2  Related Work

**Vehicle re-identification** has received increasing attention in the past few years, and many effective systems have been proposed [15,33,36,46], generally with specially designed or fine-tuned architectures. In this paper, our baseline system is built with commonly used loss functions [9,32,41] with no bells and whistles. Depending on the camera conditions, location and environment, existing vehicle re-ID datasets usually have their own distinct characteristics. For example, images in the VehicleID [18] are either captured from the car front or the back. In comparison, the VeRi-776 [20] includes a wider range of viewpoints. The recently introduced CityFlow [34] has distinct camera heights and backgrounds. Apart from dataset differences, there also exists huge differences between cameras in a single dataset [45]. For example, a camera filming a crossroad naturally has more vehicles orientation than a camera on a straight road. Because of these characteristics, within a specific dataset, we learn attributes for each camera and simulate that filming environment in a 3D engine. As a result, our proposed data simulation approach will make synthetic data more similar to the real-world in key attributes, and thus can effectively augment re-ID datasets due to its strong ability in content adaptation.

**Appearance(style)-Level Domain Adaptation.** Domain adaptation is often used to reduce the domain gaps between the distributions of two datasets. Till now, the majority of work in this field focuses on discrepancies in image style, such as real vs. synthetic [2] and real vs. sketch [24]. For example, some use the cycle generative adversarial network (CycleGAN) to reduce the style gap between two domains [7,11,29], as well as various constraints being exerted on the generative model such that useful properties are preserved. While these works

---

[1] https://www.aicitychallenge.org/.

**Fig. 2.** The VehicleX engine. (A) An illustration of the rendering platform. We adjust the vehicle orientation, light direction and intensity, camera height, and the distance between the camera and the vehicle. (B) 16 different vehicle identities are shown.

have been shown to be effective in reducing the style domain gap, a fundamental problem remains to be solved, *i.e.*, the content difference.

**Content-level domain adaptation**, to our knowledge, has been discussed by only a few existing works [14,27]. For [27], their main contribution is clever usage of the task loss to guide the domain adaptation procedure. But for the re-ID task, we will search attributes for each camera but get task loss across camera systems. That is, task loss can only be gotten when all camera attributes are set. As a result, it is hard to optimise attributes for a single camera using loss from a cross-camera system. For [14], they use Graph Convolution Neural Network (GCN) to optimise the probability grammar for scene generation (*e.g.*, detection task). Their target is to solve the relationship between multiple objects. But in re-ID settings, we only have one object (car) to optimize. As their method cannot be directly used for the re-ID task, we adopt their advantages and make new contributions. On the one hand, we adopt the idea of Ruiz *et al.* [27] that represents attributes using predefined distributions. We are also motivated by Kar *et al.* [14], who suggest that some GAN evaluation metrics (*e.g.*, KID [4]) are potentially useful to measure content differences. In practice, we propose attribute descent, which does not involve random variables and has easy-to-configure step sizes.

**Learning from 3D Simulation.** Due to low data acquisition costs, learning from 3D world is an attractive way to increase training set scale. But unlike other synthetic data (*e.g.*, images generated by GAN [43]), 3D simulation provides more accurate data labeling, flexibility in content generation and scalability in resolution, as GAN generated image may suffers from these problems. In the 3D simulation area, many applications exist in areas such as semantic segmentation [8,11,38], navigation [16], detection [12,14], object re-identification [30,33], *etc.* Usually, prior knowledge is utilized during data synthesis since we will inevitably need to determine the distribution of attributes in our defined environment. Tremblay *et al.* suggest that attribute randomness in a reasonable range is beneficial [35]. Even if it is random, we need to specify the range of random variables in advance. Our work investigates and learns these attribute distributions for vehicle re-ID.

# 3    VehicleX Engine

We introduce a large-scale synthetic dataset generator named VehicleX that includes three components: (1) vehicles rendered using the graphics engine Unity, (2) a Python API that interacts with the Unity 3D engine, and (3) detailed labels including car type and color.

**Table 1.** Comparison of some real-world and synthetic vehicle re-ID datasets. "Attr" denotes whether the dataset has attribute labels (*e.g.*, orientation). Our identities are different 3D models, thus can potentially render an unlimited number of images under different environment and camera settings. VehicleX is released open source and can be used to generate (possess) an unlimited number of images (cameras).

| Datasets | | #IDs | #Images | #Cameras | # Attr |
|---|---|---|---|---|---|
| Real | VehicleID [18] | 26,328 | 222,629 | 2 | ✗ |
| | CompCar [39] | 4,701 | 136,726 | – | ✗ |
| | VeRi-776 [20] | 776 | 49,357 | 20 | ✓ |
| | CityFlow [34] | 666 | 56,277 | 40 | ✗ |
| Synthetic | PAMTRI [33] | 402 | 41,000 | – | ✓ |
| | VehicleX | 1,362 | ∞ | ∞ | ✓ |

VehicleX has **a diverse range of realistic backbone models and textures**, allowing it to be able to adapt to the variance of real-world datasets. It has 272 backbones that are hand-crafted by professional 3D modelers. The backbones include ten mainstream vehicle types including sedan, SUV, van, hatchback, MPV, pickup, bus, truck, estate, sportscar and RV. Each backbone represents a real-world model. From these backbones, we obtain 1,362 variances (*i.e.*, identities) by adding various colored textures or accessories. A comparison of VehicleX with some existing vehicle re-ID datasets is presented in Table 1. VehicleX is three times larger than the synthetic PAMTRI dataset [33] in identities, and can potentially render an unlimited number of images from various attributes. In experiments, we will show that our VehicleX benefits real-world testing either when used alone or in conjunction with a real-world training set.

In this work, VehicleX can be set to training mode and testing mode. In training mode, VehicleX will render images with black background and these images will be used for attribute descent (see Sect. 4); in comparison, the testing mode uses random images (*e.g.*, from CityFlow [34]) as backgrounds, and generates attribute-adjusted images. In addition, to increase randomness and diversity, the testing mode contains random street objects such as lamp posts, billboards and trash cans. Figure 2 shows the simulation platform, and some sample vehicle identities.

We build the **Unity-Python interface** using the Unity ML-Agents toolkit [13]. It allows Python to modify the attributes of the environment and vehicles, and obtain the rendered images. With this API, given the attributes

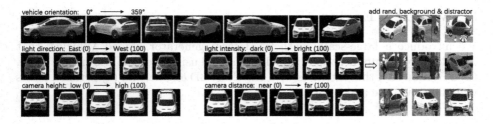

**Fig. 3. (Left:)** Attribute editing. We rotate the vehicle, edit light direction and intensity, or change the camera height and distance. Numbers in the bracket correspond to the attribute values in Unity. **(Right:)** We further add random backgrounds and distractors to the attribute-adjusted vehicles when they are used in the re-ID model.

needed, users can easily obtain rendered images without expert knowledge about Unity. The code of this API is released together with VehicleX.

VehicleX is a large scale public 3D vehicle dataset, with real-world vehicle types. We focus on vehicle re-ID task in this paper but our proposed 3D vehicle models also has potential benefits for many other tasks, such as semantic segmentation, object detection, fine-grained classification, 3D generation or reconstruction. It gives flexibility to computer vision systems to freely edit the content of the object, thus enabling new research in content-level image analysis.

## 4   Proposed Method

### 4.1   Attribute Distribution Modeling

**Important Attributes.** For vehicle re-ID, we consider the following attributes to be potentially influential on the training set simulation and testing accuracy. Figure 3 shows examples of the attribute editing process.

- **Vehicle orientation** is the horizontal viewpoint of a vehicle and takes a value between 0° and 359°. In the real world, this attribute is important because the camera position is usually fixed and vehicles usually move along predefined trajectories. Therefore, the distribute of vehicle orientation of real world dataset is usually multimodal and tend to exhibit certain patterns under a certain camera view.
- **Light direction** simulates daylight as cars are generally presented in outdoor scenes. Here, we assume directional parallel light, and the light direction is modeled from east to west, which is the movement trajectory of the sun.
- **Light intensity** is usually considered a critical factor for re-ID tasks. Factors include glass reflection and shadows will seriously influence the results. We manually defined a reasonable range for intensity from dark to light.
- **Camera height** describes the vertical distance from the ground, and significantly influences viewpoints.

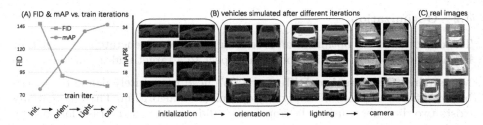

**Fig. 4.** Attribute descent visualization on the VehicleID [18]. (A) The FID-mAP curve through training iterations. The FID successively drops (lower is better) and domain adaptation mAP successively increases (higher is better) during attribute descent. For illustration simplicity, we use "light" to denote light direction and intensity, and use "cam." to denote camera height and distance. (B) We show the synthetic vehicles in each iteration. We initialize the attributes by setting orientation to right, the light intensity to dark, light direction to west, camera height to being equal to the vehicle, and camera distance to medium. The content of those images become more and more similar to (C) the target real images through the optimization procedure.

- **Camera distance** determines the horizontal distance from vehicles. This factor has a strong effect on the vehicle resolution since the resolution of the entire image is predefined as $1920 \times 1080$. Additionally, the distance has slight impacts on viewpoints.

**Distribution Modeling.** We model the aforementioned attributes with single Gaussian distributions or Gaussian Mixture Model (GMM). This modeling strategy is also used in Ruiz *et al.*'s work [27]. We denote the attribute list as: $\mathcal{A} = (a_1, a_2, ..., a_N)$, where $N$ is the number of attributes considered in the system, and $a_i, i = 1, ..., N$ is the random variable representing the $i$th attribute.

For the vehicle orientation, we use a GMM to capture its distribution. This is based on our prior knowledge that the field-of-view of a camera covers either a road or an intersection. If we do not consider vehicle turning, there are rarely more than four major directions at a crossroad. In this work, we set a GMM with 6 components. For lighting conditions and camera attributes, we use four independent Gaussian distributions. Therefore, given $N$ attributes, we optimize $M$ mean values of the Gaussians, where $M \geq N$.

We speculate that the means of the Gaussian distributions or components are more important than the standard deviations because means reflect how the majority of the vehicles look. Although our method has the ability to handle variances, this would significantly increase the search space. As such, we predefine the values of standard deviations and only optimize the means of all the Gaussians $\boldsymbol{\mu} = (\mu_1, \mu_2, ..., \mu_M)$, where $\mu_i \in \mathbb{R}, i = 1, ..., M$ is the mean of the $m$th Gaussian. As a result, given the means $\boldsymbol{\mu}$ of the Gaussians, we can sample an attribute list as $\mathcal{A} \sim G(\boldsymbol{\mu})$, where G is a function that generates a set of attributes given means of Gaussian.

## 4.2  Optimization

The objective of our optimization is to train a model to generate a dataset that has a similar content distribution with respect to a target real dataset.

**Measuring Distribution Difference.** We need to precisely define the distribution difference before we apply any optimization algorithm. There potentially exists two directions: using the appearance difference, and the task loss on the validation set. But as re-ID is a cross-camera task, it is indirect and difficult for us to optimise attributes for a single camera using loss from a cross-camera system. So we focus on the appearance difference. For the appearance difference, we use the Fréchet Inception Distance (FID) [10] to quantitatively measure the distribution difference between two datasets. Adversarial loss is not used as the measurement directly since there exists a huge appearance difference between synthetic and real data, and the discriminator would easily detect the specific detailed differences between real and generated, and yet not be useful.

Formally, we denote the sets of synthetic data and real data as $X_s$ and $X_r$ respectively, where $X_s = \{\mathcal{R}(\mathcal{A}_1), \cdots, \mathcal{R}(\mathcal{A}_K)|\mathcal{A}_k \sim G(\boldsymbol{\mu})\}$, and $\mathcal{R}$ is our rendering function through the 3D graphics engine working on a given attribute list $\mathcal{A}$ that controls the environment. $K$ is the number of images in the synthetic dataset. For the FID calculation, we employ the Inception-V3 network [32] to map an image into its feature space. We view the feature as a multivariate real-valued random variable and assume that it follows a Gaussian distribution. To measure the distribution difference between two Gaussians, we resort to their means and covariance matrices. Under FID, the distribution difference between synthetic data and real data is written as,

$$\mathrm{FID}(X_s, X_r) = \|\boldsymbol{\mu}_s - \boldsymbol{\mu}_r\|_2^2 + Tr(\boldsymbol{\Sigma}_s + \boldsymbol{\Sigma}_r - 2(\boldsymbol{\Sigma}_s \boldsymbol{\Sigma}_r)^{\frac{1}{2}}), \tag{1}$$

where $\boldsymbol{\mu}_s$ and $\boldsymbol{\Sigma}_s$ denote the mean and covariance matrix of the feature distribution of the synthetic data, and $\boldsymbol{\mu}_r$ and $\boldsymbol{\Sigma}_r$ are from the real data.

**Attribute Descent.** An important difficulty for attribute optimization is that the rendering function (through the 3D engine Unity) is not differentiable, so the widely used gradient-descent based methods cannot be readily used. Under this situation, there exist several methods for gradient estimation, such as finite-difference [14] and reinforcement learning [27]. However, these methods are developed in scenarios where there are many parameters to optimize. In comparison, our system only contains a few parameters, allowing us to design a more stable and efficient approach that is sufficiently effective in finding a close to global minimum.

We are motivated by coordinate descent, an optimization algorithm that can work in derivative-free contexts [37]. The most commonly known algorithm that uses coordinate descent is $k$-means [21]. Coordinate descent successively minimizes along coordinate directions to find a minimum of a function. The algorithm selects a coordinate to perform the search at each iteration. Compared with grid search, coordinate descent significantly reduces the search time, based on the hypothesis that each parameter is relatively independent. For our designed attributes, we study their independence in Subsect. 5.3.

Using Eq. 1 as the objective function, we propose attribute descent to optimize each single attribute in the attribute list. Specifically, we view each attribute as a coordinate in the coordinate descent algorithm. In each iteration, we successively change the value of an attribute to search for the minimum value of the objective function. Formally, for our defined parameters $\boldsymbol{\mu}$ for attributes list $\mathcal{A}$, the objective is to find

$$
\begin{aligned}
\boldsymbol{\mu} &= \arg\min_{\boldsymbol{\mu}} \mathrm{FID}(X_s, X_r), \\
X_s &= \{\mathcal{R}(\mathcal{A}_1), \cdots, \mathcal{R}(\mathcal{A}_K) | \mathcal{A}_k \sim G(\boldsymbol{\mu})\}.
\end{aligned}
\tag{2}
$$

We achieve this objective iteratively. Initially, we have

$$
\boldsymbol{\mu}^0 = (\mu_1^0, \cdots, \mu_M^0),
\tag{3}
$$

At epoch $j$, we optimize a single variable $\mu_i^j$ in $\boldsymbol{\mu}$,

$$
\begin{aligned}
\mu_i^j &= \arg\min_{z \in S_i} \mathrm{FID}(X_s, X_r), \\
X_s &= \{\mathcal{R}(\mathcal{A}_1), \cdots, \mathcal{R}(\mathcal{A}_K) | \mathcal{A}_k \sim G(\mu_1^j, \\
&\qquad \cdots, \mu_{i-1}^j, z, \mu_{i+1}^{j-1}, \cdots, \mu_M^{j-1})\},
\end{aligned}
\tag{4}
$$

where the $S_i, i = 1, ..., M$ define a specific search space for mean variable $\mu_i$. For example, the search space for vehicle orientation is from $0°$ to $330°$ by $30°$ degree increments; the search space for camera height is the equally divided editable range with 9 segments. $j = 1, \cdots, J$ are the training epochs. One epoch is defined as all attributes being updated once. In this algorithm, we perform greedy search for the optimized value of an attribute in each iteration, and achieve a local minimum for each attribute when fixing the rest.

**Discussion.** In Sect. 5.3 we show that attribute descent (non-gradient solution) is superior to our implementation of reinforcement learning (gradient-based solution). Attribute descent, inherited from the coordinate descent algorithm, is simple to implement and steadily leads to convergence. It is a new optimization tool in the learning to synthesize literature and avoids drawbacks such as difficulty in optimization and sensitivity to hyper-parameters. That being said, we note that our method is effective in small-scale environments like vehicle bounding boxes where only a small number of attributes need to be optimized. In more complex environments, we suspect that reinforcement learning algorithms should also be effective.

## 5 Experiment

### 5.1 Datasets and Evaluation Protocol

We use three real-world datasets for evaluation. **VehicleID** [18] is at a large scale, containing 222,629 images of 26,328 identities. Half of the identities are

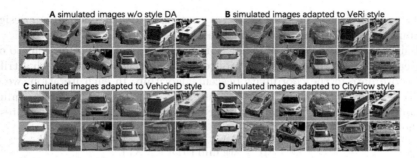

**Fig. 5.** Images w/ and w/o style domain adaptation. (A) Synthetic images without style domain adaptation. (B)(C)(D) We translate images in (A) to the style of VeRi, VehicleID and CityFlow, respectively, using SPGAN [7].

used for training, and the other half for testing. Officially there are 3 test splits. The **VeRi-776** dataset [20] contains 49,357 images of 776 vehicles captured by 20 cameras. The vehicle viewpoints and illumination cover a diverse range. The training set has 37,778 images, corresponding to 576 identities; the test set has 11,579 images of 200 identities. There are 1,678 query images. The train / test sets share the same 20 cameras. **CityFlow** [34] has more complex environments, and it has 40 cameras in a diverse environment where 34 are used in the training set. The dataset has in total 666 IDs where half are used for training and the rest for testing. We use mean average precision (mAP) and Rank-1 accuracy to measure the re-ID performance.

### 5.2   Implementation Details

**Data Generation.** For the VehicleID dataset, we only optimize a single attribute list targeting the VehicleID training set. But most re-ID datasets like VeRi-776 and CityFlow are naturally divided according to multiple camera views. Since a specific camera view usually has stable attribute features (*e.g.,* viewpoint), we perform the proposed attribute descent algorithm on each individual camera, so as to simulate images with similar content to images from each camera. For example, we optimize 20 attribute lists using the VeRi-776 training set, which has 20 cameras. Attribute descent is performed for two epochs. One epoch is defined as all attributes in the list being updated once.

**Image Style Transformation.** We apply SPGAN [7] for image style transformation, which is a state-of-the-art algorithm in style level domain adaptive re-ID. Sample results are shown in Fig. 5 and influence is shown in Table 2. Image translation models are trained using 112,042 images with random attributes as

**Table 2.** Re-ID accuracy (mAP) w/ and w/o style DA when training with synthetic data only. We clearly observe style DA brings significant improvement and thus is necessary.

| StyleDA | VehicleID | VeRi |
|---------|-----------|-------|
| ✗ | 24.36 | 12.35 |
| ✓ | **35.33** | **21.29** |

**Table 3.** Method comparison on VehicleID in data augmentation. Our method is built on IDE [41] with the cross-entropy (CE) loss. Attribute descent consistently improves over both the baseline and random attributes, and is competitive compared with the state-of-the-art. "R" means training use real data only. "R+S" denotes that both synthetic data and real data are used in training. "Small", "Medium" and "Large" refers to the number of vehicles on the VehicleID test set [18].

| Method | Data | Small | | | Medium | | | Large | | |
|---|---|---|---|---|---|---|---|---|---|---|
| | | Rank-1 | Rank-5 | mAP | Rank-1 | Rank-5 | mAP | Rank-1 | Rank-5 | mAP |
| RAM [19] | R | 75.2 | 91.5 | – | 72.3 | 87.0 | – | 67.7 | 84.5 | – |
| AAVER [15] | R | 74.69 | 93.82 | – | 68.62 | 89.95 | – | 63.54 | 85.64 | – |
| GSTE [1] | R | 75.9 | 84.2 | 75.4 | 74.8 | 83.6 | 74.3 | 74.0 | 82.7 | 72.4 |
| IDE (CE loss) | R | 77.35 | 90.28 | 83.10 | 75.24 | 87.45 | 80.73 | 72.78 | 85.56 | 78.51 |
| Ran. Attr. | R+S | 80.2 | 93.98 | 85.95 | 76.94 | 90.84 | 82.67 | 73.45 | 88.66 | 80.55 |
| Attr. Desc. | R+S | **81.50** | **94.85** | **87.33** | **77.62** | **92.20** | **83.88** | **74.87** | **89.90** | **81.35** |

**Table 4.** FID values between the generated data and VehicleID after Epoch I and II (attribute descent is performed for two epochs). Different orders of attributes are tested. 'C', 'O' and 'L' refer to camera, orientation and lighting, respectively. After Epoch II, the FID values are generally similar, suggesting that the correlation among attributes is weak, and so they are mostly independent.

| | C → O → L | C → L → O | O → L → C | O → C → L | L → C → O | L → O → C |
|---|---|---|---|---|---|---|
| FID (Epoch I) | 98.38 | 99.57 | 78.67 | 80.94 | 104.84 | 81.20 |
| FID (Epoch II) | 78.42 | 77.18 | 77.96 | 79.54 | 78.48 | 77.06 |

source domain and the training set in three vehicle datasets as target domain separately. When performing SPGAN for learned attributes data, we directly inference the learned attributes images, based on the fact that our learned attributes are a subset of the random range.

**Baseline Configuration.** For VeRi and VehicleID, we use the ID-discriminative embedding (IDE) [41]. We adopt the strategy from [22] which adds batch normalization and removes ReLU after the final feature layer. We also use the part-based convolution baseline (PCB) [31] on VeRi for improved accuracy. In PCB, we horizontally divide the picture into six equal parts and perform classification on each part. For CityFlow training, we use the setting from [22] using a combination of the cross-entropy loss and the triplet loss.

**Experiment Protocol.** We evaluate our method on both vehicleX training and joint training settings. Under vehicleX training, we train our model on VehicleX and test on real world data. Under joint training, we combine the VehicleX data and real world data and perform two-stage training; testing is on the same real-world data.

**Two-stage training** is conducted in joint training with three real-world datasets [42]. We mix synthetic dataset and a real-world dataset in the first stage and finetune on the real-world dataset only in the second stage. Taking CityFlow for example, in the first stage, we train on both real and synthetic data. We classify

**Table 5.** Comparison of the Re-ID accuracy (mAP) of two stage training when performing joint training. We can see a significant performance boost from Stage I to Stage II.

|          | VehicleID | VeRi  | CityFlow |
|----------|-----------|-------|----------|
| Stage I  | 77.54     | 69.39 | 33.54    |
| Stage II | **81.35** | **70.62** | **37.16** |

vehicle images into one of the 1,695 (333 from real +1,362 from synthetic) identities. In the second stage, we replace the classification layer with a new classifier that will be trained on the real dataset (recognizing 333 classes). Table 5 shows significant improvements with this method.

**Table 6.** Re-ID test accuracy (mAP) on VehicleID test set (large) using various training datasets with [22]. The first four training sets are generated by random attributes, random search, LTS and attribute descent, respectively. The last two training sets are real-world ones. FID measures domain gap between the training sets and VehicleID.

|     | Ran. Attr. | Ran. Sear. | LTS   | Attr. Desc. | VeRi  | Cityflow |
|-----|------------|------------|-------|-------------|-------|----------|
| FID | 134.75     | 109.94     | 95.27 | 77.96       | –     | –        |
| mAP | 22.00      | 26.35      | 32.21 | 35.33       | 38.59 | 45.57    |

**Table 7.** Method comparison when testing on VeRi-776. Both VehicleX training and joint training results are included. "R" means training with real data only, "S" represents training use synthetic data only and "R+S" denotes the joint training. VID→VeRi shows the result trained on VehicleID, test on VeRi and Cityflow→VeRi means the result trained on Cityflow, test on VeRi. In addition to some state-of-the-art methods, we summarize the results on top of two baselines, *i.e.,* IDE [41] and PCB [31].

| Experiment | Method | Data | Rank-1 | Rank-5 | mAP |
|------------|--------|------|--------|--------|-----|
| VehicleX training | ImageNet | R | 30.57 | 47.85 | 8.19 |
|  | VID →VeRi | R | 59.24 | 71.16 | 20.32 |
|  | Cityflow → VeRi | R | 69.96 | 81.35 | 26.71 |
|  | Ran. Attr. | S | 43.56 | 61.98 | 18.36 |
|  | Attr. Desc. | S | 51.25 | 67.70 | 21.29 |
| Joint training | VANet [6] | R | 89.78 | 95.99 | 66.34 |
|  | AAVER [15] | R | 90.17 | 94.34 | 66.35 |
|  | PAMTRI [33] | R+S | 92.86 | 96.97 | 71.88 |
|  | IDE | R | 92.73 | 96.78 | 66.54 |
|  | Ran. Attr. | R+S | 93.21 | 96.20 | 69.28 |
|  | Attr. Desc. | R+S | 93.44 | 97.26 | 70.62 |
|  | Attr. Desc. (PCB) | R+S | **94.34** | **97.91** | **74.51** |

## 5.3   Evaluation

**Analysis of Attribute Descent Process.** Figure 4 shows how the re-ID accuracy and FID change during along the training iterations. We observe that attributes are successively optimized when FID decreases and mAP increases. Furthermore, from the slope of the FID curve we can see that orientation has the largest impact on the distribution difference and mAP, with a huge FID drop from 147.85 to 91.14 and large mAP increase from 12.1% to 21.94%. Lighting is the second most impactful ($-7.2$ FID, $+10.7\%$ mAP), and camera attributes are the third ($-4.11$ FID, $+2.4\%$ mAP).

**Effectiveness of Learned Synthetic Data.** Learned synthetic data can be used as a training set alone, or in conjunction with real training data for data augmentation. We show the results of both cases on the three datasets in Table 3 (VehicleID), Table 7 (VeRi) and Table 8 (CityFlow). From these results we observe that when used as training data alone, learned attributes achieve much higher re-ID accuracy than random attributes. For example, on the VeRi-776 dataset, attribute descent has a $+7.69\%$ improvement in Rank-1 accuracy over random attributes. Moreover, attribute learning also benefits the data augmentation setting. For example, on CityFlow and VeRi, the improvement of learned attributes over random attributes is $+1.49\%$ and $+3.87\%$ in Rank-1 accuracy, respectively. Although this improvement looks small in number, we show that the improvement is statistical significant (Fig. 6). We note that the improvement of using synthetic data as a training set is more significant than for data augmentation. When the training set consists of only the synthetic data, a higher quality of attributes will have a more direct impact on the re-ID results.

**Few Dependencies Between Attributes.** We proceed study on dependency by testing whether the order of attributes matters. From Table 4 it is clear that attribute orders do not affect the downward trend, the only clear dependency is the relationship between orientation and camera. If we learn camera attributes before orientation, the accuracy will be influenced. But such influence will be eliminated by performing the attribute descent twice. Based on the few dependencies between attributes, we make it possible to use attribute descent rather than grid search, saving computation time.

**Attribute Descent Performs Better Than Multiple Methods: 1) Random Attribute 2) Random Search 3) LTS** [27]. For LTS, we follow their ideas but we replace the task loss with FID score, since task loss is not generalised to a re-ID task. Our reproduced LTS uses the same distribution definition and initialization as attribute descent. In order to make a fair comparison, we report values from 200 iterations of training (*i.e.,* compute FID score 200 times). Random search is a strong baseline in hyper-parameter optimization [3]. In practice, we randomly sample attribute values 200 times and choose an attribute list with the best FID score. The result comparison is shown in Table 6. First, under the same task network, all learned attributes (*i.e., random search, LTS and attribute descend*) perform better than random attributes, in both FID and mAP, showing that learned attributes significantly improves the result, and that content

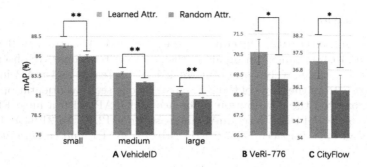

**Fig. 6.** Performance comparison between learned attributes and random attributes in joint training. We present mAP on three datasets and use statistical significance analysis to show the training stability. $*$ means statistically significant (*i.e.*, $0.01 < p$-value $< 0.05$) and $**$ denotes statistically very significant (*i.e.*, $0.001 < p$-value $< 0.01$).

**Table 8.** Method comparison on CityFlow with joint training. Our baseline is built with a combination of the CE loss and the triplet loss [22]. Rank-1, Rank-20 and the mAP are calculated by the online server.

| Method | Data | R-1 | R-20 | mAP |
|---|---|---|---|---|
| BA [17] | R | 49.62 | 80.04 | 25.61 |
| BS [17] | R | 49.05 | 78.80 | 25.57 |
| PAMTRI [33] | R+S | 59.7 | 80.13 | 33.81 |
| IDE(CE+Tri.) | R | 56.75 | 72.24 | 30.21 |
| Ran. Attr. | R+S | 63.59 | 82.60 | 35.96 |
| Attr. Desc. | R+S | **64.07** | **83.27** | **37.16** |

differences matter. Second, random search does not perform well in a limited search time. It has been shown that random search performs well when there exists many less important parameters [3]. But in our search space, all attributes contribute to the distribution differences as shown in Fig. 4, thus random search has no advantage in helping find important attributes. Third, LTS works but it does not find a better FID score than attribute descent. LTS seems to fall into a local optimum and does not reach a global one. A example of local optima is LTS outputs are either outputs of car front or rear, whereas the VehicleID contains both car front and rear. With a more hand-crafted design, we will definitely reach a better performing LTS framework. But at this stage, attribute descent is a simple realized method that finds a better solution with few iterations. It deserves to be a strong baseline in this field.

**Comparison with the State-of-the-Art.** When the synthetic data is used in conjunction with real-world training set, we achieve very competitive accuracy compared with the state-of-the-art (Table 3, Table 7 and Table 8). For example on VehicleID (Small), our method is +5.6% higher than [1] in Rank-1 accuracy. On CityFlow, our method is higher than [33] by +7.32% in Rank-1 accuracy.

# 6  Conclusion

This paper study the domain gap problem between synthetic data and real data from the content level. That is, we automatically edit the source domain image content in a graphic engine so as to reduce the content gap between the synthetic images and the real images. We use this idea to study the vehicle re-ID task, where the usage of vehicle bounding boxes decreases the set of attributes to be optimized. Fewer attributes-of-interest and low dependencies between them allow us to optimize them one by one using our proposed attribute descent approach. We show that the learned attributes bring about improvement in re-ID accuracy with statistical significance. Moreover, our experiment reveals some important insights regarding the usage of synthetic data, *e.g.*, style DA brings significant improvement and two stage training is beneficial for joint training.

**Acknowledgement.** Dr. Liang Zheng is the recipient of Australian Research Council Discovery Early Career Award (DE200101283) funded by the Australian Government.

# References

1. Bai, Y., Lou, Y., Gao, F., Wang, S., Wu, Y., Duan, L.Y.: Group-sensitive triplet embedding for vehicle reidentification. IEEE Trans. Multimed. **20**(9), 2385–2399 (2018)
2. Bak, S., Carr, P., Lalonde, J.F.: Domain adaptation through synthesis for unsupervised person re-identification. In: ECCV (2018)
3. Bergstra, J., Bengio, Y.: Random search for hyper-parameter optimization. J. Mach. Learn. Res. **13**(Feb), 281–305 (2012)
4. Binkowski, M., Sutherland, D.J., Arbel, M., Gretton, A.: Demystifying mmd gans. In: ICLR (2018)
5. Chang, A.X., et al.: Shapenet: an information-rich 3D model repository. arXiv preprint arXiv:1512.03012 (2015)
6. Chu, R., Sun, Y., Li, Y., Liu, Z., Zhang, C., Wei, Y.: Vehicle re-identification with viewpoint-aware metric learning. In: ICCV (2019)
7. Deng, W., Zheng, L., Ye, Q., Kang, G., Yang, Y., Jiao, J.: Image-image domain adaptation with preserved self-similarity and domain-dissimilarity for person re-identification. In: CVPR (2018)
8. Gaidon, A., Wang, Q., Cabon, Y., Vig, E.: Virtual worlds as proxy for multi-object tracking analysis. In: CVPR (2016)
9. Hermans, A., Beyer, L., Leibe, B.: In defense of the triplet loss for person re-identification. arXiv preprint arXiv:1703.07737 (2017)
10. Heusel, M., Ramsauer, H., Unterthiner, T., Nessler, B., Hochreiter, S.: Gans trained by a two time-scale update rule converge to a local nash equilibrium. In: NeurIPS (2017)
11. Hoffman, J., et al.: Cycada: cycle-consistent adversarial domain adaptation. In: ICML (2018)

12. Hou, Y., Zheng, L., Gould, S.: Multiview detection with feature perspective transformation. arXiv preprint arXiv:2007.07247 (2020)
13. Juliani, A., et al.: Unity: a general platform for intelligent agents. arXiv preprint arXiv:1809.02627 (2018)
14. Kar, A., et al.: Meta-sim: Learning to generate synthetic datasets. In: ICCV (2019)
15. Khorramshahi, P., Kumar, A., Peri, N., Rambhatla, S.S., Chen, J.C., Chellappa, R.: A dual path modelwith adaptive attention for vehicle re-identification. In: ICCV (2019)
16. Kolve, E., Mottaghi, R., Gordon, D., Zhu, Y., Gupta, A., Farhadi, A.: Ai2-thor: an interactive 3D environment for visual AI. arXiv preprint arXiv:1712.05474 (2017)
17. Kumar, R., Weill, E., Aghdasi, F., Sriram, P.: Vehicle re-identification: an efficient baseline using triplet embedding. arXiv preprint arXiv:1901.01015 (2019)
18. Liu, H., Tian, Y., Yang, Y., Pang, L., Huang, T.: Deep relative distance learning: tell the difference between similar vehicles. In: CVPR (2016)
19. Liu, X., Zhang, S., Huang, Q., Gao, W.: Ram: a region-aware deep model for vehicle re-identification. In: ICME (2018)
20. Liu, X., Liu, W., Ma, H., Fu, H.: Large-scale vehicle re-identification in urban surveillance videos. In: ICME (2016)
21. Lloyd, S.: Least squares quantization in PCM. IEEE Trans. Inf. Theory **28**(2), 129–137 (1982)
22. Luo, H., Gu, Y., Liao, X., Lai, S., Jiang, W.: Bag of tricks and a strong baseline for deep person re-identification. In: CVPR Workshops (2019)
23. Naphade, M., et al.: The 4th AI city challenge. In: CVPR Workshops, pp. 626–627 (2020)
24. Peng, X., Bai, Q., Xia, X., Huang, Z., Saenko, K., Wang, B.: Moment matching for multi-source domain adaptation. In: ICCV (2019)
25. Richter, S.R., Vineet, V., Roth, S., Koltun, V.: Playing for data: ground truth from computer games. In: ECCV (2016)
26. Ristani, E., Solera, F., Zou, R., Cucchiara, R., Tomasi, C.: Performance measures and a data set for multi-target, multi-camera tracking. In: Hua, G., Jégou, H. (eds.) ECCV 2016. LNCS, vol. 9914, pp. 17–35. Springer, Cham (2016). https://doi.org/10.1007/978-3-319-48881-3_2
27. Ruiz, N., Schulter, S., Chandraker, M.: Learning to simulate. In: ICLR (2019)
28. Sakaridis, C., Dai, D., Van Gool, L.: Semantic foggy scene understanding with synthetic data. Int. J. Comput. Vis. **126**(9), 973–992 (2018). https://doi.org/10.1007/s11263-018-1072-8
29. Shrivastava, A., Pfister, T., Tuzel, O., Susskind, J., Wang, W., Webb, R.: Learning from simulated and unsupervised images through adversarial training. In: CVPR (2017)
30. Sun, X., Zheng, L.: Dissecting person re-identification from the viewpoint of viewpoint. In: CVPR (2019)
31. Sun, Y., Zheng, L., Yang, Y., Tian, Q., Wang, S.: Beyond part models: person retrieval with refined part pooling (and a strong convolutional baseline). In: ECCV (2018)
32. Szegedy, C., Vanhoucke, V., Ioffe, S., Shlens, J., Wojna, Z.: Rethinking the inception architecture for computer vision. In: CVPR (2016)
33. Tang, Z., et al.: Pamtri: pose-aware multi-task learning for vehicle re-identification using highly randomized synthetic data. In: ICCV (2019)
34. Tang, Z., et al.: Cityflow: a city-scale benchmark for multi-target multi-camera vehicle tracking and re-identification. In: CVPR (2019)

35. Tremblay, J., et al.: Training deep networks with synthetic data: bridging the reality gap by domain randomization. In: CVPR Workshops (2018)
36. Wang, Z., et al.: Orientation invariant feature embedding and spatial temporal regularization for vehicle re-identification. In: ICCV (2017)
37. Wright, S.J.: Coordinate descent algorithms. Math. Programm. **151**(1), 3–34 (2015)
38. Xue, Z., Mao, W., Zheng, L.: Learning to simulate complex scenes. arXiv preprint arXiv:2006.14611 (2020)
39. Yang, L., Luo, P., Change Loy, C., Tang, X.: A large-scale car dataset for fine-grained categorization and verification. In: CVPR (2015)
40. Yao, Y., Plested, J., Gedeon, T.: Information-preserving feature filter for short-term eeg signals. Neurocomputing **408**, 91–99 (2020)
41. Zheng, L., et al.: MARS: a video benchmark for large-scale person re-identification. In: Leibe, B., Matas, J., Sebe, N., Welling, M. (eds.) ECCV 2016. LNCS, vol. 9910, pp. 868–884. Springer, Cham (2016). https://doi.org/10.1007/978-3-319-46466-4_52
42. Zheng, Z., Ruan, T., Wei, Y., Yang, Y.: Vehiclenet: learning robust feature representation for vehicle re-identification. In: CVPR Workshops (2019)
43. Zheng, Z., Zheng, L., Yang, Y.: Unlabeled samples generated by gan improve the person re-identification baseline in vitro. In: CVPR, pp. 3754–3762 (2017)
44. Zhong, Z., Zheng, L., Zheng, Z., Li, S., Yang, Y.: Camera style adaptation for person re-identification. In: CVPR (2018)
45. Zhong, Z., Zheng, L., Zheng, Z., Li, S., Yang, Y.: Camstyle: a novel data augmentation method for person re-identification. IEEE Trans. Image Process. **28**(3), 1176–1190 (2018)
46. Zhou, Y., Shao, L.: Aware attentive multi-view inference for vehicle re-identification. In: CVPR (2018)

# Author Index